THE ANNUAL DIRECTORY OF

American Bed & Breakfasts

THE ANNUAL DIRECTORY OF

American Bed & Breakfasts

Toni Sortor, *Editor*

RUTLEDGE HILL PRESS

NASHVILLE, TENNESSEE

Published in Nashville, Tennessee, by Rutledge Hill Press, Inc., 513 Third Avenue South, Nashville, Tennessee 37210.

Cover design and Book design by Harriette Bateman.
Maps and selected illustrations by Tonya Pitkin Presley, Studio III Productions.

Photograph on front cover courtesy of the Homeplace, Charlotte, NC, and used by permission.

Photograph on back cover courtesy of White Swan Inn, San Francisco, CA, and used by permission.

Manufactured in the United States of America
1 2 3 4 5 6 — 92 91 90 89

Contents

THE ANNUAL DIRECTORY OF

American Bed
& Breakfasts

Introduction

Welcome to the world of B&Bs! As you can see, there's a B&B close to almost anywhere you want to go in the U.S., whether you're on vacation, stealing a getaway weekend, or traveling on business. There are certain advantages to staying at a B&B, too. Your hosts will generally be delighted to help you with sightseeing plans — or they'll leave you alone if you prefer. Your room will be clean and comfortable, sometimes simple, but sometimes downright luxurious — at a price lower than you would find in a local motel. And you'll have breakfast right there when you wake up, so you don't have to risk a diner or find a fast-food chain.

Most of all, B&B hosts are friendly, likeable people who enjoy having company and treating their guests with every consideration. It's a pretty good deal!

How to Use This Guide

Below is a sample listing. Let's walk through it. The B&B's town is listed first, alphabetically within the state. If there's more than one B&B in town, they'll be listed alphabetically by B&B name.

An abbreviated address follows the B&B name. If you want to write to a B&B, add the town and state to the given address. The descriptions that follow the address are meant to give you some idea of the town, the house, activities and amenities available.

FRANKLIN

The Rutherford-Johnson House

Box 202, 36444
(205) 282-4423; 478-5699

A restored Victorian farmhouse, the Rutherford-Johnson House is located in Monroe County, Alabama, an area noted for its beautiful timberlands and extraordinary hunting and fishing resources. Get away from city sounds and lights — relax in a lovely rural setting! Home-cooked country breakfasts. Life the way it used to be!

Hosts: Mary Johnson & John Huff
Singles: $55
Doubles: 4 (2 PB; 2 SB) $80
Type of Beds: 1 Twin; 1 Double; 3 Queen
Full Breakfast
Minimum stay weekends & holidays: 3
Credit Cards: No
Notes: 2, 5, 6, 7, 8 (over 12), 9

NOTE: These descriptions were written by the B&B hosts themselves. The publisher has not visited these B&Bs and can't be responsible for any inaccuracies in the descriptions.

Following the descriptions are more specific notes: the hosts' names, type of rooms, baths, type of breakfast served, and so forth. In these notes, "PB" means private bath, "SB" means shared bath. Some entries may say "S2B," which means guests share two baths. Rates are for one room double occupancy, unless noted otherwise. The last line of the notes is made up of numbers that are explained at the bottom of each page. A 3 or 4 means lunch or dinner is available on the premises. For the sports entries — 10, 11, 12, 13 — the activity is within ten miles, not necessarily on the premises. If a B&B has note 14, you may book your stay through a travel agent.

You'll note that some entries have numbers or letters instead of house names, or don't list the hosts' names. These houses are booked through reservation service organizations that handle bookings for more than one house. Think of them as B&B travel agents. The advantage of booking through a service is that they have a wide variety of homes and generally do quality control. They can match your needs to the best house for you, but they do generally charge for this service.

To see where a given house is located in a state, turn to the state map and look for the town or city. Some are quite rural; others are in large cities.

Inns vs. B&Bs

This book lists inns as well as B&Bs, but the inns serve breakfast as part of the room rate. Still, check on it when you call. Most of the inns are small, family-run inns, but there is a difference between staying at an inn and a homestay B&B. You probably won't meet the inn's owners or have breakfast with them, for one thing. If relating to your host is important to you, be sure you're booking a homestay. On the other hand, an inn may have more facilities that attract you. Your choice.

How to Make a Reservation

You may either call or write to the B&B you've chosen. When you do, don't be afraid to ask questions! Will you have a private bath? If not, how many people share a bath? Is there a set time for breakfast? Does the house have all the facilities you need? Will they let you bring your children or Fido? Ask more questions than you'd ask of a hotel or motel. Your hosts will be happy to answer your questions, and many B&Bs have brochures they'll send if you request one.

Be sure to ask about payment and cancellation policies, too. Some B&Bs take credit cards, others take checks, but most prefer cash. Avoid unpleasant surprises.

When You Arrive

Plan to arrive at your B&B during their normal check-in hours, which you should ask about when you call. Arrive with the same number of people you booked for and no extraneous pets. The most important thing to remember is that you are a guest in someone's home, even though you're paying for a room and breakfast, and your hosts deserve common courtesy. If you'll be sharing a bath, remember to bring a robe and slippers. Staying at a B&B can be one of the most rewarding travel experiences you'll ever have, as Europeans who have been doing it for years will tell you, but it does take a little work on your part.

So, are you ready to go to Lawai, on the island of Kauai, Hawaii? It's in here. Have to take a high-school senior to visit Cornell? How about a family vacation on an 11,000-acre ranch in Montana? No problem. Business trip to Des Moines? It's covered. And if you're finally ready for that family trip to Washington, D.C., see our special ten-page section with tips on what to see and do in the District of Columbia. Have fun!

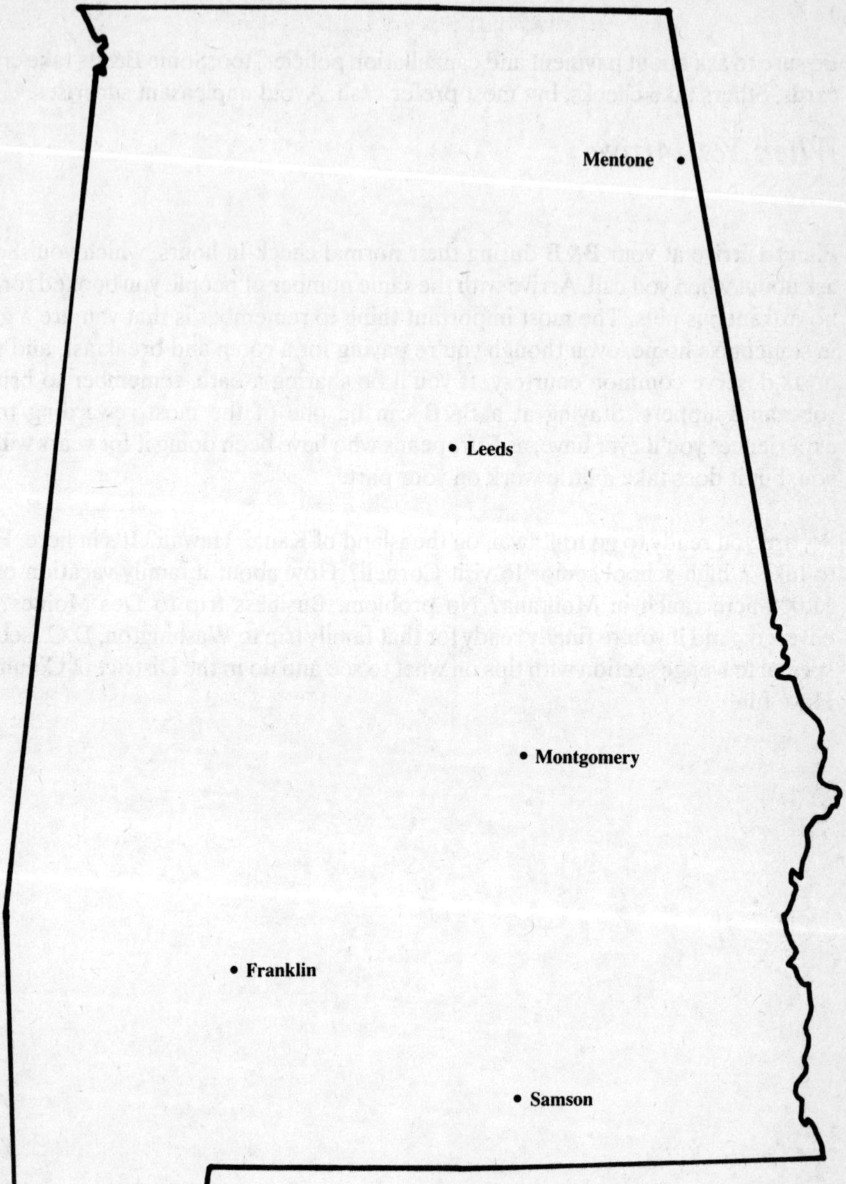

Mentone •

• Leeds

• Montgomery

• Franklin

• Samson

Mobile

ALABAMA

Alabama

The Rutherford-Johnson House

Box 202, 36444
(205) 282-4423; 478-5699

A restored Victorian farmhouse, the Rutherford-Johnson House is located in Monroe County, Alabama, an area noted for its beautiful timberlands and extraordinary hunting and fishing resources. Get away from city sounds and lights — relax in a lovely rural setting! Home-cooked country breakfasts. Life the way it used to be!

Hosts: Mary Johnson & John Huff
Singles: $55
Doubles: 4 (2 PB; 2 SB) $80
Type of Beds: 1 Twin; 1 Double; 3 Queen
Full Breakfast
Minimum stay weekends & holidays: 3
Credit Cards: No
Notes: 2, 5, 6, 7, 8 (over 12), 9

Country Sunshine

Rt. 2, Box 275, 35094
(205) 699-9841

A 4.5 acre secluded retreat with a quiet country atmosphere. Barn and pasture to board your horses. Ranch-style house with four bedrooms and four baths, TV den, fireplace, formal dining room, country dining room, outside screened patio. Guided fishing and camping is available in the area, as is horseback riding. Twenty minutes south of Birmingham, near the Botanical Gardens, Vulcan Park, and Oak Mountain State Park.

Host: Kay Ceraso
Doubles: 4 (PB and SB) $50-65
Full Breakfast
Credit Cards: A, B, C
Notes: 2, 3, 4, 5, 8 (over 13)

Mentone Inn

Highway 117, Box 284, 35984
(205) 634-4836

In an old-fashioned, relaxing, quaint old town near DeSoto Falls. Good hospitality; rock on the front porch and watch the world go by.

Host: Amelia Kirk
Doubles: 12 (PB) $40-65
Type of Beds: 4 Twin; 11 Double; 1 Queen
Full Breakfast
Credit Cards: No
Closed Nov. 1 - May 1
Notes: 2, 3, 4, 9, 10, 11, 12, 14

Vincent-Doan Home

1664 Springhill Avenue, 36604
(205) 433-7121

The Vincent Home was completed in 1827 by Captain Benjamin Vincent. It is the last remaining example of French Creole architecture in Mobile and retains its original roof line, galleries, and facade. It has been restored and furnished by its present owner and hostess. Each spacious bedroom has private bath, fireplace, and direct access to the gallery overlooking the garden. Central

---

6 Pets welcome: 7 Smoking allowed: 8 Children welcome: 9 Social drinking allowed: 10 Tennis available: 11 Swimming available: 12 Golf available: 13 Skiing available: 14 May be booked through travel agents

air-conditioning and heat have been installed. Guests receive a welcome beverage, a tour of the home, elegant accommodations, and a bountiful country breakfast with their hostess.

Host: Betty Doan
Doubles: 3 (PB) $55-77
Type of Beds: 4 Twin; 2 Double
Full Breakfast
Credit Cards: A, B
Notes: 2, 5, 6, 7, 8, 9, 10, 14

MONTGOMERY

The Colonel's Rest

Box 886, Millbrook, 36054
(205) 285-5421

A country contemporary on 60 acres just east of Montgomery and two minutes from I-85 with guest kitchenette, private entrance, pool, and terrace.

Doubles: 4 (SB) $36-40
Full Breakfast
Credit Cards: No
Notes: 2, 5, 7, 8, 9, 10, 11, 12

Crooked Creek

Box 886, Millbrook, 36054
(205) 285-5421

If you need to get away, you'll love Crooked Creek, hidden among 13 acres of towering trees and tranquility, complete with creek. Apartment with private entrance for short or extended stays. Gracious retired schoolteacher hostess.

Doubles: 2 (SB) $36-45
Full Breakfast
Credit Cards: No
Notes: 2, 5, 7, 8, 9, 10, 11, 12

1840 Cottage

Box 886, Millbrook, 36054
(205) 285-5421

Restored 1840 raised cottage filled with antiques and charm. Five minutes from I-65N, ten from downtown. Hospitable retired military officer and his wife are your hosts.

Doubles: 1 (PB) $36-40
Full Breakfast
Credit Cards: No
Notes: 2, 5, 7, 8, 9, 10, 11, 12

Federal Colonial

Box 886, Millbrook, 36054
(205) 285-5421

This lovely home features antiques and charm. Located in Prattville, it's just minutes from Montgomery and I-65N. A retired military officer and his wife offer southern hospitality and great breakfasts.

Doubles: 4 (1 PB; 3 SB) $36-40
Full Breakfast
Credit Cards: No
Notes: 2, 5, 9, 10, 11, 12

Graham House

Box 886, Millbrook, 36054
(205) 285-5421

One of Montgomery's Garden District's beautiful older homes with a large, welcoming porch, garden view, beautiful decor, great breakfasts, and friendly hosts. Fireplace in guest room; central location.

Doubles: 1 (PB) $44-48
Full Breakfast
Credit Cards: No
Notes: 2, 5, 7, 8 (call), 9, 10, 11, 12

Greek Revival

Box 886, Millbrook, 36054
(205) 285-5421

Tara was no more beautiful than this older restored mansion furnished with European and American antiques. Conveniently located near downtown and two interstates. Military officer and his musician wife offer

---

NOTES: Credit cards accepted: A Master Card; B Visa; C American Express; D Discover Card; E Diners Club; F Other: 2 Personal checks accepted: 3 Lunch available: 4 Dinner available: 5 Open all year

Southern hospitality and gourmet breakfasts. Evening meals available with advance notice. Two acres of formal gardens and lighted tennis court; elevator available.

Doubles: 2 (SB) $65-75
Full Breakfast
Credit Cards: No
Notes: 2, 4, 5, 9, 10, 11, 12

Inverrary

Box 886, Millbrook, 36054
(205) 285-5421

A delightful older restored farm home just east of Montgomery near I-85 featuring great breakfasts, pastoral scenes, a large red barn, and the hospitality of gracious retired social workers.

Doubles: 2 (PB) $36-40
Full Breakfast
Credit Cards: No
Notes: 2, 5, 7, 8, 9, 10, 11, 12

Red Bluff Cottage

Box 886, Millbrook, 36054
(205) 285-5421

A new raised cottage in one of Montgomery's oldest historical districts, conveniently located to I-65, I-85, and downtown. A great view of the Alabama River from the deep upstairs porch.

Doubles: 4 (PB) $44-48
Full Breakfast
Credit Cards: No
Notes: 2, 5, 7 (limited), 8, 9, 10, 11, 12

SAMSON

Jola Bama Guest Home

201 S. East Street, 36477
(205) 898-2478

This comfortable clapboard Victorian boasts a collection of interesting antiques. Located eighty-five miles south of Montgomery, "The Cradle of the Confederacy." North Florida beaches and the Ft. Rucker Army Aviation Museum are nearby. Your host, a tree farmer and cattle rancher, looks forward to welcoming you.

Host: Jewel M. Armstrong
Singles: 2 (PB or SB) $17-22
Doubles: 2 (PB or SB) $20-29
Continental Breakfast
Credit Cards: No
Notes: 5, 6, 7, 8 (16 and over), 9, 14

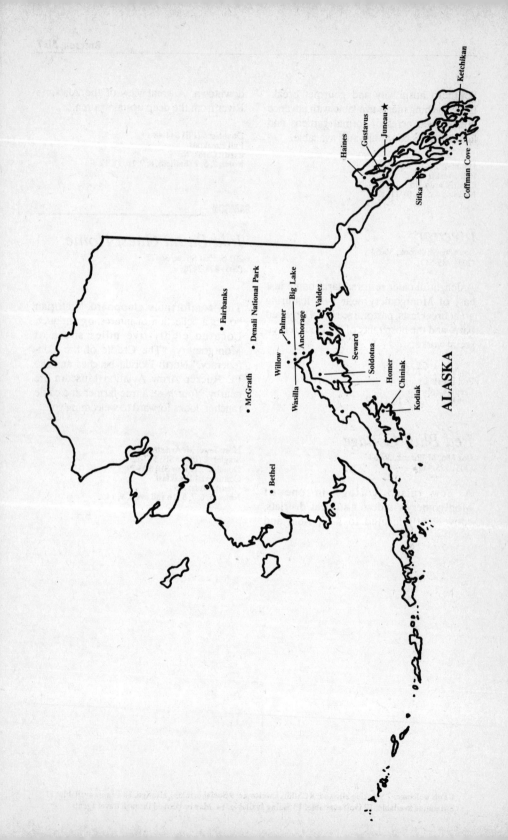

ALASKA

Ketchikan

Coffman Cove

Juneau ★

Gustavus

Haines

Sitka

Fairbanks

Denali National Park

Big Lake

Palmer

Valdez

Anchorage

Willow

Seward

McGrath

Wasilla

Soldotna

Homer

Chiniak

Kodiak

Bethel

Alaska

All the Comforts of Home
12531 Turk's Turn, 99516
(907) 345-4279

A rustic establishment with a quiet adult atmosphere. Although the "Alaskan mystique" may be intangible, our guests depart with a greater understanding of this beautiful land. Enjoy full country breakfasts while seated at an antique table in our bay window that really does overlook the bay. Year-round sauna and hot tub.

Hosts: Sydnee Mae Stiver & Frank J. McCurley
Doubles: 3 (1 PB; 2 SB) $50-75
Type of Beds: 1 Double; 2 Queen
Full Breakfast
Credit Cards: A, B
Notes: 2, 5, 9, 10, 11, 12, 13, 14

All the Comforts of Home

Butterfly B&B
Alaska Private Lodgings
Box 200047, 99520
(907) 258-1717

Hillside home with an inlet view. Guest room with private half bath. Gracious host will help make your stay pleasant. Close to Chugach Park hiking trails; ten to fifteen miles from downtown. $40-50.

Crooked Drive
Alaska Private Lodgings
Box 200047, 99520
(907) 258-1717

Hosts are long-time Alaskans. Enjoy the view from this lovely hillside home. Two guest rooms, each with queen beds. Close to hiking trails, Chugach State Park, and zoo. Ten to fifteen miles from downtown. $40-50.

11th Avenue B&B
Alaska Private Lodgings
Box 200047, 99520
(907) 258-1717

Perfect privacy in a charming, quiet location close to downtown. Long-time Alaskan will help with sightseeing suggestions. Tastefully decorated room has twin beds and private bath. Full breakfast; resident pet. $55.

5th Avenue B&B
Alaska Private Lodgings
Box 200047, 99520
(907) 258-1717

Peaceful wooded lot on a quiet street within walking distance to a large mall, restaurants, and post office. Lower level privacy. Den for guest use, TV with Alaskan videos, and

6 Pets welcome: 7 Smoking allowed: 8 Children welcome: 9 Social drinking allowed: 10 Tennis available: 11 Swimming available: 12 Golf available: 13 Skiing available: 14 May be booked through travel agents

library. Three rooms, shared bath. Continental breakfast, resident pet. $45-50.

Foraker B&B

Alaska Private Lodgings
Box 200047, 99520
(907) 258-1717

Queen-size bed to rest the weary traveler. Quiet residential area close to the inlet. No stairs. Hosts are well informed and helpful to the busy traveler. Located between the airport and the town. Private bath, full breakfast, resident pet. $45.

Forest Home B&B

Alaska Private Lodgings
Box 200047, 99520
(907) 258-1717

Cozy Alaskan log home on a wooded hillside acre. Host is a hiking enthusiast who will tell you about the good trails. Breakfast is guest's choice. Public bus service available from downtown. Shared bath. $40-45.

Forget Me Not

Alaska Private Lodgings
Box 200047, 99520
(907) 258-1717

Warm and gracious hospitality is offered by a thirty-year Alaskan resident. Quiet location with a mountain view. Former guests rave about the breakfasts! Three guest rooms, each with private bath. Full breakfast. $40-50.

Hillcrest

Alaska Private Lodgings
Box 200047, 99520
(907) 258-1717

This home offers a covered, heated swimming pool, sauna, and Jacuzzi tub. Two love-

ly guest rooms share a bath. Guests have full use of the living room. Basketball court for "jet lag" workouts. Full breakfast; resident pet. $50-55.

Homestead B&B

Alaska Private Lodgings
Box 200047, 99520
(907) 258-1717

A log homestead with private entrance to the guest room. One and one-half miles to the airport. Lovely gardens and tennis court for guests to enjoy. One room with private bath. Host has an antique doll collection you'll want to see. Full breakfast. $40-50.

Little House Downtown

Alaska Private Lodgings
Box 200047, 99520
(907) 258-1717

These modest accommodations are hosted by a gracious lady who makes her guests welcome and comfortable. Walk to Federal Building and museum. Two rooms with shared bath. Full breakfast; resident pet. $35-40.

Marsch's Manor B&B

Alaska Private Lodgings
Box 200047, 99520
(907) 258-1717

Beautiful home with deck roof garden and flowers. Terrific city location, close to bus station and museum. During summer months your retired hosts are often touring Alaska. Shared bath, full breakfast. $40-50.

Peggy's B&B

Alaska Private Lodgings
Box 200047, 99520
(907) 258-1717

NOTES: Credit cards accepted: A Master Card; B Visa; C American Express; D Discover Card; E Diners Club; F Other: 2 Personal checks accepted: 3 Lunch available: 4 Dinner available: 5 Open all year

Three lovely rooms with full kitchen, TV, phone, and private library. Walk to Muldoon Park exercise par course. Thirty minutes from airport, close to shopping center. Guests have use of the family room. Full breakfast, shared bath. $40-45.

Snug Harbor

Alaska Private Lodgings
Box 200047, 99520
(907) 258-1717

Honeymoon cottage located on the Park Strip in downtown Anchorage. Walk to bus routes, shopping, museum, and many fine restaurants. Walk the coastal trail to Earthquake Park. Cottage is adjacent to host's home and offers two guest rooms, two full baths, and living room. Good for two couples. Full breakfast. $55.

Stephens' House of Muffins

Alaska Private Lodgings
Box 200047, 99520
(907) 258-1717

Enjoy your breakfast in the sun room of this eastside home. You'll ask to take home the recipe for the host's muffins. Close to the university and hospital. Hosts are long-time Alaskans and will give good travel advice. Two guest rooms, hearty continental breakfast, shared bath, resident pet. $45.

Susitna B&B

Alaska Private Lodgings
Box 200047, 99520
(907) 258-1717

Quiet neighborhood between downtown and the airport. Wonderful host will give good travel tips. Walk to coastal trail. Double bed with private bath and no stairs. Continental breakfast. $40.

Vance Drive B&B

Alaska Private Lodgings
Box 200047, 99520
(907) 258-1717

A suite of rooms for perfect privacy, family room with TV and breakfast bar. Close to bus, university, and hospital. Two rooms with shared bath in a quiet residential neighborhood. Full breakfast. $45.

View Point Manor

10800 Stroganof Drive, 99520
(907) 346-2612

Large hillside home at an elevation of 2,000 feet. Just a few steps from Chugach State Park, where trails are available for hiking, horseback riding, and cross-country skiing. Just 15-20 minutes from the Alaska Zoo, equestrian center, shopping, and restaurants.

Hosts: Jay & Irene Jemison
Singles: 1 (PB) $35-60
Doubles: 2 (PB) $55-85
Type of Beds: 1 Double; 1 Queen; 1 King
Full Breakfast
Credit Cards: A, B, C, D
Notes: 5, 9, 10, 11, 12, 13, 14

Wildwood

Alaska Private Lodgings
Box 200047, 99520
(907) 258-1717

Across the lagoon from downtown, this lovely room has twin beds and a private bath. Hot tub and sitting room available. Walk the nearby coastal trail to downtown; watch the sunsets from this lovely home. Full breakfast. $45-50.

6 Pets welcome: 7 Smoking allowed: 8 Children welcome: 9 Social drinking allowed: 10 Tennis available: 11 Swimming available: 12 Golf available: 13 Skiing available: 14 May be booked through travel agents

BETHEL

Bentley's Porterhouse Bed & Breakfast

624 First Avenue, Box 529, 99559
(907) 543-3552

Located on the beautiful Kuskokwim River in southwest Alaska, offering comfortable rooms with cable TV. Full elegant breakfast is served on fine china — great sourdough waffles and bread! Special dietary accommodations on advance notice. Reservations advisable; brochure available.

Hosts: Bette Goodwine & Millie Bentley
Singles: 2 (SB) $63
Doubles: 7 (SB) $89.25
Type of Beds: 9 Twin; 3 Double; 1 Queen
Full Breakfast
Credit Cards: A, B (for reservations)
Notes: 2, 5, 7, 8, 9

BIG LAKE

Jeanie's on Big Lake

Box 520598, 99652
(907) 892-7594

Comfortable Alaskan hand-hewn log home on a five-mile-long recreation lake. Wraparound sun deck with sunken hot tub; panoramic view of lake and mountains. Waterskiing and fishing from the dock. Float-plane charters. Weekend/vacation rental for small groups.

Host: Jeanie McCown
Singles: $35
Doubles: 4 (SB) $50
Type of Beds: 2 Queen; 2 King
Minimum stay weekends: 3
Credit Cards: No
Notes: 2, 4, 5, 7, 8 (12 and over), 9, 11, 12, 14

CHINIAK

Road's End Lounge

Box 5629 - Mile 42, 99615
(907) 486-2885

On a coastal dirt road with the sea and mountains. Whale and sea otter watching; eagles galore. A friendly, fun place to stay. Fantastic fishing; deer hunting in season.

Hosts: Dorothy & Ernest Hopper
Singles: 2 (PB) $25
Doubles: 2 (PB) $30
Type of Beds: 4 Twin; 1 Queen; 1 King
Minimum stay weekdays: 5 ; weekends & holidays: 2
Credit Cards: No
Notes: 2 (Alaskan), 4, 5, 6, 7, 8, 9

COFFMAN COVE

Coffman Cove Bunkhouse & Skiff Rental

306 Harbor Avenue, 99950
(907) 329-2219

On Prince of Wales Island, one of the most exciting fishing areas of the world, about two hours by air from Seattle. Coffman Cove is an active logging camp providing breakfast and dinner in the cookhouse and a carry-out lunch, or breakfast only. Perfect for bear and deer hunters, fishermen, photographers, nature lovers.

Hosts: Jerry & Caroline Hedges
Doubles: 13 (SB) $35 (breakfast only)-$55 (all meals)
Full Breakfast
Credit Cards: No
Closed Dec.-March
Notes: 2, 3, 4, 6, 7, 8, 9

DENALI NATIONAL PARK

Camp Denali

Denali National Park, 99755
(907) 683-2290

Cozy cabins in the heart of Denali National Park with spectacular views of Mt. Mc-Kinley. All-inclusive package: all meals, lodging, round-trip transportation from park entrance (180 miles), hiking, canoeing, wildlife observation, photography, cycling, rafting, gold panning, evening programs. Naturalists on staff.

NOTES: Credit cards accepted: A Master Card; B Visa; C American Express; D Discover Card; E Diners Club; F Other: 2 Personal checks accepted: 3 Lunch available: 4 Dinner available: 5 Open all year

Hosts: Wallace & Jerryne Cole
Double Cabins: 12 (SB) $200/person; youth $150
Family Cabins (sleep 3-6): 6 (SB) $200/person; youth
$150. 10% discount for 3 or more family members in
same cabin.
Minimum stay; fixed arrival & departure dates
Type of Beds: 25 Twin; 9 Double; 2 Queen
Credit Cards: No
Closed Sept.-May
Notes: 2, 3, 4, 8, 14

Nenana Cabin

Alaska Private Lodgings
Box 200047, Anchorage, 99520
(907) 258-1717

Don't let the outhouse and no running water
frighten you! This is the fanciest outhouse
you ever saw, and water is supplied. Breakfast in the main house. Cabin sleeps four.
$50-75.

North Face Lodge

Denali National Park, 99755
(907) 683-2290

Country inn located in the heart of Denali
National Park, with view of Mt. McKinley.
Vacation price includes: all meals, lodging,
round-trip transportation from park
entrance (180 miles), hiking, canoeing, fishing, cycling, nature photography, wildlife observation, and evening natural-history
programs.

Hosts: Wallace & Jerryne Cole
Doubles: 13 (PB) $205-255/person; youth $154-204
Triples: 1 (PB)
Family Suite (sleeps 4) (PB)
Type of Beds: 31 Twin; 1 Queen
Full Breakfast
Minimum stay: 2-3; fixed arrival & departure dates
Credit Cards: No
Closed Sept.-May
Notes: 2, 3, 4, 8, 14

Rock Creek B&B

Alaska Private Lodgings
Box 200047, Anchorage, 99520
(907) 258-1717

If you are driving to or from Fairbanks or
Denali Park, this B&B is a must! Twenty

miles north of the park entrance and one-
third less cost. Unique log home on the
banks of the Nenana River. Two guest
rooms with shared bath. Animal pet/wild-
game display on walls. Sled-dog-mushing
host will be a great source of information.
Full breakfast, shared bath. $50-60.

FAIRBANKS

Eleanor's Inn

Alaska Private Lodgings
Box 200047, Anchorage, 99520
(907) 258-1717

Close to town and within walking distance to
the Visitors' Center. Host has lots of good
ideas for seeing Fairbanks. Full breakfast is
served. Three guest rooms, shared bath and
private bath. $36-48.

Fairbanks Bed & Breakfast

Box 74573, 99707
(907) 452-4967

We are an old Alaskan family, active gold
miners, with rooms in two different houses
close to town and the bus stop. Our rooms
vary from single to king with a private bath.
We encourage the use of our spacious living
room, yard, and deck, and you can pan gold
if you feel so inclined. Laundry facilities
available for a small fee. Two miles from the
university; four from the airport. Special
dietary needs accommodated.

Hosts: Greg & Barbara Neubauer
Singles: (SB) $36 plus tax
Doubles: (SB) $48 plus tax
Rooms with private bath: $68 plus tax
Type of Beds: 4 Twin; 2 Double; 2 Queen; 1 King
Full Breakfast
Credit Cards: A, B
Notes: 2, 5, 8, 10, 11, 14

Joan's Bed & Breakfast

5101 Electra, 99709
(907) 479-6918

Comfortable rooms three minutes from the airport. Near the riverboat *Discovery*, University of Alaska. Free pick up at the airport, bus, or train, and a senior citizen discount is offered.

Doubles: 4 (SB) $30-40
Type of Beds: 1 Twin; 3 Queen
Full Breakfast
Credit Cards: No
Notes: 2, 5, 7, 8, 9

Glacier Bay Country Inn

GUSTAVUS

Glacier Bay Country Inn

Box 5-ND, 99826
(907) 697-2288

Peaceful storybook accommodations away from the crowds in a wilderness setting. Cozy comforters, warm flannel sheets. Superb dining features local seafood, garden-fresh produce, home-baked breads, spectacular desserts. Fishing, whale watching, sightseeing aboard our deluxe 42-foot yacht. Glacier Bay boat/plane tours.

Hosts: Al & Annie Unrein
Singles: 1(SB) $89 AP
Doubles: 6(1 SB; 5 PB) $168 AP
Type of Beds: 7 Twin; 1 Double; 4 Queen
Full Breakfast
Credit Cards: No
Dinner included in daily rate
Notes: 2, 4, 5, 8, 9, 13

Gustavus Inn

Box 60, 99826
(907) 697-2254

Glacier Bay's historic homestead, newly renovated, full-service inn accommodates twenty-six. Family-style meals, seafood, garden produce, wild edibles. Boat tours of Glacier Bay, charter fishing, and air transportation from Juneau arranged. Bikes and airport transfers included in the daily rates. American Plan also available.

Hosts: David & Jo Ann Lesh
Doubles: 12 (7 PB; 5 SB) $70/person
Type of Beds: 16 Twin; 3 Double; 8 Queen
Full Breakfast
Credit Cards: A, B
Closed Sept. 20 - May 1
Notes: 2, 3, 4, 7, 8, 14

Gustavus Inn

Puffin's Bed & Breakfast

1/4 Mile Logging Road, Box 3, 99826
(907) 697-2260; winter: (907) 789-9787

Your own modern cottage on a 4 acre, partially wooded homestead carpeted in wild flowers and berries. Special diets accommodated. Hike beaches or bicycle miles of country roads. See marine life from a charter cruiser or kayak. Courtesy transportation; Glacier Bay tours, travel services available.

Hosts: Chuck & Sandy Schroth
Cottages: 3 (PB) $30-40; children under 12: $5; under 2: free
Full Breakfast

NOTES: Credit cards accepted: A Master Card; B Visa; C American Express; D Discover Card; E Diners Club; F Other: 2 Personal checks accepted: 3 Lunch available: 4 Dinner available: 5 Open all year

Credit Cards: A, B, C
Closed Oct. 15-April 15
Notes: 3, 4, 6, 7, 8, 9, 14

HAINES

The Summer Inn Bed & Breakfast

247 Second Avenue, Box 1198, 99827
(907) 766-2970

The Summer Inn Bed & Breakfast is a five-bedroom historical house with a live-in Innkeeper. Located near the heart of downtown, it is within walking distance to the sights of Haines and close to the Chilkat Bald Eagle Preserve.

Hosts: Mary Ellen & Bob Summer
Doubles: 5.5 (SB) $57.75 (US)
Type of Beds: 7 Twin; 2 Double
Full Breakfast
Credit Cards: A, B
Notes: 2, 5, 8, 10, 11, 12, 13, 14

Brass Ring Bed and Breakfast

HOMER

Brass Ring Bed & Breakfast

987 Hillfair Court, 99603
(907) 235-5450

Our traditional log home offers a country atmosphere with five individually decorated rooms. We feature a full Alaskan breakfast each morning, including sourdough blueberry pancakes and reindeer sausage. Guests will enjoy the convenient location near the airport, waterfront, and downtown shops and restaurants. We are only minutes from some of the best salmon and halibut fishing in the world.

Hosts: Guy & Renee Doyle
Doubles: 5 (S2.5B) $50-60
Full Breakfast
Credit Cards: A, B
Notes: 2 (in advance), 5, 7 (outdoors), 8 (5 and over), 10, 11, 12, 13, 14

Homer Magic Canyon

Alaska Private Lodgings
Box 200047, Anchorage, 99520
(907) 258-1717

There's a superb view of Kachemak Bay from this unique B&B five miles from Homer. Host is Alaska historian, anthropologist, and hand weaver. Hike the ranch property or take a guided nature walk. Host will arrange fishing or sightseeing tours. Farm-fresh breakfast; hot tub. Two rooms, one with shared bath, one with private. $60-75.

Seaside Farm B & B

HCR 58335 East End Road, 99603
(907) 235-7850

Charming furnished housekeeping cottages on a working pioneer farm. Spectacular views of the ocean, mountains, glaciers. Friendly Morgan horses, children's pony, ducklings, cocker spaniels. Enjoy bird watching, bald eagles, wild flowers, raspberry picking, beachcombing, picnicking, fishing, riding along a fifteen-mile beach. Relaxing family getaway.

Hosts: Mairiis Hollister
Cabins: 5 (SB) $40-45
Continental Breakfast
Minimum stay weekends & holidays: 2
Children under 12 free

6 Pets welcome: 7 Smoking allowed: 8 Children welcome: 9 Social drinking allowed: 10 Tennis available: 11 Swimming available: 12 Golf available: 13 Skiing available: 14 May be booked through travel agents

Credit Cards: B
Closed Oct.-April
Notes: 2, 6, 7, 8, 9, 11

JUNEAU

The Lost Chord

2200 Fritz Cove Road, 99801
(907) 789-7296

This music business on an exquisite private beach has expanded to become a homey B&B. Breakfast with the proprietors, who have been in Alaska since 1946. Since we are located in the country twelve miles from Juneau, a car is suggested.

Hosts: Jesse & Ellen Jones
Singles: 1 (SB) $35
Doubles: 2 (1 PB; 1 SB) $45
Suite: 1 (PB) $75
Type of Beds: 2 Twin; 2 Double
Full Breakfast
Credit Cards: No
Notes: 2, 5, 6 (small), 7 (limited), 8, 10, 11, 12, 13

KETCHIKAN

North Tongass B & B

Box 684, 99928
(907) 247-2467

Friendly Alaskan hospitality, just minutes from Ketchikan. Near fine restaurants, grocery stores, and boat harbors. Lovely beach home with private guest quarters, entry, deck, and sitting room. Also quaint two-bedroom apartment nestled in the woods. Freezers available for your catch.

Hosts: Doug & Lynda Ruhl, Daryle & Wanda Vandergriff
Singles: 6 (SB) $40
Doubles: 4 (SB) $60
Continental Breakfast
Credit Cards: No
Notes: 2, 5, 6, 8, 9, 11, 14

KODIAK

Kalsin Bay Inn

Box 1696, 99615
(907) 486-2659

We are centrally located in the heart of fishing and hunting territory, near fossil beds and World War II bunkers. Satellite TV, laundry facilities, package store, and restaurant.

Hosts: Virginia Sargent & Wayne Sargent
Doubles: 10 (SB) $40-55
Full Breakfast
Credit Cards: No
Notes: 2, 3, 4, 5, 6, 7, 8

PALMER

Pollens' Bed & Breakfast

HC 01, Box 6005D, 99645
(907) 745-8920

One mile from Palmer in quiet woods; clean, modern, and private. Choose continental breakfast or sourdough pancakes and eggs; both included in rate. Lifelong Alaskan hosts offer you genuine hospitality. Bike trail for jogging and hills for hiking close by.

Hosts: Ben & Sally Pollen
Doubles: 1 (PB) $40-45
Continental or Full Breakfast
Credit Cards: No
Notes: 2, 5, 8

SEWARD

Moose River B&B

Alaska Private Lodgings
Box 200047, Anchorage, 99520
(907) 258-1717

Ninety-seven miles from Anchorage and twenty-nine miles from Seward. Enjoy the view of Trail Lake, hike part of the historic Iditarod trail, or go fishing. Full breakfast. Shared bath. $40-45.

NOTES: Credit cards accepted: A Master Card; B Visa; C American Express; D Discover Card; E Diners Club; F Other: 2 Personal checks accepted: 3 Lunch available: 4 Dinner available: 5 Open all year

White House B&B

Alaska Private Lodgings
Box 200047, Anchorage, 99520
(907) 258-1717

Delightful place to stay when you take the unforgettable Kenai Fjords trip into Resurrection Bay. Hosts are a hardworking young couple who will help you have a pleasant stay. Three guest rooms, shared bath, full breakfast. $40-50.

SITKA

Helga's Bed & Breakfast

Box 1885, 99835
(907) 747-5497

Helga's B&B is located directly on Sitka Sound, on the bus route to the ferry. Outside barbecue is available for the guests, and some rooms have mini-kitchens. Our two-bedroom apartment is perfect for families or two couples traveling together. Joe will take you out on a fishing charter in the evenings or weekends, or on a photo or sightseeing trip, if you prefer.

Host: Helga Garrison & family
Doubles: 5 (2 PB; 3 SB) $40-50
Type of Beds: 4 Twin; 2 Double; 1 Queen
Full Breakfast
Credit Cards: A, B
Notes: 2, 5, 7, 8, 9

Karras Bed & Breakfast

230 Kogwanton Street, 99835
(907) 747-3978

Centrally located, overlooking Sitka Sound, the fishing fleet, and the Pacific Ocean. Walk to Sitka's main historical attractions, restaurants, and shopping. Telescope-equipped family room for lounging, reading, visiting, and watching the endlessly fascinating marine traffic. No smoking or alcoholic beverages allowed in the house.

Hosts: Pete & Bertha Karras
Singles: 9 (SB) $32.40-37.80
Doubles: 5 (SB) $48.60-54
Type of Beds: 9 Twin; 1 Double; 1 Queen
Full Breakfast
Credit Cards: No
Notes: 2, 5

SOLDOTNA

Riverside B&B

Alaska Private Lodgings
Box 200047, Anchorage, 99520
(907) 258-1717

On the banks of the famous Kenai River, this wonderful log home can be the highlight of your trip. Make your reservation early if a King Salmon is part of your travel plan. Young hosts will even show you how to clean and cook your catch. Free pick up at Soldotna airport. Full breakfast. $75.

VALDEZ

Chalet Alpine View

Alaska Private Lodgings
Box 200047, Anchorage, 99520.
(907) 258-1717

Walk from the ferry to this home. German-speaking host offers wonderful hospitality in an alpine canyon setting. Two rooms, continental breakfast, shared bath. $55-65.

The Garden House

Box 2017, 99686
(907) 835-2957

Indoor garden atmosphere with a spectacular view of the mountains. Close to the ferry terminal. Excellent hiking right out the back door up to Mineral Creek Canyon or down to the shores of Prince William Sound.

Host: Theresa Svancara
Doubles: 4 (1 PB; 3 SB) $50-55
Type of Beds: 2 Twin; 2 Queen; 1 King
Continental Breakfast
Credit Cards: No

---

6 Pets welcome: 7 Smoking allowed: 8 Children welcome: 9 Social drinking allowed: 10 Tennis available: 11 Swimming available: 12 Golf available: 13 Skiing available: 14 May be booked through travel agents

Closed Oct. - April
Notes: 2, 8, 9, 10, 11

Johnson House

Box 364, 99686
(907) 835-5289

Five rooms share three baths. Cable TV in rooms; sauna; large-screen TV. Tennis, indoor swimming pool nearby. Free airport and ferry transfers. We offer a discount for cash payment.

Host: Brian K. Johnson
Singles: 2 (PB avail) $50-70
Doubles: 3 (PB avail) $50-70
Continental Breakfast
Credit Cards: A, B
Notes: 2, 5, 8, 9

WASILLA

Wasilla Lake

Alaska Private Lodgings
Box 200047, Anchorage, 99520
(907) 258-1717

There are two guest rooms in this wonderful lakeside home. Host is an enthusiastic gardener. Pontoon boat rides available. Full breakfast, shared bath. $40-50.

Yukon Don's

HC 315086, 99687
(907) 376-7472

Yukon Don's is an extraordinary B&B inn. Each room is decorated in a specific Alaskan theme (Iditarod, fishing, hunting, Klondike, etc.). Our 900-square-foot Alaska room is the guest lounge, furnished with an Alaskana collection, pool table, foosball, darts, Alaska video library, and more. The 270-degree view of the Chugach and Talkectna Mountains is unequaled.

Hosts: Don & Kristan Tanner & Aaron Jesse Kristi
Singles: 2 (SB) $45
Doubles: 4 (1 PB; 3 SB) $55
Suite: 1 (PB) $65
Type of Beds: 4 Twin; 2 Double; 4 Queen
Continental Breakfast
Credit Cards: No
Notes: 2, 5, 11, 12, 13, 14

WILLOW

Wilderness B&B

Alaska Private Lodgings
Box 200047, Anchorage, 99520
(907) 258-1717

A spacious wilderness log home you can stop at on the way to or from Denali National Park. Your host will share fishing stories and travel adventures with you. Two guest rooms, each with private bath. Front-yard airstrip. Full breakfast. $40-50.

Willow Trading Post Lodge

Willow Station Road, Box 49, 99688
(907) 495-6457

The ideal place to stop on your way to Mt. McKinley and explore the Susitna Valley. Old Alaskan charm, just off the Parks Highway. Beautiful flowers, wonderful local fishing, view of Mt. McKinley. Favorite meeting place for local residents. Ask for special B&B rates.

Hosts: Stella & Helen
Doubles: 13 (5 PB; 7 SB) $31.50-131.50
Type of Beds: 23 Twin; 6 Double
Continental Breakfast
Credit Cards: No
Notes: 4, 5, 6, 7, 8, 9

Arizona

AJO

AJO101

B&B in Arizona
Box 85252, Scottsdale, 85252
(602) 995-2831

A mine manager's home built at the turn of the century and completely renovated in the style of the period. Breakfast is lavish. If you fly in, hosts will, by prearrangement, pick you up at the airport in their antique Packard. Golf course nearby. All four rooms have private baths. $49-89.

APACHE JUNCTION

AJ102

B&B in Arizona
Box 85252, Scottsdale, 85252
(602) 995-2831

A ranch family used this guest ranch as headquarters for their cattle operation in the White Mountains. A two-hour horseback ride and full breakfast is included with the B&B rate. Full American Plan is also available. Smoking permitted. Open Oct. 1 - May 1. $74-117.

BISBEE

BE102

B&B in Arizona
Box 85252, Scottsdale, 85252
(602) 995-2831

An 1890 brick home built by the town judge. The hosts are most friendly and serve a whopping breakfast. This country home with sun porch and family room has country decor. One double room and one twin room with connecting bath. $45-55.

BE106

B&B in Arizona
Box 8628, Scottsdale, 85252
(602) 995-2831

Descended from the original settlers of Bisbee, this delightful host couple know the lore and tradition of the area. Breakfasts feature fresh bread and goodies of your choice (the hostess owns a bakery and a restaurant). The spacious 1912 home faces a park, so tennis and golf are only a few steps away. All bedrooms are upstairs. Luxurious room with queen waterbed, large private bath, and terrace: $51-75. Room with double bed, private hall bath, and terrace: $35-50. No children or pets; resident cat.

CAVE CREEK

Mi Casa Su Casa #233

Box 950, Tempe, 85280
(800) 456-0682

Located eight miles east of I-17 near New River Road, on 10 acres. A variety of high Sonoran desert flora and fauna and old gold diggings can be found on the property, which is adjacent to state land. Some German spoken. Within a half hour are a living museum; Pioneer Village; Lake Pleasant; Black Canyon Gun Club; riding stables; gliding; hot-air ballooning; Dave Creek Museum; and the town of Carefree, with its

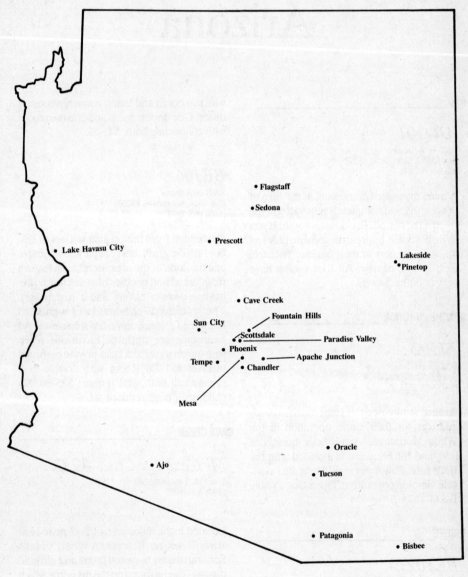

- Flagstaff
- Sedona
- Prescott
- Lake Havasu City
- Lakeside
- Pinetop
- Cave Creek
- Fountain Hills
- Sun City
- Scottsdale
- Paradise Valley
- Phoenix
- Apache Junction
- Tempe
- Chandler
- Mesa
- Oracle
- Ajo
- Tucson
- Patagonia
- Bisbee

ARIZONA

shopping, dining, and scenic drives. Resident car, dogs, horses.

Doubles: 1 (PB) $45-50
Type of Beds: 1 Queen
Full Breakfast
Minimum stay: 2
Credit Cards: No
Notes: 5, 7, 9, 10, 11, 12, 14

CHANDLER

Cone's Tourist Home

2804 W. Warner Road, 85224
(602) 839-0369

Our lovely contemporary home is situated on 2 acres and is 18 miles southeast of downtown Phoenix (15 miles from Sky Harbor Airport). The main guest room has a private hall bath, television, VCR, and telephone.

Hosts: Howard & Beverly Cone
Doubles: 1 (PB) $30
Type of Beds: 1 Double; 1 Queen
Continental Breakfast
Minimum stay: 2
Credit Cards: No
Closed June 1 - Sept. 15
Notes: 7, 8, 9, 10, 11, 12

FLAGSTAFF

Arizona Mountain Inn

685 Lake Mary Road, 86001
(602) 774-8959

Our Old English Tudor-style inn and cottages are located about three miles from Flagstaff. We have 13 wooded acres surrounded by national forest. Our rooms are decorated in antiques, crystal, and lace in a beautiful mix of European charm and classic Southwestern elegance.

Hosts: The Wanek Family
Doubles: 5 (1 PB; 4 SB) $50-100
Type of beds: 3 Twin; 1 Double; 1 Queen; 2 King
Credit Cards: A, B
Notes: 2, 5, 9, 13

Dierker House

423 West Cherry, 86001
(602) 774-3249

In beautiful mountain-pine country. Guest rooms are on the second floor of a spacious, historic home. A private entrance leads to a sitting TV room and pleasant, sunny guest kitchen. Quiet and extremely comfortable antique decor with many generous extras.

Host: Dorothea Dierker
Singles: 1 (SB) $26
Doubles: 2 (SB) $40
Type of Beds: 2 Twin; 1 Double; 2 King
Full Breakfast
Credit Cards: No
Notes: 2, 5, 6, 8 (over 12), 9, 10, 13

Dierker House

FS101

B&B in Arizona
Box 8628, Scottsdale, 85252
(602) 995-2831

This beautiful Tudor-style home boasts elegance and comfort among the pines in a prestigious area of Flagstaff. The TV balcony area looks down on a large living room with fireplace, or you may enjoy the view from the patio. The hostess is a great cook. Three upstairs bedrooms share a hall bath. One has a queen bed, one has two queen beds, and the last has two twins. $35-75.

6 Pets welcome: 7 Smoking allowed: 8 Children welcome: 9 Social drinking allowed: 10 Tennis available: 11 Swimming available: 12 Golf available: 13 Skiing available: 14 May be booked through travel agents

FS102

B&B in Arizona
Box 85252, Scottsdale, 85252
(602) 995-2831

Nestled in the pines at the base of the San Francisco Mountains, near hiking trails through thousands of acres of national forest. Private master suite with kitchenette, wet bar, king bed, and spa. Twenty minutes to Northern Arizona University. Resident dog and cat; continental breakfast. $65.

FS105

B&B in Arizona
Box 85252, Scottsdale, 85252
(602) 995-2831

Lovely, spacious home with contemporary design in the forest. Hostess is a native Arizonan and very helpful. Large living room with grand piano, Southwestern artifacts, and art. One room with double bed, one with single; shared hall bath. Smoking is permitted; older children allowed; full breakfast. $25-50.

FS106

B&B in Arizona
Box 8628, Scottsdale, 85252
(602) 995-2831

This home has a guest suite with double bed and private bath and a bedroom with a single bed. Third person in party may have this for substantially less than the single-room rate. Hosts are next-door neighbors to FS105, thus allowing a large party to stay together. Married couples only; children welcome. Not available from November to April. $35-50.

Mi Casa Su Casa #100

Box 950, Tempe, 85280
(800) 456-0682

Near Beal Road, this split ranch-style home is in one of Flagstaff's nicest areas, among tall pines near the San Francisco Peaks and the scenic route to the Grand Canyon. First-floor guest rooms, rec room with cable TV, VCR, and fireplace. Five to ten minutes to park, tennis courts, Northern Arizona University, museums, art galleries, historical observatory. Within easy driving distance of Sunset Crater, Walnut Canyon, Meteor Crater, Montezuma Castle, Sedona, Oak Creek Canyon, Grand Canyon, Painted Desert, Petrified Forest.

Doubles: 2 (SB) $35-45
Type of Beds: 2 King; 2 Sofabed
Full Breakfast
Minimum stay: 2
Credit Cards: No
Notes: 5, 7 (outside), 8, 9, 10, 11, 12, 14

Mi Casa Su Casa #190

Box 950, Tempe, 85280
(800) 456-0682

Near I-40 and Butler Avenue, this Tudor mansion in the Country Club area has an hospitable, helpful hostess. Resident chocoholic dog.

Doubles: 4 (1 PB; 3 SB) $45-60
Type of Beds: 2 Twin; 4 Queen
Continental Breakfast
Minimum stay: 2
Credit Cards: No
Notes: 5, 8, 9, 11, 12, 14

FOUNTAIN HILLS

FH102

B&B in Arizona
Box 85252, Scottsdale, 85252
(602) 995-2831

A true palace on a hilltop in the desert, four miles from the Mayo Clinic. Two bedrooms, one with a motionless queen waterbed and private hall bath, another with a four-poster bed and connecting bath. Pool, patio, garden, and tennis court on the premises. Full breakfast. $85-110.

NOTES: Credit cards accepted: A Master Card; B Visa; C American Express; D Discover Card; E Diners Club; F Other: 2 Personal checks accepted: 3 Lunch available: 4 Dinner available: 5 Open all year

FH103

B&B in Arizona
Box 85252, Scottsdale, 85252
(602) 995-2831

Spanish territorial style home hosted by a retired European importer and fashion designer who speaks German, French, Italian, and English. Guests may use the athletic club with tennis, gym, and pool. Huge bath with chaise lounge, tub, and shower. Room with queen sofa bed and another with queen bed and connecting bath. Smoking is permitted. Full breakfast. $60-80.

LAKE HAVASU CITY

LH101

B&B in Arizona
Box 85252, Scottsdale, 85252
(602) 995-2831

This home is a delight! The host has hosted B&Bs elsewhere in the world, and he'll go out of his way to orient you and make you comfortable. Master suite with two twins that can make one king, full kitchen, private bath, private entrance. Full breakfast. Small pool in the backyard. $55-65.

LH102

B&B in Arizona
Box 85252, Scottsdale, 85252
(602) 995-2831

A very nice Spanish-style home right on a golf course tee. The back patio has a pool. The view looks across the golf-course green to the raw desert mountain ranges on the other side of the lake. Private downstairs suite with queen hideabed, private entrance, private bath. Upstairs king bedroom with private bath. Full breakfast. $50-60.

LAKESIDE-PINETOP

LS101

B&B in Arizona
Box 85252, Scottsdale, 85252
(602) 995-2831

The full breakfast here is outstanding! Homemade biscuits with sausage gravy, two kinds of muffins, three breakfast meats, eggs cooked to order, fruit compote with cream sauce, and more! This house is on the Fort Apache Indian Reservation boundary, half a mile from Zane Grey's famous Mogollon rim. Hiking and cross-country ski trails are right out the door; downhill skiing is thirty miles away. One queen room with private bath, plus double and queen rooms with a shared bath. $45-65.

MESA

ME101

B&B in Arizona
Box 8628, Scottsdale, 85252
(602) 995-2831

Spanish-style home furnished with antiques. Breakfast is served on the covered patio by your hostess, who is a professional caterer. Pool, heated spa, fireplace. Master suite has a queen waterbed and large connecting bath. One double-bedded room has a hall bath. A queen and a double room share the hall bath. $35-50.

ME102

B&B in Arizona
Box 8628, Scottsdale, 85252
(602) 995-2831

Lovely airy townhome in a retirement community. Private suite with twin beds, connecting bath, and dressing area. The bedroom's Arcadia door looks out on green grass, palm trees, and a pool. Golf is a stroll away. Not far from Superstition Mountain wilderness. Full breakfast; smoking permitted. Not available June, July, and August. $35-50.

ME103

B&B in Arizona
Box 8628, Scottsdale, 85252
(602) 995-2831

Guest house with queen bed, private entrance, and pool. Beautiful view of the lake. Small refrigerator, microwave, coffee maker, and electric skillet. Private bath; gazebo. Continental breakfast on weekdays and full on weekends. Children welcome. $51075.

Mi Casa Su Casa #113

Box 950, Tempe, 85280
(800) 456-0682

Near Lindsay and McKellips, this new Spanish style home is furnished with Minnesota antiques and Southwest decor. The hostess is a professional caterer and great cook. Pool (not heated) and heated spa; fireplace in family room. Two small resident dogs .Only twenty minutes to the surrounding cities.

Doubles: 2 (SB) $40-55
Type of Beds: 1 Double; 2 Queen
Full Breakfast
Credit Cards: No
Notes: 5, 7, 8, 9, 10, 11, 14

Mi Casa Su Casa #220

Box 950, Tempe, 85280
(800) 456-0682

Warm, hospitable, retired couple from Minnesota welcomes guests to their shining ranch-style home in a quiet neighborhood. The hostess, an excellent cook, offers a large variety of full breakfasts. Crib available, light kitchen and laundry facilities. Twenty minutes to the surrounding cities.

Singles: 1 (SB) $25
Doubles: 2 (1 PB; 1 SB) $35
Type of Beds: 1 Double; 1 Queen
Full Breakfast
Minimum stay: 2
Credit Cards: No
Notes: 2, 5, 8, 9, 10, 11, 14

ORACLE

OR101

B&B in Arizona
Box 85252, Scottsdale, 85252
(602) 995-2831

Original homestead ranch with a number of cottages, great conversation, and an ample breakfast that is announced by the smell of fresh-baked homemade cinnamon rolls. Cozy ivy-covered cottage with queen room and private bath. Hilltop house overlooking the ranch and the Catalina Mountains has three bedrooms with private bath. $45-85.

PARADISE VALLEY

Mi Casa Su Casa #134

Box 950, Tempe, 85280
(800) 456-0682

Near Lincoln and Scottsdale Road, this house is a spacious Spanish colonial, beautifully landscaped with a desert front yard and tropical backyard with mountain views. Heated diving pool, lacy white gazebo, croquet lawn, extra-large patio. Guests have lunch and dinner privileges at the Mansion Club. Hostess will arrange for tennis and golf privileges. Near fine shopping and restaurants. Resident cat.

Doubles: 3 (2 PB; 1 SB) $55-85
Type of Beds: 3 King or 6 Twin
Full Breakfast
Credit Cards: No
Notes: 5, 6, 7, 8 (over 10), 9, 10, 11, 12, 14

PV103

B&B in Arizona
Box 8628, Scottsdale, 85252
(602) 995-2831

NOTES: Credit cards accepted: A Master Card; B Visa; C American Express; D Discover Card; E Diners Club; F Other: 2 Personal checks accepted: 3 Lunch available: 4 Dinner available: 5 Open all year

Adobe inn built on the slopes of the Phoenix Mountain Preserve, a short drive from the Mayo Clinic, Paradise Valley Mall, golf, and Scottsdale. All accommodations have private entrances, private baths, small refrigerators, and coffee pots. Pool. A private three-bedroom guest house: $76-150. Several rooms in main house: $76-150. Not available in the summer months.

PATAGONIA

PA101

B&B in Arizona
Box 85252, Scottsdale, 85252
(602) 995-2831

A charming adobe home rebuilt from the floor up while preserving the Mexican influence of the region. Your hosts provide a gourmet breakfast and helpful directions to the locale. Guest house with two rooms. One room has twin beds and is wheel chair compatible. The other has a queen bed. Each room has a connecting private bath, private entrance, and fireplace. Two-night minimum. $40-50.

PHOENIX

Bed 'N' Breakfast in Arizona

5995 East Orange Blossom Lane, 85018
(602) 994-3759

Marjorie's charming, magazine-featured home is located in the exclusive Arizona Country Club area. It is furnished in contemporary eclectic furnishings, and you may enjoy the swimming pool. Marjorie's delicious breakfast features Belgian waffles, Swedish pancakes with crepe suzette sauce, and cinnamon raisin French toast with three-berry sauce. Near Scottsdale shopping, A.S.U., and Desert Botanical Gardens.

Host: Marjorie Ann Lindmark
Doubles: 3 (2 PB; 1 SB) $45-55
Type of Beds: 3 Queen; 1 King
Full Breakfast
Minimum stay: 2
Credit Cards: No
Notes: 2, 5, 7, 9, 10, 11, 14

Mi Casa Su Casa #82

Box 950, Tempe, 85280
(800) 456-0682

Near 24th Street and Camelback, in east-central Phoenix, in the Biltmore area, near the best shopping, dining, theaters, airport, and public transportation. Handsome, very large ranch on a double lot with many trees and shrubs, set far back from the street. Pool, antiques, art. Guest room has private entrance and TV. Small room for a third party who will share the bath. Resident dog.

Singles: 1 (SB) $60
Doubles: 1 (PB) $60
Type of Beds: 1 Twin; 1 King
Full Breakfast
Minimum stay: 2
Credit Cards: No
Notes: 5, 7 (outside), 8 (over 10), 9, 10, 11, 12, 13, 14

Mi Casa Su Casa #125A

Box 950, Tempe, 85280
(800) 456-0682

Near Lincoln and Tatum, this restored historic adobe home sits on 2.5 acres of beautiful grounds at the foot of Squaw Peak Mountain. All guest rooms have private exits, baths, refrigerators. Hosts are very friendly and helpful.

Doubles: 5 (PB) $35-75
Type of Beds: 2 Twin; 2 Double; 3 Queen
Continental Breakfast
Minimum stay: 2
Credit Cards: No
Notes: 5, 6, 7, 8, 9, 10, 11, 12, 14

6 Pets welcome: 7 Smoking allowed: 8 Children welcome: 9 Social drinking allowed: 10 Tennis available: 11 Swimming available: 12 Golf available: 13 Skiing available: 14 May be booked through travel agents

Mi Casa Su Casa #155

Box 950, Tempe, 85280
(800) 456-0682

Near Thomas and 5th Avenue, this Spanish-style home was built in the 1930s. It's in a quiet, well-preserved area of Phoenix, five minutes from the Civic Center and within walking distance of restaurants, churches, shopping mall, and city transportation. Resident dog.

Singles: 1 (SB) $40
Doubles: 2 (SB) $45
Type of Beds: 1 Twin; 2 Queen
Full Breakfast
Minimum stay: 2
Credit Cards: No
Notes: 5, 7, 8 (6 and over), 9, 10, 11, 12, 14

Mi Casa Su Casa #207A

Box 950, Tempe, 85280
(800) 456-0682

Near 56th Street and Lafayette Blvd., this large home is on a quiet street known for its handsome homes, large yards, and big trees. Your English hosts serve large, varied breakfasts. Pool and spa.

Doubles: 4 (2 PB; 2 SB) $45-60
Type of Beds: 2 Twin; 1 Queen; 1 King
Full Breakfast
Credit Cards: No
Notes: 5, 7, 8, 9, 10, 11, 12, 14

Mi Casa Su Casa #210

Box 950, Tempe, 85280
(800) 456-0682

Between Northern and Dunlap, near 7th Avenue, this Southwestern contemporary is on an extra-large lot with pool in a quiet area. Hostess enjoys fixing Spanish, French, Scandinavian, and New England breakfasts. Guests have their own den and TV. Resident mini Schnauzer, Himalayan cat, two cockatiels. Five minutes from the freeway; fifteen to downtown Phoenix.

Doubles: 2 (PB) $35-45
Type of Beds: 2 Twin; 1 King waterbed
Full Breakfast
Minimum stay: 2
Credit Cards: No
Notes: 5, 7 (outside), 8 (8 and over), 14

Mi Casa Su Casa #226

Box 950, Tempe, 85280
(800) 456-0682

Near 24th Street and Camelback, in the Biltmore area, near the best shopping, dining, theaters, airport, and city transportation. Beautifully landscaped two-story condominium area with gate guard. Palm trees, green grass, shrubs. Your hostess lives on the second floor. Tennis courts, exercise room , and heated pool are available.

Doubles: 1 (PB) $45-55
Type of Beds: 1 Queen
Continental Breakfast
Credit Cards: No
Notes: 5, 7, 10, 11, 12, 14

PX105

B&B in Arizona
Box 8628, Scottsdale, 85252
(602) 995-2831

A completely restored fifty-year-old home just minutes from downtown and a short walk from the bus lines, St. Joseph's Hospital, and world-famous Barrow Neurological Institute. An urban haven with antiques and warm, friendly hosts. Full breakfast. Queen room with private hall bath and single room. Hosts rent to one party at a time. $35-75.

PX106

B&B in Arizona
Box 8628, Scottsdale, 85252
(602) 995-2831

Sixty-year-old home near the Phoenix country club's golf and tennis. High-ceilinged "great room" with huge fireplace. Charming hosts make their guests feel at home. Pool, large yard with palm trees.

NOTES: Credit cards accepted: A Master Card; B Visa; C American Express; D Discover Card; E Diners Club; F Other: 2 Personal checks accepted: 3 Lunch available: 4 Dinner available: 5 Open all year

Close to downtown area and short walk to bus lines. Twin beds in two rooms; private bath for each room. $35-50.

PX115

B&B in Arizona
Box 8628, Scottsdale, 85252
(602) 995-2831

A never-never land filled with stained glass and antiques, this home has been featured in a number of national and local articles on interior design. Your hostess fixes the breakfast of your choice. Backyard with gazebo, open-pit fireplace, and Jacuzzi is an oasis in the midst of the city. Strategically located between downtown and the Biltmore area. Double-bed room with private hall path. $35-50.

PX117

B&B in Arizona
Box 8628, Scottsdale, 85252
(602) 995-2831

Quiet desert-landscaped home in the midst of the Phoenix North Mountain Area. Well-traveled hostess does B&B in the old British style, serving a full breakfast. Infants or self-sufficient children are accepted. Several golf courses and a trace track are only minutes away. Double-bed and single-bed rooms with private hall bath. Resident dog and cat. $35-50.

PX118

B&B in Arizona
Box 8628, Scottsdale, 85252
(602) 995-2831

Spotless southwestern home on the north slopes of the Phoenix Mountain Preserve, in "horse country." Easy drive to the Mayo Clinic, Paradise Valley Mall. Often the smell of baking bread fills the house. Lovely pool and patio area for sunning and eating out

when the weather is nice, which is most of the time. Master suite with queen bed and connecting bath. Other bedrooms with private hall bath. Not available in mid-summer. $35-50.

PX121

B&B in Arizona
Box 8628, Scottsdale, 85252
(602) 995-2831

English hostess is very gracious and well traveled. One room with two single beds, private bath. This is a shopper's delight near bus lines, Metrocenter, several golf courses. Full breakfast; children welcome. The hostess is out during the day, so you have considerable privacy. $35-50.

PX123

B&B in Arizona
Box 8628, Scottsdale, 85252
(602) 995-2831

Fresh, light ambience in a patio home with common park and large pool guests may use. The delightful hostess loves company and takes good care of her guests. Near the American Graduate School of International Management, Metrocenter, several golf courses. Married couples or single women guests only. Double-bedded room, shared bath. $35-50.

PX125

B&B in Arizona
Box 8628, Scottsdale, 85252
(602) 995-2831

Quiet, immaculate home near the American Graduate School of International Management, Metrocenter, several golf courses. Hosts are very helpful in orienting guests to the area. Homemade cinnamon and pecan rolls, plus a full breakfast. One bedroom with twin beds, one with a double bed; hall bath. $35-50.

PX126

B&B in Arizona
Box 8628, Scottsdale, 85252
(602) 995-2831

Quiet home with antiques, spotlessly maintained by a very friendly hostess. Between Christown Mall and Park Central Malls. Double-bedded room with private bath; twin-bedded room with private bath. Full breakfast. No unmarried couples, please; children welcome. $35-50.

PX137

B&B in Arizona
Box 8628, Scottsdale, 85252
(602) 995-2831

This elegantly furnished condo in the heart of Phoenix is just your cup of tea for culture, conventions, or business. It's a stone's throw from the Civic Plaza, the Phoenix Art Museum, and Symphony Hall. Minutes from the airport, the courts, and Government Mall. Your hostess was born in Ireland and brought up in London and Europe. Upstairs accommodations include twin beds with a connecting bath. No children or pets. Full breakfast. $51-75.

Westways "Private" Resort

Valley of the Sun, Box 41624, 85080
(602) 582-3868

Located in northwest Phoenix, Westways is adjacent to Thunderbird Park and Arrowhead Ranch. Lounge with large-screen TV, VCR, games, library, and fireplace; guest wet bar/refrigerator and microwave available. Radio, TV, and sitting area in each guest room; diving pool, whirlpool, court-yard for guest use. Use of Arrowhead Country Club facilities.

Hosts: Darren Trapp & Brian Curran
Doubles: 6 (PB) $79-130; special rates available
Type of Beds: 2 Double; 4 Queen
Full Breakfast
Reservations necessary
Credit Cards: A, B, C, D
Notes: 2, 4, 5, 9, 10, 11, 12, 14

PRESCOTT

Lynx Creek Farm Bed & Breakfast

Box 4301, 86302
(602) 778-9573

Secluded country setting on beautiful Lynx Creek. Our organic orchard and garden supply fresh fruit and vegetables for scrumptious breakfasts. Spacious suites are filled with antiques and country knick-knacks. Places to visit nearby include the Grand Canyon, Sedona, Jerome, and Phoenix. Spa, croquet, volleyball, horse-shoes, swing set, animals. Gold panning, horseback riding, antique shopping, and fine dining in Prescott.

Host: Greg Temple
Doubles: 3 (PB) $70-90
Type of Beds: 4 Twin; 2 Queen; 3 King
Full Breakfast
Credit Cards: A, B
Notes: 2, 5, 6, 7 (limited), 8, 9, 10, 11, 12, 14

PR105

B&B in Arizona
Box 85252, Scottsdale, 85252
(602) 995-2831

Magnificent house on a hill, a Queen Anne that has been handsomely restored. Full breakfast is served in the main dining room. On the first floor there's a two-room suite with a double bed in each room and connecting bath. Upstairs, there are two queen rooms with private baths and a large king room with private bath. $75-120.

NOTES: Credit cards accepted: A Master Card; B Visa; C American Express; D Discover Card; E Diners Club; F Other: 2 Personal checks accepted: 3 Lunch available: 4 Dinner available: 5 Open all year

PR103

B&B in Arizona
Box 85252, Scottsdale, 85252
(602) 995-2831

Charming multi-story Victorian on the National Register. Two bedrooms upstairs, one with double bed, the other with twins. Ruffled curtains and handmade quilts, all done by the hostess. Crackling fires in the fireplaces warm you in the winter. In the summer you can relax on the porch swing or walk to the courthouse square. Full breakfast. $35-45.

PR 104

B&B in Arizona
Box 85252, Scottsdale, 85252
(602) 995-2831

Meticulously restored lodging house near the courthouse square. Original oak planking is refinished, and the walls are covered with period wallpapers. Bedrooms with twin or queen beds, private baths. Continental breakfast. Smoking permitted. $45-75.

SCOTTSDALE

Mi Casa Su Casa #46

Box 950, Tempe, 85280
(800) 456-0682

Near 68th and McDowell. Your friendly Canadian host lives near a canal with jogging path, the Botanical Gardens, and the Phoenix Zoo. Quick access to Phoenix, Tempe, or central Scottsdale. Guests have the use of the den, TV, and telephone.

Doubles: 1 (PB) $35
Type of Beds: 1 Double
Full Breakfast
Minimum stay: 2
Credit Cards: No
Notes: 5, 7 (outside), 9, 10, 11, 12, 14

Mi Casa Su Casa #66

Box 950, Tempe, 85280
(800) 456-0682

Near Hayden and McDonald. Walk to lighted tennis courts, jog on the canal bank; pool and Jacuzzi across the street. Resident cat. Light kitchen and laundry privileges. Five minutes to shopping and restaurants; ten to Old Scottsdale.

Doubles: 2 (1 PB; 1SB) $30-45
Type of Beds: 1 Double; 1 Queen
Full Breakfast
Credit Cards: No
Notes: 5, 7, 9, 10, 11, 12, 14

Mi Casa Su Casa #189

Box 950, Tempe, 85280
(800) 456-0682

Near Camelback and Scottsdale Road, this tri-level townhouse has a swimming pool and is within walking distance of resorts, art galleries, shopping, and the Civic Center.

Doubles: 1 (PB) $50
Type of Beds: 2 Twin; 1 Hideabed
Full Breakfast
Minimum stay: 2
Credit Cards: No
Notes: 5, 6 (small dog), 7, 9, 10, 11, 14

Mi Casa Su Casa #217

Box 950, Tempe, 85380
(800) 456-0682

Near Shea Blvd. and 104th Street, this contemporary home with pool has a beautiful view of the McDowell Mountains. Near Taliesen West and the Mayo Clinic. Living room with billiard table; wine and hors d'oeuvres served nightly; VCR tapes available.

Doubles: 2 (1 PB; 1 SB) $50-58
Type of Beds: 1 Queen; 1 King
Full Breakfast weekends; Continental weekdays
Minimum stay: 2
Credit Cards: No
Notes: 5, 8 (over 14), 9, 10, 11, 12, 14

6 Pets welcome: 7 Smoking allowed: 8 Children welcome: 9 Social drinking allowed: 10 Tennis available: 11 Swimming available: 12 Golf available: 13 Skiing available: 14 May be booked through travel agents

Mi Casa Su Casa #227

Box 950, Tempe, 85280
(800) 456-0682

Near Pinnacle Peak Road and Pima Road, this architect-designed adobe home sits on 2 acres with landscaped desert flora. Gambel quail and other wildlife come to visit. Pool. Near Fountain Hills, Taliesen West, Mayo Clinic, Tournament Players Club; forty-five minutes to the airport. Personable Irish sheep dog in residence.

Doubles: 1 (PB) $55-65
Type of Beds: 2 Twin
Full Breakfast
Minimum stay: 2
Credit Cards: No
Notes: 5, 9, 10, 11, 12, 14

SD101

B&B in Arizona
Box 8628, Scottsdale, 85252
(602) 995-2831

Desert-landscaped, spotless home with a hostess who loves to bake and serves your breakfast of choice. Pool and covered patio where you can watch the hummingbirds feed. Two blocks to the bus line, minutes to Scottsdale Civic Center, Desert Botanical Garden, Phoenix Zoo, and Papago Park. Fifteen minutes to Sky Harbor Airport. Twin beds with private guest bath; trundle bed available for extra charge. Children welcome. $35-50.

SD107

B&B in Arizona
Box 8628, Scottsdale, 85252
(602) 995-2831

This house always gets rave reviews. Interesting hosts have traveled widely and know how to run a B&B. The pool can be heated at additional cost; free bicycles and golf clubs are available. Seven golf courses are within five minutes of this delightful home, plus many exclusive shops and superb restaurants. Full breakfast. Full breakfast. King-bed master suite with private connecting bath. Groups of three or four can stay in two queen rooms with shared hall bath. $35-50.

SD120

B&B in Arizona
Box 8628, Scottsdale, 85252
(602) 995-2831

Split-level home. Immaculate lower-level suite with queen bed, private bath, sitting area adjacent to dining area. Refrigerator for snacks and drinks. Gracious hostess is a ballet instructor who serves your breakfast of choice with home-baked bread in your suite at a prearranged time. Pool. Minutes to Scottsdale Civic Center, the Borgata and Fashion Square shopping malls, and art galleries. $51-75.

SD124

B&B in Arizona
Box 8628, Scottsdale, 85252
(602) 995-2831

Contemporary home with pool in north Scottsdale, four miles from the Mayo Clinic, offers a beautiful view of the McDowell Mountains. Upstairs bedroom with king bed that can convert to two twins. Refrigerators stocked with soda. Private hall bath with tub and shower. Upstairs room with queen bed is available for parties of four people willing to share the bath. Each room leads into a pool-table area and balcony with private entrance. Continental breakfast on weekdays; full on weekends. $35-75.

SD126

B&B in Arizona
Box 8628, Scottsdale, 85252
(602) 995-2831

NOTES: Credit cards accepted: A Master Card; B Visa; C American Express; D Discover Card; E Diners Club; F Other: 2 Personal checks accepted: 3 Lunch available: 4 Dinner available: 5 Open all year

Southwest adobe home on two acres of desert with a cactus garden. Twin adjustable electric beds with private entrance overlooking the pool; private hall bath. Desert vistas from your window or next to the pool on a covered patio with table and chairs. Enjoy a gourmet breakfast with the lovely host couple. Fifteen minutes from the Mayo Clinic and downtown. $51-75.

SD127

B&B in Arizona
Box 8628, Scottsdale, 85252
(602) 995-2831

Trilevel townhouse with swimming pool, within walking distance of Fashion Square and art galleries. Very nice hostess who will cook you whatever you want for breakfast. She picks oranges off her trees and makes her own marmalade. Cool lower-level studio with sitting area, two twin beds, small refrigerator, cable TV, and stereo. Sitting area with couch and table. Private bath with shower. Enjoy a glass of wine before bed, if you like. $35-75.

SEDONA

Briar Patch Inn

Star Rt. 3, Box 1002, 86336
(602) 282-2342

Eight acres of beautiful grounds along Oak Creek in spectacular Oak Creek Canyon. Rooms and cottages are all delightfully furnished with Southwest charm. A haven for those who appreciate nature amid the wonders of Sedona's mystical beauty. Suitable for small workshops.

Hosts: JoAnn & Ike Olson
Doubles: 15 (PB) $89.62-142.42
Type of Beds: 5 Queen; 10 King
Continental-plus Breakfast
Credit Cards: A, B
Notes: 2, 5, 7, 8, 9, 10, 11, 12, 14

Garland's Oak Creek Lodge

Box 152, 86336
(602) 282-3343

What a delightful surprise this lodge is, tucked away in Oak Creek Canyon eight miles north of Sedona. An oasis of green lawns, gardens, and fruit trees, with fifteen log cabins. Fabulous fresh food graces the tables of the elegant, rustic dining room. Dinner and breakfast are included in the daily rate.

Hosts: Gary & Mary Garland
Cabins: 15 (PB) $128-148 MAP
Type of Beds: 2 Twin; 23 Double; 4 King
Full Breakfast
Credit Cards: A, B
Closed Nov. 15 - March 30
Notes: 2, 4, 7, 8, 9, 10, 11

Graham's B&B Inn

Graham's Bed & Breakfast Inn

150 Canyon Circle Drive, 86336
(602) 284-1425

Graham's Bed & Breakfast Inn was built specifically as an B&B inn, in the modified Suthwest style. Fine paintings and sculpture created by local artists are on display throughout the house. Large, spacious living room with games, books, TV, stereo, etc. Inviting pool and spa in beautifully landscaped grounds. Five guest rooms, each of which has a private bath and private balcony with a view of the spectacular Red

Rock formations that have made Sedona famous. Excellent local restaurants, art galleries, and shops.

Hosts: Bill & Marni Graham
Doubles: 5 (PB) $85-115
Type of Beds: 1 Twin; 2 Queen; 2 King
Full Breakfast
Minimum stay weekends: 2 ; holidays: 2-3
Credit Cards: A, B
Closed Jan. 2-31
Notes: 2 (in advance), 8 (over 12), 10, 11, 12

Mi Casa Su Casa #211

Box 950, Tempe, 85280
(800) 456-0682

Near Soldier Pass Road, this large classic country French house with passive solar design is just five minutes from downtown Senoia. Nestled in an evergreen forest with views of the Red Rock formations from the decks. Guest rooms have their own private wing and patio, remote-control TVs. Sightseeing, hiking, fishing, golf in the area.

Doubles: 2 (1 PB; 1 SB) $70-80
Type of Beds: 1 Double; 1 Queen
Full Breakfast
Minimum stay: 2
Credit Cards: No
Notes: 5, 8, 9, 11, 14

Mi Casa Su Casa #216

Box 950, Tempe, 85280
(800) 456-0682

Near Coffee Pot Drive and highway 89, this home has an outstanding collection of music boxes and is set far back from the road. Friendly retired hosts from Indiana have a lively interest in people and a good sense of humor.

Doubles: 3 (PB) $40-50
Type of Beds: 2 Queen; 1 King
Full Breakfast
Credit Cards: No
Notes: 5, 11, 14

Mi Casa Su Casa #244

Box 950, Tempe, 85280
(800) 456-0682

Near Dry Creek Road and highway 89, this home is located in a quiet evergreen area with many views. Private guest entrance, living room with TV, VCR, a game table, roll-top desk, wood-burning stove, and small kitchen. Heated Jacuzzi.

Doubles: 2 (PB) $75
Type of Beds: 1 Queen; 1 Daybed
Full Breakfast
Minimum stay: 2
Credit Cards: No
Notes: 5, 9, 10, 11, 14

SE114

B&B in Arizona
Box 85252, Scottsdale, 85252
(602) 995-2831

Magnificent view overlooking the Red Rocks and juniper of Sedona. The hostess is a gourmet chef who serves a continental breakfast you won't forget. Late afternoon wine and tea is served with homemade goodies. One suite has a queen bed, dressing room, and a superb view. A second room has twin beds, French doors opening onto a private rose garden. Each room has a private connecting bath and fireplace. Two resident dogs; children welcome; two-night minimum. $83-98.

SUN CITY

Mi Casa Su Casa #222

Box 950, Tempe, 85380
(800) 456-0682

Near Thunderbird and 103rd Avenue, this home is right on a golf course. Previously resort owners, they specialize in serving delicious breakfasts. Citrus trees are on the spacious grounds in this active retirement community. Hosts can arrange for tennis,

NOTES: Credit cards accepted: A Master Card; B Visa; C American Express; D Discover Card; E Diners Club; F Other: 2 Personal checks accepted: 3 Lunch available: 4 Dinner available: 5 Open all year

golf, bowling, and swimming. Day trips to Wildlife Zoo, Laughlin, Sedona, Grand Canyon.

Doubles: 1 (PB) $45-50
Type of Beds: 2 Twin or 1 Queen
Full Breakfast
Minimum stay: 2
Credit Cards: No
Notes: 5, 9, 10, 11, 12, 14

SC104

B&B in Arizona
Box 8628, Scottsdale, 85252
(602) 995-2831

Desert-landscaped home in a clean, quiet neighborhood of Sun City. Friendly host couple serve a full breakfast of choice. Hostess is a national champion doll maker and collector. Pick your own citrus fruit for breakfast when it's in season and eat it on the patio. Twin-bedded room with private hall bath. $35-50.

TEMPE

Mi Casa Su Casa #86

Box 950, 85280
(800) 456-0682

Near McClintock and Baseline, this attractive home in "The Lakes" is minutes from Arizona State University, the freeway, and shopping. Club-house privileges include a heated pool, Jacuzzi, sauna, exercise room, tennis, and racquet-ball courts.

Doubles: 1 (PB) $40
Type of Beds: 2 Twin
Continental Breakfast
Minimum stay: 2
Credit Cards: No
5, 7, 9, 10, 11, 12, 14

Mi Casa Su Casa

Box 950, 85280
(800) 456-0682

Near Southern and Price, this attractive home is minutes from Arizona State and Mesa Community College. Near two large shopping malls and five minutes from Superstition freeway, the home has a tranquil, pleasant atmosphere, with a fireplace in the family room. Guest room has a TV, sliding-glass doors to the patio and pool.

Doubles: 1 (PB) $45-55
Type of Beds: 1 King
Full Breakfast
Minimum stay: 2
Credit Cards: No
Notes: 5, 9, 10, 11, 12, 14

TE103

B&B in Arizona
Box 8628, Scottsdale, 85252
(602) 995-2831

Modern home with unusual decor in the Lakes subdivision, ten minutes from ASU. Artist hostess is experienced in B&B; offers sherry and fruit to welcome the weary traveler. Twin-bedded room with private hall bath. Jacuzzi, sauna, tennis, pool, weight room, and handball courts available to guests. Smoking is permitted; hostess doesn't smoke. Continental breakfast. Special diet requests accommodated. $51-75.

Valley O' the Sun Bed & Breakfast

Box 2214, Scottsdale, 85252
(602) 941-1281

Located on the Scottsdale-Tempe border, within walking distance of Arizona State University. Near restaurants, theaters, and shopping. Swimming, golf, horseback riding, and tennis nearby. Within minutes are the Phoenix Zoo, desert botanical gardens, greyhound dog racing, ASU campus, and the Fiesta Bowl.

Host: Kay Curtis
Doubles: 2 (SB) $25-35
Full or Continental Breakfast
Credit Cards: No
Notes: 5, 7 (limited), 8 (over 12), 9, 10, 11, 12, 14

TUCSON

La Posade Del Valle

1640 N. Campbell Avenue, 85719
(602) 795-3840

An elegant 1920s inn nestled in the heart of
the city with five guest rooms with private
baths and outside entrances. Mature orange
trees perfume the air as guests enjoy a gourmet breakfast and sip tea each afternoon on
the patio overlooking the gardens.

Hosts: Charles & Debbi Bryant
Doubles: 5 (PB) $80-100
Type of Beds: 2 Twin; 2 Queen; 2 King
Full breakfast weekends; continental weekdays
Credit Cards: A, B
Closed July 1 - 31
Notes: 2, 4, 8 (over 12), 9, 10, 11, 12, 14

The Lodge on the Desert

Box 42500, 85733
(800) 456-5634

A small in-town resort hotel providing the
finest in food and accommodations. The
lodge has been under the same family
ownership for over fifty-three years. Close to
golf, tennis, and shopping. One-half hour
from Arizona-Sonora Living Desert
Museum, old Tucson movie location,
Coronado National Forest. Three miles
from the University of Arizona.

Host: Schuyler W. Lininger
Singles: 3 (SB) $44-51
Doubles: 37 (PB and SB) $46-117
Type of Beds: 28 Twin; 24 Queen; 5 King
Continental Breakfast
Credit Cards: A, B, C, E, F
Notes: 2, 3, 4, 5, 6 (call), 7, 8, 9, 10, 11, 12, 14

Mi Casa Su Casa #22

Box 950, Tempe, 85280
(800) 456-0682

Near Ina Road and First Avenue, this large
home in the Catalina Foothills has mountain
and city views and is just fifteen minutes
from the University of Arizona. Pool. Host
smokes. Thirty-five minutes from Sonora
Desert Museum and Old Tucson.

Doubles: 2 (PB) $35-45
Type of Beds: 4 Twin
Full Breakfast
Minimum stay: 2
Credit Cards: No
Notes: 5, 7, 8 (over 14), 9, 10, 11, 12, 14

Mi Casa Su Casa #169

Box 950, Tempe, 85280
(800) 456-0682

Near 22nd Street and Camino Seco, this
comfortable Mediterranean style
townhouse features contemporary decor in
a very quiet neighborhood. Hostess speaks
German fluently. Two pools available, one
of which is heated. Resident cat. Near
Sabino Canyon, Colossal Cave; fifteen
minutes from the University of Arizona.

Doubles: 2 (PB) $35-50
Type of Beds: 2 Queen; 1 Sofabed
Full Breakfast
Credit Cards: No
Notes: 5, 7 (outside), 8, 9, 10, 11, 12, 14

Mi Casa Su Casa #212

Box 950, Tempe, 85280
(800) 456-0682

Near Ina Road and La Canada, this architect-designed guest cottage is heated and
air -conditioned. Heatolator stone fireplace,
kitchen, TV, radio, and phone; private
entrance. Wheel chair accessible. Solar-
heated pool is surrounded by a patio and
citrus trees. Fifteen minutes from the
University of Arizona; thirty-five from
Sonora Desert Museum and Old Tucson.

NOTES: Credit cards accepted: A Master Card; B Visa; C American Express; D Discover Card; E Diners
Club; F Other: 2 Personal checks accepted: 3 Lunch available: 4 Dinner available: 5 Open all year

Doubles: 1 (PB) $60-75
Type of Beds: 1 Twin; 1 King
Full Breakfast
Minimum stay: 2
Credit Cards: No
Notes: 5, 8, 10, 11, 12, 14

Mi Casa Su Casa #223

Box 950, Tempe, 85280
(800) 456-0682

Near Catalina Highway and Houghton Road, this adobe hacienda is one mile east of Tucson. Located on 18 acres, the home overlooks the night lights of Tucson and has a panoramíc view of the mountains. Courtyard with fountain; fireplace.

Doubles: 2 (PB) $75
Type of Beds: 2 Twin; 1 Queen
Full Breakfast
Minimum stay: 2
Credit Cards: No
Notes: 5, 9, 10, 11, 12, 13, 14

Mi Casa Su Casa #242

Box 950, Tempe, 85280
(800) 456-0682

Near Sabino Canyon Road and Sunrise, this prize-winning -design townhouse is just one mile from Sabino Canyon. Upstairs guest wing with two guest rooms, both of which have mountain views. Pool, heated Jacuzzi.

Doubles: 2 (SB) $55
Type of Beds: 2 Queen
Full Breakfast
Minimum stay: 2
Credit Cards: No
Notes: 5, 8, 9, 10, 11, 12, 13, 14

Mi Casa Su Casa #243

Box 950, Tempe, 85280
(800) 456-0682

Near Grant and Campbell, this handsome architect-designed house was built around a large courtyard. Located in a very nice neighborhood three miles northeast of the downtown business district and within walking distance of the University of Arizona and the University Medical Center; near fine dining and public transportation. Pool, private entrance, private guest living room, TV. Two resident cats.

Doubles: 5 (PB) $65
Type of Beds: 2 Twin; 4 Queen
Full Breakfast
Credit Cards: No
Notes: 5, 8 (over 10), 9, 10, 11, 12, 13, 14

Old Pueblo HomeStays #3

Box 13603, Tucson, AZ, 85732
(602) 790-2399

Mesquite Retreat offers desert quiet near the base of Mt. Lemmon, yet easy access to the city — ten minutes to fine dining. This spacious, ranch-style house on over an acre of land is decorated with a blend of traditional and antique furnishings. Guests share living areas with hosts: two TV areas, fireplace, mountain-view patio with pool and spa, laundry facilities. Full breakfast; resident cat and patio dog. Children over twelve welcome; restricted smoking. $40-45.

Old Pueblo HomeStays #4

Box 13603, Tucson, AZ, 85732
(602) 790-2399

Beautiful town house offers a warm, friendly atmosphere in a very quiet neighborhood. Hosts make their own jams and jellies from desert fruit. Fluent German spoken; airport pick up for a small fee. A pool is available from May through October. Your cheery, spacious upstairs suits has a queen bed and sleeper sofa, cable TV, and a private or shared bath. Downstairs room has a queen bed, TV, and private bath. Resident cat. Children over fourteen are welcome. $45-50.

Old Pueblo HomeStays #5

Box 13603, Tucson, AZ, 85732
(602) 790-2399

6 Pets welcome: 7 Smoking allowed: 8 Children welcome: 9 Social drinking allowed: 10 Tennis available: 11 Swimming available: 12 Golf available: 13 Skiing available: 14 May be booked through travel agents

A panoramic view of the Catalina Mountains welcomes you at this newly remodeled home nestled on 2 acres of quiet, lush desert within walking distance of the bus, church, and shopping centers. Two large rooms are available, each with queen beds, TV, walk-in closets, and a bottle of wine. The bath is shared by guests, who may enjoy the pool and waterfall, piano, TV, VCR, stereo, and kitchen/laundry privileges. Children over twelve are welcome; limited smoking. $50-55.

Old Pueblo HomeStays #6

Box 13603, Tucson, AZ, 85732
(602) 790-2399

A lovely townhouse in the Golf Links/Pantano area on the southeast side of Tucson. One large room with twin beds and a private bath. Enclosed patio; pool available May through October. Choice of full or continental breakfast; share family TV; kitchen privileges. $35-45.

Old Pueblo HomeStays #7

Box 13603, Tucson, AZ, 85732
(602) 790-2399

True western atmosphere with separate guest quarters done in southwestern decor. Double bed and private bath. Mules are kept on the property for training; peacocks, dogs, and other critters abound. Many mountain trails for hiking, or walk to a nearby park with an artesian stream. TV and refrigerator in room; breakfast served on a private porch or in the home. Children welcome. $45-50.

Old Pueblo HomeStays #9

Box 13603, Tucson, AZ, 85732
(602) 790-2399

Luxurious self-contained guest house with heat and air-conditioning in a quiet neighborhood. King bed and one twin, fireplace, TV, radio, telephone, private entrance. Accessible by wheel chair. The solar-heated pool is surrounded by a lovely patio. A full breakfast and morning paper are served in the guest house or on the patio. Children over twelve welcome; outdoor smoking only. $60-75.

Old Pueblo HomeStays #10

Box 13603, Tucson, AZ, 85732
(602) 790-2399

The Swan/Sunrise foothills area is considered by most people in Tucson to be the nicest area, due to its being nestled against the Catalina Mountains high above the city, with wonderful views. This townhouse is set in a lush desert-growth area. One room with a king waterbed, private bath, and TV. A pool adjacent to the house is handy for summer enjoyment, and another pool is heated all winter. The Jacuzzi is available all year. Continental breakfast weekdays, full on weekends. Two night minimum, outdoor smoking only. $40-45.

Old Pueblo HomeStays #14

Box 13603, Tucson, AZ, 85732
(602) 790-2399

A warm welcome awaits you at this non-smoking B&B in a quiet residential area in NE Tucson. Guests have a birds-eye view of the mountains from their private garden patio. The suite consists of two bedrooms with double and twin beds, a small sitting room with TV and refrigerator, private bath, and separate entrance. A continental-plus breakfast is served. Resident dog; children over twelve welcome. $35-45.

Old Pueblo HomeStays #15

Box 13603, Tucson, AZ, 85732
(602) 790-2399

Come share the desert solitude in this new home set in the Tucson Mountains on 3 acres. Great city lights and beautiful mountain views. The guest room is furnished with a queen bed, private bath, radio, TV, private entrance with patio. Begin your morning with a desert hike and end your day in the Jacuzzi under the stars. Your selection of breakfast and gourmet coffee with your host. Can accommodate up to four. Smoking outside only; no children. $45-55.

Old Pueblo HomeStays #22

Box 13603, Tucson, AZ, 85732
(602) 790-2399

Nestled snugly under the Tucson Mountains, this home offers a very relaxed, friendly atmosphere. Two rooms, one with a double bed and one with a single. The hostess sets out a very special continental breakfast. Easy access to desert and mountain trails, community center, downtown Tucson, and the University of Arizona. Hall bath for guests' use. Share family room, TV, and pool. Children over twelve welcome. $25-35.

Old Pueblo HomeStays #23

Box 13603, Tucson, AZ, 85732
(602) 790-2399

A neighborhood park surrounded by pleasant homes is the location of this inviting home. One room with twin beds and a private bath, separate entrance, and enclosed patio. Close to shopping, restaurants, theaters, and doctors. Neighborhood pool available for a small fee. Four miles to the University of Arizona. Dog in residence. $25-35.

Old Pueblo HomeStays #24

Box 13603, Tucson, AZ, 85732
(602) 790-2399

Double K Guesthouse. A warm welcome awaits you at this family-oriented, suburban ranch estate. The guest area has a private entrance, patio, bath, two single trundle beds, a double hidabed, and a rollaway. TV, radio, phone, and cozy Ben Franklin fireplace. Pets in residence. Close to a desert oasis, Aqua Caliente Park, with an artesian stream; desert walks and mountain trails. Children welcome, restricted smoking. $45-55.

Old Pueblo HomeStays #26

Box 13603, Tucson, AZ, 85732
(602) 790-2399

If you're looking for plain, old-fashioned hospitality, this is it. Two cozy rooms with double beds share a bath. Guests enjoy the "open door" policy and sharing the host's home, fireplace, pets, and hobbies. Conveniently located near the airport, seven miles from the University of Arizona; close to bus lines and restaurants. Full breakfast served; children welcome. $25-35.

6 Pets welcome: 7 Smoking allowed: 8 Children welcome: 9 Social drinking allowed: 10 Tennis available: 11 Swimming available: 12 Golf available: 13 Skiing available: 14 May be booked through travel agents

Old Pueblo HomeStays #30

Box 13603, Tucson, AZ, 85732
(602) 790-2399

Located in Santo Tomas Village, just north of Green Valley, a short drive from Tubac and only 45 miles from Nogales, the gateway to Mexico. Twin beds, private bath, pool. The family room has TV. Children welcome, outdoor smoking only. $40-45.

Old Pueblo HomeStays #33

Box 13603, Tucson, AZ, 85732
(602) 790-2399

Redbud House is in a quiet NE neighborhood within walking distance of the park, shops, good restaurants, and transportation. Cozy atmosphere with a mountain view, use of the living room with fireplace. Two cheerful bedrooms with twin beds, private bath, and TV. Full or light breakfast offered. Sack lunches prepared at minimal cost. Host speaks some German and Polish. Outdoor smoking only. $34-40.

Old Pueblo HomeStays #35

Box 13603, Tucson, AZ, 85732
(602) 790-2399

Central location on a quiet residential street, convenient to downtown and the University of Arizona via city buses. Walk to mall, restaurants, Reid Park, tennis, golf, and pool. Two rooms with queen bed and twins; guests share hall bath, family room, bumper pool table, color TV, kitchen, patio. Full breakfast with Blue Cornbread. Closed during the summer; children welcome, outdoor smoking only; crib available. $25-35.

Old Pueblo HomeStays #34

Box 13603, Tucson, AZ, 85732
(602) 790-2399

Double Palm Bed & Breakfast is the home of a naturalist, a university faculty member, and a charming toddler. Centrally located near major bus lines, a lovely zoo, Randolph Park, El Con, and the university. Expect whole-grain pancakes, fresh-squeezed orange juice, and fresh-ground coffee for breakfast. The guest room has a mountain view, adjacent private bath, and separate entrance from a covered patio. Children can be accommodated in the family room on a queen hideabed. $25-35.

Old Pueblo HomeStays #36

Box 13603, Tucson, AZ, 85732
(602) 790-2399

The Peppertrees is a unique Victorian built in 1905, dominated by two large pepper trees as old as the house. The rooms have been decorated with furniture that belonged to the hostess' family in England. French doors lead to a quiet patio, across which are two guest houses, each with two bedrooms, living room, full kitchen, and full bath. Within walking distance of the university; two miles to the downtown business district. Full breakfast is offered, plus a midafternoon tea. Children over twelve welcome; smoking outdoors only. $55-100.

Old Pueblo HomeStays #40

Box 13603, Tucson, AZ, 85732
(602) 790-2399

Las Naranjas is nestled in the heart of the university area. Guests have a separate unit with double bed, private bath, and entrance complete with a lovely secluded, washed-brick patio. You are free to entertain your friends or retreat to your own place in the sun and relax. Deluxe continental breakfast. Children welcome; outdoor smoking only. $55.

The Peppertrees, TU115

Old Pueblo HomeStays #52

Box 13603, Tucson, AZ, 85732
(602) 790-2399

Coyote Corners rests in the shadows of the breathtaking Santa Catalina Mountains on a beautiful golf course where guests may play for an added fee. Cable TV, VCR, compact disc and tape player are available in the family room by the fireplace. The pool is available from May to October; cabana, picnic table, and gas barbecue for guest use. Two cozy twin bedrooms, each with their own bath, make for comfortable sleeping. Fresh-ground coffee accompanies your full or continental breakfast. Children welcome. $25-45.

TU102

B&B in Arizona
Box 8628, Scottsdale, 85252
(602) 995-2831

Luxurious contemporary 1100 Square foot guest house with solar-heated pool, patio, and gorgeous views of the mountains. Near gold course and Catalina Mountains. Full kitchen, breakfast bar, stone fireplace, king bed, TV, and own phone. Private connecting bath. Wheel-chair accommodations. Host cat. $51-150.

TU103

B&B in Arizona
Box 8628, Scottsdale, 85252
(602) 995-2831

East Tucson home with great breakfasts! Unheated pool and patio for sunning. Private master suite with double bed and private connecting bath. Double and queen bedrooms share hall bath; also has room with trundle bed. Smoking permitted. $35-75.

TU105

B&B in Arizona
Box 8628, Scottsdale, 85252
(602) 995-2831

German-born hostess serves a full breakfast with homemade breads and rolls and her special jams and preserves. Airport pick up can be provided for a small fee. This townhome boasts two pools, one heated. Queen room with private hall bath. Cheery, spacious suite upstairs with queen bed and queen sofa bed. Connecting bath. Children over fourteen are welcome. Smoking permitted. $35-50.

TU111

B&B in Arizona
Box 8628, Scottsdale, 85252
(602) 995-2831

Charming old southwestern territorial-style home in mid Tucson, near the University of

Arizona. Ranch or continental breakfast, as desired. This home is something of an urban oasis, with flower gardens, fruit trees, and petting animals: two Labs, cat, angora bunnies, and chickens. Small pool. Guest room has a double bed and shared hall bath. $51-75.

TU112

B&B in Arizona
Box 8628, Scottsdale, 85252
(602) 995-2831

Sophisticated, well-traveled hosts have lots to share. Extensive continental breakfast. Home is decorated in authentic Mexican style, reflecting a knowledgeable appreciation of the arts. Situated on 3 acres in the desert in northwest Tucson, where you can watch the wildlife as you soak in the Jacuzzi. City and mountain views. Easy access to the city. Queen bedroom with private hall bath, private patio. $51-75.

TU114

B&B in Arizona
Box 8628, Scottsdale, 85252
(602) 995-2831

This small ranch is high in the Sonoran Desert foothills above Tucson. You can explore ancient Hohokam sites on the hosts' private trail or venture off on nearby National Forest trails. Hosts offer a full ranch breakfast featuring their own fresh eggs. Husband is a physician; wife is a pottery artist. Private guest house with Ben Franklin

stove, private bath, twin and double beds. Jacuzzi and pool available; tennis is five minutes away. Children and pets are welcome. Guests may smoke outside. $51-75.

TU115

B&B in Arizona
Box 8628, Scottsdale, 85252
(602) 995-2831

You will enjoy your stay with this English hostess who lives in a completely restored 1900s house filled with period pieces. Two-minute walk to the University of Arizona campus. The sunny Veranda Room has a queen bed, hall bath: $51-75. A guest house has two bedrooms, one queen and one double bed, and a hall bath. Children eight and over are welcome: $51-75. Hostess has a shy outside dog.

TU116

B&B in Arizona
Box 8628, Scottsdale, 85252
(602) 995-2831

The Desert Yankee is located in a quiet neighborhood in central Tucson, within walking distance of the University of Arizona and the University Medical Center. A continental breakfast of homemade sweet rolls, muffins, and bread is served in the dining room or in a lovely courtyard with flowers and greenery. Guests are invited to enjoy the pool. Mount Lemon is thirty minutes away, and Old Mexico is an hour. Three rooms with private baths; children sixteen and up are welcome. $51-75.

Arkansas

A304

Ozark Mountain Country B&B
Box 295, Branson, MO, 65616
(417) 334-4720

Private upstairs suite for two in a country atmosphere on highway 62 between Alpena and Green Forest, twenty-five miles from Eureka Springs. The home offers a large suite with queen bed (plus additional bed), private bath, lounging area, and ceiling fans.

Doubles: 1 (PB) $30-35
Type of Beds: 1 Twin; 1 Queen
Full Breakfast
Closed Dec. - March
Credit Cards: No

Arkansas & Ozarks B&B
ABV01

Route 1, Box 38
Calico Rock, Arkansas, 72519
(501) 297-8764

A restored 1870s Victorian home beautifully decorated with antique and contemporary furnishings. Your sitting room/bedroom has an old-fashioned queen four-poster bed, and there's an adjoining library and private bath. Complimentary cheese and wine, full breakfast in your room or the dining room. Arkansas College is in Batesville, and the White River winds through town. $55.

The Great Southern Hotel

127 West Cedar, 72021
(501) 734-4955

Grand times and true Southern hospitality await you at the Great Southern Hotel. Restored in true Victorian elegance, with rooms that reflect a quaint, homey atmosphere reminiscent of bygone days. Fine dining in the award-winning Victorian Tearoom.

Hosts: Stanley & Dorcas Prince
Doubles: 4 (PB), $38.18-$42.40
Type of Beds: 4 Double
Full Breakfast
Credit Cards: A, B, C, D, F
Notes: 2 (for reservation confirmation), 4, 5, 8, 9

Arkansas & Ozarks B&B
ACR01

Route 1, Box 38
Calico Rock, Arkansas, 72519
(501) 297-8764

Isolated country home on a 300-foot bluff overlooking the beautiful White River. A large country breakfast is served on a deck outside your room so you can enjoy the view of the mountains and mist-filled valley below. Your host can arrange trout fishing and river float trips or direct you to Blanchard Springs Caverns and the Ozark Folk Center. Wheel chair accessible house. $28-35.

6 Pets welcome: 7 Smoking allowed: 8 Children welcome: 9 Social drinking allowed: 10 Tennis available: 11 Swimming available: 12 Golf available: 13 Skiing available: 14 May be booked through travel agents

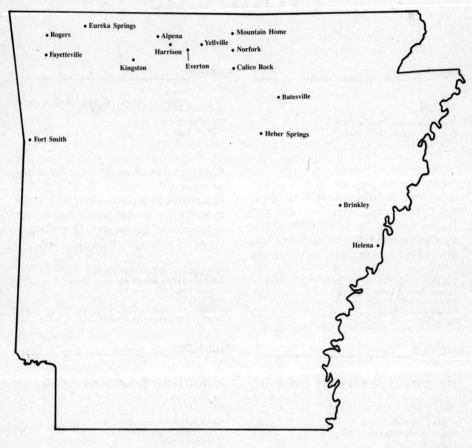

- Eureka Springs
- Rogers
- Fayetteville
- Alpena
- Mountain Home
- Harrison
- Yellville
- Norfork
- Kingston
- Everton
- Calico Rock
- Batesville
- Fort Smith
- Heber Springs
- Brinkley
- Helena

ARKANSAS

Arkansas & Ozarks B&B
ACR03

Route 1, Box 38
Calico Rock, Arkansas, 72519
(501) 297-8764

This new contemporary home in a secluded woodland setting offers amenities bound to please even the most demanding. A delicious full breakfast is served in the private sun room adjoining your quarters, or you may join the family in the dining room. There's a large family room, TV, a hot tub, a pool table. A year-round spring-fed creek is a short walk away (sometimes suitable for tubing). Children are welcome here. $30-35.

EUREKA SPRINGS _____

A302-B

Ozark Mountain Country B&B
Box 295, Branson, MO, 65616
(417) 334-4720

This quaint cottage is convenient to the historic district but in a secluded, private setting. Furnished with English country antiques, collectibles, Oriental rugs, and paintings. Guests can relax and watch the birds from the tree-top deck or enjoy the rock gardens from the front-porch swing.

Doubles: 2 (SB) $55
Type of Beds: 1 Double; 1 Queen
Continental Breakfast
Credit Cards: No
Notes: 6, 8

A305

Ozark Mountain Country B&B
Box 295, Branson, MO, 65616
(417) 334-4720

This restored country Victorian is whimsically decorated with antiques and unexpected treasures. Breakfast is served on the balcony overlooking the fantasy garden below. Air-conditioning, homemade quilts, brass and iron bedsteads, ceiling fans, and fresh flowers.

Doubles: 4 (2 PB; 2 SB) $55-65
Type of Beds: 3 Twin; 3 Double; 1 Rollaway
Full Breakfast
Credit Cards: No
Notes: 8 (weekdays only)

A306

Ozark Mountain Country B&B
Box 295, Branson, MO, 65616
(417) 334-4720

Nine miles north of Eureka Springs on highway 23 is this home that is fully equipped for totally disabled persons: railings, ramps, and a "drive in" shower. The comfortable ranch home offers two large guest rooms with hall bath and TV. Continental breakfast. $50.

Bridgeford Cottage Bed & Breakfast

263 Spring Street, 72632
(501) 253-7853

Nestled in the heart of Eureka Springs' historic residential district, Bridgeford Cottage is an 1884 Victorian delight. Outside are shady porches that invite you to pull up a chair and watch the world go by on Spring Street. Each room has a private entrance, antique furnishings, and private bath. Fresh coffee in your suite, a selection of fine teas, color TV, air-conditioning, and a mouth-watering breakfast.

Hosts: Ken & Nyla Sawyer
Doubles: 4 (PB) $65-85
Type of Beds: 1 Twin; 4 Queen
Continental Breakfast
Credit Cards: A, B
Notes: 2, 5, 7, 9, 10, 11, 12, 14

Dairy Hollow House

515 Spring Street, 72632
(501) 253-7444

6 Pets welcome: 7 Smoking allowed: 8 Children welcome: 9 Social drinking allowed: 10 Tennis available: 11 Swimming available: 12 Golf available: 13 Skiing available: 14 May be booked through travel agents

Welcome to Dairy Hollow House, a tiny, irresistible country inn and restaurant nestled in a serene, wooded valley. Just one mile from Eureka's historic downtown, we offer two houses, each with the prettiest rooms and suites imaginable. Waiting for you are fireplaces, landscaped hot tub, fresh flowers, regional antiques, and our own Ozark wildflower soaps.

Hosts: Crescent Dragonwagon & Ned Shank
Doubles: 5 (PB) $95-125
Type of Beds: 2 Twin; 4 Double; 1 Queen
Full Breakfast
Credit Cards: A, B, C, D, E
Closed Jan. & Feb.
Notes: 2, 4, 7, 8, 9, 10, 11, 12, 14

Heart of the Hills Inn

5 Summit Street, 72632
(501) 253-7468

This historic home was built in the 1800s and offers three rooms with air-conditioning, refrigerator, TV, and private baths. There are also two completely equipped cottages with decks overlooking the woods. Eureka Springs is noted for its Passion Play, outstanding restaurants, fine museums, and trolley system.

Host: Jan Jacobs Weber
Doubles: 3 (PB) $55-70
Type of Beds: 2 Twin; 1 Double; 2 Queen; 2 King
Full Breakfast
Credit Cards: A, B
Closed January
Notes: 2, 8, 9, 10, 11, 14

Heartstone Inn Bed & Breakfast & Cottages

35 Kings Highway, 72632
(501) 253-8916

Nine rooms plus two charming guest cottages in the historic district of Eureka Springs. Turn-of-the-century charm, plus modern conveniences. Antiques, air-conditioning, private entrances, limited smoking.

Hosts: Iris & Bill Simantel
Doubles: 9 (PB) $51-89 plus tax
Cottages: 2 (PB)
Type of Beds: 5 Double; 6 Queen; 2 King
Full Breakfast
Minimum stay holidays: 2
Credit Cards: A, B
Closed Christmas
Notes: 2, 8, 9, 11, 12

Heartstone Inn B&B Cottages

Redbud Manor

7 Kings Highway, 72632
(501) 253-9649

See the Passion Play, visit shops of yesteryear, listen to Ozark mountain music, or take a horse-and-buggy ride in this historic town. Nearby lake for water activities and fishing.

Host: Evelyn Kintz
Doubles: 3 (PB) $55-65
Full Breakfast
Credit Cards: A, B, C, D, E
Closed March 19 - Nov. 20
Notes: 2

EVERTON

Corn Cob Inn

Rt. 1, Box 183, 72633
(501) 429-6545

NOTES: Credit cards accepted: A Master Card; B Visa; C American Express; D Discover Card; E Diners Club; F Other: 2 Personal checks accepted: 3 Lunch available: 4 Dinner available: 5 Open all year

Originally a corn-cob-pipe factory, this native stone house sits on the banks of Clear Creek, surrounded by the beauty of the Ozarks. Fishing, swimming, hiking, canoeing, and horseback riding available. Or just relax and enjoy the peace and quiet.

Hosts: David & Anna Borg
Singles: 2 (SB) $30
Doubles: 3 (SB) $45
Type of Beds: 1 Twin; 3 Double; 1 Queen
Full Breakfast
Credit Cards: No
Notes: 2, 4, 5, 7, 8, 9, 11, 14

FAYETTEVILLE

Arkansas & Ozarks B&B AFV01

Route 1, Box 38
Calico Rock, Arkansas, 72519
(501) 297-8764

Persian rugs, cathedral ceiling, and a woodburning fireplace reflect the interior-decorating interests of the hostess. As a former tour guide, she can direct you to the local attractions, including the University of Arkansas. Enjoy a patio overlooking a park, private baths, continental breakfast, and a private sitting room. $35-40.

FORT SMITH

Arkansas & Ozarks B&B AFS01

Route 1, Box 38
Calico Rock, Arkansas, 72519
(501) 297-8764

Featuring the atmosphere of yesteryear and the luxury of today, this restored historic home offers private double suites with kitchenette, wet bar, living room, local art, and antiques. A continental breakfast, whirlpool, bikes to ride, and a horse-drawn carriage ride (weekends) are provided. Convenient to the Fort Smith District, race tracks, Arkansas wine country, golf courses, museums, and art gallery. $59-79.

HARRISON-YELLVILLE

Arkansas & Ozarks B&B AHR01

Route 1, Box 38
Calico Rock, Arkansas, 72519
(501) 297-8764

A large native-stone house, originally built as a general store in this old mining community. The house is located on a creek with private beach and swimming area. There are cows, goats, chickens, two friendly dogs, and two lively young boys on this small 18 acre farm. Large country breakfasts are served in the dining room or on the patio. Picnic lunches and dinners are available on request. Your hostess speaks French. The entire second floor, with three bedrooms and a shared bath, is reserved for guests. $25-35.

Oak Tree Inn

HEBER SPRINGS

Oak Tree Inn

Vinegar Hill and 110 West, 72543
(501) 362-7731

---

6 Pets welcome: 7 Smoking allowed: 8 Children welcome: 9 Social drinking allowed: 10 Tennis available: 11 Swimming available: 12 Golf available: 13 Skiing available: 14 May be booked through travel agents

An inn for nonsmoking adults, each room with its own private whirlpool bath; five have wood-burning fireplaces. Located near 45,000 acre Greers Ferry Lake. Dessert and a full breakfast are served daily. Tennis courts, swimming pool, and hot tub. Lakeside condos and river cottage also available; children and smokers are welcome in these units.

Host: Freddie Lou Lodge
Doubles: 6 (PB) $65-70
Type of Beds: 6 Queen
Full Breakfast
Credit Cards: No
Notes: 2, 5, 10, 11, 12, 14

HELENA

Martha's Vineyard

810 Columbia, 72342
(501) 338-3814

Our brick, ten-room cottage was built in 1908 and has three guest rooms, a large great room with fireplace, antiques, and telephone service. Dinner or lunch is also available by reservation. There are lots of French windows, a cozy backyard; in the historic district of town.

Host: Martha Heidelberger
Doubles: 3 (PB) $39-45
Continental Breakfast
Credit Cards: A, B, C
Closed Dec. 18-30
Notes: 2, 3 (by reservation), 4 (by reservation), 7, 8, 9, 10, 11, 12

KINGSTON

A308

Ozark Mountain Country B&B
Box 295, Branson, MO, 65616
(417) 334-4720

A modern home high on a mountain near Kingston, close to the Buffalo River. Two upstairs guest rooms with antique furnishings, double beds, shared hall bath. Guests are welcome to use the large living room with TV, the spacious deck with hot tub, and the screened deck with a view of the Boston Mountains. Hearty breakfast is served in the dining area or on the screened porch. Children welcome. $25-30.

MOUNTAIN HOME

A307

Ozark Mountain Country B&B
Box 295, Branson, MO, 65616
(417) 334-4720

This charming 1905 two-story home has been remodeled and beautifully redecorated. The "sittin' " porch and the deck are surrounded by huge oak trees. Guests enjoy a special gourmet continental breakfast. Four air-conditioned rooms with private baths, ceiling fans, cable TV, and central air. $32-45.

NORFORK

Arkansas & Ozarks B&B ANF01

Route 1, Box 38
Calico Rock, Arkansas, 72519
(501) 297-8764

A mountain retreat with a country-club setting, this lodge sits on the banks of the White River and overlooks the beauty of the Ozark National Forest. A complete breakfast is served, and evening meals can be arranged for an extra charge. The bedrooms are done in antiques and have their own entrances onto an open courtyard. Fly-fishing schools and White River and lake guide services are available. The White River provides some of the best year-round trout fishing in the country. $50-62.50.

NOTES: Credit cards accepted: A Master Card; B Visa; C American Express; D Discover Card; E Diners Club; F Other: 2 Personal checks accepted: 3 Lunch available: 4 Dinner available: 5 Open all year

ROGERS

Arkansas & Ozarks B&B
ARO01
Route 1, Box 38
Calico Rock, Arkansas, 72519
(501) 297-8764

This country charmer is nestled among oak, dogwood, and redbud trees and is intended for adult travelers. Queen beds, private baths, fruit and homemade candy are just a few of the features. Full breakfast is served in the spacious country dining room or on the veranda where birds, wildlife, and natural beauty may be enjoyed. Only minutes from boating, fishing, swimming, golf, and a variety of shopping and craft areas. $35-55.

YELLVILLE

Arkansas & Ozarks B&B
AYV01
Route 1, Box 38
Calico Rock, Arkansas, 72519
(501) 297-8764

This is an elegant Victorian home with six rooms and a honeymoon suite. A breakfast buffet of Belgian waffles, French toast, and other goodies is served in the large dining room. Later in the day, homemade cakes and other delights are served as snacks. No children under 5; limited smoking. $27.50-50.

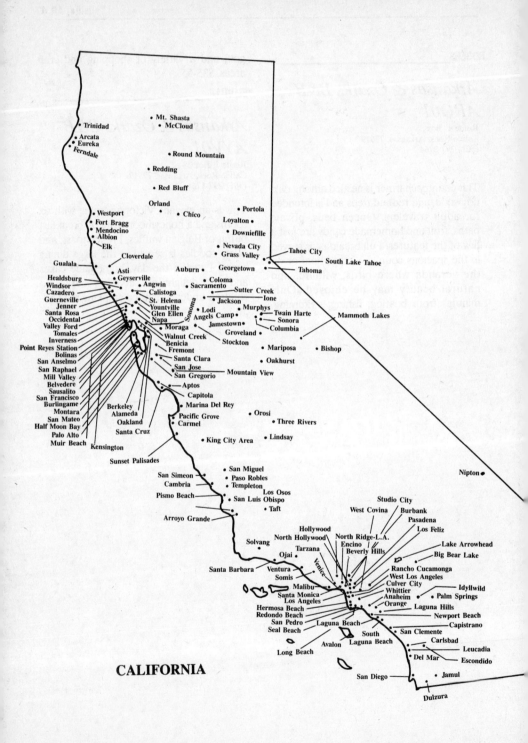

Trinidad
Arcata
Eureka
Ferndale

Mt. Shasta
McCloud

Round Mountain

Redding

Red Bluff

Orland
Chico
Portola
Loyalton
Downiefille

Westport
Fort Bragg
Mendocino
Albion
Elk

Cloverdale
Nevada City
Grass Valley
Tahoe City

Gualala
Asti
Geyserville
Auburn
Georgetown
South Lake Tahoe
Tahoma

Healdsburg
Windsor
Cazadero
Guerneville
Jenner
Santa Rosa
Occidental
Valley Ford
Tomales
Inverness
Point Reyes Station
Bolinas
San Anselmo
San Raphael
Mill Valley
Belvedere
Sausalito
San Francisco
Burlingame
Montara
San Mateo
Half Moon Bay
Palo Alto
Muir Beach

Angwin
Calistoga
St. Helena
Yountville
Glen Ellen
Napa
Moraga
Walnut Creek
Benicia
Fremont
Santa Clara
San Jose
San Gregorio
Aptos
Capitola
Marina Del Rey

Coloma
Sacramento
Sutter Creek
Ione
Jackson
Lodi
Angels Camp
Murphys
Jamestown
Sonora
Columbia
Groveland
Stockton

Twain Harte

Mammoth Lakes

Mariposa
Oakhurst

Bishop

Mountain View

Berkeley
Alameda
Oakland
Santa Cruz

Pacific Grove
Carmel

Orosi
Three Rivers

Kensington

King City Area
Lindsay

Sunset Palisades

San Simeon
Cambria
Pismo Beach

San Miguel
Paso Robles
Templeton
Los Osos
San Luis Obispo
Taft

Nipton

Arroyo Grande

Studio City
West Covina
Burbank
Pasadena
Los Feliz

Hollywood
North Hollywood
Tarzana
Solvang
Ojai
Ventura
Somis
Malibu
Santa Monica
Los Angeles
Hermosa Beach
Redondo Beach
San Pedro
Seal Beach

North Ridge-L.A.
Encino
Beverly Hills

Lake Arrowhead
Big Bear Lake

Rancho Cucamonga
West Los Angeles
Culver City
Whittier
Anaheim
Orange

Idyllwild
Palm Springs

Laguna Hills
Newport Beach
Capistrano

Venice

Santa Barbara

Laguna Beach
South
Laguna Beach

San Clemente
Carlsbad
Leucadia
Escondido
Del Mar

Long Beach
Avalon

San Diego
Jamul

Dulzura

CALIFORNIA

California

Garratt Mansion

900 Union Street, 94501
(415) 521-4779

This 1893 Victorian makes time stand still on the tranquil island of Alameda. Only ten miles to Berkeley or downtown San Francisco. We will help maximize your vacation plans or leave you alone to regroup. Our rooms are large and comfortable, and our breakfasts are nutritious and filling.

Hosts: Royce & Betty Gladden
Doubles: 6 (3 PB; 3 SB) $60-110
Type of Beds: 2 Twin; 2 Double; 3 Queen
Full Breakfast
Credit Cards: C
Notes: 2, 5, 8, 10, 12, 14

Garratt Mansion

Fensalden Inn

Box 99, 95410
(707) 937-4042

A restored 1860s stagecoach way station with antique furnishings; several units with fireplaces. Quiet country setting with pastoral and ocean views. Enjoy strolling country lanes where grazing deer share the crisp morning air, or the evening panorama of the setting sun over a crimson-stained ocean.

Hosts: Frances & Scott Brazil
Singles: 7 (PB) $75
Doubles: 2 (PB) $135
Type of Beds: 6 Queen; 1 King
Full Breakfast
Minimum stay weekends: 2; holidays: 3
Credit Cards: A, B
Notes: 2, 5, 8 (over 11), 9, 10, 11, 12

B&B Registry
#CA-92802ANA

Box 8174, St. Paul, MN, 55108
(612) 646-4238

This elegant little inn is graced with bevelled leaded-glass windows, lace curtains, and charming turn-of-the-century furnishings. Guests may relax in the quiet upstairs reading area, the comfortable Victorian living room, or on one of the airy porches.

Singles: 1 (SB) $40-85
Doubles: 8 (1 PB; 7 SB) $40-85
Type of Beds: 3 Twin; 4 Double; 2 Queen
Full Breakfast
Credit Cards: A, B, C, D
Notes: 5, 8 (over 11), 12

Southern Comfort

B&B of LA, 32074 Waterside La., Westlake Village, 91361
(818) 889-8870

---

6 Pets welcome: 7 Smoking allowed: 8 Children welcome: 9 Social drinking allowed: 10 Tennis available: 11 Swimming available: 12 Golf available: 13 Skiing available: 14 May be booked through travel agents

Retired couple with a spacious home near tourist attractions offers two rooms and an upstairs suite (living room, fireplace, balcony, TV, mini kitchen). Nicely decorated in country antiques. Spa in yard. Full breakfast. Three doubles: one private bath; two shared. $27-45.

ANAHEIM

Anaheim Country Inn

856 S. Walnut, 92802
(714) 778-0150

A 1910 Princess Anne style home with spacious grounds and gardens in a quiet neighborhood about one mile from Disneyland and the Anaheim Convention Center. Easy access to beaches, Knotts Berry Farm, the *Queen Mary,* and the *Spruce Goose.* We can accommodate executive seminars, small family reunions, and small weddings.

Hosts: Lois Ramont & Marily Watson
Doubles: 6 (5 PB; 1 SB) $32-75
Full Breakfast
Credit Cards: A, B, C, D
Notes: 2, 5, 8 (12 and over), 9, 10, 11, 12, 14

ANGELS CAMP

Cooper House Bed & Breakfast Inn

Box 1388, 95222
(209) 736-2145

Beautiful turn-of-the-century home in California's historic gold country. Quiet location surrounded by manicured gardens. Spacious rooms with private baths and air-conditioning. Sumptuous full breakfast. Near caverns, wineries, giant sequoias, Columbia State Park, gourmet dining.

Hosts: Mark & Jeannette Chandler
Doubles: 3 (PB) $67.60-78
Type of Beds: 1 Double; 1 Queen; 1 King
Full Breakfast
Credit Cards: A, B
Notes: 2, 5, 7 (limited), 8, 9, 10, 11, 12, 13

ANGWIN

Big Yellow Sunflower Bed & Breakfast

235 Sky Oaks, 94508
(707) 965-3885

In the heart of the Napa Valley wine country, this home offers a fireplace, private entrance and deck, piano, kitchenette. Home-baked goodies and a bountiful full breakfast. Cozy and romantic, with some of the lowest rates in the area.

Hosts: Dale & Betty Clement
Doubles: 2 (PB) $45-85
Type of Beds: 2 Queen
Full breakfast in the suite; continental in the room
Credit Cards: No
Notes: 2, 5, 6, 7 (outdoors), 8, 9, 10, 11, 12, 14

Forest Manor

415 Cold Springs Road, 94508
(707) 965-3538

Secluded 20-acre English Tudor estate tucked among forest and vineyards in famous Napa Wine country. Described as "one of the most romantic country Inns...A small exclusive resort." Fireplaces, verandas, 53-foot pool, spas, spacious suites (one with Jacuzzi), refrigerators, coffee makers, homebaked breakfast. Close to over 200 wineries, ballooning, hot springs, and a lake.

Hosts: Harold & Corlene Lambeth
Doubles: 3 (PB) $95-175
Type of Beds: 1 Queen; 2 King
Continental-plus Breakfast
Credit Cards: A, B
Notes: 2, 5, 9, 10, 11, 12, 14

APTOS

Apple Lane Inn

6265 Soquel Drive, 95003-3117
(408) 475-6868

NOTES: Credit cards accepted: A Master Card; B Visa; C American Express; D Discover Card; E Diners Club; F Other: 2 Personal checks accepted: 3 Lunch available: 4 Dinner available: 5 Open all year

Apple Lane Inn is an historic Victorian farmhouse restored to the charm and tranquility of an earlier age. It's located just south of Santa Cruz on 3 acres of grounds, gardens, and fields. Explore the many miles of beaches within walking distance. Golf, hiking, fishing, shopping, and dining are all close by.

Host: Ann Farley
Doubles: 5 (3 PB; 2 SB) $65-105
Type of Beds: 3 Double; 3 Queen
Full Breakfast
Credit Cards: A, B
Notes: 2, 5, 7 (limited), 9, 10, 11, 12, 14

Mangels House

Box 302, 95001
(408) 688-7982

A large southern colonial situated on 4 acres of lawn and orchard, Mangels House is bounded by a 10,000-acre redwood forest and is only 3/4 mile from the beach. The five large, airy rooms are eclectic in decor and European in feel, reflecting the owners' background.

Hosts: Jacqueline & Ronald Fisher
Doubles: 5 (3 PB; 2 SB) $97.16-110.65
Type of Beds: 4 Twin; 2 Double; 2 Queen; 1 King
Full Breakfast
Credit Cards: A, B
Closed Dec. 24-26
Notes: 2, 4, 7 (limited), 8 (over 12), 9, 10, 11, 12, 13, 14

ARCATA

The Plough and Stars Country Inn

1800 27th Street, 95521
(707) 822-8236

The Plough and Stars is an 1860s farmhouse on 2 pastoral acres at the edge of the coastal university town of Arcata. The inn and hosts welcome you to the pleasures of country living and the pampering of home-style

hospitality. Quiet, spacious, comfortable, and warm.

Hosts: Bill & Melissa Hans
Doubles: 5 (2 PB; 3 SB) $50-$85
Type of Beds: 2 Twin; 2 Double; 2 Queen
Full Breakfast
Credit Cards: No
Closed Dec. 21 - Feb. 1
Notes: 2, 7 (limited), 8 (over 12), 9, 11, 12

ARROYO GRANDE

The Guest House

120 Hart Lane, 93420
(805) 481-9304

A charming colonial home built in 1865 and furnished with many rare antiques of that era. Beautiful, old-fashioned gardens, in which a hearty breakfast and afternoon libations are enjoyed. A short walk to the interesting shops and restaurants in the old village of Arroyo Grande.

Hosts: Mark Miller & Jim Cunningham
Doubles: 2 (SB) $45-60
Type of Beds: 1 Double; 1 Queen
Full Breakfast
Credit Cards: No
Notes: 2, 5, 7 (restricted), 9, 10, 11, 12

The Village Inn

407 El Camino Real, 93420
(805) 489-5926

The Village Inn blends Victorian charm and hospitality with modern comfort and convenience. Decorated in English country style with antiques, fine reproductions, Laura Ashley prints and wallpaper. Arroyo Grande is in the heart of California's central coast, halfway between Los Angeles and San Francisco. Near several wineries, Pismo Beach State Park, Lopez Lake; less than one hour to Hearst Castle at San Simeon. Late afternoon beverages and hors d'oeuvres are served in the parlor where you'll also find games, puzzles, TV, and a VCR for your enjoyment.

6 Pets welcome: 7 Smoking allowed: 8 Children welcome: 9 Social drinking allowed: 10 Tennis available: 11 Swimming available: 12 Golf available: 13 Skiing available: 14 May be booked through travel agents

Hosts: Jude & Don Stalker
Doubles: 7 (PB) $65-85
Type of Beds: 1 Twin; 8 Queen
Full Breakfast
Minimum stay holidays: 2
Credit Cards: A, B, C, D
Notes: 2, 3, 5, 8 (over 10), 9, 11, 12, 14

ASTI

B&B International 1

1181-B Solano Avenue
Albany, 94706
(415) 525-4569

An historic building located on a working ranch and vineyard in the heart of a prime wine-growing region. Hosts raise llamas, Black Angus cattle, and sheep. Peacocks strut around the luxurious swimming pool, and canoes can be rented nearby to use on the Russian River.

Doubles: (PB and SB) $78
Full Breakfast
Minimum stay: 2
Credit Cards: Major
Notes: 7, 8 (swimmers only), 9, 11

AUBURN-NEVADA CITY

B&B International 2

1181-B Solano Avenue
Albany, 94706
(415) 525-4569

Luxurious three-story A-frame house on Lake Combi off historic highway 49. Large property, wilderness setting, views of the lake from each room. Sun deck, fireplace, swimming, boating, fishing. Guest room and studio apartment.

Doubles: 2 (SB) $94
Full Breakfast
Minimum stay: 2
Credit Cards: Major
Notes: 8 (over 12), 9, 11

Gull House

AVALON

Gull House

344 Whittley Avenue, Box 1381, 90704
1-800-442-4884; (213) 510-2547

For honeymooners and those celebrating anniversaries. AAA approved contemporary house with swimming pool, spa, barbecue, gas-log fireplaces, morning room with refrigerator, color TV. Close to bay beaches and all water activities. Deposit or full payment in advance reserves taxi pickup and return.

Hosts: Bob & Hattie Michalis
Suites: 2 (PB) $110-125
Continental Breakfast
Minimum stay: 2
Credit Cards: No
Closed Nov.-April
Notes: 2, 7, 9, 12

BELVEDERE

B&B International 3

1181-B Solano Avenue
Albany, 94706
(415) 525-4569

NOTES: Credit cards accepted: A Master Card; B Visa; C American Express; D Discover Card; E Diners Club; F Other: 2 Personal checks accepted: 3 Lunch available: 4 Dinner available: 5 Open all year

Scenes for Goldie Hawn's film "Foul Play" were shot in this elegant hilltop home over-looking San Francisco Bay. Guest room opens onto patio. Near yacht harbor and Angel Island boat terminal; fifteen minutes from San Francisco.

Doubles: 1 (PB) $70
Full Breakfast
Minimum stay: 2
Credit Cards: Major
Notes: 7, 8, 9, 10

Union Hotel

BENICIA

Union Hotel
401 First Street, 94510
(707) 746-0100

Built in 1882 and active as a twenty-room bordello until the early 1950s. The Union Hotel was completely renovated in 1981 into a twelve-room hotel and B&B. Each of the twelve rooms is decorated with a theme and named accordingly. Each room has a queen or king bed, individual room-temperature controls, Jacuzzi bathtubs, and television. The superb stained-glass picture windows in the bar and dining room are worth a trip on

their own. Restaurant on premises. Ideally located for visiting the wine country (20 minutes); 45 minutes from San Francisco; 20 minutes from the ferry to Fisherman's Wharf.

Hosts: Sherene Ross
Doubles: 12 (PB) $75-$135
Type of Beds: 11 Queen; 1 King
Continental Breakfast
Credit Cards: A, B, C, D, E
Notes: 2, 3, 4, 5, 7, 8, 9, 14

BERKELEY

B&B International 4
1181-B Solano Avenue
Albany, 94706
(415) 525-4569

Photographs of the unique pool and hot tub area of this Mediterranean-style home have appeared in magazines. Guest rooms have a panoramic view of the Golden Gate Bridge. Grand piano. Close to U.C. Berkeley.

Doubles: (PB) $54
Full Breakfast
Minimum stay: 2
Credit Cards: Major
Notes: 7, 8 (swimmers only), 9, 11

BEVERLY HILLS

Beverly Hills Guest House
B&B of LA, 32074 Waterside La., Westlake Village, 91361
(818) 889-8870

Small cottage to the rear of the main house. Small refrigerator, TV; doors open to grassy sitting area. Bus line two blocks. One double, private bath. $40-45.

Canyon Cottage
B&B of LA, 32074 Waterside Lane, Westlake Village, 91361
(818) 889-8870

English country atmosphere with an-tique furnishings and a massive fireplace. Just a

6 Pets welcome: 7 Smoking allowed: 8 Children welcome: 9 Social drinking allowed: 10 Tennis available: 11 Swimming available: 12 Golf available: 13 Skiing available: 14 May be booked through travel agents

mile downhill to Sunset Blvd. Two doubles, private bath, $50-65.

El Camino Real Bed & Breakfast #1

Box 7155, Northridge, 91327
(818) 363-6753

This is the legendary Beverly Hills — home of movie stars and millionaires. Walk to Rodeo Drive; convenient to the finest shops and restaurants. Guest quarters are separate from the main house and contain two three-room apartments consisting of bedroom, living room, kitchen, and bath. Swimming pool and hot tub.

2 Apartments (PB) $115
Type of Beds: 1 Double; 1 King
Continental Breakfast
Credit Cards: No
Notes: 8, 10, 11

BIG BEAR LAKE

Eagle's Nest Bed & Breakfast

Box 1003, 92315
(714) 866-6465

The Eagle's Nest B&B is ideally situated in the heart of a four-seasons resort. The lodge offers elegance in a rustic setting. The main house is a recently built two-story log cabin lodge. Five cozily decorated rooms all have private baths, queen beds, and warm goose-down comforters.

Hosts: James Joyce & Jack Draper
Doubles: 5 (PB) $65-95
Type of Beds: 5 Queen
Continental-plus Breakfast
Credit Cards: No
Notes: 2, 5, 8, 9, 10, 11, 12, 13, 14

Knickerbocker Mansion

Box 3661, 92315
(714) 866-8221

A turn-of-the-century vertical log mansion on 2 acres surrounded by national forest. Warm, peaceful retreat for fun or business. Country and antique furnishings, hearty breakfast, and "Grandma's Kitchen" for snacks during the day. Indoor and outdoor Jacuzzis. Close to skiing, horseback riding, and all water sports; member of local athletic club.

Host: Phyllis M. Knight
Doubles: 10 (5 PB; 5 S3B) $85-150
Type of Beds: 8 Queen; 2 King
Full Breakfast
Credit Cards: No
Notes: 2, 5, 8, 9, 10, 11, 12, 13, 14

BISHOP

The Matlick House

1313 Rowan Lane, 93514
(619) 873-3133

A 1906 ranch house, completely renovated, nestled at the base of the eastern Sierra Nevada Mountains. Close to year-round fishing, hiking, skiing, trail rides. Telephones available, air-conditioning, wine and hors d'oeuvres; antiques throughout.

Host: Nanette Robedaix
Doubles: 5 (PB) $55-75
Type of Beds: 1 Twin; 4 Queen
Full Breakfast
Notes: 2, 5, 7 (limited), 8 (over 14), 9, 10, 11, 12, 13

Thomas' White House Inn

BOLINES_____

Thomas' White House Inn
118 Kale Road, 94924
(415) 868-0279

A New England style inn near Pt. Reyes National Seashore in West Marin. Located in one of the most beautiful areas on the California coast. Two lovely rooms with window seats offer panoramic views of the mountains and the Pacific Ocean.

Hosts: Jacqueline Thomas
Doubles: 2 (SB) $81-$91.80
Type of Beds: 1 Double; 1 Queen
Continental Breakfast
Credit Cards: No
Notes: 2, 4, 5, 7, 8, 9, 10

BURBANK_____

The Hills of Burbank
B&B of LA, 32074 Waterside La., Westlake Village, 91361
(818) 889-8870

Lovely home with wonderful screened patio and a view across the valley. Share TV with hosts. Car essential. Children over 10 welcome. One double, private bath, $30.

BURLINGAME_____

B&B International 5
1181-B Solano Avenue
Albany, 94706
(415) 525-4569

Hilltop home with a panoramic view of San Francisco Bay, located between San Francisco and the airport — a twenty-minute drive either way. Guest room suite of this contemporary home has a separate entrance and opens onto the landscaped swimming pool. Aviary. Hosts from The Netherlands serve delicious breakfasts.

Doubles: (PB) $68
Full Breakfast
Minimum stay: 2
Credit Cards: Major
Notes: 7, 8 (swimmers only), 9, 11

CALISTOGA_____

Foothill House
3037 Foothill Blvd., 94515
(707) 942-6933

"The most romantic inn of the Napa Valley," according to the *Chicago Tribune* travel editor. In a country setting, Foothill House offers spacious suites individually decorated with antiques, each with private bath and entrance, fireplace, and small refrigerator.

Hosts: Susan & Michael Clow
Doubles: 3 (PB) $80-105
Type of Beds: 1 Twin; 1 Double; 3 Queen
Continental-plus Breakfast
Minimum stay weekends & holidays: 2
Credit Cards: A, B
Notes: 2, 5, 8 (over 12), 9, 10, 11, 12

The Pink Mansion
1415 Foothill Blvd., 94515
(707) 942-0558

A 110-year-old Victorian in the heart of the Napa Valley wine country. Within biking distance to several wineries; walking distance to Calistoga's many spas and restaurants. Fully air-conditioned; indoor pool; complimentary wine and cheese. Each room has a wonderful view.

Hosts: Jeff Seyfried
Doubles: 5 (PB) $72-$154
Type of Beds: 1 Twin; 5 Queen
Full Breakfast
Minimum Stay Weekends & Holidays: 2
Credit Cards: A, B
Notes: 2, 5, 8 (over 12), 9, 10, 11, 12

Quail Mountain Bed & Breakfast
4455 North St. Helena Highway, 94515
(707) 942-0316; 942-0315

---

6 Pets welcome: 7 Smoking allowed: 8 Children welcome: 9 Social drinking allowed: 10 Tennis available: 11 Swimming available: 12 Golf available: 13 Skiing available: 14 May be booked through travel agents

Quail Mountain is a secluded luxury B&B located on 26 wooded and vineyard acres. Three guest rooms, each with king bed, private bath, and private deck. Complimentary wine, pool, spa. Lovely breakfast. Close to Napa Valley tourist attractions.

Hosts: Don & Alma Swiers
Doubles: 3 (PB) $81.25-108.50
Type of Beds: 3 King
Full Breakfast
Minimum stay weekends & holidays: 2
Credit Cards: A, B
Notes: 2, 5, 7 (limited), 9, 10, 11, 12, 14

Scarlett's Country Inn

3918 Silverado Trail, 94515
(707) 942-6669

Secluded 1890 farmhouse, set in the quiet of green lawns and tall pines, overlooking the vineyards. Three exquisitely appointed suites, one with fireplace and wet bar. Breakfast in your room or by the woodland swimming pool. Close to wineries, spas.

Hosts: Scarlett & Derek Dwyer, Melissa Mapes
Doubles: 3 (PB) $70.35-113.70
Continental Breakfast
Credit Cards: A, B
Closed Thanksgiving & Christmas
Notes: 2, 5, 7, 8, 9, 10, 11, 12, 14

Trailside Inn

4201 Silverado Trail, 94515
(707) 942-4106

A charming 1930s farmhouse, centrally located in the country, with three very private suites (two in a renovated barn). Each suite has its own entrance, porch or deck, bedroom, bath, fireplace, and air-conditioning. Fresh home-baked breads provided in your fully equipped kitchen.

Hosts: Randy & Lani Gray
Suites: 3 (PB) $85-110
Type of Beds: 4 Twin; 2 Double; 1 Queen
Continental Breakfast
Credit Cards: No
Notes: 2, 5, 7, 8, 9, 10, 11, 12, 14

Wayside Inn

1523 Foothill Blvd., 94515
(707) 942-0645

Enjoy cozy down comforters, the gentle music of water fountains, and wind chimes. Gourmet breakfast served on the patio in summer and in front of an open fire in winter. Jacuzzi and bicycles also available at this 70-year-old Spanish hacienda.

Host: Pat Shebanow
Doubles: 3 (1 PB; 2 SB) $70-89
Type of Beds: 1 Queen; 2 King
Full Breakfast
Children welcome on weekdays
Credit Cards: A, B
Closed January
Notes: 2, 8, 9

Zinfandel House

1253 Summit Drive, 94515
(707) 942-0733

Zinfandel House is in a wooded setting on a western hillside with a spectacular view of the famous Napa Valley vineyards. Halfway between St. Helena and Calistoga. Choose among three tastefully decorated rooms with a private or shared bath. Lovely breakfasts served on the deck or in the solarium.

Hosts: Bette & George Starke
Doubles: 3 (PB or SB) $60-$85
Type of Beds: 1 Double; 1 Queen; 1 King
Full Breakfast
Credit Cards: No
Notes: 2, 5, 9, 10, 11, 12, 14

CAMBRIA

Beach House

6360 Moonstone Beach Drive, 93428
(805) 927-3136

The Beach House is located on the ocean front, with beautiful views, decks, and patios. Some rooms have fireplaces. Large common room with large deck facing the ocean; watch our gorgeous sunsets. Hearst Castle six miles away. Bicycles available.

NOTES: Credit cards accepted: A Master Card; B Visa; C American Express; D Discover Card; E Diners Club; F Other: 2 Personal checks accepted: 3 Lunch available: 4 Dinner available: 5 Open all year

Hosts: Penny Hitch & Tigg Morales
Doubles: 7 (PB) $100.70-132.50
Type of Beds: 6 Queen; 1 King
Continental Breakfast
Credit Cards: A, B
Notes: 2, 5, 8 (over 12), 9, 10, 11, 12

Cambria Pines by the Sea

B&B of LA, 32074 Waterside La., Westlake Village,
91361
(818) 889-8870

Elegant accommodation with white-water
ocean view. Color TV, no smoking. Wildlife
preserve and beautiful walks along the
coastline. Only one mile to town. Children
welcome. One double, private bath, $65-75.

Eye Openers #1

Box 694, Altedena, 91001
(213) 684-4428

An English couple host this elegant B&B
located near Hearst Castle and the midcoast
beaches. First floor is entirely for guests and
includes a large bedroom/sitting room with
fireplace and wet bar.

Doubles: 1 (PB) $62-65
Type of Beds: 2 Twin or 1 King
Continental-plus Breakfast
Credit Cards: A, B
Notes: 2, 5, 10, 11, 12

The J. Patrick House

2990 Burton Drive, 93428
(805) 927-3812

Every room is individually decorated with
the personal comfort of the guest in mind.
Each has a wood-burning fireplace, full
private bath; there is no TV, radio, or
telephone to disturb your privacy. Near the
ocean and pine forest in a quiet, rural area.
Wine tasting and Hearst Castle are minutes
away.

Host: Molly Lynch
Doubles: 8 (PB) $85-125

Type of Beds: 7 Queen; 1 King
Continental Breakfast
Credit Cards: A, B
Notes: 2, 3, 5, 8 (over 15), 9, 10, 11, 14

Megan's Friends B&B Service #1

1776 Royal Way, San Luis Obispo, 93401
(805) 544-4406

Cozy, quiet retreat in the pines north of the
West Village, adjacent to shops, restaurants,
art galleries, and beaches. Friendly hostess
provides guests with two rooms and a bath,
radio, and books. Continental breakfast.
Visit Hearst Castle in San Simeon, five miles
north. $50.

Musical Memories

B&B of LA, 32074 Waterside La., Westlake Village,
91361
(818) 889-8870

Two homes, just across the street from each
other, offer guest rooms with color TV,
views, refrigerator, wine and fresh flowers.
Pleasant lodging while exploring this unique
coastal village. Two doubles, private bath,
$65.

Olallieberry Inn

B&B of LA, 32074 Waterside La., Westlake Village,
91361
(818) 889-8870

An 1873 home built in the Greek Revival
style and restored to its original elegance.
TV on request; early evening appetizers included. Seven miles to Hearst Castle. Six
doubles, $65-85 plus tax.

The Pickford House Bed & Breakfast

2555 MacLeod Way, 93428
(805) 927-8619

6 Pets welcome: 7 Smoking allowed: 8 Children welcome: 9 Social drinking allowed: 10 Tennis available: 11
Swimming available: 12 Golf available: 13 Skiing available: 14 May be booked through travel agents

Only eight miles from Hearst Castle, Pickford House is decorated with antiques reminiscent of the golden age of film. Three rooms have fireplaces and a view of the mountains. Parlor with a 1860 bar is used for wine and tea bread at 5:00 P.M.

Host: Anna Larsen
Doubles: 8 (PB) $65-95 plus tax
Type of Beds: 2 Queen; 5 King
Full Breakfast
Credit Cards: A, B
Notes: 5, 7 (limited), 9, 14

CAPISTRANO

Country Bay Inn

B&B of LA, 32074 Waterside La., Westlake Village, 91361
(818) 889-8870

Motel-style inn just across the highway from the sand and surf. Each room has a small patio, TV, and fireplace. Breakfast served daily in the garden restaurant. Twenty-eight doubles, private baths, $85-105 plus tax.

Pelican Cove Inn

CAPITOLA

Summer House

216 Monterey Avenue, 95010
(408) 475-8474

A rustic summer house located on Depot Hill overlooking Capitola Village and beautiful Monterey Bay. A short walk to the beach, restaurants, theater, and unique shopping. Enjoy a redwood -paneled suite with its own private entrance opening onto a sun deck where your continental breakfast is served.

Hosts: Patricia M. Dooling
Singles: 2 (SB) $15 per child
Doubles: 1 (SB) $54
Type of Beds: 2 Twin; 1 Double
Continental Breakfast
Credit Cards: No
Closed 9/15 - 10/15
Notes: 2, 6, 8, 9, 10, 12

CARLSBAD

Pelican Cove Inn

320 Walnut Avenue, 92008
(619) 434-5995

Pelican Cove Inn features: featherbeds, fireplaces, private entries, private baths, lovely antiques, a sun deck, balconies, and a gazebo. Walk to the beach and restaurants. Palomar Airport and Amtrak pick up. Beach chairs, towels, picnic baskets available. Afternoon refreshments, flowers, fruit, and candy provided. New and beautiful.

Hosts: Bob & Celeste Hale
Doubles: 4 (PB) $75-125
Type of Beds: 2 Twin; 2 Queen; 1 King
Continental Breakfast
Minimum stay weekends & holidays: 2
Credit Cards: A, B
Notes: 2, 5, 7, 8 (over 12), 9, 10, 11, 12

CARMEL

Carmel Hide-Away

B&B of LA, 32074 Waterside La., Westlake Village, 91361
(818) 889-8870

Cute guest house built under the main home with views to the forest and golf course. Five blocks to town and nine to the beach. Deck, living area, full kitchen. Furnished in antiques with lots of charm. Weekly rental in summer. Two doubles, shared bath, $85.

Carmel Valley

B&B of LA, 32074 Waterside La., Westlake Village, 91361
(818) 889-8870

Just a short drive inland from Carmel is a two-bedroom, two-bath house with Jacuzzi tub in the master bath, modern kitchen, and sliding glass doors opening to views of the trees, mountains, and Carmel River. Two doubles, private bath, $85.

Carriage House Inn

Junipero between 7th & 8th, 93921
1-800-433-4732; 1-800-422-4732 (CA)

Fresh flowers and country-inn flavor. Continental breakfast and newspaper delivered to your room each morning. Wood-burning fireplaces, down comforters. Spacious rooms, many with open- beam ceilings and sunken tubs. A very romantic getaway!

Host: Gary Luce
Doubles: 13 (PB) $125-170
Type of Beds: 13 King
Continental Breakfast
Minimum stay weekends & holidays: 2
Credit Cards: All Major
Notes: 2, 5, 7, 9, 14

Cobblestone Inn

Junipero between 7th & 8th, 93921
(408) 625-5222

Situated in the heart of Carmel, the Cobblestone is an English country inn with a flowering garden and central courtyard. Each room is individually decorated with print wallpaper, fluffy comforters, pine furniture, fireplace, bathrobes, and fresh fruit. Enjoy a full breakfast and afternoon wine and hors d'oeuvres.

Host: Shelley Post
Doubles: 24 (PB) $99-187
Type of Beds: 19 Queen; 5 King
Full Breakfast
Credit Cards: A, B, C
Notes: 2, 5, 8, 9, 10, 11, 12, 14

Cobblestone Inn

Happy Landing Inn

Box 2619, 93921
(408) 624-7917

Delightful little B&B inn in the heart of downtown Carmel. Beautiful antiques, stained-glass windows, fresh flowers. Breakfast served in your room. This inn looks like a page out of a Beatrix Potter book; you'll love it.

Hosts: Carl & Jeannine George
Doubles: 7 (PB) $99-135
Type of Beds: 1 Double; 4 Queen; 2 King
European Breakfast
Minimum stay weekends: 2
Credit Cards: A, B
Notes: 2, 5, 8 (over 12), 9, 10, 12

Monte Verde Inn

Box 394, 93921
(408) 624-6046

6 Pets welcome: 7 Smoking allowed: 8 Children welcome: 9 Social drinking allowed: 10 Tennis available: 11 Swimming available: 12 Golf available: 13 Skiing available: 14 May be booked through travel agents

A charming country inn nestled in the heart of Carmel. Ten warmly furnished rooms with a lovely garden neatly tucked away for guests to enjoy. Wonderful continental breakfast delivered to your room.

Host: John Nahas
Doubles: 10 (PB) From $75-145
Continental Breakfast
Credit Cards: A, B, C
Notes: 2, 5, 7, 8, 9, 10, 11, 12, 14

Stonehouse Inn

Box 2517, 93921
(408) 624-4569

Victorian house (1906), furnished in antiques, within walking distance of the beach, shops, restaurants. Living room with large fireplace is the gathering spot for guests to enjoy spirits and snacks before dinner. Breakfast is served in the bright and cheery dining room each morning.

Host: Virginia Carey
Doubles: 6 (SB) $88-115.50
Type of Beds: 1 Twin; 2 Double; 2 Queen; 1 King
Full Breakfast
Credit Cards: A, B
Notes: 2, 5, 8 (14 and over), 10, 12, 14

Valley Lodge

Box 93, 93924
(408) 659-2261; in CA (800) 641-4646

A quiet country inn nestled on 3 lovely acres in peaceful Carmel Valley, the sunbelt of the Monterey Peninsula. Relax and unwind in a garden patio room or a cozy fireplace cottage. Enjoy our heated pool, hot spa, sauna, game area, and fitness center. Walk to fine restaurants and quaint shops.

Hosts: Peter & Sherry Coakley
Doubles: 31 (PB) $76-182
Type of Beds: 6 Twin; 33 Queen; 3 King
Continental-plus Breakfast
Credit Cards: A, B, C, D
Notes: 2, 5, 6, 7, 8, 9, 10, 11, 12, 14

CAZADERO

House of a Thousand Flowers

11 Mosswood Circle, 95421
(707) 632-5571

A quiet bed and breakfast house hidden away in a redwood forest. Spectacular vistas from every window; shoji screens; a bubbling spa, and an abundance of flowers make this a perfect secluded getaway.

Hosts: Dave Silva
Doubles: 2 (SB) $55-68.50
Type of Beds: Queen
Full Breakfast
Credit Cards: A, B
Notes: 2, 5, 8 (with prior arrangement), 9

CHICO

Bullard House Bed & Breakfast Inn

256 E. 1st Avenue, 95926
(916) 342-5912

Bullard House is a charming country Victorian in a university town, centrally located to downtown. Tree-lined streets for wonderful biking; close to hunting and fishing areas.

Hosts: Patrick & Patricia Macarthy
Doubles: 5 (SB) $50-60
Type of Beds: 1 Twin; 4 Double
Continental Breakfast
Credit Cards: No
Notes: 2, 5, 9, 10, 11, 12, 14

NW B&B #509

NW Bed & Breakfast Travel Unlimited
610 SW Broadway, Portland, OR, 97205
(503) 243-7616

Attractive new home with pool. The host, a fisherman and fourth-generation resident, is knowledgeable about the area. His wife, a music specialist, plays piano and guitar. Both play bridge. Pick up at train and airport. Crib available.

Doubles: 2 (SB) $30-45
Type of Beds: 2 Twin; 1 King
Continental Breakfast
Credit Cards: No
Notes: 7

CLOVERDALE

Vintage Towers Bed & Breakfast Inn
302 N. Main Street, 95425
(707) 894-4535

This lovely Queen Anne Victorian mansion was built in 1901 with three architecturally unique towers that now house some of the guest suites. Located near 52 wineries in the serene Sonoma Valley and the Russian River Basin. Gourmet breakfast prepared by a French pastry chef.

Hosts: Jim Mees & Garret Hall
Doubles: 7 (5 PB; 2 SB) $70-115
Type of Beds: 2 Twin; 3 Double; 1 Queen; 2 King
Full Breakfast
Minimum stay weekends & holidays: 2
Credit Cards: A, B, C
Closed January
Notes: 2, 7 (restricted), 8, 9, 10, 11, 12

Ye Olde' Shelford House
29955 River Road, 95425
(707) 894-5956

An 1885 country Victorian in the wine country. The inn is surrounded by vineyards and hills and has a hot tub, bikes, and pool. All rooms are decorated with family antiques, homemade quilts, and fresh flowers. Full breakfast, refreshments, and beverages. Enjoy "Surrey & Sip" — a horse-drawn surrey ride with a delicious picnic lunch following sipping wine at local wineries ($55.00 extra a couple, by reservation).

Hosts: Ina & Al Sauder
Singles: 6 (4 PB; 2 SB) $82.65-$93.55
Doubles: 6 (4 PB; 2 SB) $92.65-103.55
Type of Beds: 1 Twin; 5 Queen; 1 King
Full Breakfast
Credit Cards: A, B
Notes: 2, 3, 5, 8, 9, 10, 11, 14

COLOMA

Coloma Country Inn
2 High Street, Box 502, 95613
(916) 622-6919

Surrounded by the 300-acre Gold Discovery State Park, this 1852 farmhouse provides quiet comfort and close access to Sutter's Mill, museum, and attractions. White-water raft and balloon with hosts. Featured in the June 1988 issue of *Country Living* magazine.

Hosts: Cindi & Alan Ehrgott
Doubles: 5 (3 PB; 2 SB) $68-75
Type of Beds: 5 Double
Continental-plus Breakfast
Credit Cards: No
Notes: 2, 5, 8 (over 6), 9

COLUMBIA

Columbia City Hotel
Box 1870, 95310
(209) 532-1479

Centrally located in Columbia, a historic Gold Rush town preserved and protected by the State of California, this impeccable inn is surrounded by relics of the past. All rooms have been restored to reflect the 1850s. Downstairs, the highly acclaimed restaurant and always inviting What Cheer Saloon provide a haven for travelers seeking comfort and gracious hospitality. All rooms have half baths; hall showers.

Host: Tom Bender
Doubles: 9 (PB) $64.80-81
Type of Beds: 1 Twin; 6 Double; 2 Queen
Continental Breakfast

Credit Cards: A, B, C
Closed Christmas Eve, Christmas Day, mid-week in January
Notes: 2, 3, 4, 7 (limited), 8, 9, 10, 11, 12, 14

CULVER CITY

El Camino Real Bed & Breakfast #2

Box 7155, Northridge, 91327
(818) 363-6753

Convenient to downtown and all Hollywood points of interest. Fifteen minutes from Los Angeles airport; easy drive to Venice. Babies and children are welcome; playpen, high chair, and car seat available.

Doubles: 1 (PB) $40-44
Type of Beds: 1 Twin; 1 Trundle
Continental Breakfast
Credit Cards: No
Notes: 5, 7, 8, 10, 11, 12

Sculpture Gardens

B&B of LA, 32074 Waterside La., Westlake Village, 91361
(818) 889-8870

Built on the original MGM lot, this two-story home has artwork and sculptures displayed in the house and garden. TV. Sliding glass doors open to garden. Spanish spoken. Bus lines two blocks away. One double, private bath, $40-45.

DEL MAR

Gull's Nest

12930 Via Esperia, 92014
(619) 259-4863

Gull's Nest is a contemporary wood home surrounded by pines with a beautiful ocean view from two upper decks. Close to state beach and golf course, Scripps Clinic. Five minutes from La Jolla and Del Mar, close to I-5, and just twenty-five minutes from the San Diego Zoo and airport. Within two hours of Disneyland and Knotts Berry Farm.

Hosts: Michael & Constance Segel
Doubles: 2 (PB) $50-65
Full Breakfast
Teenagers welcome
Credit Cards: No
Notes: 2, 5, 7 (limited), 9, 11, 12

Rock Haus Inn

410 15th Street, 92014
(619) 481-3764

This California-style bungalow is an historic landmark in the quaint village of Del Mar, overlooking the ocean and the town. Everything is within walking distance. Two blocks to the beach; one block to the town. Tennis is within one mile, and golf within ten miles.

Host: Doris Holmes
Doubles: 10 (4 PB; 6 SB) $75-135
Type of Beds: 1 Twin; 7 Queen; 2 King
Continental Breakfast
Minimum stay May 15 - Oct. 15
Credit Cards: A, B, C
Notes: 2, 5, 9, 10, 11, 12, 14

DOWNIEVILLE

Sierra Shangri-La

Box 285, Highway 49, 95936
(916) 289-3455

A small resort on the North Fork of the Yuba River in the Sierra Nevada Range. At 3,100 feet elevation on the site of a former mining camp. Three rooms in the main lodgem, with balconies overlooking magnificent views over the river, which is known for its rainbow and German brown trout angling.

Hosts: Fran & Frank Carter
Doubles: 3 (PB) $55-65
Continental Breakfast
Credit Cards: A, B
Notes: 2, 5, 7, 8, 9, 11, 13 (XC), 14

DULZURA

Brookside Farm Bed & Breakfast Inn

1373 Marron Valley Road, 92017
(619) 468-3043

A country farmhouse furnished with collectibles, handmade quilts, and stained glass. Tree-shaded terraces by a stream; farm animals; gardens; hot tub in the grape arbor. Perfect for country walks. Close to Tecate, Mexico, and thirty-five minutes from San Diego.

Hosts: Ed & Judy Guishard
Doubles: 9 (6 PB; 3 SB) $37.75-70.10
Full Breakfast
Minimum stay holidays: 2
Credit Cards: No
Dinner available on weekends only
Closed Christmas-New Years
Notes: 2, 4, 9, 14

ELK

Elk Cove Inn

6300 S. Highway 1, 95432
(707) 877-3321

An 1883 Victorian atop a bluff with spectacular ocean views — some cabins with fireplaces. Full gourmet breakfast is served in our ocean-view dining room. Ready access to an expansive, driftwood-strewn beach. Beds have the subtle luxury of sun-dried linens. Relaxed, romantic atmosphere in a rural coastal village.

Host: Hildrun-Uta Triebess
Doubles: 7 (PB) $88-138
Type of Beds: 7 Queen; 1 King
Full Breakfast
Minimum stay weekends: 2; holidays: 3
Credit Cards: No
Notes: 2, 5, 8 (over 12), 9, 11, 12

Greenwood Lodge

Box 172, 95432
(707) 877-3422

1920s coastal cottages, four with private decks and three with spectacular ocean views. All with private entrances, private baths, sitting rooms with wood-burning stoves. About three hours and a century away from San Francisco. Rugged coastline, beaches, hiking, fishing, horseback riding, whale watching. Breakfast is delivered to each cottage on a tray.

Hosts: Bill & Kathleen Erwin
Oceanfront: 3 (PB) $125
Garden: 4 (PB) $95-105
Type of Beds: 4 Double; 2 Queen; 1 King
Full Breakfast
Credit Cards: No
Notes: 2, 5, 7 (outside), 9, 10, 11, 12

ENCINO

B&B International 9

1181-B Solano Avenue
Albany, 94706
(415) 525-4569

A spacious ranch-style home twenty minutes from UCLA. Swimming pool, garden, fine art. Your host is a psychologist.

Doubles: (PB) $66
Full Breakfast
Minimum stay: 2
Credit Cards: Major
Notes: 7, 8 (over 12), 9, 11

ESCONDIDO

Halbig's Hacienda

432 South Citrus Avenue, 92027
(619) 745-1296

The Hacienda is a large, family-built adobe ranch house on a knoll, with fruit trees, patios, and garden. Valley and hills surround the property. The acreage provides a country atmosphere, but we are located on the edge of town.

Hosts: George & Mary Jane Halbig
Doubles: 2 (SB) $35-40
Type of Beds: 2 Double
Continental Breakfast
Credit Cards: No
Notes: 5, 6, 7, 8, 9, 10, 11, 12, 14

EUREKA

Carter House & Hotel Carter

301 L Street, 95501
(707) 444-8062

Spectacularly re-created landmark Victorians in scenic Old Town Eureka; near the famed Carson Mansion. Original art and antique appointments. Bay and marina vistas, fireplaces, whirlpool baths, featherbeds, truly elegant dining. Dinners featured in *Bon Appetit*. "Best breakfast in California" — *California Magazine*.

Hosts: Mark & Christi Carter
Singles: 29 (27 PB; 2 SB) $55-$250
Doubles: 29 (27 PB; 2 SB) $65-$350
Type of Beds: 9 Doubles; 20 Queen
Full Breakfast
Credit Cards: A, B, C
Notes: 2 (on approved credit), 4, 5, 7, 8 (over 8), 9, 10, 11, 12, 14

Chalet de France

Star Rt. Box 20-A, 95549
(707) 443-6512; 444-3144

Traditional Swiss-Tyrolean chalet on 3,000-foot mountaintop overlooking the Pacific Ocean. Spectacular 40-mile views of 1,000 square miles of wilderness. Unique Alpine wood-sculptured architecture and elaborately painted folk scenes blend with warm European charm and quiet luxury.

Hosts: Doug & Lily Vieyra
Doubles: 2 (SB) $95-195
Type of Beds: 1 Double; 1 Queen
Full Breakfast
Credit Cards: No
Notes: 2, 4, 5, 9, 11, 14

Old Town Bed & Breakfast Inn

1521 Third Street, 95501
(707) 445-3951

Built in 1871 in the Redwood Empire, this historic Victorian home features a uniquely warm atmosphere, Teddy Bears, Rubber Duckies. Guests write: "The best....Breakfast to die for....Like Grandma's house."

Hosts: Leigh & Diane Benson
Doubles: 5 (3 PB; 2 SB) $64-115
Type of Beds: 1 Twin; 1 Double; 3 Queen; 1 King
Full Breakfast
Credit Cards: A, B, C
Notes: 2, 5, 8 (over 10), 9, 10, 11, 12, 14

The Gingerbread Mansion

FERNDALE

The Gingerbread Mansion

400 Berding Street, 95536
(707) 786-4000; (800) 441-0407

The West Coast's most photographed inn, located in northern California's Victorian village of Ferndale — a state historic landmark near redwood parks and Eureka — offers fireplaces, bicycles, English gardens. Four parlors, spectacular baths with "his and her" claw-foot tubs — unsurpassed elegance for you to enjoy.

Hosts: Wendy Hatfield & Ken Torbert
Doubles: 9 (PB) $75-150
Type of Beds: 2 Twin; 9 Queen
Continental Breakfast

NOTES: Credit cards accepted: A Master Card; B Visa; C American Express; D Discover Card; E Diners Club; F Other: 2 Personal checks accepted: 3 Lunch available: 4 Dinner available: 5 Open all year

Minimum stay weekends & holidays: 2
Credit Cards: A, B
Notes: 2, 5, 8 (over 10), 9, 10, 11, 12, 14

Shaw House Inn

Box 1125, 703 Main Street, 95536
(707) 786-9958

This 1854 Carpenter Gothic is cottage-like
in design, very cozy and bright. Like sleeping
in Grandma's attic. We have lots of antiques
and good reading in our library for our
guests to enjoy. This is an all-redwood/one-
wall-construction home. Afternoon tea at
check-in, 3:00 to 6:00 P.M.

Hosts: Ken & Norma Bessingpas
Doubles: 5 (1 PB; 4 SB) $58.30-100.70
Type of Beds: 1 Twin; 2 Double; 4 Queen
Continental-plus Breakfast
Credit Cards: A, B
Notes: 2, 5, 7 (limited), 8 (over 10), 10, 14

FORT BRAGG

Glass Beach Bed & Breakfast Inn

726 N. Main Street, 95437
(707) 964-6774

Nine rooms with private baths and hot tub.
A full country breakfast is served every
morning. Near the famous Skunk Train,
beautiful beaches, shopping, and magnificent redwoods. Ask about our special
winter rates.

Hosts: Ray & Betty McVay
Doubles: 9 (PB) $54-84
Type of Beds: 3 Double; 6 Queen
Full Breakfast
Credit Cards: A, B
Notes: 2, 5, 7, 8 (12 and over), 9, 10, 11, 12

Grey Whale Inn

615 North Main Street, 95437
(707) 964-0640; 1-800-382-7244 (CA)

A 1915 old-growth redwood inn on the Mendocino Coast. One room has a fireplace;

four have ocean views; one has a whirlpool
tub and sun deck; one has wheel chair access. Lounge with fireplace; TV room with
VCR; recreation room with pool table.
Mini-conference facilities. Whale watching,
fishing party boats, Skunk Train trips arranged.

Hosts: John & Colette Bailey
Doubles: 14 (PB) $48.60-135
Type of Beds: 2 Twin; 4 Double; 8 Queen; 4 King
Full Breakfast
Minimum stay weekends: 2; holidays: 3-4
Credit Cards: A, B, C
Notes: 2, 4, 5, 8 (over 12), 9, 10, 11, 12, 14

Pudding Creek Inn

700 N. Main Street, 95437
(707) 964-9529

Two Victorian homes connected by an
enclosed garden court. Ten rooms
decorated in country decor, with private
baths. Some rooms have fireplaces. Within
walking distance of Glass Beach, Pudding
Creek, and the Skunk Train depot. There
are many shops and restaurants nearby to
enjoy, and tennis courts within a few blocks.

Hosts: Eugene & Marilyn Gundersen
Doubles: 10 (PB) $42-85
Type of Beds: 2 Double; 5 Queen; 3 King
Full Breakfast
Credit Cards: A, B
Closed Jan. 8-27
Notes: 2, 9, 10, 11, 12, 14

FREMONT

Lord Bradley's Inn

43344 Mission Blvd., 94539
(415) 490-0520

This Victorian is nestled below Mission
Peak, adjacent to the Mission San Jose.
Numerous olive trees on the property were
planted by the Ohlone Indians. Common
room; garden, patio. Parking in rear. Take
the bus or Bay Area Rapid Transit to San
Francisco for a day.

6 Pets welcome: 7 Smoking allowed: 8 Children welcome: 9 Social drinking allowed: 10 Tennis available: 11
Swimming available: 12 Golf available: 13 Skiing available: 14 May be booked through travel agents

Hosts: Keith & Anne Bradley Medeiros
Doubles: 8 (PB) $55-$65
Type of Beds: 4 Twin; 6 Double
Continental Breakfast
Credit Cards: A, B
Notes: 2, 5, 6, 8, 9

GEORGETOWN

American River Inn

Orleans Street, Box 43, 95634
(916) 245-6566; (800) 245-6566, CA only

This "Jewel of the Mother Lode" is a totally
restored 1853 miners' boarding house. Each
room is individually decorated with Victorian and turn-of-the-century antiques.
Gorgeous natural gardens; a refreshing
mountain stream; pool with Jacuzzi; a dove
aviary; bicycles. Enjoy a full breakfast in the
morning, local wines and treats in the evening. Antique shop on the premises.
Facilities for the handicapped. Georgetown
is a Sierra foothills village with real flavor and
six historical buildings to explore.

Hosts: Will & Maria, Neal & Carol
Doubles: 25 (12 PB; 13 SB) $63-$85
Type of Beds: 25 Queen, 2 King
Full Breakfast
Credit Cards: A, B, C
Notes: 2, 5, 7, 8 (over 8) 9, 11, 12, 13

American River Inn

GEYSERVILLE

B&B Registry #CA-95441ISI

Box 8174, St. Paul, MN, 55108
(612) 646-4238

This B&B lodge and retreat center is on 10
acres of lush grounds that includes a theater.
Garden has pool, spa, sauna, and outdoor
fireplace. Mini-zoo with llama, sheep, goats,
swan, peacock. Also available for weddings,
bicycle groups, retreat groups.

Doubles: 16 (4 PB; 12 SB) $50-90
Full Breakfast
Credit Cards: A, B
Notes: 3, 4, 5, 6 (call), 11, 12

Campbell Ranch Inn

1475 Canyon Road, 95441
(707) 857-3476

Thirty-five-acre country setting in the heart
of Sonoma County wine country. Spectacular view, beautiful gardens, tennis court,
swimming pool, hot tub, bicycles. Full breakfast served on the terrace; homemade evening dessert.

Hosts: Mary Jane & Jerry Campbell
Doubles: 5 (PB) $86-108
Type of Beds: 5 King
Full Breakfast
Minimum stay weekends Mar-Nov: 2; major holiday
weekends: 3
Teenagers welcome
Credit Cards: A, B
Notes: 2, 5, 7 (limited), 9, 10, 11, 14

The Hope-Merrill House/The Hope-Bosworth House

Box 42, 95441
(707) 857-3356

Vintage Victorian turn-of-the-century inns
welcome travelers in grand style to the
California wine country. Twelve rooms with
private baths (two with Jacuzzi tubs), beautiful gardens, gazebo, vineyards, and swimming pool will make your stay a memorable
experience. Featured in *Country Homes,*
Sunset, House Beautiful magazines.

NOTES: Credit cards accepted: A Master Card; B Visa; C American Express; D Discover Card; E Diners
Club; F Other: 2 Personal checks accepted: 3 Lunch available: 4 Dinner available: 5 Open all year

Hosts: Bob & Rosalie Hope
Doubles: 12 (10 PB; 2 SB) $60-115
Type of Beds: 1 Double; 11 Queen
Full Breakfast
Credit Cards: A, B, C
Notes: 2, 5, 8, 9, 10, 11, 12, 14

GLEN ELLEN

Glenelly Inn

5131 Warm Springs Road, 95442
(707) 996-6720

Charming country inn located in the Sonoma wine country near Jack London Park. Restored turn-of-the-century inn with spacious lawn and oak trees. Boutique, wineries, and good restaurants nearby. One hour north of San Francisco.

Hosts: Gray & Addie Mattox
Doubles: 8 (PB) $75-120
Type of Beds: 1 Twin; 1 Double; 6 Queen
Full Breakfast
Minimum stay weekends & holidays, May-Oct.: 2
Credit Cards: A, B
Closed Christmas
Notes: 2, 9, 10, 11, 12, 14

GRASS VALLEY

Domike's Inn

220 Colfax Avenue, 95945
(916) 273-9010

Our Victorian home atmosphere encourages our guests to enjoy themselves. We serve a hearty, homemade breakfast at our guests' convenience. Lie back in our old-fashioned claw-foot tubs; relax in the lounge, porch, or yard whenever you wish.

Hosts: Joyce & Don Domike
Doubles: 5 (3 PB; 2 SB) $54-76.60
Type of Beds: 1 Twin; 3 Queen; 2 King
Full Breakfast
Minimum stay holidays: 2
Credit Cards: A, B
Notes: 2, 5, 7, 8, 9, 10, 11, 12, 14

GROVELAND

Eye Openers #2

Box 694, Atladena, 91001
(213) 684-4428

This large A-frame building with open-beamed ceilings sits on a tree-filled hillside above a private lake, just twenty minutes west of Yosemite. Loft bedroom/sitting room and second guest room. Enjoy your breakfast on the deck with its wonderful view of the Yosemite Park mountains.

Doubles: 2 (SB) $45-50
Type of Beds: 1 Queen; 1 King
Full Breakfast
Credit Cards: No
Notes: 2, 3, 4, 5, 8, 10, 11, 12

GUALALA

North Coast Country Inn

34591 S. Highway 1, 95445
(707) 884-4537

A cluster of rustic redwood buildings with ocean views. Our rooms feature queen beds, fireplaces, kitchenettes, private baths, decks, and private entries. The inn has a hot tub and gazebo. Full breakfast is served in guest rooms. Nearby golf, hiking, horseback riding, fishing, and beaches.

Hosts: Loren & Nancy Flanagan
Doubles: 4 (PB) $91.80-124.20
Type of Beds: 4 Queen
Full Breakfast
Minimum stay weekends: 2; holidays: 3
Credit Cards: A, B
Notes: 2, 5, 9, 10, 11, 12, 14

Whale Watch Inn

35100 Highway 1, 95445
(707) 884-3667

Serene oceanside retreat consisting of eighteen rooms, some with two-person whirlpool tubs, most with fireplaces, some with kitchens. All have ocean views. Breakfast is served in your room. Beach access.

6 Pets welcome: 7 Smoking allowed: 8 Children welcome: 9 Social drinking allowed: 10 Tennis available: 11 Swimming available: 12 Golf available: 13 Skiing available: 14 May be booked through travel agents

Doubles: 18 (PB) $135-210
Type of Beds: 18 Queen
Full Breakfast
Minimum stay weekends: 2; holidays: 3
Credit Cards: A, B, C
Notes: 2, 5, 8 (over 15), 10, 12

GUERNEVILLE

The Estate Inn

1355 Highway 116, 95446
(707) 869-9093

A Sonoma County historic landmark reborn
as an elegant bed & breakfast inn, The Estate is ideally located in the beautiful Russian River Valley just minutes from
award-winning wineries, Armstrong State
Redwood Reserve, and the dramatic Pacific
Coast.

Hosts: Jim Caron
Doubles: 10 (PB) $75-$150
Type of Beds: Queen
Full Breakfast
Credit Cards: A, B, C
Notes: 2, 5, 9, 10, 11, 12, 14

Santa Nella House

12130 Highway 116, 95446
(707) 869-9488

In the heart of the redwood, Russian River,
and champagne country. Located in a redwood forest with a quiet, comfortable,
homelike atmosphere. Wood-burning
fireplaces, private baths, large, delicious
breakfasts. Only eighteen miles from the
ocean. Reservations suggested.

Hosts: Ed & Joyce Ferrington
Doubles: 4 (PB) $75-90
Type of Beds: 1 Twin; 4 Double
Full Breakfast
Credit Cards: A, B
Closed Jan. & Feb.
Notes: 2, 8, 10, 11, 12

HALF MOON BAY

Little Creek Ranch

B&B San Francisco

Box 349, San Francisco, 94101
(415) 931-3083

A Texas millionaire opens his doors to bed
& breakfast guests. Located off Highway 1
forty-five minutes south of San Francisco,
this country mansion is filled with rare
Oriental antiques. All rooms are beautifully
decorated, have featherbeds and private
baths with whirlpool tubs. Beautiful country
setting. Golf, horseback riding, beach, restaurants nearby.

Doubles: 5 (PB) $75-200
Type of Beds: 2 Queen; 3 King
Full Breakfast
Credit Cards: A, B, C
Notes: 2, 5, 9, 10, 11, 12, 14

Mill Rose Inn

615 Mill Street, 94019
(415) 726-9794

An intimate country retreat hidden away
from the road, yet within walking distance of
the ocean and the historic Old Town district
of Half Moon Bay. The Mill Rose Inn invites
you to spend a night or weekend in the comfortable luxury of an English country garden
by the sea.

Hosts: Eve & Terry Baldwin
Doubles: 6 (PB) $145-215
Type of Beds: 1 Double; 3 Queen; 2 King
Full Breakfast
Minimum stay weekends & holidays: 2
Credit Cards: A, B, C
Notes: 2, 5, 9

Old Thyme Inn

779 Main Street, 94019
(415) 726-1616

This 1890 Victorian is on historic Main
Street, just forty minutes south of San Francisco on the Pacific Ocean. Some rooms
have double-size whirlpool tubs in private
bathrooms, fireplaces, and antiques. Stroll in

NOTES: Credit cards accepted: A Master Card; B Visa; C American Express; D Discover Card; E Diners
Club; F Other: 2 Personal checks accepted: 3 Lunch available: 4 Dinner available: 5 Open all year

Anne's herb garden and take cuttings. Complimentary beverages. Great breakfasts.

Hosts: Anne & Simon Lowings
Doubles: 7 (5 PB; 2 SB) $59-$162
Type of Beds: 1 Twin; 2 Double; 5 Queen
Full Breakfast
Credit Cards: A, B, C
Notes: 2, 5, 6, 8, 9, 10, 11, 12, 14

HEALDSBURG

Frampton House

489 Powell Avenue, 95448
(707) 433-5084

Located in the heart of Sonoma wine country, Frampton House offers personalized service and privacy. All-terrain bikes, Ping-Pong, exercycle, pool, spa, sauna, fireplace, wine and cheese. Custom-made tubs for two. Relax in any season.

Hosts: Paula & Chase Bogle
Doubles: 3 (PB) $75.60-91.80
Type of Beds: 1 Twin; 1 Double; 2 Queen
Full Breakfast
Credit Cards: A, B
Notes: 2, 5, 7 (limited), 8 (over 14), 9, 10, 11, 12

Jane's Place

B&B San Francisco
Box 349, San Francisco, 94101
(415) 931-3083

Jane's Place is located in rustic Healdsburg in the heart of the wine country, close to the Russian River beaches and resorts and only a half hour from the Pacific Coast. There are three quaintly furnished rooms with private baths on this estate overlooking vineyards. You may be entertained by wild turkeys while you enjoy your breakfast.

Doubles: 3 (PB) $75
Type of Beds: 3 Double
Full Breakfast
Credit Cards: A, B, C
Notes: 2, 5, 7, 8, 9, 11, 14

Madrona Manor

1001 Westside Road, 95448
(707) 433-4231; FAX: 433-0703

This twenty-room inn, in a national historic district, is distinguished by its sense of homey elegance that combines the graciousness one might feel at a friend's home with luxurious European amenities: thick terry robes, an expansive breakfast buffet, stately furniture, elegant decor.

Hosts: John & Carol Muir
Singles: 2 (PB) $89.50
Doubles: 18 (PB) $94.50-$140.40
Type of Beds: 4 Twin; 5 Double; 13 Queen; 2 King
Full Breakfast
Credit Cards: A, B, C, E
Notes: 2, 4, 5, 6, 7, 8, 10, 11, 12, 14

Madrona Manor

The Raford House

10630 Wohler Road, 95448
(707) 887-9573

A Victorian farmhouse sitting among the vineyards in a country setting that offers seven guest rooms, most with private baths, two with fireplaces. County historic landmark.

Hosts: Alan Baitinger & Beth Foster
Doubles: 7 (5 PB; 2 SB) $50-74.07
Type of Beds: 1 Twin; 6 Double; 1 Queen

6 Pets welcome: 7 Smoking allowed: 8 Children welcome: 9 Social drinking allowed: 10 Tennis available: 11
Swimming available: 12 Golf available: 13 Skiing available: 14 May be booked through travel agents

Full Breakfast
Credit Cards: A, B
Notes: 2, 5, 7 (limited), 8 (over 12), 9, 10, 11, 12, 14

HEALDSBURG/WINDSOR

Country Meadow Inn
11360 Old Redwood Hwy, 95492
(707) 431-1276

This restored 1890 Victorian farmhouse sits on 6.5 acres in the heart of Sonoma County's wine country. Guest rooms are decorated with carefully selected antiques that add to the warm, welcoming atmosphere. Fireplaces, whirlpool tubs, terraced gardens, and a gourmet breakfast enhance the peaceful country setting.

Hosts: Sandy & Barry
Doubles: 5 (PB) $80.80-113.20
Type of Beds: 4 Queen; 1 King
Full Breakfast
Credit Cards: A, B
Notes: 2, 5, 8, 9, 10, 11, 12, 14

HERMOSA BEACH

El Camino Real Bed & Breakfast #3
Box 7155, Northridge, 91327
(818) 363-6753

This house is seconds from the beach in this lovely beach community. The street looks like a European village, with flower boxes in all the windows. Children and babies welcome; dog run on the premises.

Doubles: 3 (S2B) $60-65
Type of Beds: 2 Twin; 1 Double; 1 Queen
Full Breakfast
Credit Cards: No
Notes: 5, 6 (inquire), 8, 10, 11, 12

HOLLYWOOD

El Camino Real Bed & Breakfast #4
Box 7155, Northridge, 91327
(818) 363-6753

Central location with easy access to tour buses and public transportation to places of interest. Fifteen to twenty minutes to studio tours, beaches, Hollywood Bowl, Chinatown, Little Tokyo, and more.

Doubles: 1 (PB) $35-40
Type of Beds: 1 Double; 1 Rollaway
Continental Breakfast
Credit Cards: No
Notes: 5, 7, 8, 10, 11, 12

Hollywood Celebrity Hotel
B&B of LA, 32074 Waterside La., Westlake Village, 91361
(818) 889-8870

Just around the corner from Mann's Chinese Theater. Art Deco style with airport and city bus lines nearby. TV, telephone; newspaper and breakfast delivered to your room daily. Free valet parking. Doubles, private bath, $60 and up.

IDYLLWILD

Wilkum Inn
Box 1115, 92349
(714) 659-4087

Nestled among the pines in a rustic mountain village, this two-story shingle-sided inn offers rooms that are individually furnished with the innkeepers' antiques and collectibles. Knotty-pine paneling and a river-rock fireplace enhance the hospitality of the common room.

Hosts: Annamae Chambers & Barbara Jones
Doubles: 4 (1 PB; 3 SB) $55-65
Type of Beds: 2 Twin; 1 Double; 2 Queen

NOTES: Credit cards accepted: A Master Card; B Visa; C American Express; D Discover Card; E Diners Club; F Other: 2 Personal checks accepted: 3 Lunch available: 4 Dinner available: 5 Open all year

Continental-plus Breakfast
Credit Cards: No
Notes: 2, 5, 9, 11, 14

INVERNESS

The Arc

180 Highland Way, Box 273, 94937
(415) 663-9338

The Arc is a charming two-room cottage sleeping up to six people, with bath and full kitchen. The ultimate in romantic seclusion, one hour north of San Francisco next to the magnificent Pt. Reyes National Seashore.

Hosts: Suzanna Storch
Singles: (PB) $102.60-118.80
Doubles: (PB) $108-124.20
Type of Beds: 2 Twin; 1 Double; 1 Queen
Full Breakfast
Credit Cards: No
Notes: 2, 5, 7, 8, 9

Ten Inverness Way

10 Inverness Way, Box 63, 94937
(415) 669-1648

The L.A. *Times* calls it "one of the niftiest inns in Northern California." Hearty breakfasts, private baths, ebullient garden, handmade quilts, Oriental rugs, stone fireplace. A redwood-shingled haven for hikers and rainy-day bookworms.

Hosts: Mary Davies
Doubles: 4 (PB) $90.72-107.88
Type of Beds: 1 Twin; 1 Double; 3 Queen
Full Breakfast
Credit Cards: A, B
Notes: 2, 5, 9, 11, 12, 14

IONE

The Heirloom

214 Shakeley Lane, 95640
(209) 274-4468

Travel down a country lane to our romantic English garden. Our petite colonial mansion (circa 1863) is shaded by century-old trees and scented by magnolias and gardenias.

Furnished with heirloom antiques, fireplaces, and balconies. Breakfast has a friendly flair. Come enjoy gracious hospitality.

Hosts: Patricia Cross & Melisande Hubbs
Doubles: 6 (4 PB; 2 SB) $50-80
Type of Beds: 2 Twin; 2 Double; 2 Queen; 2 King
Full Breakfast
Credit Cards: No
Closed Thanksgiving, Dec. 24 & 25
Notes: 2, 8 (over 10), 9, 10, 11, 12, 14

JACKSON

Gate House Inn

1330 Jackson Gate Road, 95642
(209) 223-3500

Charming turn-of-the-century Victorian in the country on an acre of garden property with swimming pool. Behind the main house is the Summer House, our finest accommodation because of its privacy and intimacy of its very special bathroom.

Hosts: Stan & Bev Smith
Doubles: 5 (PB) $75-105
Type of Beds: 5 Queen
Full Breakfast
Credit Cards: A, B
Notes: 2, 5, 8 (over 16), 9, 10, 11, 12, 14

The Wedgewood Inn

11941 Narcissus Road, 95642
(209) 296-4300

Charming Victorian replica tucked away on wooded acreage. Antique decor, afternoon refreshments, porch swing, balcony, wood-burning stoves, full gourmet breakfast. In the heart of the gold country, close to excellent dining, shopping, and sightseeing.

Hosts: Vic & Jeannine Beltz
Doubles: 6 (PB) $53-100.70
Type of Beds: 1 Double; 5 Queen
Full Breakfast
Credit Cards: A, B
Notes: 2, 5, 7 (limited), 8 (over 12), 9

6 Pets welcome: 7 Smoking allowed: 8 Children welcome: 9 Social drinking allowed: 10 Tennis available: 11 Swimming available: 12 Golf available: 13 Skiing available: 14 May be booked through travel agents

JAMESTOWN

The National Hotel
Box 502, 95327
(209) 984-3446

Historic National Hotel B&B, an eleven-room Gold Rush hotel (1859). Fully restored, with an outstanding restaurant and the original saloon. Classic cuisine and gracious service are only part of our charm.

Host: Stephen Willey
Singles: 2 (1 PB; 1 SB) $35-59.40
Doubles: 9 (4 PB; 5 SB) $35-59.40
Type of Beds: 4 Twin; 9 Queen
Continental Breakfast
Credit Cards: A, B
Notes: 2, 4, 5, 7, 8 (9 and over), 9, 11, 12, 13

The Palm Hotel Bed & Breakfast
10382 Willow St., Box 515, 95327
(209) 984-5657

Built as a home in the 1890s and later turned into a rooming house for railroad and mining men by adding more sleeping rooms. The current owners have turned this completely remodeled historic building into a bed and breakfast inn with one room arranged to accommodate people using wheel chairs. The marble-topped bar in the lobby is used as a reception desk and for serving the continental breakfast each morning from 8:30 to 10:30. Locally there is gourmet dining, antique shopping, and gold panning. The inn is convenient to Columbia State Historic and Railtown 1897 State Historic parks.

Hosts: Jacob & Pam Barendregt
Doubles: 9 (5 PB; 4 SB) $43.5-108
Type of Beds: 2 Double; 6 Queen; 1 King
Continental Breakfast
Credit Cards: A, B, C
Notes: 2(with major cc), 5, 7(in lobby), 8, 9, 10, 11, 12, 13

JAMUL

B&B Registry #CA-92035LIO
Box 8174, St. Paul, MN, 55108
(612) 646-4238

Expansive Spanish villa home overlooking the valley, with breathtaking views of San Diego, the ocean, and Mexico. Lounge in the living room, enjoy the hot tub, or take a tour into Mexico for a lobster dinner and bargains.

Doubles: 4 (PB) $40-70
Type of Beds: 3 Queen; 2 King; 1 Cot
Full Breakfast
Credit Cards: No
Notes: 3, 4, 5, 6 (call), 8, 12

JENNER

Murphys Jenner Inn
10400 Coast Highway One, 95450
(707) 865-2377

Our lovingly and quaintly furnished accommodations all have private entrances and baths. Most offer restful river, ocean, or coastal views. The absence of TV and telephones in the rooms sets the mood for relaxing amid one of nature's most wonderfully abundant and harmonious settings. Just a short walk to the rugged coastline and restaurants with fine California cuisine.

Hosts: Richard & Sheldon Murphy
Doubles: 9 (PB) $45-125
Type of Beds: 3-4 Twin; 5 Double; 3 Queen; 1 King
Continental Breakfast
Credit Cards: A, B, C
Notes: 2, 3, 4, 5, 7 (outside), 8, 9, 10, 11

KENSINGTON

B&B International 12
1181-B Solano Avenue
Albany, 94706
(415) 525-4569

NOTES: Credit cards accepted: A Master Card; B Visa; C American Express; D Discover Card; E Diners Club; F Other: 2 Personal checks accepted: 3 Lunch available: 4 Dinner available: 5 Open all year

Panoramic view of the Golden Gate in an older Tudor-style home that has been renovated with extraordinary design elements. Hot tub, fruit trees, art collection. Convenient bus to U.C. Berkeley.

Doubles: (PB) $54-65
Full Breakfast
Minimum stay: 2
Credit Cards: Major
Notes: 8, 9

KING CITY AREA

Megan's Friends B&B Service #2
1776 Royal Way, San Luis Obispo, 93401
(805) 544-4406

Solar designed country home 2.5 miles from Highway 101 in Pine Canyon with a 360-degree view of the valleys and hills. There are back roads for hiking and interesting places to visit: Lakes San Antonio and Nacimiento, Pinnacles National Monument, and Mission San Antonio. Queen bedroom with private bath. Dinner is available by advance request. $40.

LAGUNA BEACH

B&B International 13
1181-B Solano Avenue
Albany, 94706
(415) 525-4569

Hillside home overlooking Bluebird Canyon, a few minutes from the beach. Architect designed, sunny, spacious rooms. Decks, waterfall, and a sense of privacy.

Doubles: (PB) $64
Full Breakfast
Minimum stay: 2
Credit Cards: Major
Notes: 7, 8

The Carriage House

The Carriage House
1322 Catalina Street, 92651
(714) 494-8945

The Carriage House features all private suites with living room, bedroom, bath, and kitchen facilities. Some two-bedroom suites available. All surround a courtyard of plants and flowers, two blocks from the ocean. Close to art galleries, restaurants, and shops.

Hosts: Vern, Dee, & Tom Taylor
Suites: 6 (PB) $91.80-135
Type of Beds: 4 Twin; 3 Double; 3 Queen; 2 King
Continental Breakfast
Minimum stay weekends & holidays: 2
Credit Cards: No
Notes: 2, 5, 7, 8, 9, 10, 11, 12

Casa Laguna Inn
2510 South Coast Highway, 92651
(714) 494-2996

A Spanish mission-style inn on an ocean-view hillside setting with tropical gardens and courtyards, heated pool, aviary, observation bell tower, and cozy library. Complimentary afternoon tea with wine, pates, cheeses, caviar, and hors d'oeuvres. Near Los Angeles and Disneyland.

Hosts: Jerry & Luanne Siegel
Doubles: 20 (PB) $91.80-210.60
Type of Beds: 8 Twin; 17 Queen; 4 King
Continental Breakfast
Minimum stay weekends: 2; holidays: 2-3
Credit Cards: A, B, C, D, E
Notes: 2, 5, 7, 8, 9, 10, 11, 12, 14

6 Pets welcome: 7 Smoking allowed: 8 Children welcome: 9 Social drinking allowed: 10 Tennis available: 11 Swimming available: 12 Golf available: 13 Skiing available: 14 May be booked through travel agents

Eiler's Inn

741 S. Coast Highway, 92651
(714) 494-3004

Located in the heart of Laguna, just a few steps from the Pacific Ocean. Tennis, shops, and restaurants are within walking distance. The inn offers elegant yet casual sophistication, with all rooms furnished in antiques, ocean views from the sun deck, fireplaces, and a flower-scented brick courtyard with bubbling fountain.

Hosts: Henk & Annette Wirtz
Singles: 8 (PB) $100-165
Doubles: 4 (PB) $100-165
Type of Beds: 1 Twin; 3 Double; 9 Queen; 1 King
Full Breakfast
Credit Cards: A, B, C
Notes: 2, 5, 7, 8, 9, 10, 11, 12, 14

LAGUNA HILLS

B&B of LA

32074 Waterside La.
Westlake Village, 91361
(818) 889-8870

Outside stairs lead to guest rooms sharing a balcony overlooking the pool. Breakfast delivered to your door. Children over 16 welcome. French and Italian spoken. Two doubles, shared bath, $40.

LAKE ARROWHEAD

Bluebelle House Bed & Breakfast

Box 2177, 92352
(714) 336-3292

Enjoy cozy elegance in an alpine setting. Five rooms, decorated in themes from European travels or favorite things. Walk to lake, village, beach, shops, restaurants. Three-star AAA rating. Your hosts love to pamper their guests. Evening refreshments.

Hosts: Rick & Lila Peiffer
Doubles: 5 (3 PB; 2 SB) $65-95

Type of Beds: 5 Queen
Continental-plus Breakfast
Credit Cards: A, B
Closed Dec. 24-27
Notes: 2, 5, 10, 11, 12, 13

Eagle's Landing

Box 1510, Blue Jay, CA 92317
(714) 336-2642

Eagle's Landing is a contemporary mountain home furnished with antiques and arts and crafts from around the world, featuring an emphasis on hospitality, scrumptious breakfasts, a view of beautiful Lake Arrowhead, and an alpine forest. Chosen the number one B&B in Southern California by KABC's radio travel show in 1987.

Hosts: Dorothy & Jack Stone
Doubles: 4 (PB) $75-120
Full Breakfast
Credit Cards: No
Closed Dec. 24-26
Notes: 2, 5, 9, 10, 11, 12, 13, 14

Bluebelle House Bed and Breakfast

NOTES: Credit cards accepted: A Master Card; B Visa; C American Express; D Discover Card; E Diners Club; F Other: 2 Personal checks accepted: 3 Lunch available: 4 Dinner available: 5 Open all year

LEUCADIA

El Camino Real Bed & Breakfast #5

Box 7155, Northridge, 91327
(818) 363-6753

Located 27 miles north of San Diego, this home is in the country and overlooks the beach. A short drive to all San Diego has to offer: Sea World, San Diego Zoo, and the trolley to Mexico.

Doubles: 2 (SB) $40-50
Type of Beds: 2 Twin; 1 Queen; 1 Rollaway
Full Breakfast
Credit Cards: No
Notes: 5, 8, 10, 11, 12

Seascapes

B&B of LA, 32074 Waterside La., Westlake Village, 91361
(818) 889-8870

Private home overlooking the Pacific, just minutes from the beach. TV, patio, pool, spa, tennis courts. Snacks in the late afternoon. No smoking, adults only. One suite, private bath, full breakfast. $65.

LINDSAY

El Camino Real Bed & Breakfast #6

Box 7155, Northridge, 91327
(818) 363-6753

Just a thirty-minute drive from Sequoia National Park, this restored 1901 Victorian is a beautifully furnished small inn with a swimming pool and honeymoon suite. Nearby golf course.

Doubles: 4 (SB) $55-60
Type of Beds: 1 Twin; 3 Double; 1 King
Full Breakfast
Credit Cards: No
Notes: 5, 7 (limited), 11, 12

LODI

Wine & Roses Country Inn

2505 W.Turner Road, 95242
(209) 334-6988

Converted to a charming, romantic B&B and country French restaurant, our 1902 estate is secluded on 2.5 acres of towering trees and old-fashioned flower gardens. Handmade comforters, antiques, collectibles, fresh flowers. We serve evening wine and appetizers and a delightful breakfast. Pool, horse, and carriage on the premises; golf, tennis, lake within five minutes.

Hosts: Kris Cromwell & Del Smith
Doubles: 9 (PB) $75-105 and up
Type of Beds: 9 Queen
Full Breakfast
Credit Cards: A, B
Notes: 2, 4 (weekends), 5, 9, 10, 11, 12, 14

LONG BEACH

Appleton Place

B&B of LA, 32074 Waterside La., Westlake Village, 91361
(818) 889-8870

Once the home of Captain James Appleton and his family, now completely renovated. Bus line one block away. Telephones in each room. Ten blocks to the ocean. Pick-up at the Long Beach airport can be arranged; car rental available. Children over 12 welcome. No TV. Five doubles, full breakfast, $60-80.

B&B International 15

1181-B Solano Avenue
Albany, 94706
(415) 525-4569

Beachfront home in the city's most desirable location, not far from the *Queen Mary*. Hosts have a large swimming pool, ocean view from the veranda and the pool. High-

---

6 Pets welcome: 7 Smoking allowed: 8 Children welcome: 9 Social drinking allowed: 10 Tennis available: 11 Swimming available: 12 Golf available: 13 Skiing available: 14 May be booked through travel agents

quality 1930s home with a fountain in the living room.

Doubles: (PB) $52
Full Breakfast
Minimum stay: 2
Credit Cards: Major
Notes: 7, 8, 11

LOS ANGELES

B&B Registry #CA-90004HER

Box 8174, St. Paul, MN, 55108
(612) 646-4238

Located in the heart of Los Angeles, between Hollywood and the mid-Wilshire area, this comfortable two-story home provides a wonderful place to relax after a hectic day of sightseeing or business. Very private. Patio and fireplace for guests' use.

Doubles: 2 (SB) $30-40
Type of Beds: 4 Twin; 1 Double; 1 Queen
Continental Breakfast
Credit Cards: No
Notes: 5, 6 (call), 8, 12

Eastlake Victorian Inn

1442 Kellam Avenue, 90026
(213) 250-1620

Beautifully restored and furnished historic monument located in L.A.'s first preservation district. Situated on a residential hilltop, we have views and the best central location near downtown, theaters, shopping, restaurants, Dodger Stadium, and Universal Studios. Close to Disneyland and the beaches. "Incomparably romantic," says the L.A. *Times.*

Hosts: Planaria Price & Murray Burns
Singles: 1 (SB) $45
Doubles: 8 (3 PB; 5 SB) $125
Type of Beds: 5 Twin; 7 Double; 3 Queen
Full Breakfast
Minimum stay weekends: 2; holidays: 2-4
Credit Cards: A, B, C
Notes: 2, 4, 5, 8 (over 10), 9, 10, 11, 12, 14

Eye Openers #3

Box 694, Altadena, 91003
(213) 684-4428

Convenient to West Los Angeles, Beverly Hills, and beaches, this condo in Westwood offers comfortable quarters.

Doubles: 1 (PB) $60
Type of Beds: 1 Double
Continental Breakfast
Credit Cards: A, B
Notes: 2, 5, 10, 11, 12

Terrace Manor

B&B of LA, 32074 Waterside La., Westlake Village, 91361
(818) 889-8870

Time stands still in this 1902 home facing a park. Leaded-glass windows, paneling, and period furnishings create an atmosphere of genteel living. Complimentary wine in the parlor, locked parking, and a library with books, games, and TV. Children over 10 welcome. Five doubles, full breakfast, private baths. $60-90.

LOS FELIZ

El Camino Real Bed & Breakfast #7

Box 7155, Northridge, 91327
(818) 363-6753

Ten minutes to downtown; fifteen to Pasadena. Near the Music Center, Chinatown, Little Tokyo, theaters, museums, and the Rose Parade.

Doubles: 2 (SB) $44
Type of Beds: 4 Twin
Continental Breakfast
Credit Cards: No
Notes: 5, 10, 12

NOTES: Credit cards accepted: A Master Card; B Visa; C American Express; D Discover Card; E Diners Club; F Other: 2 Personal checks accepted: 3 Lunch available: 4 Dinner available: 5 Open all year

LOS OSOS

Gerarda's B&B

1056 Bay Oaks Drive, 93402
(805) 528-3973

The ideal place to stop between San Francisco and Los Angeles. On the coast with ocean and mountain views. Close to Hearst Castle, Morro Bay, and San Luis Obispo; golf, tennis, hiking, and shopping. Dutch hospitality; your host speaks several languages.

Host: Gerarda Ondang
Singles: 1: $27
Doubles: 2 (1 PB; 1 SB) $42
Type of Beds: 2 King
Full Breakfast
Credit Cards: No
Notes: 2, 4, 5, 6, 8, 9, 10, 11, 12

Megan's Friends B&B Service #3

1776 Royal Way, San Luis Obispo, 93401
(805) 544-4406

Large hillside house with a stunning view of the valley, mountains, bay, and Pacific Ocean. Two miles from sand dunes and Montana de Oro State Park. Meticulous Dutch housekeeping and hospitality. Queen room with a separate entrance and twin room. Downstairs family suite with king bed, bath, and color TV in the adjoining living room. Children welcome downstairs. $45-55.

Megan's Friends B&B Service #4

1776 Royal Way, San Luis Obispo, 93401
(805) 544-4406

Just south of Morro Bay and near Montana de Oro State Park, this bayside Cape Cod home offers a spacious, tastefully furnished bedroom with separate entrance, king bed, antiques, TV, fireplace, and private bath.

Guest sitting room with fireplace and view of the bay. Private deck and patio, canoe available. $55-70.

LOYALTON

Clover Valley Mill House

Box 928, 96118
(916) 993-4819

Heirlooms, Irish lace, comfortable antiques, and a fireplace in one of Sierra County's fine old residences. Located in a pioneer sawmill town in the heart of cowboy country. Explore a hundred lakes and a thousand miles of streams, or just curl up with a favorite book or an old-time movie.

Host: Leslie Hernandez
Singles: 1 (SB) $35
Doubles: 3 (1 PB; 2 SB) $55-70
Type of Beds: 1 Twin; 1 Double; 3 Queen
Full Breakfast
Credit Cards: A, B
Notes: 2, 5, 9, 10, 11, 14

MALIBU

Casa Larrone

Box 86, 90265
(213) 456-9333

This is a private home on a private beach one mile from famous Surfers' Beach and the sport-fishing pier. The ocean suite has kitchenette, fireplace, ceiling fan, TV, phone, and 40 feet of glass overlooking its private deck. The locals call this beach Millionaires' Row.

Hosts: Jim & Charlou Larronde
One ocean suite w/bath: $60 single occupancy; $75 double
Type of Beds: King
Full Breakfast:
Credit Cards: No
Notes: 2, 7, 8, 9, 10, 11

6 Pets welcome: 7 Smoking allowed: 8 Children welcome: 9 Social drinking allowed: 10 Tennis available: 11 Swimming available: 12 Golf available: 13 Skiing available: 14 May be booked through travel agents

El Camino Real Bed & Breakfast #8

Box 7155, Northridge, 91327
(818) 363-6753

Beautiful art-filled home with 180-degree view of the Pacific Ocean. Beaches, Getty Museum, restaurants all nearby. Upstairs suite with sitting room; two rooms on the first floor.

Doubles: 3 (1 PB; 2 SB) $40-50
Type of Beds: 2 Twin; 1 Double; 1 King; 1 Rollaway
Continental Breakfast
Credit Cards: No
Notes: 5, 8 (over 5), 10, 11, 12

MAMMOTH LAKES

Snow Goose Bed & Breakfast Inn

Box 946, 93546
(619) 934-2660

Home away from home in the European tradition. Enjoy a full breakfast each morning. Sierra Mountains winter ski resort and summer getaway. Ice skating, snow mobiling, hot-air ballooning, fishing, hiking, wind surfing. Walk to restaurants, shops, and entertainment.

Hosts: Wes & Laurie Johnson
Doubles: 15 (PB) $69-95
Suites: 3 (two bedrooms) PB $148-170
Type of Beds: 9 Twin; 1 Double; 19 Queen; 1 King
Full Breakfast
Minimum stay weekends: 2; holidays: 3
Credit Cards: A, B, C, D
Notes: 2, 4, 5, 6, 7, 8, 9, 10, 11, 13

MARINA DEL REY

Sea Lodge

B&B of LA, 32074 Waterside La., Westlake Village, 91361
(818) 889-8870

European-style hotel just a few blocks from the ocean, ten minutes from the airport, and twenty minutes from town. Restaurants and shops nearby. Breakfast in the courtyard; wine and cheese in the evenings. Forty-two doubles, $76.50-115.

MARIPOSA

Oak Meadows, too

5263 Highway 140N, Box 619, 95338
(209) 742-6161

Located in the historic gold-rush town of Mariposa, this B&B has turn-of-the-century charm. New England architecture: rooms decorated with handmade quilts, wallpaper, and brass headboards. Close to Yosemite. Home of the California State Mining & Mineral Museum.

Hosts: Dot & George Saunders
Doubles: 6 (PB) $49-59
Type of Beds: 4 Twin; 3 Queen; 1 King
Continental-plus Breakfast
Credit Cards: A, B
Notes: 2, 5, 14

The Pelennor

3871 Highway 49 South, 95338
(209) 966-2832

Country atmosphere about 45 minutes from Yosemite National Park. After a day of sightseeing, you may want to take a few laps in our lap pool, unwind in the spa, enjoy the available games, and listen to an occasional tune played on the bagpipes.

Hosts: Dick & Gwen Foster
Singles: $30; Doubles: $35
Type of Beds: 2 Twin; 1 Double; 2 Queen
Full Breakfast
Credit Cards: No
Notes: 2, 5, 6, 8, 9, 10, 11

McCLOUD

McCloud Guest House

606 W. Colombero Drive, 96057
(916) 964-3160

Built in 1907, this beautiful old country home is nestled among stately oaks and lofty

---

NOTES: Credit cards accepted: A Master Card; B Visa; C American Express; D Discover Card; E Diners Club; F Other: 2 Personal checks accepted: 3 Lunch available: 4 Dinner available: 5 Open all year

pines on the lower slopes of majestic Mt. Shasta. On the first floor is one of Siskiyou County's finer dining establishments. The second floor has a large parlor surrounded by our five guest rooms, each individually decorated.

Hosts: Bill & Patti Leigh, Dennis & Pat Abreu
Doubles: 5 (PB) $70-90
Type of Beds: 5 Queen
Continental Breakfast
Minimum stay holidays: 2
Credit Cards: A, B
Closed Thanksgiving & Christmas
Notes: 2, 4, 11, 12, 13

MENDOCINO

Brewery Gulch Inn
9350 Coast Highway One, 95460
(707) 937-4752

An authentic country B&B farm located on the rugged coast just one mile from the village of Mendocino. The lovely old white farmhouse is furnished in the Victorian style with queen beds, homemade quilts, and down pillows. Each guest room window provides views of the gardens and meadows beyond.

Hosts: Leo & Gen Pallanck
Doubles: 5 (3 PB; 2 SB) $70-110
Type of Beds: 5 Queen
Full Breakfast
Credit Cards: A, B
Notes: 2, 5, 10, 11, 12

Cypress House
Box 303, 95460
(707) 937-1456

A private romantic garden cottage just for two, overlooking Mendocino Bay and village. Adjacent to an 80 acre oceanfront state park. All the special touches for a special getaway: fireplace, fresh flowers, down comforter, stereo, and much more. Country quiet, yet only five minutes to Mendocino Village.

Hosts: Roger & Pamela Weerts
Cabin: 1 (PB) $125
Type of Beds: 1 Queen
Continental Breakfast
Credit Cards: No
Notes: 2, 5, 9, 10, 11, 12

Cypress House
Box 303, 95460
(707) 937-1456

A private romantic garden cottage just for two, overlooking Mendocino Bay and village. Adjacent to an 80-acre oceanfront state park. All the special touches for a special getaway: fireplace, fresh flowers, down comforter, stereo, and much more. Country quiet, yet only five minutes to Mendocino Village.

Hosts: Roger & Pamela Weerts
Cabin: 1 (PB) $125
Type of Beds: 1 Queen
Continental Breakfast
Credit Cards: No
Notes: 2, 5, 9, 10, 11, 12

The Headlands Inn
Box 132, 95460
(707) 937-4431

The Headlands Inn is centrally located within Mendocino Village on California's scenic north coast, minutes from redwoods and wineries. Gourmet breakfasts are served to your room. All rooms have wood-burning fireplaces; spectacular ocean views overlooking our English-style garden. Two parlors, many unusual antiques.

Hosts: Pat & Rod Stofle
Doubles: 5 (PB) $89-125
Type of Beds: 3 Queen; 2 King
Full Breakfast
Minimum stay weekends: 2; holidays: 3
Credit Cards: No
Notes: 2, 5, 8 (16 and over), 9, 10, 11, 12

6 Pets welcome: 7 Smoking allowed: 8 Children welcome: 9 Social drinking allowed: 10 Tennis available: 11 Swimming available: 12 Golf available: 13 Skiing available: 14 May be booked through travel agents

MacCallum House Inn

45020 Albion Street, 95437
(707) 937-0289

An 1882 Victorian with unique garden cottages located in the center of Mendocino. Bar and restaurant on the premises.

Hosts: Melanie & Joe Reding
Doubles: 20 (8 PB; 12 SB) $49-140
Type of Beds: 14 Double; 5 Queen; 1 King
Continental Breakfast
Minimum stay May-Dec. weekends: 2; holidays: 2-3
Credit Cards: A, B
Notes: 2, 4, 5, 7, 8, 9, 10, 11, 12

Mendocino Farmhouse

Box 247, 95460
(707) 937-0241

Mendocino Farmhouse is a small B&B with all the comforts of home. We are surrounded by redwood forest, beautiful gardens, a pond, and meadow. Choose among our comfortable rooms decorated with country antiques for a quiet night's rest and enjoy a sumptuous farmhouse breakfast in the morning.

Hosts: Margie & Bud Kamb
Doubles: 5 (PB) $60-85
Type of Beds: 1 Twin; 4 Queen; 1 King
Full Breakfast
Credit Cards: No
Notes: 2, 5, 6 (call), 8 (call), 10, 11, 12

Mendocino Village Inn

Main Street, Box 626, 95460
(707) 937-0246

A well-done bed and breakfast inn featuring hummingbirds, Picassos, French roast coffee, fuchsias, fireplaces, Vivaldi. This 1882 Victorian is filled with everything necessary for charm and gracious living, including four-poster beds, Bokharas, fresh blackberries, migrating whales, Chardonnay.

Hosts: Sue & Tom Allen
Doubles: 12 (10 PB; 2 SB) $55-110
Type of Beds: 7 Double; 4 Queen
Full Breakfast
Minimum stay weekends: 2; holidays: 3
Credit Cards: A, B
Notes: 2, 5, 8 (over 10), 9, 10, 11, 12

Whitegate Inn

Box 150, 95460
(707) 937-4892

Everything you look for in a B&B experience: antiques, fireplaces, ocean views, and all private baths. Elegant 1880 Victorian, located in the center of the historic preservation village of Mendocino. Shops, galleries, and nationally acclaimed restaurants are just steps away. A perfect setting for romantic trysts, weddings, or rest and relaxation.

Host: Patricia Patton
Doubles: 5 (PB) $75-100
Type of Beds: 2 Double; 3 Queen
Full Breakfast
Credit Cards: No
Notes: 2, 5, 9, 10, 11, 12, 13

Mendocino Village Inn

Whitegate Inn

MILL VALLEY

B&B International 17

1181-B Solano Avenue
Albany, 94706
(415) 525-4569

Japanese-style home with a garden and fish pond, an easy drive to Muir Redwoods, Marin hiking trails. Picturesque town fifteen minutes by car from San Francisco.

Doubles: (PB) $54
Full Breakfast
Minimum stay: 2
Credit Cards: Major

Mill Valley B&B

B&B Exchange of Marin
45 Entrata, San Anselmo, 94960
(415) 485-1971

Enjoy the warmth and charm of old Marin. We're tucked away on the hillside overlooking the charming town of Mill Valley. The lower floor of the house is a private guest suite that can accommodate up to four people. It has a private deck with view, sitting room with TV, and private entrance.

Doubles: 1 (PB) $80
Continental Breakfast
Notes: 2, 5, 6, 8, 9, 10, 11, 12, 14

MONTARA

The Goose & Turrets

835 George Street, Box 937, 94037
(415) 728-5451

A 1908 Italian villa in a garden setting with its own mascot geese. Thirty minutes to San Francisco; half a mile to the Pacific. Near restaurants, horseback riding, tide pools, antiques, golf. We pick up at Prince-ton Harbor and Half Moon Bay Airport. Nous parlons francais.

Hosts: Raymond & Emily Hoche-Mong
Doubles: 5 (2 PB; 3 S2B) $70-85
Type of Beds: 2 Twin; 2 Double; 1 Queen; 1 King
Full Breakfast
Credit Cards: A, B, C
Closed Easter
Notes: 2, 8, 9, 10, 11, 12, 14

Montara B & B

1125 Tamarind Street, 94037
(415) 728-3946

Just twenty miles south of San Francisco on the scenic California coast. Semi-rural area with nearby hiking, beaches, and horseback riding. Private entrance, private bath, ocean view, fireplace, TV, stereo, telephone, sun deck. Business travelers welcome.

Hosts: Bill & Peggy Bechtell
Doubles: 1 (PB) $55-65
Type of Beds: Twin or King
Full Breakfast
Minimum stay weekends & holidays: 2
Credit Cards: A, B
Notes: 2, 4, 5, 9, 10, 11, 12

MORAGA

B&B Registry #CA-94556HAL

Box 8174, St. Paul, MN, 55108
(612) 646-4238

6 Pets welcome: 7 Smoking allowed: 8 Children welcome: 9 Social drinking allowed: 10 Tennis available: 11 Swimming available: 12 Golf available: 13 Skiing available: 14 May be booked through travel agents

Attractive California contemporary home on a quiet cul-de-sac in beautiful Moraga Valley, just thirty minutes from downtown San Francisco. Take a refreshing dip in the pool or relax in the redwood hot tub. Good public transportation to San Francisco on BART.

Doubles: 2 (SB) $45-50
Type of Beds: 2 Queen
Full Breakfast
Credit Cards: No
Notes: 5, 8 (must swim), 11

MOUNTAIN VIEW

B&B International 19

1181-B Solano Avenue
Albany, 94706
(415) 525-4569

Two-story modern house on a quiet cul-de-sac has a bedroom/sitting room suite. Japanese garden with hot tub. Your hosts are a secretary and mechanical engineer.

Doubles: (PB) $48
Full Breakfast
Minimum stay: 2
Credit Cards: Major
Notes: 7, 8, 9, 11

MT. SHASTA

Mt. Shasta Ranch

1008 W.A. Barr Road, 96067
(916) 926-3870

We are a 1923 lodge-type B&B with a recreation room with pool table, Ping-Pong, and other games. Our suites are large rooms with private baths, just one mile from the lake and town center. Large living room with massive rock fireplace for your enjoyment.

Hosts: Bill & Mary Larsen
Doubles: 9 (4 PB; 5 SB) $55-65
Type of Beds: 9 Queen
Full Breakfast
Credit Cards: A, B
Notes: 2, 5, 7, 9, 10, 11, 12, 14

Ward's Big Foot Ranch B&B

1530 Hill Road, Box 585, 96067
(916) 926-5170

A delightful secluded hideaway surrounded by forest with an unparalleled view of majestic Mt. Shasta. A truly unique setting complete with hospitality, serenity, and charm. Located near ski areas, lakes, hiking trails, excellent restaurants, and a friendly, warm community. "Our home is your home!"

Hosts: Barbara & Phil Ward
Doubles: 2 (SB) $45
Guest Cottage: sleeps 6 (PB) $75 per couple
Type of Beds: 2 Twin; 1 Queen; 1 King
Full Breakfast
Credit Cards: No
Closed during Christmas (cottage open)
Notes: 2, 8, 9, 10, 11, 12, 13

MUIR BEACH

B&B of LA

32074 Waterside La.
Westlake Village, 91361
(818) 889-8870

Contemporary country home with large windows, open beams, and a balcony overlooking the ocean. Guest quarters overlook San Francisco and the Pacific. Fireplace, private entrance, sitting room. Muir Woods five minutes away. Dog in residence. One double, full breakfast. $95.

MURPHYS

Dunbar House, 1880

271 Jones Street, Box 1375, 95247
(209) 728-2897

You can explore the Gold Country during the day and enjoy a glass of lemonade on the wide porches in the afternoon. Inviting fireplaces and down comforters in your antique-filled room. Breakfast may be served

NOTES: Credit cards accepted: A Master Card; B Visa; C American Express; D Discover Card; E Diners Club; F Other: 2 Personal checks accepted: 3 Lunch available: 4 Dinner available: 5 Open all year

in your room, the dining room, or in the century-old gardens.

Hosts: Bob & Barbara Costa
Doubles: 5 (PB) $79.50-90.10
Type of Beds: 3 Double; 2 Queen
Full Breakfast
Minimum stay holidays: 2
Credit Cards: A, B
Notes: 2, 5, 8 (over 10), 9, 10, 11, 12, 13, 14

Dunbar House, 1880

NAPA

Arbor Guest House

1436 G Street, 94559
(707) 252-8144

This 1906 home and carriage house is furnished with period antiques and located in a quiet garden setting. The inn is a lovely retreat where you are pampered by thoughtful innkeepers. Fresh baked breads, seasonal fruits, juice, and beverages are served in the dining room or at patio tables.

Hosts: Bruce & Rosemary Logan
Doubles: 5 (PB) $70-110
Type of Beds: 5 Queen
Continental Breakfast
Credit Cards: A, B, C
Notes: 2, 5, 10, 11, 12, 14

Churchill Manor Bed & Breakfast Inn

485 Brown Street, 94559
(707) 253-7733

An 1889 grand mansion on a beautifully landscaped acre. Carved wood ceilings and columns, leaded-glass windows, and seven fireplaces. Furnished with antiques, Oriental rugs, and a grand piano. Buffet breakfast includes homemade breads, muffins, croissants, quiches, cheeses, and fresh fruits. Evening wine. Play croquet or ride our complimentary tandem bicycles.

Host: Joanna Guidotti
Doubles: 8 (PB) $60-145
Type of Beds: 4 Queen; 4 King; 3 Rollaways
Continental-plus Breakfast
Credit Cards: A, B
Closed Christmas & Easter
Notes: 2, 5, 9, 10, 11, 12, 14

Country Garden Inn

1815 Silverado Trail, 94558
(707) 255-1197

The Country Garden is an 1860s carriage house decorated in English pine an-tiques and family heirlooms. Riverside setting on 1.5 acres of gardens. Afternoon tea, happy hour, wine in rooms, and dessert.

Hosts: George and Lisa Smith
Doubles: 7 (PB) $100-$150
Type of Beds: 6 Queen; 1 King
Full Breakfast
Credit Cards: A, B, C
Notes: 2, 5, 8 (over 16), 9, 10, 12

The Crossroads Inn

6380 Silverado Trail, 94558
(707) 944-0646

Luxury, privacy, and sweeping Napa Valley views are yours at The Crossroads Inn, a singular retreat for appreciating the beauty and life-style of the wine country. Its commanding view of vineyards and mountains has no equal. Three spacious guest suites provide visitors with every amenity, including private spas.

Hosts: The Scott-Maxwell Family
Doubles: 3 (PB) $150-200
Type of Beds: 3 King
Continental Breakfast
Credit Cards: A, B
Closed Jan.
Notes: 2, 7 (outside), 8 (over 16), 9, 10, 11, 12

6 Pets welcome: 7 Smoking allowed: 8 Children welcome: 9 Social drinking allowed: 10 Tennis available: 11 Swimming available: 12 Golf available: 13 Skiing available: 14 May be booked through travel agents

Eye Openers #4

Box 694, Altadena, 91001
(213) 684-4428

Cozy, well-appointed cottage adjacent to the hosts' home features half-canopy bed and sitting area with fireplace. This 3.5 acre farm has a swimming pool and is close to vineyards and wine tasting.

Doubles: 1 (PB) $75-85
Type of Beds: 1 Queen
Continental Breakfast
Credit Cards: A, B
Notes: 2, 5, 7, 10, 11, 12

Napa Inn

1137 Warren Street, 94559
(707) 257-1444

The Napa Inn offers you a comfortable, quiet stay in an elegant Victorian home located in the heart of the Napa Valley wine country. Living, dining, and bedrooms are decorated with unusual antiques. Come and experience the elegance of the Victorian Era.

Hosts: Doug & Carol Morales
Doubles: 4 (PB) $90-100
Full Breakfast
Credit Cards: A, B
Closed Christmas
Notes: 2, 8 (over 12)

The Old World Inn

Wine Country

1301 Jefferson Street, 94559
(707) 257-0112

Elegant Victorian built in 1900. Eight rooms with private bath, one with private Jacuzzi, feature decor inspired by the colors of Swedish artist Carl Larsson. Enjoy afternoon tea and cookies, complimentary wine, international cheese board, a substantial breakfast, and our custom-built Jacuzzi. We look forward to welcoming you to our inn.

Hosts: Janet & Geoffrey Villiers
Doubles: 8 (PB) $92-127
Type of Beds: 7 Queen; 1 King
Continental-plus Breakfast
Credit Cards: A, B, C
Notes: 2, 5, 9, 10, 11, 12, 14

The Red Castle Inn

109 Prospect Street, 95959
(916) 265-5135

High on a forested hillside, breezes linger on wide verandas, strains of Mozart echo through lofty hallways, chandeliers sparkle, the aura of another time prevails. In Gold Country, the four-story Gothic Revival inn "would top my list of places to stay. Nothing else quite compares with it"—*Gourmet.*

Hosts: Mary Louise & Conley Weaver
Doubles: 8 (6 PB; 2 SB) $65.20-102.60
Type of Beds: 4 Double; 4 Queen
Full Breakfast
Credit Cards: A, B
Notes: 2, 5, 7 (outside), 8 (over 10), 9, 10, 11, 12, 13 (XC), 14

B&B Registry #CA-92663VIL

Box 8174, St. Paul, MN, 55108
(612) 646-4238

Lovely contemporary home on Lido Island with a patio on the bay. Sensational view of the yacht harbor. Walk to the wonderful shops and restaurants on the bay. Close to all southern California attractions.

Doubles: 2 (PB) $86
Type of Beds: 2 Twin; 1 Queen
Continental-plus Breakfast
Credit Cards: No
Closed June-Aug.
Notes: 11, 12

NOTES: Credit cards accepted: A Master Card; B Visa; C American Express; D Discover Card; E Diners Club; F Other: 2 Personal checks accepted: 3 Lunch available: 4 Dinner available: 5 Open all year

Red Castle Inn

El Camino Real Bed & Breakfast #9

Box 7155, Northridge, 91327
(818) 363-6753

This lovely condo is just a bicycle ride from the beach and twenty minutes from Disneyland. Great Fashion Isle shopping. Laundry facilities, swimming pool, bike trails. Owner has a special plan for dieters who want to go away to lose a few pounds or adjust their eating habits.

Doubles: 1 (SB) $44
Type of Beds: 1 Queen
Continental Breakfast
Credit Cards: No
Notes: 3, 4, 5, 7 (limited), 8, 10, 11, 12

Eye Openers #5

Box 694, Altadena, 91003
(213) 684-4428

Crow's nest with a 360-degree view tops this tri-level beach home. Third level is a large guest deck with bbq and refrigerator.

Stained glass is featured throughout the house. Perfectly located for beach and bay activities; bicycles and beach chairs available. Beach one-half block away. Close to Laguna Beach, Orange County Cultural Center, good restaurants, and shopping.

Doubles: 2 (PB) $50
Type of Beds: 1 Double; 1 Queen
Full Breakfast
Credit Cards: A, B
Notes: 2, 5, 7, 10, 11, 12

NIPTON

Hotel Nipton

72 Nipton Road, 92364
(619) 856-2335

Hotel Nipton, originally built in 1904, was completely restored in 1986. Located in the east Mojave National Scenic Area 65 miles south of Las Vegas. The hotel offers a panoramic view of the New York Mountains, outside Jacuzzi for star gazing, and is thirty minutes from Lake Mojave. Historic rock and cactus garden in front of hotel.

Hosts: Jerry & Roxanne Freeman
Doubles: 4 (SB) $44.94
Type of Beds: 1 Twin; 3 Double
Continental Breakfast
Credit Cards: A, B
Notes: 5, 7, 8, 9

NORTH HOLLYWOOD

B&B International 22

1181-B Solano Avenue
Albany, 94706
(415) 525-4569

Sunny guest room opens onto the swimming pool of this California ranch-style home. Air-conditioning, kitchen privileges; close to Universal Studio tour.

Doubles: (PB) $56
Full Breakfast
Minimum stay: 2
Credit Cards: Major
Notes: 7, 8 (swimmers), 11

6 Pets welcome: 7 Smoking allowed: 8 Children welcome: 9 Social drinking allowed: 10 Tennis available: 11 Swimming available: 12 Golf available: 13 Skiing available: 14 May be booked through travel agents

NORTHRIDGE-LA

El Camino Real Bed & Breakfast #10

Box 7155, Northridge, 91327
(818) 363-7155

A lovely suburban home with freeway access to all points of interest. Close to CSUN, Universal Tours, Hollywood Bowl, Magic Mountain.

Doubles: 1 (PB) $52
Type of Beds: 1 King
Continental Breakfast
Credit Cards: No
Notes: 5, 10, 12

OAKHURST

B&B International 23

1181-B Solano Avenue
Albany, 94706
(415) 525-4569

Spacious contemporary mountain home in a wooded setting twenty minutes to Yosemite, with swimming pool. Near golf course, boating and fishing on Bass Lake. Guest suite has TV, fireplace, Jacuzzi tub, private entrance.

Doubles: (PB) $50-58
Full Breakfast
Minimum stay: 2
Credit Cards: Major
Notes: 7, 8 (swimmers), 11

OAKLAND

B&B International 24

1181-B Solano Avenue
Albany, 94706
(415) 525-4569

English Tudor mansion with eight bedrooms, six baths, massive stone fireplace, ornate and gilded ceilings. Extensive gardens. Two guest rooms plus coach house apartment.

Doubles: (PB) $58
Full Breakfast
Minimum stay: 2
Credit Cards: Major
Notes: 7, 8

OCCIDENTAL

Heart's Desire Inn

3657 Church Street, 95465
(707) 874-1311

In the redwoods near the spectacular Sonoma coast and wine country, Heart's Delight Inn is a completely renovated 1867 Victorian with European ambience. With antique furnishings and goose-down comforters, each room features fresh flowers and a private bath. A courtyard garden, the parlor's fireplace, and a sumptuous breakfast are all for your enjoyment.

Hosts: Justina & Howard Selinger
Doubles: 8 (PB) $81-102; Suite $145
Type of Beds: 1 Twin; 2 Double; 5 Queen
Continental Breakfast
Minimum Stay weekends & holidays: 2
Credit Cards: A, B, C
Notes: 2, 3, 4, 5, 9, 10, 11, 12

OJAI

Ojai B & B

921 Patricia Court, 93023
(805) 646-8337

Quiet, beautifully appointed home: artwork, mineral baths, Jacuzzi. Trails, bike path are minutes from the house, which is one mile to the village at the altitude of 7,000 feet. Rooms have mountain views, excellent restaurants are nearby, and cultural activities are available almost every weekend. Home-baked scones and jam and fruit from our orchard are featured at breakfast.

NOTES: Credit cards accepted: A Master Card; B Visa; C American Express; D Discover Card; E Diners Club; F Other: 2 Personal checks accepted: 3 Lunch available: 4 Dinner available: 5 Open all year

Host: Tiba Willner
Doubles: 3 (SB) $65-75
Full Breakfast
Minimum stay holidays: 2
Credit Cards: No
Notes: 2, 5, 8 (over 12), 9

ORANGE

B&B Registry #CA-92669COU

Box 8174, St. Paul, MN, 55108
(612) 646-4238

Located near Disneyland, Knott's Berry Farm, Angels Stadium, beaches. Close to Los Angeles. A lovely home noted for its unique glass architecture offers guests country hospitality. Rise early for juice and coffee by the pool. Relax in the evening in the spa or by the fireplace.

Doubles: 4 (1 PB; 3 SB) $48-68
Type of Beds: 2 Queen; 1 King; 1 Daybed
Full Breakfast
Credit Cards: No
Notes: 5, 8, 11

ORLAND

The Inn at Shallow Creek Farm

Route 3, Box 3176, 95963
(916) 865-4093

A gracious two-story farmhouse offering spacious rooms furnished with antiques — a blend of nostalgia and comfortable country living. Three miles off Interstate 5. The Inn is known for its orchard and fresh garden produce. Breakfast features old-fashioned baked goods and local fruits and juices.

Hosts: Kurt & Mary Glaeseman
Doubles: 4 (2 PB; 2 SB) $45-$75
Type of Beds: 2 Twin; 3 Queen
Full Breakfast
Credit Cards: No
Notes: 2, 4, 5, 9, 11, 12, 14

OROSI

Valley View Citrus Ranch B&B

14801 Avenue 428, 93647
(209) 528-2275

This house features bougainvillaeas and clusters of boulders in a colorful garden with gazebo; views of the valley or hill from every window. An interesting Spanish-style house less than an hour from Sequoia National Park.

Hosts: Tom & Ruth Flippen
Doubles: 2 (PB) $55-60.50
Type of Beds: 2 Twin; 1 Queen; 2 King
Full Breakfast
Notes: 2, 5, 7 (restricted), 8, 9, 10, 14

PACIFIC GROVE

Gosby House Inn

643 Lighthouse Avenue, 93950
(408) 375-1287

The Gosby House Inn sits in the heart of the quaint town of Pacific Grove. Its magnificent Queen Anne Victorian architecture will enchant you, as will its individually decorated sleeping rooms, antique doll collection, and gracious staff. A bountiful breakfast and afternoon wine and hors d'oeuvres are served. Fluffy robes, complimentary beverages, and a heaping cookie jar.

Host: Kelly Short
Doubles: 22 (20 PB; 2 SB) $93.50-137.50
Type of Beds: 5 Double; 17 Queen
Full Breakfast
Credit Cards: A, B, C
Notes: 2, 5, 8, 9, 10, 11, 12, 14

Green Gables Inn

104 5th Street, 93950
(408) 375-2095

This is a 100-year-old Queen Anne Victorian mansion set on the dramatic

Monterey coastline. Each room is individually decorated with antiques. Guests receive full breakfast, afternoon wine and hor d'oeuvres, newspaper, complimentary beverages, bathrobes, fruit, and cookies. One of the first B&Bs in California.

Host: Claudia Long
Doubles: 11 (7 PB; 4 SB) $110-181.50
Type of Beds: 1 Double; 10 Queen
Full Breakfast
Credit Cards: A, B, C
Notes: 2, 5, 8, 9, 10, 11, 12, 14

Gosby House Inn

Maison Bleu

Box 51371, 93950
(408) 373-2993

A home away from home in the country French tradition. Canopy queen and king beds, gourmet breakfasts. Walk to theater, shops, restaurants, golf, beach, the Monterey Bay Aquarium, and Cannery Row. Carmel and Monterey are less than ten minutes away, as are Laguna Seca Racetrack and the Pebble Beach golf courses. Big Sur is half an hour.

Host: Jeanne E. Coles
Doubles: 3 (2 PB; 1 SB) $95-115
Type of Beds: 3 Queen; 2 King; 1 Rollaway
Full Breakfast
Credit Cards: A, B, C, E
Notes: 2, 5, 7 (restricted), 8, 9, 10, 11, 12

Seven Gables Inn

555 Ocean View Blvd., 93950
(408) 372-4341

Seven Gables Inn is a century-old Victorian mansion situated on a rocky promontory overlooking scenic Monterey Bay. Furnished throughout with elegant, fine Victorian antiques. All rooms have panoramic ocean views and private baths. A very generous light breakfast and four o'clock High Tea are included. Smoking in the garden only. Seven Gables provides easy access to the Monterey Aquarium, Cannery Row, Seventeen-Mile Drive, Carmel, and numerous other scenic sites in the Monterey area.

Hosts: The Flatley Family
Doubles: 14 (PB), $85-$165
Type of Beds: 1 Double; 13 Queen
Continental-plus Breakfast
Credit Cards: A, B
Notes: 2, 5, 8, 9, 10, 11, 12, 14

PALM SPRINGS

B&B International 25

1181-B Solano Avenue
Albany, 94706
(415) 525-4569

Condominium a few blocks from the main street in a spacious, landscaped setting with tennis courts and swimming pool. Rooms open onto patio.

Doubles: (PB) $54
Full Breakfast
Minimum stay: 2
Credit Cards: Major
Notes: 7, 10, 11

NOTES: Credit cards accepted: A Master Card; B Visa; C American Express; D Discover Card; E Diners Club; F Other: 2 Personal checks accepted: 3 Lunch available: 4 Dinner available: 5 Open all year

The Garbo Inn

B&B of LA, 32074 Waterside La., Westlake Village, 91361
(818) 889-8870

Desert hideaway of Greta Garbo. Recently redecorated, air-conditioned. Six suites with color TV/VCR, refrigerators. Some with fireplaces, and most with a view of the spacious lawns and gardens. Refreshments served by the pool in the afternoon. Full kitchen available for guests' use. Just a few blocks from the Tram in the heart of Palm Springs. Six doubles, private baths, full breakfast. $85-95 plus tax.

Japanese Bed & Breakfast

B&B of LA, 32074 Waterside La., Westlake Village, 91361
(818) 889-8870

Leave your shoes at the door and relax in your kimono while you sip saki. Spacious home with heated pool. Airport pick-up can be arranged. Adults only. Doubles with private bath, $45-75.

Villa Royale

B&B of LA, 32074 Waterside La., Westlake Village, 91361
(818) 889-8870

An international atmosphere, with objects from Morocco, France, and England. Brick paths lead you through the courtyards and gardens to the two pools. On 3.5 acres. Adults only. Thirty-one doubles, private baths, $49-200.

PALO ALTO

Adella Villa

Box 4528, Stanford, 94309
(415) 321-5195

A 1920s Tyrolean estate on one parklike acre just twenty-five minutes from San Francisco. Four lovely guest rooms with private baths and Jacuzzi tubs. Color TV and sherry in each room. Our music room features a Steinway grand piano. Full breakfast, swimming pool, security gates, very quiet.

Hosts: Allen & Ann McKinney
Doubles: 4 (PB) $85
Type of Beds: 2 Twin; 2 Queen; 1 King
Full Breakfast
Credit Cards: A, B, C
Notes: 2, 5, 8 (over 12), 9, 10, 11, 12, 14

B&B International 26

1181-B Solano Avenue
Albany, 94706
(415) 525-4569

This new house won an award for innovative solar heating and has been pictured in *Sunset* and *Better Homes & Gardens*. It features a lap swimming pool in the solarium.

Doubles: (PB) $65
Full Breakfast
Minimum stay: 2
Credit Cards: Major
Notes: 11

The Victorian on Lytton

555 Lytton Avenue, 94301
(415) 322-8555

Special amenities include down comforters, Battenberg lace canopies, botanical prints, and claw-foot tubs. Wander through the English country garden with over 700 perennial plants. Relax with a picture book or novel in the parlor with a cup of tea while listening to classical music.

Hosts: Maxwell & Susan Hall
Doubles: 10 (PB) $99-148.50
Type of Beds: 4 Twin; 3 Queen; 5 King
Continental Breakfast
Credit Cards: A, B, C
Notes: 2, 5, 9, 10, 11, 12, 14

6 Pets welcome: 7 Smoking allowed: 8 Children welcome: 9 Social drinking allowed: 10 Tennis available: 11 Swimming available: 12 Golf available: 13 Skiing available: 14 May be booked through travel agents

PASADENA

Eye Openers #6
Box 694, Altadena, 91003
(213) 684-4428

Located along Pasadena's scenic tour drive, this gracious Spanish home has a lovely garden with fruit trees and pool. Your German host loves to spoil guests with an elegant breakfast served on the terrace or in the sun-filled dining room. Pet cat. Near Huntington Library and Gardens, California Institute of Technology, Jet Propulsion Laboratory, Art Center School of Design, Norton Simon Museum. Twenty minutes to LA, Hollywood, Universal Studios.

Doubles: 2 (PB) $35-50
Type of Beds: 2 Twin; 1 King
Full Breakfast
Credit Cards: A, B
Notes: 2, 5, 9, 10, 11, 12

PASO ROBLES

Megan's Friends B&B Service #5
1776 Royal Way, San Luis Obispo, 93401
(805) 544-4406

Early 1900s California farmhouse, where guests enjoy a separate cabin with two bedrooms and bath, living room, and kitchen. This quiet retreat is six miles east of town, near wineries, lakes. Nature trails are provided over the 40 acres of farmland. Continental breakfast. $75-85.

PISMO BEACH

B&B International 27
1181-B Solano Avenue
Albany, 94706
(415) 525-4569

Contemporary house in Sunset Palisades that overlooks the Pacific Ocean. Fine modern furniture and art collection.

Doubles: (PB) $68
Full Breakfast
Credit Cards: Major
Notes: 7, 8

POINT REYES STATION

The Country House
B&B Exchange of Marin
45 Entrata, San Anselmo, 94960
(415) 485-1971

Great breakfasts! A country setting, in the middle of an apple orchard with an English garden. Light kitchen privileges, wood stove, great hosts will guide you to hiking trails, good restaurants, etc.

Doubles: 3 (2 PB; 1 SB) $80
Type of Beds: 1 Double; 2 Queen
Full Breakfast
Credit Cards: No
Notes: 2, 5, 6, 8, 9, 10

Jasmine Cottage
11561 Coast Highway One, 94956
(415) 663-1166

This charming guest cottage was built in 1879 for the original Point Reyes schoolhouse. Secluded, romantic cottage sleeps four, has a library, woodstove, full kitchen, beautiful pastoral views, private patios, and gardens. Five minutes' walk down the hill to town; five minutes' drive to spectacular Point Reyes National Seashore. A crib and high chair are available.

Hosts: Karen Gray
Cottage: 1 (PB) $92-124
Type of Beds: 2 Twin; 1 Queen
Full Breakfast
Credit Cards: No
Notes: 2, 4, 5, 6, 8, 9, 11

NOTES: Credit cards accepted: A Master Card; B Visa; C American Express; D Discover Card; E Diners Club; F Other: 2 Personal checks accepted: 3 Lunch available: 4 Dinner available: 5 Open all year

Marsh Cottage Bed & Breakfast
Box 1121, 94956
(415) 669-7168

The privacy of your own peaceful bay-side retreat near Inverness and spectacular Point Reyes National Seashore. Exceptional location and views, tasteful interior, fireplace, fully equipped kitchen, complete bath. Breakfast provided in the cottage. Ideal for romantics and naturalists. Hiking and other sports nearby.

Host: Wendy Schwartz
Doubles: 1 (PB) $91.80-102.60
Type of Beds: 1 Twin; 1 Queen; portacrib
Full Breakfast
Minimum stay weekends & holidays: 2
Credit Cards: No
Notes: 2, 5, 8, 9, 11

Thirty-nine Cypress
39 Cypress Street, 94956
(415) 663-1709

This redwood house on 3.5 acres has been furnished with family antiques, original art, and an eclectic library. It has an English country garden for guests to enjoy, plus a state-of-the-art spa with massaging jets outside. Spectacular view of Point Reyes peninsula and the upper reaches of Tomales Bay. Near beaches.

Host: Julia Bartlett
Doubles: 3 (SB) $80-95
Type of Beds: 1 Double; 1 Queen; 1 King
Full Breakfast
Credit Cards: No

PORTOLA

Upper Feather Bed & Breakfast
256 Commercial Street, Box 1528, 96122-1528
(916) 832-0107

Small-town comfort and hospitality in casual country comfort style. No TV or radio, but we have board games, puzzles, and popcorn for relaxing. Walk to the railroad museum, restaurants, wild and scenic river, and national forest lands. Only one hour from Reno entertainment.

Hosts: Jon & Lynne Haman
Doubles: 5 (SB) $42.40
Suites: 1 (2 rooms SB) $63.60
Type of Beds: 6 Twin; 4 Double; 1 Crib
Full Breakfast
Credit Cards: A, B
Notes: 2, 5, 6, 8, 10, 11, 12, 13

RANCHO CUCAMONGA

Christmas House Bed & Breakfast Inn
9240 Archibald Avenue, 91730
(714) 980-6450

A 1904 Victorian mansion with seven fireplaces, intricate woodwork, and stained glass throughout. Located 40 miles east of Los Angeles, close to Ontario International Airport and freeway close to all of Southern California's attractions. Gracious turn-of-the-century surroundings and hospitality.

Hosts: Jay & Janice Ilsley
Doubles: 5 (2 PB; 3 SB) $60-126
Type of Beds: 4 Double; 1 Queen
Full Breakfast
Credit Cards: No
Notes: 2, 4, 5, 8 (over 12), 9, 10, 11, 12, 13, 14

RED BLUFF

The Faulkner House
1029 Jefferson Street, 96080
(916) 529-0520

An 1890s Queen Anne Victorian, furnished in antiques. Screened porch looks out on a quiet, tree-lined street for relaxing, or let us help you discover our area. Go hiking and skiing at Laseen National Park, visit Ide Adobe or a Victorian museum, enjoy Sacramento River fishing.

6 Pets welcome: 7 Smoking allowed: 8 Children welcome: 9 Social drinking allowed: 10 Tennis available: 11 Swimming available: 12 Golf available: 13 Skiing available: 14 May be booked through travel agents

Hosts: Harvey & Mary Klinger
Doubles: 4 (1 PB; 3 SB) $43-60
Type of Beds: 1 Double; 3 Queen
Full Breakfast
Credit Cards: No
Notes: 2, 5, 7 (on porches), 9, 12, 13, 14

REDDING

Palisades Paradise B&B

1200 Palisades Ave., 96003
(916) 223-5305

You'll love the breath-taking view of the
Sacramento River, city, and surrounding
mountains from this beautiful contemporary home with its garden spa, fireplace,
wide-screen TV-VCR, and homelike atmosphere. Palisades Paradise is a serene setting
for a quiet hideaway, yet conveniently located one mile from shopping and Interstate
5, with water skiing and river rafting nearby.

Hosts: Gail Goetz
Doubles: 2 (SB) $50-$60
Type of Beds: 2 Twin; 1 Double
Continental-plus Breakfast weekdays, Full on
weekends
Credit Cards: A, B
Notes: 2, 5, 7 (restricted), 8, 9, 10, 11, 12, 13, 14

REDONDO BEACH

Ocean Breeze B&B

122 South Juanita Avenue, 90277
(213) 316-5123

Near the beach, between Los Angeles and
Long Beach, close to all freeways and attractions. Private entry, spa bathtub, and hospital beds with heated mattress covers.
Remote TV, microwave oven, toaster, coffee maker in large rooms. Rooms are new
and luxurious, but cost one-third to one-half
of local hotels.

Hosts: Norris & Betty Binding
Doubles: 2 (PB) $30-50
Type of Beds: 1 Queen; 1 King
Continental Breakfast
Minimum stay weekends & holidays: 2
Credit Cards: No
Notes: 2, 5, 7, 8 (over 5), 9, 10, 11, 12

ROUND MOUNTAIN

NW B&B #578

NW Bed & Breakfast Travel Unlimited
610 SW Broadway, Portland, OR, 97205
(503) 243-7616

Large log home, formerly a hunting lodge,
in the foothills of the Cascades between Mt.
Shasta and Mt. Lassen. Just one mile east of
Redding, this is a lovely retreat in the woods
with mountain views. The hosts raise cattle,
turkeys, and peacocks on their 30 acres.
Hosts speak English and Spanish.

Singles: 1 (SB) $35
Doubles: 2 (SB) $45
Type of Beds: 1 Twin; 1 Double; 1 Queen
Continental Breakfast
Credit Cards: No
Notes: 4, 7

Amber House

SACRAMENTO

Amber House Bed & Breakfast

1315 22nd Street, 95816
(916) 444-8085

NOTES: Credit cards accepted: A Master Card; B Visa; C American Express; D Discover Card; E Diners
Club; F Other: 2 Personal checks accepted: 3 Lunch available: 4 Dinner available: 5 Open all year

This 1905 mansion is elegantly appointed with antiques, original art, Oriental rugs, and fresh flowers. Relax in front of the fireplace or enjoy the cozy library. Guest rooms feature private baths — one with Jacuzzi tub — private telephones, radios, TVs. Full gourmet breakfast.

Hosts: Michael & Jane Richardson
Doubles: 5 (PB) $72-138
Type of Beds: 2 Double; 3 Queen
Full Breakfast
Credit Cards: A, B, C
Notes: 2, 5, 9, 10, 11, 12, 14

B&B International 28

1181-B Solano Avenue
Albany, 94706
(415) 525-4569

California ranch-style home in a residential area south of the Capitol. Japanese garden in back. Air-conditioning, fireplace.

Doubles: (PB) $48
Full Breakfast
Minimum stay: 2
Credit Cards: Major
Notes: 7, 8

The Briggs House

2209 Capitol Avenue, 95816
(916) 441-3214

The Briggs House is just a few blocks from the state capitol. European and American antiques help create a setting of quiet, peaceful splendor with rich wood paneling, inlaid hardwood floors, Oriental rugs, and delicate lace curtains. Relax in the sauna in the backyard or soak in your an-tique bathtub. Expertly arranged flowers grace your room, and breakfast will be served on fine china.

Hosts: Leslie Hopper & Pam Giordano
Doubles: 7 (5 PB; 2 SB) $60-95
Type of Beds: 2 Twin or 1 King; 2 Double; 4 Queen
Full Breakfast
Credit Cards: A, B, C
Notes: 2, 5, 8, 9, 10, 11, 12, 14

ST. HELENA

B&B Registry #CA-94574JUD

Box 8174, St. Paul, MN, 55108
(612) 646-4238

Situated within walking distance of town, yet with a quiet country atmosphere surrounded by vineyards. Bring your suit for a dip in the pool. There are over 100 wineries to visit in the area.

Doubles: 1 (PB) $65-85
Type of Beds: 1 Queen
Continental Breakfast
Credit Cards: No
Notes: 5, 8, 11, 12

B&B Registry #CA-94574RAN

Box 8174, St. Paul, MN, 55108
(612) 646-4238

Quiet, exclusive 7-acre ranch-style home with magnificent view of the countryside. Centrally located for quick access to the entire valley — wineries, mud baths, balloon rides, restaurants. Unwind in the Jacuzzi or relax in front of the fireplace.

Doubles: 3 (PB) $85-95
Type of Beds: 2 Queen; 1 King
Continental Breakfast
Credit Cards: No
Notes: 5, 8, 12

B&B Registry #CA-94574SPA

Box 8174, St. Paul, MN, 55108
(612) 646-4238

Spanish villa nestled in a wooded valley just outside of St. Helena and near the world-famous wineries of the Napa Valley. Villa features replicas of Tiffany lamps

6 Pets welcome: 7 Smoking allowed: 8 Children welcome: 9 Social drinking allowed: 10 Tennis available: 11 Swimming available: 12 Golf available: 13 Skiing available: 14 May be booked through travel agents

throughout, has a large sitting room with arched windows looking out on the patio.

Doubles: 1 (PB) $85-95
Type of Beds: 1 King
Continental Breakfast
Credit Cards: No
Notes: 5

Elsie's Conn Valley Inn

726 Rosse Road, 94574
(707) 963-4614

Nestled in lush garden surroundings with views of vineyards and rolling hills — peaceful, quiet, and romantic. In-room refrigerators, air-conditioning, antiques. Common room with fireplace, library, TV, piano. Complimentary wine, fruit, cheese and crackers. Lots of country roads for strolling or jogging.

Host: Elsie Hudaka
Doubles: 3 (1 PB; 2 SB) $75-85
Type of Beds: 1 Double; 1 Queen; 1 King
Continental-plus Breakfast
Credit Cards: No
Notes: 2, 5, 9, 10, 11, 14

Erika's Hillside

285 Fawn Park, 94574
(707) 963-2887

Enjoy a peaceful and romantic retreat nestled on a hillside overlooking the Silverado Trail with inspiring views of the Napa Valley and its vineyards.

Host: Erika Cunningham
Doubles: 3 (PB & SB) $65-150
Type of Beds: 3 Queen
Continental Breakfast
Credit Cards: No
Notes: 2, 5, 8, 9, 10, 11, 12, 14

Villa St. Helena

2727 Sulphur Springs Avenue, 94574
(707) 963-2514

Secluded hilltop Mediterranean villa that combines quiet country elegance with

panoramic views of the Napa Valley. Romantic, antique-filled rooms with private entrances, private baths; some with fireplaces. Twenty-acre estate with walking trails and a spacious courtyard pool. Complimentary wine is served.

Hosts: Ralph & Carolyn Cotton
Doubles: 3 (PB) $145-225
Continental Breakfast
Minimum stay weekends & holidays: 2
Credit Cards: A, B
Notes: 2, 5, 7, 8 (over 12), 9, 10, 11, 12, 14

The Wine Country Inn

The Wine Country Inn

1152 Lodi Lane, 94574
(707) 963-7077

Perched on a knoll overlooking manicured vineyards and the nearby hills, this country inn offers twenty-five individually decorated guest rooms. The Smiths used local antiques, family-made quilts, fireplaces, and balconies to create and atmosphere of unparalleled comfort.

Hosts: Jim Smith & Sheila Ticer
Doubles: 25 (PB) $110-133
Continental Breakfast
Credit Cards: A, B
Closed Christmas
Notes: 2, 5, 7, 9, 10, 11, 12, 14

NOTES: Credit cards accepted: A Master Card; B Visa; C American Express; D Discover Card; E Diners Club; F Other: 2 Personal checks accepted: 3 Lunch available: 4 Dinner available: 5 Open all year

SAN ANSELMO

San Anselmo B&B

B&B Exchange of Marin
45 Entrata, San Anselmo, 94960
(415) 485-1971

Private guest quarters with separate kitchen and pool. On a tree-lined lane near the heart of the old-fashioned town of San Anselmo. Walk to fine restaurants, hiking trails, many antique stores, and a lake. Fifteen miles north of San Francisco and forty-five minutes to the wine country.

Doubles: 1 (PB) $55-75
Full Breakfast
Credit Cards: No
Notes: 2, 5, 6, 8, 9, 10, 12, 14

Casa de Flores Bed and Breakfast

SAN CLEMENTE

Casa de Flores Bed & Breakfast

184 Ave. La Cuesta, 92672
(714) 498-1344

Situated midway between Los Angeles and San Diego, offering the finest in accommodations. The views of the Pacific Ocean and Dana Point Harbor are spectacular. Orchids on the property enjoy our perfect climate. Beautiful beaches and fine restaurants are within a five-minute drive.

Hosts: Marliee & Robert Arsenault
Doubles: 4 (2 PB; 2 SB) $45-$100 seasonal
Type of Beds: 1 Twin; 3 King
Full Breakfast
Minimum stay holidays: 2
Credit Cards: No
Notes: 2, 5, 7, 9, 10, 11, 12, 14

SAN DIEGO

Carole's B&B

3227 Grim Avenue, 92104
(619) 280-5258

A friendly, congenial home close to all major attractions. Only 1.5 miles to the San Diego Zoo and Balboa Park. This house, built in 1904, is decorated with antiques and has a large swimming pool. Complimentary wine and cheese are also served.

Hosts: Carole Dugdale & Michael O'Brien
Doubles: 8 (SB) $50
Continental Breakfast
Credit Cards: No
Notes: 5, 7, 9, 10, 11, 12, 14

The Cottage

3829 Albatross Street, 92103
(619) 299-1564

Located between the zoo and Sea World, The Cottage is a quiet retreat in the heart of a downtown residential neighborhood. The turn-of-the-century furnishings throughout evoke visions of a bygone era. Each morning you will be served a breakfast of freshly baked bread, fruit, and beverage.

Hosts: Robert & Carol Emerick
Doubles: 2 (PB) $45-70
Type of Beds: 2 King
Continental Breakfast
Credit Cards: A, B
Notes: 2, 5, 8, 10, 11, 12, 14

Eye Openers #7

Box 694, Altadena, 91003
(213) 684-4428

---

6 Pets welcome: 7 Smoking allowed: 8 Children welcome: 9 Social drinking allowed: 10 Tennis available: 11 Swimming available: 12 Golf available: 13 Skiing available: 14 May be booked through travel agents

Enjoy this large home with newly decorated rooms, all with views of the forest. The backyard has many varieties of plant and wildlife, tables, and bbq. Convenient to San Diego and its tourist attractions.

Doubles: 3 (1 PB; 2 SB) $37-57
Type of Beds: 1 Double; 1 Queen; 1 King
Continental-plus Breakfast
Credit Cards: A, B
Notes: 8, 10, 11, 12

Heritage Park Bed & Breakfast Inn

2470 Heritage Park Row, 92110
(619) 295-7088

A Queen Anne Victorian, circa 1889, situated on a beautiful 7-acre Victorian park in historic Old Town. Five minutes to the zoo, Sea World, and airport. Nine antique-filled rooms, private baths. Romantic candlelight dinners are available, and a full homemade breakfast is included. Free parking.

Hosts: Lori Chandler
Singles: 2 (SB) $70.15
Doubles: 7 (5 PB; 2 SB) $124.15
Type of Beds: 3 Double; 6 Queen
Full Breakfast
Minimum stay weekends & holidays: 2
Credit Cards: A, B
Notes: 4, 5, 8 (over 14), 9, 10, 11, 12

Keating House Inn

2331 Second Ave., 92101
(619) 239-8585

An elegant antique-filled historically designed Queen Anne Victorian residence three blocks west of Balboa Park with its museums, theaters, and the San Diego Zoo. Sun and shade patios provide relaxing settings. Also enjoy our fresh flowers, complimentary sherry and wine, and turn-down chocolate truffles.

Hosts: George Pearn & Jason Price
Doubles: 4 (2 PB; 2 SB) $57.24-$70.20
Type of Beds: 1 Twin; 1 Double; 2 Queen
Continental Breakfast
Credit Cards: A, B
Notes: 2, 5, 7 (limited), 8 (over 12), 9, 10, 11, 12, 14

SAN FRANCISCO

Alamo Square Inn

B&B of LA, 32074 Waterside La., Westlake Village, 91361
(818) 889-8870

This immaculately restored Victorian mansion overlooks the park at Alamo Square, between the Civic Center and the Golden Gate Park. Five beautifully furnished guest rooms with private baths. Downstairs rooms available for meetings or other small groups. No smoking.

Doubles: 5 (PB) $85-110 plus tax
Full Breakfast
Credit Cards: A, B

Art Center Bed & Breakfast Suites, Wamsley

1902 Filbert Street, 94123
(415) 567-1526

Personal comfort and family privacy with kitchens, baths, queen beds, fireplaces, and art in four suites. Accessibility to all events, theaters, restaurants, shopping by bus. Northern California tours start from this quiet residential marina area between the Bay Bridge and the Golden Gate. No smoking, please.

Hosts: George & Helvi Wamsley
Doubles: 4 (PB), $65-85
Full Breakfast
Credit Cards: All
Notes: 2, 5, 8, 9, 10, 12, 14

NOTES: Credit cards accepted: A Master Card; B Visa; C American Express; D Discover Card; E Diners Club; F Other: 2 Personal checks accepted: 3 Lunch available: 4 Dinner available: 5 Open all year

B&B Registry #CA-94123ARA

Box 8174, St. Paul, MN, 55108
(612) 646-4238

A lovely 1890 Victorian located in Pacific Heights near Fisherman's Wharf, Ghiradelli Square, Aquatic Park, and the Palace of Fine Arts. One block from unique Union Street shops and restaurants and bus that goes to the cable car and North Beach area.

Singles: 1 (SB) $50-55
Doubles: 2 (SB) $70
Type of Beds: 2 Double; 1 King
Continental Breakfast
Credit Cards: No
Notes: 5, 8

Casita Blanca

330 Edgehill Way, 94127
(415) 564-9339

Casita Blanca is a guest cottage high on a hill, close to Golden Gate Park. A delightful studio nestled in the trees, it has its own bath, kitchen, and fireplace.

Host: Joan Bard
Double: 1 (PB) $70
Type of Beds: Twin
Continental Breakfast
Minimum stay: 2
Credit Cards: No
Notes: 2, 5

Country Cottage

B&B San Francisco
Box 349, San Francisco, 94101
(415) 931-3083

A cozy country-style B&B in the heart of town, located at the end of a quiet street away from the city noise. There is a small patio with trees and birds for the guests to enjoy. Breakfast is served in the sunny kitchen each morning.

Doubles: 3 (S2B) $45-55
Type of Beds: 1 Double; 2 Queen
Full Breakfast

Credit Cards: No
Notes: 2, 5

Crooked Lombard Street

B&B San Francisco
Box 349, San Francisco, 94101
(415) 931-3083

Fisherman's Wharf and the wonderful restaurants of North Beach are within walking distance. Guests have their own keys to this private cottage, where they enjoy a queen brass bed, color TV, fireplace, private bath, and view of the bay.

Doubles: 1 (PB) $125
Type of Beds: 1 Queen
Full Breakfast
Credit Cards: A, B, C
Notes: 2, 5, 9, 10, 11, 12, 14

Dolores Park Inn

3641 17th Street, 94114
(415) 621-0482

This 1874 Italianate Victorian inn is located in the sunny part of the city near international restaurants and transportation. A lush subtropical garden and patio with birds and a fountain give this charming and much-photographed home a special flair. Three rooms have fireplaces.

Hosts: Bernie & Leslie
Doubles: 6 (2 PB; 4 SB) $50-75
Type of Beds: 1 Twin; 2 Double; 3 KIng
Continental or Full Breakfast
Minimum stay weekends & holidays: 2
Credit Cards: A, B
Notes: 2, 5, 8 (over 12), 9, 10

Edward II

B&B of LA, 32074 Waterside La., Westlake Village, 91361
(818) 889-8870

European-style hotel in the Marina District near many tourist attractions. Rooms with

---

6 Pets welcome: 7 Smoking allowed: 8 Children welcome: 9 Social drinking allowed: 10 Tennis available: 11 Swimming available: 12 Golf available: 13 Skiing available: 14 May be booked through travel agents

private or shared baths are available, as well as suites. Limited parking.

Doubles (PB): $60-70
Doubles (SB): $45-50
Suites (PB): $125-200
Continental Breakfast
Credit Cards: A, B

Eye Openers #8

Box 694, Altadena, 91003
(213) 684-4428

This hilltop home has a glorious view of the bay and city from its two-story living room. Each bedroom has its own small balcony.

Doubles: 3 (SB) $35-45
Type of Beds: 4 Twin; 1 Double
Full Breakfast
Credit Cards: A, B
Notes: 2, 5, 7, 10, 11, 12

Golden Gate Park

B&B San Francisco
Box 349, San Francisco, 94101
(415) 931-3083

Golden Gate Park is just a couple of blocks away, and U.C. Medical Center is also close by. The entire loft of this house is available, with a wonderful ocean view from its deck, fireplace, and kitchenette. Wonderful for a family, as it's large and beautifully decorated.

Doubles: 1 (PB) $60-90
Type of Beds: 1 Queen; 1 King
Full Breakfast
Credit Cards: A, B, C
Notes: 2, 8, 9, 10, 12, 14

Gold Mine Hill

B&B San Francisco
Box 349, San Francisco, 94101
(415) 931-3083

A scenic location with a panoramic view. Each guest room has a fantastic view overlooking Glen Canyon Park and a TV. The spacious family room also has a sitting area and piano. Excellent parking is available.

Family suite: 1 (PB) $60-90
Doubles: 2 (SB) $50-60
Type of Beds: 1 Twin; 2 Double; 2 Queen
Full Breakfast
Credit Cards: A, B, C
Notes: 2, 5, 8, 9, 10, 14

The Grove Inn

890 Grove Street, 94117
(415) 929-0780

The Grove Inn is a charming, intimate, and affordable B&B. Centrally located and convenient to public transportation, it has two suites for the convenience of families with children. The owners and managers are always available for information, help in renting cars, booking shuttles to the airport, and city tours.

Hosts: Klaus & Rosetta Zimmermann
Singles: 1 (SB) $38
Doubles: 17 (14 PB; 3 SB) $45-65
Type of Beds: 4 Twin; 1 Double; 12 Queen
Continental Breakfast
Credit Cards: A, B, C
Notes: 5, 8, 9, 10, 14

The Inn San Francisco

943 South Van Ness Avenue, 94110
(415) 641-0188

Restored historic 27-room Italianate Victorian mansion, circa 1872. Ornate woodwork, Oriental carpets, marble fireplaces, and period antiques combined with modern hotel conveniences. Relax in the redwood hot tub in the garden or reserve a room with a private spa tub — the perfect romantic escape!

Host: Joel Daily
Doubles: 15 (12 PB; 3 SB) $70.50-199.26
Type of Beds: 2 Twin; 5 Double; 12 Queen
Continental-plus Breakfast
Minimum stay weekends & holidays: 2-4
Credit Cards: A, B, C
Notes: 2 (in advance), 5, 7 (limited), 8, 10, 11, 12, 14

NOTES: Credit cards accepted: A Master Card; B Visa; C American Express; D Discover Card; E Diners Club; F Other: 2 Personal checks accepted: 3 Lunch available: 4 Dinner available: 5 Open all year

Kathiren's Bed & Breakfast

B&B of LA, 32074 Waterside La., Westlake Village,
91361
(818) 889-8870

An easy stroll to Pier 39 or the cable car stop,
this home offers two guest rooms with TV.
Futon available. Children over 16 welcome;
no smoking.

Doubles: 2 (SB) $55-65
Type of Beds: 1 Double; 1 King
Full Breakfast
Minimum stay weekends: 2
Credit Cards: A, B

Kathy's Fisherman's Wharf

B&B San Francisco
Box 349, San Francisco, 94101
(415) 931-3083

Quiet, spacious, tastefully decorated room
with fireplace, fresh flowers, and a fruit basket. Breakfast is served by the bay window.
Fisherman's Wharf and the cable car are
only two blocks away. Additional small
double room available.

Doubles: 2 (SB) $55-65
Type of Beds: 1 Double; 1 King
Full Breakfast
Credit Cards: A, B, C
Notes: 2, 5, 8, 9, 10, 11, 12

Le Petit Manoir

B&B of LA, 32074 Waterside La., Westlake Village,
91361
(818) 889-8870

A 1902 Edwardian house, elegantly furnished, with a glass-enclosed deck by the
redwood hot top. Your host is a well-known
restaurateur who serves an inspired breakfast.

Singles: $50
Doubles: $60
Full Breakfast

The Monte Cristo

600 Presidio Avenue, 94115
(415) 931-1875

The elegantly restored Monte Cristo was
originally built in 1875 as a saloon and hotel.
It has served as a bordello, a refuge after the
1906 earthquake, and a speakeasy. Only two
blocks from Victorian shops, restaurants,
and antique stores on Sacramento Street;
ten minutes to any other point in the city.

Host: Frances Allan
Doubles: 14 (12 PB; 2 SB) $53-98
Full Breakfast
Minimum stay weekends & holidays: 2-3
Credit Cards: A, B, C, E
Notes: 2, 5, 7, 8, 10, 11, 12

Nob Hill

B&B San Francisco
Box 349, San Francisco, 94101
(415) 931-3083

Located on famous Nob Hill, near the Fair-
mont Hotel, this is a private cottage with
wood-burning fireplace. Cable cars, Union
Square, Chinatown are all only steps away.

Doubles: 1 (PB) $125
Type of Beds: 1 Queen
Full Breakfast
Credit Cards: A, B, C
Notes: 2, 5, 9, 10, 14

The No Name Bed & Breakfast

B&B San Francisco
Box 349, San Francisco, 94101
(415) 931-3083

Located in the Alamo Square Historic District, this 1890 Victorian offers a warm,
friendly, hospitable stay. Guest rooms all
have private baths and fireplaces and share
a deck and hot tub.

Doubles: 3 (PB) $75
Type of Beds: 3 Queen
Full Breakfast
Credit Cards: A, B, C
Notes: 2, 5, 8, 9, 10, 12, 14

6 Pets welcome: 7 Smoking allowed: 8 Children welcome: 9 Social drinking allowed: 10 Tennis available: 11
Swimming available: 12 Golf available: 13 Skiing available: 14 May be booked through travel agents

Petite Auberge

Petite Auberge

863 Bush Street, 94108
(415) 928-6000

A French country inn in the heart of San Francisco. Each room is individually decorated; many have fireplaces. Guests enjoy a full buffet breakfast, afternoon wine and hor d'oeuvres, valet parking, fresh fruit, and homemade cookies. Truly romantic ambience.

Host: Carolyn Vaughan
Doubles: 26 (PB) $116.55-172
Type of Beds: 26 Queen
Full Breakfast
Credit Cards: A, B, C
Notes: 2, 5, 7 (limited), 8, 9, 10, 12, 14

Red Victorian Bed & Breakfast Inn

1665 Haight Street, 94117
(415) 864-1978

Built at the turn of the century as a country resort hotel serving nearby Golden Gate Park, the Red Victorian now enjoys an international clientele of globally minded, friendly people. From the aquarium bathroom to the Flower Child Room to the Redwood Forest Room to the Peace Gallery where breakfast is served among Transformational paintings, the Red Victorian exudes color and joy to its global family.

Hosts: Sami Sunchild, Michael Lach, Barbara Cooke & Jeffrey Hirsch
Suite: 1 (PB) $120-125
Doubles: 13 (4 PB; 10 SB) $55-100
Type of Beds: 3 Twin; 6 Double; 7 Queen; 1 King
Continental-plus Breakfast
Credit Cards: A, B, C
Notes: 2, 5, 10, 11, 12, 14

Spencer House

B&B San Francisco
Box 349, San Francisco, 94101
(415) 931-3083

Built in 1896 by the famous architect Rabin, this Queen Anne is one of the city's most beautiful Victorians. Located close to Golden Gate Park and downtown, with guest rooms feature silk wallpaper, stenciled ceilings, and European antiques. The owners are in the wine business.

Doubles: 6 (PB) $95-155
Type of Beds: 3 Double; 2 Queen; 1 King
Full Breakfast
Credit Cards: A, B, C
Notes: 2, 5, 9, 10, 12, 14

Victorian Inn on the Park

301 Lyon Street, 94117
(415) 931-1830

Queen Anne Victorian built in 1987, located near Golden Gate Park and decorated with

---

NOTES: Credit cards accepted: A Master Card; B Visa; C American Express; D Discover Card; E Diners Club; F Other: 2 Personal checks accepted: 3 Lunch available: 4 Dinner available: 5 Open all year

Victorian antiques. Many rooms have fireplaces, and the Belvedere Room features a private balcony overlooking the park. The inn features fireplaces, dining room with oak paneling, and a parlor with fireplace. Complimentary wine served nightly; fresh breads baked daily.

Hosts: Lisa & William Benau
Doubles: 12 (PB) $81-138
Type of Beds: 1 Twin; 1 Double; 10 Queen
Continental-plus Breakfast
Credit Cards: A, B, C
Notes: 2, 5, 7, 8, 9, 10, 11, 12, 14

White Swan Inn

White Swan Inn

845 Bush Street, 94108
(415) 775-1755

In the heart of San Francisco, a bit of London resides. Each oversized guest room has a fireplace, wet bar, sitting area, color TV, radio, bathrobes, fresh fruit, and soft drinks. Enjoy a full breakfast, afternoon wine and hor d'oeuvres, newspaper, valet parking,

concierge, laundry, FAX machine, living room, library, and gracious service.

Host: Carolyn Vaughan
Doubles: 26 (PB) $161-177.60
Type of Beds: 12 Queen; 14 King
Full Breakfast
Credit Cards: A, B, C
Notes: 2, 5, 7 (limited), 8, 9, 10, 12, 14

The Willows B&B Inn

710 14th Street, 94114
(415) 431-4770

The warmth and comfort of an English country inn awaits you at The Willows. Begin your day with the pampered touch of breakfast in bed. Afternoon cheese and bed turn down. Convenient neighborhood location with shops, restaurants, and subway surrounding the inn. Limited off-street parking.

Hosts: Brad Goessler & Tim Farquhar
Doubles: 11 (SB) $56-82
Type of Beds: 6 Double; 6 Queen
Continental Breakfast
Credit Cards: A, B, C
Notes: 5, 6, 8, 10, 11, 12

SAN GREGORIO

Rancho San Gregorio

5086 San Gregorio Road, Box 21, 94074
(415) 747-0722

Five miles inland from the Pacific is an idyllic rural valley where Rancho San Gregorio welcomes travelers to share relaxed hospitality. Picnic, hike, or bike in wooded parks or ocean beaches. Country breakfast. Located forty-five minutes from San Francisco, Santa Cruz, and the Bay Area.

Hosts: Bud & Lee Raynor
Doubles: 4 (PB) $50-85
Type of Beds: 4 Twin; 1 Double; 2 Queen; 1 King
Full Breakfast
Credit Cards: No
Notes: 2, 5, 7 (restricted), 8, 9, 12, 14

6 Pets welcome: 7 Smoking allowed: 8 Children welcome: 9 Social drinking allowed: 10 Tennis available: 11 Swimming available: 12 Golf available: 13 Skiing available: 14 May be booked through travel agents

SAN JOSE

B&B International 35

1181-B Solano Avenue
Albany, 94706
(415) 525-4569

Contemporary two-story home in a pleasant southwest neighborhood. Country kitchen, guest sitting room, TV, easy parking.

Doubles: (PB) $50
Full Breakfast
Minimum stay: 2
Credit Cards: Major
Notes: 7, 8

The Briar Rose Bed & Breakfast Inn

897 E. Jackson Street, 95112
(408) 279-5999

An 1875 Victorian, fabulously restored to its former grandeur. Large rooms, appointed with period furnishings. Wrap-around porch overlooking the delightful gardens, a pond, and arbor. Quaint cottage. Quiet neighborhood setting with a good central location. Ten minutes from San Jose Airport.

Hosts: James & Cheryl Fuhring
Doubles: 6 (4 PB; 2 SB) $55-125
Full Breakfast
Credit Cards: A, B, C
Notes: 2, 5, 8, 9, 11, 14

SAN LUIS OBISPO

Heritage Inn

978 Olive Street, 93401
(805) 544-7440

Experience the romance of our turn-of-the-century inn with home-style hospitality. Antiques, fireplaces, a creekside setting, bay windows, balconies, and views of San Luis Mountain. Explore the Central Coast from this central location. Minutes from beautiful sunbathing and sport-fishing beaches, hot springs, horseback riding, wineries, and famous Hearst Castle.

Hosts: Zella & Jim Harrison
Doubles: 9 (3 PB; 6 SB) $78-88
Type of Beds: 2 Twin; 6 Double; 2 Queen
Continental-plus Breakfast
Credit Cards: A, B
Notes: 2, 5, 9, 10, 11, 12, 14

Megan's Friends B&B Service #6

1776 Royal Way, 93401
(805) 544-4406

Seven miles north of town off highway 101. Hosts have a 50-acre ranch providing their guests with a cabin amid tall oak and pine trees near a creek. Two bedrooms and bath, living room, and fully furnished kitchen. Bird watch, walk, relax and enjoy the serenity of nature. $75-95.

SAN MATEO

B&B International 36

1181-B Solano Avenue
Albany, 94706
(415) 525-4569

Luxurious mission-style home on spacious grounds surrounded by an adobe wall. Professionally decorated rooms, stained-glass windows, indoor fountain. Fine neighborhood, convenient to the airport and San Francisco.

Doubles: (PB) $64
Full Breakfast
Minimum stay: 2
Credit Cards: Major
Notes: 7, 8

SAN MIGUEL

Victorian Manor Bed & Breakfast

3200 N. Mission, Box 8, 93451
(805) 467-3306

NOTES: Credit cards accepted: A Master Card; B Visa; C American Express; D Discover Card; E Diners Club; F Other: 2 Personal checks accepted: 3 Lunch available: 4 Dinner available: 5 Open all year

Victorian Manor is located in California's central coast wine-growing area. Enjoy our full library and game room with its pool table and TV. Breakfast is served in the formal dining room.

Hosts: Catherine & Ed Allen
Doubles: 5 (1 PB; 4 SB), $50
Type of Beds: 3 Double; 2 King
Continental Breakfast
Credit Cards: No
Notes: 2, 5, 7 (restricted), 8, 9

SAN PEDRO

The Grand Cottages
B&B of LA, 32074 Waterside La., Westlake Village, 91361
(818) 889-8870

Three cute cottages, used in the movie "Swing Shift," next door to the elegant Grand House Restaurant. Small living room, TV/VCR, patio. Breakfast at the Grand House patio, or it will be delivered to your door. Convenient to Catalina and San Pedro harbor terminals. Children over 14 welcome.

Doubles: 3 (PB) $75-90
Full Breakfast
Credit Cards: A, B

SAN RAPHAEL

B&B International 37
1181-B Solano Avenue
Albany, 94706
(415) 525-4569

Dignified historical colonial near Dominican College. A warm and friendly house with seven bedrooms and four baths. Nice places to sit on the landscaped grounds.

Doubles: (PB) $68
Full Breakfast
Minimum stay: 2
Credit Cards: Major
Notes: 7, 8

SAN SIMEON

Megan's Friends B&B Service #7
1776 Royal Way, San Luis Obispo, 93401
(805) 544-4406

Comfortable, quiet home in a pine-covered area close to the Pacific Ocean. Sophisticated art galleries, gourmet restaurants, and fine specialty shops are located in this charming central coast town. One of California's most beautiful coastal parks provided opportunities for walking, beach combing, and picnics. One room with private entrance to deck, queen bed, private bath, color TV. $60.

SANTA BARBARA

The Arlington Inn
1136 De LaVina Street, 93101
(805) 965-6532

A restored 1926 Victorian hotel with a rich history of royal guests. Offering European hospitality in the Santa Barbara tradition, we serve a full breakfast and early evening wine and cheese. Many of our individually decorated rooms have kitchens

Host: Ronald D. Lopez
Doubles: 42 (39 PB; 3 SB) $80-90
Type of Beds: 9 Twin; 4 Queen; 29 King
Full Breakfast
Credit Cards: A, B, C
Notes: 2, 5, 7, 8 (under 12 free), 9, 10, 11, 12, 14

B&B Registry #CA-93101VIL
Box 8174, St. Paul, MN, 55108
(612) 646-4238

Old Spanish Mediterranean inn offers the ultimate getaway. Fireplaces, rough-hewn beams, louvered doors, views of the ocean, mountains, and garden. Pool and Jacuzzi. Complimentary wine and hors d'oeuvres in the evening. Just a few steps to the beach.

Doubles: 18 (PB) $90-185
Continental Breakfast
Credit Cards: A, B, C
Notes: 5, 7, 8 (over 14), 11

B&B Registry #CA-93105VIL

Box 8174, St. Paul, MN, 55108
(612) 646-4238

Two large bedrooms with elegant private baths adjoining a large reception hall with massive fireplace, beautiful antiques, and grand piano await you at this Italian villa.

Doubles: 2 (PB) $110-140
Full Breakfast
Credit Cards: No
Notes: 5, 11, 12

B&B Registry #CA-93108VAL

Box 8174, St. Paul, MN, 55108
(612) 646-4238

Contemporary ranch-style house features fireplace, grand piano, sunny deck, and mountain view. Located near beaches, mountains, golf courses, and tennis courts. Gourmet breakfast in bed, on patio, or by fireplace.

Doubles: 2 (PB) $55-66
Type of Beds: 1 Double; 1 Queen
Full Breakfast
Credit Cards: No
Notes: 3, 5, 8, 11, 12

The Bayberry Inn

111 W. Valerio Street, 93101
(805) 682-3199

Enjoy a stroll on our spacious grounds; play croquet or badminton; retreat from the

world in our beautifully appointed in-town inn. Experience the comfort and splendor of another era. Gourmet breakfast. Many guest rooms have fireplaces.

Host: Keith Pomeroy
Doubles: 8 (PB) $75-150
Type of Beds: 8 Double
Full Breakfast
Minimum stay weekends: 2
Credit Cards: A, B, C
Closed Dec. 24-26
Notes: 2, 6 (call), 9, 10, 11, 12, 14

Blue Quail Inn & Cottages

1908 Bath Street, 93101
(805) 687-2300

Relax and enjoy the quiet country atmosphere of the Blue Quail Inn and Cottages, so close to town and beaches. Linger over a delicious home-baked breakfast served on the patio or in the main house dining room. Let us pack a picnic lunch for your day of adventure on our bicycles. Sip hot spiced apple cider in the evening before enjoying a very restful sleep in your cottage, suite, or guest room.

Hosts: Jeanise Suding Eaton
Doubles: 8 (6 PB; 2 SB), $74.25-110
Type of Beds: 7 Queen; 1 King; 2 Daybeds
Continental-plus Breakfast
Credit Cards: A, B
Closed Dec. 24 & 25
Notes: 2, 8 (over 12), 9, 10, 11, 12, 14

Eye Openers #9

Box 694, Altadena, 91003
(213) 684-4428

This architect-designed contemporary home is nestled among oaks in a rural environment, yet is only two blocks from Santa Barbara Mission and five from beach and shopping.

Doubles: 1 (PB) $45-50
Type of Beds: 1 Double
Full Breakfast
Credit Cards: A, B
Notes: 2, 5, 10, 11, 12

NOTES: Credit cards accepted: A Master Card; B Visa; C American Express; D Discover Card; E Diners Club; F Other: 2 Personal checks accepted: 3 Lunch available: 4 Dinner available: 5 Open all year

Harbour Carriage House

420 W. Montecito, 93101
(805) 962-8447

A renovated 1895 house, tastefully decorated with French and English antiques. Fireplaces and spas in six rooms. Breakfast is served in the sunny solarium, and evening refreshments are served fireside. Two blocks from the harbor, the house adjoins the gardens of two historic homes.

Host: Jo Ann Adorno
Doubles: 9 (PB) $85-165
Type of Beds: 6 Queen; 3 King
Full Breakfast
Minimum stay weekends: 2
Credit Cards: A, B
Closed Christmas Eve & Day
Notes: 2, 8, 9, 11, 12, 14

Hidden Valley Home

939 Barcelona Drive, 93105
(805) 687-8799

Ellie and Kurt live one mile from the beach and four miles from downtown. Guests are invited to relax on the patio or in the spacious living room. Share the piano and our love of Santa Barbara (The American Riviera).

Hosts: Ellie & Kurt Pilgram
Doubles: 1 (PB) $55-75
Type of Beds: 1 King
Continental Breakfast
Minimum stay weekends & holidays: 2
Credit Cards: No
Notes: 2, 4, 5, 8, 9, 10, 11, 12, 14

Ocean View House

Box 20065, 93102
(805) 966-6659

A wonderful location in Santa Barbara in a quiet private home within walking distance of the ocean. Two rooms with antique charm, TV, interesting books, and collections. A special delight are the oranges, apples, and melons that are presented with breakfast on the patio.

Hosts: Caroly Canfield
Singles: 1 (PB) $45
Doubles: 1 (PB) $50
Type of Beds: 1 Double; 1 Queen
Continental-plus Breakfast
Credit Cards: No
Notes: 2, 5, 7 (limited), 8, 9, 10, 11, 12, 14

Old Mission House

435 E. Pedregosa, 93103
(805) 569-1914

This is a Craftsman house, built in 1895, with fireplaces in all rooms. Within walking distance of the Santa Barbara Mission, parks, downtown stores, museums, and ten minutes by car to the beach.

Host: Marie Miller
Doubles: 2 (SB) $45
Type of Beds: 2 Twin; 3 Queen
Continental Breakfast
Credit Cards: No
Notes: 2, 5, 8, 9, 10, 11, 12

Old Yacht Club Inn

B&B of LA, 32074 Waterside La., Westlake Village, 91361
(818) 889-8870

Only one-half block from the beach, this 1912 home has been lovingly restored. Sinks in every room. Five-course gourmet dinners available weekends. Bikes and beach chairs available.

Doubles: 9 (5 PB; 4 S2B) $70-115 plus tax
Continental Breakfast
Credit Cards: A, B
Notes: 7 (limited), 8 (over 13)

The Olive House

1604 Olive Street, 93101
(805) 962-4902

Enjoy quiet comfort and gracious hospitality in a lovingly restored 1904 Craftsman-style house replete with redwood paneling, bay windows, window seats, coffered ceilings,

6 Pets welcome: 7 Smoking allowed: 8 Children welcome: 9 Social drinking allowed: 10 Tennis available: 11 Swimming available: 12 Golf available: 13 Skiing available: 14 May be booked through travel agents

and a fireplace in the living room. Breakfast is served in the large, sunny dining room that also houses a studio grand piano. Enjoy mountain and ocean views from the sun deck and several guest rooms.

Hosts: Lois & Bob Poire
Doubles: 6 (PB) $65-100
Type of Beds: 5 Queen; 1 King
Continental-plus Breakfast
Credit Cards: A, B
Notes: 2, 5, 10, 11, 12

Old Yacht Club Inn

The Parsonage

1600 Olive Street, 93101
(805) 962-9336

Charming 1892 Victorian, furnished beautifully with antiques and Oriental rugs. Romantic honeymoon suite with city and ocean views. Enjoy breakfast on the spacious sun deck. Centrally located within walking distance of the mission, shops, restaurants, and theaters.

Host: Hilde Michelmore
Doubles: 6 (PB) $75-140
Type of Beds: 4 Queen; 2 King
Full Breakfast
Credit Cards: A, B
Notes: 2, 5, 10, 11, 12, 14

Simpson House Inn

121 East Arrellaga, 93101
(805) 963-7067

Elegant 1874 Victorian home, secluded in an acre of English gardens, only a five-minute walk to downtown historic sights, theaters, restaurants, and shops. Furnished with antiques, fine art, Oriental carpets, and English lace. Complimentary wine.

Hosts: Gillean Wilson, Glyn & Linda Davies
Doubles: 6 (5 PB; 1 SB) $65-145
Type of Beds: 1 Double; 4 Queen; 1 King
Full Breakfast
Minimum stay weekends & holidays: 2
Credit Cards: A, B
Notes: 2, 5, 7 (restricted), 8 (over 12), 9, 10, 11, 12, 14

Tiffany Inn

1323 De la Vina, 93101
(805) 963-2283

Built in 1898, the Tiffany Inn is one of Santa Barbara's especially charming old Victorians. The MacDonalds have placed exquisite antiques throughout the house to give it old-fashioned romantic appeal. Four of the six rooms have cozy wood-burning fireplaces; one has a Jacuzzi for two. Carol prepares a full breakfast for her guests each morning. The ocean, mission, museums, wineries, and fine restaurants are just minutes away.

Hosts: Carol & Larry MacDonald
Doubles: 6 (SB) $85-155
Type of Beds: 6 Queen
Full Breakfast
Credit Cards: A, B, C
Notes: 2, 5, 9, 10, 11, 12, 14

The Upham Hotel & Garden Cottages

1404 De la Vina Street, 93101
(800) 727-0876

Established in 1871, this beautifully restored Victorian hotel is situated on an acre of gardens. Guest rooms and suites are tastefully decorated with period furnishings and antiques. Complimentary continental breakfast and afternoon wine and cheese. Walk to museums, galleries, historic attractions, shops, and restaurants in downtown Santa Barbara. One and a half miles to the beach.

Hosts: Andrea Gallant
Doubles: 49 (PB) $80-200
Continental Breakfast
Credit Cards: A, B, C, D, E
Notes: 2, 4, 5, 7, 8, 9, 10, 11, 12, 14

Valli's View

340 N. Sierra Vista, 93108
(805) 969-1272

Just three miles from the center of Santa Barbara in the Monecito foothills, this lovely private home, with its garden setting, deck, patios, and ever-changing mountain views, has an ambience of tranquility and comfort. Enjoy lounges for sunning, a porch swing for relaxing, and all nearby tourist attractions. In the evening, enjoy a cup of cafe mocha or a glass of wine by the grand piano and fireplace in the spacious living room that overlooks the mountains.

Hosts: Valli & Larry Stevens
Doubles: 3 (PB) $45-95
Type of Beds: 1 Double; 1 Queen; 1 King
Full Breakfast
Minimum stay weekends: 2
Credit Cards: No
Notes: 2, 5, 6 (outside), 7 (outside), 8, 9, 10, 11, 12, 14

SANTA CLARA

Madison Street Inn

1390 Madison Street, 95050
(408) 249-5541

Just ten minutes from San Jose Airport and five minutes from Santa Clara University, this elegant Victorian sits peacefully in the heart of Silicon Valley. Telephones in rooms; dinner available by arrangement.

Hosts: Ralph & Theresa Wigginton
Singles: 2 (SB) $55-75
Doubles: 5 (3 PB; 2 SB) $55-75
Type of Beds: 2 Double; 3 Queen
Full Breakfast
Credit Cards: A, B, C, E
Notes: 2, 4, 5, 8, 9, 10, 11, 12, 14

SANTA CRUZ

Babbling Brook Inn

1025 Laurel Street, 95060
(408) 427-2437

Waterfalls and a brook meander through the gardens of this twelve-room inn with French decor. Each room has a private bath, telephone, TV, fireplace, private deck, private entrance. Two have deep soaking bathtubs. Walk to beaches, the boardwalk, a garden mall, or tennis. Full breakfast and complimentary wine and cheese.

Hosts: Helen & Tom King
Doubles: 12 (PB) $85-125
Full Breakfast
Type of Beds: 11 Queen; 2 King; 1 Rollaway
Minimum stay weekends: 2
Credit Cards: A, B, C, D
Notes: 2, 5, 8 (over 12), 9, 10, 11, 12, 14

Chateau Victorian

118 First Street, 95060
(408) 458-9458

Chateau Victorian was built in 1885 for a family wanting to be near the water and was converted to an elegant inn in 1983. All rooms have private baths, fireplaces, queen beds, and are decorated individually in Victorian themes.

Hosts: Franz & Alice-June Benjamin
Doubles: 7 (PB) $85-115
Type of Beds: 7 Queen
Continental-plus Breakfast
Credit Cards: A, B, C
Notes: 2, 5, 9, 10, 11, 12

Valley View

Box 66593, 95066
(415) 321-5195

Magnificent forest/glass house with hot spa on the large deck that overlooks the 20,000-acre redwood valley below. Barbecue, stereo, cable TV, beautiful stone fireplace, piano. Hosted or no host for total privacy. Very peaceful. Only ten minutes to beaches.

Hosts: Scott & Tricia Young
Doubles: 2 (PB) $95
Type of Beds: 1 Queen; 1 King
Full Breakfast
Credit Cards: A, B, C, E
Notes: 2, 5, 8 (over 12), 9, 10, 11, 12, 14

SANTA MONICA

B&B International 39

1181-B Solano Avenue
Albany, 94706
(415) 525-4569

A 1931 Spanish Revival home restored and furnished in 1920-1930 style. Guest room with many windows faces the backyard. Refrigerator in room. An excellent neighborhood for tourists who want to see L.A. Walk to bus.

Doubles: (PB) $64
Full Breakfast
Minimum stay: 2
Credit Cards: Major
Notes: 7, 8

SANTA ROSA

The Gables

4257 Petaluma Hill Road, 95404
(707) 585-7777

Historical landmark, architecturally classic Gothic, located one hour from San Francisco. Gateway to the redwoods, Sonoma/Napa Valley wineries, and the marvelous California north coast. Three sculptured marble fireplaces, spiral stairs.

Honeymooners' favorite, with country elegance and good taste.

Hosts: Pamela & Mike Wood
Doubles: 5 (PB) $80-95
Type of Beds: 1 Double; 3 Queen; 1 King
Continental-plus Breakfast
Credit Cards: A, B, C
Notes: 5

Melitta Station Inn

5850 Melitta Road, 95409
(707) 538-7712

Rustic American country B&B on a country road in the Valley of the Moon near everything. Within minutes of three state parks, hiking, biking, horseback riding, boating, fishing, hot-air balloons, gliders, hot baths, and massages. Many fine restaurants.

Hosts: Vic A. Stadter & Diane Crandon
Doubles: 4 (2 PB; 2 SB) $80-90
Type of Beds: 4 Double; 2 Queen
Full Breakfast
Credit Cards: A, B
Notes: 2, 5, 8 (10 and over), 9, 10, 11, 12, 14

Vintners Inn

4350 Barnes Road, 95403
(707) 575-7350

A European-style inn, located in the middle of our own 50-acre vineyard, with the highly acclaimed John Ash & Co. restaurant on the premises. Just sixty miles north of San Francisco, in the heart of the Sonoma wine country.

Hosts: John & Francisca Duffy
Doubles: 44 (PB) $105.84-167.40
Continental Breakfast
Credit Cards: A, B, C, E, F
Notes: 2, 4, 5, 6, 7, 8, 9, 10, 11, 12, 14

SAUSALITO

Blue Heron Houseboat

B&B Exchange of Marin
45 Entrata, San Anselmo, 94960
(415) 485-1971

NOTES: Credit cards accepted: A Master Card; B Visa; C American Express; D Discover Card; E Diners Club; F Other: 2 Personal checks accepted: 3 Lunch available: 4 Dinner available: 5 Open all year

Stay on a houseboat in picturesque Sausalito! Two rooms, breakfast on the deck. Walk to the boat along a flower-filled dock. The bath has an indoor Jacuzzi tub. This is a real adventure that has had many repeat customers.

Doubles: 2 (SB) $75-90
Continental Breakfast
Credit Cards: No
Notes: 2, 5, 8, 9, 10, 11, 12, 14

SEAL BEACH

El Camino Real Bed & Breakfast #12
Box 7155, Northridge, 91327
(818) 363-7155

This home is right on the beach. Walk out the back door, through the garden, and onto the sand. Ocean-view balcony; hot tub.

Doubles: 2 (PB) $75
Type of Beds: 2 Twin; 1 King
Full Breakfast
Credit Cards: No
Notes: 7 (limited), 8, 10, 11

The Seal Beach Inn & Gardens
212 5th Street, 90740
(213) 493-2416

The Seal Beach Inn and Gardens is a French Mediterranean style bed and breakfast country inn located in the quaint seaside village of Seal Beach. Ideally located between Orange and Los Angeles counties. A lavish gourmet breakfast is served.

Host: Marjorie Bettenhausen
Doubles: 23 (PB) $96-160
Type of Beds: 5 Twin; 10 Double; 8 Queen; 8 King
Full Breakfast
Minimum stay weekends & holidays: 2
Credit Cards: A, B, C
Notes: 2, 5, 8, 10, 11, 12, 14

Villa Pacifica
204 Ocean Avenue, 90740
(213) 594-0397

On a beach! A winding walk out our private rear gate, past our greenhouses and grape arbor, puts you right on the sand and the last remaining California dunes. Jacuzzi, fireplace, all water sports available. Close to Disneyland, Knott's Berry Farm, the *Queen Mary,* and the *Spruce Goose.*

Hosts: Bruce Stark & Michelle Brendel
Doubles: 2 (PB) $110-$125
Type of Beds: King
Full Breakfast
Minimum Stay: 2 days
Credit Cards: No
Notes: 2 (with reservation), 5, 10, 11, 12, 14

SOLVANG

El Ranchito
B&B LA, 32047 Waterside La., Westlake Village, 91361
(818) 889-8870

One-room cottages with private baths and deck/balcony overlooking pastures and vineyards. Swimming pond, waterfall, peacocks, llamas, and dogs on property. Very secluded, Mediterranean style, with French country antiques. Limited smoking.

Doubles: 2 (PB) $95
Full Breakfast
Minimum stay: 2
Credit Cards: A, B

Megan's Friends B&B Service #8
1776 Royal Way, San Luis Obispo, 93401
(805) 544-4406

Lovely home graciously furnished in contemporary style with Oriental accessories and original oil paintings. Located in one of the major tourist meccas, between the Santa Ynez and San Rafael Mountain ranges. The twin bedroom suite has a dressing room and

6 Pets welcome: 7 Smoking allowed: 8 Children welcome: 9 Social drinking allowed: 10 Tennis available: 11 Swimming available: 12 Golf available: 13 Skiing available: 14 May be booked through travel agents

The Hidden Oak

private bath; view of the hills and garden through the sliding glass doors to the patio. $45-55.

Trout Farm

B&B LA, 32074 Waterside La., Westlake Village, 91361
(818) 889-8870

Marvelous restored 1880s farmhouse with a large fishing pond, lawns, porches, swing, and hammock. Private entrance, fireplace, snacks. Llamas on property and dog. Limited smoking. Children welcome.

Doubles: 2 (PB) $95
Full Breakfast
Credit Cards: A, B

SOMIS

Rancho De Somis

6441 La Cumbre Road, 93066
(805) 987-8455

One hundred avocado and fruit trees surround this house, complete with resident birds and country flowers. Telescope available for viewing the heavens. Fifty-foot deck on the second level provides relaxation and sunning. There is a hot tub set to 104 degrees to enhance your pleasure, and breakfast is served in the fern arbor, your room, or on the sun deck. On a country road, with no lights or sidewalks. Five resident golden retrievers. Picnic lunches available.

Hosts: Davis-Friedman
Doubles: 4 (PB) to $95
Type of Beds: 4 Queen
Continental Breakfast
Credit Cards: No
Notes: 2, 3, 5, 7 (outdoors), 8 (16 and over), 9, 11, 12

SONOMA

The Hidden Oak

214 E. Napa Street, 95476
(707) 996-9863

The Hidden Oak is a large, two-story Craftsman bungalow in the historic neighborhood of Sonoma, one block from the Plaza. We have three exquisitely decorated rooms with queen beds and private baths. We include full breakfast and have complimentary bicycles. Located near the wineries, shopping, restaurants, art galleries, and historic sites.

Host: Catherine Cotchett
Doubles: 3 (PB) $85-160
Type of Beds: 3 Queen
Full Breakfast
Credit Cards: No
Notes: 2, 5

NOTES: Credit cards accepted: A Master Card; B Visa; C American Express; D Discover Card; E Diners Club; F Other: 2 Personal checks accepted: 3 Lunch available: 4 Dinner available: 5 Open all year

Trojan Horse Inn
19455 Sonoma Highway, 95476
(707) 996-2430

A lovely nineteenth-century farmhouse furnished with beautiful antiques. Located one mile from the historic Sonoma Plaza and mission. Close to wineries, state parks, restaurants, shops, tennis, golf, horseback riding. Beautiful garden patio and Jacuzzi. Complimentary cocktail hour. Bicycles available.

Hosts: Brian & Susan Scott
Doubles: 8 (4 PB; 4 SB) $86.40-102.60
Type of Beds: 8 Queen
Full Breakfast
Credit Cards: A, B, C
Notes: 2, 5, 8 (over 12), 9, 10, 12, 14

Victorian Garden Inn
316 East Napa Street, 95476
(707) 996-5339

Lush gardens with private nooks; classic rooms from storybooks; private entrances, private baths; rooms overlooking garden paths; gourmet breakfast, lunch, and breaks; midweek conferences at competitive rates; romantic getaways, excursions, and tours; all of these and more are yours.

Host: Donna Lewis
Singles: 1 (SB) $45
Doubles: 5 (3 PB; 2 SB) $69-125
Type of Beds: 1 Twin; 1 Double; 3 Queen
California Breakfast
Minimum stay weekends & holidays: 2
Credit Cards: A, B, C
Notes: 2, 5, 7, 8 (over 13), 9, 10, 11, 12, 14

SONORA

Jameson's
22157 Feather River Drive, 95370
(209) 532-1248

Jameson's is set in a wooded area: Large red cedars and 200-year-old oak trees surround a natural waterfall and creek. Lots of deck. Gateway to Yosemite. Game room with

large stone fireplace and pool table. Exotic bridal suite.

Hosts: Virg & Jean Birdsall
Doubles: 4 (SB) $48.50-64.70
Type of Beds: 1 Twin; 1 Double; 1 Queen; 1 King
Full Breakfast
Minimum stay holiday weekends: 2
Teenagers welcome
Credit Cards: No
Notes: 2, 5, 7 (limited), 14

Lavender Hill B&B
683 S. Barretta Street, 95370
(209) 532-9024

Delightfully restored 1900 Victorian with three lovely guest rooms, one with private bath. Formal parlor, dining room, antiques, porch swing, and beautiful grounds. Within walking distance of shops and restaurants in the heart of the Gold Country. Old-time charm with modern convenience.

Host: Alice Byrnes
Doubles: 3 (1 PB; 2 SB) $54-65
Type of Beds: 3 Queen
Full Breakfast
Credit Cards: No
Notes: 2, 5, 7 (restricted), 9, 10, 12

SOUTH LAGUNA BEACH

La Casa Alegre
B&B LA, 32074 Waterway La., Westlake Village, 91361
(818) 889-8870

Guest quarters on the lower level of the home with private entrance to living room with fireplace. Ocean views, TV, off-street parking. Two blocks to beach. Decorated in antiques and wicker. Adults only.

Doubles: 2 (PB) $75
Full Breakfast
Minimum stay: 2
Credit Cards: A, B

SOUTH LAKE TAHOE

The Christiania Inn

Box 18298, 95706
(916) 544-7337

The entire inn is furnished in a Swiss-country decor with antiques throughout. Also located at the inn is a restaurant with the freshest available foods and a lounge. The inn is located five minutes from the lake, 100 yards from Heavenly Valley ski lifts, and eight minutes from Tahoe's nightlife. Our suites feature fireplaces, wet bars, saunas, and complimentary brandy on arrival.

Hosts: Maggie Mershon & Jane Hollingsworth
Singles: 2 (PB) $75
Doubles: 4 (PB) $150
Continental Breakfast
Credit Cards: A, B, C
Closed May 8 - May 24
Notes: 4, 6, 8, 9, 10, 11, 12, 13

STOCKTON

The Old Victorian Inn

207 West Acacia, 95203
(209) 462-1613

A beautifully restored 1891 Victorian home decorated and appointed with unusual concern for authenticity and detail. When you enter this house, you step back into the Victorian Era. There is a lovely porch in the backyard to enjoy.

Host: Rex Buethe
Singles: 8 (3 PB; 5 SB) $75-105
Suites: 2 (two room) $150
Type of Beds: 6 Double; 2 Queen
Continental Breakfast
Credit Cards: A, B
Notes: 2, 5, 9, 10, 11, 12

STUDIO CITY

El Camino Real Bed & Breakfast #13

Box 7155, Northridge, 91327
(818) 363-6753

Home of Universal Studio Tours, Studio City is near the Hollywood Bowl and the Greek theater. Fifteen minutes to downtown museums, Chinatown, Little Tokyo, and the Pasadena Rose Bowl and parade. Kitchen privileges available.

Doubles: 1 (PB) $50-70
Type of Beds: 1 Twin; 1 Queen
Continental Breakfast
Credit Cards: No
Notes: 5, 7 (limited), 8 (over 14), 10, 11, 12

SUNSET PALISADES

Megan's Friends B&B Service #9

1776 Royal Way, San Luis Obispo, 93401
(805) 544-4406

Serene ocean view from the living room of this spacious home with beach access. You may breakfast on the deck that overlooks the surf. Nearby attractions include Avila Plunge, massage, spa, hot tubs. Super breakfasts — special diets on request, and dinner with wine is available with advance notice. Double bed with adjoining bath. $45-50.

SUTTER CREEK

The Foxes in Sutter Creek

Box 159, 95685
(209) 267-5882

In the heart of historic Gold Rush country, this inn has six large, elegant suites with private baths, queen beds, air-conditioning, wood-burning fireplaces, and covered parking. Breakfast, cooked to your order, is delivered on silver service to your room. Beautiful gardens and a gazebo. Walk to shops and restaurants. Three-star Mobil rating. Hospitality is our specialty.

Hosts: Pete & Min Fox
Doubles: 6 (PB) $80-120
Type of Beds: 6 Queen
Full Breakfast

NOTES: Credit cards accepted: A Master Card; B Visa; C American Express; D Discover Card; E Diners Club; F Other: 2 Personal checks accepted: 3 Lunch available: 4 Dinner available: 5 Open all year

Credit Cards: A, B
Notes: 2, 5, 7 (outside), 9, 10, 11, 14

Sutter Creek Inn

Box 385, 95685
(209) 267-5606

The Sutter Creek Inn has nineteen rooms, all with private baths, many with fireplaces. During the summer, guests enjoy the lawns and gardens, with their hammocks and lawn furniture. The lovely old living room is for use of the guests. Several fine restaurants are in the area.

Host: Jane Way
Doubles: 19 (PB) $50-125
Type of Beds: 4 Twin; 3 Double; 12 Queen
Full Breakfast
Credit Cards: No
Closed Thanksgiving & Christmas
Notes: 2, 5, 7 (limited), 8 (over 15), 9, 10, 11, 14

Sutter Creek Inn

TAFT

B&B Registry #CA-93268LAR

Box 8174, St. Paul, MN, 55108
(612) 646-4238

Custom-built split-level home in the foothills. Sun deck with a million-dollar view and swimming pool; fireplace; citrus trees.

Doubles: 3 (SB) $30-40
Type of Beds: 2 Double; 1 Queen
Continental-plus Breakfast
Credit Cards: No
Notes: 5, 11, 12

TAHOE CITY

Mayfield House

236 Grove Street, Box 5999, 95730
(916) 583-1001

Snug and cozy 1930s Tahoe home, half a block from the beach. Premium skiing within ten miles. Full light breakfast, homemade baked goods. Within walking distance of shops and restaurants in Tahoe City. Off-street parking.

Host: Janie Kaye
Singles: 1 (SB) $65
Doubles: 5 (SB) $65-100
Type of Beds: 1 Twin; 2 Queen; 3 King
Full Breakfast (light)
Minimum stay weekends: 2
Credit Cards: A, B
Notes: 2, 5, 7 (limited), 8 (over 10), 9, 10, 11, 12, 13

TAHOMA

The Captain's Alpenhaus

6941 West Lake Blvd., 95733
(916) 525-5000; 525-5266

A refreshing European-style country inn across the street from beautiful Lake Tahoe. Our restaurant features a full breakfast menu, luncheon, and gourmet dinners. Tahoma is situated on the west shore of Lake Tahoe and is known for its quiet beauty. We have a beautiful swimming pool and an outdoor spa. Family reunion haven.

Hosts: Joel & Phyllis Butler
Doubles: 7 (PB) $70-95
Two-bedroom Suites: 2
Two-bedroom Cottages: 5
Four-bedroom Cottage: 1
Type of Beds: 15 Twin; 8 Double; 4 Queen; 1 King
Full Breakfast
Minimum stay holidays: 2
Credit Cards: A, B, C
Notes: 2, 3, 4, 5, 6, 7, 8, 9, 10, 11, 12, 13, 14

TARZANA

El Camino Real Bed & Breakfast #14

Box 7155, Northridge, 91327
(818) 363-6753

This house has excellent freeway access and is just ten minutes from Universal Studios. Swimming pool, paddle court, and air-conditioning. Private sitting room for guest use.

Doubles: 1 (PB) $50
Type of Beds: 1 King
Continental Breakfast
Credit Cards: No
Notes: 8 (over 12), 11, 12

TEMPLETON

Country House Inn

91 Main Street, 93465
(805) 434-1598

An 1886 Victorian farmhouse — designated historic site — in an old western town with many restored buildings. Quiet country setting with wine tasting and tour nearby. Full breakfast features crepes, quiches, souffles, homebaked breads, and fresh fruit.

Host: Dianne Garth
Doubles: 7 (4 PB; 3 SB) $60-80
Full Breakfast
Credit Cards: A, B
Notes: 2, 5, 8, 10, 11, 12, 14

THREE RIVERS

Cort Cottage

B&B LA, 32074 Waterside La., Westlake Village, 91361
(818) 889-8870

A little cottage with full kitchen, living room with hide-a-bed, and panoramic view of the mountains. Breakfast brought to your door. Four hours from Los Angeles. Limited smoking. Two cats in residence. Children welcome.

Doubles: 1 (PB) $60
Type of Beds: 1 Double; 1 Hide-a-Bed
Full Breakfast
Credit Cards: A, B

TOMALES

Byron Randall's Tomales Guest House

25 Valley Street, 94971
(707) 878-9992

Byron Randall's famous Victorian guest house and art gallery is a lovely, tranquil retreat. Secluded by trees and surrounded by gardens, patios, and lily ponds on the outskirts of a tiny village, it provides the consummate country experience. Come enjoy!

Host: Byron Randall
Doubles: 8 (7 SB; 1 PB) $50-85
Type of Beds: 1 Twin; 7 Double
Buffet Continental Breakfast
Credit Cards: No
Notes: 2, 5, 7, 8 (over 10), 9

TRINIDAD

Trinidad Bed & Breakfast

Box 849, 95570
(707) 677-0840

Our Cape Cod-style home overlooks beautiful Trinidad and offers spectacular views of the coastline and harbor. Surrounded by dozens of beaches, trails, and redwood parks; within walking distance of restaurants and shops. Three upstairs bay-view rooms with warm wood paneling. Family-style breakfast is served in the ocean-view kitchen.

Hosts: Paul & Carol Kirk
Doubles: (PB) $65-110
Type of Beds: 2 Twin; 3 Queen
Full Breakfast

NOTES: Credit cards accepted: A Master Card; B Visa; C American Express; D Discover Card; E Diners Club; F Other: 2 Personal checks accepted: 3 Lunch available: 4 Dinner available: 5 Open all year

Credit Cards: No
Closed Dec.
Notes: 2, 8 (over 10), 9, 10, 12

TWAIN HARTE

Twain Harte's Bed & Breakfast
Box 1718, 95383
(209) 586-3311

Welcome to a vacation hideaway in a quaint mountain village offering a wooded setting, large decks, and walkways, recreation room, and antiques. Two honeymoon suites and one family suite with private baths. Four rooms with queen beds share two full baths. Excellent dining within walking distance.

Hosts: El & Pat Pantaleoni
Singles: 1 (SB) $40
Doubles: 6 (2 PB; 4 SB) $45-70
Full Breakfast
Credit Cards: A, B, C
Notes: 2, 5, 8, 9, 10, 11, 12, 13, 14

Twain Harte

VALLEY FORD

The Inn at Valley Ford
Box 439, 94972
(707) 876-3182

The inn is a 120-year-old farmhouse furnished with antiques. Each room commemorates an author and includes a collection of his work. Valley Ford, located in the pastoral hills of western Sonoma County, is just minutes from the Pacific. Nearby are galleries, antiques, wineries, restaurants, bird watching, bicycling, and hiking.

Hosts: Nicholas Balashov & Sandra Nicholls
Singles: 1 (SB) $50
Doubles: 4 (SB) $63-68
Type of Beds: 1 Twin; 4 Double; 1 Queen
Continental-plus Breakfast
Credit Cards: A, B
Notes: 2, 5, 7 (outside), 9, 10, 11, 12, 14

VENICE

Venice Beach House
B&B LA, 32074 Waterside La., Westlake Village, 91361
(818) 889-8870

Completely restored turn-of-the-century home with each room decorated in a different motif. Sunny living room with fireplace where breakfast is served. Children over 10 welcome. Bus line 1.5 blocks.

Doubles (SB): $50-70
Doubles (PB): $90-140
Full Breakfast
Minimum stay weekends: 2
Credit Cards: A, B

VENTURA

Bella Maggiore Inn
67 Sl California Street, 93001
(805) 652-0277

One hour north of Los Angeles and three blocks to the ocean promenade and beaches. Within easy walking distance to

6 Pets welcome: 7 Smoking allowed: 8 Children welcome: 9 Social drinking allowed: 10 Tennis available: 11 Swimming available: 12 Golf available: 13 Skiing available: 14 May be booked through travel agents

fine restaurants, shops, the old mission, and the fairgrounds. We have a garden courtyard with flowers and a fountain, a lobby with fireplace and piano, complimentary appetizers, full breakfast, and scenic trolley tour.

Host: Thomas J. Wood
Singles: 3 (PB) $50-55
Doubles: 27 (PB) $65-150
Type of Beds: 3 Double; 19 Queen; 8 King
Full Breakfast
Credit Cards: A, B, C, D, E
Notes: 2, 5, 7, 8 (13 and over), 9, 10, 11, 12, 14

La Mer

411 Poli Street, 93001
(805) 643-3600

Nestled in a green hillside, this Cape Cod-style Victorian overlooks the heart of historic San BuenaVentura and the California coastline. Originally built in 1890, a historical landmark, La Mer has each individually decorated, antique-filled room furnished to capture a specific European country, all with private baths and entrances, plus ocean view.

Host: Gisela Flender Baida
Doubles: 5 (PB) $85-125
Type of Beds: 2 Twin; 1 Double; 3 Queen
Full Breakfast
Minimum stay weekends & holidays: 2
Credit Cards: A, B
Closed Christmas
Notes: 2, 7 (limited), 8 (over 13), 9, 10, 11, 12, 14

WALNUT CREEK

Gasthaus zum Baren

3112 Blackstone Drive, 94598
(415) 934-8119

Located in a quiet neighborhood near the foot of Mt. Diablo, Gasthaus zum Baren is only forty minutes from downtown San Francisco. Country decor, antiques, and an international collection of bears create Old

World "Gemutlichkeit" in this California home with every modern amenity.

Hosts: Lois D. Martin
Doubles: 3 (1 PB; 2 SB) $40-$50
Type of Beds: 2 Twin; 1 Queen; 1 King
Full Breakfast
Credit Cards: No
Notes: 2, 5, 8 (swimmers over 6), 9, 10, 11, 12, 14

WEST COVINA

Hendrick Inn

2124 East Mercer Avenue, 91791
(810) 919-2125

This large, rambling house will give you a real taste of the California life-style with its gorgeous deck, swimming pool, Jacuzzi. Centrally located for visiting Disneyland, L.A., the mountains, and the desert. Forty-five minutes to L.A.X.; 20 to Ontario Airport.

Hosts: Mary & George Hendrick
Singles: 1 (SB) $30
Doubles: 2 (SB) $40-45
Suite: 1 (PB) $50
Type of Beds: 3 Twin; 1 Double; 1 King
Full Breakfast
Credit Cards: No
Notes: 2, 4 (with notice), 5, 7, 8 (5 and over), 9, 10, 11, 12

WEST LOS ANGELES

Salisbury House

B&B LA, 32074 Waterside La., Westlake Village, 91361
(818) 889-8870

Beautifully restored Craftsman style home offering five guest rooms and gourmet breakfasts. Car essential; no children.

Doubles (PB): $70-75
Doubles (SB): $60
Full Breakfast
Credit Cards: A, B

NOTES: Credit cards accepted: A Master Card; B Visa; C American Express; D Discover Card; E Diners Club; F Other: 2 Personal checks accepted: 3 Lunch available: 4 Dinner available: 5 Open all year

Wilshire Crest Inn

B&B LA, 32074 Waterside La., Westlake Village, 91361
(818) 889-8870

Only two blocks from Beverly Hills, near the museums. Friendly, older, but elegant inn tucked in a residential neighborhood. Attractive rooms with color TV, phones, and air-conditioning. Relax in the parlor or on the patio. Breakfast served in the dining area daily.

Singles: $66 plus tax
Doubles: $74 plus tax
Full Breakfast
Credit Cards: A, B

Howard Creek Ranch

Bowen's Pelican Lodge & Inn

38921 N. Highway 1, 95488
(707) 964-5588

A Victorian western inn reminiscent of the 1890s. In a remote location with the sea in its front yard, the mountain in back, and miles of virtually untouched wilderness all around. The nearest town, Fort Bragg, is fifteen miles away. A place to get away from it all, hike secluded beaches, explore the hills, or just unwind. Full bar & restaurant, home cooking.

Host: Velma Bowen
Doubles: 6 (4 PB; 2 SB) $48.60-81
Continental Breakfast
Minimum stay holidays: 2
Credit Cards: A, B
Notes: 2, 4, 5, 7, 9

Howard Creek Ranch

Box 121, 95488
(707) 964-6725

An historic 1867 farm on 20 acres, only 100 yards from the beach. A rural retreat adjoining wilderness. Suite and cabins; views of ocean, mountains, creek, or gardens; fireplace/wood stoves; period furnishings; wood-heated hot tub, sauna, pool; horseback riding nearby. Gift certificates available.

Hosts: Charles (Sunny) & Sally Grigg
Doubles: 6 (3 PB; 3 SB) $54-$91.80
Type of Beds: 2 Double; 3 Queen; 1 King
Full Breakfast
Credit Cards: A, B
Notes: 2, 5, 7 (limited), 8 (reservations requested), 9, 11

Coleen's California Casa

11715 S. Circle Drive, 90601
(213) 699-8427

Take your children to Disneyland, Knott's Berry Farm, and Universal Studios, then come back to a luxurious home. Bedrooms are decorator designed with elegant private baths. From the deck you can see L.A., Long Beach, and Catalina Island. Hosts will help you plan your tours, provide baby-sitting, and pick you up at the airport for a small charge.

---

6 Pets welcome: 7 Smoking allowed: 8 Children welcome: 9 Social drinking allowed: 10 Tennis available: 11 Swimming available: 12 Golf available: 13 Skiing available: 14 May be booked through travel agents

Host: Coleen Davis
Singles: 1 (PB) $45-55
Doubles: 3 (PB) $55-70
Type of Beds: 3 Twin; 1 Double; 2 King
Full Breakfast
Minimum stay: 2; holidays: 3
Credit Cards: No
Notes: 2, 3, 4, 5, 7(conditional), 8, 9, 10, 11, 12, 14

YOUNTVILLE

Oleander House

7433 St. Helena Highway, 94599
(707) 944-8315

Country French charm, located at the very entrance of the wine country. Spacious, high-ceiling rooms done in Laura Ashley fabric and wallpaper and antiques. Breakfast is served in the large dining room on the main floor. All rooms have fireplaces, private baths, and their own decks.

Host: Jean A. Brunswick
Doubles: 4 (PB) $85-120
Type of Beds: 4 Queen
Full Breakfast
Minimum stay weekdays & holidays: 2
Credit Cards: A, B
No smoking
Closed Christmas
Notes: 2, 9, 10, 11, 12

NOTES: Credit cards accepted: A Master Card; B Visa; C American Express; D Discover Card; E Diners Club; F Other: 2 Personal checks accepted: 3 Lunch available: 4 Dinner available: 5 Open all year

Colorado

Cottonwood Inn

B&B Colorado, Box 12206, Boulder, 80303
(800) 373-4995

A lovely turn-of-the-century home with original art and antiques. Visit the Great Sand Dunes, ride the Cumbres-Toltec Railway, bike, hike, fish, hunt, or visit one of the nearby sanctuaries to bird watch.

Doubles: 3 (SB) $34-50
Type of Beds: 1 Twin; 1 Double; 1 Queen; 1 King
Continental-plus Breakfast weekdays; Full weekends, summers, & holidays
Credit Cards: No
Notes: 8 (over 11), 13

Ecklund's Bed & Breakfast

B&B Colorado, Box 12206, Boulder, 80303
(800) 373-4995

Located nineteen miles north of Alamosa, thirty minutes from the Great Sand Dunes and one hour from the Cumbres-Toltec Railway, in the midst of potato and barley farms. The Rio Grande is twenty miles south.

Cabin: 2 bedrooms (PB) $30-60
Type of Beds: 1 Double; 1 King
Continental-plus Breakfast
Credit Cards: No
Notes: 6, 7, 13

Altamira Ranch

B&B Colorado, Box 12206, Boulder, 80303
(800) 373-4995

A contemporary brick home on a 167-acre working ranch. Excellent cross-country skiing and hiking. The Roaring Fork River borders the ranch and offers great trout fishing and river sports. Fifteen miles north of Aspen. Resident dog.

Doubles: 2 (SB) $40-60
Type of Beds: 2 Double
Full Breakfast
Minimum stay holidays: 2
Credit Cards: No
Notes: 6 (horses), 8, 11, 13

The Ambience Inn

B&B Colorado, Box 12206, Boulder, 80303
(800) 373-4995

A contemporary chalet-style home located in the beautiful Crystal Valley between Aspen and Glenwood Springs. Within walking distance of quaint shops and restaurants. Fishing, white-water rafting, riding are within minutes. Aspen and Snowmass are 35 minutes away.

Doubles: 3 (PB) $50-75
Type of Beds: 3 Queen
Full Breakfast
Credit Cards: No
Notes: 4 (with reservations),7 (limited), 11, 12, 13

An Aspen Home

B&B Rocky Mountains.
Box 804, Colorado Springs, CO, 80901
(719) 630-3433

Twin beds in a cheerful room, private bath. Two resident mellow dogs. Only one-quarter of a mile from the free ski shuttle. Share the TV and fireplace with your hosts

6 Pets welcome: 7 Smoking allowed: 8 Children welcome: 9 Social drinking allowed: 10 Tennis available: 11 Swimming available: 12 Golf available: 13 Skiing available: 14 May be booked through travel agents

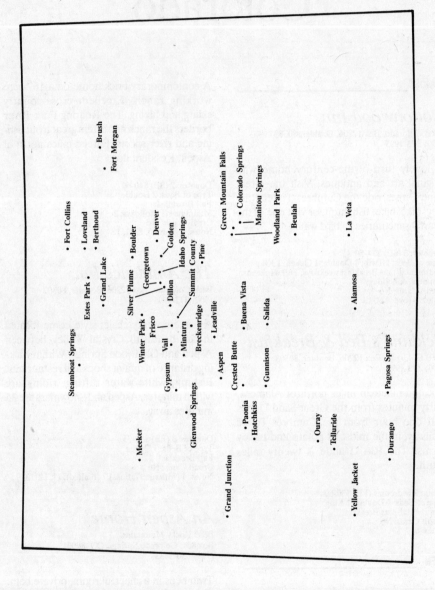

COLORADO

Fort Collins
Loveland
Berthoud
• Brush
Fort Morgan

Estes Park
Grand Lake
Boulder
Denver
Golden
Idaho Springs
Pine
Green Mountain Falls
Colorado Springs
Manitou Springs
Woodland Park
Beulah

Silver Plume
Georgetown
Dillon
Summit County

Steamboat Springs

Winter Park
Frisco
Vail
Minturn
Breckenridge
Leadville
Buena Vista
Salida
La Veta

Gypsum

Aspen
Crested Butte
Gunnison
Alamosa

Meeker

Glenwood Springs
Paonia
Hotchkiss

Grand Junction

Ouray
Telluride
Pagosa Springs

Yellow Jacket
Durango

and enjoy a special full breakfast in the morning. $55-60.

Cozy Log Home

B&B Rocky Mountains.
Box 804, Colorado Springs, CO, 80901
(719) 630-3433

Built in 1865, this room offers two large upstairs rooms with private bath and private entrance. Twenty miles from Aspen, twenty to Glenwood, twenty to Snowmass. A quiet, rural setting. House offers a wood-burning stove in the family room, phone, laundry facilities. Continental breakfast. Near fishing, golf, river rafting, Jeep tours, riding. $45-60.

The Gingerbread House

B&B Colorado, Box 12206, Boulder, 80303
(800) 373-4995

Four blocks from Aspen Mountain and 2.5 blocks from the downtown mall, this house has the perfect location for those without a car. After a day of skiing, hiking, or visiting the Music Festival, soak in the indoor hot tub or relax on the deck. One dog in residence.

Doubles: 2 (SB) $55
Type of Beds: 2 Double
Full Breakfast
Credit Cards: No
Notes: 13

Little Red Ski Haus

118 E. Cooper Street, 81611
(303) 925-3333

Charming 100-year-old Victorian three blocks from the center of town. No TV, but interesting conversation always. One could travel the world just sitting in our living room. The house is very popular with Australians. Exceptionally clean and friendly, especially suited to those traveling alone.

Hosts: Marge Riley & Irene Zydek
Quad: 1 (5 rooms SB) $20-30
Doubles: 15 (3 PB; 12 SB) $48-90
Full breakfast winter; continental summer
Credit Cards: A, B
Closed April 10 - May 31
Notes: 8, 9, 10, 11, 12, 13, 14

Little Red Ski Haus

Mountain Meadow House

B&B Colorado, Box 12206, Boulder, 80303
(800) 373-4995

A restored farmhouse outside Aspen in a high meadow with spectacular panoramic mountain views. There's an inviting fireplace for your after-skiing pleasure, or unsurpassed hiking and fishing. One friendly resident dog.

Doubles: 3 (1 PB; 2 SB) $60-120
Type of Beds: 2 Twin; 1 Queen; 1 King
Continental-plus Breakfast
Credit Cards: No
Notes: 10, 12, 13

Rocky Mts. #83

B&B Rocky Mountains.
Box 804, Colorado Springs, CO, 80901
(719) 630-3433

New eleven-room inn with beautifully appointed rooms, just a minute's walk from mall. King suites with queen sleeper sofa and two TVs, wet bar, refrigerator, and private bath. Smaller queen rooms also available. Four blocks from the gondola. Balcony or

6 Pets welcome: 7 Smoking allowed: 8 Children welcome: 9 Social drinking allowed: 10 Tennis available: 11 Swimming available: 12 Golf available: 13 Skiing available: 14 May be booked through travel agents

deck in most rooms. Full breakfast during ski season, continental other times. $70-130.

Snow Queen Victorian Lodge

124 East Cooper Street, 81611
(303) 925-8455

The Snow Queen is a quaint family-operated Victorian ski lodge built in the 1880s. The charming parlor has a fireplace and color TV for guests. We have a variety of rooms, most with private baths, plus two kitchen units. We are located in town, within walking distance of restaurants, shops, and the ski area. We also have a nice outdoor hot tub.

Hosts: Norma Dolle & Larry Ledingham
Doubles: 6 (4 PB; 2 SB) $46-135
Type of Beds: 4 Twin; 2 Double; 2 Queen; 1 King
Continental Breakfast
Credit Cards: A, B, C
Closed April 15 - May 15
Notes: 2, 7, 8, 9, 10, 11, 12, 13, 14

Stapleton Spurr

B&B Colorado, Box 12206, Boulder, 80303
(800) 373-4995

A working cattle ranch located four miles west of Aspen, one and one-half miles from Snowmass Village, and two miles from the Aspen Airport. Guinea hens, ducks, horses, and 150 head of cattle. From the living room there is a lovely view of Daly, Aspen, and Buttermilk Mountains. Large deck, fireplace, sauna. Rafting, snowmobiling, fishing, and hiking nearby. Three resident cats and two dogs.

Doubles: 4 (S2B) $50-95 plus tax
Type of Beds: 4 Twin; 1 Double; 2 Daybeds
Continental Breakfast
Credit Cards: No
Notes: 8, 13

BERTHOUD

Parrish's Country Squire

B&B Colorado, Box 12206, Boulder, 80303
(800) 373-4995

Large log home on a working cattle ranch near Estes Park and Carter Lake. Hike or ride over some of the 3000 acres of land; fish the fully stocked pond. Outside deck with a wonderful view.

Doubles: 2 (PB) $35-55
Type of Beds: 2 Double
Full Breakfast
Credit Cards: No
Closed second half of Dec.
Notes: 7, 8 (over 5)

BEULAH

Double K

B&B Colorado, Box 12206, Boulder, 80303
(800) 373-4995

Two creeks run through the 67 acres of this 1870 homestead house; a 600-acre mountain park adjoins the property, with hiking trails and streams. Fishing at Lake Isabel is a short drive, as are the famed Royal Gorge and the Old West movie town of "Buckskin Joe."

Doubles: 2 (SB) $32-50
Type of Beds: 3 Twin; 1 Double; Crib
Continental Breakfast
Credit Cards: No
Notes: 7

BOULDER

The Bluebell

B&B Colorado, Box 12206, 80303
(800) 373-4995

This contemporary two-story home is in a quiet residential area just south of the CU Law School. Many nearby hiking trails.

Doubles: 2 (SB) $32-40
Type of Beds: 1 Queen; 1 Three-quarter
Full Breakfast

NOTES: Credit cards accepted: A Master Card; B Visa; C American Express; D Discover Card; E Diners Club; F Other: 2 Personal checks accepted: 3 Lunch available: 4 Dinner available: 5 Open all year

Credit Cards: No
Notes: 8

The Blue Spruce

B&B Colorado, Box 12206, 80303
(800) 373-4995

Located in historic Mapleton Hill, this lovely two-story home is only six blocks from the downtown Boulder Mall. In the summer, breakfast is served on the outdoor deck by the creek bordering the property.

Singles: 1 (SB) $32
Doubles: 1 (SB) $40
Type of Beds: 1 Twin; 1 Double
Full Breakfast
Credit Cards: No
Notes: 8 (over 6)

Briar Rose B&B Inn

Briar Rose Bed & Breakfast Inn

2151 Arapahoe, 80302
(303) 442-3007

Genuine comfort at Boulder's original guest house. The guest rooms are comfortable, with period furniture and flowers. Sit back and enjoy tea with homemade shortbread cookies while watching the antics at the bird feeder, or sit by a crackling fire.

Hosts: Kit Riley & Emily Hunter
Doubles: 11 (6 PB; 5 SB) $53.49-106.98
Type of Beds: 2 Twin; 1 Double; 9 Queen
Continental Breakfast
Credit Cards: A, B, C, E
Notes: 2, 4, 5, 6, 7, 8, 9, 10, 11, 12

The Dodge House

B&B Colorado, Box 12206, 80303
(800) 373-4995

This charming Victorian is located in the Mapleton Historic District and has been lavishly restored. Sitting area, plant-filled solarium, breathtaking mountain views.

Doubles: 2 (SB) $50-60
Type of Beds: 2 Double
Continental-plus Breakfast
Credit Cards: No

The Flatirons

B&B Colorado, Box 12206, 80303
(800) 373-4995

Contemporary home on a cul-de-sac just below the Flatirons. A very quiet setting, yet only minutes from downtown Boulder. Private sitting room with fireplace and a lovely view of the city.

Doubles: 1 (PB) $35-45
Type of Beds: 2 Twin
Continental Breakfast
Credit Cards: No

Frazier House

B&B Colorado, Box 12206, 80303
(800) 373-4995

The stonemason for the University of Colorado built this home for his family in 1896. Antiques and contemporary Indian art blend with family pieces for a pleasant, restful stay. One resident dog.

Doubles: 2 (SB) $40
Type of Beds: 2 Double

6 Pets welcome: 7 Smoking allowed: 8 Children welcome: 9 Social drinking allowed: 10 Tennis available: 11 Swimming available: 12 Golf available: 13 Skiing available: 14 May be booked through travel agents

Full Breakfast
Credit Cards: No

The Greenwood

B&B Colorado, Box 12206, 80303
(800) 373-4995

The second floor of this home is just for you.
The bedroom has a great view of the mountains, and you can relax in your private sitting room or in front of the fireplace in the main living room. Within walking distance of Ball Aerospace and the 55th Street business complex.

Doubles: 1 (PB) $30-38
Type of Beds: 1 Double
Continental Breakfast
Credit Cards: No

Home Port West

B&B Colorado, Box 12206, 80303
(800) 373-4995

This very large brick home is situated on 10 acres in a quiet rural area fifteen minutes from downtown Boulder. Greenhouse, sun porch, patio, outdoor pool. One large but friendly resident dog.

Doubles: 2 (SB) $30-40
Type of Beds: 1 Twin; 2 Double
Full Breakfast
Credit Cards: No
Notes: 8, 11

Kalmia House

B&B Colorado, Box 12206, 80303
(800) 373-4995

This contemporary home is in north Boulder, with easy access to IBM. Baby grand piano and large backyard deck for summer evenings. Next door to a city park; private sitting room for guests.

Doubles: 1 (PB) $30-38
Type of Beds: 1 Double
Continental Breakfast
Credit Cards: No

Ray and Danny's Place

B&B Colorado, Box 12206, 80303
(800) 373-4995

Large colonial home on 5 acres twenty minutes from Boulder and thirty to Denver. Fantastic view of the entire front range — mountains and plains. Large, garden-level suites. Your choice of gourmet, ranch, or continental breakfast, served in a large sunny kitchen or by the pool. TV, pool table, fireplace, indoor pool, and spa.

Doubles: 1 (PB) $35-45
Type of Beds: 1 Queen
Choice of Breakfast
Credit Cards: No
Notes: 8, 11

Red Rocks

B&B Colorado, Box 12206, 80303
(800) 373-4995

Located on the quiet west side of Pearl Street, this ground-floor condominium is close to downtown Boulder and the Dakota Ridge hiking area. The Rolf Institute is only two blocks away. Good public transportation nearby. Two resident cats.

Doubles: 1 (PB) $25-32
Type of Beds: 2 Twin
Continental Breakfast
Credit Cards: No

Rinn's Nest

B&B Rocky Mountains.
Box 804, Colorado Springs, CO, 80901
(719) 630-3433

A contemporary ranch-style home in a country setting just twelve miles from Boulder. Large yard with flower garden and gazebo. One guest room with a double bed and private bath. Resident dog. Full breakfast. $40.

NOTES: Credit cards accepted: A Master Card; B Visa; C American Express; D Discover Card; E Diners Club; F Other: 2 Personal checks accepted: 3 Lunch available: 4 Dinner available: 5 Open all year

The Sunset House

B&B Colorado, Box 12206, 80303
(800) 373-4995

This contemporary brick home sits on a ridge overlooking the city. The terraced backyard has a large, secluded deck with a lovely view. Nine blocks north of the downtown mall. Private entrance, sitting area with fireplace, TV, bicycles available.

Doubles: 2 (SB) $32-40
Type of Beds: 4 Twin
Full Breakfast
Credit Cards: No

Valkommen

B&B Colorado, Box 12206, 80303
(800) 373-4995

Located on the original Cripple Creek to Cheyenne stagecoach line, Valkommen is a hiker's and cross-country skier's paradise. The Continental Divide is only six miles away with all its trails and wilderness areas. Forty-five minutes northwest of Boulder; twenty minutes to Rocky Mountain National Park.

Doubles: 2 (SB) $65
Type of Beds: 2 Bunks; 1 Double
Continental Breakfast
Credit Cards: No
Notes: 8

A Writer's Point of View

B&B Colorado, Box 12206, 80303
(800) 373-4995

An intimate homestay that pampers its guests and is the perfect base for experiencing all that Boulder has to offer. Within walking distance of mountain parks and downtown.

Doubles: 1 (PB) $37-45
Type of Beds: 1 Double
Full Breakfast
Credit Cards: No

BRECKENRIDGE_____

Crown Mountain

B&B Colorado, Box 12206, Boulder, 80303
(800) 373-4995

This lovely contemporary cedar home sits in a large, peaceful forest 1.5 miles south of the Breckenridge ski area. Guests have their own private entrance, a large sitting room with a full-size pool table, color TV, and a wood-burning stove. Back-country cross-country skiing and hiking trails.

Doubles: 1 (PB) $55-65
Type of Beds: 1 Double
Continental Breakfast weekdays; Full on weekends
Credit Cards: No

One Wellington Square

B&B Colorado, Box 12206, Boulder, 80303
(800) 373-4995

This new Victorian-style home is perfectly situated for those without cars. Minutes from downtown and the ski shuttle; less than one mile to the slopes. In the warmer months, enjoy 40 miles of bicycle trails, fishing, golf, and hiking.

Doubles: 2 (SB) $25-50
Type of Beds: 1 Double; 2 Queen
Continental Breakfast
Credit Cards: No
Notes: 8 (over 12), 12, 13

Rocky Mts. #109

B&B Rocky Mountains.
Box 804, Colorado Springs, CO, 80901
(719) 630-3433

A three-story twelve-room inn, on the bus line, with private or shared baths. Several rooms can accommodate six to eight people. On route of the free shuttle to all nearby ski areas. Hot tub, steam room, TV, wood-burning stove in the living room. Continental buffet breakfast. $45-83.

6 Pets welcome: 7 Smoking allowed: 8 Children welcome: 9 Social drinking allowed: 10 Tennis available: 11 Swimming available: 12 Golf available: 13 Skiing available: 14 May be booked through travel agents

Summit House

B&B Colorado, Box 12206, Boulder, 80303
(800) 373-4995

This contemporary mountain home has a hot tub and sauna and is centrally located to all major ski areas. Summer visitors can enjoy hiking and biking in the area. Two resident cats.

Doubles: 2 (PB) $38-44
Type of Beds: 2 Twin; 1 King
Continental Breakfast
Credit Cards: No

BUENA VISTA

The Adobe Inn

B&B Colorado, Box 12206, Boulder, 80303
(800) 373-4995

Capture the flavor of an old southwest adobe hacienda; relax in the Mexican tiled solarium; play the piano; drowse before the Indian fireplace. Ideally situated for summer and winter sports.

Doubles: 5, $45-65
Full Breakfast
Credit Cards: No
Notes: 8

COLORADO SPRINGS

Alumni's Hideaway

B&B Rocky Mountains.
Box 804, Colorado Springs, CO, 80901
(719) 630-3433

A modest one-story home in an older neighborhood offers a private entrance, private bath, and a large queen bedroom. Resident small dog. Within walking distance of Colorado College; one mile from downtown. Guests have use of laundry facilities, TV, and bumper pool in family room. $50.

Broadmoor Valley

B&B Colorado, Box 12206, Boulder, 80303
(800) 373-4995

This handsome Spanish-style townhouse sits in the exclusive Broadmoor area of the city. From the patio, guests can view Cheyenne Mountain and Pikes Peak. City bus stops two blocks away; excellent access to I-25.

Doubles: 1 (PB) $38-44
Type of Beds: 1 Queen
Continental Breakfast
Credit Cards: No
Notes: 7

Brownswalk

B&B Rocky Mountains.
Box 804, Colorado Springs, CO, 80901
(719) 630-3433

Just fifteen minutes from the Air Force Academy, twelve from the airport, this house offers a three-room suite that sleeps six. Private lower level with laundry facilities; full breakfast. $39 for two.

Country Cousins Suite

B&B Rocky Mountains.
Box 804, Colorado Springs, CO, 80901
(719) 630-3433

The second floor of a very nice townhome includes a double bed with sitting area, small den, and large private bath. Small resident dog. In the northeast section of the city, ten minutes from the Air Force Academy. Share the TV and fireplace with your hosts; patio with barbecue for guest use; full breakfast. $50.

El Shadmeir

B&B Rocky Mountains.
Box 804, Colorado Springs, CO, 80901
(719) 630-3433

NOTES: Credit cards accepted: A Master Card; B Visa; C American Express; D Discover Card; E Diners Club; F Other: 2 Personal checks accepted: 3 Lunch available: 4 Dinner available: 5 Open all year

This solar home overlooks the Air Force Academy and Pikes Peak. Two bedrooms, each with queen beds and private baths. Resident cat. Located twenty miles north of Colorado Springs. Hot tub available for guest use. $48.

Griffin's Hospitality House
4222 N. Chestnut Street, 80907
(719) 599-3035

The Griffins welcome singles, couples, and families. We are close to a park with tennis courts and on a bus line. Relax on our deck or in our spacious family room. Pikes Peak is right out the back door. Guests are encouraged to stay for at least three days, as there are so many sights to see. Extended-stay discounts available. Places to visit include the Air Force Academy, United States Olympic Training Center, Garden of the Gods, and more.

Hosts: Diane & John Griffin
Singles: 1 (SB) $25
Doubles: 2 (SB) $35
Type of Beds: 1 Twin; 1 Queen; 1 King
Full Breakfast
Credit Cards: No
Notes: 2, 5, 8, 9, 10, 11, 12, 13, 14

Holden House — 1902
1102 W. Pikes Peak Avenue, 80904
(719) 471-3980

A 1902 storybook Victorian, lovingly filled with antiques and family treasures. Guest rooms boast heirloom quilts, down pillows, period furnishings, and private baths. Relax fireside on winter evenings or enjoy mountain views on the veranda during the summer months. Friendly resident cat named Mingtoy.

Hosts: Sallie & Welling Clark
Doubles: 3 (PB) $50-59.35
Type of Beds: 1 Double; 2 Queen
Full Breakfast
Minimum stay holidays & special events: 2-3
Credit Cards: A, B
Notes: 2, 5, 9, 10, 11, 12, 14

Katies Korner
1304 N. El Paso, 80903
(719) 630-3322

A two-story yellow Victorian on the corner of a quiet residential area only one mile from downtown. Front porch, private guest entrance, and living room area with stereo. On bus line. Resident friendly dog in residence (not allowed in guest quarters). Full breakfast by request, otherwise a hearty continental breakfast is served.

Host: Katie Robertson
Doubles: 3 (1 PB; 1 SB) $30-55
Type of Beds: 2 Double
Continental Breakfast
Credit Cards: A, B
Closed Oct.-May
Notes: 8 (8 and over), 9, 10, 11, 12, 14

Now & Then
B&B Rocky Mountains.
Box 804, Colorado Springs, CO, 80901
(719) 630-3433

An 1890s Victorian restored to contemporary comfort, with two guest rooms on the second floor. One has a king waterbed with private bath; the other has a double bed and shares the bath. Within walking distance of Colorado College and downtown; easy freeway access. Each room offers cable TV, down comforters, and alarm clocks. Share the hot tub, fireplace, stereo, VCR, and washer/dryer. Full breakfast on weekends; continental on weekdays. $25-52.

On a Ledge
B&B Colorado, Box 12206, Boulder, 80303
(800) 373-4995

This house, built in 1912, is located on a hill overlooking Manitou Springs. Unusual copper hardware, a large copper fireplace, lovely hardwood floors, view of Pikes Peak.

Doubles: 4 (PB) $60-85
Type of Beds: 3 King; 1 Daybed

6 Pets welcome: 7 Smoking allowed: 8 Children welcome: 9 Social drinking allowed: 10 Tennis available: 11 Swimming available: 12 Golf available: 13 Skiing available: 14 May be booked through travel agents

Full Breakfast
Credit Cards: No
Notes: 7 (limited), 8

Parkside

B&B Colorado, Box 12206, Boulder, 80303
(800) 373-4995

This contemporary tri-level home offers books, brochures, travel tapes, and the host's wide knowledge of the area. The quiet park across the street frames a magnificent view of Pikes Peak. Excellent access to I-25 and public transportation.

Doubles: 1 (PB) $30-35
Type of Beds: 1 Double
Continental Breakfast
Credit Cards: No
Notes: 10, 12

The Portland Inn

B&B Colorado, Box 12206, Boulder, 80303
(800) 373-4995

Located between Pikes Peak and the Sangre de Cristo Mountains, at an elevation of 10,000 feet in one of the few authentic mining towns left in the state. The inn was built in 1898 and reflects the flavor of its era. Hiking, fishing, cross-country skiing; sun deck and outdoor hot tub. Horse corrals available.

Doubles: 4 (SB) $30-38
Type of Beds: 5 Double; 1 Daybed
Continental Breakfast
Credit Cards: No
Notes: 8, 13 (XC)

Rocky Mts. #107

B&B Rocky Mountains.
Box 804, Colorado Springs, CO, 80901
(719) 630-3433

A three-story home thirty minutes west of Colorado Springs in the mountains, surrounded by pines. Two bedrooms on the lower level, each of which opens onto a spacious patio. Rooms have one queen bed in each and share one bath. A refreshment bar

for soda, tea, and coffee whenever you want it. Wonderful continental breakfast. $55-65.

The Claim Jumper

B&B Colorado, Box 12206, Boulder, 80303
(800) 373-4995

This beautiful old log house is decorated in "high Victorian," filled with family heirlooms and antiques collected during a lifetime of traveling and working abroad. Town park across the street; free ski shuttle handy. Cable TV, indoor hot tub, and sauna.

Doubles: 3 (1 PB; 2 SB) $40-55
Type of Beds: 3 Queen
Continental Breakfast
Credit Cards: No

Purple Mountain Lodge

Box 897, 81224
(303) 349-5888

Our guests often enjoy sharing their adventures and discussing plans in the living room by a fire in the massive stone fireplace. If conversation slows, cable TV is available. Our spa, in the sun room, offers welcome relief to tired muscles. Crested Butte is located in a high (8,885 feet) open valley, surrounded by the Elk Mountains. It has many trails and roads to explore by foot, mountain bike, horseback, or four-wheel drive automobile. Nearby mountain lakes and streams provide canoeing, kayaking, rafting, and fishing. A nearby shuttle bus will take you to the ski area in winter.

Hosts: Walter & Sherron Green
Singles: 1 (SB) $28-44
Doubles: 6 (SB) $35-55
Type of Beds: 6 Twin; 2 Double; 2 Queen
Full breakfast in ski season; continental in summer
Credit Cards: A, B
Closed April, May, Oct. & Nov.
Notes: 2, 7 (restricted), 8, 9, 10, 12, 13, 14

NOTES: Credit cards accepted: A Master Card; B Visa; C American Express; D Discover Card; E Diners Club; F Other: 2 Personal checks accepted: 3 Lunch available: 4 Dinner available: 5 Open all year

DENVER

Balsam

B&B Rocky Mountains.
Box 804, Colorado Springs, CO, 80901
(719) 630-3433

A two-story home in a quiet residential area near the foothills west of Denver. Near bike trails and picnic area. Two rooms with double beds share one bath. Large backyard with hot tub, barbecue, patio; family room with fireplace, TV, and popcorn. Baby sitting available. Hearty western breakfast is served in the formal dining room. $27-38.

Cliff House Lodge

B&B Colorado, Box 12206, Boulder, 80303
(800) 373-4995

Located in the center of downtown Morrison just outside Denver, the Cliff House is surrounded with all the ambience of a small mountain town. Antique shops, art galleries, walking trails along the river, charming restaurants and beautiful views are all within walking distance. Originally built in 1873, the Cliff House has been awarded a National Historical title. A wide variety of winter and summer sports and recreation areas are in close proximity. Each guest cabin and room is warm, cozy and charmingly furnished.

Lodge: 2 Doubles (SB) $29-89
Cottage: 1 Double, 1 Twin $29-89
Continental Breakfast
Credit Cards: A, B (for deposit only)
Notes: 2 (deposit only)

The Gourmet

B&B Colorado, Box 12206, Boulder, 80303
(800) 373-4995

This large English Tudor home is located on the quiet west side of Denver, less than a fifteen-minute drive from Larimer Square. The home has an unusual antique collection and a thriving greenhouse. Good public transportation.

Doubles: 1 (PB) $40-45
Type of Beds: 1 King
Full Breakfast
Credit Cards: No

Marion Place

B&B Colorado, Box 12206, Boulder, 80303
(800) 373-4995

This gracious home offers turn-of-the-century elegance with its fine woodwork, art, and period antiques. Private patio, three working fireplaces. Within walking distance to Cheeseman Park and Botanical Gardens; excellent public transportation.

Doubles: 1 (PB) $42-48
Type of Beds: 1 King
Continental Breakfast
Credit Cards: No

Mary and Mal's

B&B Colorado, Box 12206, Boulder, 80303
(800) 373-4995

This charming house offers an Early American bedroom with a circa 1860 quilt on the wall, a small writing desk, rocking chair, and braided rug. Downtown Denver is a ten-minute drive away. Easy access to I-70, public transportation, and airport.

Doubles: 2 (SB) $30-40
Type of Beds: 2 Double; 1 Rollaway
Full Breakfast
Credit Cards: No
Notes: 7, 8

Queen Anne Inn

2147 Tremont Place, 80205
(303) 296-6666

Award-winning 1879 Victorian in downtown historic district. The luxurious, designer-quality surroundings and upscale amenities are among the most elegant anywhere. Already named "Best B&B in Town" and "Colorado Company of the Year." Listed by several editors as one of "America's Top Ten." Horse-drawn carriage rides,

6 Pets welcome: 7 Smoking allowed: 8 Children welcome: 9 Social drinking allowed: 10 Tennis available: 11 Swimming available: 12 Golf available: 13 Skiing available: 14 May be booked through travel agents

museums, art galleries, shopping, cultural events, historic districts, lakes, streams, bike paths, and parks are available.

Hosts: Ann & Chuck Hillestad
Singles: 1 (PB) $54-89 plus tax
Doubles: 9 (PB) $69-99 plus tax
Type of Beds: 4 Twin; 4 Double; 4 Queen; 2 King
Continental-plus Breakfast
Credit Cards: A, B, C
Notes: 2, 4 (with advance notice), 5, 9

Rocky Mts. #68

B&B Rocky Mountains.
Box 804, Colorado Springs, CO, 80901
(719) 630-3433

Beautifully restored 1879 historic home with ten bedrooms, each with private bath. Four short blocks from the heart of the business district, with air-conditioning, fresh fruit and flowers, complimentary soft drinks, wine, and sherry. Continental-plus breakfast. $70-110.

Seventh Avenue Manor

B&B Colorado, Box 12206, Boulder, 80303
(800) 373-4995

Built in 1895, the manor offers fireplaces, balconies, terraced gardens, and an elegant dining room. Dinner may be catered. Concierge service available; on-premises parking, high tea, full use of the "butler's pantry" and kitchen.

Doubles: 7, $50-150
Continental Breakfast
Credit Cards: No
Notes: 8

Southwestern

B&B Colorado, Box 12206, Boulder, 80303
(800) 373-4995

This two-story home in southwest Denver is located just north of Chatfield Dam and is just fifteen minutes from Martin-Marietta.

The hostess has collected many fine sets of dinnerware for your breakfast enjoyment.

Doubles: 2 (PB) $24-34
Type of Beds: 2 Double
Continental Breakfast
Credit Cards: No

The Walter House

B&B Rocky Mountains.
Box 804, Colorado Springs, CO, 80901
(719) 630-3433

Built in 1888, this house is within walking distance of fine restaurants, the Denver Zoo, Natural History Museum, hospitals. Three rooms on the second floor share one bath. Continental breakfast is served in the main dining room or on private balconies. $45-50.

Zel's Soda Bar

B&B Colorado, Box 12206, Boulder, 80303
(800) 373-4995

A lovely tri-level ranch that boasts an old-fashioned soda fountain, large patio. The location is ideal for those attending meetings in the Denver Tech area. TV, resident singing canary.

Doubles: 2 (PB) $32-39
Type of Beds: 2 Twin; 1 Double
Full Breakfast
Credit Cards: No
Notes: 8

DILLON

Home and Hearth

B&B Colorado, Box 12206, Boulder, 80303
(800) 373-4995

Country antiques abound on the interior barnwood walls of the large kitchen/living area. Enjoy the beautiful mountain view and the warmth of the huge stone fireplace after a day on the slopes or great fishing on the Blue River. Dinner and free pick-up service available with notice. Six miles to Keystone,

NOTES: Credit cards accepted: A Master Card; B Visa; C American Express; D Discover Card; E Diners Club; F Other: 2 Personal checks accepted: 3 Lunch available: 4 Dinner available: 5 Open all year

14 to Breckenridge and Copper Mt. One resident dog.

Doubles: 4 (S2B) $25-55
Type of Beds: 2 Twin; 2 Double; 2 Bunks
Full Breakfast
Credit Cards: No
Notes: 7, 8, 13

Paradox Lodge

B&B Colorado, Box 12206, Boulder, 80303
(800) 373-4995

Paradox Lodge is located on 37 acres secluded on the Snake River and surrounded by national forest. From this 10,000-foot elevation there are vistas of mountain peaks and alpine forests. Direct access to bicycling, hiking, and cross-country ski trails. Close to all ski resorts.

3 Cabins: Each sleeps 6 (PB) $60-100
Doubles: 4 (SB) $45-85
Type of Beds: 10 Queen; 3 Hideabeds
Continental Breakfast
Credit Cards: No

Snowberry Hill

B&B Colorado, Box 12206, Boulder, 80303
(800) 373-4995

Located between Dillon and Keystone, within a ten-minute drive of Keystone Ski Area. Other major slopes within a half-hour drive. Cross-country skiing, hiking, and other recreational activities nearby.

1 Suite with full kitchen sleeps 4; $60-100
Type of Beds: 1 Queen; 1 Sofa sleeper
Full Breakfast
Credit Cards: No
Notes: 8 (no charge under 18), 13

DURANGO

Blue Lake Ranch

16919 St. Hwy. 140, Hesperus 81326
(303) 385-4537

Overlooking trout-filled Blue Lake, with mountain views, this authentic, luxurious, cozy log cabin is an idyllic and romantic hideaway with all the amenities. Own kitchen and outdoor grill. Gourmet European breakfast; elegant Saturday-night dinners at the main ranch.

Hosts: David & Tia Alford
Cabin: 1 (2 PB) $134
Type of Beds: 1 Double; 2 Queen
Full Breakfast
Credit Cards: No
Closed: Oct. 31-April 30
Notes: 2, 4 (occasionally), 8, 9, 11, 14

Gable House

B&B Rocky Mountains.
Box 804, Colorado Springs, CO, 80901
(719) 630-3433

A huge three-story Victorian on a tree-lined street in an established neighborhood just five blocks from the train depot and within walking distance to restaurants and downtown shops. Two spacious rooms with double beds share one bath down the hall. Full breakfast. Open summers only. $45.

Lil's

B&B Colorado, Box 12206, Boulder, 80303
(800) 373-4995

Hosted by a local school teacher, this contemporary home is simple furnished and offers guests good public transportation to downtown to catch the Silverton/Durango Narrow Gauge Train. Purgatory Ski Area is just a thirty minute drive and a picnic along the Million Dollar Highway is a "must" during the summer.

Siagle: (PB) $28
Doubles: (PB) $34
Type of Beds: 2 Double in one room
Continental Breakfast
Credit Cards: A, B (for deposit only)
Notes: 2 (deposit only), 7, 8, 13

Logwood Inn B&B

B&B Colorado, Box 12206, Boulder, 80303
(800) 373-4995

The serenity of the Logwood Inn takes its
guests back to "the Good Old Days" when
one took time for rejuvenation of self. Picture yourself in a restful hammock or sitting
on the quiet porch taking in the fresh air and
listening to peaceful sounds of a cool stream.
Rest your eyes on a tall ponderosa pine while
you smell the inviting aroma of good home
cooking.

Doubles: 5 (PB) $45-65
Type of Beds: 1 Double; 4 Queen
Full Country Breakfast
Credit Cards: A, B (for deposit only)
Notes: 2 (deposit only), 13

Penny's Place

B&B Rocky Mountains.
Box 804, Colorado Springs, CO, 80901
(719) 630-3433

A remodeled Cape Cod house with a great
view just twenty minutes from Durango.
Large bedroom with king bed, private bath,
and kitchenette. Hot tub, pond, and stream,
on 26 acres of land; TV, Ping-Pong table,
barbecue grill. $45-50.

Rocky Mt. #48

B&B Rocky Mountains.
Box 804, Colorado Springs, CO, 80901
(719) 630-3433

Located on 10 acres of land three miles out
of Durango, this house offers four
bedrooms with shared baths. VCR, sauna,
fireplace, cable TV; delightful view. Enjoy
yourself with the pool table or look over the
host's big-game-hunting trophies. $45-55.

Scrubby Oaks

B&B Colorado, Box 12206, Boulder, 80303
(800) 373-4995

Located on 10 acres overlooking the Animas
Valley and surrounding mountains, Scrubby
Oaks has a quiet country feeling with the
convenience of being only three miles from
downtown Durango and one-half hour from
the Purgatory Ski Area. All of the rooms are
spacious and comfortably furnished with antiques, artwork and good books. Guests can
relax at any time on the patios which are
framed with trees and gardens. Winter finds
guests gathered around one of the three
fireplaces for morning coffee or evening fun.
Guests are welcome to play pool, take a
sauna, watch TV or a movie on the VCR or
play one of many of the board games available. Homemade bread and jams. No smoking, please.

Singles: $30-40
Doubles: 7 (SB) $45-55
Suites: 3 (PB)
Type of Beds: 2 Twin; 3 Double; 1 Queen size
waterbed; 1 King
Full Country Breakfast
Credit Cards: A, B (for deposit only)
Notes: 2 (deposit only), 8, 13

ESTES PARK

Allenspark Lodge

B&B Colorado, Box 12206, Boulder, 80303
(800) 373-4995

Virtually every charm and beauty of the high
mountain world is yours to enjoy as a guest
of Allenspark Lodge. The rustic lodge offers
cordial, individualized hospitality, combined
with modern comforts and attractive rates.
You will find the old-fashioned western
lobby with its huge fireplace and charming
setting for friendly conversations often
transforms strangers into friends. Seasonal
activities include hiking, scenic mountain
picnics, fishing, hunting, cross-country and
downhill skiing. A complimentary continental breakfast is served and gourmet brown-

bag lunches are available at nominal cost. Hot tub and game room. No smoking, please.

Singles: 1 $28.95
Doubles: 11 (5 PB) $44.95-54.95
Doubles and Twins: 3
Type of Beds: 7 Twin; 14 Double
Continental Breakfast
Credit Cards: A, B (for deposit only)
Notes: 2 (deposit only), 3, 8, 13

Emerald Manor

B&B Colorado, Box 12206, Boulder, 80303
(800) 373-4995

Ironed sheets, homemade Irish soda bread and hand-crocheted tablecloths are only a part of the real Irish hospitality that greets you at the Emerald Manor. Your bed will be warmed with a soft-covered hot water bottle and your breakfast so hearty that you won't be hungry for the rest of the day. The real home atmosphere is further enhanced when you watch the early morning deer saunter through the property. Situated on a hill with wonderful views of the mountains, you are only a short walk to shops or golfing and just four miles to Rocky Mountain National Park. You can even take a morning swim in the indoor pool or relax in the sauna after a day of cross-country skiing. No smoking, please.

Singles: $38-50
Doubles: 4 (SB) $40-60
Type of Beds: 2 Double; 2 Queen; 1 King
Continental Breakfast
Credit Cards: A, B (for deposit only)
Notes: 2 (deposit only), 8 (over 15), 13

Riversong, Bed & Breakfast Inn

B&B Colorado, Box 12206, Boulder, 80303
(800) 373-4995

This romantic mountain Inn is nestled at the end of a winding, country lane on 27 wooded acres. Very secluded and offers spectacular, snow-capped vistas of nearby Rocky Moun-

tain National Park. Built in the 1920's and decorated with a blend of family antiques and modern, country furniture, the Inn manages to be elegant, yet comfortable and cozy. It has its own hiking trails and trout stream. Such delights as apple pan dowdy or pecan rolls are baked fresh each morning and served in the cheery, round breakfast room. Great location for year-round hiking, snowshoeing, ice-skating, cross-country skiing, wildlife watching and just relaxing. Eight romantic rooms with full baths; includes two cottages, one carriage house; five have fireplaces or wood stoves, several with large tubs. No smoking, please.

Singles: $40-85
Doubles: $50-95
Continental Breakfast
Credit Cards: A, B (for deposit only)
Notes: 2 (deposit only), 13 (XC)

Rocky Mt. #91

B&B Rocky Mountains.
Box 804, Colorado Springs, CO, 80901
(719) 630-3433

Turn-of-the-century home furnished with antiques, wallpapers, and quilts has four bedrooms and one private log cabin in the heart of Estes Park. Your host is a chef and will arrange private dinner parties at additional cost if you ask him. Full gourmet breakfast. $50-85.

Sapphire Rose

B&B Colorado, Box 12206, Boulder, 80303
(800) 373-4995

The Sapphire Rose is a beautifully re-stored 1909 home located one block from the Village of Estes Park and within minutes of scenic Rocky Mountain Park. Awake each morning to the fresh aroma of a special country breakfast being prepared just for you. Relax in the evenings before a crackling fire in the sitting room. In the spring and summer enjoy fishing, hiking, boating, golf, tennis and horseback riding. In the winter enjoy downhill and cross-country skiing, snowmobiling, sleigh rides or ice skating. Special gourmet dinners prepared on request by your host who is a master chef. Bedrooms are decorated with the romance of the past and furnished with fine antiques. All have color TV. Also available is a one bedroom cabin with full cooking facilities. No smoking, please.

Hosts: Harry and Nancy Marsden
Doubles: 4 (SB) $50
Cabin: $70; extra adult $12; extra child $7
Type of Beds: Queen
Country Breakfast
Credit Cards: A, B (for deposit only)
Notes: 2 (deposit only), 4, 8, 13 (XC)

Wanek's Lodge at Estes
Box 898, 80517
(303) 586-5851

A modern mountain inn on a ponderosa-pine-covered hillside just a few miles from Rocky Mountain National Park. There is a resident cat, clean, cozy rooms, fireplace, plants, beautiful vistas from picture windows. Hosts are former teachers and very much interested in the environment.

Hosts: Jim & Pat Wanek
Doubles: 3 (SB) $33.50-46
Type of Beds: 1 Twin; 1 Double
Continental Breakfast
Credit Cards: No
Notes: 2, 4 (weekends), 5, 8 (over 10), 9, 10, 11, 12, 13

FORT COLLINS

Elizabeth Street Guest House
B&B Colorado, Box 12206, Boulder, 80303
(800) 373-4995

This beautifully restored 1905 house is located in the historic district, one block from Colorado State University and within walking distance to restored Old Town. The turn-of-the-century ambience is enhanced with

antiques, porcelain dolls and other country handicrafts made and collected by the owner. Day trips: one hour to Estes Park and Rocky Mountain National Park. Scenic hiking and fishing up the Poudre River twenty minutes away. Enjoy a full breakfast with homebaked specialties, homemade jams and a special granola in the lovely dining room where leaded glass windows are a distinctive feature. Sitting room with desk and telephone; TV, games and reading in the parlor.

Singles: $30
Doubles: 3 (SB) $38; child with parents $8
House: $115, 2 day minimum
Type of Beds: 2 Twin; 2 Double; 1 Queen
Full Breakfast
Credit Cards: A, B (for deposit only)
Notes: 2 (deposit only), 7 (limited), 8 (over 4)

Elizabeth Street Guest House

FORT MORGAN/BRUSH

Little House on the Prairie
B&B Colorado, Box 12206, Boulder, 80303
(800) 373-4995

Hospitality and privacy prevail at this modest country spread 1.5 hours east of Denver. Breakfast at the lovely outdoor pool in warm weather or at the cozy fireplace on cooler days. Well-behaved pets welcome

NOTES: Credit cards accepted: A Master Card; B Visa; C American Express; D Discover Card; E Diners Club; F Other: 2 Personal checks accepted: 3 Lunch available: 4 Dinner available: 5 Open all year

at additional cost. Two friendly terriers in residence.

Doubles: 1 (PB) $18-29
Type of Beds: 1 Double
Continental Breakfast
Credit Cards: A, B (for deposit only)
Notes: 2 (deposit only)

FRISCO

Twilight Inn

B&B Colorado, Box 12206, Boulder, 80303
(800) 373-4995

Located in downtown Frisco between Dillon and Vail, with convenient access to all ski areas. Within walking distance of all shuttle stops, restaurants, night clubs, and horse and buggy rides. Two living rooms, hot tub, steam room, and locked storage room for guest equipment. Kitchen available.

Doubles: 12 (8 PB; 4 SB) $31-69
Type of Beds: 2 Twin; 7 Double; 5 Queen; 3 Sofa
sleepers; 6 Bunks
Continental-plus Breakfast
Credit Cards: No

GEORGETOWN

The Hardy House

B&B Colorado, Box 12206, Boulder, 80303
(800) 373-4995

Located in the historic mining town of Georgetown, only an hour's drive from Denver, this charming Victorian is just one-half block from Main Street shops. A ten- to forty-five-minute drive will take you to five major ski areas, and great fishing in Clear Creek is just a stone's throw away. Use our custom-made, six-speed tandem mountain bike; hot toddies in winter and wine in summer; gourmet dinners served on request. One resident cat.

Doubles: 3 (1 PB; 2 S2B) $35-65
Type of Beds: 2 Twin; 2 Queen; 1 King
Full Breakfast
Credit Cards: No
Notes: 8 (over 9), 13

GLENWOOD SPRINGS

Adducci's Inn Bed & Breakfast

B&B Colorado, Box 12206, Boulder, 80303
(800) 373-4995

The Adduccis welcome you to their turn-of-the-century home, which has been refurbished with antiques. Enjoy games in the parlor or relax with an old book and a complimentary glass of wine. Off-street parking, train and bus pickup. Within walking distance to downtown, the Hot Springs Pool, and the free ski shuttle.

Doubles: 5 (PB) $25-48
Type of Beds: 3 Twin; 3 Double; 2 Queen
Full Breakfast
Credit Cards: No
Notes: 7 (limited), 8, 9, 13

Sojourner's Inn

1032 Cooper, 81601
(303) 945-7162

Sojourner's Inn is a large turn-of-the-century home retaining the flavor of the past. We feature spacious rooms and wonderful breakfasts. Downtown Glenwood Springs and the world's largest hot springs pool are just a short distance from the inn.

Hosts: Clay & Darlene Carrington
Doubles: 4 (PB) $29-48.47
Full Breakfast
Credit Cards: A, B, F
Notes: 2, 5, 8, 9, 12

Talbot House and The House Next Door

B&B Colorado, Box 12206, Boulder, 80303
(800) 373-4995

Two neighboring houses with fir flooring, Oriental rugs, and antiques. Enjoy the solar-powered hot tub; walk to the Hot Springs Pool, stores, and restaurants. Nordic and

6 Pets welcome: 7 Smoking allowed: 8 Children welcome: 9 Social drinking allowed: 10 Tennis available: 11 Swimming available: 12 Golf available: 13 Skiing available: 14 May be booked through travel agents

Alpine skiing at nearby Ski Sunlight; climbing and hiking year-round.

Singles: 1 (SB) $27-35
Doubles: 6 (3 PB; 3 SB) $42-50
Type of Beds: 3 Twin; 5 Double
Full Breakfast
Credit Cards: No
Notes: 8 (Talbot House), 13

GOLDEN

The Dove Inn

711 14th Street, 80401
(303) 278-2209

Charming Victorian inn located in the foothills of west Denver, yet in the small-town atmosphere of Golden. Close to Coors tours, Rocky Mountain National Park; one hour to ski areas. No unmarried couples, please.

Hosts: Ken & Jean Sims
Doubles: 6 (4 PB; 2 SB) $36-57.40
Type of Beds: 2 Double; 5 Queen
Full Breakfast
Credit Cards: A, B, C, E
Notes: 2, 5, 8, 9, 10, 11, 12, 13, 14

Foothills

B&B Colorado, Box 12206, Boulder, 80303
(800) 373-4995

This contemporary ranch-style home is only fifteen minutes from downtown Denver. Close to I-70, Red Rocks, or the Federal Center.

Doubles: 2 (SB) $30-38
Type of Beds: 2 Twin; 1 Queen
Continental Breakfast
Credit Cards: No

GRAND JUNCTION

Gate House Bed & Breakfast

B&B Colorado, Box 12206, Boulder, 80303
(800) 373-4995

Built in 1899 and meticulously restored, the Gate House offers the warmth and elegance of a fine English country inn. The grounds are filled with fruit trees, flowers, and a vine-covered arbor. The living area has large picture windows looking out into the gardens, oak floors, French love seats, and a native stone fireplace.

Doubles: 4 (2 PB; 1 SB) $28-52
Type of Beds: 2 Queen; 2 King; 1 Trundle
Full Breakfast
Credit Cards: No
Notes: 8 (over 12), 13

Junction Country Inn

B&B Colorado, Box 12206, Boulder, 80303
(800) 373-4995

A beautifully restored 1907 mansion with hardwood floors, picture windows, leaded glass, and a beautiful staircase. Enjoy evening snacks and conversation in one of the two comfortable parlors. Only a short walk to shops, restaurants, museums, and the sports stadium.

Doubles: 3 (1 PB; 2 SB) $17-47
Type of Beds: 2 Twin; 2 Double; 1 Queen
Full Breakfast
Credit Cards: No
Notes: 8, 13

GRAND LAKE

Onahu Lodge

B&B Rocky Mountains.
Box 804, Colorado Springs, CO, 80901
(719) 630-3433

A hand-hewn log lodge in a unique area with a spectacular view of the "never Summer Range" overlooking Rocky Mountain National Park land. Watch elk at the salt lick from your patio overlooking the river below. Two bedrooms with private or semiprivate bath. Nearby stables for rental horses; fishing, boating. No TV. Lovely continental-plus breakfast. $45-55.

NOTES: Credit cards accepted: A Master Card; B Visa; C American Express; D Discover Card; E Diners Club; F Other: 2 Personal checks accepted: 3 Lunch available: 4 Dinner available: 5 Open all year

GREEN MOUNTAIN FALLS

Outlook Lodge

Box 5, 80819
(719) 684-2303

This house was originally the parsonage for The Little Church in the Wildwood and is now celebrating its centennial with extensive restorations. Near Colorado Springs, with many major attractions within five miles. Enjoy hiking, horseback riding, swimming, tennis, fishing, sightseeing — or relax on our large veranda. Outlook Lodge provides nostalgia and enjoyment for all.

Hosts: Rod & Sherri Ramsey
Doubles: 9 (6 PB; 3 SB) $32-65
Type of Beds: 2 Twin; 8 Double; 1 Queen
Continental-plus Breakfast
Credit Cards: A, B
Notes: 2, 3, 5, 8, 9, 10, 11, 12, 14

GUNNISON

Waunita Hot Springs Ranch

8007 County Road 887, 81230
(303) 641-1266

A summer dude ranch that welcomes B&B guests from Sept. - May. Located near cross-country ski trails; forty minutes to Monarch ski area; seventy-five to Crested Butte ski area. Comfortable lodge accommodations. Hot springs pool available year round. This lodge has been family owned and operated for twenty-seven years.

Hosts: The Pringle Family
Doubles: 22 (PB) $37.50-55
Type of Beds: 6 Twin; 6 Double; 13 Queen
Full Breakfast
Credit Cards: No
Closed 4/15-5/10; 11/20-12/5
Notes: 2, 4, 8, 11

GYPSUM

7W Guest Ranch

3412 County Road 151, 81637
(303) 524-9328

Built in 1916, Colorado's second-oldest guest ranch offers a relaxed, unregimented program ideal for families and couples looking for a variety of daily options. Horseback heaven for the novice or expert rider. High-country fishing trips, hay rides, square dancing, hiking, quaint and cozy cabins, and blue-ribbon country gourmet dining.

Hosts: Missy Taylor, Layne Wing, John & Frances Mills
Cabins: 6 (PB) $75-85
Type of Beds: 4 Twin; 8 Double; 2 Queen
Full Breakfast
Credit Cards: No
Closed Sept. 24 - June 1
Notes: 2, 3, 4, 7, 8, 9, 11, 13, 14

HOTCHKISS

Ye Olde Oasis

B&B Colorado, Box 12206, Boulder, 80303
(800) 373-4995

Located on Rogers Mesa (elevation 5,200 feet), this small working farm is filled with family antiques, handmade quilts, and other touches of the past. The hosts raise Sheltie Collies, have several horses and a pet turkey. Enjoy a country breakfast cooked on the antique wood stove and the quietness of this area, which is known for its gold-medal fishing and hunting. Llama treks and rafting are also nearby.

Doubles: 3 (S2B) $25-45
Type of Beds: 2 Twin; 1 Queen; 1 King
Full Breakfast
Credit Cards: No
Notes: 4 (by arrangement), 7 (limited), 8 (over 6)

IDAHO SPRINGS

St. Mary's Glacier B&B

B&B Rocky Mountains.
Box 804, Colorado Springs, 80901
(719) 630-3433

From the deck of this mountain retreat you can enjoy majestic views of the Continental Divide, a waterfall, and lake. Your suite features a queen-size brass bed (with Teddy bear) and down comforter. Relax in a private hot tub or enjoy a roaring fire in a wood-burning stove in the living room. A remote location in the woods one hour west of Denver. Full breakfast. $48.

LA VETA

1899 Bed & Breakfast Inn

B&B Colorado, Box 12206, Boulder, 80303
(800) 373-4995

Located next to the library and Fort Francisco Museum in a small, rustic town in the heart of the Spanish Peaks and Sangre de Cristo Mountains. A wood-burning stove in the parlor will warm you after a day of cross-country skiing. Excellent restaurants in town; horseback riding, fishing, hiking, skiing are nearby.

Doubles: 5 (2 PB; 3 SB) $22.50-32.50
Type of Beds: 2 Twin; 3 Double; 2 King
Full Breakfast
Credit Cards: No
Notes: 7, 8, 13

LEADVILLE

Hilltop House

B&B Colorado, Box 12206, Boulder, 80303
(800) 373-4995

This stately Queen Anne overlooks the main street of historic Leadville. Relax and enjoy the panoramic views of the Sawatch Mountain Range from the gracefully curved front porch. Ski box lunches are available, and gourmet dinners are available with advance notice. One resident dog.

Doubles: 2 (SB) $40-65
Type of Beds: 2 Queen
Full Breakfast
Credit Cards: No
Notes: 3, 4, 8 (over 10), 13

Leadville Country Inn

B&B Colorado, Box 12206, Boulder, 80303
(800) 373-4955

This large 1893 Victorian Queen Anne boasts a magnificent view of Mt. Massive and Mt. Elbert, Colorado's highest mountains. Within walking distance of downtown; Ski Cooper is just twenty minutes away, and Copper Mountain, Keystone, Arapahoe Basin, Breckenridge, and Vail are less than an hour away. A horse-drawn sleigh and surrey are available. Afternoon tea is served.

Doubles: 10 (PB & SB) $35-65
Full Breakfast
Credit Cards: No
Notes: 8, 13

Rocky Mts. #88

B&B Rocky Mountains.
Box 804, Colorado Springs, 80901
(719) 630-3433

A stately 1907 Victorian overlooking the old mining town of Leadville. One romantic bedroom with sitting room shares a bath with a second room. Two outside dogs in residence. If you request it, you may have your full breakfast in your four-poster bed. $48-68.

LOVELAND

The Lovelander Bed & Breakfast

B&B Colorado, Box 12206, Boulder, 80303
(800) 373-4995

Located in the heart of Loveland, an arts-oriented community nestled against the Rocky Mountain foothills, just minutes away from Rocky Mountain National Park. The Lovelander is a rambling Victorian built in 1902. Afternoon tea or wine is served in

NOTES: Credit cards accepted: A Master Card; B Visa; C American Express; D Discover Card; E Diners Club; F Other: 2 Personal checks accepted: 3 Lunch available: 4 Dinner available: 5 Open all year

the dining room, library, or on the terrace. Facilities for the handicapped.

Doubles: 8 (7 PB; 1 SB) $35-90
Type of Beds: 7 Queen; 1 King; 1 Daybed
Full Breakfast
Credit Cards: No
Notes: 8 (over 10), 13

Mountains and Plains

B&B Colorado, Box 12206, Boulder, 80303
(800) 373-4995

This new, owner-designed home outside Loveland has wonderful vistas and an open feeling. Between the universities in Greeley and Ft. Collins and a short thirty minutes from Estes Park.

Doubles: 2 (SB) $35
Type of Beds: 2 Twin; 1 Double
Full Breakfast
Credit Cards: No
Notes: 8 (older)

MANITOU SPRINGS

1889 House

B&B Rocky Mountains.
Box 804, Colorado Springs, 80901
(719) 630-3433

A small restored two-story home with a guest suite. Private entrance, queen bed, small sitting area, and European wood-burning stove. Private bath. Guests may enjoy the hot tub by appointment. Continental breakfast. $75.

Ogilbee House

B&B Rocky Mountains.
Box 804, Colorado Springs, 80901
(719) 630-3433

A beautiful turn-of-the-century home in the heart of the historic district. Two newly decorated guest rooms are furnished with original antiques, and both have private baths. Cats in residence. Enjoy the sitting

room with fireplace, library, family room with TV and VCR, front porch swing, and backyard barbecue area. Continental breakfast. $50-55.

Rocky Mts. #29

B&B Rocky Mountains.
Box 804, Colorado Springs, 80901
(719) 630-3433

A three-story Queen Anne Victorian in one of the largest National Historic Districts west of the Mississippi. Ten rooms, some with private and some with shared baths, large common area with games, puzzlers, piano, and VCR. Full breakfast. $40-60.

MEEKER

The Snow Goose Bed & Breakfast

B&B Colorado, Box 12206, Boulder, 80303
(800) 373-4995

A turn-of-the-century brick house in historic Meeker with guest rooms furnished in a combination of contemporary and Victorian. Convenient for fishing, hunting, cross-country skiing, and snow mobiling.

Doubles: 3 (S2B) $27-37
Type of Beds: 2 Twin; 1 Double; 1 Queen
Continental Breakfast
Credit Cards: No
Notes: 8 (older), 13 (XC)

MINTURN

Eagle River Inn

145 N. Main St., Box 100, 81645
(303) 827-5761

Lovely twelve-room inn decorated in the Southwestern style. All guest rooms have a private bath. Enjoy a gourmet continental breakfast in our sunny breakfast room; in the evenings, relax in front of the fireplace while you enjoy wine, cheese, and classical music. Located seven miles from the Vail ski resort.

Hosts: Beverly Rude and Richard Galloway
Singles: 2 (PB) $63.86-$135.25
Doubles: 10 (PB) $74.65-$146.05
Type of Beds: 4 Twin; 10 King
Continental Breakfast
Minimum stay holidays: 2
Credit Cards: A, B, C
Closed May and October
Notes: 2, 8 (over 12), 9, 10, 11, 12, 13, 14

OURAY

The House of Yesteryear

B&B Colorado, Box 12206, Boulder, 80303
(800) 373-4995

A magnificent view and the sound of a rushing river may keep you on the front porch of this inn all day. Your hosts will make arrangements for a Jeep tour or for the Silverton-Durango Railroad Tour.

Doubles: 8 (2 PB; 6 SB) $29-49
Continental Breakfast
Credit Cards: A, B
Closed Oct. - May
Notes: 7, 8

The Manor Bed & Breakfast

B&B Colorado, Box 12206, Boulder, 80303
(800) 373-4995

The Manor is nestled 7,800 feet high in the San Juan Mountains but is just one block off Main Street and within walking distance to Ouray's unique shops and restaurants. Jeep, hike, and backpack year-round. Relax in the natural hot springs pool. In winter, you may cross-country ski and ice climb. Parlor with TV and fireplace; balcony, patio, croquet courts.

Doubles: 5 (2 PB; 3 SB) $35-60
Type of Beds: 2 Twin; 5 Double
Continental-plus Breakfast
Credit Cards: No

PAGOSA SPRINGS

Davidson's Country Inn B&B

Box 87, 81147
(303) 264-5863

A three-story log inn decorated with antiques and family heirlooms located on a 32-acre ranch in the foothills of the Rocky Mountains. Game room, outdoor activities, children's corner. Full country breakfast. Hiking, stream and lake fishing, rafting, skiing, and beautiful scenic drives are all nearby.

Hosts: Gilbert & Evelyn Davidson
Singles: 3 (PB and SB) $36
Doubles: 6 (PB and SB) $43.50-55
Type of Beds: 6 Twin; 1 Double; 7 Queen; 1 King
Full Breakfast
Credit Cards: A, B
Notes: 2, 5, 6, 8, 9, 10, 13, 14

Echo Manor Inn Bed & Breakfast

B&B Colorado, Box 12206, Boulder, 80303
(800) 373-4995

Echo Manor is across from beautiful Echo Lake, where just about any time in the spring, summer, and fall you can drop a line and come up with a variety of fish. Gift shops, theater, restaurants, hot springs, fishing, hunting, snow mobiling, cycling, water skiing, backpacking, skiing, and white-water rafting are all nearby. Ten minutes from the local airport; thirty from Wolf Creek Ski Area. Hot tub and spa, game room, and three large conference rooms are on the premises.

Doubles: 9 (5 PB; 4 SB) $40-70
Full Breakfast
Credit Cards: No

NOTES: Credit cards accepted: A Master Card; B Visa; C American Express; D Discover Card; E Diners Club; F Other: 2 Personal checks accepted: 3 Lunch available: 4 Dinner available: 5 Open all year

Hill House Manor

B&B Colorado, Box 12206, Boulder, 80303
(800) 373-4995

A completely restored Victorian located near the downtown area. Sit in the Widow's Watch room overlooking the San Juan River, or walk to the hot springs. Each room has been lovingly decorated. One room is handicapped accessible.

Doubles: 4 (1 PB; 3 SB) $38-56
Type of Beds: 3 Double; 1 Queen
Continental Breakfast
Credit Cards: No
Notes: 7 (limited)

PAONIA

Miss Mary's

B&B Rocky Mountains.
Box 804, Colorado Springs, 80901
(719) 630-3433

A renovated farmhouse with two upstairs bedrooms that share one bath. Charming wallpapers, crafts by Miss Mary decorate every room. Located just east of Delta, on the way to Aspen. Dog and two cats in residence. Fireplace in the living room, sunny breakfast area, and special dinners by request. $35-38.

PINE

Meadow Creek Bed & Breakfast

B&B Colorado, Box 12206, Boulder, 80303
(800) 373-4995

This rustic mountain retreat was built in 1929 from stone found on the property. Located at the end of a paved road on 35 acres, Meadow Creek features a secluded meadow with stone outcroppings, tall pines, and a spring-fed creek, yet is an easy 45-minute drive from Denver. Large parlor with native stone fireplace, outdoor deck, and hot tub for your relaxation.

Doubles: 6 (PB) $59-69
Type of Beds: 1 Queen; 5 King
Full Breakfast
Credit Cards: No
Notes: 7 (limited), 8 (over 12)

SALIDA

Poor Farm Country Inn

B&B Colorado, Box 12206, Boulder, 80303
(800) 373-4995

The Poor Farm was built in 1892 to serve the county's poor. Later it was the city's grange hall. Large living area with twelve-foot ceilings, library with books from 1863. Located on 11 acres on the west bank of the Arkansas River; younger children have their own stocked trout pond. Monarch ski area is just eighteen miles away, and Salida is nearby.

Doubles: 5 (2 PB; 3 S2B) $29-49
Dorm: sleeps 10 (SB) $14
Type of Beds: 14 Twin; 3 Queen; 1 King
Full Breakfast in rooms; continental in dorm
Credit Cards: No
Notes: 7 (limited), 8

SILVER PLUME

Brewery Inn Bed & Breakfast

B&B Colorado, Box 12206, Boulder, 80303
(800) 373-4995

This charming mountain retreat in the historic mining town of Silver Plume has been restored with antiques and lovely wallpapers. The large suite with fireplace makes a perfect weekend getaway. The museum is just a short walk, and the famous Georgetown Loop train stops nearby to take passengers on a scenic trip to Georgetown.

Doubles: 4 (1 PB; 3 SB) $35-60
Type of Beds: 2 Twin; 2 Double; 3 Queen
Continental-plus Breakfast
Credit Cards: No

STEAMBOAT SPRINGS

Aspen Tree Cottage

B&B Colorado, Box 12206, Boulder, 80303
(800) 373-4995

This contemporary home is within ten minutes of skiing, hiking, and snowshoeing and within walking distance of restaurants, shops, and Old Steamboat ambience.

Doubles: 1 (PB) $50-60
Type of Beds: 1 Queen
Continental Breakfast
Credit Cards: No
Notes: 13

L'Abri

B&B Vail Valley
Box 491, Vail, 81658
(313) 949-1212

Located just fifteen minutes from the ski slopes, this house is listed on the National Historic Register. It has hidden rooms from Indian invasion, abundant antiques, views of Steamboat ski area and the Yampa Valley. Sauna available.

Doubles: 1 (PB) $50-60
Type of Beds: 1 Double; 1 Daybed
Continental Breakfast
Credit Cards: A, B

Rocky Mt. #97

B&B Rocky Mountains.
Box 804, Colorado Springs, 80901
(719) 630-3433

One bedroom with private bath right in the heart of Steamboat Springs, just four blocks from downtown. Near jogging trail, park, and natural hot-spring pools. $40-50.

Rocky Mt. #104

B&B Rocky Mountains.
Box 804, Colorado Springs, 80901
(719) 630-3433

An hour from Steamboat in the sleepy little town of Craig, this house has four rooms with shared baths and a gift shop with local crafts for sale. Full breakfast. Children and smokers are welcome here, and the low rate draws folks from Steamboat. $32.

Rocky Mt. #105

B&B Rocky Mountains.
Box 804, Colorado Springs, 80901
(719) 630-3433

A rustic log lodge built of native spruce and furnished with antiques, on 400 acres of land adjacent to a national forest. Three bedrooms with private or shared bath. Three resident dogs. Located forty-five minutes from Steamboat, on the east side of Rabbit Ears Pass. Near hiking, trout fishing. Ranch animals and stocked trout pond for children, nature hikes, treasure hunts. Gourmet dinners are available with reservations. Full breakfast. $50-60.

SUMMIT COUNTY

Hummingbird House

B&B Rocky Mountains.
Box 804, Colorado Springs, 80901
(719) 630-3433

English Tudor house with a beautiful mountain view and private guest entrance. Three bedrooms, large common sitting room with TV and stereo. Only 1.5 miles to the base of ski area and free shuttle to all four Summit County ski areas. Golf, tennis, and bicycling nearby. Jacuzzi, wood stove, wet bar, small refrigerator. Full breakfast. $30-60.

Rocky Mt. #86

B&B Rocky Mountains.
Box 804, Colorado Springs, 80901
(719) 630-3433

NOTES: Credit cards accepted: A Master Card; B Visa; C American Express; D Discover Card; E Diners Club; F Other: 2 Personal checks accepted: 3 Lunch available: 4 Dinner available: 5 Open all year

Three-story log Victorian in the heart of the historic district with two rooms — one for adults and one for children. Within walking distance of downtown Breckenridge and near free shuttle to ski areas. Host will teach you skiing or lead you on cross-country tours for a fee. Use of nearby athletic club with sauna and hot tub. Hearty breakfast with organic foods; special diet foods on request. $75-90.

TELLURIDE

Bear Creek Bed & Breakfast

B&B Colorado, Box 12206, Boulder, 80303
(800) 373-4995

Come stay in Telluride's first bed and breakfast. Fireplace in the common area; roof deck overlooking main street and its surrounding mountains. Whether you come to Telluride to ski, enjoy the festivals, hike, or just relax, you'll enjoy Bear Creek. Afternoon tea and apres-ski refreshments are served. Cable TV, private phones, daily maid service, steam room, and sauna.

Doubles: 8 (PB) $55-95
Type of Beds: 2 Twin; 1 Double; 7 Queen
Full Breakfast
Credit Cards: No
Notes: 8 (over 10), 13

The San Sophia

B&B Colorado, Box 12206, Boulder, 80303
(800) 373-4995

In Telluride's historic district, surrounded by 13,000-foot peaks, the San Sophia is an elegant inn serving gourmet breakfast and afternoon tea. One block from the ski life and the downtown area. Cable TV, observatory, library, garden, gazebo with Jacuzzi.

Doubles: 16 (PB) $60-170
Full Breakfast
Credit Cards: No
Notes: 8 (over 10)

VAIL

Arrowtree

B&B Colorado, Box 12206, Boulder, 80303
(800) 373-4995

A newly constructed oak post-and-beam situated on the sixteenth fairway of the Singletree Golf Course in the heart of Vail's year-round recreational activities. Twelve miles to Vail; four to Beavercreek.

Doubles: 3 (PB) $55-75
Type of Beds: 2 Double; 1 Queen waterbed
Full Breakfast
Minimum stay: 2
Credit Cards: No
Notes: 8 (over 6), 13

Bird's Nest

B&B Vail Valley
Box 491, Vail, 81658
(313) 949-1212

This completely private guest accommodation is great for two traveling couples or those who like a little more privacy. There's a kitchen, bath, cozy living room with pullout double bed, and a large moss rock fireplace. Breakfast includes fresh baked goods and smoked meats from the family-owned smokehouse. Guests have a private entrance, parking, and ski storage. Sleeps six comfortably.

Doubles: 2 (SB) $80-120
Type of Beds: 2 Twin; 1 Double; 1 Sofabed
Full Breakfast
Credit Cards: A, B

Brown Palace

B&B Vail Valley
Box 491, Vail, 81658
(313) 949-1212

Local skiing family who has lived in the valley for twenty-five years and have plenty of skiing tips to share with their guests. Located on the bus route ten minutes from Vail, or

6 Pets welcome: 7 Smoking allowed: 8 Children welcome: 9 Social drinking allowed: 10 Tennis available: 11 Swimming available: 12 Golf available: 13 Skiing available: 14 May be booked through travel agents

the host will drive skiers to the area in the morning.

Doubles: 1 (SB) $30-50
Type of Beds: 2 Twin
Full Breakfast
Credit Cards: A, B
Notes: 6, 7

Cottonwood Falls

B&B Vail Valley
Box 491, Vail, 81658
(313) 949-1212

In a sunny, secluded location on the free bus route, with cross-country skiing and bike path nearby, a rock fireplace, kitchen, private entrance. Tennis courts are within walking distance, and you may use an athletic club's facilities for a minimal fee. Located outside Vail, this mountain hideaway is surrounded by aspen trees, mountain creeks, and waterfalls.

Doubles: 1 (PB) $70-100
Type of Beds: 1 Double
Full Breakfast
Credit Cards: A, B
Notes: 7

European B&B

B&B Rocky Mountains.
Box 804, Colorado Springs, 80901
(719) 630-3433

A lovely host home tucked away on the golf course and surrounded by trees. Two bedrooms share one bath. Just a half mile from downtown Vail and the gondola. Fireplace, TV, and living room to share; full breakfast. $50.

The Guesthouse at Vail

B&B Colorado, Box 12206, Boulder, 80303
(800) 373-4995

This large loft guest house offers private entrances and private baths for each room. Flannel sheets and cozy down comforters keep you warm on the coldest of nights. The interior is tastefully decorated with lots of thriving green plants. Sauna, washer/dryer, two fireplaces, kitchen, and recreation loft.

Doubles: 5 (PB) $40-110
Type of Beds: 2 Twin; 3 Queen; 1 King
Continental Breakfast
Credit Cards: No

Rocky Mt. #81

B&B Rocky Mountains.
Box 804, Colorado Springs, 80901
(719) 630-3433

A quiet mountain retreat just five minutes from Vail, this twelve-room inn is decorated in Southwest style. Downstairs there's a sunny breakfast room and comfortable parlor with an authentic beehive fireplace. Guest rooms offer a river view, cozy flannel sheets, cable TV, and a private bath. Four restaurants nearby, along with the free ski shuttle. Continental breakfast, plus evening wine and cheese. $49-100.

WINTER PARK

Englemann Pines Bed & Breakfast

B&B Colorado, Box 12206, Boulder, 80303
(800) 373-4995

Enjoy old-fashioned elegance and contemporary comfort in this spacious home. Spectacular views of pines and mountain tops. Just ten minutes from Winter Park ski area. A free shuttle will take you there from the inn; Amtrak station one mile away. Summer hiking, golf, biking, and fishing. Great Room with full kitchen for guests with fireplace, TV, VCR; some rooms have Jacuzzi tubs.

6 Doubles: $35-75
Type of Beds: 4 Twin; 4 Queen
Full Breakfast
Credit Cards: No

NOTES: Credit cards accepted: A Master Card; B Visa; C American Express; D Discover Card; E Diners Club; F Other: 2 Personal checks accepted: 3 Lunch available: 4 Dinner available: 5 Open all year

Rocky Mt. #17

B&B Rocky Mountains.
Box 804, Colorado Springs, 80901
(719) 630-3433

Quiet, scenic, peaceful (no TV), this house is surrounded by pine forests and wild-flower meadows. Either B&B or Modified American Plan is available in winter. Seven rooms with private baths, games, cards, fireplace in the main lodge. Eight miles from Winter Park. On the premises you'll find a well-disciplined dog, two cats, and five llamas. Full breakfast. $47-77.

Rocky Mt. #22

B&B Rocky Mountains.
Box 804, Colorado Springs, 80901
(719) 630-3433

This 38-room inn offers Modified American Plan during the ski season and B&B accommodations off-season. Indoor pool and sauna, free transportation to and from Winter Park slopes in winter, spa, restaurant, lounge, TV, patio. Full breakfast. $50-120.

Walden

B&B Rocky Mountains.
Box 804, Colorado Springs, 80901
(719) 630-3433

A passive solar home nestled in a wooded area outside Winter Park. Two second-floor rooms, each with a balcony opening into a solar greenhouse and hot tub below, private bath. Resident cat and dog. Approximately fifteen minutes from Winter Park and Mary Jane ski areas, near golf, wonderful hiking,

and cross-country skiing. Dinner is available with notice. Full breakfast. $58.

WOODLAND PARK

Rocky Mt. #105

B&B Rocky Mountains.
Box 804, Colorado Springs, 80901
(719) 630-3433

Rolling hills and picturesque dirt roads for walking, hiking, or bike riding. Two rooms each have one double bed. In this newly built home, guests enjoy a private living room with wood stove and TV. Box lunches available at nominal extra charge; guided hiking, fishing, or birding trips at reasonable prices. Continental breakfast. $40-50.

YELLOW JACKET

Wilson's Pinto Bean Farm

House No. 21434 Rd. 16, 81335
(303) 562-4476

Our farm is located in Montezuma County, forty miles from the 4-Corners where the four western states join. Waving wheat, fragrant alfalfa, pinto beans, and mountains are visible in every direction. The farmhouse sits among elm trees, with orchards and gardens around. There are farm animals to enjoy, home-cooked meals, eggs to hunt, a cow to help milk, and fruits to pick in season. We can show children of all ages the delights of farm animals and country living.

Hosts: Arthur & Esther M. Wilson
Singles: 1 (PB) $26
Doubles: 1 (SB) $33
Full Breakfast
Credit Cards: No
Closed March-Nov.
Notes: 2, 4, 6, 7, 8, 9

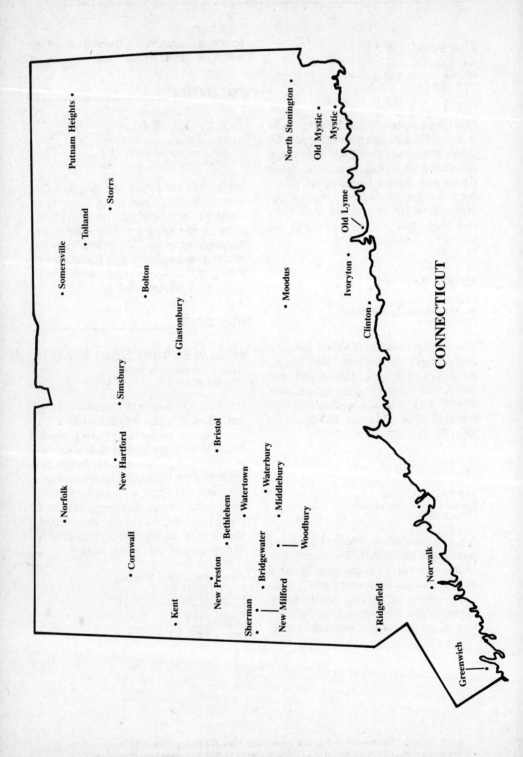

CONNECTICUT

Putnam Heights •

North Stonington •

Storrs •

Old Mystic •

Tolland •

Mystic •

Somersville •

Old Lyme

Bolton •

Ivoryton •

Glastonbury •

Moodus •

Clinton •

Simsbury •

Norfolk •

Bristol •

New Hartford •

Watertown •

Waterbury •

Cornwall •

Bethlehem •

Middlebury •

New Preston •

Woodbury

Bridgewater •

Kent •

Sherman

New Milford •

Ridgefield •

Norwalk •

Greenwich

Connecticut

BETHLEHEM

Eastover Farm

Covered Bridge
Box 447, Norfolk, CT, 06058
(203) 542-5944

Nestled in the foothills of the Berkshires on 70 acres of hills and fields with grazing cows, this home was built in 1773. You can still see an original large stone fireplace, complete with baking oven, crane, and pot hooks. A total of five fireplaces, a tennis court, guest cottage, flagstone terrace, and glassed-in porches are yours to enjoy. Near antique shops, ski areas, White Memorial Park, White Flower Farm.

Singles: 1 (SB) $55
Doubles: 6 (2 PB; 4 SB) $75-85
Continental Breakfast
Credit Cards: No
Notes: 2, 5, 7, 8, 9, 10, 11, 12, 13, 14

BOLTON

Jared Cone House

25 Hebron Road, 06043
(203) 643-8538

Enjoy the charm of our historic country home. We have spacious bedrooms with queen beds and scenic views of the countryside. Bicycle and canoe available. We serve a full breakfast featuring our own maple syrup when it's available. Fine dining nearby, and we're a short distance from berry farms, antiques, herb farms, and parks.

Hosts: Jeff & Cinde Smith
Singles: 1 (SB) $55-70

Doubles: 2 (SB) $45-60
Type of Beds: 1 Queen; 2 Rollaways
Full Breakfast
Credit Cards: No
Notes: 2, 5, 8, 10, 11, 12

BRIDGEWATER

Sanford/Pond House

Box 306, 06752
(203) 355-4677

A gracious Federal Greek revival mansion with stately, uniquely decorated bedrooms with sitting rooms or sitting areas and private baths. Relax in elegant style. "The Versailles of the region's B&Bs"—*Travel & Leisure* magazine. Excellent restaurants, antique shops, art galleries, and boutiques in the area.

Hosts: George & Charlotte Pond
Doubles: 5 (PB) $85-115
Type of Beds: 2 Double; 3 Queen
Continental-plus Breakfast
Credit Cards: A, B
Notes: 2, 5, 8, 10, 11, 12, 13, 14

BRISTOL

Chimney Crest Manor

5 Founders Drive, 06010
(203) 582-4219

English Tudor mansion with four suites — two with fireplace, two with kitchen. Twenty minutes from Hartford or Waterbury, three miles from Lake Compounce.

Hosts: Dan & Cynthia Cimadamore
Doubles: 4 (PB) $69.89-112
Type of Beds: 1 Double; 3 Queen
Full Breakfast
Minimum stay holidays: 2

6 Pets welcome: 7 Smoking allowed: 8 Children welcome: 9 Social drinking allowed: 10 Tennis available: 11 Swimming available: 12 Golf available: 13 Skiing available: 14 May be booked through travel agents

Credit Cards: A, B
Notes: 5, 7 (limited), 8, 10, 11, 12, 13

CLINTON

Captain Dibbell House
Covered Bridge
Box 447, Norfolk, CT, 06058
(203) 542-5944

This 1865 Victorian sea captain's home of-fers a charming coastal retreat just two blocks from Clinton Harbor and a short drive from the town beach. Four guest rooms, all decorated in antiques, and a living room with a fireplace are available for guests. Enjoy a full breakfast in the dining room or outside in the gazebo.

Doubles: 4 (PB) $65
Full Breakfast
Credit Cards: A, B
Notes: 2, 5, 8, 9, 10, 11, 12, 14

CORNWALL

Hilltop House
Covered Bridge
Box 447, Norfolk, CT, 06058
(203) 542-5944

Enjoy panoramic views from this secluded 64-acre wooded hilltop estate close to the village of West Cornwall and the Housatonic River. The house is furnished throughout with Victorian and Oriental antiques. A cheery conservatory overlooking the Housatonic Valley, and a library with a five-foot stone fireplace are available for guests.

Doubles: 2 (PB) $95
Type of Beds: 2 Double
Full Breakfast
Credit Cards: A, B
Notes: 2, 5, 9, 11, 13, 14

GLASTONBURY

Butternut Farm
1654 Main Street, 06033
(203) 633-7197

An eighteenth-century architectural jewel furnished in museum-quality period an-ti-ques. Estate setting with ancient trees, herb gardens, prize dairy goats, barnyard chick-ens, and pigeons. Ten minutes from Hartford. All Connecticut is within one and one-half hours.

Host: Don Reid
Doubles: 4 (2 PB; 2 S2B) $68.80-83.85
Type of Beds: 2 Twin; 3 Double
Full Breakfast
Credit Cards: A, B
Notes: 2, 5, 8, 9, 10, 11, 12, 13

GREENWICH

The Stanton House Inn
76 Maple Avenue, 06830
(203) 869-2110

This inn has thirty rooms and is situated in the heart of Greenwich on nearly 2.5 acres. The building is a Stanford White-designed turn-of-the-century mansion with original moldings and craftsmanship preserved wherever possible. Fireplaces (nonworking) and high ceilings prevail. Decorated in a Laura Ashley English inn motif with period antique reproductions.

Hosts: Tog & Doreen Pearson
Singles: 10 (SB) From $45.15
Doubles: 20 (PB) From $55.90
Type of Beds: 10 Twin; 15 Double; 3 Queen; 2 King
Continental Breakfast
Minimum stay holidays: 2
Credit Cards: A, B, C
Notes: 5, 8 (over 8), 9, 10, 11, 12

IVORYTON

The Copper Beech Inn
46 Main Street, 06442
(203) 767-0330

Gracious gardens and rustic woodlands set the stage for this handsome inn. A gallery offers antique Oriental porcelain, and the dining room is noted for fine country French cuisine. Beautiful countryside, quaint vil-

NOTES: Credit cards accepted: A Master Card; B Visa; C American Express; D Discover Card; E Diners Club; F Other: 2 Personal checks accepted: 3 Lunch available: 4 Dinner available: 5 Open all year

lages, museums, antique shops, theater, and water sports distinguish the area.

Hosts: Eldon & Sally Senner
Doubles: 13 (PB) $80.65-145.15
Type of Beds: 4 Twin; 1 Double; 9 Queen; 1 King
Continental Breakfast
Minimum stay weekends & holidays, April-Oct.: 2
Credit Cards: A, B, C, E
Closed Mondays, Christmas, New Years Day
Notes: 2, 4, 8 (over 8), 10, 11, 12

KENT

Bloom's B&B

Covered Bridge
Box 447, Norfolk, CT, 06058
(203) 542-5944

Charming eighteenth-century house is one of the oldest in Kent and is a splendid example of Federal architecture and decor. Living room with fireplace is available for guests; upstairs suite has an ornately carved four-poster canopy bed.

Doubles: 2 (PB) $85-120
Type of Beds: 1 Twin; 1 Double
Continental Breakfast
Credit Cards: A, B, C
Closed Nov. - mid-May
Notes: 2, 8, 9, 11, 12, 13, 14

OLD LYME

Old Lyme Inn

85 Lyme Street, 06371
(203) 434-2600

Outside, wild flowers bloom all summer; inside, fireplaces burn all winter, beckoning you to enjoy the romance and charm of this thirteen-room Victorian country inn with an award-winning, 3-star New York *Times* dining room. Within easy reach of the state's attractions, yet tucked away in an old New England art colony.

Host: Diana Field Atwood
Doubles: 13 (PB) $85-125
Type of Beds: 3 Twin; 10 Queen
Continental Breakfast
Credit Cards: A, B, C, D, E

Closed first two weeks of January
Notes: 2, 3, 4, 6, 7, 8, 9, 10, 11, 12, 14

MIDDLEBURY

Tucker Hill Inn

96 Tucker Hill Road, 06762
(203) 758-8334

Tucker Hill Inn is a large center-hall colonial just down from the village green in Middlebury. It was built around 1920 and was a restaurant and catering house for almost forty years. Our period rooms are large and spacious. Nearby are antiques, country drives, music and theater, golf, tennis, water sports, fishing, hiking, and cross-country skiing.

Hosts: Richard & Susan Cabelenski
Doubles: 4 (2 PB; 2 SB) $60-70
Type of Beds: 2 Twin; 1 Double; 2 Queen
Full Breakfast
Credit Cards: A, B
Closed Christmas Day
Notes: 2, 7 (restricted) 8, 9, 11, 12, 14

The Fowler House

MOODUS

The Fowler House

Plains Road, Box 432, 06469
(203) 873-8906

The Fowler House is an exquisite example of 1890 Victorian architecture, set on the town green. It has original stained-glass windows, eight working Italian ceramic fireplaces, hand-carved woodwork, elegant wallcoverings. Afternoon tea is served on the wraparound porch or in the library or parlor. Concierge service, dinner and theater reservations, complimentary arrival beverage, romantic turn-down service. Fine dining, antiquing, and shops are nearby. Year-round recreational activities.

Hosts: Barbara Ally & Paul Seals
Doubles: 6 (4 PB; 2 SB) $69.88-96.75
Type of Beds: 2 Twin; 4 Double; 1 Queen
Continental-plus Breakfast
Credit Cards: A, B
Notes: 2, 4, 5, 7, 8 (over 12), 9, 10, 11, 12, 13, 14

MYSTIC

The Adams House

382 Cowhill Road, 06355
(203) 572-9551

This circa 1790 inn is situated in a quaint country setting less than two miles from Mystic drawbridge. Homey colonial atmosphere is enhanced by three old-fashioned fireplaces, lush greenery, and flower gardens. Guests may choose from four bedrooms with shared baths in the main house or a completely private guest suite in an adjacent building that features private bath, sauna, refrigerator, and wet bar.

Hosts: Ron & Maureen Adams
Doubles: 6 (1 PB; 5 SB) $60-125
Type of Beds: 1 Twin; 5 Double
Continental Breakfast
Minimum stay weekdays & weekends: 2; holidays: 3
Credit Cards: A, B
Notes: 2, 5, 10, 11, 12

Comolli's House

36 Bruggeman Place, 06355
(203) 536-8723

Ideal for vacationers touring historic Mystic or the businessperson who desires a homey respite while traveling. This immaculate home, situated on a quiet hill overlooking the Mystic Seaport complex, is convenient to Olde Mistick Village and the Aquarium. Sightseeing, sporting activities, shopping, and restaurant information is provided by your hosts. Off-season rates are available.

Host: Dorothy M. Comolli
Singles: 1 (PB) $70
Doubles: 1 (PB) $85
Type of Beds: 2 Double
Continental Breakfast
Credit Cards: No
Notes: 2

Red Brook Inn

Box 237, Old Mystic 06372
(203) 572-0349

Beautiful country inn on 7 acres of woods. Lovely rooms, furnished with an-tiques. Many working fireplaces throughout the inn and guest rooms. A quiet colonial atmosphere within three miles of Mystic Seaport Museum.

Host: Ruth Keyes
Singles: 2 (PB) $65 plus tax
Doubles: 9 (PB) $150 plus tax
Type of Beds: 3 Twin; 10 Double; 2 Queen
Full Breakfast
Minimum stay weekends & holidays: 2
Credit Cards: A, B
Notes: 2 (in advance), 5, 8, 9, 10, 11, 12

NEW HARTFORD

Cobble Hill

Covered Bridge
Box 447, Norfolk, 06058
(203) 542-5944

A 1700s colonial farmhouse set on 40 magnificent acres with spring-fed pond for swimming and fishing; a barn for horses; chickens,

---

NOTES: Credit cards accepted: A Master Card; B Visa; C American Express; D Discover Card; E Diners Club; F Other: 2 Personal checks accepted: 3 Lunch available: 4 Dinner available: 5 Open all year

pigs, and beautiful flower gardens. There are several old brick fireplaces for guests to enjoy, a large living room with a sun porch, and a big old country kitchen. Guest rooms are decorated with antiques; two have canopy beds.

Doubles: 5 (1 PB; 4 SB) $85-150
Full Breakfast
Credit Cards: A, B, C
Closed Nov. - mid-May
Notes: 2, 8, 9, 10, 11, 12, 13, 14

Highland Farm

Covered Bridge
Box 447, Norfolk, 06058
(203) 542-5944

A grand, fourteen-gabled Victorian in a very secluded setting, yet not far from the very charming village on the Farmington River. Close to skiing, all water sports, hiking, and shopping. There is a sitting room with TV and living room with fireplace which guests are welcome to enjoy. A continental-plus breakfast is served in the elegant dining room or on the huge porch overlooking the grounds.

Doubles: 4 (SB) $65-90
Continental-plus Breakfast
Credit Cards: A, B, C
Notes: 2, 5, 7, 8 (over 12), 9, 10, 11, 12, 13, 14

NEW MILFORD

The Homestead Inn

5 Elm Street, 06776
(203) 354-4080

Enjoy warm hospitality in our charming Victorian inn located near the village green in the heart of the Litchfield Hills. Stroll to the village and enjoy the shops, restaurants, and movie theater. We have eight inn rooms and six motel rooms, all recently redecorated. Most have country antiques, private bath, color TV, air-conditioning, and phone.

Hosts: Rolf & Peggy Hammer
Singles: 1 (PB) $55-65
Doubles: 13 (PB) $65-75
Type of Beds: 5 Twin; 14 Double; 2 Queen
Continental-plus Breakfast
Credit Cards: A, B, C, D
Notes: 2, 5, 7, 8, 9, 10, 11, 12, 13 (XC), 14

NEW PRESTON

The Birches Inn

233 West Shore Road, Lake Waramaug 06777
(203) 868-0229

Secluded, cozy country inn with Old World Austrian decor and atmosphere, overlooking Lake Waramaug. Lodgings are in waterfront cottages and lake-view guest house, some with kitchenettes. Private beach, canoes, boats, water sports, and winter sports. Continental gourmet cuisine and cocktail lounge with a piano bar.

Host: Heinz Holl
Singles: 2 (PB) $70-80
Doubles: 8 (PB) $88-98
Type of Beds: 2 Twin; 8 Queen
Full Breakfast
Credit Cards: A, B
Notes: 2 (Conn. only), 4, 5, 7, 8 (over 4), 9, 10, 11, 12, 13, 14 (weekdays only)

NORFOLK

Manor House

Maple Avenue, Box 447, 06058
(203) 542-5690

Victorian elegance awaits you at our historic Tudor/Bavarian estate. Antique-decorated guest rooms, several with fireplaces, canopies, and balconies, offer a romantic retreat. Enjoy a sumptuous breakfast in our Tiffany-windowed dining rooms or treat yourself to breakfast in bed.

Hosts: Hank & Diane Tremblay
Doubles: 8 (6PB; 2SB) $65-$145
Type of Beds: 2 Twin; 4 Double; 1 Queen; 3 King
Full Breakfast
Credit Cards: A, B, C
Notes: 2, 5, 8 (over 12), 9, 10, 11, 12, 13, 14

---

6 Pets welcome: 7 Smoking allowed: 8 Children welcome: 9 Social drinking allowed: 10 Tennis available: 11 Swimming available: 12 Golf available: 13 Skiing available: 14 May be booked through travel agents

Manor House

Mountain View Inn

Rt. 272, 06058
(203) 542-5595; 542-6991

Tucked away in the village of Norfolk, with its bell towers and postcard landscapes, Mountain View Inn offers eleven charming guest rooms, full dining and bar service, recreational, musical, and cultural attractions. Mountain View is the perfect location for a country vacation at its best.

Hosts: Michele & Alan Sloane
Doubles: 11 (8 PB; 3 SB) $53.75-107.50
Type of Beds: 11 Double; 3 Twin
Full Breakfast
Minimum stay holidays: 2
Credit Cards: A, B
Notes: 2, 4, 5, 7, 8, 9, 10, 11, 12, 13

Weaver's House

Route 44, 06058
(203) 542-5108

An 1898 house overlooking the estate of the Norfolk Summer Chamber Music Festival. Simple hospitality in a village of forested hills, with four mapped areas of hiking trails.

Village woodland pond for swimming. Cross-country skiers may warm themselves by the coal stove in the sitting room.

Hosts: Judy & Arnold Tsukroff
Doubles: 4 (4 S2B) $43-65
Type of Beds: 4 Twin; 3 Double; 1 King
Full Breakfast
Minimum stay weekdays & weekends: 2; holidays: 3
Credit Cards: A, B
Notes: 2, 5, 8, 11, 13, 14

NEW MILFORD

The Quid

Covered Bridge
Box 447, Norfolk, 06058
(203) 542-5944

Vistas for viewing, woods for walking, hills for cross-country skiing, streams for fishing, flower gardens, a tennis court, and a pool are some of the attractions of this sprawling estate three miles outside town. On the first floor there is a large guest room with a private deck; upstairs there is another guest room.

Singles: 1 (SB) $55
Doubles: 2 (PB) $60-95
Full Breakfast
Credit Cards: A, B, C
Notes: 2, 5, 7, 8, 9, 10, 11, 12, 13, 14

The Weaver's House

NOTES: Credit cards accepted: A Master Card; B Visa; C American Express; D Discover Card; E Diners Club; F Other: 2 Personal checks accepted: 3 Lunch available: 4 Dinner available: 5 Open all year

NORTH STONINGTON

Antiques & Accommodations

Covered Bridge
Box 447, Norfolk, 06058
(203) 542-5944

An 1861 Victorian set in a charming, historic seacoast town close to Mystic. Fond memories of years spent traveling in England inspired the hosts to furnish their home in the Georgian manner, with formal antiques and accessories, many of which are for sale. The guest rooms have four-poster canopy beds. A full English breakfast is served in the elegant dining room.

Doubles: 3 (1 PB; 2 SB) $90-120
Type of Beds: 3 Double
Full Breakfast
Credit Cards: A, B, C
Notes: 2, 5, 9, 10, 11, 12, 14

NORWALK

Sheila & Irv's Place

11 Brenner Road, 06851
(203) 227-6330

Quiet country home near Westport and Wilton, ideal for walks and biking. Close to town, shops, restaurants, theaters, and beaches. Easy access to I-95. Excellent base for enjoying New York City, Maritime Center, Lockwood Mansion, and the fall foliage. Helpful hosts in immaculate surroundings.

Hosts: Sheila & Irv Tishler
Singles: 2 (PB & SB) $45
Doubles: 1 (PB & SB) $60-65
Type of Beds: 2 Twin; 1 Double
Continental Breakfast
Credit Cards: No
Notes: 5, 8, 10, 11, 12, 14

OLD MYSTIC

Old Mystic Inn

58 Main Street, 06372
(203) 572-9422

Early American decorative art trays and theorems by Lois Taylor enhance the charm of this converted 1800s bookstore just minutes from Mystic Seaport. Read by the fire in a room named for a famous New England author. Sumptuous country breakfasts.

Hosts: Lois & Karl Taylor
Doubles: 8 (PB) $75-115
Type of Beds: 8 Queen
Full Breakfast:
Minimum stay weekends & holidays: 2
Credit Cards: A, B, C
Notes: 2, 5, 8, 9, 10, 11, 12, 13

PUTMAN HEIGHTS

The Felshaw Tavern

Five Mile River Road, 06260
(203) 928-3467

A noble center-chimney colonial, built in 1742 as a tavern and restored in the 1980s. Frequented by Revolutionary militia, including Israel Putman, of Bunker Hill fame. Furnished in antiques with working fireplaces in guest rooms and a beehive oven in the keeping room. Peaceful setting, perfect for walking, bicycling, and unwinding. One-half hour from Worcester and Providence; one hour to Boston and Hartford; two and a half hours to New York City.

Hosts: Herb & Terry Kinsman
Doubles: 2 (PB) $75
Type of Beds: 2 Queen
Full Breakfast
Credit Cards: No
Notes: 2, 5, 7 (limited), 11, 12, 13, 14

RIDGEFIELD

Epenetus Howe House

91 N. Salem Road, 06877
(203) 438-HOWE

Step back in time to colonial New England, just 1.5 hours from New York City and 35 minutes from Stamford, Connecticut. We welcome you to our 264-year-old historic home. Many fine restaurants, an-tique shops, contemporary museum, and outdoor activities are located nearby.

Hosts: John & Diane Armato
Doubles: 2 (SB) $55-85
Type of Beds: 2 Twin; 1 Double
Continental Breakfast
Credit Cards: A, B, C
Notes: 2, 5, 8, 9, 10, 11, 12, 13, 14

Pineapple Hospitality CT 317

Box F-821, New Bedford, MA 02742-0821
(508) 990-1696

A 1960s raised ranch in a quiet, wooded spot ten minutes north of the Danbury Airport. Ample off-street parking before a huge yard with seasonal blossoms which, along with widespread Barlow Mountain beyond, provides a restful, picturesque view from the sun porch and dining room. Enjoy their collection of big-band, Broadway, symphony, and comedy tapes, their art treasures and collectibles, and their extensive library.

Doubles: 1 (PB) $50-60
Type of Beds: 2 Twin
Continental Breakfast
Credit Cards: No
Notes: 2, 5, 8, 9, 11, 13

SHERMAN

Barnes Hill Farm

Covered Bridge
Box 447, Norfolk, CT, 06058
(203) 542-5944

Circa 1835, this B&B was a rest stop for travelers throughout the 1800s and has been restored for that purpose. All rooms are decorated with antiques and special country accents to take you back to yesteryear.

Doubles: 3 (PB) $85
Type of Beds: 3 Queen
Full Breakfast
Credit Cards: A, B, C
Notes: 2, 5, 8, 9, 10, 11, 13, 14

SIMSBURY

Simsbury 1820 House

731 Hopmeadow St., 06070
(203) 658-7658

An authentic early nineteenth-century country inn with thirty-four individually designed guest rooms with private baths. Fine dining daily in our restaurant. Within walking distance of the charming town of Simsbury; twenty minutes to downtown Hartford and Bradley International Airport.

Hosts: Kelly Hohengarten
Doubles: 34 (PB) $92-$133
Type of Beds: 4 Twin; 15 Queen; 15 King
Continental Breakfast
Credit Cards: A, B, C, D, E
Notes: 2, 3, 4, 5, 7, 8, 9, 10, 11, 12, 14

SOMERSVILLE

The Old Mill Inn

63 Maple Street, Box 443, 06072
(203) 763-1473

Originally built in the mid-eighteen hundreds, the house was enlarged and renovated in the mid-nineteen hundreds by the mill owner. Antique shops, boutiques, and restaurants are only minutes away. Two golf courses are only five minutes away; polo, theater, museums, and historic houses are also close. Only twenty minutes from Bradley International Airport and Hartford.

Hosts: Ralph & Phyllis Lumb
Doubles: 4 (2 PB; 2 SB) $48.38-53.75
Type of Beds: 2 Twin; 3 Double
Continental Breakfast
Credit Cards: No
Notes: 2, 5, 8 (over 5), 9, 10, 11, 12

NOTES: Credit cards accepted: A Master Card; B Visa; C American Express; D Discover Card; E Diners Club; F Other: 2 Personal checks accepted: 3 Lunch available: 4 Dinner available: 5 Open all year

STORRS

Farmhouse on the Hill Above Gurleyville
418 Gurleyville Road, 06268
(203) 429-1400

An elegant farmhouse located in a college town. The Kollets raise purebred Columbia sheep. Sturbridge, Mass., Worcester, Mass., Mystic, Hartford, and New London, Conn. are less than an hour away. Don't forget to try Elaine's muffins! Cribs, high chairs, and carriages available for children.

Hosts: Bill & Elaine Kollet
Doubles: 4 (4 PB; 1 SB) $25-30 plus tax
Type of Beds: 2 Twin; 4 Double
Full Breakfast
Credit Cards: No
Closed January
Notes: 2, 4 (by arrangement), 7, 8, 9, 10, 11, 12, 13

TOLLAND

The Tolland Inn
63 Tolland Green, 06084-0717
(203) 872-0800

Built in 1800, The Tolland Inn stands in the northwest corner of the Tolland village green, a half-mile from I-84. Located midway between Boston and New York City, the inn is convenient to the University of Connecticut, Old Sturbridge, Caprilands, Hartford, and Brimfield Fair.

Hosts: Susan & Stephen Beeching
Singles: 1 (SB) $32.25-43
Doubles: 4 (3 PB; 1 SB) $43-53.75
Type of Beds: 2 Twin; 3 Double; 1 three-quarter
Continental Breakfast
Credit Cards: A, B
Notes: 2, 5, 8 (over 10) 9, 10, 12

WATERBURY

House on the Hill
Covered Bridge
Box 447, Norfolk, 06058
(203) 542-5944

This 1888 Victorian is on the National Register of Historic Places and sits on an acre in the historic district. There are several common rooms, including an antique-decorated living room with fireplace. A full breakfast and high tea are served in the wood-paneled dining room.

Doubles: 5 (3 PB; 2 SB) $85-125
Full Breakfast
Credit Cards: A, B, C
Notes: 2, 5, 8, 9, 10, 11, 12, 13, 14

The Parsonage Bed & Breakfast
18 Hewlett Street, 06710
(203) 574-2855

Sumptuous breakfasts, gracious period furnishings, and personal service welcome you in an aura of bygone gentility. This 1910 Colonial Revival home offers bright, sunny rooms off a gracious central foyer, or a private third-floor suite. Business travelers find us a convenient five minutes from major highways.

Host: Lonetta Baysinger
Singles: 1 (SB) $45-60
Doubles: 4 (2 PB; 2 SB) $55-70
Type of Beds: 1 Twin; 3 Double; 1 Queen
Full Breakfast
Credit Cards: No
Notes: 2, 5, 7 (restricted), 8, 9, 10, 11, 12, 13, 14

WATERTOWN

1849 House
Covered Bridge
Box 447, Norfolk, 06058
(203) 542-5944

A nineteenth-century New England home less than a mile from Taft School, secluded at the end of a long driveway and surrounded by old maples, willows, and pines. This fourteen-room white colonial is warmly furnished with antiques and a varied art collection. Enjoy summer breakfasts on the lovely patio, amid abundant flowers.

6 Pets welcome: 7 Smoking allowed: 8 Children welcome: 9 Social drinking allowed: 10 Tennis available: 11 Swimming available: 12 Golf available: 13 Skiing available: 14 May be booked through travel agents

Singles: 1 (SB) $50
Doubles: 3 (SB) $65-75
Full Breakfast
Credit Cards: A, B, C
Notes: 2, 5, 7, 8, 9, 10, 11, 12, 13, 14

WOODBURY

Curtis House

506 Main Street, 06798
(203) 263-2101

Connecticut's oldest inn, in operation since 1754, in a quaint New England town famous for antique shops. The inn features canopied beds and a popular restaurant serving regional American fare, amply portioned and moderately priced.

Hosts: The Hardisty Family
Doubles: 18 (12 PB; 6 SB) $30-45
Type of Beds: 8 Twin; 8 Double; 2 Queen
Continental Breakfast
Credit Cards: A, B
Closed Christmas Day
Notes: 2, 3, 4, 5, 7, 9, 10, 11, 12, 13

NOTES: Credit cards accepted: A Master Card; B Visa; C American Express; D Discover Card; E Diners Club; F Other: 2 Personal checks accepted: 3 Lunch available: 4 Dinner available: 5 Open all year

Delaware

Sea-Vista Villas
773-C Salt Pond Circle, Box 62, 19930
(302) 539-3354

Small townhouse villas set on 33 pine acres
six blocks from beautiful Atlantic Beach.
Tennis and pool on premises. Lakeside terrace for full breakfast and complimentary
happy hour. Midway between Rehoboth
Beach, Delaware, and Ocean City,
Maryland, on the Delmarva-Lous Peninsula.

Host: Dale M. Duvall
Doubles: 3 (PB) $52-62.40
Type of Beds: 6 Twin
Full Breakfast
Minimum stay weekends & holidays: 2 (Thanksgiving: 4)
Credit Cards: No
Closed Dec. 1-April 15
Notes: 2, 7, 9, 10, 11

LAUREL

Amanda's B&B Reservation Service #1
1428 Park Avenue, Baltimore, MD, 21217
(301) 225-0001

Step back in time and enjoy the charm of an
eighteenth-century country manor listed in
the National Register of Historic Places.
Near ocean beaches and the Chesapeake
Bay, with secluded ponds nearby for fishing,
wooded nature trails, quaint shipbuilding
towns to explore in the area. Bicycles and
picnic lunches are available.

Suite: 1 (PB) $65
Doubles: 4 (S2B) $45

Continental Breakfast
Credit Cards: No
Notes: 2, 5, 8 (8 and over), 9, 10, 11, 12, 13, 14

LEWES

Savannah Inn Bed & Breakfast
330 Savannah Road, 19958
(302) 645-5592

Quaint village location; ocean and bay
beaches, state park, resorts nearby. Casual,
comfortable bedrooms with fans, books,
piano, backyard, airy porch. Delicious
vegetarian breakfasts; resident cat in
owners' quarters. Hosts enjoy nature, outdoor sports, organic gardening.

Hosts: Dick & Susan Stafursky
Doubles: 7 (SB) $37.10-53
Type of Beds: 2 Twin; 8 Double
Continental Breakfast
Minimum stay weekends: 2; holidays:3
Credit Cards: No
Weekday Discount of 15% for extended stays
Breakfast served May 1-Sept. 30
Notes: 2, 7 (limited), 8, 9, 10, 11

Savannah Inn Bed and Breakfast

6 Pets welcome: 7 Smoking allowed: 8 Children welcome: 9 Social drinking allowed: 10 Tennis available: 11
Swimming available: 12 Golf available: 13 Skiing available: 14 May be booked through travel agents

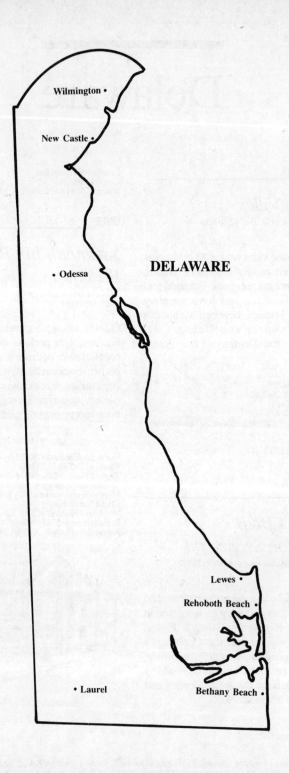

DELAWARE

Wilmington •

New Castle •

• Odessa

Lewes •

Rehoboth Beach •

• Laurel

Bethany Beach •

NEW CASTLE

William Penn Guest House

206 Delaware Street, 19720
(302) 328-7736

Choose one of four rooms in our beautifully restored 1682 guest house in the center of historic New Castle. Twenty minutes from museum and public gardens.

Hosts: Richard & Irma Burwell
Doubles: 4 (SB) $40
Type of Beds: 2 Twin; 2 Double
Continental Breakfast
Credit Cards: A, B
Notes: 2, 5, 7 (limited), 8 (10 and over), 9, 10

ODESSA

Cantwell House

107 High Street, 19730
(302) 378-4179

Odessa was an important trading port on the Delaware River until the 1890s. The town contains fine examples of colonial, Federal, and Victorian architecture, including three museums owned by Winterthur. Cantwell House (circa 1840) has been completely restored and furnished in country antiques.

Host: Carole F. Coleman
Doubles: 3 (1 PB; 2 SB) $45-65
Type of Beds: 2 Double; 1 Queen
Continental Breakfast
Credit Cards: No
Notes: 2, 4, 5, 7 (restricted), 8, 9, 10, 14

REHOBOTH BEACH

Tembo Guest House

100 Laurel Street, 19971
(302) 227-3360

Tembo, located 750 feet from the beach, offers a casual atmosphere with warm hospitality. Relax among Early American furnishings, antiques, oil paintings, waterfowl carvings, and Gerry's elephant collec-

tion. Immaculately clean bedrooms are bright and airy, with firm beds.

Hosts: Don & Gerry Cooper
Doubles: 6 (1 PB; 5 SB) $58.30-84.80
Type of Beds: 4 Twin; 3 Double; 1 King
Continental Breakfast
Minimum stay weekends: 2; holidays: 3
Credit Cards: No
Notes: 2, 5, 6 (off-season), 8 (6 and over), 9, 10, 11, 12

WILMINGTON

The Boulevard Bed & Breakfast

1909 Baynard Blvd., 19802
(302) 656-9700

Beautifully restored city mansion, originally built in 1913. Impressive foyer and magnificent staircase leading to a landing complete with window seat and large leaded-glass windows flanked by fifteen-foot columns. Breakfast is served on the screened porch, weather permitting. Close to the business district and all area attractions. Brochure on request.

Hosts: Charles & Judy Powell
Singles: 1 (SB) $50
Doubles: 5 (4 PB; 1 SB) $55-70
Type of Beds: 3 Twin; 2 Double; 2 Queen; 1 Queen sofabed; 1 Cot
Full Breakfast
Credit Cards: A, B, C
Notes: 2, 5, 7, 8, 9, 10, 11, 12, 14

The Pink Door

8 Francis Lane, 19803
(302) 478-8325

Our beautiful contemporary ranch nestles in a quiet cul-de-sac and backs into a woods. We're located just minutes away from all of Brandywine Valley's chief attractions: Longwood Gardens, Winterthur, Hagley and Nemours mansions, Brandywine River Museum, etc. Breakfast is served in our Queen Anne dining room or on the outside deck.

6 Pets welcome: 7 Smoking allowed: 8 Children welcome: 9 Social drinking allowed: 10 Tennis available: 11 Swimming available: 12 Golf available: 13 Skiing available: 14 May be booked through travel agents

Host: Mary Wehner
Singles: 1 (SB) $40-45
Doubles: 1 (SB) $45-55
Type of Beds: 3 Twin
Full Breakfast
Credit Cards: No
Notes: 2, 5, 7 (restricted), 9

Small Wonder Bed & Breakfast

213 West Crest Road, 19803
(302) 764-0789

At I-95 exit 9. Convenient to duPont mansions and Gardens; Hagley, Eleutherian Mills, Longwood, Winterthur, Nemours, Bellevue, and historic New Castle, Brandywine River Museum, Rockwood, and more. Air-conditioning, pool, hot tub.

Hosts: Dot & Art Brill
Doubles: 2 (1 PB; 1SB) $45-70
Type of Beds: 1 Twin; 1 Double; 2 King
Full Breakfast
Credit Cards: A, B, C
Notes: 5, 8 (over 9), 9, 10, 11, 12, 14

What to See and Do In Washington, D. C.

Visitors to our nation's capital will find a lively, sophisticated city, teeming with things to do and see. You can tour the home of the President, see lawmakers in action at the Capitol, watch history take shape at the Supreme Court, see the original Constitution at the National Archives, tour exciting museums, enjoy ethnic food, and shop at exclusive boutiques.

If you're planning a summer trip, check out the Smithsonian's Festival of American Folklife (357-2700) and free military band concerts on the Washington Monument grounds (Navy, 433-6090; Marines, 433-4011; Army, 696-3399; Air Force, 767-5658). In winter, enjoy the Pageant of Peace, featuring the national Christmas tree and ice skating on the Mall (347-9041). All telephone numbers are area code 202.

Climate

Washingtonians enjoy all four seasons, with a vast range of temperatures. January and February tend to be cold (high 44, low 27) and sometimes snowy; July and August are hot (high 85, low 67), with oppressive humidity. The remainder of the year is temperate, with spring highs from 53 to 82 and fall highs from 55 to 78. Bring your umbrella for April and November, your woolens for the winter, and your coolest cottons for the summer.

Traveling in Washington

If you opt not to use your own car or to rent a car, you can take public transportation. The Metro system, which includes both buses and subway, is clean, reliable, and convenient. The subway, known as Metrorail, travels all over Washington and into the Maryland and Virginia suburbs as well (637-7000).

Taxis are relatively inexpensive, and fares are based on how many zones you travel through. There are rush-hour surcharges and additional charges for extra passengers.

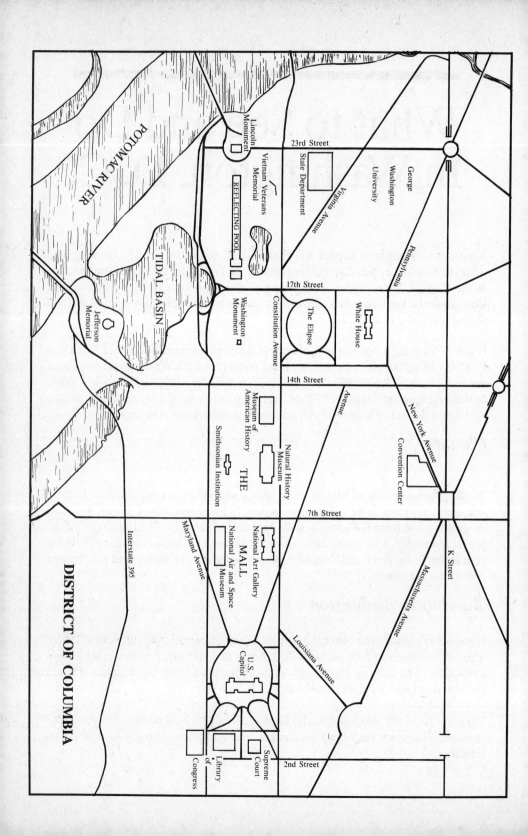

The Tourmobile provides a guided tour of Washington landmarks, including the White House, Washington Monument, five Smithsonian museums, the Capitol, Jefferson Memorial, Kennedy Center, and Lincoln Memorial. You may get off at each stop, tour at your leisure, and reboard at no extra charge (554-7950).

When Planning Your Trip

The Washington, D.C., Convention and Visitors Association can answer your questions and provide free brochures. Call or write 1575 I Street N.W., Room 250, Washington, D.C., 20005 (202-789-7000). Once in Washington, call their daily tourist information tape (737-8866). And the D.C. Department of Recreation will send *Do You Know,* listing free outdoor entertainment, craft shows, and park events. Send a self-addressed, stamped envelope to 3149 16th Street N.W., Washington, D.C., 20010 or call (202) 673-7660.

If you'd like a VIP tour of the House or Senate in session, the Capitol, White House, Kennedy Center, or FBI, write your congressman and request passes for VIP tours. Because ticket supplies are limited, write as soon as possible — six months or more prior to your trip. Include the exact dates of your trip and the number of passes you need, and address it to your representative or senator, U.S. House of Representatives (or Senate), Washington, D.C., 20515.

Once in Washington

The Washington Tourist Information Center, located between 14th and 15th Streets on Pennsylvania Avenue N.W., offers brochures and promotional literature, as well as maps (789-7000).

The Travelers Aid Society, a national nonprofit organization dedicated to helping travelers in trouble, has an office at 1015 12th Street N.W. Their phone is answered by professionals 24 hours a day (347-0101).

Foreign visitors can get brochures and information about Washington in their own language from the International Visitors Information Service at 733 15th Street N.W. (783-6540).

There are a number of publications that provide insight about Washington life and attractions. *Washingtonian* magazine, published monthly, lists a calendar of events in its "Where & When" column, including dance, theater, films, music, art galleries, lectures, workshops, sports, and special events.

The Washington Post includes current information on special happenings in its Weekend magazine, published on Friday. Also check out *City Paper,* a free newspaper that includes information on clubs, performances, galleries, and restaurants.

Museums Not to Miss

No visit to Washington would be complete without a stop at the Smithsonian Institution. The nine Smithsonian museums cover eleven square blocks of land known as the Mall. Admission is free for all Smithsonian exhibits, and most have cafeterias and gift shops (357-2700).

The most popular of the Smithsonian museums is the National Air and Space Museum, Independence Avenue and Sixth Street, S.W. The Apollo 11 command module, the *Spirit of St. Louis,* and the original Wright flyer are housed here. The films at the first-floor theater, including "To Fly" and "Hail Columbia!" (admission fee) are wonderful. Air and Space has a new cafeteria downstairs and a café upstairs.

The National Museum of American History at 14th Street and Constitution Avenue N.W. houses American memorabilia from first ladies' gowns to Fonzie's jacket from "Happy Days." The original Star-Spangled Banner hangs in the first-floor lobby and is displayed every hour on the half hour. An old-fashioned confectionery shop on the first floor serves ice cream, milk shakes, and malteds. American History also has the best of the museum shops, with a vast inventory of books, crafts, toys, and jewelry.

Next door, at 10th and Constitution Avenue N.W., in the National Museum of Natural History, are the Hope Diamond and thousands of specimens of fossils, mammals, and sea life. There is a Discovery Room with hands-on exhibits and games for children, and an Insect Zoo upstairs.

The National Gallery of Art at Sixth Street and Constitution Avenue N.W. is actually two buildings with distinctively different exhibits. The West Wing houses American and European painting and sculpture. In the East Wing, the art is more modern. You may need advance tickets to see a popular exhibition; check at the information desk on the main level. The two buildings are linked by an underground concourse with a buffet, café, and gift shop. There is also a cafe on the upper level of the East Wing.

The Arts and Industries Building at 900 Jefferson Drive S.W. houses eighteenth-century artifacts and Victorian inventions from the 1876 Centennial. Its Discovery Theater offers dance, puppet shows, and theater (admission fee). A wonderful carousel, open during the summer, carries on the Victorian flavor across the street.

Modern-art aficionados should not miss the Hirshhorn Museum and Sculpture Garden at Independence Avenue and 7th Streets, S.W. Works by Rodin, Dali, Mondrian, Eakins, Warhol, Calder, Matisse, and others are on display. An outdoor café serves light fare in summer.

New additions to the Smithsonian include the Arthur M. Sackler Gallery and the National Museum of African Art. Located beneath the Enid A. Haupt Garden, the Sackler has Near Eastern and Asian art. African Art is the only U.S. museum dedicated exclusively to the collection, study, and exhibition of African art. Nineteenth- and twentieth-century works are featured.

The Smithsonian also has several museums that are located away from the Mall proper and are worth a visit. The Anacostia Museum at 1901 Fort Place S.E. is dedicated to Afro-American culture and history and includes free educational programs and activities (357-2700).

The National Museum of American Art at 8th and G Streets N.W. houses more than 200 years of American art history in paintings, folk art, sculpture, photographs, and graphic art (357-2700).

In the National Portrait Gallery at 8th and G Streets N.W., history is chronicled from the Revolutionary era to modern day with paintings, sculpture, and photographic portraits of political, military, scientific, and cultural figures (357-2700).

The Renwick Gallery at Pennsylvania Avenue and 17th Streets N.W. features crafts from the early 1900s to the present in ceramics, metal, glass, and fiber. The Octagon Room and the Grand Salon have been restored and furnished in authentic Victorian period style (357-2700).

The National Zoological Park at the 3000 block of Connecticut Avenue N.W. is home to over 2,800 animals, including the famous giant pandas. The Zoo offers three hands-on learning labs for visitors. There are several gift shops and food kiosks. Parking lots fill quickly (fee), or take Metro to the Woodley Park/Zoo stop.

Capital Children's Museum, 800 3rd Street N.E. (Union Station Metro). Hands-on exhibits include grinding Mexican chocolate, playing metric shopkeeper, and wandering through a maze (543-8600).

Corcoran Gallery of Art, 17th and New York Avenue N.W. (Farragut West Metro). Private art collection with American, Dutch, and Flemish masterpieces (638-1439).

Dumbarton Oaks, 1703 32nd Street N.W. Beautiful winding gardens, pre-Columbian art, Byzantine art and civilization artifacts (338-8278).

National Aquarium, lower level of the Commerce Building, 14th Street between Constitution Avenue and E Streets N.W. Freshwater and marine animals. Call for shark-feeding schedule (377-2825).

National Geographic Explorers Hall, 17th and M Streets N.W. (Farragut North Metro). History of the planet and man's exploration of it are explained in photographs, tapes, and films (857-7588 weekdays; 857-7000 weekends).

The Phillips Collection, 1600 21st Street N.W. (DuPont Circle Metro). Permanent collection of modern art, including works by Van Gogh, Matisse, Degas, Picasso. Films, lectures, and free concerts (387-0961).

Washington Dolls' House and Toy Museum, 5236 44th Street N.W. Dolls, doll houses, toys and games, zoos and Noah's arks. Museum shop with dolls and doll-house supplies (244-0024).

Memorials and Other Points of Interest

The Washington Monument, at 15th Street and Constitution Avenue, (Smithsonian Metro stop), offers one of the best views of the city, especially at night. Although visitors are transported to the top via elevator, you can take a "Down the Steps" tour (all 897 of them) if staff is available (426-6839).

The Lincoln Memorial, west of the Mall at 23rd Street N.W. (Foggy Bottom Metro stop), is a great place to watch the fireworks on the Fourth of July. The Under the Lincoln tour takes visitors beneath the monument's foundation. Book as far ahead as possible by calling (202) 426-6841 or writing to the National Park Service, Mall Operations, 900 Ohio Drive S.W, Washington, D.C., 20242 (426-6895).

The Jefferson Memorial sits on the Tidal Basin, a small body of water encircled by cherry trees that are gorgeous in the spring. In the warmer months, pedal boats are available for rent opposite the memorial. The Jefferson is located at the bottom of 15th Street N.W. (426-6821).

The White House, at 1600 Pennsylvania Avenue N.W. (McPherson Square Metro stop), opens five rooms to tourists. The wait for tours is long, and the tour itself is quite brief. Candlelight tours are given at Christmas and also attract long lines. Contact your congressman or senator for VIP tickets (456-7041 or 456-2200).

The Capitol's entrance is on East Capitol Street and 1st Street N.W. (Capitol South Metro stop). House and Senate chambers are open only to those with VIP tour tickets. Otherwise, guided tours are available every fifteen minutes from the rotunda. *The Post* runs a "Today in Congress" column that lists which committee meetings are open to the public (225-6827).

The Supreme Court, between East Capitol Street and Maryland Avenue at 1st Street N.E. (Capitol South or Union Station Metro stops), meets from October through April. Check the *Post* "Court Calendar" for specifics. When the Court is not in session, lectures on Court procedure and architecture are given (479-3030).

The Library of Congress has a seemingly infinite collection of books and periodicals. Located on 1st Street S.E., between Independence Avenue and East Capitol Street (Capitol South Metro), tours leave hourly on weekdays. Over 80 million items are housed here (707-6400).

The National Archives, at Constitution Avenue between 7th and 9th Streets N.W. houses the Declaration of Independence, the Constitution, and the Bill of Rights. The Archives is also a center for genealogical research (523-3000, general information; 523-3220, research information).

The Federal Bureau of Investigation, E Street between 9th and 10th Streets N.W., offers weekday tours. VIP passes are available from senators and congressmen (324-3447).

The Vietnam Veterans Memorial, located across from the Lincoln Memorial between 21st and 22nd Streets N.W., is inscribed with names of those who lost their lives in this conflict (426-6700).

Washington's Culinary Delights

From traditional American grills to nouvelle cuisine, Thai to Nepali, Washington has it. We suggest you call first to confirm restaurant hours and check out changing prices. Most Washington B&Bs have a list of recommended restaurants available for their guests.

American Café, 1211 Wisconsin Avenue N.W. (944-9464); 227 Massachusetts Avenue N.E. (547-8500); 5252 Wisconsin Avenue N.W. (363-5400; 1331 Pennsylvania Avenue N.W. (626-0770). Creative American cuisine, homemade soups, sandwiches, entrees, desserts.

Armand's Chicago Pizzeria, 4231 Wisconsin Avenue N.W. (686-9450); 226 Massachusetts Avenue N.E. (547-6600). Best deep-dish pizza in town.

Au Pied de Cochon, 1335 Wisconsin Avenue N.W. (333-5440). French bistro.

Bacchus, 1827 Jefferson Place N.W. (785-0734). Middle Eastern/Lebanese.

Bombay Palace, 1835 K Street N.W. (331-0111). Indian, including lamb vindaloo, tandoori prawns, "butter chicken."

Bootsie, Winky and Miss Maud, 2026 P Street N.W. (887-0900). American cuisine with a French twist.

Cantina D'Italia, 1214A 18th Street N.W. (659-1830). Northern Italian, homemade pasta.

Charlie Chiang's, 19121 I Street N.W. (293-6000); 4250 Connecticut Avenue N.W. (966-1916). Hunan and Szechuan.

Churreria Madrid, 2505 Champlain Street N.W. (483-4441). Spanish, featuring homemade soups and churros.

Clyde's, 3236 M Street N.W. (333-0294). Classic American cuisine, burgers, and sandwiches. Wonderful atrium room.

Csiko's, 3601 Connecticut Avenue N.W. (362-5624). Hungarian.

Dar Es Salam, 3056 M Street N.W. (342-1925). Moroccan, prix-fixe dinners of three, five, or six courses.

Duke Zeibert's, 1050 Connecticut Avenue N.W. in Washington Square (466-3730). Home of the power lunch. Famous for meat-and-potatoes fare, matzo ball soup.

Enriqueta's — Georgetown, 2811 M Street N.W. (338-7772). Mexican, featuring mussels with chili sauce, chicken with chili-and-chocolate-mole sauce.

F. Scott's, 1232 36th Street N.W. (965-1789). Continental cuisine. Named by *Esquire* as one of the best bars in Washington.

Florida Avenue Grill, 1100 Florida Avenue N.W. (265-1586). Southern American soul food.

Foggy Bottom Café, 924 25th Street N.W. (338-8707). Creative American dishes.

Georgetown Bagelry, 3245 M Street N.W. (965-1011). Locally made bagels, bagel sandwiches. Great orange butter.

Hisago, 3020 K Street N.W. (944-4181). Japanese, including kaiseki menus: multi-course meals of seasonal foods.

Joe and Mo's, 1211 Connecticut Avenue N.W. (659-1211). Popular American-style steak house.

Katmandu, 1800 Connecticut Avenue N.W. (483-6470). Napali/Kashmiri cuisine, featuring pork fried in mustard oil and mixed seafood in yogurt sauce.
La Colline, 400 N. Capitol Street N.W. (737-0400). French, including saute of veal with Armagnac, gratin of crayfish, grilled salmon with beurre blanc.

Las Pampas, 3291 M Street N.W. (333-5151). Argentine, featuring grilled chicken, short-rib steak, and Argentine-style sausage.

Le Lion D'Or, 1150 Connecticut Avenue N.W. (296-7972). On everyone's best-restaurant list. Nouvelle French cuisine: lobster stew, wild mushroom soup, pigeon with shiitake mushrooms, and quail in puff pastry.

Madurai, 3318 M Street N.W. (333-0997). Vegetarian cuisine from South India, including lotus root curry and dosas filled with curried potatoes.

Market Inn, 200 E Street S.W. (554-2100). Extensive seafood menu, including Maine lobster.

Meskerem, 2434 18th Street N.W. (462-4100). Ethiopian.

Morton's of Chicago, 3251 Prospect Street N.W. (342-6258). Famous for some of the best steaks in town. Call ahead if you want prime rib.

Occidental and the Occidental Grill, 1475 Pennsylvania Avenue N.W. (783-1475). Modern American dishes; burgers and sandwiches also available at the Grill.

Old Europe, 2434 Wisconsin Avenue N.W. (333-7600). German favorites, seasonal asparagus, May wine.

Omega, 1856 Columbia Road N.W. (745-9158). Cuban, specializing in shrimp sauteed with garlic and paella.

Sholl's Cafeteria, 1990 K Street N.W. in the Esplanade Mall (296-3065). Home cooking at very low prices. Jammed at lunchtime.

Take Me Home, 32120 O Street N.W. (298-6818). Gourmet sandwich shop.

Taverna the Greek Islands, 307 Pennsylvania Avenue S.E. (547-8360). Greek.

Tony Cheng's Mongolian Restaurant, 619 H Street N.W. (842-8669). All-you-can-eat Mongolian barbecue and Mongolian hot pot.

Washington After Dark

Washington is an exciting place to be when the sun goes down. There are theatrical productions, music and jazz performances, bars, and comedy clubs to enjoy. Double-check *The Washington Post* and *Washingtonian* magazine for performance schedules, sporting events, children's events, and seasonal specialties.

TICKETplace between 12th and 13th Streets N.W. on F Street Plaza is a great place to buy discount tickets the day of the show.

Arena Stage at 6th Street and Maine Avenue S.W. (488-3300) offers productions on three stages. Don't miss "Banjo Dancing."

The Shakespeare Theater at the Folger, 201 E. Capitol Street S.E. (546-4000) offers plays in an Elizabethan inn courtyard, weekend concerts, and free children's programs, concerts, and poetry readings Thursday noons.

Ford's Theater, 511 10th Street N.W. (347-4833) offers experimental productions and productions bound for Broadway.

The John F. Kennedy Center for the Performing Arts houses five theaters. For information and advance tickets, call (800) 424-8504. In Washington, call 254-3600 for information; 857-0900 to charge tickets. The Kennedy Center is located at New Hampshire Avenue and Rock Creek Parkway.

The Concert Hall is the home of the National Symphony Orchestra. Chamber music societies, headliners, and choral groups also perform here (254-3776).

The National Theater, 1321 Pennsylvania Avenue N.W. (628-6161) is a great place to see shows from or on their way to Broadway. Saturday morning children's theater is also held at the National.

Clubs, Bars, and Discos

Following is a representative sampling of nightspots in Washington. Many have cover charges. Call for information about shows, seating, and hours, as they change nightly.

Anton's 1201 Club, 1201 Pennsylvania Avenue N.W. (783-1201). Jazz club with big-name pianists and vocalists.

Café Lautrec, 2431 18th Street N.W. (265-6436). Piano/cabaret atmosphere.

Cagney's, 1 Dupont Circle N.W. (659-8820). New-wave music.

Club Soda, 3433 Connecticut Avenue N.W. (244-3189). Oldies music, bands.

The Comedy Café, 1520 K Street N.W. (638-JOKE). Local and national comedians. Open mike Thursday nights.

Deja Vu, 2119 M Street N.W. (452-1966). Mostly oldies, three dance floors, six bars in a Victorian setting.

Dubliner, 4 F Street N.W. (737-3773). Irish folk music in an authentic pub-style atmosphere.

Garvin's Comedy Club, L Street between 13th and 14th Streets (726-1334). Young comedians perform weekends. Open mike on Tuesdays.

Kilimanjaro, 1724 California Street N.W. (328-3838). African, Caribbean, Latin disco, plus Calypso and reggae.

Rumors, 1900 M Street N.W. (466-7378); 1716 H Street N.W. (342-6433). Singles bar/ dance club.

Ten-63, 1063 Wisconsin Avenue N.W. (338-8880). Dancing to top 40 hits.

Shopping

If you're a shopper by hobby or searching for souvenirs, Washington is the place to be.

Mazza Gallerie, 5300 Wisconsin Avenue N.W. at the D.C./Maryland border, has 52 luxury boutiques, plus Neiman-Marcus, F.A.O. Schwartz, Kron Chocolatier, Williams Sonoma, and several restaurants (966-6114)

The Pavilion at the Old Post Office, 1100 Pennsylvania Avenue N.W. has a number of boutiques, restaurants, and a food court with a wide variety of delicacies. The Observation Tower offers a view of D.C. from over 300 feet in the air (289-4224).

Union Station, 50 Massachusetts Avenue N.E. not only serves as an Amtrak and Metro station, but now has a food court and trendy boutiques (289-1908).

The Shops at National Place, between 13th and 14th Streets at F Street, is a collection of boutiques around the corner from the theater district.

Georgetown Park, Wisconsin and M Streets N.W., is a three-story Victorian-style mall in the heart of Georgetown. It houses Ann Tayor, Godiva Chocolatier, Liberty of London, Conran's, and Ralph Lauren. Several restaurants (342-8190).

Eastern Market, 7th and C Streets S.E. (Eastern Market Metro stop), is a farmers' market selling produce, eggs, baked goods, and flowers on Saturdays during warm weather.

District of Columbia

Adams Inn

1749 Lanier Place NW, 20009
(202) 745-3600

Convenient, home-style atmosphere near the Metro and bus, restaurants, shopping, museums, government buildings, convention sites. Economical for the tourist and business traveler.

Hosts: Gene & Nancy Thompson
Doubles: 25 (11 PB; 14 SB) $39.56-78
Type of Beds: 15 Twin; 10 Double
Continental Breakfast
Minimum stay weekends: 2
Credit Cards: A, B, C, E
Notes: 2, 5, 8, 14

Amanda's B&B Reservation Service #2

1428 Park Avenue, Baltimore, MD, 21217
(301) 225-0001

Located in Arlington, VA, just ten minutes from Washington, DC, this inviting frame house is located on a spacious corner lot in what used to be East Falls Church. Most exterior gingerbread is original to the house, and the house is being meticulously restored to its former beauty and charm.

Doubles: 1 (PB) $60
Type of Beds: 1 Twin; 1 Double
Full Breakfast
Credit Cards: No
Notes: 2, 5, 8, 9, 14

The B&B League #1

Box 9490, 20016
(202) 363-7767

A very large Victorian home located in Cleveland Park, an area noted for its large number of period homes originally built as summer homes. Trees and flowers abound, and the Metro stop is an easy seven-minute walk from the house, as are numerous shops and restaurants.

Doubles: 1 (PB) $55
Type of Beds: 1 Double; 1 Twin foldaway
Continental Breakfast
Credit Cards: A, B, C
Notes: 2, 5, 7, 8, 9

The B&B League #2

Box 9490, 20016
(202) 363-7767

A charming home on Capitol Hill, built in 1855. One block from the Library of Congress, a five-minute walk to the Capitol, and 1.5 blocks to the Metro; a superb location. The host is an international economist; the hostess is a real-estate agent who specializes in the Capitol Hill Historic District.

Doubles: 2 (SB) $45-55
Type of Beds: 2 Queen
Continental Breakfast
Credit Cards: A, B, C
Notes: 2, 5, 8, 9

The B&B League #3

Box 9490, 20016
(202) 363-7767

A warm, cozy 1910s home just one block to the Eastern Market Metro and a ten-minute walk to the Capitol. Your English hostess, a caterer, serves a full English breakfast. Her recipes have been featured in several

6 Pets welcome: 7 Smoking allowed: 8 Children welcome: 9 Social drinking allowed: 10 Tennis available: 11 Swimming available: 12 Golf available: 13 Skiing available: 14 May be booked through travel agents

newspaper articles. One friendly, gentle dog in residence.

Singles: 1 (SB) $33
Doubles: 3 (SB) $38-60
Type of Beds: 4 Twin; 2 Double
Full Breakfast
Credit Cards: A, B, C
Notes: 2, 5, 9

The B&B League #4

Box 9490, 20016
(202) 363-7767

A 150-year-old brick house full of antiques and travel mementos on a quiet street just six blocks from all the shops and restaurants in Georgetown and only a ten-minute walk to the DuPont Circle Metro. Three friendly cats in residence.

Doubles: 2 (PB) $55-65
Type of Beds: 2 Double
Continental Breakfast
Credit Cards: A, B, C
Notes: 2, 5, 9

The B&B League #5

Box 9490, 20016
(202) 363-7767

A beautifully restored 1910 home, elegant and gracious, within walking distance of Du-Pont Circle and the Metro. The high-ceilinged rooms provide a perfect backdrop for the owners' antiques and Oriental rugs. She is a psychiatric social worker, and he is the author of several books.

Doubles: 4 (SB) $50-60
Type of Beds: 4 Twin; 1 Double; 1 Queen
Continental Breakfast
Credit Cards: A, B, C
Notes: 2, 5, 9

B&B of Washington, DC #100

Box 12011, 20005
(202) 328-3510

A 100-year-old Victorian mansion, carefully and extensively restored. The house features original wood paneling, stained glass, chandeliers, Victorian lattice porch. Central air-conditioning, color TV in each room, player piano, security and fire system, laundry facilities. French and English are spoken. Off-street parking available for a fee if reserved in advance.

Singles: $56-67
Doubles: $67-78
Continental Breakfast
Credit Cards: A, B, C, E
Notes: 2 (in advance), 5, 8, 10, 11, 12, 14

B&B of Washington, DC #112

Box 12011, 20005
(202) 328-3510

A restored 1910 in-town residence across the street from the Washington Hilton and within walking distance of Dupont Circle. Elegant and gracious, the high-ceiling rooms provide a perfect backdrop for their antiues and Oriental rugs. One block off Connecticut Avenue. There is no off-street parking.

Singles: $56
Doubles: 4 (S2B) $67
Continental Breakfast
Credit Cards: A, B, C, E
Notes: 2, 5, 10, 11, 12, 14

B&B Washington, DC #135

Box 12011, 20005
(202) 328-3510

This corner rowhouse at Dupont Circle was built in the late 1890s. With its wide stone facade, balconies, and turret, the house has a castle appearance. Great care was taken to retain the original details of the house when it was renovated. Off-street parking is available for a fee. Dupont Circle is in the heart of Washington, midway between the National Cathedral and the Capitol. Convenient to public transportation.

NOTES: Credit cards accepted: A Master Card; B Visa; C American Express; D Discover Card; E Diners Club; F Other: 2 Personal checks accepted: 3 Lunch available: 4 Dinner available: 5 Open all year

Doubles: 4 (2 PB; 2 SB) $67-94.50
Type of Beds: 4 Twin; 2 Double; 1 Queen
Continental Breakfast
Credit Cards: A, B, C, E
Notes: 2, 5, 10, 11, 12, 14

B&B Washington, DC #145

Box 12011, 20005
(202) 328-3510

A quintessential Washington townhouse in a prestigious tree-lined district on Capitol Hill. The elegantly restored and appointed residence is renowned among preservationists as the earliest (1891) and finest local example of Colonial Revival architecture. Pets in residence. No off-street parking is available.

Doubles: 3 (SB) $56-67
Type of Beds: 2 Twin; 2 Double; 1 Rollaway
Continental Breakfast
Credit Cards: A, B, C, E
Notes: 2, 5, 10, 11, 12, 14

B&B Washington, DC #170

Box 12011, 20005
(202) 328-3510

A Victorian townhouse furnished with American antiques. Guests are invited to use the Florida room, where breakfast is served, as well as the living room and garden. There is no off-street parking available. The house is located on southeast Capitol Hill, just off Pennsylvania Avenue. Public transportation and restaurants in the area.

Doubles: 2 (SB) $61.50-72.50
Type of Beds: 2 Double
Continental Breakfast
Credit Cards: A, B, C, E
Notes: 2, 5, 10, 11, 12, 14

B&B Washington, DC #173

Box 12011, 20005
(202) 328-3510

Built in 1912, this house was one of the early, gracious row houses in the Mt. Pleasant area. Major renovations in 1985 added modern conveniences and a new kitchen, but kept the original details of the house. Situated 1.5 miles north of the White House, between 16th Street and the National Zoo. Public transportation is one block away.

Doubles: 2 (SB) $61.50-72.50
Type of Beds: 2 Double
Continental Breakfast
Credit Cards: A, B, C, E
Notes: 2, 5, 10, 11, 12, 14

Crystal Bed & Breakfast

2620 South Fern Street, Arlington 22202
(703) 548-7652

Two homes side by side with large, sunny rooms and lovely gardens. Minutes by subway from downtown museum area of D.C. Handmade quilts, antique furnishings, gourmet muffins, and large breakfasts. Recommended in nationwide travel column.

Host: Susan Swain
Singles: 2 (1 PB; 1 SB) $43.80
Doubles: 4 (SB) $54.75
Type of Beds: 2 Twin; 4 Queen
Continental Breakfast weekdays; Full on weekends
Credit Cards: No
Notes: 2, 5, 7, 8, 9

Embassy Inn

1627 16th St. NW, 20009
(202) 234-7800

A European-style hotel located nine blocks north of the White House featuring a quiet, relaxed atmosphere and personalized service. We offer a complimentary continental breakfast each morning and sherry each evening.

Hosts: Susan Araujo
Singles: 3 (PB) $76.90
Doubles: 36 (PB) $98.90
Type of Beds: 3 Twin; 36 Double
Continental Breakfast
Credit Cards: A, B, C, D, E, F
Notes: 2, 5, 7, 8, 9, 14

6 Pets welcome: 7 Smoking allowed: 8 Children welcome: 9 Social drinking allowed: 10 Tennis available: 11 Swimming available: 12 Golf available: 13 Skiing available: 14 May be booked through travel agents

Kalorama Guest House at Woodley Park

2700 Cathedral Ave., NW, 20008
(202) 328-0860

This turn-of-the-century Victorian townhouse offers you a downtown residential home away from home. Decorated in period antiques, the guest house is a short walk to the underground Metro, restaurants, and shops. Only ten minutes from the Smithsonian and White House, yet offering you the relaxation and hospitality of a country inn. Enjoy our complimentary continental breakfast and evening aperitif.

Hosts: Lynn Foley
Doubles: 19 (12 PB; 7 SB) $40-85
Type of Beds: 6 Twin; 14 Double; 2 Queen
Continental Breakfast
Credit Cards: A, B, C, E
Notes: 2, 5, 7, 8, 9, 10, 11, 12, 14

Norris House Inn

108 Loudoun Street SW, Leesburg, VA, 22075
(703) 777-1806

Located within one hour's drive of Washington and the Shenandoah Mountains, this house was built in 1806 and is located in the heart of historic Leesburg. Candlelight accommodations amid elegant surroundings. Guest rooms and suites are fully air-conditioned; some have fireplaces and canopy beds. Lovely gardens and veranda to enjoy after a day of sightseeing in the city.

Host: Laura Walton
Suites: 2 (PB) $115
Doubles: 6 (S3B) $60-115
Type of Beds: 2 Twin; 6 Double; 1 Queen; 2 Hidabeds
Full Breakfast
Credit Cards: No
Closed Thanksgiving, Christmas
Notes: 2, 5, 8 (8 and over), 9, 10, 11, 12, 14

The Reeds

Box 12011, 20005
(202) 328-3510

A 100-year-old Victorian mansion that has been carefully and extensively restored. Original wood paneling, stained glass, chandeliers, porch. Each room has a color television; laundry facilities are available. Adjoins Logan Circle Historic District, with excellent transportation and easy parking. Ten blocks from the White House. Your hosts speak English and French.

Hosts: Charles & Jackie Reed
Doubles: 5 (SB) $45-82.50
Type of Beds: 3 Double; 2 Queen
Continental Breakfast
Credit Cards: A, B, C, E (surcharge)
Notes: 2 (two weeks before), 5, 8, 9

The Reeds

Victorian Accommodations

1221 12th Street NW; 1304 Rhode Island Avenue NW, 20005
(202) 234-6292

NOTES: Credit cards accepted: A Master Card; B Visa; C American Express; D Discover Card; E Diners Club; F Other: 2 Personal checks accepted: 3 Lunch available: 4 Dinner available: 5 Open all year

Victorian Accommodations represents renovated Victorian in-town houses with interesting architectural detail in the heart of Washington. Our luxurious rooms are decorated with art and antiques and include the comforts of home. We have convenient access to public transportation.

Host: Ronald D. Morgan
Doubles: 14 (7 PB; 7 SB) $67-105.50
Type of Beds: 4 Twin; 10 Double; 1 Queen
Continental Breakfast
Credit Cards: A, B
Notes: 2, 5, 7 (limited), 8, 9

Windsor Inn
1842 16th St., NW, 20009
(202) 667-0300

A European-style hotel located eleven blocks north of the White House featuring a quiet, relaxed atmosphere and personalized service. We offer a complimentary continental breakfast each morning and sherry each evening.

Hosts: Susan Araujo
Singles: 10 (PB) $76.90
Doubles: 36 (PB) $98.90
Type of Beds: 4 Twin; 27 Double; 5 Queen
Continental Breakfast
Credit Cards: A, B, C, D, E
Notes: 2, 5, 7, 8, 9, 10, 11, 12, 14

6 Pets welcome: 7 Smoking allowed: 8 Children welcome: 9 Social drinking allowed: 10 Tennis available: 11 Swimming available: 12 Golf available: 13 Skiing available: 14 May be booked through travel agents

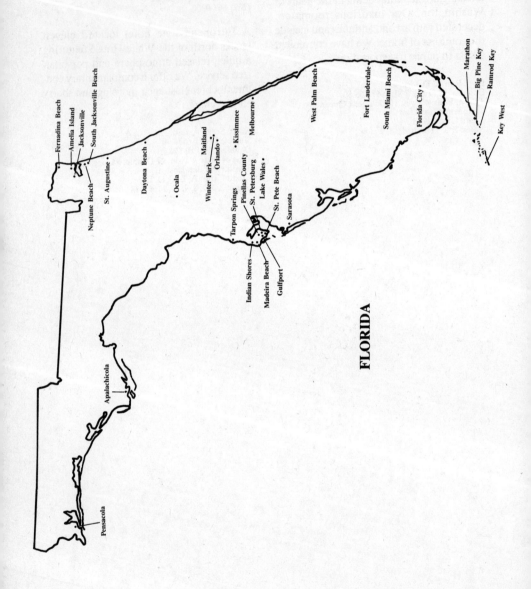

FLORIDA

Fernadina Beach
Amelia Island
Jacksonville
South Jacksonville Beach
Neptune Beach
St. Augustine
Daytona Beach
Ocala
Maitland
Winter Park
Orlando
Kissimmee
Melbourne
Tarpon Springs
Pinellas County
St. Petersburg
Lake Wales
St. Pete Beach
Sarasota
Indian Shores
Madeira Beach
Gulfport
West Palm Beach
Fort Lauderdale
South Miami Beach
Florida City
Marathon
Big Pine Key
Ramrod Key
Key West
Apalachicola
Pensacola

Florida

The Bailey House
28 S. 7th St., Fernandina Beach, 32034
(904) 261-5390

Elegant 1895 Victorian filled with an-tiques; air-conditioning, private baths. On National Historic Register in the center of town, a short walk to restaurants, shops, marina, lighted tennis. Five minutes to Ft. Clinch, the beach, golf, and horseback riding. Bicycles available. Transportation available from the marina & municipal airport, with advance notice.

Hosts: Tom & Diane Hay
Doubles: 4 (PB) $65-$95
Type of Beds: 3 Double; 1 Queen
Expanded Continental Breakfast
Credit Cards: C
Notes: 2, 5, 7 (veranda only), 8 (over 10), 9, 10, 11, 12, 14

The 1735 House
584 S. Fletcher Avenue, 32034
(904) 261-5878

An ocean-front country inn on a Florida beach. Antique nautical decorations enhance your private ocean view. Full suites, private bath, fresh-baked pastries, and morning newspaper. One suite located in a lighthouse, with two bedrooms, bath, galley, working light, and observation deck.

Hosts: Gary & Emily Grable
Suites: 6 (PB) $55-125
Type of Beds: 5 Twin; 3 Double; 3 Queen
Continental Breakfast
Credit Cards: A, B, C
Notes: 2, 5, 7, 8, 9, 10, 11, 12, 14

The Gibson Inn
Box 221, 32320
(904) 653-2191

All rooms are decorated with period furnishings: four-poster beds, ceiling fans, an-tique armoires, and pedestal lavatories with wide basins and porcelain fixtures. Shelling, boating, and fishing are close, plus four barrier islands to explore. Apalachicola is a seafood lover's paradise.

Hosts: Michael Koun & Jo Ann Dearing
Doubles: 30 (PB) $60-$80
Type of Beds: 18 Twin; 14 Queen; 7 King
Full Breakfast
Minimum stay holidays: 2
Credit Cards: A, B, C
Notes: 2, 4, 5, 6, 7, 8, 9, 14

The Barnacle
Rt. 1, Box 780A, 33043
(305) 872-3298

Enjoy the ambience of a home-stay bed and breakfast, along with every amenity. A unique experience on the ocean, surrounded by lush, verdant foliage, where you can enjoy peace and quiet, yet be only thirty miles from the attractions of Key West.

Hosts: Wood & Joan Cornell
Doubles: 3 (PB) $65-85
Type of Beds: 3 Queen
Full Breakfast
Credit Cards: No
Notes: 2, 5, 7, 9, 11, 14

---

6 Pets welcome: 7 Smoking allowed: 8 Children welcome: 9 Social drinking allowed: 10 Tennis available: 11 Swimming available: 12 Golf available: 13 Skiing available: 14 May be booked through travel agents

The Barnacle

Deer Run

Long Beach Road, Box 431, 33043
(305) 872-2015; 872-2800

Deer Run is a Florida-cracker-style house nestled among lush native trees on the ocean. Breakfast is served on the large veranda overlooking the ocean. Dive at Looe Key National Marine Sanctuary, fish the Gulf Stream, or lie on the beach.

Host: Sue Abbott
Doubles: 2 (PB) $65-75
Type of Beds: 1 Double; 1 King
Full Breakfast
Minimum stay: 2
Credit Cards: No
Notes: 2, 5, 9, 11

DAYTONA BEACH

Captains Quarters Inn

3711 S. Atlantic Avenue, 32019
(904) 767-3119

The inn features new oceanfront suites with private balconies overlooking the Atlantic Ocean and our swimming pool. Daily maid service, old English charm with poster beds. Only minutes from Disney World. Enjoy our old-fashioned coffee shoppe and Rebecca's Place, full of gifts and antiques. We welcome you with wine and cheese, and deliver a daily newspaper to your door. AAA rated excellent.

Hosts: Beckey Sue Morgan
Doubles: 25 (PB) $75-110

Type of Beds: 8 Double; 17 Queen
Full Breakfast
Credit Cards: A, B, C
Notes: 2, 5, 7, 8, 9, 10, 11, 12, 14

FERNADINA BEACH

B&B Suncoast #1

8690 Gulf Blvd., St. Pete Beach, 33706
(813) 360-1753

Private entrance, walk to the ocean. VCR available, old radio tapes, and surf-casting great. Refrigerator stocked with goodies.

Doubles: 2 (PB) $60-90
Type of Beds: 1 Twin; 1 Double; 1 Queen
Continental Breakfast
Credit Cards: No
Notes: 5, 9, 10, 11, 12

FLORIDA CITY

Grandma Newtons B&B

40 N.W. 5th Ave., 33034
(305) 247-4413

Visit Grandma and the relaxed country atmosphere of her 1914 two-story renovated country home. Minutes from national parks, the Florida Keys, and Miami. Spacious rooms with air-conditioning insure a peaceful rest that sets your appetite for our huge country breakfast.

Hosts: Mildred T. Newton
Singles: 4 (2 PB; 2 SB) $33.30-$49.95
Doubles: 4 (2 PB; 2 SB) $39.95-$61.50
Type of Beds: 2 Twin; 3 Double; 1 King
Full Breakfast
Minimum stay holidays: 2
Credit Cards: No
Notes: 2 (for deposit only), 5, 7, 8, 9, 10, 11, 12, 14

FORT LAUDERDALE

The Dolan House

1401 N.E. 5 Court, 33301
(305) 462-8430

We are centrally located for the beach, shopping, businesses, and full park exercise

NOTES: Credit cards accepted: A Master Card; B Visa; C American Express; D Discover Card; E Diners Club; F Other: 2 Personal checks accepted: 3 Lunch available: 4 Dinner available: 5 Open all year

facilities. Each room is equipped with ceiling fans and individual air-conditioners. Our garden and patio areas are great for enjoying the Florida sun, or you may want to slip into the hot tub spa.

Hosts: Tom & Sandra Dolan
Doubles: 4 (2 PB; 2 SB) $49.05-$54.50, 20% disc.
July & Aug.
Type of Beds: 4 Twin; 2 Queen
Continental Breakfast
Minimum stay: 2
Credit Cards: No
Closed Aug. & Sept.
Notes: 2, 7 (restricted), 9, 10, 11

GULFPORT

B&B Suncoast #2

8690 Gulf Blvd., St. Pete Beach, 33706
(813) 360-1753

This unit has a swimming pool and sitting area for guests with TV. Closed March 15-April 15. One full bed with private bath. Continental breakfast. $45-60.

INDIAN SHORES

Meeks B&B on the Gulf Beaches

19506 Gulf Blvd., 34635
(813) 596-5425

Our luxurious beach condo overlooks the pool and Gulf beaches. Sumptuous breakfast served. Nearby shopping and restaurants; easy drive to Busch Gardens and Disney World. A private cottage on the beach is also available.

Hosts: Bob & Greta Meeks
Singles: 1 (PB) $35
Doubles: 2 (PB & SB) $50
Type of Beds: 2 Twin; 2 Double
Full Breakfast
Credit Cards: No
Notes: 2, 5, 7 (limited), 8, 9, 10, 11, 12

JACKSONVILLE

House on Cherry Street

1844 Cherry Street, 32205
(904) 384-1999

Historic restored home on the St. John's River near downtown Jacksonville. Antiques, elegant breakfast, wine, snacks, and bicycles for guest use.

Host: Carol Anderson
Doubles: 4 (2 PB; 2 SB) $60.50-82.50
Type of Beds: 1 Twin; 1 Double; 2 Queen
Full Breakfast
Minimum stay during special events: 2-3
Credit Cards: No
Notes: 2, 5, 8 (6 and over), 9, 10, 12, 14

KEY WEST

Eaton Lodge, Traditional Inn

511 Eaton Street, 33040
(305) 294-3800

Designed for those who appreciate personal attention, dignified comfort, and the unique atmosphere of a nineteenth-century residence on the National Register of Historic Places. All rooms feature antique furnishings from England, refrigerator, air-conditioning, and a patio or veranda overlooking the lush tropical grounds.

Hosts: Denison Temple & Sam Maxwell
Singles: 1 (PB) $66-99 seasonal
Doubles: 7 (PB) $99-140 seasonal
Suites: 2 (2 bedrooms; PB)
Type of Beds: 6 Twin; 6 Double; 3 Queen; 2 King
Continental Breakfast
Minimum stay in season: 3; holidays: 4 to 6
Credit Cards: A, B
Notes: 2, 5, 7, 8, 9, 10, 11, 12, 14

Garden House of Key West

329 Elizabeth Street, 33040
(305) 296-5368

Located in the heart of Old Town. Shop on Duval St., two blocks away. Spend a quiet afternoon in the hammock or around the pool/waterfall. Daily wine social hour. Large sun deck. Rooms contain air-conditioning, telephones, ceiling fans, and radios, Scandinavian and German languages spoken.

Hosts: David & Tor
Doubles: 10 (8 PB; 2 SB) $43-109
Type of Beds: 4 Double; 7 Queen
Continental-plus Breakfast
Credit Cards: A, B, C, D, E
Notes: 2 (reservations only), 5

Heron House

512 Simonton Street, 33040
(305) 294-9227

Heron House consists of three homes. One, built in 1856, represents the few remaining classic "Conch" houses. Location is in the very heart of the historical district, one block from the main tourist street and three blocks from the nearest beach.

Doubles: 17 (PB) $49.50-148.50
Type of Beds: 19 Double; 3 Queen
Continental Breakfast
Credit Cards: A, B, C
Notes: 2 (for deposit), 5, 7, 9, 10, 11, 12, 14

Merlinn Guest House

811 Simonton Street, 33040
(305) 296-3336

Lush tropical pool, sun decks, and gardens in the heart of Old Town. Complimentary quiche breakfast and sunset cocktails. Eighteen cathedral-ceilinged rooms with private baths, air-conditioning, and TV. You'll never want to leave!

Hosts: Pat Hoffman
Singles: 1 (PB) $54-93 seasonal
Doubles: 17 (PB) $65-103 seasonal
Type of Beds: 5 Twin; 15 Double; 3 Queen; 1 King
Full Breakfast
Minimum stay holidays: 3
Credit Cards: A, B, C
Notes: 2 (deposit only), 5, 6, 7, 8, 9, 11, 14

Whispers B&B Inn

Whispers Bed & Breakfast Inn

409 William Street, 33040
(305) 294-5969

As owner-managers, we take great pride in our service, hospitality, and the romance of our historic 1866 Inn. Each room is unique and appointed with antiques. Included in the room rate is a full breakfast served in our tropical gardens.

Hosts: Les & Marilyn Tipton
Singles: 6 (S3B) $55-75
Doubles: 6 (S3B) $65-85
Type of Beds: 2 Twin; 7 Double; 1 King
Full Breakfast
Credit Cards: A, B, C
Notes: 2, 5, 7, 9, 10, 11, 12, 14

NOTES: Credit cards accepted: A Master Card; B Visa; C American Express; D Discover Card; E Diners Club; F Other: 2 Personal checks accepted: 3 Lunch available: 4 Dinner available: 5 Open all year

Wicker Guesthouse

913 Duval, 33040
(305) 296-4275

The Wicker Guesthouse, a compound of restored Conch homes, is ideally located on colorful Duval Street, within easy walking distance of beaches, restaurants, shops, and attractions. A 41' sailboat and 26' power boat are available for day trips to the coral reef.

Hosts: Mark & Libby Curtis
Singles: 1 (SB) $40.70-82.50
Doubles: 15 (2 PB; 13 SB) $49.50-93.50
Type of Beds: 8 Twin; 9 Double; 4 Queen
Continental Breakfast
Credit Cards: A, B, C
Notes: 2 (advance deposit only), 5, 7, 8, 9, 10, 11, 12, 14

KISSIMMEE

The Unicorn Inn English Bed & Breakfast

8 S. Orlando Avenue, 32741
(407) 846-1200

Beautifully restored 1900 Victorian house in downtown Kissimmee. This unique English bed and breakfast hotel is in a quiet setting, but close to Disney and Epcot. Also very close to Lake Toho, with some of the best fishing in Florida. Enjoy some English hospitality!

Hosts: Graham & Amanda Camplin
Doubles: 4 (PB) $32.70-54.50
Type of Beds: 3 Twin; 4 Queen
Full Breakfast
Credit Cards: No
Notes: 2, 5, 7, 14

LAKE WALES

Chalet Suzanne Country Inn & Restaurant

P.O. Drawer AC, 33859
(800) 676-6011

Discover Europe in the heart of Florida. This historic country inn is located on 70 acres surrounded by orange groves. Thirty charming guest rooms with private baths. Award-winning dining overlooking Lake Suzanne. Forty-five minutes southwest of the Orlando area.

Hosts: Carl & Vita Hinshaw
Doubles: 30 (PB) $75-155
Type of Beds: 5 Twin; 14 Double; 11 King
Full Breakfast
Credit Cards: A, B, C, D, E
Notes: 2, 3, 4, 5, 6, 7, 8, 9, 10, 11, 12, 14

Chalet Suzanne Country Inn

6 Pets welcome: 7 Smoking allowed: 8 Children welcome: 9 Social drinking allowed: 10 ... able: 11 ... Swimming available: 12 Golf available: 13 Skiing available: 14 May be booked throu...

MADEIRA BEACH

B&B Suncoast #3

8690 Gulf Blvd., St. Pete Beach, 33706
(813) 360-1753

On the bay with a dock and swimming pool.
Two rooms with full beds, private bath. Continental breakfast. Open all year. No smoking; children are welcome. $45-65.

MAITLAND

A&A B&B of Florida #9

Box 1316, Winter Park, 32790
(407) 628-3233

Large, two-story home by Lake Sybelia with
accommodations on the first floor. Lovely
hostess, good with children. Can accommodate a party of four. Full breakfast. One
double, private bath, $45-55.

MARATHON

B&B of the Florida Keys #90

Box 1373, 33050
(305) 743-4118

This home is located on a canal, just a short
walk to the beach. The first room has a
private entrance and bath, plus a deck overlooking the ocean. The second room also has
a private bath. Perfect for two couples
traveling together.

Doubles: 2 (PB) $40-60
Type of Beds: 2 Twin; 1 King
Full Breakfast
Credit Cards: A, B
Notes: 8 (over 12), 9, 10, 11, 12

B&B of the Florida Keys #34

Box 3050
(305) 8

This home is located on the open water — a
perfect spot for swimming or watching the
boats go by. Breakfast is served on the porch
overlooking the water.

Doubles: 1 (PB) $40-60
Type of Beds: 1 Double
Full Breakfast
Credit Cards: A, B
Notes: 5, 7, 10, 11, 12

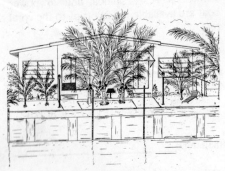

Hopp-Inn Guest House

Hopp-Inn Guest House

5 Man-O-War Drive, 33050
(305) 743-4118

We are located in the heart of the Florida
Keys. Every room has a water view. Charter
fishing on premises aboard the *Sea Wolf*.
Families welcome in villas.

Hosts: The Hopp Family
Doubles: 5 (PB) $49.50-93.50
Villas: 3 (PB)
Type of Beds: 4 Twin; 3 Double; 3 Queen; 3 King
Full Breakfast
Credit Cards: A, B
Notes: 2 (for deposit), 5, 7 (limited), 8, 10, 11, 12

MELBOURNE

The Guest Room

Southern Comfort Reservations
2856 Hundred Oaks Avenue, Baton Rouge, LA, 70808
(504) 346-1928

Pleasant modern home with one bedroom
and private bath. Breakfast is served in the

dining area or on the beautiful screened lanai. Close to Kennedy Space Center, Atlanta beaches; only 45 minutes from Disney World and Epcot Center.

Doubles: 1 (PB) $45-50
Type of Beds: 2 Twin or 1 King
Full Breakfast
Credit Cards: A, B, C
Closed May 1 - Nov. 1
Notes: 2, 9

NEPTUNE BEACH

B&B Suncoast #4

8690 Gulf Blvd., St. Pete Beach, 33706
(813) 360-1753

Walk to ocean, shops. Complete two-bedroom apartment with private bath. Apartment is stocked; guests prepare own breakfast. Three twin beds. Smoking allowed. $50-90.

OCALA

Doll House B&B

719 S.E. 4th St., 32671
(904) 351-1167

An 1899 Victorian in the historic district of downtown Ocala. Oriental rugs decorate the house, as well as an extensive doll collection. Homemade Irish scones come with breakfast. Close to Gainesville, ninety minutes to Disney/Epcot. Near Silver Springs (glass bottom boats), Cross Creek, and historic McIntosh and Micanopy for antique buffs. Our white Angora cat, Ashley, lives on the premises.

Host: Marcie Gauntlett
Doubles: 1 (PB) $30-$35
Type of Beds: 1 Double
Full Breakfast
Credit Cards: No
Closed Christmas
Notes: 2, 4, 8 (over 12), 9, 12

The Ritz

Southern Comfort Reservations
2856 Hundred Oaks Avenue, Baton Rouge, LA, 70808
(504) 346-1928

An Art Deco inn of the 1920s on the National Register of Historic Places. Thirty-two designer suites all include living room with sleeper sofa, TV, phone, bedroom, large dressing room, stocked mini refrigerator. Beautiful pool, complimentary cocktail, newspaper.

Doubles: 32 (PB) $65-85
Type of Beds: 4 Twin; 22 Queen; 8 King
Continental Breakfast
Credit Cards: A, B, C
Notes: 2, 3, 4, 5, 6, 7, 8, 9, 10, 11, 12

ORLANDO

A&A B&B of Florida #1

Box 1316, Winter Park, 32790
(407) 628-3233

Beautiful, large, four-bedroom home with lots of flowers. Screened patio with exercise bike and other workout items. Only minutes to the airport and ten minutes from Disney World and Epcot. Airport pick-up available. Full breakfast. One single: $45. One double: $45. Private bath.

A&A B&B of Florida #2

Box 1316, Winter Park, 32790
(407) 628-3222

Studio apartment in a nice location. Hostess is an interior decorator. Small kitchen, private entrance. Easy access to I-4, which takes you to Disney and Epcot. Full breakfast. One double, private bath, $45-65.

A&A B&B of Florida #3

Box 1316, Winter Park, 32790
(407) 628-3233

---

6 Pets welcome: 7 Smoking allowed: 8 Children welcome: 9 Social drinking allowed: 10 Tennis available: 11 Swimming available: 12 Golf available: 13 Skiing available: 14 May be booked through travel agents

Contemporary-style home located on a wide canal with a view of Orlando's beautiful lakes. You may use their pool, take in some sunshine, and relax. Host and hostess are in their fifties and smoke. Full breakfast. One double, private bath. $35-45.

A&A B&B of Florida #4

Box 1316, Winter Park, 32790
(407) 628-3233

Smaller home in a nice area with lakefront and a beautiful garden. Breakfast is served on the nice, bright patio when weather permits. Full breakfast. One double, private bath, $30-40.

A&A B&B of Florida #6

Box 1316, Winter Park, 32790
(407) 628-3233

Ten minutes away from Disney and Epcot, this home is in a nice area. Guests have a private sitting room with TV, air-conditioning. Near shopping area. Full breakfast. One double, private bath, $35-45.

A&A B&B of Florida #14

Box 1316, Winter Park, 32790
(407) 628-3233

Lovely home west of I-4 offers a mother-in-law apartment for guests. Nonsmokers only; no children, dogs, or birds. Small kitchen and laundry facilities included. Continental breakfast. One double, private bath, $45-55.

A&A B&B of Florida #15

Box 1316, Winter Park, 32790
(407) 628-3233

Lovely condo on Lake Eola, overlooking the city and its activities. Use of kitchen at any time. Host works, and guests have a lot of privacy. Pool and tennis court are available. Full breakfast. One double, private bath, $45-55.

A&A B&B of Florida #11

Box 1316, Winter Park, 32790
(407) 628-3233

Old English home with lots of antiques, Laura Ashley linens, private entrance, sunning area, ample parking. Continental breakfast. Two doubles, private bath, $55-65.

B&B Suncoast #5

8690 Gulf Blvd., St. Pete Beach, 33706
(813) 360-1753

Thirteen miles north of Disney area, with a swimming pool on the premises. One room with private bath, continental breakfast, king bed. Open all year; children welcome. $45-65.

Esther's Bed & Breakfast

2411 Virginia Drive, 32803
(407) 896-9916

Located near Epcot Center and Disney World. A continental breakfast of homemade coffee cake or muffins, cheese, fruit, and coffee is served, plus evening wine or homemade ice cream in the midst of Esther's needlepoints of old masters' paintings. Swimming pool.

Hosts: Esther M. Allen
Doubles: 2 (SB) $37.10- $47.70; cot $10.60
Type of Beds: Double
Continental Breakfast
Credit Cards: No
Notes: 2 (deposit only), 5, 8 (over 10), 9, 10, 11, 12

The Rio Pinar House

532 Pinar Drive, 32825
(407) 277-4903

NOTES: Credit cards accepted: A Master Card; B Visa; C American Express; D Discover Card; E Diners Club; F Other: 2 Personal checks accepted: 3 Lunch available: 4 Dinner available: 5 Open all year

A quiet, spacious, private home, furnished with antiques, featuring a breakfast porch overlooking a yard of trees and flowers. Located in a golf course community, convenient to the airport, downtown Church Street Station, Disney and Epcot, the Space Center, and Expressway exits.

Hosts: Delores & Vic Freudenburg
Singles: 2 (PB) $40
Doubles: 1 (PB) $45
Type of Beds: 2 Twin; 1 Double; 1 Queen
Full Breakfast
Credit Cards: No
Notes: 2 (if sent in advance), 5, 8, 9

The Spencer Home Bed & Breakfast

313 Spencer Street, 32809
(407) 855-5603

Our suite with private entrance consists of one or two bedrooms with a queen and double bed and living room with queen sofabed. TV, swimming pool, kitchen, laundry are all available. Convention Center and most of Central Florida's attractions are within fifteen to thirty minutes away. Brochure available.

Hosts: Neal & Eunice Schattauer
Doubles: 1-2 (PB) $50-100
Type of Beds: 1 Double; 2 Queen
Full Breakfast
Credit Cards: No
Notes: 2, 3, 4, 5, 8, 9, 10, 11, 12

PENSACOLA

The Homestead Inn

7830 Pine Forest Road, 32506
(904) 944-4816

This beautiful bed-and-breakfast inn combines the charm and grace of yesteryear with modern comfort and convenience. Personal attention is the order of the day in an atmosphere of intimate elegance. Guest rooms are individually appointed with private bath, color TV, and telephone. Some come with

skylight and fireplace, and one extra-special room boasts a private courtyard and luxurious hot tub. Guests enjoy complimentary desserts each evening and awake to a six-course gourmet breakfast. A hot tub & billiard table are available to our guests.

Hosts: Neil & Jeanne Liechty
Singles: 2 (PB) $55
Doubles: 2 (PB) $65
Suites: 2 (PB) $70
Type of Beds: 2 Twin; 2 Double; 4 Queen; 2 King
Full Breakfast
Credit Cards: A, B, C
Notes: 2, 5, 8, 9, 10, 11, 12, 14

PINELLAS COUNTY

B&B Suncoast #6

8690 Gulf Blvd., St. Pete Beach, 33706
(813) 360-1753

Waterfront dock, heated spa, private shower bath, refrigerator, cable TV, air-conditioning, heat. Gulf beach .5 mile away. Phone in room; additional room available for families. Kitchen and laundry privileges. Tennis and golf nearby. Busch Gardens, 45 minutes; Sunken Gardens, 20 minutes.

Singles: 1 (SB) $30-45
Doubles: 3 (SB) $35-65
Type of Beds: 1 Twin; 2 Double; 1 Queen
Continental Breakfast
Credit Cards: No
Notes: 2 (for deposit), 5, 7, 8, 9, 10, 11, 12, 14 (May-Dec.)

RAMROD KEY

Knightswood

Box 151, Summerland Key, 33042
(305) 872-2246

Knightswood overlooks one of the loveliest views in the Keys. Accommodations include a guest room with private bath or an apartment with bedroom, bath, kitchenette, rec room, and screened porch. Guests enjoy private dock, swimming pool, and separate spa. Located 27.5 miles from Key West.

Hosts: Chris & Herb Pontin
Doubles: 2 (PB) $71.50-82.50
Full Breakfast
Minimum stay: 2
Credit Cards: No
Notes: 2, 5, 9, 10, 11, 12

ST. AUGUSTINE

Carriage Way Bed & Breakfast

70 Cuna Street, 32084
(904) 829-2467

An 1883 Victorian in the historic district, within walking distance of the waterfront, shops, restaurants, and historic sites. Complimentary cordials, newspaper, cookies, and breakfast. The atmosphere here is leisurely and casual.

Host: Karen Burkley-Kovacik
Doubles: 5 (PB) $49-85
Continental Breakfast
Credit Cards: A, B
Notes: 2, 5, 8, 9, 10, 11, 14

Casa de la Paz

22 Avenida Menendez, 32084
(904) 829-2915

Overlooking historic Matanzas Bay in the heart of Old St. Augustine, this three-story Mediterranean revival home provides both single rooms and elegant suites. Furnished with antiques, the rooms also include ceiling fans, central air and heat, fine linens and mattresses, cable TV, and complimentary sherry or wine and chocolates. Guests may enjoy the bayfront parlor and library, a private walled courtyard, and the convenient location to all historic sites and attractions, which are within walking distance.

Hosts: The Staffords
Singles: 3 (PB) $75-110
Suites: 2 (PB) $110-150
Type of Beds: 2 Twin; 2 Double; 3 Queen; 1 King
Continental-plus Breakfast
Minimum stay weekends: 2; holidays: 3
Credit Cards: A, B, C
Notes: 2, 5, 8 (over 9), 9, 10, 11, 12

Casa de Solana B&B Inn

Casa de Solana Bed & Breakfast Inn

21 Aviles St., 32084
(904) 824-3555

Circa 1763. Four antique-filled suites with cable TV, private bath, enclosed courtyard. Full breakfast is served in the formal dining room; a decanter of sherry is presented on arrival. The inn is downtown, with all the quaint shops, museums, restaurants, and horse and buggies to help you in your tour of Saint Augustine, our oldest city.

Hosts: Jim & Faye McMurry
Doubles: 4 (PB) $108
Type of Beds: 2 Double; 1 Queen; 1 King
Full Breakfast
Minimum stay weekends & holidays: 2
Credit Cards: A, B, C
Notes: 2, 5, 8, 9

The Kenwood Inn

38 Marine Street, 32084
(904) 824-2116

Local maps and early records show the inn was built between 1865 and 1885 and was functioning as a private boarding house as early as 1886. Located in the historic district, the inn is within walking distance of many fine restaurants and all historic sights. One block from the Intracoastal Waterway, with its passing fishing trawlers, yachts at anchor, and the classic Bridge of Lions. Beautiful ocean beaches are just across the bridge.

Hosts: Mark, Kerrianne & Caitlin Constant
Doubles: 12 (PB) $45-75
Type of Beds: 5 Double; 4 Queen; 3 King
Continental Breakfast
Credit Cards: A, B
Notes: 2, 5, 7 (restricted), 9, 10, 11, 12

St. Francis Inn

279 St. George Street, 32084
(904) 824-6068

The qualities that make the St. Francis special include the varied selection of accommodations, the warmth and peacefulness of the inn, the ideal location, and the quality of guests it attracts. Its architectural charm and modern amenities also contribute to its overall appeal and comfort.

Host: Marie Register
Doubles: 14 (PB) $44-90
Type of Beds: 1 Twin; 10 Double; 1 Queen; 2 King
Continental Breakfast
Credit Cards: A, B
Notes: 2, 5, 8, 9, 10, 11, 12

Westcott House

146 Avenida Menendez, 32084
(904) 824-4301

Circa 1890, restored in 1983, in the historic district within walking distance to historical sights. All rooms have private baths, king-sized beds, cable television, private telephone, and are furnished in antiques. Year-round climate control. On Matanzaz Bayfront, one-half block from the city's yacht pier.

Hosts: Ruth & Fred Erminelli
Doubles: 8 (PB) $70.20-108 weekdays; $91.80-145.80 weekends
Type of Beds: King
Continental Breakfast
Credit Cards: A, B
Notes: 2, 5, 8, 9, 10, 11, 12, 14

ST. PETERSBURG

B&B Suncoast #8

8690 Gulf Blvd., 33706
(813) 360-1753

Separate entrance. Pick grapefruit off the tree in season. TV, air-conditioning. One twin room with private bath. $45-55.

Bayboro House Bed & Breakfast

1719 Beach Drive SE, 33701
(813) 823-4955

Turn-of-the-century Queen Anne home furnished in antiques. Old-fashioned porch swing to enjoy sea gulls and sailboats on Old Tampa Bay. Minutes from the Dali Museum, pier, Bayfront Center, Al Lange Stadium. Many fine restaurants in the area.

Hosts: Gordon & Antonia Powers
Doubles: 3 (PB) $54.50-70.85
Type of Beds: 1 Twin; 2 Double; 1 Queen
Continental Breakfast
Credit Cards: A, B
Notes: 2, 5, 7 (limited), 9, 10, 11, 12

ST. PETE BEACH

B&B Suncoast #9

8690 Gulf Blvd., 33706
(813) 360-1753

Short drive to Passe Grille Beach. One room with twin beds and private bath. Open all year. $45-55.

SARASOTA

B&B Suncoast #10

8690 Gulf Blvd., St. Pete Beach, 33706
(813) 360-1753

Directly on the Gulf with swimming pool, great views. Five rooms: four twin beds, three full; continental breakfast. Visa accepted. Open all year. $75-85.

B&B Suncoast #11

8690 Gulf Blvd., St. Pete Beach, 33706
(813) 360-1753

Swimming pool on premises; short drive to
beaches, Ringling Museum. One room with
private bath, full bed. Open all year, continental breakfast. $45-55.

SOUTH JACKSONVILLE BEACH

B&B Suncoast #12

8690 Gulf Blvd., St. Pete Beach, 33706
(813) 360-1753

Three blocks to ocean beach. Two rooms
with bath on the second floor for families.
Continental breakfast. One room has twin
beds; the other has a full bed. Children welcome. $45-65.

SOUTH MIAMI BEACH

Avalon Hotel

700 Ocean Dr., 33139
(305) 538-0133

A newly restored Art Deco hotel commanding a magnificent beach-front location. Our
restored rooms feature all amenities including cable TV, compact refrigerators, high-
quality linens, and complimentary
continental breakfast. Just minutes from
Miami International Airport, Port of Miami,
and I-95.

Hosts: Susan Machin & Beth Hoban
Doubles: 60 (PB) $45-$95
Type of Beds: Twin & Queen
Continental Breakfast
Credit Cards: A, B, C
Notes: 2, 4, 5, 7, 8, 9, 10, 11, 12, 14

TARPON SPRINGS

East Lake Bed & Breakfast

421 Old East Lake Road, 34689
(813) 937-5487

A lovely private home on 2.5 acres, located
on a quiet road along Lake Tarpon. Your
hosts are retired business people who enjoy
new friends and are well informed about the
area. A full home-cooked breakfast is
served.

Hosts: Marie & Dick Fiorito
Doubles: 1 (PB) $35-40
Type of Beds: 1 Double
Full Breakfast
Credit Cards: No
Notes: 2, 4, 5, 7, 9, 10, 11, 12, 14

Spring Bayou Inn

32 W. Tarpon Avenue, 34689
(813) 938-9333

A large, comfortable home built around the
turn of the century. Unique in architectural
detail, reflecting the elegance of the past
with modern-day conveniences. Located in
historical district within walking distance of
downtown and Spring Bayou.

Hosts: Ron & Cher Morrick
Doubles: 5 (PB) $49.05-70.85
Type of Beds: 1 Twin; 1 Double; 3 Queen
Continental-plus Breakfast
Minimum stay weekends & holidays: 2
Credit Cards: No
Notes: 2, 5, 9, 10, 11, 12

WEST PALM BEACH

Hibiscus House

Box 2612, 33402
(407) 863-5633

Hibiscus House is located in a charming,
historic neighborhood with easy access to
the ocean, Palm Beach Airport, and the
fabulous shopping of the city. Guest rooms
are individually furnished to provide an intimate, relaxed atmosphere. Some rooms

have private terraces overlooking the pool; all have private baths. A full or continental breakfast is served in the dining room or by the pool.

Host: Raleigh Hill
Doubles: 5 (PB) $55-65
Type of Beds: 1 Double; 4 Queen
Full or Continental Breakfast
Credit Cards: No
Notes: 2, 4, 5, 6 (small), 7, 8, 9, 10, 11, 12, 14

WINTER PARK

A&A B&B of Florida #5

Box 1316, Winter Park, 32790
(407) 628-3233

Inviting contemporary two-story home on a quiet cul-de-sac. Close to downtown Winter Park, with its famous Park Avenue shops. Lakefront home with pool, refrigerator. Full breakfast. Two doubles, shared bath. $45-55.

A&A B&B of Florida #6

Box 1316, Winter Park, 32790
(407) 628-3233

Contemporary brick home in downtown Winter Park, right by the golf course. Host and hostess are well traveled. Home has a pool and is one block from the fourth fairway. Full breakfast. Two doubles, private bath. $45-55.

A&A B&B of Florida #10

Box 1316, Winter Park, 32790
(407) 628-3233

Recently built colonial, with circular staircase, has beautifully appointed rooms. Swimming, fishing, and horseback riding all close. A dip in the beautiful Florida-shaped pool is very inviting in the morning or evening. Full breakfast. Two doubles, private bath. $55-65.

A&A B&B of Florida #12

Box 1316, Winter Park, 32790
(407) 628-3233

Located on beautiful Lake Killarney, this large, nicely furnished home has a lovely sun deck, and you may fish from the host's pier. Host offers guests a ride on his pontoon boat by request. Full breakfast. One double, private bath. $35-55.

A&A B&B of Florida #13

Box 1316, Winter Park, 32790
(407) 628-3233

The Whitaker Inn is located west of I-4, only minutes from the interstate that takes you to Disney and Epcot. Pool and hot tub overlook the lake; good fishing. Continental breakfast. Singles: $45. Doubles: $55.

6 Pets welcome: 7 Smoking allowed: 8 Children welcome: 9 Social drinking allowed: 10 Tennis available: 11 Swimming available: 12 Golf available: 13 Skiing available: 14 May be booked through travel agents

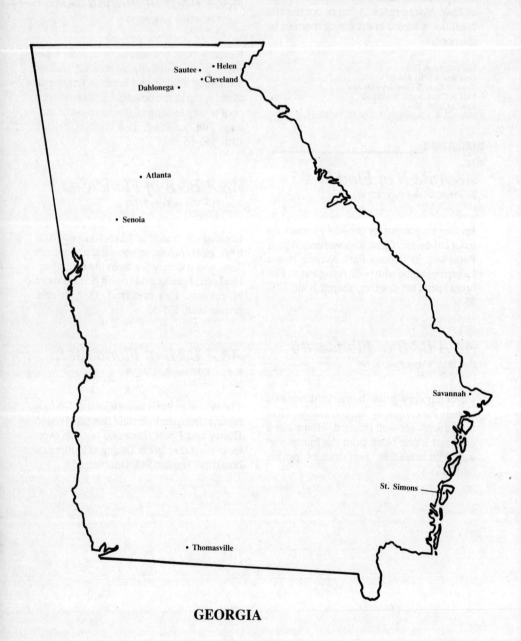

Sautee • • Helen
Dahlonega • • Cleveland

• Atlanta

• Senoia

Savannah •

St. Simons

• Thomasville

GEORGIA

Georgia

Atlanta B&B Services #1

2472 Lauderdale Drive, 30345
(404) 493-1930

Genial Southern hospitality and central location, plus a private entrance, serve to provide a special home away from home.

Doubles: 1 (PB) $20-75
Type of Beds: 2 Twin
Full Breakfast
Credit Cards: No

B&B Atlanta #2

1801 Piedmont Avenue NE, 30324
(404) 875-0525

Ten minutes from downtown Atlanta and two blocks from Peachtree Road. Public transportation makes all of Atlanta readily accessible. Antiques, cable TV, telephone, elevator. The lovely terraced rear garden has been featured in *Southern Accents*. A well-regarded cat resides here.

Doubles: 1 (PB) $60-68
Type of Beds: 1 King
Full Breakfast
Credit Cards: A, B, C

B&B Atlanta #4

1801 Piedmont Avenue NE, 30324
(404) 875-0525

This house is two to three miles from downtown, with excellent public transportation. Walk to many points of interest. An architecturally interesting home built about 1910 in a neighborhood of beautiful winding streets on the Historic Register. Sitting area, cable TV, telephone. Resident dog. No smoking, please.

Doubles: 2 (SB) $60-72
Type of Beds: 2 Twin; 1 King
Continental-plus Breakfast
Credit Cards: A, B, C

B&B Atlanta #2

B&B Atlanta #5

1801 Piedmont Avenue NE, 30324
(404) 875-0525

Located in one of Atlanta's historic neighborhoods, this home is two to three miles from downtown. Excellent public transportation; within walking distance of many points of interest, restaurants, shops, etc. Deck, pool, nearby park. Three small dogs in residence.

Doubles: 1 (PB) $44-52
Type of Beds: 1 Double; 1 Queen
Continental Breakfast
Credit Cards: A, B, C

6 Pets welcome: 7 Smoking allowed: 8 Children welcome: 9 Social drinking allowed: 10 Tennis available: 11 Swimming available: 12 Golf available: 13 Skiing available: 14 May be booked through travel agents

B&B Atlanta #6

1801 Piedmont Avenue NE, 30324
(404) 875-0525

This air-conditioned traditional two-story house with swimming pool is located on 16 beautiful wooded acres in northeast Atlanta.

Doubles: 2 (SB) $40-48
Continental-plus Breakfast
Credit Cards: A, B, C

B&B Atlanta #7

1801 Piedmont Avenue NE, 30324
(404) 875-0525

The swimming pool in the rear of this NW Atlanta home is a few feet from the banks of the Chattahoochee River. Wonderful location for antiquing, shopping, sightseeing, or reaching downtown meetings by car. Large screened porch.

Doubles: 2 (SB) $60-68
Type of Beds: 4 Twin
Continental-plus Breakfast
Credit Cards: A, B, C

B&B Atlanta #8

1801 Piedmont Avenue NE, 30324
(404) 875-0525

Glass, light, and high style prevail in this stunning contemporary house. Rooms are on a private ground-floor hall, allowing total privacy if desired. Contemporary furniture, phone, and TV in each room, use of sauna and pool. Nonsmokers, please.

Doubles: 2 (PB) $56-72
Type of Beds: 1 Queen; 1 King
Continental Breakfast
Credit Cards: A, B, C

B&B Atlanta #9

1801 Piedmont Avenue NE, 30324
(404) 875-0525

Lovely secluded street, spacious split-level home, large Jacuzzi on the rear patio. The guest suite is by itself on the lower level for privacy.

Doubles: 1 (PB) $40-48
Type of Beds: 1 King
Continental or Full Breakfast
Credit Cards: A, B, C

B&B Atlanta #11

1801 Piedmont Avenue NE, 30324
(404) 875-0525

This close-in older neighborhood attracts Atlanta's trendsetters with it many restaurants, shops, and galleries. This new home features a grand piano and sixteen-foot ceilings in the living room, overlooking the wooded yard. Nonsmokers only.

Doubles: 1 (PB) $36-44
Type of Beds: 1 Queen
Continental-plus Breakfast
Credit Cards: A, B, C

B&B Atlanta #13

1801 Piedmont Avenue NE, 30324
(404) 875-0525

A two-story brick traditional facade conceals a Victorian haven filled with fine an-tiques and collectibles in the historic Ansley Park neighborhood of Atlanta. Main-floor guest rooms are totally separate from host quarters. Sliding-glass doors open to a large deck overlooking the rear garden and a tree-filled park.

Doubles: 1 (PB) $44-48
Type of Beds: 1 Double
Continental Breakfast
Credit Cards: A, B, C

B&B Atlanta #14

1801 Piedmont Avenue NE, 30324
(404) 875-0525

NOTES: Credit cards accepted: A Master Card; B Visa; C American Express; D Discover Card; E Diners Club; F Other: 2 Personal checks accepted: 3 Lunch available: 4 Dinner available: 5 Open all year

Built in 1928 by one of Atlanta's most renowned architects, this is a true English Tudor of stone and brick, located on a private road atop a secluded wooded hill in Morningside. Public transportation is excellent, and most downtown destinations are only a ten-minute drive away. Pool, patio, and garden. Nonsmokers only.

Doubles: 2 (SB) $60-72
Type of Beds: 1 Queen; 1 King
Continental Breakfast
Credit Cards: A, B, C

B&B Atlanta #15

1801 Piedmont Avenue NE, 30324
(404) 875-0525

Conveniently located to some of the city's finest neighborhoods and most elegant shopping, this Georgian townhouse is in an exclusive area entered through a gate from Northside Parkway. Nonsmokers only.

Doubles: 1 (PB) $52
Type of Beds: 1 Queen
Continental Breakfast
Credit Cards: A, B, C

B&B Atlanta #16

1801 Piedmont Avenue NE, 30324
(404) 875-0525

Twenty miles south of downtown, ten miles south of Atlanta Airport, this large California contemporary is located in an elegant rural neighborhood on a 600-acre lake. Additional meals available by arrangement. Ideal for those traveling on I-75 and sports fans attending Atlanta's stadium.

Doubles: 2 (SB) $40-48
Type of Beds: 2 Twin; 1 Double; 1 Sofabed
Full Breakfast
Credit Cards: A, B, C

B&B Atlanta #17

1801 Piedmont Avenue NE, 30324
(404) 875-0525

This spacious, rambling Cape Cod home is located in the Peachtree Battle area of Atlanta. Private entry, patio, pool. Dog and cat in residence; no smoking.

Doubles: 1 (PB) $48-56
Type of Beds: 2 Twin
Continental Breakfast
Credit Cards: A, B, C

Beverly Hills Inn

65 Sheridan Drive, 30305
(404) 233-8520

A charming city retreat located one-half block from public transportation, 1.5 miles from Lenox Square, and 5 minutes from the Atlanta Historical Society. Full kitchens, library, free parking, color TV, continental breakfast.

Hosts: Bonnie & Lyle Kleinhans
Doubles: 18 (PB) $59-74
Type of Beds: 18 Queen
Continental Breakfast
Credit Cards: A, B, C
Notes: 2, 5, 7, 8, 9, 10, 11, 12, 14

Woodruff Cottage

100 Waverly Way NE, 30307
(404) 688-9498

The "Honeymoon Cottage" of Robert Woodruff, Atlanta's famous anonymous donor and soft-drink magnate. Totally restored Victorian located on a park in historic Inmon Park. One block from the subway station, close to dining. Twelve-foot ceilings, heart-pine woodwork, fireplaces, antiques, a screened porch, and private garden are yours to enjoy.

Host: Eleanor Matthews
Doubles: 3 (PB) $45-60
Full Breakfast
Credit Cards: No
Notes: 2 (deposit), 5, 6, 7, 8, 9, 10, 11

CLEVELAND

The Schlemmer's Lodging

Rt. 4, Box 4655, 30528
(404) 865-5897

This chalet is nestled in the woods at the Chattahoochee River and offers tubing, canoeing, and trout fishing. The bedrooms are attractively furnished, each with private bath and outside entrance. Alpine Helen, with quaint shops, restaurants, and friendly people, is only fifteen minutes away.

Hosts: Hans & Karla Schlemmer
Singles: 1 (SB) $55
Doubles: 4 (PB) $55
Type of Beds: 2 Twin; 1 Double; 3 King
Continental Breakfast
Minimum stay weekends & holidays: 2
Credit Cards: No
Closed Nov. 15-May 15
Notes: 2, 8, 9

DAHLONEGA

Mountain Top Lodge at Dahlonega

Rt. 3, Box 173, 30533
(404) 864-5257

Share the magic of a secluded country inn surrounded by towering trees and spectacular views. Enjoy antique-filled rooms, cathedral-ceiling great room, spacious decks, and porches. Generous country breakfast with home-made biscuits.

Host: David Middleton
Doubles: 8 (PB) $62.40
Suite (PB) $72.80
Type of Beds: 2 Twin; 7 Double
Full Breakfast
Minimum stay holidays: 2
Credit Cards: A, B, C
Notes: 2, 5, 7, 8 (12 and over), 9

The Smith House

202 South Chestatee, 30533
(404) 864-3566

Experience country hospitality in an 1884 inn. Old-time charm combined with new-fangled comforts. All rooms have TV and private baths. Enjoy our famous family-style meals: three meats and nine to ten vegetables served daily.

Hosts: Fred, Shirley, Chris & Freida Welch
Doubles: 18 (PB) $52-60
Continental Breakfast
Credit Cards: A, B, C, D
Closed Christmas Day
Notes: 3, 4, 5, 7, 8, 10, 11, 14

The Smith House

HELEN

Hilltop Haus

Chattahoochee Street, Box 154, 30545
(404) 878-2388

Contemporary split-level overlooking alpine Helen and the Chattahoochee River. Near the foothills of the Smoky Mountains, six miles from the Appalachian Trail. Rich wood paneling and fireplaces create a homey atmosphere for the traveler. Home-made biscuits and preserves.

Host: Ms. Frankie Tysor
Doubles: 5 (3 PB; 2 SB) $50-60
Type of Beds: 2 Double; 3 Queen
Full Breakfast
Minimum stay weekends & holidays: 2
Credit Cards: A, B
Notes: 2, 5, 7, 8 (over 10), 9, 10, 11, 12, 13

NOTES: Credit cards accepted: A Master Card; B Visa; C American Express; D Discover Card; E Diners Club; F Other: 2 Personal checks accepted: 3 Lunch available: 4 Dinner available: 5 Open all year

ST. SIMONS

Little St. Simons Island

Box 1078, 31522
(912) 638-7472

Privately owned 10,000-acre barrier island retreat with six miles of pristine beaches. Comfortable accommodations, bountiful regional meals with hors d'oeuvres and wine, horseback riding, fishing, boating, canoeing, bird watching, naturalist expeditions. A very unique experience in an unspoiled, natural environment.

Hosts: Ben Gibbens & Debbie McIntyre
Doubles: 12 (10 PB; 2 SB) $250-375
Full Breakfast
Credit Cards: A, B
Closed Nov. 15-Feb. 15
Notes: 2, 4, 7, 8 (5 and over), 9, 11, 14

SAUTEE

The Stovall House

Rt. 1, Box 1476, 30571
(404) 878-3355

Our 1837 farmhouse beckons you for a country experience in the historic Sautee Valley near Helen. The award-winning restoration and personal touches here will make you feel at home. Enjoy mountain views in all directions. Our restaurant, recognized as one of the top fifty in Georgia, features regional cuisine with a fresh difference.

Hosts: Ham & Kathy Schwartz
Doubles: 5 (PB) $68.75
Type of Beds: 3 Double; 2 King
Continental Breakfast
Credit Cards: A, B
Notes: 2, 3, 4, 5, 7 (limited), 8, 9, 10, 11, 12

SAVANNAH

Bed and Breakfast Inn

117 West Gordon Street, 31401
(912) 238-0518

We are located in a 1853 townhouse in the historic district of Savannah, amid old mansions, museums, restaurants, churches, and antique shops. Within easy walking distance to most major attractions and River Street.

Host: Robert T. McAlister
Doubles: 12 (4 PB; 8 SB) $33-71.50
Type of Beds: 6 Twin; 15 Queen
Full Breakfast
Credit Cards: A, B, C
Notes: 2, 5, 7, 8, 9, 14

Eliza Thompson House

5 West Jones Street, 31401
(912) 236-3620

Built in 1847, this elegant Federal Style inn is in the heart of Savannah's historic district. A wine and cheese reception is held daily between 5:00-7:00 P.M. Our friendly staff will assist with reservations for tours and meals.

Host: David Barrow
Doubles: 25 (PB) $85.80-118.80
Continental Breakfast
Minimum stay March St. Patrick's Day: 2
Children under 5 free
Credit Cards: A, B, C
Notes: 2, 5, 7, 8, 9, 10, 12, 14

The Forsyth Park Inn

102 West Hall Street, 31401
(912) 233-6800

Circa 1893 Victorian Queen Anne mansion with sixteen-foot ceilings, fourteen-foot doors. Ornate woodwork, floors, stairways, fireplaces, antiques. Whirlpool baths, courtyard cottage. Faces 23-acre park in large historic district. Complimentary wine, social hour; fine dining, tours, beaches all nearby.

Hosts: Virginia & Hal Sullivan
Singles: 1 (PB) $66
Doubles: 9 (PB) $82-143
Type of Beds: 3 Twin; 8 Queen; 2 King
Continental Breakfast
Minimum stay holidays: 2-3
Credit Cards: A, B, C
Notes: 2 (as deposit), 5, 7, 8, 9, 10, 12

6 Pets welcome: 7 Smoking allowed: 8 Children welcome: 9 Social drinking allowed: 10 Tennis available: 11 Swimming available: 12 Golf available: 13 Skiing available: 14 May be booked through travel agents

Jesse Mount House

209 W. Jones Street, 31401
(912) 236-1774

The Jesse Mount House, built in 1854, is in the historic district of Savannah. There are two three-bedroom suites accommodating from one to six people in a party. The house and suites have many rare antiques and reproductions. The garden suite has a full kitchen and access to the walled rose garden. The upper suite has high, four-poster beds with canopies. Gilded harps are in the parlor and dining room, since your hostess is a concert harpist.

Hosts: Howard Crawford & Lois Bannerman
Suites: 2-3 (PB) $85 for 2
Continental-plus Breakfast
Credit Cards: No
Notes: 2, 5, 6 (limited), 7, 8, 9, 10, 11, 12, 14

Liberty Inn -- 1834

Liberty Inn — 1834

128 W. Liberty Street, 31401
(912) 233-1007; 1-800-637-1007

Two- and three-room luxury suites with family rooms, kitchenettes, private baths, queen-size beds, period and antique furnishings, private phones, cablevision, VCRs. Eight-foot heated spa. Located in the heart of Savannah's historic district.

Hosts: Frank & Janie Harris
Suites: 5 (PB) $95-120
Type of Beds: 10 Queen
Continental Breakfast
Credit Cards: A, B, C
Notes: 2, 5, 7, 8, 9, 12, 14

Presidents' Quarters

225 E. President Street, 31401
(912) 233-1600

A premier historic inn in the heart of the historic district, offering deluxe accommodations at affordable prices. Amenities include a full afternoon tea, complimentary continental-plus breakfast, Georgia wine. Suites feature Jacuzzi bathtubs, color cable TV with VCRs, gas-log fireplaces, ceiling fans. Balconies overlook our secluded courtyard and private walled parking. AAA four diamond rated.

Hosts: Muril L. Broy & Sallie Tyran
Doubles: 16 (7 PB; 9 SB) $85-175
Type of Beds: 14 Double; 3 Queen; 6 King
Continental Breakfast
Credit Cards: A, B, C, E
Notes: 2, 5, 7, 8, 9, 10, 11, 12, 14

SENOIA

The Culpepper House

35 Broad Street, 30276
(404) 599-8182

Treat yourself to a whimsical Victorian adventure in this restored home located in a picturesque country town just thirty minutes south of Atlanta's airport.

Host: Mary A. Brown
Doubles: 4 (1 PB; 3 SB) $50-55
Type of Beds: 1 Twin; 2 Double; 1 Queen
Continental or Full Breakfast
Credit Cards: No
Notes: 2, 5, 7 (limited), 8 (infants or over 10), 9, 10, 12

The Veranda

252 Seavy Street, 12345
(404) 599-3905

NOTES: Credit cards accepted: A Master Card; B Visa; C American Express; D Discover Card; E Diners Club; F Other: 2 Personal checks accepted: 3 Lunch available: 4 Dinner available: 5 Open all year

Beautifully restored spacious Victorian rooms in a 1907 hotel on the National Register. Just thirty miles south of Atlanta airport. Freshly prepared Southern gourmet meals by reservation. Unusual gift shop featuring kaleidoscopes. Memorabilia and 1930 Wurlitzer player piano pipe organ. One room has a whirlpool bath.

Hosts: Jan & Bobby Boal
Doubles: 9 (PB) $55-85
Type of Beds: 2 Twin; 8 Queen
Full Breakfast
Credit Cards: A, B
Notes: 2, 4, 5, 8, 14

THOMASVILLE

Quail Country #1
Quail Country B&B
1104 Old Monticello Road, Thomasville, 31792
(912) 226-7218

Quaint Williamsburg guest house with pool and an eighteenth-century garden overlooking other dependencies. Private bath, dressing room, and full kitchen.

Doubles: 1 (PB) $50
Type of Beds: 2 Twin; 1 Sofabed
Continental Breakfast
Credit Cards: No
Notes: 2, 5, 8, 9, 10, 11, 12

Quail Country #2
Quail Country B&B
1104 Old Monticello Road, Thomasville, 31792
(912) 226-7218

Located in the Thomasville Historic District and built in 1885, this two-story Victorian was converted into charming apartments in 1940. Complete apartment has a fully equipped kitchen, bedroom, and living room with queen sofa bed.

Doubles: 1 (PB) $60
Type of Beds: 1 Queen; 1 Queen sofabed
Continental Breakfast
Credit Cards: No
Notes: 2, 5, 8, 9, 10, 11, 12

Quail Country #3
Quail Country B&B
1104 Old Monticello Road, Thomasville, 31792
(912) 226-7218

Charming Cape Cod style house on a tree-lined street in a quiet residential area. Enjoy coffee on the terrace that overlooks the attractive garden.

Singles: 1 (SB) $30
Doubles: 1 (PB) $40
Type of Beds: 1 Twin; 1 Queen
Continental Breakfast
Credit Cards: No
Notes: 2, 5, 8, 9, 10, 11, 12

Quail Country #4
Quail Country B&B
1104 Old Monticello Road, Thomasville, 31792
(912) 226-7218

Built in 1900 and located in pecan groves, this neo-classical house features porches with large columns on three sides. Each bedroom has a bath and fireplace. Floors are pine, and the rooms are furnished with antiques.

Doubles: 2 (PB) $30-40
Type of Beds: 1 Double; 1 Queen
Continental Breakfast
Credit Cards: No
Notes: 2, 5, 8, 9, 10, 11, 12

Quail Country #5
Quail Country B&B
1104 Old Monticello Road, Thomasville, 31792
(912) 226-7218

This twenty-five-year-old bungalow in a lovely residential neighborhood has one bedroom with twin beds and private bath.

Doubles: 1 (PB) $30-40
Type of Beds: 2 Twin
Continental Breakfast
Credit Cards: No
Notes: 2, 5, 8, 9, 10, 11

6 Pets welcome: 7 Smoking allowed: 8 Children welcome: 9 Social drinking allowed: 10 Tennis available: 11 Swimming available: 12 Golf available: 13 Skiing available: 14 May be booked through travel agents

Quail Country #6

Quail Country B&B
1104 Old Monticello Road, Thomasville, 31792
(912) 226-7218

Surrounded by natural woodland of oak and pine, this charming country French provincial house is conveniently located near a shopping center and restaurants. Excellent area for walking and bird watching.

Doubles: 1 (PB) $30-40
Type of Beds: 3 Twin
Continental Breakfast
Credit Cards: No
Notes: 2, 5, 8, 9, 10, 11, 12

Quail Country #7

Quail Country B&B
1104 Old Monticello Road, Thomasville, 31792
(912) 226-7218

Located in a lovely residential area, this second-story garage apartment overlooks a beautiful swimming pool. Two bedrooms, bath, kitchen, and living area. Crib available. Your host is an antique-car enthusiast.

Doubles: 2 (SB) $50
Type of Beds: 2 Twin; 2 Double
Continental Breakfast
Credit Cards: No
Notes: 2, 5, 8, 9, 10, 11, 12

Quail Country #8

Quail Country B&B
1104 Old Monticello Road, Thomasville, 31792
(912) 226-7218

Lovely neo-classical house built in 1903, located in the Thomasville Historic District. Guest wing with private entrance includes full bath, queen bed, and small screened porch.

Doubles: 1 (PB) $30-40
Type of Beds: 1 Queen
Continental Breakfast
Credit Cards: No
Notes: 2, 5, 8, 9, 10, 11, 12

Hawaii

B&B Honolulu (Statewide) 1

3242 Kaohinani Drive
Honolulu, HI 96817
(800) 288-4666; (808) 595-7533

Only a short drive to the "night life" in Waikiki, this Japanese/American home has three guest rooms. Each room has TV and a lovely view of the mountain canyons; two have their own lanai. Close to shopping and entertainment; three blocks to the beach. Breakfast is "Minshuku style" (Japanese), unless otherwise requested. Children welcome; smoking outside only. $50.

B&B Honolulu (Statewide) H1

3242 Kaohinani Drive
Honolulu, HI 96817
(800) 288-4666; (808) 595-7533

On the slopes above the "Place of Refugee" in Hanaunau. Unobstructed view of the ocean from the hot tub on the lanai. TV, VCR, refrigerator, microwave. Three light, airy rooms decorated with local art. The hostess is an archery champion who loves to swim and ski on Mauna Kea. $30.

B&B Honolulu (Statewide) M2

3242 Kaohinani Drive
Honolulu, HI 96817
(800) 288-4666; (808) 595-7533

Homestay with three B&B guest rooms, one with a king bed and two with twins. All have private baths and entrances, and the home offers a panoramic view of Haleakala and the ocean. It sits on 2 secluded acres. The hostess is very willing to tell you about her island and prefers adults. $50.

B&B Honolulu (Statewide) M3

3242 Kaohinani Drive
Honolulu, HI 96817
(800) 288-4666; (808) 595-7533

Modern cedar chalet in Paniolo (cowboy) country. The hostess provides beach mats, towels, and picnic supplies for the beach and warm clothing for trips to Haleakala Crater. Enjoy the tropical setting from the comfortable lanai. Her hobbies are music, art, and pampering a retired race horse whose buddy is a fiesty burro. She enjoys sharing anecdotes of our islands. $40.

Haikuleana

69 Haiku Road, 96708
(808) 575-2890

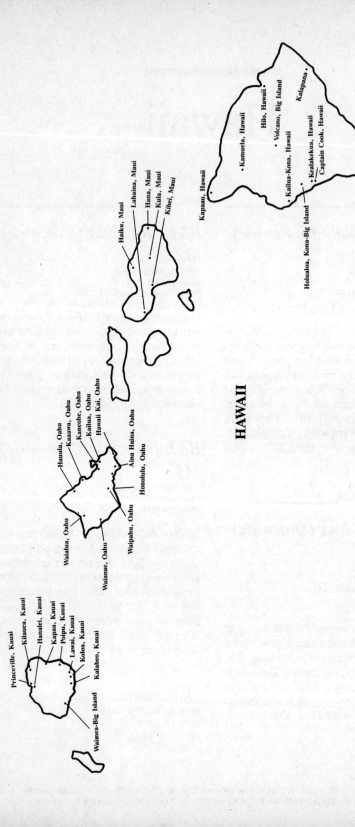

HAWAII

Kamuela, Hawaii
Hilo, Hawaii
Volcano, Big Island
Kailua-Kona, Hawaii
Kalapana
Kealakekua, Hawaii
Captain Cook, Hawaii
Holualoa, Kona-Big Island
Kapaau, Hawaii

Haiku, Maui
Lahaina, Maui
Hana, Maui
Kula, Maui
Kihei, Maui

Hauula, Oahu
Kaaawa, Oahu
Kaneohe, Oahu
Kailua, Oahu
Hawaii Kai, Oahu
Aina Haina, Oahu
Honolulu, Oahu
Waialua, Oahu
Waipahu, Oahu
Waianae, Oahu

Princeville, Kauai
Kilauea, Kauai
Hanalei, Kauai
Kapaa, Kauai
Poipu, Kauai
Lawai, Kauai
Koloa, Kauai
Kalaheo, Kauai
Waimea-Big Island

Hawaiian country life, situated among pineapple fields, close to fine dining, shopping, and super beaches. Only fifteen minutes from the airport, on the way to Hana and Haleakala crater. Cool nights, warm days.

Hosts: Clark & Denise Champion
Doubles: 2 (SB) $70.85
Type of Beds: 1 Twin; 1 Queen
Continental (Hawaiian) Breakfast
Credit Cards: No
Notes: 2, 5, 7, 8, 9, 10, 11, 12, 14

Haikuleana

HANA, MAUI

Kaia Ranch & Co.

Box 404, 96713
(808) 248-7725

Experience the real Hawaii. Secluded tropical flower farm with animals and friends you'll never forget. Do-nothingness and serenity at its best. Tropical ranch home with large guest area. Casual and clean. Kerosene lamps and rain on a tin roof.

Hosts: JoLoyce & John Kaia
Doubles: 1 (SB) $50
Type of Beds: 2 Twin; 1 Queen
Full Breakfast
Minimum stay: 2
Credit Cards: No
Notes: 5, 10, 11

HANALEI, KAUAI

B&B Honolulu (Statewide) K1

3242 Kaohinani Drive
Honolulu, HI 96817
(800) 288-4666; (808) 595-7533

One room in a two-bedroom, two-bath condo. the hostess serves a continental breakfast. Take a short walk down the path to a very private, lovely sandy beach. Enjoy the peace and tranquility of paradise. $55.

Haena Hideaway

Go Native...Hawaii, Box 13115, Lansing, MI, 48901
(517) 349-9598

Luxuriate in the splendor of a lovely tropical home only one block from a sandy beach. The home, reminiscent of a plantation estate, is spacious and sits in a garden of lush vegetation. A cozy bedroom is offered in the main home, or you may prefer the charming studio cottage, which has a stove and refrigerator. Within walking distance of Charo's restaurant.

Doubles: 2 (PB) $50-65
Type of Beds: 2 Double
Continental Breakfast
Credit Cards: No
Notes: 2, 5, 9, 10, 11, 12

HAUULA, OAHU

B&B Honolulu (Statewide) 2

3242 Kaohinani Drive
Honolulu, HI 96817
(800) 288-4666; (808) 595-7533

If you wish a quiet time in luxurious, lush, secluded surrounding, you will enjoy this oceanside estate on the North Shore of Oahu. Choose one of the three suites in the main house. Pick your own bananas and papayas; macadamia nuts provided in the rooms. Swimming pool, Jacuzzi, TV. Near the Polynesian Cultural Center, Waimea Falls, North Shore surfing, and the historic town of Hale'iwa. $60.

HAWAII KAI, OAHU

B&B Honolulu (Statewide) 3

3242 Kaohinani Drive
Honolulu, HI 96817
(800) 288-4666; (808) 595-7533

Attached studio. Enjoy the fantastic ocean view from the private lanai overlooking Molokai, Lanai and Haleakaua Mountain on the island of Maui. Also has a charcoal grill for your use on the lanai. Golf, shopping, restaurants are nearby. Just fifteen minutes to Waikiki; two miles to sandy beach. Full cooking facilities; very quiet. $50.

HILO, HAWAII

B&B Honolulu (Statewide) H2

3242 Kaohinani Drive
Honolulu, HI 96817
(800) 288-4666; (808) 595-7533

This beautiful home was used to film "Black Widow." Jacuzzi and pool; all rooms have ocean view. The guest rooms adjoin the guest family room. No drapes anywhere, but you have complete privacy, since the house is built so no one can see in. Enjoy a relaxed vacation on a bluff overlooking the beach. Host has a dog and cat. $50.

B&B Honolulu (Statewide) H3

3242 Kaohinani Drive
Honolulu, HI 96817
(800) 288-4666; (808) 595-7533

Two-story "Sugar Plantation, Camp Style," with private bath and entrance. Guest room has TV, refrigerator, not pot. View the entire coastline at breakfast from the 1,000 foot elevation, and enjoy cool nights. Rainbow Falls, the pools below, boiling ports, and caves close by. Very country, very quiet. $35.

B&B Honolulu (Statewide) H4

3242 Kaohinani Drive
Honolulu, HI 96817
(800) 288-4666; (808) 595-7533

Hale Alani is on an acre of landscaped yard with towering coconut trees overlooking Hilo Bay and less than a quarter mile from downtown Hilo. Two rooms accommodate two people each and share a bath. Your hostess is Hawaiian born and happy to help. Ten minutes to the airport. Enjoy the sun and moon rise from the back deck; view the ocean from the large porch, or have a sit in the hot tub. $35.

B&B Honolulu (Statewide) H5

3242 Kaohinani Drive
Honolulu, HI 96817
(800) 288-4666; (808) 595-7533

Two miles out of Hilo on a cliff overlooking Hilo Bay, this Hawaiian-type home has a private yard with lovely pool. The yard is beautifully landscaped, and there's also a charming tea house on the grounds. Children who can swim and smokers are accepted. $40.

HOLUALOA, KONA-BIG ISLAND

Bell's Bed & Breakfast
Go Native...Hawaii, Box 13115, Lansing, MI, 48901
(517) 349-9598

NOTES: Credit cards accepted: A Master Card; B Visa; C American Express; D Discover Card; E Diners Club; F Other: 2 Personal checks accepted: 3 Lunch available: 4 Dinner available: 5 Open all year

A lovely B&B site 1,000 feet above the Kona resort in the quaint art community of Holualoa. Expansive mountain and ocean views. The new deluxe suite has a private entry, spacious bedroom high among the trees, a bath of native Koa, sitting room with three decks. Japanese furo for your enjoyment. This is the real Hawaii, only eight miles above the ocean with spectacular views of the coastline.

Doubles: 1 (PB) $80
Type of Beds: 1 King
Continental Breakfast
Credit Cards: No
Notes: 2, 5, 7, 8, 9, 10, 11, 12

Holualoa Inn

Box 222N, 96725
(808) 324-1121

This architectural masterpiece features a spectacular view of the Kona coast. Located in the Kona coffee district on a 40-acre estate, the inn is a peaceful retreat, yet within a short drive of Kailua Village and many activities.

Hosts: Desmond & Karen Twigg-Smith
Doubles: 4 (PB) $54.50-119.90
Type of Beds: 2 Twin; 1 Queen; 2 King
Continental Breakfast
Minimum stay: 2
Credit Cards: A, B, E, F
Notes: 2, 5, 8 (12 and over), 9, 10, 11, 12, 14

HONOLULU, OAHU

B&B Honolulu (Statewide) 4

3242 Kaohinani Drive
Honolulu, HI 96817
(800) 288-4666; (808) 595-7533

This home is located on a high ridge about fifteen minutes from Waikiki by car. The bedrooms offer a beautiful view of the ocean and Koko Marina. Hanauma Bay (Oahu's best snorkeling beach), two shopping centers, and other tourist attractions are all within a five-minute drive. The bedrooms are large and have private baths. $50.

B&B Honolulu (Statewide) 5

3242 Kaohinani Drive
Honolulu, HI 96817
(800) 288-4666; (808) 595-7533

Located in Waikiki, a short ten-minute walk to the beach. The host offers a guest room with queen bed and a private bath. The hostess provides a continental tropical breakfast. You are welcome to use her kitchen, washer, and dryer. Enjoy the Beta machine or the piano. Wheel chair accessible. $50.

B&B Honolulu (Statewide) 6

3242 Kaohinani Drive
Honolulu, HI 96817
(800) 288-4666; (808) 595-7533

This ten -by-twenty foot Waikiki studio, attached to the host's home, is very convenient for the guests. One block to the zoo, two blocks to the beach, .5 block to the convenience store. Enjoy sunbathing in the yard. Hostess provides books, games, and picnic supplies; children welcome. $40.

B&B Honolulu (Statewide) 7

3242 Kaohinani Drive
Honolulu, HI 96817
(800) 288-4666; (808) 595-7533

This Oahu home is about two miles from Pearl Harbor and the *Arizona* memorial. Two rooms available, kitchen privileges, laundry facilities. Color TV in the living room. The hosts enjoys sharing island information with visitors. Children and smokers accepted. $30.

6 Pets welcome: 7 Smoking allowed: 8 Children welcome: 9 Social drinking allowed: 10 Tennis available: 11 Swimming available: 12 Golf available: 13 Skiing available: 14 May be booked through travel agents

B&B Honolulu (Statewide) 8

3242 Kaohinani Drive
Honolulu, HI 96817
(800) 288-4666; (808) 595-7533

Centrally located on the island of Oahu, this host home offers a complete private studio with full kitchen, TV, and phone. In the lush, cool, tropical setting of Nuuanu, yet only twenty minutes from Waikiki or thirty to Kailua, on the opposite side of the island. $45.

B&B Honolulu (Statewide) 9

3242 Kaohinani Drive
Honolulu, HI 96817
(800) 288-4666; (808) 595-7533

This comfortable guest room is located in the Makiki/University area. Twin or king beds. The host is a lively, happy person who goes out of her way for her guests. The bath is shared with the hosts. You are welcome to use the kitchen. Close to a major bus line. $25.

B&B Honolulu (Statewide) 10

3242 Kaohinani Drive
Honolulu, HI 96817
(800) 288-4666; (808) 595-7533

Host offers extra bedroom in his condo on the slopes of Punchbowl. Panoramic sunrise-to-sunset views from Diamond Head to the Waianae Range. The Kama'aina host will share his knowledge of Hawaiiana. Tastefully furnished in traditional Hawaiian rattan and Oriental carpets. Artwork depicting old Hawaii. Use of kitchen, TV, laundry, pool. $50.

B&B Honolulu (Statewide) 11

3242 Kaohinani Drive
Honolulu, HI 96817
(800) 288-4666; (808) 595-7533

Two blocks from Waikiki Beach, this tasteful condo offers two guest rooms. Enjoy the view of downtown Waikiki and the beach in the day and the beautiful stars and sunsets in the evening. Easy walking distance to shopping, restaurants, shows, and all the color of Waikiki. Or take a quiet stroll along the Ala Wai Canal. $37.50.

Hale O' Kahala

Go Native...Hawaii, Box 13115, Lansing, MI, 48901
(517) 349-9598

In the Hale O' Kahala compound, two cottage units are available, both with full kitchens and baths. This delightful location captures the romantic spirit of Carmel, California, and the beautiful Hawaiian Islands. All units surround the brick covered lanai adorned with hanging flower baskets and shaded by large avocado and banyan trees.

Doubles: 2 (PB) $55-75
Type of Beds: 2 Double
Continental Breakfast
Minimum stay: 3
Credit Cards: No
Notes: 2, 5, 9, 10, 11, 12

The Manoa Valley Inn

2001 Vancouver Drive, 96822
(800) 634-5115

An intimate country inn located in lush Manoa Valley, just two miles from Waikiki Beach. Furnished in antiques, each room is individually decorated to enhance its charm and personality. Continental breakfast buf-

NOTES: Credit cards accepted: A Master Card; B Visa; C American Express; D Discover Card; E Diners Club; F Other: 2 Personal checks accepted: 3 Lunch available: 4 Dinner available: 5 Open all year

fet, wine and cheese tasting served daily on the shady lanai.

Host: Marianne Schultz
Doubles: 8 (5 PB; 3 SB) $87.20-158.05
Type of Beds: 5 Double; 2 Queen; 2 King
Continental Breakfast
Credit Cards: A, B
Notes: 2, 5, 7, 8 (14 and over), 9, 10, 11, 12

Rainbow Bed & Breakfast

Go Native...Hawaii, Box 13115, Lansing, MI, 48901
(517) 349-9598

A large five-bedroom bed & breakfast home in the Pacific Heights area of Honolulu. The breathtaking view of the city and ocean is magnificent! Huge common living room for guests.

Singles: 1 (SB) $30
Doubles: 4 (3 PB; 1 SB) $35-45
Type of Beds: 2 Twin; 1 Double; 2 Queen
Continental Breakfast
Credit Cards: No
Notes: 2, 5, 8, 9, 10, 11, 12

B&B Honolulu (Statewide) 12

3242 Kaohinani Drive
Honolulu, HI 96817
(800) 288-4666; (808) 595-7533

North Shore Oahu. Host offers a 940 square foot upstairs apartment above his home. Queen hideabed in the living room; kitchen equipped for light cooking; TV; full bath. Weekly maid service. Enjoy the view of the cerdant Koolaus (mountains) and the crystal-blue Pacific from the front and back lani's. One-half block to the beach. Post office, shopping, restaurants are within half a mile. $60.

B&B Honolulu (Statewide) H6

3242 Kaohinani Drive
Honolulu, HI 96817
(800) 288-4666; (808) 595-7533

Four beautiful, scenic, oceanview rooms, each with its own patio, color TV, and the special Kona breeze. Convenient — two blocks to Magic Sands Beach, .5 mile to Kahaluu Beach and its famous snorkeling. Near golf and shopping areas. Snorkel and beach gear provided; BBQ pavilion available for cookouts. Adults only. $50.

B&B Honolulu (Statewide) 13

3242 Kaohinani Drive
Honolulu, HI 96817
(800) 288-4666; (808) 595-7533

This home is only fifty yards from the beach. It has a lovely patio and yard area for guest use. Breakfast is served on a covered lanai. $40.

B&B Honolulu (Statewide) 14

3242 Kaohinani Drive
Honolulu, HI 96817
(800) 288-4666; (808) 595-7533

On the Windward side of Oahu, this attached studio is on the grounds of an estate. It has its own entrance, will sleep four, and has light cooking facilities. You're welcome to use the pool. The hostess has lived on Oahu since shortly after WWII and is glad to provide tips to plan your time. The privacy of this location makes a car necessary. Children and smokers accepted. $40.

6 Pets welcome: 7 Smoking allowed: 8 Children welcome: 9 Social drinking allowed: 10 Tennis available: 11 Swimming available: 12 Golf available: 13 Skiing available: 14 May be booked through travel agents

B&B Honolulu (Statewide) 15
3242 Kaohinani Drive
Honolulu, HI 96817
(800) 288-4666; (808) 595-7533

This lovely studio is attached to the host's home. Complete cooking facilities, a lanai with view of the pool, which you are welcome to use. Enjoy pool-side sunning. Offers lots of privacy. Cool, airy unit with TV, phone. Less than two miles to the beach, close to shopping and golf. $50.

B&B Honolulu (Statewide) 16
3242 Kaohinani Drive
Honolulu, HI 96817
(800) 288-4666; (808) 595-7533

Located on the windward side of Oahu, this lovely home offers a comfortable guest room with king bed, private bath, and a lovely view of the ocean. The hosts provides a continental breakfast. Located close to shopping, golf, restaurants, and only four blocks to the beach. $45.

B&B Honolulu (Statewide) 17
3242 Kaohinani Drive
Honolulu, HI 96817
(800) 288-4666; (808) 595-7533

This host offers an attached studio for the B&B traveler. Color TV, light cooking facilities, private bath, queen bed, and a futon sofa for extra guests. One block to the beach. Away from the bustle of Waikiki, the unit offers a quiet vacation in a convenient location for touring the island. $55.

B&B Honolulu (Statewide) 18
3242 Kaohinani Drive
Honolulu, HI 96817
(800) 288-4666; (808) 595-7533

A private compound less than a block from Kailua Bay Beach, the wind-surfing capital of the world. The host offers a studio and a cottage. Wake up to the fragrance of tropical fruits, flowers, and the sound of birds. The grounds are landscaped with lush tropical flora. $65.

B&B Honolulu (Statewide) 19
3242 Kaohinani Drive
Honolulu, HI 96817
(800) 288-4666; (808) 595-7533

This host offers a large and a small cottage located on the grounds of his home. The larger cottage is a full one-bedroom unit; the other is a studio. One block to the beach, completely private, with color TV. $50.

B&B Honolulu (Statewide) 20
3242 Kaohinani Drive
Honolulu, HI 96817
(800) 288-4666; (808) 595-7533

An original beach estate one hundred feet from world-renowned Kailua Bay. Completely renovated. The white sands of Kailua Beach are a quiet respite from the noise and congestion of Waikiki. The gentle wash of the bay's breaking surf will lull you to sleep at night. Walk to the center of Kailua Town. Two cottages; two guest rooms. $55.

NOTES: Credit cards accepted: A Master Card; B Visa; C American Express; D Discover Card; E Diners Club; F Other: 2 Personal checks accepted: 3 Lunch available: 4 Dinner available: 5 Open all year

B&B Honolulu (Statewide) 21

3242 Kaohinani Drive
Honolulu, HI 96817
(800) 288-4666; (808) 595-7533

A delightful, fully furnished, spacious garden studio just a one-minute walk from one of the most beautiful swimming and windsurfing beaches on Oahu. Oriental rugs, comfortable chairs, TV, and radio. Tub and shower. Has its own lanai and parking space. Wheel chair accessible. $55.

B&B Honolulu (Statewide) 23

3242 Kaohinani Drive
Honolulu, HI 96817
(800) 288-4666; (808) 595-7533

Away from the bustle of Waikiki Beach, this host has a guest wing with three units, family room with TV, and pool. The home is casual and relaxed. Enjoy the view of the golf course or stroll down to the boat dock on the quiet canal that runs just beyond the landscaped lawn. Ice maker and host's refrigerator available for your beverages. Children who can swim are welcome. $45.

B&B Honolulu (Statewide) 24

3242 Kaohinani Drive
Honolulu, HI 96817
(800) 288-4666; (808) 595-7533

One-bedroom detached cottage, just a five-minute walk from the beach and next door to a park. The bedroom is air-conditioned, the living room has two twin beds. Fully equipped kitchen, phone, cable TV, radio. Children welcome. $65.

B&B Honolulu (Statewide) 25

3242 Kaohinani Drive
Honolulu, HI 96817
(800) 288-4666; (808) 595-7533

This attractively decorated single-family home offers two rooms for guests, one with TV. Limited kitchen and refrigerator privileges. The host offers warm hospitality, maps, and snorkeling gear. Enjoy a hearty continental breakfast on the lanai with a view of Mt. Olomana. Five minutes to Kailua Beach by car, although a car is not essential. $35.

Bed & Breakfast Pacific-Hawaii

19 Kai Nani Place, 96734
(800) 263-4848

Beachfront executive home. Separate guest entrance, private bath, cooking facilities, phone, TV. Located on four miles of white sand beach in a nontouristy, safe, residential neighborhood. Ideal swimming; walk to shops and restaurants.

Host: Doris Epp
Doubles: 2 (PB) $75
Continental Breakfast
Credit Cards: No
Notes: 5, 7, 8,, 9, 10, 11, 12, 14

Hawaiian Dreams Bed & Breakfast

Go Native...Hawaii, Box 13115, Lansing, MI, 48901
(517) 349-9598

Wake up to the fragrance of tropical fruit and the sound of birds. A delightful location in Kailua, landscaped with lush tropical

6 Pets welcome: 7 Smoking allowed: 8 Children welcome: 9 Social drinking allowed: 10 Tennis available: 11 Swimming available: 12 Golf available: 13 Skiing available: 14 May be booked through travel agents

flora. The room in the main house has its own entrance, bath, color TV.

Doubles: 1 (PB) $65
Type of Beds: 1 Double
Continental Breakfast
Credit Cards: No
Notes: 2, 5, 7, 9, 10, 11, 12

Kailua Bed & Breakfast

Go Native...Hawaii, Box 13115, Lansing, MI, 48901
(517) 349-9598

Beautiful home with a swimming pool, located beside a quiet stream and golf course and within walking distance to Kailua Beach Park. A master bedroom in the main house is available with a separate entrance. Also available is a lovely cottage with living room, bedroom, and kitchenette. Large whirlpool bath.

Cottage: 1 (PB) $65
Doubles: 1 (PB) $40
Type of Beds: 1 Double; 1 Queen
Continental Breakfast
Credit Cards: No
Notes: 2, 5, 9, 11, 12

Mauna'Ikina Bed & Breakfast

Go Native...Hawaii, Box 13115, Lansing, MI, 48901
(517) 349-9598

This almost-new, two-story cedar home is about three miles above Kailua town center. Guest quarters are located on the lower level of the home and include a two-bedroom apartment unit, private bath, complete kitchen, and living area with a large deck. Hot tub, color cable TV, and radio.

Doubles: 2 (PB) $55
Type of Beds: 2 Twin; 1 Double
Continental Breakfast
Credit Cards: No
Notes: 2, 5, 8, 9, 10, 11, 12

KALAHEO, KAUAI

B&B Honolulu (Statewide) K2

3242 Kaohinani Drive
Honolulu, HI 96817
(800) 288-4666; (808) 595-7533

Kalaheo countryside! Three delightful self-contained cottages adjacent to the host's custom-built home. They feature antique stained and leaded windows from New Zealand. Full kitchens, TV, daily linen service. Ten minutes to the golden beaches; five to golf and tennis. $40.

KALAPANA

Kalani Honua

RR. 2, Box 4500, 96778
Reservations (800) 367-8047, ext. 669
Information (808) 965-7828

Kalani Honua welcomes guests to a pleasant country retreat. Four cedar lodges provide simple, comfortable accommodations on 20 secluded, oceanfront, landscaped acres of paradise on the Big Island. Our cafe serves delicious, healthy cuisine at reasonable rates. The spirit of aloha awaits you!

Host: Richard Koob
Singles: 19 (SB) $35-72
Doubles: 16 (9 PB; 7 SB) $20-72
Type of Beds: 32 Twin; 15 Double; 1 King
Full Breakfast
Credit Cards: A, B, C, E, F
Notes: 2, 3, 4, 5, 7, 8, 9, 10, 11, 14

KAMUELA, HAWAII

B&B Honolulu (Statewide) H7

3242 Kaohinani Drive
Honolulu, HI 96817
(800) 288-4666; (808) 595-7533

NOTES: Credit cards accepted: A Master Card; B Visa; C American Express; D Discover Card; E Diners Club; F Other: 2 Personal checks accepted: 3 Lunch available: 4 Dinner available: 5 Open all year

This lovely B&B adjoins the Parker Ranch in Waimea. The unit is cool, comfortable, quiet, and private. Sleeps four. Room TV and refrigerator. The host serves a true country breakfast. Enjoy the mountain stream with is ohia, giner, and ferns. Thirty minutes to the beach, ten to the airport. $30.

B&B Honolulu (Statewide) H8

3242 Kaohinani Drive
Honolulu, HI 96817
(800) 288-4666; (808) 595-7533

Hawaiian missionary-style home in Parker Ranch country. Acre lot beside a quiet, meandering stream. Guest quarters and sitting room are completely private, with a 360-degree mountain-ocean view. The host is a sailing enthusiast. The hostess, a nature lover, makes soft sculptured Hawaiian nene (geese). $40.

KANEOHE, OAHU

B&B Honolulu (Statewide) 26

3242 Kaohinani Drive
Honolulu, HI 96817
(800) 288-4666; (808) 595-7533

Two guest rooms, one with private bath and a king bed, and one with a shared bath and twin beds. An island home with louvered walls. You can enjoy viewing Kaneohe Bay and Chinaman's Hat. Ginger, banana, tangerine, and other fruit-bearing trees and tropical garden. $36.

B&B Honolulu (Statewide) 28

3242 Kaohinani Drive
Honolulu, HI 96817
(800) 288-4666; (808) 595-7533

Large, spacious, airy room with bay view and veranda. TV, radio, and refrigerator in the room. Also a small studio with a small price: double hot plate, refrigerator, and microwave. Nice view. $35.

House of Blue Ginger

Go Native...Hawaii, Box 13115, Lansing, MI, 48901
(517) 349-9598

A lovely island-style home on Oahu's windward side with panoramic views of the majestic Koolau mountains and Kaneohe Bay. Home features lots of windows, three guest rooms. Your hostess, a writer from Scotland, serves afternoon tea.

Doubles: 3 (1 PB; 2 SB) $40-50
Type of Beds: 3 Double
Continental Breakfast
Credit Cards: No
Notes: 2, 5, 8, 9, 10, 11, 12

Kaneohe Bed & Breakfast

Go Native...Hawaii, Box 13115, Lansing, MI, 48901
(517) 349-9598

A delightful tropical home with a wonderful ambience. Located in the bedroom community of Kaneohe, the home features one guest room with private bath, beautifully furnished with antiques. The home has a swimming pool and overlooks Kaneohe Bay and the ancient Heeia Fish Pond. Friendly, caring hosts.

Doubles: 1 (PB) $45
Type of Beds: 1 Double
Continental Breakfast
Credit Cards: No
Notes: 2, 5, 9, 10, 11, 12

Queen Emma's Bed & Breakfast

Go Native...Hawaii, Box 13115, Lansing, MI, 48901
(517) 349-9598

6 Pets welcome: 7 Smoking allowed: 8 Children welcome: 9 Social drinking allowed: 10 Tennis available: 11 Swimming available: 12 Golf available: 13 Skiing available: 14 May be booked through travel agents

A modern, spacious island home featuring five guest rooms with access to kitchen, dining area, color TV, and lounge. Located in beautiful Temple Valley on the windward side of Oahu, approximately twenty-five minutes from Waikiki Beach. Private entrance, gracious hosts.

Doubles: 5 (2 PB; 3 SB) $35-45
Type of Beds: 2 Twin; 2 Queen; 1 King
Continental Breakfast
Credit Cards: No
Notes: 2, 5, 8, 9, 10, 11, 12

KAPAA, KAUAI

Kay Barker's Bed & Breakfast
Box 740, 96746
(808) 822-3073

The home is in a lovely garden setting, in a quiet rural area, with pastoral and mountain views. There is a large living room, TV room, extensive library, and lanai for you to enjoy. Brochures are available.

Host: Kay Barker
Doubles: 4 (PB) $54.50
Type of Beds: 2 Twin; 1 Double; 1 Queen; 1 King
Continental Breakfast
Credit Cards: No
Notes: 2, 5, 7, 8, 9, 10, 11, 12, 14

Wailua Bed & Breakfast
Go Native...Hawaii, Box 13115, Lansing, MI, 48901
(517) 349-9598

In a beautiful residential neighborhood looking down on the lovely Wailua River. Two complete studio units attached to the main home, both built of expensive Koa wood. Impressive views from each apartment, both of which have a small kitchen. There's also a charming courtyard.

Doubles: 2 (PB) $45-55
Type of Beds: 1 Double; 1 Queen
Continental Breakfast

Credit Cards: No
Notes: 2, 5, 8, 9, 10, 11, 12

KAPPAAU, HAWAII

B&B Honolulu (Statewide) H9
3242 Kaohinani Drive
Honolulu, HI 96817
(800) 288-4666; (808) 595-7533

This large old plantation-manager's home has landscaped grounds, two guest rooms and shared bath. The rooms are bright and airy. Resident dog and cat. Only a half-hour drive to Mauna Kea or the the whale-watching areas. $50.

KEALAKEKUA, HAWAII

B&B Honolulu (Statewide) H10
3242 Kaohinani Drive
Honolulu, HI 96817
(800) 288-4666; (808) 595-7533

This home has an expanse of emerald lawn with palms and exotic fruit trees. Fenced with head-high poinsiettas surrounded by a wall of banana trees. Near groves of coffee and macadamias. Swim in the pool; tennis nearby; beaches only a few miles away. Enjoy bicycling, ping pong, or hiking with your hosts. $35.

KIHEI, MAUI

B&B Honolulu (Statewide) M4
3242 Kaohinani Drive
Honolulu, HI 96817
(800) 288-4666; (808) 595-7533

The queen bedroom in this house has an ocean view and a sitting room. The king room also has a private bath and private entrance. Color TV. Enter the units through

NOTES: Credit cards accepted: A Master Card; B Visa; C American Express; D Discover Card; E Diners Club; F Other: 2 Personal checks accepted: 3 Lunch available: 4 Dinner available: 5 Open all year

a gate into the courtyard, with its gardens and trees. Sit and enjoy the quietness of nature of view the ocean from the lanai. A hearty breakfast is served on the lanai. $50.

B&B Honolulu (Statewide) M5

3242 Kaohinani Drive
Honolulu, HI 96817
(800) 288-4666; (808) 595-7533

This new two-story home is .5 mile from the beach. It offers two bedrooms and a living room with queen hideabed. The bath is shared by the guests. Your continental breakfast is served either on your private patio or upstairs on the deck, with its ocean view. Children are welcome. $55.

B&B Honolulu (Statewide) M6

3242 Kaohinani Drive
Honolulu, HI 96817
(800) 288-4666; (808) 595-7533

This host offers two studios and a room with a private bath and entrance. The studios have light cooking facilities and refrigerator. The host serves a full breakfast. There is an ocean view from the units; only six blocks to the beach; wheel chair accessible. $45.

Corbin Bed & Breakfast

Go Native...Hawaii, Box 13115, Lansing, MI, 48901
(517) 349-9598

On a quiet cul-de-sac just one quarter mile from Kealia Beach in north Kihei, your delightful hosts welcome you to a studio apartment or two-bedroom cottage adjacent to the main house. Completely private, the studio features a kitchen with microwave, small refrigerators, and color cable TV. The cottage accommodates up to four people in two bedrooms, with complete kitchen, bath, living room with a view and cable TV. Large patio and gas barbecue.

Singles: 2 (PB) $40-50
Doubles: 2 (PB) $55-60
Type of Beds: 2 Twin; 2 Double
Continental Breakfast
Credit Cards: No
Notes: 2, 5, 8, 9, 10, 11, 12

KILAUEA, KAUAI

Hale Ho'o Maha Bed & Breakfast

Go Native...Hawaii, Box 13115, Lansing, MI, 48901
(517) 349-9598

Hale Ho'o Maha (House of Rest) is located on the north shore at Kilihiwai Bay. Nestled in a tropical garden, this home is ten steps from one of Hawaii's most beautiful beaches. Hike or boat up the river to waterfalls with lovely pools for swimming. Only minutes away from riding stables, golf, shopping, and good restaurants. The home has one cozy bedroom with a seven-foot round bed and fully equipped kitchen. Boats, gas grill, washer, and cable TV.

Doubles: 1 (SB) $50
Type of Beds: 2 Twin; 1 Queen
Continental Breakfast
Credit Cards: No
Notes: 2, 5, 7, 9, 10, 11, 12

Slippery Slide Bed & Breakfast

Go Native...Hawaii, Box 13115, Lansing, MI, 48901
(517) 349-9598

A marvelous tropical-style two-story redwood home strategically located on the north shore for breathtaking views of Kauai's mountains, valleys, and oceanscapes. Adjacent to "Slippery Slide" Estate and within sound of tranquil water-

6 Pets welcome: 7 Smoking allowed: 8 Children welcome: 9 Social drinking allowed: 10 Tennis available: 11 Swimming available: 12 Golf available: 13 Skiing available: 14 May be booked through travel agents

falls. Each room has a private entrance. Portable Jacuzzi, delightful hosts.

Singles: 1 (SB) $35
Doubles: 2 (SB) $40
Type of Beds: 3 Twin; 1 Double; 1 Queen; Futons
Continental Breakfast
Credit Cards: No
Notes: 2, 5, 8, 9, 10, 11, 12

KOLOA, KAUAI

B&B Honolulu (Statewide) K5

3242 Kaohinani Drive
Honolulu, HI 96817
(800) 288-4666; (808) 595-7533

A residential 1200 square foot daylight basement in panoramic Poipu Beach. Enjoy ocean and mountain views from this spacious, light, airy unit. There is a queen sofa and color TV in the living room. Full shower/tub; fully equipped kitchen. A continental breakfast is provided. $67.

B&B Honolulu (Statewide) K6

3242 Kaohinani Drive
Honolulu, HI 96817
(800) 288-4666; (808) 595-7533

Two lovely guest rooms, well located for easy sightseeing. Room refrigerator, color TV, private patio with tropical view, complete with running stream. Host offers pleasant company and will help with travel plans. Golf, tennis, hiking all nearby. The sandy beaches of Poipu are two miles away. Three-night minimum stay. $35.

Koloa Bed & Breakfast

Go Native...Hawaii, Box 13115, Lansing, MI, 48901
(517) 349-9598

A delightful Japanese-hosted guest house in the countryside. Only two miles from Poipu Beach. Bedroom with private entrance, refrigerator, TV, and small patio. Lush tropical yard with stream.

Doubles: 1 (PB) $35-40
Type of Beds: 2 Twin
Continental Breakfast
Minimum stay: 3
Credit Cards: No
Notes: 2, 5, 9, 10, 11, 12

Poipu Bed & Breakfast

Go Native...Hawaii, Box 13115, Lansing, MI, 48901
(517) 349-9598

Experience Kauai hospitality and relax in the luxurious surroundings of another time and place in an authentic renovated plantation house only one block from Poipu Beach. All rooms have private baths (some with whirlpool tubs), color TV, and refrigerators. Beautifully decorated with white Victorian wicker, fine antiques, and carousel horses. Suites also available; afternoon tea is served.

Doubles: 4 (PB) $65-100
Type of Beds: 4 Twin; 4 King
Continental Breakfast
Credit Cards: A, B
Notes: 2, 5, 8, 9, 10, 11, 12

KULA, MAUI

B&B Honolulu (Statewide) M8

3242 Kaohinani Drive
Honolulu, HI 96817
(800) 288-4666; (808) 595-7533

Two wonderful upstairs suites furnished in antiques and collectibles with room TV and a panoramic view of the islands. Shared bath. Guests have full use of the living room with fireplace. Sprawling grounds with small vineyard, macadamia nut, avocada, loquat trees. Pick your fruit at a moment's whim. $55.

NOTES: Credit cards accepted: A Master Card; B Visa; C American Express; D Discover Card; E Diners Club; F Other: 2 Personal checks accepted: 3 Lunch available: 4 Dinner available: 5 Open all year

B&B Honolulu (Statewide) M9

3242 Kaohinani Drive
Honolulu, HI 96817
(800) 288-4666; (808) 595-7533

Lush, cool, upcountry Maui. Guest room has 300 square feet, plus private entrance and bath, room TV. Savor a breakfast of fresh home-made bread, juice, coffee, and fruit. Host is an orchid grower and conservation enforcement officer. Sit by the fireplace and enjoy viewing Haleakala. $55.

Bloom Cottage Bed & Breakfast

RR 2, Box 229, 96790
(808) 878-1425

The perfect getaway spot, located one-third of the way up Haleakala Crater. Spectacular view; cool mountain climate; surrounded by herb and flower gardens. Antique Hawaiian quilt on four-poster bamboo bed; old wicker in breakfast nook, original art on the walls. The two-bedroom cottage has a full kitchen, large living room with fireplace, breakfast nook, bathroom. Hosts stock your refrigerator; you fix your own breakfast.

Hosts: Herb & Lynne Horner
Cottage: 1, $81.75-92.65
Type of Beds: 1 Twin; 1 Queen
Continental Breakfast
Credit Cards: No
Notes: 2, 5, 8 (by arrangement), 9, 14

Kilohana Bed & Breakfast

Go Native...Hawaii, Box 13115, Lansing, MI, 48901
(517) 349-9598

A "home away from home," plantation style, on the slopes of Haleakala Volcano. Built by an Australian between 55-85 years ago, the lovely home is reminiscent of his heritage and the ambience of the English countryside. Features two wonderful

upstairs suites furnished in antiques and collectibles. Guests have full use of the living room with fireplace and the grounds overlooking the island, a small vineyard, and macadamia nut, avocado, and loquat trees, each bearing fruit you may pick.

Doubles: 2 (SB) $55-65
Type of Beds: 2 Double
Continental Breakfast
Credit Cards: No
Notes: 2, 5, 9, 10, 11, 12

Kula Lodge

Go Native...Hawaii, Box 13115, Lansing, MI, 48901
(517) 349-9598

A marvelous rustic retreat that hugs the mountainside and blends with the astonishing ambience of Upcountry Maui. At 3,200 feet, the lodge sits in a garden of flowers as nearby flower farms color the earth with carnations, protea, and other blossoms. Five chalet-like cabins afford a panoramic view of the West Maui mountains, distant towns, and the Pacific Ocean. Fine dining available at the restaurant on the grounds.

Doubles: 5 (PB) $80-125
Type of Beds: 5 Twin; 1 Double; 4 Queen
Full Breakfast
Credit Cards: A, B
Notes: 2, 3, 4, 5, 8, 9, 14

LAHAINA, MAUI

The Lahaina Hotel

127 Lahainaluna Road, 96761
(808) 661-0577

Located in the heart of Lahaina Town, the Lahaina Hotel is convenient to natural and recreational attractions as well as fine restaurants and shops. The small hotel is lavishly furnished with turn-of-the-century antiques for a look and feel of the period's elegance. Guests enjoy breakfast on the balconies overlooking the bustle of activity on the street below.

Doubles: 12 (PB) $92.65-147.15
Type of Beds: 12 Double
Continental Breakfast
Credit Cards: A, B
Notes: 2, 4, 5, 8 (14 and over), 9, 10, 11, 12

Laha 'Ole Bed & Breakfast

Go Native...Hawaii, Box 13115, Lansing, MI, 48901
(517) 349-9598

A wonderful new (1989) oceanfront home in Lahaina right at the water's edge. Hosts offer one bedroom in the main house with a queen bed, day bed, TV, private bath, and ocean view (sleeps 2).

Doubles: 1 (PB) $55
Type of Beds: 1 Queen
Continental Breakfast
Credit Cards: No
Notes: 2, 5, 8, 9, 10, 11, 12

LAWAI, KAUAI

B&B Honolulu (Statewide) K7

3242 Kaohinani Drive
Honolulu, HI 96817
(800) 288-4666; (808) 595-7533

A 500 square foot studio with TV, kitchen, private lanai with BBQ grill. Enjoy a great view of the mountains and sea, or join the host in a game of bridge. Three acres of country surroundings with horses, dogs and cats. Five minutes to small private beach. $55.

Victoria's Place

Go Native...Hawaii, Box 13115, Lansing, MI, 48901
(517) 349-9598

In a lovely, spacious skylit home perched high in the lush hills of southern Kauai, overlooking thick jungle, whispering cane field, and the beckoning Pacific. All rooms open directly through glass doors onto a pool sur-

rounded by flowering walls of hibiscus, gardenia, ginger, and bougainvillaea. On the pool deck there's a small refrigerator for drinks.

Singles: 1 (SB) $45-55
Doubles: 2 (PB) $55-75
Type of Beds: 2 Twin; 1 Double; 1 Queen
Continental Breakfast
Credit Cards: No
Notes: 2, 5, 9, 10, 11, 12

PAIA, MAUI

B&B Honolulu (Statewide) M11

3242 Kaohinani Drive
Honolulu, HI 96817
(800) 288-4666; (808) 595-7533

Located in the heart of historic Wailuku Town. Meticulously restored 1920s plantation house, surrounded by citrus trees and the blossoming gardens of its residential neighborhood. Minutes from historic sites, shops, and restaurants. Midway between Maui's finest beaches, tourist, and scenic attractions. Ten minutes to the airport. $55.

POIPU, KAUAI

Sprouting Horn Bed & Breakfast

Go Native...Hawaii, Box 13115, Lansing, MI, 48901
(517) 349-9598

An intimate oceanfront retreat offering the paradise you've always dreamed about. Nestled beside lush green fields of sugar cane only one short mile from sunny Poipu Beach, the house is a convenient distance from all of Kauai's noted attractions and activities. Each guest room is uniquely decorated, some with brass beds, antique armoires, and lovely country comforters. Color cable TV, refrigerator, ceiling fan. Formal breakfast with fine china and crystal.

NOTES: Credit cards accepted: A Master Card; B Visa; C American Express; D Discover Card; E Diners Club; F Other: 2 Personal checks accepted: 3 Lunch available: 4 Dinner available: 5 Open all year

Doubles: 5 (2 PB; 3 SB) $50-85
Type of Beds: 2 Twin; 4 Queen; 1 King
Continental Breakfast
Credit Cards: No
Notes: 2, 5, 9, 10, 11, 12

PRINCEVILLE, KAUAI

Hale 'Aha Hospitality House

Box 3370, Princeville, Kauai, Hawaii, 96722
(808) 826-6733; (800) 826-6733

Newly built on 1.5 acres of resort property, this gracious home offers the serenity of 480 feet of fabulous fairway frontage overlooking the ocean and lush mountains of Kauai. Hale 'Aha hospitality also offers honeymoon privacy with separate decks and entrances. Our 1,000-square-foot "Executive Penthouse Suite" has its own balcony, with open beams and views (including "Bali Hai") on three sides.

Hosts: Herb & Ruth Bockelman
Doubles: 3 (PB) $80-220
Type of Beds: 1 Queen; 2 King or 4 Twin
Full Breakfast
Credit Cards: A, B
Notes: 5, 10, 11, 12, 14

VOLCANO, BIG ISLAND

Volcano Bed & Breakfast

Go Native...Hawaii, Box 13115, Lansing, MI, 48901
(517) 349-9598

An historical home, restored to it former grandeur, from the early missionary era. Known as "Heleohu," this three-story home is a historian's delight: hand-poured glass panes in the windows; Franklin Fireplace made in 1867; stairway rails of natural untreated Koa wood branches.

Singles: 1 (SB) $40
Doubles: 4 (1 PB; 3 SB) $50
Type of Beds: 9 Twin; 1 Double; 2 Queen
Continental Breakfast
Credit Cards: No
Notes: 2, 5, 8, 9, 10, 12

Volcano Heart Chalet

Box 404, Hana, Maui 96713
(808) 248-7725

Cozy, comfy, two-story cedar retreat surrounded by exotic native flora. A good base for exploring Volcano National Park and many other attractions. Exercise/sitting room, tree-view porch, light cooking, laundry facilities available at a small fee. Cool nights; flannel sheets!

Hosts: JoLoyce & John Kaia
Doubles: 3 (PB) $50
Type of Beds: 2 Twin; 2 Queen
Continental Breakfast
Minimum stay: 2
Credit Cards: No
Notes: 5, 12

WAIALUA, OAHU

B&B Honolulu (Statewide) 29

3242 Kaohinani Drive
Honolulu, HI 96817
(800) 288-4666; (808) 595-7533

A warm hostess with three guest rooms five minutes from the famous beaches of the North Shore. Guests are welcome to use the TV in the living room or swim in the pool. Enjoy the serene view of the sweeping mountains and valleys. Wailua-town still holds much of the old Hawaiian history. Children over twelve welcome. $45.

WAIANAE, OAHU

B&B Honolulu (Statewide) 30

3242 Kaohinani Drive
Honolulu, HI 96817
(800) 288-4666; (808) 595-7533

On the quiet side of Oahu. The hosts offer a guest room with a double bed and private bath. Enjoy sitting in the yard taking in the sun or take a short walk to the beach. The hosts speak German and Japanese. Children are welcome to share the guest room on a futon. Smoking is allowed on the patio. $45.

WAIMEA, KAUAI

B&B Honolulu (Statewide) K8

3242 Kaohinani Drive
Honolulu, HI 96817
(800) 288-4666; (808) 595-7533

This attached studio is only .5 mile from Waimea Canyon, "The Grand Canyon of the Pacific." It's completely private, with refrigerators, microwave, and coffee maker. Bright and airy, with many windows. Across from the beach. Hostess provides continental breakfast, beach chairs, and ice chests. $50.

NW B&B #2400

NW Bed & Breakfast Travel Unlimited
610 SW Broadway, Portland, OR, 97205
(503) 243-7616

Pleasant, private garden suite in the lovely Parker Ranch area of northern Hawaii. The home is in a quiet residential neighborhood surrounded by pasture land, and has an unsurpassed view of the mountains. The 3,150-foot elevation makes this a cool, comfortable location. Short drive to beautiful white, sandy beaches and championship golf courses.

Doubles: 1 (PB) $36-42
Type of Beds: 1 Double; 1 Double hideabed
Continental Breakfast
Credit Cards: No

WAIPAHU, OAHU

B&B Honolulu (Statewide) 31

3242 Kaohinani Drive
Honolulu, HI 96817
(800) 288-4666; (808) 595-7533

This guest room is located in the Aiea/Waipahu area. Enjoy the Hawaiian sun by the pool or take a leisurely hike down the nearby trail. Enjoy the view of Diamond Head from the front yard. The bath is shared with this lovely German couple. $35.

NOTES: Credit cards accepted: A Master Card; B Visa; C American Express; D Discover Card; E Diners Club; F Other: 2 Personal checks accepted: 3 Lunch available: 4 Dinner available: 5 Open all year

Idaho

BOISE

Idaho Heritage Inn

B&B of Idaho, 109 West Idaho Street, 83702
(208) 342-8066

Built in 1904, this home has been used as a governor's residence and the home of Senator Frank Church. Located in Boise's historic Warm Springs District just five blocks from downtown and adjacent to the park system and Boise State University. Guest rooms are comfortably provided with period furniture.

Doubles: 5 (S2B) $45-75
Type of Beds: 2 Double; 4 Queen
Continental Breakfast
Credit Cards: A, B, C, D
Notes: 2, 5, 7 (limited), 8 (16 and over), 9, 10, 11, 12, 14

COEUR D'ALENE

Greenbriar Bed & Breakfast Inn

315 Wallace, 83814
(208) 667-9660

A three-story brick mansion built in 1908 and furnished with eclectic antiques. Easy walk to Lake Coeur d'Alene. Year-round outdoor spa; summer canoe and tandem bike rentals. Six-course gourmet dinners served Fridays and Saturdays; baby-sitting often available.

Hosts: Kris McIlvenna & Charlene Soucy
Doubles: 7 (4 PB; 3 SB) $35-59
Type of Beds: 4 Double; 2 Queen; 2 King
Full Breakfast
Credit Cards: A, B, C, D
Notes: 2, 4 (Fri. & Sat.), 5, 8, 9, 10, 11, 12, 13, 14

Inn the First Place

509 N 15th Street, 83814
(208) 667-3346

An ex-grocery store? Yes, but now a cozy home. Lots of books, artwork, magazines, and wonderful breakfasts insure a delightful stay. Close to the freeway, downtown shopping, restaurants, and two swimming beaches. Two cats in residence. Reservations suggested.

Hosts: Tom & Lois Knox
Doubles: 3 (S2B) $37.45
Type of Beds: 1 Twin; 1 Double; 1 Queen
Full Breakfast
Credit Cards: A, B
Notes: 2, 5, 7 (limited), 8 (over 10), 9, 10, 11, 12

IDAHO CITY

Idaho City Hotel

Box 70, 83631
(208) 392-4290

Located in an historic gold-mining town, the hotel is furnished with antiques, phones, cable TV and HBO in each room. Near warm springs pool, hiking, fishing, skiing snow mobiling.

Host: Don Campbell
Doubles: 5 (PB) $28-36
Type of Beds: 5 Double
Full Breakfast
Credit Cards: A, B, C, D
Notes: 2, 5, 6, 7, 8, 9, 10, 11, 13, 14

McCALL

Northwest Passage

B&B of Idaho, 109 West Idaho Street, Boise, 83702
(208) 342-8066

6 Pets welcome: 7 Smoking allowed: 8 Children welcome: 9 Social drinking allowed: 10 Tennis available: 11 Swimming available: 12 Golf available: 13 Skiing available: 14 May be booked through travel agents

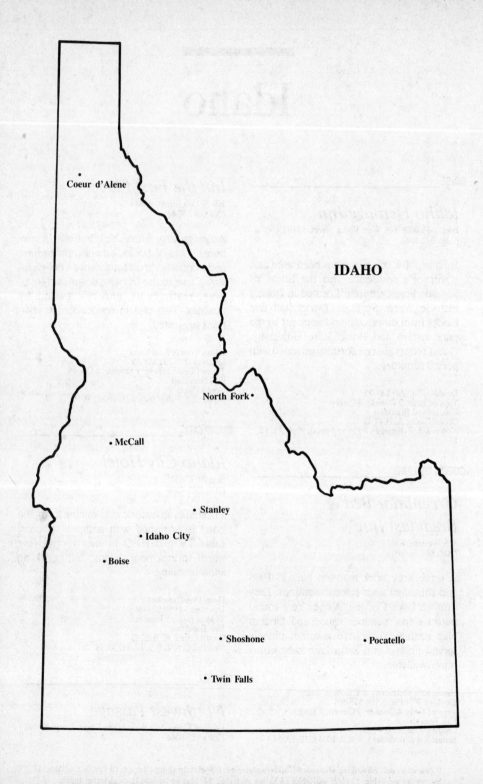

IDAHO

Coeur d'Alene

North Fork

McCall

Stanley

Idaho City

Boise

Shoshone

Pocatello

Twin Falls

Cozy accommodations close to beautiful Payette Lake, Ponderosa State Park, skiing, snowmobile runs, golf, hunting, fishing, and horseback riding.

Doubles: 5 (2 PB; 3 SB) $37.50-45
Type of Beds: 5 Double
Full Breakfast
Credit Cards: A, B
Notes: 2, 5, 7, 8, 9, 10, 11, 12, 13

Indian Creek Guest Ranch

NORTH FORK

Indian Creek Guest Ranch

Rt. 2, Box 105, 83466
Phone Salmon, Idaho, operator and ask for 24F211

Four private modern cabins surrounding a restored 1895 lodge called the Red Onion Bar in gold-mining days. Very isolated, on the border of the central Idaho wilderness. Horseback riding, 4x4 rides, float trips on the Salmon River, fishing, fall hunting, backpacking. There's another beautiful view with every corner you turn.

Host: Jack Briggs
Doubles: 4 (PB) $30-60
Type of Beds: 4 Twin; 3 Double
Full Breakfast
Credit Cards: No
Notes: 2, 3, 4, 5, 6, 7, 8, 9, 13, 14

POCATELLO

Holmes Retreat

178 N. Mink Creek Road, 83204
(208) 232-5518

Breakfast is served on the deck, near songbirds and hummingbirds, with crystal goblets, fresh strawberries, first-prize bran muffins. Fishing, horseshoes, nature walk, and barbecue dinners with soft music and a bonfire. Horseback riding can be arranged. Near a dinosaur exhibit and Old West Fort, with elk, deer, and bison. Three hours from Salt Lake City and Yellowstone Park.

Hosts: Shirley & Acel Holmes
Doubles: 2 (SB) $49-59
Type of Beds: 1 Double; 1 Queen; 2 Airbeds
Full Breakfast
Credit Cards: A, B
Notes: 2, 3, 4, 5, 6 (outside), 8, 10, 11, 12, 13, 14

SHOSHONE

Governor's Mansion Bed & Breakfast Inn

B&B of Idaho, 109 West Idaho Street, Boise, 83702
(208) 342-8066

This mansion was built by a former governor of Idaho and is on the list of National Historic Sites. Complimentary pick up and return to Shoshone Amtrak Station and Twin Falls Airport. Shoshone is within easy traveling distance to Sun Valley, Ketchum, Craters of the Moon, Balanced Rock, the Ice Caves. The region is famous for its trout fishing, big game, and migratory bird hunting.

Doubles: 4 (1 PB; 3 SB) $35-65
Type of Beds: 1 Twin; 3 Double; 1 Queen
Full Breakfast
Credit Cards: A, B, C, D
Notes: 2, 5, 6, 7, 8, 9, 12, 13

6 Pets welcome: 7 Smoking allowed: 8 Children welcome: 9 Social drinking allowed: 10 Tennis available: 11 Swimming available: 12 Golf available: 13 Skiing available: 14 May be booked through travel agents

STANLEY

Sawtooth Hotel
West End of Ace of Diamonds, 83278
(208) 774-9947

Stanley's first bed & breakfast. Warm western hospitality with an uninterrupted view of the Sawtooth Mountains, with their endless recreational opportunities. Enjoy world-famous sourdough pancakes and cinnamon rolls, country-style ham, sausage or bacon, fresh fruit, and other delights.

Hosts: Steve & Kathy Cole
Doubles: 8 (SB) $35-50
Type of Beds: 2 Twin; 7 Double
Full Breakfast
Credit Cards: A, B

Closed Nov. 1-March 1
Notes: 2, 7, 8, 9, 13 (XC)

TWIN FALLS

Hedgerow Manor
B&B of Idaho, 190 West Idaho Street, Boise, 83702
(208) 342-8066

Historic home on Blue Lakes Blvd, tastefully restored with turn-of-the-century furniture. Within walking distance of numerous restaurants, shops, and theaters.

Doubles: 4 (SB) $45
Type of Beds: 4 Double
Continental Breakfast
Credit Cards: No
Notes: 2, 5, 9, 10, 11, 12

NOTES: Credit cards accepted: A Master Card; B Visa; C American Express; D Discover Card; E Diners Club; F Other: 2 Personal checks accepted: 3 Lunch available: 4 Dinner available: 5 Open all year

Illinois

Holden's Guest House
East Main Street, 61419
(309) 927-3500

Opened in 1988, this restored 1869 farmstead is situated on 1.5 acres adjacent to your hosts and within blocks of the Bishop Hill historic district. Originally a commune, the village is a national landmark, offering five museums, restaurants, and over two dozen shops. It's truly a Utopia on the prairie.

Hosts: Linda & Steve Holden
Single suite: 1 (SB) $125
Doubles: 3 (1 PB; 2 SB) $50-60
Type of Beds: 2 Twin; 3 Double; 1 King
Full Breakfast
Credit Cards: A, B
Notes: 2, 4, 5, 6, 7, 8, 9

The Wright Farmhouse
RR 3, 62321
(217) 357-2421

Comfortable, quiet rooms with period furnishings in a restored nineteenth-century home on a working farm. Country charm plus private baths, air-conditioning, and private guest entrance. Nearby attractions include historic town square and courthouse and the scenic Mississippi River.

Hosts: John & Connie Wright
Doubles: 4 (PB) $26.50-37.10
Type of Beds: 2 Double; 1 Queen; 2 Three-quarter size
Continental Breakfast
Credit Cards: No
Notes: 5, 8, 9, 10, 11, 12

Grandma Joan's Homestay
2204 Brett Drive, 61821
(217) 356-5828

This comfortable contemporary home with two fireplaces, large deck, and collection of modern and folk art, is located ten minutes from the University of Illinois. Grandma will pamper you with cookies and milk at bedtime and a healthy breakfast. Let this be your home away from home.

Host: Joan Erickson
Doubles: 3 (SB) $40
Type of Beds: 1 Twin; 1 Double; 1 Queen
Continental Breakfast
Credit Cards: No
Closed Dec. 20 - Jan. 10
Notes: 2, 7, 9, 10, 11, 12

B&B of Chicago #5
Box 14088, 60614
(312) 951-0085

A traditionally furnished three-story townhouse where guests are welcome to enjoy the family room, fireplace. Your host is a seasoned traveler who works as a legal assistant and is a part-time graduate student. Easy access to public transportation, restaurants, shops, theaters, and pubs. Air-conditioning, TV. One double, shared bath, $40-150.

6 Pets welcome: 7 Smoking allowed: 8 Children welcome: 9 Social drinking allowed: 10 Tennis available: 11 Swimming available: 12 Golf available: 13 Skiing available: 14 May be booked through travel agents

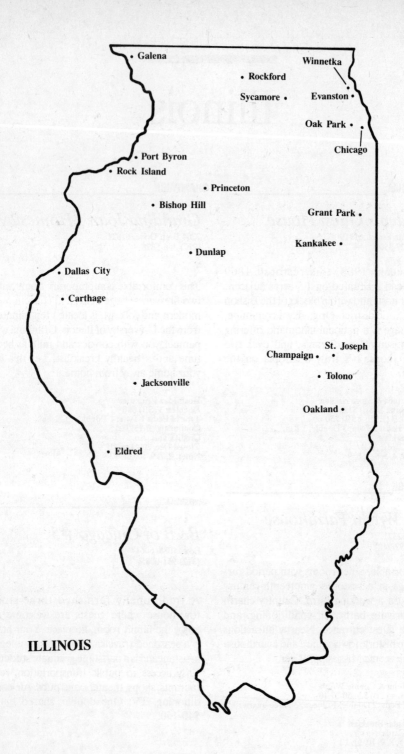

- Galena
- Winnetka
- Rockford
- Sycamore
- Evanston
- Oak Park
- Chicago
- Port Byron
- Rock Island
- Princeton
- Bishop Hill
- Grant Park
- Dunlap
- Kankakee
- Dallas City
- Carthage
- St. Joseph
- Champaign
- Tolono
- Jacksonville
- Oakland
- Eldred

ILLINOIS

B&B of Chicago #17
Box 14088, 60614
(312) 951-0085

Easily accessible to downtown and just a few blocks from Lincoln Park, this large second-floor Victorian apartment offers a sunny room with separate phone line, ceiling fan, and a nice selection of books and magazines. Your host is an interior designer and artist. One single, private bath, $50.

B&B of Chicago #28
Box 14088, 60614
(312) 951-0085

Spacious two-bedroom, two-bath apartment located on Lake Shore Drive near the Drake Hotel and Oak Street Beach. Wonderful lake and city views. Your host is a project management consultant in data processing. Air-conditioning, TV. Women or couples only; no smoking. One double, private bath, with trundle bed, $55-60.

B&B of Chicago #29
Box 14088, 60614
(312) 951-0085

On North Michigan Avenue, close to the John Hancock Building, Water Tower Place, and the Ritz Carlton. This lovely condo apartment on Chicago's premier shopping street, is close to restaurants and museums. Overlooking Michigan Avenue, it boasts antique furnishings. Your host is a semi-retired businessman active in community affairs. Air-conditioning, TV. Gentlemen only; no smokers. One single with private bath, $65.

B&B of Chicago #55
Box 14088, 60614
(312) 951-0085

This house, originally built in the 1920s as a chauffeur's garage, has been converted into a contemporary home. A catwalk on the second level allows open space between the first and second floors. The home is furnished with antiques and features skylights, recessed lighting, Oriental rugs, and fireplace. Women or couples only; no smoking. Two doubles (twins and double), $55-65.

B&B of Chicago #58
Box 14088, 60614
(312) 951-0085

This beautifully restored turn-of-the-century sandstone has hardwood floors, fireplaces, recessed lighting, VCRs, and cable TV. Just one block from the "el" with excellent access to Downtown and other parts of the city. No smoking. One double, private bath, $55-65.

B&B of Chicago #61
Box 14088, 60614
(312) 951-0085

A lovingly restored Victorian with guest sitting area, color TV. Use of the elegantly furnished living room with twenty-foot ceiling and wood-burning stove, as well as the reading room and formal dining room where breakfast is served. Hostess is a business administrator for Northwestern University; host is an attorney. One double, private bath, $55-65.

B&B of Chicago #67
Box 14088, 60614
(312) 951-0085

Located just north of the Chicago River and west of Michigan Avenue, this contemporary loft apartment is filled with charming,

6 Pets welcome: 7 Smoking allowed: 8 Children welcome: 9 Social drinking allowed: 10 Tennis available: 11 Swimming available: 12 Golf available: 13 Skiing available: 14 May be booked through travel agents

homey touches. Parquet floors, fireplace, and antiques, plus air-conditioning and TV. Your host is in real-estate management and sales. One double trundle bed, $55-65.

Hyde Park House

5210 South Kenwood Avenue, 60615
(312) 363-4595

Ours is a Victorian house with a veranda, porch swing, rear deck, two Steinways, attic greenhouse, near the University of Chicago, Museum of Science and Industry. Twenty minutes from downtown by bus along the Lake Michigan shore. Also within walking distance are excellent sushi, Tai, Cantonese, Greek, Italian, and continental restaurants, gift shops, and art galleries.

Host: Irene Custer
Doubles: 3 (1 PB; 2 SB) $45-50
Type of Beds: 1 Double; 2 Queen
Continental Breakfast
Credit Cards: No
Notes: 2, 5, 7, 8, 9, 10, 11, 12, 13

DALLAS CITY

1850s Guest House

RR 1, Box 267, 62330
(217) 852-3652

On 4 landscaped acres. Large comfortable rooms, seventy-foot portico, gift shop, outdoor pool, and fountain. Built in 1850 of stone, with interesting history and architecture. Full breakfast and a conducted tour of the house are included.

Hosts: Fred & Virginia Massie
Doubles: 8 (PB and SB) $47.70-58.30
Type of Beds: 8 Twin; 6 Double; 1 Queen
Full Breakfast
Credit Cards: A, F
Notes: 2, 5, 7 (limited), 10, 11, 12

DUNLAP

Eagle's Nest

11125 North Trigger Road, 61525
(309) 243-7376

Country Georgian home, filled with interesting antiques, situated in a tranquil rural setting on 2.5 wooded acres. Swimming pool on premises; hiking, cross-country skiing. Continental breakfast is served on the screened porch in nice weather. Jubilee College and Wildlife Prairie Park are readily accessible. Ten minutes from Peoria.

Hosts: John & Lou Ann Williams
Doubles: 2 (PB) $30-35
Type of Beds: 4 Twin
Continental Breakfast
Credit Cards: No
Notes: 2, 4, 5, 8, 9, 10, 11, 12

ELDRED

Hobson's Bluffdale

RR 1, 62027
(217) 983-2854

Our ancestral farm has been in our family for eight generations on 320 acres of beautiful bluffs near the Illinois River. Built of rock, the home is one of the oldest in the state. Six fireplaces, beehive oven, working farm with animals, horseback riding, pool, hot tub, hay rides. Scenic and restful, with bountiful meals.

Hosts: Bill & Lindy Hobson
Singles: 1 (PB) $40
Doubles: 8 (PB) $53
Type of Beds: 18 Twin; 8 Double
Full Breakfast
Credit Cards: A, B
Closed Thanksgiving & Christmas
Notes: 2, 3, 4, 8, 9, 11, 12, 14

EVANSTON

B&B of Chicago #30

Box 14088, Chicago, 60614
(312) 951-0085

NOTES: Credit cards accepted: A Master Card; B Visa; C American Express; D Discover Card; E Diners Club; F Other: 2 Personal checks accepted: 3 Lunch available: 4 Dinner available: 5 Open all year

Listed on the National Register and located in Evanston's historic district, this architecturally interesting Victorian townhouse is the center unit of a five-unit rowhouse built in 1892. Lake Michigan and Northwestern University are within walking distance; public transportation into Chicago is only a few blocks away. Resident cat and dog. Two doubles share bath, $55-65.

B&B of Chicago #35

Box 14088, Chicago, 60614
(312) 951-0085

This centrally located bed and breakfast is just two blocks from Northwestern, Kendall College, and the Chicago "el." Downtown Evanston and Lake Michigan are only five minutes away. Complimentary sherry; radio, classical music, TV/VCR, terry robes, shampoo, iron. No smokers. Two doubles share bath, $50-60.

B&B of Chicago #52

Box 14088, Chicago, 60614
(312) 951-0085

This Victorian is located one block west of Northwestern's campus and three blocks from the "el." Your hosts, a family with two daughters, two cats, a cocker spaniel, and two guinea pigs, warmly welcome you to relax and watch TV in their living room. Breakfast often includes pancakes and waffles. Limited smoking. Two doubles share bath, $40-50.

B&B of Chicago #56

Box 14088, Chicago, 60614
(312) 951-0085

This Victorian in Evanston's Lake Shore Historic District is one mile south of Northwestern and a short walk to fine restaurants and public transportation. Fea-tured in several local and national magazines, it is furnished with a blend of antiques and art. No smokers. Individuals or married couples only. One single, shared bath, $55; one double, shared bath, $65.

GALENA

Amber Creek Farm

Box 5, 61036
(815) 598-3301

Romantic country lodging on 300 wooded acres with hiking trails, ponds, streams, and abundant wildlife. Lovely one-bedroom suites are furnished with antiques, king beds, fireplaces, and several have whirlpool baths. Special honeymoon and anniversary packages available, plus discounts for midweek reservations. Wonderful homemade breakfasts.

Hosts: Doug & Kate Freeman
Doubles: 3 (PB) $75-105
Type of Beds: 3 King
Full Breakfast
Credit Cards: A, B, C, D
Notes: 2, 5, 6, 8, 9, 10, 11, 12, 13, 14

Avery Guest House

606 South Prospect Street, 61036
(815) 777-3883

Located within Galena's historic district, this pre-Civil War home is a short walk from antique shops and historic buildings. Enjoy the scenic view from our porch swing; feel free to play the piano or just visit. Breakfast is served in the sunny dining room with a bay window overlooking the Galena River valley.

Hosts: Flo & Roger Jensen
Doubles: 4 (S2B) $40-60
Type of Beds: 1 Twin; 4 Queen
Continental-plus Breakfast
Minimum stay weekends & holidays: 2
Credit Cards: A, B
Notes: 2, 5, 8, 9, 10, 11, 12, 13

6 Pets welcome: 7 Smoking allowed: 8 Children welcome: 9 Social drinking allowed: 10 Tennis available: 11 Swimming available: 12 Golf available: 13 Skiing available: 14 May be booked through travel agents

Belle Aire Mansion Guest House

11410 Rt. 20 West, 61036
(815) 777-0893

Belle Aire Mansion is a pre-Civil War home
set on 16 beautiful acres only minutes from
historic Galena. Our rooms are large and
comfortable. Our guests say, "It's just like
visiting friends." We say, " Welcome home
— to our home."

Hosts: Jan & Lorraine Svec
Doubles: 4 (2 PB; 2 SB) $59.95-81.75
Type of Beds: 2 Twin; 2 Double; 1 King
Minimum stay holidays: 2
Credit Cards: No
Closed Christmas
Notes: 2, 8, 9, 11, 12, 13

The Comfort Guest House

1000 Third Street, 61036
(815) 777-3062

An 1856 Greek Revival brick home now
serving as a Euopean-style bed and breakfast. Rooms are furnished in antiques, with
hand-tied quilts. Guests enjoy the living
room, where there is a marble fireplace; play
cribbage in the front parlor; or enjoy the
front porch swing, TV, VCR. Breakfast is
served on antique dishes in the formal dining
room. The hostess is a master gardener and
will share perennial gardening tips.

Host: Connie Sola
Doubles: 3 (S2B) $55-60
Type of Beds: 1 Twin; 3 Double
Continental-plus Breakfast
Credit Cards: A, B
Notes: 2, 5, 7 (restricted), 9, 10, 11, 12, 13, 14

DeSoto Guest Hotel

230 South Main Street, 61036
(815) 777-0090; (800) 343-6562

Legendary 134-year-old hotel in historic
Galena that is noted for its deluxe accommodations and superior service. General
Grant, Abraham Lincoln, and many other
famous people have been guests of the De-
Soto Hotel. Guests are invited to tour with
our General Grant look-a-like. Full breakfast and two-hour libation reception nightly
included in our rates. Enter and ascend our
grand staircase.

Host: George Bush
Doubles: 55 (PB) $65-115
Type of Beds: 33 Double; 22 King
Full Breakfast
Credit Cards: A, B, C, D, E
Notes: 2, 3, 4, 5, 7, 8, 9, 10, 11, 12, 13, 14

DeSoto Guest Hotel

Farster's Executive Inn

305 N. Main Street, 61036
(815) 777-9125

Farster's Executive Inn is located on
Galena's historic Main Street, close to many
major sites and restaurants. Originally an
1845 general store, the inn has been restored

NOTES: Credit cards accepted: A Master Card; B Visa; C American Express; D Discover Card; E Diners
Club; F Other: 2 Personal checks accepted: 3 Lunch available: 4 Dinner available: 5 Open all year

to its turn-of-the-century elegance, with today's conveniences. Jacuzzi, game room, and private off-street parking.

Hosts: Bob & Sandy Farster
Singles: 2 (SB) $55
Suites: 5 (SB) $80 and up
Type of Beds: 7 Double
Continental Breakfast
Credit Cards: A, B, C, D
Notes: 2, 5, 6, 7, 8, 9, 10, 11, 12, 13, 14

Stillman's Country Inn

513 Bouthillier, 61036
(815) 777-0557

Restored 1858 Victorian mansion adjacent to General U. S. Grant's home. Five lovely guest rooms with private baths, color TVs, air-conditioning; three have working fireplaces. On-premise fine dining, lounge, and weekend 1950s and 1960s entertainment.

Hosts: Bill & Pam Lozeau
Doubles: 5 (PB) $60-90
Type of Beds: 2 Double; 3 Queen
Continental Breakfast
Credit Cards: A, B, C, D
Closed Christmas Eve
Notes: 2, 3, 4, 5, 7, 9, 10, 11, 12, 13, 14

Stillman's Country Inn

GRANT PARK

Bennett-Curtis House

302 W. Taylor Street, 60940
(815) 465-6025

The Bennett-Curtis House offers two rooms, one with continental breakfast and one with full breakfast. Restaurant on the premises. One room has two double beds with canopies; the other is in a separate building.

Hosts: Sam & Charlotte VanHook
Singles: 1 (PB) $50
Doubles: 1 (SB) $75
Type of Beds: 2 Double
Full or Continental Breakfast
Credit Cards: A, B, C
Closed February
Notes: 2, 3 (Tues.-Sat.), 4 (weekends), 5, 6, 7, 8

JACKSONVILLE

The 258 Inn

Monton at Church Street, 62650
(217) 245-2588; 245-6665

One-hundred-fifty-year-old Victorian home, decorated with quilts and antiques, featuring home-baked breads and delicious breakfasts. Shop in store: antiques, quilts, bath shop, wicker store. Thirty miles west of Springfield. Very unique.

Hosts: Rosalee & Ray McKinley
Doubles: 3 (PB) $52.55
Type of Beds: 2 Double; 1 King
Full Breakfast
No smoking
Credit cards: No
Notes: 2, 5, 8 (over 12), 9, 12, 14

KANKAKEE

Norma's B&B

429 S. Fourth Avenue, 60901
(815) 937-1533

A clean, friendly, homey atmosphere away from home. Enjoy our front porch for visiting and relaxing. Located a block and one-

6 Pets welcome: 7 Smoking allowed: 8 Children welcome: 9 Social drinking allowed: 10 Tennis available: 11 Swimming available: 12 Golf available: 13 Skiing available: 14 May be booked through travel agents

half from the Kankakee River, with water skiing, canoeing, and fishing for the sportsman. Parks, hospitals, and tennis courts are within walking distance.

Host: Norma Gall
Doubles: 5 (PB and SB) $25-40
Type of Beds: 3 Twin; 3 Double
Continental Breakfast
Credit Cards: No
Notes: 2, 3, 4, 5, 9, 10

OAKLAND

Inn-on-the-Square

3 Montgomery, 61943
(217) 346-2289; 346-2653

Restored colonial inn offering a potpourri of the "village experience." Antiques, gifts, flowers, crafts, and ladies' apparel shop to pique your curiosity. Our Tea Room offers simple but elegant luncheons. Golf, swimming, conservation park, Amish settlement, and historical sites nearby.

Hosts: Max & Caroline Coon
Singles: 4 (3 PB; 1 SB) $42.80
Doubles: 4 (3 PB; 1 SB) $ 48.15
Type of Beds: 6 Double
Full Breakfast
Credit Cards: A, B
Closed major holidays only
Notes: 2, 3, 5, 7 (limited), 8 (over 2), 9 (served by hosts), 10, 11, 12, 13 (XC)

OAK PARK

Toad Hall Bed & Breakfast House

301 N. Scoville Avenue, 60302
(312) 386-8623

A 1909 colonial five miles from downtown Chicago in the Frank Lloyd Wright Historic District. Old-world atmosphere and service. Antiques, Oriental rugs, Laura Ashley furnishings, telephones, TV, air-conditioning. Walk to twenty-five Wright masterpieces,

lovely shops, restaurants, public transportation.

Hosts: Cynthia & Jerry Mungerson
Suites: 1 (PB) $50-90
Doubles: 2 (PB) $40-50
Type of Beds: 2 Twin; 3 Double; 1 Queen
Full Breakfast
Credit Cards: No
Notes: 2, 5, 9, 10, 11, 12

PORT BYRON

The Olde Brick House

502 N. High Street, 61275
(309) 523-3236

Restored 1855 Greek Revival located on 1.5 acres in a quiet, picturesque Mississippi River town. Once owned by Cyrus McCormick and a station in the underground railroad. Rich historic area with antique and craft shops, water sports, and activities.

Hosts: Fred & LaVerne Waldbusser
Doubles: 3 (SB) $31.69-36.97
Type of Beds: 3 Queen
Continental Breakfast
Credit Cards: A, B
Notes: 2, 5, 8, 10, 11, 12

PRINCETON

Yesterday's Memories

303 East Peru Street, 61356
(815) 872-7753

Comfortable and homelike, the house is located one mile from I-80 in central Illinois. Within walking distance to most points of interest and excellent shopping. Free pick up from Amtrak. Uniquely furnished; organic gardens; country breakfasts with homegrown food.

Hosts: Marilyn & Robert Haslam
Doubles: 2 (SB) $40 plus tax
Type of Beds: 2 Twin; 1 Double
Full Breakfast
Credit Cards: No
Notes: 2, 5, 8 (by arrangement), 11, 12

NOTES: Credit cards accepted: A Master Card; B Visa; C American Express; D Discover Card; E Diners Club; F Other: 2 Personal checks accepted: 3 Lunch available: 4 Dinner available: 5 Open all year

ROCKFORD

Victoria's Bed & Breakfast Inn

201 North 6th Street, 61107
(815) 963-3232

Opulence, elegance, and generous hospitality await you in this turn-of-the-century mansion. Walk out the door and enter "Victorian Village," seventy unique stores and eateries. Return and enjoy a cozy fire in a Victorian parlor or retire to your suite with its heart-shaped Jacuzzi.

Hosts: Carol & Marty Lewis
Doubles: 4 (PB) $74.52-172.80
Type of Beds: 2 Double; 1 Queen; 1 King; 1 Round
Continental Breakfast
Credit Cards: A, B
Notes: 2, 5, 9, 10, 11, 12, 13

ROCK ISLAND

Top O' the Morning

1505 19th Avenue, 61201
(309) 786-3513

Sam and Peggy welcome you to their brick mansion on the bluffs overlooking the Mississippi River. Fantastic view, day or night. Three-acre wooded estate with winding drive, orchard, and gardens. Air-conditioned bedrooms, whirlpool tub, natural fireplaces.

Hosts: Sam & Peggy Doak
Doubles: 2 (PB)$35-45
Type of Beds: 2 Double
Full Breakfast
Credit Cards: No
Notes: 2, 5, 7, 8, 9, 10, 11, 12, 13

ST. JOSEPH

Home At Last

RR 2, Box 273, 61873
(217) 469-2402

Contemporary home featuring Shaker-style rustic kitchen, Victorian and country guest rooms. In a small-town setting by a country stream and wooded river. Located just off Rt. 74, fifteen minutes from the University of Illinois at Urbana-Champaigne.

Hosts: Alice & Ed Vernon
Doubles: (PB) $35
Full Breakfast
Credit Cards: No
Closed Thanksgiving & Christmas Day
Notes: 2, 5, 10, 11, 12

SYCAMORE

Country Charm Inn

Rt. 2, Box 154, Quigley Road, 60178
(815) 895-5386

Understated elegance is the hallmark of our three-story country farm home. Pit fireplace, 2,000-book library, mini petting zoo, trick horse (Champ), breakfast on the cozy front porch. Howard and Donna are former AFS hosts, and Donna, the oldest of fourteen children, loves people!

Hosts: Howard & Donna Petersen
Doubles: 4 (PB) $32.50-58.30
Type of Beds: 1 Double; 1 Queen; 2 King
Continental-plus Breakfast
Minimum stay holidays: 2
Credit Cards: No
Closed Dec. 20-April 1
Notes: 2, 7 (restricted), 8, 9, 10, 11, 12

TOLONO

Aunt Zelma's Country Guest House

RR 1, Box 129, 61880
(217) 485-5101; 485-8925

Located near Tolono, eight miles from Champaign and the University of Illinois. Just three miles from Willard Airport. This one-story country home is furnished with family antiques, and quilts are displayed as bedspreads.

Hosts: Zelma Weibel
Doubles: 3 (1 PB; 2 SB) $36.10-42.40
Type of Beds: 2 Twin; 2 Double
Full Breakfast
Credit Cards: No
Notes: 2, 5, 8, 12

WINNETKA

Chateau des Fleurs

552 Ridge Road, 60093
(312) 256-7272

Chateau des Fleurs is an elegant respite from the world that welcomes you with light, beauty, warmth, and lovely views of magnificent trees, gardens, and a swimming pool. A French country home filled with antiques, four fireplaces, fifty-inch television, and a grand piano. Located by a private road for jogging or walking, it is only four blocks from shops and restaurants and a thirty-minute train ride to Chicago's Loop. Ten minutes from Northwestern University.

Host: Sally H. Ward
Doubles: 3 (PB) $70-80
Type of Beds: 2 Twin; 1 Double; 1 King
Continental-plus Breakfast
Minimum stay weekends & holidays: 2
Credit Cards: No
Notes: 2, 5, 8 (over 16), 9, 10, 11, 12, 13, 14

Indiana

BEVERLY SHORES

Dunes Shore Inn

Lake Shore County Road, Box 807, 46301
(219) 879-9029

A B&B in the Gasthof tradition; quiet, informal. One block to Lake Michigan. A four-season oasis for those who wish to relax in the natural beauty of the Indiana dunes. Ideal stopping-off place for exploring this unique area.

Hosts: Rosemary & Fred Braun
Singles: 1 (SB) $32-38
Doubles: 11 (S4B) $43-50
Type of Beds: 4 Twin; 10 Double
Continental Breakfast
Minimum stay weekends & holidays: 2
Credit Cards: A, B
Closed March
Notes: 2, 8, 9, 10, 11, 12, 13

CHESTERTON

Gray Goose Inn

350 Indian Boundary Road, 46304
(219) 926-5781

English style country house located on 100 wooded acres overlooking a private lake. Walking trails, paddle boat, rowboat, bikes are available for guests. Minutes from Dunes State and National Lakeshore; fifty minutes from Chicago.

Hosts: Tim Wilk & Chuck Ramsey
Doubles: 5 (PB) $60-75
Type of Beds: 2 Double; 2 Queen; 2 King
Full Breakfast
Credit Cards: A, B, C, D
Notes: 2, 5, 7, 8 (12 and over), 9, 10, 11, 12, 13, 14

CORYDON

Kentucky Homes B&B C001

1432 St. James Court
Louisville, KY 40208
(502) 635-7341

Cedar Glade is a beautiful plantation home now occupied by the fourth generation of the same family. It predates the Capitol by about five years. Twin and double bedrooms share a bath; private bath if only one room is taken. $60-65.

Kintner House Inn

101 South Capitol Avenue, 47112
(812) 738-2020

Completely restored inn (circa 1873), a National Historic Landmark. Fourteen rooms, each with private bath, furnished in Victorian and country antiques. Serves full breakfast. Also two apartment suites adjacent to inn, completely furnished and decorated, that are ideal for families. Fine Italian restaurant across the street; sports available at the Corydon Country Club.

Host: Mary Jane Bridgwater
Doubles: 16 (PB) $59.40-91.80
Type of Beds: 2 Twin; 13 Double; 1 Queen; 1 King
Full Breakfast
Credit Cards: A, B, C, E
Notes: 2, 5, 8, 9, 10, 11, 12

---

6 Pets welcome: 7 Smoking allowed: 8 Children welcome: 9 Social drinking allowed: 10 Tennis available: 11 Swimming available: 12 Golf available: 13 Skiing available: 14 May be booked through travel agents

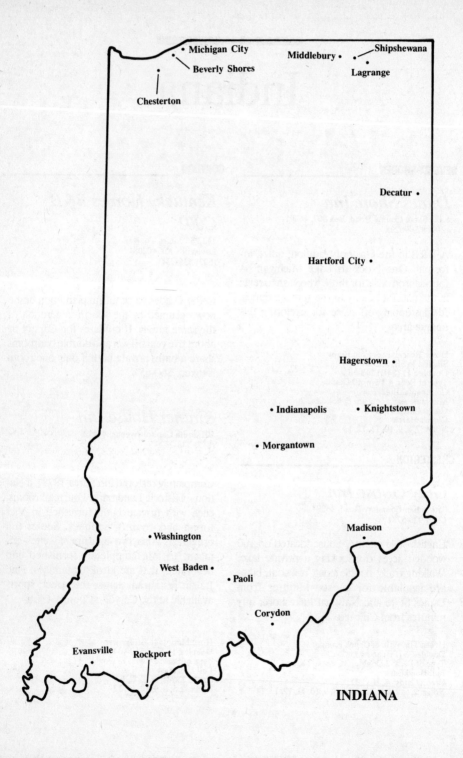

Michigan City

Beverly Shores

Chesterton

Middlebury •

Shipshewana

Lagrange

Decatur •

Hartford City •

Hagerstown •

• Indianapolis

• Knightstown

• Morgantown

Madison

• Washington

West Baden •

• Paoli

Corydon

Evansville

Rockport

INDIANA

DECATUR

Cragwood Inn Bed & Breakfast

303 N. Second Street, 46733
(219) 728-2000

Elegant 1900 Queen Anne home with beveled-glass windows and magnificent woodwork, tin ceiling, and four fireplaces. Spacious guest rooms blend the charm of the past and comfort of the present. Just south of Ft. Wayne, near a large Amish community.

Hosts: George & Nancy Craig
Suite: 1 (PB) $75
Doubles: 4 (2 PB; 2 SB) $45-55
Type of Beds: 1 Twin; 5 Double; 1 Queen
Continental-plus Breakfast
Credit Cards: No
Notes: 2, 5, 10, 11, 12, 14

EVANSVILLE

Brigadoon Bed & Breakfast Inn

1201 SE Second Street, 47713
(812) 422-9635

Romantic white-frame Victorian with 1892 parquet floors, four fireplaces, and stained glass. Enjoy the rainbows cast every sunny morning in the lace-curtained parlor. Large antique-furnished guest rooms are Scottish, English, Irish, and Welsh.

Host: Kathee Linda Forbes
Doubles: 4 (2 PB; 2 SB) $35-40
Type of Beds: 2 Double; 2 Queen
Full Breakfast
Credit Cards: A, B
Notes: 2, 5, 6, 7, 8, 9, 10, 11, 12, 14

HAGERSTOWN

Teetor House

300 West Main Street, 47346
(317) 489-4422

An elegant converted home with historical significance in the automotive industry on 10 landscaped acres with many unique amenities. Full breakfast included; excellent restaurants nearby. All rooms are fully air-conditioned, and some have TV.

Hosts: Jack & Joanne Warmoth
Doubles: 4 (PB) $66-93.50
Type of Beds: 3 Twin; 1 King
Full Breakfast
Credit Cards: A, B
Notes: 2, 5, 7 (limited), 8, 9, 10, 11, 12, 14

HARTFORD CITY

De'Coy's Bed & Breakfast

1546 West 100N, 47348
(317) 348-2164

Recently restored country home, completely furnished with antiques. Relaxing rural setting close to three universities. Each room demonstrates its own character, comfortable and unique. There is a cat in residence. Experience a friendly, pleasant getaway!

Hosts: Chris & Tiann Coy
Doubles: 4 (1 PB; 3 SB) $30.45-42
Type of Beds: 2 Twin; 2 Double; 1 Queen
Full Breakfast
Credit Cards: No
Notes: 2, 5, 8, 9, 12, 14

INDIANAPOLIS

Kentucky Homes B&B IN01

1432 St. James Court
Louisville, KY 40208
(502) 635-7341

This home is on the bank of the White River on the north side of the city, within 45 minutes of everything. Guest suite with a double bedroom, sitting room with queen sofabed, bath, and small greenhouse. Walk out on ground level to the river's edge. Open March to November. $50-55. Honeymoon suite: elegant bedroom with double bed, whirlpool bath in suite: $85.

6 Pets welcome: 7 Smoking allowed: 8 Children welcome: 9 Social drinking allowed: 10 Tennis available: 11 Swimming available: 12 Golf available: 13 Skiing available: 14 **May be booked through travel agents**

Old Hoosier House

The moment guests see the large red-brick exterior and walk through the wooden front door of the 1886 Inn, they are surrounded by historical charm and elegance. The house was originally built in 1886 as the home of a Civil War veteran and prominent politician and features a raised stone foundation and high, arching windows. Your hosts are glad to share the history and many unusual aspects of their home over breakfast.

Hosts: Duane & Gloria Billman
Singles: 1 (PB) $39
Doubles: 3 (PB) $55
Type of Beds: 2 Twin; 6 Double; 2 Queen
Continental-plus Breakfast
Credit Cards: A, B
Notes: 2, 5, 8, 10, 11, 12, 13

KNIGHTSTOWN

"Old Hoosier House"

Rt. 2, Box 299-1, 46148
(317) 345-2969

This historic brick house looks just as it did when ex-president Martin Van Buren visited here in 1844. Real Indiana country setting where you may sit on the deck and watch the golfers or shop the many nearby antique stores. You will sleep in a large, air-conditioned room and awake to a delicious Hoosier breakfast.

Hosts: Jean & Tom Lewis
Doubles: 4 (3 PB; 1 SB) $41-$61
Type of Beds: 2 Twin; 2 Queen; 1 King
Full Breakfast
Credit Cards: No
Closed Nov. 1 - May 1
Notes: 2, 8, 9, 10, 11, 12, 14

LAGRANGE

The 1886 Inn

212 Factory Street, 46761
(219) 463-4227

MADISON

Cliff House Bed & Breakfast

122 Fairmount Drive, 47250
(812) 265-5272

This outstanding Victorian home was built in 1885 and is furnished with lovely antiques. Located on a bluff high above the town of Madison and the mighty Ohio River. Guests can relax and watch the river roll by. There are canopy beds in the rooms and a candlelight breakfast is served in the morning.

Host: Jae Breitweiser
Doubles: 6 (PB) $55-82.50
Type of Beds: 2 Twin; 3 Double; 3 Queen
Continental-plus Breakfast
Credit Cards: A, B
Notes: 2, 4, 5, 7 (limited), 8, 9, 10, 11, 12, 13, 14

Clifty Inn

Clifty Falls State Park, 47250
(812) 265-4135

Clifty Inn has welcomes generations of visitors to southern Indiana. Rooms include motor-lodge and riverview styles. Our full-service dining room offers a family-pleasing

---

NOTES: Credit cards accepted: A Master Card; B Visa; C American Express; D Discover Card; E Diners Club; F Other: 2 Personal checks accepted: 3 Lunch available: 4 Dinner available: 5 Open all year

menu. Clifty Inn combines great food, comfortable lodging, and gracious hospitality with breathtaking scenery to create a relaxing environment. Guests desiring B&B accommodations should specify so when they call for reservations.

Doubles: 72 (PB) $39-42 plus tax
Type of Beds: 62 Twin; 10 Double
Full Breakfast
Credit Cards: A, B, C
Notes: 3, 4, 5, 7, 8, 9, 10, 11, 12, 13, 14

Cliff House B&B

MICHIGAN CITY

Plantation Inn

651 E. 1500 North, 46360
(219) 874-2418

A luxury country inn on several landscaped acres near the Indiana Dunes National Lakeshore recreation area. Two miles to the beaches, sport fishing marinas, bird and wildlife sanctuaries. Close to restaurants, shopping, golf, theater, and other entertainment.

Host: Ann C. Stephens
Doubles: 5 (PB) $55-80
Full Breakfast
Credit Cards: A, B, C
Notes: 2, 4, 5, 7, 8 (12 and over), 9, 10, 11, 12, 13, 14

MIDDLEBURY

Patchwork Quilt Country Inn

11748 CR 2, 46540
(219) 825-2417

Patchwork Quilt is a centennial farm growing soy beans or corn. Restaurant on the premises, and the three bedrooms are decorated in quaint country style.

Hosts: Maxine Zook & Susan Thomas
Singles: 2 (SB) $49.95
Doubles: 1 (SB) $54.95
Continental Breakfast
Credit Cards: A, B
Closed Jan. 1-15 and Sundays
Notes: 2, 3, 4, 8 (5 and over), 11, 12

MORGANTOWN

The Rock House

380 West Washington Street, 46160
(812) 597-5100

An 1894 Victorian built of concrete block, each block decorated with rocks, geodes, dice, doorknobs, dishes — even the skull of a wild boar! Visitors to Nashville/Brown County, Indiana University, and Lake Monroe are served a full breakfast before taking a "binocular" tour of the home's exterior (the only way to find all the embedded treasures).

Hosts: Doug & Marcia Norton
Doubles: 6 (2 PB; 4 SB) $50-65
Type of Beds: 2 Twin; 4 Double; 1 Queen
Full Breakfast
Credit Cards: No
Notes: 2, 5, 7 (limited), 8, 9, 12, 13

PAOLI

Braxtan House Inn Bed & Breakfast

210 N. Gospel, 47454
(812) 723-4677

Braxtan House is a twenty-one-room Queen Anne Victorian, lovingly restored and furnished in antiques. The inn overlooks the historic courthouse square and is near Paoli Peaks ski resort, Patoka Lake, and antique and craft shops in picturesque southern Indiana hill country.

Hosts: Terry & Brenda Cornwell
Doubles: 6 (4 PB; 2 SB) $31.50-73.50
Type of Beds: 1 Twin; 6 Double; 1 Queen
Full Breakfast
Minimum stay holidays: 2
Credit Cards: A, B (with surcharge)
Notes: 2, 5, 7, 8 (12 and over), 9, 10, 11, 12, 13

ROCKPORT

The Rockport Inn

Third at Walnut, 47635
(812) 649-2664

The Rockport Inn, built as a private residence in 1855, is now operated as a country inn with six guest rooms and four dining rooms. It is known for its turn-of-the-century ambience and excellent cuisine.

Hosts: Carolyn & Emil Ahnell
Doubles: 6 (PB) $32-45
Type of Beds: 8 Double
Continental Breakfast
Credit Cards: No
Notes: 2, 3, 4, 5, 7, 8, 9, 10, 11, 12

SHIPSHEWANA

Green Meadow Ranch

Rt. 2, Box 592, 46565
(219) 768-4221

You're a stranger only once at Green Meadow. Nestled in the center of Amish and Mennonite country, two miles from Shipshewana, home of the Amish-Mennonite Visitors Center, the Shipshewana Auction and many shops and attractions. We offer tours of the Amish country.

Hosts: Paul & Ruth Miller
Doubles: 11 (8 PB; 3 SB) $25
Continental-plus Breakfast
Credit Cards: A, B
Closed Jan. & Feb.
Notes: 2, 8, 11, 12

WASHINGTON

Kentucky Homes B&B WA01

1432 St. James Court
Louisville, KY 40208
(502) 635-7341

Two hours from Louisville and Indianapolis, this large, rambling contemporary home offers a hot tub in the solarium, easy walking on 10 acres, or bird watching on the patio. There's a spacious party and card room on the lower level. Three double bedrooms, two baths. Smokers welcome. $45-50.

WEST BADEN

Kentucky Homes B&B WB01

1432 St. James Court
Louisville, KY 40208
(502) 635-7341

A large turn-of-the-century home featuring stained glass, pocket doors, and hardwood mantels and woodwork. Two large porches with rocking chairs invite you to relax. Many of the spa facilities a mile away are available to guests. Well-disciplined children are welcome. Three large double bedrooms, each with private bath. $40-45.

NOTES: Credit cards accepted: A Master Card; B Visa; C American Express; D Discover Card; E Diners Club; F Other: 2 Personal checks accepted: 3 Lunch available: 4 Dinner available: 5 Open all year

Iowa

Bed & Breakfast in Iowa #1
Box 430, Preston, 52069
(319) 689-4222

This 1860 brick farmhouse has been renovated and charmingly decorated with period furniture. Fireplace, stained-glass windows, and glass chandeliers add atmosphere. The South Raccoon River borders the farm on the north and east, where canoeing and fishing for catfish await. Hunters are welcome. Full breakfast. Two doubles, $30-40.

The Shaw House
509 South Oak, 52205
(319) 462-4485

Enjoy a relaxing step back in time in this three-story 1872 Italianate mansion on a hilltop overlooking scenery immortalized in the paintings of native son Grant Wood. Located on a 45-acre farm within easy walking distance of town. State park, canoeing, antiques are nearby.

Hosts: Connie & Andy McKean
Singles: 1 (PB) $25-35
Doubles: 3 (2 PB; 1 SB) $35-50
Type of Beds: 1 Twin; 3 Double
Full Breakfast
Credit Cards: No
Notes: 2, 5, 8, 9, 10, 11, 12, 13

Victorian Bed & Breakfast Inn
Box 249, 51521
(712) 343-6336

Fully restored 1904 Victorian inn with the original golden pine woodwork, large modern baths, antique furnishings, detailed columns, and grand-scaled windows. Elegant dinners by appointment. An immaculately maintained journey back in time. Golf and antique shops nearby. Ninety-one miles from Des Moines and forty-five from Omaha.

Hosts: Gene & Jan Kuehn
Doubles: 4 (1 PB; 3 SB) $44
Type of Beds: 1 Double; 3 Queen
Full Breakfast
Credit Cards: A, B
Closed Christmas
Notes: 2, 3, 4, 5, 7 (outdoors), 8 (12 and over), 9, 11, 12, 14

Victorian B&B Inn

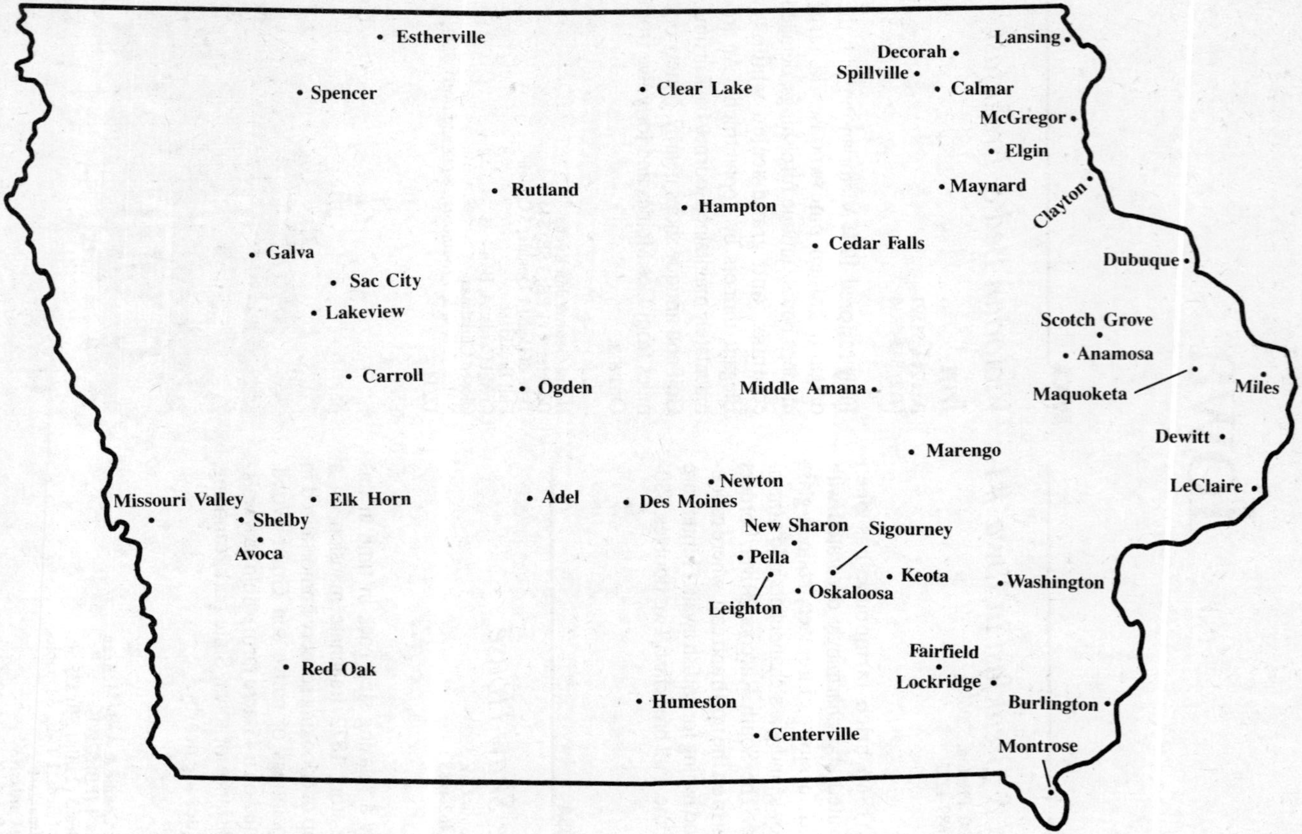

IOWA

Lansing
Decorah
Spillville
Calmar
McGregor
Elgin
Maynard
Clayton
Dubuque
Scotch Grove
Anamosa
Maquoketa
Miles
Dewitt
LeClaire
Washington
Burlington
Montrose
Cedar Falls
Clear Lake
Hampton
Marengo
Middle Amana
Sigourney
New Sharon
Pella
Keota
Oskaloosa
Leighton
Fairfield
Lockridge
Newton
Des Moines
Humeston
Centerville
Rutland
Ogden
Adel
Estherville
Spencer
Sac City
Lakeview
Carroll
Galva
Elk Horn
Shelby
Avoca
Red Oak
Missouri Valley

BURLINGTON

Bed & Breakfast in Iowa #2
Box 430, Preston, 52069
(319) 689-4222

Roads-Gardner House is a brick home built in 1854, located at the top of the Heritage Hill. Marble fireplaces adorn the library and one guest room. Antiques are the furnishings, including a four-poster bed. Hunters welcome. Two doubles, full breakfast, $35-40.

CALMAR

Calmar Guesthouse
RR 1, Box 206, 52132
(319) 562-3851

Newly remodeled Victorian home with antiques, located near Luther College and NITI Community College. Close to world-famous Bily Clocks in Spillville, Niagara Cave, Lakes Meyer, and much more. Wake up to a fresh country breakfast. Air-conditioned. Good variety of restaurants in the area.

Hosts: Art & Lucille Kriese
Doubles: 5 (1 PB; 4 SB) $30-35
Type of Beds: 5 Queen
Full Breakfast
Credit Cards: No
Notes: 2, 5, 7 (restricted), 8, 9, 10, 11, 12, 13

CARROLL

Bed & Breakfast of Iowa #3
Box 430, Preston, 52069
(319) 689-4222

A lovely 1900 home, remodeled, includes a fireplace in the family room. On an attractive farm that raises certified seed. Located on some of Iowa's finest soils. Your host has a private air strip next to the home. Hunters welcome. Two doubles, full breakfast, $25-35.

CEDAR FALLS

Bed & Breakfast of Iowa #4
Box 430, Preston, 52069
(319) 689-4222

A scenic, secluded, wooded acreage along the West Fork of the Cedar and Shell Rock River (called the Turkey Foot area). Near the University of Northern Iowa, Wartburg College, Star Clipper Dinner Train, John Deere Tractor Works, Waverly Horse Sale Barns, and many historical attractions. Contemporary eleven-year-old home, where you may enjoy breakfast overlooking the river. Full breakfast. Two doubles, $35-40.

CENTERVILLE

Paint 'n Primitives
107 E. Washington, 52544
(515) 856-8811

This Victorian-style home, located one block north of the world's largest square, houses an arts and crafts store and three charmingly decorated rooms. Near Lake Rathbun, boating, fishing, fish hatchery, museums.

Hosts: Joe & Mary Murphy
Doubles: 3 (SB) $35-40
Type of Beds: 3 Double
Full Breakfast
Credit Cards: A, B
No smoking
Notes: 2, 5, 8, 11, 12

CLAYTON

Cklaytonian Bed & Breakfast Inn
RR 2, Box 125A, 52049
(319) 964-2776

Enjoy the beauty of the majestic Mississippi River from the window of every room or from our veranda. We are one mile off the

---

6 Pets welcome: 7 Smoking allowed: 8 Children welcome: 9 Social drinking allowed: 10 Tennis available: 11 Swimming available: 12 Golf available: 13 Skiing available: 14 May be booked through travel agents

Great River Road, in the village of Clayton, which is surrounded by many historic sites, recreation areas, antique shops, and a rural warmth not found in other areas.

Host: Karilyn Bonomold
Singles: 2 (SB) $50
Doubles: 3 (PB) $50
Full Breakfast
Credit Cards: A, B
Notes: 2, 5, 7, 8, 10, 11, 12, 14

CLEAR LAKE

Bed & Breakfast of Iowa #5
Box 430, Preston, 52069
(319) 689-4222

Modern accommodations near the lake. Hosts are active young grandparents who will make arrangements for boating or fishing for you. Many activities in the area are free. A wood-burning fireplace is relaxing for the cool evenings. Full breakfast. Two doubles, $30-45.

DECORAH

Montgomery Mansion Bed & Breakfast
812 Maple Avenue, 52101
(319) 382-5088

An 1850s restored brick Victorian located in a quiet residential neighborhood. Large, comfortable rooms, air-conditioning. Quiet sitting room upstairs with TV and library. Conveniently located for canoeing, tubing, trout fishing, hiking, shops, and museums.

Hosts: Bob & Diane Ward
Doubles: 4 (1 PB; 3 SB) $35-40
Type of Beds: 2 Twin; 2 Double; 1 Queen
Full Breakfast
Credit Cards: A, B
Notes: 2, 5, 7 (limited), 8, 9, 10, 11, 12, 13, 14

DES MOINES

Bed & Breakfast of Iowa #6
Box 430, Preston, 52069
(319) 689-4222

Close to I-235 near the state capitol. A Federal style home, furnished in modern furniture with a fireplace in the living room. A formal dining room lets you enjoy the quiet neighborhood. Both hosts are retired, but active with volunteer work. Full breakfast. Two doubles, $25-35.

Brownswood
5938 SW 48th Avenue, 50321
(515) 285-4135

On acreage with quiet country charm only minutes away from I-80 and I-35, with easy access to historic Valley Junction's twenty-four antique shops, Adventureland, Living History Farms, Art Center, and nature walks through Brown's Woods. Air and water purification systems.

Hosts: Elaine & John Walser
Doubles: 2 (SB) $30-40
Type of Beds: 2 Twin; 1 Queen
Full Breakfast
Credit Cards: No
Notes: 2, 5, 6 (horses), 7, 8, 9, 10, 11, 12, 13 (XC)

DEWITT

Bed & Breakfast of Iowa #7
Box 430, Preston, 52069
(319) 689-4222

Relax as you visit with this farm couple about farming in the Heartland. You are twenty minutes from Davenport river excursions; thirty minutes from Clinton showboat (live theater in the summer); forty minutes from Moline horse racing. Hunters are welcome. One-room suite with gas fireplace. Full breakfast. One double, $35-40.

NOTES: Credit cards accepted: A Master Card; B Visa; C American Express; D Discover Card; E Diners Club; F Other: 2 Personal checks accepted: 3 Lunch available: 4 Dinner available: 5 Open all year

DUBUQUE

F. D. Stout House

1105 Locust Street, 52001
1-800-331-5454

A gracious and elegant restored lumber baron's home now offers travelers a rare opportunity to relax in grand style. Seasonal packages available.

Host: Debbie Griesinger
Doubles: 6 (2 PB; 4 S2B) $50.14-109
Continental-plus Breakfast
Minimum stay May 1-Nov. weekends: 2
Credit Cards: A, B, C, E
Notes: 2, 4, 5, 7, 8, 9, 10, 11, 12, 13, 14

The Hancock House

1105 Grove Terrace, 52001
(319) 557-8989

Perched on the bluffs of the mighty Mississippi, the Hancock House offers a panoramic view with old-fashioned elegance. Built in 1891 and restored to its original grandeur, all rooms are furnished in period antiques. Complimentary beverages are always available. Find yourself at home with us. Corporate rates available.

Hosts: Jim & Julie Gross
Doubles: 6 (3 PB; 3 SB) $55-110
Type of Beds: 6 Queen
Full Breakfast
Credit Cards: A, B
Notes: 2, 5, 7 (restricted), 8, 9, 10, 11, 12, 13

ELGIN

Country Swiss Guest House

404 Mill Street, RR 2, Box 55, 52141
(319) 426-5712

Country Swiss Guest House is a classic home overlooking a Swiss setting with a river valley and streams stocked with trout. Nearby is a conservation park with skiing, canoe access, hiking trails for the blind, deer, pheasant, and wild turkey hunting. Quaint Amish stores and antique shops also nearby.

Hosts: Sue & Ray Crammond
Singles: 1 (SB) $25
Doubles: 1 (PB) $45
Type of Beds: 2 Queen
Full Breakfast
Closed Christmas
Credit Cards: No
Notes: 2, 8 (over 12), 10, 11, 12, 13

ELK HORN

Rainbow H. Lodginghouse

RR 1, Box 89, 51531
(712) 764-8272

Visitors will enjoy the spacious setting of this grand brick home. Adults can enjoy a game of horseshoes or watch a crackling fire in the large recreation room. Children will enjoy having the room to explore outdoors and view the varied livestock, including some of the nation's finest Texas Longhorn cattle, which they may help feed. The house has air-conditioning, private guest entrance, outdoor patio, color TV, and private guest bath. Choose a hearty breakfast or eat as light as you wish.

Hosts: Mark & Cherie Hensley
Doubles: 2 (PB) $26-35
Type of Beds: 2 Twin; 1 Double
Full Breakfast
Credit Cards: No
Notes: 2, 7, 8, 11

The Travelling Companion

4314 Main Street, 51531
(712) 764-8932

Velkommen (Welcome) to The Travelling Companion. Delightful accommodations await you in this 1909 home nestled in the peaceful Danish town of Elk Horn. The Ortgies chose the house's name from one of Hans Christian Andersen's fairy-tale stories. Each guest room is named after a different fairy tale.

Hosts: Duane & Karolyn Ortgies
Doubles: 3 (SB) $42.80
Type of Beds: 4 Double
Full Breakfast

6 Pets welcome: 7 Smoking allowed: 8 Children welcome: 9 Social drinking allowed: 10 Tennis available: 11 Swimming available: 12 Golf available: 13 Skiing available: 14 May be booked through travel agents

Credit Cards: No
Notes: 2, 4, 5, 8, 10, 11, 12

ESTHERVILLE

Bed & Breakfast of Iowa #8

Box 430, Preston, 52069
(319) 689-4222

Hoffman Guest House is a charming 1912 home with an open stairway, fireplace, lead-glass windows, and oak woodwork throughout. Ask for the three-quarter bed with a featherbed for a real treat in sleeping pleasure. The hostess is a secretary who will help you use her computer word processor if you ask her. Hunters welcome. Three doubles. Continental breakfast. $20-40.

FAIRFIELD

Bed & Breakfast of Iowa #9

Box 430, Preston, 52069
(319) 689-4222

Clark House is Prairie School architecture at its best. Built in 1915, fully restored, and furnished with many original unique pieces. The original chandeliers are still in use in the living room. The history of this home is any architect's delight. Amtrack stops in Fairfield. Three doubles, full breakfast, $30-55.

GALVA

Pioneer Farm Bed & Breakfast

RR 1, Box 96, 51020
(712) 282-4670

Pioneer Farm is a working farm raising hogs, corn, and soybeans. You may don your "grubbies" and help with the chores or field work, if you wish. Pheasant and Hungarian partridge wander over the farm and adjoining lands, and hunters are welcome. Join us for fresh air, sunrises, and sunsets!

Hosts: Darold & JoAnn Jacobson
Singles: 1 (SB) $30
Doubles: 2 (SB) $35
Type of Beds: 2 Twin; 2 Double
Full Breakfast
Credit Cards: No
Closed Jan. - April
Notes: 2, 3, 6, 7, 8, 9, 10, 11, 12

HAMPTON

Bed & Breakfast of Iowa #10

Box 430, Preston, 52069
(310) 689-4222

Retired farm couple will show you Iowa hospitality in their Victorian home furnished with antiques. Features a foyer, fireplace, and two guest rooms. Ten miles east of I-35. Area is prime farmland, small manufacturing, and horticultural nurseries. Two doubles, $25-35.

HUMESTON

Bed & Breakfast of Iowa #11

Box 430, Preston, 52069
(319) 689-4222

Two-story frame home, circa 1900, in small town. Many areas available in state parks for hiking, back-packing, or hunting. Excellent restaurant near. Lake Rathbun and Red Haw Lake less than thirty miles. Three doubles, $30-45. Full breakfast.

KEOTA

Elmhurst

Rt. 1, Box 3, 52248
(515) 636-3001

This 1905 Victorian mansion retains much of its original grandeur: stained-glass and curved windows, circular solarium, parqueted floors, beamed ceilings, marble

---

NOTES: Credit cards accepted: A Master Card; B Visa; C American Express; D Discover Card; E Diners Club; F Other: 2 Personal checks accepted: 3 Lunch available: 4 Dinner available: 5 Open all year

fireplace mantles, ballroom, two grand stairways, leather wall coverings, and more. Golf course across the road.

Host: Marjie Schantz-Koehler
Singles: 2 (SB) $31
Doubles: 2 (SB) $36.40
Type of Beds: 7 Double
Full Breakfast
Credit Cards: No
Notes: 2, 5, 9, 10, 11, 12

LAKEVIEW

Bed & Breakfast of Iowa #12

Box 430, Preston, 52069
(319) 689-4222

Lovely brick home one block from 900-acre Blackhawk Lake. An old historical home is 1.5 blocks away. Many activities around the lake, and five parks are in the area. The Fourth of July Parade of Boats is spectacular. Full breakfast. One double, $30-45.

LANSING

FitzGerald's Inn

160 N. 3rd Street, Box 157, 52151
(319) 538-4872

Century-old Victorian country home of unusual charm, situated on one of Lansing's hilly residential streets. Terraced grounds rise dramatically to a bluff-top view of the Mississippi River at one of its most beautiful stretches. Ideal setting for relaxation, canoeing, boating, hiking, bird watching, skiing.

Hosts: Maire & Jeff FitzGerald
Doubles: 5 (3 PB; 2 SB) $52-67.60
Type of Beds: 2 Twin; 2 Double; 3 Queen
Full Breakfast
Credit Cards: No
Notes: 2, 5, 7, 8, 9, 10, 11, 12, 13, 14

Lansing House

Box 97, 52151
(319) 538-4263

Lansing House, a handsome riverfront home, is situated next to the picturesque Blackhawk Bridge and offers its guests an atmosphere of comfort and elegance — plus a picture-window view of the Great River. The area offers hikes in the woods and walks along the river. Rental boats are available for sight-seeing in the back waters and fishing.

Hosts: Chris & Margaret Fitz Gerald
Doubles: 2 (SB) $50
Type of Beds: 2 Twin; 1 Queen
Full Breakfast
Credit Cards: No
Notes: 2, 5, 11, 13

LeCLAIRE

Mohr Haus

21710 Great River Road N., 52753
(319) 289-4503

Located in a century-old farmhouse overlooking the Mississippi River one-half mile north of LeClaire. The old is blended with the new to offer you a very enjoyable stay in air-conditioned comfort. Many points of interest within an hour's drive.

Hosts: Leona & Joe Mohr
Doubles: 3 (SB) $35
Type of Beds: 1 Double; 1 Queen; 1 King
Continental Breakfast
Credit Cards: No
Closed Nov. 1 - May 27
Notes: 2, 7 (restricted), 9, 10, 11, 12

LEIGHTON

Heritage House

Rt. 1, Box 166, 50143
(515) 626-3092

A 1918 house that has been renovated, airconditioned, and beautifully decorated. Over 2,600 acres nearby for hunting deer,

6 Pets welcome: 7 Smoking allowed: 8 Children welcome: 9 Social drinking allowed: 10 Tennis available: 11 Swimming available: 12 Golf available: 13 Skiing available: 14 May be booked through travel agents

quail, pheasant, and turkey, plus facilities to dress game and keep it refrigerated. Come for the Tulip Time Festival the second week in May, or visit Pella's historical village museum tours all year. For breakfast, enjoy homemade cinnamon rolls, scrambled eggs, bacon pie, or caramel French toast.

Host: Iola Vander Wilt
Doubles: 2 (SB) $28-35
Type of Beds: 2 Double
Full Breakfast
Credit Cards: No
Closed Jan.
Notes: 2, 8, 9, 11

LOCKRIDGE

Bed & Breakfast of Iowa #13

Box 430, Preston, 52069
(319) 689-4222

A private 4.5 acre pond is available for fishing, or you may visit your hosts' hog farm. Visit the clock museum, with over forty hand-crafted clocks, each with a unique story. Near Mt. Pleasant and the Midwest Old Threshers' Reunion over Labor Day. Bikers, hikers, and hunters welcome. Full breakfast. Three doubles, $25-35.

MARENGO

Loy's Bed & Breakfast

RR #1, Box 82, 52301
(319) 642-7787

Modern farm home on a large grain and hog farm. Recreation room and farm tour available. Close to the Amana Colonies and many other interesting places. Small conference retreat. Farm breakfast with hot breads.

Hosts: Loy & Robert Walker
Doubles: 3 (SB) $32.70-49.05
Type of Beds: 4 Twin

Full Breakfast
Credit Cards: No
Notes: 2, 4, 5, 8, 9, 10, 11, 12

MAYNARD

Boedeker's Bungalow/WestSide Bed & Breakfast

125 7th Street North, 50655
(319) 637-2711

Just off Highway 150, you'll have a hearty breakfast after a quiet rest and a country view from your private upstairs quarters. You're in the center of things in Fayette County, and right in northeast Iowa's famous hills and rivers territory. Air-conditioning and TV.

Host: Mrs. Margaret I. Boedeker
Singles: 2 (SB) $20.80-31.20
Doubles: 1 (PB) $36.40
Type of Beds: 2 Twin; 1 Double
Full Breakfast
Credit Cards: No
Notes: 2, 5, 8, 9, 11, 12, 13

MAQUOKETA

Bed & Breakfast of Iowa #14

Box 430, Preston, 52069
(319) 689-4222

A modern home of unique design that blends into the natural surroundings of the countryside. Visit the Hurtsville Lime Kilns, Maquoketa Caves State Park, Banowetz Antiques, or the dog races in Dubuque. The guest rooms are on the lower level and include an electric fireplace in the family room and a private bath. Full breakfast. One double, $25-55.

NOTES: Credit cards accepted: A Master Card; B Visa; C American Express; D Discover Card; E Diners Club; F Other: 2 Personal checks accepted: 3 Lunch available: 4 Dinner available: 5 Open all year

The Rettig House

An invitation to relax in a peaceful, comfortable atmosphere, in a house decorated in beautiful Amana antiques. Located in historic Middle Amana, we have taken a touch of the past and accented it with a greenhouse, spacious deck, and Jacuzzi.

Hosts: Bradley & Lynn Hahn
Singles: 1 (PB) $38.15
Doubles: 3 (PB) $41.42
Type of Beds: 2 Twin; 3 Double
Continental Breakfast
Credit Cards: A, B
Notes: 2, 5, 7, 8, 9, 12

McGREGOR

Little Switzerland Inn
Box 195, 52157
(319) 873-3670

The building housing the inn was constructed in 1862 as the home for Iowa's oldest weekly newspaper. Since then, it has undergone renovation. The newest addition to the inn is an authentic log cabin that was moved onto the property and furnished for guests with a large Jacuzzi and beautiful stone fireplace. The Mississippi River is less than a block away, and guests will enjoy watching its traffic from the balcony of the inn.

Hosts: Bud & Chris Jameson
Doubles: 6 (5 PB; 1 SB) $20-55
Type of Beds: 1 Twin; 2 Double; 2 Queen; 2 King
Full Breakfast
Credit Cards: A, B
Notes: 2, 4, 5, 6, 7, 8, 10, 11, 13, 14

MIDDLE AMANA

Dusk to Dawn Bed & Breakfast
Box 124, 52307
(319) 622-3029

The Rettig House
52307
(319) 622-3386

Found in peaceful Middle Amana, one of seven historic villages. Constructed in 1893, The Rettig House served as one of the original community kitchen houses in old communal Amana. Charming old-world ambience with antiques and heirlooms in every room.

Hosts: Ray & Marge Rettig
Doubles: 5 (3 PB; 2 SB) $42-50
Type of Beds: 4 Twin; 3 Double
Continental Breakfast
Credit Cards: No
Notes: 2, 5

MILES

Bed & Breakfast of Iowa #15
Box 430, Preston, 52069
(319) 689-4222

A working dairy farm where you may watch while they milk, if you wish. The home was designed and built with wood cut on the farm. A sunken living room and a sunken bathtub contrast with the antique organ and furnishing. The game room has a fireplace and pool table. Ten miles to the Mississippi River. Hunters are welcome. Continental-plus breakfast. One double, $25-35.

6 Pets welcome: 7 Smoking allowed: 8 Children welcome: 9 Social drinking allowed: 10 Tennis available: 11 Swimming available: 12 Golf available: 13 Skiing available: 14 May be booked through travel agents

Bed & Breakfast of Iowa #16

Box 430, Preston, 52069
(319) 689-4222

A modern ranch-style home with a view of Iowa's rolling farmland. The Mississippi River is five miles away; Dubuque dog races are thirty minutes; Galena, IL, is less than an hour away. Hunters welcome. This farm has livestock that includes Belgian horses. Full breakfast. Two doubles, $30-40.

MISSOURI VALLEY

Apple Orchard Inn

RR 3, Box 129, 51555
(712) 642-2418

This country home on a 26-acre apple orchard is situated on a hill overlooking the beautiful Boyer Valley. Gourmet cooking featuring fresh-ground wheat in homemade breads and jellies. Comfortable rooms, a keeping room, and a Jacuzzi room. German and Spanish are spoken here.

Hosts: Dr. Electa & John Strub
Doubles: 3 (SB) $39-43
Type of Beds: 3 Double
Full Breakfast
Credit Cards: B
Notes: 2, 4, 5, 8, 10, 11, 12, 13

MONTROSE

Bed & Breakfast of Iowa #17

Box 430, Preston, 52069
(319) 689-4222

This remodeled cabin has a spectacular view of the Mississippi River from the top of a 300-foot bluff. Nauvoo, IL, is across the river. The history of the Mormon people, including the winery, makes Nauvoo and interesting visit. Have breakfast on the deck that overlooks the river, or in the dining room behind glass doors. Continental-plus breakfast. Two doubles, $30-40.

NEW SHARON

Bed & Breakfast of Iowa #18

Box 430, Preston, 52069
(319) 689-4222

This 600-acre farm grows grains and livestock that includes a 3,000 hog confinement project. Your hosts have traveled extensively. Hunters are welcome to hunt on the farm. Pella Tulip Festival in May. The balloon races are in Indianola the first week of August. Full breakfast. Two doubles, $25-35.

Bed & Breakfast of Iowa #19

Box 430, Preston, 52069
(319) 689-4222

Modern, beautiful brick ranch home that stands at the edge of a small, rural town. Busy host and hostess will show you their horses and/or stable your horse. They will also willingly share their interests concerning their careers. Three guest rooms for up to five people. One-half mile off Rt. 63, near Pella. Full breakfast. Three doubles, $25-45.

NEWTON

La Corsette Maison Inn

629 1st Avenue East, 50208
(515) 792-6833

Historic turn-of-the-century Mission-style mansion. Charming French bedchambers; fireplaces; gourmet dining in a style of elegance. On I-80, thirty minutes from Des

NOTES: Credit cards accepted: A Master Card; B Visa; C American Express; D Discover Card; E Diners Club; F Other: 2 Personal checks accepted: 3 Lunch available: 4 Dinner available: 5 Open all year

Moines. Close to horse track and other points of interest.

Host: Kay Owen
Doubles: 4 (PB) $50-85
Type of Beds: 1 Double; 1 Queen; 1 King
Full or Continental Breakfast
Credit Cards: No
Notes: 2, 4, 5, 6 (call), 7 (restricted), 8 (call), 9, 11, 12

OGDEN

Bed & Breakfast of Iowa #20

Box 430, Preston, 52069
(319) 689-4222

Visit 280-acre Century Farm, which has been home to three generations. Livestock and grain are raised here. Farm visitors are welcome, as well as hunters. Your host may have time to hunt with you. Boone is twenty miles away, where you may visit Mamie Eisenhower's birthplace, the Kate Shelly bridge, or "Puffer Bills Days" in September. Full breakfast. Two doubles, $20-40.

OSKALOOSA

Bed & Breakfast of Iowa #21

Box 430, Preston, 52069
(319) 689-4222

Several colleges are in the Oskaloosa-Pella area, with the usual college activities for students and parents. The 1844 Nelson Homestead has a home and barn that are designated National Historic Sites. It is open for tours during the summer months. The Pella Tulip Festival is in May. This home is a ranch-style house on the outskirts of town, with a view of farmland from the deck. Hunters welcome. Full breakfast. Two doubles, $25-35.

PELLA

Bed & Breakfast of Iowa #22

Box 430, Preston, 52069
(319) 689-4222

Flowers abound inside and out at this lovely home. Your host is a carpenter who will show you his workshop and projects. Your hostess is a busy volunteer worker who loves to cook. The guest rooms include cooking facilities; hunters are welcome. Full breakfast. One double, $25-40.

RED OAK

Usher's Bed & Breakfast

711 Cornine Street, 51566
(712) 623-3222

A restored turn-of-the-century home furnished with antiques. Two guest rooms with hared bath, private study, and home-cooked Iowa breakfast in our formal dining room or on the sun deck. Nestled in the heart of town, with restaurants, shopping, and a walking tour of historical homes nearby. Reservations, please.

Hosts: Marti & Denny Usher
Doubles: 2 (SB) $38.50-48.50
Type of Beds: 2 Double
Full Breakfast
Credit Cards: A, B
Notes: 2, 5, 7, 8, 9, 10, 11, 12

RUTLAND

Bed & Breakfast of Iowa #23

Box 430, Preston, 52069
(319) 689-4222

Your hosts are native Iowans who have spent their entire lives in Humboldt County. After twenty-four years of farming, they moved to the small town of Rutland in northwest Iowa, on the west fork of the Des Moines River. Visit the West Bend Grotto and Humboldt Museum. Your host is now working as a carpenter; she is interested in restoring older homes and furniture. Their home is decorated in country style. Hunters are welcome. Full breakfast. Two doubles, $25-35.

SAC CITY

Brick Bungalow Bed & Breakfast

1012 Early Street, 50583
(712) 662-7302

A warm welcome greets you in this brick house in a quiet neighborhood. This is a solid 1930s house with beautiful dark oak wood-work and beams. Guests are invited to use all of the house and spacious backyard. Families are especially welcome. Guest rooms have golden pine paneling, separate baths, electric blankets, and central air.

Host: Phyllis Hartman
Dorm: 1 (PB) $35
Doubles: 1 (PB) $35
Type of Beds: 5 Twin; 1 Double
Full Breakfast
Credit Cards: No
Notes: 2, 4, 5, 7 (limited), 8, 10, 11, 12

SCOTCH GROVE

The Grove

RR 1, 52331
(319) 465-3858

Have a mini vacation or an overnight at this peaceful rural working farm. Charming 135-year-old home. Hard-surface roads to within one-quarter of a mile. Big country breakfast featuring homemade rolls. Close to famous Grant Wood Country in Jones County.

Hosts: Robert & Ruth Zirkelbach
Doubles: 2 (SB) $26-36.40
Type of Beds: 2 Double
Full Breakfast

Credit Cards: No
Notes: 2, 5, 6 (if tied), 8, 9, 10, 11, 12

SHELBY

Bed & Breakfast of Iowa #24

Box 430, Preston, 52069
(319) 689-4222

Enjoy the beautiful views from the picture windows of this farm home, which was designed and built with remnants of a rustic barn. Elkhorn and the Danish windmill are twenty miles away. Your king bed is in the loft. Full breakfast. Two doubles, $25-35.

Hannah Marie Country Inn

SIGOURNEY

Bed & Breakfast of Iowa #25

Box 430, Preston, 52069
(319) 689-4222

A turn-of-the-century family home with ex-quisite furnishings. Your hosts have grown children now on their own. Interesting an-tique pieces, fireplace, dolls, and quilts add to the pleasant, quiet environment. The sale barn has weekly livestock sales. Come and visit friendly people in a friendly town. Continental-plus breakfast. Two doubles, $30-40.

SPENCER

Hannah Marie Country Inn

RR 1, Hwy. 71 South, 51301
(712) 262-1286; 332-7719

A lovingly restored farm home offering romantic country strolls, a good night's rest, and a hearty, gourmet breakfast. Be pampered by our private baths, air-conditioning, afternoon hors d'oeuvres; relax in a whirlpool or hot shower. Afternoon theme teas Tues.-Sat. Iowa Great Lakes, twenty miles.

Hosts: Mary Nichols, Dave Nichols
Doubles: 3 (PB) $46.80-62.40
Type of Beds: 1 Double; 2 Queen
Full Breakfast
Credit Cards: A, B
Closed mid-Nov. - April
Notes: 2, 6 (in barn), 7 (restricted), 8, 9 (limited), 10, 11, 12

SPILLVILLE

The Old World Inn

331 South Main, 52168
(319) 562-3739: 562-3186

Lodge and dine at the Old World Inn while exploring this picturesque Czech village where Antonin Dvorak and the Bily Brothers were inspired to compose music and carve clocks. National Historic Register building, built in 1871, renovated in 1987, features Czech cuisine, gifts, crafts, and lodging. All rooms are air-conditioned.

Host: Juanita J. Loven
Doubles: 4 (PB) $36.40-46.80
Type of Beds: 2 Twin; 3 Double
Full or Continental Breakfast
Credit Cards: A, B
Notes: 2, 3, 4, 5, 8, 9, 10, 11, 12, 13

WASHINGTON

Antiques and Old Lace

RR 2, Box 34K, 52353
(319) 653-6486

Loys' Bed & Breakfast

Enjoy bed and breakfast in a Victorian country setting with a beautiful panoramic view. Fresh flowers, wine and cheese on arrival. Golf and fishing within walking distance. Country club nearby for evening meal. Furnished with antiques.

Hosts: JoAnn & Dale Torpey
Doubles: 1 (PB) $31.20-36.40
Type of Beds: 1 Double
Continental or Full Breakfast
Credit Cards: No
Notes: 2, 5, 7, 8 (over 5), 9, 12

Little Switzerland Inn

Quiet Sleeping Rooms

125 Green Meadows Drive, 52353
(319) 653-3736

Modern home with old-fashioned hospitality! Private entrance, central air, TV, and refrigerator. Area interests include antique shops, quilts, Amish culture, Amana colonies, the University of Iowa, and the Old Threshers Reunion on Labor Day weekend.

Hosts: Glen & Lois Williams
Doubles: 4 (SB) $30-35
Type of Beds: 2 Twin; 1 Double; 1 Queen
Full Breakfast
Credit Cards: No
Notes: 2, 5, 6, 7, 8, 10, 11, 12

Kansas

Heritage Inn
300 Main Street, 67056
(316) 835-2118

Heritage Inn is an extraordinary 1922 bed and breakfast inn, located in the heart of Kansas. The moment you step through the doors of the Heritage Inn, you'll feel the comfort and relaxed charm of the 1920s, yet enjoy the convenience of the 1990s.

Hosts: Bill & Merle Olos
Singles: 5 (4PB; 1 SB) $19
Doubles: 10 (9 PB; 1 SB) $22
Type of Beds: 4 Twin; 11 Double
Full Breakfast
Credit Cards: A, B, C
Notes: 2, 4, 5, 7, 8, 9, 10, 11, 12, 14

The Dauddy Haus
Route 2, Box 273, 67543
(no telephone)

Spend an evening back in time! Nice Amish farm with a variety of animals. A small harness shop is on the premises. This is an excellent place for a family or group of friends who need four bedrooms, plus small living room and kitchenette. A bakery, craft shops, variety store, and cafe are within two miles.

Hosts: Robert & Velma Schroek
Singles: 2 (SB) $35
Doubles: 3 (SB) $40
Type of Beds: 2 Twin; 1 Double; 2 Queen
Continental or Full Breakfast
Credit Cards: No
No alcoholic beverages, cameras, or smoking in house
Notes: 2, 5, 8

Pomeroy Inn
224 West Main, 67642
(913) 674-2098

This two-story old limestone building was built in 1886 with walls that are twenty-six inches thick. We have a large lobby with two big picture windows; a big TV; couches, chairs, and tables for coffee and homemade Amarath and whole-wheat cinnamon rolls. Located on highway 24, one block east of the intersection of highways 24 & 283. Very comfortable; reasonable rates. Each room is unique, with handmade quilts.

Hosts: Don & Mary Worcester
Singles: 6 (3 PB; 3 SB) $24.95
Doubles: 3 (PB) $24.95
Type of Beds: 1 Twin; 6 Double; 4 Queen; 1 King
Continental Breakfast
Credit Cards: A, B
Notes: 2, 5, 6, 7, 8, 9, 10, 11, 12

Auntie Emm's
318 N. 2nd, 67301
(316)331-8937 (after 6 P.M.)

This is a restored Queen Anne Victorian home in the lake district of southeast Kansas. We are between Elk Lake and Big Hill Lake, two hours southeast of Wichita, two hours north of Tulsa, three hours south of Kansas City.

Host: Eleanor Woodall
Singles: 1 (SB) $30
Doubles: 1(SB) $35
Type of Beds: 1 Twin; 1 Double
Credit Cards: No

---

6 Pets welcome: 7 Smoking allowed: 8 Children welcome: 9 Social drinking allowed: 10 Tennis available: 11 Swimming available: 12 Golf available: 13 Skiing available: 14 May be booked through travel agents

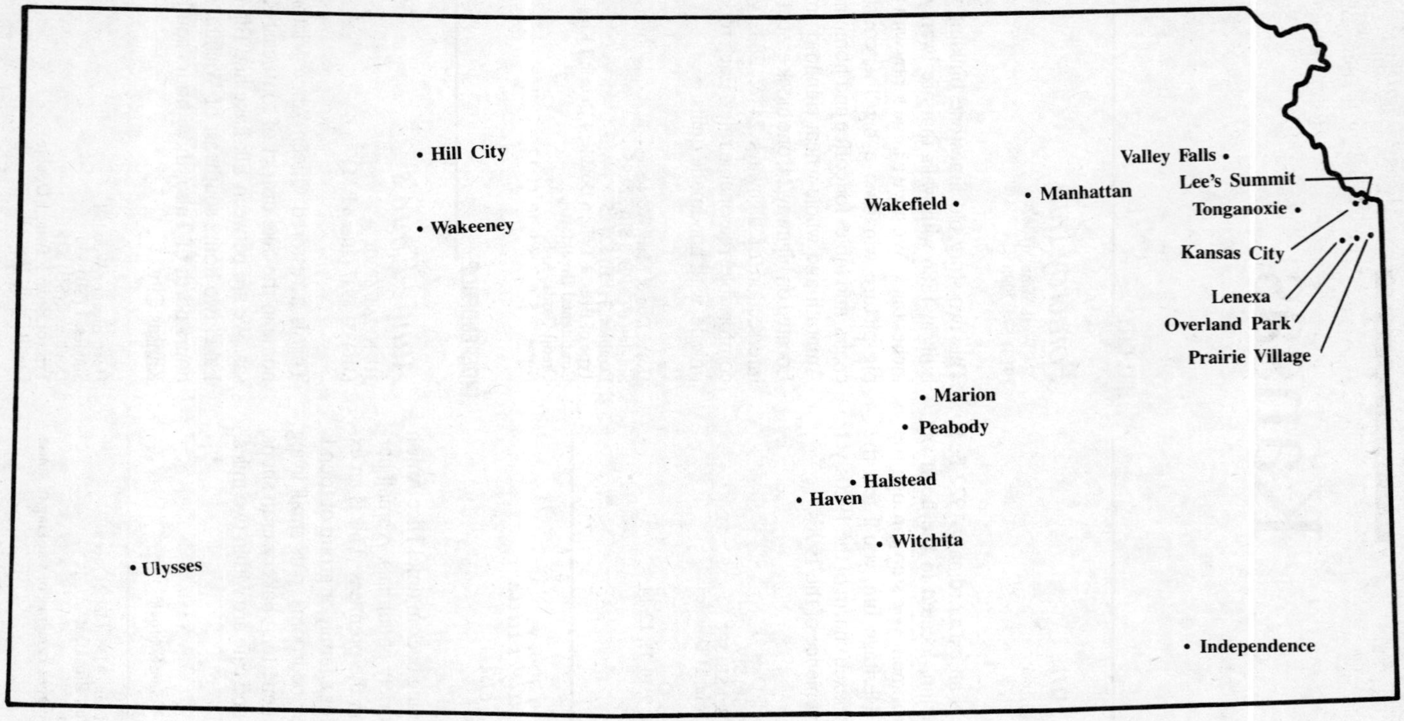

KANSAS

- Valley Falls
- Lee's Summit
- Tonganoxie
- Kansas City
- Lenexa
- Overland Park
- Prairie Village
- Independence

- Manhattan
- Wakefield
- Marion
- Peabody
- Halstead
- Haven
- Witchita

- Hill City
- Wakeeney

- Ulysses

Closed Christmas & July
Notes: 2, 7, 8, 9, 11

KANSAS CITY

B&B Kansas City FO81

Box 14781, Lenexa, Kansas, 66215
(913) 888-3636

A 1935 two-story detached home, adjacent to hosts. A full breakfast is served with your hosts. Family rates available. $35-55.

Auntie Emm's

LEE'S SUMMIT

B&B Kansas City RI36

Box 14781, Lenexa, Kansas, 66215
(913) 888-3636

Traditional brick home, built in 1977 on a lake. Library/TV room adjacent to three bedrooms with private baths. Full breakfast is served in the sun room or breakfast area. Fishing and gold are nearby. No smoking, children, or pets, please. $50-55.

LENEXA

B&B Kansas City MA13

Box 14781, Lenexa, Kansas, 66215
(913) 888-3636

Handsome, spacious builder's home offers a four-poster double bed with antique sheets and quilt. Large room with private bath. A second bedroom shares the bath. Crib and high chair available; full breakfast. $35-40.

B&B Kansas City MO70

Box 14781, Lenexa, Kansas, 66215
(913) 888-3636

Contemporary condo offers a king bedroom with balcony, cathedral ceilings, full breakfast on the patio or elegant dining room. Private bath, double vanity, shower. Swimming and tennis. $45.

MANHATTAN

Kimble Cliff Bed & Breakfast

6782 Anderson Avenue, 66502
(913) 539-3816

Located in the Flinthills region of Kansas, this 1894 stone farmhouse was built of limestone quarried nearby and fashioned by hand. A visit to Australia and New Zealand inspired the hosts, a veterinarian and antique dealer, to open their B&B in 1983. Manhattan is the home of Kansas State University.

Hosts: Betty & Neil Anderson
Doubles: 2 (SB) $40
Type of Beds: 1 Double; 2 Rollaways; 1 Crib
Continental Breakfast
Credit Cards: No
Closed August
Notes: 2, 8, 10, 11, 12

MARION

Haven of Rest

Route 1, Box 120A, 66861
(316) 382-2286

We have a lovely home just off highway 56 and only one-half mile from large Marion

Lake. We have two large lounge areas, fireplaces, TV, pool, and Ping-Pong. We are five miles from a golf course. Swimming, water skiing, and fishing are only one-half mile away.

Hosts: Don & Alice Thompson
Single: $36 plus tax
Double: 44 plus tax
Type of Beds: 2 Double; 1 Queen; 1 King
Full Breakfast
Credit Cards: No
Closed Dec.
Notes: 2, 4, 10, 11, 12

Kimble Cliff

OVERLAND PARK

B&B Kansas City RO11

Box 14781, Lenexa, Kansas, 66215
(913) 888-3636

Contemporary style house with antiques and country decorations. Two rooms share a bath. Full breakfast; dinners also available. South of College Blvd. $45-50.

B&B Kansas City RO12

Box 14781, Lenexa, Kansas, 66215
(913) 888-3636

New home with Victorian decor, several levels. Queen room with private bath and twin room. Full breakfast. $45-50.

PEABODY

Jones Sheep Farm Bed & Breakfast

RR 2, Box 185, 66866
(316) 983-2815

Enjoy an entire turn-of-the-century home in a pastoral setting. Situated on a working sheep farm "at the end of the road," the house is furnished in 1930s style (no phone or TV). Quiet, private. Historic small town nearby.

Hosts: Gary & Marilyn Jones
Guest House: 1 (2 bedrooms, 1 bath) $32-37
Type of Beds: 2 Twin; 1 Double; 1 Crib
Credit Cards: No
Notes: 2, 5, 6, 10, 11, 12

PRAIRIE VILLAGE

B&B Kansas City HA51

Box 14781, Lenexa, Kansas, 66215
(913) 888-3636

Retired minister and his wife travel all over the world and enjoy entertaining other travelers. King bedroom with private bath, color TV, full breakfast. $45-50.

TONGANOXIE

Almeda's Bed & Breakfast

220 South Main Street, 66086
(913) 845-2295

Located in a picturesque small town made an historical site in 1983, the inn dates back to World War I. You are welcome to sip a cup of coffee at the stone bar once used as a bus stop in 1930. In fact, this room was the inspiration for the play "Bus Stop."

Hosts: Almeda & Richard Tinberg
Singles: 5 (PB and SB) $30
Doubles: 2 (PB and SB) $40
Continental Breakfast
Credit Cards: No
Notes: 2, 5, 9, 11, 12

NOTES: Credit cards accepted: A Master Card; B Visa; C American Express; D Discover Card; E Diners Club; F Other: 2 Personal checks accepted: 3 Lunch available: 4 Dinner available: 5 Open all year

ULYSSES

Fort's Cedar View
RR #3, Box 120B, 67880
(316) 356-2570

Fort's Cedar View is located in the heart of the world's largest natural-gas field. We are on the Santa Fe Trail, eight miles north of famed Wagon Bed Springs, the first source of water after crossing the Cimarron River west of Dodge City, which is eighty miles northeast.

Host: Lynda Fort
Doubles: 4 (1 PB; 3 SB) $25-35
Type of Beds: 4 Double
Full Breakfast
Credit Cards: No
Notes: 2, 5, 7 (limited), 10, 11, 12

VALLEY FALLS

The Barn Bed & Breakfast Inn
RR 2, Box 87, 66088
(913) 945-3303

In the rolling hills of northeast Kansas you can sleep in a barn that is 98 years old. We serve you supper when you arrive and homemade bread made from the wheat raised on our farm along with a full breakfast in the morning. There's also an exercise room and heated year-round pool for you to enjoy.

Hosts: Tom, Marcella & Patricia Ryan
Doubles: 16 (PB) $54
Type of Beds: 16 King
Full Breakfast
Credit Cards: A, B
Notes: 2, 3, 4, 5, 8, 9, 10, 11, 12, 14

WAKEENEY

Thistle Hill Bed & Breakfast
Route 1, Box 93, 67672
(913) 743-2644

Located halfway between Kansas City and Denver along I-70, this two-story country bed & breakfast has a large front porch and is decorated with antiques. An old-fashioned breakfast is served next to the brick fireplace in the oak-floored dining room.

Hosts: Dave & Mary Hendricks
Doubles: 3 (2 PB; 1 SB) $35-40
Type of Beds: 3 Double
Full Breakfast
Credit Cards: No
Notes: 2, 5, 8, 9, 10, 11, 12,

WAKEFIELD

Bed 'n' Breakfast — Still Country
Rt. 1, Box 297, 67487
(913) 461-5596

Wakefield, which is on Milford Lake with a population of 800, is a great place for a getaway. This is my twenty-ninth year of inviting new friends to spend a spell with me. Nearby are an arboretum, museum, antiques, drafts, quilts, space, and peace.

Host: Pearl Thurlow
Doubles: 2 (SB) $20-30
Type of Beds: 2 Double
Full Breakfast
Credit Cards: No
Notes: 2, 5, 6, 8, 10, 11

WICHITA

B&B Kansas City HE95
Box 14781, Lenexa, Kansas, 66215
(913) 888-3636

Small 1920s home with one double room, full gourmet breakfast. Located on the Arkansas River, with a lovely patio, yard, and view. $35-40.

Max Paul ... an inn
3910 East Kellogg, 67218
(316) 689-8101

6 Pets welcome: 7 Smoking allowed: 8 Children welcome: 9 Social drinking allowed: 10 Tennis available: 11 Swimming available: 12 Golf available: 13 Skiing available: 14 May be booked through travel agents

Rooms are furnished with European antiques, feather beds, cable TV, and private baths. Executive suites have vaulted ceilings, wood-burning fireplaces, and features like skylights and private balconies. There is a Jacuzzi/exercise room. Weekends, breakfast may be served to the room or in the garden.

Centrally located for the airport, downtown, shopping, and local attractions.

Hosts: Jill & Roberta Eaton
Doubles: 14 (PB) $50-100
Type of Beds: 5 Twin; 7 Double; 7 Queen; 4 King
Breakfast weekends only
Credit Cards: A, B, C, E
Closed Christmas Day
Notes: 2, 5, 7, 9, 10, 11, 12

Kentucky

Kentucky Homes B&B AG01

1432 St. James Court
Louisville, KY 40208
(502) 635-7341

This 1880s brick Georgian is five blocks from the Ohio River. Your hosts enjoy antiques, sports, and cooking. The pioneer towns of Washington and Maysville are nearby. Three bedrooms, one with fireplace, share two baths. $45-50.

Kentucky Homes B&B BD01

1432 St. James Court
Louisville, KY 40208
(502) 635-7341

A 200 acre working tobacco and dairy farm that's just the place to bring the family for a relaxing farm stay. Fish pond, animals, real farm breakfast. Two double bedrooms (one with crib) and guest bath. $45-50.

Kentucky Homes B&B BE01

1432 St. James Court
Louisville, KY 40208
(502) 635-7341

Berea is the home of the unique college for students of the Appalachian region and a famous craft center. Just .5 mile off I-75, this spacious 1919 house has a front porch filled with wicker furniture. One Art Deco king bedroom can be opened to the second twin room to make a suite. A third room features a cherry double bed. All rooms share 1.5 baths. $40-45.

Bowling Green Bed & Breakfast

659 E. 14th Avenue, 42101
(502) 781-3861

A 1939 gray shingled home on a shaded corner. A lounge, front porch, or picnic area help you relax in this comfortable family home near I-65. The restored town square and Western Kentucky University are nearby. Your hosts enjoy travel, photography, antiques, music, reading, and writing. They serve as foreign exchange counselors and teach at Western Kentucky University. Mammoth Cave National Park is forty minutes north; Opryland sixty minutes south.

Hosts: Ronna Lee & Norman Hunter
Doubles: 3 (1 PB; 2 SB) $30-40
Type of Beds: 3 Double
Continental-plus Breakfast
Credit Cards: No
Notes: 2, 4 (advance reservations), 5, 9, 10, 11, 12

---

6 Pets welcome: 7 Smoking allowed: 8 Children welcome: 9 Social drinking allowed: 10 Tennis available: 11 Swimming available: 12 Golf available: 13 Skiing available: 14 May be booked through travel agents

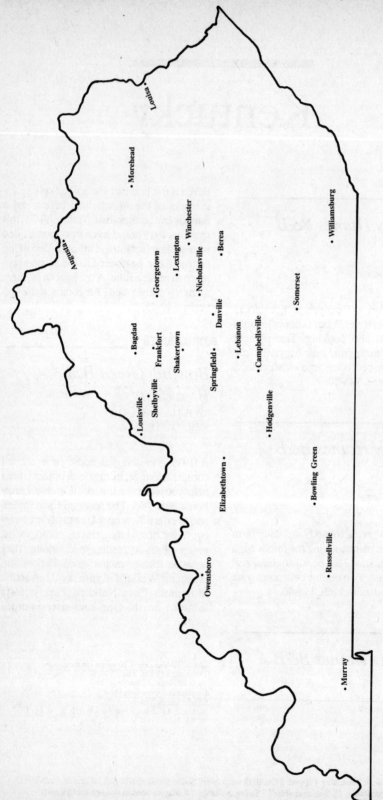

KENTUCKY

Louisa

Morehead

Augusta

Winchester
Georgetown • Lexington
• Nicholasville
• Berea
Somerset

Williamsburg

Bagdad
Shakertown • Danville
Frankfort
Shelbyville Springfield• • Lebanon
• Louisville • Campbellsville

Hodgenville

Elizabethtown •

• Bowling Green

Owensboro •

• Russellville

• Murray

Kentucky Homes B&B
BG01

1432 St. James Court
Louisville, KY 40208
(502) 635-7341

Discover this Swiss chalet-style home on a hill just 2.5 miles from midtown that sits on several acres, with deer stands, gazebo, screened porch, and deck. Cathedral ceiling and fireplace in living room. The hosts are musicians with a music studio on the premises. First floor: two double rooms with shared guest bath: $45. Second floor: sitting room with TV separates two suites: $50-60.

CAMPBELLSVILLE_____

Kentucky Homes B&B
CA01

1432 St. James Court
Louisville, KY 40208
(502) 635-7341

Hospitality comes naturally to this retired benefits counselor. The cherry acorn-post twin beds in her guest room were handmade by a local artisan. She has totally redecorated this contemporary home in Early American, with Oriental rugs and all the right details. $40-45.

DANVILLE_____

Kentucky Homes B&B
DV01

1432 St. James Court
Louisville, KY 40208
(502) 635-7341

This charming white frame 1906 home features an ornate porch wrapped around the front and side. In the gently rolling landscape of central Kentucky, it is one mile from historic Centre College, three from Danville's industrial complex, and forty-five miles south of Lexington via U.S. 127. Smokers and children are welcome; resident dog. Twin downstairs room has a private bath, while a large room upstairs has a queen bed and single bed with private bath. $45-75.

Kentucky Homes B&B DV02

Kentucky Homes B&B
DV02

1432 St. James Court
Louisville, KY 40208
(502) 635-7341

An eye-catching home with classic Italianate windows reaching to the floor. Two large queen rooms, each with private bath. Antique fanciers revel in this tastefully furnished home. $50-65.

Kentucky Homes B&B
DV03

1432 St. James Court
Louisville, KY 40208
(502) 635-7341

Danville is known for its lovely homes, and this one is no exception. Gray shingled and red roofed, it was built in 1902 and is decorated with antiques. Second-floor twin and double bedrooms share a guest bath. $45-50.

6 Pets welcome: 7 Smoking allowed: 8 Children welcome: 9 Social drinking allowed: 10 Tennis available: 11 Swimming available: 12 Golf available: 13 Skiing available: 14 May be booked through travel agents

ELIZABETHTOWN

Kentucky Homes B&B
ET01

1432 St. James Court
Louisville, KY 40208
(502) 635-7341

Four miles west of Elizabethtown, this mansion was built by a former governor in 1830, then served as a girls' school. Vestiges of the school remain in its large conference room, which is available for business gatherings. There's also a large chapel for weddings, receptions, and balls. First-floor room with outside entrance, queen bed, working fireplace, private bath. A second-floor room has a queen bed and private bath. On the third floor, one room has a double bed with private bath and the bridal suite has a queen bed, huge bath with bubble tub, and shower. $60-75.

FRANKFORT

Kentucky Homes B&B
FR01

1432 St. James Court
Louisville, KY 40208
(502) 635-7341

This eastside suburban home is convenient to Keeneland. Ranch-style home, attractively done in antiques and traditional decor. Resident cat. One twin room with private bath; one double with hall bath. $45-50.

GEORGETOWN

Kentucky Homes B&B
GT01

1432 St. James Court
Louisville, KY 40208
(502) 635-7341

A charming two-story gray clapboard home at the edge of a college campus. The original small brick building is now almost completely encased by late nineteenth-century remodeling. One twin bedroom and a room with an unusual bunk-bed set on the second floor. These two rooms share a guest bath. For special occasions, take the king suite with sitting area and large bath with twin lavatories, which closes off from the rest of the floor for privacy. $60-80.

Log Cabin Bed & Breakfast

350 N. Broadway, 40324
(502) 863-3514

Enjoy this Kentucky log cabin (circa 1809) with its shake roof, chinked logs, and period furnishings. Completely private. Two bedrooms, fireplace, fully equipped kitchen, only five miles to Kentucky Horse Park and twelve miles north of Lexington. Children welcome.

Hosts: Clay & Janis McKnight
Cabin: (PB) $60
Continental Breakfast
Credit Cards: No
Notes: 2, 5, 6, 7, 8, 9, 10, 11, 12, 14

HODGENVILLE

Kentucky Homes B&B
HV01

1432 St. James Court
Louisville, KY 40208
(502) 635-7341

Watch the changing seasons at this stately colonial home on a diversified farm in the heart of Lincoln country. Six miles from Lincoln National Historical Park; children welcome. The downstairs separate guest wing features air-conditioning, a bedroom with a four-poster bed, and private bath; an upstairs single or double bedroom shares a bath. $55-60.

NOTES: Credit cards accepted: A Master Card; B Visa; C American Express; D Discover Card; E Diners Club; F Other: 2 Personal checks accepted: 3 Lunch available: 4 Dinner available: 5 Open all year

LEBANON

Kentucky Homes B&B
LN01

1432 St. James Court
Louisville, KY 40208
(502) 635-7341

Located sixty miles from Louisville or Lexington, this southern colonial home was built circa 1833. Splendidly situated on 2 wooded acres with three large guest rooms, two full baths, unusual architectural details. Lots to see within a few miles: distilleries, historic Catholic landmarks, Lincoln country. $60-65.

LEXINGTON

Kentucky Homes B&B
LX01

1432 St. James Court
Louisville, KY 40208
(502) 635-7341

Cozy white frame and stucco home on two bus lines, with good restaurants within five to six blocks. Ten miles to Kentucky Horse Park; convenient to I-64 and I-75. Children are welcome. One room has a double bed and private bath. From April to November, a double room is available with a single bed. $40-45.

Kentucky Homes B&B
LX02

1432 St. James Court
Louisville, KY 40208
(502) 635-7341

If you'd like to stay on a real Bluegrass horse farm, this is the place. Ten miles from Lexington, the farm also hosts an award-winning Jersey dairy herd. You may, on request, have a guided tour of the foaling barns and see the horse industry in action. This two-story brick home has vast acreage; children welcome. Upstairs twin and double bedrooms share a guest bath. Downstairs, a double room has a half-bath. Hostess smokes. $60-65.

Kentucky Homes B&B
LX03

1432 St. James Court
Louisville, KY 40208
(502) 635-7341

This 1890s home is near Gratz Park and downtown. The decor is an interesting mix of traditional and antique furnishings and art. A handsome broad staircase rises from the spacious foyer. Children welcome. One double room with window air-conditioner, and a second room is available during the school year with a double bed and private bath. $55-60.

LOUISA

Kentucky Homes B&B
LA01

1432 St. James Court
Louisville, KY 40208
MS(502) 635-7341

This typical eastern Kentucky country home is in a valley surrounded by hills, on 5 acres. Peace and quiet, abundant wildlife and wild flowers in the woods. Three dogs outside, two cats inside. Ten miles south of I-64, twenty-five miles from Ashland. Double-bed guest room upstairs, shared bath downstairs. $40-45.

6 Pets welcome: 7 Smoking allowed: 8 Children welcome: 9 Social drinking allowed: 10 Tennis available: 11 Swimming available: 12 Golf available: 13 Skiing available: 14 May be booked through travel agents

LOUISVILLE

Kentucky Homes B&B
G002

1432 St. James Court
Louisville, KY 40208
(502) 635-7341

A stunning 1810 mansion on a working 1700 acre horse farm. The bricks for the house were fired on the site. There's a pool in the summer, with peaceful landscaped gardens. Enjoy the extensive library in the stone addition built in 1930. There's a twin bedroom upstairs with private bath and a double room with private bath. Three dogs and one cat are in residence. Children over twelve are welcome. $60-65.

Kentucky Homes B&B
G003

1432 St. James Court
Louisville, KY 40208
(502) 635-7341

About twenty-three miles east of Louisville is a magnificent 10,000 square foot contemporary home on 25 acres in horse country. Sparkling decor, heated pool, and tennis court. You can conduct business from here by sharing the host's office, including the FAX machine. Hostess smokes. There is a queen bedroom with private bath, plus one double bedroom and one twin room with a shared bath. $80-90.

Kentucky Homes B&B
LU03

1432 St. James Court
Louisville, KY 40208
(502) 635-7341

A real find! Twenty-one miles from mid-city, this unique contemporary is built in the "tobacco barn" style, board and batten, on three levels, all very open, with a majestic stone chimney and fireplaces on all levels. Located on a hillside surrounded by trees. There's a twin bedroom suite including a sitting room with fireplace and private bath. A queen bedroom suite with a sitting/dining area is also available. $75-80.

Kentucky Homes B&B
LU06

1432 St. James Court
Louisville, KY 40208
(502) 635-7341

Only three blocks from I-264, this contemporary cottage is on a quiet cul-de-sac. Double and single bedrooms share a guest bath; perfect for a party of three. $35-50.

Kentucky Homes B&B
LU07

1432 St. James Court
Louisville, KY 40208
(502) 635-7341

Renovation of this 1893 home is now in its final stages. Two queen rooms share an old-fashioned bath upstairs. Attractive back garden and deck, off-street parking. Children and smokers are welcome, as are well-disciplined pets. $50-55.

Kentucky Homes B&B
LU08

1432 St. James Court
Louisville, KY 40208
(502) 635-7341

Cherokee Triangle is one of the city's most desirable close-in neighborhoods. Stay one block from the park's edge in a 1920s first-floor duplex with high ceilings, spacious rooms, antiques, and good art. Glassed-in porch. Two double bedrooms with private baths. $50-55.

Kentucky Homes B&B
LU10

1432 St. James Court
Louisville, KY 40208
(502) 635-7341

A 1920s Dutch colonial overlooking Cherokee Park offers informality and cordiality with antique and traditional decoration. There's a sun porch for relaxation and conversation. Two double bedrooms share a guest bath. $50-55.

Kentucky Homes B&B
LU12

1432 St. James Court
Louisville, KY 40208
(502) 635-7341

This opulent home was designed by William Dodd and was once owned by a member of the DuPont family. It's a professionally decorated antique showplace. Two double-bed rooms on the second floor, each with private bath. Sitting room available if a suite is needed. On the third floor there's a suite with queen and double bedrooms, kitchen, full bath, private entrance. $70-120.

Kentucky Homes B&B
LU15

1432 St. James Court
Louisville, KY 40208
(502) 635-7341

You'll have access to the neighborhood's own pool when staying at this charming one-story home on a corner lot with trees. The decor reflects the hostess's love of blues, greens, and peach. One twin bedroom and two double rooms share 1.5 baths. $40-45.

Kentucky Homes B&B
LU17

1432 St. James Court
Louisville, KY 40208
(502) 635-7341

For a party of three wishing to stay in one room, this hostess is located about .5 mile off I-264. The bedroom has double and single beds. $40-45.

Kentucky Homes B&B
LU18

1432 St. James Court
Louisville, KY 40208
(502) 635-7341

A charming Cape Cod home located about ten scenic miles out from midtown, built when the hostess's parents married. Park in the garage or carport. King and twin bedrooms share the guest bath. $40-45.

Kentucky Homes B&B
LU19

1432 St. James Court
Louisville, KY 40208
(502) 635-7341

This stately Georgian showplace is the only presidential home in the country that is privately owned; Zachary Taylor's boyhood was spent here. Furnishings are of the period, yet comfort abounds. Fifteen to twenty minutes to midtown. Two double bedrooms share the guest bath, and there is another double room with private bath. $80-90.

Kentucky Homes B&B
LU20

1432 St. James Court
Louisville, KY 40208
(502) 635-7341

6 Pets welcome: 7 Smoking allowed: 8 Children welcome: 9 Social drinking allowed: 10 Tennis available: 11 Swimming available: 12 Golf available: 13 Skiing available: 14 May be booked through travel agents

This home is made of two historic structures connected by a second-floor hallway. The original pre-1800 ten-room mansion was styled "a French Retreat" by the owner. The "new" eighteen-room house is a fine example of the Greek Revival style. There is a two-bedroom suite with sitting room, bath, double and twin beds. Children and well-discipled pets are welcome. Also available is a stunning double bedroom with private bath. $80-90.

Kentucky Homes B&B
LU23

1432 St. James Court
Louisville, KY 40208
(502) 635-7341

Your high-school science teacher host offers a beautifully decorated room with ornate white iron double bed and private bath. Interesting, eclectic collection of Americana — even the wallpaper borders are unusual and fun. Resident cat. $50-55.

Kentucky Homes B&B
LU25

1432 St. James Court
Louisville, KY 40208
(502) 635-7341

In this posh East End location you will find a solar-covered pool and landscaped backyard. The hostess collects and deals in antique quilts; host is a pilot. The area is good for biking (loaners available). There is an antique double bed in one guest room and a twin with trundle in another; the guest bath is shared if both rooms are taken. $50-55.

Kentucky Homes B&B
LU27

1432 St. James Court

Louisville, KY 40208
(502) 635-7341

A large second-floor twin bedroom in a massive home near the fountain, decorated in antiques and traditional furnishings. The private bath has an oversize antique tub on legs. Host smokes; hostess is a food pro, teacher, and cookbook author. $50-55.

Kentucky Homes B&B
LU28

1432 St. James Court
Louisville, KY 40208
(502) 635-7341

A two-story brick home on a curving, tree-lined street near I-264. Super Southern hospitality! Upstairs, a queen and a double room share a bath. Two single bedrooms are available for members of the same party, and there is also a queen room with private bath. $45-55.

Kentucky Homes B&B
LU29

1432 St. James Court
Louisville, KY 40208
(502) 635-7341

A handsome 1920s Beaux Arts apartment building gone condo in the Cherokee Triangle area. The hostess, famed for her breakfast muffins, will meet you in the Art Deco lobby and show you to your twin-bedded room with private bath. $50-55.

Kentucky Homes B&B
LU31

1432 St. James Court
Louisville, KY 40208
(502) 635-7341

Laura's Log & Stone Inn is deep in the country but convenient to I-64 and I-65.

NOTES: Credit cards accepted: A Master Card; B Visa; C American Express; D Discover Card; E Diners Club; F Other: 2 Personal checks accepted: 3 Lunch available: 4 Dinner available: 5 Open all year

Eighteen miles to Watterson X-way, airport, Fair-Expo Center; 22 to mid-city. The two-story stone center section of the house replicates the original Kentucky home of Squire Boone. Two-story wings on each side are made of logs salvaged from old houses. Some furniture dates from the late 1700s. Huge stone fireplaces, home-made jams at breakfast. Upstairs there are queen and double rooms sharing a full bath. On the lower level there is a queen room with private bath. $50-55.

Kentucky Homes B&B LU32

1432 St. James Court
Louisville, KY 40208
(502) 635-7341

This is one of the up-and-coming blocks in Old Louisville, as renovation fever spreads to the east. The house is a three-story buff brick 1890s Queen Anne with two antique-filled bedrooms on the second floor and a shared guest bath. Children are welcome. $50-55.

Kentucky Homes B&B LU34

1432 St. James Court
Louisville, KY 40208
(502) 635-7341

There's a loveseat in the round bay window of this large, delightful second-floor double overlooking the fountain. Antiques include a huge tub in the private bath. $55-60.

Kentucky Homes B&B LU35

1432 St. James Court
Louisville, KY 40208
(502) 635-7341

This spacious second-floor suite has a sitting room/queen bedroom with a working fireplace. It opens onto a redwood deck overlooking a charming city garden. Private bath. An adjacent double room is also available. Children and smokers welcome. $75.

Kentucky Homes B&B LU36

1432 St. James Court
Louisville, KY 40208
(502) 635-7341

In the Middletown area, near the University of Louisville's Shelby campus and a large shopping mall. This attractive two-story brick home is accented by fine art from the host's native country of Poland. Single women or couples only. Twin or queen bedroom with private bath. $45-50.

Kentucky Homes B&B LU37

1432 St. James Court
Louisville, KY 40208
(502) 635-7341

Two vivacious hostesses preside here in a Bedford stone home in a lovely suburban setting. Their collection of old oak furniture, quilts, and other homey touches make this house a delight. Dogs and cat in residence. There's an upstairs suite with a double bedroom, sitting room, and full bath. Downstairs there are two double bedrooms, each with a half bath and a shared full bath. Children over twelve are welcome. $45-50.

Kentucky Homes B&B LU38

1432 St. James Court
Louisville, KY 40208
(502) 635-7341

Located across the street from LU06, these two hosts will work together to accommodate a large party. The host here is a Lutheran minister. On the first floor there's a queen bedroom with private bath. On the lower level, there is a single bed, baby bed, and sofabed. $45-50.

Kentucky Homes B&B
LU39

1432 St. James Court
Louisville, KY 40208
(502) 635-7341

This 1890s three-story renovation offers two immaculate rooms on the third floor. The larger room has twin beds, the smaller a double. The old-fashioned bath is on the second floor. $40-45.

Kentucky Homes B&B
LU40

1432 St. James Court
Louisville, KY 40208
(502) 635-7341

This spacious, handsome 1907 building was once home to a Louisville mayor. Two bedrooms on the third floor, one with twin beds, one with a double bed. Guest bath between. Freshly and tastefully decorated throughout with antiques. $50-55.

Kentucky Homes B&B
LU41

1432 St. James Court
Louisville, KY 40208
(502) 635-7341

Early twentieth-century apartment building gone condo. This unit has antiques, large rooms, high ceilings. A double-bed room shares 1.5 baths with the hosts. Resident cat. $40-45.

Kentucky Homes B&B
LU42

1432 St. James Court
Louisville, KY 40208
(502) 635-7341

A one-story contemporary home on a lovely landscaped acre offers two double bedrooms with private baths. Decor is country French, with antiques. The hostess smokes. $50-55.

Kentucky Homes B&B
LU43

1432 St. James Court
Louisville, KY 40208
(502) 635-7341

Antiques and long shelves of books help make this one of the most gracious homes on gas-lit Belgravia Court. There's a large room with a queen bed and bath. Or, for a party of two desiring twin beds, there are two smaller bedrooms, each with one single. $70-75.

Kentucky Homes B&B
LU44

1432 St. James Court
Louisville, KY 40208
(502) 635-7341

This beautifully restored Victorian combines Haitian art, antiques, and modern furniture with imagination. There are two guest rooms on the second floor, one double with private bath and one twin room with a private bath on the first floor. On the third floor there is a suite with a twin bedroom and a queen bedroom, bath, kitchen. Dog and cat in residence. $60-80.

Kentucky Homes B&B
LU45

1432 St. James Court
Louisville, KY 40208
(502) 635-7341

An elegant townhouse with deck and garden that overlook the golf course in an exclusive country-club setting. Hosts smoke. Upstairs there is a queen bedroom with private bath and a double room with a private bath on the first floor. $70-75.

Kentucky Homes B&B
PV01

1432 St. James Court
Louisville, KY 40208
(502) 635-7341

In historic Pewee Valley, sitting in the midst of woodland, you'll find a cozy stone cottage that looks like it belongs in the Cotswolds in England. Formal garden; leaded, diamond-paned windows. Hostess smokes. Beautifully decorated second-floor suite is closed off from the rest of the house by a sliding door: double bedroom, sitting room, and bath with tub. $90.

MOREHEAD

Kentucky Homes B&B
M001

1432 St. James Court
Louisville, KY 40208
(502) 635-7341

Morehead is the ideal stopover for entering and leaving the state on I-64, and you'll never meet more interesting hosts. Crib available. Two upstairs guest rooms with shared guest bath. $40-45.

MURRAY

Kentucky Homes B&B
MY01

1432 St. James Court
Louisville, KY 40208
(502) 635-7341

This Victorian inn in the heart of town opened in 1986 after extensive decoration. Children are welcome; pets may be allowed by arrangement. Near Murray State University and the National Museum of the BSA. Two queen and one double guest rooms share a bath. $35-40.

NICHOLASVILLE

Kentucky Homes B&B
NV01

1432 St. James Court
Louisville, KY 40208
(502) 635-7341

Your charming, world-traveling hostess dispenses true Bluegrass hospitality in this charming 1805 home eight miles south of Lexington. Small-town ambience with convenience. Fine antiques throughout the house and great food. Children over twelve are welcome. One upstairs room has a double bed and antique sleigh bed for a third person. Two additional rooms are available spring and fall; share guest bath. $60-65.

RUSSELLVILLE

Kentucky Homes B&B
RU01

1432 St. James Court
Louisville, KY 40208
(502) 635-7341

A one-of-a-kind hideway in the country. The log house is 100 feet from end to end, made of several ancient log cabins, sitting on 15 acres of woodland. Five bedrooms, each with private bath. The decor is country antique. Hot tub on the lower back porch; upper porch with rockers and swing looks into the tall trees. $65-70.

SHAKERTOWN

Kentucky Homes B&B
HB01

1432 St. James Court
Louisville, KY 40208
(502) 635-7341

A retired attorney now turned sheep farmer and his wife welcome you to their circa 1800 Flemish Bond brick Georgian home only 1.9 miles from town. Children love the goats and dogs outside and the inside cats. Spring-fed pool for cooling swims; hiking is great here. A double and a twin room share one bath. $50-55.

SHELBYVILLE

Kentucky Homes B&B
SH01

1432 St. James Court
Louisville, KY 40208
(502) 635-7341

Shelbyville is famed for its beautiful old homes, and this downtown 1825 mansion is no exception. One double bedroom with working fireplace and private bath. Patio for breakfast in sunny weather. The hostess smokes. $40-45.

SOMERSET

Kentucky Homes B&B
ST01

1432 St. James Court
Louisville, KY 40208
(502) 635-7341

There's more to Kentucky than Bluegrass, as you'll find when you visit this dynamic young family at their contemporary home three miles out of Somerset in the foothills of the Cumberlands. Ten miles from Lake Cumberland and Daniel Boone National Forest; 24 miles from Cumberland Falls. Separate guest entrance to the double guest room with private bath. $45-50.

SPRINGFIELD

Kentucky Homes B&B
SP01

1432 St. James Court
Louisville, KY 40208
(502) 635-7341

This country home with large acreage is twelve miles from Bardstown and five miles from Lincoln Park Homestead. An antique-fancier's dream, the late 1700s home also features hand-crafted reproductions made by the host. Lavish country breakfast! Enjoy the stillness of country living in an atmosphere of luxury. Careful smokers and children over twelve are welcome. Twin bedroom, canopied double room, cannon ball room, and antique double room; all with private baths. $70-75.

WILLIAMSBURG

Kentucky Homes B&B
WB01

1432 St. James Court
Louisville, KY 40208
(502) 635-7341

At Kentucky's southern edge, Williamsburg is convenient to I-75. A lively retired teacher is your hostess here. The home features a rear deck with a view of the Cumberland River when the leaves have fallen. Two upstairs rooms available, one with three twin

NOTES: Credit cards accepted: A Master Card; B Visa; C American Express; D Discover Card; E Diners Club; F Other: 2 Personal checks accepted: 3 Lunch available: 4 Dinner available: 5 Open all year

beds, the other with two double beds. Guest bath is shared. $40-45.

WINCHESTER

Kentucky Homes B&B WI01

1432 St. James Court
Louisville, KY 40208
(502) 635-7341

This farm sits on a hill — the perfect picture of the antebellum classic Greek Revival home. Sixteen miles east of Lexington and three miles south of Boonesboro. High ceilings and spacious rooms, beautiful stairway. One room has a queen and single beds, fireplace, and window air-conditioner. One double room shares the guest bath. $45-55.

Kentucky Homes B&B SP01

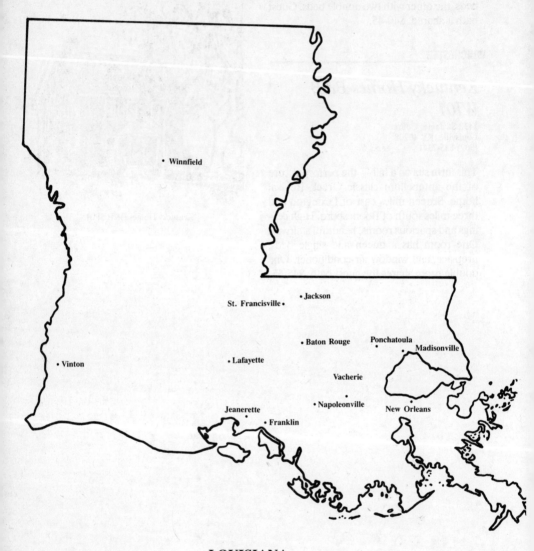

• Winnfield

• Jackson

St. Francisville •

• Baton Rouge   Ponchatoula

• Vinton   • Madisonville

• Lafayette

Vacherie

• Napoleonville   New Orleans

Jeanerette

• Franklin

LOUISIANA

Louisiana

BATON ROUGE

Joy's Bed & Breakfast

Southern Comfort Reservations
2856 Hundred Oaks Avenue, 70808
(504) 346-1928

Two upstairs bedrooms have one bath, sitting room, refrigerator, microwave, HBO and VCR. Kitchenette available. Beautiful antiques; centrally located.

Doubles: 2 (1 PB; 2 SB) $35-55
Type of Beds: 3 Double
Full Breakfast
Credit Cards: A, B, C
Notes: 5, 8 (over 12), 9, 10

Sandy Inn

Southern Comfort Reservations
2856 Hundred Oaks Avenue, 70808
(504) 346-1928

Semi-retired hosts enjoy pampering guests in this attractive, centrally located modern home. Large upstairs bedroom has an eight-foot desk that's perfect for business travelers. Your choice of breakfast; bike riding, walking available; den and kitchen privileges.

Doubles: 1 (PB) $40-45
Type of Beds: 1 Double
Full Breakfast
Credit Cards: A, B, C
Notes: 5, 8, 9

FRANKLIN

Laurel Ridge Country Inn

Southern Comfort Reservations
2856 Hundred Oaks Avenue, Baton Rouge, 70808
(504) 346-1928

Superbly restored 1880s raised cottage in a tranquil setting on the banks of Bayou Teche, near sugar-cane fields. Make it headquarters for your fishing, tennis, golf, fine Cajun food, swamp tours, and more. Fluent French spoken.

Suite: 1 (PB) $125
Doubles: 3 (PB) $75-125
Type of Beds: 1 Twin; 3 Double
Continental Breakfast
Credit Cards: A, B, C
Notes: 5, 7 (restricted), 8, 9, 10, 11, 12

JACKSON

Milbank

Southern Comfort Reservations
2856 Hundred Oaks Avenue, Baton Rouge, 70808
(504) 346-1928

This National Register property has been a home and a bank, and was occupied by Union troops. Now it's been restored to its former elegance and furnished with period antiques. Two sitting rooms and complete kitchens; front and back verandas on the first and second floors.

Doubles: 5 (2 PB; 3 SB) $65-75
Type of Beds: 2 Twin; 2 Double; 1 Queen
Full Breakfast
Credit Cards: A, B, C
Notes: 2, 3, 4, 5, 9, 12

JEANERETTE

Bed & Breakfast on Bayou Teche

2148 1/2 W. Main Street, 70544
(318) 276-5061

---

6 Pets welcome: 7 Smoking allowed: 8 Children welcome: 9 Social drinking allowed: 10 Tennis available: 11 Swimming available: 12 Golf available: 13 Skiing available: 14 May be booked through travel agents

Contemporary residence with separate guest cottage containing one large room with three single beds, complete kitchen, TV, carport, use of washer, dryer, and barbecue pit. Ideal for families with two or three children. Minutes from Jungle Gardens, and many other must-sees in Cajun Country.

Hosts: Warren & Barbara Patout
Doubles: 1 (PB) $40
Type of Beds: 3 Twin
Continental-plus Breakfast
Credit Cards: No
Notes: 2, 5, 7, 8, 9, 10, 12

LAFAYETTE

Bois des Chenes Inn

Southern Comfort Reservations
2856 Hundred Oaks Avenue, Baton Rouge, 70808
(504) 346-1928

This authentically restored Acadian raised mansion, circa 1820, has rooms in the mansion and in the Victorian carriage house, plus one of the finest existing collections of furniture handcrafted of native Louisiana woods. Chocolates and after-dinner drinks are offered in the evening. Pet kennel on premises.

Suite: 1 (PB) $90-110
Doubles: 6 (PB) $55-95
Type of Beds: 2 Twin; 3 Double; 3 Queen
Full Breakfast
Credit Cards: A, B, C
Notes: 5, 6, 7 (restricted), 8, 9

MADISONVILLE

River Run Bed & Breakfast

Southern Comfort Reservations
2856 Hundred Oaks Avenue, Baton Rouge, 70808
(504) 346-1928

Century-old house seven miles from Lake Pontchartrain Causeway leading to New Orleans. Big porches, wide hallways, high ceilings, bright, airy rooms give the house a casual atmosphere. Just steps to Tchefuncte River for crabbing, fishing, and water sports.

Doubles: 3 (SB) $40-45
Type of Beds: 3 Double; 1 Rollaway
Full Breakfast
Credit Cards: A, B, C
Notes: 5, 7, 8, 9

NAPOLEONVILLE

Madewood Plantation House

Rt. 2, Box 478, 70390
(504) 369-7151 (10 A.M.-3 P.M.)

A National Historic Landmark Greek Revival plantation house seventy-five miles from downtown New Orleans. Antiques, canopied beds, wine and cheese. Candlelight dining is available. Oak trees and sugar-cane fields. Featured in *Country Home, Travel and Leisure, Vogue,* and *Southern Living.* Modified American Plan also available.

Hosts: Keith & Millie Marshall
Doubles: 9 (PB) $85 (B&B); 150 (MAP)
Type of Beds: 1 Twin; 5 Double; 4 Queen
Continental Breakfast in cottages; Full in main house
Credit Cards: A, B, C
Closed Christmas Eve & Day, New Year's Eve,
Thanksgiving Eve & Day
Notes: 2, 4, 8, 9, 14

NEW ORLEANS

B&B New Orleans #1

Box 52257, 70152
(504) 525-4640

Modest guest apartment in uptown home in a lovely residential neighborhood of historic homes. Universities are close by, as well as the Audubon Zoological Gardens. Only fifteen minutes from the French Quarter by car. Hosts live upstairs and guests occupy the first floor with its own entrance.

Doubles: 2 (SB) $50-100
Type of Beds: 2 Twin; 1 Double
Continental Breakfast

NOTES: Credit cards accepted: A Master Card; B Visa; C American Express; D Discover Card; E Diners
Club; F Other: 2 Personal checks accepted: 3 Lunch available: 4 Dinner available: 5 Open all year

Credit Cards: No
Notes: 5, 7, 8, 9, 10, 11, 12, 14

B&B New Orleans #2

Box 52257, 70152
(504) 525-4640

Modest home near Audubon Park, just a thirty-minute streetcar ride from downtown. Visit nearby Audubon Zoological Gardens with its walk-through Louisiana Swamp exhibit.

Doubles: 2 (SB) $25-40
Type of Beds: 2 Double
Continental Breakfast
Credit Cards: No
Notes: 5, 8, 9, 10, 11, 12, 14

B&B New Orleans #5

B&B New Orleans #3

Box 52257, 70152
(504) 525-4640

Modest guest suite in a Victorian cottage. Built in 1896, this home displays the gingerbread ornamentation so typical of New Orleans cottages. Private guest entrance; self-service breakfast.

Doubles: 1 (PB) $40-56
Type of Beds: 1 Queen
Continental Breakfast
Credit Cards: No
Notes: 5, 7, 8, 9, 10, 11, 12, 14

B&B New Orleans #5

Box 52257, 70152
(504) 525-4640

Modest guest suites in a nineteenth-century cottage in the French Quarter. Self-serve breakfast. English hosts are restoring the cottage themselves while becoming local music experts.

Doubles: 3 (PB) $45-100
Type of Beds: 4 Twin; 1 Double
Continental Breakfast
Credit Cards: No
Notes: 5, 6, 7, 8, 9, 10, 11, 12, 14

B&B New Orleans #4

Box 52257, 70152
(504) 525-4640

Modest Garden District home where guests are warmly welcomed. Streetcar arrives downtown in ten minutes. Beloved pets in residence. Tour New Orleans' unique cemeteries for a special treat.

Doubles: 2 (SB) $35-50
Type of Beds: 4 Twin
Continental Breakfast
Credit Cards: No
Notes: 5, 7, 8, 9, 10, 11, 12, 14

B&B New Orleans #6

Box 52257, 70152
(504) 525-4640

Modern English Tudor home in an exclusive subdivision. The house is filled with collectibles. Venture forth along River Road into antebellum Louisiana plantation country to discover traces of the past. The French Quarter is just a twenty-minute drive away.

Doubles: 2 (PB) $30-45
Type of Beds: 2 Double
Continental Breakfast
Credit Cards: No
Notes: 5, 8, 10, 11, 12, 14

6 Pets welcome: 7 Smoking allowed: 8 Children welcome: 9 Social drinking allowed: 10 Tennis available: 11 Swimming available: 12 Golf available: 13 Skiing available: 14 May be booked through travel agents

B&B New Orleans #7

Box 52257, 70152
(504) 525-4640

Bellaire home with swimming pool. Your hostess is a German teacher. By car, the house is ten minutes from downtown. Experience exotic Swamfari — ride in a piroque (Louisiana-style canoe) through moss-draped swamps, catching sight of native wildlife.

Doubles: 1 (PB) $30-45
Type of Beds: 1 Double
Continental Breakfast
Credit Cards: No
Notes: 5, 7, 8, 9, 10, 11, 12, 14

B&B New Orleans #8

Box 52257, 70152
(504) 525-4640

University area home that provides a comfortable, homey flavor. Restaurants, specialty shops, and music clubs are near at hand. A pleasurable forty-minute streetcar ride will take you downtown (fifteen minutes by car).

Doubles: 1 (PB) $30-70
Type of Beds: 1 Twin; 1 Double
Continental Breakfast
Credit Cards: No
Notes: 5, 6, 7, 8, 9, 10, 11, 12, 14

B&B New Orleans #9

Box 52257, 70152
(504) 525-4640

Guest suite in a Greek Revival home nestled in an historic community just across the Mississippi from the French Quarter. Guests have a private apartment overlooking the swimming pool. Walk or drive to the free ferry for a romantic ride, or drive over the nearby bridge.

Doubles: 1 (PB) $30-70
Type of Beds: 1 Queen; 1 Sofabed
Continental Breakfast

Credit Cards: No
Notes: 5, 6, 7, 8, 9, 10, 11, 12, 14

B&B New Orleans #10

Box 52257, 70152
(504) 525-4640

Uptown home with a pool in the shade of a magnificent live oak tree. Feel at home in a big family atmosphere. The host will even take you canoeing through the swamps and bayous. Downtown is fifteen minutes away by car or peak-time express bus; fifty minutes at other times.

Doubles: 3 (S2.5B) $25-40
Type of Beds: 3 Double
Continental Breakfast
Credit Cards: No
Notes: 5, 10, 11, 12, 14

B&B New Orleans #11

Box 52257, 70152
(504) 525-4640

Napoleon Avenue home, recently renovated by the hosts. After an exciting day of sightseeing or conventioneering, guests relax on the wide front veranda. Guest rooms are apart from hosts' rooms. By car it's five minutes to downtown; by bus, fifteen.

Doubles: 4 (1 PB; 3 S1.5B) $40-70
Type of Beds: 1 Twin; 3 Double; 1 Queen
Continental Breakfast
Notes: 5, 7, 8, 9, 10, 11, 12, 14

B&B New Orleans #12

Box 52257, 70152
(504) 525-4640

A room with a view! The host, an antique-shop owner, loves to tell the history of his home, originally a petite maisonette. His family has lived here for generations. The tiny second-floor bedroom has a romantic view of the French Quarter's rooftops.

NOTES: Credit cards accepted: A Master Card; B Visa; C American Express; D Discover Card; E Diners Club; F Other: 2 Personal checks accepted: 3 Lunch available: 4 Dinner available: 5 Open all year

Doubles: 1 (SB) $50-70
Type of Beds: 1 Double
Continental Breakfast
Credit Cards: No
Notes: 5, 7, 8, 9, 10, 11, 12, 14

B&B New Orleans #13

Box 52257, 70152
(504) 525-4640

Artist's guest atelier. A cozy studio apartment with a balcony overlooking a walkway famous for fencing masters of the past. Natural brick walls and original artworks. Walk half a block to Royal Street's antique shops and art galleries.

Doubles: 1 (PB) $75-85
Type of Beds: 1 King
Continental Breakfast
Credit Cards: No
Notes: 5, 6, 7, 8, 9, 10, 11, 12, 14

B&B New Orleans #14

Box 52257, 70152
(504) 525-4640

Bourbon Street suite in a residential section. Your host, a New Orleans native, enjoys sharing his vast knowledge of the special spots you should see.

Doubles: 1 (PB) $65-100
Type of Beds: 1 King
Continental Breakfast
Credit Cards: No
Notes: 5, 7, 8, 9, 10, 11, 12, 14

B&B New Orleans #15

Box 52257, 70152
(504) 525-4640

Creole cottage, restored by your host, with lovely antiques. Lush patio. French Quarter walking tours and Cajun dancing (even lessons) are available to guests. Just steps to the French Quarter and the mini-bus.

Doubles: 1 (PB) $50-70
Type of Beds: 1 Double
Continental Breakfast

Credit Cards: No
Notes: 5, 6, 7, 8, 9, 10, 11, 12, 14

B&B New Orleans #16

Box 52257, 70152
(504) 525-4640

Originally a slave building, this private guest cottage with nice antique pieces has a balcony and French doors opening onto a landscaped courtyard. Guests can easily stroll to the French Quarter and then return to relax in the furnished courtyard.

Cottage: 1 (2 bedrooms, 1 bath) $75-150
Type of Beds: 2 Double
Continental Breakfast
Credit Cards: No
Notes: 5, 6, 7, 8, 9, 10, 11, 12, 14

B&B New Orleans #17

Box 52257, 70152
(504) 525-4640

Designer guest cottage, originally the studio of a famous Southern sculptor. A short streetcar ride to galleries, antiques, restaurants, the French Quarter. Hosts live in the 1876 main house.

Cottage: 1 (PB) $95-135
Type of Beds: 2 Twin; 1 Queen
Continental Breakfast
Credit Cards: No
Notes: 5, 6, 7, 8, 9, 10, 11, 12, 14

B&B New Orleans #18

Box 52257, 70152
(504) 525-4640

French Quarter guest cottage with private entrance. A short walk takes you to Royal Street's antique shops and famous restaurants.

Cottage: 1 (PB) $75-105
Type of Beds: 1 Double; 1 Sofabed
Continental Breakfast
Credit Cards: No
Notes: 5, 8, 10, 11, 12, 14

6 Pets welcome: 7 Smoking allowed: 8 Children welcome: 9 Social drinking allowed: 10 Tennis available: 11 Swimming available: 12 Golf available: 13 Skiing available: 14 May be booked through travel agents

B&B New Orleans #20

Box 52257, 70152
(504) 525-4640

French Quarter guest maisonette on an intimate courtyard. This historic two-story guest cottage offers guests a private home in the residential area of world-famous Bourbon Street. Two bedrooms, one bath; sleeps 4.

Cottage: 1 (PB) $200-300
Type of Beds: 2 Double
Continental Breakfast
Credit Cards: No
Notes: 5, 7, 8, 9, 10, 11, 12, 14

B&B New Orleans #21

Box 52257, 70152
(504) 525-4640

French Quarter home filled with lovely artwork and antiques. Architecturally, this is a Louisiana gem. Two guest bedrooms, each with its own sitting room, are located on the second floor apart from the hosts' quarters. Guests can also relax on the brick patio.

Suite: 1 (PB) $65-170
Type of Beds: 2 Twin; 1 Double; 1 Daybed
Continental Breakfast
Credit Cards: No
Notes: 5, 7, 8, 9, 10, 11, 12, 14

B&B New Orleans #22

Box 52257, 70152
(504) 525-4640

French Quarter petit guest cottage, just off Bourbon Street. In a quiet residential neighborhood with the excitement of jazz clubs and celebrated restaurants nearby. A walk to the riverfront streetcar offers a trip along the mighty Mississippi past historic Jackson Square's artists and street performers to the new Riverwalk Shopping Center.

Cottage: 1 (1 bedroom, PB) $75-100
Type of Beds: 1 Queen; 1 Futon
Continental Breakfast

Credit Cards: No
Notes: 5, 8, 9, 10, 11, 12, 14

B&B New Orleans #23

Box 52257, 70152
(504) 525-4640

Garden District guest suite with three lovely antique beds, living room, and kitchen. Enjoy the special flavors of New Orleans style cooking at the nearby bistros.

Suite: 1 (2 bedrooms, PB) $50-80
Type of Beds: 3 Twin
Continental Breakfast
Credit Cards: No
Notes: 5, 7, 8, 9, 10, 11, 12, 14

B&B New Orleans #26

Box 52257, 70152
(504) 525-4640

Guest garret suite in an historic home, formerly the private residence of an interior designer. In the Garden District, with the streetcar at hand for touring; ten-minute walk to downtown convention centers and the French Quarter.

Suite: 1 (1 bedroom, PB) $65-95
Type of Beds: 2 Twin; 1 King
Continental Breakfast
Credit Cards: No
Notes: 5, 7, 8, 9, 10, 11, 12, 14

B&B New Orleans #27

Box 52257, 70152
(504) 525-4640

Guest suite in historic Garden District home with private entrance. Overlooks the swimming pool. Streetcar ride downtown takes only ten minutes. A short walk takes guest to Magazine Street antique shops.

Suite: 1 (1 bedroom, PB) $50-90
Type of Beds: 1 King; 1 Sofabed
Continental Breakfast
Credit Cards: No
Notes: 5, 7, 9, 10, 11, 12, 14

NOTES: Credit cards accepted: A Master Card; B Visa; C American Express; D Discover Card; E Diners Club; F Other: 2 Personal checks accepted: 3 Lunch available: 4 Dinner available: 5 Open all year

B&B New Orleans #28

Box 52257, 70152
(504) 525-4640

An historic home of national significance, this house's title dates back to 1775. Guests occupy a well-appointed room with antiques. The hosts are longtime French Quarter residents who enjoy sharing their knowledge with guests.

Doubles: 1 (PB) $60-80
Type of Beds: 2 Twin
Continental Breakfast
Credit Cards: No
Notes: 5, 7, 8, 9, 10, 11, 12, 14

B&B New Orleans #29

Box 52257, 70152
(504) 525-4640

Le Garconiere guest suite in the French Quarter. Antique shops, restaurants, and jazz clubs are just a short walk from this quiet neighborhood. Private two-story guest cottage overlooking the tropical courtyard offers a balcony and full kitchen.

Cottage: 1 (1 bedroom, PB) $70-85
Type of Beds: 1 King
Continental Breakfast
Credit Cards: No
Notes: 5, 7, 8, 9, 10, 11, 12, 14

B&B New Orleans #30

Box 52257, 70152
(504) 525-4640

Quaint guest cottages, flavored with antiques and architectural details, look onto a patio and antique swing. The streetcar is downtown at the French Quarter in just fifteen minutes. Nearby antique shops, bistros, and music.

Cottage: 2 (1 bedroom each, PB) $50-95
Type of Beds: 1 Twin; 2 Queen
Continental Breakfast
Credit Cards: No
Notes: 5, 7, 8, 9, 10, 11, 12, 14

B&B New Orleans #31

Box 52257, 70152
(504) 525-4640

Queen Anne Victorian home, recently renovated, with original artwork and fabric-dressed walls. The Garden District mansions are just steps away, as are restaurants, antiques, and art galleries.

Doubles: 3 (SB) $40-60
Type of Beds: 7 Twin; 1 Double; 1 Queen; 3 King
Continental Breakfast
Credit Cards: No
Notes: 5, 7, 8, 9, 10, 11, 12, 14

B&B New Orleans #30

6 Pets welcome: 7 Smoking allowed: 8 Children welcome: 9 Social drinking allowed: 10 Tennis available: 11 Swimming available: 12 Golf available: 13 Skiing available: 14 May be booked through travel agents

B&B New Orleans #31

B&B New Orleans #32

Box 52257, 70152
(504) 525-4640

Victorian cottage offers peaceful, intimate
guest rooms with private entrance onto the
patio. Nearby is the old French Market and
the Mississippi River Walk.

Doubles: 3 (PB) $55-70
Type of Beds: 3 Double
Continental Breakfast
Credit Cards: No
Notes: 5, 7, 8, 9, 10, 11, 12, 14

Bernard B&B

New Orleans B&B, Box 8128, 70182
(504) 822-5046; 822-5038

In this pretty little uptown cottage right next
to the Universities (Tulane, Newcomb,
Loyola), you can have either a bedroom with
a double bed or a bedroom with twin beds.
Private bath. Near bus lines that will take
you into Canal Street and the French
Quarter. Also very near Audubon Park and
Zoological Gardens. Long term rates available. A very good bargain for one or two
persons.

$45-50
Continental Breakfast
Credit Cards: A, B, C (for deposit only)
Notes: 7, 14

Brown B&B

New Orleans B&B, Box 8128, 70182
(504) 822-5046; 822-5038

In this delightful brick home you can choose
an elegant, airy room decorated in rose, with
an art-deco look and private bath; a spacious
bedroom with double bed which shares a
bath with another lovely room with twin
beds; a pretty garage apartment with twin
beds and a trundle bed in the living area.
Loads of off street parking, and two buses
stop just steps away to take you to the
French Quarter, the Fairgrounds (Jazz Fest
country), or wherever you wish to go. A safe,
convenient residential ares. The two rooms
which share a bath may be booked as a suite;
if only one is booked, guest has a private
bath. The garage apartment can accommodate four persons, and includes private
bath and a kitchenette.

$40-50
Type of Beds: 4 Twin; 1 King
Continental Breakfast
Credit Cards: A, B, C (for deposit only)
Notes: 7, 14

Burke B&B

New Orleans B&B, Box 8128, 70182
(504) 822-5046; 822-5038

In a stately old family home on St. Charles
Avenue, complete with four poster beds and
antique armoires; two second floor
bedrooms make a suite, one with double
bed, one with twins, and bath between.
Across the hall is a small room with double
bed and private bath. On the third floor
(there's an elevator) is a great "garden"

NOTES: Credit cards accepted: A Master Card; B Visa; C American Express; D Discover Card; E Diners
Club; F Other: 2 Personal checks accepted: 3 Lunch available: 4 Dinner available: 5 Open all year

room, ringed with windows overlooking the treetops. Deluxe in every way. On the St. Charles Ave. streetcar line; across from Tulane and Loyola Universities, and very near Audubon Park and Zoological Gardens. The streetcar will have you at Canal St. and the French Quarter in 20-25 minutes. For Old New Orleans atmosphere, this home is hard to beat.

Doubles: 4 (2 PB; 2S1) $65-75
Type of Beds: 2 Twin; 3 Double
Continental Breakfast
Credit Cards: A, B, C (for deposit only)
Notes: 14

B&B New Orleans #32

Cartier B&B

New Orleans B&B, Box 8128, 70182
(504) 822-5046; 822-5038

Across the lake (Pontchartrain) from New Orleans, here's a very comfortable guest house with a large bedroom, a liv/din/kit combo with a pull out sofa bed; 1.5 baths. Upstairs is a gym with half bath. Also there is an Allegro motor home with a big bedroom having a king size bed, a kitchen, and a bath. There is a 20 X 40 pool and tennis courts; and only a half block to the lake. Very relaxing, great for a family; but,

no pets. please. The guest house has cable TV and a VCR.

Motor Home: $55 for 2
Guest house: $65 for 2, $10 each additional person
Continental Breakfast
Credit Cards: A, B, C (for deposit only)
Notes: 7, 8, 10, 11, 14

Carrollton Cottage

Southern Comfort Reservations
2856 Hundred Oaks Avenue, Baton Rouge, 70808
(504) 346-1928

In a pleasant older subdivision, this cottage is near universities, parks, museums, the French Quarter, and downtown. Easy access to highways. Hostess speaks fluent Spanish. Cat in residence. Off-street parking.

Doubles: 2 (SB) $37.50-47
Type of Beds: 2 Twin; 1 Double
Continental Breakfast
Credit Cards: A, B, C
Notes: 5, 6 (small), 7, 9

The Columns Hotel

3811 Saint Charles Avenue, 70115
(504) 899-9308

One of the stateliest remaining examples of turn-of-the-century Louisiana architecture, The Columns Hotel offers a return to old-age elegance and one of the best entrees into the New Orleans of today. Despite its elegance, The Columns is affordable and comfortable. Its nineteen rooms range from modest comfort to the very grand; each features some delight for the experienced traveler.

Hosts: Jacques & Claire Creppel
Doubles: 19 (9 PB; 10 SB) $50-105
Type of Beds: 7 Twin; 14 Double; 1 King
Continental Breakfast
Credit Cards: A, B, C
Notes: 2, 3, 4, 5, 7, 8, 9, 10, 11, 12, 14

Dauzat House

337 Burgundy Street, 70130
(504) 524-2075

6 Pets welcome: 7 Smoking allowed: 8 Children welcome: 9 Social drinking allowed: 10 Tennis available: 11 Swimming available: 12 Golf available: 13 Skiing available: 14 May be booked through travel agents

An historic oasis in the French Quarter offering townhouse suites, lush courtyard with pool, homemade amaretto, wood-burning fireplaces, superb antiques, and the personal attention you can't find in larger hotels.

Hosts: Richard L. Nicolais & Donald E. Dauzat
Suites: (PB) from $160
Continental Breakfast
Credit Cards: No
Notes: 2, 5, 6, 9, 11, 12, 14

Davenport B&B

New Orleans B&B, Box 8128, 70182
(504) 822-5046; 822-5038

A lovely little cottage behind the main house in mid-French Quarter; pleasant and comfortable. Downstairs is a living-dining area and a kitchenette; upstairs is a bedroom with twin beds and a bath. The brick-paved courtyard with trees and flowers invite you to sit and relax. Your hosts are talented, knowledgeable, and well-traveled. A deluxe accommodation in every sense; very well located near major hotels, Convention Center, Canal Street, and all French Quarter attractions.

Single: $75
Double: $85
Triple: $95
Credit Cards: A, B, C (for deposit only)
Notes: 14

Davis B&B

New Orleans B&B, Box 8128, 70182
(504) 822-5046; 822-5038

Lovely three-room condo with courtyard in the heart of the French Quarter; a sofa bed in the living room and a queen size bed in the bedroom. Your continental breakfast will be in the refrigerator. Very pleasant, pretty and comfortable. Parking is available at an extra charge.

Doubles: $80 for 2; $100 for 4
Continental Breakfast

Credit Cards: A, B, C (for deposit only)
Notes: 11, 14

Dey B&B

New Orleans B&B, Box 8128, 70182
(504) 822-5046; 822-5038

A spacious apartment in an historic area within walking distance to Bayou St. John, New Orleans Museum of Art, and City Park, where guests can jog, play tennis, golf, or just stroll under the ancient oaks. With a private entrance, private bath, a well equipped kitchenette, TV, and off street parking this apartment has a double bed and a sofa bed. It is near bus lines to Canal Street and the French Quarter and is very convenient to the Fairgrounds, where the Jazz Fest is held. There is a pleasant outdoor sitting area and your hosts are very hospitable.

$45 for 2; $65 for 4
Continental Breakfast
Credit Cards: A, B, C (for deposit only)
Notes: 14

Dumaine Guest House

Southern Comfort Reservations
2856 Hundred Oaks Avenue, Baton Rouge, 70808
(504) 346-1929

Romantic hideaway in a French Quarter patio with lush semitropical plants. Private entrance. Built in 1824, it now has all modern conveniences. First floor has sitting room and kitchenette; second has bath, bedroom, and balcony. English, Spanish, and Portuguese are spoken.

Cottage: 1 (PB) $80
Type of Beds: 2 Twin; 1 Sofabed
Continental-plus Breakfast
Credit Cards: A, B, C
Notes: 5, 9

Fowler B&B

New Orleans B&B, Box 8128, 70182
(504) 822-5046; 822-5038

NOTES: Credit cards accepted: A Master Card; B Visa; C American Express; D Discover Card; E Diners Club; F Other: 2 Personal checks accepted: 3 Lunch available: 4 Dinner available: 5 Open all year

A courtyard apartment that is private, safe, and convenient. Downstairs is a living room with a sofa bed, a dining area, and a kitchenette; upstairs has a bedroom with a double bed and a balcony overlooking the courtyard. Bright airy and fresh with your hosts on premises. Your hostess is gracious and knowledgeable about the city. Continental breakfast will be in the refrigerator. The lovely location in the French Quarter is near major hotels, parking, transportation to Convention Center, Rivergate, Riverwalk, etc.

$75 for 2; 125 for 4
Continental Breakfast
Credit Cards: A, B, C (for deposit only)
Notes: 14

Fowler B&B #2

New Orleans B&B, Box 8128, 70182
(504) 822-5046; 822-5038

In this charming French Quarter home with exposed brick, hand-hewn cypress, French doors are two bedrooms with a private entrance; one bedroom has twin beds, the other has a double bed. Each bedroom has a sitting area; the bath is between. Unless guests know each other, only one room is available so that guests will have a private bath. A continental breakfast is served in the sun room overlooking the patio. Well located, this home is near major hotels, restaurants, antique shops, transportation to Convention Center, Rivergate, and Riverwalk.

$75 each room
Continental Breakfast
Credit Cards: A, B, C (for deposit only)
Notes: 7, 14

Gibson B&B

New Orleans B&B, Box 8128, 70182
(504) 822-5046; 822-5038

In a lovely uptown home with serene and traditional atmosphere, here's a large two-bedroom-and-bath suite — one bedroom with twin beds and one with double bed. With a private entrance, hot tub, and patio you are just steps away from St. Charles Avenue and the streetcar so you can be in the French Quarter in minutes. This home is in the Garden District — Old New Orleans' prestigious residential section of great homes. You are near the universities (Tulane and Loyola) and Audubon Park and Zoological Gardens.

Doubles: (2S1B) $75 each room
Type of Beds: Twin; Double
Continental Breakfast
Credit Cards: A, B, C (for deposit only)
Notes: 14

Griest B&B

New Orleans B&B, Box 8128, 70182
(504) 822-5046; 822-5038

In this lovely home, c. 1840, on the fringe of the Garden District, your convivial hosts have created an Old New Orleans atmosphere complete with beautiful rooms and antiques. All five bedrooms have private baths; most have queen or king size beds. Also available is a spacious attic bedroom with a king size bed and a Louisiana antique bed (NOT for tall people!) and private bath. You're one block from the St. Charles Avenue streetcar, which will have you in the French Quarter in 15 to 20 minutes, or the University section and Audubon Park and Zoological Gardens in an equally short time. Deluxe in every way. Cocktail parties and dinners may be arranged with the host. Hosts can entertain business groups, wedding parties, etc., in a sit-down dinner.

Doubles: 6 (PB) $65-85
Type of Beds: Double; Queen; King
Continental Breakfast
Credit Cards: A, B, C (for deposit only)
Notes: 7, 8, 14

6 Pets welcome: 7 Smoking allowed: 8 Children welcome: 9 Social drinking allowed: 10 Tennis available: 11 Swimming available: 12 Golf available: 13 Skiing available: 14 May be booked through travel agents

Jensen's Bed & Breakfast

1631 Seventh Street, 70115
(504) 897-1895

A 100-year-old Queen Anne Victorian beautifully decorated with antiques, stained glass, twelve-foot alcove ceilings, and cypress doors. Located across the street from the Garden District, and area famed for its lovely homes. The trolley is one block away and provides easy access to the French Quarter and Audubon Park and Zoo. All rooms are air-conditioned.

Hosts: Shirley, Bruce & Joni
Doubles: 5 (SB) $40-50
Type of Beds: 2 Twin; 1 Double; 1 Queen; 2 King
Continental Breakfast
Credit Cards: No
Notes: 2, 5, 8, 9, 10, 12

Josephine Guest House

Southern Comfort Reservations
2856 Hundred Oaks Avenue, Baton Rouge, 70808
(504) 346-1928

Lower Garden District late-nineteenth-century Italianate mansion has six rooms with TVs, balconies, unusual antiques. Hosts' hobbies are gourmet cooking, an-tique collecting, and helping guests see New Orleans. French and Spanish spoken; resident terrier.

Suite: 1 (PB) $135 and up
Doubles: 6 (PB) $65-135 and up
Type of Beds: 4 Twin; 2 Double; 1 Queen; 1 King
Continental Breakfast
Minimum stay weekends, Oct. - May: 2
Credit Cards: A, B, C
Notes: 5, 7, 8, 9

Kellin B&B

New Orleans B&B, Box 8128, 70182
(504) 822-5046; 822-5038

This half of a Creole double house is at ground floor level, easily accessible to anyone who cannot manage stairs. It is very fresh, clean, and airy with a living room, bedroom, kitchen, and courtyard. The living room has a queen size sofa bed, the bedroom has a double bed. This is a great bargain, well located, pleasant, comfortable, and smack-dab in the middle of the French Quarter — within walking distance to all attractions, major hotels, and Convention Center.

$60 for 2; 85 for 4 people
Continental Breakfast
Credit Cards: A, B, C (for deposit only)
Notes: 8

Mazant Guest House

906 Mazant Street, 70117
(504) 944-2662

We are an informal, self-catering, modestly priced and happy household located only two miles from the French Quarter. A small kitchen is available to guests during their stay, and we offer advice about restaurants and the best places to hear local New Orleans music.

Hosts: Jane Henderson & Robyn Halvorsen
Doubles: 11 (2 PB; 9 SB) $15-25
Suites available to sleep 4-5; $40-45
Type of Beds: 1 Twin; 8 Double; 1 Queen; 1 King
Continental Breakfast
Minimum stay during Mardi Gras: 5
Notes: 2, 5, 6, 7, 8, 9, 10, 11, 12

Prigmore B&B

New Orleans B&B, Box 8128, 70182
(504) 822-5046; 822-5038

A gracious hostess welcomes you to this fine old Victorian home, one block from the St. Charles Avenue streetcar, in the middle of the lovely Garden District — an area of fine Old New Orleans homes. One great bedroom with two double beds, two bedrooms with king size beds, one bedroom with twin beds, and a lovely downstairs bedroom with a queen size bed; all with private baths. There are also available three cozy and comfortable "budget rooms", two with double beds and one with twin beds; all with private baths. This home is fine for

NOTES: Credit cards accepted: A Master Card; B Visa; C American Express; D Discover Card; E Diners Club; F Other: 2 Personal checks accepted: 3 Lunch available: 4 Dinner available: 5 Open all year

parents visiting Tulane or Loyola students, or guests can be in the French Quarter in minutes via streetcar. On-street parking.

Budget Rooms: 3 (PB) $45
Doubles: 4 (PB) $65-85
Type of Beds: 4 Twin; 3 Double; 1 Queen; 2 King
Continental Breakfast
Credit Cards: A, B, C (for deposit only)
Notes: 14

Richmond B&B

New Orleans B&B, Box 8128, 70182
(504) 822-5046; 822-5038

This very old building has been completely renovated into deluxe condos and corporate apartments with rooftop garden and courtyard. A delightful three-room apartment with living room (double sofa bed), complete kitchen, bath, and a bedroom with twin beds which may be made into one king size bed. Convivial, well-traveled hosts. Your continental breakfast will be in the refrigerator. Well located in the heart of the French Quarter; watch the city skyline at night; walk to all French Quarter attractions; near major hotels, transportation to Convention Center, Rivergate, and Riverwalk Mall.

$85 for 2
Continental Breakfast
Credit Cards: A, B, C (for deposit only)

Sanchez B&B

New Orleans B&B, Box 8128, 70182
(504) 822-5046; 822-5038

Here's a commercial building converted into a comfortable, sparkling-clean, attractive home. Very friendly hosts offer one large bedroom with two double beds, a smaller bedroom (double bed) and bath between the two rooms. There are two more small rooms with double beds share a hall bath. There is an attractive sitting area with a refrigerator and coffee hot plate where guests can relax and watch TV. Offering off street parking and city busses to the business

district and the French Quarter there is also an airport bus stop at your front door. No smoking or small children, please.

Singles: $35-45
Doubles: 4 (SB) $45-55
Type of Beds: Double
Continental Breakfast
Credit Cards: A, B, C (for deposit only)
Notes: 14

Sporl B&B

New Orleans B&B, Box 8128, 70182
(504) 822-5046; 822-5038

Two lovely little efficiency apartments in a fine old 1807 house with a swimming pool. It's about 20 minutes by the Magazine Street bus to the French Quarter. These are deluxe accommodations, private, very comfortable, and with off street parking. One apartment has twin beds, the other has a double bed.

$65-75 each apartment
Continental Breakfast
Credit Cards: A, B, C (for deposit only)
Notes: 7, 14

Terrell House

1441 Magazine Street, 70130
(504) 524-9859

Built in 1858 by cotton broker Richard Terrell, this house was restored and opened as an inn in 1984. Balconies, galleries, authentic antique furnishings, and a courtyard make this a true New Orleans home filled with atmosphere. All rooms have private baths, telephones, and TV. Terrell House is a five-minute drive from the French Quarter and three blocks from the St. Charles streetcar in the historic Lower Garden District. Complimentary cocktail, soft drinks, sherry in parlor.

Host: Counce Hightower
Rooms: 9 (PB) start at $65.60 per person
Type of Beds: 1 Twin; 6 Double; 2 Queen
Continental Breakfast
Minimum stay during Sugar Bowl, Mardi Gras, and Jazz Festival

6 Pets welcome: 7 Smoking allowed: 8 Children welcome: 9 Social drinking allowed: 10 Tennis available: 11 Swimming available: 12 Golf available: 13 Skiing available: 14 May be booked through travel agents

Credit Cards: A, B, C
Notes: 2, 5, 7, 8, 9, 14

Theriot B&B

New Orleans B&B, Box 8128, 70182
(504) 822-5046; 822-5038

Two bedrooms with queen size beds and
private baths in this nice New Orleans suburb; very comfortable, near shopping, but
you'll need a car.

Doubles: 2 (PB) $50
Type of Beds: 2 Queen
Continental Breakfast
Credit Cards: A, B, C (for deposit only)
Notes: 7, 8, 14

Wilkinson B&B

New Orleans B&B, Box 8128, 70182
(504) 822-5046; 822-5038

Here's lush, plush Victorian ambience in a
two-story cottage on a quiet, secluded courtyard just off Royal Street. The living room
with a double sofa bed and the kitchen are
on the first floor, the bedroom with a queen
size bed and the bath are on the second, all
done in turn-of-the-century elegance. Add
to this an absolutely beautiful courtyard —
cool, green, and very inviting — in the
beautiful French Quarter. Walk to attractions, major hotels, Convention Center, etc.

$85 for 2; $125 for 4
Continental Breakfast
Credit Cards: A, B, C (for deposit only)

PONCHATOULA

Taste of Bavaria

Southern Comfort Reservations
2856 Hundred Oaks Avenue, Baton Rouge, 70808
(504) 346-1928

A touch of Europe 45 miles north of New
Orleans and 45 miles east of Baton Rouge,

this home and business operates as a German Gasthaus. The charming home is built
of all old wood and furnished with unique
antiques.

Doubles: 2 (PB) $40-50
Type of Beds: 2 Double; 1 Sofabed
Full Breakfast
Credit Cards: A, B, C
Notes: 5, 8

ST. FRANCISVILLE

Barrow House

524 Royal Street, Box 1461, 70775
(504) 635-4791

Sip wine in a wicker rocker on the front
porch while you enjoy the ambience of a
quiet neighborhood of antebellum homes.
Rooms are all furnished in antiques from
1840-1870. Gourmet candlelight dinners
are available, as is breakfast in bed. A cas-
sette walking tour of the historic district is
available for our guests.

Hosts: Shirley & Lyle Dittloff
Doubles: 3 (PB) $40-55
Suite: 1 (PB)
Type of Beds: 3 Double; 1 Queen; 1 King
Continental Breakfast, Full Breakfast Available
Credit Cards: No
Closed Dec. 23-25
Notes: 2, 4, 5, 7, 8, 9, 12, 14

The Guest Quarters

Southern Comfort Reservations
2856 Hundred Oaks Avenue, Baton Rouge, 70808
(504) 346-1928

Complete guest accommodations including
kitchen, dining area overlooking a lake,
living room, large bedroom, washer, and
dryer. Two weeks' notice required for reservations. This is the home of one of the state's
most famous citizens, and reservations are
only taken when he is at home.

Doubles: 1 (PB) $80-100
Type of Beds: 1 Queen; 1 Sofabed
Full Breakfast
Credit Cards: A, B, C
Notes: 2, 8, 9, 12

NOTES: Credit cards accepted: A Master Card; B Visa; C American Express; D Discover Card; E Diners
Club; F Other: 2 Personal checks accepted: 3 Lunch available: 4 Dinner available: 5 Open all year

The St. Francisville Inn

118 N. Commerce, 70775
(504) 635-6502

In the heart of Louisiana Plantation Country, the St. Francisville Inn has nine antique-furnished guest rooms opening onto a lovely New Orleans-style brick courtyard where guests may relax. The restored main house, circa 1880, has a restaurant, a sitting room for guests, porches, and swings for rocking, and an original spectacular ceiling medallion with Mardi Gras mask design. On the edge of the historic district.

Hosts: Florence & Dick Fillet
Doubles: 9 (PB) $38.50-60.50
Type of Beds: 4 Twin; 8 Double; 3 King
Continental Breakfast
Credit Cards: A, B, C, D
Notes: 2, 3, 4, 5, 7, 8, 9, 12

The St. Francisville Inn

VACHERIE

Mississippi River Plantation

Southern Comfort Reservations
2856 Hundred Oaks Avenue, Baton Rouge, 70808
(504) 346-1928

Guest cottages on the grounds of a plantation overlooking the Mississippi River. Cottages have central air and heat, private baths.

Cottages: 6 (PB) $75-100
Continental Breakfast
Credit Cards: A, B, C
Notes: 2, 3, 5, 8, 9

VINTON

Old Lyons House

1335 Horridge Street, 70668
(318) 589-2903

Queen Anne Victorian in the downtown area of a small rural town, restored and furnished with antiques. The hosts will make you welcome and do everything possible to insure that when you leave, you know the meaning of the words *southern hospitality*. Horse racing, fishing, swimming, canoeing, nature, old homes, and more, are all within a few minutes' drive.

Hosts: Danny Cooper & Ben Royal
Doubles: 2 (SB) $25-35
Type of Beds: 2 Double
Full Breakfast
Credit Cards: No
Notes: 2, 5, 7, 8, 9, 10, 11

WINNFIELD

Southern Colonial

Southern Comfort Reservations
2856 Hundred Oaks Avenue, Baton Rouge, 70808
(504) 346-1928

Built in the days of high ceilings, wide halls, and big front porches, this home has three upstairs bedrooms, two baths, and a sitting area. Thirty miles from historic Natchitoches, Winnfield is home of the colorful Long family, famous in Louisiana politics.

Doubles: 3 (SB) $40-45
Type of Beds: 3 Double
Full Breakfast
Credit Cards: A, B, C
Notes: 5, 8, 9, 10, 11, 12

6 Pets welcome: 7 Smoking allowed: 8 Children welcome: 9 Social drinking allowed: 10 Tennis available: 11 Swimming available: 12 Golf available: 13 Skiing available: 14 May be booked through travel agents

Bingham •

Newport •

Eastport
Dennyville •
Lubec
Machias •

Blue Hill
Cherryfield
Bucksport •
Castine
Sunset
Searsport •
Hancock
Belfast •

Bethel •
Bryant Pond •

Chamberlain •

Camden •
Waldboro •
Rockport •
Bar Harbor
Southwest Harbor
Bass Harbor
South Brooksville

Center Lovell •

Fryeburg •

Wiscasset •
Bridgton •
Newcastle •
Bristol Mills
Bath
Topsham
Brunswick
Freeport •
Harpswell

Isle Au Haut
Thomaston
Spruce Head
Pemaquid Falls
Damariscotta, Damariscotta Mills
Georgetown
East Boothbay
Boothbay Harbor Capitol Island

Cornish •

Bailey Island
South Harpswell

Sanford •
Arundel •
Biddeford Pool
Kennebunkport

Isle Au Haut •

Wells Beach
Wells
Ogunquit
Eliot •
York
York Beach
York Harbor
Kittery Point

MAINE

Maine

ARUNDEL

Arundel Meadows Inn

Route 1
Mail to: Box 1129, Kennebunk, 04043
(207) 985-3770

This 165-year-old farmhouse features an extensive art collection and antiques in each of the six uniquely decorated rooms. Several rooms feature working fireplaces. One owner is a professor at Boston University; the other is a professional chef. The inn is bordered by the Kennebunk River on the south and 3 acres of meadows to the east.

Hosts: Mark Bachelder & Murray Yaeger
Doubles: 6(PB) $70-95
Type of Beds: 2 Double; 4 Queen
Full Breakfast plus afternoon tea
Minimum stay from May 1-Oct. 15
Credit Cards: A, B
Notes: 2, 5, 7, 8 (over 12), 9, 10, 11, 12

BAILEY ISLAND

Katie's Ketch

Box 105, 04003
(207) 833-7785

Your host Albert is a retired lobsterman of forty years who hand carves duck decoys. Katie's plants abound in their Dutch colonial home. Bailey Island is a lobster-fishing community providing fishing, swimming, sailing, ferry rides, plus scrumptious fare from the sea that is served in nearby restaurants.

Hosts: Albert & Catherine Johnson
Singles: 1 (SB) $35, plus tax
Doubles: 3 (1 PB; 2 SB) $45-60, plus tax
Type of Beds: 1 Twin; 2 Double; 1 Queen waterbed
Full Breakfast
Minimum stay weekends & holidays: 2

Credit Cards: No
Closed Jan. 1-May 1
Notes: 2, 10, 11, 12

The Lady & The Loon

Box 98, Main Street, 04003
(207) 833-6871

Built in the late 1800s, this house on Bailey Island sits high overlooking the Atlantic Ocean toiling among Casco Bay. Private stairs down to the sea, a picnic table overlooking the islands. A small island appliqued with New England Shore restaurants, people, architecture, flora and fauna. Your hostess is a wildlife artist and naturalist who loves antiques and crafts.

Host: Gail Sprague
Doubles: 2 (PB) $60-65
Type of Beds: 1 Double; 1 Queen
Continental Breakfast
Credit Cards: A, B,
Closed winter
Notes: 2, 9, 11, 12

Castlemaine Inn

6 Pets welcome: 7 Smoking allowed: 8 Children welcome: 9 Social drinking allowed: 10 Tennis available: 11 Swimming available: 12 Golf available: 13 Skiing available: 14 May be booked through travel agents

BAR HARBOR

Castlemaine Inn

39 Holland Avenue, 04609
(207) 288-4563

Castlemaine Inn is nestled on a quiet side street in the village of Bar Harbor, which is surrounded by the magnificent Acadia National Park. Our rooms are well-appointed, with canopy beds and fireplaces. A delightful buffet-style breakfast is served.

Hosts: Terence O'Connell & Norah O'Brien
Doubles: 12 (PB) $65-150
Full Breakfast
Credit Cards: A, B
Notes: 2, 5, 8 (over 10), 9, 10, 11, 12

Hearthside Inn B&B

Hearthside Inn Bed & Breakfast

7 High Street, 04609
(207) 288-4533

Built as a private residence in 1907, Hearthside Inn is now a beautiful and luxuriously appointed B&B. Our rooms feature a blend of country and Victorian furnishings, and most have queen beds and private baths. We are conveniently located on a quiet side street, within easy walking distance of shops, restaurants, and picturesque Frenchman's Bay. A short car ride from Acadia National Park.

Hosts: Susan & Barry Schwartz
Doubles: 9 (7 PB; 2 SB) $60-95
Type of Beds: 4 Double; 5 Queen
Continental Breakfast
Credit Cards: A, B
Notes: 2, 5, 8 (over 10), 9, 10, 11, 12, 13

Holbrook House

74 Mt. Desert Street, 04609
(207) 288-4970

A nineteen-room Victorian inn with chintz, lace, and flowers. Full buffet breakfast. Just a five-minute walk to the ocean, shops, and restaurants; one mile to Acadia National Park. Sun room, library, and parlor.

Hosts: Dorothy & Mike Chester
Doubles: 10 (PB) $80-95
Type of Beds: 1 Twin; 5 Double; 4 Queen
Full Breakfast
Minimum stay: 2
Credit Cards: A, B
Closed Oct. 15 - June 10
Notes: 2, 8 (8 and over), 9, 10, 11, 12

Manor House Inn

106 West Street, 04609
(207) 288-3759

Enjoy our 1887 Victorian summer cottage listed on the National Register of Historic Places. Located near Acadia National Park and within walking distance of downtown Bar Harbor.

Hosts: Jan Matter & Rosemary Hamblen
Doubles: 14 (PB) $79.18-149.80
Type of Beds: 4 Twin; 8 Double; 1 Queen; 4 King
Continental Breakfast
Minimum stay July, Aug., and holidays: 2
Credit Cards: A, B, C
Closed Nov.-mid April
Notes: 2, 7, 8 (over 8), 9, 10, 11, 12

Manor House Inn

The Maples "A Victorian Inn"

16 Roberts Avenue, 04609
(207) 288-3443

Discover why the rich and famous stayed and played in Bar Harbor. Recapture the charm, elegance, and enjoyment of a bygone era at this family-operated inn. Walk to the harbor, shops, and restaurants. Five-minute drive to Acadia National Park or the Nova Scotia ferry terminal. Fishing, sailing, hiking, climbing, boating, cycling, wind surfing, and whale watching will fill your days.

Hosts: Michele & Richard Suydam
Doubles: 10 (8 PB; 2 SB) $53.50-85.60
Type of Beds: 2 Twin; 8 Double
Continental-plus Breakfast
Minimum stay holidays: 2
Credit Cards: A, B
Notes: 2, 5, 10, 11, 12, 13

Mira Monte Inn

69 Mt. Desert Street, 04609
(207) 288-4263

Built in 1864, this gracious eighteen-room Victorian mansion is renovated in the simpler style of Bar Harbor's elegance, featuring period furnishings, library, fireplaces, porches, and 1.5 acres of estate grounds. Friendly, informative staff.

Host: Marian Burns
Doubles: 11 (PB) $80-125
Type of Beds: 2 Twin; 2 Double; 7 Queen; 2 King
Continental-plus Breakfast
Minimum stay: 2
Credit Cards: A, B, C
Closed Oct. 25-May 10
Notes: 2, 7, 8, 9, 10, 11, 12

Stratford House Inn

45 Mount Desert Street, 04609
(207) 288-5189

Stratford House Inn features English Tudor architecture with a likeness to Queen Elizabeth's summer home. Beautiful bedrooms, each one different. Easy walk to stores, restaurants, or waterfront. Acadia National Park is close by with beauty and activities for all.

Hosts: Barbara & Norman Moulton
Doubles: 10 (8 PB; 2 SB) $70-135
Type of Beds: 6 Double; 3 Queen; 1 King
Continental Breakfast
Minimum stay weekends & holidays: 2
Credit Cards: A, B, C
Closed Nov.-May
Notes: 2, 7, 8, 9, 10, 11, 12

BASS HARBOR

The Bass Harbor Inn

Shore Road, 04653
(207) 244-5157

On beautiful Mt. Desert Island, the Bass Harbor Inn offers you a lovely harbor view and choice of lodging ranging from rooms with private or half bath, fireplace, to suite with full kitchen and bath or housekeeping cottage. Write for brochure.

Hosts: Carl & Leslie
Doubles: 9 (PB and SB) $50-90
Type of Beds: 2 Twin; 2 Double; 7 Queen
Continental Breakfast
Credit Cards: No

Pointy Head Inn
Rt. 102A, 04653
(207) 244-7261

Relax on the quiet side of Mount Desert Island near Acadia National Park, in an old sea captain's home on the shore of a picturesque harbor, where schooners anchor overnight. Haven for artists and photographers. Minutes to lighthouse, trails, restaurants, stores.

Hosts: Doris & Warren Townsend
Singles: 1 (SB) $37.45
Doubles: 5 (1 PB; 4 SB) $58.85
Type of Beds: 4 Twin; 3 Double; 1 Queen
Full Breakfast
Minimum stay: 2
Credit Cards: No
Closed Nov.-mid May
Notes: 2, 8 (over 5), 10, 11, 12

BATH

Fairhaven Inn
RR 2, Box 85, 04530
(207) 443-4391

This classic, comfortable, quiet colonial, built in 1790, stands on the bank of the Kennebec River surrounded by 27 acres of meadows, lawns, and dark pine woods. Renowned for its breakfasts. Hiking and cross-country skiing on the premises; beaches nearby.

Hosts: George & Sallie Pollard
Singles: 1 (SB) $42.80-48.15
Doubles: 8 (PB and SB) $53.50-74.90
Type of Beds: 2 Twin; 4 Double; 2 Queen
Full Breakfast
Credit Cards: No
Notes: 2, 5, 6, 7 (limited), 8, 9, 10, 11, 12, 13

Glad II
60 Pearl Street, 04530
(207) 443-1191

A comfortable 138-year-old Victorian home near the center of town and convenient to Maritime Museum, beaches, Freeport shopping, L.L. Bean, and Boothbay Harbor. Nicholas, my four-legged concierge, and I love to welcome new friends.

Host: Gladys Lansky
Doubles: 3 (SB) $37.45-48.15
Type of Beds: 2 Twin; 1 Double
Continental-plus Breakfast
Minimum stay weekends & holidays: 2
Credit Cards: No
Notes: 2, 5, 8 (over 12), 9, 10, 11, 12, 13, 14

BELFAST

Londonderry Inn
Belmont Avenue, 04915
(207) 338-3988

Restored 1803 farmhouse with five spacious guest rooms furnished with country charm. Besides the large country kitchen where a full breakfast is served, guests can enjoy two sitting rooms, a library with piano, and a sun porch. There are 2.5 shared baths. A quiet country setting with fields, woods, and pond for the connoisseur of life's simple pleasures.

Hosts: Suzanne & Buzz Smedley
Doubles: 5 (S2.5B) $42-50
Type of Beds: 4 Double; 1 Queen
Full Breakfast
Credit Cards: A, B
Minimum stay weekends & holidays: 2
Closed Jan. 1-Memorial Day
Notes: 2, 7 (limited), 8 (over 12), 9, 12, 13, 14

Penobscot Meadows Inn
Rt. 1, 04915
(207) 338-5320

Penobscot Meadows is a small, completely renovated, turn-of-the-century inn in quiet Belfast. Conveniently located for day trips to Acadia, Camden, Islesboro, Blue Hill, etc.

NOTES: Credit cards accepted: A Master Card; B Visa; C American Express; D Discover Card; E Diners Club; F Other: 2 Personal checks accepted: 3 Lunch available: 4 Dinner available: 5 Open all year

Featuring four-star dining on our deck overlooking Penobscot Bay; extensive wine list.

Hosts: Dini & Bernie Chapnick
Doubles: 7 (PB) $41.73-95.23
Type of Beds: 2 Twin; 4 Double; 1 Queen
Continental Breakfast
Credit Cards: A, B, D
Notes: 2, 4, 5, 6, 7, 8, 9, 10, 11, 12, 13 (XC)

The Chapman Inn

BETHEL

The Chapman Inn

Box 206, 04217
(207) 824-2657

An 1865 Federal in a National Historic District, facing the village common. Friendly, homelike atmosphere; large, sunny rooms. Delicious breakfasts features fresh fruits, muffins, and a variety of main courses. Private saunas, game room, cable color TV in sitting room. Dorm accommodations also available.

Hosts: Doug & Robin Zinchuk, David Weston, Lori Kennagh
Doubles: 8 (3 PB; 5 SB) $55-65
Type of Beds: 6 Twin; 10 Double
Full Breakfast
Credit Cards: A, B, C
Notes: 2, 5, 6, 7, 8, 9, 10, 11, 12, 13, 14

The Douglass Place

Star Rt. Box 90, 04217
(207) 824-2229

A four-season, nineteenth-century, Early American/Victorian home situated between two major ski areas and the White Mountains of New Hampshire. Marvelous location for antiquing, summer sports, and hiking. Gardens and gazebo in summer; game room, cozy fireplace in winter.

Hosts: Dana & Barbara Douglass
Doubles: 4 (SB) $37.45-48.15
Type of Beds: 3 Twin; 1 Queen; 1 Sofabed
Continental Breakfast
Minimum stay weekends & holidays: 2
Credit Cards: C
Closed Christmas & 2 weeks in April
Notes: 2, 6, 7, 8, 9, 10, 11, 12, 13

BIDDEFORD POOL

Pineapple Hospitality ME 436

Box F-821, New Bedford, MA 02742-0821
(508) 990-1696

This white clapboard ranch-style home is perched on a knoll overlooking the sand, the sea, and the rugged terrain of coastal Maine. Walk to Biddeford Pool or relax on the private beach. The entire home is like a museum, with art objects, Oriental, Persian, and African carpets, antiques and fine artifacts. Your hostess speaks five languages.

Doubles: 2 (SB) $50-70
Type of Beds: 2 Twin; 1 Double
Continental Breakfast
Credit Cards: No
Notes: 2, 7, 8, 9, 10, 11

BINGHAM

Mrs. G's Bed & Breakfast

Box 389, 04920
(207) 672-4034

An old Victorian home on the picturesque Kennebec River, where white-water rafting is popular. Hiking on the Appalachian Trail, beautiful waterfalls, shopping, tennis, and golf are all nearby. Fifty miles from skiing at Sugarloaf.

6 Pets welcome: 7 Smoking allowed: 8 Children welcome: 9 Social drinking allowed: 10 Tennis available: 11 Swimming available: 12 Golf available: 13 Skiing available: 14 May be booked through travel agents

Arcady Down East

Host: Frances M. Gibson
Loft: 9 beds (SB) $20
Doubles: 4 (SB) $24
Type of Beds: 11 Twin; 3 Double
Full Breakfast
Credit Cards: No
Notes: 2, 3, 4, 5, 6, 7, 8, 9, 10, 11, 12, 13, 14

BLUE HILL

Arcady Down East

South Street, 04614
(207) 374-5576

This Victorian mansion, listed on the National Register, is filled with period antiques. Coastal location on a ridge overlooking Blue Hill Bay, Mount Desert Island, and Acadia National Park. Sailing, fishing, hiking, biking, antiquing, crafts, and nearby historic attractions.

Hosts: Tommie & Andy Duncan
Doubles: 8 (5 PB; 3 SB) $50-90
Type of Beds: 3 Twin; 2 Double; 1 Queen; 2 King
Full Breakfast
Credit Cards: No
Closed Oct. 15 - June 15
Notes: 2, 7, 8 (over 12), 9, 10, 11, 12

BOOTHBAY HARBOR

Anchor Watch

3 Eames Road, 04538
(207) 633-2284

With a shorefront location on a scenic, quiet lane, the Anchor Watch is just a short walk to town for shopping, dining, and boat trips. From the breakfast room you will see lobstermen hauling their traps, lighthouses flashing, and ducks feeding along the shore.

Hosts: Diane & Bob Campbell
Doubles: 3 (SB) $52-66
Type of Beds: 3 Twin; 3 Double
Continental Breakfast
Credit Cards: No
Notes: 2, 5, 9, 12

Captain Sawyer's Place

87 Commercial Street, 04538
(207) 633-2290

Enjoy the Maine elegance of an 1878 sea captain's home in one of Maine's most beautiful fishing villages. Ten guest rooms with private baths. Only a few steps from sailing and cruise boats, shops, galleries, fine restaurants, and theater.

Doubles: 10 (PB) $65-120
Type of Beds: 2 Twin; 8 Queen
Continental Breakfast
Credit Cards: A, B
Closed Nov.-April
Notes: 8 (over 12), 9, 10, 11, 12

Hilltop Guest House

44 McKown Hill, 04538
(207) 633-2941

This home is only a three-minute walk to all activities: boat trips, restaurant, dinner theater, and shops, and has ample parking facilities, a large porch, and a tree swing for the young and old.

Hosts: Georgia Savory & Virginia Brewer
Doubles: 6 (2 PB; 4 SB) $32-42
Continental Breakfast
Credit Cards: No
Notes: 2, 5, 6, 7, 8, 9, 10, 11, 12, 14

The Howard House Motel

Route 27, 04538
(207) 633-3933

Each spacious room has a private bath, cable color TV, and its own balcony. Early American furnishings, high-beamed ceilings, and natural wood walls. Shopping, sightseeing, boating, and fine restaurants are all nearby.

Hosts: The Farrins
Doubles: 15 (PB) $35-75
Type of Beds: 4 Double; 8 Queen; 4 King
Continental-plus Breakfast
Credit Cards: No
Closed Dec.-Feb.
Notes: 2, 8, 9, 10, 11, 12

Newagen Seaside Inn

Rt. 27 South, Cape Newagen, 04552
(207) 633-5242

Lobsters, lighthouses, fresh flowers, fog horns, sea spray, spruce forests, fresh and salt-water pools, tennis courts, delicious meals, and cocktails. Rooms and suites with private baths. A gracious, fun, authentic New England inn 3.5 hours north of Boston and 6 miles out to sea from Boothbay Harbor. Accessible by car or boat.

Hosts: Peter & Heidi Larsen
Singles: 10 (PB) $75
Doubles: 22 (PB) $85-150
Type of Beds: 20 Twin; 13 Double; 2 Queen
Full breakfast July & Aug; continental June & Sept.
Credit Cards: A, B
Closed Oct. 15 - May 15
Notes: 2, 3, 4, 8, 9, 10, 11, 14

Topside — "The Inn on the Hill"

McKown Hill, 04538
(207) 633-5404

Overlooking beautiful Boothbay Harbor on top of McKown Hill. Just a two-minute walk to all the activities on the waterfront, shops, restaurants, and dinner theater. Excellent accommodations. All rooms with private baths.

Hosts: Faye & Newell Wilson
Singles: 1 (PB) $50-75
Doubles: 29 (PB) $75-95
Type of Beds: 58 Queen; 5 King
Continental Breakfast
Credit Cards: A, B
Closed Nov. - mid-May
Notes: 2, 7, 8, 9, 10, 11, 12

BRIDGTON

The Noble House Bed & Breakfast

37 Highland Road, Box 180, 04009
(207) 647-3733

Romantic turn-of-the-century manor, set amid stately old oaks and towering pines. Private lake frontage on scenic Highland Lake, with barbecue, canoe, and hammock. Cross-country and downhill skiing nearby. Sumptuous full breakfast, whirlpool baths, and family suites.

6 Pets welcome: 7 Smoking allowed: 8 Children welcome: 9 Social drinking allowed: 10 Tennis available: 11 Swimming available: 12 Golf available: 13 Skiing available: 14 May be booked through travel agents

Middlefield Farm

Hosts: Jane & Dick Starets
Doubles: 10 (6 PB; 4 SB) $58-110, plus tax
Type of Beds: 4 Twin; 6 Double; 3 Queen
Full Breakfast
Minimum stay weekends & holidays: 2
Credit Cards: No
Closed Christmas
Notes: 2, 7 (limited), 8, 9, 10, 11, 12, 13, 14

BRISTOL MILLS

Middlefield Farm B&B

Box 4, Upper Round Pond Road, 04539
(207) 529-5439

Spend a night with us in this elegant circa
1800 Federal farmhouse, set on 180 acres of
woods and fields. Huge shade trees lines the
drive, and there are many cool places to read
or relax on the grounds. A quiet rural setting
less than a mile from the water.

Hosts: Ned & Leslie Helm
Doubles: 3 (PB) $70
Type of Beds: 2 Twin; 3 Queen
Full Breakfast
Credit Cards: A, B
Notes: 2, 5, 9, 11, 12, 13, 14

BRUNSWICK

The Samuel Newman House

7 South Street, 04011
(207) 729-6959

Adjoining the Bowdoin College campus, this
handsome Federal house was built in 1821

and is comfortably furnished in an-tiques.
Hearty continental breakfasts include freshly baked muffins/pastry and homemade
granola. Brunswick is a culturally rich college town just ten minutes north of
Freeport.

Host: Anne Greacen
Doubles: 7 (SB) $37.45-53.50
Type of Beds: 3 Twin; 7 Double
Continental Breakfast
Credit Cards: A, B
Notes: 2, 5, 8, 9, 10, 11, 12, 13 (XC)

BRYANT POND

Glen Mountain House

B&B Marblehead & North Shore
Box 172, Beverley, MA, 01915
(508) 921-1336

An attractive Victorian with interesting
period pieces. Close to Sunday River Ski
Area (12 miles) and Mount Abram Ski Area
(4 miles). Good cross-country touring nearby. In summer, Lake Christopher is good for
swimming, boating, fishing. Canoe rental
four miles. One dog and two cats in
residence.

Singles: 1 (SB) $40-45
Doubles: 4 (SB) $50-55
Type of Beds: 2 Twin; 4 Double; 2 Rollaways
Full Breakfast
Credit Cards: No
Notes: 2, 5, 6 (call), 7, 8, 9, 10, 11, 12, 13, 14

NOTES: Credit cards accepted: A Master Card; B Visa; C American Express; D Discover Card; E Diners
Club; F Other: 2 Personal checks accepted: 3 Lunch available: 4 Dinner available: 5 Open all year

BUCKSPORT

L'Ermitage

219 Main Street, 04416
(207) 469-3361

All rooms are large and suitably furnished with antiques. The inn is an 1830 captain's home facing the Penobscot River. Small, excellently rated restaurant features French cuisine for dinner only. Cocktails available; excellent wine list.

Hosts: Richard & Veronique Melsheimer
Doubles: 3(SB) $37.45-42.80
Type of Beds: 3 Double
Full Breakfast
Credit Cards: A, B
Notes: 4, 5, 7, 9

CAMDEN

Blackberry Inn

82 Elm Street, 04843
(207) 236-6060

Blackberry Inn is a restored Italianate Victorian with large, spacious rooms decorated in period style. Stroll to Camden's harbor and fine restaurants, or relax in our comfortable parlors. Wonderful full breakfasts. Featured in *Daughters of Painted Ladies: America's Resplendent Victorians.*

Hosts: Vicki & Edward Doudera
Doubles: 8 (3 PB; 5 private half baths) $42.8096.30
Type of Beds: 1 Twin; 3 Double; 4 Queen
Full Breakfast
Credit Cards: A, B
Notes: 2, 5, 8, 9, 10, 11, 12, 13

Edgecombe-Coles House

HCR 60, Box 3010, 04843
(207) 236-2336

Edgecombe-Coles House is a classic Maine summer home on a quiet hillside with magnificent views of Penobscot Bay. Each room is furnished with country antiques and has a private bath. Our generous breakfasts have been praised nationwide.

Hosts: Louise & Terry Price
Doubles: 6 (PB) $64.20-128.40
Full Breakfast
Credit Cards: A, B, C, E
Notes: 2, 5, 7, 8 (over 7), 9, 10, 11, 12, 13, 14

Hawthorn Inn

9 High Street, 04843
(207) 236-8842

An elegant family-run Victorian inn with harbor view, spacious grounds, large deck. Walk through the back garden to shops and restaurants. Full breakfast and afternoon tea served. Carriage house bedrooms with private Jacuzzi and balconies.

Hosts: Pauline & Bradford Staub
Doubles: 11 (9 PB; 2 SB) $75-125
Full Breakfast
Minimum stay July & Aug.: 2
Credit Cards: A, B
Notes: 2, 5, 7, 8, 9, 10, 11, 12, 13

Windward House

6 High Street, 04843
(207) 236-9656

An historic 1854 Greek revival on stately High Street above picturesque Camden Harbor. Our five tastefully appointed guest rooms are furnished with period antiques and have private baths. Several common rooms, gardens, full gourmet breakfast. Only a short walk to shops, restaurants, and the harbor.

Hosts: Jon & Mary Davis
Doubles: 5 (PB) $60-90
Type of Beds: 2 Twin; 2 Double; 2 Queen
Full Breakfast
Credit Cards: A, B
Notes: 2, 5, 7 (outside), 9, 10, 11, 12, 13, 14

CAPITOL ISLAND

Albonegon Inn

04538
(207) 633-2521

---

6 Pets welcome: 7 Smoking allowed: 8 Children welcome: 9 Social drinking allowed: 10 Tennis available: 11 Swimming available: 12 Golf available: 13 Skiing available: 14 May be booked through travel agents

Located on a private island four miles from Boothbay Harbor, the inn is perched on the edge of the rocks, with water views from every room. It is very simple, in the cottage style; the perfect place for quiet relaxation.

Hosts: Bob & Kin Peckham
Singles: 4 (SB) $44.95
Doubles: 11 (3 PB; 8 SB) $85.60
Type of Beds: 4 Singles; 4 Twin; 6 Double
Continental Breakfast
Credit Cards: No
Closed Nov.-May
Notes: 2, 8, 10, 11, 12

CASTINE

The Manor

Battle Avenue, 04421
(207) 326-4861

A romantic stone and shingle mansion located in what the *Washington Post* described as "Maine's most beautiful seaside village." Tranquil setting, spacious rooms with ocean views, private baths, candlelit fireside dining, marble-topped bar and fine wines. Near Acadia National Park.

Hosts: Paul & Sara Brouillard
Doubles: 12 (10 PB; 2 SB) $90-150
Type of Beds: 4 Twin; 7 Double; 2 Queen; 1 King
Continental Breakfast
Credit Cards: A, B
Closed Dec. - April
Notes: 2, 4, 6, 7, 8, 9, 10, 11, 12

CENTER LOVELL

Center Lovell Inn

Route 5, Box 261N, 04016
(207) 925-1575

Built in 1805, this house originally had two stories; a third was added in the mid-1800s. Center Lovell is situated in western Maine, within half an hour of four ski areas. Great fishing, canoeing, hiking, and bird watching area, with miles of quiet, unspoiled forest to explore.

Hosts: Bil & Susie Mosca
Singles: 2 (PB) $46.75-65

Doubles: 11 (7 PB; 4 SB) $63-97.50
Type of Beds: 3 Twin; 11 Double
Full Breakfast
Credit Cards: A, B, C
Closed 10/30-5/1
Notes: 2, 4, 7, 8, 9, 10, 11, 12, 13, 14

Center Lovell Inn

Westways on Kezar Lake

Rt. 5, 04016
(207) 928-2663

Kezar Lake lies at the foothills of the White Mountains, with one-half mile of lakefront, swimming, canoeing, sailing, tennis, nature walks, playing fields, indoor rec room with Ping-Pong, billiards, bowling, and handball. Gourmet porch dining overlooking the lake.

Host: Nancy Tripp
Doubles: 7 (3 PB; 4 SB) $80-125
Full Breakfast
Credit Cards: A, B, C
Closed November
Notes: 2, 4, 8, 9, 10, 11, 12

CHAMBERLAIN

Ocean Reefs on Long Cove

Rt. 32, 04541-3530
(207) 677-2386

Watch the waves break over the reefs, lobstermen hauling traps, or the shoreline between tides. Hike or bicycle roads along the rocky coast. Pemaquid Beach, Pemaquid lighthouse, Fort William Henry, and the boat to Monhegan Island are all within five miles.

NOTES: Credit cards accepted: A Master Card; B Visa; C American Express; D Discover Card; E Diners Club; F Other: 2 Personal checks accepted: 3 Lunch available: 4 Dinner available: 5 Open all year

Doubles: 4 (PB) $50
Continental Breakfast
Credit Cards: No
Closed Sept. 30 - Memorial Day
Notes: 2, 7, 9, 10, 11, 12

CHERRYFIELD

Ricker House

Park Street, Box 256, 04622
(207) 546-2780

This comfortable 1803 Georgian colonial borders the Narraguagus River and offers guests a central place for enjoying the many wonderful activities in Downeast Maine. Reasonably priced restaurants offer great menus, and all feature fabulous local lobster.

Hosts: William & Jean Conway
Doubles: 3 (SB) $37.45-42.80
Type of Beds: 3 Twin; 2 Double
Full Breakfast
Credit Cards: No
Notes: 2, 5, 8, 9, 10, 11, 12, 13 (XC)

CORNISH

The Cornish Inn

Main Street, 04020
(207) 625-8501

Comfortable lodging in warm, informal surroundings. Located in an unspoiled Maine village amid mountain and river scenery. Seventeen hand-stenciled rooms, wraparound porch, comfortable library, and parlor available.

Hosts: Judie & Jim Lapak
Doubles: 17 (10 PB; 7 SB) $40-75
Type of Beds: 9 Twin; 17 Double
Full Breakfast
Credit Cards: A, B, C
Notes: 2, 4, 5, 7 (limited), 8, 9, 10, 11

DAMARISCOTTA

Brannon-Bunker Inn

HCR 64, Box 045X, 04543
(207) 563-5941

Quaint bed and breakfast inn decorated in different periods from colonial to Victorian located in a 1820 cape, 1880 converted barn, and 1900 carriage house. Country view of the Damariscotta River. Ten minutes to lighthouse, fort, beach, antique and craft shopping.

Hosts: Jeanne & Joe Hovance
Doubles: 7 (4 PB; 3 SB) $42.80-58.85
Type of Beds: 3 Twin; 3 Double; 3 Queen
Continental Breakfast
Credit Cards: A, B
Notes: 2, 5, 8, 9, 10, 11, 12, 13

DENNYSVILLE

Lincoln House Country Inn

Routes 1 & 86, 04628
(207) 726-3953

The centerpiece of northeastern coastal Maine. A lovingly restored colonial on 95 acres bordering beautiful Cobscook Bay. Eagles, osprey, seals, whale watching. Choice accommodations. Rates include breakfast and dinner. Serves as a B&B only in the winter; reduced rates.

Hosts: Mary & Jerry Haggerty
Singles: 1 (S4B) $70-80
Doubles: 5 (S4B) $140-160
Type of Beds: 5 Twin; 3 Double
Full Breakfast
Credit Cards: A, B, C
Notes: 2, 4, 7, 8 (over 10), 9, 10, 11, 13

DAMARISCOTTA MILLS

The Mill Pond Inn

Rt. 215, 04553
(207) 563-8014

Whimsical and cozy 1780 home offering an excellent atmosphere for viewing the wonder of Maine's wildlife. The breakfast room with fireplace and deck faces a pond. Swim or canoe onto Damariscotta Lake across the street and see its loons and eagles. Near Pemaquid, Boothbay, and Camden. Artists welcome.

6 Pets welcome: 7 Smoking allowed: 8 Children welcome: 9 Social drinking allowed: 10 Tennis available: 11 Swimming available: 12 Golf available: 13 Skiing available: 14 May be booked through travel agents

Hosts: Sherry & Bobby Whear
Doubles: 6 (PB) $55-65
Type of Beds: 6 Twin; 3 Double; 1 Cot
Full Breakfast
Credit Cards: No
Notes: 2, 3, 4, 5, 6, 7, 8, 10, 11, 12, 14

EAST BOOTHBAY

Five Gables Inn

Murray Hill Road, 04544
(207) 633-4551

Five Gables Inn is a completely restored Victorian, circa 1865, located on Linekin Bay. All rooms have an ocean view and five have fireplaces. A gourmet breakfast is served in the large common room or on the spacious wraparound veranda.

Hosts: Ellen & Paul Morissette
Doubles: 15 (PB) $80-120
Type of Beds: 4 Double; 10 Queen; 1 King
Full Breakfast
Minimum stay weekends: 2; holidays: 3
Credit Cards: A, B
Closed Nov. 16-May 15
Notes: 2, 8 (over 12), 9, 10, 11, 12

EASTPORT

Kilby House

122 Water Street, 04631
(207) 853-4791

Beautiful 1883 Victorian inn nestled in an historic coastal village. Within walking distance of quaint shops, restaurants, and the ferry landing. Board the ferry and explore the magnificent islands of Canada, or experience a whale-watching cruise. Picnic lunches are available.

Hosts: Betty Woodworth & Jeff Puliafico
Doubles: 3 (SB) $42.80-$58.85
Type of Beds: 1 Double; 2 Queen
Full Breakfast

Credit Cards: No
Notes: 2, 5, 7, 8, 9, 11, 14

EASTPORT

Todd House

1 Caper Avenue, 04631
(207) 853-7232

Todd House, circa 1775, located on Todd Head, is a typical New England large cape with center chimney and a unique "good morning" staircase. Magnificent views of sunrises and sunsets over Passamaquoddy Bay; deck barbecue facilities. Well-behaved pets and children welcome, handicapped accessible rooms.

Host: Ruth McInnis
Singles: 1 (SB) $32.10
Doubles: 6; (2 PB; 4 SB) $37.45-69.55
Type of Beds: 5 Twin; 2 Double; 2 Queen
Continental-plus Breakfast
Credit Cards: No
Notes: 2, 5, 6, 8, 9, 10, 11, 14

Weston House

26 Boynton Street, 04631
(207) 853-2907

Built in 1810, this imposing Federal-style house overlooks Passamaquoddy Bay across to Campobello Island. Listed on the National Register of Historic Places; located in a lovely downeast coastal village. Grounds include an expansive lawn suitable for croquet and a flower garden for quiet relaxation. Picnic lunches available.

Hosts: Jett & John Peterson
Doubles: 5 $37.45-58.85
Type of Beds: 2 Twin; 1 Double; 2 Queen; 1 King
Full Breakfast
Credit Cards: No
Notes: 2, 5, 7 (restricted), 8, 9, 10

NOTES: Credit cards accepted: A Master Card; B Visa; C American Express; D Discover Card; E Diners Club; F Other: 2 Personal checks accepted: 3 Lunch available: 4 Dinner available: 5 Open all year

ELIOT

High Meadows Bed & Breakfast
Route 101, 03903
(207) 439-0590

A colonial house built in 1736 by a ship builder and captain. On 6 acres of land in the country, but only 4.5 miles to Route 1, fine restaurants, beaches, whale watching, and factory outlets.

Host: Elaine Raymond
Doubles: 5 (3 PB; 2 SB) $50-60
Type of Beds: 2 Twin; 2 Double; 2 Queen
Continental-plus Breakfast
Credit Cards: No
Closed Jan. 1 - April 1
Notes: 2, 6, 8, 9, 10, 11, 12

FREEPORT

Captain Josiah Mitchell House
188 Main Street, 04032
(207) 865-3289

Located in the town of Freeport just a five-minute walk from L.L. Bean on tree-shaded sidewalks, past beautiful old sea captain's homes. From the moment you arrive you'll know you've discovered a very special place. Furnished with antiques, four-posters, canopies; walls filled with oil paintings and floors covered with a large collection of Oriental rugs. Breakfast in the formal dining room with its magnificent chandelier. No smoking.

Hosts: Loretta & Alan Bradley
Doubles: 6 (PB) $73
Type of Beds: 2 Twin; 4 Double
Full Breakfast
Credit Cards: A, B
Notes: 5, 9, 11, 12, 13, 14

Harraseeket Inn
162 Main Street, 04032
(207) 965-9377

Luxury B&B inn two blocks north of L.L. Bean's. Antiques, fireplaces, Jacuzzi, steam or standard baths, cable TV, air-conditioning, tavern on premises. Afternoon tea served.

Hosts: Nancy & Paul Gray
Doubles: 54 (PB) $65-225
Type of Beds: 22 Double; 9 Queen; 23 King
Full Breakfast
Credit Cards: A, B, C, D, E
Notes: 4, 5, 7, 8, 9, 10, 11, 12, 13 (XC)

Holbrook Inn
7 Holbrook Street, 04032
(207) 865-6693

Exceptionally comfortable and spacious accommodations. Each room has a queen bed, cable color TV, and private bath. Enjoy a hearty breakfast in our "Recipe Room." Just park your car and walk downtown to visit the many outlet shops.

Hosts: Ralph & Beatrice Routhier
Doubles: 3 (PB) $64.20-69.55
Type of Beds: 3 Queen
Full Breakfast
Credit Cards: No
Notes: 2, 5, 8 (over 10), 9, 11, 12, 13 (XC)

The Isaac Randall House
Independence Drive, 04032
(207) 865-9295

Comfortable, charming, antique-furnished rooms in an 1823 farmhouse. Oriental rugs and lovely old quilts. Located on 5 wooded acres with a spring-fed pond. Just a few blocks from L.L. Bean and downtown Freeport. Hearty breakfasts and evening snacks. Resident cats. Smoking discouraged.

Hosts: Glynrose & Jim Friedlander
Doubles: 10 (8 PB; 2 SB) $48.15-107.00
Type of Beds: 3 Twin; 4 Double; 4 Queen; 1 King
Full Breakfast
Credit Cards: No
Notes: 2, 4, 5, 6, 8, 9, 11, 12

6 Pets welcome: 7 Smoking allowed: 8 Children welcome: 9 Social drinking allowed: 10 Tennis available: 11 Swimming available: 12 Golf available: 13 Skiing available: 14 May be booked through travel agents

181 Main Street

181 Main Street, 04032
(207) 865-1226

Cozy, antique-filled 1840 cape just a five-minute walk to L.L. Bean and over 120 luxury outlets. In-ground pool, ample parking. On U.S. 1, a short drive from the beaches and rock-bound coast, Portland, Brunswick, and Bowdoin College.

Hosts: Ed Hassett & David Cates
Doubles: 7 (PB) $85
Type of Beds: 7 Double
Full Breakfast
Credit Cards: A, B
Notes: 2, 5, 7 (limited), 9, 10, 11, 12, 13

FRYEBURG

The Oxford House Inn

105 Main Street, 04037
(207) 935-3442

Charming Edwardian home built in 1913 in a quaint colonial village. Year-round activities nearby: swimming, canoeing, boating, skiing, hiking. Nine miles from fantastic tax-free factory outlet shopping. Unique gourmet dining available in an elegant atmosphere with wonderful mountain views.

Hosts: John & Phyllis Morris
Doubles: 5 (3 PB; 2 SB) $45-75
Type of Beds: 2 Twin; 5 Double; 1 Queen
Full Breakfast
Credit Cards: A, B, C, E
Notes: 2, 4, 5, 7, 8, 9, 10, 11, 12, 13

GEORGETOWN

The Grey Havens

Box 308, 04548
(207) 371-2616

"All you can see is sea and sky," wrote one guidebook. Listed on the National Register as "The last 'Shingle-style' hotel on the Maine coast." Turrets, veranda, 1904 interior. Peaceful and informal. Row to island

sanctuary, walk long, quiet beaches, shop at Bean's and other famous outlets.

Hosts: The Hardcastle Family
Doubles: 14 (10 PB; 4 SB) $60-125
Type of Beds: 3 Twin; 8 Double; 3 Queen; 1 King
Continental-plus Breakfast
Credit Cards: No
Closed Nov. - May
Notes: 2, 4, 7, 8 (by arrangement), 9, 11, 14

Guilford Bed & Breakfast

Elm & Prospect Streets, 04443
(207) 876-3477

A lovely 1905 post-Victorian with a half-wrap porch, situated high on a knoll within walking distance of the town and its shops. Hearty breakfast of homemade muffins, pancakes, eggs, and so forth. On the Moosehead Trail for fishing, the Appalachian Trail for hiking, or Squaw Mountain for skiing.

Hosts: Pat & John Selicious
Doubles: 3 (SB) $40-53.50
Type of Beds: 3 Double
Full Breakfast
Credit Cards: A, B
Notes: 3, 5, 7, 9, 12

Glen Mountain House

Crocker House

HANCOCK

Crocker House Country Inn
Hancock Point Road, 04640
(207) 422-6806

Quiet coastal country inn and restaurant on scenic Hancock Point. Ten rooms, each with a private bath; gourmet restaurant with full liquor license. "A little out of the way, and way out of the ordinary." Featured in *Country Inns and Back Roads*.

Hosts: Richard & Elizabeth Malaby
Doubles: 10 (PB) $50-68
Type of Beds: 2 Twin; 8 Double; 1 Queen
Full Breakfast
Credit Cards: A, B, C
Closed Jan. 1 - April 27; Mon.-Wed., Columbus Day - New Years
Notes: 2, 4, 7, 9, 10, 11, 12

ISLE AU HAUT

The Keepers House
04645
(207) 367-2261

Remote island lighthouse station located in the undeveloped wilderness area of Acadia National Park. Guests arrive on the mail boat from Stonington. No phones, cars, TV, or crowds. Osprey, seal, deer, rugged trails, spectacular scenery, seclusion, peace, and inspiration. Three elegant meals included in rate.

Hosts: Jeff & Judi Burke
Doubles: 5 (SB) $185-205
Type of Beds: 5 Double
All Meals
Minimum stay July-Aug.:2
Credit Cards: No
Closed Nov. 1-April 30
Notes: 2, 3, 4, 8, 9, 11

KENNEBUNKPORT

The Breakwater Inn
Box 1160, 04046
(207) 967-3118

A seaside inn at the mouth of the Kennebunk River offering views of the Atlantic. A short walk to Dock Square, close to beaches, and one mile from the "summer White House." Offering breakfast and dinner in a common dining room with fireplace and friendly faces.

Hosts: The Lambert Family
Doubles: 20 (PB) $65-125
Type of Beds: 9 Twin; 11 Double; 9 Queen
Full Breakfast May-Oct.
Credit Cards: A, B, C
Closed January
Notes: 2, 4, 7, 8, 9, 10, 11, 12, 14

The Captain Lord Mansion
Box 800, 04046
(207) 967-3141

An intimate Maine Coast inn featuring large, luxurious rooms, working fireplaces, private baths, queen four-poster beds, and antiques. Has received the coveted AAA 4 Diamond rating for seven consecutive years. Named in the top ten U.S. inns by *Country Inns Bed & Breakfast* magazine, January 1989.

Hosts: Bev Davis & Rick Litchfield
Doubles: 24 (PB) $100-200
Type of Beds: 5 Double; 17 Queen; 4 King
Full Breakfast
Credit Cards: A, B, D
Notes: 2, 5, 9, 10, 11, 12

6 Pets welcome: 7 Smoking allowed: 8 Children welcome: 9 Social drinking allowed: 10 Tennis available: 11 Swimming available: 12 Golf available: 13 Skiing available: 14 May be booked through travel agents

The Captain Lord Mansion

A waterfront inn nestled on the rocky shore of picturesque Cape Porpoise Harbor, a quiet fishing village a few miles east of bustling Kennebunkport. Luxuriate in the peace of changing tides and wheeling gulls. Lighthouses, lobster boats, luscious breakfasts.

Hosts: Joan & Dave Sutter
Doubles: 4 (PB) $95-135
Type of Beds: 3 Queen; 1 King
Full Breakfast
Credit Cards: A, B, D
Notes: 2, 5, 9, 11, 12, 14

1802 House

Locke Street, 04046
(207) 967-5632

A pleasant, cozy interlude that you will long remember.

Hosts: Patricia Ledda
Doubles: 6 (PB) $75-$123
Type of Beds: 1 Twin; 4 Double; 2 Queen
Full Breakfast
Credit Cards: A, B, C
Notes: 2, 4, 5, 7, 9, 10, 11, 12, 14

The Green Heron Inn

Box 2578, 04046
(207) 967-3315

This inn, with its inviting porch, is located between the river and the ocean in this colonial resort village. Ten guest rooms and a cottage all have private baths, air-conditioning, cable television.

Hosts: Charles & Elizabeth Reid
Doubles: 10 (PB) $56-78 plus tax
Full Breakfast
Credit Cards: No
Closed mid-Dec. - mid-April; open various off-season weekends & holidays
Notes: 2, 6 (restricted), 7, 8, 9, 11, 12

The Inn at Harbor Head

RR 2, Box 1180, Pier Road, 04046
(207) 967-5564

The Inn on South Street

Box 478A, 04046
(207) 967-5151

Enjoy the comfortable elegance of this nineteenth-century Greek Revival house. Three beautifully decorated guest rooms and one luxury suite. Private baths, fireplaces. A sumptuous breakfast is served each morning in the sunny kitchen with views of the water. Located on a quiet street, within walking distance of restaurants, shops, and water.

Hosts: Jacques & Eva Downs
Doubles: 3 (PB) $75-110
Type of Beds: 2 Twin; 4 Queen
Full Breakfast
Credit Cards: C
Notes: 2, 5, 7 (restricted), 8 (over 8), 9, 10, 11, 12, 13, 14

Kilburn House

Chestnut Street, 04046
(207) 967-4762

Kilburn House is an 1890s Victorian home located one block from the center of downtown Kennebunkport. Kennebunkport is a colonial New England village with many fine restaurants, beaches, and shops.

Hosts: Samuel A. Minier & Muriel Friend
Singles: 1 (SB) $42.80
Doubles: 3 (2 PB; 1 SB) $74.90
Type of Beds: 1 Twin; 3 Double

NOTES: Credit cards accepted: A Master Card; B Visa; C American Express; D Discover Card; E Diners Club; F Other: 2 Personal checks accepted: 3 Lunch available: 4 Dinner available: 5 Open all year

Continental Breakfast
Minimum stay weekends & holidays: 2
Credit Cards: A, B
Closed Nov. 1-May 15
Notes: 2, 8, 9, 10, 11, 12

Kylemere House

South Street, Box 1333, 04046
(207) 967-2780

Kylemere House, located in the historic district, is a quiet haven just a minute's walk from the beach, shops, galleries, and restaurants. Come and relax in a friendly atmosphere in our beautifully appointed roms. Enjoy a "Down East" breakfast in our formal dining room overlooking the gardens.

Hosts: Bill & Mary Kyle
Doubles: 3 (2 PB; 1 SB) $65-86
Type of Beds: 4 Twin; 2 Queen; 1 King
Full Breakfast
Minimum stay weekends: 2
Credit Cards: C
Closed Jan.-April
Notes: 2, 7 (restricted), 8 (over 12), 9, 10, 11, 12, 13

Lake Brook Guest House B&B

Western Avenue, RR 3, Box 218, 04046
(207) 967-4069

Charming rooms, fresh-cut flowers, great full breakfasts. Lovely perennial garden. Rooms overlook a tidal marsh and brook. Lake Brook is centrally located only one-half mile from downtown, with its shops, restaurants, galleries. Just over one mile to the beach.

Host: Carolyn A. McAdams
Doubles: 4; (1 PB; 3 SB) $48.15-$74.90
Type of Beds: 3 Double; 1 Queen
Full Breakfast
Credit Cards: No
Notes: 2, 5, 8, 9, 10, 11, 12

Maine Stay Inn & Cottages

Box 500 A, 04046
(207) 967-2117

Elegant inn rooms and delightful cottage units located in the quiet surroundings of Kennebunkport's National Register of Historic Homes. Complimentary continental breakfast, afternoon tea, New England desserts. Color cable TV; private baths. Easy walking distance to restaurants, galleries, shops, and harbor. One mile to beach and golf.

Hosts: Jacques & Carol Gagnon, Suzanne Gagnon
Doubles: 17 (17 PB) $75-105
Type of Beds: 2 Twin; 17 Double; 10 Queen
Continental-plus Breakfast
Credit Cards: A, B
Closed Jan.; open weekends & holidays only from Nov.-March
Notes: 2, 4, 7 (limited), 8, 9, 10, 11, 12, 14

Old Fort Inn

Old Fort Inn

Box M-30, 04046
(207) 967-5353

Discover the hospitality of a luxurious New England Inn that combines all yesterday's charm with today's conveniences. From the daily buffet breakfast to the comfort and privacy of our antique-appointed room. Includes pool, tennis court, color TV, and a charming antique shopall in a secluded setting.

Hosts: David & Sheila Aldrich
Doubles: 16 (PB) $95-195
Type of Beds: 1 Twin; 12 Full; 10 Queen; 4 King

Full Breakfast
Credit Cards: A, B, C, D
Closed mid-Dec. - mid-April
Notes: 2, 7, 8 (over 12), 9, 10, 11, 12, 14

Port Gallery Inn

Corner of Spring and Main Streets, Box 1367, 04046
(207) 967-3728

Circa 1860s, elegant Victorian mansion located in village center within walking distance to shops, restaurants, galleries, fishing, whale watching. The inn features comfortable rooms done in period furniture with hidden secrets like — color TV in a closed hutch, marine art gallery — baby grand piano, stained-glass sun porch with white wicker for savoring your morning in Maine.

Hosts: Francis & Lucy Morphy
Doubles: 7 (PB) $84.53-214.00
Type of Beds: 2 Double; 5 Queen
Continental Breakfast
Credit Cards: A, B, C
Notes: 5, 7, 8, 9, 10, 11, 12, 14

KITTERY POINT

Harbour Watch Bed & Breakfast

Follett Lane, 03905
(207) 439-3242

Colonial sea captain's house, in same family since 1797. Wonderful view, quiet atmosphere. Within five miles to outlet shops, theaters, beaches, fabulous restaurants, whale-watching excursions, harbor cruises. Evening musicales with harpsichord and baroque instruments. Just an hour's drive from Boston.

Hosts: Marian & Robert Craig
Doubles: 4 (S2B) $55
Type of Beds: 2 Twin; 2 Double; 1 Queen
Continental Breakfast
Minimum stay weekends: 2; holidays: 2
Credit Cards: No
Closed Nov.-April
Notes: 2, 9, 10, 11, 12

LUBEC

Breakers By The Bay

37 Washington, 04652
(207) 733-2487

One of the oldest houses in the 200-year-old town of Lubec, which is a small fishing village. Three blocks to Campobello Island, the home of Franklin D. Roosevelt. All rooms have hand-crocheted table cloths and hand-quilted bedspreads. Two rooms have private decks for viewing the bay. All rooms that share a bath have their own washstands in them.

Host: E. M. Elg
Doubles: 5 (PB; 3 SB) $42.80-53.50
Full Breakfast
Credit Cards: No
Closed Oct.-May
Notes: 2, 4, 12

Home Port Inn

45 Main Street, 04652
(207) 733-2077

Charming 1880 inn in the heart of Lubec. Five antique-furnished rooms, all with private bath. Lubec area includes Quoddy Head State Park, Roosevelt International Park on nearby Campobello Island, unique bird watching, and whale watching. AAA and Mobil rated.

Hosts: Claire & Bob Studley
Doubles: 5 (PB) $60-75
Type of Beds: 1 Twin; 7 Double
Continental Breakfast
Credit Cards: A, B
Closed Nov.-April
Notes: 2, 8 (over 7), 9, 12

MACHIAS

Clark Perry House

59 Court Street, 04654
(207) 255-8458

An 1868 Victorian in a quiet coastal town. Within easy walking distance of shops, restaurants, places of worship, library, and historic sites. Rogue Bluffs State Park, Jasper Beach, and the University of Maine at Machias are nearby.

Hosts: Robin & David Rier
Singles: 1 (SB) $40
Doubles: 1 (SB) $50
Type of Beds: 2 Twin; 1 Double
Full Breakfast
Credit Cards: B
Closed Jan. & Feb.
Notes: 2, 8, 10, 11, 12, 13

NEWCASTLE

The Captain's House B&B

Box 242, 04553
(207) 563-1482

The Captain's House B&B is a Greek Revival home overlooking the Damariscotta River. On your arrival you will be overwhelmed with our river view, and inside you'll find out large, sunny rooms warm and inviting. Enjoy a leisurely walk to town for fine dining and carefree shopping. We serve homemade breads, blueberry pancakes, French toast, and farm-fresh eggs for a breakfast you'll never forget.

Hosts: Susan Rizzo & Joe Sullivan
Doubles: 5 (SB) $65
Type of Beds: 6 Double
Full Breakfast
Credit Cards: No
Notes: 2, 5, 7, 8, 9, 10, 11, 12

Glidden House

RR 1, Box 740, 04553
(207) 563-1859

A lovely mansard-roofed Victorian (Second Empire) overlooking the Damariscotta River. A memorable house that's attractively furnished, comfortable, and quiet. Excellent breakfasts. Within walking distance of restaurants, shops, galleries, and historical sites.

Host: Doris E. Miller
Doubles: 3 (PB) $45

Type of Beds: 2 Twin; 1 Double; 1 Queen
Full Breakfast
Credit Cards: B
Notes: 2, 5, 7 (restricted), 8, 9, 10, 11, 12, 13 (XC)

The Markert House

Glidden Street, 04553
(207) 563-1309

Four rooms with two shared baths in a hillside 1900 Victorian overlooking the Damariscotta River. Your host is an artist, photographer, gourmet cook, and gardener. Reproduction Victorian veranda, antique furnishings, tasteful art.

Host: William P. Markert
Doubles: 4 (SB) $40-55
Type of Beds: 3 Double; 1 Queen
Full Breakfast
Minimum stay weekends: 2
Credit Cards: A, B, C
Notes: 2, 5, 9, 12

The Newcastle Inn

River Road, 04553
(207) 563-5685

A romantic country inn situated on the Damariscotta River — one of the longest-operating inns in the region. All fifteen rooms have private baths, and some have canopy beds. In the dining room, elegant candlelight dinners and multi-course breakfasts are served. The living room has a fireplace, and the porch overlooks the river.

Hosts: Ted & Chris Sprague
Doubles: 15 (PB) $70-90
Type of Beds: 2 Twin; 7 Double; 5 Queen; 1 King
Full Breakfast
Credit Cards: A, B
Notes: 2, 4, 5, 11, 12, 13 (XC), 14

NEWPORT

Lake Sebasticook Bed & Breakfast

8 Sebasticook Avenue, Box 502, 04953
(207) 368-5507

6 Pets welcome: 7 Smoking allowed: 8 Children welcome: 9 Social drinking allowed: 10 Tennis available: 11 Swimming available: 12 Golf available: 13 Skiing available: 14 May be booked through travel agents

Take a step back in history in our 1903 Victorian home located on a quiet street. Relax on the second-floor sun porch or comfortable wraparound porch and enjoy the sounds of ducks and loons on Lake Sebasticook. Take a short walk to the lake park, or play tennis at the city park a block away. In the morning, savor a full country breakfast including homemade breads.

Hosts: Bob & Trudy Zothner
Doubles: 3 (S2B) $37.45-53.50
Type of Beds: 2 Twin; 1 Double; 1 Queen
Full Breakfast
Credit Cards: No
Notes: 2, 5, 10, 11, 12, 13

OGUNQUIT

The Gazebo

Box 668, 03907
(207) 646-3733

A 150-year-old farmhouse with swimming pool, where you will enjoy a full gourmet breakfast (stuffed French toast with apricot orange sauce). Located on the trolley line; short walk to the beach.

Host: Tony Fontes
Doubles: 8 (SB) $85-100
Full Breakfast
Credit Cards: A, B
Closed January
Notes: 2, 7, 9, 10, 11, 12

Hartwell House

116 Shore Road, 03907
(207) 646-7210

In the tradition of fine European country inns, the Hartwell House offers its guests rooms and suites tastefully furnished with Early American and English antiques. Breakfast is included. Perkins Cove, Ogunquit Beach, and the Marginal Way are all within a few steps from the house.

Hosts: Jim & Trisha Hartwell
Singles: 2 (PB) $65-175
Doubles: 14 (PB) $65-175
Type of Beds: 2 Twin; 1 Double; 13 Queen

Full or Continental Breakfast (seasonal)
Minimum stay weekends & holidays: 1-3
Credit Cards: A, B, C
Notes: 2, 5, 7, 8 (14 or older), 9, 10, 11, 12

The Morning Dove

Box 1940, 03907
(207) 646-3891

Elegant 1860s farmhouse, featuring bright, airy rooms with antiques, art, and European accents. Breakfast is served on the Victorian porch reminiscent of sidewalk cafes. Amenities include down comforters, air-conditioning, welcoming wine, chocolates, plush towels, and soaps. Short stroll to the beaches, cove, restaurants, and playhouse. Reservations appreciated.

Hosts: Peter & Eeta Sachon
Doubles: 8 (4 PB; 4 SB) $60-95
Type of Beds: 4 Twin; 1 Double; 4 Queen; 1 King
Continental-plus Breakfast
Minimum stay in season: 2; weekends: 3
Credit Cards: A, B, C
Closed weekdays Nov. 1 - May 1
Notes: 2, 7, 8 (10 and over), 9, 10,11, 12, 13 (XC), 14

The Trellis House

2 Beachmere Place, 03907
(207) 646-7909

A turn-of-the-century beach house, appointed with an eclectic blend of antiques. All rooms have private baths, and a full cottage breakfast is served. Walk to all that's special in Ogunquit.

Host: Jim Pontolilo
Doubles: 4 (PB) $90
Full Breakfast
Credit Cards: A, B
Closed January & February
Notes: 2, 7 (limited), 9, 10, 11, 12

PEMAQUID FALLS

B&B Registry
#ME-04558LIT

Box 8174, St. Paul, MN, 55108
(612) 646-0174

An 1840 Cape farmhouse on the banks of a river across from an old lumber mill with the original water wheel. Surrounded by spruce forest. A laid-back, folksy place with plenty of yard for children's play. Minutes from the lighthouse, beach, harbor, galleries.

Doubles: 7 (2 PB; 5 SB) $45-55
Type of Beds: 7 Double; 1 Hideaway
Full Breakfast
Credit Cards: A, B
Notes: 5, 7, 8, 11

ROCKPORT

Sign of the Unicorn
Box 99, 191 Beauchamp Avenue, 04856
(207) 236-8789

"We spoil you rottener than you are!" On a quiet lane overlooking Rockport Harbor, near all sports, sailing, antiquing, wildlife refuge, concerts, restaurants — and lobster. With over thirteen years' experience running a B&B, we also are realtors and make Nantucket Lightship Baskets of museum quality.

Hosts: Winnie & Howard Jones
Singles: 1 (SB) $37.45-48.15
Doubles: 4 (2 PB; 2 SB) $57.75-85.60
Type of Beds: 6 Twin; 3 Double
Full Breakfast
Credit Cards: No
Closed Christmas
Notes: 2, 7 (outside), 8, 9, 10, 11, 12, 13, 14

SANFORD

Oakwood Inn & Motel
279 Main Street, 04073
(207) 324-2160

Oakwood is located in the heart of Sanford, yet it is private, with a lovely courtyard and grounds. The inn boasts of many famous visitors. Handy to both ocean and mountains. At Oakwood you will find old-fashioned, turn-of-the-century charm.

Hosts: Sherri Biasin & Stephen Clark
Singles: 2 (SB) $35-45

Doubles: 5 (2 PB; 3 SB) $45-65
Type of Beds: 6 Twin; 23 Double
Continental Breakfast
Credit Cards: A, B, C
Notes: 2, 5, 7, 8, 9, 10, 11, 12

SEARSPORT

The Carriage House Inn
Box 238, 04974
(207) 548-2289

Built in 1874, this classic Victorian has been beautifully maintained, and the large, cheerful rooms offer a restful night's stay. Located in the center of the "Antique Capital of Maine," within walking distance of restaurants, flea markets, the museum, and oceanfront town park.

Hosts: Brad & Cathy Bradbury
Doubles: 4 (3 PB; 1 SB) $58.85-69.55
Type of Beds: 1 Twin; 3 Double
Continental Breakfast
Credit Cards: A, B
Closed March & April
Notes: 2, 7, 8, 9, 10, 11, 12

The Carriage House Inn

SOUTH BROOKSVILLE

Breezemere Farm Inn
Box 290, Breezemere Farm Road, 04617
(207) 326-8628

Picturesque 1850 farmhouse plus nine cottages on 60 acres on Orcutt Harbor, East Penobscot Bay. Spruce to smell, islands to explore, water to sail, trails to hike, berries to pick, mussels to rake. Bikes, beach, boats.

Saturday night lobster clam bakes, May through October. Free brochure.

Hosts: Joan & Jim Lippke
Cottages: 6 (PB) $100
Doubles: 7 (S4.5B) $65-80
Type of Beds: 9 Twin; 10 Double; 1 Queen
Full Breakfast
Credit Cards: A, B
Closed Nov. 1 - April
Notes: 2, 4 (Sat.), 8 (cottages), 9, 10, 11, 12, 14

SOUTH HARPSWELL

Lookout Point House

141 Lookout Point Road, 04079
(207) 833-5509

Victorian inn (circa 1761) located on a hill overlooking the ocean. Minutes from L.L. Bean and outlet shopping. Full range of outdoor activities available: boating, swimming, hiking, bicycling, etc. Beautiful grounds, huge great room with fireplace, elegant living room and dining room for guests to enjoy.

Hosts: The Sewalls
Singles: 1 (SB) $55
Doubles: 12 (2 PB; 10 SB) $90
Type of Beds: 6 Twin; 6 Double; 2 Queen; 2 King
Full Breakfast
Credit Cards: A, B
Notes: 2, 5, 7, 8 (over 6), 9, 10, 11, 12, 13

SOUTHWEST HARBOR

The Island House

Box 1006, 04679
(207) 244-5180

Relax in a gracious, restful seacoast home on the quiet side of the island. We serve such Island House favorites as blueberry coffee cake and sausage/cheese casserole. Charming private loft apartment available. Acadia National Park is just a five-minute drive away. The house is located across the street from the harbor, with swimming, sailing, biking, and hiking nearby.

Host: Ann Gill
Doubles: 5 (1 PB; 4 SB) $50-95

Type of Beds: 5 Twin; 2 Double; 1 Queen; 1 Double daybed
Full Breakfast
Credit Cards: No
Closed Nov. - mid-April
Notes: 2, 8 (over 12), 9, 10, 11, 12, 14

Island Watch B&B

Box 1359, 04679
(207) 244-7229

Overlooking the great harbor of Mount Desert Island and the village of Southwest Harbor, Island Watch sits atop Freeman Ridge on the quiet side of the island. The finest panoramic views, privacy, and comfort. Walk to Acadia National Park and the fishing village of Southwest Harbor.

Host: Maxine M. Clark
Doubles: 7 (4 PB; 3 SB) $45-55
Type of Beds: 2 Twin; 4 Double; 2 Queen; 1 King
Full Breakfast
Credit Cards: No
Notes: 5, 8 (12 and over), 9, 10, 11, 12, 14

The Kingsleigh Inn

100 Main Street, Box 1426, 04679
(207) 244-5302

Located in the heart of Acadia National Park overlooking the picturesque harbor. A romantic and intimate inn that will surround you with charm the moment you walk through the door. Many rooms enjoy spectacular harbor views and all are very tastefully decorated.

Hosts: Jim & Kathy King
Doubles: 8 (PB) $58.85-101.65
Type of Beds: 2 Double; 6 Queen
Full Breakfast
Credit Cards: No
Closed Jan.-March
Notes: 2, 8 (over 10), 9, 10, 11, 12, 13

Lindenwood Inn

Clark Point Road, Box 1328, 04679
(207) 244-5335

A lovely sea captain's home overlooking the harbor on the quiet side of Acadia National

Park. Offers a warm, cozy atmosphere and full breakfast. Explore Mt. Desert Island, relax in the parlor, or play our harpsichord. Brochure available.

Hosts: Gardiner & Marilyn Brower
Doubles: 7 (3 PB; 4 SB) $42.80-90.95
Cottage: 1 (PB) $80.25-101.65
Types of Beds: 4 Twin; 5 Double; 2 Queen
Full Breakfast
Children over 6 welcome in cottage; over 12 in inn
Notes: 2, 5, 8, 9, 10, 11, 12, 13

SPRUCE HEAD

Craignair Inn
Clark Island Road, 04859
(207) 594-7644

Craignair Inn is located on 4 acres of shore front, set on a granite ledge rising from the sea. Miles of coastline to explore, clam flats, offshore islands, tidal pools. Short drive to the ferry for Monhegan Island; near Owls Head Lighthouse and State Park. A deep saltwater quarry pool, surrounded by spruce and birch, provides warm-water swimming for our guests.

Hosts: Terry & Norman Smith
Singles: 2 (S3B) $47.08-52.97
Doubles: 19 (5 PB; 12 S3B) $70.62-94.16
Full Breakfast
Minimum stay holidays: 2
Credit Cards: A, B
Closed Feb.
Notes: 2, 4, 6, 7, 8, 9, 10, 11, 12, 13

SUNSET

Goose Cove Lodge
Goose Cove Road, 04683
(207) 348-2508

Seventy acres of nature trails and one-half mile of ocean frontage with beaches. Cottages and rooms are rustic, with private baths, fireplaces, and sun decks overlooking the ocean. Modified American Plan mid-June to mid-September; B&B in the spring and fall. One-week minimum stay in July and August.

Hosts: George & Elli Pavloff
Singles: 2 (PB) $50
Doubles: 8 (PB) $70-80
Cottages: 11 (PB) $90
Type of Beds: 24 Twin; 15 Double; 10 Queen; 2 King
Full breakfast summer; continental spring & fall
Credit Cards: No
Closed Oct. 15 - May 1
Notes: 2, 3, 4, 8, 9, 10, 11, 12

THOMASTON

Cap'n Frost's Bed & Breakfast
241 West Main Street, 04861
(207) 354-8217

Our 1840 cape is furnished with country antiques, some of which are for sale. If you are visiting our midcoast area, we are a comfortable overnight stay, close to Monhegan Island and a two-hour drive to Acadia National Park. Reservations are helpful.

Hosts: Arlene & Harold Frost
Rooms: 3 (1 PB; 2 SB) $40
Full Breakfast
Credit Cards: A, B
Notes: 2

TOPSHAM

Middaugh B & B
36 Elm Street, 04086
(207) 725-2562

Located in the historic district and listed on the National Register of Historic Places, this 150-year-old Federal Greek Revival home is ten minutes from L.L. Bean and Freeport. Centrally located between Camden, Boothbay Harbor, and Portland. A Maine coastal route home with a family atmosphere.

Hosts: Dewey & Mary Kay Nelson
Doubles: 2 (PB) $50-60
Type of Beds: 1 Queen; 1 King
Full Breakfast
Closed Christmas
Credit Cards: No
Notes: 2, 8 (over 4), 10, 12

6 Pets welcome: 7 Smoking allowed: 8 Children welcome: 9 Social drinking allowed: 10 Tennis available: 11 Swimming available: 12 Golf available: 13 Skiing available: 14 May be booked through travel agents

Broad Bay Inn & Gallery

WALDOBORO

Broad Bay Inn and Gallery B&B

Box 607, 04572
(207) 832-6668

Lovingly restored 1830 inn, handsomely appointed with Victorian furnishings, canopy beds, paintings, and so forth. Breakfast banquet feasts and afternoon tea or sherry on the deck. Established art gallery in the barn. Walk down to the river, to tennis, theater, antique shops. A short drive to the lighthouse, Audubon sanctuary, and fishing villages. Send for your free brochure.

Hosts: Jim & Libby Hopkins
Doubles: 5 (S3B) $35-65
Full Breakfast
Credit Cards: A, B
Closed Jan.
Notes: 2, 4, 7 (limited), 8 (over 10), 9, 10, 11, 12, 13, 14

The Roaring Lion

Box 756, 04572
(207) 832-4038

A 1905 Victorian home with tin ceilings; elegant woodwork throughout. We cater to special diets and serve miso soup, sourdough bread, homemade jams and jellies. Hosts are well traveled and lived two years in West Africa. Their interests are books, gardening, art, and cooking.

Hosts: Bill & Robin Branigan
Doubles: 4 (1 PB; 3 SB) $42.80-64.20
Type of Beds: 2 Twin; 2 Double; 1 Queen
Full Breakfast
Credit Cards: No
Notes: 2, 5, 8, 10, 11, 12, 13

WELLS

Purple Sandpiper Guest House

RR 3, Box 226C, 04090
(207) 646-7990

NOTES: Credit cards accepted: A Master Card; B Visa; C American Express; D Discover Card; E Diners Club; F Other: 2 Personal checks accepted: 3 Lunch available: 4 Dinner available: 5 Open all year

We are located on Rt. 1, minutes from the beach. Our rooms are comfortably furnished with private baths, cable TV, and refrigerators. Continental breakfast includes fresh-baked muffins and coffeecakes. Miniature golf, tennis, and restaurants are within walking distance.

Hosts: Paul & Sandi Goodwin
Doubles: 6 (PB) $35-60
Type of Beds: 5 Twin; 4 Double; 1 Queen; 1 King
Continental Breakfast
Credit Cards: No
Closed mid-Oct. - mid-May
Notes: 2, 7, 8, 9, 10, 11, 12, 14

WELLS BEACH

B&B Registry #ME-04090BAY

Box 8174, St. Paul, MN, 55108
(612) 646-4238

An 1890s restored carriage house with view of the ocean from all guest rooms. Deck overlooking bird sanctuary. House is decorated with comforters, colonial curtains. Walk to restaurant.

Doubles: 5 (SB) $50-105
Continental-plus Breakfast
Credit Cards: No
Notes: 5, 8 (over 12), 10, 11

WISCASSET

The Squire Tarbox Inn

RR 2, Box 620, 04578
(207) 882-7693

A handsome antique farmhouse on a country road near midcoast Maine harbors, beaches, antique shops, and museums. The proper balance of history, quiet country, good food, and relaxation. Serves a delicious homemade goat cheese by the fire before dinner. Known primarily for rural privacy and five-course dinners. Daily rate includes all taxes, breakfast, five-course dinner, and gratuities.

Hosts: Karen & Bill Mitman
Doubles: 11 (PB) $100-189
Type of Beds: 3 Twin; 4 Double; 5 Queen; 2 King
Continental-plus Breakfast
Credit Cards: A, B, C
Closed late Oct. - mid-May
Notes: 2, 4, 7 (limited), 8 (over 14), 9, 14

The Stacked Arms

RR2, Box 146, 04578
(207) 882-5436

All bedrooms decorated in different styles, each with a small refrigerator; ceiling fans in all upstairs rooms. Within thirty minutes of many day trips to museums, beaches, boat trips, shopping outlets, L.L. Bean, quaint fishing villages, and the Bath Iron Works, where naval vessels are built.

Hosts: Dee, Karen & Sean Maquire
Doubles: 5 (SB) $45-60
Full Breakfast
Credit Cards: A, B
Closed January
Notes: 2, 4, 7 (limited), 8 (over 5), 9, 10, 11, 12, 13, 14

YORK

A Summer Place

RFD #1, Box 196, 03909
(207) 363-5233

Secluded country setting with woods, lawns, gardens, and a river view. Only ten minutes to miles of sandy beaches; many excellent restaurants nearby. Visit historic York's colonial building, famous Kittery, and other discount malls within five miles.

Hosts: John & Harriet Simonds
Doubles: 1 (PB) $50
Type of Beds: 2 Twin
Continental Breakfast
Credit Cards: No
Notes: 2, 7 (limited), 9, 11, 12

Dockside Guest Quarters

Harris Island Road, Box 205, 03909
(207) 363-2868

6 Pets welcome: 7 Smoking allowed: 8 Children welcome: 9 Social drinking allowed: 10 Tennis available: 11 Swimming available; 12 Golf available: 13 Skiing available: 14 May be booked through travel agents

The Dockside Guest Quarters is a small resort on a private peninsula in York Harbor. Panorama of ocean and harbor activities. Spacious grounds with privacy and relaxing atmosphere. Accommodations are in an early seacoast lodge and modern, multi-unit cottages.

Hosts: The Lusty Family
Doubles: 21 (19 PB: 2 SB) $46-110
Type of Beds: 39 Twin; 7 Double; 3 Queen; 3 King
Continental-plus Breakfast
Minimum stay weekdays & weekends: 2 ; holidays: 3
Credit Cards: A, B
Closed Oct. 22 - May 1
Notes: 2, 3, 4, 6, 7, 8, 9, 10, 11, 12, 14

Scotland Bridge Inn

One Scotland Bridge Road, 03909
(207) 363-4432

Escape to the beautiful coast of Maine and spend hours of pleasure at the Scotland Bridge Inn, where we provide an elegant country setting with tasty, tempting breakfasts and mid-afternoon teas.

Host: Sylvia S. Batchelder
Doubles: 3 (1 PB; 3 SB) $42.80-90.95
Type of Beds: 4 Twin; 3 Double
Full Breakfast
Minimum stay weekends & holidays: 2
Credit Cards: A, B
Notes: 2, 4, 5, 8, 9,10, 11, 12, 13 (XC)

The Wild Rose of York

78 Long Sands Road, 03909
(207) 363-2532

An 1814 captain's house on a hill, with large porch and columns, very colonial, with a working fireplace in one room and a four-poster bed. Another room is smaller, with an attached sun porch, nonworking fireplace, and 100-year-old high-back oak bed. The third room is on the first floor with a queen bed and single bed. The house is located just over a mile from the beach.

Hosts: Fran & Frank Sullivan
Doubles: 3 (PB) $45-55 plus tax

Full Breakfast
Credit Cards: No
Closed some winter months
Notes: 2, 8, 9, 10, 11, 12, 13 (XC)

YORK BEACH

B&B Registry #ME-03903CAN

Box 8174, St. Paul,MN, 55108
(612) 646-4238

A comfortable Victorian inn with a homey atmosphere. Beautiful ocean views. Within easy strolling distance of beaches, shops, and amusement park. Listen to the roar of the ocean while you relax on the sun deck or front porch.

Doubles: 10 (SB) $55-65
Type of Beds: 11 Twin; 8 Double
Continental Breakfast
Credit Cards: No
Closed Sept. 6 - June 30
Notes: 7, 8, 11

YORK HARBOR

York Harbor Inn

Box 573, Rt. 1A, 03911
(207) 363-5119

Coastal country inn overlooking beautiful York Harbor, located in an exclusive residential neighborhood. thirty-two air-conditioned rooms with antiques and ocean views, seven working fireplaces. Fine dining with ocean views year-round, and there's an English pub on the premises with entertainment. The beach is within walking distance, and boating, fishing, antique shops are all nearby.

Hosts: Joe, Jean, Garry & Nancy Dominguez
Singles: 3 (PB) $49-60
Doubles: 29 (PB) $55-120
Type of Beds: 32 Double
Continental Breakfast
Credit Cards: A, B, C
Notes: 2, 3, 4, 5, 7, 8, 9, 10, 11, 12, 14

NOTES: Credit cards accepted: A Master Card; B Visa; C American Express; D Discover Card; E Diners Club; F Other: 2 Personal checks accepted: 3 Lunch available: 4 Dinner available: 5 Open all year

Maryland

ANNAPOLIS_____

Gibson's Lodgings
110 Prince George Street, 21401
(301) 268-5555

Historic twenty-room bed and breakfast inn
with a new conference parlor for business
and private gatherings. Group discount for
six or more rooms Sundays through
Thursdays. Located half a block from the
city dock.

Host: Holly Perdue
Doubles: 20 (7 PB; 13 SB) $55-120
Type of Beds: 5 Twin; 9 Double; 6 Queen
Continental Breakfast
Credit Cards: A, B, C
Notes: 2, 5, 7, 8, 9, 12

Heron Watch
The Traveller In Maryland
Box 2277, Annapolis, 21404
(301) 269-6232

Waterfront home minutes from the Historic
District. Quiet contemporary with Oriental
and country antiques. Two waterfront
bedrooms with private bath, sitting room
and terrace overlooking the water, Japanese
garden.

Doubles: 2 (PB) $75
Type of Beds: 1 Double; 1 King
Continental Breakfast
Credit Cards: No
Notes: 2, 5, 8 (12 and over), 9, 10, 11, 12

The Jonah Williams House, 1830
101 Severn Avenue, 21403
(301) 269-6020

Convenient to shopping, restaurants, and
boating, just one block to the water taxi and
two minutes to the city dock and the Naval
Academy. Plenty of parking. A Laura Ashley
historic environment.

Hosts: Dorothy & Hank Robbins
Singles: 2 (SB) $65
Doubles: 4 (1 PB; 3 SB) $70
Type of Beds: 2 Twin; 1 Queen; 2 King
Continental Breakfast
Credit Cards: No
Notes: 2, 5, 8 (10 and over), 9, 10, 11, 12

Magnolia House
The Traveller In Maryland
Box 2277, Annapolis, 21404
(301) 269-6232

Three-story Georgian Revival brick
residence in the Historic District. Located
just outside the Naval Academy, within
walking distance of historic homes, the State
Capitol, antique shops, and restaurants. Intimate, private garden with a majestic
Southern magnolia tree.

Doubles: 2 (PB) $65-75
Type of Beds: 2 Double
Full Breakfast
Credit Cards: No
Notes: 2, 5, 8 (12 and over), 10, 11

Prince George Inn B&B
232 Prince George Street, 21401
(301) 263-6418

This Victorian townhouse in the historic district offers antique-filled guest rooms and
immaculate shared baths. A charming parlor with fireplace, sunny breakfast porches,
and lovely garden are for guests' enjoyment.

6 Pets welcome: 7 Smoking allowed: 8 Children welcome: 9 Social drinking allowed: 10 Tennis available: 11
Swimming available: 12 Golf available: 13 Skiing available: 14 May be booked through travel agents

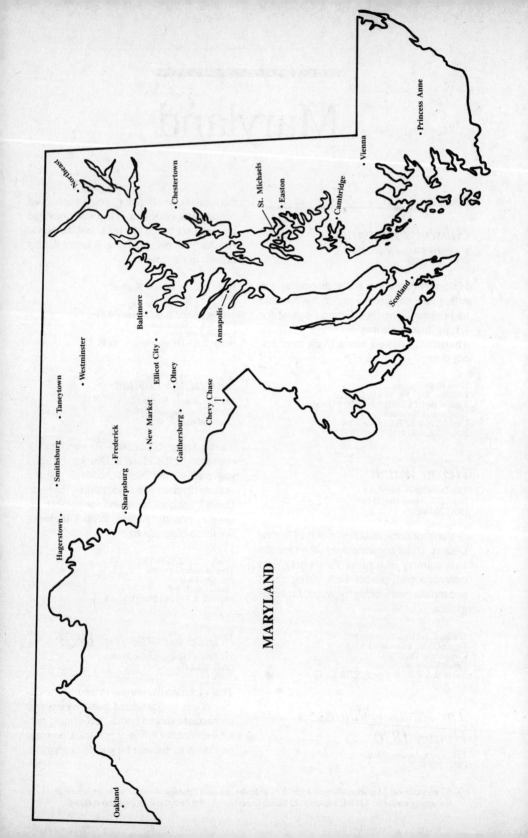

MARYLAND

Northeast

Chestertown

St. Michaels
Easton
Cambridge
Vienna
Princess Anne
Scotland

Baltimore
Annapolis

Westminster
Ellicot City
Olney

Taneytown

Smithsburg
Frederick
New Market
Gaithersburg
Chevy Chase

Hagerstown
Sharpsburg

Oakland

Easy walk to nearby shops, restaurants, dock, and Naval Academy.

Hosts: Norma & Bill Grovermann
Single: (SB) $52.50
Doubles: 4 (SB) $68.25
Type of Beds: 2 Twin; 2 Double; 1 Queen
Continental Breakfast
Credit Cards: A
Notes: 2, 8 (12 and over), 9, 10, 12

Shaw's Fancy Bed & Breakfast

161 Green Street, 21401
(301) 268-9750

Shaw's Fancy is located in the heart of historic Annapolis. Walk to boutique shopping, sailing, great restaurants, or an evening of live jazz. Decorated in a mix of graceful Victorian furniture, lace, and fantasy art. Enjoy complimentary sherry under our magnolia or in our hot tub.

Hosts: Jack House & Lilith Ren
Singles: 1 (SB) $47.50
Doubles: 3 (2 PB; 1 SB) $68.50-131.25
Suites available to sleep up to 4
Continental Breakfast
Credit Cards: A, B, C
Notes: 2, 5, 8 (over 10), 9

William Page Inn B&B

The Traveller In Maryland
Box 2277, Annapolis, 21404
(301) 269-6232

A renovated social club built in 1908, furnished in antiques with period reproductions to accentuate a quiet splendor. Centrally located two blocks from the Annapolis city docks and Naval Academy. Honeymoon suite available.

Doubles: 5 (PB and SB) $70-120
Type of Beds: 5 Queen
Continental Breakfast
Credit Cards: No
Notes: 2, 5, 9, 10, 11, 12

BALTIMORE

Admiral Fell Inn

888 S. Broadway, 21231
(301) 522-7377

The Admiral Fell Inn consists of seven buildings constructed between 1770 and 1910, all restored and decorated in charming Federal period antiques. Each room has been uniquely decorated and has a private bath. Restaurant and English pub are located on the premises.

Host: Jim Widman
Singles: 25 (PB) $89
Doubles: 15 (PB) $110
Type of Beds: 9 Twin; 18 Double; 13 King
Continental Breakfast
Credit Cards: A, B, C
Notes: 2, 4, 5, 7, 8, 9, 12, 14

Amanda's B&B Reservation Service #3

1428 Park Avenue, 21217
(301) 225-0001

In the heart of the Fell's Point waterfront community, this handsomely renovated nineteenth-century townhouse recalls the spirit of Baltimore's seafaring past while offering the best in modern conveniences. Stocked kitchenette, roof deck with sweeping views of the city skyline, free parking.

Doubles: 1 (PB) $80-85
Type of Beds: 2 Twin or 1 King
Continental Breakfast
Credit Cards: A, B, C
Notes: 2, 5, 7, 10, 11, 12, 14

Amanda's B&B Reservation Service #4

1428 Park Avenue, 21217
(301) 225-0001

Located in the historic neighborhood of Fell's Point, this charming row house is decorated with antiques. One bedroom has

6 Pets welcome: 7 Smoking allowed: 8 Children welcome: 9 Social drinking allowed: 10 Tennis available: 11 Swimming available: 12 Golf available: 13 Skiing available: 14 May be booked through travel agents

a fireplace. Wholesome breakfast; cat in residence.

Doubles: 3 (PB) $65
Full Breakfast
Credit Cards: A, B, C
Notes: 2, 5, 8, 9, 10, 11, 12, 14

Amanda's B&B Reservation Service #5

1428 Park Avenue, 21217
(301) 225-0001

A 45-foot Gulf Star yacht with gourmet kitchen, excellent stereo, TV, beautiful stateroom. Travel into town by water taxi. Deli on shore.

Doubles: 1 (PB) $140
Type of Beds: 1 King
Continental Breakfast
Credit Cards: A, B, C
Closed Dec. - March
Notes: 2, 8, 9, 10, 11, 12, 14

Amanda's B&B Reservation Service #6

1428 Park Avenue, 21217
(301) 225-0001

A circa 1830 Federal townhouse with leaded-glass transoms and entrance-fan windows, courtyard, grand piano, fireplace. Parking available on the property at no charge. Within walking distance of many of Baltimore's points of interest.

Doubles: 4 (PB) $65
Type of Beds: 4 Double
Full Breakfast
Credit Cards: A, B, C
Notes: 2, 5, 9, 10, 11, 12, 14

Betsy's Bed & Breakfast

1428 Park Avenue, 21217
(301) 383-1274
A four-story townhouse in downtown Baltimore, just seven minutes from the Inner Harbor area. Large, spacious rooms in an interestingly decorated home. Center stairway opens to skylight; hot tub available for guest use. Historic residential neighborhood. Off-street parking available.

Host: Betsy Grater
Doubles: 3 (1 PB; 2 SB) $47.25-68.25
Full Breakfast
Credit Cards: A, B, C
Notes: 2, 5, 8, 9, 10, 11, 12, 14

Mulberry House

111 W. Mulberry Street, 21201
(301) 576-0111

An 1830 townhouse in downtown Baltimore with antiques, stained glass, crystal and brass chandeliers, Oriental rugs, grand Steinway piano, and fireplaces. Walk to most points of interest and all the best restaurants, including Harborplace, the convention center, and the aquarium.

Hosts: Charlotte & Curt Jeschke
Doubles: 4 (S2B) $65
Type of Beds: 4 Double
Full Breakfast
Credit Cards: No
Notes: 2, 5, 8 (over 16), 9

Shirley Madison Inn

205 W. Madison Street, 21201
(301) 728-6550

Built in 1880, our historically registered urban inn recreates the past with elegant antique furniture, fourteen-foot ceilings, original woodwork, and floor-to-ceiling windows. Our downtown location in Baltimore's historic Mt. Vernon residential district is a short walk to the Inner Harbor, "antique row," museums, and a host of dining alternatives. Enjoy our complimentary continental breakfast and evening aperitif.

Hosts: Herman Lantz, Stanley Gondzar, Irene Borowicz
Doubles: 25 (PB) $55-105

NOTES: Credit cards accepted: A Master Card; B Visa; C American Express; D Discover Card; E Diners Club; F Other: 2 Personal checks accepted: 3 Lunch available: 4 Dinner available: 5 Open all year

Type of Beds: 4 Twin; 10 Double; 8 Queen; 8 King
Continental Breakfast
Credit Cards: A, B, C, E
Notes: 2, 4, 5, 7, 8, 9, 14

Society Hill Hotel

58 W. Biddle Street, 21201
(301) 837-3630

A delightful converted townhouse within walking distance of the Meyerhoff Symphony Hall and Lyric Opera House, antique and boutique rows. This fifteen-room inn offers the exciting combination of a B&B and an American country inn. Brass beds, fresh flowers, rich Victorian furniture, breakfast served to your room. The hotel has a bar and restaurant on the premises, as well as a jazz piano bar.

Hosts: Kate Hopkins & Cheryl Maszczycki
Singles: 4 (PB) $75
Doubles: 11 (PB) $95-115
Type of Beds: 4 Twin; 3 Full; 6 Queen; 2 King
Continental Breakfast
Credit Cards: A, B, C, E
Notes: 2, 3, 4, 5, 7, 8, 9, 10, 11, 12, 14

Twin Gates B&B Inn

308 Morris Avenue, 21093
(301) 252-3131; 1-800-635-0370

Experience serene elegance in this Victorian mansion near the National Aquarium, Harborplace, and Maryland Hunt Country. Friendly hosts, wine and cheese, and gourmet breakfasts.

Hosts: Gwen & Bob Vaughan
Doubles: 7 (3 PB; 4 SB) $85
Type of Beds: 2 Twin; 6 Queen
Full Breakfast
Minimum stay weekends & holidays: 2
Credit Cards: A, B
Notes: 2, 5, 9, 10, 12, 14

CAMBRIDGE

Sarke Plantation Inn

6033 Todd Point Road, 21613
(301) 228-7020

An Eastern Shore waterfront property of 27 country acres with a spacious house that is furnished tastefully with many antiques. There is a large pool room with a regulation table, and the living room has a large fireplace, a good stereo system, and a grand piano for your enjoyment.

Host: Genevieve Finley
Doubles: 5 (3 PB; 2 SB) $40-90
Type of Beds: 5 Twin; 3 Double; 1 Queen
Continental Breakfast
Credit Cards: C
Closed New Year's Eve
Notes: 2, 6, 7, 8 (over 10), 9, 11

Twin Gates B&B Inn

CHESTERTOWN

The Inn at Mitchell House

Rd 2, Box 329, 21620
(301) 778-6500

Nestled on 10 rolling acres, surrounded by woods and overlooking a pond, this historic manor house, built in 1743, greets you with warmth and affords a touch of tranquility. A mere half mile from the Chesapeake, this six-bedroom inn, with parlors and numerous fireplaces, provides a casual, friendly atmosphere.

Hosts: Jim & Tracy Stone
Doubles: 6 (PB) $75-90
Type of Beds: 1 Twin; 5 Double; 1 King
Full Breakfast
Credit Cards: A, B
Notes: 2, 5, 7, 8, 9, 10, 11, 12

The Inn at Mitchell House

CHEVY CHASE

Chevy Chase Bed & Breakfast

6815 Connecticut Avenue, 20815
(301) 656-5867

Enjoy the convenience of being close to the sights of Washington, D.C., in a relaxing country-style house in historic Chevy Chase. Furnished with rare tapestries, Oriental rugs, baskets, copperware, and native crafts from around the world.

Host: S. C. Gotbaum
Singles: 2 (PB) $45-55
Type of Beds: 3 Twin; 1 King
Continental Breakfast
Credit Cards: No
Notes: 2, 5, 7, 8, 10, 11, 12

EASTON

Amanda's B&B Reservation Service #7

1428 Park Avenue, Baltimore, 21217
(301) 225-0001

A charming Victorian B&B in the colonial capital of Maryland's Eastern Shore. Built circa 1890, the house has a high octagonal tower, a roof hipped with dormers, and a porch that runs across the front and part of the south side. All rooms have air-conditioning, ceiling fans, and private baths. Within walking distance of the Tidewater Inn and other historic points of interest.

Doubles: 3 (PB) $50-65 plus tax
Type of Beds: 1 Double; 1 Queen; 1 King
Continental Breakfast
Credit Cards: A, B, C
Notes: 2, 5, 8 (weekdays), 9, 10, 11, 12, 14

ELLICOT CITY

Amanda's B&B Reservation Service #8

1328 Park Avenue, Baltimore, 21217
(301) 225-0001

This picturesque town offers a mix of history and commerce, with old shops and antique stores that make it resemble an old European mountain village. The stately Federal-period stone farmhouse is situated on 2 acres with a pond. All rooms are air-conditioned.

Doubles: 4 (2 PB; 2 SB) $65-85 plus tax
Type of Beds: 2 Double; 2 Queen
Continental Breakfast
Credit Cards: A, B
Notes: 2, 5, 14

FREDERICK

Tran Crossing

121 East Patrick Street, 21701
(301) 663-8449

Delight in Maryland hospitality in a beautifully restored nineteenth-century townhouse. An elegant Victorian home combining comfort with period charm. Guests enjoy the serenity of the garden as they sip their morning coffee or relax from a

NOTES: Credit cards accepted: A Master Card; B Visa; C American Express; D Discover Card; E Diners Club; F Other: 2 Personal checks accepted: 3 Lunch available: 4 Dinner available: 5 Open all year

day of sightseeing in Frederick's historic district.

Hosts: Becky & Fred Tran
Suites: 1 (PB) $80
Type of Beds: 1 Double; 1 Queen
Continental-plus Breakfast
Credit Cards: No
Notes: 2, 5, 7, 8, 9, 10, 11, 12, 14

Tran Crossing

Turning Point Inn

3406 Urbana Pike, 21701
(301) 874-2421

Turning Point Inn is a lovely 1910 Edwardian estate home with Georgian features. Less than an hour from the Washington, D.C., Baltimore, Gettysburg, and Antietam areas, this inn is ideally situated for a getaway weekend of sightseeing, shopping, antiquing, hiking, or exploring nearby historic towns and battlefields.

Hosts: Ellie & Bernie Droneburg & Charlie Seymour
Doubles: 5 (PB) $75-85
Type of Beds: 3 Double; 2 Queen; 1 King
Full Breakfast
Credit Cards: A, B
Notes: 2, 3 (Tues.-Fri.), 4 (Tues.-Sun.), 5, 7 (limited), 8, 9, 10, 11, 12

GAITHERSBURG

Gaithersburg Hospitality Bed & Breakfast

18908 Chimney Place, 20879
(301) 977-7377

Located in Montgomery Village, near restaurants, shopping, and recreation, this luxury home is furnished in family pieces with your comfort and pleasure in mind. It offers all amenities and is convenient (30 minutes) to Washington, D.C., via the Metro or your car. Home cooking!

Hosts: Joe & Suzanne Danilowicz
Doubles: (PB) $50 + Singles: (PB) $40
Type of Beds: 4 Twin; 2 Double
Full Breakfast
Credit Cards: No
Closed Jan. 15-Feb. 15
Notes: 2, 8, 9, 10, 11, 12, 14

HAGERSTOWN

Lewrene Farm Bed & Breakfast

RD 3, Box 150, 21740
(301) 582-1735

Close to I-70 and I-81 on a quiet 125 acre farm near Antietam Battlefield, Harper's Ferry, the C&O Canal. Baltimore and Washington, DC, are only seventy miles away. Colonial-style home with antique furnishings, large living room, fireplace, deluxe bedrooms. Hostess speaks English and Spanish.

Hosts: Lewis & Irene Lehman
Doubles: 6 (3 PB; 3 SB) $44-68
Type of Beds: 5 Double; 1 Queen
Full Breakfast
Credit Cards: No
Notes: 2, 4, 5, 8, 10, 11, 12

NEW MARKET

National Pike Inn

9 West Main Street, Box 299, 21774
(301) 865-5055

6 Pets welcome: 7 Smoking allowed: 8 Children welcome: 9 Social drinking allowed: 10 Tennis available: 11 Swimming available: 12 Golf available: 13 Skiing available: 14 May be booked through travel agents

This Federal house, built in the early 1800s, offers a special charm that must be shared. Each guest room has its own special decor. Shop for antiques, dine in excellence, or simply stroll the streets of this quaint village fifteen minutes from Frederick and thirty minutes from Harpers Ferry.

Hosts: Tom & Terry Rimel
Singles: 1 (SB) $60-65
Doubles: 4 (2 PB; 2 SB) $65-100
Type of Beds: 2 Twin; 1 Double; 3 Queen
Continental-plus Breakfast
Credit Cards: A, B
Notes: 2, 5, 7, 8 (over 5), 10, 12, 13

Turning Point Inn

The Strawberry Inn

17 Main Street, Box 237, 21774
(301) 865-3318

An 1840 Maryland farmhouse that's completely restored. Each guest room has its own private bath, and rooms are tastefully furnished with comfortable antiques. Common room with wood-burning fireplace for wine or tea after a day of antique shopping in "The Antique Capital of Maryland." Restaurant across the street.

Hosts: Jane & Ed Rossig
Doubles: 5 (PB) $55-85
Type of Beds: 2 Twin; 1 Double; 2 Queen
Continental Breakfast
Credit Cards: No
Notes: 2, 5, 7, 9, 10, 11, 12

NORTHEAST

Amanda's B&B
Reservation Service #9

1428 Park Avenue, Baltimore, 21217
(301) 225-0001

Originally a mill and mill-owner's house built about 1710, this home is full of history and colonial charm. After a full breakfast, you may want to walk around the grounds and enjoy the wild flowers in the marsh between the mill run and the river. Less than an hour from the Baltimore Inner Harbor, Pennsylvania Dutch country, Winterthur Museum, Brandywine River Museum, and Longwood Gardens.

Doubles: 2 (SB) $55
Type of Beds: 2 Double
Full Breakfast
Credit Cards: A, B, C
Closed Nov. 1 - Feb. 28
Notes: 2, 9, 10, 11, 12, 14

OAKLAND

Red Run Inn

Rt. 5, Box 268, 21550
(301) 387-6606

Nestled in a natural wooded setting, Red Run overlooks the expansive blue waters of Deep Creek Lake. On 18 acres, with a large swimming pool, two tennis courts, cross-country ski trail, horseshoe pits, and dock facilities.

Host: Ruth M. Umbel
Doubles: 6 (PB) $65-100
Type of Beds: 2 Twin; 5 Double; 1 King
Continental Breakfast
Credit Cards: A, B, C
Closed Nov. 15-May 1
Notes: 7, 8, 9, 10, 11, 12

NOTES: Credit cards accepted: A Master Card; B Visa; C American Express; D Discover Card; E Diners Club; F Other: 2 Personal checks accepted: 3 Lunch available: 4 Dinner available: 5 Open all year

PRINCESS ANNE

Elmwood c. 1770 Bed & Breakfast

Box 220, Locust Point Road, 21853
(301) 651-1066

This historic manor house has a wonderful setting on 160 acres of fields, woods, and lawn, with a mile of waterfront and commanding view of the Manokin River. The goal of the innkeepers is to surround their guests with the life-style of the nineteenth century and tranquility.

Hosts: Helen & Steve Monick
Cottages: 2 (PB) $75-109.25
Doubles: 4 (SB) $75-109.25
Full Breakfast
Credit Cards: A, B
Closed mid-Dec. - mid-Jan.
Notes: 2, 7 (limited), 8 (12 and over), 9, 10, 14

Elmwood c. 1770 B&B

OLNEY

Amanda's B&B Reservation Service #11

1428 Park Avenue, Baltimore, 21217
(301) 225-0001

Nestled in the rolling hills just outside of Washington, DC, this 175-acre B&B also features thoroughbred horses on the premises. Relax and enjoy pleasant walks in the countryside, swim in the pool, warm up in the hot tub, or read in the comfortable sitting room. Near restaurants, a very good theater, horseback riding, picnic areas, falls, a canal, and rafting.

Doubles: 5 (3 PB; 2 SB) $45-70
Type of Beds: 2 Twin; 3 King; 1 Trundle bed
Full Breakfast
Credit Cards: A, B, C
Notes: 2, 5, 8, 9, 10, 11, 12, 14

ST. MICHAELS

Kemp House Inn

412 Talbot Street, 21663
(301) 745-2243

Built in 1805 by Col. Joseph Kemp, who commanded the local militia in the War of 1812 (Robert E. Lee was a guest in the house). Four-poster beds with trundle beds underneath, period furnishings, fireplaces, candlelight, tab curtains, and flannel nightshirts.

Hosts: Diane & Steve Cooper
Doubles: 7 (3 PB; 4 SB) $50-100
Type of Beds: 3 Twin; 4 Double; 3 Queen
Continental Breakfast
Minimum stay weekends: 2 ; holidays: 3
Credit Cards: A, B
Notes: 2, 5, 7, 8, 9, 12, 14

Parsonage Inn

210 N. Talbot Street, 21663
(301) 745-5519

Elegantly furnished Victorian with brass beds, Laura Ashley linens, private baths, and working fireplaces in three of seven rooms. Guests enjoy sumptuous continental breakfasts in the dining room. Parlor, deck, front porch, and bikes available. Within the historic district; two blocks to museum and shops.

Hosts: Betty & Charles Oler
Doubles: 7 (PB) $72-102
Type of Beds: 2 Double; 4 Queen; 2 King

6 Pets welcome: 7 Smoking allowed: 8 Children welcome: 9 Social drinking allowed: 10 Tennis available: 11 Swimming available: 12 Golf available: 13 Skiing available: 14 May be booked through travel agents

Continental Breakfast
Notes: 2, 5, 9, 12

SCOTLAND

St. Michael's Manor Bed & Breakfast

St. Michael's Manor & Vineyard, 20687
(301) 872-4025

St. Michael's Manor (1805) was originally patented to Leonard Calvert in 1637. The house, located on Long Neck Creek, is furnished with antiques. Boating, canoeing, wine-tasting are available. Near Pt. Lookout State Park, Civil War monuments, and historic St. Mary's City.

Hosts: Joseph & Nancy Dick
Doubles: 3 (SB) $35-55
Type of Beds: 4 Twin; 1 Double
Full Breakfast
Credit Cards: No
Notes: 2, 5, 7 (limited), 8, 9, 10, 11

The Inn at Antietam

SHARPSBURG

Inn at Antietam

Box 119, 21782
(301) 432-6601

The Inn at Antietam is a classic turn-of-the-century Victorian with a wraparound porch that provides views of the Antietam National Battlefield, the village of Sharpsburg, and the Blue Ridge Mountains. The inn has five guest rooms, all with private baths, and is furnished with antiques.

Hosts: Betty & Cal Fairbourn
Doubles: 5 (PB) $65-95
Type of Beds: 1 Twin; 3 Double; 1 Queen
Continental-plus Breakfast
Credit Cards: C
Closed 2 weeks at Christmas
Notes: 2, 7 (restricted), 8 (over 6), 9, 10, 11, 12, 14

SMITHSBURG

Blue Bear Bed & Breakfast

Rt. 2, Box 378, Holiday Drive, 21783
(301) 824-2292

Country charm and warm, friendly hospitality await you at the Blue Bear. There are two beautifully decorated and air-conditioned rooms with a shared bath. Enjoy a delicious breakfast of fresh fruits, breads and pastries, and quiche. We want you to feel at home here.

Host: Ellen Panchula
Doubles: 2 (SB) $30-40
Type of Beds: 2 Double
Continental Breakfast
Credit Cards: No
Closed Sept. - June weekdays
Notes: 2, 8 (over 12), 10, 11, 12

TANEYTOWN

Glenburn

3515 Runnymede Road, 21787
(301) 751-1187

Glenburn is a circa 1840 Georgian home with Victorian additions. Guest rooms overlook pasture, lawns, woods with creek. European and American antiques. Exceptional setting for a getaway. Close to Gettysburg; sixty miles from Washington, DC. Agricultural and recreational area with historic interest.

Hosts: Robert & Elizabeth Neal
Doubles: 5 (3 PB; 2 SB) $55-75
Type of Beds: 1 Twin; 3 Double; 1 Queen

NOTES: Credit cards accepted: A Master Card; B Visa; C American Express; D Discover Card; E Diners Club; F Other: 2 Personal checks accepted: 3 Lunch available: 4 Dinner available: 5 Open all year

Full Breakfast
Minimum stay holidays: 2
Credit Cards: No
Notes: 2, 5, 7 (restricted), 9, 10, 11, 12, 13

VIENNA

The Tavern House

Box 98, 21869
(301) 376-3347

A colonial tavern on the Nanticoke River featuring the simple elegance of colonial living and special breakfasts that are a social occasion. A glimpse into Michener's *Chesapeake* for those who love colonial homes, the peace of a small town, or watching osprey in flight.

Hosts: Harvey & Elise Altergott
Doubles: 4 (SB) $50-65
Type of Beds: 2 Twin; 3 Double
Full Breakfast
Credit Cards: A, B
Notes: 2, 5, 7, 8 (over 12), 9, 10, 14

WESTMINSTER

Amanda's B&B Reservation Service #12

1428 Park Avenue, Baltimore, 21217
(301) 225-0001

A brick Georgian manor house on several acres of land just a few minutes off the main highway. Listed on the National Historic Register (circa 1765). Westminster is an historic college town with a wonderful farm museum, shops, golf, and antiques.

Doubles: 1 (PB) $65
Type of Beds: 1 King
Full Breakfast
Credit Cards: A, B, C
Notes: 2, 5, 8, 9, 10, 11, 12, 14

The Winchester Country Inn

430 South Bishop Street, 21157
(301) 876-7373

Built in the 1760s by the founder of Westminster, the Winchester Country Inn is one of Carroll County's oldest buildings. Various recreational facilities and historic points of interest abound around the inn, which is centrally located in Maryland. The refurbished interior makes this one of the most delightful and refreshing country inns open to the public.

Host: Estella Williams
Doubles: 5 (3 PB; 2 SB) $55-70
Type of Beds: 2 Twin; 2 Double; 2 Queen; 1 King
Full Breakfast
Credit Cards: A, B
Notes: 2, 5, 7 (limited), 8 (6 and over), 9, 10, 11, 12

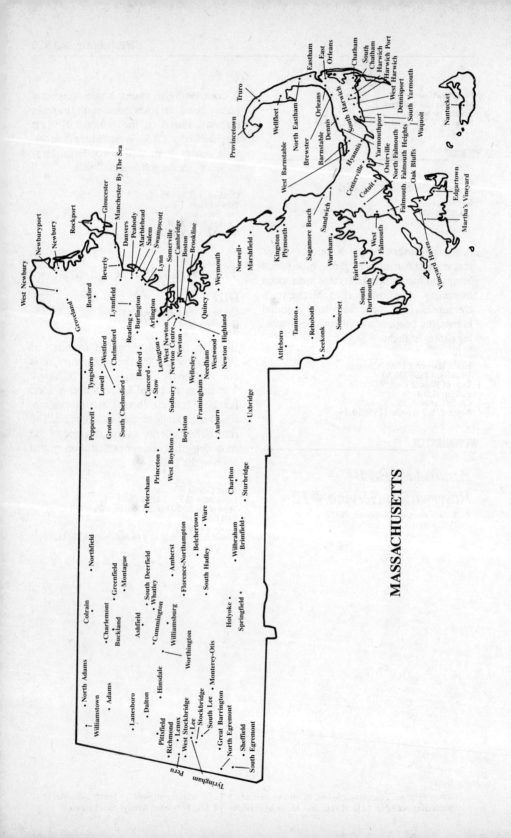

MASSACHUSETTS

Massachusetts

Bascom Lodge

Box 686, Lanesboro, 02137
(413) 743-1591

A rustic stone-and-wood lodge on the summit of Mt. Greylock, fifty feet from the great Appalachian Trail, that features an all-you-can-eat breakfast and dinner, bunk-style dormitory, private accommodations, and 100-mile views.

Hosts: Appalachian Mountain Club
Bunks: 26 (SB) $26
Doubles: 3 (SB) $48
Type of Beds: 2 Twin; 2 Double; 26 Bunks
Full Breakfast
Credit Cards: A, B
Closed Oct. 24-May 12
Notes: 2, 4, 8, 11, 12

Berkshire PV14

Berkshire B&B Homes
Box 211, Williamsburg, MA, 01096
(413) 268-7244

1984 Cape Cod with contemporary and country furnishings, one mile from the University of Massachusetts, two from Amherst College, five from Hampshire College, and minutes from Smith College.

Doubles: 2 (SB) $45-50
Type of Beds: 1 Double; 1 Queen
Full breakfast weekends, continental weekdays
Credit Cards: No
Notes: 2, 5, 8 (10 and over), 10, 11, 12

B&B Registry
#MA-02174ORN

Box 8174, St. Paul, MN, 55108
(612) 646-4238

Small 1925 New England home within walking distance of town center. Living room fireplace. Arlington is on the trail of Paul Revere's ride, just north of Cambridge. Public transportation to downtown Boston every thirty minutes stops across the street.

Singles: 1 (SB) $45
Doubles: 1 (SB) $55
Type of Beds: 1 Double; 1 Cot
Continental Breakfast weekdays; Full weekends
Credit Cards: No
Notes: 3, 4, 5, 8, 11, 12, 13

Ashfield Inn

Box 129, 01330
(413) 628-4571

A gracious Georgian mansion situated in the foothills of the Berkshires. The house is located on over 9 acres of land overlooking Ashfield Lake. Close to historic Deerfield, the Mohawk Trail; 35 miles to Stockbridge and Tanglewood. Antique shopping, cross-country and downhill skiing; in the heart of maple-syrup country.

Hosts: Stacy & Scott Alessi
Doubles: 8 (S4B) $52.85-84.56
Type of Beds: 1 Twin; 7 Double; 1 Queen
Full Breakfast on weekends; Continental on weekdays
Minimum stay Sept. 15-Oct. 15 & major holidays: 2

6 Pets welcome: 7 Smoking allowed: 8 Children welcome: 9 Social drinking allowed: 10 Tennis available: 11 Swimming available: 12 Golf available: 13 Skiing available: 14 May be booked through travel agents

Credit Cards: A, B, C
Notes: 2, 4, 5, 8 (10 and up), 9, 10, 11, 12, 13

ATTLEBORO

B&B Rhode Island #MA-238

Box 3291-ND, Newport, R.I., 02840
(401) 849-1298

Comfortable country decor creates a homey atmosphere in this new colonial. Interesting collections of folk art and advertising memorabilia. Relax in a traditional parlor, an informal sitting room with wood stove, or on the backyard deck. Swing set for children. Located on a quiet cul-de-sac close to major routes and the Amtrak station.

Doubles: 2 (SB) $45-65
Type of Beds: 2 Double
Full Breakfast
Credit Cards: No
Notes: 5, 8, 9, 10, 11, 12, 14

Ashley Manor

AUBURN

Capt. Samuel Eddy B&B Inn

609 Oxford Street South, 01501
(508) 832-5282

Come join us and step back in time to the warmth and charm of the eighteenth century in our 1765 inn. Antiques throughout, canopy beds, and common rooms with fireplaces. Breakfast is served in the sun room overlooking the herb gardens and pool area. Close to Sturbridge Village, thirteen colleges, and Boston. Visit our Country Shop.

Hosts: Jack & Carilyn O'Toole
Doubles: 5 (PB) $48-75
Full Breakfast
Credit Cards: A, B
Notes: 2, 3, 4, 5, 8, 9, 10, 11, 12, 14

BARNSTABLE

Ashley Manor

Box 856, 02630
(508) 362-8044

Ashley Manor is a very special place, a gracious 1699 mansion on a 2-acre estate in Cape Cod's historic district. Romantic rooms and suites feature private baths and fireplaces. Elegant public rooms with antiues, Oriental rugs. Delicious full breakfast. Walk to the beach and village.

Hosts: Donald & Fay Bain
Doubles: 6 (PB) $100-145
Type of Beds: 2 Double; 3 Queen; 1 King
Full Breakfast
Minimum stay weekends: 2
Credit Cards: A, B, C
Notes: 2, 5, 7 (limited), 8 (over 14), 9, 10, 11, 12, 14

B&B Registry #MA-02630HEN

Box 8174, St. Paul, MN, 55108
(612) 646-4238

Gracious two-story center chimney colonial built circa 1800 as a residence and tavern. Filled with authentic country antiques and fine reproductions finished in the host's own shop. Three large fireplaced common rooms to warm you at night. Screened porch, sprawling grounds.

Singles: 1 (SB) $40-75
Doubles: 3 (SB) $50-75
Type of Beds: 1 Twin; 1 Double; 2 Queen
Continental-plus Breakfast

NOTES: Credit cards accepted: A Master Card; B Visa; C American Express; D Discover Card; E Diners Club; F Other: 2 Personal checks accepted: 3 Lunch available: 4 Dinner available: 5 Open all year

Credit Cards: A, B
Notes: 5, 8 (over 12), 11, 12

Charles Hinckley House
Box 723, 02630
(508) 362-9924

Small, intimate country inn in historic
Barnstable. Circa 1809 Federal gem listed
on the National Register. Fireplace suites
with private baths, four-poster beds, and
English country breakfasts. A five-minute
walk down a country lane to Cape Cod Bay;
1.5 miles to Barnstable harbor and all boating activities. Golf and tennis are within
minutes, and museums, beaches, antique
and craft shops are abundant.

Hosts: Les & Miya Patrick
Doubles: 4 (PB) $98-135
Type of Beds: 1 Double; 3 Queen
Full Breakfast
Credit Cards: No
Notes: 2, 3, 4, 5, 9, 10, 11, 12, 14

Cobb's Cove
Box 208, 02630
(508) 362-9356

Our colonial timbered manor overlooks
Barnstable Village, the harbor, and Cape
Cod Bay. Walk to the beach and whale-
watch boat. All rooms have a full bath with
whirlpool tub and toweling robes. Enjoy our
keeping room, with its huge Count Rumford
fireplace, and breakfast on the peaceful garden patio.

Hosts: Evenlyn Chester & Henri-Jean
Doubles: 6 (PB) $139-169
Type of Beds: 4 Queen; 2 King
Full Breakfast
Credit Cards: No
Notes: 2, 5, 7, 9, 10, 11, 12, 14

Crocker B&B
B&B Cape Cod, Box 341, W. Hyannisport, 02672
(508) 775-2772

This 1790 colonial is in the heart of the
village's national registry district. Once a
tavern, it was restored in 1986. Cape Cod
Bay views can be seen from the house; water
is .5 mile away. Cider or tea served after-
noons. Walk to whale-watch boats, village
shops, restaurants.

Doubles: 3 (SB) $75
Type of Beds: 1 Twin; 1 Double; 2 Queen
Continental Breakfast
Credit Cards: No
Notes: 2, 5, 9, 10, 11, 12, 14

Genny's B&B
B&B Cape Cod, Box 341, W. Hyannisport, 02672
(508) 775-2772

A few steps off the Old Kings Highway sits
this 1852 renovated Victorian with decorative wall coverings, period furnishings, and
fresh flowers. Outside wraparound porch
provides a place to relax after a day at the
beach or shopping in the nearby antique
store. Quiet, rural setting.

Doubles: 4 (PB) $55
Type of Beds: 2 Twin; 2 Double
Continental Breakfast
Credit Cards: No
Notes: 2, 9, 10, 11, 12, 14

Honeysuckle Hill
591 Main Street, 02668
(508) 362-8418

Charming restored farmhouse, circa 1810,
on the National Registry of Historic Places.
Features feather beds, English country
breakfast, afternoon tea on the screened
porch. All rooms have private baths with
fluffy terry-cloth robes and homemade
cookies at bedside. Large great room with
TV. Near beautiful Sandy Neck Beach.
Bicycles and beach towels are available for
guests.

Hosts: Barbara & Bob Rosenthal
Doubles: 3 (PB) $90-105
Type of Beds: 2 Queen; 1 King

6 Pets welcome: 7 Smoking allowed: 8 Children welcome: 9 Social drinking allowed: 10 Tennis available: 11 Swimming available: 12 Golf available: 13 Skiing available: 14 May be booked through travel agents

Full Breakfast
Credit Cards: A, B, C
Notes: 2, 5, 7, 9, 10, 11, 12, 14

Talo Ystava B&B

B&B Cape Cod, Box 341, W. Hyannisport, 02672
(508) 775-2772

Nestled in a wooded rural area next to Garrett Pond in West Barnstable. Contemporary home built to owner's specs, it features a light and airy living room, fireplace, and open atrium to second floor. Post-and-beam construction. Guests have use of the entire first floor.

Doubles: 1 (PB) $75
Type of Beds: 1 Queen
Continental Breakfast
Credit Cards: No
Notes: 2, 5, 9, 10, 11, 12, 14

Thomas Huckins House

2701 Main Street, Box 515, 02630
(508) 362-6379

Experience the charm of old Cape Cod. Sleep in canopy beds next to working fireplaces in this restored 1705 house. Breakfast in the antique-filled keeping room, walk to the ocean and village through the historic district on the Cape's picturesque and less-crowded North Shore.

Hosts: Burt & Eleanor Eddy
Doubles: 3 (PB) $55-85
Type of Beds: 2 Double; 1 Queen
Full Breakfast
Minimum stay weekends & holidays: 2
Credit Cards: A, B
Notes: 2, 5, 7, 8 (over 6), 9

BASS RIVER

Old Cape House

108 Old Main Street, 02664
(508) 398-1068

Enjoy warm hospitality in the English tradition in our circa 1815 Greek Revival house. All rooms are furnished New England style, with lacy curtains and quilts. Garden and porch for relaxation. Enjoy a plentiful breakfast of home-baked muffins and breads. Close to several fine beaches, golf, sailing, fishing, shops, and restaurants.

Hosts: George & Linda Arthur
Doubles: 5 (3 PB; 2 SB) $30-65
Type of Beds: 1 Single; 3 Double; 1 Queen
Continental Breakfast
Credit Cards: No
Closed Oct. 20 - May 20
Notes: 2 (for deposits), 8 (over 15), 9, 10, 11, 12

Old Cape House

BEDFORD

B&B Folks 1

48 Springs Road, MA 01730
(617) 275-9025

Charming 150-year-old colonial in the center of the historic district of this old New England town. Close to Boston, Cambridge, New Hampshire, and the ocean. Reduced rate for long-term stays.

Doubles: 1 (SB) $40-50
Type of Beds: 1 Double
Continental Breakfast
Credit Cards: No
Notes: 2, 4, 5, 6, 7, 8, 9, 10, 11, 12

NOTES: Credit cards accepted: A Master Card; B Visa; C American Express; D Discover Card; E Diners Club; F Other: 2 Personal checks accepted: 3 Lunch available: 4 Dinner available: 5 Open all year

BELCHERTOWN

Berkshire PV5

Berkshire B&B Homes
Box 211, Williamsburg, MA, 01096
(413) 268-7244

1839 Victorian on the green in this charming New England town. Living room with fireplace. Close to the five-college area, Quabbin Reservoir, and the Brimfield Flea Market.

Singles: 1 (SB) $30
Doubles: 2 (1 PB; 1 SB) $35-50
Type of Beds: 1 Twin; 2 Double
Continental Breakfast
Credit Cards: No
Notes: 2, 5, 8 (12 and over), 10, 11, 12, 13

BEVERLY

Beverly Cove B&B

B&B Marblehead & North Shore
Box 172, 01915
(508) 921-1336

Attractive, immaculate split level just a two-minute walk from a private beach in a quiet, prestigious area close to Endicott College. The hosts are English and enjoy entertaining in the best B&B tradition. Hostess enjoys music, singing, cooking.

Doubles: 3 (SB) $40-54
Type of Beds: 4 Twin; 1 Double
Full Breakfast
Credit Cards: No
Notes: 2, 5, 7 (restricted), 8 (over 9), 9, 10, 11, 12, 13 (XC), 14

Oceanview Dutch Colonial

B&B Marblehead & North Shore
Box 172, 01915
(508) 921-1336

Dutch colonial family home facing the ocean and decorated in antiques. One or more teenage sons at home. Hostess is a consultant on nonprofit fund raising and is particularly interested in local history and politics. She speaks some Spanish and Hebrew.

Singles: 1 (SB) $36-38
Doubles: 3 (1 PB; 2 SB) $45-65
Type of Beds: 3 Twin; 1 Double; 1 Queen
Continental Breakfast
Credit Cards: No
Notes: 2, 6 (call), 8, 9, 10, 11, 12, 14

BOSTON

Bed & Breakfast Associates #M103

Box 166, Babson Park, Boston, 02157
(617) 449-5302

Only three blocks from the Boston Common or Copley Square, this cozy first-floor studio apartment offers guests a separate entrance and the use of a quiet garden patio. The refrigerator will be stocked for you, or the hostess will deliver a full breakfast. Kitchen, telephone, color TV.

Doubles: 1 (PB) $90
Type of Beds: 1 Double
Stocked refrigerator or full breakfast
Minimum stay: 3
Credit Cards: A, B, C
Notes: 5, 7 (restricted), 11, 12

Bed & Breakfast Associates #M123

Box 166, Babson Park, 02157
(617) 449-5302

Located on Beacon Hill, this lovely private home offers guests a large garden-level guest room with a private bath. Public transportation is only two blocks away, and guests can easily walk to Fanueil Hall, Quincy Marketplace, or the Public Gardens.

Doubles: 1 (PB) $95
Type of Beds: 1 Queen
Continental Breakfast
Credit Cards: A, B, C
Notes: 5, 7, 8, 11, 12, 14

6 Pets welcome: 7 Smoking allowed: 8 Children welcome: 9 Social drinking allowed: 10 Tennis available: 11 Swimming available: 12 Golf available: 13 Skiing available: 14 May be booked through travel agents

Bed & Breakfast Associates #M309

Box 166, Babson Park, Boston, 02157
(617) 449-5302

Classic Victorian townhouse in Boston's up-and-coming South end. Your hostess is a retired secretary who enjoys gardening, music, and antiques. Small refrigerator in each room; parking garage several blocks away; resident cat.

Doubles: 2 (PB) $70-75
Type of Beds: 4 Twin
Continental Breakfast
Minimum stay: 3
Credit Cards: A, B, C
Notes: 5, 6, 7, 8 (over 6), 10, 11, 12

Bed & Breakfast Associates #M314

Box 166, Babson Park, Boston, 02157
(617) 449-5302

Located in the heart of Boston, only 2.5 blocks from Copley Square, guests are welcome in this fine 1860 brick townhouse. Antique armoires and hardwood floors with Oriental rugs add charm to the large third-floor guest rooms.

Doubles: 2 (PB) $90
Full Breakfast
Minimum stay: 3
Credit Cards: A, B, C
Notes: 5, 8 (over 10), 11, 12

Bed & Breakfast Associates #M319

Box 166, Babson Park, Boston, 02157
(617) 449-5302

Tucked away on a quiet, pretty street only 2.5 blocks from Copley Square, this brick townhouse offers guests a blending of Victorian and contemporary atmospheres.

Doubles: 2 (1 PB; 1 SB) $60-78
Type of Beds: 2 Queen

Continental Breakfast
Minimum stay: 3
Credit Cards: A, B, C
Notes: 5, 8, 10, 11, 12

Bed & Breakfast Associates #M350

Box 166, Babson Park, Boston, 02157
(617) 449-5302

Two self-contained studios, each with private entry, kitchenette, private bath, and charming brick walls. On the third floor of a renovated South End brownstone in an urban neighborhood just a few blocks from the Sheraton Hotel and the new Copley Place, with the finest shops in Boston.

Doubles: 2 (PB) $60-80
Type of Beds: 2 Queen
Continental Breakfast
Minimum stay: 3
Credit Cards: A, B, C
Notes: 5, 6, 7, 8, 10, 11, 12

Bed & Breakfast Associates #M485

Box 166, Babson Park, Boston, 02157
(617) 449-5302

This fabulous new three-level waterfront condo overlooks Boston Harbor and is located within walking distance of Quincy Marketplace. The hosts offer a large, pleasant room with an expansive view of the city skyline.

Doubles: 1 (PB) $85
Type of Beds: 1 Double
Continental Breakfast
Minimum stay: 3
Credit Cards: A, B, C
Notes: 5, 10, 11, 12

B&B Registry #MA-02115CUM

Box 8174, St. Paul, MN, 55108
(612) 646-4238

NOTES: Credit cards accepted: A Master Card; B Visa; C American Express; D Discover Card; E Diners Club; F Other: 2 Personal checks accepted: 3 Lunch available: 4 Dinner available: 5 Open all year

Located in a restored neighborhood in the heart of the city, close to Boston's historic and cultural attractions. This lovely brick and brownstone townhouse has two guest rooms with antiques and a studio apartment that opens to the patio.

Doubles: 3 (2 PB; 1 SB) $55-70
Type of Beds: 3 Twin; 2 Double
Full Breakfast
Credit Cards: No
Notes: 5, 8, 11

B&B Registry #MA-02116LAW

Box 8174, St. Paul, MN, 55108
(612) 646-4238

Historic South End neighborhood within easy walking distance of Copley Square, subway, restaurants, shops. Quiet residential side street with brick sidewalks, old-style street lamps, and restored 1860s homes.

Doubles: 2 (1 PB; 1 SB) $55-70
Type of Beds: 2 Twin; 1 Double; 1 Queen
Continental-plus Breakfast
Credit Cards: No
Notes: 5, 8 (over 5)

B&B Registry #MA-02118CLA

Box 8174, St. Paul, MN, 55108
(612) 646-4238

Adjacent to Copley Square and Back Bay, close to downtown. Beautiful tree-lined side street with brick sidewalks and restored brick townhouses. Close to Metro, symphony, city center.

Doubles: 1 (PB) $75
Type of Beds: 1 Twin; 1 Double
Continental Breakfast
Credit Cards: No
Notes: 5, 7, 8

Greater Boston Hospitality #7

Box 1142, Brookline 02146
(617) 277-5430

Historic, romantic, elegant, filled with antiques, all rooms are air-conditioned, have private telephones, and feature breakfast in your room plus high tea in the library from 4-4:30. Limited smoking.

Doubles: 4 (2 PB; 2 SB) $125-135
Type of Beds: 1 Double; 2 Queen; 1 King
Full Breakfast
Credit Cards: No

Greater Boston Hospitality #12

Box 1142, Brookline 02146
(617) 277-5430

A registered historic home built in 1799, this petite grey quarry-stone townhouse boasts pumpkin pine floors and authentic Williamsburg colors. Fireplace in guest room, air-conditioning, TV. Walking distance to Quincy Market, Faneuil Hall, and the Freedom Trail. No smoking; children welcome.

Doubles: 2 (SB) $80
Type of Beds: 2 Twin; 1 Double
Full Breakfast
Credit Cards: No

Greater Boston Hospitality #14

Box 1142, Brookline 02146
(617) 277-5430

This inn is located on a major street two miles from downtown and directly on a public transportation line. Seven decorative fireplaces, high ceilings, washer and dryer available. Parking at a nominal fee.

6 Pets welcome: 7 Smoking allowed: 8 Children welcome: 9 Social drinking allowed: 10 Tennis available: 11 Swimming available: 12 Golf available: 13 Skiing available: 14 May be booked through travel agents

Doubles: 9 (PB) $54-72
Type of Beds: 9 Double
Continental Breakfast
Credit Cards: No

Greater Boston Hospitality #19

Box 1142, Brookline 02146
(617) 277-5430

Beautiful custom home set back on 2 acres of grounds. Large rooms, high ceilings, and enormous French windows. Close to Boston College, Boston University, Pine Manor, Harvard Medical Area. Ample parking; close to public transportation. Smokers accepted.

Doubles: 2 (PB) $42-75
Type of Beds: 1 Twin; 1 Double; 1 Queen
Full Breakfast
Credit Cards: No

Greater Boston Hospitality #21

Box 1142, Brookline 02146
(617) 277-5430

A classic 1890 brownstone in the Back Bay area, minutes from the garden, fine shops, and scores of restaurants. Each room is decorated with eighteenth-century furniture; grand piano, TV, air-conditioning. Lunch and dinner available by reservation. Children welcome, smoking permitted.

Doubles: 4 (PB) $80
Type of Beds: 8 Twin
Continental Breakfast
Credit Cards: No

Greater Boston Hospitality #22

Box 1142, Brookline 02146
(617) 277-5430

An elegant turn-of-the-century brownstone in the Back Bay area with high ceilings, nice appointments, prime location. Lunch and dinner available by reservation. Adults only; parking extra.

Singles: 2 (SB) $60
Continental Breakfast
Credit Cards: No

Greater Boston Hospitality #24

Box 1142, Brookline 02146
(617) 277-5430

Surrounded by Copley Place, the Prudential Center, elegant shops, galleries, and fine restaurants, this B&B is in one of Boston's luxury high-rise apartments. Air-conditioning. Parking available in garage.

Doubles: 1 (PB) $74-81
Type of Beds: 2 Twin
Continental Breakfast
Credit Cards: No

Greater Boston Hospitality #26

Box 1142, Brookline 02146
(617) 277-5430

Modeled after a small European inn, these two renovated townhouses comprise an intimate B&B in the heart of the Back Bay area, minutes from the Prudential Center, Copley Square, and the Christian Science Center. Central air-conditioning, private phones, color TV. Smoking permitted. Adults only.

15 Doubles: $57-84
Continental Breakfast
Credit Cards: No

Greater Boston Hospitality #28

Box 1142, Brookline 02146
(617) 277-5430

NOTES: Credit cards accepted: A Master Card; B Visa; C American Express; D Discover Card; E Diners Club; F Other: 2 Personal checks accepted: 3 Lunch available: 4 Dinner available: 5 Open all year

Stunning brick Federal home with nine fireplaces offers rooms with oak floors, Laura Ashley and Pied Deux fabrics. No smoking. Walk everywhere from this location. Children welcome.

Doubles: 3 (1 PB; 2 SB) $93-108
Type of Beds: 1 Twin; 2 Double
Continental-plus Breakfast
Credit Cards: No

Greater Boston Hospitality #29

Box 1142, Brookline 02146
(617) 277-5430

Located on one of the most prestigious, gas-lit, brick streets of historic Back Bay, this mammoth 1864 red brick English townhouse offers a room with a fireplace, roof deck with view of the city. Walk to public gardens, shops, art galleries, and the Freedom Trail. Limited smoking. Children over 12 welcome.

Doubles: 1 (PB) $90
Type of Beds: 2 Twin or 1 King
Continental Breakfast
Credit Cards: No

Greater Boston Hospitality #32

Box 1142, Brookline 02146
(617) 277-5430

Built in 1928, this spacious red brick home is in the National Register of Historic Places. Piano, living room, dining room. Children welcome; one dog and two cats in residence. Short walk to Harvard Medical area and the Museum of Fine Arts. Parking included. No smoking.

Doubles: 3 (SB) $47-54
Type of Beds: 2 Twin; 2 Queen
Full Breakfast
Credit Cards: No

Greater Boston Hospitality #36

Box 1142, Brookline 02146
(617) 277-5430

Conveniently located for driving in or out of Boston and near public transportation, this brick colonial offers a den, patio, TV, piano. Children over 18 welcome, parking included; no smoking.

Doubles: 2 (SB) $55-59
Type of Beds: 2 Twin; 1 Queen
Continental Breakfast
Credit Cards: No

Greater Boston Hospitality #37

Box 1142, Brookline 02146
(617) 277-5430

A converted Georgian carriage house located on a cul-de-sac in an outstanding neighborhood close to the museum and medical area. Private sitting room, tree-enclosed patio, parking. Adults only.

Doubles: 2 (PB) $78-84
Type of Beds: 2 Twin; 1 Queen
Full Breakfast
Credit Cards: No

Greater Boston Hospitality #40

Box 1142, Brookline 02146
(617) 277-5430

This meticulously maintained, unusual double mansard home has easy access to public transportation. Parking included.

Doubles: 2 (SB) $52-85
Type of Beds: 2 Twin; 1 Double
Continental Breakfast
Credit Cards: No

Greater Boston Hospitality #44

Box 1142, Brookline 02146
(617) 277-5430

This 1894 Victorian guest house is in a quiet neighborhood of Victorian homes in the Dorchester section of Boston. Children welcome; crib available. Guests are welcome to use the living room, library. Close to the World Trade Center, Bayside Exposition Center, Kennedy Library, the University of Massachusetts. Twenty minutes by train to M.I.T. and Harvard. Ample parking. Smoking allowed in the library.

6 Doubles: $50-70
Continental Breakfast
Credit Cards: No

Greater Boston Hospitality #47

Box 1142, Brookline 02146
(617) 277-5430

Lovely center-hall colonial in a quiet residential neighborhood minutes from the Longwood Medical area and the Museum of Fine Arts. Parking included; close to public transportation. Older children welcome.

Double: 3 (1 PB; 2 SB) $47-57
Type of Beds: 3 Twin; 1 King
Continental Breakfast
Credit Cards: No

Greater Boston Hospitality #125

Box 1142, Brookline 02146
(617) 277-5430

This 100-year-old condominium building has been completely renovated and is located across the street from one of Boston's wharves. Walk to Quincy Market, Faneuil Hall, the North End, or just watch the boats in the harbor. Stunning modern room; no smoking.

Doubles: 1 (PB) $70-75
Type of Beds: 1 Double
Continental Breakfast
Credit Cards: No

Greater Boston Hospitality #181

Box 1142, Brookline 02146
(617) 277-5430

The whole second floor of this 1868 brick townhouse is available for guests. Just minutes from the Hynes Convention Center, Copley Place, and the Prudential Center. TV, refrigerator, toaster oven, coffee maker, den, telephone. No smoking; children welcome.

Singles: 1 (SB) $40
Doubles: 1 (PB) $75
Type of Beds: 1 Twin; 1 Double
Continental Breakfast
Credit Cards: No

Greater Boston Hospitality #185

Box 1142, Brookline 02146
(617) 277-5430

Beautiful 1916 stucco home with five fireplaces in an historic area offers a large room with working fireplace. Children over 8 welcome, parking included; no smoking.

Doubles: 1 (PB) $65
Type of Beds: 2 Twin
Continental-plus Breakfast
Credit Cards: No

Host Homes of Boston #1

Box 117, Waban Branch, 02168
(617) 244-1308

Beacon Hill B&B, an immense Victorian townhouse in the heart of historic Boston

NOTES: Credit cards accepted: A Master Card; B Visa; C American Express; D Discover Card; E Diners Club; F Other: 2 Personal checks accepted: 3 Lunch available: 4 Dinner available: 5 Open all year

near Hynes Convention Center and Massachusetts General Hospital.

Doubles: 2 (PB) $80
Type of Beds: 1 Double; 1 Queen
Continental Breakfast
Minimum stay: 2
Credit Cards: A, B, C
Notes: 2, 5, 8 (over 10), 9

Host Homes of Boston #2
Box 117, Waban Branch, 02168
(617) 244-1308

Downtown duplex near Faneuil Hall, the waterfront, and downtown. Fifth- and sixth-floor walk-up with brick and beam decor, balcony, antiques, skylight, air-conditioning. No parking.

Doubles: 1 (PB) $68
Type of Beds: 1 Double
Continental Breakfast
Minimum stay: 2
Credit Cards: A, B, C
Notes: 2, 5, 9

Host Homes of Boston #3
Box 117, Waban Branch, 02168
(617) 244-1308

The Boston Common, Public Garden, fine shops, hotels, and subway are steps away from this nineteenth-century private professional club. Parlor, antiques, elaborate architecture, elevator, air-conditioning, fireplace, telephone.

Singles: 4 (SB) $60
Doubles: 3 (PB) $90
Continental Breakfast
Minimum stay: 2
Credit Cards: A, B, C
Notes: 2, 5, 7, 8 (6 and over), 9

BOXFORD

Day's End B&B
B&B Marblehead & North Shore
Box 172, Beverly, MA, 01915
(508) 921-1336

A beautiful architect-designed contemporary home in a country setting, with swimming pool and large grounds. The guest rooms can be rented individually or as a suite.

Doubles: 3 (1 PB; 2 SB) $45-60
Type of Beds: 2 Twin; 2 Double; 1 Queen
Continental Breakfast
Credit Cards: No
Notes: 2, 5, 6, 7, 8, 9, 10, 11, 12, 14

BOYLSTON

French's Bed & Breakfast
5 Scar Hill Road, 01505
(508) 869-2666

We're in the historic district of an unspoiled New England village. Our home, built for Norm's grandparents, is an oasis of New England hospitality, where guests are invited to browse through tin-types, old photo albums, and other collections. Rooms are furnished with a blend of family antiques and newer traditional pieces. Breakfast is served overlooking the gardens. We're on the shores of the Wachusett Reservoir; great for hiking or cross-country skiing. Just eight miles north of downtown Worcester. 3.5 miles from I-290.

Hosts: Norm & Margot French
Doubles: 2 (SB) $50
Type of Beds: 2 Twin; 1 Double
Continental or Full Breakfast
Minimum stay during foliage season: 2
Infants and children over 10 welcome
Credit Cards: A, B
Closed March 15-31 & Dec. 15-31
Notes: 2 (for deposit), 8, 9, 10, 11, 12, 13, 14

BREWSTER

Barbara's B&B
B&B Cape Cod, Box 341, W. Hyannisport, 02672
(508) 775-2772

In 1739 this house was built following Cape Cod style designs of that day. Sited in a remote area with birds and plants offering a natural wonderland. Your host is a Cordon Bleu trained chef.

Doubles: 1 (PB) $75
Type of Beds: 2 Twin
Continental Breakfast
Credit Cards: No
Notes: 5, 8 (over 12), 9, 10, 11, 12, 14

The Deck House

Orleans B&B Assoc., Box 1312, Orleans, 02653
(508) 255-3824

Enjoy your own deck by watching gorgeous sunsets gild the waters of 250-acre Upper Mill Pond. This custom-designed house has two large guest rooms on the second floor. Sliders provide private entrances. Swimming, canoeing, sailing, and wind surfing are all are your doorstep. Two and a half miles to salt water. Two doubles, $65.

Isaiah Clark House & Rose Cottage

1187 Main Street, 02631
(508) 896-2223

Built in 1780, this inn was once the mansion of a famous sea captain and is set on 5 acres of land. The main-house guests are served breakfast on a deck overlooking a private pond. Rose Cottage guests have private gardens and a huge hearth in the center of the keeping room. Host was formerly a Swiss-trained hotelier. Special welcome for honeymooners.

Host: Charles Phillipe DeCesare
Doubles: 12 (8 PB; 4 SB) $58-92
Continental-plus Breakfast
Credit Cards: A, B, C
Notes: 5, 7 (limited), 8, 9, 10, 11, 12, 14

Lois's B&B

B&B Cape Cod, Box 341, W. Hyannisport, 02672
(508) 775-2772

This is a large Civil War era Greek Revival style home offering wide shaded porches, broad rolling lawns, and a wooded setting where 25 varieties of birds have been counted. Shops, restaurants, beaches, and summer theater are close.

Singles: 1 (SB) $35
Doubles: 2 (1 PB; 1 SB) $45-54
Type of Beds: 1 Twin; 2 Double
Continental Breakfast
Credit Cards: No
Notes: 2, 7, 8 (over 3), 9, 10, 11, 12, 14

Quail Hollow

Orleans B&B Assoc., Box 1312, Orleans, 02653
(508) 255-3824

A secluded eighteenth-century Cape nestled in the woods between two ponds. Inviting front parlor and common room with wood-burning fireplace and TV. Guest rooms have water view. Resident black Labrador. Canoe to freshwater beach; bike trail and ocean and Bay beaches nearby. One single: $25. One double: $50.

Old Sea Pines Inn

2553 Main Street, 02631
(508) 896-6114

Lovely old turn-of-the-century mansion, once the "Sea Pines School of Charm and Personality for Young Women," now a newly renovated and redecorated country inn. Furnished with antiques, some of the rooms have working fireplaces. Situated on 3.5 acres of land, with a wraparound porch looking out over the lawn, trees, and flowers. Complimentary beverage on arrival.

Hosts: Stephen & Michele Rowan
Doubles: 14 (9 PB; 5 SB) $40-85
Type of Beds: 8 Twin; 8 Double
Full Breakfast
Minimum stay in-season weekends & holidays: 2-3
Credit Cards: A, B, C, E, F
Notes: 2, 5, 7, 8 (over 8), 9, 11, 12, 13(XC), 14 (off-season only)

NOTES: Credit cards accepted: A Master Card; B Visa; C American Express; D Discover Card; E Diners Club; F Other: 2 Personal checks accepted: 3 Lunch available: 4 Dinner available: 5 Open all year

Stoneybrook

Orleans B&B Assoc., Box 1312, Orleans 02653
(508) 255-3824

A pre-1776 restored colonial home with a storybook setting next to the old grist mill and famous Stony Brook Herring Run. Private entrance to upstairs: large bedroom with fireplace, private bath, and sitting room. TV and air-conditioning; outdoor sitting area overlooking the mill pond. Small, modern kitchenette. One double, $60.

The Skep Garden

Orleans B&B Assoc., Box 1312, Orleans, 02653
(508) 255-3824

Ideally located for exploring the unique charms of historic Rt. 6A, with its many fascinating antique, craft, and gift shops, as well as fine restaurants. Off the beaten path in quiet surroundings at the end of a dead-end street. The Cape Cod Rail Trail bike path, tennis, and golf are minutes away; short walk to a private bay beach. Two doubles, $50.

BRIMFIELD

Berkshire ST4

Berkshire B&B Homes
Box 211, Williamsburg, MA, 01096
(413) 268-7244

A beautifully restored 1798 Connecticut Valley colonial with antique furnishings. Five minutes to Sturbridge/Brimfield Flea Market; antique shop on the premises.

Singles: 1 (SB) $70
Doubles: 4 (1 PB; 3 SB) $65-95
Type of Beds: 1 Twin; 1 Double; 3 Queen
Continental Breakfast
Credit Cards: No
Notes: 2, 5, 6, 8, 10, 11, 12

BROOKLINE

Bed & Breakfast Associates #M611

Box 166, Babson Park, Boston, 02157
(617) 449-5302

Located in a quiet residential neighborhood, this traditionally decorated townhouse offers two sunny guest rooms and driveway parking. A short walk to public transportation will give guests access to the nearby hospital area of Boston. Two cats in residence.

Doubles: 2 (SB) $68
Type of Beds: 2 Twin; 1 Double
Continental Breakfast
Minimum stay: 3
Credit Cards: A, B, C
Notes: 5, 8, 10, 11, 12

B&B Registry #MA-02146BEA

Box 8174, St. Paul, MN, 51108
(612) 646-4238

A perfect location for visiting Boston. Only ten minutes from downtown by subway, this brick Victorian townhouse is in a charming neighborhood within walking distance of restaurants.

Doubles: 15 (8 PB; 7 SB) $35-55
Continental Breakfast
Credit Cards: A, B, D, E
Notes: 5, 7, 8

Host Homes of Boston #4

Box 117, Waban Branch, Boston, 02168
(617) 244-1308

A traditional center-entrance brick colonial (1930) in a fashionable, quiet area. Parking available; subway half a mile. Near Boston

College, Pine Manor, Longwood medical area, Back Bay.

Doubles: 2 (SB) $60
Type of Beds: 1 Double; 1 Queen
Continental Breakfast
Minimum stay: 2
Credit Cards: A, B, C
Notes: 2, 5, 8 (8 and over), 9, 10

Host Homes of Boston #5

Box 117, Waban Branch, Boston, 02168
(617) 244-1308

Boston is ten minutes door-to-door via subway from the artist's bright, tidy home on Beacon Street. Near Boston College, B.U., Longwood medical area, and restaurants. Parking nearby.

Singles: 1 (PB) $56
Type of Beds: 1 Twin
Continental Breakfast
Minimum stay: 2
Credit Cards: A, B, C
Notes: 2, 5

Host Homes of Boston #6

Box 117, Waban Branch, Boston, 02168
(617) 244-1308

Country atmosphere in a colonial house set on an acre of rolling lawn. English hostess, resident outdoor cat. Parking available; subway one-half mile away; Boston five miles. Near Pine Manor, B.C., Longwood medical area.

Doubles: 2 (SB) $67
Type of Beds: 2 Twin; 1 Queen
Continental Breakfast
Minimum stay: 2
Credit Cards: A, B, C
Notes: 2, 5, 8, 9, 10

Host Homes of Boston #7

Box 117, Waban Branch, Boston, 02168
(617) 244-1308

This 1928 Williamsburg attached house is listed in the National Register of Historic Places. TV in each room. Resident cat and

dog; parking. Subway three blocks, Boston one mile. Near Fenway Park and the Back Bay; walk to Longwood medical area.

Doubles: 3 (SB) $57
Type of Beds: 2 Twin; 2 Queen
Continental Breakfast
Minimum stay: 2
Credit Cards: A, B, C
Notes: 2, 5, 8 (over 10), 9, 10

Host Homes of Boston #8

Box 117, Waban Branch, Boston, 02168jD
(617) 244-1308

This older colonial sits on 2 shady acres and features antiques, a huge deck, childrens' equipment, TV, and parking. Subway one-half mile; parking available. Near B.C., Pine Manor, Longwood medical area.

Doubles: 2 (1 PB; 1 SB) $54-67
Type of Beds: 2 Twin; 1 Double; 1 Queen
Continental Breakfast
Minimum stay: 2
Credit Cards: A, B, C
Notes: 2, 5, 7, 8, 9, 10, 12

Host Homes of Boston #9

Box 117, Waban Branch, Boston, 02168
(617) 244-1308

Bright, spacious third-floor suite has skylights, stereo, huge living area, refrigerator, and microwave. Subway two blocks, Boston one mile. Parking available. Near Fenway Park, the Back Bay.

Doubles: 1 (PB) $68
Type of Beds: 1 Queen
Continental Breakfast
Minimum stay: 2
Credit Cards: A, B, C
Notes: 2, 5, 8, 9

Host Homes of Boston #10

Box 117, Waban Branch, Boston, 02168
(617) 244-1308

Elegant 1916 French Riviera style home with a walled garden and a city skyline view.

NOTES: Credit cards accepted: A Master Card; B Visa; C American Express; D Discover Card; E Diners Club; F Other: 2 Personal checks accepted: 3 Lunch available: 4 Dinner available: 5 Open all year

Subway one mile; parking available. Near the Museum of Fine Arts, Longwood medical area, the Back Bay.

Doubles: 1 (PB) $67
Type of Beds: 2 Twin
Continental-plus Breakfast
Minimum stay: 2
Credit Cards: A, B, C
Notes: 2, 5, 8 (over 10), 10

Host Homes of Boston #11

Box 117, Waban Branch, Boston, 02168
(617) 244-1308

This modern townhouse has a sweeping view from its glass-walled living room and deck. Two cats in residence. Parking available; subway three blocks. Near Back Bay the medical area, B.C., B.U., Fenway Park.

Doubles: 2 (SB) $57
Type of Beds: 2 Twin; 1 Double
Continental Breakfast
Minimum stay: 2
Credit Cards: A, B, C
Notes: 2, 5, 8 (8 and over), 9

The Pleasant Pheasant

296 Heath Street, 02167
(617) 566-4178

The Pleasant Pheasant is located on 2 secluded acres. It boasts comfortable accommodations, complete amenities with full breakfast, and a hostess happy to make your stay a pleasant one. Located five miles west of Boston, near Boston College, Pine Manor College, Longwood Hospital, Harvard Medical School, and Boston University.

Host: Marian Ferguson
Doubles: 2 (1 PB; 1 SB) $40-60
Type of Beds: 2 Twin; 1 Double; 1 Queen
Full Breakfast
Credit Cards: No
Closed Christmas week
Notes: 2, 5, 7, 8, 9, 10, 11, 12

BUCKLAND

1797 House

Upper Street-Clarlemont Road, 01338
(413) 625-2975

Our eighteenth-century home is located in a peaceful rural area, yet is convenient to many attractions and all points in New England. Large rooms, private baths, down quilts, and a lovely screened porch insure your comfort. We offer a modicum of civilization in an increasingly uncivilized world.

Host: Janet Turley
Doubles: 3 (PB) $47-60
Type of Beds: 1 Twin; 3 Double
Full Breakfast
Credit Cards: No
Closed Nov. & Dec.
Notes: 2, 9, 10, 11, 12, 13

BURLINGTON

Carmen's B&B

B&B Marblehead & North Shore
Box 172, Beverly, MA, 01915
(508) 921-1336

A very pretty, spacious ranch home on a large wooded lot in a quiet, attractive suburb. Close to the Route 128 high-tech region and the Lahey Clinic. The Monroe Tavern, Battle Green, Lexington are all five miles away. The Old North Bridge in Concord is nine miles away.

Doubles: 4 (SB) $45-65
Type of Beds: 4 Twin; 2 Queen; 2 Double sofabeds
Continental Breakfast
Credit Cards: No
Notes: 2, 5, 7 (limited), 8, 9, 10, 11, 12, 13, 14

CAMBRIDGE

Bed & Breakfast Associates #M817

Box 166, Babson Park, Boston, 02157
(617) 449-5302

6 Pets welcome: 7 Smoking allowed: 8 Children welcome: 9 Social drinking allowed: 10 Tennis available: 11 Swimming available: 12 Golf available: 13 Skiing available: 14 May be booked through travel agents

Located on the north perimeter of Harvard University, this roomy Victorian offers guests two pleasant rooms. The widely traveled hosts can converse with the guests in six different languages. One dog and two cats in residence.

Doubles: 2 (SB) $50-60
Type of Beds: 4 Twin
Continental Breakfast
Minimum stay: 3
Credit Cards: A, B, C
Notes: 5, 7, 8, 10, 11, 12

Greater Boston Hospitality #30

Box 1142, Brookline 02146
(617) 277-5430

Located literally in the heart of Harvard University, this red brick 1920 house is in the finest section of Cambridge. Harvard envelops you, and history surrounds you. Women guests only.

Singles: $40
Continental Breakfast
Credit Cards: No

Greater Boston Hospitality #38

Box 1142, Brookline 02146
(617) 277-5430

This lovely 1890 Victorian is in a fine residential area only a fifteen-minute walk from Harvard Square. Large den with working fireplace; resident Siamese cat. Children over 14 welcome; no smoking. Air-conditioned.

Doubles: 2 (SB) $63-68
Type of Beds: 1 Twin; 1 Double
Continental-plus Breakfast
Credit Cards: No

Greater Boston Hospitality #42

Box 1142, Brookline 02146
(617) 277-5430

Treat yourself to a stay in this gorgeous classic Colonial Revival built in 1892. Sitting area for guests' use, fully air-conditioned, parking available. Close to Harvard and Porter squares.

9 Doubles: $90-137
Full Breakfast
Credit Cards: No

Host Homes of Boston #12

Box 117, Waban Branch, Boston, 02168
(617) 244-1308

This large home, built in 1855, is on a quiet road only three blocks from bustling Harvard Square. Guest sitting room, desk, sofa, air-conditioning, off-street parking. Subway three blocks.

Doubles: 1 (PB) $80
Type of Beds: 1 Queen
Continental Breakfast
Minimum stay: 2
Credit Cards: A, B, C
Notes: 2, 5

Host Homes of Boston #13

Box 117, Waban Branch, Boston, 02168
(617) 244-1308

Just a short walk from Harvard Square, Harvard Yard, Brattle Street, and the subway, in a quiet, shady location. TV, air-conditioning, street parking. Host smokes.

Doubles: 1 (SB) $60
Type of Beds: 1 Double
Continental Breakfast
Minimum stay: 2
Credit Cards: A, B, C
Notes: 2, 5, 7

NOTES: Credit cards accepted: A Master Card; B Visa; C American Express; D Discover Card; E Diners Club; F Other: 2 Personal checks accepted: 3 Lunch available: 4 Dinner available: 5 Open all year

Host Homes of Boston #14

Box 117, Waban Branch, Boston, 02168
(617) 244-1308

This Victorian jewel sits on a quiet hill between Harvard and Porter squares. Street parking permit; subway and train three blocks away; bus one block.

Doubles: 2 (SB) $56
Type of Beds: 1 Double; 1 Queen; 1 Cot
Continental Breakfast
Minimum stay: 2
Credit Cards: A, B, C
Notes: 2, 5, 8

CENTERVILLE

Copper Beech Inn

497 Main Street, 02632
(508) 771-5488

Built in 1830, this historic sea captain's house is one-half mile from Craigville Beach, three miles from Hyannis, and close to fine restaurants, shopping, and the Cape Cod Melody Tent. Enjoy the ambience of the historic district and mid-cape convenience.

Host: Joyce Diehl
Doubles: 3 (PB) $65-75
Type of Beds: 2 Double; 1 King
Full Breakfast
Minimum stay from May 25-Oct. 10: 2
Credit Cards: A, B, C
Notes: 2, 5, 7, 8 (12 and over), 9, 10, 11, 12

Gallo's B&B

B&B Cape Cod, Box 341, W. Hyannisport, 02672
(508) 775-2772

An elegant 1830s mansion, formerly the home of Cardinal Spellman, with grounds designed by Frederick Law Olmstead. This Victorian has been totally restored and is in a marvelous location close to Craigville Beach. Hyannis and the island ferry is a five-minute drive.

Doubles: 7 (PB) $95-175
Type of Beds: 2 Twin; 4 Queen; 1 King
Full Breakfast
Credit Cards: No
Notes: 2, 5, 9, 10, 11, 12, 14

Sandman Inn

B&B Cape Cod, Box 341, W. Hyannisport, 02672
(508) 775-2772

High on a hill overlooking the largest fresh-water lake on the Cape. Walk a block to the fresh-water beach for a morning swim. Hyannis, the island ferry, shops, and restaurants are all near.

Doubles: 1 (SB) $55
Type of Beds: 1 King
Continental Breakfast
Credit Cards: No
Notes: 2, 5, 8, 9, 10, 11, 12, 14

CHARLEMONT

Forest Way Farm

Jacksonville Stage Road, 01337
(413) 337-8321

This carefully restored circa 1812 mountain-top country inn reflects the ambience of rural New England. Family heirlooms, nicely decorated rooms, and farm breakfasts with homemade fixin's and grits make your stay an unforgettable experience.

Hosts: Jimmie & Paul Snyder
Doubles: 6 (S2.5B) $45-65
Type of Beds: 2 Twin; 3 Double; 1 King
Full Breakfast
Minimum stay holidays: 2
Credit Cards: C
Notes: 2, 5, 7, 8, 9, 11, 12, 13, 14

The Inn at Charlemont

Rt. 2, 01339
(413) 339-5796

Built in 1787, the Inn at Charlemont has served Mohawk Trail travelers for over 200 years. Located at the foot of the Berkshires, the inn is surrounded by cultural and sport-

6 Pets welcome: 7 Smoking allowed: 8 Children welcome: 9 Social drinking allowed: 10 Tennis available: 11 Swimming available: 12 Golf available: 13 Skiing available: 14 May be booked through travel agents

ing activities and the most colorful fall foliage in New England.

Hosts: Linda, Marcia, & Mary
Singles: 2 (SB) $38
Doubles: 12 (SB) $58
Type of Beds: 7 Twin; 6 Double; 1 Queen
Continental Breakfast
Minimum stay holidays: 2
Credit Cards: All Major
Notes: 4, 5, 6 (by arrangement), 7, 8, 9, 11, 12, 13

CHARLTON

The Prindle House

71 Prindle Hill Road, RFD 1 Southbridge, 01550
(508) 248-3134

Enjoy the charm of our country farmhouse with six fireplaces, beautiful views, and a country setting. Located just six miles east of Old Sturbridge Village, forty miles east of Hartford, twelve miles west of Worcester. Nearby you'll find golf, fishing, swimming, cross-country skiing, and antique-lovers' Brimfield Flea Market.

Hosts: Richard & Roberta DeLeo
Singles: 1 (SB) $45
Doubles: 2 (SB) $45-50
Type of Beds: 1 Twin; 1 Double; 1 Queen
Continental Breakfast
Credit Cards: No
Notes: 2, 5, 7 (restricted), 8, 9, 10, 11, 12, 13 (XC)

CHATHAM

B&B Registry #MA-02633VIE

Box 8174, St. Paul, MN, 51108
(612) 646-4238

Large, gracious brick colonial with breathtaking views of the Atlantic. The home is filled with furniture from the hosts' travels. Breakfast on the porch, in the dining room, or in front of the fireplace. Walk to beach, golf course.

Singles: 1 (SB) $60
Doubles: 2 (SB) $75
Type of Beds: 1 Twin; 4 Double
Full Breakfast

Credit Cards: No
Closed Nov. 16 - May 14
Notes: 7, 8 (over 16), 11, 12

The Bronze Bell

Orleans B&B Assoc., Box 1312, Orleans, 02653
(508) 255-3824

Gracious hospitality awaits you in this inviting reproduction of a full classic Cape. On a quiet village street one-half mile from town and 3/4 mile from the beach. Generous continental breakfast includes home-baked breads and muffins served in country room or on the patio. One double, $60.

Chatham Bow B&B

B&B Cape Cod, Box 341, W. Hyannisport, 02672
(508) 775-2772

Ten-year-old house with Early American Cape Cod design. Wide board floors, a huge fireplace in the common room, braided rugs. Walk to the village, the fish pier, and the beach, all less than one mile away.

Doubles: 2 (SB) $50
Type of Beds: 2 Double
Continental Breakfast
Credit Cards: No
Notes: 2, 5, 8, 9, 10, 11, 12, 14

Crow's Nest

Orleans B&B Assoc., Box 1312, Orleans 02653
(508) 225-3824

Your private hideaway high above the treetops in a quiet cul-de-sac. Private bath, kitchen, TV, deck. Only one-half mile from lovely Nantucket Sound beach. For maximum privacy, you may request the refrigerator be stocked and make your own breakfast, or the hostess will serve breakfast on your private deck. One double, $65.

NOTES: Credit cards accepted: A Master Card; B Visa; C American Express; D Discover Card; E Diners Club; F Other: 2 Personal checks accepted: 3 Lunch available: 4 Dinner available: 5 Open all year

Harbor View

Orleans B&B Assoc., Box 1312, Orleans, 02653
(508) 255-3824

Quiet residential area overlooking Pleasant Bay. Breakfast is served on a glass-enclosed porch with a view of the Atlantic and a golf course. Sandy beach and busy fish pier at the end of the street. Short walk to all activities. Two doubles, $75.

Joy's B&B

B&B Cape Cod, Box 341, W. Hyannisport, 02672
(508) 775-2772

This two-story Garrison colonial stands three miles from the village center along a warm-water sound and is only .2 mile from the beach. The rear deck overlooks a salt-water marsh.

Doubles: 3 (1 PB; 2 SB) $55-65
Type of Beds: 4 Twin
Continental Breakfast
Credit Cards: No
Notes: 2, 5, 8 (over 8), 9, 10, 11, 12, 14

Marian's B&B

B&B Cape Cod, Box 341, W. Hyannisport, 02672
(508) 775-2772

This twenty-year-old, beautifully decorated Cape Cod home features wide board floors, two fireplaces, and a den for guest use. Walk down the lane to the ocean inlet and see the lighthouse in the distance. Fine restaurants, shops, and Atlantic Ocean beaches are one mile away.

Doubles: 3 (1 PB; 2 SB) $60-68
Type of Beds: 5 Twin; 1 Double
Continental Breakfast
Credit Cards: No
Notes: 2, 5, 8 (over 12), 9, 10, 11, 12, 14

Mass Appeal

Orleans B&B Assoc., Box 1312, Orleans, 02653
(508) 255-3824

Set on a lovely, quiet cul-de-sac, less than a quarter mile from School House Pond and one mile to Pleasant Bay, this graciously decorated newer home has a spacious den with cable TV. Ideal for two or more couples traveling together. Breakfast served in the lovely dining room or on the deck. Siamese cat in residence. Three doubles, shared bath, $55.

Nickerson's B&B

B&B Cape Cod, Box 341, W. Hyannisport, 02672
(508) 775-2772

This large Victorian, built in 1839 by Moses Nickerson, is one of Chatham's historic treasures. Wide board floors, paneled walls, fireplaces, and wide porches. Centrally located to the beach, fishing pier, village, and many fine restaurants and shops.

Doubles: 6 (PB) $85
Type of Beds: 2 Twin; 5 Double
Continental Breakfast
Credit Cards: No
Notes: 2, 5, 7, 8 (over 12), 9, 10, 11, 12, 14

Port View

Orleans B&B Assoc., Box 1312, Orleans, 02653
(508) 255-3824

Charming, comfortable Cape Cod cottage overlooking Nantucket Sound. Just a short walk to Cockle Cove beach. Stroll through Chatham center, with its interesting shops, art galleries, and fine restaurants. One double, private bath, $50.

Salt Marsh House

Orleans B&B Assoc., Box 1312, Orleans, 02653
(508) 255-3824

Fresh breezes ruffle the white curtains in this pristine house only a two-minute walk from Nantucket Sound. Buffet-style breakfast when you wake up. Relax and enjoy yourself;

6 Pets welcome: 7 Smoking allowed: 8 Children welcome: 9 Social drinking allowed: 10 Tennis available: 11 Swimming available: 12 Golf available: 13 Skiing available: 14 May be booked through travel agents

great place for families. Three doubles. One private bath; two shared. $55-65.

The Ships Inn at Chatham
364 Old Harbor Road, 02633
(508) 495-5859

A quiet, romantic country inn, originally built in 1839 for whaling captain Moses Nickerson. Wide planked floors, original Sandwich Window glass, antique furnishings, and Oriental rugs. Light, airy guest rooms, some with fireplaces, porch, or bay window seat. Walk to the quaint village of Chatham, with its fine shops, art galleries, and restaurants.

Hosts: Elsie & Carl Piccola
Doubles: 7 (PB) $85-100
Continental Breakfast
Credit Cards: A, B, C
Notes: 2, 5, 9, 10, 11, 12, 14

The Sleepy Whale
Orleans B&B Assoc., Box 1312, Orleans, 02653
(508) 255-3824

A separate entrance brings you into a huge, high-ceilinged family room with many windows giving country views. Private deck for sunning and relaxing, private bath, wet bar with refrigerator, color TV. Less than half-mile from a sandy beach on Nantucket Sound. One double, private bath, $65.

Sunny Hours
Orleans B&B Assoc., Box 1312, Orleans, 02653
(508) 255-3824

A charming Cape Cod cottage overlooking a salt marsh. Walk or bike to lovely Harding's Beach on Nantucket Sound. Full breakfast on the sunny deck, screened porch, or dining room. Two doubles, shared bath, $50.

CHELMSFORD

B&B Folks 2
48 Springs Road, Bedford, MA 01730
(617) 275-9025

Charming home on a lake with boating, fishing, and swimming at your door, yet still close enough to tour Boston. Relax in indoor spa. Reduced rate for long-term stays.

Singles: 2 (SB) $55
Doubles: 2 (SB) $65
Type of Beds: 2 Twin; 1 Double; 1 Queen
Full Breakfast
Credit Cards: No
Notes: 2, 4, 7, 8, 9, 10, 11, 12

COLRAIN

Maple Shade Farm B&B
Rt. 1, Box 469, 01340
(413) 624-3931

Enjoy our peaceful eighteenth-century farmhouse in the shade of giant maple trees that are over 100 years old. We are set on 80 acres of fields and woodland just 6.5 miles from I-91 in picturesque Colrain. Nearby are Old Deerfield, Glacial Pot Holes, Bridge of Flowers, Covered Bridge, and Northfield Mountain Recreation.

Hosts: Freda Sessler & Audrey Stockwell
Doubles: 3 (SB) $30-40
Continental Breakfast
Credit Cards: No
Notes: 2, 6, 9, 11, 12

CONCORD

Anderson-Wheeler Homestead
154 Fitchburg Tpk., 01742
(508) 369-3756

An 1890 Victorian with wraparound veranda, tastefully decorated with antiques accentuated with window seats and fireplaces. A popular area for canoeing, bird watching, and cross-country skiing. Rural, but convenient to two restaurants and a grocery store. Only three miles from historic Concord center, Walden Pond, and the Audubon Center.

Hosts: David & Charlotte Anderson
Doubles: 5 (2 PB; 3 SB) $65-75
Type of Beds: 2 Twin; 3 Double; 1 King
Continental-plus Breakfast
Credit Cards: A, B, C, E
Notes: 2, 5, 7 (limited), 8, 9, 10, 11, 12, 13 (XC), 14

Colonial Inn

48 Monument Square, 01742
(508) 369-9200

Located in the heart of Concord Center and host to guests since 1716, this 57-room inn offers charming accommodations with telephones, television, and air-conditioning. Walk to many historical attractions and experience traditional New England fare in our dining room.

Host: Jurgen Demisch
Doubles: 57 (55 PB; 2 SB) $104.22-142.61
Full Breakfast
Credit Cards: A, B, C, E
Notes: 4, 5, 7, 8, 9, 14

Hawthorne Inn

462 Lexington Road, 01742
(508) 369-5610

Built circa 1870 on land once owned by Ralph Waldo Emerson, Nathaniel Hawthorne, and the Alcotts. Located alongside the "Battle Road" of 1775 and within walking distance of authors' homes, battle sites, and Walden Pond. Furnished with antiques, handmade quilts, original artwork, Japanese prints, and sculpture.

Hosts: G. Burch & M. Mudry
Doubles: 7 (PB) $75-150
Type of Beds: 2 Twin; 6 Double
Continental Breakfast
Credit Cards: No
Notes: 2, 5, 6, 7 (limited), 8, 9, 10, 11, 12, 13 (XC), 14

Host Homes of Boston #15

Box 117, Waban Branch, Boston, 02168
(617) 244-1308

Contemporary on a wooded hill overlooking a pond. A serene, Thoreau-like setting in historic Concord. Rooms have large window-walls and balcony facing the pond. Three miles to the village and its museums. Visit Old North Bridge, Walden Pond.

Singles: 1 (SB) $49
Doubles: 1 (SB) $56
Type of Beds: 2 Twin; 1 Queen
Continental Breakfast
Minimum stay: 2
Credit Cards: A, B, C
Notes: 2, 5, 8, 9

COTUIT

Klund's B&B

B&B Cape Cod, Box 341, W. Hyannisport, 02672
(508) 775-2772

Built about twenty years ago, this comfortable home features a family room with TV and an enclosed porch for guest use. The patio and yard are great for relaxing after a day at the nearby beach. Situated on a quiet, tree-lined beach in the heart of the village.

Doubles: 1 (PB) $60
Type of Beds: 2 Twin
Continental Breakfast
Credit Cards: No
Notes: 5, 8, 9, 10, 11, 12, 14

Salty Dog Inn

451 Main Street, 02635
(508) 428-5228

A circa 1850 house once owned by a cranberry farmer in quaint Cotuit on Cape Cod. Warm-water beaches are nearby and may be reached on one of our complimentary bikes. Enjoy the fine restaurants and theater at

Hyannis or Falmouth. Island boats are a short drive away.

Hosts: Lynn & Jerry Goldstein
Doubles: 4 (1 PB; 3 SB) $30-65
Type of Beds: 2 Double; 1 Queen; 1 King
Continental Breakfast
Minimum stay Memorial Day-Labor Day: 2
Credit Cards: A, B (5% service charge)
Notes: 2, 5, 8 (over 12), 10, 11, 12

CUMMINGTON

Cumworth Farm

RR 1, Box 110, Rt. 112, 01026
(413) 634-5529

A 200-year-old house with a sugar house and blueberry and raspberry fields on the premises. Pick your own berries in season. The farm raises sheep and is close to Tanglewood, Smith College, the William Cullen Bryant Homestead, cross-country skiing, and hiking trails.

Hosts: Ed & Mary McColgan
Singles: 2 (SB) $35
Doubles: 6 (SB) $50
Type of Beds: 4 Twin; 4 Double
Full Breakfast
Credit Cards: No
Notes: 2, 5, 8, 10, 11, 12, 13, 14

Windfields Farm

Windsor Bush Road, RR 1, Box 170, 01026
(413) 684-3786

Secluded, spacious Federal homestead on a dirt road amid fields and forests. Guests have their own entrance, book-lined living room, fireplace, piano, dining room. Family antiques, paintings, flowers. Windfields organic produce, eggs, maple syrup, raspberries, wild blueberries enrich the hearty breakfasts. Near Tanglewood, six colleges.

Hosts: Carolyn & Arnold Westwood
Doubles: 2 (SB) $40-50
Type of Beds: 1 Double; 1 Queen
Full Breakfast
Minimum stay weekends & holidays: 2
Credit Cards: No
Closed March & April
Notes: 2, 8 (over 12), 9, 11, 13

DALTON

The Dalton House

955 Main Street, 01226
(413) 684-3854

The main house has five rooms plus a large sitting room with fireplace where breakfast is served. The carriage house has been restored and now has four rooms and two large suites. All rooms have private baths, air-conditioning, and thermostats. In the warm months, breakfast may be enjoyed outside on the deck. There is also a picnic area and swimming pool.

Hosts: Gary & Bernice Turetsky
Singles: 5 (PB) $48-68
Doubles: 6 (PB) $48-90
Type of Beds: 9 Twin; 9 Double
Continental Breakfast
Credit Cards: A, B, C
Notes: 2, 5, 8 (over 7), 9, 10, 11, 12, 13, 14

DANVERS

The Antique Sleigh

B&B Marblehead & North Shore
Box 172, Beverly, MA, 01915
(508) 921-1336

A beautiful 1854 Federal landmark colonial with beamed ceilings, old-fashioned kitchen fireplace, and antique kitchen utensils. Situated in a historic district one-half mile from Route 1, very close to I-95. The hostess serves breakfast on pewter and picks fresh blueberries from her own garden for homemade muffins.

Doubles: 3 (SB) $75
Type of Beds: 1 Twin; 3 Queen; 2 Rollaways
Full Breakfast
Credit Cards: No
Notes: 2, 5, 6 (call), 7, 8, 9, 10, 11, 12, 14

DENNIS

The Four Chimneys Inn

946 Main Street, 02638
(508) 385-6317

A comfortable, spacious 1881 Victorian home with lovely gardens, located on historic Rt. 6A across from Scargo Lake. Short walk to Cape Cod Bay, the playhouse, Fine Arts Museum, restaurants, shops. Golf, tennis, bike trails within two miles. Centrally located, convenient to all of Cape Cod.

Hosts: Christina Jervant & Diane Robinson
Doubles: 9 (7 PB; 2 SB) $39-90
Type of Beds: 4 Twin; 6 Double; 3 Queen
Continental Breakfast
Credit Cards: A, B, C
Closed Jan. & Feb.
Notes: 2, 7, 8 (over 8), 9, 10, 11, 12

Isaiah Hall B&B Inn

Isaiah Hall B&B Inn

152 Whig Street, 02638
(508) 385-9928

Enjoy country ambience and hospitality in the heart of Cape Cod. Lovely 1857 farmhouse quietly located within walking distance of the beach and village shops, restaurants, museums, cinema, and playhouse. Nearby bike trails, tennis, and golf.

Hosts: Marie & Dick Brophy
Doubles: 11 (10 PB; 1 SB) $46-88
Type of Beds: 4 Twin; 5 Double; 6 Queen
Continental-plus Breakfast
Minimum stay in season & holidays: 2
Credit Cards: A, B, C
Closed mid Nov.-mid March
Notes: 2, 7, 8 (over 8), 9, 10, 11, 12, 14

DENNISPORT

B&B Registry #MA-02639DEN

Box 8174, St. Paul, MN, 55108
(612) 646-4238

Comfortable, small inn within a short walk of beaches and just minutes from downtown Hyannis. A blend of the old and new, rustic and restful.

Doubles: 5 (SB) $45-50
Type of Beds: 2 Twin; 5 Double
Continental Breakfast
Credit Cards: A, B, C
Notes: 5, 8, 11, 12

B&B Registry #MA-02639WES

Box 8174, St. Paul, MN, 55108
(612) 646-4238

White Cape with four guest rooms and three cottages. B&B guests are served breakfast in the dining room with china and silver. The large grounds have a picnic area with grills.

Singles: 1 (SB) $30-35
Doubles: 4 (2 PB; 2 SB) $45-60
Type of Beds: 4 Twin; 2 Double; 1 Cot
Continental Breakfast
Credit Cards: No
Closed Nov. - April
Notes: 7, 8, 11

The Rose Petal B&B

152 Sea Street, Box 974, 02639
(508) 398-8470

Lovely accommodations and complete homemade breakfast in an attractively restored 1872 historic home in the heart of Cape Cod. Walk to beach, shops, dining, or relax in our guest parlor or beautifully landscaped yard. We are a short drive to the ferries to Nantucket and Martha's Vineyard. Enjoy the diverse recreation, beautiful

6 Pets welcome: 7 Smoking allowed: 8 Children welcome: 9 Social drinking allowed: 10 Tennis available: 11 Swimming available: 12 Golf available: 13 Skiing available: 14 May be booked through travel agents

scenery, and interesting history of Cape Cod. Brochures are available.

Hosts: Dan & Gayle Kelly
Doubles: 4 (SB) $37-50
Type of Beds: 4 Twin; 2 Queen
Full Breakfast
Minimum stay holidays: 2
Credit Cards: A, B
Reservations preferred
Notes: 2, 5, 7 (restricted), 8, 9, 10, 11, 12

1721 House

B&B Cape Cod, Box 341, W. Hyannisport, 02672
(508) 775-2772

The warm-water beach can be seen from two of the three bedrooms on the second floor of this antique colonial house built in 1721. Characteristic low ceilings are part of the charm of this restored house. Golf, tennis, and fine restaurants are a short walk away.

Doubles: 4 (SB) $60-70
Type of Beds: 2 Twin; 3 King
Continental Breakfast
Credit Cards: No
Notes: 2, 5, 7, 8, 9, 10, 11, 12, 14

EASTHAM

Chester Woods

Orleans B&B Assoc., Box 1312, Orleans, 02653
(508)255-3824

Half-Cape country house in a wooded area with charm, comfort, and convenience. Loveable Springer Spaniel in residence; breakfast served in an interesting country kitchen. Near the National Seashore Visitor's Center, bike path, and ocean beaches. Two doubles, shared bath, $50-60.

Fort Hill House

Orleans B&B Assoc., Box 1312, Orleans, 02653
(508) 255-3824

In a superb location facing the Atlantic at historic Fort Hill, this wonderful new house

combines Cape Cod tradition with all that's best in contemporary design. Watch the heron from the wide decks overlooking the marsh. Three doubles. One private bath; two share. $50-70.

Great Oak

Orleans B&B Assoc., Box 1312, Orleans, 02653
(508) 255-3824

Charming Cape residence located on a pleasant, quiet street 1.5 miles from the National Seashore Beaches and Cape Cod Bay. Private ground-level entrance to a fireplaced living room with TV and stereo, private bath with shower. Breakfast is served in either your sitting room or on the sunny screened porch. One double, private bath, $50.

Kamen's B&B

B&B Cape Cod, Box 341, W. Hyannisport, 02672
(508) 775-2772

Located a half mile from the National Seashore, this rambling home overlooks beautiful Minister Pond. Furnished with a comfortable mix of antiques and traditional decor. Bike trail very close to house; hostess will assist with bike rentals.

Doubles: 2 (1 PB; 1 SB) $52-55
Type of Beds: 1 Double; 1 Queen
Full Breakfast
Credit Cards: No
Notes: 2, 7, 8, 9, 10, 11, 12, 14

The Over Look Inn

Rt. 6, Box 771, 02642
(508) 255-1886

Located on the beautiful outer cape, across from Cape Cod National Seashore. Full breakfast, afternoon tea. Victorian billiard room, library, parlour, porches. Near biking, hiking, fine dining. Scottish hospitality.

NOTES: Credit cards accepted: A Master Card; B Visa; C American Express; D Discover Card; E Diners Club; F Other: 2 Personal checks accepted: 3 Lunch available: 4 Dinner available: 5 Open all year

Hosts: Ian & Nan Aitchison
Doubles: 8 (PB) $60-100
Type of Beds: 1 Twin; 2 Double; 5 Queen
Full Breakfast
Notes: 2, 5, 7 (limited), 8 (12 and over), 9, 14

Pilgrim's Place

Orleans B&B Assoc., Box 1312, Orleans, 02653
(508) 255-3824

In a quiet neighborhood just up from a
secluded bay beach. Within walking distance
to paths circling two ponds; close to the bike
trail. Cable TV, VCR, sitting area. Two
doubles, shared bath, $60.

Soft Winds

Orleans B&B Assoc., Box 1312, Orleans, 02653
(508) 255-3824

Staying here is like having your own comfortable apartment. Private guest wing with
living room, kitchen, bath, bedroom, and
your own deck. Cable TV with HBO. All the
makings for a good breakfast will be on-hand
for you. Next to bike path and convenient to
beaches and ponds. One double, private
bath, self-prepared breakfast. $70.

Spindrift

Orleans B&B Assoc., Box 1312, Orleans, 02653
(508) 255-3824

Delightful wing on an old house, just five
minutes' walk to Coast Guard Beach. Close
to bike path. Private entrance into library/-
sitting room with large window facing the
ocean. Patio. Hosts offer privacy or
hospitality, as you wish. The host is a potter
with a shop in Orleans. Two doubles, private
bath, $80.

Tory Hill

Orleans B&B Assoc., Box 1312, Orleans, 02653
(508) 255-3824

An old Cape with a private guest wing. Enjoy
the attractive parlor or patio. Owners have
an interesting antique business in an adjacent barn, and everything reflects their
lively interests. Walk to the ice-cream parlor.
Bay beach 3/4 mile; ocean, 2 miles. One
double, private bath, $65.

Nauset House Inn

EAST ORLEANS

Nauset House Inn

143 Beach Dr., Box 774, 02643
(508) 255-2195

The Nauset House Inn is a place where the
gentle amenities of life are still observed , a
quiet place removed from the cares of the
workaday world, a place where sea and
shore, orchard and field all combine to create a perfect setting for tranquil relaxation.
The Nauset House Inn is ideally located
near one of the world's great ocean beaches,
yet is close to antique and craft shops, restaurants, art galleries, scenic paths, and
remote places for sunning, swimming, and
picnicking.

Hosts: Diane & Al Johnson
Doubles: 14 (8 PB; 6 SB) $40-85
Type of Beds: 2 Twin; 9 Double; 1 Queen; 2 King
Full Breakfast
Credit Cards: A, B
Closed Nov. 1 - March 31
Notes: 2, 9, 10, 11, 12

6 Pets welcome: 7 Smoking allowed: 8 Children welcome: 9 Social drinking allowed: 10 Tennis available: 11
Swimming available: 12 Golf available: 13 Skiing available: 14 May be booked through travel agents

Ship's Knees Inn

80 Beach Road, Box 756, 02643
(508) 255-1312

Built over 150 years ago, the inn offers an intimate setting that's only a short walk to scenic Nauset Beach. Many of the bright guest rooms have beamed ceilings, quilts, and old four-poster beds. Several rooms have an ocean view, and the master suite has a working fireplace.

Doubles: 21(8 PB; 13 SB) $45-75
Continental Breakfast
Minimum stay summer weekends: 2
Credit Cards: No
Notes: 2, 5, 7, 8 (over 12), 9, 10, 11, 12

Ship's Knees Inn

EDGARTOWN, MARTHA'S VINEYARD

The Arbor

222 Upper Main Street, Box 1228, 02539
(508) 627-8137

Circa 1890 turn-of-the-century guest house on the bicycle path in historic Edgartown. Short walk to downtown and the harbor. Guests may relax in the hammock, have tea in the courtyard, or walk the unspoiled beaches of Martha's Vineyard.

Host: Peggy Hall
Singles: 1 (PB) $75-110 plus tax

Doubles: 9 (7 PB; 2 SB) $75-110 plus tax
Type of Beds: 2 Twin; 2 Double; 6 Queen
Continental Breakfast
Minimum stay in season: 3
Credit Cards: A, B
Closed Nov. 1-April 30
Notes: 2, 7, 8 (over 12), 9, 10, 11, 12, 14

Arlene's B&B

B&B Cape Cod, Box 341, W. Hyannisport, 02672
(508) 775-2772

This attractive inn in Edgartown retains the casual elegance of a restored whaling captain's home. Many rooms have four-poster canopy beds; some have balconies overlooking the harbor or an English garden.

Doubles: 14 (PB) $107-177
Type of Beds: 5 Double; 4 Queen; 5 King
Full Breakfast
Credit Cards: No
Notes: 2, 5, 7, 8, 9, 10, 11, 12, 14

Ashley Inn

Box 650, 02539
(508) 627-9655

Among spacious lawns, rose gardens, and apple trees, the Ashley Inn offers and attractive 1860s captain's home with country charm. Conveniently located on Edgartown's historic Main Street, the inn is a leisurely stroll to shops, beaches, and fine goods. Each room is tastefully decorated with period antiques, brass, and wicker. Join us for breakfast and relax in our hammocks. We hope to make your visit to Martha's Vineyard a memorable one.

Hosts: Jude Cortese & Fred Hurley
Doubles: 10 (8 PB; 2 SB) $85-160
Type of Beds: 5 Double; 5 Queen
Continental Breakfast
Credit Cards: A, B, C
Notes: 2, 5, 7, 8 (under 12), 9, 10, 11, 12, 14

The Daggett House

54 N. Water Street, Box 1333, 02539
(508) 627-4600

NOTES: Credit cards accepted: A Master Card; B Visa; C American Express; D Discover Card; E Diners Club; F Other: 2 Personal checks accepted: 3 Lunch available: 4 Dinner available: 5 Open all year

The only bed and breakfast in Edgartown that is on the water. The rooms in this circa 1660 home were all redecorated in 1988-1989. Open all year.

Hosts: Sue Cooper-Street
Singles: 1 (PB) $71.30
Doubles: 22 (PB) $153.58
Suites: 2 (PB) $208.43
Type of Beds: 1 Twin; 6 Double; 10 Queen; 8 King
Continental Breakfast
Credit Cards: A, B
Notes: 2, 5, 7, 8, 9, 10, 11, 12

The Governor Bradford Inn

128 Main Street, 02539
(508) 627-9510

The atmosphere at this restored 1865 whaling captain's home is one of casual elegance. Guests can walk to the many shops and restaurants in Edgartown, bicycle to beaches, or simply relax. Freshly baked treats are served at breakfast and afternoon tea. Guest rooms are decorated with antiques and ceiling fans.

Hosts: Mark & Helen Anderson
Doubles: 16 (PB) $60-195
Type of Beds: 2 Twin; 1 Queen; 15 King
Continental Breakfast

Credit Cards: A, B, C, E
Notes: 2, 5, 7, 8 (over 10), 9, 10, 11, 12, 14

Point Way Inn

Box 128, 02539
(508) 627-8633

Our delightful country inn provides a warm, relaxed retreat, with working fireplaces in eleven rooms. Tea and scones are provided in the winter; in the summer, lemonade and oatmeal cookies are served in the gazebo overlooking the croquet court, lawn, and gardens.

Hosts: Linda & Ben Smith
Doubles: 15 (PB) $70-205
Type of Beds: 4 Twin; 5 Double; 8 Queen
Continental Breakfast
Minimum stay holidays: 2
Credit Cards: A, B, C
Notes: 2, 5, 7, 8, 9, 10, 11, 12, 14

EGREMONT

Berkshire SC8

Berkshire B&B Homes
Box 211, Williamsburg, MA, 01096
(413) 268-7244

Governor Bradford Inn

An 1803 country farmhouse on 3 acres, furnished with country and antiques. Parlor and dining room with fireplaces, air-conditioning. All rooms have private baths. Near Jacob's Pillow, Stockbridge Playhouse, Butternut and Catamont ski areas.

Singles: 1 (PB) $70
Doubles: 5 (PB) $65-85
Type of Beds: 3 Twin; 3 Double; 1 Queen
Full Breakfast
Credit Cards: No
Notes: 2, 5, 10, 11, 12, 13

FAIRHAVEN

Edgewater Bed & Breakfast

2 Oxford Street, 02719
(508) 997-5512

A gracious waterfront house located in the early whaleship building area of historic Fairhaven. Spectacular views of neighboring New Bedford Harbor, close to historic areas, beaches, factory outlets; five minutes from I-195. Five rooms, each with private bath (two with fireplaces). Sitting rooms.

Host: Kathy Reed
Doubles: 5 (PB) $30-65
Continental Breakfast
Credit Cards: A, B
Notes: 2, 5, 9, 10, 11, 12, 14

FALMOUTH

Capt. Tom Lawrence House

75 Locust Street, 02540
(508) 540-1445

An 1861 Victorian, former whaling captain's residence, in the historic village of Falmouth. Comfortable, spacious corner guest rooms. Firm beds — some with canopies. Steinway piano and working fireplace. Gourmet breakfast consists of fresh fruit, breads, pancakes made from freshly ground

organic grain, and a variety of other delicious specialties. German spoken.

Singles: 1 (PB) $45-55
Doubles: 5 (PB) $65-88
Type of Beds: 4 Twin; 4 Queen; 1 King
Full Breakfast
Minimum stay: 2
Credit Cards: A, B
Notes: 2, 5, 7 (restricted), 8 (over 12), 9, 11, 12

Capt. Tom Lawrence House

Gladstone Inn

219 Grand Avenue South, 02540
(508) 548-9851

An oceanfront Victorian inn overlooking Martha's Vineyard. Established in 1910. Light, airy guest rooms have period furniture and their own wash stations. Buffet breakfast is served on our glassed-in porch that also provides a cozy place to read, watch cable TV, or relax. Refrigerators, bikes, and gas grill are provided for our guests to use.

Hosts: Jim & Gayle Carroll
Singles: 2 (SB) $27.50
Doubles: 14 (1 PB; 13 SB) $45-65
Type of Beds: 12 Twin; 7 Double; 1 Queen; 2 King
Full Breakfast
Credit Cards: No
Closed Oct. 15 - May 15
Notes: 2, 7, 8 (12 and over), 9, 10, 11, 12

NOTES: Credit cards accepted: A Master Card; B Visa; C American Express; D Discover Card; E Diners Club; F Other: 2 Personal checks accepted: 3 Lunch available: 4 Dinner available: 5 Open all year

Grafton Inn

261 Grand Avenue, South, 02540
(508) 540-8688

Oceanfront Victorian inn with miles of beautiful beach and breathtaking views of Martha's Vineyard. Sumptuous breakfasts are served on a lovely enclosed porch. Private baths, airy, comfortable rooms furnished with period antiques, thoughtful amenities. Picnic lunches and bicycles are available, as is ample parking. short walk to restaurant, shops, and ferry. Ask about off-season rates and package plans.

Hosts: Liz & Rudy Cvitan
Doubles: 11 (PB) $60-80
Type of Beds: 3 Twin; 6 Double; 4 Queen; 1 King
Full Breakfast
Credit Cards: A, B
Closed Dec. 1 - March 1
Notes: 2, 9, 10, 11, 12, 14

Mostly Hall B&B Inn

27 Main Street, 02540
(508) 548-3786

Romantic 1849 southern-plantation-style Cape Cod home with wraparound veranda and widow's walk. Set back from the road on an acre of beautiful gardens with a gazebo. Close to restaurants, shops, beaches, island ferries. Spacious corner rooms, gourmet breakfast, bicycles.

Hosts: Caroline & Jim Lloyd
Doubles: 6 (PB) $60-110
Type of Beds: 2 Twin; 6 Queen
Full Breakfast
Minimum stay Memorial Day-Columbus Day: 2; selected holidays: 2-3
Credit Cards: No
Closed Jan.-mid Feb.
Notes: 2, 8 (16 and over), 9, 10, 11, 12

Palmer House Inn

81 Palmer Avenue, 02540
(508) 548-1230

Turn-of-the-century Victorian bed and breakfast located in the historic district. An-
tique furnishings return you to the romance of Grandma's day. Full gourmet breakfast featuring Pain Perdue, Belgian waffles, cheese blintzes. Close to island ferries, beaches, shops. Bicycles available.

Hosts: Phyllis & Bud Peacock
Doubles: 8 (PB) $75-110
Type of Beds: 2 Twin; 6 Double
Full Breakfast
Minimum stay: 2
Credit Cards: A, B, E, F
Notes: 2, 5, 7, 8 (over 14), 9, 10, 11, 12

Sea Winds

Box 1333, 02360
(508) 548-3459

Charming Cape Cod home, ideally located on the Vineyard Sound. Walk to beach; less than one mile to ferry to Martha's Vineyard. Boston is 73 miles away; Plymouth 30.

Hosts: Mary Gill & Diane Gillis
Singles: 1 (SB) $38
Doubles: 1 (SB) $50
Continental Breakfast
Minimum stay: 2
Credit Cards: A, B, C
Notes: 5, 7 (restricted), 8, 9, 11

Village Green Inn

40 W. Main Street, 02540
(508) 548-5621

Gracious old Victorian, ideally located on historic Village Green. Walk to fine shops and restaurants, bike to beaches, tennis, and the picturesque bike path to Woods Hole. Enjoy nineteenth-century charm and warm hospitality in elegant surroundings. Four lovely guest rooms and one romantic suite all have private baths. Discounted rates from Nov.-May.

Hosts: Linda & Don Long
Doubles: 5 (PB) $70-95
Type of Beds: 1 Twin; 2 Double; 3 Queen; 1 Cot
Full Breakfast
Credit Cards: No
Notes: 2, 5, 7 (outside), 8 (16 or older), 9, 10, 11, 12

---

6 Pets welcome: 7 Smoking allowed: 8 Children welcome: 9 Social drinking allowed: 10 Tennis available: 11 Swimming available: 12 Golf available: 13 Skiing available: 14 May be booked through travel agents

Wyndemere House at Sippewissett

718 Palmer Ave. at Goodings Way, 02540
(508) 540-7069

Located in Sippewissett, a tiny, quiet village within Falmouth proper, Wyndemere House is for those who enjoy the peaceful charm and congeniality of an English country house but also desire the modern conveniences of an American inn. Five minutes from downtown Falmouth.

Host: Carole Railsback
Doubles: 6 (PB) $75-105
Type of Beds: 2 Twin; 2 Double; 2 King
Full Breakfast
Minimum stay weekdays & weekends: 2 ; holidays: 3
Credit Cards: No
Closed Oct.-April
Notes: 2, 7 (limited), 8 (12 and over), 9, 10, 11

FALMOUTH HEIGHTS

The Moorings Lodge

207 Grand Avenue S., 02540
(508) 540-2370

A Victorian sea captain's home, within walking distance of the beach, restaurants, and island ferries. Complimentary homemade breakfast buffet served overlooking Vineyard Sound and the islands. Call us your home while you tour the Cape.

Hosts: The Benard Family
Doubles: 8 (6 PB; 2 SB) $49.30-71.22
Type of Beds: 3 Twin; 5 Double
Full Breakfast
Minimum stay weekdays & weekends: 2; holidays: 3
Credit Cards: No
Closed Columbus Day-May 15
Notes: 2, 7, 8 (over 10), 9, 10, 11, 12

FLORENCE-NORTHAMPTON

Berkshire PV10

Berkshire B&B Homes
Box 211, Williamsburg, MA, 01096
(413) 268-7244

Turn-of-the-century home on 17 acres with antique furnishings, shared baths with tub. Located in the five-college area, minutes from a swimming pool, picnic area, and tennis courts.

Doubles: 4 (SB) $45-50
Type of Beds: 2 Twin; 3 Double
Full Breakfast
Credit Cards: No
Notes: 2, 5, 10, 11, 12

FRAMINGHAM

Host Homes of Boston #16

Box 117, Waban Branch, Boston, 02168
(617) 244-1308

In the Boston countryside near historic Wayside Inn, this century-old house resembles a Currier & Ives print with its stone walls, winding wooded roads, field, and barn. Near I-90, I-495.

Doubles: 1 (PB) $60
Type of Beds: 1 King
Continental Breakfast
Minimum stay: 2
Credit Cards: A, B, C
Notes: 2, 5, 9

GLOUCESTER

Ginny's B&B

B&B Cape Cod, Box 341, W. Hyannisport, 02672
(508) 775-2772

An 1898 Victorian on the Annisquam River, thirty miles north of Boston at Cape Ann, with a marvelous water view. Watch the ocean-bound ships pass by your bedroom window.

Doubles: 4 (SB) $50-60
Type of Beds: 2 Twin; 2 Double; 1 Queen
Continental Breakfast
Credit Cards: No
Notes: 2, 7, 8, 9, 10, 11, 12, 14

NOTES: Credit cards accepted: A Master Card; B Visa; C American Express; D Discover Card; E Diners Club; F Other: 2 Personal checks accepted: 3 Lunch available: 4 Dinner available: 5 Open all year

Greater Boston Hospitality #111

Box 1142, Brookline 02146
(617) 277-5430

An 1889 waterfront home with private beach on a warm river that's great for swimming. Rooms are decorated with Laura Ashley prints, and all have water views. Whale watch, shop, eat fantastic seafood dinners in nearby restaurants.

Doubles: 4 (S2B) $70-78
Continental Breakfast
Credit Cards: No

Mill River B&B

B&B Marblehead & North Shore
Box 172, Beverly, MA, 01915
(508) 921-1336

A pretty antique-furnished home on a river, close to Rockport. First-floor porch facing the river, sitting room with TV. One small dog in residence.

Doubles: 2 (SB) $50-70
Type of Beds: 2 Double; 1 Rollaway
Continental Breakfast
Credit Cards: No
Notes: 2, 5, 8, 9, 10, 11, 12, 14

Riverview B&B

B&B Marblehead & North Shore
Box 172, Beverly, MA, 01915
(508) 921-1336

A beautiful 1898 riverfront home on the Annisquam River with wonderful views of the boats and bird life. Explore Cape Ann's harbors and beautiful coast. Whale-watching cruises and deep-sea fishing charter boats operate from the harbor.

Doubles: 4 (S2B) $60-75
Type of Beds: 2 Twin; 2 Double; 1 Queen; 2 Rollaways
Continental Breakfast
Credit Cards: No
Closed Oct. 31 - May 15
Notes: 2, 7, 8 (over 10), 9, 10, 11, 12, 14

GREAT BARRINGTON

Elling's B&B Guest House

RD 3, Box 6, 01230
(413) 528-4103

Our 1746 homestead, with porches, lawns, flower gardens with views of hills and corn fields, offers six charming guest rooms. Large guest living room with fireplace, and a generous buffet breakfast. Our guest return to enjoy Tanglewood, ballet, the playhouses, and winter sports. We've been hosts for eighteen years now.

Hosts: Jo & Ray Elling
Doubles: 6 (2 PB; 4 SB) $55-80
Type of Beds: 3 Double; 1 Queen; 1 King
Continental Breakfast
Credit Cards: No
Notes: 2, 5, 10, 11, 12, 13

Littlejohn Manor

1 Newsboy Monument Lane, 01230
(413) 528-2882

Victorian charm recaptured in this uniquely personable home. Antiques grace four warmly furnished guest rooms — two with fireplaces. Guest parlor with color TV and fireplace. Full English breakfast and afternoon tea. Set on spacious, landscaped grounds, with extensive herb and flower beds. Scenic views. Within five miles of Butternut Basin and Catamount.

Hosts: Herbert Littlejohn, Jr., & Paul A. DuFour
Doubles: 4 (SB) $50-75
Type of Beds: 2 Twin; 2 Double; 1 King
Full Breakfast
Minimum stay weekends: 2; holidays: 3
Credit Cards: No
Notes: 2, 5, 7 (limited), 9, 10, 11, 12, 13

Round Hill Farm

17 Round Hill Road, 01230
(413) 528-3366

A haven for nonsmokers. Classic nineteenth-century hilltop horse farm

6 Pets welcome: 7 Smoking allowed: 8 Children welcome: 9 Social drinking allowed: 10 Tennis available: 11 Swimming available: 12 Golf available: 13 Skiing available: 14 May be booked through travel agents

Round Hill Farm

overlooking 300 acres, on a dirt road 2.6 miles from town. Miles of tended fields, trails, trout stream, with panoramic views of the Berkshire Hills. Please call for our brochure.

Hosts: Thomas & Margaret Whitfield
Singles: 1 (PB) $65
Doubles: 8 (3 PB; 5 SB) $65-140
Type of Beds: 2 Twin; 6 Double; 2 Queen
Full Breakfast
Horses welcome
Credit Cards: A, B
Nonsmokers only, please
Notes: 2, 5, 8 (over 16), 9, 10, 11, 12, 13, 14

Seekonk Pines Inn

142 Seekonk Cross Road, 01230
(413) 528-4192

Restored 1830s homestead, located in a rural Berkshire setting. Large guest living room with fireplace and grand piano. Full country breakfast changes daily. Special diets accommodated. Convenient to Tanglewood and other cultural events, museums, shops, hiking. Features antique quilts, stenciling, original watercolors, and gardens.

Hosts: Linda & Chris Best
Doubles: 7 (2 PB; 4 S1B) $47.57-89.85
Type of Beds: 1 Twin; 4 Double; 2 Queen
Full Breakfast
Credit Cards: No
Notes: 2, 5, 8, 9, 10, 11, 12, 13

The Turning Point Inn

3 Lake Buel Road, 01230
(413) 528-4777

An eighteenth-century former stagecoach inn. Full, naturally delicious breakfast. Featured in the New York *Times, Boston Globe,* *L.A. Times.* Adjacent to Butternut Ski Basin; near Tanglewood and all Berkshire attractions. Hiking, cross-country ski trails. Sitting rooms with fireplaces, piano, cable TV. Groups and families welcome.

Hosts: Shirley, Irving & Jamie Yost
Singles: 1 (SB) $50-60
Doubles: 8 (3 PB; 5 SB) $75-100
Type of Beds: 3 Twin; 3 Double; 1 Queen; 2 King
Full Breakfast
Minimum stay weekends: 1-2; holidays: 2-3
Credit Cards: No
Notes: 2, 5, 8, 9, 10, 11, 12, 13

GREENFIELD

Berkshire PV32

Berkshire B&B Homes
Box 211, Williamsburg, MA, 01096
(413) 268-7244

Turn-of-the-century colonial Revival with antique and Victorian furnishings, living room fireplace, and library with pool table. Minutes to historic Deerfield, Northfield, and the five-college area.

NOTES: Credit cards accepted: A Master Card; B Visa; C American Express; D Discover Card; E Diners Club; F Other: 2 Personal checks accepted: 3 Lunch available: 4 Dinner available: 5 Open all year

Doubles: 5 (2 PB; 3 SB) $70-85
Type of Beds: 3 Twin; 1 Double; 1 Queen
Full Breakfast
Credit Cards: No
Notes: 2, 5, 10, 11, 12, 13

GROTON

B&B Folks 3

48 Springs Road, Bedford, MA 01730
(617) 275-9025

Colonial house in rural Massachusetts that's close to New Hampshire and forty minutes from Boston. Reduced rates for long-term stays.

Singles: 1 (SB) $40
Doubles: 1 (SB) $50
Type of Beds: 1 Double
Continental Breakfast
Credit Cards: No
Notes: 4, 8, 9, 10, 11, 12

GROVELAND

The Seven Acres Farm

B&B Marblehead & North Shore
Box 172, Beverly, MA, 01915
(508) 921-1336

Antique Victorian on a herb farm in a very historic area next to the wide Merrimack River. The colonials in the area date to the 1600s, and a stroll through the historic district is well worth your while. Close to Newburyport and I-95.

Doubles: 1 (SB) $50-65
Type of Beds: 1 Double; 1 Double sofabed
Continental breakfast weekdays; full on weekends
Credit Cards: No
Notes: 2, 5, 7 (restricted), 8, 9, 10, 11, 12, 13, 14

HARWICH

Bel-Aire

Orleans B&B Assoc., Box 1312, Orleans, 02653
(508) 255-3824

Step out of your private entrance and relax on the porch with a view of Nantucket Sound. Or step across the road lined with hedges and roses and walk down a short path to the fine warm-water beach. Your private suite on the first floor includes a sitting room with TV and bath with shower. One double, private bath, $75.

Freshwater Whale

Orleans B&B Assoc., Box 1312, Orleans, 02653
(508) 255-3824

Charming antique-filled cottage has view from every room of a large, clear pond that's excellent for swimming. Full breakfast with hot, homemade breads is served on the deck or in the country kitchen. Family room with fireplace and TV, patio, old-fashioned garden, sandy beach. Canoe and beach towels provided. Five minutes to ocean beach, bike path, golf, and tennis. Two doubles, full breakfast, $70.

Hank's B&B

B&B Cape Cod, Box 341, W. Hyannisport, 02672
(508) 775-2772

This Cape style home sits 100 yards from a fresh-water pond. Located on the Cape Cod Bike Trail, it's a great spot for riders. The pond is available for swimming and fishing; one mile to the beach.

Doubles: 2 (SB) $48
Type of Beds: 2 Twin; 1 Double
Continental Breakfast
Credit Cards: No
Notes: 8 (over 8), 9, 10, 11, 12, 14

The Larches

97 Chatham Road, 02645
(508) 432-0150

A charming 1835 Greek Revival with contemporary wing surrounded by flower and vegetable gardens. Close to swimming, bike tails, art galleries, little theater, and summer

6 Pets welcome: 7 Smoking allowed: 8 Children welcome: 9 Social drinking allowed: 10 Tennis available: 11 Swimming available: 12 Golf available: 13 Skiing available: 14 May be booked through travel agents

stock. Continental breakfast is served in gracious surroundings, on patio, if preferred.

Hosts: Dr. & Mrs. Edwin O. Hook
Doubles: 2 (1 PB; 1 SB) $50-60
Type of Beds: 2 Twin; 1 King
Continental Breakfast
Minimum stay: 2
Credit Cards: No
Closed Christmas & Thanksgiving
Notes: 9, 10, 11, 12

Pinniped Inn

Orleans B&B Assoc., Box 1312, Orleans, 02653
(508) 255-3824

A warm and comfortable circa 1800 Greek Revival country home lovingly re-stored. Minutes to beaches, bike trails, good restaurants, golf. Attractively furnished with antiques and collectibles. Resident affectionate golden retrievers. Three doubles, full breakfast, $50.

Serendipity

Orleans B&B Assoc., Box 1312, Orleans, 02653
(508) 255-3824

Peace and quiet "on golden pond." Private beach with excellent swimming. All rooms have a beautiful water view. Color TV, generous breakfast; minutes to ocean beach, tennis, golf, and bike path. Singles: $30. Doubles: $60.

Windchimes

Orleans B&B Assoc., Box 1312, Orleans, 02653
(508) 255-3824

Central Cape location in a quiet residential area. Three-four minute walk to fine Nantucket Sound beach. Bicycle path nearby. New spacious guest suite with full bath, living room area with color TV, and front and rear private entrances. Your hosts are enthusiastic sailors. One double, $70.

HARWICH PORT

Alyce's B&B

B&B Cape Cod, Box 341, W. Hyannisport, 02672
(508) 775-2772

This Dutch colonial was built in 1922 and has served as a small inn for thirty years. The house stands 300 feet from a private beach on Nantucket Sound. Large sun porch, living room with fireplace, and large dining area.

Doubles: 8 (PB) $65-90
Type of Beds: 2 Double; 5 Queen; 2 King
Continental Breakfast
Credit Cards: No
Notes: 2, 5, 7, 8, 9, 10, 11, 12, 14

The Coach House

74 Sisson Road, 02646
(508) 432-9452

Delightful old cape home, once an estate barn, offering quiet, comfortable elegance. Conveniently located for day trips to Martha's Vineyard and Nantucket, whale watching, and 21-mile bike trail through woodlands and cranberry bogs to the National Seashore.

Hosts: Sara & Cal Ayer
Doubles: 3 (2 PB; 1 SB) $65-70
Type of Beds: 1 Queen; 2 King
Continental Breakfast
Minimum stay weekends & holidays: 2
Credit Cards: A, B, C
Closed Nov.-April
Notes: 2, 7, 9, 10, 11, 12

Eagles Nest B&B

B&B Cape Cod, Box 341, W. Hyannisport, 02672
(508) 775-2772

Bank Street Beach, village shops, fine restaurants, and two public golf courses are very close to this 1960s restored Victorian. Guests have their own private entrance.

Doubles: 2 (SB) $60
Type of Beds: 2 Twin; 1 Double

NOTES: Credit cards accepted: A Master Card; B Visa; C American Express; D Discover Card; E Diners Club; F Other: 2 Personal checks accepted: 3 Lunch available: 4 Dinner available: 5 Open all year

Continental Breakfast
Credit Cards: No
Notes: 2, 5, 7, 8 (12 and over), 9, 10, 11, 12, 14

Harborwalk B&B

B&B Cape Cod, Box 341, W. Hyannisport, 02672
(508) 775-2772

Wychmere Harbor is across the street from this 1880 rambling guest house. Short walk to one of the best seafood restaurants on the Cape. The beaches, village shops, and recreational activities are a short distance away.

Doubles: 7 (PB and SB) $45-60
Type of Beds: 2 Twin; 2 Double; 2 Queen; 1 King
Continental Breakfast
Credit Cards: No
Notes: 2, 8 (4 and over), 9, 10, 11, 12, 14

The Inn on Bank Street

88 Bank Street, 02646
(508) 432-3206

A bed & breakfast in the center of lovely Harwich Port. Five minute walk to ocean beach. Close to good restaurants, quaint shops, picturesque harbors. Enjoy breakfast on the sun porch of this charming Cape Cod country inn.

Hosts: Janet & Arky Silverio
Doubles: 6 (PB) $57-77
Type of Beds: 4 Twin; 3 Double; 1 Queen; 2 King
Continental Breakfast
Minimum stay weekends & holidays: 2
Credit Cards: A, B (for deposit only)
Closed Dec.-March
Notes: 2, 7, 8, 9, 10, 11, 12

The Shoals Guesthouse

3 Sea Street, 02646
(508) 432-3837

On a beautiful sandy beach on Nantucket Sound. Quiet residential area, central to all of Cape Cod. Very comfortable rooms with private baths; delicious continental buffet. Walk to village, restaurants, and shops.

Hosts: Dottie & John Girard
Singles: 2 (PB) $44-85
Doubles: 6 (PB) $44-85
Type of Beds: 4 Twin; 6 Double
Continental Breakfast
Minimum stay weekends & holidays: 2
Credit Cards: No
Notes: 2, 5, 7, 8, 9, 10, 11, 12

HINSDALE

Berkshire NC10

Berkshire B&B Homes
Box 211, Williamsburg, MA, 01096
(413) 268-7244

A 1770s central-hall colonial with an-tique and country furnishings. Comfortable parlor with piano and carved chess set. Screened-in porch for warm summer evenings; ceiling fans in each guest room. Close to summer camps, lakes, cross-country skiing, hiking, and Tanglewood's cultural activities.

Doubles: 4 (1 PB; 3 SB) $55-65
Type of Beds: 2 Twin; 2 Double; 1 Queen
Full Breakfast
Credit Cards: No
Notes: 2, 5, 8, 10, 11, 12

The Inn on Bank Street

HOLYOKE

Yankee Pedlar Inn

1866 Northampton Street, 01040
(413) 532-9494

Our New England Inn with guest accom-modations and restaurant is located in western Massachusetts, in the scenic Connecticut River Valley. Fall foliage is breath-taking, and antiquing is excellent. Skiing, golf, tennis, water slides, and other sports facilities are nearby. Museums and Old Deerfield are some historical points of interest. We're close to many educational institutions.

Hosts: Frank & Claire Banks
Singles: 30 (PB) $55-65
Doubles: 16 (PB) $65-75
Type of Beds: 14 Twin; 13 Double; 14 Queen; 5 King
Continental Breakfast
Credit Cards: A, B, C, D, E
Notes: 2, 3, 4, 5, 7, 8, 9, 10, 11, 12, 13, 14

HYANNIS

B&B Registry #MA-02601CRA

Box 8174, St. Paul, MN, 55108
(612) 646-4238

This Cape is situated beside a cranberry bog just outside Hyannis. Guests can enjoy the small private beach nearby and the town beach five minutes away. Within walking distance of the local night spots, restaurants, ferries.

Doubles: 2 (SB) $75
Type of Beds: 2 Twin; 1 Double
Continental-plus Breakfast
Credit Cards: No
Notes: 5, 8, 11, 12

Elegance By-The-Sea

162 Sea Street, 02601
(508) 775-3595

Romantic 1880 Queen Anne Victorian home, furnished with antiques in the European style. Walk to beaches, restaurants, island ferries. Great location as a base for visiting all of Cape Cod. Many common areas available to guests: porch, breakfast greenhouse room, formal dining room with separate tables, fireplace and parlor with TV and piano.

Hosts: Clark & Mary Boydston
Doubles: 6 (PB) $59.80-75
Type of Beds: 1 Twin; 3 Double; 2 Queen
Full Breakfast
Minimum stay weekends & holidays: 2
Credit Cards: A, B, C
Closed January
Notes: 2, 8 (over 16), 9, 10, 11, 12

Gloria's B&B

B&B Cape Cod, Box 341, W. Hyannisport, 02672
(508) 775-2772

This contemporary home overlooks Snow Creek and Hyannis Harbor. Large living room with fireplace.

Doubles: 2 (SB) $60
Type of Beds: 2 Twin; 1 Queen
Continental Breakfast
Credit Cards: No
Notes: 5, 8 (10 and over), 9, 10, 11, 12, 14

Hansen's B&B

B&B Cape Cod, Box 341, W. Hyannisport, 02672
(508) 775-2772

A townhouse condominium located in a quiet section of Hyannis. The first floor features a sitting area with TV for guest use. Patio, wall-to-wall carpeting, guest parking. A great location for people traveling to Cape Cod without cars.

Doubles: 1 (SB) $60
Type of Beds: 1 Queen
Continental Breakfast
Credit Cards: No
Notes: 5, 9, 10, 11, 12, 14

The Inn On Sea Street

358 Sea Street, 02601
(508) 775-8030

Romantic, elegant Victorian inn, just steps from the beach and the Kennedy compound. Antiques, Persian carpets, fireplace.

NOTES: Credit cards accepted: A Master Card; B Visa; C American Express; D Discover Card; E Diners Club; F Other: 2 Personal checks accepted: 3 Lunch available: 4 Dinner available: 5 Open all year

Six unique guest rooms; gourmet breakfast of homemade delights, fruit, and cheese.

Hosts: Lois M. Nelson & J. B. Whitehead
Doubles: 6 (4 PB; 2 SB) $60.34-87.76
Type of Beds: 1 Twin; 4 Double; 2 Queen
Full Breakfast
Credit Cards: A, B, C
Closed Nov. 15-April 1
Notes: 2, 4, 7 (limited), 8 (over 16), 9, 10, 11, 12

Laura's B&B

B&B Cape Cod, Box 341, W. Hyannisport, 02672
(508) 775-2772

Centrally located colonial that's just a short walk from either the train or bus. Walk to beaches, restaurants, shops, the Cape Cod Melody Tent, and island ferries.

Doubles: 3 (SB) $50
Type of Beds: 3 Double
Continental Breakfast
Credit Cards: No
Notes: 2, 8 (12 and over), 9, 10, 11, 12, 14

KINGSTON

Be Our Guest B&B, Ltd. #1

Box 1333, Plymouth, 02360
(617) 837-9867

Antique Federal colonial less than five miles to Plymouth Center. Adjoining guest rooms, each with a double bed, share a bath. Ideal for families or parties traveling together. Beautifully decorated throughout.

Doubles: 2 (SB) $38-50
Type of Beds: 2 Double
Full Breakfast
Credit Cards: A, B, C
Notes: 5, 8, 9, 11, 14

LANESBORO

Berkshire NC1

Berkshire B&B Homes
Box 211, Williamsburg, MA, 01096
(413) 268-7244

A 200-year-old colonial farmhouse at the foot of Mt. Greylock on a working sheep farm with a small bake shop. Rooms furnished with country charm. Near ski areas, Cummington Farm, and Pontoosuc Lake.

Singles: 2 (SB) $30
Doubles: 3 (SB) $35-50
Type of Beds: 2 Twin; 3 Double
Continental Breakfast
Credit Cards: No
Notes: 2, 5, 7 (limited), 8, 10, 11, 12, 13

Berkshire NC12

Berkshire B&B Homes
Box 211, Williamsburg, MA, 01096
(413) 268-7244

A 1979 contemporary post-and-beam-style home with country and contemporary furnishings. Master bedroom has a king bed, private bath, and Jacuzzi. Second guest room have twin beds with shared bath. This home is located on 100 acres with views of the Greylock and Berkshire mountain ranges. Twenty minutes to Tanglewood.

Doubles: 2 (1 PB; 1 SB) $70-90
Type of Beds: 2 Twin; 1 King
Continental Breakfast
Credit Cards: No
Notes: 2, 10, 11, 12

LEE

Haus Andreas

Stockbridge Road, 01238
(413) 243-3298

Completely restored colonial mansion with heated pool, tennis, lawn sports, bicycle, air-conditioning. Fireplaces in some rooms. Library, piano, TV room, guest pantry.

Hosts: Gerhard & Lilliane Schmid
Doubles: 8 (PB) $69-212
Type of Beds: 5 Queen; 3 King
Full or Continental Breakfast
Credit Cards: A, B
Notes: 2, 5, 7, 8 (over 10), 9, 10, 11, 12, 13

LENOX

Amity House

Covered Bridge
Box 447, Norfolk, CT, 06058
(203) 542-5944

An 1800s colonial within walking distance of
the village center. There are several common rooms for the guests, including a living
room with wood-burning stove. The seven
guest rooms are decorated with the owner's
collection of antique quilts. A continental
breakfast is served in the pleasant dining
room.

Doubles: 7 (2 PB; 5 SB) $65-100
Continental Breakfast
Credit Cards: A, B, C
Notes: 2, 5, 8, 9, 10, 11, 12, 13

Apple Tree Inn

224 West Street, 01240
(413) 637-1477

Situated on 22 hilltop acres directly across
the road from the Tanglewood Festival, this
100-year-old main house features charming
country bedrooms. Some have fireplaces,
most have private baths, and all are air-conditioned. Enjoy excellent cuisine and a
panoramic view of the surrounding hills in
our circular dining room or snack in our
oak-beamed tavern. Additional rooms are
located in the guest cottage. There is a clay
tennis court and large heated pool.

Hosts: Aurora & Greg Smith
Main House: 13 (11 PB; 2 SB) $55-260
Guest Lodge: 20 (16 PB; 4 SB) $75-130
Type of Beds: 9 Twin; 38 Double; 4 Queen; 2 King
Continental Breakfast
Credit Cards: A, B, C, E, F
Closed March 15 - April 25
Notes: 2, 4, 7, 9, 10, 11, 12, 13, 14

Brook Farm Inn

15 Hawthorne Street, 01240
(413) 637-3013

There is poetry here. Large library, poets on
tape. Near Tanglewood (Boston Symphony), theater, ballet, shops. Pool, gardens,
fireplaces in winter. Cross-country and
downhill skiing close in the winter. Relax and
enjoy.

Hosts: Bob & Betty Jacob
Doubles: 12 (PB) $55-135
Type of Beds: 6 Twin; 4 Double; 5 Queen
Full Breakfast
Minimum stay weekends & holidays: 2
Credit Cards: A, B
Notes: 2, 5, 7 (restricted), 8 (15 or older), 9, 10, 11,
12, 13

Cliffwood Inn

25 Cliffwood Street, 01240
(413) 637-3330

An 1890s mansion of "Belle Epoque"
beauty built for an ambassador to France.
Seven rooms with private baths and
fireplaces. Complimentary wine, hors
d'oeuvres, copious continental breakfast.
Heated pool open June-August. Forty
performing-arts groups in the area; hiking,
downhill and cross-country skiing.

Hosts: Joy & Scottie Farrelly
Doubles: 7 (PB) $70-160
Type of Beds: 1 Double; 1 Queen; 5 King
Continental Breakfast
Minimum stay weekends & holidays: 2
Credit Cards: No
Notes: 2, 5, 7, 8 (over 13), 9, 10, 11, 12, 13

The Gables Inn

103 Walker Street, 01240
(413) 637-3416

Former home of authoress Edith Wharton.
Queen Anne style with period furnishings,
pool, tennis, fireplaces, and theme rooms.

Hosts: Mary & Frank Newton
Doubles: 14 (PB) $60-135
Type of Beds: 2 Twin; 4 Double; 8 Queen
Continental Breakfast
Minimum stay weekends & holidays: 2-3
Notes: 2, 5, 7, 8 (over 12), 9, 10, 11, 12, 13

NOTES: Credit cards accepted: A Master Card; B Visa; C American Express; D Discover Card; E Diners
Club; F Other: 2 Personal checks accepted: 3 Lunch available: 4 Dinner available: 5 Open all year

Gateways Inn & Restaurant

71 Walker Street, 01240
(413) 637-2532

Stay and dine in this elegantly restored inn located in the heart of Lenox. Close to Tanglewood and many cultural attractions. Mobil four-star rated.

Host: Vito Perulli
Doubles: 9 (PB) $60-125
Type of Beds: 1 Twin; 2 Double; 4 Queen; 2 King
Country Breakfast
Minimum stay summer weekends: 3
Credit Cards: A, B, C, E
Notes: 2, 4, 5, 9, 10, 12, 13

Rookwood Inn

Box 1717, 01240
(413) 637-9750

Capture the spirit of a bygone era at our gracious Victorian inn. Originally built in 1885, Rookwood has seventeen guest rooms, all decorated with period antiques. Our unique location is peaceful and secluded, yet only half a block from town center. We serve full breakfast and afternoon tea, and we are near shopping, restaurants, and all sports.

Hosts: Tom & Betsy Sherman
Doubles: 17 (PB) $55-150
Type of Beds: 4 Twin; 4 Double; 9 Queen
Full Breakfast
Credit Cards: A, B
Notes: 2, 5, 8, 9, 10, 11, 12, 13, 14

Underledge Inn

76 Cliffwood Street, 01240
(413) 637-0236

Underledge offers elegance and country charm in a Victorian mansion. Large air-conditioned parlor bedrooms are decorated with an air of bygone days. Stroll down the street to discover Lenox Village's fine restaurants, boutiques, galleries, and quaint shops. Minutes from Tanglewood,

Berkshire Theater, Jacob's Pillow, Edith Wharton, the opera, and Shakespeare.

Host: Marcie Kanoue
Doubles: 9 (PB) $60-130
Continental Breakfast
Credit Cards: A, B, C
Notes: 5, 7, 8 (over 10), 9, 10, 11, 12, 13

Walker House

Walker House

74 Walker Street, 01240
(413) 637-1271

Reflecting the owners' tastes and passions, each guest room is named and decorated for a classical composer. The large parlor contains a piano that has been the focal point of many concerts and recitals and the inspiration for many visitors to return to, or try for the first time, the keyboard.

Hosts: Richard & Peggy Houdek
Doubles: 8 (PB) $52.85-142.70
Type of Beds: 2 Twin; 3 Double; 5 Queen
Continental-plus Breakfast
Minimum stay weekends: 2-3; holidays: 3
Credit Cards: No
Notes: 2, 5, 6, 8 (12 and over), 9, 10, 11, 12, 13

Whistlers' Inn

5 Greenwood Street, 01240
(413) 637-0975

Historic 1820 Tudor mansion on 7 acres of woodland just three blocks from the town center. Antique-filled home has eight fireplaces, English library, baronial dining room, and Louis XVI music room with

Steinway and chandeliers. Home-baked breakfast, afternoon sherry/tea.

Hosts: Joan & Richard Mears
Doubles: 11 (PB) $63.42-179.69
Type of Beds: 11 Twin; 6 Double; 1 Queen; 1 King
Continental-plus Breakfast
Credit Cards: A, B, C
Notes: 2, 5, 7, 8, 9, 10, 11, 12, 13

LEXINGTON

B&B Folks 4

48 Springs Road, Bedford, MA 01730
(617) 275-9025

A private three-room suite with living room, bedroom, and kitchen, within walking distance of historic Lexington sights. Only fifteen miles to Boston and Cambridge, twenty to New Hampshire. Reduced rates for long-term stays.

Doubles: 1 (PB) $70
Type of Beds: 1 Double
Continental Breakfast
Credit Cards: No
Notes: 2, 4, 8, 9, 10, 11, 12

Carol's B&B

B&B Marblehead & North Shore
Box 172, Beverly, MA, 01915
(508) 921-1336

Many historic sites, including the Monroe Tavern and Battle Green, are located in Lexington, first settled in the seventeenth century. Two traditional New England commons, one with bandstand and the other where the confrontation between the Minutemen and Redcoats occurred.

Doubles: 3 (SB) $55-60
Type of Beds: 2 Twin; 2 Double
Continental Breakfast
Credit Cards: No
Notes: 2, 5, 8

Greater Boston Hospitality #86

Box 1142, Brookline 02146
(617) 277-5430

In picturesque Lexington, close to Mitre, Raytheon, Itek, and scores of other companies. One cat and one dog in residence. Use of other rooms, laundry facilities; swimming available in a nearby neighborhood pool. Smoking okay.

Singles: 1 (SB) $47
Doubles: 2 (1 PB; 1 SB) $52
Type of Beds: 5 Twin
Full Breakfast
Credit Cards: No

Red Cape Bed & Breakfast

61 Williams Road, 02173
(617) 862-4913

Historic area with easy access to public transportation to downtown Boston. B&B in a quiet neighborhood; bedroom with private bath is decorated with handmade quilts. Hostess is a retired secretary, interested in quilting and other handwork. Resident friendly cat.

Hosts: Ruby & Dick Transue
Doubles: 1 (PB) $50-60
Type of Beds: 2 Twin; 1 Rollaway Cot
Full Breakfast
Credit Cards: No
Notes: 2, 5, 7, 8, 9, 10, 11, 12

LOWELL

B&B Registry #MA-01851SHE

Box 8174, St. Paul, MN, 55108
(612) 646-4238

Shaded by sugar maples and featuring an old-fashioned front porch, this old Victorian is the perfect place to spend a few days. The home is filled with select antique furnishings and Oriental rugs. Guests may lounge in front of the parlor fireplace or in the upstairs sitting room.

Doubles: 3 (SB) $45-50
Type of Beds: 2 Twin; 2 Double
Continental-plus Breakfast

NOTES: Credit cards accepted: A Master Card; B Visa; C American Express; D Discover Card; E Diners Club; F Other: 2 Personal checks accepted: 3 Lunch available: 4 Dinner available: 5 Open all year

Credit Cards: No
Notes: 5, 8, 12

Pineapple Hospitality MA 1024A

Box F-821, New Bedford, MA 02742-0821
(508) 990-1696

A circa 1893 restored Queen Anne Victorian with two guest rooms and shared bath. The house has antiques, stained glass, a friendly ghost, and a wraparound porch. A formal front parlor and back parlor filled with antiques, plus an upstairs sitting room with TV, are available to guests.

Doubles: 2 (SB) $45-55
Type of Beds: 2 Twin; 1 Double
Full Breakfast
Credit Cards: No
Notes: 2, 5, 8, 9, 10, 12

Sherman-Berry House

163 Datmouth Street, 01851-2425
(508) 459-4760

Charmingly restored Queen Anne Victorian in a national historic district with stained glass, a player piano, antiques, and a friendly ghost. Near Rt. 495 and Rt. 3, Lowell Historic Parks, the New England Quilt Museum, Lexington and Concord.

Hosts: Susan Scott-Strohmeyer & David Strohmeyer
Singles: 1 (SB) $45
Doubles: 2 (SB) $50
Type of Beds: 2 Twin; 2 Double
Full Breakfast
Credit Cards: No
Notes: 2, 5, 7, 8, 9, 10, 11, 12, 13

LYNN

B&B Registry #MA-01902CAR

Box 8174, St. Paul, MN, 55108
(612) 646-4238

Large 1870 Victorian one-half block from the beach, with biking, walking, and jogging paths and beautiful dunes with rose hips.

The house has four fireplaces and most of its original fixtures. Large porch for sunny mornings and afternoon tea.

Doubles: 3 (SB) $60-70
Type of Beds: 2 Twin; 2 Double
Continental-plus Breakfast
Credit Cards: A, B, C
Notes: 5, 8 (over 5), 11

LYNNFIELD

Willow Tree Farm

B&B Marblehead & North Shore
Box 172, Beverly, MA, 01915
(508) 921-1336

A very attractive, restored, second-floor barn apartment that is separate from the main house. Built circa 1802, the apartment is on a hobby farm with Nubian goats, rabbits, ducks, chickens, and geese.

Doubles: 1 (PB) $60-65
Type of Beds: 1 Twin; 1 Queen sofabed
Full Breakfast
Credit Cards: No
Notes: 2, 4, 5, 6, 8, 9, 10, 11, 12, 13 (XC), 14

MANCHESTER BY THE SEA

The Corner Inn

B&B Marblehead & North Shore
Box 172, Beverly, MA, 01915
(508) 921-1336

Situated about a mile from the town and harbor, this comfortable old inn has attractive rooms on the second and third floors, some with working fireplaces, and a sitting room with TV.

Singles: 1 (SB) $60
Doubles: 9 (6 PB; 3 SB) $60-85
Type of Beds: 5 Twin; 6 Double; 1 Queen; 1 Double sofabed
Continental Breakfast
Credit Cards: No
Notes: 2, 5, 7, 8, 9, 10, 11, 12, 14

6 Pets welcome: 7 Smoking allowed: 8 Children welcome: 9 Social drinking allowed: 10 Tennis available: 11 Swimming available: 12 Golf available: 13 Skiing available: 14 May be booked through travel agents

Federal Revival

B&B Marblehead & North Shore
Box 172, Beverly, MA, 01915
(508) 921-1336

An antique-furnished colonial with an
English garden just one block from the harbor. The host is an artist and designer involved in the theater as an actor and
director. Three cats in residence.

Doubles: 2 (SB) $55-65
Type of Beds: 2 Double
Full Breakfast
Credit Cards: No
Notes: 2, 5, 8, 9, 10, 11, 12, 14

The Victorian

B&B Marblehead & North Shore
Box 172, Beverly, MA, 01915
(508) 921-1336

A beautifully decorated Victorian just a
short walk from Singing Beach. The home
has been in the family for generations and
has been restored. Situated on large grounds
in an estate area, surrounded by colonial
estate homes and horse paddocks. One dog
in residence.

Doubles: 2 (1 PB; 1 SB) $75-85
Type of Beds: 2 Twin; 1 Double
Continental Breakfast
Credit Cards: No
Notes: 2, 5, 7 (restricted), 8 (under 6 months and over
4 years), 9, 10, 11, 12, 14

MARBLEHEAD

Greater Boston Hospitality #89

Box 1142, Brookline 02146
(617) 277-5430

One hundred yards from the ocean, this
95-year-old Victorian is owned by a charming couple from New Zealand, a black Lab,
and two cats. Two houses from one of the
best beaches in New England. Children over
2 welcome; smoking outdoors only.

Doubles: 3 (1 PB; 2 SB) $58-68
Type of Beds: 4 Twin; 1 Double
Full Breakfast
Credit Cards: No

Harborside House

23 Gregory Street, 01945
(617) 631-1032

An 1840 colonial in the historic district overlooking Marblehead Harbor, the nation's
yachting capital. Near quaint shops, historic
sites, beach. Enjoy our breakfast porch,
third-story sun deck, antique dining room,
resident cat. Hostess is a professional
dressmaker and competitive swimmer.

Host: Susan Blake
Doubles: 2 (SB) $50-65
Type of Beds: 2 Twin; 1 Double
Continental Breakfast
Credit Cards: No
Notes: 2, 5, 8 (over 10), 10, 11

Host Homes of Boston #17

Box 117, Waban Branch, Boston, 02168
(617) 244-1308

This airy Victorian on a quiet road just up
from the beach has spacious rooms and porches, nooks and crannies, lawn, garden.
Private guest entrances off the shared deck.
Resident cat and dog.

Doubles: 3 (1 PB; 2 SB) $54-70
Type of Beds: 2 Twin; 2 Double
Continental Breakfast
Minimum stay: 2
Credit Cards: A, B, C
Notes: 2, 5, 10, 11, 12

Marblehead Cape

B&B Marblehead & North Shore
Box 172, Beverly, MA, 01915
(508) 921-1336

This is an attractive Cape Cod home in a
pretty suburban area close to the Salem line.
Guest rooms are separate from the host's
quarters. TV in living room downstairs. You

NOTES: Credit cards accepted: A Master Card; B Visa; C American Express; D Discover Card; E Diners
Club; F Other: 2 Personal checks accepted: 3 Lunch available: 4 Dinner available: 5 Open all year

may participate in the hostess's Yoga classes if you wish to.

Doubles: 2 (SB) $55-70
Type of Beds: 3 Twin; 1 Double
Continental Breakfast
Credit Cards: No
Notes: 2, 5, 8 (babies and children over 6), 9, 10, 11, 12, 14

Oceanview Tudor

B&B Marblehead & North Shore
Box 172, Beverly, MA, 01915
(508) 921-1336

Oceanfront Tudor on a cliff overlooking the Atlantic Ocean, a short walk from a sandy beach. In the Clifton area three miles south of Old Town. Guest living room and dining area facing the ocean; BYOB bar.

Doubles: 5 (PB) $105-145
Type of Beds: 1 Double; 1 Queen; 3 King
Continental Breakfast
Credit Cards: A, B, C
Notes: 2, 5, 7, 8 (over 6), 9, 10, 11, 12, 14

Old Town Victorian

B&B Marblehead & North Shore
Box 172, Beverly, MA, 01915
(508) 921-1336

An attractive Victorian in historic Old Town, a quaint, well-manicured area one block from the harbor, above the Boston Yacht Club. One dog in residence.

Doubles: 4 (PB) $85
Type of Beds: 2 Twin; 1 Double; 2 Queen
Continental Breakfast
Credit Cards: No
Notes: 2, 5, 8, 9, 10, 11, 12, 14

1752 House

B&B Marblehead & North Shore
Box 172, Beverly, MA, 01915
(508) 921-1336

Located in historic Old Town, near two beaches and cooled by sea breezes all summer. Your hostess is chairman of the Marblehead historical commission. One dog and one cat in residence.

Doubles: 1 (PB) $60-65
Type of Beds: 2 Twin; 1 Queen
Continental Breakfast
Credit Cards: No
Notes: 2, 5, 8, 9, 10, 11, 12, 14

Ten Mugford Street

10 Mugford Street, 01945
(617) 639-0343; 631-5642

Located in the historic district, we offer five two-room suites with private baths, plus four double rooms with shared baths. Two units have kitchens, and three have private living rooms with king size pull-out couches. Two antique buildings, newly renovated, allow for comfort and charm.

Hosts: Liz & Mike Mentuck
Doubles: 4 (SB) $65-75
Suites: 5 (PB) $75-95
Type of Beds: 6 Twin; 3 Double; 4 Queen; 1 King; 2 Sofabeds
Continental Breakfast
Credit Cards: A, B
Notes: 2, 5, 7, 8, 9, 10, 11, 12

MARSHFIELD

Be Our Guest B&B, Ltd. #2

Box 1333, Plymouth, 02360
(617) 837-9867

Antique Federal colonial over 200 years old, set on a scenic road less than one mile from the public beach. White wicker room on the first floor with a private bath. On the second floor, two rooms share a bath. One room has mahogany twin sleigh beds, while the other has a fireplace and antique brass bed.

Doubles: 3 (1 PB; 2 SB) $38-50
Type of Beds: 2 Twin; 1 Double; 1 Queen
Full Breakfast
Credit Cards: A, B, C
Notes: 5, 8, 9, 10, 11, 12, 14

6 Pets welcome: 7 Smoking allowed: 8 Children welcome: 9 Social drinking allowed: 10 Tennis available: 11 Swimming available: 12 Golf available: 13 Skiing available: 14 May be booked through travel agents

MEDFORD

Bed & Breakfast Associates #IN220

Box 166, Babson Park, 02157
(617) 449-5302

This large home has three gracious porches and irresistible appeal. Located near Tufts University, you're only fifteen minutes from Boston via the commuter train at the corner. On-street free parking. Dog in residence.

Singles: 1 (SB) $50
Doubles: 2 (SB) $55-65
Type of Beds: 1 Twin; 2 Double
Continental Breakfast
Minimum stay: 3
Credit Cards: A, B, C
Notes: 5, 6 (dog), 7, 8, 10, 11, 12

MONTAGUE

Berkshire PV34

Berkshire B&B Homes
Box 211, Williamsburg, MA, 01096
(413) 268-7244

A 1851 Victorian on the green, with antique and country furnishings. Working fireplace in parlor, dining room, and kitchen. Minutes to the five-college area, Northfield Mountain, historic Deerfield, Mohawk Trail, cross-country skiing, and hiking.

Doubles: 2 (SB) $60
Type of Beds: 2 Twin; 1 Double
Continental Breakfast
Credit Cards: No
Notes: 2, 3, 5, 7, 10, 11, 12, 13

MONTEREY-OTIS

Berkshire SC6

Berkshire B&B Homes
Box 211, Williamsburg, MA, 01096
(413) 268-7244

A 100-year-old country farmhouse with a wood-burning stove in the breakfast room, parlor with TV, games, and books. Guest rooms are on the second floor with semi-private baths. Third floor accommodates four guests with a separate sitting area and private bath. Wraparound screened-in porch, where breakfast is served in warm weather.

Doubles: 4 (SB) $65-70
Type of Beds: 6 Twin; 1 Queen; 3 King
Full Breakfast
Credit Cards: No
Notes: 2, 5, 8, 10, 11, 12, 13

NANTUCKET

B&B Registry #MA-02564WAD

Box 8174, St. Paul, MN, 55108
(612) 646-4238

Summer retreat with private beach on the east side of Nantucket Island. Siasconset, a small seventeenth-century village, is within walking distance.

Doubles: 1 (SB) $50-77
Type of Beds: 1 Double
Continental Breakfast
Minimum stay: 3
Credit Cards: No
Closed Oct. - April
Notes: 7, 8, 11, 12

Carlisle House Inn

26 N. Water Street, 02554
(508) 228-0720

Built in 1765, The Carlisle House has been a quality inn for more than 100 years. Located just off the center of town, the inn has been carefully restored. Hand-stenciled wallpapers, inlaid pine paneling, wide board floors, rich Oriental carpets.

Hosts: Peter Conway & Sue Arnold
Singles: 3 (SB) $35
Doubles: 11 (8 PB; 4 SB) $125
Type of Beds: 4 Twin; 2 Double; 8 Queen
Continental Breakfast
Minimum stay 6/15-10/15: 3
Credit Cards: C
Notes: 2, 5, 7, 8 (over 10), 9, 14

NOTES: Credit cards accepted: A Master Card; B Visa; C American Express; D Discover Card; E Diners Club; F Other: 2 Personal checks accepted: 3 Lunch available: 4 Dinner available: 5 Open all year

The Century House

Enjoy bed and breakfast accommodations in a 1771 sea captain's home. Overlooking scenic Nantucket town and harbor, a short walk from the many fine restaurants, art galleries, and shops on Main Street. Beautiful English country decor! See us in *Country Homes Magazine*, August 1988.

Hosts: Mary & Perry Patton
Singles: 1 (PB) $45
Doubles: 11 (PB) $50-140
Type of Beds: 2 Twin; 5 Double; 1 Queen; 4 King
Continental Breakfast
Credit Cards: A,B
Notes: 2, 5, 7, 8 (over 7), 9, 10, 11, 12, 14

The Century House

10 Cliff Road, 02554
(508) 228-0530

The Century House is located in the residential section of the Old Historic District on prestigious Cliff Road, a short walk from Jetties Beach, Steamboat Wharf, and Main Street. Most of our rooms have private baths, and six have old fireplaces. This gracious home was constructed in 1833 in the Late Federal style, and features a handsome veranda along its frontage. $50-120.

The Four Chimneys

38 Orange Street, 02554
(508) 228-1912

Captain's mansion, with canopy beds, fireplace in the drawing room, harbor views, fine antiques, porches. In the historic district. Continental breakfast is served in your room; cocktail snack at 5:00 P.M.

Host: Betty York
Doubles: 10 (PB) $98-155
Type of Beds: 5 Double; 5 Queen
Continental Breakfast
Minimum stay weekends & holidays: 3
Credit Cards: A, B, C
Closed early Dec. - late April
Notes: 2, 7, 9, 10, 11, 12

Grieder Guest House

43 Orange Street, 02554
(508) 228-1399

House built in the early 1700s on the "street of whaling captains." Rooms with four-poster beds, antiques, exposed beams made from ships' knees. Only several minutes' walk from Main Street. Parking permits and refrigerators provided. Large off-street yard.

Hosts: Ruth & Bill Grieder
Doubles: 2 (SB) $55-80
Types of Beds: 4 Twin
Continental Breakfast
Minimum stay weekends & holidays: 2

The Cliff Lodge

The Cliff Lodge

9 Cliff Road, 02554
(508) 228-9480

6 Pets welcome: 7 Smoking allowed: 8 Children welcome: 9 Social drinking allowed: 10 Tennis available: 11 Swimming available: 12 Golf available: 13 Skiing available: 14 May be booked through travel agents

Credit Cards: No
Closed Oct. 15-May 15
Notes: 2, 7, 8 (over 3), 9, 10, 11, 12

House of Seven Gables

32 Cliff Road, 02554
(508) 228-4706

Located in the old historic district of Nantucket. A continental breakfast is served to your room. Most rooms in this 100-year-old Victorian have a view of Nantucket Sound.

Hosts: Sue & Ed Walton
Doubles: 10 (8 PB; 2 SB) $80-125
Continental Breakfast
Credit Cards: A, B, C
Notes: 2, 5, 7, 8 (over 16), 9, 10, 11, 12

The Four Chimneys

La Petite Maison

132 Main Street, 02554
(508) 228-9242

An owner-managed European inn quietly located ten minutes from the center of town. Breakfast on the sun porch with homemade baked goods, stimulating conversation, and new friends. Relax in your yard and experience this year's vegetable garden.

Host: Holli Martin
Singles: 3 (SB) $39-60

Doubles: 9 (SB) $55-108
Suite: 1 (PB) $185
Type of Beds: 10 Twin; 6 Double; 1 Queen
Continental Breakfast
Credit Cards: No
Closed Nov. 1 - April 30
Notes: 6, 7, 8 (over 10), 9, 10, 11

Lee's B&B

B&B Cape Cod, Box 341, W. Hyannisport, 02672
(508) 775-2772

Built in 1830, this neoclassic Greek Revival house is located five blocks from the ferry. Facing the narrow cobblestone street is a large entry foyer with a formal parlor, music room, TV room. No car is necessary.

Doubles: 2 (PB) $90
Type of Beds: 2 Twin; 1 King
Continental Breakfast
Credit Cards: No
Notes: 2, 7, 8 (3 and over), 9, 10, 11, 12, 14

Seven Sea Street Inn

7 Sea Street, 02554
(508) 228-3577

Seven Sea Street is a red oak, post-and-beam country inn newly constructed with an authentic Nantucket ambience. All guest rooms come with a queen canopy bed, cable TV, small refrigerator, and private bath. Additional amenities include a full-size indoor Jacuzzi whirlpool and widow's walk deck with view of Nantucket Harbor. Ideally located in the historic district.

Hosts: Matthew & Mary Parker
Doubles: 8 (PB) $65-155
Type of Beds: 8 Queen
Continental Breakfast
Minimum stay weekends: 2; holidays: 3
Credit Cards: A, B, C
Notes: 2, 4, 5, 8 (over 8), 9, 10, 11, 12

76 Main Street

76 Main Street, 02554
(508) 228-2533

All the quiet and subtle beauty of Nantucket is yours to explore while you make yourself

---

NOTES: Credit cards accepted: A Master Card; B Visa; C American Express; D Discover Card; E Diners Club; F Other: 2 Personal checks accepted: 3 Lunch available: 4 Dinner available: 5 Open all year

comfortable in our 1883 Victorian home in the historic district, on elm-shaded and cobblestoned Main Street. We are dedicated to your enjoyment of the island and look forward to accommodating you.

Hosts: Mitch Blake & Shirley Peters
Doubles: 18 (PB) $100-130
Continental Breakfast
Credit Cards: A, B, C
Notes: 2, 5, 8 (in annex), 9, 10, 11, 12, 14

NEEDHAM

Greater Boston Hospitality #100

Box 1142, Brookline 021465
(617) 277-5430

This immaculately maintained suburban Williamsburg Cape is minutes away from Wellesley or Babson colleges, close to I-95 by car and public transportation. Children welcome.

Doubles: 1 (PB) $50-55
Type of Beds: 2 Twin or 1 King
Continental Breakfast
Credit Cards: No

Greater Boston Hospitality #102

Box 1141, Brookline 02146
(617) 277-5430

Close to Dedham, West Roxbury, and Wellesley, this is a beautiful Williamsburg Cape with a gracious host and hostess.

Doubles: 2 (SB) $55
Type of Beds: 2 Twin; 1 Double
Continental-plus Breakfast
Credit Cards: No

Host Homes of Boston #18

Box 117, Waban Branch, Boston, 02168
(617) 244-1308

Typical New England colonial cape with a spacious interior and antiques. First-floor guest parlor, parking. One-half mile to train; Boston twelve miles. Near Wellesley College.

Doubles: 2 (PB) $54
Type of Beds: 2 Twin; 1 Double
Continental-plus Breakfast
Minimum stay: 2
Credit Cards: A, B, C
Notes: 2, 5, 7 (limited)

NEWBURY

The Noyes House

B&B Marblehead & North Shore
Box 172, Beverly, MA, 01915
(508) 921-1336

One mile from downtown Newburyport, in a pretty, rural setting, this authentic antique 1646 colonial is owned by a couple whose interests include skiing, travel, and gardening. One dog and one cat in residence. TV room and screened porch for relaxing.

Doubles: 1 (PB) $42-56
Type of Beds: 1 Twin; 1 Double
Continental Breakfast
Credit Cards: No
Notes: 2, 5, 8, 9, 10, 11, 12, 13 (XC), 14

NEWBURYPORT

The Homestead

B&B Marblehead & North Shore
Box 172, Beverly, MA, 01915
(508) 921-1336

An authentic 1813 colonial that has been in the family since the early 1900s. The hostess is retired and prefers couples over forty or women guests. Convenient to bus service for Boston. Guests may enjoy the piano in the living room or join the hostess in watching TV. Newburyport was settled in 1640 as a ship-building town, and has a beautiful harbor filled with sailboats. Five minutes from Plum Island Wildlife Reserve; whale-watch cruises depart from the town.

6 Pets welcome: 7 Smoking allowed: 8 Children welcome: 9 Social drinking allowed: 10 Tennis available: 11 Swimming available: 12 Golf available: 13 Skiing available: 14 May be booked through travel agents

Singles: 1 (SB) $36
Doubles: 3 (SB) $54-60
Type of Beds: 3 Twin; 2 Double
Continental Breakfast
Credit Cards: No
Notes: 2, 5, 8 (over 13), 9, 10, 11, 12, 12 (XC), 14

The Homestead

The Windsor House in Newburyport

38 Federal Street, 01950
(508) 462-3778

This eighteenth-century Federal mansion offers a rare blend of Yankee hospitality and the English bed and breakfast tradition. Spacious rooms recall the spirit of the English country house. Located in an historic seaport near a wildlife refuge, whale watching, and antiques.

Host: Judith Crumb
Doubles: 6 (3 PB; 3 SB) $85-115
Type of Beds: 3 Twin; 3 Double; 1 Queen; 1 King
Full Breakfast
Minimum stay weekends & holidays: 2
Credit Cards: A, B
Notes: 2, 5, 8, 11, 12, 14 (for 3 or more days)

NEWTON

Greater Boston Hospitality #107

Box 1142, Brookline 02146
(617) 277-5430

A large, beautifully furnished late Victorian that is handicapped accessible and close to public transportation.

Doubles: 1 (PB) $60-65
Type of Beds: 1 Double; 1 Daybed
Full Breakfast
Credit Cards: No

Greater Boston Hospitality #108

Box 1142, Brookline 02146
(617) 277-5430

A restful, well-maintained, custom-built home in the suburban town of Newton. Breakfast is served in the dining room or on a glassed-in porch overlooking the backyard in summer.

Doubles: 1 (PB) $55-63
Type of Beds: 1 Double
Full Breakfast
Credit Cards: No

Greater Boston Hospitality #109

Box 1142, Brookline 02146
(617) 277-54302

Spacious 1898 Queen Anne Victorian with two cats in residence. Owned by an English marketing manager. Fireplace in library and dining rooms.

Singles: 1 (SB) $55
Doubles: 2 (1 PB; 1 SB) $55-93
Type of Beds: 1 Twin; 3 Double
Continental Breakfast
Credit Cards: No

Host Homes of Boston #19

Box 117, Waban Branch, Boston, 02168
(617) 244-1308

Large, authentic Victorian home (1898) with air-conditioning, parking. Walk to restaurants, express bus to downtown. Quick

NOTES: Credit cards accepted: A Master Card; B Visa; C American Express; D Discover Card; E Diners Club; F Other: 2 Personal checks accepted: 3 Lunch available: 4 Dinner available: 5 Open all year

drive to the airport, Back Bay, or Cambridge.

Doubles: 2 (1 PB; 1 SB) $56
Type of Beds: 2 Twin; 1 Double
Continental Breakfast
Minimum stay: 2
Credit Cards: A, B, C
Notes: 2, 5

Host Homes of Boston #20

Box 117, Waban Branch, Boston, 02168
(617) 244-1308

In a sylvan setting along the Charles River, this colonial is replete with Early American antiques. Color TV, air-conditioning, view of river and woods. Subway five blocks away. Near Rts. 9 and I-95.

Host Homes of Boston #21

Box 117, Waban Branch, Boston, 02168
(617) 244-1308

Large colonial near Boston College is filled with the host's pottery and Mexican art collection. Host smokes. Five minute walk to Boston College or subway for Boston University, Back Bay, and downtown.

Singles: 1 (SB) $44
Doubles: 1 (SB) $54
Type of Beds: 2 Twin; 1 Double
Continental Breakfast
Minimum stay: 2
Credit Cards: A, B, C
Notes: 2, 5, 7, 9, 10

Host Homes of Boston #22

Box 117, Waban Branch, Boston, 02168
(617) 244-1308

This rambling 100-year-old home was once a farmhouse. Your hosts and four children offer a casual, friendly atmosphere where children are welcome. Resident cat. Subway one-half mile away .

Doubles: 3 (1 PB; 2 SB) $49-60
Type of Beds: 2 Twin; 1 Queen; 1 King
Continental Breakfast

Minimum stay: 2
Credit Cards: A, B, C
Notes: 2, 5, 8

Host Homes of Boston #23

Box 117, Waban Branch, Boston, 02168
(617) 244-1308

Traditional brick colonial has hill-top view, tall trees, a screened porch, and garden. TV. Host smokes. Subway is three blocks away; twenty minute ride to Boston; twelve minutes by car.

Doubles: 2 (SB) $45-50
Type of Beds: 2 Double
Continental Breakfast
Minimum stay: 2
Credit Cards: A, B, C
Notes: 2, 5, 7, 9, 12

NEWTON CENTRE

Host Homes of Boston #24

Box 117, Waban Branch, Boston, 02168
(617) 244-1308

The hosts' solar gourmet kitchen and deck attract guests for breakfast and talk. This older colonial welcomes children. Resident cat. In a quiet location two blocks from Boston College's Newton campus, one mile to the Mass. Pike or subway. Twelve-minute drive to Hynes Convention Center in the Back Bay.

Doubles: 1 (PB) $57
Type of Beds: 1 Double
Continental Breakfast
Minimum stay: 2
Credit Cards: A, B, C
Notes: 2, 5, 7, 8, 9, 10, 11, 12

Host Homes of Boston #25

Box 117, Waban Branch, Boston, 02168
(617) 244-1308

Spacious older Victorian just four blocks from the village and subway. Music room with grand piano; resident dog and two cats. Twenty minute subway ride to Boston.

6 Pets welcome: 7 Smoking allowed: 8 Children welcome: 9 Social drinking allowed: 10 Tennis available: 11 Swimming available: 12 Golf available: 13 Skiing available: 14 May be booked through travel agents

Doubles: 1 (PB) $55
Type of Beds: 2 Twin
Continental Breakfast
Minimum stay: 2
Credit Cards: A, B, C
Notes: 2, 59

Host Homes of Boston #26

Box 117, Waban Branch, Boston, 02168
(617) 244-1308

Stylish and elegant, this airy lakeside home
has antiques, high ceilings, and wood detail.
Two cats in residence. Subway four blocks;
Boston eight miles.

Doubles: 2 (PB) $61
Type of Beds: 2 Twin; 1 Double
Continental Breakfast
Minimum stay: 2
Credit Cards: A, B, C
Notes: 2, 5, 9, 11

Host Homes of Boston #27

Box 117, Waban Branch, Boston, 02168
(617) 244-1308

A contemporary home located on a quiet
road, where you can enjoy a game of billiards
in the family room. TV, air-conditioning,
parking. Resident cat. Subway and Newton
Centre are one mile away.

Doubles: 1 (PB) $54
Type of Beds: 1 Double
Continental Breakfast
Minimum stay: 2
Credit Cards: A, B, C
Notes: 2, 57, 9, 10

Host Homes of Boston #28

Box 117, Waban Branch, Boston, 02168
(617) 244-1308

Your hosts' collection of artifacts from
around the world adds spice to this century-
old home. Breakfast served where you can
relax by the fire, sip sherry, watch TV. Three

blocks to the subway, shops, and restaurants.

Doubles: 2 (SB) $54
Type of Beds: 2 Twin; 1 Double
Continental Breakfast
Minimum stay: 2
Credit Cards: A, B, C
Notes: 2, 5, 9, 10, 11

NEWTON HIGHLAND

Host Homes of Boston #29

Box 117, Waban Branch, Boston, 02168
(617) 244-1308

Stately Victorian (1882) in a prime location
with antiques, trees, and gardens. Guest parlor with TV; resident cat. Two blocks to the
lake, village, and subway; twenty-minute
subway ride to downtown Boston.

Doubles: 3 (SB) $56
Type of Beds: 2 Twin; 1 Double; 1 Queen
Continental Breakfast
Minimum stays: 2
Credit Cards: A, B, C
Notes: 2, 5, 8 (10 and over)

NORTH ADAMS

Berkshire NC5

Berkshire B&B Homes
Box 211, Williamsburg, MA, 01096
(413) 268-7244

An 1820 Georgian Victorian with an-tique
and country furnishings. Common room
with TV, piano, stereo, and wood-burning
stove. Minutes to Williams College, Williamstown Summer Playhouse, Sterling
Clarke Museum. Charming and gracious.

Doubles: 4 (1 PB; 2 SB) $70-120
Type of Beds: 2 Twin; 1 Double; 2 Queen
Full on weekends, continental on weekdays
Credit Cards: No
Notes: 2, 8, 10, 11, 12

NOTES: Credit cards accepted: A Master Card; B Visa; C American Express; D Discover Card; E Diners
Club; F Other: 2 Personal checks accepted: 3 Lunch available: 4 Dinner available: 5 Open all year

NORTH EASTHAM

Penny House
Box 238, Rt. 6, 02651
(508) 255-6632

Captain Isaiah Horton built The Penny House in 1751. Traditional wide-planked pine floors grace each room of the main house, and 200-year-old beams buttress the ceiling of the public room, where breakfast is served. Only five minutes from the majestic dunes and unspoiled Atlantic beaches of the National Seashore Park and five minutes to the warm waters of Cape Cod Bay. Near the bird sanctuary, miles of bicycle paths, nature trails, and sport fishing.

Hosts: Bill & Margaret Keith
Doubles: 11 (6 PB; 5 SB) $55-90
Type of Beds: 2 Twin; 7 Double; 2 Queen; 1 King
Full Breakfast
Credit Cards: A, B, C
Notes: 2, 5, 7 (restricted), 8 (over 12), 9, 10, 11, 12, 14

NORTH EGREMONT

Bread & Roses
Star Rt. 65, Box 50, Great Barrington, 41345
(413) 528-1099

Nestled on 8 acres with its own private pond, this 180-year-old colonial has all the right updates while still retaining its original wide plank floors and antique flavor. Only 1.5 miles from the historic village of South Egremont. Electric stairlift to second-floor guest rooms; bathrobes, books, quiet country setting, smoke-free environment.

Host: Julie Lowell
Doubles: 5 (PB) $85
Full Breakfast
Credit Cards: No

NORTH FALMOUTH

Shubal Nye B&B
B&B Cape Cod, Box 341, W. Hyannisport, 02672
(508) 775-2772

This 1806 restored farmhouse captures the flavor of a bygone era. Two beautiful beaches are within a mile of this quiet, comfortable, air-conditioned home. Bike rentals are available. Full gourmet meals available at additional charge.

Doubles: 1 (PB) $70-80
Type of Beds: 1 Double
Full Breakfast
Credit Cards: No
Notes: 4, 5, 11, 12, 14

Wingate Crossing B&B
B&B Cape Cod, Box 341, W. Hyannisport, 02672
(508) 775-2772

Built in 1793, this Cape Cod colonial was expanded through the years and restored to its original condition. Early American Primitive decor. This antique-collector's home was featured in *Cape Cod Life* magazine in 1986-87.

Doubles: 2 (PB) $85
Type of Beds: 2 Double
Full Breakfast
Credit Cards: No
Notes: 5, 7, 9, 10, 11, 12, 14

NORTHFIELD

Berkshire PV25
Berkshire B&B Homes
Box 211, Williamsburg, MA, 01096
(413) 268-7244

An 1824 Federal home with antiques and country pieces. Close to Northfield Mountain for cross-country skiing and hiking, Mt. Hermon School, the five-college area, and Deerfield.

Singles: 2 (SB) $40
Doubles: 2 (SB) $50-70
Type of Beds: 3 Twin; 2 Double
Full Breakfast
Credit Cards: No
Notes: 2, 5, 8, 10, 11, 12, 13

6 Pets welcome: 7 Smoking allowed: 8 Children welcome: 9 Social drinking allowed: 10 Tennis available: 11 Swimming available: 12 Golf available: 13 Skiing available: 14 May be booked through travel agents

Centennial House Bed & Breakfast

94 Main Street, 01360
(413) 498-5921

In its eight years as a bed and breakfast, this lovely old colonial, built in 1811, has hosted guests from throughout the country and the world. Located in one of New England's lovely villages and near the fine independent school, Northfield Mount Hermon, Centennial House looks forward to welcoming you.

Host: Marguerite Linsert Lentz
Doubles: 5 (2 PB; 3 SB) $45-65
Type of Beds: 1 Twin; 2 Double; 2 Queen
Continental Breakfast
Credit Cards: A, B
Notes: 2, 5, 10, 11, 12, 13

NORWELL

Pineapple Hospitality MA 1062

Box F-821, New Bedford, MA 02742-0821
(508) 990-1696

This single-family home is a New England colonial built in 1810 with some additions. Wide floorboards, three working fireplaces, original ceiling beams. Two lovable dogs share this home. Norwell offers several delightful antique shops and plenty of foliage.

Doubles: 3 (SB) $60
Full Breakfast
Credit Cards: No
Notes: 2, 5, 8, 9, 10, 11, 12

OAK BLUFFS, MARTHA'S VINEYARD

Arend's Samoset on the Sound

Box 847, 02557
(508) 693-5148

Charming Victorian beach house, built in 1873, on the waterfront. Five minutes' walk to the ferries, shops, restaurants, parks, tennis, bike rentals, and so forth. The house offers a living room, piano nook, dining room, sun porch, open porch, widow's walk, and an unobstructed view of the sunrise over Martha's Vineyard Sound.

Hosts: Valgerd & Stanley Arend
Doubles: 8 (2 PB; 6 S3B) $55-90
Type of Beds: 7 Double; 1 Queen
Continental Breakfast
Credit Cards: A, B
Closed Columbus Day - Memorial Day
Notes: 2 (deposit), 7, 8, 9, 10, 11, 12, 14

The Inn at Dockside

Box 1206, 02557
(508) 693-1066

Lovely Victorian rooms with private baths, queen beds, and cable TV. Located on the harbor in historic Oak Bluffs, steps away from the beach, restaurants, shops, and entertainment. Complimentary bicycles, gas grills, and picnic tables. Friendly, warm atmosphere with personalized service.

Host: Barbara Hanover
Doubles: 19 (PB) $50-125
Type of Beds: 19 Queen
Continental Breakfast in season
Credit Cards: A, B, C
Closed Oct. 15 - May 12
Notes: 2, 7, 8, 9, 10, 11, 12, 14

King's B&B

B&B Cape Cod, Box 341, W. Hyannisport, 02672
(508) 775-2772

Built in the 1800s as a summer cottage, this home is now a small B&B inn. The house overlooks a park, with the ocean and beach beyond. The ferry is only five blocks away; close to village shops, restaurants, and stores.

Doubles: 5 (SB) $65-80
Type of Beds: 2 Twin; 2 Double; 1 King
Continental Breakfast

NOTES: Credit cards accepted: A Master Card; B Visa; C American Express; D Discover Card; E Diners Club; F Other: 2 Personal checks accepted: 3 Lunch available: 4 Dinner available: 5 Open all year

Credit Cards: No
Notes: 2, 7, 8 (6 and over), 9, 10, 11, 12, 14

Narragansett House

Box 2478, 02557
(508) 693-3627

Surrounded by a white picket fence and festooned with flowers of the season, the Narragansett House offers an ideal location. Miles of beaches, restaurants, churches, retail shops, movie theaters, and activities such as fishing, boating, and tennis are close by.

Hosts: Jane & Paul Lofgren
Doubles: 12 (PB) $45-65
Type of Beds: 5 Twin; 8 Double; 3 Queen
Continental Breakfast
Credit Cards: A, B
Closed Nov. 1 - April 14
Notes: 2, 8 (over 12), 9, 10, 11, 14

The Nashua House

Box 803, 02557
(508) 693-0043

A holiday on Martha's Vineyard on a budget. Clean old rooms, continental breakfast in July and August, shared baths, steps to the beach, ferries, harbor, shuttle buses, bike rentals, restaurants, movies, the historic gingerbread campgrounds, and antique carousel by the sea.

Hosts: Harry & Son
Singles: 1 (SB) $25-55
Doubles: 14 (SB) $35-65
Type of Beds: 11 Twin; 9 Double
Continental Breakfast served July & Aug only
Minimum stay weekends: 2; holidays: 3
Credit Cards: A, B, C
Closed Oct.-April
Notes: 8 (over 10), 10, 11, 12

The Oak House

Seaview Avenue, Box 299, 02557
(508) 693-4187

Enjoy a romantic seaside Victorian holiday. Elegant oak interior in restored 1876 summer home of Governor Claflin. Furnished with antiques; most rooms have ocean view. Wide porches and stained glass sun porch. Daily maid service; afternoon tea; lovely beach; walk to ferry and downtown.

Host: Betsi Convery-Luce
Doubles: 10 (PB) $85-125
Two-room Suite: (PB) $175
Type of Beds: 7 Queen; 2 King
Continental Breakfast
Minimum stay weekdays & weekends: 2; holidays: 3
Credit Cards: A, B
Closed Oct. 16-May 15
Notes: 2, 7, 8 (10 and over), 9, 11

ORLEANS

Arey's Pond Relais

Orleans B&B Assoc., Box 1312, 02653
(508) 255-3824

A very special house filled with warmth, delightful details, and unusual collections. Private patio and entrance, small refrigerator, gourmet breakfast on an expansive deck overlooking Arey's Pond, a saltwater inlet leading to Little Pleasant Bay. Full breakfast. One double, private bath, $70.

Bird Nest

Orleans B&B Assoc., Box 1312, 02653
(508) 255-3824

Private entrance, large, airy bedroom/sitting room, color TV. Breakfast is served in the skylighted garden room overlooking colorful flower beds. Minutes away from ocean, bay, and shopping. Hosts interested in quilting, woodworking, and antiques. Resident black Labrador. Full breakfast. One double, $65.

Capt. Doane House

Orleans B&B Assoc., Box 1312, 02653
(508) 255-3824

The captain built this house in 1810 in the old Rock Harbor area of town, on a quiet lane, and the large rooms speak of an era gone by. Lovely and clean, with nice old furnishings. Large guest living room with TV and screened porch; warm Irish hospitality. On bike trail; walk to historic Rock Harbor. One single: $30. Two doubles: $50.

Coveside

Orleans B&B Assoc., Box 1312, 02653
(508) 255-3824

Right on the salt water, this contemporary saltbox is situated on beautiful Town Cove. Separate entrance, refrigerator, private waterfront patio. Enjoy cove sights: boating, clamming, bird activity, great sunsets. Spectacular view! Two doubles, $70.

The Farmhouse

163 Beach Road, 02653
(508) 569-0402

The Farmhouse at Nauset Beach is a nineteenth-century farmhouse that has been tastefully restored and furnished. Guests enjoy a blend of country life in a seashore setting. Come and enjoy.

Hosts: The Standishes
Doubles: 8 (4 PB; 4 SB) $25-90
Continental Breakfast
Credit Cards: A, B
Notes: 2, 5, 8 (6 and over), 9, 11, 12, 14

Gray Gables

Orleans B&B Assoc., Box 1312, 02653
(508) 255-3824

Fine old house set well back from the road in a very desirable neighborhood with a private guest suite. Full breakfast served on Limoges china in your room at 8:30 or continental if you should care to sleep late. Private entrance leads to sheltered yard shaded by an enormous old elm. Air-conditioning, refrigerator, and TV. One double, $60.

Helen's B&B

B&B Cape Cod, Box 341, W. Hyannisport, 02672
(508) 775-2772

Not far from Nauset Beach, this house is both private and beautiful. The village is about one mile away. A delightful and relaxing home.

Doubles: 2 (PB) $55
Type of Beds: 4 Twin
Continental Breakfast
Credit Cards: No
Notes: 2, 5, 8, 9, 10, 11, 12, 14

High Tide (Lan Mara)

Orleans B&B Assoc., Box 1312, 02653
(508) 255-3824

Guest wing in a traditional Cape situated near historic Rock Harbor on 7 acres of beautiful marsh and upland. Living room with fireplace. Half mile to bike trail and .8 mile to Bay beach. Delicious breakfasts, warm hospitality. One double, private bath, $50.

Le Louette (The Gull)

Orleans B&B Assoc., Box 1312, 02653
(508) 255-3824

This beautiful house offers exceptional hospitality and comfort in any season. Its boat house and beach are directly across the road that skirts Pleasant Bay, offering guests a deck on the water for watching the sailboats and wind surfers. Fine saltwater swimming. Two doubles, private bath, $90.

Lockwood House

Orleans B&B Assoc., Box 1312, 02653
(508) 255-3824

NOTES: Credit cards accepted: A Master Card; B Visa; C American Express; D Discover Card; E Diners Club; F Other: 2 Personal checks accepted: 3 Lunch available: 4 Dinner available: 5 Open all year

Large ancestral home lovingly maintained. Private dock on Pleasant Bay; private porch, private entrance. Hosts have two well-behaved dogs and a cat. Near famous Captains Course for golf. One double, $70.

Lodestone
Orleans B&B Assoc., Box 1312, 02653
(508) 255-3824

This traditional Cape Cod home in a quiet neighborhood has a private backyard, large, screened porch, and songbirds galore. Two doubles, shared bath, $55.

Long View
Orleans B&B Assoc., Box 1312, 02653
(508) 255-3824

High above the Town Cove, with sweeping vistas as far as the Atlantic, this house offers a private deck, wonderful walking, or biking. Two doubles. One private bath, one shared. $70.

Maison du Mer
Orleans B&B Assoc., Box 1312, 02653
(508) 255-3824

If you have dreamed of having your own secluded beach, this delightful house is for you. The beach is just across the lane. Private entrance, living room with water view, sunny dining area overlooking the seaside garden, deck. Fine dining, shopping, and bike trail nearby. One double, private bath, $70.

McKenzie B&B
B&B Cape Cod, Box 341, W. Hyannisport, 02672
(508) 775-2772

This gracious Cape home is built on a harbor in a quiet inlet. Deck, sunfish, water views. For a small additional charge, harbor cruises in the host's boat are available.

Doubles: 3 (PB) $55-75
Type of Beds: 1 Twin; 2 Double
Continental Breakfast
Credit Cards: No
Closed Oct.-May
Notes: 8 (8 and over), 9, 10, 11, 12, 14

Mayflower House
B&B Cape Cod, Box 341, W. Hyannisport, 02672
(508) 775-2772

Handsome bow house on a residential dead-end road. Two large bedrooms, each with private bath and color TV. Breakfast is served in an attractive first-floor parlor that has nice wing chairs for reading. Animal lovers especially welcome, as hosts have a friendly Doberman in their private quarters. Two doubles, private bath, $60.

Morningside
Orleans B&B Assoc., Box 1312, 02653
(508) 255-3824

Waterfront suite with private entrance in a gracious home overlooking Nauset Harbor and the Atlantic. Private beach. Huge room with sitting area faces the ocean. One double, full breakfast, $90.

The Red Geranium
Orleans B&B Assoc., Box 1312, 02653
(508) 255-3824

Located in historic East Orleans, only a bike trip away from the pure waters of Nauset Beach and a short walk to village shopping and fine dining. Rooms are decorated with heirloom treasures; individually controlled air-conditioning, cable TV. Full breakfast. Two doubles, shared bath, $60.

Roseland Cottage

Orleans B&B Assoc., Box 1312, 02653
(508) 255-3824

Old-fashioned charm awaits you as you enter this 1840 Federal house. Short stroll to beach via shaded back road. .3 mile to Skaket Beach, 4.5 miles to Nauset Beach. Off the beaten path, but close to everything. Two doubles, shared bath, $55.

Salty Ridge

Orleans B&B Assoc., Box 1312, 02653
(508) 255-3824

A handsome new Cape with a breezeway that guests love. Right on the Cape Cod Rail Trail for easy access to biking. The atmosphere in this well-kept house is relaxed and cordial; special diets accommodated. Fine dining within walking distance; one mile to Skaket Beach. Full breakfast. Two doubles, private bath, $60.

Seaside Gardens

Orleans B&B Assoc., Box 1312, 02653
(508) 255-3824

Down a private road, this lovely Cape offers a quiet retreat for weekends only. Old-fashioned formal gardens; short path to a secluded beach on Pleasant Bay. Host has a studio for decorative arts. Close to Captains Golf Course. One double, private bath, $70.

1700 House

Orleans B&B Assoc., Box 1312, 02653
(508) 255-3824

A weathered quarterboard marks this historic house. Tender, loving care and sensitive planning have made all the old features gleam. Color cable TV, exquisite decor, exciting breakfast. Short walk to Academy

Playhouse. Three doubles. One private bath, two shared bath. $65-75.

Sweet Season Retreat

Orleans B&B Assoc., Box 1312, 02653
(508) 255-3824

A delightful in-town hideaway for two. Private deck with garden furniture, kitchenette. Host owns a patisserie and catering business; count on good things at breakfast! Bike to beaches and walk to village art shows, craft fairs, ball games, restaurants, interesting shops and galleries. One double, private bath, $65.

Taffrail

Orleans B&B Assoc., Box 1312, 02653
(508) 255-3824

Located in one of the choicest areas of Orleans. Separate entrance leads up to a large room overlooking Nauset Harbor and the Atlantic. Living/sitting area with fireplace and TV; small kitchenette. Short walk to saltwater beach. One double, private bath, $85.

Treehouse

Orleans B&B Assoc., Box 1312, 02653
(508) 255-3824

You can easily bike the one mile to famous Nauset Beach from this house. Have a generous breakfast in an unusual skylighted, cathedral-ceilinged dining room. Small shops, post office, and restaurants nearby. One double, shared bath, $60.

Vollerwasser

Orleans B&B Assoc., Box 1312, 02653
(508) 255-3824

NOTES: Credit cards accepted: A Master Card; B Visa; C American Express; D Discover Card; E Diners Club; F Other: 2 Personal checks accepted: 3 Lunch available: 4 Dinner available: 5 Open all year

A private entrance leads to the second-level apartment with large living room overlooking the water, TV, and refrigerator. Enjoy the company of your hosts while breakfasting on their handsome waterfront deck at the main house. Fascinating bird life and boating on Town Cove. Choice secluded area, yet close to beaches, shopping, and restaurants. One double, private bath, $70.

The White Rose

Orleans B&B Assoc., Box 1313, 02653
(508) 225-3824

Set in beautifully landscaped, spacious grounds, with a brick terrace for sunbathing and reading, this house is close to shopping, restaurants, and beaches. Your English host knows how to provide a good breakfast and make your stay memorable. Two doubles, shared bath, $55.

Winterwell

Orleans B&B Assoc., Box 1312, 02653
(508) 255-3824

A comfortably restored eighteenth-century Cape Cod farmhouse just a .3 mile stroll to Skaket Beach. Separate entrance, private baths, living room. Breakfast is served on the enclosed porch overlooking a large yard with an active bird feeder. Two doubles, private bath, $60-80.

OSTERVILLE

Blink Bonnie B&B

B&B Cape Cod, Box 341, W. Hyannisport, 02672
(508) 775-2772

Complete with private tennis court, magnificent grounds, carriage house, and an 85-foot tower, this mansion overlooks the ocean at East Bay and scenic Dowses Beach on Nantucket Sound.

Singles: 1 (SB) $40
Doubles: 2 (SB) $65-75
Type of Beds: 3 Twin; 1 Double
Continental Breakfast
Credit Cards: No
Notes: 7, 9, 10, 11, 12, 14

June's B&B

B&B Cape Cod, Box 341, W. Hyannisport, 02672
(508) 775-2772

Situated in one of the prettiest villages on the Cape, this home sits on spacious property lined with trees and beautiful grounds. Fresh and salt-water beaches are nearby. The quaint village is filled with great shops and restaurants.

Doubles: 2 (SB) $48
Continental Breakfast
Credit Cards: No
Notes: 8, 9, 10, 11, 12, 14

Potter-Smith House

B&B Cape Cod, Box 341, W. Hyannisport, 02672
(508) 775-2772

In a very quiet setting that's convenient to most Cape activities, this ten-year-old house is a spacious colonial reflecting the artist-owners' passion for painting and creativity.

Singles: 1 (SB) $40
Doubles: 2 (1 PB; 1 SB) $45-52
Type of Beds: 2 Twin; 2 Double
Continental Breakfast
Credit Cards: No
Notes: 2, 5, 8, 9, 10, 11, 12, 14

PEABODY

1660 House

B&B Marblehead & North Shore
Box 172, Beverly, MA, 01915
(508) 921-1336

A beautifully restored historic landmark home — one of the oldest frame homes still standing. Furnished with antiques throughout; one room with fireplace. the house is close to Route 128 and the Centennial Office and Industrial Park. Small dog in residence.

Doubles: 1 (PB) $65-75
Type of Beds: 1 Double; 1 Single sofabed
Continental-plus Breakfast
Credit Cards: No
Notes: 2, 5, 6 (call), 7 (limited), 8, 9, 10, 11, 12, 14

PEPPERELL

B&B Folks 5

48 Springs Road, Bedford, MA 01730
(617) 275-9025

A 200-year-old farmhouse with farm animals. Help make maple sugar on the property, play with the animals, enjoy the New England hospitality. Reduced rate for long-term stays.

Singles: 1 (SB) $55
Doubles: 2 (SB) $65
Continental Breakfast
Credit Cards: No
Notes: 2, 5, 7, 8, 9, 10, 11, 12

PERU

Berkshire NC8

Berkshire B&B Homes
Box 211, Williamsburg, MA, 01096
(413) 268-7244

This 1830 Federal home is on the Historical Register. Common room with wood-burning stove, charming breakfast room overlooking the lovely patio and woodlands. Near cross-country and downhill skiing, Jacob's Pillow, and Tanglewood.

Doubles: 2 (1 PB; 1 SB) $50-60
Type of Beds: 2 Twin; 1 Double
Credit Cards: No
Notes: 2, 5, 8, 10, 11, 12, 13

Chalet d'Alicia

East Windsor Road, 01235
(413) 655-8292

This Swiss chalet-style home offers a private, casual atmosphere. Set in the Berkshire Mountains, it overlooks the beautiful countryside. Fresh homemade breads and muffins round off the full country breakfasts. Four resident cats and one dog make everyone welcome. Tanglewood, Jacob's Pillow, Williamstown theater, and lots of cross-country skiing are nearby.

Hosts: Alice & Richard Halvorsen
Singles: 2 (SB) $40
Doubles: 1 (PB) $45
Type of Beds: 4 Twin; 1 Double
Full Breakfast
Credit Cards: No
Notes: 2, 5, 6 (inquire), 7, 8, 9, 10, 11, 12, 13

PETERSHAM

Winterwood at Petersham

North Main Street, 01366
(508) 724-8885

An elegant sixteen-room Greek Revival mansion built in 1842, located just off the common of a classic New England town. The inn boasts numerous fireplaces and several porches for relaxing. Cocktails available. On the National Register of Historic Homes.

Hosts: Jean & Robert Day
Doubles: 5 (PB) $63.42-84.56
Type of Beds: 1 Twin; 4 Double
Continental Breakfast
Credit Cards: A, B, C
Notes: 2, 5, 7, 8, 9, 12

PITTSFIELD

Country Hearts Bed 'N' Breakfast

52 Broad Street, 01201
(413) 499-3201

NOTES: Credit cards accepted: A Master Card; B Visa; C American Express; D Discover Card; E Diners Club; F Other: 2 Personal checks accepted: 3 Lunch available: 4 Dinner available: 5 Open all year

Centrally located, Country Hearts is easily accessible to all Berkshire attractions. Nestled on a quiet residential street well known for its collection of beautifully restored "aristocrats," this lovely Painted Lady is waiting to open her doors to you.

Hosts: Jan & Steve Foose
Doubles: 3 (1 PB; 2 SB) $40-75
Type of Beds: 2 Twin; 1 Double; 1 Queen
Full Breakfast
Credit Cards: A, B
Notes: 2, 4, 8, 9, 10, 11, 12, 13

PLYMOUTH

Another Place Inn

240 Sandwich Street, 02360
(508) 746-0126

Another Place is an inn with many facets of charm and convenience. Begin your stay in this antique half-cape with an authentic seventeenth-century breakfast. Plymouth's historic sites and the ocean are all in walking distance. Near Route 3, the Cape, Boston, and Newport.

Host: Carol A. Barnes
Doubles: 1 (SB) $55-60
Type of Beds: 1 Double
Full Breakfast
Credit Cards: No
Notes: 2, 5, 8 (call), 11, 12, 14

Pineapple Hospitality MA 1060

Box F-821, New Bedford, MA 02742-0821
(508) 990-1696

A 150-year-old captain's Cape Cod house, beautifully decorated with antiques, Oriental rugs, and furnishings. Your hostess will long be remembered for her warm, bubbly, outreaching approach to life. One Persian cat shares this home.

Doubles: 3 (1 PB; 2 SB) $60-70
Type of Beds: 2 Twin; 1 Double; 1 King
Continental Breakfast
Credit Cards: No
Notes: 2, 5, 7 (limited), 8, 9, 10, 11, 12

PRINCETON

The Harrington Farm

178 Westminster Road, 01541
(508) 464-5600

Located on the western slope of Mount Wachessett, this 1763 farmhouse has the charm and antiques of old and all the modern conveniences you want. Quiet and serene, with hiking and cross-country ski trails starting at our back door.

Hosts: Linda Morgan-Yatzor, Victoria Morgan & Barry Yatzor
Doubles: 8 (1 PB; 7 SB) $57.50-75
Type of Beds: 1 Twin; 6 Double; 2 Queen
Full Breakfast
Credit Cards: A, B
Notes: 2, 4, 5, 6 (limited), 8, 9, 11, 13, 14

PROVINCETOWN

Bed'N B'Fast

44 Commercial Street, 02657
(508) 487-9555

Greek Revival, circa 1850, between the town and beach in the quiet West End. True bed 'n b'fast, serving full American b'fast till noon. BYOB Safari Bar. Predominately a gay operation, where all are welcome. At this time, second and third floors are limited to men only because they share a bath.

Hosts: Bill Gilbert & Dick B. Knudson
Doubles: 5 (SB) $32.28-86.16
Type of Beds: 1 Twin; 3 Double; 1 Queen
Full Breakfast
Credit Cards: A, B, C, E
Notes: 4, 5, 7, 9, 14

Bradford Gardens Inn

178 Bradford Street, 02657
(508) 487-1616

Beautiful antique-filled colonial country inn. Eight rooms with color TV, private baths; six

Beautiful antique-filled colonial country inn. Eight rooms with color TV, private baths; six with fireplaces. Includes maid service, firewood, parking, and full breakfast. Fully equipped cottages also available. Beaches, tennis, shops, restaurants, and galleries nearby.

Host: M. Susan Culligan
Doubles: 8 (PB) $89-104
Type of Beds: 1 Twin; 7 Double; 3 Queen
Full Breakfast
Minimum stay weekends & holidays: 2
Credit Cards: A, B, C
Notes: 2, 7, 8 (off season), 9

Captain Lysander Inn

46 Commercial Street, 02657
(508) 487-2253

An elegant home of a sea captain, the Captain Lysander Inn was built in 1852. The gracious guest rooms are decorated with a blend of antique and traditional furnishings. Befitting a sea captain, the inn is a few steps from the water, with an impressive view of Provincetown Harbor. Situated in the quiet part of this bustling town, it is within walking distance of the myriad attractions of this year-round resort area.

Hosts: Madeline & Charles Edwards
Doubles: 13 (7 PB; 6 SB) $43.20-70.20
Four-room Apartment also available
Four-room House also available
Type of Beds: 3 Twin; 12 Double; 2 Queen
Continental Breakfast
Minimum stay weekends & holidays during season
Credit Cards: A, B, C
Notes: 2, 5, 7, 8, 9, 10, 11, 12

Elephant Walk Inn

156 Bradford Street, 02657
(508) 487-2543

A romantic Edwardian inn near Provincetown's center. The spacious, well-appointed rooms offer an eclectic mixture of antique furnishings and decorations. All have private bath, color TV, and refrigerator. Enjoy our large sun deck or lounge with your morning coffee.

Host: Len Paoletti
Doubles: 8 (PB) $45-78
Type of Beds: 6 Double; 3 Queen; 1 King
Continental Breakfast
Minimum stay weekdays: 3; weekends in season: 5;
Holidays in season: 7
Closed Nov.-March
Notes: 2 (for deposit), 7, 8 (off-season), 9, 10, 11

Elephant Walk Inn

The Fairbanks Inn

90 Bradford Street, 02657
(508) 487-0386

The Fairbanks Inn is a lovingly restored 200-year-old ship captain's house filled with a collection of art, antiques, and reproduction furnishings. Rooms have four-poster or canopy beds, Oriental rugs, wide pine-planked floors. Some have working fireplaces. In the summer, a continental breakfast is served on our glass-enclosed porch that overlooks the patio and private gardens.

Host: Don Graichen
Doubles: 14 (7 PB; 7 SB) $48-90
Continental Breakfast
Credit Cards: A, B, C
Notes: 7, 9, 10, 11, 12, 14

NOTES: Credit cards accepted: A Master Card; B Visa; C American Express; D Discover Card; E Diners Club; F Other: 2 Personal checks accepted: 3 Lunch available: 4 Dinner available: 5 Open all year

Land's End Inn

22 Commercial Street, 02657
(508) 487-0706

High atop Gull Hill, Land's End Inn over-looks Provincetown and all of Cape Cod Bay. Large, airy, comfortably furnished living rooms, a large front porch, and lovely antique-filled rooms provide relaxation and visual pleasure to guests.

Host: David Schoolman
Doubles: 14 (10 PB; 4 SB) $65-108
Type of Beds: 6 Twin; 10 Double
Continental Breakfast
Minimum stay weekends: 2; holidays: 4
Credit Cards: No
Notes: 2, 5, 7, 8 (infants or over 12), 9, 10, 11, 12

Rose and Crown Guest House

158 Commercial Street, 02657
(508) 487-3332

The Rose and Crown is a classic Georgian "square rigger" built in the 1780s. The guest house sits behind an ornate iron fence, and a ship's figurehead greets visitors from her post above the paneled front door. During restoration, wide floorboards were un-covered and pegged posts and beams ex-posed. An appealing clutter of Victorian antiques and artwork fills every nook and cranny.

Hosts: Preston Babbitt, Jr.
Singles: 1(SB) $40
Doubles: 7 (PB and SB) $60-100
Type of Beds: 4 Twin; 6 Double; 2 Queen; 1 King
Continental Breakfast
Credit Cards: No
Notes: 5, 7, 9, 10, 11, 12, 14

Victoria House

5 Standish Street, 02657
(508) 487-1319

Victoria House is situated in the heart of Provincetown. Comfortable rooms with private and shared baths, color cable TV with HBO and Cinemax, refrigerators, and continental breakfast. Call for rates and reservations.

Hosts: Martin Bettencourt & Bill Woolley
Singles: 6 (SB) $45-60
Doubles: 4 (PB) $60-90
Type of Beds: 4 Double; 6 King
Continental Breakfast
Credit Cards: A, B, C, D, E
Notes: 2 (deposit), 6, 8 (over 12), 9, 10, 11, 14

White Wind Inn

174 Commercial Street, 02657
(508) 487-1526

A white Victorian, circa 1845, across the street from the beach and five minutes' walk from almost everything. Continental break-fast in season. Please write or call for brochure.

Host: Russell Dusablon
Singles: 2 (SB) $25-30
Doubles: 10 (PB) $45-100
Continental Breakfast
Credit Cards: A, B, C, D, F
Notes: 5, 6 (inquire), 10

Rose and Crown Guest House

6 Pets welcome: 7 Smoking allowed: 8 Children welcome: 9 Social drinking allowed: 10 Tennis available: 11 Swimming available: 12 Golf available: 13 Skiing available: 14 May be booked through travel agents

QUINCY

Host Homes of Boston #30

Box 117, Waban Branch, Boston, 02168
(617) 244-1308

Walk to city beach, subway, and historic mansions. Renovated colonial with color TV, Jacuzzi, parking. Near Kennedy Library, Bayside Expo Center. Fifteen minutes from downtown Boston by subway; Amtrak station ten minutes; Boston ten-minute drive on I-93. Airport limo to Quincy Center available.

Doubles: 2 (SB) $55
Type of Beds: 1 Double; 1 Queen
Continental Breakfast
Minimum stay: 2
Credit Cards: A, B, C
Notes: 2, 5, 11

READING

B&B Folks 6

48 Springs Road, Bedford, MA 01730
(617) 275-9025

A New England colonial in the center of the high-tech region. Close to Boston, the ocean, and the mountains. Reduced rate for long-term stays.

Doubles: 2 (SB) $40-50
Type of Beds: 2 Double
Continental Breakfast
Credit Cards: No
Notes: 2, 4, 7, 8, 9, 10, 11, 12

Host Homes of Boston #31

Box 117, Waban Branch, Boston, 02168
(617) 244-1308

A turn-of-the-century eleven-room home with a heated in-ground pool, guest parlor with TV, parking. Twelve miles northwest of Boston, and convenient to the airport,

Cambridge, and the North Shore. Near Burlington and Andover, Mass.

Doubles: 2 (SB) $57
Type of Beds: 2 Twin; 1 Double
Full Breakfast
Minimum stay: 2
Credit Cards: A, B, C
Notes: 2, 5, 8, 9

REHOBOTH

B&B Registry #MA-02769PER

Box 8174, St. Paul, MN, 55108
(612) 646-4238

Four acres adjacent to an old mill-pond trout stream and across the street from a public golf course. Totally renovated three-story house with sitting rooms for guests. Screened front porch for breakfast in the summer. Kitchen has a pot-belly stove. Tea or sherry every afternoon.

Doubles: 5 (3 PB; 2 SB) $40-75
Continental-plus Breakfast
Credit Cards: A, B, C
Notes: 5, 8, 12, 13 (XC)

B&B Rhode Island #MA-159

Box 3291-ND, Newport, R.I., 02840
(401) 849-1298

Enjoy a taste of country life on this 70-acre tree farm. Hike cross-country ski the many woodland trails just out the back door. Farm animals include Shetland ponies, horses, chickens, pigeons, and a rabbit. Guests may take a pony cart out for a slow-paced tour or help with the farm chores. Outdoor terrace, in-ground pool.

Doubles: 3 (SB) $45
Type of Beds: 2 Twin; 2 Double
Full Breakfast
Credit Cards: No
Notes: 5, 8, 9, 10, 11, 12, 13 (XC), 14

NOTES: Credit cards accepted: A Master Card; B Visa; C American Express; D Discover Card; E Diners Club; F Other: 2 Personal checks accepted: 3 Lunch available: 4 Dinner available: 5 Open all year

RICHMOND

Berkshire SC3

Berkshire B&B Homes
Box 211, Williamsburg, MA, 01096
(413) 268-7244

This 1987 post-and-beam colonial sits on 4 acres of land. Family room with fireplace. Guest rooms on the second floor with cathedral ceiling and skylights. Sitting area with TV and stereo; private bath. First-floor guest room also has a private bath.

Doubles: 2 (PB) $70-85
Type of Beds: 4 Twin; 1 Queen
Full Breakfast
Credit Cards: No
Notes: 2, 5, 8, 10, 11, 12, 13

ROCKPORT

Bide a Wee

B&B Marblehead & North Shore
Box 172, Beverly, MA, 01915
(508) 921-1336

Ocean-view Cape Cod style home across the road from Halibut Point State Park, a rocky promontory that juts into the ocean and provides wonderful sunset views. The house has spectacular ocean views of the cove, which is one of Cape Ann's earliest fishing grounds. One dog and one cat in residence.

Singles: 1 (SB) $55
Doubles: 2 (1 PB; 1 SB) $65-75
Type of Beds: 3 Twin; 1 Double; 1 King
Full breakfast weekends; continental weekdays
Credit Cards: No
Notes: 2, 5, 7 (restricted), 9, 10, 11, 12, 14

Eden Pines Inn

Eden Road, 01966
(508) 546-2505

Directly on the ocean in historic Rockport, and ol fishing village filled with shops. The inn is within walking distance of two picturesque beaches and affords a most spectacular view of ocean activity — lobstermen, fishermen, sailors. Spacious sun deck; private baths and sitting areas in each room.

Host: Inge Sullivan
Doubles: 6 (PB) $88-110
Continental Breakfast
Credit Cards: A, B
Closed mid-Nov. - mid-April
Notes: 2, 10, 11

Eden Pines Inn

The Inn on Cove Hill

37 Mt. Pleasant Street, 01966
(508) 546-2701

Our 200-year-old house's ambience features canopy beds and antiques, continental breakfast at our umbrella tables in the garden. The picturesque harbor unfolds from the third-floor porch vista or at dockside one block away.

Hosts: Marjorie & John Pratt
Doubles: 11 (9 PB; 2 SB) $48-91
Type of Beds: 4 Twin; 7 Double; 3 Queen
Continental Breakfast
Minimum stay: 2
Credit Cards: No
Closed late Oct.-March
Notes: 2, 8 (16 and older), 9, 10, 11, 12

Lantana House

22 Broadway, 01966
(508) 546-3535

6 Pets welcome: 7 Smoking allowed: 8 Children welcome: 9 Social drinking allowed: 10 Tennis available: 11 Swimming available: 12 Golf available: 13 Skiing available: 14 May be booked through travel agents

An in-town Victorian guest house open year round in the historic district of Rockport —a classic, picturesque, seacoast village. A one to five minute walk takes you to the beaches, art galleries, restaurants, and gift shops. Rockport is an artists' haven.

Host: Cynthia Sewell
Singles: 1 (PB) $60.53
Doubles: 4 (3 PB; 1 SB) $60.53-76.79
Type of Beds: 3 Twin; 4 Double
Continental Breakfast
Minimum stay weekdays: 1-3; weekends: 2; holidays: 3
Credit Cards: No
Notes: 2, 5, 7 (restricted), 8, 9, 10, 11, 12

Mooringstone

12 Norwood Avenue, 01966
(508) 546-2479

For nonsmokers only. Quiet, central location with home-baked muffins and breads at breakfast. Comfortable new ground-floor rooms with air-conditioning, cable TV, refrigerators. Park and walk to beach, restaurants, shops, headlands. Daily, weekly, and off season rates available. No room tax.

Hosts: David & Mary Knowlton
Doubles: 3 (PB) $65-68
Type of Beds: 2 Twin; 1 Queen; 1 King
Continental Breakfast
Minimum stay weekends & holidays: 2
Credit Cards: A, B, C
Closed mid-Oct.-mid-May
Notes: 2, 9, 10, 11, 12

Old Farm Inn

291 Granite Street, Rt. 127, 01966
(508) 546-3237

A country farmhouse inn in a seaside town. Surrounded by an ocean-front park, the inn has a warm, comfortable, peaceful setting, yet dining, shops, and beaches are only minutes away. We share our inn, knowledge of the area, and our hospitality with you.

Hosts: The Balzarini Family
Doubles: 8 (PB) $68-88
Type of Beds: 6 Twin; 2 Double; 5 Queen; 1 King
Continental-plus Breakfast

Minimum stay weekends & July-Aug.: 2; holidays: 3
Credit Cards: A, B, C
Closed Jan.-March
Notes: 2, 7, 8, 9, 10, 11, 12

Pleasant Street Inn

17 Pleasant Street, 01966
(508) 546-3915

Pleasant Street Inn sits on a knoll overlooking Rockport, just one hour north of Boston. The inn has seven guest rooms, all with private baths. Pleasant Street Inn is conveniently located to shops, galleries, restaurants, and beaches. Ample parking.

Hosts: Roger & Lynne Norris
Doubles: 7 (PB) $65-82
Type of Beds: 4 Twin; 3 Double; 4 Queen
Continental Breakfast
Credit Cards: A, B
Notes: 2, 5, 7, 8 (over 6), 9, 10, 11, 12

Ralph Waldo Emerson Inn

Ralph Waldo Emerson Inn

Box 2369, 01966
(508) 546-6321

A traditional country inn with a wide front porch overlooking the ocean, the Emerson features Greek Revival architecture, spacious public rooms, heated salt-water pool, sauna and whirlpool, and a theater with an eight-foot screen projector TV and VCR. Tennis, whale watching, and golf are available nearby. Dinner is served in season.

Host: Gary Wenyss
Singles: 3 (PB) $46-63
Doubles: 33 (PB) $74-114
Type of Beds: 19 Twin; 13 Double; 4 Queen; 1 King
Full Breakfast
Credit Cards: A, B, D
Closed Dec. 1 - March 31
Notes: 2, 4, 7, 8, 9, 10, 11, 12

Seven South Street — The Inn

7 South Street, 01966
(508) 546-6708

Built in 1750, the inn has a friendly, informal atmosphere. In a quiet setting, with gardens, deck, and pool. An ample continental breakfast is served each morning, after which the guest is free to explore the art galleries and shops within walking distance of the inn.

Hosts: Helene & George Waldschlagel
Singles: 1 (SB) $30-32
Doubles: 3 (PB) $65-70
Doubles: 2 (SB) $55-58
Type of Beds: 5 Twin; 3 Double
Continental Breakfast
Credit Cards: No
Closed Nov.-April
Notes: 2, 7, 9, 10, 11, 12

SAGAMORE BEACH

Bed & Breakfast of Sagamore Beach

One Hawes Road, 02562
(508) 888-1559

A private, peaceful home overlooking Cape Cod Bay. Sixty miles to Boston or Provincetown. Relax in the casual atmosphere in front of the fireplace or on the large porches and decks that surround the house. Walk for miles on the quiet, sandy beach. Home has been featured in *Bon Appetit* and *Better Homes & Gardens*.

Host: John F. Carafoli
Doubles: 3 (SB) $85
Type of Beds: 3 Double
Continental Breakfast
Credit Cards: No
Notes: 2, 5, 9, 10, 11, 12, 14

SALEM

Amelia Payson Guest House

16 Winter Street, 01915
(508) 744-8304

Built in 1845, this fine example of Greek Revival architecture is located in the heart of Salem's historic district. Guest rooms are furnished with canopy or brass beds and antiques. A five-minute stroll to downtown shopping, historic houses, museums, and Pickering Wharf's waterfront dining.

Hosts: Ada & Donald Roberts
Doubles: 4 (2 PB; 2 SB) $50-85
Type of Beds: 3 Twin; 3 Double
Continental Breakfast
Credit Cards: A, B, C, D
Notes: 5, 8 (over 12), 9, 10, 11, 12

The Antique Colonial

B&B Marblehead & North Shore
Box 172, Beverly, MA, 01915
(508) 921-1336

One block from the harbor and one-half block from the Salem Common, with its grand homes. The hostess works with ceramics; the host makes guitars and does stained-glass work. Third-floor guest sitting room with TV and dining area. Settled in 1626, Salem has many beautiful buildings. The Peabody Museum features whaling and seafaring exhibits. Plan a whale-watch cruise from Salem for a treat for the whole family.

Doubles: 4 (PB) $75
Type of Beds: 2 Twin; 4 Double; 2 Rollaways
Continental Breakfast
Credit Cards: No
Notes: 2, 5, 7, 8, 9, 10, 11, 12, 14

The Inn at Seven Winter St.

7 Winter Street, 01970
(508) 745-9520

6 Pets welcome: 7 Smoking allowed: 8 Children welcome: 9 Social drinking allowed: 10 Tennis available: 11 Swimming available: 12 Golf available: 13 Skiing available: 14 May be booked through travel agents

The inn is an impeccably restored French Victorian home, with each room finely appointed with period furnishings and antiues. Private baths, cable TV, phone, air-conditioning in every room. Some have fireplaces; others have a large sun deck. Excellent location in the historic district. Please write or call for our brochure. We offer a smoke-free environment.

Hosts: Sally Flint, Jill & Dee L. Cote
Doubles: 9 (PB) $65-85
Type of Beds: 4 Twin; 9 Double
Continental Breakfast
Credit Cards: A, B
Notes: 5

The Salem Inn

7 Summer Street, 01970
(508) 741-0680

Elegantly restored 1834 Federal townhouse located in the heart of historic Salem. Twenty-three spacious, comfortably appointed rooms, each uniquely different, with a blend of period detail, antique furnishings, and homey touches. Two-room suites with kitchenettes are ideal for families. Some working fireplaces. Courtyard Café offers fine dining Tuesday through Saturday.

Hosts: Richard & Diane Pabich
Doubles: 22 (PB) $76.79-104.21
Type of Beds: 3 Queen; 20 King
Continental Breakfast

Credit Cards: A, B, C, D, E, F
Notes: 2, 4, 5, 7, 8, 9, 11, 12, 14

SANDWICH

Academy Hill B&B

B&B Cape Cod, Box 341, W. Hyannisport, 02672
(508) 775-2772

This beautifully maintained sixty-year-old house sits high on Academy Hill. Classic design and traditional furnishings create a gracious, relaxing atmosphere overlooking the village of Sandwich. Walk to all town facilities.

Doubles: 2 (PB) $60
Type of Beds: 2 Twin; 1 Double
Continental Breakfast
Credit Cards: No
Notes: 2, 5, 7, 9, 10, 11, 12, 14

Capt. Ezra Nye House

152 Main Street, 02563
(508) 888-6142

A sense of history and romance fills this 1829 Federal home, built by the distinguished clipper ship captain Ezra Nye. Located in the heart of the oldest town on Cape Cod, the inn is near many famous attractions.

Hosts: Elaine & Harry Dickson
Singles: 1 (SB) $45-80
Doubles: 5 (4 PB; 1 SB) $45-80

The Dan'l Webster Inn

Type of Beds: 2 Twin; 3 Double; 1 Queen; 1 King
Continental-plus Breakfast
Minimum stay holidays: 2
Credit Cards: A, B, C
Notes: 2, 5, 8 (6 and over), 9, 10, 11, 12, 14

Capt. Ezra Nye House

Dan'l Webster Inn

149 Main Street, 02563
(508) 888-3622

The award-winning Dan'l Webster Inn is
located in Cape Cod's oldest town,
Sandwich. This four-star country inn
provides fine dining, charming accommodations, and quality service in the quaint village
of Sandwich, with its country New England
charm, museums, antique shops, and historic homes.

Hosts: The Catania Family
Doubles: 42 (PB) $65-135
Full Breakfast
Credit Cards: A, B, C, E
Notes: 2 (for deposits), 3, 4, 5, 7, 8, 9, 10, 11, 12, 14

Hawthorn Hill

Box 777, 02563
(508) 888-3333; 3336

Rambling English country house with continental hospitality. Quiet and serene, yet
close to all attractions. Situated on Shawme
Pond, adjacent to Heritage Plantation.
Large, sunny breakfast and living room,

deck, woods to roam in, rowboat for exercise. Short distance to beaches.

Host: Maxime Caron
Doubles: 2 (PB) $65
Type of Beds: 2 Queen
Full or Continental Breakfast
Credit Cards: No
Closed Winter
Notes: 2, 7, 8, 9, 10, 11, 12

Host Homes of Boston #32

Box 117, Waban Branch, Boston, 02168
(617) 244-1308

Luxury beach-front accommodations with
all the amenities. Privacy, space, romantic
setting overlooking Cape Cod Bay. Rooms
have decks and ocean view, cable TV,
phone, refrigerator, and a private beach.
Suite available with Jacuzzi. Two fireplaced
living rooms, dining room, and kitchen. Only
one hour's drive from Boston. Walk to
Sandwich's museums and historic sites.

Doubles: 3 (PB) $100-150
Type of Beds: 2 Double; 2 King
Continental-plus Breakfast
Minimum stay: 2
Credit Cards: A, B, C
Notes: 2, 5, 10, 11, 12

Quince Tree B&B

B&B Cape Cod, Box 341, W. Hyannisport, 02672
(508) 775-2772

This 1840 Federal colonial was restored in
1985. Complete with polished antiques,
period furnishings. Convenient to fine restaurants, museums, and local beaches.

Doubles: 3 (2 PB; 1 SB) $55-75
Type of Beds: 1 Double; 2 Queen
Continental Breakfast
Credit Cards: No
Notes: 2, 5, 9, 10, 11, 12, 14

Isaiah Jones Homestead

165 Main Street, 02563
(508) 888-9115

6 Pets welcome: 7 Smoking allowed: 8 Children welcome: 9 Social drinking allowed: 10 Tennis available: 11
Swimming available: 12 Golf available: 13 Skiing available: 14 May be booked through travel agents

An intimate Victorian bed and breakfast inn with beautiful antiques, fresh flowers, and candlelight. Homemade, freshly baked breakfast and afternoon tea. Walk to most points of interest. "Superior in every respect —A trip into the past."

Hosts: Kathy & Steven Catania
Doubles: 4 (PB) $71.31-120.47
Type of Beds: 4 Queen
Continental Breakfast
Minimum stay weekends & holidays: 2
Credit Cards: A, B, C
Closed Christmas Eve & Christmas Day
Notes: 2, 10, 11, 12

SEEKONK

B&B Rhode Island #MA-225

Box 3291-ND, Newport, R.I., 40145
(401) 840-1298

This 1799 Federal mansion is a National Historic Property. Nestled on a 9 acre rural knoll overlooking the fields and banks of the Palmer River. Breakfast is served in the original kitchen with its massive cooking fireplace. Each guest room features a working fireplace and antique wash stand with running water.

Doubles: 3 (SB) $38-45
Type of Beds: 4 Double
Full Breakfast
Credit Cards: No
Notes: 5, 8, 9, 10, 11, 12, 14

SHEFFIELD

A Unique Bed & Breakfast Inn

Box 729, 01257
(413) 229-3363

A most relaxing B&B. Cozy, attractively furnished and decorated. Central air-conditioning. Lounge/dining room with fireplace. Full buffet country breakfast. Twenty minutes to Tanglewood Music Festival; fifteen to Lime Rock; ten to skiing. Hand-ironed percale sheets, fresh flowers in rooms. Antique shops galore.

Host: May Stendardi
Doubles: 4 (PB) $50-105
Type of Beds: 2 Twin; 2 Double; 1 King
Full Breakfast
Minimum stay weekends & holidays: 2-3
Credit Cards: A, B (for reservations only)
Notes: 5, 8 (15 or older), 9, 10, 11, 12, 13

Centuryhurst Antiques & Bed & Breakfast

Main Street, Box 486, 01257
(413) 229-8131

Circa 1800 center-hall colonial furnished in period antiques, located in historic district. In the heart of the Berkshires, close to Tanglewood and numerous other summer theaters and cultural events. Winter recreation offers skiing at several large ski areas.

Hosts: Ronald & Judith Timm
Singles: 1 (SB) $54-58
Doubles: 3 (S2B) $58-62
Type of Beds: 2 Twin; 3 Double
Continental Breakfast
Minimum stay weekends:2 ; holidays: 3
Credit Cards: A, B, C
Notes: 2, 5, 8 (12 and over), 9, 10, 11, 12, 13

Staveleigh House

Staveleigh House

So. Main Street, 01257
(413) 229-2129

Renovated 1821 Georgian colonial in the center of the historic district. Five guest rooms furnished for maximum comfort. Full breakfast, afternoon tea. Close to all Berkshire cultural and scenic attractions. Sheffield is well-known as a center for antiques, with more than thirty shops.

Hosts: Marion Whitman & Dorothy Marosy
Doubles: 5 (2 PB; 3 SB) $63.42-89.85
Type of Beds: 4 Twin; 2 Double; 1 Queen
Full Breakfast
Minimum stay weekends: 2
Credit Cards: No
Notes: 2, 5, 8 (over 12), 9, 10, 11, 12, 13

SOMERSET

B&B Rhode Island #MA-267

Box 3291-ND, Newport, R.I., 02840
(401) 849-1298

This sea captain's home was built in 1845 on gardens that date back to the 1700s. A view of the lovely Taunton River awaits its guests. Large dining room with fireplace and period tiles; living room with fireplace and stereo. Two rooms and one suite are available; suite has a balcony and fireplace. Hosts speak English and Spanish.

Doubles: 3 (1 PB; 2 SB) $45-70
Type of Beds: 1 Double; 2 Queen
Full Breakfast
Credit Cards: No
Notes: 5, 8, 9, 10, 11, 12, 14

SOMERVILLE

Greater Boston Hospitality #131

Box 1142, Brookline 02146
(617) 277-5430

Immaculately maintained mansard Victorian serving full breakfast on weekends and continental on weekdays in the dining room or on the lovely patio. Minutes to Tufts University; a few short train stops from Harvard and M.I.T. Air-conditioned; no smoking; children welcome.

Doubles: 1 (SB) $52-62
Type of Beds: 2 Twin or 1 King
Full or Continental Breakfast
Credit Cards: No

Host Homes of Boston #33

Box 117, Waban Branch, Boston, 02168
(617) 244-1308

Spotless new home sitting on a hill near Tufts University. Breakfast is served in a glass-walled dining room. Resident dog. Walk to Tufts; close to Cambridge, Boston, Lexington.

Doubles: 1 (PB) $48
Type of Beds: 2 Twin
Continental Breakfast
Minimum stay: 2
Credit Cards: A, B, C
Notes: 2, 5

SOUTH CHATHAM

Ye Olde Nantucket House

Box 468, 02659
(508) 432-5641

Built on Nantucket in 1840 and later moved to its present location, the inn has five rooms with private baths and Victorian decor. Shopping, the Chatham lighthouse, recreational activities, and a Nantucket Sound beach are all nearby.

Hosts: Norm & Helen Anderton
Doubles: 5 (PB) $58-70
Type of Beds: 2 Twin; 4 Double
Continental-plus Breakfast
Credit Cards: A, B
Notes: 2, 5, 8 (over 8), 9, 10, 11, 14

---

6 Pets welcome: 7 Smoking allowed: 8 Children welcome: 9 Social drinking allowed: 10 Tennis available: 11 Swimming available: 12 Golf available: 13 Skiing available: 14 May be booked through travel agents

SOUTH CHELMSFORD

Westview Landing

Box 141, 01824
(508) 256-0074

Large contemporary home overlooking
Hart's Pond, located three miles from
routes 495 and 3 and thirty miles north of
Boston. Close to historic Lexington, Concord, and Lowell. Many recreational activities: swimming, boating, fishing,
bicycling. Hot spa on premises.

Hosts: Lorraine & Robert Pinette
Doubles: 3 (SB) $40-50
Type of Beds: 1 Double; 1 Queen; 2 Daybeds
Full Breakfast
Credit Cards: No
Closed Christmas & New Years
Notes: 2, 4, 5, 8, 9, 11, 12

SOUTH DARTMOUTH

Pineapple Hospitality MA 1065

Box F-821, New Bedford, MA 02742-0821
(508) 990-1696

Replica of a sea captain's home, with
hardwood floors, country eclectic furnishings, Oriental rugs, and antiques. Three-
quarters of a mile from Padanarum Harbor.
Hosts are retired and enjoy deep-sea fishing,
antiquing, and gourmet cooking. Twenty-
five minutes to Newport and forty-five to
Cape Cod.

Doubles: 3 (SB) $50
Type of Beds: 2 Twin; 1 Double; 1 Queen
Full Breakfast
Credit Cards: No
Closed Nov. 24 - Jan. 3
Notes: 2, 3, 8, 9, 10, 11, 12

SOUTH DEERFIELD

Berkshire PV30

Berkshire B&B Homes
Box 211, Williamsburg, MA, 01096
(413) 268-7244

A 1910 Georgian colonial with formal, classic furnishings. Minutes to historic Deerfield, Eaglebrook, Bemet and Mount
Hermon schools, and the five-college area.

Doubles: 3 (1 PB; 2 SB) $55-100
Type of Beds: 3 Double; 1 Queen
Continental Breakfast
Credit Cards: No
Notes: 2, 5, 7, 8 (12 and over), 10, 11, 12

SOUTH EGREMONT

The Egremont Inn

Old Sheffield Road, 01258
(413) 528-2111

Located in the historic district, this 1780 inn
has several dining rooms, public sitting
areas, bar, tavern, swimming pool, tennis
courts, and 22 guest rooms. Breakfast and
dinner included.

Host: John Black
Doubles: 22(PB) $235-400 (MAP)
Type of Beds: 22 Twin; 11 Double
Continental Breakfast
Minimum stay summer weekends: 3

SOUTH HADLEY

Berkshire PV4

Berkshire B&B Homes
Box 211, Williamsburg, MA, 01096
(413) 268-7244

This 1794 colonial has a screened porch and
dining room with fireplace and is only two
miles from Mount Holyoke College. Close
to five major colleges.

Singles: 2 (SB) $35
Doubles: 2 (SB) $55
Type of Beds: 2 Twin; 2 Double
Continental Breakfast
Credit Cards: No
Notes: 2, 5, 7, 8 (10 and up), 10, 11, 12

SOUTH HARWICH

The House on the Hill

968 Main Street, 02661
(508) 432-4321

A lovely old Cape Cod farmhouse, built in 1832 and furnished with antiques and old family pieces. Enjoy the sunny deck or our quiet patio with its pretty walled garden. Warm-water beach only one mile away. We are located at the center of Cape Cod.

Hosts: Allen & Carolyn Swanson
Singles: 1 (SB) $25-35
Doubles: 3 (2 PB; 1 SB) $40-65
Type of Beds: 3 Twin; 2 Double; 1 King
Continental Breakfast
Credit Cards: No
Closed Christmas
Notes: 2, 5, 8, 9, 10, 11, 12, 14

Merrell Tavern Inn

SOUTH LEE

Merrell Tavern Inn

Rt. 102, Main Street, 01260
(413) 243-1794

This 200-year-old brick stagecoach inn is listed on the National Register and located in a small New England village along the banks of the Housatonic River. Rooms with fireplaces, canopy beds, and antique furnish-

ings. Full breakfast is served in the original tavern room. One mile to Normal Rockwell's beloved Stockbridge.

Hosts: Charles & Faith Reynolds
Doubles: 9 (PB) $55-120
Type of Beds: 1 Twin; 8 Double
Full Breakfast
Credit Cards: A, B, C
Notes: 5, 8, 9, 10, 11, 12, 13, 14

SOUTH YARMOUTH

The Belvedere

B&B Cape Cod, Box 341, W. Hyannisport, 02672
(508) 775-2772

This 1820 sea captain's house is complete with wide board floors and widow's walk. Walk to the beach and a short distance to fine restaurants and shops. A carriage house is also available for four guests.

Singles: 1 (SB) $40
Doubles: 2 (1 PB; 1 SB) $55-65
Type of Beds: 1 Twin; 2 Double
Continental Breakfast
Credit Cards: No
Notes: 5, 8, 9, 10, 11, 12, 14

SPRINGFIELD

Berkshire PV12

Berkshire B&B Homes
Box 211, Williamsburg, MA, 01096
(413) 268-7244

A 1920s colonial revival in a residential area two miles from downtown Springfield and one mile from I-91. Twenty-five minutes to the Brimfield Flea Market and just minutes to Big E (Eastern State Exposition).

Singles: 1 (SB) $35
Doubles: 2 (SB) $45
Type of Beds: 3 Twin; 1 Double
Continental Breakfast
Credit Cards: No
Notes: 2, 5, 8, 10, 11, 12

6 Pets welcome: 7 Smoking allowed: 8 Children welcome: 9 Social drinking allowed: 10 Tennis available: 11 Swimming available: 12 Golf available: 13 Skiing available: 14 May be booked through travel agents

STOCKBRIDGE

Berkshire SC9

Berkshire B&B Homes
Box 211, Williamsburg, MA, 01096
(413) 268-7244

An 1865 Federal on 3 beautifully landscaped acres with in-ground swimming pool and patio where breakfast is served in warm weather. Guest rooms are furnished with canopy beds, sitting areas, private baths. The living room has a fireplace, and your full breakfast will be served on English china with sterling silver.

Doubles: 2 (PB) $125-150
Type of Beds: 2 Queen
Full Breakfast
Credit Cards: No
Notes: 2, 4, 5, 10, 11, 12, 13

The Berkshire Thistle Inn

Pine Street, 01262

We are located three blocks from the Norman Rockwell Museum in the center of Stockbridge. All rooms have private bath and four-poster beds, color TV. Five minutes to Tanglewood; skiing nearby.

Hosts: Jessie & Michael Cibelli, Faith Crawford
Doubles: 9 (PB) $85-140
Type of Beds: 9 Queen
Full Breakfast
Credit Cards: A, B, C
Notes: 2, 3, 4, 5, 7, 8, 9, 10, 11, 12, 13, 14

The Inn at Stockbridge

Rt. 7, Box 618, 01262
(413) 298-3337

Exquisite white-pillared colonial country inn on 12 secluded acres, set far back from the road. No children, no pets. Gourmet breakfasts are served on fine china with silver in the formal dining room. Private pool.

Hosts: Lee & Don Weitz
Doubles: $80-180

Full Breakfast
Minimum stay during Tanglewood season: 3; other weekends: 2

Woodside Bed & Breakfast

Box 1096, 01262
(413) 298-4977

Enjoy comfort and hospitality in our contemporary country home located just one mile from the center of Stockbridge, home of the Norman Rockwell Museum. Close to Tanglewood, Chesterwood, Jacob's Pillow Dance Festival. In winter, enjoy skiing at nearby resorts. Handicapped access, special diets accommodated.

Hosts: Paula Schutzmann, R.N., Sarah & Katie Harvey
Doubles: 3 (1 PB; 2 SB) $55-85
Type of Beds: 2 Twin; 2 Queen; 2 Daybeds
Full Breakfast weekends, Continental on weekdays
Credit Cards: A, B
Notes: 2, 5, 6, 7 (restricted), 8, 9, 10, 11, 12, 13

STOW

Amerscot House

61 West Action Road, 01775
(508) 897-4762

Convenient to Boston, historic Concord, and the centers of technology, this charming 1750 colonial farmhouse offers the warmth and hospitality of the past. Each guest room has a fireplace and private bath. Amerscot provides comfort, food, and pleasant surroundings for the discriminating traveler.

Host: Doreen Gibson
Doubles: 3 (PB) $80-100
Type of Beds: 1 Twin; 2 Queen
Continental Breakfast
Credit Cards: A, B
Notes: 2, 5, 8 (over 12), 9, 10, 12

STURBRIDGE

Berkshire ST1

Berkshire B&B Homes
Box 211, Williamsburg, MA, 01096
(413) 268-7244

NOTES: Credit cards accepted: A Master Card; B Visa; C American Express; D Discover Card; E Diners Club; F Other: 2 Personal checks accepted: 3 Lunch available: 4 Dinner available: 5 Open all year

An oversized Cape Cod home in a residential area. Large screened porch; fireplace in the living room. Five minutes from Sturbridge Village.

Doubles: 2 (PB) $60
Type of Beds: 2 Twin; 1 Double
Full Breakfast
Credit Cards: No
Notes: 2, 5, 8, 10, 11, 12

Bethlehem Inn

72 Stallion Hill, Box 451, 01566
(508) 347-3013

Bethlehem Inn is operated to help defray the costs of operating Bethlehem in Sturbridge. Guests share the family living room and TV.

Host: Agnes Duquette
Doubles: 2 (1 PB; 1 SB) $40-60
Continental Breakfast
Credit Cards: No
Closed December
Notes: 2, 7, 9, 10, 11, 12, 13

Colonel Ebenezer Crafts Inn

Box 187, 01566
(508) 347-3313

Restored colonial farmhouse built in 1786, featuring spacious grounds, a library, sun porch, and outdoor pool. A gracious, quiet, and peaceful inn offering grand New England views. Located 1.3 miles from the Publick House Historic Inn.

Hosts: Patricia & Henri Bibeau
Doubles: 8 (PB) $90-135
Type of Beds: 1 Twin; 3 Double; 2 Queen; 2 Suites
Continental Breakfast
Credit Cards: A, B, C, E
Notes: 2, 5, 8, 10, 11, 12, 14

Commonwealth Inn

Box 60, 01566
(508) 347-7603

A 100-year-old Victorian mansion with a large wraparound porch, fireplaces, hot tub, player piano. Located one mile from Old Sturbridge Village. Walk to restaurants, antique shops, lakes, rivers, and cross-country skiing.

Host: Kevin MacConnell
Singles: 6 (4 PB; 2 SB) $39
Doubles: 2 (1 PB; 1 SB) $59
Type of Beds: 3 Double; 7 Queen
Full Breakfast
Credit Cards: No
Notes: 2, 5, 7, 8, 9, 10, 11, 12, 13

Sturbridge Country Inn

530 Main Street, 01566
(508) 347-5503

Circa 1840 Greek Revival mansion, fully restored post-and-beam structure. Vaulted ceilings, sun porches. Each room has a fireplace and luxury bath, plus many amenities. Close to Old Sturbridge Village. Conveniently located in the heart of Sturbridge.

Host: Kevin MacConnell
Doubles: 9 (PB) $79-99
Type of Beds: 9 Queen
Continental Breakfast
Credit Cards: A, B, C, D
Notes: 2, 4, 5, 7, 8, 9, 10, 11, 12, 13

SUDBURY

Checkerberry Corner B&B

5 Checkerberry Circle, 01776
(508) 443-8660

Located in a quiet residential neighborhood, we are only a short drive to Longfellow's Wayside Inn, the Old North bridge, the Alcott, Emerson, Hawthorne, and Thoreau houses. Boston's Freedom Trail, Quincy Markets, and other attractions are easily reached within forty minutes.

Hosts: Stu & Irene MacDonald
Doubles: 3 (SB) $50-60
Type of Beds: 2 Twin; 1 Double; 1 Queen
Full Breakfast
Credit Cards: No
Notes: 2, 5, 8, 9, 10, 11, 12, 14

6 Pets welcome: 7 Smoking allowed: 8 Children welcome: 9 Social drinking allowed: 10 Tennis available: 11 Swimming available: 12 Golf available: 13 Skiing available: 14 May be booked through travel agents

Sudbury Bed & Breakfast

3 Drum Lane, 01776
(508) 443-2860

A large Garrison colonial home with traditional furnishings located on a quiet, tree-
studded acre. Close to Boston, Concord,
and Lexington. An abundance of outdoor
recreation and historical sights are near. We
offer friendly hospitality for the New
England visitor. Resident cat.

Hosts: Nancy & Don Somers
Singles: 1 (PB) $40
Doubles: 1 (PB) $50
Type of Beds: 2 Twin; 1 Double
Continental Breakfast
Credit Cards: No
Closed Christmas Day
Notes: 2, 5, 8, 9, 10, 11, 12

SWAMPSCOTT

B&B Registry #MA-01907MAR

Box 8174, St. Paul, MN, 55108
(612) 646-4238

Sit on the spacious porch and watch the
ocean in this quiet North Shore town. The
home is decorated in country style. Guests
are invited to sit in the comfortable sofas in
front of the wood-burning stove and enjoy
their evenings. Near great seafood restaurants, shops, and transit.

Singles: 1 (SB) $55-60
Doubles: 3 (SB) $60-65
Type of Beds: 1 Twin; 2 Double; 1 Queen
Continental Breakfast
Credit Cards: A, B, C
Notes: 5, 8 (over 4), 11, 12

The Maguire's

43 Hampden Street, 01907
(617) 593-5732

Located two blocks from the Atlantic Ocean
and public beaches, ten miles from historic
Boston. Public transportation available.
Horse and dog racing is held daily within

eight miles, and there are famous restaurants along the North Shore. Twenty
miles from Lexington and Concord; five
from Salem; eighteen from Gloucester and
Rockport.

Hosts: Tom & Arline Maguire
Singles: 1 (SB) $40
Doubles: 2 (SB) $50
Type of Beds: 3 Twin; 1 Double
Full breakfast weekends; continental weekdays
Credit Cards: No
Notes: 5, 7, 8, 9, 10, 11, 12

Oak Shores B&B

Oak Shores Bed & Breakfast

64 Fuller Avenue, 01907
(617) 599-7677

This 60-year-old Dutch colonial is on
Boston's lovely North Shore. Rooms are
filled with fine restored furniture. Sleep in
the comfort of old brass and iron beds, relax
in our private garden, or stroll the two blocks
to the beach. Near public transportation.

Host: Marjorie L. McClung
Singles: 1 (SB) $55
Doubles: 1 (SB) $60
Type of Beds: 2 Twin; 1 Double; 2 Cots
Continental Breakfast
Credit Cards: No
Closed Dec. 2 - March 31
Notes: 8 (9 and older), 10, 11

NOTES: Credit cards accepted: A Master Card; B Visa; C American Express; D Discover Card; E Diners
Club; F Other: 2 Personal checks accepted: 3 Lunch available: 4 Dinner available: 5 Open all year

The Victorian

B&B Marblehead & North Shore
Box 172, Beverly, MA, 01915
(508) 921-1336

This beautiful Victorian is furnished in American country decor with hand-stenciled walls. TV and refrigerator in each room; living room and covered porch downstairs. Bicycles available. Swampscott has some spectacular beaches and a number of excellent restaurants on and near the ocean. It's only fifteen minutes from Boston and Logan Airport, on the commuter rail and bus lines.

Doubles: 4 (SB) $55-70
Type of Beds: 4 Twin; 2 Double; 1 Queen; 2 Rollaways
Continental Breakfast
Credit Cards: A, B
Notes: 2, 5, 8 (over 6), 9, 10, 11, 12, 14

Vinnin Square

B&B Marblehead & North Shore
Box 172, Beverly, MA, 01915
(508) 921-1336

An attractive condominium next to a shopping mall and close to Marblehead, Swampscott, and Salem. The hostess is an insurance agent whose hobbies are tennis, swimming, and cycling. She also speaks Hebrew.

Doubles: 1 (SB) $45-55
Type of Beds: 1 Queen
Continental Breakfast
Credit Cards: No
Notes: 2, 5, 7, 8, 9, 10, 11, 12, 14

TAUNTON

Pineapple Hospitality MA 1014

Box F-821, New Bedford, MA 02742-0821
(508) 990-1696

This lovely circa 1775 Ambrose Lincoln House is listed on the National Register of Historic Places. The hip-roofed Georgian is almost entirely original, with an ample kitchen that typifies those in the homes of prosperous farmers of the period. Four working fireplaces. Open weekends only.

Doubles: 2 (PB) $50-65
Type of Beds: 2 Twin; 1 Queen
Full Breakfast
Credit Cards: No
Closed weekdays & Thanksgiving - New Years
Notes: 2, 8, 9, 10, 11, 12

TRURO, CAPE COD

B&B Registry #MA-0266PAR

Box 8174, St. Paul, MN, 55108
(612) 646-4238

Spacious 1815 Full-size Cape furnished with family antiques. Comfortable parlor for conversation and relaxing, screened porch, large yard. Beach towels available. Truro is an unspoiled little town with a beautiful bay, dunes, and ocean beaches within two miles.

Doubles: 3 (PB) $40-55
Type of Beds: 4 Double
Continental Breakfast
Credit Cards: No
Notes: 5, 7, 11

Edgewood Farm

Orleans B&B Assoc., Box 1312, Orleans, 02653
(508) 255-3824

This is authentic rural Truro, where a private lane leads to a typical old Cape and a long, low cottage. Surrounded by meadows, a trail up Great Hill leads to a view of the Atlantic. The cottage offers two bright studios; one with fireplace and kitchenette, the other with a sun room opening onto extensive lawns that are great for children. Three doubles, private bath, $65.

6 Pets welcome: 7 Smoking allowed: 8 Children welcome: 9 Social drinking allowed: 10 Tennis available: 11 Swimming available: 12 Golf available: 13 Skiing available: 14 May be booked through travel agents

Tonie's B&B

B&B Cape Cod, Box 341, W. Hyannisport, 02672
(508) 775-2772

A 250-year-old cape built by the founder of
the town of Truro, this house sits on high
ground and overlooks the Pamet River with
a distant view of Cape Cod Bay. Lush growth
and natural beauty add to the overall feeling
of this rural setting.

Doubles: 2 (PB) $60
Type of Beds: 2 Twin; 1 Double
Continental Breakfast
Credit Cards: No
Notes: 2, 7, 9, 10, 11, 12, 14

TYNGSBORO

B&B Folks 7

48 Springs Road, Bedford, MA 01730
(617) 275-9025

A modern condo with tennis and swimming
available on the perimeter. five minutes
from southern New Hampshire, forty-five to
Boston. Reduced rate for long-term stays.

Doubles: 1 (PB) $40-50
Type of Beds: 1 Queen
Continental Breakfast
Credit Cards: No
Notes: 2, 6, 8, 9, 10, 11, 12

TYRINGHAM

The Golden Goose

Main Road, 01264
(413) 243-3008

Small, friendly 1800 country inn, nestled in
Tyringham Valley in the Berkshires. Victorian antiques, sitting rooms with
fireplaces, homemade breakfast fare.
Within a half hour are Tanglewood, Stockbridge, Jacob's Pillow, Hancock Shaker Village, the Normal Rockwell Museum,
Berkshire Theater Festival, skiing, golf, tennis. The inn is on the Appalachian Trail.

Hosts: Lilja & Joe Rizzo
Doubles: 6 (3 PB; 3 SB) $55-95
Type of Beds: 1 Twin; 4 Double; 1 Queen
Continental Breakfast
Credit Cards: No
Notes: 2, 5, 7, 8 (in apartment), 9, 10, 11, 12, 13, 14

UXBRIDGE

B&B Rhode Island #MA-155

Box 3291-ND, Newport, R.I., 02840
(401) 849-1298

Elegant yet comfortable, this seventeen-
room Victorian has spacious landscaped
grounds that include a terrace and barn. The
hostess is an interior designer who has used
her skills to fill her house with tasteful antiues, lace curtains, and woven rugs.

Doubles: 3 (PB) $65
Type of Beds: 2 Twin; 2 Queen
Full Breakfast
Credit Cards: No
Notes: 5, 8 (over 8), 9, 10, 11, 12, 14

VINEYARD HAVEN, MARTHA'S VINEYARD

Captain Dexter House

Box 2457, 02568
(508) 693-6564

Built in 1843 as the home of sea captain
Rodulphus Dexter, the inn has been
meticulously restored and furnished in
period with antiques. Several rooms have
working fireplaces and four-poster,
canopied beds. Our complimentary continental breakfast (baked on the premises)
and evening aperitif set the tone of
hospitality. Walk to the beaches, the ferry,
restaurants, and shops.

Host: Alisa Lengel
Doubles: 8 (PB) $55-145
Type of Beds: 4 Double; 2 Queen; 2 King
Continental Breakfast
Minimum stay weekends in season: 3
Credit Cards: A, B, C
Notes: 2, 5, 7, 8 (12 or older), 9, 10, 11, 12, 14

NOTES: Credit cards accepted: A Master Card; B Visa; C American Express; D Discover Card; E Diners
Club; F Other: 2 Personal checks accepted: 3 Lunch available: 4 Dinner available: 5 Open all year

Hanover House

Box 2107, 02568
(508) 693-1066

A large old inn offering the conveniences of a modern hotel while retaining the personalized hospitality of the inns of yesteryear. Spacious rooms with private baths and cable TV. Within walking distance of the ferry and minutes from fine dining, beautiful beaches, and quaint shops.

Host: Barbara Hanover
Doubles: 16 (PB) $83-118
Type of Beds: 6 Double; 13 Queen; Cribs
Continental Breakfast, May-Oct.
Credit Cards: A, B, C
Notes: 2, 5, 7, 8, 9, 10, 11, 12, 14

Lothrop Merry House

Owen Park, Box 1939, 02568
(508) 693-1646

The Merry House, built in 1790, overlooks beautiful Vineyard Haven Harbor, has a private beach, expansive lawn, flower-bordered terrace. Most rooms have ocean view and fireplace. All are charming, furnished with antiques and fresh flowers. Complimentary canoe and sunfish for guests' use. Sailing also available on our 54' ketch, *Laissez Faire*.

Hosts: John & Mary Clarke
Doubles: 7 (4 PB; 3 SB) $60-150
Type of Beds: 3 Twin; 5 Double; 2 Queen
Continental Breakfast
Minimum stay weekends & holidays: 2
Credit Cards: A, B
Notes: 2 (for deposit), 5, 7, 8, 9, 10, 11, 12

Thorncroft Inn

Box 1022, 02568
(508) 693-3333

Nineteen antique-appointed rooms in four restored buildings. Private baths, working fireplaces, air-conditioning. Romantic and intimate, in a noncommercial environment. Located on 3.5 landscaped acres in an ex-clusive residential neighborhood one mile from the main ferry dock. Off-season rates available.

Hosts: Karl & Lynn Buder
Doubles: 19 (PB) $109.25-224.25
Type of Beds: 1 Twin; 5 Double; 13 Queen
Full Breakfast
Minimum stay weekends & holidays in season: 3
Credit Cards: A, B, C
Notes: 2, 5, 7 (limited), 8 (over 12), 9, 14

WAQUOIT

Host Homes of Boston #35

Box 117, Waban Branch, Boston, 02168
(617) 244-1308

On Cape Cod, this contemporary house is right on the water, with glass walls, cathedral ceilings, and a view of Vineyard Sound. Rooms have private decks, telephone, private beach. Passive solarium and bubbling spa for eight. Located between Falmouth and Hyannis.

Doubles: 2 (SB) $85
Type of Beds: 1 Twin; 1 Double; 1 King
Continental Breakfast
Minimum stay: 2
Credit Cards: A, B, C
Closed Labor Day - late June
Notes: 2, 8 (12 and over), 9, 10, 11, 12

WARE

Berkshire PV22

Berkshire B&B Homes
Box 211, Williamsburg, MA, 01096
(413) 268-7244

This 1880 colonial welcomes children (crib available). Located close to Quabbin Reservoir, Brimfield Flea Market, Sturbridge Village, the University of Massachusetts, and Hampshire College.

Doubles: 5 (SB) $55-65
Type of Beds: 2 Twin; 3 Double; 2 Queen
Full Breakfast
Credit Cards: No
Notes: 2, 5, 8, 10, 11, 12

1880 Inn

14 Pleasant Street, 01082
(413) 967-7847

A beautiful twelve-room colonial inn, complete with six fireplaces and rustic country beams. Each room is named. Enjoy afternoon tea before the cozy fireplace.

Host: Margaret Skutnik
Doubles: 5 (2 PB; 3 SB) $52.25-57.75
Type of Beds: 4 Twin; 3 Double; 2 Queen
Full Breakfast
Minimum stay weekends & holidays: 2
Credit Cards: No
Notes: 5, 8, 9, 10, 11, 12, 14

WAREHAM

Little Harbor Guest House

20 Stockton Shortcut, 02571
(508) 295-6329

Surrounded by an eighteen-hole golf course, we are a short half-hour drive to Plymouth, New Bedford, or Hyannis. In-ground pool, or walk to the beach. There are many great restaurants and quaint shops only a few miles away.

Hosts: Dennis & Ken
Doubles: 5 (SB) $57
Type of Beds: 2 Twin; 6 Double
Continental Breakfast
Credit Cards: A, B
Notes: 2, 5, 7, 8, 9, 10, 11, 12

WELLESLEY

Host Homes of Boston #35

Box 117, Waban Branch, Boston, 02168
(617) 244-1308

This 1890 home is surrounded by fields and offers quiet, gracious ambience. Breakfast is served in the guest sitting room/library with fireplace and garden vista. Resident dog. Boston only sixteen miles away; one mile to Wellesley College.

Doubles: 2 (PB) $62-72
Type of Beds: 4 Twin

Continental Breakfast
Minimum stay: 2
Credit Cards: A, B, C
Notes: 2, 5, 7

WELLFLEET

Captain Lewace House

Orleans B&B Assoc., Box 1312, Orleans, 02653
(508) 255-3824

A large, handsome, historic house, restored to perfect condition. Walk to everything, including Wellfleet Harbor Beach. Private porch, air-conditioning, sitting area. Hosts have a travel agency and are very knowledgeable about the Cape. One double, private bath, $75.

Deep Denes

Orleans B&B Assoc., Box 1312, Orleans, 02653
(508) 255-3824

Overlooking the Atlantic, set in unusual gardens, with lots of glass to take advantage of the views, this house offers peace and enrichment. Musical, artistic hosts. Sitting room with fireplace, Japanese garden; short distance to ocean beach. One double, private bath, $60.

1820 House

Orleans B&B Assoc., Box 1312, Orleans, 02653
(508) 255-3824

Authentic Cape Cod, circa 1820. Charming furnishing, original fireplaces, and a steep old Cape stairway to the second floor. Himalayan cat in residence. Two doubles, shared bath, $45.

Inn at Duck Creek

Box 364, 02667
(508) 349-9333

NOTES: Credit cards accepted: A Master Card; B Visa; C American Express; D Discover Card; E Diners Club; F Other: 2 Personal checks accepted: 3 Lunch available: 4 Dinner available: 5 Open all year

Five-acre complex with duck pond and salt marsh. Two outstanding restaurants. Within walking distance of the village of Wellfleet and within the Cape Cod National Seashore. Antique shops, fine art galleries, ocean and bay beaches, fresh-water ponds, cycling, and boating all nearby.

Hosts: Robert Morrill & Judith Pihl
Doubles: 25 (17 PB; 8 SB) $55-90
Type of Beds: 10 Twin; 15 Double
Continental Breakfast
Minimum stay weekends: 2; holidays: 3
Credit Cards: A, B, C
Closed Oct. 15-May 15
Notes: 4, 7, 8, 9, 10, 11, 12

The Inn at Duck Creek

Marsh View

Orleans B&B Assoc., Box 1312, Orleans, 02653
(508) 255-3824

Herons may be seen wading in the salt marsh beyond the sliding doors leading from your room to the private patio. TV, refrigerator. Host is knowledgeable about golf and fishing, and knows where the best oysters may be found. Hostess is an enthusiastic quilter and good cook. Harriet, the cat, is in residence. Full breakfast. One double, private bath, $50.

Owl's Nest

Orleans B&B Assoc., Box 1312, Orleans, 02653
(508) 255-3824

A Gothic contemporary located on 6 acres known as Owl Woods. Cathedral living room and dining room, filled with antiques and collectibles. Upper level, skylighted sitting and writing area. Walk down a country lane to a picturesque bay beach. A short ride to ocean or pond swimming and Wellfleet's galleries and shops. Two doubles, shared bath, $60.

WEST BARNSTABLE

Honeysuckle Hill

591 Main Street, 02668
(508) 362-8418

Charming country inn near the dunes of Sandy Neck beach. Full country breakfast and afternoon tea. Feather beds, down comforters, and homemade cookies at bedside. English toiletries and terry cloth robes in private baths. Wraparound screen porch filled with wicker, and a large great room for games and large-screen TV watching make this a perfect spot for any season.

Hosts: Bob & Barbara Rosenthal
Doubles: 3 (PB) $75-105
Type of Beds: 2 Double; 1 King
Full Breakfast
Minimum stay on seasonal weekends & holidays: 2
Credit Cards: A, B, C
Notes: 2, 5, 7, 8 (over 12), 9, 10, 11, 12

WEST BOYLSTON

The Rose Cottage

24 Worcester Street, 01583
(508) 835-4034

Enjoy the quiet elegance of a nineteenth-century cottage overlooking Wachusett Reservoir. Marble fireplaces, gaslight lamps, gabled roof, and gingerbread dormers.

Honeysuckle Hill

Browse our antique shop filled with two floors of treasures.

Hosts: Michael & Loretta Kittredge
Doubles: 5 (1 PB; 4 S2B) $65-71
Apartment: 1 fully furnished; $384/week
Type of Beds: 1 Twin; 4 Double
Full Breakfast
Minimum stay holidays: 2
Reservations required
Credit Cards: No
Notes: 2, 5, 7 (limited), 8, 9, 10, 11, 12, 13

WEST FALMOUTH

The Elms

Box 895, 02574
(508) 540-7232

Charming Victorian, built in the early 1800s, features nime beautifully appointed bedrooms, seven private baths, and antique decor throughout. A four-course gourmet breakfast is served each morning. Tour the manicured grounds to survey the flower and herb gardens or relax in the gazebo. One-half mile from the ocean.

Hosts: Betty & Joe Mazzucchelli
Doubles: 9 (7 PB; 2 SB) $70-85
Type of Beds: 4 Twin; 5 Double; 2 Queen
Full Breakfast
Credit Cards: No
Notes: 2, 5, 7, 8 (over 14), 9, 10, 11, 12

Old Silver Beach Bed & Breakfast

3 Cliffwood Lane, Box 642, 02574
(508) 540-5446

Located near Old Silver Beach, the Cape Cod Canal, and island ferries. Nearby golf, antiquing, restaurants, and shops.

Host: Beverley A. Kane
Doubles: 2 (SB) $35-55
Continental-plus Breakfast
Credit Cards: No
Notes: 2, 5, 7, 8, 9, 10, 11, 12, 14

WESTFORD

B&B Folks 8

48 Springs Road, Bedford, MA 01730
(617) 275-9025

Charming ranch home in rural Mass., near Boston and New Hampshire. Reduced rate for long-term stays.

Doubles: 4 (SB) $40-50
Continental Breakfast
Credit Cards: No
Notes: 2, 4, 8, 9, 10, 11, 12

B&B Folks 9

48 Springs Road, Bedford, MA 01730
(617) 275-9025

NOTES: Credit cards accepted: A Master Card; B Visa; C American Express; D Discover Card; E Diners Club; F Other: 2 Personal checks accepted: 3 Lunch available: 4 Dinner available: 5 Open all year

A 200-year-old home with hand-stenciled walls and an old quilt collection. Craft shop attached. Reduced rates for long-term stays.

Singles: 2 (SB) $40
Doubles: 1 (SB) $50
Type of Beds: 6 Twin
Continental Breakfast
Credit Cards: No
Notes: 2, 8, 9, 10, 11, 12

Cape Cod Sunny Pines B&B Inn

WEST HARWICH

Cape Cod Sunny Pines B&B Inn

77 Main Street, 02671
(508) 432-9628

Irish hospitality in a Victorian ambience. Family-style gourmet Irish breakfast by candlelight on bone china and crystal. All private, antique-decorated suites. Evening happy hour poolside or fireside. Walk to Nantucket Sound, fine restaurants, biking and hiking tails. Take day trips to the islands or go whale watching.

Hosts: Eileen & Jack Connell
Singles: 1 (PB) $82
Doubles: 6 (PB) $104.21
Type of Beds: 2 Twin; 4 Queen; 2 King
Full Breakfast
Minimum stay weekdays & weekends: 2 ; holidays: 3
Credit Cards: A, B, C
Notes: 2, 5, 7, 8 (over 12), 9, 10, 11, 12

Lion's Head Inn

186 Belmont Road, Box 444, 02671
(508) 432-7766

The Lion's Head Inn is a former sea captain's house dating from the 1820s. Recently renovated, it combines the charm of yesteryear with modern amenities. Located on a private residential street with a Nantucket Sound beach one-half mile away. Swimming pool on premises.

Hosts: Bill & Kathleen Lockyer
Doubles: 6 (PB) $80-99
Cottages: 1 Bedroom & 2 Bedroom
Full Breakfast
Minimum stay July & Aug.: 2
Credit Cards: A, B
Notes: 2, 5, 7, 8 (by arrangement), 9, 10, 11, 12

The Tern Inn

91 Chase Street, 02671
(508) 432-3714

Prime mid-cape location near Nantucket Sound beaches. The inn presents a cheerful atmosphere in a nostalgic original cape built two centuries ago. Wide board floors, "bean pot" cellar, and sparkling windows are complimented by antiques and hospitality.

Hosts: Bill & Jane Myers
Doubles: 5 (PB) $49.37-73.50
Type of Beds: 4 Twin; 2 Double; 1 Queen
Full Breakfast
Minimum stay weekends & holidays: 2
Credit Cards: No
Closed Dec. 1-April 1
Notes: 2, 7, 8, 9, 10, 11, 12

WEST NEWBURY

West Newbury B&B

B&B Marblehead & North Shore
Box 172, Beverly, MA, 01915
(508) 921-1336

In a country setting, where roadside produce stalls stock the most delicious green beans and corn. Beautiful antique-furnished Cape Cod home, surrounded by a few colonials and other capes in a small group. Guest

6 Pets welcome: 7 Smoking allowed: 8 Children welcome: 9 Social drinking allowed: 10 Tennis available: 11 Swimming available: 12 Golf available: 13 Skiing available: 14 May be booked through travel agents

living room with working fireplace and bar setups; swimming pool, large deck.

Doubles: 2 (SB) $55-65
Type of Beds: 2 Twin; 1 Double; 1 Rollaway
Continental Breakfast
Credit Cards: No
Notes: 2, 5, 7, 8, 9, 10, 11, 12, 13 (XC), 14

WEST NEWTON

Host Homes of Boston #36

Box 117, Waban Branch, Boston, 02168
(617) 244-1308

This exceptional 1830 home on West Newton Hill was built by Increase Sumner Withington. It's of Italianate design with a Georgian porch, and is filled with fireplaces, antiques, and quiet formality. Resident poodle. One-half mile to I-90 and a quick drive to the airport, Boston, or Cambridge.

Doubles: 2 (PB) $75
Type of Beds: 2 Twin; 1 Double
Continental Breakfast
Minimum stay: 2
Credit Cards: A, B, C
Notes: 2, 5, 9, 10

WEST STOCKBRIDGE

Card Lake Country Inn

Main Street, 01266
(413) 232-7120

Our charmingly restored guest rooms all have antiques, and many have brass beds. The atmosphere is warm, comfortable, and casual. The restaurant and tavern on the premises serve excellent food with daily specials and homemade soups and desserts. The building dates back to 1803.

Hosts: Lynn & Larry Schiffman
Doubles: 8 (4 PB; 4 SB) $50-100
Type of Beds: 2 Twin; 3 Double; 3 King
Full Breakfast
Credit Cards: A, B, C
Notes: 2, 3, 4, 5, 7, 8, 9, 10, 11, 12, 13

WESTWOOD

Host Homes of Boston #37

Box 117, Waban Branch, Boston, 02168
(617) 244-1308

A tree grows through the roof of this 1958 redwood contemporary in the woods. A stunning blend of antiques, modern art, potters, and porcelain collection. Rooms have window-walls, TV, air-conditioning. Twelve miles southwest of Boston near I-95.

Doubles: 2 (PB) $55
Type of Beds: 2 Twin; 1 Double
Continental Breakfast
Minimum stay: 2
Credit Cards: A, B, C
Notes: 2, 5, 9, 10, 12

WEYMOUTH

Host Homes of Boston #38

Box 117, Waban Branch, Boston, 02168
(617) 244-1308

Pre-revolutionary landmark on the Fore River has been revived by third-generation owners of this historic home. The suite has a fireplace, TV, river view. Third-floor room has TV and a view. Watch the boats and water life. Families welcome. Short drive to Boston, Plymouth, Cape Cod; subway or water shuttle to Boston is nearby.

Doubles: 2 (PB) $60-96
Type of Beds: 2 Twin; 1 Double; 1 Queen
Full Breakfast
Minimum stay: 2
Credit Cards: A, B, C
Notes: 2, 5, 8, 11, 12

WHATELY

Berkshire PV21

Berkshire B&B Homes
Box 211, Williamsburg, MA, 01096
(413) 268-7244

An 1870, fourteen-room farmhouse on 50 acres amid the beautiful farms along the

Connecticut River. Wraparound porch with summer furniture, plants, and a swing. Good location for biking and hiking, and convenient for Deerfield, the five-college area, I-91, Mt. Sugarloaf, and pick-you-own berry fields.

Singles: 1 (SB) $45
Doubles: 4 (SB) $60-65
Type of Beds: 7 Twin; 1 Double; 1 King
Full Breakfast
Credit Cards: No
Notes: 2, 5, 8, 10, 11, 12

WILBRAHAM

Bed & Breakfast With Barbara and Bob

15 Three Rivers Road, 01095
(413) 596-6258

This lovely 1928 Dutch colonial is located in the country. Immaculate guest rooms are on the second floor with a shared bath and Jacuzzi. Sun porch, TV, swimming pool, and patio for guests' use. Your host, an artist whose works grace the home, is a former banker, while your hostess managed an insurance agency.

Hosts: Barbara & Bob Gliddene
Singles: 1 (SB) $45
Doubles: 2 (SB) $50
Type of Beds: 3 Twin; 1 Double
Continental Breakfast
Credit Cards: No
Notes: 2, 5, 6, 8, 9, 10, 11, 12, 13

WILLIAMSBURG

Berkshire PV3

Berkshire B&B Homes
Box 211, Williamsburg, MA, 01096
(413) 268-7244

A 200-year-old farmhouse with antique and country furnishings, common room with TV, and full breakfast. Near the five-college area; seven miles to Northampton and twelve to Amherst.

Doubles: 3 (SB) $45
Type of Beds: 2 Twin; 2 Double
Full Breakfast
Credit Cards: No
Notes: 2, 5, 8, 10, 11, 12

WILLIAMSTOWN

Berkshire NC4

Berkshire B&B Homes
Box 211, Williamsburg, MA, 01096
(413) 268-7244

An 1870s farmhouse on 127 acres of land, furnished with country and natural wood. Breakfast room and sitting room with fireplace, gazebo where breakfast is served when weather permits. Near Pontoosuc Lake, Brodie, Jiminy Peak, Williams College, Sterling Clarke Museum, and summer playhouse.

Doubles: 3 (1 PB; 2 SB) $65-85
Type of Beds: 3 Double
Continental Breakfast
Credit Cards: No
Notes: 2, 5, 7, 8, 10, 11, 12, 13

Berkshire NC11

Berkshire B&B Homes
Box 211, Williamsburg, MA, 01096
(413) 268-7244

This 200-year-old house is on a 600-acre working dairy farm with beautiful views of mountains and fields. Furnished with antiues. Tours of the farm, swimming in the pond, fishing. Near hiking, skiing, Williams College, the Williamstown Summer theater, Sterling Clarke Museum. Minutes to Bennington, VT.

Doubles: 2 (SB) $40
Type of Beds: 2 Twin; 1 Double
Continental Breakfast
Credit Cards: No
Notes: 2, 5, 7, 8, 10, 11, 12, 13

Upland Meadow House

1249 Northwest Hill Road, 01267
(413) 458-3990

6 Pets welcome: 7 Smoking allowed: 8 Children welcome: 9 Social drinking allowed: 10 Tennis available: 11 Swimming available: 12 Golf available: 13 Skiing available: 14 May be booked through travel agents

Situated on the slope of the Taconic Range, this contemporary house provides a panoramic view. With 160 acres of field and woods, privacy and quiet are assured. Williams College woods offers opportunities for hiking and cross-country skiing.

Hosts: Pan & Alfred Whitmas
Doubles: 2 (SB) $55-60
Type of Beds: 1 Twin; 1 Double
Full Breakfast
Credit Cards: No
Notes: 2, 5, 10, 11, 12, 13

WORTHINGTON

American Country Collection 094

984 Gloucester Place
Schenectady, N.Y., 12309
(518) 370-4948

A new five-bedroom colonial inn and restaurant on 23 acres near the town common, in the most scenic area of the rolling Hampshire Hills and adjacent to one of the finest ski-touring centers in New England. A short ride from Pittsfield or Northampton. Gift shop and antique store on the premises.

Doubles: 5 (PB) $70
Type of Beds: 4 Twin; 3 Queen
Full Breakfast
Credit Cards: No
Notes: 2, 3, 4, 5, 7 (limited), 8 (10 and over), 9, 13, 14

Hill Gallery

HC65, Box 96, 01098
(413) 238-5914

Located on a mountaintop in the Hampshire Hills on 25 acres. Enjoy relaxed country living in an owner-built contemporary home with art gallery, fireplaces, and swimming pool. Self-contained cottage also available.

Hosts: Ellen & Walter Korzec
Doubles: 2 (PB) $30-50
Type of Beds: 1 Double; 1 King
Full Breakfast

Minimum stay holidays: 2
Credit Cards: No
Notes: 2, 5, 8 (over 5), 9, 10, 11, 12, 13

Inn Yesterday

Huntington Road, 01098
(413) 238-5529

In 1877 this restored Greek Revival home was known as Frissell's Inn. Today Inn Yesterday welcomes guests with many amenities of the past, including antiques throughout. In nice weather, a full country breakfast is served in the porch sun room.

Hosts: Janet & Robert Osborne
Doubles: 3 (SB) $45-55
Type of Beds: 2 Twin; 2 Double
Full Breakfast
Credit Cards: No
Notes: 2, 5, 8 (over 5), 9, 10, 11, 12, 13

The Worthington Inn at Four Corners Farm

Old North Road, 01098
(413) 238-4441

The Worthington Inn is a 1780 colonial listed in the National Historic Register. With wide pine floorboards, billowy soft down comforters, and British and American antiues, the Worthington is a trip into the past. A full gourmet breakfast is served at an impressive seventeenth-century table in front of a glowing fireplace. Winter offers skiing at nearby Hickory Hill Touring Center.

Hosts: Debi & Joe Shaw
Doubles: 4 (PB) $70
Type of Beds: 2 Twin; 3 Double
Full Breakfast
Credit Cards: A, B
Notes: 2, 5, 9, 11, 12, 13, 14

YARMOUTHPORT

Old Yarmouth Inn

223 Main Street, 02675
(508) 362-3191

NOTES: Credit cards accepted: A Master Card; B Visa; C American Express; D Discover Card; E Diners Club; F Other: 2 Personal checks accepted: 3 Lunch available: 4 Dinner available: 5 Open all year

The oldest inn on Cape Cod (built in 1696), on historic Rt. 6A. Charming antique homes, inns, and antique shops along the road, as well as golf, swimming, and other activities.

Host: Shane Peros
Doubles: (PB) $80-90
Full Breakfast
Credit Cards: A, B, C, D, E
Notes: 3, 4, 5, 7, 9, 11, 12

One Centre Street Inn

1 Centre Street, 02675
(508) 363-8910

This vintage colonial inn has been restored with a lot of care and is very comfortable, with country decor and antique furnishings throughout. The house boasts wide pine floors, old hutches and clocks, hook rugs, and fresh-cut flowers. We serve an excellent breakfast with freshly baked goods. AAA approved; on the National Historic Register.

Hosts: Stefanie & Bill Wright
Doubles: 5 (3 PB; 2 SB) $50-85
Type of Beds: 3 Twin; 4 Double
Full breakfast winter; continental summer
Credit Cards: A, B, C
Notes: 2, 4, 5, 8, 9, 11, 12, 14

Paddock-Thacher House

B&B Cape Cod, Box 341, W. Hyannisport, 02672
(508) 775-2772

Built 207 years ago, this unique cape house has all the character of the past reflected in its antiques and Early American decor. Walk to fresh-water beaches or to salt-water bay beaches. Restaurants, shops are a short walk away.

Doubles: 2 (SB) $60
Type of Beds: 2 Twin; 1 Double
Continental Breakfast
Credit Cards: No
Notes: 5, 7, 8, 9, 10, 11, 12, 14

Wedgewood Inn

83 Main Street, 02675
(508) 362-5157

Located in the historic area of Cape Cod, the inn is in the National Register of Historic Places and has been featured in *Country Inns of America*. Near beaches, art galleries, antique shops, golf, boating, and fine restaurants. Fireplaces and private screened porches.

Doubles: 6 (PB) $95-145
Type of Beds: 2 Twin; 1 Double; 5 Queen
Full Breakfast
Notes: 2, 5, 7 (restricted), 8 (over 10), 9, 10, 11, 12

One Centre Street Inn

6 Pets welcome: 7 Smoking allowed: 8 Children welcome: 9 Social drinking allowed: 10 Tennis available: 11 Swimming available: 12 Golf available: 13 Skiing available: 14 May be booked through travel agents

Blaney Park

Manistique

St. Ignace

Stephenson

Harbor Springs

Bay View

Charlevoix

Northport

Omena

Traverse City

Maple City-Leland

Black River

Frankfort

Harrisville

Manistee

Ludington

Pentwater

Caseville

Harbor Beach

Midland

Bay City

Caro

MICHIGAN

Frankemuth

Grand Haven

Ithaca

Clio

Spring Lake

Owosso

Lapeer

Grand Rapids

East Lansing

Grand Blanc

Holland

Fenton

Romeo

Saugatuck

Howell

Detroit

Douglas

Lansing

Allegan

Dimondale

Dearborn

South Haven

Battle Creek

Ann Arbor

Paw Paw

Albion

Brooklyn

Union Pier

Hillsdale

Tecumseh

Niles

Blissfield

Michigan

D's Bed & Breakfast

Box 1731, Dearborn, 48128
(313) 561-6041

Handsome Victorian adorned with treasured antiques. Easy walk to Albion College campus. Two double rooms, one twin, private bath. Continental breakfast; children welcome. $45.

Winchester Inn

524 Marshal, 49010
(616) 673-3621

The Winchester Inn is centrally located to Saugatuck, Holland, Grand Rapids, and Kalamazoo for both business and vacation travelers. Visitors will enjoy antiquing, skiing, tennis, swimming, golf, as well as murder mystery weekends offered at our historic 1863 Italianate mansion.

Hosts: Gail & Keith Miller, Marge & Shawn Gavan
Doubles: 6 (PB)
Type of Beds: 2 Twin; 4 Double; 1 Queen; 1 King
Full Breakfast
Credit Cards: A, B
Notes: 2, 4, 5, 7, 8, 9, 10, 11, 12, 13, 14

B&B in Michigan #AA-1

Box 1731, Dearborn, 48128
(313) 561-6041

Two-story farmhouse built in 1859. Many quaint architectural features remain. Large country kitchen; antiques, handmade quilts in each room. Large dog in residence. Children and smokers welcome. One twin room, one double, private baths: $50. One double, one single, shared bath: $45. Continental-plus breakfast.

B&B in Michigan #AA-3

Box 1731, Dearborn, 48128
(313) 561-6041

Well-traveled hosts have decorated their lovely home with mementoes from all over the world. Close to town, but country atmosphere with wooded acreage and a small stream. German spoken. No smoking, no pets; large dog in residence. One room with double bed, one with single; shared bath. Two-night minimum, continental breakfast. $45.

B&B in Michigan #AA-4

Box 1731, Dearborn, 48128
(313) 561-6041

Country Farm Park is right in the backyard of this ranch home for wild-flower walks and bird watching. Cats in residence. Continental-plus breakfast. Double bed room, twin room, queen room; shared bath. $40-50.

B&B in Michigan #AA-5

Box 1731, Dearborn, 48128
(313) 561-6041

6 Pets welcome: 7 Smoking allowed: 8 Children welcome: 9 Social drinking allowed: 10 Tennis available: 11 Swimming available: 12 Golf available: 13 Skiing available: 14 May be booked through travel agents

Spacious third-floor suite with double bed, sitting area, private bath, and small balcony. Within walking distance of the University of Michigan, downtown Ann Arbor, and university hospital. No smoking. Continental breakfast. $55.

The Homestead Bed & Breakfast

9279 Macon Road, Saline, 48176
(313) 429-9625

In the country, within fifteen minutes of Ann Arbor and Ypsilanti. Relax in the living room or parlor of our 1851 brick farmhouse furnished with comfortable antiques. Walk, cross-country ski on our 50 acres of woods, fields, and river. A traditional B&B and very special place. Ask for our brochure.

Host: Shirley Grossman
Singles: 1 (SB) $26
Doubles: 4 (SB) $45-55
Type of Beds: 1 Twin; 4 Double
Full Breakfast
Credit Cards: A, B, E
Closed Dec. 24
Notes: 2, 5, 7, 9, 10, 12, 13, 14

BATTLE CREEK

The Old Lamp-Lighter's

276 Capital Ave. NE (north M66), 49017
(616) 963-2603

Features of this magnificent home include: Fifteen-inch-thick walls, clear clay French tile roof, porch roofs and house gutters of copper, quarry tile porch floor. The two-floor foyer features the original stenciled canvas with its background restored, an elegant open oak staircase, and a large stained glass window on the west wall. The library, always available to guests, features a fireplace flanked by shelves covered with leaded glass doors depicting Aladdin's lamp. Close to the Y Center, Bailey Park, Kellogg Community College, McCamly Place, Civic Theatre, Kellogg Center Arena and Auditorium, shops, restaurants, and the linear parkway for walks and jogging.

Host: Roberta Stewart
Doubles: 6 (4PB; 2SB)
Type of Beds: 4 Twin; 8 Double
Full Breakfast
Credit Cards: A, B, C
Notes: 2, 4, 5, 8, 10, 11, 12, 13(XC), 14

BAY CITY

Wm. Clements Inn

1712 Center Avenue, 48708
(517) 894-4600

The Clements mansion has eight newly renovated guest rooms that are restful yet elegantly decorated with rich Victorian decor. Some original pieces remain. Accommodations include private baths, telephones with modems, and many other modern conveniences. The home has been restored to respond to the needs of the corporate traveler, and private meeting rooms are available for business gatherings and presentations.

Hosts: Beverley & Elden Bender
Doubles: 6 (PB) $45-89
Type of Beds: 2 Twin; 4 Queen; 1 Queen hideabed
Full Breakfast
Credit Cards: A, B, C
Notes: 2, 5, 8, 9, 10, 11, 14

BAY VIEW

Terrace Inn

Box 1478, 49770
(616) 347-2410

The Terrace Inn, a romantic Victorian hotel, was built in 1910 and retains its early twentieth-century charm. each of the 44 rooms is furnished in original period furniture and has a private bath. The dining room, open for breakfast, lunch, and dinner in season, has a reputation for fine dining.

NOTES: Credit cards accepted: A Master Card; B Visa; C American Express; D Discover Card; E Diners Club; F Other: 2 Personal checks accepted: 3 Lunch available: 4 Dinner available: 5 Open all year

Hosts: Patrick & Mary Lou Barbour
Doubles: 44 (PB) $62-68
Type of Beds: 8 Twin; 6 Double; 30 Queen
Full breakfast in season; continental off-season
Credit Cards: A, B, C
Notes: 2, 3, 4, 5, 7, 8, 9, 10, 11, 12, 13, 14

BLACK RIVER

Silver Creek Lodge Bed N' Breakfast
4361 US 23 South, 48721
(517) 471-2198; 724-6430

Unique home and antique shop on 80 tranquil wooded acres adjoining 5,200 acres of federal forest. Hiking, cross-country ski trails, hay and sleigh rides. Enjoy watching deer, turkey, and all forms of wildlife in a beautiful woodland setting.

Hosts: Kim, Jim, & Bill Moses
Singles: 2 (SB) $31.20
Doubles: 3 (1 PB; 2 SB) $52
Type of Beds: 6 Twin; 3 Double
Full Breakfast
Minimum stay holidays: 2
Credit Cards: A, B
Nearby boarding for pets
Notes: 2, 5, 7, 8 (over 5), 9, 10, 11, 12

BLANEY PARK

Celibeth House
Blaney Park Rd., Rt. 1, Box 58A, 49836
(906) 283-3409

The Celibeth House, built in 1905, offers eight lovely rooms. Each room is spacious, clean, and tastefully furnished. Guests may also enjoy the cozy living room, a guest reading room, enclosed quaint porch, and a lovely back porch overlooking 86 acres.

Host: Elsa Strom
Doubles: 8 (6PB; 2SB)
Type of Beds: 6 Twin; 4 Double; 1 Queen; 1 King
Continental Breakfast
Credit Cards: A, B
Open May 1 - Dec 1; By reservation only Dec. 1 - May 1
Notes: 2, 8, 9, 13

Hiram D. Ellis House

BLISSFIELD

Hiram D. Ellis House
B&B in Michigan, Box 1731, Dearborn, 48128
(313) 561-6041

Set in the rolling farmlands near the Michigan-Ohio border, this imposing brick home was built 100 years ago. Continental breakfast includes homebaked breads and muffins and jams made from the host's own fruit trees. TV in all rooms. Smoking, small pets, children allowed. $50-65.

BROOKLYN

The Chicago Street Inn
219 Chicago Street, 49230
(517) 592-3888

An 1880s Queen Anne Victorian, located in the Heart of the Irish HIlls. Furnished with family and area antiques. Antiquing, hiking, biking, shops, swimming, museums and more are available. Area of quaint villages.

6 Pets welcome: 7 Smoking allowed: 8 Children welcome: 9 Social drinking allowed: 10 Tennis available: 11 Swimming available: 12 Golf available: 13 Skiing available: 14 May be booked through travel agents

Hosts: Karen & Bill Kerr
Doubles: 4 (PB) $50-60
Type of Beds: 4 Full
Credit Cards: A, B
Continental-plus Breakfast
Notes: 2, 5, 7, 9, 10, 11, 12, 14

CARO

Garden Gate Bed & Breakfast

315 Pearl Street, 48723
(517) 673-2696

Built with charm in the Cape Cod colonial style, Garden Gate Bed & Breakfast is a new home designed with its guests in mind. Antiques adorn every corner of its rooms. In a quiet residential area of Caro. In summer, the yard is full of flowers and shrubs, including a large planting of New England wild flowers. On cool evenings, guests can warm up by the fireplace that adds rustic charm to the living room.

Hosts: Jim & Evelyn White
Singles: 1 (PB) $40 and up
Doubles: 4 (PB) $50 and up
Type of Beds: 1 Twin; 2 Double; 1 Queen; 1 King
Full Breakfast
Credit Cards: A, B
Smoking discouraged
Notes: 2, 4, 5, 7, 8, 9, 10, 11, 12, 13 (XC)

CASEVILLE

B&B in Michigan #C-1

Box 1731, Dearborn, 48128
(313) 561-6041

Waterfront location on Saginaw Bay offers swimming, boating, and fishing. Beamed ceiling and stone fireplace. Continental-plus breakfast is served on the glassed-in porch. Guest room with twin beds, private bath. Loft with four twin beds and shared bath for families. Children over 10 welcome. No smoking, no pets; bicycles available. $40.

CHARLEVOIX

The Patchwork Parlour

B&B in Michigan, Box 1731, Dearborn, 48128
(313) 561-6041

Built in 1890 and located right on the main street, this home is within walking distance of the beach, yacht basin, and Star of Charlevoix. Hosts will pick up at airport. Seven rooms with private baths. Children welcome, smoking allowed, continental breakfast. Open May 1 - Nov. 1. $50.

CLIO

Chandelier Guest House

1567 Morgan Road, 48420
(313) 687-6061

Relax in our country home. Your hosts, of German descent, provide a special treat on your arrival and will serve your breakfast in bed if you ask them to. One-half mile to plaza for shopping and meals. Near Michigan's main attractions: Frankenmuth, Flint, Chesaning, Birch Run. Reservations recommended.

Hosts: Al & Clara Bielert
Doubles: 2 (SB) $45-90
Type of Beds: 2 Twin; 1 Double
Full Breakfast
Credit Cards: No
Notes: 2, 5, 7, 8, 9, 10, 11, 12, 14

DEARBORN

B&B in Michigan

Box 1731, 48128
(313) 561-6041

Cozy Tudor-style brick bungalow decorated in colonial country style with antiques and collectibles. Guests may enjoy tea and cookies beside the living room fireplace. Free pick-up at Amtrak.

NOTES: Credit cards accepted: A Master Card; B Visa; C American Express; D Discover Card; E Diners Club; F Other: 2 Personal checks accepted: 3 Lunch available: 4 Dinner available: 5 Open all year

Doubles: 2 (SB) $45
Type of Beds: 1 Twin; 1 Double; 1 Queen
Full Breakfast
Credit Cards: A, B
Notes: 2, 5, 8, 10, 11, 12

DETROIT

B&B in Michigan #DT-1

Box 1731, Dearborn, 48128
(313) 561-6041

Home located in a historic area five minutes from downtown. Near GM headquarters, cultural center. Hostess has been active in the civil rights movement and NAACP and is a nationally known speaker and author. Two cats and dog in residence. No smoking. One double-bed room, one king; share bath. One twin with private half bath. Full Southern breakfast. $40.

B&B Michigan DT-2

B&B in Michigan #DT-2

Box 1731, Dearborn, 48128
(313) 561-6041

One look at the pillared portico and you understand why this is called the "little White house." Restored and modernized, it has seven double guest rooms, each with private bath. One mile from Belle Isle, with easy access to downtown Detroit. Dog in residence. Continental breakfast. No smoking; no pets; children over 12 welcome. $70-75.

B&B in Michigan #RO-1

Box 1731, Dearborn, 48128
(313) 561-6041

Friendly farm family welcomes guests to their 20 acre farm. Pick your own strawberries in season. Great place for children to see and pet farm animals. One room with double and single bed; one double room. Crib available. Share bath. Smoking allowed; stable available for horses; full breakfast. $40.

B&B in Michigan #RD-1

Box 1731, Dearborn, 48128
(313) 561-6041

Two-story brick colonial overlooking golf course. Guests may play tennis, golf, or cross-country ski at club. One room with twins, private bath. One room with double bed, shared bath. Continental breakfast. $40-45.

B&B in Michigan #BE-1

Box 1731, Dearborn, 48128
(313) 561-6041

Beautiful three-story Victorian on Belleville Lake. Fishing and boating available. Ten minutes from Ypsilanti; fifteen from Ann Arbor. No smoking. Small pets and children welcome. Three rooms with double beds; rollaway available. Shared bath. Continental-plus breakfast. $45.

B&B in Michigan #BM-3

Box 1731, Dearborn, 48128
(313) 561-6041

6 Pets welcome: 7 Smoking allowed: 8 Children welcome: 9 Social drinking allowed: 10 Tennis available: 11 Swimming available: 12 Golf available: 13 Skiing available: 14 May be booked through travel agents

Prairie-style home filled with a collection of contemporary quilts and modern art. Guest room with twin beds, private bath. No pets, no smoking; full breakfast. $45.

B&B in Michigan #BL-2

Box 1731, Dearborn, 48128
(313) 561-6041

Flower-filled atrium entrance leads to three-level townhouse on Wabeek golf course. Two guest rooms with twin beds; one can be converted to king. Crib available. Private bath. No smoking, no pets; full breakfast. $50.

B&B in Michigan #SF-1

Box 1731, Dearborn, 48128
(313) 561-6041

White brick tri-level on quiet street. Built-in swimming pool, cable TV in bedroom. Queen bedroom, shared bath; no pets, children welcome. Restricted smoking. Full breakfast. $40.

B&B in Michigan #R-1

Box 1731, Dearborn, 48128
(313) 561-6041

Custom country home on 4 acres, just five minutes from downtown Rochester. Rolling terrain, woods, pond stocked with trout. Morning paper with your continental breakfast. One single room, one double, one twin; share bath. Crib available. Infants and older children welcome. Dog in residence. Limited smoking. $45.

B&B in Michigan #R-2

Box 1731, Dearborn, 48128
(313) 561-6041

Delightful 145-year-old farmhouse on the historic register. Double room and single with adjoining half bath. Full bath shared with hostess. Stable available. Pets okay; limited smoking; older children. Continental breakfast. $40.

B&B in Michigan #R-3

Box 1731, Dearborn, 48128
(313) 561-6041

Casual, rambling home in a country setting on 3.5 wooded access. Glass-enclosed family room overlooks trout stream and pond 25 feet below. Two double rooms, shared bath. No smoking, no pets; children over 12 welcome. Two dogs in residence. Continental-plus breakfast. $40.

DIMONDALE

Bannick's Bed & Breakfast

4608 Michigan Road - M99, 48821
(517) 646-0224

Large ranch-style home features attractive decor throughout with stained-glass entrances. Our 2.75 rural acres offer a quiet escape from the fast pace of the workaday world. Located on a main highway (M99) only five miles from Lansing and close neighbor to Michigan State University.

Hosts: Pat & Jim Bannick
Doubles: 2 (SB) $20-30
Type of Beds: 2 Queen
Full Breakfast
Credit Cards: No
Notes: 2, 5, 8, 10, 11, 12, 13

DOUGLAS

Rosemont Inn

Box 857, 49406
(616) 857-2637

Our Victorian home, built in 1886, offers fourteen delightful rooms, each with private bath and air-conditioning. Nine rooms feature gas fireplaces; two of our three common rooms have wet bars and TV. We have a heated pool and are located across the street from a public beach on Lake Michigan. Unique shopping, charter fishing, golf, and cross-country skiing are nearby.

Hosts: Mike & Shelly Sajdak
Doubles: 14 (PB) $50-80
Type of Beds: 1 Twin; 1 Double; 12 Queen
Continental Breakfast
Minimum stay weekends (5/1-10/31): 2
Credit Cards: A, B
Notes: 2, 5, 7, 8, 9, 10, 11, 12, 13

Rosemont Inn

EAST LANSING

Coleman Corners

B&B in Michigan, Box 1731, Dearborn, 48128
(313) 561-6041

Contemporary home decorated in the country manner. Common room with fireplace, TV/VCR, games. Built-in swimming pool, air-conditioning. Hosts will provide transportation to MSU football games. Crib and rollaway available.

Doubles: 4 (SB) $55-65
Type of Beds: 4 Queen
Continental Breakfast
Credit Cards: No
Notes: 2, 5, 7 (restricted), 8, 11

FENTON

B&B in Michigan #FEN-1

Box 1731, Dearborn, 48128
(313) 561-6041

Five stately maple trees line the front of this three-story Victorian built in 1865. Great cross-country skiing or sailing area. One single, one double; crib available, private bath. Continental breakfast. Smoking allowed. $40.

FRANKENMUTH

Bed & Breakfast at the Pines

327 Ardussi Street, 48734
(517) 652-9019

Frankenmuth, a Bavarian village, is Michigan's number one tourist attraction. Our ranch-style home is within walking distance of tourist area and famous restaurants. Bedrooms tastefully decorated with heirloom quilts, antique accents, and ceiling fans. Enjoy homemade breads and rolls.

Hosts: Richard & Donna Hodge
Singles: 1 (SB) $26
Doubles: 2 (1 PB; 1 SB) $36.40
Type of Beds: 3 Twin; 1 Double
Continental Breakfast
Credit Cards: No
No smoking or drinking
Notes: 2, 5, 6, 8, 12

FRANKFORT

B&B in Michigan #F-1

Box 1731, Dearborn, 48128
(313) 561-6041

Your hosts have traveled extensively and are now ready to welcome guests to their summer home. Located at the entrance to Sleeping Bear Dunes National Lakeshore; tour of dunes included. One double, one twin, shared bath. Full kitchen privileges, game room, full breakfast. No smokers or pets, but children are welcome. Spanish spoken. $45.

GRAND BLANC

The Country Inn of Grand Blanc

6136 South Belsay, 48439
(313) 694-6749

Beautiful turn-of-the-century Victorian on 10 acres offers down comforters, lace spreads, croquet, and a tandem bicycle you can borrow. Picnic lunches are available on request. Hot air balloon packages available.

Hosts: Earl & Neva Pigeon
Doubles: 3 (1 PB; 2 SB) $45-65
Type of Beds: 1 Queen; 2 King
Continental Breakfast
Credit Cards: B, C
Notes: 2, 3, 4, 8, 9, 11, 12

GRAND HAVEN

Seascape Bed & Breakfast

Mail to: 20009 Breton, Spring Lake, 49456
(616) 842-8409

On the shore of Lake Michigan with a private sandy beach and panoramic view of Grand Haven harbor. Relaxing lodging in a nautical seashore cottage with all lakefront guest rooms with private baths. Stroll of cross-country ski on nearby duneland nature trails.

Host: Susan Meyer
Doubles: 3 (PB) $60-75
Type of Beds: 2 Twin; 2 Double; 1 Queen
Full Breakfast
Credit Cards: A, B
Closed Christmas
Notes: 2, 5, 7, 9, 10, 11, 12, 13, 14

GRAND RAPIDS

Fountain Hill Bed & Breakfast

222 Fountain NE, 49503
(616) 458-6621

Fountain Hill Bed & Breakfast is a 115-year-old home located in the historic Heritage Hill district overlooking downtown Grand Rapids. High ceilings and an elegant front entry with spiral staircase set off the lovely parlor and living room with fireplace. Within easy walking distance of great restaurants, shopping, and cultural center of the city.

Host: Sally Hale
Doubles: 4 (PB) $45-75
Type of Beds: 1 Twin; 3 Double
Continental-plus Breakfast
Credit Cards: A, B, C, E
Notes: 2, 5, 9, 10, 11, 12, 13

HARBOR BEACH

The Wellock Inn

404 South Huron Ave., 48441
(517) 479-3645

This restored "Dream House" of lumberman businessman John Wellock is filled with antique furniture from the early 1900 era when it was built. Oak woodwork and beveled glass enhance the beauty and provide for a very relaxing atmosphere.

Hosts: Lavonne & Bill Cloutier
Doubles: 4 (2PB; 2SB)
Type of Beds: 2 Double; 3 Queen
Continental Breakfast
Credit Cards: A, B
Notes: 2, 5, 6, 7, 8, 9, 10, 11

HARBOR SPRINGS

B&B in Michigan #HSP-3

Box 1731, Dearborn, 48128
(313) 561-6041

NOTES: Credit cards accepted: A Master Card; B Visa; C American Express; D Discover Card; E Diners Club; F Other: 2 Personal checks accepted: 3 Lunch available: 4 Dinner available: 5 Open all year

Private entrance to double room with private bath. Walking distance to shops, restaurants, and harbor. Enjoy watching the birds at the feeder while you have breakfast of French toast or other homemade goodies. No smoking, pets, or children. $45.

Red Geranium Inn B&B

Box 613, 48740
(517) 724-6153

Guests will find a homey ambience in this home that was built in 1910. In a parklike setting, it overlooks both downtown and Lake Huron, and features a 38-foot glass-enclosed porch, plus rear deck. Within minutes of shopping, restaurants, and beautiful Harbor of Refuge, yet a quiet oasis for real relaxation.

Hosts: Mary & Jim Hamather
Doubles: 5 (SB) $25-40
Type of Beds: 2 Twin; 2 Double; 2 Queen; 1 Rollaway
Continental-plus Breakfast
Credit Cards: No
Notes: 2, 7 (restricted), 8, 9, 10, 11, 12

HILLSDALE

Shadowlawn Manor

B&B in Michigan, Box 1731, Dearborn, 48128
(313) 561-6041

Dating from the Civil War, this Gothic American with gingerbread trim and spacious grounds occupies a full block. Breakfast is served on antique dishes and features homemade breads and jams. Downstairs room with private entrance and queen bed; double, twin, and single rooms. Shared baths. Cat in residence. $30-50.

HOLLAND

Old Holland Inn

133 West 11th Street, 49423
(616) 396-6601

A grand four-room inn located on a tree-lined cul-de-sac of Victorian homes. Located in Holland's historic district, our home features ten-foot ceilings, antique-filled rooms, original brass and oak. Breakfasts are special: house-blend coffee, muffins, and fruit plate, all served on china and linen. Fran, an artist, features much of her artwork within the house.

Hosts: Dave & Fran Plaggemars
Doubles: 4 (1 PB; 3 SB) $45-75
Type of Beds: 8 Twin
Continental Breakfast
Credit Cards: A, B
Notes: 2, 5, 9, 10, 11, 12, 14

The Parsonage

6 East 24th Street, 49423
(616) 396-1316

This elegant and historic B&B home is situated in a peaceful residential neighborhood close to Hope College, exceptional dining, summer theater, and Lake Michigan. We're proud of the superior rating we received from our guests. Ten minutes to Traverse City, Bloomfield Hills area.

Host: Bonnie Verwys
Doubles: 4 (2 PB; 2 SB) $50-90
Type of Beds: 1 Twin; 3 Double
Full Breakfast
Credit Cards: No
Closed Nov. 1 - April 31
Notes: 2, 8 (over 10), 9, 10, 11, 12, 14

HOWELL

B&B in Michigan #H-1

Box 1731, Dearborn, 48128
(313) 561-6041

A twenty-one room Italianate Victorian built in 1847. Many fine architectural features, walnut staircase, antiques. Five guest rooms with double and twin beds, shared baths. Children welcome, smoking allowed. Half hour from Ann Arbor or Lansing. Continental breakfast. $45.

6 Pets welcome: 7 Smoking allowed: 8 Children welcome: 9 Social drinking allowed: 10 Tennis available: 11 Swimming available: 12 Golf available: 13 Skiing available: 14 May be booked through travel agents

ITHACA

Chaffins Balmoral Farm Bed 'n Breakfast

1245 W. Washington Road, 48847
(517) 875-3410

Located on a working cash-crop farm with free tours available. The restored farmhouse, furnished with family antiques, is fronted by a fieldstone fence. Country breakfast is served in the open-beamed kitchen. The house is well kept, clean, and attractive; children are welcome. Parks, restaurants, and shopping are all nearby.

Host: Sue Chaffin
Doubles: 3 (1 PB; 2 SB) $20.80-41.60
Type of Beds: 2 Twin; 2 Double; 1 Queen
Full Breakfast
Credit Cards: No
Closed Nov. 15-May 15
Notes: 2, 8, 10, 11, 12

LANSING

Cherry Hill Bed & Breakfast

B&B in Michigan, Box 1731, Dearborn, 48128
(313) 561-6041

Built in 1875, this home in Lansing's historic district was saved from demolition and completely restored by the young couple who live here with their three children. Private guest quarters on the second floor include a breakfast area and sitting room with cable TV. Choice of Dutch, French, or American menu. Walk to state capital, museums, and cultural attractions. Three doublebed rooms, shared bath. Children over 12 welcome; no pets; no smoking. $35.

Maplewood

15945 Wood Road, 48906
(517) 485-1426

Located on a 3 acre plot overlooking the countryside, Maplewood was built in 1890. Guest rooms feature a comfortable country-style decor and are accessible through a private entrance.

Hosts: Pat & Keith Bunce
Doubles: 3 (SB) $45-55
Type of Beds: 2 Double; 1 Queen
Full Breakfast
Credit Cards: No
Notes: 2, 5, 8, 9, 10, 12, 13(XC)

LAPEER

B&B in Michigan #LA-1

Box 1731, Dearborn, 48128
(313) 561-6041

Converted cottage in a secluded wooded area, on a small, spring-fed lake. The entire first floor is for guests' use: kitchen, living room, double-bed room with attached dressing room and bath. Screened-in porch with double sofa bed. Good fishing, boating, swimming, and hiking. Two-night minimum on weekends. Children, pets, smokers welcome. Host will provide fixings for your breakfast. Two-four people: $50.

LUDINGTON

House on the Hill

B&B in Michigan, Box 1731, Dearborn, 48128
(313) 561-6041

A thoroughly romantic setting in this mauve Victorian that sits on a hill in the center of town, within walking distance to shops and beach. Two-night minimum on weekends. Dog and cat in residence. No smoking, full breakfast. King, two queens, twin room. $55-75.

Ludington House Inn

B&B in Michigan, Box 1731, Dearborn, 48128
(313) 561-6041

NOTES: Credit cards accepted: A Master Card; B Visa; C American Express; D Discover Card; E Diners Club; F Other: 2 Personal checks accepted: 3 Lunch available: 4 Dinner available: 5 Open all year

Former lumber baron's mansion, built in the 1870s in the Italianate-Gothic style. Two suites with private bath, four doubles share bath. Decorated with porcelains, vintage clothing, Victorian accessories. Fresh flowers, turndown service with mints. Full breakfast. Dog in residence. No smoking, no pets, older children welcome. $45-75.

MANISTEE

1879 E.E. Douville House

111 Pine Street, 49660
(616) 723-8654

Victorian home with ornate, hand-carved woodwork, interior shutters, a soaring staircase, and elaborate archways with pocket doors original to the house. Ceiling fans in every room. Lake Michigan beaches, fishing, golf, skiing, and historical buildings are nearby.

Hosts: Barbara & Bill Johnson
Doubles: 3 (SB) $35-40
Type of Beds: 2 Double; 1 Queen
Continental Breakfast
Credit Cards: No
Notes: 2, 5, 9, 10, 11, 12, 13

Inn Wick-a-te-wah

3813 Lakeshore Drive, 49660-9760
(616) 889-4396

Enjoy our spectacular sunsets and beautiful views of Portage Lake and Lake Michigan channel in a quiet, relaxing setting. Lakeside living, with swimming, fishing, nearby golf and shopping. The inn has light, airy bedrooms decorated with unusual period furnishings. Enjoy breakfast and lounging on the decks, screened porch, sun parlor with woodstove, or living room with fireplace.

Hosts: Len & Marge Carlson
Doubles: 4 (1 PB; 3 SB) $40-60
Type of Beds: 2 Twin; 3 Double
Continental-plus Breakfast

Credit Cards: A, B
Closed Jan. 2 - March 31
Notes: 2, 8, 9, 10, 11, 12, 13, 14

MANISTIQUE

Marina Guest House

230 Arbutus, 49854
(906) 341-5147

The 1905 house was rebuilt in 1922 and served as a B&B until 1936 for people summering in the Upper Peninsula. Most crossed Lake Michigan on car ferries that docked within view of this B&B. Located at the marina, one block from the business district, just off US 2 and M 94.

Host: Margaret A. Beach
Doubles: 7 (3 PB; 4 SB) $31.20-52
Type of Beds: 4 Twin; 2 Double; 3 Queen
Full Breakfast
Credit Cards: No
Notes: 2, 5, 8 (with reservations), 9, 10, 11, 12, 13 (XC)

MAPLE CITY - LELAND

Country Cottage Bed & Breakfast

135 E. Harbor Hwy, M22, 49664
(616) 228-5328; 228-5672

Quiet country beauty in Leelanau County, northern Michigan. Near sandy beaches, winter skiing, golf, hiking, biking, and all nature's best. Garden-fresh flowers with a continental buffet breakfast. Enjoy winery visits, fun shopping, and the quiet countryside.

Host: Karen Eitzen
Singles: 1 (SB) $40
Doubles: 3 (1 PB; 2 SB) $65
Type of Beds: 2 Twin; 3 Double; 1 Queen
Continental Breakfast
Minimum stay weekends & holidays: 2
Credit Cards: No
Notes: 2, 5, 7, 8, 9, 10, 11, 12, 13

---

6 Pets welcome: 7 Smoking allowed: 8 Children welcome: 9 Social drinking allowed: 10 Tennis available: 11 Swimming available: 12 Golf available: 13 Skiing available: 14 May be booked through travel agents

MIDLAND

Jay's Bed & Breakfast
4429 Bay City Road, 48640
(517) 496-2498

If you rest better in a quiet, residential setting, want a home away from home, and find a summertime garden deck appealing, along with cable TV, phone service, and off-street parking, then Jay's is for you!

Host: Jay Hanes
Singles: 2 (SB) $30
Doubles: 2 (SB) $35
Type of Beds: 4 Double
Continental Breakfast
Credit Cards: No
Notes: 2, 5, 10, 11, 12, 13

NILES

Yesterdays Inn B&B
518 North Fourth, 49120
(616) 683-6079

Elegant 1875 Italianate home with graceful porches, tall shuttered windows, and teardrop front door. Enjoy restful, relaxing evenings after sampling the year-round activities in the area. Golf, canoe, ski, or antique. Two blocks from shopping and restaurants.

Hosts: Dawn & Phil Semler
Singles: 2 (SB) $45
Doubles: 5 (PB) $55
Type of Beds: 4 Double; 1 Queen
Full Breakfast
Credit Cards: A, B
Notes: 2, 5, 8, 9, 10, 11, 12, 13, 14

NORTHPORT

North Shore Inn
B&B in Michigan, Box 1731, Dearborn, 48128
(313) 561-6041

Spacious estate home on the shore of Northport Bay. Complimentary beverages served every afternoon in the common room. Hostess is a gourmet cook who serves a full country breakfast. One suite with private bath, kitchen, and private patio. Double with private bath, balcony, and fireplace. King room with private bath. Double room with shared bath. $50-85.

Wood How
Rt. 1, Box 44E, 49670
(616) 386-7194

Enjoy the cabin-peaceful atmosphere of an environment that offers a unique experience in a return to a more quiet, relaxed time that mature adults can enjoy. Wood How lodge is an authentic log lodge located in a secluded 10 acres of hardwood forest at the tip of the Leelanau Peninsula in beautiful northern Michigan.

Hosts: Kay & Charly Peak
Doubles: 3 (PB) $75
Full Breakfast
Credit Cards: No
Closed Labor Day - June 30
Notes: 2, 7, 9, 11

OMENA

Haus Austrian
B&B in Michigan, Box 1731, Dearborn, 48128
(313) 561-6041

Contemporary designer house nestled in the woods on the shore of Lake Michigan. Swim in the bay, walk on the private beach, or stroll the woods. Twin and double rooms share a bath. No children, no pets, limited smoking. German spoken. Continental breakfast. $50.

OWOSSO

Mulberry House Bed & Breakfast
1251 N. Shiawassee Street, 48867
(517) 723-4890

NOTES: Credit cards accepted: A Master Card; B Visa; C American Express; D Discover Card; E Diners Club; F Other: 2 Personal checks accepted: 3 Lunch available: 4 Dinner available: 5 Open all year

Lovely restored 1890 farm home with many antiques. Breakfast is served in the beautiful dining area with a bay window or on the deck. Enjoy the large porch with swing and wicker. Many historic areas to visit within an hour's drive. A wonderful getaway for that special occasion or just to treat yourself!

Host: Carol Holmes
Doubles: 3 (1 PB; 2 SB) $45-60
Continental-plus Breakfast
Credit Cards: No
Notes: 2, 4 (by reservation), 5, 7, 8, 9, 10, 11, 12

PAW PAW

Carrington's Country House

B&B in Michigan, Box 1731, Dearborn, 48128
(313) 561-6041

Nestled among cherry orchards and grape arbors, this 150-year-old farmhouse has plenty of country charm. Large screened-in front porch; acres of land; swimming pond with beach close by. Dog and cat in residence.

Doubles: 3 (SB) $35-50
Type of Beds: 2 Twin; 1 Double; 1 Queen
Continental Breakfast
Credit Cards: No
Notes: 2, 5, 6, 8, 11

PENTWATER

The Pentwater Inn

180 E. Lowell, Box 98, 49449
(616) 869-5909

We are located twenty minutes south of Ludington, two blocks from town with a beautiful beach, unique shopping, charter boats, excellent cross-country skiing, tennis, and golf. Two large decks, Ping-Pong, game table, cable TV, and tandem available for guests. 1880 home furnished with antiques.

Host: Janet R. Gunn
Doubles: 6 (1 PB; 5S2B) $30-55

Type of Beds: 2 Twin; 4 Double
Full Breakfast
Credit Cards: A, B
Notes: 2, 5, 7, 8 (over 12), 9, 10, 11, 12, 13

ROMEO

Country Heritage Bed & Breakfast

64707 Mound Road, 48065
(313) 752-2879

A Greek Revival style home built in 1840, furnished with antiques, country accessories, and treasured family pieces. Old farm buildings remain on the 6 acres. A suite with a fireplace in both the sitting room and bedroom is a favorite. There's also a fireplace in the fining room and an outdoor pool. Arthur the peacock awaits your arrival.

Hosts: Jo Ann & Jill Celani
Doubles: 3 (1 PB; 2 SB) $50-70
Type of Beds: 2 Twin; 2 Double
Continental Breakfast
Credit Cards: No
Notes: 2, 5, 9, 10, 11, 12, 13

ST. IGNACE

Colonial House Inn

90 N. State Street, 49781
(906) 643-6900

On the National Historic Register, the Colonial House Inn was built in 1870. Today the beautifully renovated inn houses unique antiques and gifts for sale. An abundant breakfast smorgasbord is included. Just walk across the street to catch the ferry to Mackinaw Island.

Hosts: Marilyn Hurst & Letaine Lewis
Singles: 3 (SB) $48
Doubles: 19 (12 PB; 7 SB) $65
Full Breakfast
Credit Cards: A, B, C, D
Closed Oct. 30 - May 14
Notes: 2, 7, 8, 9, 10, 11, 12, 13

6 Pets welcome: 7 Smoking allowed: 8 Children welcome: 9 Social drinking allowed: 10 Tennis available: 11 Swimming available: 12 Golf available: 13 Skiing available: 14 May be booked through travel agents

SAUGATUCK

Hiatus House

B&B in Michigan, Box 1731, Dearborn, 48128
(313) 561-6041

Walk to Lake Michigan from this charming summer cottage. Game room and sitting room, two queen rooms, one double; shared bath. Private suite available with double and single bed. Nearby cottage available by day or week. Continental-plus breakfast with homemade dishes. Open May-Nov. Children, small pets, smokers welcome. $46-55.

The Maplewood Hotel

428 Butler Street, Box 1059, 49453
(616) 857-2788

The Maplewood Hotel architecture is un-mistakably Greek revival. Some rooms have fireplaces and double Jacuzzi tubs. Other areas include a library, dining room, lounge, sun room, screened porch, lap pool.

Hosts: Donald & Harriet Mitchell
Doubles: 13 (PB) $46.80-139.36
Type of Beds: 4 Double; 7 Queen; 2 King
Continental Breakfast
Minimum stay weekends: 2 ; holidays: 3
Credit Cards: A, B, C
Notes: 2, 5, 7, 8, 9, 10, 11, 12, 13

The Park House

888 Holland Street, 49453
(616) 857-4535

Saugatuck's oldest residence (1857) hosted Susan B. Anthony. Summer guests enjoy Lake Michigan, short walks to town, and air-conditioning. Winter guests relax fireside with our dog, Jimmy, curled at their feet. Tulip Festival, Victorian Christmases, Grand Escapes are favorites.

Hosts: Lynda & Joe Petty
Doubles: 8 (PB) $57.20-88.40
Minimum stay summers: 2
Continental Breakfast

Credit Cards: A, B, D
Notes: 2, 5, 7 (limited), 9, 10, 11, 12, 13, 14

Twin Gables Country Inn

900 Lake Street, 49453
(616) 857-4346

Built in 1865, this State Historic Inn is rich in history, having undergone several changes of function. Recently restored, it features fourteen charming guest rooms with private baths and antiques. Swimming pool, indoor hot tub, air-conditioning, fireplace.

Hosts: Michael & Denise Simcik
Doubles: 14 (PB) $39-92.56
Continental Breakfast
Minimum stay weekends: 2 ; holidays: 3
Credit Cards: A, B
Notes: 2, 5, 8 (over 5), 9, 10, 11, 12, 13

SOUTH HAVEN

The Last Resort Bed & Breakfast Inn

86 North Shore Drive, 49090
(616) 637-8943

This historic inn is located on a picturesque peninsula between Lake Michigan and the Harbour ... all rooms view water! Half a block to the beach, fishing, boating, and restaurants, a lovely stroll to town. Tennis, golf, wineries, and orchards are close by. The artist innkeepers share their original art and jewelry in The Inn Gallery.

Hosts: Wayne & Mary Babcock
Doubles: 12 (3 PB; 9 SB) $45-130
Type of Beds: 1 Twin; 10 Double; 5 Queen
Continental Breakfast
Credit Cards: No
Closed Nov. 1 - mid-April
Notes: 2, 7 (restricted), 9, 10, 11, 12, 14

Ross House Bed & Breakfast

229 Michigan Avenue, 49090
(616) 637-2256

NOTES: Credit cards accepted: A Master Card; B Visa; C American Express; D Discover Card; E Diners Club; F Other: 2 Personal checks accepted: 3 Lunch available: 4 Dinner available: 5 Open all year

The historic Ross House was built in 1886 by a lumber tycoon named Volney Ross. It sits on a quiet, tree-lined street on the south side of the Black River. Lake Michigan public beaches, downtown shopping area, and many fine restaurants are only blocks away.

Hosts: Cathy Hormann & Brad Wilcox
Doubles: 7 (1 PB; 6 S3B) $45-55
Type of Beds: 4 Double; 3 Queen; 2 Daybeds
Full Breakfast
Credit Cards: No
Notes: 2, 5, 9, 10, 11, 12, 13 (XC)

SPRING LAKE

Seascape Bed & Breakfast

20009 Breton Street, 49456
(616) 842-8409

On the Lake Michigan shore, offering a private, sandy beach and panoramic view of Grand Haven Harbor. All lakefront rooms with private baths. Relaxing lodging in a nautical seashore cottage. Stroll or cross-country ski on dune-land nature trails.

Host: Susan Meyer
Doubles: 3 (PB) $75
Type of Beds: 2 Twin; 2 Double; 1 Queen
Full Breakfast
Credit Cards: A, B
Closed Dec. 22-26
Notes: 2, 5, 7 (restricted), 9, 10, 11, 12, 13, 14

STEPHENSON

Top O' the Hill

Center Street, 49887
(906) 753-4757

Located in a small, quiet town in the southwest corner of the Upper Peninsula of Michigan, close to the Wisconsin border, away from the tourist traps of larger cities. There are nice restaurants, craft shops, and lots of natural beauty.

Hosts: Art & Phyllis Strohl
Doubles: 2 (1 PB; 1 SB) $30-35

Continental Breakfast
Credit Cards: No
Notes: 2, 5, 8, 9, 10, 11, 12, 13 (XC)

TECUMSEH

The Boulevard Inn

904 W. Chicago Blvd., 49286
(517) 423-5169

A Victorian inn in quaint Tecumseh. "The Inn the town helped build." Beautifully restored, warm, and inviting. Master suite has three rooms: bedroom, private sitting room, and bath with Jacuzzi. All rooms are elegant and unique. We look forward to being your getaway resting spot.

Hosts: Gary & Judy Hicks
Doubles: 5 (3 PB; 2 SB) $62.40-114.40
Full Breakfast
Credit Cards: A, B, C
Notes: 2, 5, 8 (10 and over), 9, 10, 11, 12, 14

TRAVERSE CITY

Rafael's Bed & Breakfast

B&B in Michigan, Box 1731, Dearborn, 48128
(313) 561-6041

Magnificent home in the historic area. Walk to lake, park, and shops. Craftsman-style architecture with fireplaces, antique furnishings. Three rooms: queen, double, and single. Shared bath. No smoking, no pets. Continental-plus breakfast. $65-75.

Warwickshire Inn B&B

5037 Barney Road, 49684
(616) 946-7176

This stunning turn-of-the-century gem sits on a hill surrounded by large shade trees and overlooks Traverse City. Famous for the family-style breakfast that's elegantly served on fine Wedgewood china and sterling silver.

6 Pets welcome: 7 Smoking allowed: 8 Children welcome: 9 Social drinking allowed: 10 Tennis available: 11 Swimming available: 12 Golf available: 13 Skiing available: 14 May be booked through travel agents

Close to beaches, skiing, and the Interlochen Arts Academy. Air-conditioned.

Hosts: Patricia & Dan Warwick
Doubles: 3 (PB) $45-65
Type of Beds: 2 Twin; 1 Double; 1 Queen
Full Breakfast
Credit Cards: No
Notes: 2, 5, 7 (limited), 9, 10, 11, 12, 13, 14

UNION PIER

The Inn at Union Pier
Box 222, 49129
(616) 469-4700

An elegant refurbished inn that blends barefoot informality with all the comforts of a well-appointed country home. Across from Lake Michigan. Eleven guest rooms have Swedish fireplaces; outdoor hot tub.

Hosts: Madeleine & Bill Reinke
Doubles: 15 (PB) $85-110
Full Breakfast
Credit Cards: A, B
Notes: 2, 5, 7, 9, 10, 11, 12, 13

Minnesota

Bluff Creek Inn
1161 Bluff Creek Drive, 55318
(612) 445-2735

A Victorian brick farm home built in 1864 and decorated with country antiques, porch swings, and fireplaces. Lodgings include a full three-course breakfast plus wine and a snack in the evening. Nearby are hiking and biking trails, a dinner theater, arboretum, and race track. Thirty minutes from the Metro area.

Host: Anne Karels
Doubles: 4 (PB) $65-85
Type of Beds: 3 Double; 1 Queen
Full Breakfast
Credit Cards: A, B
Notes: 2, 5, 9, 13

Bluff Creek Inn

Lunds' Guest House
500 Winona Street, 55923
(507) 867-4003

Charming 1920 bungalow, furnished in 1920s and 1930s furniture. Quaint kitchen, dining room, living room with fireplace, TV, old electric organ. Large screened front porch and small screened back porch. A quiet escape just twenty miles from Rochester and 100 miles from Minneapolis.

Hosts: Shelby & Marion Lund
Doubles: 4 (PB) $35-40
Type of Beds: 2 Twin; 3 Double
Continental Breakfast
Credit Cards: No
Notes: 2, 5, 7 (outside), 8, 9, 10, 11, 12, 13

East Bay Hotel
55604
(218) 387-2800

Old historic resort hotel in downtown Grand Marais on the shore of Lake Superior. Stroll the beach or village shops next door, downhill and cross-country ski. A good place to ease back into civilization when returning from Boundry Waters or Isle Royale pack trips.

Hosts: Jim & Lois Pedersen
Doubles: 15-20 (9 PB; 6 SB) $26-42
Full Breakfast
Credit Cards: No
Notes: 2, 3, 4, 5, 6, 7 (limited), 8, 9, 10, 11, 12, 13, 14

6 Pets welcome: 7 Smoking allowed: 8 Children welcome: 9 Social drinking allowed: 10 Tennis available: 11 Swimming available: 12 Golf available: 13 Skiing available: 14 May be booked through travel agents

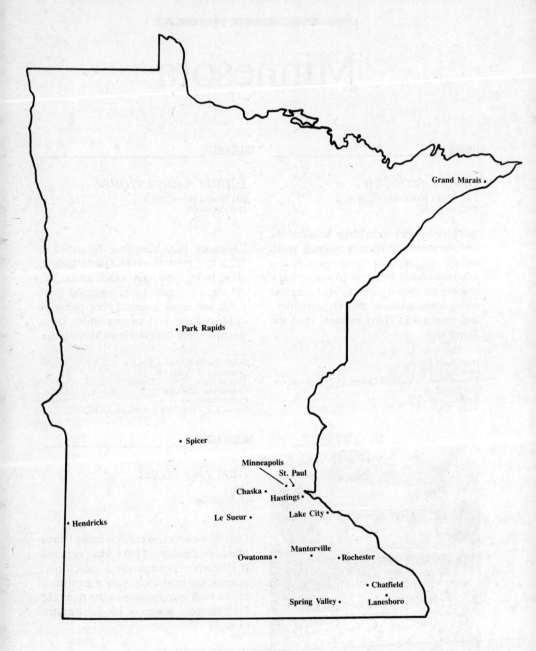

Grand Marais •

• Park Rapids

• Spicer

Minneapolis
St. Paul •
Chaska • Hastings •
Le Sueur • Lake City •
• Hendricks
Mantorville
Owatonna • • • Rochester
• Chatfield
Spring Valley • Lanesboro

MINNESOTA

Pincushion Mountain Bed & Breakfast

Box 181-E, 55604
(218) 387-1276; 1-800-542-1226

This year-round B&B sits on a ridge of Minnesota's Sawtooth Mountains overlooking the north shore of Lake Superior 1,000 feet below. New, country decor. Hiking, biking, and cross-country ski trails are at our doorstep. Twenty minutes from BWCA canoe entry points; three miles from Grand Marais.

Hosts: Scott & Mary Beattie
Doubles: 4 (1 PB; 3 SB) $50-68
Type of Beds: 3 Twin; 3 Double
Full Breakfast
Credit Cards: A, B
Closed April
Notes: 2, 8 (over 12), 9, 10, 11, 12, 13, 14

HASTINGS

Thorwood Inn

4th and Pine, 55033
(612) 437-3297

French Second Empire (1880) home with suite-sized rooms and private dining area in each. Private baths, some with double whirlpools, and fireplaces. Weekends are Modified American Plan. Located one block from Mississippi River bluff and walking tour of historic downtown. Central air-conditioning; dining packages and limousine available.

Hosts: Dick & Pam Thorsen
Doubles: 13 (PB) $49-195
Full Breakfast
Credit Cards: A, B, C
Notes: 2, 4, 5, 9, 10, 11, 12, 13, 14

HENDRICKS

Triple L Farm

Rt. 1, Box 141, 56136
(507) 275-3740

A large, remodeled 1890 white frame farmhouse on a working family farm. Guest rooms have antique furnishings, homemade quilts. Private or shared baths are available; generous home-cooked breakfast. Country road hiking, biking, and hunting in the area. Only 2.5 miles from the lake.

Hosts: Lanford & Joan Larson
Singles: 1 (SB) $30-35
Doubles: 1 (PB) $40-45
Type of Beds: 1 Twin; 2 Double; 1 Queen
Full Breakfast
Credit Cards: No
Notes: 2, 5, 6 (outside only), 7 (outside only), 8, 10, 11, 12, 13 (XC), 14

Red Gables Inn

LAKE CITY

Evergreen Knoll Acres B&B

RR 1, Box 145, 55041
(612) 345-2257

This B&B is located on a dairy farm with sixty-five milk cows, 160 acres of land 8.5 miles southwest of Lake City and thirty-five miles north of Rochester. Nearby Lake Pepin provides fishing, sailing, and waterskiing. The large, German-style country home was built in 1919 and is furnished with antiues, country crafts, air-conditioning, and a fireplace.

Hosts: Paul & Bev Meyer
Doubles: 3 (SB) $45

---

6 Pets welcome: 7 Smoking allowed: 8 Children welcome: 9 Social drinking allowed: 10 Tennis available: 11 Swimming available: 12 Golf available: 13 Skiing available: 14 May be booked through travel agents

Type of Beds: 2 Twin; 2 Double
Full Breakfast
Credit Cards: No
Closed Christmas
Notes: 2, 5, 8, 9, 10, 11, 12, 13

Red Gables Inn

403 North High Street, 55041
(612) 345-2605

Red Gables Inn is in a quiet residential section of Lake City, home of the largest small-
boat marina on the Mississippi River. The
red Victorian was built in 1865 and displays
a mixture of Italianate and Greek Revival
architecture. There are formal Victorian antiques in the parlor and dining room, while
the guest rooms have floral wallpapers and
iron, brass, and painted Victorian beds. In
early evening, guests may join the innkeepers for wine and hors d'oeuvres.

Hosts: Bill & Bonnie Saunders
Singles: 4 (2 PB; 2 SB) $43-63
Doubles: 5 (3 PB; 2 SB) $48-68
Type of Beds: 2 Double; 2 Queen; 1 King
Full Breakfast
Credit Cards: A, B
Closed Thanksgiving Day & Christmas Day
Notes: 2, 5, 7 (limited), 8 (13 and over), 9, 10, 11, 12, 13, 14

Carrolton Country Inn & Cottage

LANESBORO

Carrolton Country Inn & Cottage

RR 2, Box 139, 55949
(507) 467-2257

Carrolton Country Inn & Cottage is nestled
among hills in an open valley near historic
Lanesboro. We're located on the Root
River and Trail for outdoor fun year around,
with Amish farms nearby. Ask for our free
brochures.

Hosts: Charles & Gloria Ruen
Singles: 1 (SB) $35-40
Doubles: 4 (PB) $50-65
Type of Beds: 6 Twin; 3 Double; 2 Queen; 1 King
Full Breakfast
Credit Cards: A, B
Notes: 2, 5, 8, 9, 10, 11, 12, 13

Sconlon House Bed & Breakfast

708 Parkway South, 55949
(507) 467-2158

An 1889 Victorian listed on the National
Register with large bedroom suites appointed in period pieces. Original woodwork, stained glass, and fireplaces. We serve
a full breakfast brunch. We're in southeast
MN bluff country, near Amish tours, antique shops, fishing, hunting, eleven golf
courses, the Root River trails for cross-
country, biking, and walking.

Hosts: Mary, Gene & Kirsten Mensing
Doubles: $45-90
Full Breakfast
Credit Cards: A, B, C
Notes: 2, 3, 4, 5, 7, 8, 9, 11, 12, 13, 14

LE SUEUR

The Cosgrove Bed & Breakfast

228 S. Second Street, 56058
(612) 665-2763

NOTES: Credit cards accepted: A Master Card; B Visa; C American Express; D Discover Card; E Diners
Club; F Other: 2 Personal checks accepted: 3 Lunch available: 4 Dinner available: 5 Open all year

Located in the heart of the beautiful Minnesota River valley, the Cosgrove is a gracious Victorian home with four period rooms, two with fireplace. A full breakfast is served in the formal wood-paneled dining room. A National Historic Register home.

Host: Pam Quist
Doubles: 4 (SB) $60
Type of Beds: 3 Double; 1 Queen
Full Breakfast
Credit Cards: No
Notes: 2, 5, 7, 8, 9, 10, 11, 12, 13 (XC)

MANTORVILLE

Grand Old Mansion
Box 185, 55955
(507) 635-3231

Enjoy bed and breakfast in this lovely ornate Victorian that's filled with antiques and collectibles. Dine in an elegant atmosphere at Hubbell House, or visit the several antique and specialty shops.

Hosts: Clair & Irene Felker
Doubles: 4 (2 PB; 2 SB) $30-50
Full Breakfast
Credit Cards: No
Notes: 2, 5, 7 (limited), 9, 11, 12, 13, 14

MINNEAPOLIS

Evelo's Bed & Breakfast
2301 Bryant Avenue South, 55405
(612) 374-9656

This B&B was established in 1979 and is only ten minutes by bus from the new convention center. Spacious 1897 Victorian "urban" B&B offers comfort and convenience for a city experience. Antiques throughout; full breakfasts served in the formal dining room. Near lakes and buses, numerous restaurants, museums, shops.

Hosts: David & Sheryl Evelo
Doubles: 3 (SB) $37.30-47.95
Type of Beds: 1 Twin; 3 Double
Full Breakfast
Credit Cards: No
Notes: 2, 5, 8, 9, 10, 11, 12, 13 (XC), 14

OWATONNA

Northrop House
358 East Main Street, 55060
(507) 451-4040

One of twelve historic homes in Owatonna, this house was built in 1898. Formerly owned by Dr. Harson Atwood Northrop, candidate for U.S. Senate and Governor, this three-story home is furnished with oak woodwork, stained-glass windows, and original family heirlooms.

Host: Richard Northrop
Doubles: 4 (SB) $44-49
Type of Beds: 3 Double; 1 Waterbed
Continental Breakfast
Credit Cards: A, B
Notes: 2, 4, 5, 6, 8, 9, 10, 11, 12

PARK RAPIDS

Dickson Viking Huss Bed & Breakfast
202 E. 4th Street, 56470
(218) 732-8089

Charming contemporary elegance. Bicycle on Heartland Trail, visit Sawmill Creek, Village of the Smoky Hills, Itasca Park, or the source of the Mississippi. Near lakes, unique restaurants, and shops; tennis across the street. The living room features a vaulted ceiling and fireplace and original artwork.

Host: Helen K. Dickson
Doubles: 3 (1 PB; 2 SB) $19.50-34.50
Type of Beds: 1 Double; 1 Queen; 1 King
Continental-plus Breakfast
Credit Cards: A, B
Notes: 2, 5, 7 (limited), 8, 9, 10, 11, 12, 13 (XC), 14

ROCHESTER

Canterbury Inn Bed & Breakfast
723 2nd Street SW, 55902
(507) 289-5553

6 Pets welcome: 7 Smoking allowed: 8 Children welcome: 9 Social drinking allowed: 10 Tennis available: 11 Swimming available: 12 Golf available: 13 Skiing available: 14 May be booked through travel agents

Canterbury Inn combines the charm of an 1890 Victorian landmark with modern comforts and delightful cuisine. Gourmet breakfasts are served anytime (in bed on request), plus complimentary tea-time hors d'oeuvres and libations. We have a city location near the Mayo Clinic, off-street parking, and central air-conditioning.

Hosts: Mary Martin & Jeffrey VanSant
Doubles: 4 (PB) $60.50-71.50
Type of Beds: 2 Twin; 1 Queen; 2 King
Full Breakfast
Credit Cards: A, B
Notes: 2, 5, 7 (limited), 8 (over 10), 9, 10, 11, 12, 13 (XC)

SPICER

Spicer Castle

11600 Indian Beach Road, 56288
(507) 796-5870

Stately 1893 Tudor home with original furnishings on a beautiful 5,500 acre lake. Five acres of wooded grounds with gardens and a swimming beach. Fine restaurants, recreation, and shopping are nearby. Visit this getaway to indulge yourself in the slow pace and gentle ways of a century ago.

Hosts: Allen & Marti Latham
Doubles: 6 (PB) $60-90
Type of Beds: 6 Queen
Full Breakfast
Credit Cards: A, B, C
Open weekends year round and daily in summer
Notes: 2, 5, 7, 9, 10, 11, 12, 13, 14

SPRING VALLEY

Chase's

No. Huron Avenue, 55975
(507) 346-2850

It's life in the slow lane at our Second Empire mansion. It's flowers, birds, stars, and exploring this unglaciated area. Step back in time with a tour: Amish, Laura Ingalls Wilder, caves — or enjoy our trails and trout streams.

Hosts: Bob & Jeannine Chase
Doubles: 5 (2 PB; 3 SB) $55-65
Type of Beds: 3 Double; 1 Queen; 1 King
Full Breakfast
Minimum stay Sept. & Oct. weekends & holidays: 2
Credit Cards: A, B
Closed Jan.
Notes: 2, 8, 9, 10, 11, 12, 13

ST. PAUL

Chatsworth Bed & Breakfast

984 Ashland Avenue, 55104
(612) 227-4288

Elegantly furnished Victorian home in a quiet residential neighborhood. Fifteen minutes from the airport. Near Governor's Mansion and numerous restaurants and shops. Easy access to both downtown St. Paul and Minneapolis. Two rooms with double whirlpool baths. Licensed; smoke-free.

Hosts: Donna & Earl Gustafson
Doubles: 5 (2 PB; 3 SB) $44.52-90.10
Type of Beds: 2 Twin; 1 Double; 3 Queen; 1 King
Continental-plus Breakfast
Minimum stay weekends & holidays: 2
Credit Cards: No
Notes: 2, 5, 8, 9, 10, 11, 12, 13

NOTES: Credit cards accepted: A Master Card; B Visa; C American Express; D Discover Card; E Diners Club; F Other: 2 Personal checks accepted: 3 Lunch available: 4 Dinner available: 5 Open all year

Mississippi

ABERDEEN

Lincoln, Ltd. #43
Box 3479, Meridian, 39303
(601) 482-5483

This fine Victorian home is filled with antiues and decorated in the Victorian manner. The living room features an 1840s square grand piano and a stereoscope with a stack of cards. The guest room features an antique bed and is also decorated in the Victorian style.

Doubles: 1 (PB) $45-55
Type of Beds: 1 Double
Full Breakfast
Credit Cards: A, B
Notes: 2, 5, 6, 11, 14

BROOKHAVEN

Lincoln, Ltd. #1
Box 3479, Meridian, 39303
(601) 482-5483

A beautiful nineteenth-century home, completely restored and furnished in the Victorian style with antiques. The host is well-known as a decorator and architectural designer. Dinner is available by special arrangement and reservation. A full breakfast is served in the dining room.

Singles: 1 (PB) $80
Doubles: 3 (PB) $85-90
Type of Beds: 3 Double; 1 King
Full Breakfast
Credit Cards: A, B
Notes: 2, 4, 5, 14

CHATHAM-GREENVILLE

Lincoln, Ltd. #48
Box 3479, Meridian, 39303
(601) 482-5483

This antebellum mansion, circa 1856, is one of the finest examples of Italianate architecture in Mississippi. Located on historic Lake Washington just south of Greenville, the home is surrounded by several acres of beautiful "River Land." Sit on the front porch and enjoy the lake view or stroll the grounds.

Doubles: 4 (3 PB; 1 SB) $75
Type of Beds: 3 Double; 1 Queen
Full Breakfast
Credit Cards: A, B
Notes: 2, 5, 9, 11, 14

COLUMBUS

Lincoln, Ltd. #5
Box 3479, Meridian, 39303
(601) 482-5483

This is a Federal house — the oldest brick house in Columbus. It was built in 1828, the year Andrew Jackson was elected president. The house has been completely restored and is furnished with antiques of the period.

Doubles: 3 (PB) $60
Type of Beds: 2 Twin; 1 Double; 1 Queen
Full Breakfast
Credit Cards: A, B
Notes: 2, 5, 9, 11, 14

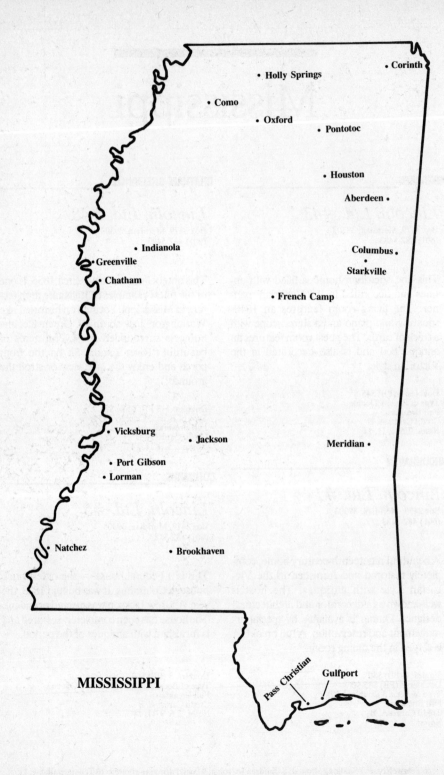

Corinth

Holly Springs

Como

Oxford

Pontotoc

Houston

Aberdeen

Indianola

Columbus

Greenville

Starkville

Chatham

French Camp

Vicksburg

Jackson

Meridian

Port Gibson

Lorman

Natchez

Brookhaven

Pass Christian

Gulfport

MISSISSIPPI

COMO

Lincoln, Ltd. #49

Box 3479, Meridian, 39303
(601) 482-5483

A very attractive guest cottage in a delightful small Mississippi town right on I-55 between Memphis and Jackson. There are also accommodations in the main house. Guests in the cottage are served a continental breakfast; full in the main house.

Doubles: 2 (PB) $60-80
Type of Beds: 1 Twin; 2 Double
Full and Continental Breakfast
Credit Cards: A, B
Notes: 2, 5, 9, 14

CORINTH

Lincoln, Ltd. #37

Box 3479, Meridian, 39303
(601) 482-5483

A beautiful Victorian home, completely furnished with antiques. Convenient to Memphis, TN, and Shiloh National Park (Civil War battlefield). A full Southern breakfast is served to guests; lunch and dinner are also available.

Doubles: 4 (PB) $65
Type of Beds: 4 Double
Full Breakfast
Credit Cards: A, B
Notes: 2, 3, 4, 5, 8, 10, 14

FRENCH CAMP

Lincoln, Ltd. #59

Box 3479, Meridian, 39303
(601) 482-5483

Enjoy the spacious view of forest and wildlife from the wide windows of this two-story home. Constructed with chinked log walls, this home was reconstructed from two log cabins over 100 years old. Awake to a tradi-

tional country breakfast and air scented with cypress and pine.

Doubles: 2 (PB) $53
Type of Beds: 2 Queen
Full Breakfast
Credit Cards: A, B
Notes: 2, 4, 5, 8, 11, 14

GULFPORT

Lincoln, Ltd. #42

Box 3479, Meridian, 39303
(601) 482-5483

A nice contemporary home in a quiet neighborhood just two blocks from the beach. Convenient to the Biloxi convention center. Private, nicely furnished bedroom with private bath. Hostess is a native of the area and will help you decide what to see and do in this growing coastal city.

Doubles: 1 (PB) $45
Type of Beds: 1 Double
Full Breakfast
Credit Cards: A, B
Notes: 2, 5, 11, 14

Lincoln, Ltd. #53

Box 3479, Meridian, 39303
(601) 482-5483

Three-story raised French cottage located 1.5 miles south of I-10 Longbeach, on 5 acres of live oaks and magnolias. Antiques, 6 fireplaces, and a 64-foot front porch with swings.

Doubles: 4 (3 PB; 1 SB) $39-69
Type of Beds: 2 Twin; 3 Double
Full Breakfast
Credit Cards: A, B
Notes: 2, 5, 8, 11, 14

HOLLY SPRINGS

Hamilton Place

105 E. Mason Avenue, 38635
(601) 252-4368

6 Pets welcome: 7 Smoking allowed: 8 Children welcome: 9 Social drinking allowed: 10 Tennis available: 11 Swimming available: 12 Golf available: 13 Skiing available: 14 May be booked through travel agents

Antebellum home built in 1838 and listed on the National Register. All rooms furnished in antiques. There is an antique shop in the carriage house, seasonal pool, and year-round hot tub for guests to enjoy. Museum, art gallery, and other historic homes are within walking distance.

Hosts: Linda & Jack Stubbs
Doubles: 4 (PB) $55-68.90
Type of Beds: 2 Twin; 1 Double; 2 Queen
Full Breakfast
Credit Cards: A, B
Notes: 2, 4, 5, 7, 8, 9, 10, 11, 12, 14

Lincoln, Ltd. #8

Box 3479, Meridian, 39303
(601) 4825483

A lovely home furnished with heirloom antiques has three guest rooms with private baths. An antique shop adjoins the house. Young executive hosts have completely restored this home themselves.

Doubles: 3 (PB) $65
Type of Beds: 2 Twin; 2 Queen
Full Breakfast
Credit Cards: A, B
Notes: 2, 5, 9, 11, 14

HOUSTON

Lincoln, Ltd. #39

Box 3479, Meridian, 39303
(601) 482-5483

A Victorian home, completely renovated that's a comfortable stop for travelers on business or pleasure in this small Mississippi town. Just one block from the town square, this home has five bedrooms, all with private bath and TV. A full Southern breakfast is served.

Doubles: 5 (PB) $40-45
Type of Beds: 2 Twin; 4 Queen
Full Breakfast
Credit Cards: A, B
Notes: 2, 5, 14

JACKSON

Lincoln, Ltd. #50

Box 3479, Meridian, 39303
(601) 482-5483

Step through the door and back 100 years, into a graceful world of sparkling chandeliers and finely crafted furnishings in this nineteenth-century home. Only minutes away from the city's central business distract and government district; convenient to much of Jackson's finest shopping, dining, and entertainment.

Doubles: 11 (PB) $65-95
Type of Beds: 4 Twin; 11 Queen
Continental-plus Breakfast
Credit Cards: A, B
Notes: 2, 5, 7 (limited), 8, 9, 14

INDIANOLA

Lincoln, Ltd. #9

Box 3479, Meridian, 39303
(601) 482-5483

Enjoy a full breakfast of country ham and homemade biscuits at this extremely attractive two-story home in the heart of the Mississippi Delta. The hosts, known for their hospitality, will take guests on a tour of the area, pointing out crops in season and directing them to well-know area restaurants.

Doubles: 1 (PB) $50
Type of Beds: 1 Queen
Full Breakfast
Credit Cards: A, B
Notes: 2, 5, 14

LORMAN

Rosswood Plantation

Rt. 552, 39096
(601) 437-4215

An authentic antebellum mansion, close to Natchez and Vicksburg, offering luxury, comfort, charm, and hospitality on a serene country estate. Once a cotton plantation, Rosswood now grows Christmas trees. Ideal for honeymoons. A Mississippi landmark, National Register, AAA recommended.

Hosts: Jean & Walt Hylander
Doubles: 4 (PB) $75-90
Type of Beds: 1 Twin; 1 Double; 2 Queen
Full Breakfast
Credit Cards: A, B
Notes: 2, 5, 7, 8, 9, 14

Hamilton Hall

MERIDIAN

Hamilton Hall

4432 State Blvd., 39307
(601) 483-8469

An 1890 Victorian private home, filled with antiques. Hostess is a caterer. Meridian is home of the Jimy Rodgers Festival, Grand Opera House of MS, Denzel Carousel, and other attractions.

Hosts: Edna & Bob Holland
Doubles: 2 (1 PB; 1 SB) $65
Type of Beds: 2 Double
Full Breakfast
Credit Cards: No
Closed Thanksgiving, Christmas, Fourth of July
Notes: 2, 4, 5, 7, 9, 12

Lincoln, Ltd. #13

Box 3479, 39303
(601) 482-5483

This restored Victorian is on 10 wooded acres within the city limits. Hostess is a noted gourmet cook and will, by special arrangement, prepare dinner for an additional charge.

Doubles: 1 (PB) $65
Type of Beds: 1 Double
Full Breakfast
Credit Cards: A, B
Notes: 2, 4, 5, 14

Lincoln, Ltd. #15

Box 3479, 39303
(601) 482-5483

This contemporary home has hosts who are very active in local and state affairs. Hostess is a well-know Mississippi artist; host is an attorney. Their home is filled with art and collections from their travels.

Doubles: 1 (PB) $45
Type of Beds: 1 Double
Full Breakfast
Credit Cards: A, B
Notes: 2, 5, 14

Lincoln, Ltd. #18

Box 3479, 39303
(601) 482-5483

In one of Meridian's loveliest neighborhoods, this home is set among flowering shrugs and dogwoods. The host and hostess have always been active in civic and cultural activities. There are two attractively furnished bedrooms with shared bath for a family or four people traveling together, or a double bedroom with private bath.

Doubles: 2 (1 PB; 1 SB) $45-70
Type of Beds: 2 Double
Full Breakfast
Credit Cards: A, B
Notes: 2, 5, 8, 14

Lincoln, Ltd. #57

Box 3479, 39303
(601) 482-5483

Nestled in the woods, this California-style
home has a bedroom with private bath and
a loft area that will sleep two additional
people traveling with the same party. Wake
to the sound of birds, have breakfast on the
patio, walk in the woods, or sun on the deck.

Doubles: 2 (1 PB; 1 SB) $55
Type of Beds: 2 Double
Full Breakfast
Credit Cards: A, B
Notes: 2, 5, 8, 11, 14

D'Evereux

Monmouth

Southern Comfort Reservations
2856 Hundred Oaks Avenue, Baton Rouge, LA, 70808
(504) 346-1928

This 1818 historic home is furnished in antiques, many original to the house.
Nineteenth-century elegance with private
baths, air-conditioning, and TV. Tour of the
house and ground is included in the rate.
Rooms are available in the house, restored
brick slave quarters, and cottages on the
grounds. One second-floor suite.

Doubles: 14 (PB) $75-150
Type of Beds: 7 Twin; 6 Double; 4 Queen; 1 King
Full Breakfast
Credit Cards: A, B, C
Notes: 2, 5, 9

The Burn

Lincoln, Ltd. #58

Box 3479, 39303
(601) 482-5483

A new contemporary inn that's convenient
to I-59 and I-20. Beautiful spacious rooms.
Meeting space for up to sixty people. Swimming pool and whirlpool on premises.

Doubles: 15 (PB) $39-43
Type of Beds: 15 Double
Continental Breakfast
Credit Cards: A, B
Notes: 2, 3, 4, 5, 6, 7, 8, 9, 12, 14

NATCHEZ

The Burn

Bed & Breakfast Pilgrimage Tours
Box 347, Natchez, MS, 39121
(800) 647-6742

Built in 1836, this is one of the earliest docu-
mented, purely Greek Revival residences in
Natchez. The three-story mansion is especially noted for its beautiful semi-spiral staircase in the central hall and the gardens with
many rare varieties of camellias.

NOTES: Credit cards accepted: A Master Card; B Visa; C American Express; D Discover Card; E Diners
Club; F Other: 2 Personal checks accepted: 3 Lunch available: 4 Dinner available: 5 Open all year

Doubles: 9 (PB) $70-125
Full Breakfast
Credit Cards: A, B, C
Notes: 2, 5, 7, 8 (6 and over), 9, 10, 12, 14

D'Evereux

Natchez Pilgrimage Tours
Box 347, Natchez, MS, 39121
(800) 647-6742

Built in 1840. Resembling a Greek temple, D'Evereux sits in the heart of a 7-acre manicured park near downtown Natchez. A broad gallery leads into the spacious home, which was designed by James Hardie. Many of the home's furnishings are original. Listed on the National Register of Historic Places.

Doubles: 1 (PB) $100
Continental Breakfast
Credit Cards: A, B, C
Closed July & August
Notes: 2, 7, 9, 10, 12, 14

Dunleith

84 Homochitto, 39120
(601) 446-8500

A National Historic Landmark located on 40 acres with formal gardens, wood-burning fireplaces in each room, color TV, and individual thermostats. Full Southern breakfast, welcome drink, tour of house, snack in room. Gift shop on premises; free brochure.

Host: Nancy Gibbs
Doubles: 11 (PB) $85-130
Type of Beds: 1 Twin; 5 Double; 5 Queen
Full Breakfast
Credit Cards: A, B, C, D
Closed Thanksgiving, Christmas, New Years
Notes: 8 (14 and over), 9, 10, 11, 12, 14

Elgin

Natchez Pilgrimage Tours
Box 347, Natchez, MS, 39121
(800) 647-6742

In a country setting just three miles from the city limits, Elgin offers accommodations in a separate 1853 building. Guests may relax in the downstairs living room or on their own upstairs gallery. Full Southern breakfast. Listed on the National Register of Historic Places.

Doubles: 3 (PB) $75-120
Full Breakfast
Credit Cards: A, B, C
Closed Jan. & Feb.
Notes: 2, 7, 8, 9, 10, 12, 14

Hope Farm

Natchez Pilgrimage Tours
Box 347, Natchez, MS, 39121
(800) 647-6742

Hope Farm was built 1775-1789 and is listed on the National Register of Historic Places. Four guest rooms are furnished with exquisite antiques and distinctive tester beds. A full Southern breakfast is served in the formal dining room, followed by a complete tour of the home.

Doubles: 4 (PB) $80
Full Breakfast
Credit Cards: A, B, C
Notes: 2, 5, 7, 8 (6 and over), 9, 10, 12, 14

Dunleith

Lincoln, Ltd. #46

Box 3479, Meridian, 39303
(601) 482-5483

---

6 Pets welcome: 7 Smoking allowed: 8 Children welcome: 9 Social drinking allowed: 10 Tennis available: 11 Swimming available: 12 Golf available: 13 Skiing available: 14 May be booked through travel agents

One of the finest examples of early Southern plantation-style architecture, this lovely home is situated on a promontory overlooking the Mississippi River. Abounding in history, the antique-filled rooms offer the guest time to relax and enjoy the very room where Jefferson Davis was married in 1845.

Doubles: 13 (PB) $90-135
Type of Beds: 4 Twin; 4 Queen; 8 King
Full Breakfast
Credit Cards: A, B
Notes: 2, 5, 8 (over 12), 9, 11, 14

Lincoln, Ltd. #22

Box 3479, Meridian, 39303
(601) 482-5483

This circa 1818 home was once the home of General John A. Quitman, an early governor of Mexican War fame. Many original Quitman pieces still furnish the home. On the National Register.

Doubles: 14 (PB) $70-155
Full Breakfast
Credit Cards: A, B
Notes: 2, 5, 8 (over 12), 9, 14

Lincoln Ltd. #29

Box 3479, Meridian, 39303
(601) 482-5483

Sleep in a canopied bed or stretch out in a hammock in this historic home whose hosts will tell you the history of Natchez and what to do and see. A full plantation breakfast is served on the sunny glass porch.

Doubles: 5 (PB) $75-85
Full Breakfast
Credit Cards: A, B
Notes: 2, 5, 9, 14

Lincoln, Ltd. #30

Box 3479, Meridian, 39303
(601) 482-5483

An outstanding historical home with a panoramic view of the Mississippi River. Furnished with an impressive collection of antiques, including the work of John Belter and P. Mallard. Welcoming beverage, tour of the home, and a large plantation breakfast are included.

Doubles: 5 (PB) $70
Type of Beds: 5 Double
Full Breakfast
Credit Cards: A, B
Notes: 2, 5, 8, 9, 14

Lincoln, Ltd. #44

Box 3479, Meridian, 39303
(601) 482-5483

This home, on the National Register of Historic Places, was built in 1858. It is situated on a bluff overlooking the Mississippi River, which can be seen from all the bedrooms. The second story of the home was removed during the Civil War by Union forces to prevent its being used to signal Confederate troops. This story was rebuilt in 1903.

Doubles: 3 (PB) $75-95
Continental Breakfast
Credit Cards: A, B
Notes: 2, 5, 8, 9, 14

Lincoln, Ltd. #45

Box 3479, Meridian, 39303
(601) 482-5483

This cottage was built in 1836 on a 500-acre working plantation 13 miles south of Natchez. Owned by descendants of the builders, it was restored in 1986 and retains some original furniture and documents. One of the oldest farms in the state; pastures, ponds.

Doubles: 3 (PB) $90-125
Type of Beds: 3 Double
Continental Breakfast
Credit Cards: A, B
Notes: 2, 5, 8, 9, 14

Linden

Southern Comfort Reservations
2856 Hundred Oaks Avenue, Baton Rouge, LA, 70808
(504) 346-1928

This home is on the National Registry of Historic Homes. Descendants of the family that purchased it in 1849 still live here. Magnificent collection of period furniture and Audubon prints. Tour of the main house is included in the rate.

Doubles: 7 (PB) $65-75
Type of Beds: 3 Twin; 5 Double; 1 Queen; 1 King
Full Breakfast
Credit Cards: A, B, C
Notes: 2, 5, 9

Melrose

Melrose

Natchez Pilgrimage Tours
Box 347, Natchez, MS, 39121
(800) 647-6742

Built in 1845 and noted for its impeccable architecture and lovely old gardens, Melrose is largely furnished with the original early nineteenth-century furnishings, which included painted floor cloths in two rooms.

Doubles: 6 (3 PB; 3 SB) $100
Full Breakfast
Credit Cards: A, B, C
Notes: 2, 5, 7, 8, 9, 10, 12, 14

Mount Repose

Natchez Pilgrimage Tours
Box 347, Natchez, MS, 39121
(800) 647-6742

Built in 1824. A lovely plantation home located on 250 acres of rolling hills, green pastures, tree-lined ponds, and magnificent live oaks. The bedrooms are in the main house, which is decorated with period antiues and family portraits.

Doubles: 2 (PB) $75
Full Breakfast
Credit Cards: A, B, C
Notes: 2, 5, 8, 9, 10, 12, 14

Shields Town House

Natchez Pilgrimage Tours
Box 347, Natchez, MS, 39121
(800) 647-6742

Built in 1860, this Greek Revival was the last fine town house built in Natchez prior to the Civil War. Exquisitely furnished in eighteenth- and early twentieth-century antiques.

Doubles: 2 (PB) $75-85
Continental Breakfast
Credit Cards: A, B, C
Notes: 2, 5, 7, 8 (12 and over), 9, 10, 12, 14

Stanton Hall

Natchez Pilgrimage Tours
Box 347, Natchez, MS, 39121
(800) 647-6742

Built in 1857, this is one of the most magnificent and palatial residences of antebellum America. Furnished with Natchez antiques and objects d'art. Across the beautifully landscaped courtyard is the famous Carriage House Restaurant.

Doubles: 4 (PB) $75-100
Continental Breakfast
Credit Cards: A, B, C
Open only in March, April & October
Notes: 2, 3, 4, 7, 8 (14 and over), 9, 10, 12, 14

6 Pets welcome: 7 Smoking allowed: 8 Children welcome: 9 Social drinking allowed: 10 Tennis available: 11 Swimming available: 12 Golf available: 13 Skiing available: 14 May be booked through travel agents

Texada

Natchez Pilgrimage Tours
Box 347, Natchez, MS, 39121
(800) 647-6742

Built in 1792 in the old Spanish Quarter, Texada has served as a tavern, hotel, and Territorial Legislative Hall. Contains American and English period furnishings.

Doubles: 5 (PB) $70
Full Breakfast
Credit Cards: A, B, C
Notes: 2, 5, 7, 8 (3 and over), 9, 10, 12, 14

Twin Oaks

Natchez Pilgrimage Tours
Box 347, Natchez, MS, 39121
(800) 647-6742

Built in 1812, this charming town house is surrounded by beautiful gardens and is noted for its furnishings. An early Greek Revival extension now forms the major portion of the home.

Doubles: 1 (PB) $75
Full Breakfast
Credit Cards: A, B, C
Notes: 2, 5, 7, 9, 10, 12, 14

OXFORD

Lincoln, Ltd. #23

Box 3479, Meridian, 39303
(601) 482-5483

Built in 1838, this lovely antebellum home is made entirely of native timber and is on the National Register. In an attic, 150 years of fashion are displayed on mannequins. Guests can enjoy cakes that are still warm and have breakfast on the balcony on warm spring mornings. Conveniently located to the University of Mississippi and the William Faulkner home.

Doubles: 3 (2 PB; 1 SB) $50-70
Type of Beds: 3 Double
Continental Breakfast

Credit Cards: A, B
Notes: 2, 5, 14

Lincoln, Ltd. #24

Box 3479, Meridian, 39303
(601) 482-5483

Charming small inn with five bedrooms with private baths. Convenient to the University of Mississippi and the Faulkner residence.

Doubles: 5 (PB) $45
Type of Beds: 5 Double
Continental Breakfast
Credit Cards: A, B
Notes: 2, 3, 4, 5, 8, 9, 14

PASS CHRISTIAN

Lincoln, Ltd. #25

Box 3479, Meridian, 39303
(601) 482-5483

Enjoy the unique opportunity of staying in a log home on 40 acres! Just 2.5 miles north of I-10 and 2.5 miles from the beach. This home has a private bedroom and bath, a loft for children, and a swimming pool. The hosts have lived in this area for over thirty-six years and will direct you to all the activities on the Mississippi coast.

Doubles: 1 (PB) $55
Type of Beds: 2 Double
Continental Breakfast
Credit Cards: A, B
Notes: 2, 5, 8, 11, 12, 14

Lincoln, Ltd. #40

Box 3479, Meridian, 39303
(601) 482-5483

A nineteenth-century beach home located just minutes from the Gulf coast beaches. Decorated in boarding-house style with antiques, this rustic home offers the traveler a comfortable summer getaway or a quiet place to relax and enjoy the coast. Sit on the porch and enjoy the harbor view or lie on the beach.

NOTES: Credit cards accepted: A Master Card; B Visa; C American Express; D Discover Card; E Diners Club; F Other: 2 Personal checks accepted: 3 Lunch available: 4 Dinner available: 5 Open all year

Doubles: 4 (PB) $45-60
Type of Beds: 2 Twin; 3 Double
Continental Breakfast
Credit Cards: A, B
Notes: 2, 5, 8, 11, 12, 14

PONTOTOC

Lincoln, Ltd. #52

Box 3479, Meridian, 39303
(601) 482-5483

A very attractive historic Victorian with
three guest rooms, all with private baths.
High ceilings in all rooms; furnished comfortably. Rock on the front porch or use the
lovely library with fireplace.

Singles: 1 (SB) $45
Doubles: 4 (PB) $55
Type of Beds: 5 Double
Continental Breakfast
Credit Cards: A, B
Notes: 2, 3, 4, 5, 12, 14

PORT GIBSON

Oak Square Plantation

1207 Church Street, 39150
(601) 437-4350; 437-5300

Antebellum mansion in the town General U.
S. Grant said was "too beautiful to burn."
Heirloom antiques, canopied beds; the
house is on the National Register of Historic
Places. AAA 4 Diamond rated.

Hosts: Mr. & Mrs. William Lum
Doubles: 10 (PB) $60-85
Type of Beds: 6 Twin; 4 Queen
Full Breakfast
Credit Cards: A, B, C
Notes: 2, 5, 8, 9, 14

STARKVILLE

Lincoln, Ltd. #56

Box 3479, Meridian, 39303
(601) 482-5483

A unique place to stay that combines the
history of a 200-year-old, hand-hewn square

logged cabin with the convenience of today.
Located in the middle of 35 acres overlooking a small lake and nestled in a grove of
cedars. The second-floor guest suite has a
large sun deck, large living room, bedroom
with fireplace and four-poster bed.

Doubles: 1 (PB) $45-55
Type of Beds: 1 Double
Continental Breakfast
Credit Cards: A, B
Notes: 2, 5, 7, 8 (over 12), 9, 11, 14

Lincoln, Ltd. #60

Box 3479, Meridian, 39303
(601) 482-5483

This special country home is in a wonderful
setting among a 15 acre Christmas-tree farm
with cows and horses. The private guest suite
is located on the second floor and contains a
living/kitchen area, bedroom, private bath.
Sleeps up to four. Convenient to Mississippi
State University.

Doubles: 1 (PB) $45-60
Type of Beds: 2 Double
Continental Breakfast
Credit Cards: A, B
Notes: 2, 5, 8, 9, 14

VICKSBURG

Anchuca

1010 First East, 39180
(601) 636-4931

Anchuca is an 1830 Greek Revival mansion
housing some of the most magnificent
period antiques and artifacts, complete with
gas-burning chandeliers. Beautiful brick
courtyards completely surround the mansion and renovated slave quarters. Overnight guests are accommodated in the slave
quarters, the guest cottage, and one room in
the main house.

Hosts: May White & Kathy Tanner
Doubles: 9 (PB) $75-105
Type of Beds: 1 Twin; 4 Double; 4 Queen
Full Breakfast

6 Pets welcome: 7 Smoking allowed: 8 Children welcome: 9 Social drinking allowed: 10 Tennis available: 11
Swimming available: 12 Golf available: 13 Skiing available: 14 May be booked through travel agents

Credit Cards: A, B, C, D
Notes: 2, 5, 6, 7, 9, 10, 11, 12, 14

Cedar Grove Mansion-Inn

2200 Oast Street, 39180
1-800-862-1300; 1-800-448-2820

Relive "Gone With the Wind" in this 1840 magnificently furnished inn. Four acres of gardens, fountains, and courtyards. Gas lights, four-poster beds, period antiques. Pool, Jacuzzi, and the terrace has a view of the Mississippi River. Chosen by *Escape In Style* as one of the most romantic inns in the world. Four diamond rated by AAA and a National Historic Property.

Host: Estelle Mackey
Doubles: 17 (PB) $65-120
Type of Beds: 2 Twin; 10 Double; 4 Queen; 1 KIng
Full Breakfast
Credit Cards: A, B
Notes: 2, 5, 7 (limited), 8 (6 and over), 9, 11, 14

The Corners

601 Klein, 39180
1-800-444-7421

Built as a wedding present in 1872, the mansion has its original parterre gardens, a 68-foot long gallery with spectacular view of the Mississippi River and Delta. Architecture combines Greek Revival, Victorian, and Steamboat Gothic. Furnished with antiques. Comfort and hospitality emphasized.

Hosts: Cliff & Bettye Whitney
Doubles: 9 (PB) $58-91
Type of Beds: 1 Twin; 4 Double; 4 Queen
Full Breakfast
Credit Cards: A, B
Notes: 2, 5, 7 (limited), 8, 9, 12

Lincoln, Ltd. #41

Box 3479, Meridian, 39303
(601) 482-5483

Elegant antebellum mansion, circa 1856, located in Vicksburg's Historic District. It's the best example of Paladian architecture in Mississippi. Used as a hospital during the Civil War, the house was shelled during the siege of Vicksburg. Listed on the National Register of Historic Places. A welcoming beverage and tour of the home are included.

Doubles: 8 (PB) $75-140
Type of Beds: 5 Double; 3 Queen; 1 King
Continental Breakfast
Credit Cards: A, B
Notes: 2, 5, 8 (over 12), 9, 14

NOTES: Credit cards accepted: A Master Card; B Visa; C American Express; D Discover Card; E Diners Club; F Other: 2 Personal checks accepted: 3 Lunch available: 4 Dinner available: 5 Open all year

Missouri

ARROW ROCK

Borgman's Bed & Breakfast

706 Van Buren, 65320
(816) 837-3350

We invite you to experience the historic town of Arrow Rock in the warmth of our century-old home. Four rooms, shared bath, no smiking. Home-baked breakfast. Arrow Rock (1829) is a National Historic Landmark town at the beginning of the Santa Fe trail and was the home of artist George Caleb Bingham.

Hosts: Kathy & Helen Borgman
Doubles: 4 (SB) $35-40
Type of Beds: 4 Double
Continental-plus Breakfast
Credit Cards: No
Notes: 2, 5, 8

Borgman's B&B

BONNE TERRE

Lamplight Inn B&B

207 E. School Street, 63628
(314) 358-4222; 358-3332

"The food at the Lamplight Inn and the antique-filled bedrooms provide a setting that could put you in several European countries. We enjoyed lovely sleeping accommodations at the Wibskov's Bed & Breakfast home. Our room was magnificent." *St. Louis Post-Dispatch.*

Hosts: Jorgen & Krista Wibskov
Doubles: 6 (PB) $58.56-79.86
Type of Beds: 6 Double
Full Breakfast
Credit Cards: A, B, C
Notes: 2, 4, 5, 7, 8, 9, 10, 11, 12

BRANSON

The Branson House

Ozark Mountain Country B&B
Box 295, Branson, MO, 65616
(417) 334-4720

This elegant early 1900s home has been lovingly restored, redecorated, and air-conditioned. Spacious parlor available for guests. Breakfast of pastries, rolls, fruits, and cheeses served in the formal dining room or on the large front porch.

Doubles: 7 (PB) $50-75
Type of Beds: 2 Twin; 7 Double
Continental Breakfast
Credit Cards: No
Closed Nov. 1 - Feb.
Notes: 2

St. Joseph

Hannibal

Weston   Parkville
Platte City
Louisiana
Liberty
Independence
Concordia
Arrow Rock
Grandview
Kansas City
Sedalia
Hermann
St. Louis
Warrensburg

Warsaw

Osage Beach

Camdenton
Bonne Terre

Springfield   Hartville
Carthage   Rogersville-Springfield
Marionville   Nixa
Lampe
Indian Point   Branson
Kimberling City   Pt. Lookout   West Plains
Hollister

MISSOURI

OMC 112-B

Ozark Mountain Country B&B
Box 295, Branson, MO, 65616
(417) 334-4720

Delightful retreat on Lake Taneycomo, across the lake from Branson. Home has recently been remodeled and redecorated. All guests have access to the swimming pool, fishing docks; rental boats available. One room has a small private deck; the other has a whirlpool tub/shower.

Doubles: 2 (PB) $40-55
Type of Beds: 2 Queen
Continental Breakfast
Credit Cards: No
Notes: 2, 7, 8, 9, 11, 13

OMC 118

Ozark Mountain Country B&B
Box 295, Branson, MO, 65616
(417) 334-4720

This contemporary home offers four guest areas, two upstairs and two on a lower level, including a large sitting area with fireplace, TV, VCR, and large sliding doors opening onto a large patio and swimming pool.

Doubles: 4 (SB) $45-95
Type of Beds: 1 Double; 1 Queen; 2 King
Full Breakfast
Credit Cards: No
Notes: 2, 5, 7 (limited), 9, 10, 11, 12, 13

OMC 119

Ozark Mountain Country B&B
Box 295, Branson, MO, 65616
(417) 334-4720

Contemporary new home on a hill above Table Rock Lake, about seven miles southwest of Branson and 1.5 miles from Silver Dollar City. One guest room with private bath. A second room has a single bed. The home is air-conditioned, and TV is available in the guest room. Full breakfast is served on the deck or in the dining room. Limited smoking; adults only. $50-65.

BRANSON-LAKES AREA

OMC 107-B

Ozark Mountain Country B&B
Box 295, Branson, MO, 65616
(417) 334-4720

Located in a secluded area two blocks from Table Rock Lake. Table Rock Dam, the state park and marina, and Lake Taneycomo are just two miles away. Easy access to Silver Dollar City and a variety of music shows. Rooms have private entrances, refrigerator, TV, and sitting area.

Doubles: 2 (1 PB; 1 SB) $45-80
Type of Beds: 1 Queen; 1 King
Full Breakfast
Credit Cards: No
Notes: 2, 8, 9, 11, 13

CAMDENTON

OMC 203-C

Ozark Mountain Country B&B
Box 295, Branson, MO, 65616
(417) 334-4720

Just fifty feet from Lake of the Ozarks, this home has cathedral ceilings and many glass doors opening onto the patio and deck. You'll be lulled to sleep by the sound of lapping water. HaHa Tonka Mansion and Trails, Bridal Cave, country music shows, antique shops, and good restaurants are close by. Air-conditioning, TV, continental breakfast. Adults only, please. $40.

OMC 207

Ozark Mountain Country B&B
Box 295, Branson, MO, 65616
(417) 334-4720

This charming home is in a quiet neighborhood. Host serves a full, hearty breakfast in the dining room or on the shady deck. Adults only; small resident dog.

Doubles: 2 (SB) $35-70
Type of Beds: 1 Double; 1 Queen

6 Pets welcome: 7 Smoking allowed: 8 Children welcome: 9 Social drinking allowed: 10 Tennis available: 11 Swimming available: 12 Golf available: 13 Skiing available: 14 May be booked through travel agents

Full Breakfast
Credit Cards: No
Closed Nov. - Feb.
Notes: 2, 11, 13

CARTHAGE

Hill House

1157 S. Main, 64836
(417) 358-6145

Hill House is a 100-year-old Victorian mansion furnished in antiques. Rooms feature feather beds and tied comforters. Family-style breakfast includes home-baked muffins and jams. Antiques and gifts are for sale on the third floor.

Hosts: Dean & Ella Mae Scoville
Doubles: 4 (PB) $26.60-42.54
Type of Beds: 4 Double
Credit Cards: No
Notes: 2, 5, 8, 10, 11, 12

Hill House

Maple Lane Farms

RR 1, 64836
(417) 358-6312

A National Register Historic Place with twenty-two rooms filled with family heir-looms. The 676 acre farm is ideal for hunting, fishing, or a family vacation. There's a barnyard full of animals, a playground for kids, and a 22-acre lake for fishermen.

Hosts: Arch & Renee Brewer
Doubles: 4 (SB) $35-40
Cottage: 2 Bedrooms
Type of Beds: 4 Twin; 3 Double
Continental Breakfast
Closed Dec. 15-Feb. 1
Notes: 2, 8

CONCORDIA

B&B Kansas City CA90

Box 14781, Lenexa, Kansas, 66215
(913) 888-3636

This inn has four rooms, all restored with antiques and private baths. Country breakfast included; dinner available from $12.50. Fifty miles to Kansas City; KCI pick up. Area is great for antiquing. $40-45.

GRANDVIEW

B&B Kansas City GA52

Box 14781, Lenexa, Kansas, 66215
(913) 888-3636

Large colonial home on 6 acres and a lake with ducks, geese, peacocks. Three country rooms with full breakfast; child's playroom. $45-55.

B&B Kansas City ST12

Box 14781, Lenexa, Kansas, 66215
(913) 888-3636

Convenient home near St. Joseph Hospital with three twin-bedded rooms. Can accommodate eight to nine people. Living room and kitchen, patio for guests. Continental breakfast. Hostess smokes; family rates available. $30-50.

NOTES: Credit cards accepted: A Master Card; B Visa; C American Express; D Discover Card; E Diners Club; F Other: 2 Personal checks accepted: 3 Lunch available: 4 Dinner available: 5 Open all year

HANNIBAL

Fifth Street Mansion

213 South Fifth Street, 63401
(314) 221-0445

Historic 1858 Italianate home of lifelong
friends of Mark Twain combines Victorian
charm with contemporary comforts. Period
furnishings, original fireplaces, stained glass,
and old-fashioned hospitality abound. Walk
to historic sites, shops, restaurants. Inquire
about special weekends.

Hosts: Donalene & Mike Andreotti
Singles: 1 (SB) $37
Doubles: 7 (4 PB; 3 SB) $42-55
Type of Beds: 3 Twin; 6 Double; 1 Queen
Full Breakfast
Credit Cards: A, B
Notes: 2, 5, 7, 8, 9, 10, 11, 12, 14

HARTVILLE

Frisco House

Box 118, 65667
(417) 741-7304

Victorian home on the National Register,
located in the noncommercial area of the
Ozarks near the Laura Ingalls Wilder home
and museum and an Amish community. The
house has been completely restored and furnished with antiques, many third and fourth
generation heirlooms, including oil paintings, Oriental rugs, hanging lamps, china,
brass, and wooden artifacts. Meals are
served on railroad dining-car china and silver.

Hosts: Charley & Betty Roberts
Doubles: 4 (SB) $30-35
Type of Beds: 3 Double; 1 Queen
Full Breakfast
Credit Cards: No
Closed part of Jan. & Feb.
Notes: 2, 9, 10, 11, 14

HERMANN

Birk's Goethe Street Gasthaus

700 Goethe Street, 65041
(314) 486-2911

Bed & Breakfast in our romantic Victorian
mansion daily, except for two weekends a
month, when you can be Agatha Christie
and try to solve the mystery of the month.

Hosts: Elmer & Gloria Birk
Doubles: 9 (7 PB; 2 SB) $50.95-61.68
Type of Beds: 6 Double; 3 King
Full Breakfast
Credit Cards: A, B, C
Closed Dec. 24-Jan. 1
Notes: 2, 7 (limited), 8 (over 16), 9, 10, 11, 12, 14

HOLLISTER

OMC 106

Ozark Mountain Country B&B
Box 295, Branson, MO, 65616
(417) 334-4720

This home offers two guest rooms twelve
miles from downtown Branson. View of
Table Rock Lake; one-quarter mile to fishing and swimming area. One mile to boat
launch, rentals, and picnic area.

Doubles: 2 (1 PB; 1 SB) $30-40
Type of Beds: 2 Double; 1 Divan
Continental Breakfast
Credit Cards: No
Closed Nov. - Feb.
Notes: 2, 7, 8, 9, 11, 13

INDEPENDENCE

B&B Kansas City WA40

Box 14781, Lenexa, Kansas, 66215
(913) 888-3636

A fascinating 1850s middle-class Victorian
home just half a block from Harry Truman's
home. Hundreds of details: antique walnut
furniture, period lighting. Two rooms with a

---

6 Pets welcome: 7 Smoking allowed: 8 Children welcome: 9 Social drinking allowed: 10 Tennis available: 11
Swimming available: 12 Golf available: 13 Skiing available: 14 May be booked through travel agents

shared bath and double beds. Full breakfast. No smoking. $42-50.

B&B Kansas City WE40

Box 14781, Lenexa, Kansas, 66215
(913) 888-3636

Spacious home adjacent to the hosts' home. Full breakfast is served;fireplace in master bedroom with double bed and a twin bedroom. House overlooks the Missouri River and Kansas City skyline; ten minutes to the stadium. $45-55.

B&B Kansas City WO12

Box 14781, Lenexa, Kansas, 66215
(913) 888-3636

Quaint, comfortable inn with TV and full breakfast. $38.50-55.

INDIAN POINT

OMC 116

Ozark Mountain Country B&B
Box 295, Branson, MO, 65616
(417) 334-4720

This home is on Indian Point, two miles from Silver Dollar City on Table Rock Lake. It offers a large, carpeted, air-conditioned guest area great for families. Private entrance, patio overlooking the lake, and a boat dock for your rental boat. Only one party at a time is accepted as guests.

Doubles: 2 (SB) $50-80
Type of Beds: 2 Double; 1 Rollaway
Full Breakfast
Credit Cards: No
Notes: 2, 7 (on patio), 8, 9, 11, 13

OMC 117

Ozark Mountain Country B&B
Box 295, Branson, MO, 65616
(417) 334-4720

A rustic, contemporary lakeside home on Indian Point, three miles from Silver Dollar City, in a quiet, secluded area. Breakfast is served at your leisure in the great room or on the deck overlooking Table Rock Lake. Guests are welcome to use the great room with fireplace and the deck; fish and swim in the lake, or watch the sunset over the lake from the deck in their room.

Doubles: 2 (PB) $45-57
Type of Beds: 1 Double; 1 King
Continental-plus Breakfast
Credit Cards: No
Closed Nov. - March
Notes: 2, 9, 11, 13

KANSAS CITY

B&B Kansas City BO33

Box 14781, Lenexa, Kansas, 66215
(913) 888-3636

Hyde Park tour home offers a third-floor suite with double bed, sofabed, TV, refrigerator, and private bath. Full breakfast. $35-50.

B&B Kansas City BO47

Box 14781, Lenexa, Kansas, 66215
(913) 888-3636

Interesting National Historic Register home that was the garener's cottage for William Rockhill Nelson Estate. King bedroom, sitting room with TV, private bath, air-conditioning. Full breakfast. Walk to Plaza. $55-60.

B&B Kansas City CL38

Box 14781, Lenexa, Kansas, 66215
(913) 888-3636

Third-floor room in an Art Deco "Painted Lady" with private bath, TV, second-floor sitting room, and continental breakfast. $35-40.

NOTES: Credit cards accepted: A Master Card; B Visa; C American Express; D Discover Card; E Diners Club; F Other: 2 Personal checks accepted: 3 Lunch available: 4 Dinner available: 5 Open all year

B&B Kansas City CO22

Box 14781, Lenexa, Kansas, 66215
(913) 888-3636

Contemporary earth-integrated home on 85 acres with a four-bedroom wing, lounge, and indoor pool. Double beds, private bath, TV. A wooded getaway with jogging paths, ponds, fishing. Full breakfast is served by the pool; lavish Sunday brunch. Children welcome. $55-65.

B&B Kansas City HA36

Box 14781, Lenexa, Kansas, 66215
(913) 888-3636

A 100-year-old Queen Anne style Hyde Park Home, furnished from estate sales, offers two double rooms and a magnificent walnut screened port. One private bath, one shared. Full breakfast. $35-40.

B&B Kansas City KE32

Box 14781, Lenexa, Kansas, 66215
(913) 888-3636

Early 1900s home — spacious and restored with lots of antiques. Three rooms, shared bath; perfect for a family. Full breakfast. Near KC Museum, nine minutes to downtown and the stadium. $30-50.

B&B Kansas City LA60

Box 14781, Lenexa, Kansas, 66215
(913) 888-3636

Stunning Plaza home with pool, twin room, king room, private bath. Full breakfast in breakfast room or on terrace. Walk to Plaza. No smoking. $70.

B&B Kansas City NU14

Box 14781, Lenexa, Kansas, 66215
(913) 888-3636

West of the Plaza. The owner is an interior designer. Breakfast room overlooks the terraced yard. King-size room and/or double-bed room. Private bath and shower; continental breakfast. Ideal for two couples. $55-60.

B&B Kansas City TH71

Box 14781, Lenexa, Kansas, 66215
(913) 888-3636

Handsome 1913 Georgian, a former mayor's home, with a top-floor suite or double room, private bath. Continental breakfast. Lovely brick home in the Hyde Park area. $40-5-.

B&B Kansas City WH60

Box 14781, Lenexa, Kansas, 66215
(913) 888-3636

Large English Tudor home with beautiful furnishings, landscaping. Two blocks from Plaza. Twin beds, balcony with private bath, full gourmet breakfast. No smoking. $55-60.

Doanleigh Wallagh Inn

Doanleigh Wallagh Inn

217 E. 37th Street, 64111
(816) 753-2667

6 Pets welcome: 7 Smoking allowed: 8 Children welcome: 9 Social drinking allowed: 10 Tennis available: 11 Swimming available: 12 Golf available: 13 Skiing available: 14 May be booked through travel agents

A turn-of-the-century mansion minutes from Crown Center, Country Club Plaza, and Westport. Antiques, telephone, and cable television with movie channels in each room. Also available for parties, weddings, and conferences. Hosts will help plan sightseeing and make restaurant reservations.

Hosts: Carolyn & Edward Kitchfield
Doubles: 12 (PB) $60-90
Type of Beds: 4 Twin; 1 Double; 6 Queen; 5 King
Full Breakfast
Credit Cards: A, B
Notes: 2, 7 (limited), 8 (by arrangement), 9, 10, 14

Dome Ridge

14360 Walker Road, 64164
(816) 532-4074

A unique geodesic dome with three guest rooms furnished with many antiques. The great room has a thirty-foot wood ceiling; custom-built woodwork and cabinets are throughout the house. A deck completely circles the house and is perfect for bird watching. In a lovely, quiet country setting twenty minutes from downtown Kansas City and ten from the airport.

Hosts: Roberta & Bill Faust
Singles: 1 (PB) $40
Doubles: 2 (PB) $45
Type of Beds: 2 Twin; 1 Double; 1 Queen
Full Breakfast
Credit Cards: No
Notes: 2, 5, 7 (limited), 9, 10, 11, 12, 14

KIMBERLING CITY

OMC 102-B

Ozark Mountain Country B&B
Box 295, Branson, MO, 65616
(417) 334-4720

Charming new log home four miles south of Kimberling City on Highway 13. Guests are welcome to use the living/dining room with TV and covered deck with a beautiful view of Table Rock Lake. Boat launch, picnic area, and swimming is just two miles from the home.

Cottage: 1 (PB) $50
Doubles: 2 (SB) $40-65
Type of Beds: 2 Double; 1 Queen; 1 Hideabed
Continental Breakfast
Credit Cards: No
Closed Dec. - Feb.
Notes: 2, 10, 11, 12, 13

LAMPE

Williams Mountain

Ozark Mountain Country B&B
Box 295, Branson, MO, 65616
(417) 334-4720

A gorgeous new home with a spectacular view of Table Rock Lake and the Ozark mountains, located ten miles south of Kimberling City. Private lakeside patio area, sitting area with game room and TV.

Doubles: 2 (PB) $55-95
Full Breakfast
Credit Cards: No
Closes Nov. - April
Notes: 2, 8, 11, 12, 13

OMC 221

Ozark Mountain Country B&B
Box 295, Branson, MO, 65616
(417) 334-4720

This 4,500-square-foot new home is located on a private lake on the southeast side of Kansas City. Offering three guest rooms, a balcony library with TV, family room with fireplace, and antiques, including an antique pipe organ. A full breakfast is served in the kitchen, sun room, or dining room. No children or pets. $50-55.

LIBERTY

B&B Kansas City LI22

Box 14781, Lenexa, Kansas, 66215
(913) 888-3636

NOTES: Credit cards accepted: A Master Card; B Visa; C American Express; D Discover Card; E Diners Club; F Other: 2 Personal checks accepted: 3 Lunch available: 4 Dinner available: 5 Open all year

Restored 1912 three-story home with porches. Two rooms share a bath. Full breakfast. Near Wm. Jewell College. $40-45.

B&B Kansas City SS3

Box 14781, Lenexa, Kansas, 66215
(913) 888-3636

Large Cape Cod Home in a country setting with stables and riding lessons (fee). Two bedrooms with elegant country furnishings share one bath. Full breakfast. $40-65.

LOUISIANA

B&B Kansas City MO12

Box 14781, Lenexa, Kansas, 66215
(913) 888-3636

Pre-Civil War two-story brick home, totally restored. Queen bedroom with private bath, two double rooms with shared bath. Private sitting room, VCR, TV. Gourmet full breakfast inside or in the garden. Lots of deck. Perfect for a family. Walk to the Mississippi River and enjoy the many antique shops along the way. $40-45

MARIONVILLE

White Squirrel Hollow Inn

Ozark Mountain Country B&B
Box 295, Branson, MO, 65616
(417) 334-4720

White Squirrel Hollow Inn is a darling Victorian built about 1896. Located about twenty-one miles southwest of Springfield, it's close to Highway 60. You can watch the rare white squirrel families at play on the grounds. Guests are welcome to use the parlor with fireplace and TV, library filled with new and antique books, formal dining

room, upstairs sitting room with TV, and spacious front porch. Adults only.

Doubles: 6 (3 PB; 3 SB) $40-55
Full Breakfast
Credit Cards: No

NIXA

Country View B&B

Ozark Mountain Country B&B
Box 295, Branson, MO, 65616
(417) 334-4720

This charming new home is furnished and accessorized with casual, country-style antiues. Located four miles south of Springfield, about twenty-five miles from Branson. Hearty country breakfast is served in the dining room on antique china or on the covered deck. Resident dogs and cats. No smokers or preteenagers. $40-95.

OSAGE BEACH

OMC 208

Ozark Mountain Country B&B
Box 295, Branson, MO, 65616
(417) 334-4720

This new home is on Lake of the Ozarks, near Osage Beach, and offers two guest rooms, each with queen bed and private bath, one with a private entrance. Sitting room adjoining the guest rooms has two day beds and a kitchenette; sliding doors open onto a private lakeside patio. Children welcome; baby-sitting arrangements can be made. Pets accepted with prior arrangement. Continental breakfast. $30-70.

PARKVILLE

Down to Earth Lifestyles Bed & Breakfast

Rt. 22, 64152
(816) 891-1018

6 Pets welcome: 7 Smoking allowed: 8 Children welcome: 9 Social drinking allowed: 10 Tennis available: 11 Swimming available: 12 Golf available: 13 Skiing available: 14 May be booked through travel agents

Unique getaway haven offering the best of midwestern country and city living. Indoor heated pool, plus 86 acres with farm animals, fishing ponds, wildlife, walking, and jogging. Full special-order breakfast served at place and time of guest's choice.

Hosts: Lola & Bill Coons
Doubles: 4 (PB) $55-65
Type of Beds: 2 Twin; 3 Double
Full Breakfast
Credit Cards: No
Notes: 2, 5, 7, 8, 9, 10, 11, 12, 13, 14

PLATTE CITY

Basswood Country Inn B&B

Rt. 1, Box 145B, 64079
(816) 431-5556

Ten minutes northeast of Kansas City International Airport. This 74-acre country estate has seven fishing lakes, wooded trails, four new country French suites, private entrances, and decks. A 1935 two-bedroom restored lakeside cottage sleeps six. Bess Truman entertained her bridge club at Basswood in the 1940s and 1950s.

Hosts: Don & Betty Soper
Doubles: 4 (PB) $52-92
Cottage (PB) $77-88
Type of Beds: 1 Double; 5 Queen; 5 King
Continental Breakfast
Minimum stay weekends & holidays: 2
Children over 7 welcome; younger in cottage
Credit Cards: A, B
Notes: 2, 5, 7, 8, 9, 11, 12, 14

PT. LOOKOUT

Cameron Craig

Ozark Mountain Country B&B
Box 295, Branson, MO, 65616
(417) 334-4720

"On a clear day you can see forever" from this lovely new home high on a bluff overlooking Lake Taneycomo and the valley beyond. The home is just three miles from Branson, just around the corner from the School of the Ozarks. The guest area includes a sitting area, private entrance off the deck, color TV, air-conditioning.

Doubles: 1 (PB) $40-45
Type of Beds: 1 Queen
Full Breakfast
Credit Cards: No
Closed Dec. - Feb.
Notes: 2, 8 (5 and over), 9, 10, 11, 12, 13

ROGERSVILLE

OMC 201-B

Ozark Mountain Country B&B
Box 295, Branson, MO, 65616
(417) 334-4720

This old-fashioned country home is about fifteen miles east of Springfield and four miles from Rogersville. If you want to get away, this lovely rock home on a 1,200 acre Arabian horse farm has a lot to offer! A completely furnished kitchen, dining room, living room and den with TV are available for guests. Hot tub is a little way up the hill from the home. You may board your horse for $5 a day and are welcome to watch the workings of the ranch, but can't ride our horses.

Doubles: 3 (2 PB; 1 SB) $30-45
Type of Beds: 5 Twin; 1 Double; 1 Queen
Continental Breakfast
Credit Cards: No
Closed Dec. - Feb.
Notes: 2, 7, 8, 9, 11

ST. JOSEPH

B&B Kansas City HA21

Box 14781, Lenexa, Kansas, 66215
(913) 888-3636

Gracious turn-of-the-century Victorian with beveled glass windows, oak woodwork, many antiques. Four double-bedded rooms share two baths. Tea or sherry is served by the fire or on the porch in season. Real American full breakfast with homemade pasteries. No smoking. $30-45.

NOTES: Credit cards accepted: A Master Card; B Visa; C American Express; D Discover Card; E Diners Club; F Other: 2 Personal checks accepted: 3 Lunch available: 4 Dinner available: 5 Open all year

ST. LOUIS

Lafayette House

2156 Lafayette Avenue, 63104
(314) 772-4429

An 1876 brick Queen Anne mansion in the center of things to do in St. Louis. Furnished with antiques, but with modern conveniences. Extensive library, many interesting collections. Complimentary soda, wine, cheese, crackers. Train, plane, and bus pick up for a small fee. Three cats in residence.

Hosts: Sarah & Jack Milligan
Doubles: 4 (1 PB; 3 SB) $35-60
Suite: 1 (PB) sleeps 6-8
Type of Beds: 5 Twin; 3 Double
Minimum stay in suite: 2
Full Breakfast
Credit Cards: No
Notes: 2, 5, 6 (by prior arrangement), 7, 8 (limited), 9, 10, 11, 12, 13, 14

Lafayette House

SEDALIA

B&B Kansas City FL4

Box 14781, Lenexa, Kansas, 66215
(913) 888-3636

A 300 acre cattle ranch with a 1905 stone colonial home with pillars. Three rooms with twin beds and antiques. Full breakfast in the dining room with chippendale and a crystal chandelier; library with cable TV. Located 1.5 hours from Kansas City. $55.

SPRINGFIELD

Walnut Street Bed & Breakfast

Ozark Mountain Country B&B
Box 295, Branson, MO, 65616
(417) 334-4720

Take a step back in time and capture the warmth and elegance of a Queen Anne Victorian inn conveniently located in the historic district. Built in 1894, the inn is listed as a National Historic Site. Try a tune on the 1862 square grand piano or enjoy the fireplace and game table.

Doubles: 7 (PB) $60-85
Type of Beds: 2 Twin; 2 Double; 3 Queen
Full Breakfast
Credit Cards: No
Notes: 2, 5, 7 (outside), 8 (over 8)

Yorkshire House

Ozark Mountain Country B&B
Box 295, Branson, MO, 65616
(417) 334-4720

A lovely two-story colonial in a quiet, rural area in southeast Springfield. The entire home is furnished and accessorized with antiques. Sightseeing trips and airport pick up can be arranged for an additional fee. Guests are welcome to use the kitchen, family room, game room with Jacuzzi, and gas grill.

Doubles: 3 (1 PB; 2 SB) $35-70
Type of Beds: 3 Double; 1 Queen
Full Breakfast
Credit Cards: No
Notes: 2, 5, 8 (over 5)

WARRENSBURG

B&B Kansas City BA21

Box 14781, Lenexa, Kansas, 66215
(913) 888-3636

6 Pets welcome: 7 Smoking allowed: 8 Children welcome: 9 Social drinking allowed: 10 Tennis available: 11 Swimming available: 12 Golf available: 13 Skiing available: 14 May be booked through travel agents

Massive three-story home built in 1915 offers big rooms, one with queen bed and a fireplace. Another queen shares the bath. Antiques, TV room, VCR. Full breakfast. $45.

B&B Kansas City SCH2

Box 14781, Lenexa, Kansas, 66215
(913) 888-3636

Rustic wooded home of a college professor offers the whole lower level, with queen hidabed, single bedroom, private bath. There's a single room with bath on the main level. Enjoy walking in to woods. Full breakfast. $30-35.

OMC 216

Ozark Mountain Country B&B
Box 295, Branson, MO, 65616
(417) 334-4720

Enjoy the natural beauty of the Ozarks as guests on a genuine farm. This restored and renovated circa 1867 farmhouse looks much as it did around 1890, except it has the comforts of today. Two century-old barns, still in use, flank the farmstead, which is in the middle of 80 acres of woods and meadows. Horses can be accommodated.

Doubles: 2 (SB) $25
Type of Beds: 1 Twin; 2 Double; 1 Three-quarter
Full Breakfast
Credit Cards: No
Notes: 2, 3, 4, 5, 7 (limited)

WARSAW

OMC 215

Ozark Mountain Country B&B
Box 295, Branson, MO, 65616
(417) 334-4720

A completely remodeled and redecorated 1900 era bungalow. A full breakfast features all you can eat of a variety of choices, including Belgian waffles. Cable TV in the guest

sitting room; central air-conditioning. Warsaw is on the headwaters of the Lake of the Ozarks and three miles from Truman Lake, Truman Dam, the Truman Lake Observatory and Visitor Center. Two rooms with private baths. $30-40.

WESTON

B&B Kansas City AP90

Box 14781, Lenexa, Kansas, 66215
(913) 888-3636

Recently restored turn-of-the-century home with six rooms, two with private baths. Many antiques, wonderful homemade breakfast. The perfect getaway. $55-65.

WEST PLAINS

Hopp's Hillside

Ozark Mountain Country B&B
Box 295, Branson, MO, 65616
(417) 334-4720

A 100-year-old colonial two blocks from the square in West Plains, decorated in comfortable country and colonial furnishings and antiques. Read in the library, watch cable TV, or stroll the garden and sit in the gazebo. Three bedrooms are available; two shared baths. Full breakfast is served, and dinner can be arranged. $30-55.

OMC 12

Ozark Mountain Country B&B
Box 295, Branson, MO, 65616
(417) 334-4720

Relax in the Ozarks on this 60-acre farm located six miles south of West Plains. The ranch-style home is air-conditioned and accessorized with antiques. Two guest rooms, continental breakfast. Well-behaved pets are welcome; resident cat. Available weekends only. No preteenagers or smoking. $20-50.

NOTES: Credit cards accepted: A Master Card; B Visa; C American Express; D Discover Card; E Diners Club; F Other: 2 Personal checks accepted: 3 Lunch available: 4 Dinner available: 5 Open all year

Montana

BIG SANDY

B&B Western Adventure

Box 20972, Billings, 59104
(406) 259-7993

Participate in ranch life by feeding and grooming the horses, feeding chickens, gathering eggs. Abundant wild game area. Two log cabins sleep four, each with bath. Another lodge offers four bedrooms sharing two full baths. Continental-plus breakfast. $26-40.

BIG SKY

Lone Mountain Ranch

Box 69, 59716
(406) 995-4644

Comfortable ranch cabin accommodations nestled in a secluded valley. Horseback riding, Yellowstone National Park interpretive trips, Orvis-endorsed fly-fishing program, kids' activities, nature hikes in summer. Cross-country skiing, sleigh-ride dinners in winter. Nationally acclaimed cuisine in our historic dining room. All meals are included in the weekly rate.

Hosts: Bob & Vivian Schaap
Singles: 3 (PB) $595-903/week/cabin
Doubles: 17 (PB) $595-903/week/cabin
Type of Beds: 28 Twin; 2 Double; 19 Queen
Full Breakfast
Credit Cards: A, B
Closed April 1-June 1; Oct. 1-Dec. 1
Notes: 2, 4, 8, 9, 10, 11, 12, 13, 14

BIG TIMBER

B&B Western Adventure #226

Box 20972, Billings, 59104
(406) 259-7993

This grand old hotel, built in 1890, has been restored to its original dignity. Seven rooms: one suite with private bath; six rooms share two full baths, two lavatories, two showers, and a sauna. Fishing, outfitters, hiking, dude ranches, snow mobiling, rafting. Full or continental breakfast. $45-75.

B&B Western Adventure #233

Box 20972, Billings, 59104
(406) 259-7993

This ranch home is in Absarokee National Forest beside Deer Creek. Antelope and deer are always in view on this cattle and sheep ranch. Lambing, shearing, and branding to watch. Six rooms share a three-bath and sauna suite. A guest house with its own bath can sleep six. Full breakfast. $45-60.

BILLINGS

B&B Western Adventure #36

Box 20972, 59104
(406) 259-7993

6 Pets welcome: 7 Smoking allowed: 8 Children welcome: 9 Social drinking allowed: 10 Tennis available: 11 Swimming available: 12 Golf available: 13 Skiing available: 14 May be booked through travel agents

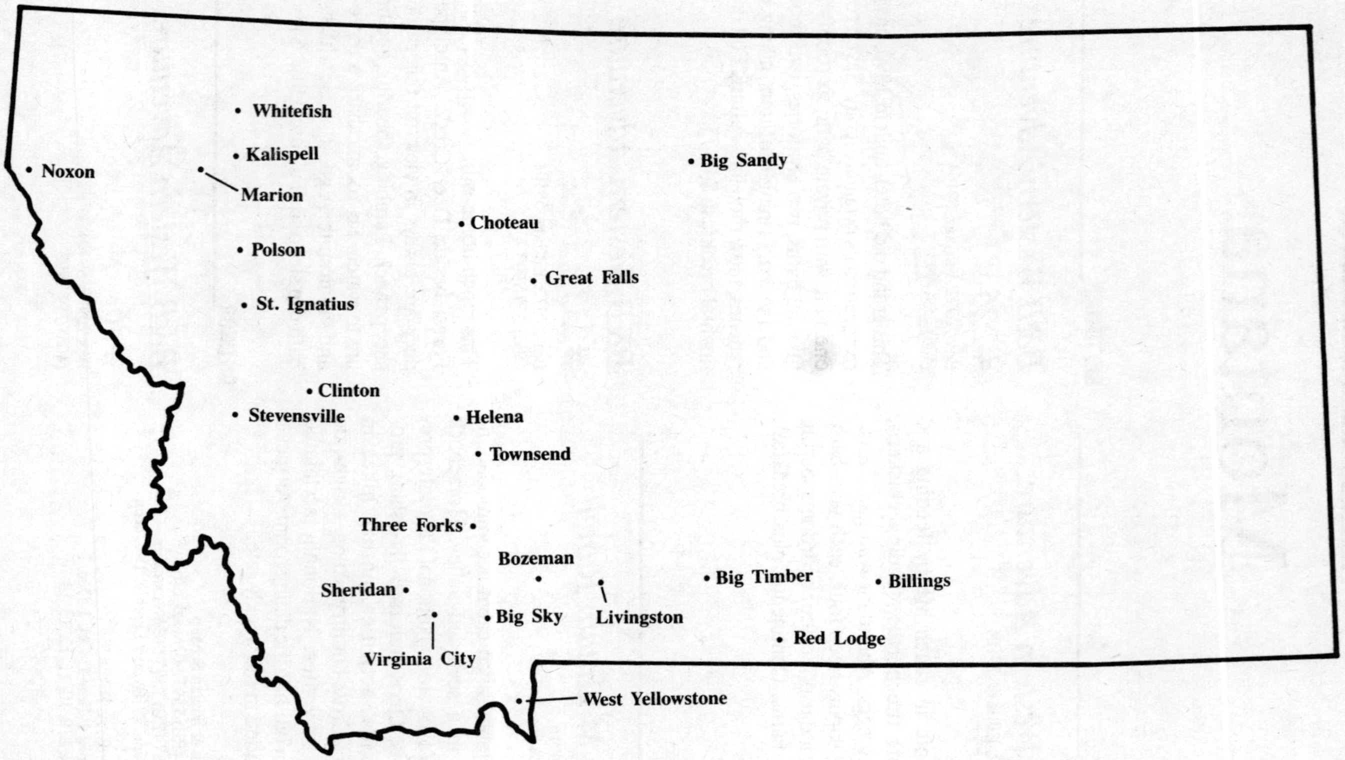

MONTANA

Big Sandy

Choteau

Great Falls

Whitefish
Kalispell
Marion
Polson
St. Ignatius

Clinton
Stevensville

Noxon

Helena
Townsend

Three Forks

Bozeman
Big Sky

Sheridan

Virginia City

Big Timber
Billings

Red Lodge

Livingston

West Yellowstone

Newly restored historic wood-frame house furnished with antiques and collectibles. Four bedrooms with sinks share master bath. Two rooms on the lower lever share a shower bath. Within walking distance of downtown shopping, restaurants, museums. Continental breakfast. $24-36/couple.

BOZEMAN

B&B Western Adventure #202

Box 20972, Billings, 59104
(406) 259-7993

A 1906 Colonial Revival home in the historic district furnished with antiques. Three bedrooms on the second floor, one with private bath, two shared. Short walk to Montana State University, museums, and downtown. No smoking. $35-45.

B&B Western Adventure #203

Box 20972, Billings, 59104
(406) 259-7993

Located on 11 acres in the beautiful Gallatin Valley with a trout stream within walking distance. Hunt in fall, ski in winter, hike, raft, and swim in summer. Three bedrooms in the home and three in the guest house. Full breakfast, children welcomed to help feed the ducks and other animals. Swimming pool. $50-100.

Hillard's B&B and Guest House

11521 Axtell Cty. Road, 59715
(406) 763-4696

Located ten miles from Bozeman in a quiet setting close to the Gallatin River and excellent trout fishing. Close to the airport, twen-ty-five miles to Bridger Bowl or Big Sky for skiing. Big-game area; seventy-five miles to West Yellowstone.

Hosts: Larry & Doris Hillard
Doubles: 2 (SB) $62.40
Guest House: 3 bedrooms & private bath
Full Breakfast
Credit Cards: No
Notes: 2, 4, 5, 6, 7, 8, 9, 11, 12, 13

Voss Inn B&B

Voss Inn Bed & Breakfast

319 South Willson, 59715
(406) 587-0982

Magnificently restored Victorian inn in the historic district with elegant guest rooms with private baths. A delightful gourmet breakfast is served in the privacy of your room. Bozeman is ninety miles north of Yellowstone Park, near skiing, fishing, hiking, snow mobiling.

Hosts: Bruce & Frankee Muller
Doubles: 6 (PB) $45-65
Type of Beds: 3 Twin; 5 Queen; 1 King
Full Breakfast
Credit Cards: A, B
Notes: 2, 5, 9, 10, 11, 12, 14

CHOTEAU

B&B Western Adventure #224

Box 20972, Billings, 59104
(406) 259-7993

6 Pets welcome: 7 Smoking allowed: 8 Children welcome: 9 Social drinking allowed: 10 Tennis available: 11 Swimming available: 12 Golf available: 13 Skiing available: 14 May be booked through travel agents

Two-story home constructed of hand-hewn logs and stone. Thick quilts, crisp linens, antiques, original artwork. Two rooms with double beds share a bath. Near the Bob Marshall Wilderness area and the Egg Mountain Fossil Beds. Bicycles and picnic baskets can be arranged with notice. Winter skiing at Teton Pass. Full breakfast. $28-35.

CLINTON

B&B Western Adventure #239

Box 20972, Billings, 59104
(406) 259-7993

A two-story colonial surrounded by 25 acres of woods and meadows. Only minutes from Missoula and the University of Montana. Three rooms share a large bath. Clark Fork River and rafting are available within one mile; twenty minutes to two ski areas. Full breakfast. $50-65.

GREAT FALLS

B&B Western Adventure #206

Box 20972, Billings, 59104
(406) 259-7993

Charming restored Victorian in the historic section of downtown. Three bedrooms share a bath and sitting room with TV. Bedroom with private bath on first floor. Ten minutes from I-15. Skiing, fishing, hiking are within one hour's drive. Full breakfast. Children over 6 are welcome; no smoking. $35-50.

B&B Western Adventure #209

Box 20972, Billings, 59104
(406) 259-7993

Stately Victorian chalet from the early 1900s with leaded and beveled glass, hardwood floors, Oriental rugs. Five bedrooms, two with private baths. Within walking distance of an indoor pool, park, museums, and downtown. Full breakfast. Restricted smoking. $35-60.

HELENA

B&B Western Adventure #208

Box 20972, Billings, 59104
(406) 259-7993

Elegantly restored 1875 Victorian with original antiques and Oriental rugs. Seven rooms each have private bath, telephone, and a view of the city. Credit cards accepted. $40-60.

KALISPELL

B&B Western Adventure #78

Box 20972, Billings, 59104
(406) 259-7993

This quaint red brick farmhouse is in the country but convenient to Kalispell, Whitefish, and Glacier National Park. Two bedrooms share a bath. Full breakfast. No smoking; children over 10 welcome. $35-45.

B&B Western Adventure #213

Box 20972, Billings, 59104
(406) 259-7993

A Victorian house in town with three bedrooms, one with private bath. Thirty miles from Glacier National Park and seven miles from Flathead Lake. Downhill and XC skiing, fishing, hunting, boating, hiking, and rafting are only minutes away. Full breakfast. Smoking allowed. $35-50.

B&B Western Adventure #214

Box 20972, Billings, 59104
(406) 259-7993

A working ranch sitting right next to the Absaroka/Beartooth Wilderness and Davis Creek. Five to ten-minute drive to trout streams and forty to Yellowstone. Two bedrooms share a private bath. Guided hiking tours, picnics, horseback riding within five miles. Full breakfast. Children are welcome. $45.

B&B Western Adventure #215

Box 20972, Billings, 59104
(406) 259-7993

This ranch home on Mill Creek has two guest cabins thirty miles north of Yellowstone, with private bath. Ideal for fishing, hiking, photography, XC skiing. Full breakfast. $45.

B&B Western Adventure #234

Box 20972, Billings, 59104
(406) 259-7993

This 1903 mansion is on the National Register of Historic Homes. Children are welcome. Four bedrooms, one with private bath; three share two baths. Five minutes from I-90 and one hour from Yellowstone. Ideal location for fly fishermen or history buffs. Full breakfast. $50-65.

B&B Western Adventure #237

Box 20972, Billings, 59104
(406) 259-7993

A working cattle ranch in the upper Rocky Mountains between the Kootenai and Lola national forests. Ideal for wildlife lovers, photographers, hikers, and sportsmen. Guest house with private bath sleeps six. Two rooms in the house sleep four. Full breakfast. $50-60/couple.

B&B Western Adventure #151

Box 20972, Billings, 59104
(406) 259-7993

A Southern plantation-style home with huge columns and porch across the front. Four bedrooms with private baths. trail rides, hiking, fishing, houseboat cruises, lake swimming, rafting. Full breakfast. Pets, smoking, and children allowed. $45-55.

B&B Western Adventure #210

Box 20972, Billings, 59104
(406) 259-7993

On Flathead Lake with a gravel beach, rock gardens, and boardwalks. Watch for osprey and bald eagles; listen for the whistle of marmots. Four bedrooms with views; one with private bath. Marina and boat-launching facilities on the premises; canoes and paddle-boats available; fall hunting; skiing. Continental-plus breakfast. Children over 16 welcome. $75-90/couple.

---

6 Pets welcome: 7 Smoking allowed: 8 Children welcome: 9 Social drinking allowed: 10 Tennis available: 11 Swimming available: 12 Golf available: 13 Skiing available: 14 May be booked through travel agents

Mission Mountain Bed 'N Breakfast

RED LODGE

B&B Western Adventure #255

Box 20972, Billings, 59104
(406) 259-7993

Charmingly restored 1896 house decorated with antique furniture and artwork. Two rooms with private baths share a private sitting room. Continental-plus breakfast. Children over 6 welcome; no smoking or pets. $35-50.

ST. IGNATIUS

Mission Mountains Bed 'N Breakfast

RR Box 183A, 59865
(406) 745-4331

Comfortable ranch home 2.5 miles north of St. Ignatius offers beautiful views of the Mission Mountains, Cabinet Mountains, National Bison Range, and Ninepipe National Bird Refuge. Year-round outdoor activities in the surrounding area. Come relax and enjoy the beauty.

Hosts: Vic & Doris Peterson
Doubles: 2 (SB) $28.08-34.32

Type of Beds: 2 Twin; 1 Queen
Full Breakfast
Credit Cards: No
Notes: 2, 4, 5, 8, 10, 11, 12

SHERIDAN

B&B Western Adventure #222

Box 20972, Billings, 59104
(406) 259-7993

Lovely two-story new home in ranch country in the Ruby River Valley. Fantastic mountain views in every direction. Arabian horses. Open June-September. Three bedrooms share two baths. Fly fishing only three miles away; mountain hiking trails within five miles. Full breakfast, limited smoking. $30-40.

STEVENSVILLE

B&B Western Adventure #77

Box 20972, Billings, 59104
(406) 259-7993

A grand Georgian colonial on the National Register with grand staircase, antique fur-

NOTES: Credit cards accepted: A Master Card; B Visa; C American Express; D Discover Card; E Diners Club; F Other: 2 Personal checks accepted: 3 Lunch available: 4 Dinner available: 5 Open all year

nishing, and four large bedrooms that share two baths. Halfway between Yellowstone and Glacier National Parks in a sleepy little town. Wildlife bird refuge and float trips are nearby; thirty miles from the University of Montana, an international airport. Full breakfast, no children or smoking. Open May-October. $35-40.

THREE FORKS

B&B Western Adventure #252
Box 20972, Billings, 59104
(406) 259-7993

Stately three-story home, restored to its original elegance, now serves as a small inn hosting 45-50 people at a time. Twenty rooms, some with private bath, some with shared. Continental breakfast, no smoking or pets. $30-50.

TOWNSEND

Hidden Hollow Ranch
211 Flynn Lane, 59644
(406) 266-3580

Hidden Hollow is an 11,000 acre ranch/farm with meadows, mountains, creeks, fields with hay, grain, livestock. Beautiful gardens, farm museum. Modest large farmhouse with a homey atmosphere.

Hosts: Frank & Rose Flynn
Singles: 4 (SB) $25
Doubles: 3 (SB) $35
Suite: (2 bedrooms, private bath) $60
Full Breakfast
Closed Nov.-April
Notes: 8, 11, 12

VIRGINIA CITY

B&B Western Adventure #238
Box 20972, Billings, 59104
(406) 259-7993

This historic inn was built in 1879 and has just been restored. Five bedrooms, all with handmade quilts and antiques, share two baths. A small dog is in residence. Gold and garnet panning can be done nearby; ride the historic train for Virginia City to Nevada City; fish the Madison River. Continental-plus breakfast; children over 7 welcome; no smoking. $33-42.

B&B Western Adventure #251
Box 20972, Billings, 59104
(406) 259-7993

Stately 1884 grey stone house with wraparound porch, antiques, quilts. Six rooms, including a suite that sleeps five. Step into the gold-rush days, cross-country ski. Full breakfast; continental for late risers. No smoking. $35-48.

WEST YELLOWSTONE

B&B Western Adventure #230
Box 20972, Billings, 59104
(406) 259-7993

A sportsman's and photographer's paradise. Deer and moose are often seen in the back-yard at dusk. Tie your own flies and enjoy the area fishing. Drift boating on the Madison and Gallatin Rivers and Hebgen Lake are within twenty miles. Cat in residence. Three bedrooms; one private bath, two share bath. Continental-plus breakfast; no smoking; children over 16 welcome. $45-50.

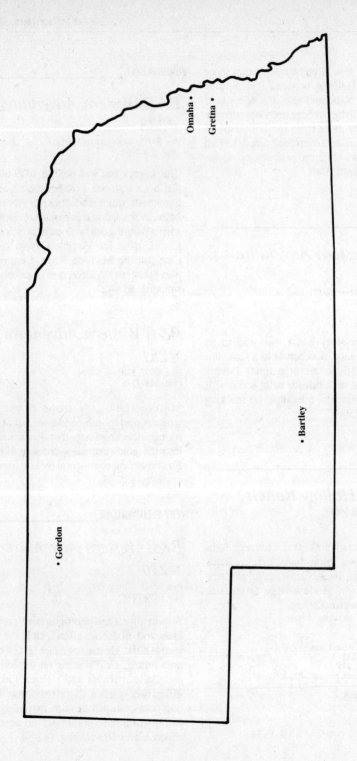

NEBRASKA

Omaha •
Gretna •

• Bartley

• Gordon

Nebraska

BARTLEY

Pheasant Hill Farm
HCR 68, Box 12, 69020
(308) 692-3278

Enjoy the good life on our southwest Nebraska farm. Unique family experience. In-season hunting for dove, quail, pheasant, deer. Fish, swim, boat on area lakes. Thirty minutes to world-class golf, shopping, and entertainment. Relax on the porch with ten-mile vistas; enjoy country cooking.

Hosts: Max & Dona Nelms
Singles: 3 (2 PB; 1 SB) $30-35
Doubles: 2 (PB) $40-45
Type of Beds: 6 Twin; 2 Double
Full Breakfast
Minimum stay weekdays: 4 ; weekends: 3 ; holidays: 2
Credit Cards: No
Notes: 2, 3, 4, 5, 7, 8, 9, 14

GORDON

Double "V" Ranch
HC 84, Box 53, 69343
(308) 282-2197

Enjoy the serene, endless panorama of the Sandhills of Nebraska. Visit "Old Jules Country," hunt, fish, hike, or just relax. Recharge your spiritual life on a Christian working ranch. Reservations, please. Send for free flyer.

Hosts: Virgil & Alice Elsberry, John & Beth Lee & family
Doubles: 2 (SB) $40
Type of Beds: 2 Double
Full Breakfast
Credit Cards: No
Notes: 2, 4, 5, 8

GRETNA

Bundy's Bed & Breakfast
16906 South 255, 68028
(402) 332-3616

Our bed and breakfast features antiques and collectibles and is an active farm home. A Christian atmosphere with a good farm breakfast is yours to enjoy. Close to Nebraska's only snow ski area and two blocks from swimming and dining.

Hosts: Bob & Dee Bundy
Doubles: 4 (SB) $15-25
Type of Beds: 4 Double
Full Breakfast
Credit Cards: No
Notes: 2, 5, 11, 13

OMAHA

The Offutt House
140 N. 39th Street, 68131
(402) 553-0951

This comfortable mansion, built in 1894, is part of the city's section of large homes built around the same time by Omaha's most wealthy residents. Rooms are comfortably spacious and furnished with antiques. Some feature fireplaces. The house is near downtown Omaha and the historic Old Market area, which offers many beautiful shops and excellent restaurants. Reservations, please.

Host: Jeannie K. Swoboda
Doubles: 7 (2 PB; 5 SB) $40-60
Type of Beds: 1 Twin; 6 Double; 1 Queen
Continental Breakfast
Credit Cards: A, B, C
Notes: 2, 5, 7, 8 (over 12), 9, 10, 11, 12, 14

---

6 Pets welcome: 7 Smoking allowed: 8 Children welcome: 9 Social drinking allowed: 10 Tennis available: 11 Swimming available: 12 Golf available: 13 Skiing available: 14 May be booked through travel agents

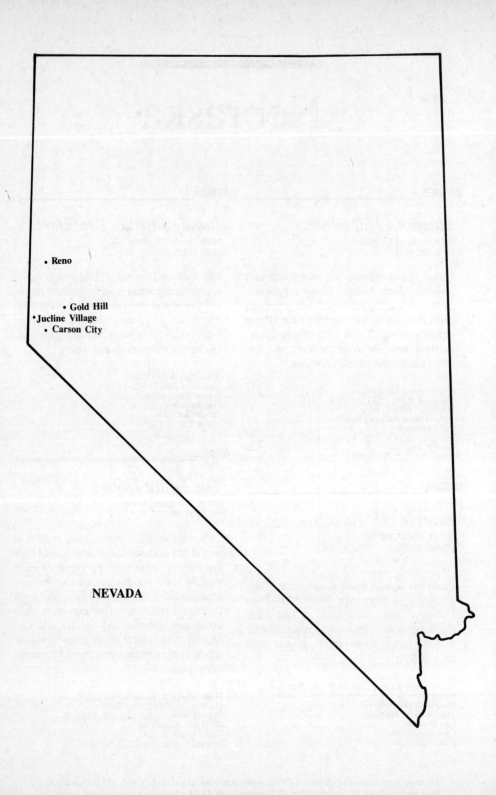

- Reno

- Gold Hill
- Jucline Village
- Carson City

NEVADA

Nevada

The Edwards House

204 N. Minnesota Street, 89703
(702) 882-4884

This gracious sandstone Victorian was built in 1877, in the heart of Carson City's historic district. Within walking distance of the Capitol, state museum, governor's mansion, legislature, and casinos. Delight in the beauty of the surrounding Sierra Nevada, Lake Tahoe, Virginia City, and Reno. Complimentary wine and sherry in your room, fresh flowers, Jacuzzi, grand piano, and one resident cat.

Host: Christina Broo
Doubles: 3 (SB) $65
Type of Beds: 1 Twin; 1 Double; 1 Queen
Full Breakfast
Credit Cards: A, B
Closed Nov. 22, 23 & Dec. 24, 25
Notes: 2, 5, 7, 8, 9, 10, 11, 12, 13, 14

GOLD HILL

House on the Hill

920 Sky Lane, 89440
(702) 847-0193

Experience whispers of the past! The elegant, three-story new Victorian, situated between Reno and Lake Tahoe, overlooks Gold Canyon, site of some of history's largest gold strikes. Only minutes to historic Virginia City.

Hosts: Kay & George Halliwell
Doubles: 3 (1 PB; 2 SB) $45-95 plus tax
Type of Beds: 3 Queen
Continental Breakfast

Credit Cards: No
Notes: 2, 5, 9

JUCLINE VILLAGE

Haus Bavaria

Box 3308, 89450
(702) 831-6122

Haus Bavaria is located on the north shore of beautiful Lake Tahoe. It's a Bavarian style chalet, established in 1980, that offers comfortable home hospitality, including a full European breakfast.

Hosts: Wolfgang & Anneliese Zimmermann
Doubles: 5 (PB) $60-70
Type of Beds: 10 Twin
Full Breakfast
Credit Cards: No
Notes: 2, 5, 9, 10, 11, 12, 13, 14

RENO

Lace & Linen Guest House

Suite 114, 4800 Kietzke Lane, 89502
(702) 826-3547

This B&B is furnished in pastels with antiques and Oriental rugs, white Victorian wicker, and European pieces. Guests may relax in the living room by the wood-burning fireplace and view the beautiful Sierra Nevadas or sit on the balcony to watch the sunset or the city lights at night.

Host: Patricia Parks
Doubles: 3 (PB) $40-45
Type of Beds: 4 Twin; 1 King
Continental Breakfast
Credit Cards: No
Notes: 3 (on request), 4 (on request), 5, 7 (limited), 9, 10, 11, 12, 13, 14

6 Pets welcome: 7 Smoking allowed: 8 Children welcome: 9 Social drinking allowed: 10 Tennis available: 11 Swimming available: 12 Golf available: 13 Skiing available: 14 May be booked through travel agents

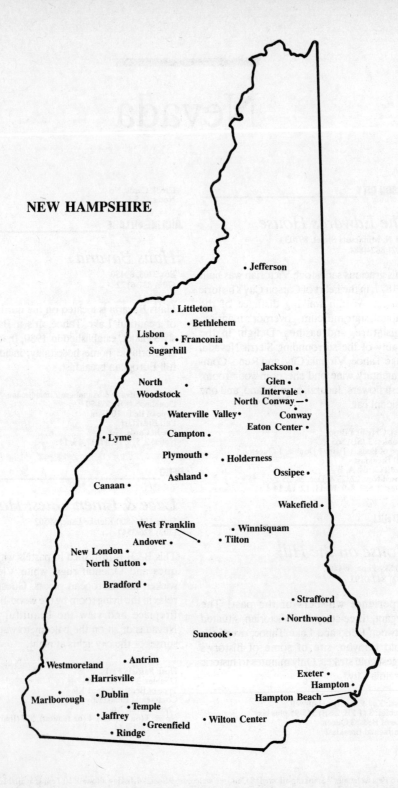

NEW HAMPSHIRE

Jefferson

Littleton
Bethlehem
Lisbon
Franconia
Sugarhill

Jackson
Glen
North Intervale
Woodstock North Conway
Waterville Valley Conway
Eaton Center

Lyme Campton
Plymouth Holderness
Ashland Ossipee
Canaan

Wakefield

West Franklin Winnisquam
Andover Tilton
New London
North Sutton

Bradford

Strafford
Northwood
Suncook

Antrim
Westmoreland
Harrisville Exeter
Hampton
Marlborough Dublin Hampton Beach
Temple
Jaffrey Wilton Center
Greenfield
Rindge

New Hampshire

ANDOVER

The English House

Box 162, 03216
(603) 735-5987

We have renovated, decorated, and furnished our home to recreate an English country house. We serve afternoon tea to our guests as well as a notable breakfast. All breads, muffins, cakes, jams, jellies, and marmalades are homemade.

Hosts: Gillian & Ken Smith
Doubles: 7 (PB) $53.50-69.55
Type of Beds: 6 Twin; 5 Queen
Full Breakfast
Minimum stay foliage weekends & holidays: 2
Credit Cards: A, B
Closed one week in mid-March
Notes: 2, 4 (by arrangement), 5, 8 (8 or older), 9, 10, 11, 12, 13, 14

ANTRIM

The Steele Homestead Inn

RR 1, Box 78, 03440
(603) 588-6772

Beautifully restored 1810 Federal-style home, furnished with the owners' collection of antiques and artwork. Tastefully decorated to retain the old feeling but provide modern necessities. Two rooms have working fireplaces. All-season activities include swimming, bicycling, hiking, skiing — all in the Monadnock region. Warm, friendly hospitality in a relaxing atmosphere.

Hosts: Barbara & Carl Beehner
Doubles: 4 (2 PB; 2 SB) $55-72
Type of Beds: 3 Twin; 1 Double; 1 Queen; 1 King
Full Breakfast

Credit Cards: A, B
Notes: 2, 5, 7 (limited), 8, 9, 10, 11, 12, 13, 14

ASHLAND

Country Options

Box 736, 03217
(603) 968-7958

An 1893 homestead offering comfortable ambience and delicious hearty breakfasts. Large common room with wood stove for winter; light, airy sun porch for summer. "In the early 80's when the movie makers went looking for a place to be Golden Pond they found everything they wanted right here" — *Yankee.* We know you will, too!

Hosts: Sandra Ray & Nancy Puglisi
Singles: 2 (SB) $37.45
Doubles: 3 (SB) $53.50
Type of Beds: 1 Twin; 5 Double
Full Breakfast
Credit Cards: No
Notes: 2, 5, 9, 10, 11, 12

The Bells

---

6 Pets welcome: 7 Smoking allowed: 8 Children welcome: 9 Social drinking allowed: 10 Tennis available: 11 Swimming available: 12 Golf available: 13 Skiing available: 14 May be booked through travel agents

The Mulburn Inn

BETHLEHEM

The Bells

Strawberry Hill Street, 03574
(603) 869-2647

Situated right in town, with an antique shop on the premises. Restaurants and golf courses within walking distance; all White Mountain attractions close. A fascinating Victorian house with unusual decor. Memorable breakfasts change daily.

Hosts: Bill & Louise Sims
Doubles: 4 (PB) $40-70
Type of Beds: 2 Twin; 3 Double
Full Breakfast
Minimum stay some holidays
Credit Cards: No
Notes: 2, 5, 7, 8, 9, 10, 11, 12, 13

The Mulburn Inn

Main Street, 03574
(603) 869-3389

A sprawling summer estate built in 1913 as a family retreat on the Woolworth Estate. Spacious, elegant rooms, stained-glass windows, and even an elevator are maintained in gracious style. Located in the heart of the White Mountains, minutes from Franconia Notch and the Mt. Washington Valley attractions.

Hosts: Bob & Cheryl Burns, Moe & Linda Mukligian
Singles: 2 (PB) $35
Doubles: 5 (PB) $50-65
Type of Beds: 4 Twin; 3 Double; 1 Queen; 1 King
Full Breakfast
Credit Cards: A, B, C
Notes: 2, 5, 8, 9, 10, 11, 12, 13, 14

BRADFORD

The Bradford Inn

Main Street, 03221
(603) 938-5309

The Bradford Inn, a restored 1898 small country hotel, features comfortable lodging and J. Albert's Restaurant, which serves exceptional regional New England cuisine. Fireplaces, large parlors, wide halls with antiques and personal mementoes. Four-season activity area.

Hosts: Connie & Tom Mazol
Doubles: 12 (PB) $64-84
Type of Beds: 4 Twin; 8 Double
Full Breakfast
Credit Cards: A, B, C, D
Notes: 2, 4, 5, 6, 7, 8, 9, 10, 11, 12, 13, 14

NOTES: Credit cards accepted: A Master Card; B Visa; C American Express; D Discover Card; E Diners Club; F Other: 2 Personal checks accepted: 3 Lunch available: 4 Dinner available: 5 Open all year

Mountain Lake Inn

Rt. 114, 03221
(603) 938-2136; 1-800-662-6005

A true New England country inn, built in 1760 on the shores of Massaseusm Lake. Our private sandy beach provides summer enjoyment. In winter, our guests snowshoe on our 167 acres. The inn is tastefully decorated with antiques and period furniture, and our country cuisine will please the most delicate palate. Peace and tranquility abound.

Hosts: Carol & Phil Fullerton
Doubles: 9 (PB) $53.50-85.60
Type of Beds: 2 Twin; 1 Double; 2 Queen; 4-6 King
Full Breakfast
Minimum stay some holiday weekends: 2
Credit Cards: A, B, D
Notes: 2, 4, 5, 7, 8, 9, 10, 11, 12, 13, 14

CAMPTON

Mountain Fare Inn

Mad River Road, 03223
(603) 726-4283

Lovely 1840s farmhouse, truly country New Hampshire — simple and welcoming. Adjacent to the White Mountain National Forest. Two hours north of Boston, and a perfect stop between Vermont and Maine. Open year round for foliage, skiing, antiquing, hiking, or resting. Hearty full breakfasts.

Hosts: Susan & Nicholas Preston
Singles: 1 (SB) $30-45
Doubles: 7 (5 PB; 2 SB) $50-75
Type of Beds: 9 Twin; 7 Double; 3 Bunks
Full Breakfast
Credit Cards: No
Notes: 2, 4, 5, 8, 9, 10, 11, 12, 13, 14

CANAAN

The "Inn" on Canaan Street

Box 92, 03741
(603) 523-7310

On one of the most beautiful streets in New Hampshire, the inn is in an historical district on 14 lakefront acres just twenty-five minutes from Hanover. Fields, flowers, fireplaces, antiques, paintings — all combine to give an atmosphere of warmth and comfort.

Hosts: Lee & Louise Kremzner
Singles: 1 (SB) $65-75
Doubles: 4 (2 PB; 2 SB) $65-85
Full Breakfast
Credit Cards: B
Notes: 2, 3 (with reservations), 4 (with reservations), 5, 9, 10, 11, 12, 13, 14

CONWAY

Darby Field Inn

Bald Hill Road, 03818
(603) 447-2181

A charming, out-of-the-way country inn that offers excellent dining, a cozy atmosphere, and spectacular mountain views. We have an outdoor pool, cross-country ski trails, and a staff that is both friendly and courteous. Reservations recommended. Rate includes breakfast, dinner, tax, and gratuity.

Hosts: Marc & Marily Donaldson
Singles: 5 (3 PB; 2 SB) $109.80
Doubles: 11 (9 PB; 2 SB) $170.80
Type of Beds: 5 Twin; 11 Double; 1 Queen
Full Breakfast
Minimum stay weekends: 2 ; holidays: 2-3
Credit Cards: A, B, C
Closed 3/19-4/27 and 10/22-11/21
Notes: 2, 4, 7, 8 (2 to 12), 9, 10, 11, 12, 13

Manner B&B

B&B Marblehead & North Shore
Box 172, Beverly, MA, 01915
(508) 921-1336

This Victorian home is just steps from a traditional covered bridge. An antique pump organ is featured in the living room, where guest may relax and plan their dinner or activities with the help of their host. Conway is noted for its skiing, outlet shopping, and excellent restaurants. Swimming pool,

---

6 Pets welcome: 7 Smoking allowed: 8 Children welcome: 9 Social drinking allowed: 10 Tennis available: 11 Swimming available: 12 Golf available: 13 Skiing available: 14 May be booked through travel agents

skating rink, river swimming, tennis, and basketball are all close at hand. One dog in residence.

Doubles: 4 (2 PB; 2 SB) $40-60
Type of Beds: 2 Double; 1 Queen; 1 King; 3 Cots
Continental breakfast weekdays; full weekends
Credit Cards: A, B
Notes: 2, 5, 7 (limited), 8, 9, 10, 11, 12, 13, 14

DUBLIN

French's Tavern Bed & Breakfast

Main Street, 03444-0283
(603) 563-8848

Come back to a time when travelers were a special breed, when innkeepers welcomed wearied souls with warmth and hospitality, offering home and hearth and the comfort of a good night's rest. You'll find such a welcome at French's Tavern.

Hosts: Mary Anne, Partick & Kei Egan
Doubles: 4 (SB) $53.50
Type of Beds: 1 Twin; 3 Double
Full Breakfast
Credit Cards: A, B
Notes: 2, 5, 9, 10, 11, 12, 13

EATON CENTER

The Inn at Crystal Lake

Rt. 153, Box 12, 03832
(603) 447-2120

Unwind in a restored 1884 inn in a quiet, scenic corner of the Mt. Washington Valley. Eleven guest rooms have Victorian antiques and private baths. There's a parlor, TV den/library, and cocktail lounge for your enjoyment. Swim, fish, sail, canoe, ski, skate, shop, or just relax! MAP available.

Hosts: Walter & Jacqueline Spink
Doubles: 11 (PB) $35-45
Type of Beds: 5 Double; 5 Queen; 1 Canopy
Full Breakfast
Credit Cards: A, B, C
Notes: 2, 4, 5, 7 (limited), 8, 9, 10, 11, 12, 12, 14

EXETER

The "G" Clef Bed & Breakfast

10 Ashbrook Road, 03833
(603) 772-8850

The "G" Clef Bed and Breakfast is a 1980 Dutch gambrel, recently decorated into an elegant bed and breakfast. Located minutes from historic downtown Exeter, the "G" Clef is just moments away from gracious dining, the famous Seacoast waterfront, and a galaxy of the finest shops in New Hampshire. Your taste for art, antiques, crafts, and outlet stores are sure to be satisfied.

Hosts: Jan & Ted Foster
Doubles: 2 (1 PB; 1 SB) $56
Type of Beds: 2 Double
Full Breakfast
Credit Cards: For deposit only
Closed Christmas
Notes: 2, 5, 8 (over 12), 9, 10, 11, 12, 13 (XC), 14

FRANCONIA

Bungay Jar Bed & Breakfast

Box 15, Easton Valley Road, 03580
(603) 823-7775

Built out of a century-old barn and nestled among woodlands in Robert Frost's Easton Valley, this mountain home offers a relaxed country setting. Secluded, yet convenient to all major attractions in the White Mountain National Forest. Fireplaced, two-story living room, library, sauna, balconies, and large guest rooms with mountain views. Hosts are a practicing landscape architect and patent attorney who are avid hikers and skiers.

Hosts: Kate Kerivam & Lee Strimbeck
Doubles: 4 (2 PB; 2 SB) $55-85
Type of Beds: 2 Twin; 2 Double; 1 King
Full Breakfast
Minimum stay weekends & holidays: 2-3
Credit Cards: A, B, C
Notes: 2, 5, 8 (over 6), 9, 10, 11, 12, 13, 14

NOTES: Credit cards accepted: A Master Card; B Visa; C American Express; D Discover Card; E Diners Club; F Other: 2 Personal checks accepted: 3 Lunch available: 4 Dinner available: 5 Open all year

Lovett's Inn by Lafayette Brook

Profile Road, Rt. 18, 03580
(603) 823-7761; 1-800-356-3802 (outside NH)

A 1784 inn on the National Register of Historic Places. Situated on 90 wooded acres within minutes of the interstate and close to several downhill ski areas and various scenic attractions: Mt. Washington Cog Railway, Cannon Mt. Aerial Tramway, Appalachian Mt. trails, etc. European Plan (no meals) or Modified American Plan (complete breakfast and full dinner). Fireplaced guest cottages. Cross-country touring center. Public restaurant with full liquor license. Package plans available. Heated swimming pool in summer; nonsmoking dining room.

Host: Lan Finlay
Doubles: 30 (19 PB; 11 SB) $45-130 (MAP) plus tax
& gratuity
Type of Beds: 44 Twin; 15 Double
Full Breakfast
Minimum stay foliage season: 2
Credit Cards: A, B, C, E, F
Closed April 1-mid May; Nov. 2 - mid Dec.
Notes: 2 (limited), 4, 7 (limited), 8, 9, 10, 11, 12, 13, 14

GLEN

B&B Registry #NH-03838BER

Box 8174, St. Paul, MN, 55108
(612) 646-4238

Cozy inn five miles from North Conway, near five major ski areas. Lovely lounge and fireplace, public dining, and Old World tap room. Finnish sauna.

Doubles: 5 (2 PB; 3 SB) $50-60
Type of Beds: 4 Twin; 4 Double; 1 Cot
Full Breakfast
Credit Cards: A, B, C
Notes: 4, 5, 8, 11, 12, 13

The Bernerhof Inn

Box 240, 03838
(800) 548-8007; (603) 383-4414

An elegant Victorian set in the foothills of the White Mountains, the Bernerhof remains true to its European tradition. Host of a Taste of the Mountains Cooking School, the inn's dining room offers a changing menu of middle European favorites, while a popular tap room offers lighter fare. Several rooms boast extra-large spa tubs for true relaxation.

Hosts: Ted & Sharon Wroblewski
Doubles: 11 (9 PB; 2 SB) $75-117
Full Breakfast
Credit Cards: A, B, C
Notes: 2, 3, 4, 5, 7 (restricted), 8, 9, 10, 11, 12, 13, 14

GREENFIELD

Greenfield B&B Inn

Box 156, 03047
(603) 547-6327

This beautifully restored Victorian on 3 acres of lawn is in the lovely valley of the Monadnick Mountains. Enjoy the relaxing mountain view from the spacious veranda with white wicker chairs and rockers. Very close to skiing, swimming, hiking, tennis, golf, biking, and antique shopping.

Hosts: Vic & Barbara Mangini
Doubles: 8 (4 PB; 4 SB) $45-60
Full Breakfast
Credit Cards: A, B
Notes: 2, 5, 6 (limited), 7 (limited), 8 (limited), 9, 10, 11, 12, 13, 14

HAMPTON

B&B Registry #NH-03842CUR

Box 8174, St. Paul, MN, 55108
(612) 646-4238

Only seven miles from the Atlantic Ocean and five beaches, located on 5 country acres in a quiet country neighborhood just three miles from the historic town of Exeter. Home was built by the host's father, a master craftsman who built many antique reproductions. Fifty miles to Boston.

Doubles: 3 (2 PB; 1 SB) $45-60
Type of Beds: 2 Twin; 1 Double; 1 Queen
Full Breakfast
Credit Cards: A, B
Notes: 4, 5, 10, 11, 12, 13 (XC)

HAMPTON BEACH

Pineapple Hospitality NH 530

Box F-821, New Bedford, MA 02742-0821
(508) 990-1696

This inn is located directly across the street from Hampton Beach, within walking distance of restaurants, shops, and other attractions. Wednesday nights there are fireworks on the beach that can be viewed from the upper deck, patio, or the beach itself. The house has a wraparound deck, self-serve bar, color TV, popcorn and ice, as well as a coffee nook with microwave. An attendant supplies towels and beach chairs on the inn's private section of the beach.

Doubles: 10 (PB) $54-90
Full Breakfast
Credit Cards: No
Closed mid-Oct. - mid-May
Notes: 2, 7, 8, 9, 11, 12

HARRISVILLE

The Harrisville Squires' Inn B&B

Keene Road, 03450
(603) 827-3925

In the historic village of Harrisville. Enjoy this beautifully restored home that is on the National Historic Register. On over 45 acres of private maintained trails for cross-country skiing or hiking. Monadnock Bicycle Touring Center and gift shop located in the inn. Four-season enjoyment!

Hosts: Doug & Pat McCarthy
Doubles: 5 (2 PB: 3 SB) $42.80-53.50
Type of Beds: 2 Twin; 2 Double; 1 Queen; 1 King
Full Breakfast
Credit Cards: No
Notes: 2, 5, 7 (limited), 8 (over 10), 11, 12, 13, 14

HOLDERNESS

The Inn on Golden Pond

Route 3, 03245
(603) 968-7269

An 1879 colonial home located on 55 wooded acres. Bright and cheerful sitting, breakfast, and game rooms. Close to major ski areas. Nearby is Squam Lake, the setting for the film "On Golden Pond."

Hosts: Bill & Bonnie Webb
Doubles: 9 (7 PB: 2 SB) $48-91
Type of Beds: 3 Twin; 1 Double; 5 Queen
Full Breakfast
Minimum stay holidays
Credit Cards: A, B
Notes: 2, 5, 8 (over 12), 9, 10, 11, 12, 13

INTERVALE

Wildflowers Guest House

Rt. 16, 03845
(603) 356-2224

Return to the simplicity and elegance of yesteryear. With our ideal location and gracefully decorated rooms, our small 1878 Victorian inn specializes in comfort and convenience for the modern-day traveler. We welcome you to enjoy and share our home.

Hosts: Dean Franke & Eileen Davies
Doubles: 6 (2 PB; 4 SB) $42.80-85.60
Type of Beds: 3 Twin; 6 Double
Continental Breakfast
Credit Cards: A, B
Notes: 2, 5, 7, 8, 9, 10, 11, 12, 13

JACKSON

Ellis River House

Rt. 16, Box 656, 03846
(603) 383-9339

A traditional B&B that boasts fine lodging and superb country dining in a turn-of-the-century farmhouse overlooking the spectacular Ellis River. Jacuzzi, antiques, minutes to all area attractions. Cross-country ski from our door. Enjoy hiking, canoeing, and outlet shopping.

Hosts: Barry & Barbara Lubao
Doubles: 5 (SB) $46.80-117
Suites: 1 (PB)
Type of Beds: 6 Twin; 4 double; 3 Queen
Full Breakfast
Minimum stay weekends: 2 ; holidays: 2-3
Credit Cards: A, B, C
Notes: 2, 4, 5, 7 (limited), 8, 9, 10, 11, 12, 13

The Inn at Jackson

The Inn at Jackson
Box H, Thornhill Road, 03846
(603) 383-4321

You'll find us on a knoll overlooking the peaceful village of Jackson. In summer you can enjoy golf, swimming, tennis, fishing, or just a walk on a quiet mountain trail. In winter enjoy cross-country skiing, alpine skiing, sleigh rides, or relax by our cozy fireplace. We offer spacious guest rooms with a relaxing atmosphere.

Hosts: Steve & Lori Tradewell
Doubles: 6 (PB) $56-78
Type of Beds: 3 Twin; 6 Double
Full Breakfast
Minimum stay weekends & holidays: 2
Credit Cards: A, B, C
Notes: 2, 5, 7, 8, 9, 10, 11, 12, 13

Nestlenook Farm by the River
Box Q, 03846
(603) 383-9443

Recently renovated, this inn has seven rooms with private baths and Jacuzzis. Some have fireplaces or wood stoves. Beautiful Victorian farmhouse with dining room pub, guest kitchen, library, and game room. On the grounds you'll find cross-country skiing, sleigh and hay rides, hiking trails, fishing, and much more.

Hosts: Tom & Chris Cormier
Doubles: 7 (PB) $95-195
Full Breakfast
Credit Cards: A, B
Notes: 2, 3, 4, 5, 8 (over 12), 9, 10, 11, 12, 13, 14

JAFFREY

B&B Registry #NH-03452GAL
Box 8174, St. Paul, MN, 55108
(612) 646-4238

Oversized Cape with a spacious yard and sun deck. Quiet woodland setting with wildlife. Located in the center of the Monadnoc Region — an ideal base for seeing all the area attractions.

Doubles: 2 (SB) $30-38
Type of Beds: 3 Twin; 2 Double
Full Breakfast
Credit Cards: No
Closed July
Notes: 8, 11, 12, 13

JEFFERSON

B&B Registry #NH-03583JEF
Box 8174, St. Paul, MN, 55108
(612) 646-4238

6 Pets welcome: 7 Smoking allowed: 8 Children welcome: 9 Social drinking allowed: 10 Tennis available: 11 Swimming available: 12 Golf available: 13 Skiing available: 14 May be booked through travel agents

An 1896 Victorian inn located in a small New England town. Hosts provide guests with old-fashioned foot warmers in the evening along with their nightly tea. Relax on the wraparound porch or stroll through the 3 acres of grounds and enjoy the White Mountains. Skiing nearby.

Doubles: 6 (SB) $31-43
Type of Beds: 4 Twin; 4 Double
Full Breakfast
Credit Cards: A, B
Notes: 5, 8, 11, 12, 13

The Jefferson Inn

RFD 1, Box 68A, 03583
(603) 586-7998

Situated among the White Mountain National Forest, the Jefferson Inn offers 360 degree views and nightly sunsets. With Mt. Washington nearby, the inn is an ideal location for hiking, cross-country and downhill skiing, and most outdoor activities. Evening tea served nightly.

Hosts: Greg Brown & Bertie Koelewijn
Doubles: 10 (5 PB; 5 SB) $44-70
Type of Beds: 1 Twin; 8 Double; 1 Queen
Full Breakfast
Minimum stay weekends & holidays: 2
Credit Cards: A, B, C
Closed Nov. & April
Notes: 2, 8, 9, 10, 11, 12, 13

LISBON

Ammonousuc Inn

Bishop Road, 03585
(603) 838-6118

Beautiful 100-year-old New England inn located in the White Mountains. Nine charming rooms with private baths. The inn has its own golf course, pool, tennis court, and cross-country skiing trails on the premises, plus a restaurant. Close to most ski areas and attractions. Great canoeing, hiking, and biking.

Hosts: Steven & Laura Bromley
Doubles: 9 (PB) $50-70
Type of Beds: 2 Twin; 7 Queen
Continental Breakfast
Credit Cards: A, B, C
Notes: 2, 4, 5, 7 (limited), 8, 9, 10, 11, 12, 13

Edencroft Manor Country Inn

LITTLETON

Edencroft Manor Country Inn

RFD #1, Rte. 135, 03561
(603) 444-6776

Edencroft Manor sets the standard for hospitality, comfort, and fine dining in the tradition of classic New England inns. Close to all White Mountain attractions and minutes from all year-round activities. Romantic atmosphere, gourmet cuisine by candlelight with classical music in the background. Mountain view from our full-service lounge. AAA three-diamond rated.

Hosts: Phil & Maryann Frasca & sons
Doubles: 6 (4 PB; 2 SB) $50-65
Type of Beds: 9 Double
Full Breakfast
Credit Cards: A, B, C
Notes: 4, 5, 6, 7, 8, 9, 10, 11, 12, 13

LYME

Loch Lyme Lodge

RFD 278, Rt. 10, 03768
(603) 795-2141

NOTES: Credit cards accepted: A Master Card; B Visa; C American Express; D Discover Card; E Diners Club; F Other: 2 Personal checks accepted: 3 Lunch available: 4 Dinner available: 5 Open all year

Loch Lyme Lodge has been hosting guests since 1924. From May through September, the twenty-five cabins and rooms in the main lodge are open for the enjoyment of summer vacationers. During the fall and winter months, the main lodge, a farmhouse built in 1784, is open. Children are welcome at any season, and the emphasis is always on comfortable, informal hospitality.

Hosts: Paul & Judy Barker
Doubles: 4 (SB) $26/person
Type of Beds: 6 Twin; 1 Double
Full Breakfast
Credit Cards: No
Closed Thanksgiving & Christmas days
Notes: 2, 3 (summer), 4 (summer), 5, 6 (summer), 8, 9, 10, 11, 12, 13

MARLBOROUGH

Peep-Willow Farm

Bixby Street, 03455
(603) 876-3807

Peep-Willow Farm is a working thoroughbred horse farm that also caters to humans. Situated on 20 acres with a view all the way to the Connecticut River Valley. Guests are welcome to help with chores or watch the young horses frolic in the fields, but there is no riding. Flexibility and serenity are the key ingredients to enjoying your stay.

Host: Noel Aderer
Doubles: 3 (SB) $20-35
Type of Beds: 2 Twin; 1 Double; 2 King
Full Breakfast
Credit Cards: No
Notes: 2, 5, 6 (by arrangement), 8, 9, 13 (XC), 14

NEW LONDON

New London Inn

Main Street, 03257
(603) 526-2791

Here you will find a classic New England inn with wide verandas overlooking this serene New Hampshire college town. The inn is comfortable and cozy, and the prize-winning gardens are glorious. "...spiffier and better

known for its dining room than ever" — *Boston Globe.*

Hosts: Maureen & John Follansbee
Doubles: 30 (PB) $77-100
Type of Beds: 3 Twin; 22 Double; 2 Queen; 3 King
Full Breakfast
Minimum stay weekends: 2
Credit Cards: A, B
Notes: 2, 4, 5, 7, 8, 9, 10, 11, 12, 13, 14

Pleasant Lake Inn

Pleasant Street, 03257
(603) 526-6271

Let us share our view with you along with our good food, warm country lodgings, and friendly atmosphere. Our 1790 inn is open year round for skiing, lake swimming, fishing, hiking, or just plain relaxing.

Hosts: Margaret & Grant Rich
Doubles: 12 (PB) $60-85
Type of Beds: 2 Twin; 7 Double; 2 Queen; 1 King
Full Breakfast
Minimum stay holidays: 2
Credit Cards: A, B
Notes: 2, 4, 5, 7, 8 (8 and over), 9, 10, 11, 12, 13

The Buttonwood Inn

NORTH CONWAY

The Buttonwood Inn

Box 3297B, Mt. Surprise Road, 03860
(603) 356-2625

Built in the 1820s as a farmhouse, the inn is tucked away on Mt. Surprise, where it's quiet and secluded, yet only two miles to the

6 Pets welcome: 7 Smoking allowed: 8 Children welcome: 9 Social drinking allowed: 10 Tennis available: 11 Swimming available: 12 Golf available: 13 Skiing available: 14 May be booked through travel agents

village and excellent dining and shopping. Minutes to Mt. Washington, skiing (cross-country from our door), hiking, fishing, and canoeing. Enjoy our outdoor pool.

Hosts: Ann & Hugh Begley
Doubles: 9 (PB and SB) $27-45/ person
Type of Beds: 5 Twin; 7 Double
Full Breakfast
Credit Cards: A, B, C
Notes: 2, 4 (winter), 5, 7, 8, 9, 10, 11, 12, 13, 14

Cranmore Mt. Lodge

Box 1194, Kearsarge Road, 03860
(603) 356-2044

Cranmore Mt. Lodge, an historic New England country inn, is the perfect place to unwind. Our atmosphere is homey, and our accommodations and reasonable rates are ideal for families and groups. Formerly owned by Babe Ruth's daughter and visited by him many times. Hiking, rock climbing, skiing, kayaking, canoeing, bicycling, tennis, golf, riding, summer theater, and fine restaurants are just some of the area's attractions.

Hosts: Dennis & Judy Helfand
Singles: 4 (SB) $26-63
Doubles: 16 (5 PB; 11 SB) $67-99/per person
Type of Beds: 49 Twin; 17 Double
Full Breakfast
Credit Cards: A, B, C, D
Notes: 2, 4, 5, 7, 8, 9, 10, 11, 12, 13

The 1785 Inn

Rt. 16, 03860
(603) 356-9025

Enjoy a relaxing retreat in the White Mountains on 6 scenic acres overlooking Mt. Washington, close to all North Conway's activities. You can experience some of the best dining and one of the finest wine lists in America in a romantic colonial setting overlooking beautiful scenery. Also awaiting you are seventeen individually decorated bedrooms, two guest living rooms with 200-year-old fireplaces, a Victorian lounge, a

swimming pool, and cross-country and downhill skiing.

Hosts: Becky & Charlie Mallar
Doubles: 17 (12 PB; 5 SB) $40-115
Type of Beds: 4 Twin; 18 Double; 1 King
Full Breakfast
Credit Cards: A, B, C, D, E
Notes: 2, 4, 5, 7, 8, 9, 10, 11, 12, 13, 14

The 1785 Inn

Sunny Side Inn

Seavey Street, 03860
(603) 356-6239

A casual, affordable country inn in a restored 1850s farmhouse. Short walk to North Conway Village and its many shops and restaurants. Enjoy mountain views from our flower-trimmed porches in summer or relax by the fireplace in winter.

Hosts: Chris & Marylee Uggerholt
Singles: 2 (SB) $27-50
Doubles: 8 (2 PB; 6 SB) $38-62
Type of Beds: 6 Twin; 9 Double
Full Breakfast
Minimum stay holidays: 2
Credit Cards: A, B
Notes: 2, 5, 7, 8, 9, 10, 11, 12, 13

NORTH SUTTON

Follansbee Inn

Box 92, 03260
(603) 927-4221

An authentic 1840 New England inn with white clapboard and green trim. Located on peaceful Kezar Lake, with an old-fashioned porch, comfortable sitting rooms, and charming antique furnishings. Nestled in a small country village, but convenient to all area activities. A healthy, no-smoking inn.

Hosts: Dick & Sandy Reilein
Doubles: 23 (11 PB; 12 SB) $65-85
Type of Beds: 8 Twin; 13 Double; 2 King
Full Breakfast
Closed parts of Nov. & April
Notes: 2, 4, 5, 8 (over 10), 9, 10, 11, 12, 13, 14

Follansbee Inn

NORTHWOOD

B&B Registry #NH-03261COM

Box 8174, St. Paul, MN, 55108
(612) 646-4238

Located on Bow Lake at the end of the road, this spacious home provides a quiet, picturesque setting. Fresh flowers in the summer. Table linens and silver with your breakfast in the morning. Close to the University of New Hampshire, antiquing, great day trips.

Doubles: 3 (2 PB; 1 SB) $25-45
Type of Beds: 2 Twin; 2 Queen
Full Breakfast
Credit Cards: No
Notes: 6 (call), 11

NORTH WOODSTOCK

Mt. Adams Inn

So. Main Street, 03262
(603) 745-2711

Historic nineteenth-century inn B&B with twenty guest rooms furnished with antiques. Fireplaced lounge and living room. Dining room, specializing in Polish and American cuisine, is open to the public. Centrally located in the heart of the White Mountains.

Hosts: Gloria & Joe Town
Singles: 14 (SB) $37.45
Doubles: 19 (SB) $44.44-54.57
Type of Beds: 14 Twin; 19 Double
Full Breakfast
Minimum stay weekends: 2 ; holidays: 3
Credit Cards: A, B
Notes: 4, 5, 7, 8 (10 and up), 9, 10, 11, 12, 13

OSSIPEE

Acorn Lodge

Duncan Lake, Box 144, 03864
(603) 539-2151

Once President Grover Cleveland's summer fishing camp, Acorn Lodge overlooks tranquil Duncan Lake. Breakfast is served on the veranda, then you may want to fish from our dock or use our motorboat, rowboat, or canoe. Enjoy a cool swim from our sandy beach or play lawn games. Close to skiing, Wolfeboro, summer theater, golf.

Hosts: Julie & Ray Terry
Singles: 1 (PB) $46
Doubles: 5 (PB) $46
Continental Breakfast
Minimum stay: 2
Credit Cards: A, B
Closed Oct. 15 - May 15
Notes: 2, 7, 8, 9, 10, 11, 12, 13, 14

PLYMOUTH

Crab Apple Inn

RR 4, Box 1955, 03264
(603) 536-4476

6 Pets welcome: 7 Smoking allowed: 8 Children welcome: 9 Social drinking allowed: 10 Tennis available: 11 Swimming available: 12 Golf available: 13 Skiing available: 14 May be booked through travel agents

This inn is an 1835 brick Federal situated beside a brook at the foot of Tenney Mountain. The grounds are complemented by an English garden and brick courtyard. Located at the gateway to the White Mountains.

Hosts: Bill & Carolyn Crenson
Doubles: 4-5 (2 PB; 2 SB) $65-80
Type of Beds: 1 Twin; 2 Double; 2 Queen
Full Breakfast
Credit Cards: A, B
Notes: 2, 7, 8 (over 10), 9, 10, 11, 12, 13

Northway House

RFD 1, US Rt. 3N, 03264
(603) 536-2838

Hospitality Plus awaits the traveler in this cozy colonial near both the lakes and the White Mountains of New Hampshire. Hiking, river, or lake activities in summer; fall foliage; winter skiing — all are a short, scenic drive. Gourmet breakfast.

Hosts: Micheline & Norman McWilliams
Singles: 1 (SB) $26.75
Doubles: 2 (SB) $40.50
Type of Beds: 2 Twin; 2 Double
Full Breakfast
Credit Cards: No
Notes: 2, 5, 6, 7, 8, 9, 11, 12, 13

RINDGE

B&B Registry #NH-03461TOK

Box 8174, St. Paul, MN, 55108
(612) 646-4238

New England Christmas-tree farm with a view of three states. Large three-story house only fifty miles from Boston. Secluded in the midst of forest, off the beaten path. Pond for swimming; woodland trails for hiking, bird watching, cross-country skiing.

Doubles: 5 (SB) $25-60
Type of Beds: 5 Twin; 2 Double; 1 King
Continental Breakfast
Credit Cards: No

Closed Dec. - April
Notes: 11, 12, 13

Grassy Pond House

03461
(603) 899-5166; 899-5167

An 1831 homestead nestled among 150 forested acres, overlooking water and gardens. Convenient to main roads, restaurants, antique marts, weekly local auctions, theater, music, and craft fairs. Hike the Grand Monadnock; ski cross country and downhill. A retreat for all seasons.

Hosts: Carmen Linares & Bob Multer
Singles: 1 (SB) $40-50
Doubles: 3 (2 PB; 1 SB) $60-65
Type of Beds: 2 Twin; 3 Double
Full Breakfast
Minimum stay during foliage: 2
Credit Cards: No
Notes: 2, 5, 9, 10, 11, 12, 13, 14

STRAFFORD

Province Inn

Box 309, 03884
(603) 664-2457

Elegant, homey antique colonial on pristine Bow Lake. Pool, tennis court, canoes on premises. On 120 acres of pine woods with waterfall. A mini resort without the crowds, midway between Portsmouth and Concord. Antiquing three miles away. Resident dog and cat.

Hosts: Steve & Corky Garboski
Doubles: 4 (SB) $67.41
Family rates available
Type of Beds: 2 Twin; 3 Double
Minimum stay Columbus Day weekend: 2
Notes: 2, 5, 7, 8, 9, 10, 11, 12, 13, 14

SUGAR HILL

The Hilltop Inn

Main Street, 03585
(603) 823-5695

NOTES: Credit cards accepted: A Master Card; B Visa; C American Express; D Discover Card; E Diners Club; F Other: 2 Personal checks accepted: 3 Lunch available: 4 Dinner available: 5 Open all year

The Hilltop Inn

An 1895 Victorian inn in the small village of Sugar Hill, which is nestled in the heart of the White Mountains. Near alpine and nordic skiing, hiking, Franconia Notch. Peaceful and homey, with beautiful sunsets and a large country breakfast.

Hosts: Meri & Mike Hern
Doubles: 4 (2 PB; 2 SB) $40-80.60
Suite: 1 (2 rooms, PB, sleeps 4)
Efficiency apartment: 1 (sleeps 2-8)
Type of Beds: 2 Twin; 4 Double; 1 Queen
Full Breakfast
Minimum stay holidays and fall foliage weekends:2
Credit Cards: A, B, C
Notes: 2, 5, 6, 7, 8, 9, 10, 11, 12, 13

Ledgeland

Sugar Hill, 03585
(603) 823-5341

Ledgeland is located in the heart of the White Mountains and features a superb view. The inn is open from late June through mid-October. Cottages with wood-burning fireplaces and kitchens surround the inn and are available all year.

Hosts: The Whipples
Singles: 4 (PB) $42-50
Doubles: 18 (PB) $58-100
Continental-plus Breakfast
Credit Cards: No
Closed late Oct. - late June
Notes: 2, 7, 8, 9, 10, 11, 12, 13

SUNCOOK

Suncook House

62 Main Street, 03275
(603) 485-8141

A brick Georgian home on 3 acres in the center of Suncook. The house has been recently renovated and is furnished in period pieces. You may relax in the formal living room, which has an organ, or in the sun parlor or den. Convenient to the White Mountains and the lakes area of New Hampshire; an easy walk to village restaurants, tennis courts. New Hampshire College and Bear Brook State Park are both a five-minute drive.

Hosts: Gerry & Evelyn Lavoie
Singles: 1 (SB) $35
Doubles: 3 (1 PB; 2 SB) $50
Type of Beds: 3 Twin; 2 Double
Full Breakfast
Credit Cards: No
Notes: 2, 5, 8 (over 12), 9, 10, 11, 12

TEMPLE

Birchwood Inn

Route 45, 03084
(603) 878-3285

6 Pets welcome: 7 Smoking allowed: 8 Children welcome: 9 Social drinking allowed: 10 Tennis available: 11 Swimming available: 12 Golf available: 13 Skiing available: 14 May be booked through travel agents

A cozy family-run inn on the National Register. Elegant dining in small dining rooms with candlelight and Rufus Porter murals on the walls. Guest rooms are filled with antiques and homemade quilts are on the beds.

Hosts: Judy & Bill Wolfe
Doubles: 7 (5 PB; 2 SB) $70
Full Breakfast
Credit Cards: No
Closed 2 weeks in April & 1 in Nov.
Notes: 2, 4, 7, 8 (over 10), 9, 10, 11, 12, 13

TILTON

The Country Place

RFD 2, Box 342, 03276
(603) 286-8551

Our beautifully maintained 100-year-old home is located on 6 acres and has lovely mountain views. An open porch runs along two sides of the house. Hearty breakfasts are served in the country kitchen. Brochures available.

Hosts: Ed & Claire Tousignant
Doubles: 4 (S2B) $48.15-53.50
Type of Beds: 2 Twin; 2 Double; 1 King
Full Breakfast
Minimum stay holidays: 2
Credit Cards: No
Notes: 2, 5, 7, 8 (12 and over), 9, 10, 11, 12, 13

WAKEFIELD

The Wakefield Inn

RR 1, Box 2185, 03872
(603) 522-8272

Located within the historic district of Wakefield Corner, along with twenty-seven other buildings. Early travelers arrived by stagecoach. The majestic mountains and cool blue lakes offer unlimited outdoor activities. Or just relax and enjoy the ambience of days gone by.

Hosts: Lou & Harry Sisson
Doubles: 6 (3 PB; 3 SB) $54-64
Type of Beds: 4 Twin; 5 Double
Full Breakfast

Minimum stay holidays: 2
Credit Cards: A, B, C
Notes: 2, 3, 4, 5, 7, 8 (over 10), 9

WATERVILLE VALLEY

The Snowy Owl Inn

Box 407, 03215
(603) 236-8383

Rustic country inn in picturesque Waterville Valley. Eighty guest rooms, some with Jacuzzis and wet bars. Indoor and outdoor pools, saunas, reading porch, and six lobbies with fireplaces. Complimentary wine and cheese party every afternoon, plus free admission to a nearby sports center and free golf, tennis, and boating.

Host: Donald Hyde
Doubles: 80 (PB) $49-129
Type of Beds: 78 Twin; 79 Double; 2 Queen; 1 King
Continental Breakfast
Credit Cards: A, B, C, E
Notes: 2, 5, 7, 8, 10, 11, 12, 13, 14

WEST FRANKLIN

Maria Atwood Inn

RFD 2, 03235
(603) 934-3666

An 1830 brick Federal colonial on 3 acres close to the lakes, mountains, shopping, auctions, Shaker villages, crafts, swimming, skiing, golf, tennis, hiking, and boating. The house has six fireplaces and is furnished with period pieces.

Hosts: Irene & Philip Fournier
Singles: 1 (PB) $50
Doubles: 6 (PB) $60
Type of Beds: 4 Twin; 5 Double; 1 Queen
Full Breakfast
Credit Cards: A, B, C, E
Notes: 2, 5, 7, 8 (12 and over), 9, 10, 11, 12, 13, 14

WESTMORELAND

Partridge Brook Inn

Box 151, 03467
(603) 399-4994

NOTES: Credit cards accepted: A Master Card; B Visa; C American Express; D Discover Card; E Diners Club; F Other: 2 Personal checks accepted: 3 Lunch available: 4 Dinner available: 5 Open all year

This historic 1790 home in a serene, pastoral setting offers visitors the best of the English bed-and-breakfast tradition. Once a tavern and a stopover for the underground railroad, the interior bears many reminders of a rich past, with mortise-and-tendon doors, original fireplaces, a handcarved fireplace mantle, detailed stenciling on the parlor floor, and Indian Shutters at the windows. Nearby you will find trout fishing, nature walks, horseback riding, swimming, boating, golf, and tennis.

Hosts: Renee & Don Strong
Doubles: 5 (PB) $65-75
Full Breakfast
Credit Cards: B
Notes: 2, 5, 8 (no babies or infants), 10, 11, 12, 12

WILTON CENTER

Stepping Stones Bed & Breakfast

Pennington Battle Trail, 03086
(603) 654-9048

Nineteenth-century house with extensive gardens and quiet comfort. Handwoven fabrics, fresh flowers, down puffs, and scrumptious breakfast, served in the solar garden room. Summer Theater, chamber music, antique shops, hiking trails, and a waterfall are all nearby. Or just relax in civilized peace.

Host: Ann Carlsmith
Doubles: 3 (1 PB; 2 SB) $25-40
Type of Beds: 2 Twin; 1 Double; 1 Queen
Full Breakfast
Credit Cards: No
Notes: 2, 5, 6, 7 (restricted), 8, 9, 11, 12

WINNISQUAM

Tall Pines Inn

Old Route 3, Box 327, 03289
(603) 528-3632

A four seasons destination on Lake Winnisquam. Spectacular lake and mountain views; boat rental and sandy beach only yards away. Winter skiing within minutes of our wood stove. Special dinners by reservation. "Almost always open."

Hosts: Kent & Kate Kern
Doubles: 3 (1 PB; 2 SB) $48-70
Type of Beds: 1 Double; 1 Queen; 1 King
Full Breakfast
Minimum stay weekends & holidays: 2
Credit Cards: A, B
Notes: 2, 4, 5, 7 (limited), 8, 9, 10, 11, 12, 13

Partridge Brook Inn

NEW JERSEY

New Jersey

ABSECON

B&B of New Jersey #499

Suite 132, 103 Godwin Avenue
Midland Park, 07432
(201)444-7409

Hospitality abounds in the friendly atmosphere of this two-story colonial. Your hosts are casino employees who will be happy to share their first-hand knowledge of all the "bests" in the Atlantic City area, one of which is the fabulous breakfast here. Guests share a bath and have a choice of comfortable, air-conditioned twin or double rooms. $55-65.

ANDOVER

Northern NJ B&B 1

11 Sunset Trail, Denville
(201)625-5129

New home on a rural 3.5 acres, with a guest room with double bed, wood-burning stove, use of hot tub; horseback riding nearby. Private bath. One dog in residence; full breakfast. $36-48.

AVON-BY-THE-SEA

Cashelmara Inn

22 Lakeside Avenue, 07717
(201) 776-8727

Oceanside/lakefront Victorian inn where you can enjoy views of the Atlantic from your bed. Rooms decorated in beautiful Victorian antiques; wicker-filled veranda overlooking the ocean; suite with fireplace also available. Only fifty-five minutes from New York City and one hour from Philadelphia.

Host: Martin J. Mulligan
Doubles: 14 (PB) $63-116
Type of Beds: 9 Double; 2 Queen; 2 King
Full Breakfast
Minimum stay summer weekends: 3 ; holidays: 4
Credit Cards: A, B, C
Notes: 2, 5, 8, 9, 10, 11, 12

BARNEGAT

B&B of New Jersey #486

Suite 132, 103 Godwin Avenue
Midland Park, 07432
(201)444-7409

A contemporary ranch beside a lagoon, this Mediterranean-styled B&B overlooks a national wildlife refuge. You'll enjoy spectacular sunsets and a respite from the hustle and bustle of everyday life. Two twin guest rooms share a bath; a third room has a private bath and sliding glass doors overlooking the lagoon and swimming pool. Central air-conditioning; individual room thermostats; TV/VCR; beach passes. Continental or full breakfast is served. $43-100.

BEACH HAVEN

B&B of New Jersey #482

Suite 132, 103 Godwin Avenue
Midland Park, 07432
(201)444-7409

This magnificent inn is just 100 feet from the water, completely Victorian, down to the doorknobs. All furnishings are authentic antiques, and each room is beautifully appointed. Your hosts formerly owned a gourmet restaurant in Philadelphia and serve five-course breakfasts. Special dinners can be prepared with advance reservations. There is a large yard with gazebo and fountain, plus complimentary bicycles. $85-115.

Bayberry Barque Bed & Breakfast Inn
117 Center Street, 08008
(609) 492-5216

Our nineteenth-century Victorian is located one block from the ocean in historic Beach Haven. The Barque is tastefully restored to its past splendor, with the open staircase illuminated by an original stained-glass window, natural pine floors, and antique furniture. Walk to restaurants, shops, theaters, fishing, and charters to Atlantic City.

Hosts: Glenn, Pat & Gladys
Doubles: 9 (2 PB; 7 SB) $40-100
Type of Beds: 4 Twin; 3 Double; 3 Queen; 1 King
Continental Breakfast
Credit Cards: A, B, C
Notes: 5, 8, 9, 10, 11

BEDMINSTER

Northern NJ B&B 2
11 Sunset Trail, Denville
(201)625-5129

A fourteen-room Georgian home on enormous grounds — very rural. Exquisitely furnished. Sitting area upstairs for guests, color TV. Four guest rooms, two with private baths; continental breakfast. $66-75.

BELMAR

B&B of New Jersey #435
Suite 132, 103 Godwin Avenue
Midland Park, 07432
(201)444-7409

The atmosphere at this seashore Dutch colonial is friendly and informal. Built around the turn of the century, the home has seven guest rooms, one with an ocean view. All are equipped with fans. Most rooms have private baths, and some can be combined to accommodate three or four guests. A full breakfast is served, and guests are welcome to use the front porch, sitting room, and sun deck. Near the Garden State Art Center, Monmouth Race Track, Great Adventure Amusement Park, and Englishtown Flea Market. $45-70.

BELMAR

B&B of New Jersey #455
Suite 132, 103 Godwin Avenue
Midland Park, 07432
(201)444-7409

There's much to enjoy in this rustic mountain lodge at the seashore. Built in 1908, it boasts original wooden beams, great stone fireplace, and wood and brick floors. The seven guest rooms have been completely redecorated, each with a private bath and a view of the lake and/or ocean. Some rooms also have a private porch or balcony. Within walking distance of Lake Como. Beach badges are available for the ocean beaches that are five minutes away. Buffet-style continental breakfast is served; children over twelve are welcome. $75-95.

BLAIRSTOWN

B&B of New Jersey #443
Suite 132, 103 Godwin Avenue
Midland Park, 07432
(201)444-7409

The homemade pastries, pies, crepes, and fritters filled with fruits grown at this B&B farm keep guests coming back again and again. Enjoy breakfast in the gazebo or on the front porch, with its 100-mile view of the

Appalachian Trail, the mountain ranges of Pennsylvania, and the Delaware Water Gap. Swimming pool and deck, antique furniture, shared bath. $50-60.

BOONTON

Northern NJ B&B 3

11 Sunset Trail, Denville
(201)625-5129

A colonial home in an established, quiet residential area. Pleasant, bright room with TV and air-conditioner, shared bath. Easily accessible to I-287 and I-80; public transportation to New York City by train or bus. Continental breakfast is served. $30.

BRIDGEWATER

Northern NJ B&B 4

11 Sunset Trail, Denville
(201)625-5129

A striking mountainside contemporary home in a serene wooded setting adjacent to a deer preserve. Three guest rooms with spacious private or semi-private baths. Use of many areas in this custom-built home for quiet reading, conversation, and cable TV. Large sunken living room with cathedral ceiling, cozy family room with raised-hearth brick fireplace, and outside deck. Seasonal snacks and beverages; continental breakfast. $42-54.

CAPE MAY

The Abbey

Columbia Avenue & Gurney Street, 08204
(609) 884-4506

The Abbey consists of the main house, which is an 1869 Gothic revival villa built for a wealthy coal baron, and the cottage, which he built in 1873 for his son. Both houses are furnished with antiques, and although the decor is formal, the atmosphere is friendly and relaxed.

Hosts: Jay & Marianne Schatz
Doubles: 14 (PB) $60-115
Type of Beds: 12 Double; 2 Queen; 1 King
Continental Breakfast (summer); Full (spring & fall)
Minimum stay June 15-Sept. 30 & major holidays: 3-4
Closed Dec. - March
Credit Cards: No
Notes: 2 (advance deposit only), 8 (over 12), 9, 10, 11, 12

Alexander's Inn

Albert G. Stevens Inn

127 Myrtle Street, 08204
(609) 884-4717

Restored 1900 Victorian built as a wedding present by a local physician for his wife. Victorian elegance in the two parlors allow the guests space to read and relax. One parlor has the original mother-of-pearl inlay parlor suite presented by Dr. Stevens to his wife. As you approach the inn, you will see a wraparound veranda that serves as the main entrance. The flowers and plants invite guests to relax leisurely on the white wicker furniture.

Hosts: Paul & Alice Linden
Doubles: 6 (4 PB; 2 SB) $74.20-100.70
Type of Beds: 6 Double
Full Breakfast
Minimum stay weekdays: 2 ; weekends & holidays: 3
Credit Cards: A, B
Notes: 2, 5, 8 (12 and over), 9, 10, 11, 12

6 Pets welcome: 7 Smoking allowed: 8 Children welcome: 9 Social drinking allowed: 10 Tennis available: 11 Swimming available: 12 Golf available: 13 Skiing available: 14 May be booked through travel agents

Alexander's Inn

653 Washington Street, 08204
(609) 884-2555

In the heart of the primary historic district, this Victorian has authentic antique furnishings in the guest rooms, parlor, and music room. Have breakfast in your air-conditioned room or on the veranda. Afternoon tea in the parlor and Sunday brunch is included. Exceptional gourmet dining is available in our public dining room.

Hosts: Larry & Diane Muentz
Doubles: 4 (PB) $75-130
Type of Beds: 4 Double
Continental Breakfast
Credit Cards: A, B, C, E
Notes: 2, 4, 5, 9, 10, 11, 12, 14

Bedford Inn

Barnard-Good House

238 Perry Street, 08204
(609) 884-5381

We are known for our breakfast. Selected as number one by *New Jersey Monthly* magazine, we continue to make it even better. We serve four courses, all gourmet and homemade. Our purple house caters to happiness and comfort with Victorian restora-

tion. The two rooms that share baths have private facilities in the room and only share tub and shower facilities.

Hosts: Nan & Tom Hawkins
Doubles: 5 (3 PB; 2 SB) $82.62-103.86
Full Breakfast
Minimum stay weekdays & weekends in season: 3 ; holidays in season: 4
Credit Cards: A, B (for deposit only)
Closed March 15-Thanksgiving
Notes: 2, 7 (restricted), 8 (14 and over), 9, 10, 11, 12

Bedford Inn

805 Stockton Avenue, 08204
(609) 884-4158

Restored Italianate Victorian inn with an unusual double staircase to the third floor. Full-width first- and second-floor verandas have comfortable antique wicker furniture and old-fashioned porch rockers. Large buffet breakfast and afternoon tea by the parlor fireplace in the winter.

Hosts: Cindy & Al Schmucker
Doubles: 11 (PB) $79.50-137.50
Type of Beds: 1 Twin; 7 Double; 3 Queen
Full Breakfast
Credit Cards: A, B
Notes: 2, 5, 7, 8 (7 and older), 9, 10, 11, 12

The Brass Bed Inn

719 Columbia Avenue, 08204
(609) 884-8075

Our individually restored rooms boast a fine collection of nineteenth-century brass beds, antiques, lace curtains, and dramatic period wall coverings. In the fall, full, hearty breakfasts by the hearth and tea or cider in the late afternoon, with lots of good conversation, complete your day.

Hosts: John & Donna Dunwoody
Doubles: 8 (4 PB; 4 SB) $70-112
Type of Beds: 4 Twin; 6 Double
Full Breakfast
Credit Cards: A, B
Closed Thanksgiving & Christmas
Notes: 2, 5, 7 (outside), 8 (over 12), 9 (moderate), 10, 11, 12

Chalfonte Hotel

Capt. Mey's Inn

202 Ocean Street, 08204
(609) 884-7793

This 1890 Victorian inn boasts Persian rugs on tabletops, a Delft Blue china collection, authentic European antiques, Eastlake paneling in the dining room, a leaded-glass bay window, and a restored fireplace with intricately carved mantle. The wraparound veranda offers wicker furniture, hanging ferns, and Victorian wind curtains for those returning from a day at the beach.

Hosts: Milly LaCanfora & Carin Fedderman
Doubles: 8 (2 PB; 6 SB) $60-125
Type of Beds: 2 Twin; 6 Double; 1 Queen
Full Breakfast
Credit Cards: A, B
Notes: 2 (for deposit), 5, 7 (outside), 10, 11

Chalfonte Hotel

301 Howard Street, 08204
(609) 884-8409

A rustic 1876 Victorian summer hotel with verandas, rocking chairs, and delicious Southern fare. Relaxing and comfortable — the pleasures of another era await you. In-

quire about workshops, children's programs, classical and jazz concerts, historic programs, tours, and special discounts. Dinner is included in the daily rate.

Hosts: Anne LeDuc & Judy Bartella
Singles: 4 (SB) $60-64
Doubles: 68 (11 PB; 57 SB) $86-129
Type of Beds: 13 Twin; 27 Double; 1 Queen; 2 King
Full Breakfast
Credit Cards: A, B
Closed Nov.-April
Notes: 2, 4, 7 (limited), 8, 9, 10, 11, 12, 14

Capt. Mey's Inn

---

6 Pets welcome: 7 Smoking allowed: 8 Children welcome: 9 Social drinking allowed: 10 Tennis available: 11 Swimming available: 12 Golf available: 13 Skiing available: 14 May be booked through travel agents

Colvmns by the Sea

1513 Beach Drive, 08204
(609) 884-2228

Elegant Victorian mansion overlooking the ocean in an historic landmark village. Large, airy rooms are decorated with antiques. Gourmet breakfast and snacks, complimentary bikes, beach towels, and badges. Relaxing, enjoyable retreat for history buffs, bird watchers, and seashore lovers. Great restaurants nearby.

Hosts: Barry & Cathy Rein
Doubles: 11 (PB) $90-132
Type of Beds: 1 Twin; 2 Double; 8 Queen, 1 King; 2 Trundle beds
Full Breakfast
Minimum stay summer weekends & holidays: 3
Credit Cards: A, B
Closed Nov.-April
Notes: 2, 7 (limited), 8 (over 12), 9, 10, 11, 12

Duke of Windsor Bed & Breakfast Inn

817 Washington Street, 08204
(609) 884-1355

Queen Anne Victorian house with a forty-five-foot tower built in 1896 and restored with Victorian furnishings. Foyer with three-story carved oak open staircase, fireplace. Sitting room, parlor with fireplace, library, dining room. Beach tags provided, hot and cold outdoor showers, and off-street parking is available.

Hosts: Bruce & Fran Prichard
Doubles: 10 (8 PB; 2 SB) $50-95
Type of Beds: 3 Twin; 9 Double; 1 Queen
Full Breakfast
Credit Cards: A, B
Closed January
Notes: 2, 8 (over 12), 9, 10, 11, 12

Gingerbread House

28 Gurney Street, 08204
(609) 884-0211

An elegantly restored 1869 Victorian cottage listed on the National Register. Enjoy the well-appointed guest rooms, listen to classical music by the fire in the parlor, or enjoy the porches in warm weather. Centrally located one-half block from the beach.

Hosts: Fred & Joan Echevarria
Doubles: 6 (3 PB; 3 SB) $60-115
Continental Breakfast
Minimum stay summers: 4
Credit Cards: No
Notes: 2, 5, 7, 8 (7 and over), 9, 10, 11, 12

The Humphrey Hughes House

29 Ocean Street, 08204
(609) 884-4428

Nestled in the heart of Cape May's historic section is one of her most authentically restored inns — perhaps the most spacious and gracious of them all. Until 1980 it was the Hughes family home, and while the house is filled with magnificent antiques, it still feels more like a home than a museum.

Hosts: Lorraine & Terry Schmidt
Doubles: 11 (9 PB; 2 SB) $65-120
Type of Beds: 8 Double; 2 Queen; 1 King
Full Breakfast
Minimum stay weekends: 3
Credit Cards: A, B
Notes: 5, 10, 11, 12

Mainstay Inn

Mainstay Inn

635 Columbia Avenue, 08204
(609) 884-8690

The Mainstay Inn and Cottage are two of Cape May's most beautiful Victorian structures, and are decorated and furnished to historic perfection. Tom and Sue welcome all visitors; community breakfast and afternoon tea are highlights of the day. All rooms are large, airy, well lighted, and very comfortable. The Mainstay is in its nineteenth season — one of the first B&Bs in America.

Hosts: Tom & Sue Carroll
Doubles: 12 (PB) $74.20-118.72
Type of Beds: 3 Double; 7 Queen; 2 King
Full Breakfast
Minimum stay weekends: 3 ; holidays: 4
Credit Cards: No
Closed mid-Dec. to mid-March
Notes: 2, 9, 10, 11, 12

Perry Street Inn

Perry Street Inn

29 Perry Street, 08204
(609) 884-4590

Charming Victorian in National Landmark City. Half a block to beaches and Victorian Mall. Near fine restaurants, unique shopping, fishing, marinas, and state park wildlife preserve. Forty miles to Atlantic City. Comfortable rooms, many ocean views, period furnishings, hearty breakfasts, and parking.

Hosts: John & Cynthia Curtis
Singles: 1 (SB) $31.80
Doubles: 9 (5 PB; 4 SB) $42.40-90.10
Type of Beds: 5 Twin; 7 Double; 1 King
Full Breakfast
Minimum stay weekends & holidays: 2

Credit Cards: A, B
Notes: 2 (call), 3 (picnic by special request), 4 (by special request), 7, 8 (over 13), 9, 10, 11, 12, 14

The Queen Victoria

102 Ocean Street, 08204
(609) 884-8702

The Wells family welcomes you as friends and treats you royally with unpretentious service and attention to detail. Four restored buildings, comfortably furnished with antiues, are in the center of the historic district. Nationally recognized for special Christmas activities.

Hosts: Dane & Joan Wells
Doubles: 17 (13 PB; 4 SB) $49-175 plus tax
Suites: 7 (PB)
Type of Beds: 1 Twin; 3 Double; 21 Queen; 1 King
Full Breakfast
Credit Cards: A, B, C
Notes: 2, 5, 8, 9, 10, 11, 12

Windward House

24 Jackson Street, 08204
(609) 884-3368

Edwardian shingle style cottage one-half block to the beach and Victorian Mall. Completely decorated in elegant antiques plus vintage collectibles, paintings, and clothing.

The Queen Victoria

Three sun and shade porches plus three common rooms. Stained and leaded, beveled glass abound throughout.

Hosts: Sandy & Owen Miller
Doubles: 8 (PB) $85-110
Type of Beds: 3 Double; 5 Queen
Full Breakfast
Minimum stay weekends: 2 ; holidays: 3-4
Credit Cards: A, B
Notes: 2, 5, 7, 8 (over 12), 9, 10, 11, 12

Woodleigh House

808 Washington Street, 08204
(609) 884-7123

Victorian, but informal. Centrally located, with off-street parking, beach bikes, comfortable parlor, courtyard, and gardens. Walk to everything: marvelous restaurants, sights galore, nearby nature preserve, outdoor summer theater, craft and antique shows.

Hosts: Jan & Buddy Wood
Doubles: 8 (5 PB; 3 SB) $60-90
Type of Beds: 8 Double
Continental Breakfast
Credit Cards: No
Notes: 2, 5, 7 (limited), 8 (over 5), 10, 11, 12, 14

CHATHAM

B&B of New Jersey #401

Suite 132, 103 Godwin Avenue
Midland Park, 07432
(201)444-7409

A four-year-old Labrador retriever will be delighted to show you the walking paths surrounding this sprawling colonial. Situated on 18 acres and tucked away at the end of a private road, the property borders on a wildlife center. There is a twin room with private bath on the second floor and a sitting room with TV. Children are welcome, and a crib is available. Continental breakfast is served. $40-55.

CLINTON

Northern NJ B&B 5

11 Sunset Trail, Denville
(201)625-5129

A beautiful 1862 Victorian inn, in an old residential neighborhood. A short stroll on wide slate sidewalks brings you to Clinton's picturebook main street. Five guest rooms with semi-private baths, air-conditioning, and ceiling fans. Continental-plus breakfast featuring the hostess's homemade coffee cake. Cat in residence. $45-65.

CLOSTER

B&B of New Jersey #428

Suite 132, 103 Godwin Avenue
Midland Park, 07432
(201)444-7409

Enjoy a continental breakfast in the greenhouse just off the kitchen or on the deck at this nicely appointed 1945 colonial. Very centrally located and convenient to public transportation, it is ideal for a traveler who wants to see New York but stay in the suburbs. Many fine restaurants are within walking distance. French, German, and English are spoken. The guest room on the first floor has a cathedral ceiling, private entrance, exposed beams, and private bath. A second room has twin beds, private bath, and private entrance. The third guest room has a queen bed; a fourth room shares the bath with this room. $70-75.

CRESSKILL

Northern NJ B&B 6

11 Sunset Trail, Denville
(201)625-5129

A traditional home with one guest room, double bed, and private bath. Loveseat and lounge chair in guest room. One cat and two

NOTES: Credit cards accepted: A Master Card; B Visa; C American Express; D Discover Card; E Diners Club; F Other: 2 Personal checks accepted: 3 Lunch available: 4 Dinner available: 5 Open all year

dogs in residence; continental breakfast. $40-50.

DENNISVILLE

Henry Ludlam Inn
RD #3, Box 298, Woodbine, 08270
(609) 861-5847

Ludlam Inn is an historic 1804 home situated on a 55-acre lake, where you can nourish your senses and sustain your soul. Sip wine in front of the fireplace in your room; sleep on a featherbed; awake to a gourmet breakfast. Near beaches, state parks, and restaurants. Come and explore.

Doubles: 5 (3 PB; 2 SB) $75-85
Type of Beds: 5 Double
Full Breakfast
Minimum stay holidays: 3
Credit Cards: A, B
Notes: 2, 4, 5, 7 (limited), 8 (over 12), 9, 10, 11, 12, 14

DENVILLE

Northern NJ B&B 7
11 Sunset Trail, Denville
(201)625-5129

A lakeside B&B situated on Indian Lake, just off I-80, midway between NYC and PA. Private guest quarters comprise the first floor: guest room with double bed, family room with color TV, private bath. Enjoy the view of the bay. Rowboat available, beach passes and snacks provided. Full breakfast. Dog in residence upstairs. $40-45.

EAST BRUNSWICK

B&B of New Jersey #469
Suite 132, 103 Godwin Avenue
Midland Park, 07432
(201)444-7409

Old-fashioned hospitality is in abundance at this lovely two-story colonial. The guest room with shared bath has a hand-stenciled border and features a queen canopy bed. Guests are welcome to use the TV in the family room. An additional bedroom can be made available for children, and a crib is available. $40-58.

EAST WINDSOR

B&B of New Jersey #478
Suite 132, 103 Godwin Avenue
Midland Park, 07432
(201)444-7409

Your hosts at this charming townhouse are famous dessert cookbook authors. Their home is filled with treasures they have collected over the years. The second-floor air-conditioned guest room has large sliding-glass windows overlooking the tennis courts and shares a bath only during the summer. Guests have access to the tennis courts and swimming pool. A full breakfast is served. $47-53.

EDISON

B&B of New Jersey #437
Suite 132, 103 Godwin Avenue
Midland Park, 07432
(201)444-7409

Guest rooms in this two-story colonial are on the second floor. A queen room offers a private bath, and the double room shares a bath. Both rooms have sitting areas. Continental breakfast is served in the dining room. An easy drive to Plainfield, Rutgers University, and Somerset; thirty minutes to Newark Airport. $40-60.

ENGLEWOOD CLIFFS

B&B of New Jersey #422
Suite 132, 103 Godwin Avenue
Midland Park, 07432
(201)444-7409

6 Pets welcome: 7 Smoking allowed: 8 Children welcome: 9 Social drinking allowed: 10 Tennis available: 11 Swimming available: 12 Golf available: 13 Skiing available: 14 May be booked through travel agents

Two private suites are available in this large home. One overlooks the secluded patio and yard and has a comfortable sitting room, fireplace, TV, bar, refrigerator, private bath. The upstairs suite has a king bed (or two twins) and the downstairs suite has a double bed and private entrance. A continental breakfast is served daily. In an exclusive, quiet neighborhood just fifteen minutes from the George Washington Bridge and Manhattan. $70-80.

FLEMINGTON

Jerica Hill

96 Broad Street, 08822
(201) 782-8234

Be warmly welcomed at this gracious Victorian country home. The bright, airy guest rooms are furnished with canopy, brass, and four-poster beds, fresh flowers, and antiues. Large living room with an open fire in the winter, and wicker-filled screened porch in the summer. Special adventures include champagne hot-air balloon flights and country winery tours.

Host: Judith Studer
Doubles: 5 (2 PB; 3 SB) $55-80
Type of Beds: 2 Twin; 3 Double; 1 Queen
Continental Breakfast
Credit Cards: A, B, C
Notes: 2, 5, 9, 10, 11, 12

FRENCHTOWN

The Old Hunterdon House

12 Bridge Street, 08825
(201) 996-3632

This Civil-War era mansion in a small Delaware River village captures the ambience of the Victorian age. Distinctive architecture, period furnishing, and attention to detail and guest comfort all combine to make for a memorable stay. Convenient to excellent dining, antique and outlet shop-

ping, and recreational activities in Bucks and Hunterdon counties.

Host: Rick Carson
Doubles: 7 (PB) $68-95
Type of Beds: 2 Twin; 4 Double; 2 Queen
Continental-plus Breakfast
Credit Cards: A, B
Notes: 2, 5, 7, 9, 10, 11

Jerica Hill

HAWORTH

B&B of New Jersey #406

Suite 132, 103 Godwin Avenue
Midland Park, 07432
(201)444-7409

If privacy is what you're after, this Dutch colonial will suit you perfectly. There is a separate driveway and entrance for guests, a large bedroom featuring a private bath, color TV, phone, and separate heat control. An additional room is available, and children are welcome. Located on a quiet street adjacent to a country club. Nearby public transportation to New York. $40-55.

HILLSBOROUGH

B&B of New Jersey #458

Suite 132, 103 Godwin Avenue
Midland Park, 07432
(201)444-7409

NOTES: Credit cards accepted: A Master Card; B Visa; C American Express; D Discover Card; E Diners Club; F Other: 2 Personal checks accepted: 3 Lunch available: 4 Dinner available: 5 Open all year

This contemporary townhouse is located in the heart of the state, with easy access to several highways. Historic Morristown and Princeton, the Meadowlands Sports Center, New York City, and the shore are all within an hour's drive. Swimming and tennis facilities are available; private gym; tennis lessons available from your host for an additional fee. The cheerful room on the second floor shares a bath with the hosts. $37-40.

HOPE

B&B of New Jersey #470
Suite 132, 103 Godwin Avenue
Midland Park, 07432
(201)444-7409

Originally the heart of the village economy, this impressive colonial grist mill complex is now a gracious country inn. It is situated on 23 acres along Beaver Brook and was built circa 1769 by Moravian pioneers. Each room has a private bath, antiques, original wide board floors, and handcrafted Oriental rugs. Area attractions include Waterloo Village, antique and craft shows, fishing or canoeing on the Delaware River, hiking, and wine tasting. Lovely continental breakfast. $49-80 plus tax.

ISLAND HEIGHTS

B&B of New Jersey #451
Suite 132, 103 Godwin Avenue
Midland Park, 07432
(201)444-7409

This unusual studio/home of a renowned artist was built in 1889 and has recently been restored. Sit on the old-fashioned porch and watch the boats sail by on Toms River. Three beaches are within walking distance, along with lots of recreational facilities and fine restaurants. Three rooms with shared baths; full breakfast. $45-81.25.

JACKSON

B&B of New Jersey
Suite 132, 103 Godwin Avenue
Midland Park, 07432
(201)444-7409

Children are always welcome to this home, which offers two bedrooms, one twin with a shared bath and a king with private entrance and bath. A sitting room is available for reading, music, or TV. Golf and tennis are within walking distance; fifteen minutes to the shore; fifteen to Great Adventure. $33-40.

LAMBERTVILLE

B&B of New Jersey #444
Suite 132, 103 Godwin Avenue
Midland Park, 07432
(201)444-7409

An impressive stone and frame colonial on 10 rolling acres with a formal garden and a boxwood maze. Guest rooms are beautifully furnished in antiques and period reproductions. All rooms have private baths, queen or king beds, air-conditioning; two have working fireplaces. A full gourmet breakfast is served in the original 1820 dining room. $85-150.

B&B of New Jersey #446
Suite 132, 103 Godwin Avenue
Midland Park, 07432
(201)444-7409

A traditional B&B built in the 1750s, filled with art and antiques. Three beautiful guest rooms include one with private bath. Continental-plus breakfast in bed, free champagne with breakfast for honeymooners, and many other extras. A horse-drawn carriage can be called for a leisurely drive around town. $65-75.

LYNDHURST

The Jeremiah J. Yereance House

410 Riverside Avenue, 07071
(201) 438-9457

This 1841 house, a state and national landmark, is five minutes from the Meadowland complex and twenty minutes from New York City. The guest rooms in the South Wing include a front parlor with fireplace, a central hall, and a small but comfortable bedroom that adjoins the parlor and private bath.

Hosts: Evelyn & Frank Pezzollar
Singles: 1 (SB) $50-70 plus tax
Doubles: 3 (1 PB; 2 SB) $55-75 plus tax
Type of Beds: 1 Twin; 3 Double
Continental Breakfast
Credit Cards: C
Notes: 2, 5, 8 (over 12), 9, 10

MADISON

Northern NJ B&B 9

11 Sunset Trail, Denville
(201)625-5129

A two-room suite featuring a bedroom with queen bed, bath, and sitting room with queen sofabed. There are fireplaces in both rooms and antiques throughout. This 1880s home features wide board floors, hand-hewn beams, and a porch overlooking the perennial garden. Continental breakfast weekdays, full on weekends. $80.

MAHWAH

B&B of New Jersey #403

Suite 132, 103 Godwin Avenue
Midland Park, 07432
(201)444-7409

This new luxury townhouse is located in a quiet neighborhood and surrounded by beautifully landscaped property. Guest ac-commodations feature white down coverlets on twin beds that can be converted to a king. The living room has a TV and stereo and includes a dining area and double sleep sofa. Private bath with stall shower. A continental-plus breakfast is served. $60-72.

MANAHAWKIN

B&B of New Jersey #483

Suite 132, 103 Godwin Avenue
Midland Park, 07432
(201)444-7409

Year-round activities abound at this new B&B inn. Seasonal beach tags are available to Long Beach Island beaches, just ten minutes away; boat rentals and deep-sea fishing trips; many fine restaurants. This little country-style inn is hosted by two ladies who serve an extended continental breakfast during the summer and full breakfast off-season. Three air-conditioned guest rooms, one with private bath. $45-60.

MARGATE

Northern NJ B&B 10

11 Sunset Trail, Denville
(201)625-5129

A lovely California-style home located right on the beach. Atlantic City is only minutes away, but unlike the hotels, here there are miles of open, clean, uncrowded beaches. Or you may find the deck or patio the place to relax and enjoy the ocean view. Six rooms, all with ocean views; continental breakfast. $60-125.

MAYS LANDING

B&B of New Jersey #480

Suite 132, 103 Godwin Avenue
Midland Park, 07432
(201)444-7409

NOTES: Credit cards accepted: A Master Card; B Visa; C American Express; D Discover Card; E Diners Club; F Other: 2 Personal checks accepted: 3 Lunch available: 4 Dinner available: 5 Open all year

A new addition, with alpine chalet architecture, complete with balconies and flower boxes, has been constructed with the comfort of guests in mind. The two air-conditioned guest suites with private baths provide a comfortable, quiet retreat. Located on 20 acres across from Estell Manor County Park, yet just fifteen minutes from the hustle and bustle of Atlantic City. Breakfast is either full or continental, as you please. Additional amenities include TV, small refrigerator, private entrance, picnic tables, and garden chairs. $50-55.

B&B of New Jersey #497
Suite 132, 103 Godwin Avenue
Midland Park, 07432
(201)444-7409

One of the most romantic inns in the Northeast is located on the river in the sleepy little town of Mays Landing. This 1845 Italianate is impeccably maintained. Of the six guest rooms appointed with antiques, four have private baths. A full breakfast is offered daily, as is afternoon tea. Just seventeen miles from Atlantic City, near many fine restaurants and public transportation. $65.

MILLINGTON

B&B of New Jersey #449
Suite 132, 103 Godwin Avenue
Midland Park, 07432
(201)444-7409

Originally built in 1764 and renovated in 1980, this historic home was recently featured on a house tour. The cozy atmosphere begins in the country kitchen, where a fireplace will make your extended continental breakfast a real treat. The three guest rooms, one with private bath, all feature antiques. $50-66.

MORRISTOWN

B&B of New Jersey #450
Suite 132, 103 Godwin Avenue
Midland Park, 07432
(201)444-7409

A tastefully decorated guest room, located in a separate wing, is featured in this twenty-two-room estate manor house located in the Country Club Area two miles from the center of town. The large carpeted room has three walls of windows, original artwork, and authentic antiques. One queen room, two double rooms with private baths. Continental breakfast. $50-60.

Northern NJ B&B 11
11 Sunset Trail, Denville
(201)625-5129

An historic home in the heart of the historic district, this twenty-one room residence was built in 1886. Within a three to five block walk are the Morristown Green, restaurants, department stores and specialty shops, a complex of ten movie theaters, and train and bus stations to Manhattan and eastern New Jersey. The two guest rooms have private baths and share a kitchen and sunken living room with TV. Continental-plus breakfast is served. $55-75.

MORRIS TOWNSHIP

B&B of New Jersey #433
Suite 132, 103 Godwin Avenue
Midland Park, 07432
(201)444-7409

This 1844 Federal house offers guest rooms on a separate level, both of which have Laura Ashley linens, wall-to-wall carpeting, cable TV, hand-made quilts, and air-conditioning. The bath is shared. Enjoy the fireplace in the guest parlor or dining room, as well as the patio. Miles of walking paths just across the street; fine shops and restaurants nearby. $50-55.

OCEAN CITY

BarnaGate
637 Wesley Avenue, 08226
(609) 391-9366

We offer a warm welcome to share our five newly redone guest rooms with private and semi-private baths. Enjoy our front porch in summer and our cozy living room all year. Located within easy reach of Atlantic City, historic attractions, and Cape May, we also have biking, walking, jogging, and swimming.

Hosts: Frank & Lois Barna
Doubles: 5 (1 PB; 4 SB) $30-60
Type of Beds: 1 Twin; 4 Double
Continental Breakfast
Minimum stay summer holidays: 2
Credit Cards: A, B
Notes: 5, 8 (10 or older), 9, 10, 11, 12

BarnaGate

The Enterprise B&B
1020 Central Avenue, 08226
(609) 398-1698

You can have it all! Combine the excitement of Atlantic City (ten minutes away) with the totally relaxing ambience of our seashore Victorian. Great beaches, boardwalk, restaurants, quaint shops are all here within walking distance.

Hosts: Stephen & Patty Hydock
Doubles: 9 (7 PB; 2 SB) $55-85
Type of Beds: 9 Double
Full Breakfast
Minimum stay weekends: 2 ; holidays: 3
Credit Cards: A, B
Notes: 2, 5, 7, 8 (over 12), 9, 10, 11, 12

Top O' The Waves
5447 Central Avenue, 08226
(609) 399-0477

You can have it all when you come to Top O' The Waves. Located right on the beach, this private vacation complex features luxury ocean-front rentals. Cozy single units and a spacious duplex with all amenities. The hosts delight in making your R&R of surf, sun, and sand special, and give everyone privacy, luxury, and service. Special off-season rates for business persons and senior citizens.

Hosts: Dolly & Des Nunan
Single Units: 10 (PB) $76-125
Double Units: 4 (SB) $76-125
Type of Beds: 4 Twin; 2 Double; 8 Queen
Continental Breakfast
Minimum stay summer single units: 3: duplexes 2 weeks
Credit Cards: A, B, C
Notes: 2 (2 weeks in advance), 4, 5, 7, 8, 9, 10, 11, 12

OCEAN GROVE

Cordova
26 Webb Avenue, 07756
(201) 774-3084 (in season); (212) 751-9577

The Cordova is a century-old Victorian located in a lovely, historic beach community with Old World charm. It's only 1.5 blocks from the white sand beach and wooden boardwalk. Selected by *NJ Magazine* as "one of the 7 best places on Jersey Shore." Family atmosphere. Many former presidents (Wilson, Cleveland, Roosevelt) have slept in Ocean Grove and spoken at the 7,000-seat

"Great Auditorium" — the largest wooden structure in the U.S.

Hosts: Doris & Vlad Chernik
Singles: 4 (SB) $26-36
Doubles: 11 (SB) $30-50
Type of Beds: 7 Twin; 8 Double
Continental-plus Breakfast
Minimum stay holidays: 3
Credit Cards: No
Closed Labor Day - Memorial Day
Notes: 2, 7 (restricted), 8, 9, 10, 11, 14

Pine Tree Inn

10 Main Avenue, 07756
(201) 775-3264

A small Victorian hotel offering a quiet interlude for visitors to the Jersey Shore. One hour from New York City and Newark Airport, and 1.5 hours from Atlantic City and Philadelphia. Beach towels, bicycles, and discounted beach passes are available on request.

Hosts: Karen Mason & Francis Goger
Singles: 3 (SB) $45-80
Doubles: 10 (5 PB; 5 SB) $55-85
Type of Beds: 5 Twin; 7 Double; 2 Queen
Continental-plus Breakfast
Minimum stay weekends: 2; Holidays: 3
Credit Cards: A, B
Notes: 2, 4, 5, 8 (over 12), 9, 10, 11, 12

PALISADES PARK

B&B of New Jersey #468

Suite 132, 103 Godwin Avenue
Midland Park, 07432
(201)444-7409

Your hosts at this red brick home are a charming young couple who are fluent in French and Spanish. The adorable and friendly dog also responds to French. The single guest room has a European flavor to it; the bath is shared with the hosts. Continental breakfast. Public transportation is just two blocks away, and major highways are nearby, providing easy access to the Meadowlands Sports Complex, shopping outlets, and New York City. No smoking. $35.

PENNS GROVE

B&B of New Jersey #487

Suite 132, 103 Godwin Avenue
Midland Park, 07432
(201)444-7409

French and Italian are often heard in this five-bedroom residence facing the Delaware River, just fifteen minutes from Wilmington, Delaware. Three guest rooms on the second floor share a bath, as do the two rooms on the third floor. Children are welcome here, and the host will escort you on guided tours of the area. $55-65.

PHILLIPSBURG AREA

B&B of New Jersey #439

Suite 132, 103 Godwin Avenue
Midland Park, 07432
(201)444-7409

Originally a miller's house, this gracious fieldstone manor is set in the middle of 16 acres of rolling hills and forests. The outdoor patio overlooks landscaped gardens with stone walkways, a huge free-form pool, and numerous outbuildings that contribute to the pastoral setting. The house has eight bedrooms, two with fireplaces, and seven baths. Each room has a four-poster bed, its own TV, and private phone. $75-85.

PITTSTOWN

B&B of New Jersey #434

Suite 132, 103 Godwin Avenue
Midland Park, 07432
(201)444-7409

A working farm, built in 1810 on over 100 acres. Many of the antiques in the house have been in the family for many years. Guests can hike in the woods, fish in the pond, go sledding, relax on the patio, or pass the time in the homey living room with a game or good book. The farm has lots of animals to enjoy: cows, sheep, pigs, chickens, ducks, and geese. Visitors are treated to a big, old-fashioned breakfast with homegrown products. The house can accommodate seven adults, two children, and an infant; shared baths. $40-65.

PRINCETON

The Peacock Inn
20 Bayard Lane, 08540
(609) 924-1707

Originally built on the Princeton campus circa 1775, the inn was moved 100 years later to its present location. Convenient, comfortable lodging in a warm, hospitable environment. Only one block from the Princeton campus, the inn has hosted illustrious guests such as Bertrand Russell, Albert Einstein, and F. Scott Fitzgerald.

Hosts: Michael Walker & Candy Lindsay
Singles: 3 (SB) $75
Doubles: 13 (12 PB; 1 SB) $105
Type of Beds: 3 Twin; 10 Double; 3 Queen
Continental-plus Breakfast
Credit Cards: A, B, C
Notes: 2, 3, 4, 5, 6, 7, 8, 9, 14

B&B of New Jersey #412
Suite 132, 103 Godwin Avenue
Midland Park, 07432
(201)444-7409

This luxury townhouse has been decorated by its interior-designer hostess with artwork and collections from around the world. The three-level unit includes a huge deck that overlooks two lakes and trees. The second floor has a balcony guest room with a great view of the lake. A larger room on this floor can serve as a sitting room or as another sleeping room. A third-floor loft with cedar ceiling and skylights is also available as a sitting/den area. The entire home is air-conditioned and carpeted. Within walking distance of restaurants, shopping, and public

transportation. A full breakfast of your choice is served. $55-66.

RIDGEWOOD

B&B of New Jersey #411
Suite 132, 103 Godwin Avenue
Midland Park, 07432
(201)444-7409

An extended continental breakfast with lots of home-baked goodies is featured in a large kitchen filled with hanging plants and copper pots. This professional couple shares their home with a gentle collie. Two guest rooms, a single and a double, have color TV and air-conditioning; shared bath. Tennis and public transportation are within walking distance. One hour from New York City. $35-45.

B&B of New Jersey #413
Suite 132, 103 Godwin Avenue
Midland Park, 07432
(201)444-7409

This traditional two-story home is located in a residential neighborhood close to public transportation to New York City. The cozy second-floor rooms include a private bath, air-conditioning, TV, and plenty of closet space. Continental breakfast. $55-60.

B&B of New Jersey #414
Suite 132, 103 Godwin Avenue
Midland Park, 07432
(201)444-7409

Your hosts here speak French and German and go out of their way to make you feel at home. Their guest room has a single bed and a shared bath (or use of the bath upstairs). A large, bright twin room on the third floor has a bath with shower. Continental breakfast, pool, and family room. $35-45.

NOTES: Credit cards accepted: A Master Card; B Visa; C American Express; D Discover Card; E Diners Club; F Other: 2 Personal checks accepted: 3 Lunch available: 4 Dinner available: 5 Open all year

B&B of New Jersey #466

Suite 132, 103 Godwin Avenue
Midland Park, 07432
(201)444-7409

If you are really interested in better health, this home may interest you. It boasts a flotation tank, Swedish massage or shiatsu, whirlpool, steam cabinet, and exercise equipment. Your hostess is a certified massage therapist who also offers yoga, life-style body wellness counseling, or European facials. The large guest room has a double bed, desk, and private bath. A second smaller room shares a bath. Vegetarian and macrobiotic diets can be arranged for breakfast, if you wish. $60.

ROCKAWAY

Northern NJ B&B 12

11 Sunset Trail, Denville
(201)625-5129

An 85-year-old manor set among flowering trees offers two rooms with private or shared bath, air-conditioning, swimming pool, kitchen, and living room with color TV. Full breakfast. $45-50.

SPRING LAKE

Ashling Cottage

106 Sussex Avenue, 07762
(201) 449-3553

Under sentinel sycamores since 1877 in a storybook setting, Ashling Cottage, a Victorian seaside inn, has served as a portal to an earlier time. A block from the ocean and just half a block from a fresh-water lake.

Hosts: Goodi & Jack Stewart
Doubles: 10 (8 PB; 2 SB) $60-108
Type of Beds: 10 Queen
Continental-plus Breakfast
Credit Cards: No
Closed Jan. & Feb.
Notes: 2, 7 (limited), 8 (over 12), 9, 10, 11, 12

Ashling Cottage

The Chateau

500 Warren Avenue, 07762
(201) 974-2000

The house may be 101 years old, but it's brand-new inside: air-conditioning, color cable TV, HBO, phones, refrigerators. Suites and parlors have living rooms, wet bars, paddle fans. Some have fireplaces and facilities for FAX machines and personal computers.

Host: Scott Smith
Doubles: (PB) $44-96
Suites: (PB) $70-142
Continental Breakfast
Credit Cards: A, B, C
Closed Nov. 1 - March 29
Notes: 2, 7, 8, 9, 10, 11, 12, 14

Johnson House Inn

25 Tuttle Avenue, 07762
(201) 449-1860

A family-style ambience awaits you just a half block from the beach. Come relax on our spacious wraparound porch with wicker chairs and rockers. Our family extends a warm invitation to your family to come visit us.

Hosts: Helen & Lou Gombos, Hellin & Joe Desiderio
Singles: 2 (SB) $40
Doubles: 16 (9 PB; 7 SB) $75-85

---

6 Pets welcome: 7 Smoking allowed: 8 Children welcome: 9 Social drinking allowed: 10 Tennis available: 11
Swimming available: 12 Golf available: 13 Skiing available: 14 May be booked through travel agents

Type of Beds: 13 Twin; 5 Double
Continental-plus Breakfast
Minimum stay weekends: 2 ; holidays: 3
Credit Cards: No
Notes: 2, 5, 8, 9, 10, 11, 12

Normandy Inn

21 Tuttle Avenue, 07762
(201) 449-7172

An 1888 Italianate villa filled with prized possessions: an 1860 signed Herter bed; woven Brussels carpet; Robert Todd Lincoln's bedroom wallpaper. If you arrive in tranquil Spring Lake by train or bus, we'll meet you at the station. Explore the wide, tree-lined streets, turn-of-the-century estates, quaint shops and boutiques, and a wide selection of fine restaurants. Ocean swimming, sunning, golf, tennis, horseback riding, fishing, and thoroughbred racing are all close by.

Hosts: Michael & Susan Ingino
Singles: 2 (PB) $65-120
Doubles: 17 (PB) $75-130
Type of Beds: 7 Twin; 12 Double
Full Breakfast
Minimum stay March-Nov.: 2 ; holiday weekends: 3 ;
July & Aug. weekends: 4
Credit Cards: A, B, C
Notes: 2, 5, 8, 9, 10, 11, 12

The Sandpiper

7 Atlantic Avenue, 07762
(201) 449-6060

A romantic Victorian hotel and restaurant overlooking the ocean. All rooms have newly tiled bathrooms, some with whirlpools, telephones, cable TV, air-conditioning, concierge service, and beach badges.

Host: Grace P. Compton
Singles: 2 (PB) $65-95
Doubles: 14 (PB) $95-155
Continental Breakfast
Minimum stay weekends: 2; holidays: 3
Credit Cards: A, B, C
Closed Jan. & Feb.
Notes: 2, 7, 8, 9, 10, 11, 12

The Sea Crest of Spring Lake

19 Tuttle Avenue, 07762
(201) 449-9031

Touching the beach and boardwalk, the Sea Crest has a wraparound porch with wicker furniture, off-street parking, private baths, TV, and air-conditioning. The Sea Crest, built in 1885, has been a bed & breakfast for 103 years.

Host: Valeria Moravek
Doubles: 14 (PB) $40-90
Continental Breakfast
Credit Cards: No
Notes: 2, 5, 8, 10, 11, 12

The Whistling Swan

STANHOPE

Whistling Swan Inn

110 Main Street, Box 791, 07874
(201) 347-6369

We are northwest New Jersey's finest Victorian bed & breakfast, located just off I-80 only 45 minutes west of the George Washington Bridge. Near Waterloo Village, International Trade Zone, skiing, antiques, shops, restaurants. "For those with more refined nesting instincts."

NOTES: Credit cards accepted: A Master Card; B Visa; C American Express; D Discover Card; E Diners Club; F Other: 2 Personal checks accepted: 3 Lunch available: 4 Dinner available: 5 Open all year

Hosts: Paula Williams & Joe Mulay
Doubles: 10 (SB) $65-80
Type of Beds: 10 Queen
Full Breakfast
Minimum stay holidays: 2
Credit Cards: A, B, C
Notes: 2, 5, 9, 10, 11, 12, 13, 14

STILLWATER

B&B of New Jersey #442

Suite 132, 103 Godwin Avenue
Midland Park, 07432
(201)444-7409

Step back into 1840 on this 15-acre working farm complete with animals, river, pond, and stream. The hostess spins and dyes wool and angora, makes her own butter, candles, breads, and grows or raises all their food. Guests are free to do nothing or participate in any of the chores. The entire home is yours to enjoy — living room with two working fireplaces, woodstove, baby grand piano, and kitchen with a fireplace. Breakfast is served in the country kitchen or on the wraparound porch. Both guest rooms have antiques and working fireplaces; shared bath. Children and smokers are welcome. $50-60.

STOCKTON

The Stockton Inn, "Colligan's"

Main and Bridge Streets, 08559
(609) 397-1250

Serving the public since 1796, this is *the* small hotel immortalized in the Rogers and Hart song, "There's a Small Hotel," and it does have a wishing well. Two restaurants, one innovative American and the other classic French. Minutes from New Hope, PA.

Hosts: Andrew McDermott & Richard Colton
Doubles: 11 (PB) $85-130
Continental Breakfast
Credit Cards: A, B, C, E, F
Closed Christmas
Notes: 3, 4, 5, 7, 9, 10, 11, 12, 13

SUCCASUNNA

B&B of New Jersey #430

Suite 132, 103 Godwin Avenue
Midland Park, 07432
(201)444-7409

Just five minutes from the heart of town, this 1963 center-hall colonial offers one room with a queen bed and shared bath. Amenities include a large deck, enclosed porch, pool, and help-yourself continental breakfast. Tennis courts are nearby, as are restaurants and shops. $50-55.

SUMMIT

B&B of New Jersey #448

Suite 132, 103 Godwin Avenue
Midland Park, 07432
(201)444-7409

Tucked away in a quiet neighborhood, this charming home offers you a place to relax and unwind. The guest room on the third floor is bright and airy, with lace curtains and a skylight. Private bath. Lounge around the pool in the lush backyard or take a stroll in the nearby park. $75.

UPPER MONTCLAIR

B&B of New Jersey #408

Suite 132, 103 Godwin Avenue
Midland Park, 07432
(201)444-7409

Travel down a tree-lined avenue, past manicured lawns and well-tended gardens, and you will come to this lovely Greek Revival home. The cozy living room features a collection of old books, TV, and stereo. An air-conditioned guest suite is located on the first floor with twin beds. Also on the first floor is a guest room with a single bed; bath is shared. An extended continental breakfast is served in the dining room or on the

6 Pets welcome: 7 Smoking allowed: 8 Children welcome: 9 Social drinking allowed: 10 Tennis available: 11 Swimming available: 12 Golf available: 13 Skiing available: 14 May be booked through travel agents

covered porch overlooking the lush back-yard. $50-60.

Northern NJ B&B 15
11 Sunset Trail, Denville
(201)625-5129

Lovely home on a quiet, tree-lined street. Two guest rooms tastefully furnished with antiques. Near Montclair State College and parks; minutes from bus and train to NYC. Private or shared bath; air-conditioning. Your friendly hostess will serve a continental breakfast in a lovely setting overlooking a wooded area. Outside deck. $50-60.

VENTNOR

B&B of New Jersey #496
Suite 132, 103 Godwin Avenue
Midland Park, 07432
(201)444-7409

This guest house has been magnificently res-tored to its original beauty. Just steps from the white, sandy beaches and boardwalk, within easy reach of all the entertainment of Atlantic City. A full breakfast is served, plus afternoon tea. There is an extra-large Jacuz-zi, sauna, and masseuse by appointment. $110-120.

WAYNE

B&B of New Jersey #419
Suite 132, 103 Godwin Avenue
Midland Park, 07432
(201)444-7409

If you want a retreat in the country but need the convenience of highway access, this turn-of-the-century redwood colonial is perfect. Located in a quiet, residential area near I-80, the home features a deck with a panoramic view. The large guest room has a queen bed, coffee maker, and small refrigerator, along with a wonderful view. Guests have use of a sitting room, living room, and TV room. The bath is shared. New York is half an hour away. $48-60.

WEST ORANGE

B&B of New Jersey #425
Suite 132, 103 Godwin Avenue
Midland Park, 07432
(201)444-7409

This charming B&B is a three-story, turn-of-the-century home on a quiet, tree-lined residential street. The upstairs guest room has a private bath, queen bed, and an alcove that provides an instant office, if needed. Adjacent to the guest room is a library where a continental breakfast is served. Exercise equipment is available in the workout room. $50-60.

WESTWOOD

B&B of New Jersey #418
Suite 132, 103 Godwin Avenue
Midland Park, 07432
(201)444-7409

This wonderful young couple will make you feel very welcome in their country home in this suburban community. The ranch home is situated in a secluded wooded area just off a main street; pool and patio are available. There is a twin room with TV and private bath on the main level. The finished base-ment is complete with bedroom, living room with color TV, eating area, and bath with shower. Continental breakfast. $40-45.

WILDWOOD

B&B of New Jersey #479
Suite 132, 103 Godwin Avenue
Midland Park, 07432
(201)444-7409

NOTES: Credit cards accepted: A Master Card; B Visa; C American Express; D Discover Card; E Diners Club; F Other: 2 Personal checks accepted: 3 Lunch available: 4 Dinner available: 5 Open all year

Relax and enjoy a cool retreat in a gracious eighty-year-old Queen Anne guest house that boasts an 1855 sofa and an 1890 Eastlake piano. Sit and relax on the veranda, walk to the beaches, the boardwalk, and shopping. Nine guest rooms, seven with private baths; full breakfast. A three-night minimum is necessary in July and August. $65-90.

WYCKOFF

B&B of New Jersey #415
Suite 132, 103 Godwin Avenue

Midland Park, 07432
(201)444-7409

Your hosts in this quiet suburban home have been taking care of guests from around the world for many years. The air-conditioned guest suite features twin beds, a dressing area, and private bath. Relax in an overstuffed chair or the needlepoint rocker while you savor the delicious continental breakfast that is delivered to your suite each morning. Smokers are welcome. New York City is within an hour's drive. $50-60.

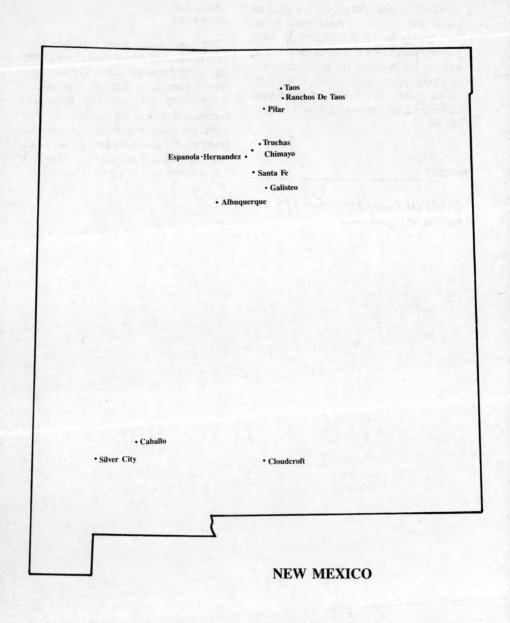

• Taos
• Ranchos De Taos
• Pilar

• Truchas
Espanola -Hernandez •   • Chimayo

• Santa Fe
• Galisteo

• Albuquerque

• Caballo
• Silver City   • Cloudcroft

NEW MEXICO

New Mexico

ALBUQUERQUE

Adobe & Roses

1011 Ontega NW, 87114
(505) 898-0654

An adobe hacienda on 2 acres in Albuquerque's North Valley, featuring a casually elegant and spacious suite with private entrance, fireplace, piano, kitchen, big windows overlooking the gardens and horse pasture. Two interior rooms with shared bath are also available. A quiet, romantic place to visit.

Host: Dorothy Morse
Singles: 1 (SB) $30
Doubles: 2 (1 PB; 1 SB) $40-60 & up
Type of Beds: 2 Twin; 2 Double; Rollaways
Continental Breakfast
Credit Cards: No
Notes: 2, 5, 6, 8, 9, 10, 12

B&B New Mexico #401

Box 2805, Santa Fe, 87504
(505) 982-3332

There's a magnificent view of the Sandia Mountains and city lights from this home located on the west side of town near the new hospital.

Doubles: 1 (PB) $40
Type of Beds: 1 Double
Continental Breakfast
Credit Cards: No

The Corner House

9121 James Place NE, 87111
(505) 298-5800

Jean welcomes you to her Southwestern-style home, decorated in a delightful mix of antiques and family mementos. The Corner House is located in a quiet residential neighborhood minutes from the Sandia Mountains and convenient to Old Town, Santa Fe, and many Indian pueblos.

Host: Jean Thompson
Doubles: 2 (1 PB; 1 SB) $35-45
Type of Beds: 2 Twin; 1 King
Full Breakfast
Credit Cards: No
Notes: 2, 4, 5, 6 (inquire), 8, 9, 10, 12, 13, 14

Tramway Vista

B&B Rocky Mountains.
Box 804, Colorado Springs, CO, 80901
(719) 630-3433

Southwest charm with mountain and city views. King room with private bath and sun room with hot tub. Two more guests can be accommodated in a second modest room. Near mountains, close to hiking, stables, golf, and Albuquerque's Old Town, with its shopping and museums. Full breakfast. $45-50.

CABALLO

B&B New Mexico #501

Box 2805, Santa Fe, 87504
(505) 982-3332

View Caballo Lake State Park and dam from the porch. Historic mining towns and hot-spring baths are close by; charter fishing, paddle and power-boat rentals are available.

6 Pets welcome: 7 Smoking allowed: 8 Children welcome: 9 Social drinking allowed: 10 Tennis available: 11 Swimming available: 12 Golf available: 13 Skiing available: 14 May be booked through travel agents

Doubles: 1 (PB) $55
Type of Beds: 1 Queen
Continental Breakfast
Credit Cards: No

CHIMAYO

La Posada De Chimayo

Box 463, 87522
(505) 351-4605

A cozy, comfortable adobe inn in a tradition-al northern New Mexico village famous for its tradition of fine Spanish weaving and its beautiful old church, El Santuario. Thirty miles north of Santa Fe on the High Road to Taos.

Host: Sue Farrington
Suites: (sitting room, bed, bath) $55-75
Type of Beds: 2 Double
Full Breakfast
Minimum stay holidays: 2-3
Credit Cards: A, B
Notes: 2, 5, 6 (with advance notice), 7, 8 (over 12), 9

CLOUDCROFT

B&B New Mexico #504

Box 2805, Santa Fe, 87504
(505) 982-3332

Large, comfortable log cabin nestled in the Sacramento Mountains with a whispering pine-tree forest surrounding it. Fireplace in living room; within ten miles of local skiing; hunting and fishing. White Sands National Park is within twenty miles.

Doubles: 5 (SB) $50-65
Type of Beds: 2 Twin; 2 Double; 2 Queen; 2 Daybeds
Continental Breakfast
Credit Cards: No

ESPANOLA

B&B New Mexico #260

Box 2805, Santa Fe, 87504
(505) 982-3332

This simply elegant adobe casita is nestled in the pink cliffs of northern New Mexico. It's filled with local handmade crafts and furni-ture; high beamed ceiling; Talevera tile and pine floors. Located near Espanola, halfway between Santa Fe and Taos, the house is within a short walk of the Chama River.

Doubles: 1 (PB) $61
Type of Beds: 2 Twin or 1 King
Full Breakfast
Credit Cards: No

La Puebla House

Rt. 3, Box 172A, 87532
(505) 753-3981

Opened in 1981, this traditional adobe with flagstone floors, vigas, and latillas, is a lovely country setting from which to explore the many attractions of northern New Mexico. Nearby are Indian pueblos and ruins, the Santa Fe opera, and the many attractions of Santa Fe, Taos, Abiquiu, and the Espanola Valley.

Host: Elvira Bain
Singles: 2 (SB) $23
Doubles: 4 (SB) $40
Continental Breakfast
Credit Cards: No
Notes: 2, 5, 6 (outside), 8, 9

GALISTEO

The Galisteo Inn

Box 4, 87540
(505) 982-1506

Visit our 200-year-old adobe hacienda in the beautiful countryside of northern New Mexico; enjoy our hot tub, sauna, pool, bicycles, and horseback riding. Our dinners feature creative southwestern cuisine. Din-ner is served nightly except for Monday and Tuesday from May though September. Reservations required.

Hosts: Dorna Andersen & Suzanne Chavez
Doubles: 10 (8 PB; 2 SB) $60-150
Type of Beds: 3 Twin; 4 Double; 4 Queen; 2 King
Continental Breakfast
Credit Cards: A, B
Notes: 2, 4, 5, 9, 11

NOTES: Credit cards accepted: A Master Card; B Visa; C American Express; D Discover Card; E Diners Club; F Other: 2 Personal checks accepted: 3 Lunch available: 4 Dinner available: 5 Open all year

HERNANDEZ

Casa del Rio

Box 92, 87532
(505) 753-2035

Casa del Rio is a private adobe guest house furnished with local handmade furniture and crafts, plus a beautiful Kiva fireplace. Set amid the pink cliffs of northern New Mexico, we are within a half hour of Santa Fe, Taos, and Los Alamos.

Hosts: Eileen & Mel Vigil
Doubles: 1 (PB) $61
Full Breakfast
Credit Cards: A, B
Notes: 2, 9, 14

PILAR

The Plum Tree

Box 1-A, Pilar, 87531
(800) 678-7586

Located in Pilar — a centuries-old village along the banks of the Rio Grande — between the cultural centers of Taos and Santa Fe. Hike the river in the Rio Grande Gorge or the mountains of Sangre de Cristo. We are centrally located for going to Indian Pueblors or natural hot springs. Join us for summer fine arts workshops, fall nature studies, and winter skiing and snow picnics.

Hosts: Dick Thibodeau & Robin Sandeen
Doubles: 5 (3 PB; 2 SB) $22-45
Type of Beds: 4 Twin; 5 Double
Continental Breakfast
Credit Cards: A, B
Notes: 2, 5, 8, 9, 11, 13, 14

RANCHOS DE TAOS

Whistling Waters

Talpa Route, Box 9, 87557
(505 758-7798

Old adobe hacienda and furniture/pottery gallery. Two courtyards, cottonwoods, stream, six fireplaces, vigas, arched door-ways. Furnished in early southwest-primitive antiques. Located in old, quiet Spanish community at the edge of Taos, with mountain views. Skiing, hunting, fishing near.

Hosts: Al & Jo Hutson
Doubles: 4 (PB) $45-75
Type of Beds: 4 Double
Full Breakfast
Minimum stay holidays: 3
Credit Cards: No
Notes: 2, 5, 8 (over 10), 9, 10, 11, 12, 13, 14

SANTA FE

B&B New Mexico #101

Box 2805, 87504
(505) 982-3332

This house is ideally located four blocks from downtown, close to the galleries, shops, and museums and just fourteen miles from Santa Fe Ski Basin. One block from the municipal pool, sports complex, and tennis courts.

Doubles: 2 (PB) $50-60
Type of Beds: 2 Twin; 1 King
Continental Breakfast
Credit Cards: No
Notes: 10, 11, 13

Casa De La Cuma Bed & Breakfast

105 Paseo De La Cuma, 87501
(505) 983-1717

Located on a hill with mountain views, we are close to the downtown plaza, shopping, restaurants, galleries, and museums. City sports facility across the street. A special continental breakfast awaits our guests in the sun room or the patio. A fireplace is in the guests' common room. Enjoy our Southwest sunsets, too. Bienvenidos!

Hosts: Norma & Al Tell
Singles: 1 (PB) $95
Doubles: 2 (SB) $65
Type of Beds: 2 Twin; 1 Double; 1 Queen; 1 King
Continental-plus Breakfast

Credit Cards: No
Closed Dec. 15 - Jan. 31
Notes: 2, 8 (12 and over), 9, 10, 11, 12, 13, 14

Dunshee's

986 Acequia Madre, 87501
(505) 982-0988

A romantic adobe getaway in the historic eastside, about a mile from the plaza. Your suite includes a living room and bedroom with Kiva fireplaces, antiques, folk art, fresh flowers, homemade cookies, refrigerator, private bath, and patio. Gourmet breakfast. Brochure available.

Host: Susan Dunshee
Doubles: 1 (PB) $72-82
Type of Beds: 1 Double
Full Breakfast
Minimum stay weekends & holidays: 2
Credit Cards: A, B
Closed Christmas
Notes: 2, 8, 9

Grant Corner Inn

El Paradero

200 W. Manhattan, 87501
(505) 988-1177

Just a short walk from the busy plaza, this 200-year-old Spanish farmhouse was restored as a charming twelve room South-

western inn. Enjoy a full gourmet breakfast, caring service, and a relaxed friendly atmosphere. The inn offers lots of common space, and a patio for afternoon tea and snacks.

Hosts: Thom Allen & Onida MacGregor
Doubles: 12 (8 PB; 4 SB) $38-95
Type of Beds: 3 Twin; 9 Queen; 3 King
Full Breakfast
Credit Cards: A, B
Notes: 2, 5, 6, 8 (over 4), 9, 10, 11, 12, 13 (17 mi.), 14

Grant Corner Inn

122 Grant Avenue, 87501
(505) 983-6678

An exquisite colonial manor home in downtown Santa Fe with an ideal location just two blocks from the historic plaza, the inn nestles among intriguing shops, restaurants, and galleries. Each room is appointed with antiques and treasures from around the world: antique quilts, brass and four-poster beds, armoires, and art work. Private phones, cable television, and ceiling fans. Complimentary wine is served in the evening.

Hosts: Louise Stewart & Pat Walter
Singles: 2 (1 PB; 2 SB) $49.33
Doubles: 11 (6 PB; 5 SB) $109.62-120.59
Type of Beds: 7 Twin; 2 Double; 3 Queen; 4 King
Full Breakfast
Credit Cards: A, B
Closed January
Notes: 2, 7, 8, 10, 11, 12, 13

Inn on the Alameda

303 East Alameda, 87501
(505) 984-2121

This delightful 38-room European-style small hotel is a stone's throw from Canyon Road and the Plaza. Handcrafted rooms, splendid breakfast buffet, and intimate library with fireplace and full-service bar.

Host: Gil Martinez
Singles: 12 (PB) $80-115
Doubles: 26 (PB) $90-125
Type of Beds: 26 Queen; 12 King
Continental Breakfast
Credit Cards: A, B, C
Notes: 2, 5, 6, 7, 8, 9, 10, 11, 12, 14

NOTES: Credit cards accepted: A Master Card; B Visa; C American Express; D Discover Card; E Diners Club; F Other: 2 Personal checks accepted: 3 Lunch available: 4 Dinner available: 5 Open all year

Preston House

106 Faithway Street, 87501
(505) 982-3465

Located downtown in a quiet garden setting, where guest may enjoy breakfast and afternoon tea on the flagstone patio among blooming lilacs or by the glowing pinon fire in the parlor. Antiques, stained-glass windows, freshly baked breads, and personalized service complete the Preston House experience.

Host: Signe Bergman
Doubles: 9 (7 PB; 2 SB) $45-125
Type of Beds: 3 Twin; 2 Double; 6 Queen; 2 King
Continental Breakfast
Credit Cards: A, B, C
Notes: 2, 5, 8 (6 and over), 9, 10, 11, 12, 13, 14

Preston House

Pueblo Bonito Bed & Breakfast Inn

138 W. Manhattan, Box 5679, 87502
(505) 984-8001

A 100-year-old adobe estate, just three blocks from the historic plaza. Private baths, fireplaces, Southwestern decor — the ultimate in Santa Fe charm! Experience old Santa Fe, with vigas, santos, sand paintings, hardwood floors, and flagstone pathways.

Hosts: Herb & Amy Behm
Doubles: 15 (PB) $50-125
Type of Beds: 2 Double; 13 Queen
Continental Breakfast
Credit Cards: A, B
Notes: 2, 5, 7, 8, 9, 10, 11, 12, 13, 14

Rocky Mt. #112

B&B Rocky Mountains.
Box 804, Colorado Springs, CO, 80901
(719) 630-3433

A handsome one-room adobe guest house with king bed, fireplace, and Mexican-tiled private bath. One resident outside dog. Located between Santa Fe and Taos a stone's throw from the Chama River. Arabian horses are raised on the farm, and boarding is available for guest horses. Full breakfast is served at the main house. $61.

Sunset House

436 Sunset, 87501
(505) 983-3523

Pueblo-style home located four blocks from downtown, close to galleries, shops, museums. The ambience is focused on warth and friendliness in an artistic atmosphere of quiet and mountain views.

Hosts: Jack & Gloria Bennett
Doubles: 2 (PB) $55-70
Type of Beds: 2 Twin; 1 Queen
Continental Breakfast
Credit Cards: A, B, C
Notes: 2, 5, 9, 10, 11, 12, 14

SILVER CITY

Bear Mountain Guest Ranch

Box 1163, 88062
(505) 538-2538

Two-story ranch house, one cottage, five-bedroom house available for guests. Elevation 6250 feet; air-conditioning unnecessary. Pinyon-juniper area. Ranch features home cooking, tours, bird watching, wild plant identification, ghost towns, archaeological sites, and prehistoric primitive pottery workshops. Rate includes breakfast, sack lunch, and dinner.

Host: Myra B. McCormick
Doubles: 16 (PB) $51.45-84.50
Type of Beds: 2 Twin; 14 Double
Credit Cards: No
Notes: 2, 3, 4, 5, 6, 7 (limited), 8, 9, 12

TAOS

B&B New Mexico #201

Box 2805, Santa Fe, 87504
(505) 982-3332

Each room in this charming home features a Kiva fireplace, private bath, and private entrance. Magnificent view of Taos mountains. Guests may use the living room with fireplace, dining room, and sun room, all with wood beamed ceilings. Brick portico, side garden, and rear redwood deck with outdoor hot tub.

Doubles: 4 (PB) $55-80
Type of Beds: 4 Twin (or 2 King); 1 Queen; 1 King
Full Breakfast
Credit Cards: No

B&B New Mexico #204

Box 2805, Santa Fe, 87504
(505) 982-3332

This adobe home is over 100 years old except for the new second story that was constructed in the old manner. Large collection of fine art. Most rooms have a small refrigerator, all have TV, and most have a VCR. During warm weather, breakfast is served on a colorful patio.

Doubles: 7 (PB) $45-85
Continental Breakfast
Credit Cards: No

The Brooks Street Inn

119 Brooks Street, Box 4954, 87571
(505) 758-1489

Selected as one of the ten best inns of North America for 1988 by "Country Inns" magazine, we're casual, fun, and just a short walk from the plaza. Our rambling main house and charming guest house feature fireplaces, reading nooks, and private baths.

Hosts: Susan Stevens & John Testore
Doubles: 6 (PB) $65.47-98.21
Type of Beds: 3 Twin; 2 Double; 5 Queen
Continental Breakfast
Credit Cards: A, B
Notes: 2, 5, 8 (over 5), 9, 13, 14

Hacienda del Sol

109 Mabel Dodge Lane, Box 177, 87571
(505) 758-0287

Once part of art patroness Mabel Dodge Luhan's estate, this spacious adobe adjoins 95,000 acres of Taos Pueblo Indian Land, providing a majestic view of Taos Mountain. Just north of Taos Plaza. Most rooms feature Kiva fireplaces and private baths.

Hosts: Carol & Randy Pelton
Doubles: 6 (4 PB; 2 SB) $38.20-103.68
Type of Beds: 2 Twin; 3 Double; 3 Queen; 1 King
Continental Breakfast
Credit Cards: A, B
Notes: 2, 5, 8, 9, 10, 11, 13, 14

La Posada de Taos

309 Juanita Lane, Box 1118, 87571
(505) 758-8164

La Posada de Taos offers guests modern comforts in a provincial adobe inn with an atmosphere of friendliness that truly makes the word *guest* valid. The hospitality is highly personal, unique, and will bring you back to Taos again.

Host: Sue Smoot
Doubles: 5 (PB) $42-80
Type of Beds: 2 Twin; 2 Double; 1 Queen; 1 King
Full Breakfast

NOTES: Credit cards accepted: A Master Card; B Visa; C American Express; D Discover Card; E Diners Club; F Other: 2 Personal checks accepted: 3 Lunch available: 4 Dinner available: 5 Open all year

Minimum stay May-Oct. weekends: 2 ; holidays: 3
Credit Cards: No
Notes: 2, 5, 6, 7, 8, 9, 10, 11, 12, 13

Mabel Dodge Luhan House

Box 3400, 87571
(505) 758-9456

A national and state historic site on 5 acres bordered by the Taos Pueblo Reservation on the north and east and well within walking distance of town. The house is sequestered behind an adobe wall whose gates are part of the original St. Francis Church in Ranchos de Taos. Huge cottonwood, beech, and elm strees shade the house and flagstone placita. All main rooms have ceilings of viga and latia construction, arched Pueblo-style doorways and fireplaces, hand-carved doors, and dark hardwood floors.

Hosts: George Otero & Susan Cook
Doubles: 10 (4 PB; 6 SB) $55-95
Type of Beds: 6 Twin; 6 Double
Full Breakfast
Credit Cards: A, B
Notes: 2, 3, 5, 6, 7 (limited), 8, 9, 10, 11, 12, 13

Mabel Dodge Luhan House

Rocky Mt. #46

B&B Rocky Mountains.
Box 804, Colorado Springs, CO, 80901
(719) 630-3433

A lovely two-bedroom suite with private bath, a large living room, and enclosed sun porch. High vigaed ceiling, Persian rug, artwork, wood stove, cable TV; crib available. Lovely private patio and semi-private entrance. Full breakfast. $70.

Rocky Mt. #95

B&B Rocky Mountains.
Box 804, Colorado Springs, CO, 80901
(719) 630-3433

An elegant location if you want a king bed and hot tub in your room under the skylight! This house is a 200-year-old adobe hacienda on the outskirts of Taos. Other rooms are available, four of which have fireplaces. Two resident cats. All rooms have private baths, private entrances, plus hors d'oeurves or pastries made by your chef host. Full gourmet breakfast. $60-95.

TRUCHAS

Rancho Arriba

Box 338, 87578
(505) 689-2374

A European-style B&B with an informal and tranquil atmosphere. This traditional adobe hacienda is located on an historic Spanish land grant. Spectacular mountain view in every direction, amid colonial villages featuring traditional arts and architecture. Adobe churches, hand weaving, wood carving, quilting.

Host: Curtiss Frank
Doubles: 4 (SB) $35-50
Type of Beds: 4 Double
Full Breakfast
Credit Cards: No
Notes: 2, 4, 5, 7 (outside), 8, 9, 13

6 Pets welcome: 7 Smoking allowed: 8 Children welcome: 9 Social drinking allowed: 10 Tennis available: 11 Swimming available: 12 Golf available: 13 Skiing available: 14 May be booked through travel agents

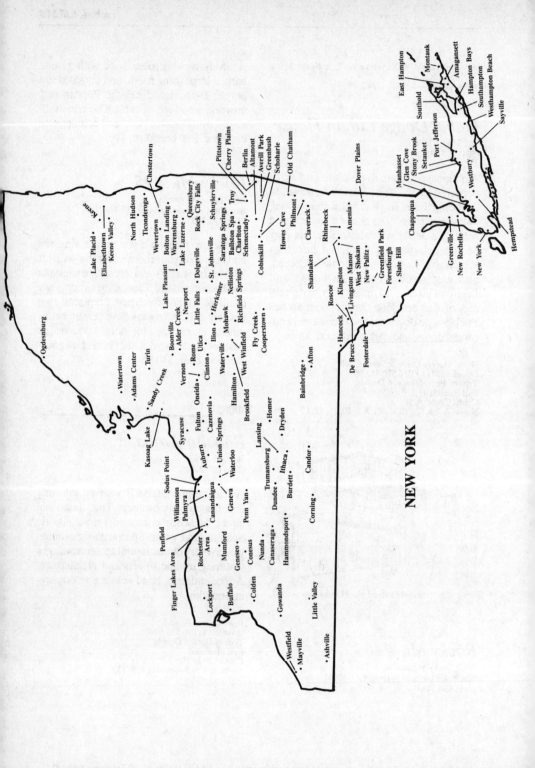

NEW YORK

New York

ADAMS CENTER

Elaine's B&B Service #1
143 Didama Street, Syracuse, 13224
(315) 446-4199

Sprawling farmhouse with two large guest rooms sharing a brand-new bath. Your hostess makes and sells quilts and pillows, does quilling and other crafts. Only ten minutes to downtown Watertown; under five minutes to Rt. 81.

Doubles: 2 (SB) $32-42
Type of Beds: 2 Twin; 1 Double
Continental Breakfast
Credit Cards: No

AFTON

Jericho Farm Inn
Bed & Breakfast Leatherstocking
389 Brockway Road, Frankfort, 13340
(315) 733-0040

Charming B&B accommodations on the picturesque Susquehanna River, handy for fishermen and hunters, golf enthusiasts, or vacationers. Five minutes from I-88, halfway between Oneonta and Binghampton, this home features a grand common room with generous fireplace and canopy bedroom suite. $35-95.

Full Breakfast
Credit Cards: No
Notes: 7, 8 (under 3), 12, 13 (XC)

ALDER CREEK

Alder Creek Country Inn
Bed & Breakfast Leatherstocking
389 Brockway Road, Frankfort, 13340
(315) 733-0040

This century-old colonial manor on a 360-acre estate reflects charm and comfort, with plenty of activities to keep you happily occupied. Golf and cross-country skiing are at the doorstep; Turin, Old Forge, and the Adirondacks are nearby. $35-95.

Continental Breakfast
Credit Cards: No
Notes: 4, 7, 13 (XC)

ALTAMONT

American Country Collection 020
984 Gloucester Place
Schenectady, N.Y., 12309
(518) 370-4948

This home, the site of the first town meeting of Guilderland, was built in 1765. It served as a tavern during colonial days and is now on the state and national historic registers. Situated at the base of the Helderburg Mountains on 6 acres of grounds that include lawns, a tennis court, a gazebo, large red barns, and a flowing brook.

Doubles: 4 (S2B) $45-60
Type of Beds: 3 Double; 1 Queen
Full Breakfast
Credit Cards: No
Notes: 2, 5, 7 (limited), 8, 10, 11, 13

6 Pets welcome: 7 Smoking allowed: 8 Children welcome: 9 Social drinking allowed: 10 Tennis available: 11 Swimming available: 12 Golf available: 13 Skiing available: 14 May be booked through travel agents

American Country Collection 045

984 Gloucester Place
Schenectady, N.Y., 12309
(518) 370-4948

This 75-year-old colonial is just twenty miles from the state capital, situated well back from the road on 15 acres that include lawns, barns, a swimming pool, patio, and orchards. Convenient access to both Albany and Schenectady; seven miles from Union College, fifteen to Albany Medical Center; forty to Saratoga Springs.

Doubles: 2 (SB) $45
Type of Beds: 1 Twin; 1 Double
Full Breakfast
Credit Cards: No
Notes: 2, 7 (limited), 8, 10, 11, 14

AMAGANSETT

Amaganset B&B

Bed & Breakfast of Long Island
Box 392, Old Westbury, 11568
(516) 334-6231

This charming two-story clapboard beach house is two blocks from the ocean. Private entrance. Sleep late and enjoy the breakfast your host has left you on the beautiful deck or in the huge dining/living room. A great location for those without a car, within walking distance of the village. Dog in residence.

Doubles: 2 (1 PB; 1 SB) $85
Type of Beds: 2 Double; 1 Cot; 1 Crib
Continental-plus Breakfast
Credit Cards: No
Closed Oct. - April
Notes: 8, 10, 11, 12

AMENIA

Troutbeck

Box 26, Leedoville Road, 12501
(914) 373-9681

Troutbeck is a world-class country inn with a regional four-star rating for its cuisine. Indoor (covered and heated) and outdoor pools, tennis courts, 442 acres, and a reputation for relaxed, attentive service. Just 2.25 hours from midtown New York City. Open only on weekends.

Hosts: Jim Flaherty & Kathy Robinson
Doubles: 34, $575-790/couple. Includes all meals from Fri. P.M.-Sunday 2:00 P.M.
Type of Beds: 12 Double; 22 Queen
Full Breakfast Sunday; Continental on Saturday
Credit Cards: C
Closed Weekdays and Christmas weekend
Notes: 2, 3, 4, 7, 8 (over 12), 9, 10, 11, 12, 13

ASHVILLE

Green Acres Bed & Breakfast

RD 1, 14710
(716) 782-4254

Green Acres features include hand-hewn beams, stone fireplaces, canopy beds, and antiques. We also have a heated pool, wooded hiking and cross-country trails, and a fish pond. Gourmet breakfast and satellite TV.

Hosts: Lowell & Mary Ann Green
Singles: 1 (SB) $40
Doubles: 2 (SB) $55
Type of Beds: 2 Twin; 1 Double
Full Breakfast
Credit Cards: No
Notes: 2, 5, 8, 10, 11, 12, 13

AUBURN

Fay's Point Beachhouse

RD 1, Box 147A, 13021
(315) 253-9525

Magnificent 1910 Adirondack cottage lodge near Owasco Lake. Spacious rooms, excellent craftsmanship, high-quality furnishings. Each room has picture windows overlooking the lake and double French doors opening onto a large screened porch filled with an-

NOTES: Credit cards accepted: A Master Card; B Visa; C American Express; D Discover Card; E Diners Club; F Other: 2 Personal checks accepted: 3 Lunch available: 4 Dinner available: 5 Open all year

tique wicker and plants. No smoking, no children under 12, no pets.

Host: Janet Rhodes
Doubles: 2 (private half baths) $75
Type of Beds: 2 Twin; 1 Queen
Continental-plus Breakfast
Credit Cards: No

AVERILL PARK

Ananas Hus Bed & Breakfast

Route 3, Box 301, 12018
(518) 766-5035

The Tomlinsons' hillside ranch home, located in West Stephentown on thirty acres, offers a panoramic view of the Hudson River Valley, natural beauty, and tranquility, plus patio dining in summer and the warmth of a fireplace in winter. Skiing and culture abound in nearby western Mass. and the Capitol District of New York State.

Hosts: Thelma & Clyde Tomlinson
Doubles: 3 (SB) $42.80-53.50
Type of Beds: 2 Twin; 2 Double
Full Breakfast
Minimum stay weekend holidays: 2
Credit Cards: No
Closed Christmas Day
Notes: 2, 8 (over 12), 9, 11, 12, 13

The Gregory House

Rt. 43, Box 401, 12018
(518) 674-3774

A charming blend of old and new, this country inn is just minutes east of Albany. Four candlelit dining rooms offer gourmet dinners as well as your included continental breakfast. A common room with fireplace is available for socializing, and an in-ground pool and patio welcome visitors in the summer. Summer theater, mountain trails, golf, skiing, historic tours, and more are nearby.

Hosts: Bette & Bob Jewell
Doubles: 12 (PB) $50-70

Type of Beds: 1 Twin; 2 Double; 9 Queen
Continental Breakfast
Credit Cards: A, B, C, E
Notes: 2, 4, 5, 7, 8 (over 6), 9, 10, 11, 12, 13, 14

BAINBRIDGE

Berry Hill Farm

Bed & Breakfast Leatherstocking
389 Brockway Road, Frankfort, 13340
(315) 733-0040

If you're looking for a serene spot to get away from it all, Berry Hill Farm is perfect for you! A quiet drive along a winding country road just seven miles off I-88 will bring you to this 1820s farmhouse with its extensive acreage. Bedrooms feature crafts and folk art blended with carefully chosen antiques and heirlooms. German, Spanish, Italian, French, and Latin are spoken here. Pet in residence. $35-95.

Full Breakfast
Credit Cards: No
Notes: 7, 8 (under 3), 13 (XC)

BALLSTON SPA

American Country Collection 009

984 Gloucester Place
Schenectady, N.Y., 12309
(518) 370-4948

A Second Empire Victorian in the historic district of this tiny village. The B&B section of the house has a private entrance, guest living room with fireplace, porch, dining room, and kitchen. Four miles to Saratoga Springs; twenty-five to Albany; fifty to Lake George. Local cross-country skiing areas.

Doubles: 3-5 (2 PB; 3 SB) $55-95
Type of Beds: 3 Double; 2 Queen
Full Breakfast
Credit Cards: No
Notes: 2, 5, 8 (over 12), 13 (XC), 14

6 Pets welcome: 7 Smoking allowed: 8 Children welcome: 9 Social drinking allowed: 10 Tennis available: 11 Swimming available: 12 Golf available: 13 Skiing available: 14 May be booked through travel agents

BERLIN

The Sedgwick Inn
Route 22, 12022
(518) 658-2334

An historic colonial inn located on 12 acres in the scenic Taconic Valley, beautifully furnished with antiques. We are close to the Williamstown Theater, the Tanglewood Festival, other Berkshire attractions, and both downhill and cross-country skiing. We have a renowned restaurant and a small motel unit behind the main house.

Hosts: Robert & Edith Evans
Doubles: 10 (PB) $55-75
Suites: 1 (PB) $90
Type of Beds: 2 Twin; 13 Double; 2 Queen
Full Breakfast
Credit Cards: A, B, C, E
Notes: 2, 3, 4, 5, 6 (motel only), 7, 8, (motel only), 9, 10, 11, 13

The Sedgwick Inn

BOLTON LANDING

Hilltop Cottage B & B
Lakeshore Drive, Box 186, 12814
(518) 644-2492

Hilltop Cottage is a European-style tourist home: clean rooms, shared bath, and ample breakfasts in a safe and comfortable private home. Bolton is in the Lake George Basin, a resort area. We are within walking distance of beaches, marinas, restaurants, museums, and tourist shops.

Hosts: Anita & Charlie Richards
Doubles: 3 (SB) $32.10-42.80
Type of Beds: 3 Doubles; 1 Queen
Full Breakfast
Credit Cards: No
Notes: 2, 5, 8 (over 4), 9, 10, 11, 12, 13

BOONVILLE

Greenmeadow
Bed & Breakfast Leatherstocking
389 Brockway Road, Frankfort, 13340
(315) 733-0040

A Victorian Italianate home situated on a 230-acre family farm south of Boonville. Streams, a pond, and rolling meadowland; perfect for hunters and fishermen — experienced guides available. Families with children are welcome to enjoy the antique and craft shops, fine restaurants, and many outdoor activities in the area. Pet in residence; family rate available. $35-95.

Full Breakfast
Credit Cards: No
Notes: 8 (under 3), 11, 12, 13 (XC)

Millcreek Inn
Bed & Breakfast Leatherstocking
389 Brockway Road, Frankfort, 13340
(315) 733-0040

Millcreek Inn is near the village green in Boonville and is named for the original Millcreek saw and grist mill built in 1796 by the town's first settlers. Sports enthusiasts from fishermen to snow mobilers, woodsmen to cross-country skiers find this the ideal retreat. Boonville has twenty miles of the best-groomed cross-country ski trails in the state, and just up the road are forty-five miles of snow mobile trails. A full breakfast is served. $35-95.

BROOKFIELD

Bivona Hill Bed & Breakfast

Bed & Breakfast Leatherstocking
389 Brockway Road, Frankfort, 13340
(315) 733-0040

This multi-level home is nestled on a hillside with a panoramic view of beautiful Beaver Creek Valley. Guest rooms are spacious, airy, and decorated in a country motif. A queen suite with fireplace and private bath is available; every room offers a spectacular view. Over 130 miles of state-marked and maintained horse trails are available, plus a trail system for snow mobiles, cross-country skiing, and hiking. Near Cooperstown, Colgate University, and Hamilton College. $35-95.

Full Breakfast
Credit Cards: No
Notes: 4, 13 (XC)

BUFFALO

B&B of Niagara Frontier

440 Le Brun Road, 14226
(716) 836-0794

A well-traveled health professional welcomes you to his elegantly furnished home with its parklike grounds. Visit Niagara Falls and the Buffalo area's attractions, yet feel at home away from home. Station pick up is available at extra cost.

Host: Virginia F. Trinidad
Singles: 1 (SB) $35-40
Doubles: 1 (SB) $45-50
Type of Beds: 2 Twin; 1 Queen
Full breakfast weekends; continental weekdays
Credit Cards: No
Notes: 2, 5, 7 (outside), 9, 11, 12, 14

Bryant House

236 Bryant Street, 14222
(716) 885-1540

Stay in a charming Victorian house — a pleasant alternative to commercial accommodations — five minutes to downtown Buffalo and the Canadian border; convenient to excellent theaters, boutiques, restaurants, and Niagara Falls. Our house features antiques and fireplaces; and, your breakfast may be served on our multi-level deck overlooking the garden.

Hosts: John & June Nolan
Doubles: 2 (PB) $39-59
Type of Beds: 2 Twin; 1 Double
Continental Breakfast
Credit Cards: No
Notes: 2 (deposit only), 5, 8, 9,

BURDETT

The Red House Country Inn

Finger Lakes National Forest Picnic Area Rd., 14818
(607) 546-8566

The only residence within 13,000+ acre Finger Lakes National Forest. Twenty-eight miles of hiking and cross-country trails. Near Watkins Glen Gorge, wineries, swimming beach. The house is a completely restored 1840s farmstead with beautifully appointed rooms, a pool, and 5 acres of lawns and gardens. Large breakfast; guest kitchen. Goats and chickens on the property.

Hosts: Joan Martin & Sandy Schmanke
Singles: 1 (S4B) $39
Doubles: 5 (S4B) $65
Type of Beds: 6 Double
Full Breakfast
Minimum stay weekends & holidays: 2
Credit Cards: A, B, C
Closed Thanksgiving & Christmas
Notes: 2, 8 (over 12), 9, 11, 13, 14

CANANDAIGUA

Wilder Tavern

5648 N. Bloomfield Road, 14425
(716) 394-8132

6 Pets welcome: 7 Smoking allowed: 8 Children welcome: 9 Social drinking allowed: 10 Tennis available: 11 Swimming available: 12 Golf available: 13 Skiing available: 14 May be booked through travel agents

An 1829 brick stagecoach inn welcomes travelers to the beautiful Finger Lakes area. Second floor is air-conditioned. Superior breakfasts with homemade breads and preserves. Other meals available by prior arrangement. Summer music festival, winery tours, historic architecture, Sonnenberg Gardens, and antique shops nearby.

Host: Linda C. Swartout
Doubles: 4 (1 PB; 3 SB) $53.50-69.55
Type of Beds: 2 Queen; 2 King
Full Breakfast
Credit Cards: A, B
Closed Christmas
Notes: 2, 3, 4, 8 (over 12), 9, 10, 11, 12, 13, 14

CANASERAGA

The Country House Bed & Breakfast

37 Mill Street, 14822
(607) 545-6439

Sample the heart of New York's Southern Tier with a stay at our century-old Victorian home. On a quiet side street in the charming rural village of Canaseraga, we are just minutes from the best skiing in the state, Letchworth State Park, Corning Glassworks, and numerous places for hunting, fishing, hiking, and scenic solitude.

Hosts: Robert & Renee Coombs
3 Doubles: (SB) $25-45
Type of Beds: 2 Twin; 1 Double; 1 Queen
Full Breakfast
Credit Cards: No
Notes: 2, 5, 6, 7, 8, 9, 10, 11, 12, 13

CANDOR

Edge of Thyme Bed & Breakfast

6 Main Street, 13743
(607) 659-5155

Turn-of-the-century Georgian house with antiques, leaded-glass windowed porch, comfortable atmosphere, and outdoor gardens with pergola. Central to the Finger Lakes, Cornell University, Ithaca College, Watkins Glen, wineries, and Corning Glass.

Hosts: Eva Mae & Frank Musgrave
Singles: 1 (SB) $35-45
Doubles: 6 (2 PB; 4 SB) $50-65
Type of Beds: 2 Twin; 4 Double; 1 Queen
Full Breakfast
Credit Cards: No
Notes: 2, 5, 8, 12, 13 (XC), 14

CAZENOVIA

Brae Loch Inn

5 Albany Street, 13035
(315) 655-3431

Family owned and operated since 1946; originally built in 1805. As close to a Scottish Inn as you will find this far west of Edinburgh! Victorian antiques, mellow tartan plaids, original stained glass, shop featuring Scottish wools and crystal on the premises. All rooms have their own private bath and shower, color TV, air-conditioning, and electric heat. Dinners available in the main-floor dining room.

Hosts: H. Grey & Doris Barr
Doubles: 12 (PB) $62.06-73.83
Type of Beds: 10 3/4 size; 4 Double; 5 King
Continental Breakfast
Minimum stay holidays: 2
Credit Cards: A, B, C, E
Notes: 2, 4, 5, 7, 8, 9, 10, 11, 12, 13, 14

Elaine's B&B Service #2

143 Didama Street, Syracuse, 13224
(315) 446-4199

This 150-year-old Federal colonial has wide plank floors, a graceful curved staircase, two fireplaces, and is decorated with antiques and Oriental carpets. Located on a quiet village street; two-minute walk to college, stores, restaurants, and lake. Resident dog.

Singles: 1 (SB) $32
Doubles: 1 (SB) $37-47
Type of Beds: 3 Twin

Continental Breakfast
Credit Cards: No

CHAPPAQUA

Crabtree's Kittle House

11 Kittle Road, 10514
(914) 666-8044

Built in 1790, Crabtree's Kittle House maintains a distinctive blend of country style and comfort. Only twenty miles from New York City, the inn is also a comfortable base from which to explore Van Cortlandt and Philipsburg Manors, Sunnyside, and Pocantico Hills. Not to be missed are the dinner specialties of the house, including crisp roast duckling and the freshest seafood available. Entertainment on weekends.

Hosts: John & Dick Crabtree
Doubles: 11, $81.55-92.45
Credit Cards: A, B, C, E
Notes: 2, 4, 5, 9, 11, 12

CHARLTON

American Country Collection 087

984 Gloucester Place
Schenectady, N.Y., 12309
(518) 370-4948

A pre-Revolutionary estate on 100 country acres just a few miles west of Saratoga Springs. The brick Federal home was constructed during the late 1700s. Formal gardens, wooded paths, private pond and pond house, stone patio, and lots of woods. Twelve miles from Saratoga Springs; ten to Schenectady. Near Skidmore College and Union College.

Doubles: 1 (PB) $60-85
Type of Beds: 1 Double
Full Breakfast
Credit Cards: No
Notes: 2, 5, 7, 8, 14

CHERRY PLAINS

Mattison Hollow

Covered Bridge
Box 447, Norfolk, CT, 06058
(203) 542-5944

This 1790 colonial, nestled in the New York Berkshires, is very secluded, yet minutes from Tanglewood and summer theaters. Hiking trails, cross-country skiing, and a pond for fishing and skating are available on the grounds. Enjoy a full breakfast and dinner, both made with natural foods.

Doubles: 4 (PB) $100 (dinner included)
Full Breakfast
Credit Cards: A, B, C
Notes: 2, 4, 5, 8, 9, 10, 11, 12, 13 (XC), 14

CHESTERTOWN

Friends Lake Inn

Friends Lake Road, 12817
(518) 494-4751

Located in the Adirondacks, overlooking Friends Lake, the inn is located twenty minutes north of Lake George. Gore Mountain Ski Center is only fifteen minutes away. Breakfast and dinner are served daily. Built in the 1860s as a boarding house, the inn has been completely restored and refurbished.

Hosts: Sharon & Greg Taylor
Singles: 3 (1 PB; 2 SB) $45-105
Doubles: 8 (PB), $70-140
Type of Beds: 4 Twin; 6 Double; 3 Queen
Full Breakfast
Minimum stay weekends:2 ; holidays: 3
Credit Cards: A, B, C,
Open weekends only from Nov.-mid-Dec.
Notes: 2, 4, 5, 7, 8, 9, 10, 11, 12, 13, 14

CLAVERACK

Meadowlark Manor

Box 588, 12513
(518) 851-9808

An 1860 Federal mansion with a traditional decor. The house has six large white pillars and has entertained many guests over the years. Located in Columbia County, it is central to many historic areas and recreational activities.

Host: Noreen Marcincuk
Doubles: 4 (2 PB; 2 SB) $30-77
Type of Beds: 2 Twin; 3 Queen
Full Breakfast
Credit Cards: A, B
Notes: 2, 5, 7, 8, 9, 11, 12, 13, 14

CLINTON

Lewago Hall

Bed & Breakfast Leatherstocking
389 Brockway Road, Frankfort, 13340
(315) 733-0040

This splendid 1855 mansion is in the center of the Clinton Village Historical Restoration Area. Ornate winding staircase, chandelier, carved window cornices, and three marble fireplaces grace the house. Hamilton College and the Kirkland Art Gallery are nearby, as are antique shops and Oneida Silversmiths. Handy to I-90. Continental breakfast; pet in residence; cross-country skiing nearby. $35-95.

The Victorian Carriage House

Bed & Breakfast Leatherstocking
389 Brockway Road, Frankfort, 13340
(315) 733-0040

Your hosts' interests in antiques and interior decorating are combined in this elegant colonial, circa 1873. Gables of diagonal wood and a lovely Victorian garden are just part of the charm of this house filled with family heirlooms and antiques. Hamilton College is located in Clinton. $35-95.

Continental Breakfast
Credit Cards: No
Notes: 4, 13 (XC)

COBLESKILL

The Gables Bed & Breakfast Inn

Bed & Breakfast Leatherstocking
389 Brockway Road, Frankfort, 13340
(315) 733-0040

A turn-of-the-century brick home with an adjacent family homestead. On the Historical Register; Queen Anne towers, gothic gables, sawn bracketure, and gingerbread. Near SUNY Cobleskill, Howe Caverns, Secret Caverns, Cooperstown. $35-90. Senior-citizen discount.

Continental Breakfast
Credit Cards: A, B
Notes: 7, 13 (XC)

COLDEN

Back of the Beyond

7233 Lower East Hill Road, 14033
(716) 652-0427

A charming country mini-estate located in the Boston Hills and ski area of western New York: twenty-five miles from Buffalo and fifty from Niagara Falls. Accommodations are in a separate chalet with three bedrooms, one bath, fully furnished kitchen, dining/living room, piano, pool table, and fireplace. A rustic post-and-beam cottage in the woods will accommodate two more. Stroll through our organic herb, flower, and vegetable gardens, swim in the pond, or hike the woods. Cross-country ski trails on the premises; commercial downhill slopes are only one mile away.

Hosts: Bill and Shash Georgi
Doubles: 3 (S1.5B) $40-45
Type of Beds: 2 Twin; 1 Double; 1 Queen; 1 Futon
Full Breakfast
Credit Cards: No
Notes: 2, 5, 8, 9, 10, 11, 12, 13, 14

NOTES: Credit cards accepted: A Master Card; B Visa; C American Express; D Discover Card; E Diners Club; F Other: 2 Personal checks accepted: 3 Lunch available: 4 Dinner available: 5 Open all year

CONESUS

Conesus Lake B&B

2388 E. Lake Road, 14435
(716) 346-6526

Located lakeside on beautiful Conesus Lake. Overnight free docking, private beach, and picnic facilities are available. Two attractive rooms with spacious decks share a bath with a double whirlpool tub. Near golf, museums, and excellent restaurants. Reservations suggested.

Hosts: Dale & Virginia Esse
Doubles: 2 (SB) $60
Type of Beds: 2 Queen
Full Breakfast
Credit Cards: A, B
Closed Thanksgiving & Christmas
Notes: 2, 5, 9, 11, 12

COOPERSTOWN

Creekside Bed & Breakfast

RD 1, Box 206, 13326
(607) 547-8203

Lovely colonial home offering beautiful furnishings, an elegant atmosphere; five minutes from the Baseball Hall of Fame and Glimmerglass Opera. Acres of lawns and a creek for fishing and swimming. Green Room, elegant bridal chamber, penthouse suite, and honeymoon cottage.

Hosts: Gwen & Fred Ermlich
Doubles: 4 (PB) $58.30-100.70
Type of Beds: 1 Double; 3 Queen
Full Breakfast
Minimum stay holidays: 2; Hall of Fame weekend: 3
Credit Cards: No
Notes: 2, 5, 8, 9, 10, 11, 12, 13

The Inn at Brook Willow

RD 2, Box 514, 13326
(607) 547-9700

An 1885 Victorian country home on 14 acres, with a fine collection of antiques in the main house and three guest rooms in the

"reborn barn." Fresh fruit, garden flowers, and a bountiful breakfast await each guest. Two fireplaces, fields, and meadows relax the traveler. Five minutes to the Baseball Hall of Fame and Otsego Lake.

Hosts: Joan & Jack Grimes
Doubles: (PB) $55-75 (Single rate upon request)
Minimum stay weekends & holidays: 2
Type of Beds: 2 Twin; 1 Double; 3 Queen
Full Breakfast
Credit Cards: No
Notes: 2, 5, 9, 10, 11, 12, 13

The J. P. Sill House

The J. P. Sill House

63 Chestnut Street, 13326
(607) 547-2633

A stately Italianate Victorian built in 1864, with original antiques, finely crafted woodwork, marble fireplaces, etched glass, and carefully reproduced, authentic, hand-printed Victorian wallcoverings. A registered historical building located in the heart of town, within walking distance of shops, museums, and Lake Otsego. Off-street parking.

Hosts: Joyce Bohlman & Bob Douglas
Doubles: 5 (SB) $50-75
Type of Beds: 5 Queen
Full Breakfast

Minimum stay weekends in season: 2; holidays: 3
Credit Cards: A, B
Notes: 2, 4, 5, 9, 10, 11, 12, 13

CORNING

DeLevan House

188 DeLevan Avenue, 14830
(607) 962-2347

Southern Colonial home/ hospitality. Over-looking Corning. Quiet surroundings, out-standing accommodations, complimentary wine.

Host: Mary M. DePumpo
Doubles: 3 (1 PB; 2 SB) $53.50-65.40
Type of Beds: 3 Double
Full Breakfast
Credit Cards: No
Notes: 2, 5, 7, 8 (over 12), 9, 11, 12

Rosewood Inn

134 East 1st Street, 14830
(607) 962-3253

Six elegantly appointed Victorian guest rooms, four with private baths. Generous breakfast served in beautiful paneled dining room. Within walking distance of Corning Glass Center, museums, restored Market Street, restaurants, and shops.

Hosts: Dick & Winnie Peer
Doubles: 6 (4 PB; 2 SB) $65-105
Type of Beds: 1 Twin; 4 Double; 1 Queen
Full Breakfast
Minimum stay on holidays
Credit Cards: A, B, E
Notes: 2, 5, 7, 8, 9

West Wind Farm Bed & Breakfast

RD 3, Box 402A; 14830
(607) 962-3979

Just ten minutes from Corning Painted Post area attractions: glass museum, Corning Glass corporate headquarters, Rockwell Museum, historic Market Street, Dresser Rand corporate headquarters. Convenient-

ly located in the beautiful Finger Lakes region, near Watkins Glen, Ithaca, and local wineries.

Host: G. Lauriston Walsh, Jr.
Doubles: 4 (1 PB; 3 SB) $55-75
Type of Beds: 2 Twin; 3 Double
Full Breakfast
Credit Cards: A, B, C, E
Dog kennel on premises
Notes: 2, 4, 5, 6, 7, 8, 9, 10, 11, 12, 13 (XC)

DE BRUCE

De Bruce Country Inn

De Bruce Road, 12758
(914) 439-3900

In a spectacular 1,000 acre natural setting within the Catskill Forest, overlooking the Willowemoc Trout Stream, the inn offers turn-of-the-century charm and hospitality. Terrace dining, wooded trails, wildlife, pool, sauna, fitness and health, fresh air and mountain water.

Hosts: Ron & Marilyn
Doubles: 15 (PB) From $60/person
Type of Beds: 8 Twin; 15 Double
Full Breakfast
Credit Cards: A, B
Closed: Dec. 15 - April 1 (except for groups)
Notes: 2 (deposit only), 4, 6 (call), 7, 8, 9, 10, 11, 12, 13

DOLGEVILLE

Adrianna Bed & Breakfast

44 Stewart Street, 13329
(315) 429-3249

Adrianna is located just off the New York Thruway at exit 29A, amid glorious views of the Adirondack foothills. Just a short ride to Cooperstown, Saratoga, Syracuse, and Utica areas. A most cozy and hospitable B&B.

Host: Adrianna Naizby
Singles: 1 (SB) $40
Doubles: 2 (1 PB; 1 SB) $45
Type of Beds: 2 Twin; 1 Double; 1 Queen
Full Breakfast
Minimum stay weekends & holidays: 2

NOTES: Credit cards accepted: A Master Card; B Visa; C American Express; D Discover Card; E Diners Club; F Other: 2 Personal checks accepted: 3 Lunch available: 4 Dinner available: 5 Open all year

Credit Cards: A, B
Closed Christmas Eve & Day
Notes: 2, 7, 8 (over 5), 9, 10, 11, 12, 13

DOVER PLAINS

The Mill Farm

66 Cricket Hill Road, 12522
(914) 832-9198

This 1850 rambling colonial makes you feel a welcomed guest. Guests enjoy panoramic views from the large sitting porch. The home is decorated with antique furniture and linens. The setting is real country, yet we are only one and one-half hours north of New York City near the Connecticut line.

Host: Margery Mill
Doubles: 4 (1 PB; 3 SB) $50-90
Type of Beds: 2 Twin; 3 Double
Full Breakfast
Minimum stay weekends and holidays: 2
Credit Cards: No
Married couples only, please
Closed Feb. & March
Notes: 2, 9, 10, 11, 12, 13

DRYDEN

Sarah's Dream

49 W. Main Street, 13053
(607) 844-4321

A place to be coddled. On the National Register of Historic Places, this 1828 homestead, furnished with antiques, is subtly elegant without being pretentious. The beds and breakfasts will make you sigh. Convenient to Ithaca, Cornell, wineries, and the Finger Lakes.

Hosts: Judi Williams & Ken Morusty
Doubles: 8 (4 PB; 4 SB) $40-85
Type of Beds: 4 Twin; 2 Double; 4 Queen
Full Breakfast
Credit Cards: A, B
Notes: 2, 5, 8 (over 10), 9, 10, 11, 12, 13

Spruce Haven B & B

9 James Street, Box 119, 13053
(607) 844-8052

This log home surrounded by tall spruce trees gives you the feeling of being in the woods while still enjoying the advantages of the village. On a quiet street, this warm and friendly home is within twelve miles of Ithaca, Cortland, lakes, golf, skiing, colleges, museums. Restaurants nearby. One night's deposit holds reservations.

Host: Margaret Thatcher Brownell
Singles: 1 (SB) $35 plus tax
Doubles: 1 (SB) $40 plus tax
Type of Beds: 2 Twin; 1 Double
Full Breakfast
Credit Cards: No
Notes: 2, 5, 8, 10, 11, 12, 13

Sarah's Dream

DUNDEE

Elaine's B&B Service #3

143 Didama Street, Syracuse, 13224
(315) 446-4199

On Seneca Lake in the Finger Lakes region, right in vineyard country. This B&B was built as an inn in 1828. Right on the lake! Breakfast is served in the spacious dining room or on the open porch overlooking the lawn and lake.

Doubles: 4 (S2B) $40-50
Type of Beds: 4 Twin; 2 Double
Continental Breakfast
Credit Cards: No
Closed Nov.-April

Lakeside Terrace Bed & Breakfast

660 East Waneta Lake Road
RD 1, Box 197, 14837
(607) 292-6606

Air-conditioned bedrooms on the lake, central to all Finger Lake attractions. Enjoy swimming, fishing, rafting, canoeing, sailing, or just relax and unwind as your mood dictates. Close to Watkins Glen Race Track and Hammondsport wineries.

Hosts: Chris & George Patnoe
Doubles: 3 (SB) $51-55
Type of Beds: 3 Queen
Continental Breakfast
Minimum stay weekends & holidays: 2
Credit Cards: A, B
Notes: 2, 5, 8 (over 10), 11

EAST HAMPTON

Mill House Inn

33 North Main Street, 11937
(516) 324-9766

A 1790 colonial located in "America's most beautiful village." Open all year so you can enjoy lemonade while overlooking the Old Hook windmill or a restful nap in our backyard hammock. In the off-season, enjoy hot cider by the fireplace or a brisk walk to the beach.

Hosts: Barbara & Kevin Flynn
Doubles: 8 (6 PB; 2 SB) $75-135
Type of Beds: 2 Twin; 4 Double; 2 Queen
Full Breakfast
Minimum stay weekends in season: 3; holidays in season: 4; holidays off-season: 2-3
Credit Cards: A, B
Notes: 2, 5, 8 (12 and over), 10, 11, 12

ELIZABETHTOWN

American Country Collection 072

984 Gloucester Place
Schenectady, N.Y., 12309
(518) 370-4948

This house dates back to the early settlement of the town, circa 1775, when it was a sawmill. The B&B, several cottages, and an art studio and gallery are on 2.5 acres bordered on two sides by the Boquet River, a favorite fishing and swimming hole. Near I-87, twenty-six miles from Lake Placid; ten minutes from Lake Champlain; twenty minutes to the ferry to Vermont.

Singles: 1 (SB) $32
Doubles: 4 (3 PB; 1 SB) $64-76
Type of Beds: 2 Twin; 4 Double
Full Breakfast
Credit Cards: No
Notes: 2, 5, 7 (limited), 8, 11, 13, 14

FINGER LAKES AREA

Hill & Hollow

B&B Rochester, Box 444, Fairport, 14450
(716) 223-8877

Beautiful new home tucked into a hollow between two hills. Small pond, peace and quiet, but only twenty minutes from downtown Rochester. Air-conditioning. Two resident cats.

Doubles: 2 (PB) $40-50
Type of Beds: 2 Twin; 1 Double
Full Breakfast
Credit Cards: No
Notes: 2, 5, 8 (older), 9, 10, 11, 12, 13

Lake Keuka Manor

B&B Rochester, Box 444, Fairport, 14450
(716) 223-8877

Gorgeous lakeside cottage with three fireplaces, inlaid wooden floors, solid wood doors, Turkish carpets, grand piano. Daily

NOTES: Credit cards accepted: A Master Card; B Visa; C American Express; D Discover Card; E Diners Club; F Other: 2 Personal checks accepted: 3 Lunch available: 4 Dinner available: 5 Open all year

wine-tasting snacks, summer weekend barbecues. Near wineries, boat launch, restaurants, Watkins Glen.

Doubles: 4 (PB) $80-90
Type of Beds: 2 Twin; 3 Queen
Full Breakfast
Credit Cards: A, B
Notes: 2, 5, 7, 9, 10, 11, 12

On the Beach
B&B Rochester, Box 444, Fairport, 14450
(716) 223-8877

If you took a careful running jump, you could hit the water from this beach-side deck! Three-level chalet-style home two miles from Keuka College, half an hour from Watkins Glen, about an hour from Corning, Ithaca, Rochester, Hammondsport.

Doubles: 4 (SB) $45-55
Type of Beds: 4 Twin; 2 Queen
Full Breakfast
Credit Cards: No
Notes: 2, 5, 9, 10, 11, 12

FLY CREEK

Lost Trolley Farm
Bed & Breakfast Leatherstocking
389 Brockway Road, Frankfort, 13340
(315) 733-0040

This pleasant 100-year-old country farmhouse is situated on 95 acres of fields, wetlands, and woods. See for yourselves where the trolley line was lost forever. Take an early morning walk to enjoy the landscape and view the wildlife in natural surroundings. Near the Baseball Hall of Fame, Farmers Museum, Fenimore House, parks, shops, restaurants. Oneonta and Hartwick Colleges are close by. Pet in residence. $35-95.

Full Breakfast
Credit Cards: No
Notes: 8 (under 3), 13 (XC)

FORESTBURGH

Inn at Lake Joseph
Box 81, Country Rd. 108, 12777
(914) 791-9506

A quiet, secluded 125-year-old Queen Anne mansion surrounded by 2,000 acres of wildlife preserve and forest, with a 250-acre private lake. Once the vacation estate of cardinals Hayes and Spellman, the house now offers swimming, boating, fishing, tennis, cross-country skiing and more on the premises. Both breakfast and dinner are included in the daily rate.

Hosts: Ivan Weinser & Merrill Kramer
Doubles: 9 (PB) $108-198
Type of Beds: 8 Queen; 1 King
Full Breakfast
Credit Cards: A, B, C
Notes: 2, 3, 4, 5, 7, 8, 9, 10, 11, 12, 13, 14

FOSTERDALE

Fosterdale Heights House
RD 1, Box 198, 12726
(914) 482-3369

Circa 1840 country Victorian B&B, just two hours from New York City. Enjoy the parlor with its grand piano; pond; Christmas tree farm; enchanted forest; and bountiful country breakfast. Informal evenings of chamber music and parlor games break out frequently. Free brochure.

Hosts: Roy & Trish Singer
Singles: 2 (SB) $38
Doubles: 10 (1 PB; 9 SB) $52-90
Type of Beds: 8 Twin; 8 Double
Full Breakfast
Minimum stay holidays: 2
Credit Cards: A, B
Notes: 2, 4, 5, 7, 9, 10, 11, 12, 13

FULTON

Battle Island Inn
RD #1, Box 176, 13069
(315) 593-3699

6 Pets welcome: 7 Smoking allowed: 8 Children welcome: 9 Social drinking allowed: 10 Tennis available: 11 Swimming available: 12 Golf available: 13 Skiing available: 14 May be booked through travel agents

Battle Island Inn is a pre-Civil War farm estate that has been restored and furnished with period antiques. The inn is across the road from a golf course that also provides cross-country skiing. Guest rooms are elegantly furnished with imposing high-back beds, TVs, phones, and private baths. Breakfast is always special in our 1840s dining room.

Hosts: Joyce & Richard Rice
Singles: 1 (SB) $48-59
Doubles: 6 (PB) $59-80
Type of Beds: 3 Twin; 4 Double; 1 Queen
Full Breakfast
Credit Cards: A, B
Notes: 2, 5, 8, 9, 12, 13, 14

Battle Island Inn

GENESEO

American House Bed & Breakfast Inn

39 Main Street, 14454
(716) 243-5483

American House is a Victorian home in the heart of the historic village of Geneseo. Nearby attractions include Letchworth State Park, Genesee Country Museum, Conesus Lake, and the National Warplane

Museum. The State University at Geneseo is one block away.

Hosts: Harry & Helen Wadsworth
Doubles: 6 (2 PB; 4 SB) $42.80-64.20
Type of Beds: 2 Twin; 4 Double; 1 Queen
Continental Breakfast
Credit Cards: No
Notes: 2, 5, 7, 8, 9, 10, 11, 12, 14

GENEVA

Geneva On The Lake

1001 Lochland Road, 14456
(315) 789-7190; 1-800-3GENEVA

Geneva On The Lake is a small resort on Seneca Lake in the Finger Lakes wine district. An Italian Renaissance villa offering luxurious suites overlooking a furnished terrace, formal gardens, pool, and lake. "The food is extraordinarily good," writes *Bon Appetit.* Friendly, attentive staff. Awarded AAA four diamonds. Suite rates include continental breakfast, complimentary bottle of wine, fresh fruit, and flowers on arrival, a wine and cheese party on Friday evenings, and a daily copy of the New York *Times.*

Host: Norbert H. Schickel, Jr.
Suites: 29 (PB) $160-324
Type of Beds: 3 Twin; 4 Double; 22 Queen
Continental and Full Breakfast
Minimum stay weekends: 2 if Sat.
Credit Cards: A, B, C, D
Notes: 2, 4, 5, 7, 8, 9, 10, 11, 12, 14

Virginia Deane's Bed & Breakfast

168 Hamilton Street, 14456
(315) 789-6152

Located across from Hobart-William Smith College, with a public tennis court nearby, this room offers two rooms with private or shared bath.

Doubles: 2 (PB or SB) $42.80-48.15
Type of Beds: 2 Double
Continental Breakfast
Credit Cards: No
Notes: 2, 5, 9, 10, 11, 12

GLEN COVE

Le Fleurs #GCB
Bed & Breakfast of Long Island
Box 392, Old Westbury, 11568
(516) 334-6231

This stunning Victorian home has been converted to a spectacular contemporary interior with atriums in the breakfast room so you can enjoy the landscaped gardens and swimming pool. Your hosts are French. Walk to village, Long Island railroad, and fabulous restaurants. Close to Post University, Theodore Roosevelt's home, Vanderbilt Planetarium, Sands Point Preserve.

Doubles: 2 (PB) $68-72
Type of Beds: 2 Double; Cot and Crib
Continental Breakfast
Credit Cards: No
Notes: 5, 8, 9 (limited), 10, 11, 12

Virginia Deane's B&B

GOWANDA

The Teepee
RD 1, Box 543, 14070
(716) 532-2168

This bed and breakfast is operated by Seneca Indians on the Cattaraugus Indian Reservation near Gowanda, New York.

Tours of the reservation and the Amish community nearby are available.

Hosts: Maxwell & Phyllis Lay
Doubles: 3 (SB) $30-35
Type of Beds: 4 Twin; 1 Double
Full Breakfast
Credit Cards: No
Notes: 2, 5, 6, 7, 8, 9, 10, 11, 12

GREENBUSH

American Country Collection 065
984 Gloucester Place
Schenectady, N.Y., 12309
(518) 370-4948

A cheery home on a tree-covered corner lot in a quiet residential area just four miles from downtown Albany. A perfect spot for businessmen and women, it provides a homey atmosphere with lots of privacy, plus the convenience of being within walking distance of the bus stop and a short distance to the train station.

Doubles: 2 (SB) $40
Type of Beds: 1 Queen; 1 King
Continental Breakfast
Credit Cards: A, B, C, D
Notes: 2, 5, 6, 7 (limited), 8, 14

GREENFIELD PARK

Greenfield Polo & Hunt Club
Birchall Road, Box 83, 12435
(914) 647-3240

Located in the foothills of the Catskill Mountains ninety miles northwest of New York City, we offer an atmosphere of relaxed country elegance and conviviality in our ranch house that can accommodate up to twelve guests. We feature English riding over 1,000 acres of cross-country trails and an introduction to the exciting sport of polo. We also have an outdoor swimming pool and tennis courts on the premises. Come join us!

Hosts: Arno, Gina, & J. D. Mares
Singles: 3 (PB) $65
Doubles: 6 (PB) $85
Type of Beds: 2 Twin; 6 Double; 1 Queen
Full or Continental Breakfast
Credit Cards: No
Closed mid-Dec. - mid-April; mid-June - mid-Aug.
Notes: 2, 3, 4, 6, 7 (limited), 8, 9, 10, 11, 12, 13

GREENVILLE

Greenville Arms

South Street, 12083
(518) 966-5219

A Victorian country inn in the northern Hudson River Valley on 2 acres of beautiful grounds with a swimming pool. Old-fashioned country cooking.

Hosts: Laura & Barbara Stevens
Singles: 1 (PB) $60
Doubles: 18 (6 PB; 12 SB) $70-110
Type of Beds: 10 Twin; 17 Double
Full Breakfast
Credit Cards: A, B, C
Closed Nov. 1 - May 1
Notes: 2, 9, 10, 11, 12, 14

Greenville Arms

HAMILTON

Colgate Inn

On the Green, 13346
(315) 824-2300

Tucked away in a pleasant university town overlooking the village green and surrounded by the beauty and history of the Upper Chenango Valley, where you can still delight in the traditional hospitality of yesterday while enjoying the comforts of today.

Singles: 1 (PB) $51.36
Doubles: 43 (PB) $77.04
Type of Beds: 50 Twin; 20 Double
Continental Breakfast
Credit Cards: A, B, C, E
Notes: 2, 4, 5, 7, 8, 9, 10, 11, 12, 13, 14

HAMMONDSPORT

The Bowman House

61 Lake Street, Box 586, 14840
(607) 569-2516

Located in the heart of New York wine country. Pleasant experience in picturesque Hammondsport. Large 1880s Queen Anne Victorian home. Privacy, sitting rooms, library, welcoming touches enhance relaxation after village shopping, visiting wineries, museums, and Finger Lakes. Unique comfort, gracious hosts.

Hosts: Manita & Jack Bowman
Doubles: 4 (2 PB; 2 SB) $50-75
Type of Beds: 2 Double; 2 Queen
Continental-plus Breakfast
Minimum stay holidays: 2
Credit Cards: No
Notes: 2, 5, 9, 10, 12, 13

Laufersweiler's Blushing Rose B&B

11 William Street, 14840
(607) 569-3402

Step back in time in a warm country house filled with antiques. Hammondsport is an historic village with shopping, dining, and great walking. Keuka Lake is just a few doors away; wineries are nearby, plus Corning Glass and Watkins Glen.

Hosts: Ellen & Frank Laufersweiler
Doubles: 4 (PB) $55-60

NOTES: Credit cards accepted: A Master Card; B Visa; C American Express; D Discover Card; E Diners Club; F Other: 2 Personal checks accepted: 3 Lunch available: 4 Dinner available: 5 Open all year

Type of Beds: 2 Double; 1 Queen; 1 King
Full Breakfast
Credit Cards: No
Closed Christmas & Easter
Notes: 2, 5, 8 (over 6), 9, 10, 11, 12

Pleasant Valley Bed & Breakfast
RD #3, Box 69, 14840
(607) 569-3472

Spend a night in a lovely old Victorian home situated in the beautiful Finger Lake country. Places of interest within walking distance include various museums, the Corning Glass Works, wineries, and the shops of the enchanting village of Hammondsport.

Hosts: Jeanne & Tom McCabe
Doubles: 3 (SB) $40-55
Type of Beds: 2 Twin; 1 Double; 1 Queen
Full Breakfast
Credit Cards: No
Notes: 2, 5, 7, 9, 11, 12

HAMPTON BAYS

House on the Water
Box 106, 11946
(516) 728-3560

Ranch house on two acres of garden on Shinnecock Bay. Quiet location. One mile to village, train, and bus. Seven miles to Southampton and Westhampton. Two miles to ocean beaches. Bicycles, wind surfers, pedal boat, barbecue, beach lounges, and umbrellas. German, Spanish, and French spoken.

Host: Mrs. Ute
Doubles: 2 (PB) $60-85
Type of Beds: 2 Twin
Full Breakfast
Minimum stay weekdays: 2; weekends: 3; holidays: 4
Credit Cards: No
Closed Nov. 1-May 1
Notes: 2, 9, 10, 11, 12

HANCOCK

Sunrise Inn B&B
RD, Box 232B, 13856
(607) 865-7254

At this nineteenth-century farmhouse nestled in the Catskills, you will enjoy homey comfort, country tranquility, a gazebo, wraparound porch, library, and wood stove. Awaken to the aroma of homemade soda bread. Browse through a quaint antique shop. Pets in residence. No smoking allowed.

Hosts: Jim & Adele Toth
Singles: 1 (SB) $30
Doubles: 3 (1PB; 2 SB) $35-58
Type of Beds: 1 Twin; 3 Double
Continental Breakfast
Credit Cards: No
Notes: 2, 5, 8, 9, 12

HEMPSTEAD

Duvall Bed & Breakfast
237 Cathedral Avenue, 11550
(516) 292-9219

Charming old Dutch colonial near airports, railroad to New York City (40 minutes), beaches, Adelphi and Hofstra universities, Nassau Coliseum. Furnished with antiques, rooms have air conditioning and color TV. On-premises parking, complimentary wine. Many nearby tourist attractions.

Hosts: Richard & Wendy Duvall
Doubles: 4 (2 PB; 2 SB) $50-75
Type of Beds: 4 Twin; 1 Queen; 1 King
Full Breakfast
Minimum Stay weekends: 2; Holidays: 3
Credit Cards: No
Checks for deposit in advance only; cash or traveler's checks on arrival
Notes: 4, 5, 8, 9, 12

HERKIMER

Bellinger Woods
Bed & Breakfast Leatherstocking
389 Brockway Road, Frankfort, 13340
(315) 733-0040

6 Pets welcome: 7 Smoking allowed: 8 Children welcome: 9 Social drinking allowed: 10 Tennis available: 11 Swimming available: 12 Golf available: 13 Skiing available: 14 May be booked through travel agents

Built in the 1860s, Bellinger Woods is located in the village of Herkimer, nestled along the Mohawk River. It has been carefully restored and furnished with antiques and traditional pieces. The main parlors have working marble fireplaces. Near I-90. $35-95.

Full Breakfast
Credit Cards: No
Notes: 8 (under 3), 13 (XC)

HOMER

David Harum House

80 South Main Street, 13077
(607) 749-3548

Famous Federal period house built circa 1815 located in the historic district. Eleven by thirty-four foot entrance foyer with beautiful spiral staircase. David Harum memorabilia on display. Half mile from I-81.

Hosts: Ed & Connie Stone
Doubles: 2 (1 PB; 1 SB) $28-42
Type of Beds: 2 Double
Full Breakfast
Credit Cards: No
Notes: 2, 5, 8, 9, 10, 11, 12, 13

HOWES CAVE

Cavern View

Bed & Breakfast Leatherstocking
389 Brockway Road, Frankfort, 13340
(315) 733-0040

This Italianate home, built in the 1870s, is located on 47 acres of rolling farmland. Your hosts are former museum curators with extensive knowledge of antiques and genealogy. Cavern View is near the Bramanville Grist Mill, Old Stone Fort, Iroquois Indian Museum, and SUNY Cobleskill, 2.5 miles from I-88 and 1 mile west of Howes Caverns. $35-95.

Full Breakfast
Credit Cards: A, B
Notes: 8 (under 3), 13 (XC)

ILION

The Chesham Place

Bed & Breakfast Leatherstocking
389 Brockway Road, Frankfort, 13340
(315) 733-0040

The Chesham Place was built in 1872 and combines Second Empire and late Victorian Italianate with exquisitely detailed furnishings. Crystal chandeliers, marble fireplaces, stained-glass windows, black-walnut circular staircase. A full breakfast is served. Pet in residence; smoking allowed. $35-95.

ITHACA

Buttermilk Falls Bed & Breakfast

110 E. Buttermilk Falls Road, 14850
(607) 273-3947

This 1814 Federal brick has been the family homestead for five generations. Built at the foot of Buttermilk Falls, where you can swim and hike wooded gorge trails. Just 3.5 miles from Cornell University and Cayuga Lake. Hot whole-grain cereals with fruit and nut toppings are served.

Host: Margie Rumsey
Doubles: 6 (PB) $60-105
Full Breakfast
Credit Cards: A, B (as deposit)
Notes: 2, 5, 7 (limited), 8, 9, 10, 11, 12, 13, 14

Glendale Farm Bed & Breakfast

224 Bostwick Road, 14850
(607) 272-8756

Our large, comfortable home is furnished with antiques, Oriental carpets, and beamed ceilings. During the winter there is always a fire burning in the fireplace. In the summer the large screened porch provides a place to relax with a book or pleasant conversation.

NOTES: Credit cards accepted: A Master Card; B Visa; C American Express; D Discover Card; E Diners Club; F Other: 2 Personal checks accepted: 3 Lunch available: 4 Dinner available: 5 Open all year

Glendale Farm B&B

Near Cornell University and Ithaca College, state parks, wineries, Corning Glass, Cayuga Lake. Close to Watkins Glen Racetrack.

Host: Jeanne Marie Tomlinson
Singles: 6 (2 PB; 4 SB) $60
Doubles: 6 (3 PB; 3 SB) $75
Type of Beds: 3 Twin; 5 Double; 1 King

Full Breakfast
Credit Cards: A, B, C
Notes: 2, 4, 5, 8, 9, 10, 11, 12, 13

Log Country Inn

Box 581, 14851
(607) 589-4771

Enjoy the rustic charm of a log house at the edge of a 7,000-acre state forest. Modern accommodation in the spirit of international hospitality. Three rooms, all-you-can-eat European breakfast. Hiking, skiing, sauna, afternoon tea. Convenient to Ithaca, Cornell, Corning, wineries, and antique shopping.

Host: Wanda Grunberg
Doubles: 3 (1 PB; 2 SB) $40-65
Type of Beds: 2 Twin; 1 Double; 1 Queen
Full Breakfast
Credit Cards: A, B
Notes: 2, 4, 5, 8, 9, 10, 11, 12, 13

Peirce House B&B

218 South Albany Street, 14850
(607) 273-0824

Willard Peirce built this turn-of-the-century downtown residence in a style befitting a proper Victorian family. Our lovingly restored home features period furniture, fireplaces, stained glass, fine woodwork, Oriental rugs, and whirlpool baths. Near numerous state parks, wineries, skiing, and boating. One mile to Cornell, Ithaca College, and Cayuga Lake.

Hosts: Cathy Emilian & Joe Daley
Doubles: 4 (PB) $70-100
Type of Beds: 4 Double
Full Breakfast
Credit Cards: A, B, C
Notes: 2, 5, 9, 10, 11, 12, 13

Peregrine House Victorian Inn

140 College Avenue, 14850
(607) 272-0919

An 1874 brick home with sloping lawns and pretty gardens, just three blocks from Cornell University. Down pillows, fine linens, and air-conditioned bedrooms with Victorian decor. In the center of Ithaca, one mile from Cayuga Lake with its boating, swimming, summer theater, and wineries. Wonderful breakfasts, free snacks.

Hosts: Nancy Falconer & Susan Vance
Doubles: 8 (PB) $69-99
Type of Beds: 2 Twin; 4 Double; 3 Queen
Full Breakfast

6 Pets welcome: 7 Smoking allowed: 8 Children welcome: 9 Social drinking allowed: 10 Tennis available: 11 Swimming available: 12 Golf available: 13 Skiing available: 14 May be booked through travel agents

Credit Cards: A, B
Notes: 2, 5, 7, 8 (over 10), 9, 10, 11, 12, 13, 14

Rose Inn

Box 6576, 14851
(607) 533-7905

An elegant 1840s Italianate mansion on 20 landscaped acres. Fabulous circular staircase of Honduran mahogany. Prix fixe dinner served with advance reservations.

Hosts: Sherry & Charles Rosemann
Doubles: 15 (PB) $85-125
Suites: $150-200
Type of Beds: 2 Twin; 4 Double; 3 Queen; 6 King
Full Breakfast
Minimum stay weekends & holidays: 2
Credit Cards: A, B, C
Notes: 2, 4, 5, 8 (over 12), 9, 10, 11, 12, 13, 14

KASOAG LAKE

JayHawkers Bunkhouse

C.C. Rd., Box B2, Altmar, 13302
(315) 964-2557

Ten miles east of Pulaski, on Rts. 11 and 81. A quiet, rustic getaway retreat in the country, convenient to Lake Ontario; 45 minutes to Syracuse or Watertown. Easy drive to Salmon River; great for snowmobilers and fishermen. Efficiencies sleeping up to six, hot tub, handicap access. Each unit has full kitchen with microwave and fixings for breakfast. Owners raise horses and Australian shepherds.

Hosts: Shirl & R. Guenthner
Cabins: $22/person
Stocked refrigerator
Credit Cards: No

KEENE

The Bark Eater

Box 139, 12942
(518) 576-2221

Originally a stagecoach stopover, the Bark Eater has been in operation since the early 1800s. The atmosphere still reflects these early times, with its wide board floors, stone fireplaces, and rooms filled with antiques.

Hosts: Joe-Pete & Harley Wilson
Singles: 1 (SB) $45
Doubles: 16 (4 PB; 12 SB) $100
Type of Beds: 6 Twin; 8 Double; 2 Queen; 6 King
Full Breakfast
Minimum stay weekends: 2 ; holidays: 3-4
Credit Cards: C
Notes: 2, 4, 5, 7, 8, 9, 10, 11, 12, 13, 14

KEENE VALLEY

Champagnes High Peaks Inn

Rt. 73, Box 701, 12943
(518) 576-2003

A warm and comfortable inn located in the scenic High Peaks region of the Adirondacks. Relax and enjoy the view from our wraparound porch or sit by the large stove fireplace in our spacious living room. Quality meals and genuine hospitality await our guests. Near endless outdoor activity; twenty miles south of Lake Placid and the Olympic facilities there.

Hosts: Norman & Sherry Champagne
Doubles: 8 (2 PB; 6 SB) $55-70
Type of Beds: 4 Twin; 3 Double; 2 Queen; 1 King
Full Breakfast
Credit Cards: A, B
Closed early April & Nov.
Notes: 2, 5, 8, 9, 10, 11, 12, 13

KINGSTON

Rondout B&B

88 W. Chester Street, 12401
(914) 331-2369

Spacious and gracious 1905 mansion on 2 acres in a quiet neighborhood near the historic district, between the Hudson River and the Catskill Mountains. Hearty breakfasts, evening refreshments, hospitable and knowledgeable hosts. Excellent restaurants, cruises, antiques, museums, galleries, theaters, and five colleges are nearby. Kingston, rich in history and architectural variety, is an Urban Cultural Park.

Hosts: Adele & Ralph Calcavecchio
Doubles: 2 (SB) $42.80-58.85
Type of Beds: 2 Double
Full Breakfast
Credit Cards: No
Notes: 2, 5, 8, 9, 10, 11, 12, 14

LAKE LUZERNE

The Lamplight Inn

2129 Lake Avenue, Box 70, 12846
(518) 696-5294

Romantic 1890 Victorian inn. Warm, friendly atmosphere: fireplaces, country breakfasts, freshly ground coffee, antiques, Oriental rugs, chess. Perfect getaway for couples. One block from Lake Luzerne in the southern Adirondacks. Ten minutes to Lake George; twenty to Saratoga Springs.

Hosts: Gene & Linda Merlino
Doubles: 10 (PB) $59-119
Type of Beds: 5 Double; 5 Queen
Full Breakfast
Minimum stay weekends & holidays: 2
Credit Cards: C
Closed Christmas
Notes: 2, 8 (over 12), 9, 10, 11, 12, 13

LAKE PLACID

Highland House Inn

3 Highland Place, 12946
(518) 523-2377

Peaceful central location in the village of Lake Placid. Each room is equally appealing, all having been recently redecorated. The full breakfast includes our special blueberry pancakes. Fully efficient country cottage also available adjacent to inn.

Hosts: Teddy & Cathy Blazer
Singles: 1 (SB) $32-48
Doubles: 8 (6 PB; 2 SB) $43-60
Type of Beds: 10 Twin; 8 Double
Full Breakfast
Minimum stay weekends: 2
Holidays: 3

Credit Cards: A, B
Notes: 2, 5, 7, 8, 9, 10, 11, 12, 13

Interlaken Inn and Restaurant

15 Interlaken Avenue, 12946
(518) 523-3180

A Victorian inn in the heart of Lake Placid featuring a gourmet restaurant and twelve uniquely decorated rooms. The inn has tin ceilings, a cozy fireplace in the living room, lots of lace and charm. Nearby you can enjoy golf, skiing, or any of the pleasures of the Adirondacks.

Hosts: Roy & Carol Johnson
Doubles: 12 (PB) $50-140, plus gratuity
Type of Beds: 2 Twin; 8 Double; 2 Queen; 2 King
Full Breakfast
Minimum stay weekends & holidays: 2
Credit Cards: A, B, C
Closed Nov. and April
Notes: 2, 4, 7, 8 (over 5), 9, 10, 11, 12, 13

Interlaken Inn

Spruce Lodge Bed & Breakfast

31 Sentinel Road, 12946
(518) 523-9350

A large, private home owned by the Wescott family since 1949. Located in Lake Placid, within a ten-mile radius of all area activities.

6 Pets welcome: 7 Smoking allowed: 8 Children welcome: 9 Social drinking allowed: 10 Tennis available: 11 Swimming available: 12 Golf available: 13 Skiing available: 14 May be booked through travel agents

Hosts: Michael & Beth Quinn
Doubles: 6 (1 PB; 5 SB) $39.59
Suite: 1 (PB) $50.29
Type of Beds: 10 Twin; 4 Double
Continental Breakfast
Minimum stay holidays: 2
Credit Cards: A, B
Notes: 2, 5, 8, 9, 10, 11, 12, 13

LAKE PLEASANT

Hummingbird Hill

Bed & Breakfast Leatherstocking
389 Brockway Road, Frankfort, 13340
(315) 733-0040

This rustic lodge is nestled in the Adirondack Mountains, where the hummingbirds migrate in the spring, overlooking Oxbow Lake. One bedroom with private bath and sitting room. A fieldstone fireplace covers one wall of the family room. Just seven miles from Speculator; a pleasant drive from Gore Mountain, Indian Lake, or the Adirondack Museum. Fine dining in nearby restaurants and all the outdoor activity you could want. $35-95. Senior discount available.

Full Breakfast
Credit Cards: No
Notes: 11, 12, 13

LANSING

The Bay Horse

813 Ridge Road, 14482-8805
(607) 533-4612

Victorian home, furnished with antiques. First floor handicap accessible. Afternoon tea is served weekdays from November through April by advance reservation. Stalls available for horses. Finger Lakes region of upstate New York.

Hosts: Mary & David Flinn
Doubles: 5 (SB) From $35-60
Suite: 1 (PB) $70-85
Type of Beds: 4 Twin; 4 Double; 1 Queen; 2 King

Full Breakfast
Credit Cards: A, B, C, D
Notes: 2, 5, 6, 8, 9, 10, 11, 12, 13 (XC), 14

LITTLE FALLS

Buttermilk Bear

Bed & Breakfast Leatherstocking
389 Brockway Road, Frankfort, 13340
(315) 733-0040

A truly charming colonial home nestled on the bluffs overlooking the city of Little Falls. In a quiet residential section, the house is decorated with antique and traditional furnishings, satin oak flooring, Oriental carpeting, and collectible bears. Just off I-90 and the Barge Canal, this is a perfect stop for visiting Herkimer Junior College, Cooperstown, Utica, or the Adirondack Park. Pet in residence. Senior discount available.

Doubles: 1 (SB) $35-95
Full Breakfast
Credit Cards: No
Notes: 13 (XC)

LITTLE VALLEY

Napoli Stagecoach Inn

Napoli Corners, 14755
(716) 938-6735

A real stagecoach inn from 1830-1880. The family room has a fireplace, and the library contains 3,000 volumes. Comfort and easy hospitality are memorable, with access to skiing and golf at Holiday Valley, history at Seneca Indian Museum, culture at Chautauqua Institution, and nature at Allegheny State Park.

Hosts: Marion & Emmett Waite
Doubles: 3 (SB) $27-37.80
Type of Beds: 1 Twin; 2 Double
Full Breakfast
Credit Cards: No
Notes: 2, 4, 5, 8 (10 and over), 10, 11, 12, 13, 14

NOTES: Credit cards accepted: A Master Card; B Visa; C American Express; D Discover Card; E Diners Club; F Other: 2 Personal checks accepted: 3 Lunch available: 4 Dinner available: 5 Open all year

LIVINGSTON MANOR

Lanza's Country Inn
RD 2, Box 446, 12758
(914) 439-5070

Catskill Mountain outdoor enjoyment: rivers, streams, lakes, woods, mountains, country roads, and quaint villages. Comfortable antique-filled rooms, great food. Invigorating, relaxing, with friendly, personal service. You'll love our "Covered Bridge Country."

Hosts: Dick, Pat, & Mickey Lanza
Doubles: 8 (PB) $52-80
Type of Beds: 1 Twin; 5 Double; 1 Queen; 1 King
Full Breakfast
Minimum stay holidays: 2
Credit Cards: A, B, C
Notes: 2, 4, 5, 7, 8, 9, 10, 11, 12, 13

LOCKPORT

Chestnut Ridge Inn
7205 Chestnut Ridge Road, 14094
(716) 439-9124

An 1826 Federal mansion with 8 acres of gardens and lawns, circular staircase, library, fireplaces, and antique furniture. On the historic Niagara frontier, within minutes of Niagara Falls, Canada, and Fort Niagara. Country auctions, lush fruit farms, fairs, summer theaters.

Hosts: Frank & Lucy Cervoni
Suite: 1 (PB) $75-85
Doubles: 2 (PB) $70-75
Type of Beds: 2 Twin; 1 Double; 2 Queen
Full Breakfast
Credit Cards: No
Notes: 2, 3, 5, 8, 9, 10, 11, 12, 13

MANHASSET

The Manor House #MM
Bed & Breakfast of Long Island
Box 392, Old Westbury, 11568
(516) 334-6231

The second oldest house in the area, built in 1840. Huge dining room with three chandeliers and a table that seats thirty, original carved fireplace, original brass door hinges. Walk to the railroad for a quick trip to the city or to local restaurants and movies. Minutes to luxurious shopping in designer boutiques, Bonwit Tellers, Lord & Taylor. Near the U.S. Merchant Marine Academy, North Shore University, and Long Island Jewish hospitals.

Singles: 1 (PB) $65
Doubles: 3 (PB) $75
Type of Beds: 2 Twin; 2 Double; 1 King
Full Breakfast
Credit Cards: No
Notes: 5, 8, 9, 10, 11, 12

Plumbush

MAYVILLE

Plumbush
RD 2, Box 332, 14757
(716) 789-5309

Newly restored circa 1865 Italian villa hilltop country home surrounded by 125 acres. Just one mile from Chautauqua Institute.

6 Pets welcome: 7 Smoking allowed: 8 Children welcome: 9 Social drinking allowed: 10 Tennis available: 11 Swimming available: 12 Golf available: 13 Skiing available: 14 May be booked through travel agents

Bluebirds and wildlife abound. Bicycles available; cross-country ski trail. Sunny rooms, wicker, antiques, and a touch of elegant charm.

Hosts: George & Sandy Green
Doubles: 4 (PB) $55-80
Type of Beds: 2 Twin; 3 Double
Continental Breakfast
Credit Cards: A, B
Notes: 2, 5, 8 (over 12), 9, 10, 11, 12, 13, 14

MOHAWK

Country Hills

Bed & Breakfast Leatherstocking
389 Brockway Road, Frankfort, 13340
(315) 733-0040

A spacious 1860s farmhouse amid rolling lawns and private woods overlooking the Mohawk Valley. Choose between two cozy suites with full baths, complete kitchens, and Murphy beds for children. Nearby attractions include Herkimer Diamonds, Russian Orthodox Seminary, and many Revolutionary historic sites.

Suites: 2 (PB) $35-95
Type of Beds: 1 Double; 1 Queen
Full Breakfast
Credit Cards: A, B
Notes: 8 (under 3), 13

MONTAUK

Greenhedges Oceanside Villa B & B

Essex Street, Box 122, 11954
(516) 668-5013

Two blocks from the public beach, this 1926 brick and stucco Tudor is on a private acre surrounded by green hedges. Sunken living room, cathedral ceilings, two fireplaces, lovely gardens, solarium, gazebo. One block to village. Tennis, restaurants, golf, surfing, fishing, horseback riding, and health spa nearby.

Hosts: Ellie & Warren Adams
Doubles: 3 (PB) $59-96.75
Type of Beds: 2 Queen; 1 King
Continental Breakfast
Minimum stay weekends: 2 ; holidays: 3
Credit Cards: No
Closed mid-Nov.- mid-March
Notes: 2, 7, 8 (over 7), 9, 10, 11, 12, 14

MUMFORD

Genesee Country Inn

948 George Street, 14511
(716) 538-2500

This historic stone mill is located on 6 quiet acres of woods and waterfalls. Lovingly restored, with all timely conveniences and nine individually decorated guest rooms. Many oversized beds; balconies; rooms overlooking water; fireplaces; lots of historic stenciling. Tea and full breakfast are served. Nearby is a museum, fine restaurants. Niagara Falls is one hour away.

Doubles: 9 (PB) $80-95
Full Breakfast
Credit Cards: A, B
Closed Dec. 1 - March 1
Notes: 2, 8, 9, 11, 12, 13

NELLISTON

The Historian

Bed & Breakfast Leatherstocking
389 Brockway Road, Frankfort, 13340
(315) 733-0040

This Victorian stone house, built in 1842, overlooks the Mohawk River and is listed in the National Registry of Historic Homes. Lovingly restored with crystal chandeliers, inside-window shutters, tiled fireplaces, and hand-painted ceilings. A fifty-foot deck overlooks the river. Pet in residence. $35-95.

Full Breakfast
Credit Cards: No
Notes: 7

NOTES: Credit cards accepted: A Master Card; B Visa; C American Express; D Discover Card; E Diners Club; F Other: 2 Personal checks accepted: 3 Lunch available: 4 Dinner available: 5 Open all year

NEW PALTZ

Nana's

54 Old Ford Road, 12561
(914) 255-5678

Nana's B&B is in the Hudson River fruit belt near two beautiful resorts. Enjoy the mountains, three lakes, swimming, boating, hiking, mountain climbing, cross-country skiing, etc. Nana's is in a country setting on 20 acres. Antique furnishings, full country breakfast. Many places of interest nearby.

Host: Kathleen Maloney
Doubles: 2 (SB) $37.45-53.50
Type of Beds: 2 Double
Full Breakfast
Credit Cards: No
Notes: 2, 8, 9, 11, 12, 13

NEWPORT

Roesler's Bed & Breakfast

Bed & Breakfast Leatherstocking
389 Brockway Road, Frankfort, 13340
(315) 733-0040

This Greek Revival mansion, with its circular porch, is adjacent to a private pond and surrounded by maples. North of Herkimer on sprawling farmland adjacent to West Canada Creek, the house is near the Adirondacks. Fishing, hiking, and skiing are within fifteen minutes. Pet in residence. $35-95.

Full Breakfast
Credit Cards: No
Notes: 8 (under 3), 13

NEW ROCHELLE

Rose Hill Guest House

44 Rose Hill Avenue, 10804
(914) 632-6464

This beautiful and intimate French Normandy home's hostess is a real estate agent and bridge Life Master. Weather permitting, enjoy breakfast on the flowered patio or in the chandeliered library/dining room.

Thirty minutes to Manhattan by train or car. Safe parking behind house.

Host: Marilou Mayetta
Doubles: 2 (SB) $48.50-64.65
Type of Beds: 4 Twin; 1 Double
Continental Breakfast
Minimum stay holidays: 2
Credit Cards: No
Notes: 2, 5, 7, 8, 9, 10, 11, 12, 14

NEW YORK

Al B's B&B

B&B Network of NY
134 W. 32nd Street, 10001
(212) 645-8134

Luxury doorman building with courtyard in the heart of midtown on the east side. Minutes from Grand Central Station, United Nations, and Bloomingdale's. Air-conditioning, cable TV, laundry facilities.

Doubles: 1 (PB) $90
Type of Beds: 2 Twin
Continental Breakfast
Credit Cards: No
Notes: 5, 8

Alden's B&B

B&B Network of NY
134 W. 32nd Street, 10001
(212) 645-8134

Nicely furnished loft in an eighteenth-century warehouse. Original wooden beams and windows, cast-iron columns, exposed brick. TV, stereo, air-conditioning, ceiling fans, laundry facilities. Only one-half block from historic South Street Seaport. Near Wall Street, Battery Park, Statue of Liberty, and Chinatown.

Doubles: 1 (SB) $60-80
Type of Beds: 2 Twin
Continental Breakfast
Credit Cards: No
Notes: 5, 7, 8

Ariel's B&B

B&B Network of NY

6 Pets welcome: 7 Smoking allowed: 8 Children welcome: 9 Social drinking allowed: 10 Tennis available: 11 Swimming available: 12 Golf available: 13 Skiing available: 14 May be booked through travel agents

134 W. 32nd Street, 10001
(212) 645-8134

Beautifully furnished penthouse apartment near Broadway theaters, Lincoln Center, Central Park, and Carnegie Hall. Unique jeweled canopy bed, terrace, telephone, air-conditioning. Laundry on premises.

Doubles: 2 (1 PB; 1 SB) $80
Type of Beds: 1 Double; 1 Queen
Continental Breakfast
Credit Cards: No
Notes: 5, 8

Beatrice's B&B

B&B Network of NY
134 W. 32nd Street, 10001
(212) 645-8134

Beautiful duplex penthouse on the upper east side. Guests have bottom floor with cable TV, stereo, air-conditioning, laundry in building, telephone, lovely views.

Doubles: 1 (PB) $90
Type of Beds: 1 Double
Continental Breakfast
Credit Cards: No
Notes: 5, 7, 8

Bevy's B&B

B&B Network of NY
134 W. 32nd Street, 10001
(212) 645-8134

Large Soho artist's loft. Guest room on upper level. European feeling, nicely furnished. Near galleries, shops, restaurants. Cat on premises.

Doubles: 1 (PB) $60-80
Type of Beds: 1 Queen
Continental Breakfast
Credit Cards: No
Notes: 5, 7, 8

Carnegie House

New World Bed & Breakfast
150 Fifth Avenue, Suite 711, 10011
(800) 443-3800

Super-luxury building with doorman has guest room on the eighteenth floor. Very private, clean, and well-kept, with excellent views. Hostess is in the theater. Excellent location by Carnegie Hall, Central Park, Fifth Avenue shops, and Broadway theaters.

Doubles: 1 (PB) $70-90
Type of Beds: 1 Queen
Continental Breakfast
Credit Cards: A, B
Notes: 5, 9, 10, 11

Central Park South

New World Bed & Breakfast
150 Fifth Avenue, Suite 711, 10011
(800) 443-3800

Charming couple have a single room available in their luxury apartment facing Central Park. Small, private, and super convenient to Midtown business district, Carnegie Hall, Lincoln Center, Broadway theaters, and shopping. Cat in residence.

Singles: 1 (PB) $65
Type of Beds: 1 Twin
Continental Breakfast
Credit Cards: A, B
Notes: 5, 9, 10, 11

Columbus Circle

New World Bed & Breakfast
150 Fifth Avenue, Suite 711, 10011
(800) 443-3800

Luxury doorman hi-rise apartment house across the street from Central Park has a guest room on the upper floor with views to the west. Large room in a big apartment with a congenial hostess. One block from a Visitor's Information Bureau. Walking distance from Broadway theaters, Lincoln Center, Fifth Avenue shops.

Doubles: 1 (PB) $65-80
Type of Beds: 1 King
Continental Breakfast
Credit Cards: A, B, C
Notes: 5, 7, 8, 9, 10, 11

NOTES: Credit cards accepted: A Master Card; B Visa; C American Express; D Discover Card; E Diners Club; F Other: 2 Personal checks accepted: 3 Lunch available: 4 Dinner available: 5 Open all year

Dawn's B&B

B&B Network of NY
134 W. 32nd Street, 10001
(212) 645-8134

Gorgeous duplex penthouse apartment on the upper west side overlooking the Museum of Natural History and Central Park. Wraparound terrace with greenhouse, air-conditioning, TV, laundry facilities. Two cats in residence.

Doubles: 2 (PB) $90
Type of Beds: 2 Full
Continental Breakfast
Credit Cards: No
Notes: 5, 7, 8

DeForrest House

New World Bed & Breakfast
150 Fifth Avenue, Suite 711, 10011
(800) 443-3800

Landmark apartment house in Greenwich Village has a beautifully furnished guest room. Hostess is a designer. Terrace garden in summer. Well worth walking up five flights of stairs, this apartment is close to Washington Square and New York University.

Doubles: 1 (SB) $60-80
Type of Beds: 1 Double
Continental Breakfast
Credit Cards: A, B, C
Notes: 5, 9, 10, 11

East End House

New World Bed & Breakfast
150 Fifth Avenue, Suite 711, 10011
(800) 443-3800

Luxury doorman building has guest room in the home of a single business woman. Clean and private, especially convenient to the Upper East Side and Bloomingdale's. A safe neighborhood for visitors.

Doubles: 1 (PB) $65-80
Type of Beds: 1 Double
Continental Breakfast

Credit Cards: A, B, C
Notes: 5, 9, 10, 11

Frick House

New World Bed & Breakfast
150 Fifth Avenue, Suite 711, 10011
(800) 443-3800

Luxury doorman hi-rise has an apartment with room for a single lady visitor. Share bath with hostess in this lovely apartment close to the Upper East Side museums, Central Park zoo, Madison Avenue shopping, and art galleries.

Singles: 1 (SB) $65
Type of Beds: 1 Twin
Continental Breakfast
Credit Cards: A, B, C
Notes: 5, 7, 9, 10, 11

Gramercy Park Loft

New World Bed & Breakfast
150 Fifth Avenue, Suite 711, 10011
(800) 443-3800

Artist's loft in a beautifully renovated elevator building just off Gramercy Park in an elegant downtown setting close to restaurants and clubs for music and dance. Playwright hostess provides a large, sunny room. Close to Madison Square, New York University, and Greenwich Village.

Doubles: 1 (PB) $65-80
Type of Beds: 1 Queen
Continental Breakfast
Credit Cards: A, B, C
Notes: 5, 9, 10, 11

Ingeborg's B&B

B&B Network of NY
134 W. 32nd Street, 10001
(212) 645-8134

Gorgeous duplex in a 1910 Stanford White brownstone on Park Avenue. Air-conditioning, two fireplaces, TV, stereo, terrace, dish-

6 Pets welcome: 7 Smoking allowed: 8 Children welcome: 9 Social drinking allowed: 10 Tennis available: 11 Swimming available: 12 Golf available: 13 Skiing available: 14 May be booked through travel agents

washer, laundry facilities. Original artwork, lots of light. Cat in residence.

Singles: 1 (PB) $60
Doubles: 1 (PB) $90
Type of Beds: 1 Twin; 1 Double
Continental Breakfast
Credit Cards: No
Notes: 5, 7, 8

Japanese Writer's B&B

B&B Network of NY
134 W. 32nd Street, 10001
(212) 645-8134

One-half block from Central Park on the upper west side. Private studio with TV, air-conditioning, ceiling fan. Full Japanese breakfast on request. Laundry on premises, garden. One dog and two cats in residence.

Doubles: 1 (PB) $120
Type of Beds: 2 Twin
Full Breakfast
Credit Cards: No
Notes: 7, 8

Jim R's B&B

B&B Network of NY
134 W. 32nd Street, 10001
(212) 645-8134

Seven-story, twenty-room mansion from 1899 overlooking the Hudson River and Riverside Park. Backyard with barbecue. Eight fireplaces, pool room, exercise room, Victorian furnishings, stained glass, roof garden, Jacuzzi, steam bath, elevator.

Singles: 1 (SB) $65
Doubles: 4 (3 PB; 1 SB) $135
Type of Beds: 1 Twin; 4 Double
Continental Breakfast
Credit Cards: No
Notes: 7, 8

Joan & Leonard's B&B

B&B Network of NY
134 W. 32nd Street, 10001
(212) 645-8134

Incredible 2000 square-foot, 4-level, 8-room houseboat docked at an upper westside marina. Five minutes' walk to shopping, restaurants, transportation. Air-conditioning, TVs, stereos, fireplace. Master bedroom has a sauna and Jacuzzi, skylights.

Singles: 1 (SB) $50
Doubles: 2 (1 PB; 1 SB) $90-150
Type of Beds: 1 Twin; 1 Double; 1 Queen
Continental Breakfast
Credit Cards: No
Notes: 7, 8

Julius's B&B

B&B Network of NY
134 W. 32nd Street, 10001
(212) 645-8134

Luxury doorman building on the upper east side near Central Park, museums, shopping, express subway. TV and air-conditioning, terrace with views and sun all day. Health club with pool; laundry on premises. Host has NYC guide license.

Doubles: 1 (PB) $60-90
Type of Beds: 2 Twin
Continental Breakfast
Credit Cards: No
Notes: 5, 7, 8

Karen K's B&B

B&B Network of NY
134 W. 32nd Street, 10001
(212) 645-8134

Doorman building on the upper west side. Room has a river view, TV, stereo, desk. Across from Riverside Park, near shopping, restaurants, transportation, and Columbia University. Cat in residence. No children or single men.

Doubles: 1 (PB) $60-80
Type of Beds: 1 Queen
Continental Breakfast
Credit Cards: No
Notes: 5, 7

NOTES: Credit cards accepted: A Master Card; B Visa; C American Express; D Discover Card; E Diners Club; F Other: 2 Personal checks accepted: 3 Lunch available: 4 Dinner available: 5 Open all year

La Casa del Pueblo

New World Bed & Breakfast
150 Fifth Avenue, Suite 711, 10011
(800) 443-3800

A little bit of Santa Fe in Greenwich Village. Southwest-style interior is combined with the charm of a New York brownstone. Guest room has high ceilings and Native American art. Close to New York University, Washington Square. Easy access to SoHo art galleries.

Doubles: 1 (PB) $70-90
Type of Beds: 1 Double
Continental Breakfast
Credit Cards: A, B, C
Notes: 5, 8, 9, 10, 11

Lexington House

New World Bed & Breakfast
150 Fifth Avenue, Suite 711, 10011
(800) 443-3800

Luxury doorman hi-rise on the Upper East Side has a guest room with private bath. Host family is involved with the theater. Close to Madison Avenue shopping, art galleries, Frick Museum, Park Avenue. Easy transportation to midtown.

Doubles: 1 (PB) $65-80
Type of Beds: 1 Queen
Continental Breakfast
Credit Cards: A, B, C
Notes: 5, 8, 9, 10, 11

Lincoln House

New World Bed & Breakfast
150 Fifth Avenue, Suite 711, 10011
(800) 443-3800

Luxury doorman hi-rise has a guest room in the home of a business lady. Excellent views from this high floor close to Central Park and Lincoln Center. Just off bustling Broadway, this is an excellent area of Manhattan for transportation and entertainment.

Doubles: 1 (SB) $65-80
Type of Beds: 2 Twin
Continental Breakfast
Credit Cards: A, B, C
Notes: 5, 8, 9, 10, 11

Linda K's B&B

B&B Network of NY
134 W. 32nd Street, 10001
(212) 645-8134

Beautifully furnished home of an interior designer. One block from Bloomingdale's. Luxury highrise with doorman. TV, air-conditioning, phones, garage, and laundry in building.

Doubles: 2 (1 PB; 1 SB) $60-90
Type of Beds: 4 Twin
Continental Breakfast
Credit Cards: No
Notes: 5, 7, 8

London Terrace

New World Bed & Breakfast
150 Fifth Avenue, Suite 711, 10011
(800) 443-3800

Lady travel writer has a guest room available in the Chelsea neighborhood. The doorman building is a landmark location, close to Javits Convention Center, Madison Square, and the garment district. Easy access to Greenwich Village.

Doubles: 1 (SB) $55-70
Type of Beds: 2 Twin
Continental Breakfast
Credit Cards: A, B, C
Notes: 5, 8, 9, 10, 11

Mary G's B&B

B&B Network of NY
134 W. 32nd Street, 10001
(212) 645-8134

In the heart of Greenwich Village, this host has two rooms for guests. Air-conditioning, TV, nicely furnished. Only 1.5 blocks from Washington Square Park.

6 Pets welcome: 7 Smoking allowed: 8 Children welcome: 9 Social drinking allowed: 10 Tennis available: 11 Swimming available: 12 Golf available: 13 Skiing available: 14 May be booked through travel agents

Singles: 1 (SB) $50
Doubles: 1 (PB) $80
Type of Beds: 2 Twin; 1 Queen
Continental Breakfast
Credit Cards: No
Notes: 5, 7, 8

Museum House

New World Bed & Breakfast
150 Fifth Avenue, Suite 711, 10011
(800) 443-3800

Beautifully renovated studio apartment
with a modern kitchen and bath. Completely
private unit in an Upper West Side
brownstone. On a residential street one
block from Central Park West. Close to Lincoln Center, Museum of Natural History,
and Columbus Avenue shopping.

Doubles: 1 (PB) $100
Type of Beds: 1 Twin; 1 Queen
Continental Breakfast
Credit Cards: A, B, C
Notes: 5, 8, 9, 10, 11

Nancy & Ed's B&B

B&B Network of NY
134 W. 32nd Street, 10001
(212) 645-8134

Artist's loft in Soho with lots of original
artwork by your hosts. Ceiling fans, twelve-foot ceilings, TV, stereo, laundry facilities.
Two dogs on premises.

Doubles: 1 (PB) $60-80
Type of Beds: 1 Twin; 1 Double
Continental Breakfast
Credit Cards: No
Notes: 5, 7, 8

Olivier's B&B

B&B Network of NY
134 W. 32nd Street, 10001
(212) 645-8134

Lovely duplex penthouse apartment in midtown Manhattan near Sutton Place.
Wraparound terrace with garden, incredible
views. Guest room has sauna, working

fireplace, air-conditioning, separate
entrance, refrigerator, skylight, telephone.
One cat, two dogs in residence.

Doubles: 1 (PB) $135
Type of Beds: 1 Queen
Continental Breakfast
Credit Cards: No
Notes: 5, 7, 8

Perry Street

New World Bed & Breakfast
150 Fifth Avenue, Suite 711, 10011
(800) 443-3800

An 1890s Queen Anne Revival Style apartment house with a B&B room in a sixth-floor walk-up apartment. The room is sunny
and faces west. In the heart of Greenwich
Village on a tree-lined block.

Doubles: 1 (SB) $55-70
Type of Beds: 1 Double
Continental Breakfast
Credit Cards: A, B, C
Notes: 5, 8, 9, 10, 11

Peter Cooper Village House

New World Bed & Breakfast
150 Fifth Avenue, Suite 711, 10011
(800) 443-3800

Hi-rise apartment with East River views offers a large, clean room in a safe area
downtown on the East Side. Close to New
York University Medical Center, the School
of Visual Arts, the East Village. Easy access
to the United Nations.

Doubles: 1 (PB) $50-70
Type of Beds: 2 Twin
Continental Breakfast
Credit Cards: A, B, C
Notes: 5, 8, 9, 10, 11

Rae M's B&B

B&B Network of NY
134 W. 32nd Street, 10001
(212) 645-8134

NOTES: Credit cards accepted: A Master Card; B Visa; C American Express; D Discover Card; E Diners
Club; F Other: 2 Personal checks accepted: 3 Lunch available: 4 Dinner available: 5 Open all year

Luxury doorman building opposite Lincoln Center and near Central Park. Air-conditioning, cable TV, piano, stereo, original artwork, beautiful furnishings.

Singles: 1 (PB) $60
Continental Breakfast
Credit Cards: No

Rita L's B&B

B&B Network of NY
134 W. 32nd Street, 10001
(212) 645-8134

Upper east side doorman building. Host is an actress. Nicely furnished guest room has TV, air-conditioning. Near shopping, museums, Central Park, express subway. Laundry in building.

Doubles: 1 (PB) $60-90
Type of Beds: 2 Twin
Continental Breakfast
Credit Cards: No
Notes: 5, 7, 8

SoHo Loft

New World Bed & Breakfast
150 Fifth Avenue, Suite 711, 10011
(800) 443-3800

Artists' loft just off the lower Broadway art-gallery district. Loft bed and private bath in a big, open space. Charming hosts. Close to many restaurants and galleries; also near Little Italy and Greenwich Village.

Singles: 1 (SB) $60
Doubles: 1 (PB) $80
Continental Breakfast
Credit Cards: A, B, C
Notes: 5, 8, 9, 10, 11

Tribeca House

New World Bed & Breakfast
150 Fifth Avenue, Suite 711, 10011
(800) 443-3800

Artist's loft space in downtown Manhattan has clean, sunny room for guests with a loft bed, beautifully finished floors, some an-

tiues. "Triangle Below Canal" neighborhood is famous for art, restaurants, and experimental theaters. Close to SoHo and the World Trade Center. Host has a small friendly dog.

Doubles: 1 (SB) $60-75
Type of Beds: 1 Double
Continental Breakfast
Credit Cards: A, B, C
Notes: 5, 9, 10, 11

Urban Ventures #1036

Box 426, 10024
(212) 594-5650

A triplex apartment in a brownstone that sparkles with artwork. Caring New Yorkers live here, making the best of all combinations. On West 95th, half a block from Central Park. One double, $58-70.

Urban Ventures #1044

Box 426, 10024
(212) 594-5650

In 1887, this brownstone cost $12,000 to build. Constant care has kept it a showplace with a pond trickling through a beautifully planted garden. Third floor has three bedrooms and bath, with washer and dryer. Three doubles, shared bath, $48-75.

Urban Ventures #2043

Box 426, 10024
(212) 594-5650

Your host is a most interesting person who also happens to live in center city in a splendid apartment. Brass bed, mirrors, and lots of room to be comfortable in. On East 69th. One double, private bath, $70/person.

Urban Ventures #2078

Box 426, 10024
(212) 594-5650

6 Pets welcome: 7 Smoking allowed: 8 Children welcome: 9 Social drinking allowed: 10 Tennis available: 11 Swimming available: 12 Golf available: 13 Skiing available: 14 May be booked through travel agents

Twins and a private bath are what you get in this doorman elevator building. Terrace with view and a host who is a former New York City guide and speaks German, French, and Hungarian. On East 86th. One double, private bath, $65-125.

Washington Mews

New World Bed & Breakfast
150 Fifth Avenue, Suite 711, 10011
(800) 443-3800

Fourth-floor walk-up apartment has a guest room with microwave. Room overlooks an historic mews close to Washington Square, New York University. Easy access to SoHo art galleries.

Doubles: 1 (SB) $55-70
Type of Beds: 2 Twin
Continental Breakfast
Credit Cards: A, B, C
Notes: 5, 8, 9, 10, 11

West End House

New World Bed & Breakfast
150 Fifth Avenue, 10011
(800) 443-3800

Pre-war apartment house with a doorman has a guest room with clean, comfortable accommodations hosted by a retired professional lady. Close to the upper Broadway shops; easy access to Columbia University and Lincoln Center.

Doubles: 1 (PB) $65-80
Type of Beds: 2 Twin
Continental Breakfast
Credit Cards: A, B, C
Notes: 5, 9, 10, 11

Yorkville House

New World Bed & Breakfast
150 Fifth Avenue, Suite 711, 10011
(800) 443-3800

Upper East Side luxury doorman building has a guest room with full amenities. High

floor offers excellent views. Close to the Metropolitan Museum, good restaurants, art galleries. Good transportation to midtown Bloomingdale's area. Hostess is a writer and has a cat.

Doubles: 1 (PB) $65-80
Type of Beds: 2 Twin
Continental Breakfast
Credit Cards: A, B, C
Notes: 5, 7, 8, 9, 10, 11

NORTH HUDSON

Pine Tree Inn B&B

Route 9, 12855
(518) 532-9255

Small century-old classic Adirondack inn. Full breakfast served, featuring homemade breads, in the dining room with its original tin ceiling. Period furniture decorates the country-comfortable rooms. Centrally located for year-round activities.

Hosts: Peter & Patricia Schoch
Doubles: 5 (S2B) $37.45-53.50
Type of Beds: 2 Twin; 3 Double
Full Breakfast
Minimum stay holidays: 2-3
Credit Cards: No
Notes: 2, 4 (winter only), 5, 7, 8 (over 6), 9, 10, 11, 12, 13

NUNDA

Butternut B&B

44 East Street, 14517
(716) 468-5074

A stately Victorian situated in the Genesee Valley, five minutes from Letchworth Park. Picnic baskets packed and bikes provided. Skiing is minutes away at Swain. Fireplaces, natural woodwork, bathrooms with clawfoot tubs, screened porches, gracious rooms with many antiques. Cozy, comfortable full and queen bedrooms.

Hosts: Barb & Bob Lloyd
Doubles: 4 (2 PB; 2 SB) $45-55
Type of Beds: 2 Double; 2 Queen
Full Breakfast

NOTES: Credit cards accepted: A Master Card; B Visa; C American Express; D Discover Card; E Diners Club; F Other: 2 Personal checks accepted: 3 Lunch available: 4 Dinner available: 5 Open all year

Credit Cards: No
Notes: 2, 3, 4, 5, 7 (restricted), 8, 9, 10, 11, 12, 13, 14

OGDENSBURG

Maple Hill Country Inn
Riverside Drive, Box 21
(315) 383-3961

Charming Cape Cod home situated amid fifty-year-old maples overlooking the beautiful St. Lawrence River. Decorated with antiques and wicker. Open all year, with special winter packages available.

Host: Marilyn Jones
Doubles: 4 (SB) $40-65
Type of Beds: 4 Twin; 2 Double
Full Breakfast
Credit Cards: No
Notes: 2, 4, 5, 6, 8, 9, 12, 13

OLD CHATHAM

American Country Collection 037
984 Gloucester Place
Schenectady, N.Y., 12309
(518) 370-4948

A cozy 175-year-old Greek Revival home on a half acre with antiques, wild flowers, birds, stone wall, and lawns to relax you. Located just west of Massachusetts, with Tanglewood eighteen miles away, Stockbridge twenty-five, and Albany twenty.

Doubles: 1 (PB) $40
Type of Beds: 2 Twin
Continental Breakfast
Credit Cards: A, B
Notes: 2, 5, 7 (limited), 14

ONEIDA

The Pollyanna
Bed & Breakfast Leatherstocking
389 Brockway Road, Frankfort, 13340
(315) 733-0040

A charming Victorian Italianate villa in Oneida's historic district. Crystal chandeliers, marble fireplaces, crafts, and antiues. Near numerous colleges, the cities of Syracuse, Rome, and Utica, Oneida Lake, and Vernon Downs. Pet in residence. $35-95. Full breakfast is served.

PALMYRA

Canaltown Bed & Breakfast
119 Canandaigua Street, 14522
(315) 597-5553

Savor a delicious country breakfast in this 1850s historic Greek Revival home. Located close to antique stores and local museums in this locale area for the founding of the Mormon religion. One hundred yards to the Erie Canal Hiking Trail; canoe rentals nearby.

Hosts: Robert & Barbara Leisten
Doubles: 2 (SB) $42.50
Full Breakfast
Credit Cards: No
Notes: 2, 5, 8, 10, 11

PENN YAN

The Wagener Estate Bed & Breakfast
351 Elm Street, 14527
(315) 536-4591

Centrally located in the Finger Lakes, we offer bed & breakfast in an historic 1796 home furnished with antiques and country charm and nestled on 4 acres. Hospitality, comfort, and an elegant breakfast await you.

Hosts: Norm & Evie Worth
Singles: 1 (SB) $45-55
Doubles: 4 (2 PB; 2 SB) $55-65
Type of Beds: 2 Twin; 1 Double; 2 Queen; 1 King
Full Breakfast
Credit Cards: A, B, C
Closed January
Notes: 2, 8 (over 5), 9, 10, 11, 12

6 Pets welcome: 7 Smoking allowed: 8 Children welcome: 9 Social drinking allowed: 10 Tennis available: 11 Swimming available: 12 Golf available: 13 Skiing available: 14 May be booked through travel agents

PHILMONT

American Country Collection 066

984 Gloucester Place
Schenectady, N.Y., 12309
(518) 370-4948

Set back from the country road, this spacious lodge-style contemporary B&B is enveloped by 8 acres of woods, yet is conveniently located just one mile from the Taconic Parkway and thirty miles from Tanglewood.

Doubles: 4 (2 PB; 2 SB) $55-65
Type of Beds: 4 Twin; 1 Double; 1 King
Full Breakfast
Credit Cards: A, B, C
Notes: 2, 5, 7 (limited), 8, 13, 14

PITTSTOWN

Maggie Towne's B&B

Box 82, Rd 2, Valley Falls, 12185
(518) 663-8369

An old colonial located amid beautiful lawns and trees fourteen miles east of Troy. Enjoy tea or wine before the fireplace in the family room. Use the music room or read on the screened porch. Your hostess will prepare lunch for you to take on tour or enjoy at the house. It's twenty miles to historic Bennington, Vermont, and thirty to Saratoga Springs, New York.

Host: Maggie Towne
Doubles: 2 (SB) $25-35
Full Breakfast
Credit Cards: No
Notes: 2, 3, 5, 6, 8, 9

PORT JEFFERSON

House in the Glen

Bed & Breakfast of Long Island
Box 392, Old Westbury, 11568
(516) 334-6231

Situated right in this picturesque town with its harbor and quaint boutiques and craft shops, guests can walk everywhere from this charming home that's almost 100 years old. The unusual rotunda foyer with a winding staircase leads to the guest rooms. Little goodies, like baskets of toiletries, are left in the rooms. Theater playhouse in town; excellent restaurants.

Doubles: 2 (SB) $48-58
Type of Beds: 2 Twin; 1 Queen
Continental Breakfast
Credit Cards: No
Notes: 5, 8, 9, 11, 12

QUEENSBURY

Crislip's Bed & Breakfast

RD 1, Box 57, 12804
(518) 793-6869

Located just minutes from Saratoga Springs and Lake George, this landmark Federal home provides spacious accommodations complete with period antiques, four-poster beds, and down comforters. The country breakfast menu features buttermilk pancakes, scrambled eggs, and sausages. Your hosts invite you to relax on the porches and enjoy the mountain view of Vermont.

Hosts: Ned & Joyce Crislip
Singles: 1 (SB) $45
Doubles: 3 (2 PB; 1 SB) $65-75
Type of Beds: 2 Double; 1 King
Full Breakfast
Credit Cards: A, B
Notes: 2, 5, 6 (with prior approval), 8 (no infants), 9, 10, 11, 12, 13

RHINEBECK

The Heller's

91 Astor Drive, 12572
(914) 876-3468

We are located atop a little knoll on a country road one and one-half miles from historic Beekman-Arms Inn. Our guests

---

NOTES: Credit cards accepted: A Master Card; B Visa; C American Express; D Discover Card; E Diners Club; F Other: 2 Personal checks accepted: 3 Lunch available: 4 Dinner available: 5 Open all year

enjoy a quiet atmosphere and delicious breakfasts by "chef" John. The Catskill Mountains are nearby.

Hosts: John & Cecilia Heller
Doubles: 2 (SB) $35-40
Type of Beds: 1 Twin; 1 Double
Full Breakfast
Credit Cards: No
Notes: 2, 5, 6, 7, 8, 10, 11, 12

RICHFIELD SPRINGS

Country Spread Bed & Breakfast

Bed & Breakfast Leatherstocking
389 Brockway Road, Frankfort, 13340
(315) 733-0040

Country warmth blended with generous measures of hospitality and interesting conversation. The house has been child proofed for the relaxation of its guests, who enjoy a family suite with private bath. Easy access to I-90. Shared and private baths, $35-95.

Full Breakfast
Credit Cards: No
Notes: 8 (under 3), 13 (XC)

Jonathan House

Bed & Breakfast Leatherstocking
389 Brockway Road, Frankfort, 13340
(315) 733-0040

An echo of the splendid 1880s, this Eastlake-style Victorian features solid cherry paneling and carved woodwork. Crystal chandeliers, gilt mirrors, and Oriental rugs enhance the charm of the breathtaking antique furnishings. You may choose a suite comprised of bedroom, sitting room, and bath, or a room with a canopied bed. Minutes from Canadarago Lake, the great Mohawk Valley, and Cooperstown. Shared and private baths. $35-95.

Full Breakfast
Credit Cards: A, B
Notes: 4, 7

Summerwood

Bed & Breakfast Leatherstocking
389 Brockway Road, Frankfort, 13340
(315) 733-0040

Summerwood is a unique Queen Anne Victorian with stained-glass windows and period furnishings on 3 acres of grassy slopes. Local activities include free concerts in the park, craft shows, and great fishing in Canadarago Lake. Refrigerator, laundry facilities, game table, TV. Shared and private baths are available; pet in residence.

Doubles: 4, $35-95
Full Breakfast
Credit Cards: No
Notes: 4, 7

ROCHESTER AREA

Dartmouth House

B&B Rochester, Box 444, Fairport, 14450
(716) 223-8877

Spacious, centrally located, turn-of-the-century Tudor near boutiques, restaurants, antique shops, and the Park Avenue area. Easy access to museums, concerts, colleges, business section. Near bus lines and I-490. Air-conditioned.

Doubles: 3 (1 PB; 2 SB) $50-55
Type of Beds: 2 Twin; 1 Queen; 1 King
Full Breakfast
Credit Cards: No
Notes: 2, 5, 8 (older), 9, 10, 11, 12

Durand Park

B&B Rochester, Box 444, Fairport, 14450
(716) 223-8877

Contemporary home on the edge of Durand Eastman Park, near Lake Ontario. Fifteen minutes from downtown; ten from Kodak. Close to the zoo, Rochester Yacht Club, Charlotte Beach, fishing. Guest rooms on a separate level from the family.

6 Pets welcome: 7 Smoking allowed: 8 Children welcome: 9 Social drinking allowed: 10 Tennis available: 11 Swimming available: 12 Golf available: 13 Skiing available: 14 May be booked through travel agents

Singles: 1 (SB) $40
Doubles: 1 (SB) $50
Type of Beds: 3 Twin
Full Breakfast
Credit Cards: No
Notes: 2, 5, 8, 9, 10, 11, 12

Singles: 1 (SB) $45
Doubles: 1 (SB) $55
Type of Beds: 3 Twin
Full Breakfast
Credit Cards: No
Notes: 2, 5, 7 (outside), 8, 9, 10, 11, 12, 13

Fonda House

B&B Rochester, Box 444, Fairport, 14450
(716) 223-8877

Lovely early 1800s Italianate home in a small village in the country. Large, shaded yard has many specimen trees. Easy access to skiing at Bristol, great antiquing, Genesee Country Museum, Naples, and the Finger Lakes.

Doubles: 3 (SB) $35-45
Type of Beds: 2 Twin; 1 Double; 2 Day beds
Continental Breakfast
Credit Cards: No
Notes: 2, 5, 6, 7, 8, 9, 10, 11, 12, 13

Highland House

B&B Rochester, Box 444, Fairport, 14450
(716) 223-8877

Large city home on the east side, centrally located for easy access to museums, colleges, central city. On a bus line, off-street parking. Quiet, tree-lined street, spacious lawns and gardens. Air-conditioned.

Singles: 1 (SB) $45
Doubles: 3 (PB) $45-50
Type of Beds: 2 Twin; 1 Double; 1 King
Full Breakfast
Credit Cards: No
Notes: 2, 5, 7, 8, 9, 10, 11, 12

Mendon Wood

B&B Rochester, Box 444, Fairport, 14450
(716) 223-8877

Beautifully decorated contemporary ranch home recently featured on Smith College tour of homes, centered in 8 acres of woods. Tennis court and naturally landscaped in-ground pool. Driving time to downtown Rochester is 20-25 minutes. Two cats, two dogs in residence.

Rice's Little Acres

B&B Rochester, Box 444, Fairport, 14450
(716) 223-8877

Sprawling ranch house, easily accessible for the handicapped. Comfortably furnished with traditional furniture, in a country setting with a scenic view of the lake. Close to Xerox, Irondequoit Bay, Lake Ontario, Webster Park. One lazy brown dog in residence.

Singles: 2 (SB) $40
Doubles: 1 (SB) $40-50
Type of Beds: 2 Twin; 1 Double
Full Breakfast
Credit Cards: No
Notes: 2, 5, 6, 7 (outside), 8, 9, 10, 11, 12

Windy Shores

B&B Rochester, Box 444, Fairport, 14450
(716) 223-8877

New contemporary built on the edge of a cove — the water wraps around it. About thirty minutes from Kodak; twenty-eight from I-90. A superb location for a getaway weekend, winter or summer.

Singles: 1 (SB) $40
Doubles: 1 (SB) $40-50
Type of Beds: 1 Twin; 1 Double
Continental Breakfast
Credit Cards: No
Notes: 2, 5, 7, 8, 9, 10, 11, 12

Woods Cabin

B&B Rochester, Box 444, Fairport, 14450
(716) 223-8877

Charming small hideaway in the woods. Living room has large fireplace; complete kitchen; washer/dryer; antique furnishings.

NOTES: Credit cards accepted: A Master Card; B Visa; C American Express; D Discover Card; E Diners Club; F Other: 2 Personal checks accepted: 3 Lunch available: 4 Dinner available: 5 Open all year

Only twenty minutes from downtown Rochester, near Exit 45 on I-90.

Doubles: 1 (PB) $75
Type of Beds: 1 Queen; 1 Queen sofa bed
Continental Breakfast
Credit Cards: No
Notes: 2, 5, 7, 8, 9, 10, 11, 12, 13

Woods Edge

B&B Rochester, Box 444, Fairport, 14450
(716) 223-8877

Home nestled in the woods where deer can be seen; hiking, XC skiing on premises. Shopping and restaurants nearby. Air-conditioned. Near exit 45 on I-90; twenty minutes to downtown Rochester. One resident cat.

Doubles: 2 (SB) $40-50
Type of Beds: 2 Twin; 1 Double
Full Breakfast
Credit Cards: No
Notes: 2, 5, 8, 9, 10, 11, 12, 13

ROCHESTER-PENFIELD

Strawberry Castle

1883 Penfield Road, 14526
(716) 385-3266

A suburban Rochester landmark Victorian Italianate on 3 acres with pool and patio. Brass or Empire beds in large, air-conditioned rooms. Fine restaurants and golf courses nearby. A relaxing retreat for your traveling pleasure.

Hosts: Cynthia & Charles Whited
Doubles: 3 (SB) $49.50-82.50
Type of Beds: 3 Double
Continental Breakfast
Credit Cards: A, B, C
Notes: 2, 5, 7, 8 (12 and over), 9, 11, 14

ROCK CITY FALLS

The Mansion Inn

Box 77, 12863
(518) 885-1607

Elegant Victorian/Italianate, twenty-one-room mansion built in 1866. Furnished with period antiques, original brass and copper chandeliers, exquisite thirteen-foot mirrored marble fireplaces, distinctive woodwork and moldings. Two parlors, library, summer porches, spacious grounds, antique barns, views of Kayaderosseras Creek, hills, and magnificent pines. Adjacent to Saratoga Springs: horse racing, health spas, Performing Arts Center. The Mansion Inn was featured in the 1987-88 winter edition of *Country Inns* magazine and the February 1989 issue of *Victorian Accents* magazine.

Hosts: Tom Clark & Alan Churchill
Doubles: 5 (PB) $75-135
Type of Beds: 1 Twin; 4 Double; 1 Queen
Full Breakfast
Credit Cards: No
Notes: 2, 5, 7, 9, 10, 11, 12, 13

ROME

Maple Crest

Bed & Breakfast Leatherstocking
389 Brockway Road, Frankfort, 13340
(315) 733-0040

A modern split-level three miles west of Rome. Guests enjoy the comfort of a well-appointed family room with fireplace. Breakfast is served in a pleasant dining room or on the spacious deck overlooking the garden. Within minutes of Fort Stanwix, the Erie Canal Village, Fort Rickey Game Farm, Revere Ware Factory Store, and the Oneida Community silverware outlet. Shared bath, airport pick up.

Full Breakfast
Credit Cards: A, B

ROSCOE

Huff House

RD #2, 12776
(914) 482-4579

---

6 Pets welcome: 7 Smoking allowed: 8 Children welcome: 9 Social drinking allowed: 10 Tennis available: 11 Swimming available: 12 Golf available: 13 Skiing available: 14 May be booked through travel agents

A 100-year-old B&B resort under fourth-generation ownership and management. Located on 180 acres in the scenic western Catskill mountains, with on-premise golf, tennis, heated pool, and stocked trout pond. Centrally located between the famous Beaverkill, Willowemac, and Delaware rivers. Excellent food and wine cellar.

Hosts: Joseph & Joanne Forness
Singles: 1 (PB) $55
Doubles: 3 (PB) $85
Full Breakfast
Credit Cards: C
Closed Nov. - April
Notes: 2, 3, 4, 6 (restricted), 7, 8, 9, 10, 11, 12, 14

ST. JOHNSVILLE

Five Acre Farm

Bed & Breakfast Leatherstocking
389 Brockway Road, Frankfort, 13340
(315) 733-0040

This contemporary ranch is nestled on wooded farmland in the center of the Herkimer Diamond Area famous for fine quartz crystal. Small animals on the premises include sheep, chickens, geese, and dogs. The organic garden supplies fresh fruits and vegetables. SUNY colleges at Herkimer and Fulton-Montgomery are nearby, as area historic sites, museums, and cross-country skiing. $35-90.

Full Breakfast
Credit Cards: No
Notes: 7, 8 (under 3), 13 (XC)

SANDY CREEK

Evelyn's Pink House Inn

9125 S. Main Street, Box 85, 13145
(315) 387-3276

We're just 2.5 miles from Lake Ontario and 5 from the Salmon River, the greatest salmon, steelhead, and trout fishing area in the North Country. Wonderfully maintained cross-country skiing and snow-mobile trails,

and beautiful state parks are within ten miles.

Host: Evelyn Sadowski
Doubles: 5 (SB) $21
Full Breakfast
Credit Cards: No
Notes: 5, 7, 8 (over 10), 9, 10, 11, 12

SARATOGA SPRINGS

American Country Collection 062

984 Gloucester Place
Schenectady, N.Y., 12309
(518) 370-4948

This ten-year-old home is situated on a quiet street within five miles of the Performing Arts Center, Skidmore College, and the raceway. There's a private yard with flower and rock gardens and an above-ground pool. The air-conditioned two-room guest suite is on the lower level of the home, with sitting area, small refrigerators, Jacuzzi, and stone fireplace.

Doubles: 1 (PB) $65-95
Type of Beds: 1 Queen
Continental Breakfast
Credit Cards: A, B, C
Notes: 2, 5, 11, 14

The Inn on Bacon Hill

200 Wall Street, Schuylerville, 12871
(518) 695-3693

Relax in the peacefulness of elegant country living in this restored 1865 Victorian just twelve minutes from historic Saratoga Springs and its race tracks. Enjoy the inn's double parlors, each with marble fireplace, library of books, high ceilings, baby grand piano, original moldings, and antique chandeliers.

Host: Andrea Collins-Breslin
Doubles: 4 (2 SB; 2 PB) $55-85
Type of Beds: 2 Twin; 3 Double
Full Breakfast
Minimum stay: 2 days during August

NOTES: Credit cards accepted: A Master Card; B Visa; C American Express; D Discover Card; E Diners Club; F Other: 2 Personal checks accepted: 3 Lunch available: 4 Dinner available: 5 Open all year

Credit Cards: A, B
Notes: 2, 5, 8 (over 16), 9, 10, 11, 12, 13

The Westchester House

102 Lincoln Avenue, 12866
(518) 587-7613

Gracious Queen Anne Victorian featuring elaborate fireplaces, beautiful wainscotting, antique furnishing, and modern comforts. All the charm and excitement of historic Saratoga Springs are at our doorstep. Walk to the museums, race tracks, shops, restaurants, and the springs that made Saratoga famous.

Hosts: Bob & Stephanie Melvin
Doubles: 7 (5 PB; 2 SB) $54-$97.20
Type of Beds: 2 Twin; 5 Double; 1 King
Continental Breakfast
Minimum stay weekends & holidays: 2
Credit Cards: A, B, C
Closed January
Notes: 2, 8 (over 12), 9, 10, 11, 12, 13(XC), 14

The Westchester House

SAYVILLE

House on the Bay

Bed & Breakfast of Long Island
Box 392, Old Westbury, 11568
(516) 334-6231

This spectacular waterfront contemporary is filled with antiques, brass beds, Tiffany lamps, oak pieces, and Oriental rugs. Guests have their own private entrance and often are taken sailing by the hosts. Two golf courses nearby; free tennis courts; hiking areas; horseback riding. Short walk to excellent restaurants.

Doubles: 2 (SB) $68-75
Type of Beds: 2 Double; Cot available
Full Breakfast
Credit Cards: No
Notes: 5, 8 (over 10), 9, 10, 11, 12

SCHENECTADY

American Country Collection 043

984 Gloucester Place
Schenectady, N.Y., 12309
(518) 370-4948

This house served as a tavern during the late 1700s on a narrow street in the heart of the city's historic Stockade district. The two guest rooms have TV, air-conditioning; one has a working fireplace, and the shared bath has a Jacuzzi. For guests' use there is also a gourmet kitchen with cathedral ceiling, dining room, and living room with fireplace.

Singles: 1 (SB) $45-50
Doubles: 3 (1 PB; 3 SB) $75-85
Type of Beds: 1 Twin; 2 Double; 1 Queen
Full Breakfast
Credit Cards: A, B, C
Notes: 2, 5, 7, 8, 10, 11, 12, 13, 14

SCHOHARIE

The Marsh House

374 Main Street, 12157
(518) 295-7981

6 Pets welcome: 7 Smoking allowed: 8 Children welcome: 9 Social drinking allowed: 10 Tennis available: 11 Swimming available: 12 Golf available: 13 Skiing available: 14 May be booked through travel agents

The Marsh House

A 1920 Federal home, decorated in period furnishings. In summer, breakfast is served on the stone patio overlooking grounds that include a wedding gazebo and flower arbor. Surroundings give guests the feeling of stepping back into the days of yesteryear.

Hosts: Jack & Laurie Knoll
Doubles: 3 (SB) $40-50
Suite: 1 (PB) $75
Type of Beds: 4 Twin; 4 Double
Continental Breakfast
Minimum stay holidays: 2
Credit Cards: B
Notes: 2, 5, 7 (limited), 9, 10, 11, 12, 13

SETAUKET

The Farmhouse

Bed & Breakfast of Long Island
Box 392, Old Westbury, 11568
(516) 334-6231

A beautifully restored circa 1800 farmhouse furnished with antiques. Host has an antique lighting-fixture business, and the beamed, country kitchen displays many of these exquisite lamps. TV in each bedroom. Minutes to Stonybrook University and town; two miles to the beach.

Doubles: 2 (SB) $68
Type of Beds: 2 Twin; 1 Double
Continental Breakfast
Credit Cards: No
Notes: 5, 9, 10, 11, 12

SHANDAKEN

Two Brooks

Route 42, 12480
(914) 688-7101

A spacious, rustic, nineteenth-century lodging house in a secluded natural setting with two trout brooks, a spring-fed fountain, organic garden. Bountiful breakfast served every morning before you set out to explore the area. Woodstock is only seventeen miles away; hike the many mountains in the area; cross-country and downhill skiing (nine miles to Belleayre; seventeen to Hunter); fly fishing in the Esopus. Three dogs and three cats on the premises.

Hosts: Doris & Jerry Bartlett
Doubles: 4 (S2B) $52-58
Full Breakfast
Credit Cards: A, B (with surcharge)
Minimum stay: 2 ; holidays: 3
Notes: 2, 5, 6 (call ahead), 8, 9, 11, 13

NOTES: Credit cards accepted: A Master Card; B Visa; C American Express; D Discover Card; E Diners Club; F Other: 2 Personal checks accepted: 3 Lunch available: 4 Dinner available: 5 Open all year

SLATE HILL

American Country Collection 064
984 Gloucester Place
Schenectady, N.Y., 12309
(518) 370-4948

This 1850 farmhouse was once part of the Civil War underground railway. Its owners operate an English-style hunt club and have six thoroughbred horses and a tack shop on the premises. A game room with billiard table and a Jacuzzi with exercise equipment are available. Located about five miles from I-84, eighteen miles from New Paltz.

Doubles: 5 (S3B) $65-75
Type of Beds: 3 Twin; 3 Double; 1 Queen
Full Breakfast
Credit Cards: A, B, C
Notes: 2, 7 (limited), 8, 13

SODUS POINT

Carriage House Inn
8375 Wickham Blvd., 14555
(315) 483-2100

Stay in our Victorian house, circa 1870, or our stone carriage house, circa 1880. All rooms have private baths. Situated on 4 acres in a quiet residential area overlooking an historic lighthouse and Lake Ontario. Beach access. Suite and efficiency also available.

Host: James denDecker
Doubles: 8 (PB) $40-50
Type of Beds: 16 Twin
Full or Continental Breakfast
Credit Cards: A, B
Notes: 2, 4, 5, 6 (in our kennel), 7, 8, 9, 10, 11, 12, 13

Silver Waters Guesthouse B&B
8420 Bay Street, 14555
(315) 483-8098

This historic home, built after the War of 1812, was an inn at one time. Located in the heart of Sodus Point — a vacation and world-class fishing resort. Stroll the sandy beach, enjoy the sand bluffs and beautiful sunsets.

Host: Zaida Bruno
Doubles: 4 (SB) $45-70
Type of Beds: 8 Double
Continental Breakfast
Credit Cards: No
Notes: 2, 4, 5, 8, 9, 10, 11, 12, 13

SOUTHAMPTON

Village Latch Inn
101 Hill Street, 11068
(516) 283-2160

Village Latch Inn is known internationally for its charming ambience. A 37-room mansion on 5 glorious acres, right in town, within walking distance of the famous Jobs Lane boutiques. Swimming and tennis; all rooms have private bath. Rent your own mansion for group celebrations, corporate outings, and weddings.

Hosts: Marta & Martin White
Doubles: 70 (PB) $79-175
Continental Breakfast
Minimum stay weekends: 2
Credit Cards: All major
Notes: 2, 5, 6, 7, 8, 9, 10, 11, 12, 14

SOUTHOLD

Goose Creek Guesthouse
1475 Waterview Drive, 11971
(516) 765-3356

Quiet, secluded guest house on Long Island's North Fork — resort, farming, and vineyard area. Pre-Civil War farmhouse in 7 acres of woods on Goose Creek. Near ferries to New London or, via Shelter Island, to the South Shore, then to Block Island. Tennis, golf, beaches, wineries, museums, antiques, and shopping.

Host: Mary Mooney-Getoff
Singles: 2 (SB) $45
Doubles: 2 (SB) $60
Type of Beds: 4 Twin; 1 Queen
Full Breakfast
Credit Cards: No
Notes: 2 (for deposit), 5, 7 (outside), 8, 9, 10, 11, 12

STONY BROOK

Three Village Inn

150 Main Street, 11790
(516) 751-0555

The Three Village Inn is truly a unique location, offering historic colonial charm with magnificent views of Stony Brook Harbor on Long Island Sound. We offer the finest in food, service, and hospitality. Our dining rooms are open daily; weekend live music in our tap room. We have a variety of accommodations, ranging from rooms in the original 1751 inn to rooms in our country cottages — each with private bath, phone, and cable TV.

Hosts: Jin & Lous Miaritis
Doubles: 32 (PB) $85-110
Full Breakfast
Credit Cards: A, B, C
Closed Christmas
Notes: 3, 4, 5, 8, 9, 10, 11, 12, 14

Goose Creek Guesthouse

SYRACUSE

Elaine's B&B Service #4

143 Didama Street, 13224
(315) 446-4199

In the East Side of Syracuse, convenient to Syracuse University and LeMoyne, is a delightful knotty pine basement apartment that can sleep two and has full eat-in kitchen. Color TV, desk, easy chairs, game table, patio, and yard.

Doubles: 1 (PB) $60-70
Continental Breakfast
Credit Cards: No

Ivy Chimney

143 Didama Street, 13224
(315) 446-4199

Circa 1920 colonial conveniently located in Syracuse with easy access to Syracuse University, LeMoyne College, hospitals, major highways, shopping, restaurants, all sports and cultural activities. Attractive, quiet guest rooms have good double beds and share beautiful new bath. Friendly, clean, and secure.

Host: Elaine N. Samuels
Singles: $32-40
Doubles: 2 (SB) $42-50
Type of Beds: 2 Double
Continental-plus Breakfast
Credit Cards: No
Notes: 2, 5, 8 (over 15), 9, 10, 11, 12

TICONDEROGA

American Country Collection 046

984 Gloucester Place
Schenectady, N.Y., 12309
(518) 370-4948

Capture the romance of a moonlit winter evening with a horsedrawn sleigh ride along the wooded paths of this 52-acre farm. Or go cross-country skiing on a sunny afternoon. There are chickens, pigs, a cow, four horses, a dog, a few cats, and a rooster who hasn't learned to tell time. Canoeing, fishing, and swimming on beautiful Lake George are two miles away; Lake George Village, thirty miles.

Singles: 1 (SB) $30
Doubles: 3 (SB) $40
Type of Beds: 1 Twin; 3 Double
Full Breakfast
Credit Cards: A, B, C
Notes: 2, 5, 8, 11, 13, 14

TROY

American Country Collection 018

984 Gloucester Place
Schenectady, N.Y., 12309
(518) 370-4948

Built in 1810 as a farmhouse, this house still contains a cooking fireplace in the kitchen and original wide-plank floors. There are manicured lawns, flowers, an in-ground pool, and plenty of off-street parking for guests. Just fifteen minutes to downtown Albany; near RPI and Russell Sage colleges, and ten miles from SUNY-Albany.

Doubles: 2 (PB) $40-55
Type of Beds: 2 Double
Full Breakfast
Credit Cards: A, B, C
Notes: 2, 5, 8

Drawing by Paula Horrigan

Sage Cottage

TRUMANSBURG

Sage Cottage

112 East Main Street, 14886
(607) 387-6449

Unwind in the homey elegance of our Gothic Revival home. Savor a full breakfast complemented by homemade herb breads and jams. Explore our flourishing herb gardens and historic village. Four cozy guest rooms with private baths. Taughannock Falls, wineries, Ithaca are nearby.

Host: Dorry Norris
Doubles: 4 (PB) $40-50
Type of Beds: 1 Twin; 1 Double; 1 Queen; 1 King
Full Breakfast
Minimum stay holiday weekends: 2
Notes: 2, 5, 9, 11, 12, 13

TURIN

Towpath Inn

Box E, West Road, 13473
(315) 348-8122

Located at the base of Snow Ridge Ski Area and across from an eighteen-hole golf course. Free HBO, 40-foot game room, sauna. This house, originally a stagecoach stop, now has white linens and stemware in three dining rooms, original oil paintings, ladder-back chairs, antiques, and an ambience of understated elegance. Rates include breakfast and dinner.

Hosts: Roger & Ann Abbey
Singles: 3 (SB)
Doubles: 9 (8 PB; 1 SB) $91-106 plus gratuity & tax
Type of Beds: 6 Twin; 9 Double
Full Breakfast
Credit Cards: A, B
Closed 4/15-5/29
Notes: 2, 4, 7, 8, 9, 11, 12

UNION SPRINGS

Ludwig's B & B

Box 453, 13160
(315) 889-5940

Boat dock, fishing, movies. Rooms have private baths, microwaves, and refrigerators. Cayuga Wine Trail and Corning glass factory nearby. Children's play equipment. Beach fires at night with marshmallows and popcorn. Beautiful sunsets. Reservations requested.

Hosts: Jean & George Ludwig
Doubles: 2 (PB) $58.85
Type of Beds: 2 Double
Full Breakfast
Credit Cards: No
Closed 10/15-5/15
Notes: 7, 8, 9, 11, 12

UTICA

Heartcross

Bed & Breakfast Leatherstocking
389 Brockway Road, Frankfort, 13340
(315) 733-0040

Situated on a residential street off Genesee Street, this home reflects traditional styling enhanced by a glass-paneled wall that savors the sun. Within easy access of Hamilton College, Utica College, or Mohawk Valley Community College. Just twenty minutes from Adirondack Park. Animal in residence. Full breakfast is served, and smoking is allowed. $35-95.

VERNON

Elaine's B&B Service #5

143 Didama Street, Syracuse, 13224
(315) 446-4199

A sprawling Victorian/Italianate manor house atop a knoll of 7 acres. Filled with antiques, the house has been featured in several local historical books. Children and well-behaved pets are welcome. No smoking in the bedrooms. Your hosts, a young couple and their son, also raise Russian Wolfhounds in their kennel.

Doubles: 4 (SB) $40-50
Type of Beds: 4 Double
Continental Breakfast
Credit Cards: No

Lavender Inn

Bed & Breakfast Leatherstocking

389 Brockway Road, Frankfort, 13340
(315) 733-0040

This Federal-style home was built in 1799 and boasts a nine-foot entry hall opening into the parlor with fireplace. The dining room has a bread oven, large brick fireplace, and slate hearth. Activities in the area include visits to Oriskany battlefield, Fort Stanwix, Erie Canal Village, antique and craft shops. $35-95.

Full Breakfast
Credit Cards: No
Notes: 4, 7, 8 (under 3), 13 (XC)

WARRENSBURG

Country Road Lodge

HCR1, Box 227, 12885
(518) 623-2207

The Adirondack Mountain/Hudson River view hasn't changed since 1905, when the now-abandoned railroad bridge was built. Minutes from Lake George, we've offered seclusion and casual comfort since 1974. Homemade bread, hiking, skiing, horseshoes, badminton, books, board games. Antiquing, fine restaurants nearby.

Hosts: Steve & Sandi Parisi
Doubles: 4 (S2B) $42-52
Type of Beds: 2 Twin; 2 Double
Full Breakfast
Minimum stay holidays: 2
Credit Cards: No
Closed Nov. & April
Notes: 2, 7, 9, 10, 11, 12, 13

White House Lodge

53 Main Street, 12885
(518) 623-3640

An 1847 Victorian in the heart of the Adirondacks — an antiquer's paradise! The home is furnished with many antiques. Only five minutes to Lake George Village, historic Fort William Henry, and Great Escape. Walk to restaurants, antique shops, and shopping areas. Enjoy the comfort of the

---

NOTES: Credit cards accepted: A Master Card; B Visa; C American Express; D Discover Card; E Diners Club; F Other: 2 Personal checks accepted: 3 Lunch available: 4 Dinner available: 5 Open all year

air-conditioned TV lounge or rock on the front porch. Twenty minutes to Gore Mountain Ski Lodge and the Adirondack Balloon Festival.

Hosts: James & Ruth Gibson
Singles: 1 (SB) $60
Doubles: 4 (SB) $70
Type of Beds: 1 Twin; 4 Double
Continental Breakfast
Credit Cards: A, B
Notes: 5, 7, 8 (over 7), 10, 11, 12, 13, 14

WATERLOO

The Historic James Russell Webster Mansion Inn
115 E. Main Street, 13165
(315) 539-3032

A New Age Inn in the Finger Lakes region. Like living in a major museum. Two private palatial suites include air-conditioning, marble fireplaces and bathrooms, seventeenth, eighteenth, and nineteenth-century treasures, and a cat figurine museum. Haute cuisine dinners and breakfast; member, Master Chefs Institute.

Hosts: Leonard & Barbara N. Cohen
Suites: 2 (PB) $267.50
Type of Beds: 2 Double Period Canopy
Continental Breakfast
Minimum stay weekends: 2
Credit Cards: A, B
Notes: 2, 4 (advanced notice), 5, 9 (in moderation), 10, 11, 12, 13 (XC), 14

WATERTOWN

Starbuck House
253 Clinton Street, 13601
(315) 788-7324

Seventeen-room Italianesque mansion built in 1869. Completely restored and updated, the inn offers accommodations for nine guests in five comfortable rooms, one of which is a suite. Breakfast is served in an elegant formal dining room; guests socialize in the living room.

Host: Marsha Brown
Singles: $55-60
Doubles: $65-70
Suite: $70-75
Full Breakfast
Credit Cards: A, B
Notes: 2

WATERVILLE

The Bed & Breakfast of Waterville
Bed & Breakfast Leatherstocking
389 Brockway Road, Frankfort, 13340
(315) 733-0040

This lovely Victorian home is situated in Waterville's historic triangle. Each room artistically displays the hostess' talents with quilts and needlework. Within minutes of Colgate University, Hamilton College, SUNY Morrisville, Oneonta, and Cazenovia.

Doubles: 3 (1 PB; 2 SB) $35-95
Type of Beds: 1 Twin; 2 Double
Full Breakfast
Credit Cards: No
Notes: 6, 7, 8 (under 3)

WESTBURY

Welcome House #WR
Bed & Breakfast of Long Island
Box 392, Old Westbury, 11586
(516) 334-6231

Convenient to Adelphi, Hofstra, Post universities and Naussau Community College, as well as Nassau coliseum for sports and cultural events. Minutes from Old Westbury Gardens; ten-minute drive to the Syosset and Woodbury commercial complexes.

Doubles: 2 (SB) $50-60
Type of Beds: 4 Twin

Full Breakfast
Credit Cards: No
Notes: 3 (inquire), 5, 8 (over 8), 9, 10, 11, 12

WESTFIELD

William Seward Inn

RD 2, South Portage Road, 14787
(716) 326-4151

"A country inn well done." Formerly the home of Lincoln's secretary of state, this 1821 Greek Revival mansion features ten rooms with period antiques and private baths. Comfortable elegance close to Westfield's wineries and national antique center. Minutes from the world-famous Chautauqua Institution and both downhill and cross-country skiing.

Hosts: Peter & Joyce Wood
Doubles: 10 (PB) $58-84
Type of Beds: 2 Twin; 7 Double; 2 Queen; 2 King
Full Breakfast
Credit Cards: A, B
Notes: 2, 4 (winter), 5, 8 (over 12), 9, 10, 11, 12, 13

WESTHAMPTON BEACH

Seafield House

2 Seafield Lane, 11978
1-800-346-3290

Seafield House, a one-hundred-year-old country retreat, is only ninety minutes from Manhattan on Westhampton Beach's exclusive Seafield Lane. A swimming pool and tennis court are on the premises, and it's only a short walk to the beach. The Hamptons offer numerous outstanding restaurants and shops. Indoor tennis is available locally, as is a health spa at Montauk Point.

Host: Elsie Pardee Collins
Doubles: 2 (PB) $90-175
Type of Beds: 2 Double
Full Breakfast
Minimum stay: 2
Credit Cards: No
Notes: 2, 5, 9, 10, 11

WEST SHOKAN

Glen Atty Farm

Box 578, Moonhaw Road, 12494
(914) 657-8110

An 1840s farmhouse and working farm with horses, sheep, pigs, chickens, ducks, etc. Relaxing country atmosphere with many walking trails and stream. Two bedrooms, one with a fireplace and one with a king bed and two twins. Close to Woodstock and many fine restaurants. Two cats and one small dog in residence.

Hosts: Susan & Tom Kizis
Doubles: 2 (SB) $40-65
Type of Beds: 2 Twin; 1 Double; 1 King
Full Breakfast
Minimum stay: 2
Credit Cards: No
Notes: 2, 5, 7, 8 (over 6), 9, 10, 11

WEST WINFIELD

The Five Gables

Bed & Breakfast Leatherstocking
389 Brockway Road, Frankfort, 13340
(315) 733-0040

This historic Victorian, circa 1890, is in the village near the park. The sweeping porch with its white wicker furniture and hanging flowers is the perfect spot for breakfast. Jacuzzi, hand-stenciled wall, bay windows. Near the colleges of Colgate, Hamilton and state land that offers horse trails, hiking, and biking. Many antique shops in the area.

Suite: 1 (PB) $35-95
Type of Beds: 1 Queen
Full Breakfast
Credit Cards: No
Notes: 10, 12, 13 (XC)

Victoria Lodge

Bed & Breakfast Leatherstocking
389 Brockway Road, Frankfort, 13340
(315) 733-0040

NOTES: Credit cards accepted: A Master Card; B Visa; C American Express; D Discover Card; E Diners Club; F Other: 2 Personal checks accepted: 3 Lunch available: 4 Dinner available: 5 Open all year

This Victorian is decorated with antiques and family keepsakes; high ceilings, hand-rubbed woodwork, and circular cherry stairway. Village tennis courts and park near many antique shops. Near Cooperstown, the Automobile Museum, the Musical Museum, Hamilton, Colgate colleges. Private bath, full breakfast, pet in residence. $35-95.

WEVERTOWN

Mountainaire Adventures
Rt. 28, Box A, 12886
(518) 251-2194

Newly renovated private lodge and chalet in the Adirondack Park near Lake George and Gore Mountain Ski Center. Jacuzzi, sauna, beer and wine, bikes and boats. Custom adventure trips, such as white-water rafting, are available. Ideal for private meetings with audio-visual services available.

Host: Douglas Cole
Doubles: 8 (6 PB; 2 SB) $37.45-74.90
Type of Beds: 12 Twin; 4 Queen
Full Breakfast
Minimum stay weekends & holidays: 2
Credit Cards: A, B
Notes: 2, 4, 5, 6, 7, 8, 9, 10, 11, 12, 13

WILLIAMSON

Jediah Pound Homestead
7127 Townline Road, 14589
(315) 589-9119

Enjoy a touch of country elegance in this circa 1850 cobblestone house. Two bedrooms with period furnishings and wall stenciling. Minutes from the Seaway Trail, historic Pultneyville, country shops, and Lake Ontario. Convenient parking for boat trailers.

Hosts: Louis & Anne Pepin
Doubles: 2 (SB) $45
Type of Beds: 2 Double
Continental-plus Breakfast
Credit Cards: A, B
Notes: 2, 5, 10, 11, 12

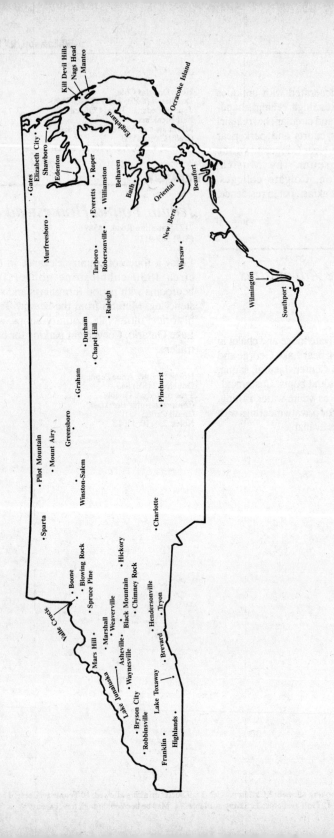

NORTH CAROLINA

North Carolina

Flint Street Inns

100 & 116 Flint Street, 28801
(704) 253-6723

Two lovely old homes on an acre lot with century-old trees. Comfortable walking distance to town. Guest rooms are furnished with antiques and collectibles, are air-conditioned, and some have fireplaces. The inns provide wine, bicycles, and restaurant menus. Breakfast is full Southern style, featuring home-baked breads and iron -skillet biscuits.

Hosts: Rick, Lynne & Marion Vogel
Doubles: 8 (PB) $70
Type of Beds: 8 Double
Full Breakfast
Credit Cards: A, B, C, D
Notes: 2, 5, 7 (limited), 14

Heritage Hill

64 Linden Avenue, 28801
(704) 254-9336

A 1908 colonial with wraparound porch for summer eating and rocking. Antiques, working fireplaces, books, and large conservatory kitchen for winter dining. Private grounds with century-old trees. Six blocks to downtown and three miles to the Biltmore Estate. Welcome!

Hosts: Linda & Ross Willard
Singles: 1 (PB) $28
Doubles: 8 (PB) $63
Type of Beds: 3 Twin; 4 Double; 4 King; 1 Sofabed
Full Breakfast
Minimum stay fall season: 2

Credit Cards: A, B
Notes: 2, 5, 7 (limited), 8 (over 12), 9, 10, 11, 12, 14

The Old Reynolds Mansion

100 Reynolds Heights, 28804
(704) 254-0496

Bed and breakfast in an antebellum mansion listed on the National Registry. Beautifully restored with furnishings from a bygone era. In a country setting with acres of trees, mountain views from all rooms. Wood-burning fireplaces, two-story verandas, pool.

Hosts: Fred & Helen Faber
Doubles: 10 (8 PB; 2 SB) $40-65 plus tax
Type of Beds: 2 Twin; 9 Double; 1 Queen
Continental Breakfast
Minimum stay weekends & holidays: 2
Credit Cards: No
Open weekends only Jan.-March
Notes: 2, 7, 8 (6 and over), 9, 10, 11, 12

Reed House

119 Dodge Street, 28803
(704) 274-1604

Come stay with us in our comfortable Victorian home built in 1892. Near Biltmore House. We have working fireplaces in every room. Breakfast, featuring home-made, low-sodium muffins, is served on the wraparound porch. Relaxing rocking chairs everywhere. Furnished in period decor.

Host: Marge Turcot
Doubles: 5 (1 PB; 4 SB) $35-50
Type of Beds: 3 Twin; 4 Double
Continental Breakfast
Credit Cards: A, B
Closed Nov. 1-May 1
Notes: 2, 7, 8, 9, 10, 11, 12

6 Pets welcome: 7 Smoking allowed: 8 Children welcome: 9 Social drinking allowed: 10 Tennis available: 11 Swimming available: 12 Golf available: 13 Skiing available: 14 May be booked through travel agents

BATH

Bayview

B&B in the Albemarle
Box 248, Everetts, 27825
(919) 792-4584

Bayview, a summer retreat overlooking the lovely Pamlico River, is the place for a quiet, relaxing weekend. You can share the shady patio while you view the river. Only minutes from Old Bath Town on the historic Albemarle Tour Route.

Doubles: 2 (SB) $25-30
Type of Beds: 2 Double
Continental Breakfast
Credit Cards: No
Closed Aug. 16-June 14
Notes: 2, 11

BEAUFORT

The Cedars At Beaufort

305 Front Street, 28516
(919) 728-7036

This lovingly restored eighteenth-century inn offers twelve elegantly appointed rooms with private baths and fireplaces. The dining room boasts the finest cuisine on the Carolina coast. Daily tours of historic Beaufort and the Outer Banks are available in season. Special weekly rate for Sunday night through Thursday night including breakfast and dinner — $525 plus tax.

Hosts: Bill & Pat Kwaak
Doubles: 12 (PB) $75-105
Type of Beds: 1 Twin; 6 Double; 3 Queen; 2 King
Full Breakfast
Minimum stay in-season weekends: 2 ; holidays: 3
Credit Cards: A, B
Notes: 2, 4, 5, 7, 8, 9, 10, 11, 12

1854 Shotgun House

406 Ann Street, 28516
(919) 728-6248

A completely restored 1854 Greek Revival in the center of historic Beaufort, one block from the boardwalk, where you can see yachts and watch the wild ponies graze on Shackleford Shoals. Come and be pampered with designer sheets, down comforters, antique furniture, and clean, modern baths.

Host: Becky Koonce
Singles: 1 (SB) $55
Doubles: 3 (PB) $65
Type of Beds: 2 Twin; 1 Double; 1 Queen
Full Breakfast
Credit Cards: A, B
Notes: 2, 5, 9, 10, 11, 12

Inlet Inn

601 Front Street, 28516
(919) 728-3600

Comfortable, reconstructed nineteenth-century inn with unsurpassed view of historic Beaufort Harbour, Cape Lookout Lighthouse, the ocean, and wild horses on nearby islands. Oversized rooms have heavy yellow pine furnishings. Evening wine and cheese; fireplaces in six rooms.

Host: Betty Shannon
Doubles: 37 (PB) $49.79
Type of Beds: 20 Queen; 17 King
Continental Breakfast
Minimum stay weekends: 2
Credit Cards: A, B, C
Notes: 2, 5, 7, 8, 9, 10, 11, 12, 14

Langdon House

135 Craven Street, 28516
(919) 728-5499

The Langdon House, circa 1733, has witnessed Beaufort as it was pillaged by pirates in 1747, plundered by the British in 1782, occupied by the Union forces in 1862, and pounded by the great hurricane of 1879. The small inn is furnished with antiques that support the colonial atmosphere. Jimm Prest practices the art of innkeeping — genuinely caring for his guests, providing them a special experience they will long remember, and doing whatever is necessary to assure their comfort and enjoyment.

NOTES: Credit cards accepted: A Master Card; B Visa; C American Express; D Discover Card; E Diners Club; F Other: 2 Personal checks accepted: 3 Lunch available: 4 Dinner available: 5 Open all year

Host: Jimm Prest
Doubles: 4 (PB) $73-115
Type of Beds: 4 Queen
Full Breakfast
Credit Cards: No
Notes: 2, 5, 8 (12 and over), 9, 10, 11

BELHAVEN

River Forest Manor & Marina

600 East Main Street, 27810
(919) 943-2151

An elegant mansion located on the Pungo River. Besides being a wonderful country inn with leaded cut-glass windows and crystal chandeliers, River Forest Manor is also a fully equipped marina. A famous smorgasbord is served nightly during the season; dinner from a menu the balance of the year. The grand old manor offers a carefully preserved feeling of Victorian times.

Hosts: Ms. Melba G. Smith & Axson Smith, Jr.
Doubles: 6 (PB) $60-75
Suites: 3 (2 bedrooms; PB) $40
Type of Beds: 3 Twin; 1 Double; 1 Queen; 1 King
Continental Breakfast
Credit Cards: A, B
Notes: 4, 5, 7, 9, 10, 11

BLACK MOUNTAIN

Bed & Breakfast Over Yonder

269 North Fork Road, 28711
(704) 669-6762

This comfortable old mountain home, furnished with antiques, has views of mountains and the surrounding woods from its landscaped decks and terrace. Secluded on 40 acres, it is two miles from I-40 and Black Mountain, which has antique and craft shopping. Close to the Blue Ridge Parkway and Asheville's Biltmore House. Our breakfast specialty is fresh mountain brown trout.

Host: Wilhelmina Headley
Doubles: 5 (3 PB; 2 SB) $36.75-52.50

Type of Beds: 2 Twin; 1 Double; 2 Queen; 1 King
Full Breakfast
Credit Cards: No
Closed Dec.-May
Notes: 2, 7 (limited), 8, 9, 10, 11, 12

BLOWING ROCK

Ragged Garden Inn

Box 1927, Sunset Drive, 28605
(704) 295-9703

A cozy, European, chestnut-bark-covered home with a romantic candlelit dining room downstairs. Located on 1 acre just half a block from the quaint village of Blowing Rock, near the Blue Ridge Parkway. Rooms are individually decorated with interesting artwork and artifacts.

Hosts: Joe & Joyce Villani
Doubles: 7 (PB) $40-75
Type of Beds: 1 Double; 1 Queen; 5 King
Full Breakfast
Credit Cards: A, B, C
Closed Jan. & Feb.
Notes: 2, 4, 7, 8 (over 12), 9, 10, 11, 12, 13, 14

Ragged Garden Inn

BOONE

Overlook Lodge

Box 1327, 28607
(704) 963-5785

Cozily secluded mountain house in the heart of the Blue Ridge Mountains. Spectacular

6 Pets welcome: 7 Smoking allowed: 8 Children welcome: 9 Social drinking allowed: 10 Tennis available: 11 Swimming available: 12 Golf available: 13 Skiing available: 14 May be booked through travel agents

view from two large decks. Adjacent to National Forest and the Blue Ridge Parkway. Great Room with fireplace. Golf, skiing, hiking, whitewater rafting, antique and craft shopping, outdoor drama all nearby.

Host: Nancy Garrett
Doubles: 5 (3 PB; 2 SB) $55-100
Type of Beds: 3 Twin; 7 Double; 1 Queen
Full Breakfast
Credit Cards: A, B
Notes: 2, 5, 7, 8, 9, 10, 12, 13, 14

BREVARD

The Red House Inn

412 W. Probart Street, 28712
(704) 884-9349

The Red House was built in 1851 and has been lovingly restored and furnished in turn-of-the-century period antiques. Located in the Blue Ridge Mountains, with the wonderful Brevard Music Center every night during the summer.

Hosts: Lynne Ong & Mary MacGillycuddy
Doubles: 6 (PB and SB) $32-47
Type of Beds: 4 Twin; 4 Double
Full Breakfast
Credit Cards: No
Closed Nov. 15 - May 15
Notes: 2, 9, 11, 12, 14

BRYSON CITY

Folkstone Inn

767 W. Deep Creek Road, 28713
(704) 488-2730

Enjoy the romance of an old world inn, the charm and nostalgia of the long-forgotten life-style of gracious country living. The inn is located in the Great Smoky Mountains, in Swain Country, which is 86 percent parkland. You may hike, fish, sail, raft, or horseback ride.

Hosts: Norma & Peter Joyce
Doubles: 6 (PB) $59
Type of Beds: 6 Double
Full Breakfast
Credit Cards: No

Closed Jan. & Feb.
Notes: 2, 10

Fryemont Inn

Box 459, 28713
(704) 488-2159

Overlooking the Great Smoky Mountains National Park. All rooms have private bath. Dinner and breakfast are included in the daily rate, and the house is on the National Register of Historic Places. Featured in *Bon Appetit*.

Hosts: Sue & George Brown
Doubles: 39 (PB) $75-158
Type of Beds: 9 Twin; 35 Double; 9 King
Full Breakfast
Credit Cards: A, B
Closed Nov. - mid-April
Notes: 2, 4, 7, 8, 9, 10, 11, 14

Fryemont Inn

CHAPEL HILL

The Fearrington House

Fearrington Village Center
Pittsboro, 27312
(919) 542-2121

The Fearrington Inn and Restaurant is located just eight miles outside of Chapel Hill in the countryside. Each of the fourteen rooms is individually decorated and furnished throughout with pine antiques from England.

NOTES: Credit cards accepted: A Master Card; B Visa; C American Express; D Discover Card; E Diners Club; F Other: 2 Personal checks accepted: 3 Lunch available: 4 Dinner available: 5 Open all year

Hosts: Jenny & R. B. Fitch
Doubles: 14 (PB) $99.75-183.75
Type of Beds: 6 Double; 11 Queen
Continental Breakfast
Credit Cards: A, B
Notes: 2, 4, 5, 8 (12 or over), 9, 10, 11, 12

The Inn at Bingham School

Mebane Oaks Road at NC 54W, 27514
(919) 563-5583

Restored headmaster's home, listed on National Register of Historic Places. Furnished with eighteenth-century family antiques; four bedrooms have fireplaces. Convenient to the University of North Carolina and Duke University. Full Southern breakfast and afternoon wine and cheese provided. Situated on 10 acres in piedmont North Carolina.

Hosts: Jane & Bob Kelly
Doubles: 6 (PB) $68-115
Type of Beds: 2-3/4; 2 Double; 3 Queen
Full Breakfast
Minimum stay football & graduation weekends: 2
Credit Cards: No
Closed last two weeks of Dec.
Notes: 2, 7, 8 (over 12), 9, 10, 12, 14

The Homeplace

CHARLOTTE

The Inn on Providence

6700 Providence Road, 28226
(704) 366-6700

A three-story colonial nestled on 2 acres amid gardens and a pool in south Charlotte. The rooms are all decorated with Early American antiques, quilts, and family heirlooms. A full home-cooked breakfast features special egg dishes, souffles, Apple Pannekoeken, homemade breads and muffins and is served on our veranda in good weather.

Hosts: Dan & Darlene McNeill
Doubles: 5 (3 PB; 2 SB) $59.40-81
Type of Beds: 2 Twin; 1 Double; 2 Queen; 1 King
Full Breakfast
Minimum stay holidays: 3
Credit Cards: A, B
Notes: 2, 5, 8 (over 12), 10, 11, 12, 14

The Homeplace

5901 Sardis Road, 28226
(704) 365-1936

Restored 1902 Country/Victorian on 2.5 acres with garden gazebo and wraparound porch. Victorian elegance and old-fashioned charm with a full home-cooked breakfast. A quiet setting and unique experience for the traveler, business executive, or connoisseur of fine older homes.

Hosts: Peggy & Frank Dearien
Doubles: 4 (2 PB; 2 SB) $54-70.20
Type of Beds: 2 Twin; 1 Double; 2 Queen
Full Breakfast
Minimum stay holidays: 2
Credit Cards: A, B, C
Notes: 2, 5, 8 (over 10), 10, 12, 14

CHIMNEY ROCK

The Gingerbread Inn

Box 187, 28720
(704) 625-4038

The Gingerbread Inn is located on the Rocky Broad River. The rooms are country finished — ruffled curtains, dust ruffles, quilts, etc. There are two decks located on the river with chairs for relaxing while listening to the flowing water.

6 Pets welcome: 7 Smoking allowed: 8 Children welcome: 9 Social drinking allowed: 10 Tennis available: 11 Swimming available: 12 Golf available: 13 Skiing available: 14 May be booked through travel agents

Hosts: Tom & Janet Sherman
Singles: 1 (SB)
Doubles: 4 (2 PB; 2 SB) $35-45
Type of Beds: 1 Twin; 3 Double; 1 Queen
Continental Breakfast
Credit Cards: No
Notes: 2, 5, 7, 8, 9

DURHAM

Arrowhead Inn

106 Mason Road, 27712
(919) 477-8430

This restored 1775 manor hour, on 4 rural
acres, offers homey hospitality in an atmosphere that evokes colonial Carolina. But
along with eighteenth-century architecture,
decor, and furnishings, Arrowhead Inn features contemporary comfort, sparkling
housekeeping, and bounteous, home-
cooked breakfasts.

Hosts: Jerry & Barbara Ryan
Doubles: 8 (4 PB; 4 SB) $48.60-97.20
Type of Beds: 2 Twin; 3 Double; 4 Queen
Full Breakfast
Credit Cards: A, B, C
Closed Dec. 22-Jan.1
Notes: 2, 5, 7, 8, 9, 10, 11, 12, 14

EDENTON

The Lords Proprietors' Inn

300 North Broad Street, 27932
(919) 482-3641

Establishing a reputation for the finest accommodations in North Carolina, the inn
offers twenty elegantly appointed rooms
with private baths and spacious parlors for
gathering for afternoon tea by the fire. Inquire about special weekend programs that
include dinner and tour.

Hosts: Arch & Jane Edwards
Doubles: 20 (PB) $47.25-68.25
Continental-plus Breakfast (Full on Sundays)
Credit Cards: No
Dinner available on special weekends
Closed Christmas
Notes: 2, 7, 8, 9, 10, 11, 12

Sound Side

B&B in the Albemarle
Box 248, Everetts, 27825
(919) 792-4584

A new two-story white clapboard colonial on
Albemarle Sound about ten minutes from
Edenton. This home has a wide front porch
with old-fashioned rockers for your comfort
and a beautiful view of the adjoining golf
course. Spacious deck, air-conditioning,
swimming on the premises. Tennis and golf
at the adjoining golf club.

Doubles: 1 (PB) $60
Type of Beds: 2 Twin
Continental Breakfast
Credit Cards: No
Notes: 2, 8, 9, 10, 11

The Trestle House Inn

Rt. 4, Box 370, 27932
(919) 482-2282

Located south of Albemarle's colonial capital, off Rt. 32 and Soundside Road.
Luxurious, immaculate accommodations include: private bath, free HBO, exercise
room with steam bath, game room with billiards and shuffleboard, sun deck, private
stocked 15-acre fishing lake. Overlooks a
60-acre wildlife preserve.

Hosts: Harlan & Louise Worthley
Doubles: 4 (PB) $50
Type of Beds: 1 Twin; 2 Double; 1 Queen
Continental Breakfast
Credit Cards: A, B, C
Notes: 2, 5, 7 (limited), 8 (over 11), 9, 12

ELIZABETH CITY

White House #106

B&B in the Albermarle
Box 248, Everetts, 27825
(919) 792-4584

This home is just 1.5 blocks to downtown, 2
blocks to the Pasquotank River, and 54
miles to the Outer Banks (Dare County and

Manteo). Guests have their own private sitting room with TV and air-conditioning.

Singles: 2 (SB) $30
Doubles: 1 (SB) $35
Type of Beds: 4 Twin; 1 Three-quarter
Continental Breakfast
Credit Cards: No
Notes: 2, 5

ENGLEHARD

Hunters Paradise

B&B in the Albemarle
Box 248, Everetts, 27825
(919) 792-4584

This B&B is located in the loft of an old barn that's now being used as the host's business shop. It has a private entrance with outside deck, air-conditioning, living room and kitchen. In the historic district of Hyde Country with many fine homes to explore; crabbing, fishing, and hunting are nearby; bird watching.

Singles: 1 (SB) $50
Doubles: 2 (SB) $50
Continental Breakfast
Credit Cards: No
Notes: 2, 5

EVERETTS

Beaver Dam Farm

B&B in the Albemarle
Box 248, 27825
(919) 792-4584

Federal-style country farmhouse located centrally in the Triangle area of North Carolina and Nags Head/Manteo. Excellent location for visiting on the historic Albermarle Tour. Air-conditioned; 1.5 hours from the ocean.

Singles: 1 (SB) $35
Doubles: 1 (SB) $40
Type of Beds: 2 Twin; 1 Queen
Full Breakfast
Credit Cards: No
Notes: 2, 5, 6, 7, 8, 9, 10, 11, 12

FRANKLIN

Buttonwood Inn

190 Georgia Road, 28734
(704) 369-8985

A quaint, small mountain inn awaits those who prefer a cozy country atmosphere. Before hiking, golfing, gem mining, or horseback riding, enjoy a breakfast of puffy scrambled eggs and apple sausage ring or eggs benedict, Dutch babies, blintz souffle, strawberry omelet, or stuffed French toast. Relax, enjoy, return!

Host: Liz Oehser
Doubles: 4 (2 PB; 2 SB) $50.76-64.80
Type of Beds: 2 Twin; 3 Double
Full Breakfast
Credit Cards: No
Closed Dec. - March
Notes: 2, 9, 10, 11, 12

GATES

State Line House

B&B in the Albemarle
Box 248, Everetts, 27825
(919) 792-4584

Restored 1817 country farmhouse on 500 acres of land, listed on the National Register of Historic Places. The house is divided by the NC/VA state line and is on the Albemarle Tour route ten minutes from Merchants Millpond State Park. One hour to Norfolk and Virginia Beach.

Doubles: 2 (SB) $30-40
Type of Beds: 2 Double
Continental Breakfast
Credit Cards: No
Notes: 2, 5

GRAHAM

Leftwich House

215 E. Harden Street, 27253
(919) 226-5978

6 Pets welcome: 7 Smoking allowed: 8 Children welcome: 9 Social drinking allowed: 10 Tennis available: 11 Swimming available: 12 Golf available: 13 Skiing available: 14 May be booked through travel agents

Let us pamper you with Southern hospitality in the European tradition of B&B. Whether you enjoy a relaxed, old-fashioned breakfast with all the trimmings or a light meal, we guarantee you will enjoy visiting Leftwich House. Located within ten minutes of over 200 factory outlets and convenient to five major universities.

Host: Carolyn Leftwich Morrow
Singles: 1 (SB) $25
Doubles: 2 (SB) $35
Full Breakfast
Credit Cards: No
Notes: 2, 5, 8, 10, 11, 12, 14

Leftwich House

GREENSBORO

The Greenwich Inn Bed & Breakfast

111 West Washington Street, 27401
(919) 272-3474

An intimate British-style small hotel nestled in historic Old Greensborough. In the middle of things, but still a peaceful haven. Valet parking, free wine and cheese, complimentary daily paper with your in-room continental breakfast. Refrigerators in each room. Near University of N.C., Bennett College, Guilford College, malls, amusement park, zoo.

Hosts: Bill & Barb MacKinnon
Singles: 12 (PB) $70.20-86.40
Doubles: 13 (PB) $81-91

Type of Beds: 23 Double; 10 Queen; 4 King; 4 Four-poster Queens; 4 King canopy
Continental Breakfast
Credit Cards: A, B, C
Notes: 2, 4, 5, 7, 8, 9, 10, 11, 12, 14

Greenwood

205 N. Park Drive, 27401
(919) 274-6350

Enjoy the warm hospitality of our 1905 home on the park in the historic district of Greensboro. Three minutes from downtown; three miles from I-85 and I-40. Air-conditioning, two fireplaces in living rooms, swimming pool, TV room, guest kitchen. Hearty continental breakfast is served.

Host: Jo Anne Green
Doubles: 5 (3-4 PB; 2 SB) $32.40-75.60
Type of Beds: 2 Twin; 3 Queen; 1 King
Continental-plus Breakfast
Minimum stay Southern Furniture Market: 3
Credit Cards: A, B, C
Notes: 2, 5, 7, 8 (over 4), 9, 10, 11, 12, 14

HENDERSONVILLE

Claddagh Inn

755 North Main Street, 28739
(704) 697-7778; 1-800-225-4700

The Claddagh Inn is located in downtown Hendersonville, just two blocks from the beautiful Main Street Shopping Promenade. The inn has undergone extensive remodeling. The guest rooms are tastefully decorated, and our guests awake to a delicious full country breakfast.

Hosts: Marie & Fred Carberry
Doubles: 18 (14 PB; 4 SB) $25-59 plus tax
Type of Beds: 8 Twin; 15 Double; 1 Queen; 1 King
Full Breakfast
Credit Cards: A, B, C, D
Notes: 2, 5, 7, 8, 9, 10, 11, 12, 14

Echo Mountain Inn

2849 Laurel Park Highway, 28739
(704) 693-9626

NOTES: Credit cards accepted: A Master Card; B Visa; C American Express; D Discover Card; E Diners Club; F Other: 2 Personal checks accepted: 3 Lunch available: 4 Dinner available: 5 Open all year

Built in 1896, located in the peace and tranquility of an established residential neighborhood at three thousand feet overlooking Hendersonville and beyond to the Blue Ridge. Turn-of-the-century charm, gourmet dining. Convenient to Carl Sandburg's home, Flat Rock Playhouse, Biltmore House, Chimney Rock, and many other N.C. attractions.

Hosts: Marion & Dick Mulford
Singles: 3 (PB) $45-56
Doubles: 28 (PB) $56-106
Types of Beds: 18 Twin; 31 Double; 1 King
Continental Breakfast
Credit Cards: A, B, C
Closed Jan.-March
Notes: 2, 3, 4, 7, 8, 9, 10, 11, 12

HICKORY

The Hickory Bed & Breakfast

464 7th Street SW, 28602
(704) 324-0548

Early turn-of-the-century space, with modern comfort. We offer more than hospitality. Major furniture sales, mountain sports, and a central location for this arts mecca lure visitors to Hickory. Antique and year-round flea markets nearby.

Hosts: Bill & Jane Mohney
Doubles: 4 (2 PB; 2 SB) $35-50
Type of Beds: 2 Twin; 2 Double; 1 Queen
Full Breakfast
Credit Cards: No
Notes: 2, 5, 7, 8, 9

The Old Mill

Box 252, 28710
(704) 625-4256

1920s Bavarian chalet style B&B perched on the banks of a rushing mountain stream in scenic Hickory Nut Gorge. Attractions within thirty minutes include: Flat Rock, Hendersonville, Asheville, Biltmore House, Black Mountain, Green River, and the Blue Ridge Parkway.

Host: Walt Davis
Doubles: 5 (PB) $55-65
Type of Beds: 4 Twin; 3 Double; 1 Queen; 1 King
Continental-plus Breakfast
Credit Cards: A, B
Closed Dec. 15 - March 15 open for groups only
Notes: 2, 9, 10, 11, 12

Colonial Pines Inn

HIGHLANDS

Colonial Pines Inn

Rt. 1, Box 22B, 28741
(704) 526-2060

A quiet country guest house with lovely mountain view. Comfortably furnished with antiques and many nice accessories. Half a mile from Highlands' fine dining and shopping area. Full breakfast includes egg dishes, homemade breads, fresh fruit, coffee, juice.

Hosts: Chris & Donna Alley
Singles: 2 (PB) $55-65
Doubles: 4 (PB) $60-75
Apartment: 1 (PB, kitchen; sleeps 4)
Full Breakfast
Credit Cards: A, B
Notes: 2, 5, 8, 9, 10, 11, 12, 13

LAKE JUNALUSKA

Providence Lodge

1 Atkins Loop, Lake Junaluska, 28745
(704) 456-6486

Providence Lodge is located near the Blue Ridge Parkway and is an easy drive from the Cherokee Indian Reservation, Great Smoky Mountain National Park, or the Biltmore Estate in Asheville. Rustic, with period furniture, comfortable beds, claw-foot tubs,

6 Pets welcome: 7 Smoking allowed: 8 Children welcome: 9 Social drinking allowed: 10 Tennis available: 11 Swimming available: 12 Golf available: 13 Skiing available: 14 May be booked through travel agents

and big porches. Delicious family-style meals feature the best in country cooking.

Hosts: Ben & Wilma Cato
Singles: 2 (1 PB; 1 SB) $40
Doubles: 14 (7 PB; 7 SB) $60
Type of Beds: 12 Twin; 20 Double
Full Breakfast
Credit Cards: No
Closed Sept. - May
Notes: 2, 4, 8, 9, 10, 11, 12

KILL DEVIL HILLS

The Figurehead

B&B in the Albemarle
Box 248, Everetts, 27825
(919) 792-4584

A lovely two-story beach home sitting on a high dune overlooking the sound, with a view of the ocean from the upper deck. A short walk to the ocean or the sound, and the nature trails of Nags Head Woods are nearby. Good surfing and fishing, fine food and golf nearby. Bird watchers will find lots of waterfowl on Pea Island. Living room, TV/VCR, air-conditioning, Jacuzzi in one room.

Singles: 1 (SB) $40-50
Doubles: 2 (PB) $55-75
Continental Breakfast
Minimum stay: 2
Credit Cards: No
Notes: 2, 5, 9, 10, 11, 12

Ye Olde Cherokee Inn

500 North Virginia Dare Trail, 27948
(919) 441-6127

Large pink beach house with cypress-wood interior five hundred feet from ocean beach. Quiet, restful. Ideal for relaxing and romance. Close to fine restaurants, golf, hang gliding, scuba diving, wind surfing, deep-sea fishing, and shopping. Be as active or inactive as you wish.

Hosts: Bob & Phyllis Combs
Doubles: 6 (PB) $55-81
Type of Beds: 2 Twin; 6 Double
Continental Breakfast

Minimum stay holidays: 3
Credit Cards: A, B, C
Closed Nov.-March
Notes: 2, 9, 10, 11, 12

LAKE TOXAWAY

The Greystone Inn

Greystone Lane, 28747
(704) 966-4700

The Greystone Inn, an early 1900s restored Swiss revival-style mansion, is listed on the National Register of Historic Places. Golf and tennis, swimming, boating, and fishing on the largest private lake in North Carolina.

Hosts: Tim & Harriet Lovelace
Doubles: 34 (PB) $80-145/person
Type of Beds: 2 Twin; 16 Double; 8 Queen; 9 King
Full or Continental Breakfast
Credit Cards: A, B, C
Closed Nov.-April
Notes: 2, 4, 7, 8, 9, 10, 11, 12, 14

MANTEO

Scarborough Inn

Box 1310, 27954
(919) 473-3979

The comforts of the present: private baths, TV, refrigerator, room telephone, and in-room coffee. Plus memorable touches from the past: family heirlooms, antiques, and collectibles, all carefully chosen and lovingly managed by natives Sally and Phil, of historic Roanoke Island.

Hosts: Phil & Sally Scarborough
Doubles: 10 (PB) $37.80-48.60
Type of Beds: 14 Double; 3 Queen
Continental Breakfast
Minimum stay holidays: 3
Credit Cards: A, B, C, E, F
Notes: 4, 5, 7, 8, 9, 10, 11, 12

MARSHALL

Marshall House

5 Hill Street, 28753
(704) 649-9205

NOTES: Credit cards accepted: A Master Card; B Visa; C American Express; D Discover Card; E Diners Club; F Other: 2 Personal checks accepted: 3 Lunch available: 4 Dinner available: 5 Open all year

Built in 1903, the inn overlooks the peaceful town of Marshall and the waters of the French Broad River. The house is a twenty-room country inn, decorated with fancy chandeliers, mirrors, and pictures. Historically, the house has played a major roll in the development of the town. Come spend a relaxing time in the mountains and enjoy Marshall House.

Host: Ruth Boylan
Doubles: 8 (2 PB; 6 SB) $30-50
Continental Breakfast
Credit Cards: A, B, C, D, E
Notes: 2, 5, 7, 8, 9, 10, 11, 12, 13, 14

MARS HILL

Baird House, Ltd.
121 South Main Street, 28754
(704) 689-5722

Five guest rooms—one with a working fireplace two with private bath — are featured in an old brick, antique-filled bed and breakfast inn that once was the grandest house in this pastoral corner of the western North Carolina mountains.

Host: Mrs. Yvette Wessel
Doubles: 5 (2 PB; 3 SB) $36.75-52.50
Type of Beds: 2 Twin; 2 Double; 3 Queen
Full Breakfast
Credit Cards: C
Closed Dec.
Notes: 2, 7, 8, 9, 10, 11, 12, 13, 14

MOUNT AIRY

Pine Ridge Inn
2893 West Pine Street, 27030
(919) 789-5034

Built in 1948, this southern mansion offers private bedroom suites, swimming pool with sun deck, large indoor hot tub, exercise room. Lunch and dinner available Tuesday-Sunday.

Hosts: Ellen & Manford Haxton
Doubles: 7 (5 PB; 2 SB) $50-85
Type of Beds: 2 Twin; 3 Double; 2 Queen

Continental Breakfast
Credit Cards: A, B, C
Notes: 2, 3, 4, 5, 7, 8, 9, 10, 11, 12, 14

MURFREESBORO

Winborne House
333 Jay Trail, 27855
(919) 398-5224

A retired army couple are your hosts in this restored Greek Revival built in 1818 and 1840. In a small college town; historical tours led by your hosts, who are local docents, are available. Friendly, casual atmosphere in a house filled with antiques and collectibles. Good food.

Hosts: Richard & Edna Hammel
Doubles: 2 (SB) $30-35
Type of Beds: 2 Twin; 1 Queen
Full Breakfast
Credit Cards: No
Notes: 2, 5, 6, 7 (limited), 8, 9

NAGS HEAD

First Colony Inn
Rt. 1, Box 748, 27959
(919) 441-2343

Enjoy Southern hospitality in our historic inn with direct ocean access to a beach and sound views. Convenient to all historic and natural attractions. Renovations will be complete in the spring of 1990. Efficiencies, wet bars, luxury baths, wonderful porches with rockers and hammocks.

Hosts: Richard & Camille Lawrence
Doubles: 26 (PB) $90-185
Continental Breakfast
Credit Cards: A, B
Notes: 2, 5, 7 (limited), 8, 9, 10, 11, 12, 14

Ocean Side
Box 248, Everetts, 27825
(919) 792-45484D

A lovely cedar-shingle Nags Head cottage, with large wraparound porches, just 50 yards

6 Pets welcome: 7 Smoking allowed: 8 Children welcome: 9 Social drinking allowed: 10 Tennis available: 11 Swimming available: 12 Golf available: 13 Skiing available: 14 May be booked through travel agents

First Colony Inn

from the shore with a beautiful view of the Atlantic. Sit on the large back deck and watch the hang gliders. Beach chairs and umbrellas available; spacious lounge with TV and piano; fireplace. Available *weekdays only from April 15 - November 1.*

Doubles: 4 (SB) $55
Type of Beds: 3 Twin; 5 Double
Continental Breakfast
Credit Cards: No

NEW BERN

The Aerie

509 Pollock Street, 28560
(919) 636-5553

A Victorian inn one block from Tryon Palace. Individually decorated rooms are furnished with antiques and reproductions; sitting room with player piano. Bicycles are available for guests who want to tour New Bern's historic district.

Hosts: Rick & Lois Cleveland
Doubles: 7 (PB) $52-75
Type of Beds: 4 Twin; 5 Queen
Full Breakfast
Credit Cards: A, B
Notes: 2, 5, 7, 8, 9, 12, 14

Harmony House Inn

215 Pollock Street, 28560
(919) 636-3810

This circa 1850 Greek Revival inn provides comfortable elegance in the historic district. Unusual spaciousness, antiques, a guest parlor, rocking chairs and swings on the front porch, and a parking area add to guests' enjoyment. Near Tryon Palace, restaurants, and shops.

Hosts: A.E. & Diane Hansen
Doubles: 9 (PB) $52.92-75.60
Type of Beds: 4 Twin; 5 Queen
Full Breakfast
Credit Cards: A, B, C
Notes: 2, 5, 7, 8, 9, 10, 12, 14

Kings Arms Inn

212 Pollock Street, 28560
(919) 638-4409

The King's Arms Inn, named for an old New Bern tavern reputed to have hosted members of the First Continental Congress, upholds a heritage of hospitality and graciousness as New Bern's "first and foremost" in bed and breakfast accommodations. Spacious rooms with comfortable four-poster, canopy, or brass beds,

NOTES: Credit cards accepted: A Master Card; B Visa; C American Express; D Discover Card; E Diners Club; F Other: 2 Personal checks accepted: 3 Lunch available: 4 Dinner available: 5 Open all year

fireplaces, private baths, and elegant decor harbor travelers who want to escape the present and steep themselves in colonial history. Home-baked breakfasts include: banana or zucchini bread, blueberry, lemon ginger, apple streusel, or sweet potato muffins, Smithfield ham and biscuits, fresh fruit, juice, and cinnamon coffee or tea — all delivered to your room with the morning paper.

Hosts: David & Diana Parks
Doubles: 9 (PB) $49-69
Type of Beds: 2 Twin; 8 Double; 3 Queen
Continental-plus Breakfast
Credit Cards: A, B, C
Notes: 2, 5, 7, 8, 9, 10, 12, 14

New Berne House Inn

709 Broad Street, 28560
(919) 636-2250

Particularly pleasing English country house decor in New Bern's only authentically restored B&B. Antique beds with piles of pillows and crisp eyelet sheets; private vintage baths; outstanding breakfasts; afternoon tea; complimentary champagne, tandem bikes; hammocks; carriage rides. Closest accommodations to Tryon Palace.

Hosts: Shan & Joel Wilkins
Doubles: 6 (PB) $54-81
Type of Beds: 2 Twin; 2 Double; 2 Queen; 1 King
Full Breakfast
Credit Cards: A, B, C
Notes: 2, 5, 6, 7, 8 (over 6), 9, 10, 11, 12, 13, 14

OCRACOKE ISLAND

Oscar's House

Rt. 12, Box 206, 27960
(919) 928-1311

Oscar's House offers friendly accommodations in a comfortable 1940s home on Ocracoke Island. The home is one block from the harbor and one mile from the Atlantic Ocean, within easy walking distance to shops, restaurants, and historic sites. The full breakfast is healthy, and special diets are catered to.

Host: Ann Ehringhaus
Singles: 1 (SB) $35-45
Doubles: 2 (1 PB; 1 SB) $45-55
Type of Beds: 2 Twin; 1 Double; 1 Queen
Full Breakfast
Credit Cards: A, B
Closed Nov.-April
Notes: 2, 7 (restricted), 8 (over 3), 9, 11

ORIENTAL

The Tar Heel Inn

Box 176, 28571
(919) 249-1078

This quiet fishing village is located on the Neuse River and the Pamlico Sound and is known as the sailing capital of N.C. This quaint circa 1890 inn has been restored to capture the feeling of an old English-style country inn with comfortable common rooms. The patios and gardens are yours to enjoy, and you can even borrow bikes to pedal around town. Excellent restaurants and shops, sailing, golf, tennis, and fishing are within walking or biking distance.

Hosts: Dave & Patti Nelson
Doubles: 6 (PB) $40-65
Type of Beds: 2 Twin; 4 Queen; 1 King
Full Breakfast
Credit Cards: No
Notes: 2, 5, 8 (over 12), 9, 10, 11, 12, 14

PILOT MOUNTAIN

Pilot Knob Inn

Box 1280, 27041
(919) 325-2502

Individual 100-year-old log tobacco barns, nestled in the woods on the side of Pilot Mountain. The perfect place for two to rough it in comfort. Each cabin has a stone fireplace, whirlpool for two, upstairs bedroom, bathrobes, flowers, fruit. Also on premises: dry sauna and swimming pool.

Host: James Rouse
Doubles: 5 (PB) $63-105
Type of Beds: 2 Double; 3 Queen
Continental Breakfast
Credit Cards: A, B
Notes: 2, 5, 7, 9, 11, 12, 14

PINEHURST

The Magnolia Inn

Box 266, Magnolia Road, 28374
(919) 295-6900

The Magnolia Inn was built in 1896, has ten guest rooms with private baths, and serves a full breakfast. Located in town, where shopping is available, but most of all, there are fifteen golf courses only a short distance away.

Hosts: Sue & Earl Payne & Ann Martin
Singles: 1 (PB) $20
Doubles: 9 (PB) $34
Full Breakfast
Credit Cards: A, B
Closed December
Notes: 2, 7, 8, 10, 11, 12

RALEIGH

The Oakwood Inn

411 North Bloodworth Street, 27604
(919) 832-9712

The Oakwood Inn is an 1871 Victorian listed on the National Register and located in a downtown historic district. Its Victorian heritage is seen in the carefully restored decor, period architecture, and details such as names scratched on a windowpane in 1875.

Host: Diana Newton
Singles: 1 (PB) $60-70
Doubles: 5 (PB) $70-80
Type of Beds: 2 Double; 3 Queen; 1 King
Full Breakfast
Credit Cards: A, B, C
Closed Christmas week
Notes: 2, 7, 8 (over 12), 14

ROBBINSVILLE

Blue Boar Lodge

200 Santeetlah Road, 28771
(704) 479-8126

Secluded mountain retreat cooled by mountain breezes. Hiking, fishing, hunting, bird watching, and canoeing are all very close by. Rustic but modern house. Meals served family style on our lazy Susan table. Located away from all city traffic, ten miles NW of Robbinsville. Quiet and peaceful. Rate includes breakfast and dinner.

Hosts: Roy & Kathy Wilson
Doubles: 7 (PB) $90
Type of Beds: 2 Twin; 1 Double; 4 King
Full Breakfast
Minimum stay holidays: 2
Credit Cards: A, B
Closed April 1-mid-Oct.
Notes: 4, 7

ROBERSONVILLE

Kilpatrick House

B&B in the Albemarle
Box 248, Everetts, 27825
(919) 792-4584

This large, comfortable home is in a quiet small town. Located on a lovely tree-shaded street one block from downtown, in the heart of tobacco country. Warehouse tours are available in the fall. Also near Anheuser-Bush, Eagle Snacks, Robersonville Products/Hallmark Products, Perdue, Southern Apparel, and Generation II.

Doubles: 3 (1 PB; 2 SB) $30-35
Type of Beds: 2 Twin; 2 Double
Continental Breakfast
Credit Cards: No
Notes: 2, 5

Magnolia Place

B&B in the Albemarle
Box 248, Everetts, 27825
(919) 792-4584

NOTES: Credit cards accepted: A Master Card; B Visa; C American Express; D Discover Card; E Diners Club; F Other: 2 Personal checks accepted: 3 Lunch available: 4 Dinner available: 5 Open all year

Located in a quiet residential area of one of North Carolina's unique small towns. Only eight miles to Hamilton. Magnolia Place is within walking distance of all churches and the downtown business district. Piano, family room with fireplace, TV.

Doubles: 5 (1 PB; 4 SB) $35-50
Continental Breakfast
Credit Cards: No

ROPER

Soundview

B&B in the Albemarle
Box 248, Everetts, 27825
(919) 792-4584

Ranch home within 100 yards of Albemarle Sound and a three-minute walk to the nearest restaurant. Edenton is just a fifteen-minute drive; Pettigrew State Park and Sommerset Place are twenty minutes. You may drive to the Outer Banks in one hour.

Doubles: 2 (SB) $38-40
Full Breakfast
Credit Cards: No
Notes: 2, 5, 6 (outside), 8

SHAWBORO

Shawboro Farm

B&B in the Albemarle
Box 248, Everetts, 27825
(919) 792-4584

This grain, produce, and livestock farm is located one mile off the main beach road from Norfolk, Virginia to the Outer Banks/Nags Head area. It's a sixty-five-year-old, two-story farmhouse near Currituck Sound, which is famous for hunting and fishing.

Doubles: 2 (SB) $30-35
Type of Beds: 2 Double
Continental Breakfast
Credit Cards: No

SOUTHPORT

Dosher Plantation House

Rt. 5, Box 100, 28461
(919) 457-5554

The Dosher House, originally the home of Dr. J. Arthur Dosher, founder of the local hospital, was restored in 1986. Sandy beaches are within five minutes; Orton Plantation, ten minutes; historic Southport five minutes. Also near Old Brunswick and Fort Fisher Ferry. Come and enjoy.

Hosts: George & Ola Inman
Doubles: 3 (PB) $49-54
Type of Beds: 2 Twin; 1 Double; 1 Queen
Full Breakfast
Credit Cards: A, B, C
Notes: 2, 5, 10, 11, 12

SPARTA

Turby-villa

East Whitehead Street, 28675
(919) 372-8490

This B&B is located on twenty acres of beautiful mountain farmland. Breakfast is selected from a menu and served on a glassed-in porch with a beautiful view of the mountains. We are ten miles from the Blue Ridge Parkway, which is maintained by the National Park Service.

Hosts: Maybelline & R.E. Turby Turbiville
Doubles: 3 (PB) $26.25-42
Type of Beds: 2 Twin; 2 Double
Full Breakfast
Credit Cards: No
Notes: 2, 5, 7, 8, 9, 10, 12

SPRUCE PINE

The Fairway Inn Bed & Breakfast

110 Henry Lane, 28777
(704) 765-4917

Beautiful country home with a scenic view. Located on highway 226, three miles north of the Blue Ridge Parkway. Gourmet breakfast and homemade breads. Wine and cheese in the afternoon. Restaurants nearby.

Hosts: Margaret & John P. Stevens
Singles: 2 (PB) $50
Doubles: 4 (PB) $60-70
Type of Beds: 4 Twin; 1 Queen; 3 King
Full Breakfast
Minimum stay weekends and holidays: 2
Credit Cards: No
Closed Jan.-April
Notes: 2, 7, 8, 9, 10, 12, 13, 14

TARBORO

Little Warren

304 East Park Avenue, 27886
(919) 823-1314

Large, gracious, Edwardian family home, renovated and modernized, located within a quiet neighborhood in the historic district. Deeply set wraparound front porch overlooks the town common, which is one of two originally chartered commons remaining in the United States. Antiques available.

Hosts: Patsy & Tom Miller
Doubles: 3 (PB) $50.40-68.25
Type of Beds: 4 Twin; 1 Double
Continental and Full Breakfast
Credit Cards: A, B, C
Notes: 2, 5, 7, 8 (over 6), 9, 10

TRYON

Mill Farm Inn

Box 1251, 28782
(800)-545-6992

The disappointments of travel are forgotten at Mill Farm Inn! Emphasis is on important amenities: a homelike atmosphere, the warmth of bedrooms with private baths, and cozy, relaxing living and dining rooms that make our special guests feel at home.

Hosts: Chip & Penny Kessler
Doubles: 8 (PB) $42-50.40

Continental Breakfast
Credit Cards: No
Notes: 2, 5, 7, 8, 9, 10, 11, 12, 14

Stone Hedge Inn

Box 366, 28782
(704) 859-9114

Grand old estate on 28 acres at the base of Tryon Mountain. Lodging in the main building, cottage, and guest house. Private baths, TV, antiques, and wonderful views. Some rooms have kitchens and some have fireplaces. A full breakfast is served in the dining room by the picture windows; our restaurant serves fine continental country-inn cuisine.

Hosts: Ray & Anneliese Weingartner
Doubles: 6 (PB) $56-75
Type of Beds: 2 Twin; 4 Double; 1 Queen
Full Breakfast
Credit Cards: A, B
Notes: 2, 4, 5, 7, 8 (over 6), 9, 10, 11, 12

Mill Farm Inn

VALLE CRUCIS

Mast Farm Inn

Box 704, 28691
(704) 963-5857

Recently restored eleven-room inn on the National Register of Historic Places. Vegetables and berries for the dining room are grown on the 18-acre farm located in North Carolina's High Country near the Blue Ridge Parkway. Country cooking with

NOTES: Credit cards accepted: A Master Card; B Visa; C American Express; D Discover Card; E Diners Club; F Other: 2 Personal checks accepted: 3 Lunch available: 4 Dinner available: 5 Open all year

Mast Farm Inn

a gourmet touch. Golf, hiking, swimming, fishing, and skiing are nearby. Breakfast and dinner are included in the daily rate.

Hosts: Sibyl & Francis Pressly
Doubles: 11 (9 PB; 2 SB) $46-124 MAP
Type of Beds: 3 Twin; 7 Double; 3 Queen; 1 King
Continental Breakfast
Credit Cards: A, B
Closed March 6 - April 25 & Nov. 6 - Dec. 26
Notes: 2, 4, 9, 10, 11, 12, 13

WARSAW

The Squire's Vintage Inn

Rt. 2, Box 130R, 28398
(919) 296-1831

The Squire's Vintage Inn is located in the heart of Duplin County, as is its companion restaurant, The Country Squire, noted for its delicious cuisine and good taste. The rural setting adds to the privacy, intimacy, and relaxation for an overall feeling of "getting away from it all." Located near historic Kenansville.

Host: Iris Lennon
Doubles: 12 (PB) $44.10-51.45
Type of Beds: 11 Double; 1 King

Continental Breakfast
Credit Cards: A, B, C, E
Notes: 2, 4, 5, 7, 8, 9, 12

WAYNESVILLE

Grandview Lodge

809 Valley View Circle Road, 28786
(704) 456-5212

A country inn in the western North Carolina mountains; open all year. Southern home cooking, with breakfast featuring homemade breads, jams, and jellies. Dinner includes fresh vegetables, freshly baked breads, and desserts. Meals served family style; included in the rates. Private bath and cable TV.

Hosts: Stan & Linda Arnold
Doubles: 15 (PB) $75-85
Type of Beds: 8 Twin; 21 Double; 1 Queen
Full Breakfast
Credit Cards: No
Notes: 2, 4 (included), 5, 7, 8, 9, 10, 11, 12, 13, 14

Hallcrest Inn

299 Halltop Circle, 28786
(704) 456-6457

---

6 Pets welcome: 7 Smoking allowed: 8 Children welcome: 9 Social drinking allowed: 10 Tennis available: 11 Swimming available: 12 Golf available: 13 Skiing available: 14 May be booked through travel agents

The homelike atmosphere here encourages a relaxing stay at this 1880s farmhouse on a mountaintop. Southern-style meals are served around large, lazy Susan tables. All rooms have private baths. There's a beautiful view from the front porch, where rocking chairs await you. Near area attractions. The daily rate includes both breakfast and dinner.

Hosts: Russell & Margaret Burson
Doubles: 12 (PB) $70
Type of Beds: 12 Double
Full Breakfast
Credit Cards: No
Closed Nov. - late May
Notes: 2, 3 (by arrangement), 4, 7, 8, 9, 10, 11, 12, 14

Heath Lodge

900 Dolan Road, 28786
(704) 456-3333

Our inn offers the charm of the past along with contemporary comforts. Enjoy cool mountain air from rockers on the porches of our stone and poplar buildings, set on a wooded hillside. Bountiful breakfasts and country gourmet dinners are included in our inviting rates.

Hosts: David & Bonnie Probst
Singles: 1 (PB) $50 MAP
Doubles: 21 (PB) $75-90 MAP
Full Breakfast
Credit Cards: No
Closed Nov.-April
Notes: 2, 4, 7, 8, 9, 10, 11, 12, 13

The Palmer House

108 Pigeon Street, 28786
(704) 456-7521

Built before the turn of the century, The Palmer House is one of the last of Waynesville's once numerous tourist homes. Within one block of Main Street. Relaxing environment, beautiful mountains, good food, a home away from home.

Hosts: Jeff Minick & Kris Gillet
Doubles: 7 (PB) $35-49
Type of Beds: 3 Twin; 3 Double; 3 Queen

Full and Continental Breakfast
Credit Cards: No
Notes: 2, 5, 7, 8, 9, 10, 12

WEAVERVILLE

Dry Ridge Inn

26 Brown Street, 28787
(704) 658-3899

Large comfortable farmhouse, circa 1849, furnished with many antiques and handmade quilts. We try to keep our home in the manner of the time it was built: no TV, but plenty of books, games, an old Victrola, and good conversation.

Hosts: John & Karen VanderElzen
Doubles: 5 (PB) $42-47.25
Type of Beds: 7 Double
Full Breakfast
Minimum stay fall weekends and holidays: 2
Credit Cards: A, B
Notes: 2, 4, 5, 7, 8, 9, 11, 12, 13

The Five Star Guest House

WILLIAMSTON

Colonial House

B&B in the Albemarle

Box 248, Everetts, 27825
(919) 792-4584

This spacious colonial, decorated in the Williamsburg tradition, is in an historic area on a lovely tree-shaded street. A large, comfortable front porch is available for relaxing, and it's an easy drive to the nearby Fort Branch restoration.

Doubles: 2 (PB) $30-35
Type of Beds: 2 Double
Continental Breakfast
Notes: 2, 5, 8, 9, 10, 11, 12

WILMINGTON

Anderson Guest House

520 Orange Street, 28401
(919) 343-8128

An 1851 Italianate townhouse with separate guest quarters overlooking our private garden. Furnished with antiques, ceiling fans, working fireplaces; drinks on arrival. A delightful gourmet breakfast is served.

Hosts: Landon & Connie Anderson
Doubles: 2 (1 PB; 1 SB) $50-60
Type of Beds: 1 Double; 1 Queen
Full Breakfast
Credit Cards: No
Notes: 2, 5, 6, 7 (limited), 8, 9, 10, 11, 12

The Five Star Guest House

14 N. Seventh Street, 28401
(919) 763-7581

The Five Star Guest House was built in 1908 and is just minutes from beaches, restaurant, shops, and galleries. It features spacious bedrooms furnished with antiques and private baths with deep claw-foot tubs. Listed with AAA.

Hosts: Harvey & Ann Crowther
Doubles: 3 (PB) $50-60
Type of Beds: 4 Double; 1 Queen
Full Breakfast
Credit Cards: A, B, C
Notes: 2, 5, 7, 8 (over 12), 9, 10, 11, 12, 14

Murchison House

305 South 3rd Street, 28401
(919) 343-8580

Located in the historic Wilmington residential district, this modified Victorian Gothic mansion features four spacious rooms with private baths, clawfoot tubs, four back verandas overlooking the enclosed formal garden and brick courtyard. Two blocks from Cape Fear River and numerous shops and restaurants. Horse-drawn carriage rides available.

Hosts: Mr. & Mrs. Joseph P. Curry
Doubles: 4 (PB) $60-65
Type of Beds: 2 Twin; 3 Double
Full Breakfast
Credit Cards: A, B, C, D
Notes: 2, 5, 7, 8, 9, 10, 11, 12

Colonel Ludlow Inn

Worth House

412 S. Third Street, 28401
(919) 762-8562

The Worth House is an elegant old Queen Anne that looks like a beautifully decorated wedding cake. Be pampered with lush towels, fine linens, imported soaps, and attentive personal service. Enjoy a gourmet breakfast in bed, on a private veranda, or in our dining room. Delicious beach and fireside baskets available.

Hosts: Terry Meyer & Kate Walsh
Doubles: 4 (PB) $65-70
Type of Beds: 1 Double; 2 Queen; 1 King
Full Breakfast
Credit Cards: No
Notes: 2, 3, 4, 5, 7, 8 (over 12), 10, 11, 12, 14

WINSTON-SALEM

Colonel Ludlow Inn

W. 5th & Summit, 27101
(919) 777-1887

A blend of the elegance of yesteryear and the convenience of today. The Victorian rooms are furnished with period antiques skillfully combined with two-person whirlpool baths, stereo systems with tapes, bar refrigerators with refreshments, microwaves, telephones, and cablevision. This National Register Inn is located in the historic district of West End, within walking distance of restaurants, shops, and parks.

Host: Terri L. Jones, Mgr.
Doubles: 12 (PB) $45-125
Type of Beds: 2 Double; 2 Queen; 8 King
Continental-plus Breakfast
Credit Cards: A, B, C, D, E
Notes: 2, 5, 7, 8 (over 10), 9, 10, 11, 12, 14

North Dakota

FORT RANSOM

Old West B&B Service 3
Box 211, Regent, N.D.

This contemporary split-level home with a relaxed atmosphere is in a beautiful open area. One of the guest rooms on the second floor is done in tones of mauve and rose, with an antique decor. The downstairs bedroom is done in tones of blue and purple and has a private bath. There is also a second-floor den with queen hideabed for children. No smoking in guest rooms; Ukrainian is spoken. $30-35.

GOODRICH

Old West B&B Service 6
Box 211, Regent, N.D.

Warmly decorated frame home with hand-made quilts and wall hangings. Horseback riding available. Duck and deer hunting in the area. No household pets; some German spoken. $20-25.

KENMARE

Farm Comfort
RR 2, Box 71, 58746
(701) 848-2433

True farm atmosphere in an area noted for excellent goose, duck, upland game, deer, and antelope hunting, fishing, and bird watching. The Canadian border is just thirty miles away. Large family room, TV, kitchenette.

Hosts: Delmer & Marion Nelson
Doubles: 2 (SB) $20-25
Type of Beds: 2 Double
Full Breakfast
Credit Cards: No
Notes: 5, 6, 7, 8, 9, 10, 11, 12

KILLDEER

Old West B&B Service 7
Box 211, Regent, N.D.

Located in the foothills of the scenic Killdeer Mountains, twenty miles from Theodore Roosevelt National Park. There are Indian relics in the area, as well as a battlefield where Indians and Army fought. Children are welcome. No smoking in the guest rooms. $20-25.

LIDGERWOOD

Kaler Bed & Breakfast
Rt. 2, Box 151, 58053
(701) 538-4848

Enjoy country living on this 640 acre small grain farm, situated in the pheasant heartland. This older farm home has five beautiful bedrooms upstairs. A delicious full breakfast is served, and children are most welcome.

Hosts: Mark & Dorothy Kaler
Doubles: 5 (SB) $25-30
Type of Beds: 4 Double; 1 Queen
Full Breakfast
Credit Cards: No
Notes: 2, 5, 7, 8, 9, 10, 11, 12

---

6 Pets welcome: 7 Smoking allowed: 8 Children welcome: 9 Social drinking allowed: 10 Tennis available: 11 Swimming available: 12 Golf available: 13 Skiing available: 14 May be booked through travel agents

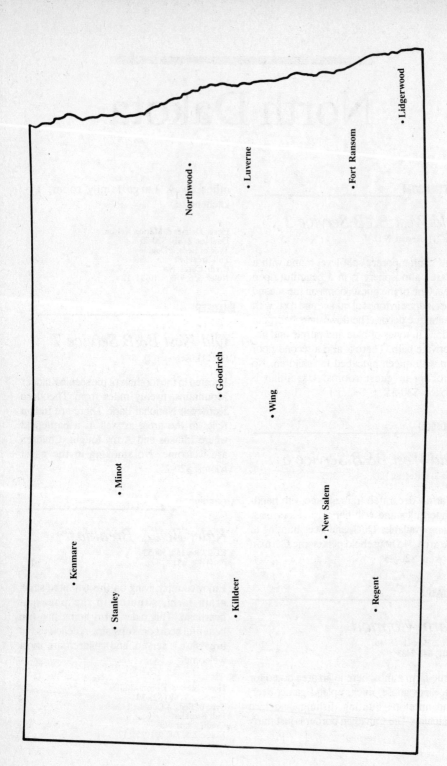

NORTH DAKOTA

Old West B&B Service 8

Box 211, Regent, N.D.

A very comfortable older home with a choice of bedrooms on the second floor and a private bath. Children are welcome, and the hosts can accommodate a pet. $25-35.

LUVERNE

Old West B&B Service 12

Box 211, Regent, N.D.

Scandinavian hosts, retired after 27 years in the Air Force, welcome you to their country home, which is decorated with antiques and family pieces. They serve a Scandinavian breakfast from their farm and garden, including Swedish pancakes and Danish Ableskiver. $30-50.

MINOT

Old West B&B Service 10

Box 211, Regent, N.D.

Located a few blocks from Minot State College, this air-conditioned home offers second-floor bedrooms with complete privacy. Children are welcome, and smoking is allowed except for the guest rooms. $25-35.

NEW SALEM

Old West B&B Service 11

Box 211, Regent, N.D.

A Scandinavian-style log home built by Finnish craftsmen in a quiet country setting four miles off I-94. Forty minutes from Bismarck and 100 miles from the Badlands. Guest rooms consist of one large room with a queen bed and private bath, and a family room with fireplace, wet bar, refrigerator,

TV, full bed, and private entrance. Ideal for two couples. There is also one large room upstairs with two full beds and a half bath. Children are welcome; smoking in the family room. $20-25.

NORTHWOOD

Old West B&B Service 9

Box 211, Regent, N.D.

Visit a diversified farm operation, and bring your binoculars for bird watching. The hosts are craft oriented and offer some pieces for sale. Children over twelve are welcome. Riding horses are available, and Norwegian is spoken. $30-35.

REGENT

Old West B&B Service 4

Box 211, Regent, N.D.

Not far from Medora and the Badlands, this house has an outdoor heated pool in the summer. Two bedrooms with double beds. No smoking or children under twelve, please. $25-35.

STANLEY

Old West B&B Service 1

Box 211, Regent, N.D.

This ranch-style home is located in the Little Knife River Valley. The area is close to Lake Sakakawea, with swimming, fishing, and boating, and fifteen miles from Fort Berthold Indian Reservation. During many summer weekends, there are rodeos and Indian powwows. The guest quarters consist of two large bedrooms, private bath, family room with fireplace, pool table, games, and semi-private entry. Guests may not smoke in guest rooms. $25-30.

---

6 Pets welcome: 7 Smoking allowed: 8 Children welcome: 9 Social drinking allowed: 10 Tennis available: 11 Swimming available: 12 Golf available: 13 Skiing available: 14 May be booked through travel agents

WING

Eva's Bed & Breakfast

HCR 1, Box 10, 58494
(701) 943-2461

Your hosts are retired farmers who built a new house on their third-generation grain and cattle ranch four miles from Mitchel Lake. Good fishing, swimming, boating, and picnic areas. One mile from Haystack Butte.

Forty-five minutes to the state capital, Heritage Center, zoo, museums, and many other points of interest.

Hosts: Harold & Eva Williams
Doubles: 2 (SB) $20-25
Type of Beds: 2 Double
Full Breakfast
Credit Cards: No
Notes: 2, 3, 4, 5, 8, 11, 14

Ohio

Portage House

601 Copley Road, 44320
(216) 535-1952

A large, gracious Tudor home in Portage — the site of the portage route between the Cuyahoga and Tuscarawas rivers. Five second-floor rooms and two baths, large living room. Breakfast is served in the formal dining room or at the large center island in the modern kitchen. Homemade breads and jams. Your host is a retired physics professor.

Hosts: Jeanne & Harry Pinnick
Singles: 1 (SB) $22
Doubles: 4 (1 PB; 3 SB) $28
Type of Beds: 2 Twin; 3 Double; 1 Queen; cots & cribs
Full Breakfast
Credit Cards: No
Closed Dec. & Jan.
Notes: 2, 6, 7 (limited), 8, 9, 10, 11, 12, 13

BELLVILLE

The Frederick Fitting House

72 Fitting Avenue, 44813
(419) 886-2863

An 1863 Victorian home in a quaint country village between Columbus and Cleveland. Gourmet breakfast served in hand-stenciled dining room, garden gazebo, or country kitchen. Near Mohican and Malabar Farm state parks, downhill and cross-country skiing, canoeing, Kenyon and Wooster colleges.

Hosts: Ramon & Suzanne Wilson
Doubles: 3 (SB) $40-50
Type of Beds: 1 Twin; 1 Double; 1 Queen
Full Breakfast
Credit Cards: No
Closed Thanksgiving & Christmas
Notes: 2, 4, 7, 8 (over 7), 9, 10, 11, 12, 13

The Frederick Fitting House

BLUE ROCK

McNutt Farm II

6120 Cutler Lake Road, 43720
(614) 674-4555

We are a country B&B, and for people trailering horses, we offer bed, breakfast, and barn. For city folk, we offer a quiet country night, beautiful scenery, fishing, swimming, buggy rides, farm chores, and more. There's a canoe for you to use, archery and rifle ranges, but no rental horses are available.

Hosts: Don & Patty McNutt
Doubles: (SB) $20
Continental Breakfast
Credit Cards: A, B
Notes: 5, 7, 8, 10, 11, 12

6 Pets welcome: 7 Smoking allowed: 8 Children welcome: 9 Social drinking allowed: 10 Tennis available: 11 Swimming available: 12 Golf available: 13 Skiing available: 14 May be booked through travel agents

- Geneva-On-The-Lake
- Marblehead
- Kinsman
- Cleveland Area
- Sandusky
- Pennisula
- Medina
- Akron
- Poland
- Wooster
- Loudonville
- Zoar
- Bellville
- Dellroy
- Mount Vernon
- Delaware
- Old Washington
- Troy
- Westerville
- West Milton
- Granville
- East Fultonham
- Blue Rock
- Lewisville
- Marietta
- Morrow

OHIO

CLEVELAND

Private Lodgings — Fairview Park

Box 18590, Cleveland, 44118
(216) 321-3213

A century-old home with lovely details. Your hosts are delightful people, friendly and knowledgeable of the neighborhood. No smoking; off-street parking. One double, private bed, $45-55.

Private Lodgings — Notre Maison

Box 18590, Cleveland, 44118
(216) 321-3213

A French chateau in a lovely suburb east of Cleveland. the house is furnished in wonderful antiques. The owner is French and speaks nine languages. No smoking; driveway parking. Two doubles, shared bath, $55-65.

Private Lodgings — Olmsted Falls

Box 18590, Cleveland, 44118
(216) 321-3213

A large Victorian farmhouse on 2 acres of land that was built in 1872 and has been lovingly renovated. Off-street parking; resident dog, cat, and goose. Two doubles, shared bath, $40-46.

Private Lodgings — Peninsula

Box 18590, Cleveland, 44118
(216) 321-3213

A "little Maine" cabin in the woods. Total privacy is assured with a laid-in breakfast.

There is a fireplace to laze in front of with a glass of wine in hand. Self-prepared breakfast. One double, private bath, $85.

Private Lodgings — Rocky River

Box 18590, Cleveland, 44118
(216) 321-3213

This guest room is large, with a private bath across the hall. The owners are bank managers active in the community. No smoking; off-street parking. One double, private bath, $45-55.

DELAWARE

Camelot at Heater's Run

6761 Taggart Road, 43015
(614) 548-4555

A nearly new chalet perched above a creek on 13 wooded acres only twenty-five minutes from Columbus. Hiking, fishing, cycling, and restful surroundings. Near Ohio State, Ohio Wesleyan, Otterbein, Battelle Institute, the Columbus Zoo, and Olentangy Indian Caverns. Perfect parking for camper, boat. Dog in residence.

Hosts: Don & Sally Hollenback
Doubles: 2 (PB) $35-50
Type of Beds: 2 Double
Full Breakfast
Credit Cards: No
Notes: 2, 5, 9, 10, 11, 12, 14

DELLROY

Pleasant Journey Inn

4247 Roswell Road SW, 44620
(216) 735-2987

An elegant fourteen-room post-Civil War mansion decorated in antiques and centrally located in Ohio's lake country. Nearby

6 Pets welcome: 7 Smoking allowed: 8 Children welcome: 9 Social drinking allowed: 10 Tennis available: 11 Swimming available: 12 Golf available: 13 Skiing available: 14 May be booked through travel agents

horseback riding, golf, fishing, swimming, boating, and Amish country visits.

Hosts: Jim & Marie Etterman
Doubles: 3 (1 PB; 2 SB) $46-56
Type of Beds: 2 Twin; 6 Double
Continental Breakfast
Credit Cards: A, B
Notes: 2, 5, 9, 10, 11, 12, 13, 14

EAST FULTONHAM

Hill View Acres

7320 Old Town Road, 43735
(614) 849-2728

Located ten miles southwest of Zanesville off U.S. 22. Large, spacious home on 21 rolling acres with pond. Guest rooms on first floor are handicapped accessible. Area popular for antiquing, pottery, hunting, and fishing. Honeymoon or getaway package available. Country cooking a specialty.

Hosts: Jim & Dawn Graham
Doubles: 2 (SB) $25-32
Type of Beds: 2 Double
Full Breakfast
Credit Cards: No
Notes: 2, 3, 4, 5, 7, 8, 9, 10, 11, 12

GENEVA-ON-THE-LAKE

The Otto Court Bed & Breakfast

5653 Lake Road, 44041
(216) 466-8668

Hotel and cottage complex overlooking Lake Erie. Within walking distance of the famous Geneva-on-the-Lake amusement center, Geneva State Park and Marina, and the Old Firehouse Winery. Conveniently located near the historic Ashtabula Harbor area and thirteen covered bridges.

Host: Mrs. C. Joyce Otto
Doubles: 12 (8 PB; 4 SB) $27-40
Type of Beds: 7 Twin; 10 Double; 1 Queen; 1 King
Full Breakfast
Minimum stay weekends & holidays: 2

Credit Cards: A, B
Notes: 2, 4, 5, 7, 8, 9, 10, 11, 12, 13 (XC), 14

GRANVILLE

Buxton Inn — 1812

313 E. Broadway, 43023
(614) 587-0001

Quiet elegance and cozy charm describe Buxton Inn's four guest rooms, all authentically furnished in period antiques. We have five dining rooms, a tavern, and wine cellar. The adjacent Warner House — 1815 — houses eleven period rooms. Breakfast, lunch, and dinner are available daily.

Hosts: Orville & Audrey Orr
Doubles: 15 (PB) $59.95-87.20
Type of Beds: 3 Twin; 18 Double; 2 Queen
Continental Breakfast
Credit Cards: A, B, C, E, F
Closed Christmas
Notes: 2, 3, 4, 5, 7, 8, 9, 10, 11, 12

KINSMAN

Hidden Hollow

9340 Rt. 5, 44428
(216) 876-8686

We are built on a hillside, with an eighty-foot balcony up and down. Very country; very private. Breakfast by the pool or in the large kitchen. Lots of birds and wildlife.

Hosts: Bob & Rita White
Doubles: 4 (PB) $32.50
Full Breakfast
Notes: 2, 5, 6, 7, 8, 9, 11, 12

LEWISVILLE

Grandma Betty's Bed & Breakfast

35226 Route 78, 43754
(614) 567-3465

Stay in the Scenic Switzerland of Ohio in a lovely country home. Relax in a family room or play pool in the game room. On warm summer days, enjoy a dip in the swimming pool. Sleep in a waterbed or a regular one. Wake up to a full country breakfast.

Hosts: Coy & Betty Hogue
Doubles: 3 (PB) $25-35
Type of Beds: 3 Double
Full Breakfast
Credit Cards: A, B
Notes: 2, 5, 7, 8, 9, 10, 11, 12

LOUDONVILLE

The Blackfork Inn

303 North Water Street, Box 149, 44842
(419) 994-3252

Elegantly restored Victorian townhouse near Mohican and Malabar state parks and Amish Country. A picturesque region with numerous restaurants, cheese shops, quilt coops, cabinetmakers. Two Victorian parlors for guests' use and a formal dining room serving home-grown raspberries and Amish specialties.

Hosts: Sue & Al Gorisek
Doubles: 6 (PB) $45-75
Type of Beds: 2 Twin; 2 Double; 2 Queen
Continental Breakfast
Credit Cards: A, B
Notes: 2, 4, 5, 6, 7, 8, 9, 10, 11, 12, 13

MARBLEHEAD

Old Stone House on the Lake

133 Clemons Street, 43440
(419) 798-5922

Stately stone mansion, built in 1861, gracing the shoreline of Lake Erie's western basin. Overlooks Kelleys Island and is located between the Kelleys ferry and Marblehead lighthouse. Patio on the water, library sitting room with cable TV, and games. Craft and gift shop in summer kitchen. Shopping, sightseeing, marinas, and restaurants are all

nearby. Seasonal executive fishing-charter service available.

Hosts: Pat Parks & Dorothy Bright
Doubles: 14 (2 PB; 12 SB) $55-85
Continental-plus Breakfast
Credit Cards: A, B
Notes: 2, 5, 7, 9, 10, 11, 12, 14

MARIETTA

Folger's Bantam Farm Bed & Breakfast

Rt. #6, Mitchell Lane, 45750
(614) 374-6919

A special welcome awaits you at Folger's Bantam Farm B&B, one mile north of I-77. This modern farm home has two cozy bedrooms, shared bath, living room, and a delicious country breakfast featuring Freida's homemade whole-wheat cinnamon rolls, fresh fruit, coffee, and more. Stroll our 22-acre farm, fish in the pond, swim in the pool, enjoy the calves, kittens, and other farm animals.

Hosts: Freida & Bill Folger
Doubles: 2 (SB) $35-45
Type of Beds: 2 Queen
Full Breakfast
Credit Cards: No
Closed Dec. 1-April 1
Notes: 2, 4, 8, 10, 11

Old Stone House on the Lake

MEDINA

Oakwood B&B

226 North Broadway, 44256
(216) 723-1162

Cozy country Victorian, furnished with antiques. Within walking distance of the restored Victorian town square; thirty miles south of Cleveland. Small-town atmosphere.

Hosts: David & Lonore Charboneau
Doubles: 2 (SB) $35
Type of Beds: 2 Double
Continental Breakfast
Credit Cards: No
Closed New Year's, Thanksgiving, Christmas
Notes: 2, 7, 8 (12 and over), 12

MORROW

Country Manor B & B

6315 Zoar Road, 45152
(513) 899-2440

Country Manor sits on a quiet 55 acres overlooking a valley, yet is conveniently located in an active area of southern Ohio that features Kings Island Amusement Park, Jack Nicklaus Golf Course, and Lebanon Raceway. Large, comfortable rooms feature 1868 elegance with modern conveniences.

Hosts: Rhea Hughes & Bobby Salyers
Doubles: 3 (1 PB; 2 SB) $32-58
Type of Beds: 2 Twin; 2 Double; 1 Double Sofa Bed;
1 Rollaway Single
Full Breakfast
Credit Cards: No
Closed Thanksgiving & Christmas
Notes: 2, 6 (outdoor facilities), 8 (over 11), 9, 10, 11, 12

MOUNT VERNON

The Russell-Cooper House

115 East Gambier Street, 43050
(614) 397-8638

History lives! Landmark circa 1829 Victorian mansion restored to 1880s grandeur. Nestled in America's Hometown — Mount Vernon — central Ohio's vacation headquarters. Antiques abound, luxurious guest rooms with baths, full breakfast, gift/craft shop, and more. Discover Ohio's best-kept secret; a memory you'll always cherish.

Hosts: Tim & Maureen Tyler
Doubles: 6 (PB) $45-60
Type of Beds: 2 Twin; 4 Double; 1 Queen
Full Breakfast
Credit Cards: A, B
Notes: 2, 3, 4, 5, 7, 8 (over 13), 9, 10, 11, 12, 13, 14

The Russell-Cooper House

OLD WASHINGTON

Zane Trace Bed & Breakfast

Box 115, Main Street, 43768
(614) 489-5970 (service)

Brick Victorian built in 1859. In-ground swimming pool, extra-large rooms, beautiful woodwork with high ceilings, antique furnishings. The quaint, quiet village of Old Washington is seven miles east of Cambridge, Ohio. Write for your free brochure.

Host: Ruth Wade
Doubles: 4 (SB) $32-60
Type of Beds: 2 Twin; 2 Double; 1 Queen
Continental Breakfast
Credit Cards: No
Closed Nov.-April
Notes: 2, 7, 8 (over 10), 9, 11, 12

NOTES: Credit cards accepted: A Master Card; B Visa; C American Express; D Discover Card; E Diners Club; F Other: 2 Personal checks accepted: 3 Lunch available: 4 Dinner available: 5 Open all year

PENINSULA

Centennial House
5995 Center Street, Box 67, 44264
(216) 657-2506

This gracious Victorian house is located in an historic village surrounded by the Cuyahoga Valley Park. Sports and music centers are nearby. The hosts restored and now share their century-old house following careers abroad in the American diplomatic service.

Hosts: Mona & Jay Ruoff
Doubles: 4 (2 PB; 2 SB) $30-50
Type of Beds: 4 Double
Full Breakfast
Notes: 2, 5, 6, 8, 9, 10, 11, 12, 13

POLAND

Inn at the Green
500 S. Main Street, 44514
(216) 757-4688

A classically proportioned Victorian townhouse on the south end of the green in preserved Connecticut Western Reserve Village. Featuring large moldings, twelve-foot ceilings, five Italian marble fireplaces, original poplar floors, and interior-shuttered windows.

Hosts: Ginny & Steve Meloy
Doubles: 4 (2 PB; 2 SB) $35-50
Type of Beds: 4 Twin; 3 Double
Continental Breakfast
Credit Cards: A, B
Notes: 2, 5, 7, 8 (over 7), 9, 10, 11, 12, 14

SANDUSKY

Bogarts Corner Bed & Breakfast
1403 East Bogart Road, 44870
(419) 627-2707

A home away from home. Relax in one of our many rocking chairs on the porch or in

the rooms. Easy access to interstates 80, 90, and U.S. 2. We're in the center of Lake Erie vacationland and all the activities Lake Erie has to offer: dinner cruises, island hopping, swimming and sunning on Lake Erie.

Hosts: Zendon & Davilee Willis
Singles: 2 (SB) $20-25
Doubles: 3 (2 PB; 1 SB) $40-50
Type of Beds: 2 Twin; 4 Queen
Full Breakfast
Credit Cards: No
Closed Oct. 15-May 1
Notes: 2, 6, 7, 8, 10, 11, 12, 14

Allen Villa B&B

TROY

Allen Villa B & B
434 South Market Street, 45373
(513) 335-1181

This B&B has seven fireplaces and is decorated in period antiques. Each room has a private bath, TV, telephone, and central air-conditioning. There is a self-serve snack bar for your evening pleasure, and a bountiful breakfast is served on the fifteen-foot antique dining room table that seats twelve guests.

Hosts: Robert & June Smith
Doubles: 5 (PB) $42.40-63.60
Type of Beds: 2 Twin; 3 Double; 1 King
Full Breakfast
Credit Cards: A, B, C
Notes: 2, 5, 9, 10, 11, 12, 14

6 Pets welcome: 7 Smoking allowed: 8 Children welcome: 9 Social drinking allowed: 10 Tennis available: 11 Swimming available: 12 Golf available: 13 Skiing available: 14 May be booked through travel agents

WESTERVILLE

Priscilla's Bed & Breakfast

5 South-West Street, 43081
(614) 882-3910

Located in an historic area adjacent to Otterbein College, this 1854 New England style home is surrounded by a white picket fence. The interior abounds with antiques and collectibles. Guests are welcome to borrow bicycles, use the patio, enjoy concerts in the adjoining park, walk to the Benjamin Hanby Museum or the quaint shops.

Host: Priscilla Haberman Curtiss
Singles: 1 (SB) $30 plus tax
Doubles: 1 (SB) $35 plus tax
Type of Beds: 1 Twin; 1 Double
Continental Breakfast
Credit Cards: No
Notes: 5, 7 (limited), 9, 12

WEST MILTON

Locust Lane Farm B & B

5590 Kessler Cowlesville Road, 45383
(513) 698-4743

Delightful old Cape Cod home in a rural setting. Air-conditioned bedrooms. Relax in the library or in front of the fireplace. Full breakfast served on the lovely screened porch in the summer. Browse through local antique shops, enjoy the nature center, golf, or canoeing.

Hosts: Ruth & Don Shoup
Doubles: 2 (1 PB; 1 SB) $35-40
Type of Beds: 1 Double; 1 Queen
Full Breakfast
Credit Cards: No
Notes: 2, 5,8, 10, 12

WOOSTER

Howey House

340 N. Bever Street, 44691
(216) 264-8231

A 139-year-old restored Victorian home furnished in period furniture. We're close to the College of Wooster, QARDC, ATI, and picturesque Amish country. Air-conditioned, with TV.

Hosts: James & Jo Howey
Doubles: 4 (1 PB; 3 SB) $24-34
Type of Beds: 2 Twin; 4 Double
Full Breakfast
Credit Cards: No
Notes: 2, 5, 8 (12 and over), 9

ZOAR

Haven at 4th N' Park

Box 467, 44697
(216) 874-4672

Designated a Heritage House on the corner of Zoar's beautiful formal garden in the center of the historic 1800s village. Brick and timber hallways lead to art gallery and keeping room with stone fireplace. Shops, restaurants, and museums within walking distance.

Hosts: Dick & Koki Maloney
Doubles: 3 (SB) $35-45
Type of Beds: 3 Double
Full Breakfast
Minimum stay holidays: 2
Credit Cards: A, B, C
Notes: 2, 5, 8 (over 5), 11, 12

The Weaving Haus

Box 431, 44697
(216) 874-3318

Built in the early 1830s and used as a shop for weaving flax and wool, The Weaving Haus still contains reminders of its former use in its drying room, dying vat, and vaulted fruit cellar that is now a German lunchroom called the Kaffe Stube. Conveniently located for strolling around the village and exploring other historic buildings.

Hosts: Dale & Bev Dessecker
Doubles: 3 (2 PB; 1 SB) $35-50
Type of Beds: 1 Twin; 1 Double; 1 Queen
Credit Cards: A, B
Notes: 2, 3, 4, 5, 8, 12

NOTES: Credit cards accepted: A Master Card; B Visa; C American Express; D Discover Card; E Diners Club; F Other: 2 Personal checks accepted: 3 Lunch available: 4 Dinner available: 5 Open all year

Oklahoma

Harrison House Inn

124 West Harrison, 73044
(405) 282-1000

Twenty-three rooms furnished in Victorian style with antiques and quilts. All have private baths. Central heat and air with thermostats in every room. Located next door to the theater in central downtown Guthrie. Featured in *Glamour, Insider,* and *Southern Living.*

Host: Phyllis Murray
Doubles: 23 (PB) $60-80
Type of Beds: 15 Double; 8 King
Continental-plus Breakfast
Credit Cards: A, B, C, D, E
Notes: 2, 5, 6, 7, 8, 9, 10, 11, 12, 14

The Grandison Inn

1841 N.W. 15th Street, 73106
(405) 521-0011

Three stories furnished with antiques in the Victorian style. Built originally in 1896, the house has lots of windows, fruit-bearing trees, and a gazebo. Central heat and air. Convenient to downtown Oklahoma City and Interstates 40 and 35.

Hosts: Claudia & Bob Wright
Doubles: 5 (PB) $40-90
Type of Beds: 4 Double; 1 Queen
Continental Breakfast
Credit Cards: No
Notes: 2, 5, 7, 8 (over 12), 9, 10, 11

Newton & Joann Flora

23312 W.W.46, 73112
(405) 840-3157

This house, furnished with antiques and collectibles, has a large patio off the living-room area that overlooks downtown Oklahoma City. TV, radio, and library are available for guests. Easy access to the Cowboy Hall of Fame, Remington Park Race Track, Omniplex, and other points of interest. Many good eating places in the vicinity.

Hosts: Newton W. & Joann Flora
Doubles: 2 (PB) $35-45
Type of Beds: 2 Double
Continental Breakfast
Credit Cards: No
Notes: 2, 5, 7, 8, 9 (light), 12

6 Pets welcome: 7 Smoking allowed: 8 Children welcome: 9 Social drinking allowed: 10 Tennis available: 11 Swimming available: 12 Golf available: 13 Skiing available: 14 May be booked through travel agents

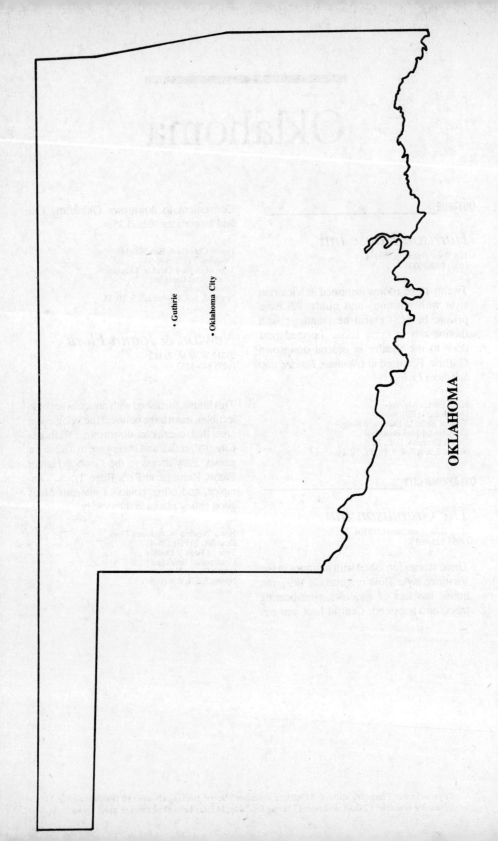

Oregon

Country Willows

1313 Clay Street, 97520
(503) 488-1590

A quiet, relaxing hideaway on 5 white-fenced acres with a beautiful view of the Siskiyou Mountains. This 1905 house was elegantly rebuilt with your comfort in mind, including air-conditioning and private baths. Enjoy a full breakfast on the porch or relax by the pool and spa.

Hosts: Bill & Barbara Huntley
Doubles: 5 (PB) $75-90
Type of Beds: 3 Twin; 4 Queen; 1 King
Full Breakfast
Credit Cards: A, B
Notes: 2, 5, 8 (12 and over), 9, 10, 11, 12, 13, 14

Cowslip's Belle

Cowslip's Belle

159 N. Main Street, 97520
(503) 488-2901

Fluffy down comforters, fresh flowers, antiques, chocolate truffles all await you at the 1913 craftsman home with stained glass, antique quilts, scrumptious breakfasts, and a willow swing. Just three blocks to the Shakespeare Festival and plaza. The Cowslip's Belle offers four cozy air-conditioned guest rooms for your comfort.

Hosts: Jon & Carmen Reinhardt
Doubles: 4 (PB) $48-78
Full Breakfast
Credit Cards: A, B
Notes: 2, 5, 9, 10, 11, 12, 13, 14

Hersey House

Hersey House

451 N. Main Street, 97520
(503) 482-4563

Gracious living in an elegantly restored Victorian with a colorful English country garden. Sumptuous breakfasts. Central air-conditioning. Walk to Plaza and three Shakespeare theaters. Nearby: white-water rafting on the Rogue River, Jacksonville Na-

---

6 Pets welcome: 7 Smoking allowed: 8 Children welcome: 9 Social drinking allowed: 10 Tennis available: 11
Swimming available: 12 Golf available: 13 Skiing available: 14 May be booked through travel agents

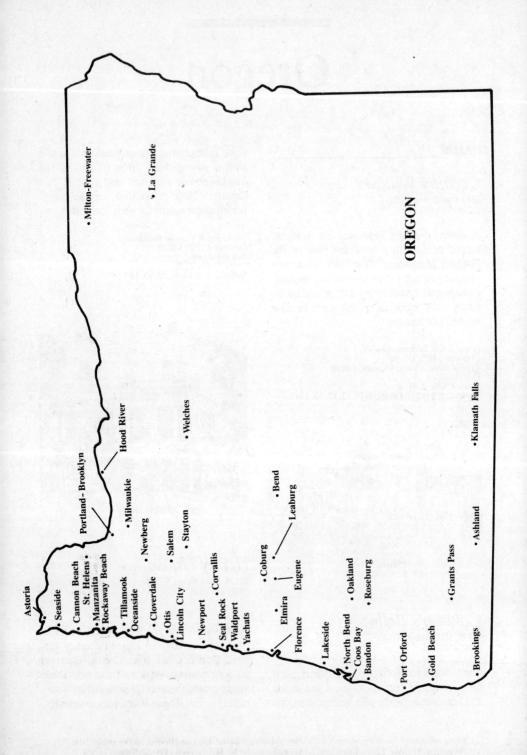

OREGON

Milton-Freewater

La Grande

Hood River

Portland - Brooklyn

Welches

Milwaukie

Bend

Newberg

Leaburg

Salem

Stayton

Tillamook

Oceanside

Coburg

Cloverdale

Corvallis

Eugene

Otis

Newport

Lincoln City

Seal Rock

Elmira

Oakland

Klamath Falls

Waldport

Florence

Roseburg

Astoria

Yachats

Lakeside

Ashland

Seaside

North Bend

Cannon Beach

Coos Bay

Grants Pass

St. Helens

Bandon

Manzanita

Port Orford

Rockaway Beach

Gold Beach

Brookings

tional Historic District, Britt Music Festival, Crater Lake National Park.

Hosts: K. Lynn Savage & Gail Orell
Doubles: 4 (PB) $63.10-78.40
Type of Beds: 2 Twin; 4 Queen
Full Breakfast
Credit Cards: No
Closed Nov. 1- April 20
Notes: 2, 8 (12 and over), 10, 11, 12, 13, 14

The Iris Inn

59 Manzanita Street, 97520
(503) 488-2286

A 1905 Victorian furnished with antiques. Elegant breakfasts feature eggs benedict, and cheese-baked eggs. Mountain views, quiet neighborhood. Nearby are the Oregon Shakespeare theater and the Rogue River for rafting.

Host: Vicki Lamb
Doubles: 5 (1 PB; 4 SB) $55-64
Type of Beds: 1 Twin; 1 Double; 4 Queen
Full Breakfast
Credit Cards: A, B
Notes: 2, 5, 7 (outside), 8, 9, 10, 11, 12

The Morical House

668 North Main Street, 97520
(503) 482-2254

A superbly restored 1880s farmhouse on 1.5 acres of beautifully landscaped grounds, The Morical House offers nineteenth-century elegance and hospitality with twentieth-century comfort. Five gracious guest rooms with private baths, large complimentary breakfast, afternoon treats.

Hosts: Pat & Peter Dahl
Doubles: 5 (PB) $45-80
Type of Beds: 2 Twin; 1 Double; 3 Queen; 1 Rollaway
Full Breakfast
Credit Cards: A, B
Notes: 2, 5, 8 (over 12), 10, 11, 12, 13, 14

Romeo Inn

295 Idaho Street, 97520
(503) 488-0884

Mobil gives us a three-star rating. A quiet, elegant, lovely Cape Cod amid pines with a valley view. Four spacious rooms with central air-conditioning; some rooms have fireplaces. A luxurious suite has a fireplace and whirlpool tub. There's a beautiful spa and pool, gardens, and gourmet breakfast. Walk to the Oregon Shakespeare Theaters and town.

Hosts: Margaret & Bruce Halverson
Doubles: 5 (PB) $86-145
Type of Beds: 5 King
Full Breakfast
Credit Cards: A, B

Romeo Inn

ASTORIA

Franklin House Bed & Breakfast Inn

1681 Franklin Avenue, Box 804, 97103
(503) 325-5044

A feeling of elegance will charm you when you enter the Franklin House Bed & Breakfast Inn, built in the late 1800s. Nearby you will find the Columbia River Maritime

Museum, Captain George Flavel House, and two beaches. Full breakfast and a gift shop on the premises.

Host: Karen N. Nelson
Doubles: 5 (PB) $48-65
Full Breakfast
Minimum stay summer & holidays: 2
Credit Cards: A, B
Closed 2 days for Thanksgiving & Christmas
Notes: 2, 8

Grandview Bed & Breakfast

1574 Grand Avenue, 97103
(503) 325-0000; 325-5555

Wonderful views of the Columbia River; close to the best maritime museum on the West Coast and other museums, churches, and Victorian homes. Tour domestic and foreign ships in port. Light, airy, three-story Victorian with hardwood floors.

Host: Charleen Maxwell
Doubles: 3 (PB) $40.28-63.60
Suites: 3 (2 bedrooms, PB) $68.90-93.28
Type of Beds: 5 Twin; 8 Queen
Continental Breakfast
Credit Cards: A, B, D
Notes: 2, 5, 8 (over 10), 10, 11, 12

BANDON

Lighthouse B&B

650 Jetty Road, Box 24, 97411
(503) 347-9316

Contemporary home located on the beach across from the historic Bandon lighthouse. Unequaled jetty, lighthouse, and ocean views. Walk to Old Town, shops, galleries, and fine restaurants. November through March, a lighthouse studio with kitchen is available.

Hosts: Bruce & Linda Sisson
Doubles: 4 (PB) $65-75
Type of Beds: 3 Queen; 1 King
Full Breakfast
Credit Cards: A, B, D
Notes: 2, 5, 8 (over 12), 9, 10, 12, 14

Seabird Inn

3165 Beach Loop Drive, 97411
(503) 347-2056

A contemporary home located within easy walking distance of one of Oregon's most dramatic beaches. Spacious, well-appointed rooms with private baths adjoin a large, light-filled solarium — all tastefully decorated in soft pastels. Evening wine and cheese; full gourmet breakfast.

Hosts: Carol & Ollie Sapousek
Doubles: 2 (PB) $63.60
Type of Beds: 1 Queen; 1 King
Full Breakfast
Credit Cards: No
Closed Christmas
Notes: 2, 9, 12

BEND

Mirror Pond House

1054 NW Harmon Blvd., 97701
(503) 389-1680

A small inn at water's edge where wild ducks and geese glide ashore. Near downtown in a quiet residential area, we serve complimentary wine and full breakfasts with homemade bread. Relaxing — surrounded by numerous activities — starting with our guest canoe.

Host: Beryl Kellum
Doubles: 2 (PB) $63.01-84.41
Type of Beds: 2 Twin; 2 Queen; 1 King
Full Breakfast
Credit Cards: No
Notes: 2, 5, 7, 8 (over 12), 9, 10, 11, 12, 13

BROOKINGS

The Ward House B&B

Box 86, 97415
(503) 469-5557

A 1917 vintage home built in the "craftsman style" architecture by Wm. Ward. Restored and furnished with antiques and treasures. Large parlor, hot tub/sauna, spacious

NOTES: Credit cards accepted: A Master Card; B Visa; C American Express; D Discover Card; E Diners Club; F Other: 2 Personal checks accepted: 3 Lunch available: 4 Dinner available: 5 Open all year

bedrooms upstairs. Ocean view; just a few blocks from the river and harbor. Gourmet breakfast, including Norwegian waffles.

Hosts: Sheldon & Gro
Doubles: 2 (PB) $55
Type of Beds: 2 Queen
Full Breakfast
Credit Cards: A, B
Notes: 2, 5, 8 (over 12), 9, 10, 11, 14

BROOKLYN

Holmes Sea Cove Bed & Breakfast

17350 Holmes Drive, 97415
(503) 469-3025

A delightful seacoast hideaway with a spectacular ocean view, private guest entrances, and a tasty continental breakfast served to your room. Enjoy beach combing and whale watching.

Hosts: Jack & Lorene Holmes
Doubles: 3 (PB) $70-85
Type of Beds: 3 Queen
Continental-plus Breakfast
Credit Cards: A, B
Notes: 2, 5, 7 (limited), 9, 10

CANNON BEACH

Tern Inn

3663 S. Hemlock, Box 952, 97110
(503) 436-1528

European-style B&B with an ocean view. Light goose-down quilts for year-round comfort, full bath, and color TV. Fresh home-baked goods are served, including vegetarian and low cholesterol foods. Rooms are suitable for up to four adults or may be combined for seven adults. Special off-season and weekly rates; gift certificates.

Hosts: Chris & Enken Friedrichsen
Doubles: 2 (PB) $68.25-99.75
Type of Beds: 1 Twin; 1 Double; 2 Queen
Full Breakfast
Minimum stay June 15-Labor Day: 2-3

Credit Cards: No
Closed January
Notes: 2, 9, 10, 11, 12

CLOVERDALE

Sand Lake Country Inn

8505 Galloway Road, 97112
(503) 965-6745

This state historic registry 1894 farmhouse is the perfect hideaway for first or second honeymoons. Private garden spa, honeymoon suite (four rooms) with private luxury bath, deck, view of Cape Lookout, parlor, vintage movies. Full breakfast in bed. Just a mile to the beach; picnic baskets available.

Hosts: Margo & Charles Underwood
Doubles: 2 (PB) $40-75
Type of Beds: 2 Queen
Full Breakfast
Credit Cards: No
Notes: 2, 3, 4, 5, 14

COBURG

Wheeler's Bed & Breakfast

Box 8201, 97401
(503) 344-1366

Modern country home located one-half mile off I-5, seven miles north of Eugene and just a few minutes from Autzen Stadium. Guest quarters include the entire upstairs of the house. Hiking, swimming, antique shops, century-old homes are nearby. Children over ten are welcome, and small pets only with their own kennels.

Hosts: Joe & Isabel Wheeler
Doubles: 3 (SB) $30-40
Type of Beds: 1 Twin; 2 Double
Full Breakfast
Credit Cards: A, B
Closed Dec.-April
Notes: 2, 6, 8, 9, 10, 11, 12

6 Pets welcome: 7 Smoking allowed: 8 Children welcome: 9 Social drinking allowed: 10 Tennis available: 11 Swimming available: 12 Golf available: 13 Skiing available: 14 May be booked through travel agents

COOS BAY

Captain's Quarters Bed & Breakfast

265 South Empire Blvd., Box 3231, 97420
(503) 888-6895

An 1892 Victorian lovingly restored to its original beauty. Former home of Captain McGenn of the *Breakwater*. Bedrooms face the colorful bay and North Spit. One can watch the ships come in. Close to beaches, parks, boat charters. No smoking. Full homemade breakfasts are served in the dining room or on the sun porch.

Hosts: John & Jean Griswold
Doubles: 2 (SB) $45
Type of Beds: 2 Double
Full Breakfast
Credit Cards: No
Notes: 2, 8 (over 12), 9, 10, 11, 12

This Olde House Bed & Breakfast

202 Alder Avenue, 97420
(503) 267-5224

Charming Victorian built in 1893 overlooking the bay, just off highway 101 in Coos Bay. The house has inlaid wooden floors and double stairways. Short drive to Charleston Fishing Village, Sunset Beach, and Shore Acres Botanical Gardens of the Coast. Hosts are collectors of antiques.

Hosts: Edward & Jean Mosieur
Doubles: 4 (1 PB; 3 SB) $47-55
Type of Beds: 1 Double; 1 Queen; 2 King
Full Breakfast
Credit Cards: No
Notes: 2, 5, 8 (12 and over), 9, 10, 11, 14

CORVALLIS

Huntington Manor

3555 NW Harrison Blvd., 97330
(503) 753-3735

Huntington Manor is a beautiful 65-year-old Williamsburg Colonial that has been completely refurbished and is elegantly furnished with American and European antiques. Guest rooms feature down comforters and color TV.

Host: Ann Sink
Doubles: 3 (PB) $50
Type of Beds: 2 Double; 1 Queen
Full Breakfast
Credit Cards: No
Notes: 2, 4, 5, 7, 8 (over 12), 9, 10, 11, 12, 13

Madison Inn Bed & Breakfast

660 SW Madison, 97333
(503) 757-1274

The Madison Inn is an historical home facing Central Park in downtown Corvallis. Oregon State University is within walking distance. This four-story Victorian offers comfortable guest rooms and a variety of breakfasts, including Madison Inn scones, individual puffed pancakes, fresh fruit, and juice.

Hosts: Richard & Paige Down
Doubles: 7 (1 PB; 6 SB) $53.50
Type of Beds: 2 Twin; 6 Queen
Full Breakfast
Credit Cards: A, B
Notes: 2, 5, 10, 11

ELMIRA

McGillivray's Log Home Bed & Breakfast

88680 Evers Road, 97437
(503) 935-3564

West of Eugene, Oregon, you will find the best of yesterday with the comforts of today. Situated on 5 wooded acres, this air-conditioned log home has wheel-chair access.

The hearty breakfasts are often prepared on an antique wood cook stove.

Host: Evelyn R. McGillivray
Doubles: 2 (PB) $36.50-62.40
Type of Beds: 2 Queen
Full Breakfast
Credit Cards: A, B
Notes: 2, 5, 8, 9, 11

EUGENE

Kjaer's House in the Woods
814 Lorane Highway, 97405
(503) 343-3234

A 1910 craftsman-style home in a peaceful setting on a quiet, countrylike road ideal for walking, jogging, hiking, deer and bird watching. Antiques, Oriental carpets, fireplace, square grand piano available for guests. "Urban convenience/suburban tranquility."

Hosts: George & Eunice Kjaer
Singles: 1 (SB) $40.50
Doubles: 1 (SB) $58.75
Type of Beds: 1 Twin; 1 Double; 1 Queen
Full Breakfast
Minimum stay weekends: 2
Children under 2 or over 12 welcome
Closed Dec. 22-Jan. 3
Credit Cards: No
Notes: 2, 8, 9, 10, 11, 12, 14

Kjaer's House in the Woods

Krumdieck Kottage
858 Washington, 97401
(503) 484-0208

Your very own cottage, with total privacy, in one of Eugene's oldest and most charming neighborhoods. Studio with downstairs living area, 1920s charm, complete with a full kitchen, double bed, two hideabeds. Close to downtown, fairgrounds, and Hutt Center.

Hosts: Richard & Karen Krumdieck
Doubles: 2 (SB) $45
Type of Beds: 2 Double; 1 Queen
Continental Breakfast
Credit Cards: A, B
Notes: 2, 5, 8, 9, 10, 11, 12, 14

FLORENCE

The Johnson House
Box 1892, 97439
(503) 997-8000

The Johnson House, the oldest house in Florence, was built in 1892. The structure and details in this splendid old Victorian are original. Antique furnishings in every room evoke the atmosphere of warm, plain living on the Oregon coast nearly a century ago.

Hosts: Jayne & Ron Fraese
Doubles: 5 (1 PB; 4 S3B) $55-65
Type of Beds: 5 Double
Full Breakfast
Credit Cards: A, B
Notes: 2, 5, 9, 10, 11, 12, 14

GOLD BEACH

High Seas Inn
105 Walker Street, Box 3, 97444
(503) 247-6524

Sitting high on a hill overlooking the town of Gold Beach and the Pacific Ocean, the High Seas Inn offers a breathtaking view of the ocean. Built in 1911, the inn is now the home of your hosts. Each morning a hearty breakfast is served in the dining room: caramel rolls or Belgian waffles, fine cheese, fresh fruit, juice, hot drinks. Savor a beautiful sunset on the front porch swing or enjoy a guided salmon trip up the Rogue River.

Hosts: Steve & Jane Yeiter
Doubles: 2 (SB) $53
Type of Beds: 2 Twin; 2 Queen
Continental-plus Breakfast
Credit Cards: A, B
Notes: 2, 5, 8, 9, 10, 12

The Johnson House

GRANTS PASS

AHLF House Bed & Breakfast

762 NW 6th Street, 97526
(503) 474-1374

1902 Queen Anne Victorian, architecturally interesting. Largest historic residence in Grants Pass. Furnished with lovely antiques, this beautifully appointed home offers travelers pleasing accommodations. Featured on the walking tour of National Historic Buildings. A Victorian evening, with music and refreshments, is special.

Hosts: Herbert & Betty Buskirk, Rosemary Althaus
Doubles: 3 (SB) $50-60
Type of Beds: 3 Double
Full Breakfast

Credit Cards: No
Notes: 2, 5, 9

Mt. Baldy Bed & Breakfast

678 Troll View Road, 97527
(503) 479-7998

Ranch-style home, high on Mt. Baldy, provides a spectacular view of Grants Pass and the Rogue Valley. Two rooms with private bath and entrance. Full breakfast: fresh-squeezed orange juice, fresh-ground coffee. Jet boating and white-water rafting available. Free brochure on request.

Hosts: John & June Gustafson
Doubles: 2 (PB) $55-60
Type of Beds: 2 Queen
Full Breakfast
Credit Cards: A, B
Closed Nov.-March
Notes: 2, 8 (7 and up), 9, 10, 11, 12, 14

The Washington Inn

1002 Washington Blvd., 97526
(503) 476-1131

A charming 1864 historical Victorian home, where each guest room offers individual charms. Fireplaces, queen beds, private baths, view of the mountains. Bicycles offered; shops and restaurants within walking distance. Fishing, rafting, and jet-boat rides can be enjoyed on the Rogue River. Fabulous continental breakfast.

Hosts: Maryan & Bill Thompson
Doubles: 3 (2 PB; 1 SB) $30-65
Type of Beds: 3 Queen
Continental Breakfast
Credit Cards: A, B
Notes: 2, 5, 7 (limited), 8 (10 and over), 9, 10, 11, 12, 14

HOOD RIVER

Hackett House

922 State Street, 97031
(503) 386-1014

A classic three-story Dutch colonial home near downtown. The hearty "Buckaroo

Breakfast" may be enjoyed in the country kitchen, the dining rom, or on the sun deck. Guests are invited to enjoy the house, listen to music, or browse the library.

Hosts: Alice Rosebrook & Sam Dunlap
Singles: 2 (SB) $37.25
Doubles: 2 (SB) $58.50
Type of Beds: 2 Twin; 2 Double
Full Breakfast
Credit Cards: A, B, C
Notes: 2, 5, 8, 10, 11, 12, 13, 14

KLAMATH FALLS

Thompsons' Bed & Breakfast by the Lake

1420 Wild Plum Court, 97601
(503) 882-7938

A new home in a serene mountain setting overlooking the lake. Adjacent to a wilderness park, with hiking, fishing, boating, abundant wildlife — bald eagles, deer, rabbits, etc. Three king-size bedrooms each with private bath, family room, one single bedroom with private entrance. Open all year.

Hosts: Mary & Gil
Singles: 1 (SB) $37.10
Doubles: 3 (PB) $47.70-58.30
Type of Beds: 1 Twin; 3 King
Full Breakfast
Credit Cards: No
Notes: 2, 5, 7, 8, 9, 10, 11, 12, 13, 14

LA GRANDE

Stange Manor

1612 Walnut Street, 97850
(503) 963-2400

Large early 1920s Georgian colonial home on beautiful grounds with lovely views. The home has lovely furnishings and a comfortable atmosphere. Guest baths feature large, old-fashioned tubs. One suite available with a marvelous old fireplace.

Hosts: Steve & Gail Hart; Gene & Bernadine Curry
Doubles: 5 (3 PB; 2 SB) $35-60
Type of Beds: 2 Twin; 2 Double; 4 Queen

Full Breakfast
Credit Cards: A, B, C
Notes: 2, 5, 9, 10, 11, 12, 13

LAKESIDE

Country Lane Bed & Breakfast

777 Country Lane, Box Y, 97449
(503) 759-3869

Protected from coastal winds and fog, this chalet-style homestead retreat is located on 18 secluded acres in a magnificent forest setting. Enjoy forest trails, country lanes, badminton, hammock, nearby beaches, dune buggies, golfing, sport fishing on famous Tenmile Lakes.

Hosts: Roy & Carolyn Sindell
Doubles: 2 (SB) $40-45
Type of Beds: 2 Twin (or King); 1 Queen
Full Breakfast
Credit Cards: No
Notes: 2, 5, 8 (over 12), 11, 12

LEABURG

Marjon Bed & Breakfast

44975 Leaburg Dam Road, 97489
(503) 896-3145

Pamper yourself at Marjon, featured in *Women's Day* magazine (January, 1988).Enjoy a gourmet breakfast while viewing the river a few feet away past flowers, ferns, and woods. Relax in the huge, magnificently furnished rooms with oversized beds and spacious baths. Private fishing dock, water sports, hiking. Restaurants near. Twenty-five miles from downtown Eugene, but in another world.

Host: Marguerite Haas
Doubles: 2 (PB) $65-80
Type of Beds: 1 Queen; 1 King
Full Breakfast
Credit Cards: A, B
Notes: 2, 5, 7, 9, 11, 12, 14

6 Pets welcome: 7 Smoking allowed: 8 Children welcome: 9 Social drinking allowed: 10 Tennis available: 11 Swimming available: 12 Golf available: 13 Skiing available: 14 May be booked through travel agents

LINCOLN CITY

Pacific B&B 1

Pacific B&B Agency
701 NW 60th, Seattle, WA, 98107
(206) 784-0539

Just one block from the beach, this house has three main-floor guest rooms, each with private bath and private entrance, and one upstairs room with a fireplace. A full or continental breakfast is served in the lounge beside the fireplace. Limited smoking, indoor heated pool; small dog in residence. Arabic, French, and German are spoken. $50-65.

Marjon B&B

Stahlrose Bed & Breakfast Inn

646 NW Inlet, 97367
(503) 994-7932

Private entrance, your own key, plus a wide deck for relaxing and watching the ocean tides or sunsets. Queen bed, private bath, fireplace, TV, and a small refrigerator. In the morning, a gourmet continental breakfast is served in your room with the morning paper. Just a few steps down from the house

is a superb beach; golf, fishing, and good restaurants are close by.

Hosts: Dede & Bob McKay
Doubles: 1 (PB) $68.60
Type of Beds: 1 Double
Full Breakfast
Credit Cards: No
Notes: 2 (in some cases), 5, 6, 7 (limited), 8, 9, 10, 11, 12, 14

MANZANITA

The Manzanita Inn B&B

Box 117, 97130
(503) 368-5499

Clean, comfortable, traditional B&B with great breakfasts! Fireplace, library, large deck with BBQ. Close to shopping and seven miles of beach. Golf, fish, hike, beach comb, bike, wind surf, whale watch, or just relax.

Hosts: Tom & Vicki Strang
Doubles: 4 (1 PB; 3 SB) $47.25-63
Type of Beds: 3 Double; 2 Queen
Full Breakfast
Minimum stay holidays: 2
Credit Cards: A, B
Notes: 2, 5, 7, 8, 9, 10, 11, 12

MILTON-FREEWATER

Birch Tree Manor

615 S. Main Street, 97862
(503) 938-6455

A handsome brick home surrounded by birch trees that offers guests pleasant, personable accommodations. Located at the foot of the Blue Mountains in eastern Oregon, where travelers can experience year-round outdoor activities. Full breakfast with local fruit and berries, along with homemade breads and pastries.

Hosts: Ken & Priscilla Dauble
Doubles: 3 (1 PB; 2 SB) $35-45
Type of Beds: 2 Twin; 1 Double; 1 Queen
Full Breakfast
Minimum stay holidays: 2
Credit Cards: A, B
Notes: 2, 5, 8, 10, 11, 12, 13, 14

NOTES: Credit cards accepted: A Master Card; B Visa; C American Express; D Discover Card; E Diners Club; F Other: 2 Personal checks accepted: 3 Lunch available: 4 Dinner available: 5 Open all year

MILWAUKIE

Historic Broetje House

3101 SE Courtney, 97222
(503) 659-8860

An 1890 Queen Anne/Craftsman style estate with four-story water tower on 2 acres of picturesque grounds. Gazebo under 100-year-old trees. Inside, the decor is elegant with a touch of country. Rooms with period furnishing.

Host: Lorraine Hubbard
Doubles: 3 (1 PB; 2 SB) $45-75
Type of Beds: 1 Twin; 2 Queen
Full Breakfast
Credit Cards: No
Notes: 2, 4, 5, 8, 9, 10, 11, 12, 12, 14

NEWBERG

Secluded Bed & Breakfast

19719 NE Williamson Road, 97132
(503) 538-2635

Secluded beautiful country home located on 10 acres. The ideal retreat in the woods for hiking, country walks, and observing wildlife. Ten minutes' drive to several wineries; about one hour to the coast. Breakfast is a special occasion. Many antiques in the home. Located near George Fox College and Linfield College.

Hosts: Durell & Del Belanger
Doubles: 2 (1 PB; 1 SB) $29-50
Type of Beds: 1 Double; 1 Queen
Full Breakfast
Credit Cards: No
Closed January
Notes: 2, 8 (under 6 months or over 6 years), 10, 11, 12, 14

NEWPORT

Ocean House B&B

4920 NW Woody Way, 97365
(503) 265-6158

Ocean House, overlooking beautiful gardens and surf at Agate Beach, is a special place to relax and enjoy the many coastal pleasures. Newport's historic bay front, restaurants, and shops are nearby, and magnificent scenery stretches north and south.

Hosts: Bette & Bob Garrard
Doubles: 4 (2 PB; 2 SB) $45-80
Type of Beds: 1 Twin; 1 Double; 1 Queen; 1 King
Full Breakfast
Credit Cards: A, B
Closed Dec. 15-Jan. 7
Notes: 2, 9, 10, 11, 12

Sylvia Beach Hotel

267 NW Cliff, 97365
(503) 265-5428

Oceanfront B&B for book lovers. No smoking. Each room is named after a different author and decorated individually. Some have fireplaces. Hot spiced wine is served in the library at 10:00 P.M. Dinner served nightly. Not suitable for young children.

Hosts: Goody Cable & Sally Ford
Doubles: 20 (PB) $45-110
Type of Beds: 3 Twin; 6 Double; 10 Queen; 1 King
Full Breakfast
Credit Cards: A, B
Notes: 2, 4, 5, 8 (over 10), 9, 10, 11, 12

NORTH BEND

Sherman House

2380 Sherman Avenue, 97459
(503) 756-3496

This 1903 Pennsylvania Dutch home located two blocks from Highway 101 offers harbor and mountain views. Close to the rugged coast, sand dunes, botanical gardens, waterfalls, and recreational activities. Antique furnishings include an extensive toy collection.

Hosts: Phillip & Jennifer Williams
Doubles: 3 (2 PB; 1 SB) $48-55
Type of Beds: 3 Double; 1 Child's
Full Breakfast
Credit Cards: No
Notes: 2, 5, 7, 8, 9

6 Pets welcome: 7 Smoking allowed: 8 Children welcome: 9 Social drinking allowed: 10 Tennis available: 11 Swimming available: 12 Golf available: 13 Skiing available: 14 May be booked through travel agents

OAKLAND

The Pringle House B & B
Locust & 7th Streets, Box 578, 97462
(503) 459-5038

A gracious 1880 Queen Anne Victorian home, on National Register, overlooking historic town. Comfortable, quiet, charming rooms with antiques, quilts, and doll collection. Cozy common rooms. Near fine dining, antiques, fishing, boating, six wineries, wildlife park. Brochure available.

Hosts: Jim & Demay Pringle
Doubles: 2 (SB) $30-45
Type of Beds: 2 Twin; 2 Double
Full Breakfast
Credit Cards: No
Notes: 2, 5, 8 (over 11), 9, 10, 11, 12

The Pringle House B&B

OCEANSIDE

Sea Haven Inn
Box 203, 97134
(503) 842-3151

Sea Haven Inn is a new inn with nine rooms, five suites, and an annex of seven ocean-front cabins. All accommodations have private baths and color TV, and barbecues are available. Suites have refrigerators. The inn is all ocean front, on a cliff 250 feet high.

Suites: 5 (PB) $70-75
Doubles: 4 (PB) $55
Type of Beds: 6 Double; 3 Queen
Full Breakfast
Credit Cards: A, B
Notes: 2, 3, 5, 7 (limited), 8, 9, 10, 11, 12, 14

OTIS

Salmon River Lodge
5622 Salmon River Highway, 97368
(503) 994-2639

Our coastal locale gives you a break from both summer's heat and winter's chill. Shops and galleries are plentiful. Winter brings agates to the shore and steelhead to the Salmon River. Salmon, crabs, kite flying, and boating are available in the summer. As a local native says, "We've got so many ways you're sure to like some of them!"

Hosts: Marvin & Paunee Pegg
Singles: 1 (SB) $30-40
Doubles: 3 (PB and SB) $35-40
Type of Beds: 2 Twin; 2 Double; 1 Queen
Full Breakfast
Credit Cards: No
Closed Dec. 24-25
Notes: 2, 5, 6 (outside), 7 (outside), 8, 9, 10, 11, 12, 14

PORTLAND

Cape Cod B&B
5733 SW Dickinson Street, 97219
(503) 246-1839

We are conveniently located seven miles south of Portland off I-5. Our 1939 Cape Cod home is furnished with traditional and antique furniture collected over a forty-year period. An outdoor spa, in the ivy-hedged enclosed gardens, relaxes you for the next day's activities.

Hosts: John & Marcelle Tebo
Doubles: 2 (SB) $38.15-43.60
Type of Beds: 2 Twin; 1 Double
Full Breakfast
Minimum stay weekends: 2
Credit Cards: No
Closed Nov.-end Feb.
Notes: 2 (one month in advance), 8 (over 5), 10, 12, 14

NOTES: Credit cards accepted: A Master Card; B Visa; C American Express; D Discover Card; E Diners Club; F Other: 2 Personal checks accepted: 3 Lunch available: 4 Dinner available: 5 Open all year

General Hookers Bed & Breakfast

125 SW Hooker, 97201
(503) 222-4435

Portland's premier Victorian B&B, a romantic Queen Anne, lovingly restored, in a quiet historic district near downtown. Preferred by business travelers for its superb location and amenities: air-conditioning, cable TVs, VCRs, use of a local fitness club. Call or write for illustrated brochure. Fully licensed.

Host: Lori Hall
Doubles: 4 (1 PB; 3 SB) $55-85
Type of Beds: 2 Twin; 1 Double; 1 Queen; 1 King
Continental Breakfast
Minimum stay holidays: 2
Credit Cards: A, B, C
Notes: 2, 5, 8 (over 10), 9, 10, 11, 12, 14

John Palmer House

4314 N. Mississippi Avenue, 97217
(503) 284-5893

Forty-five minutes from Columbia Gorge, Mt. Hood, wine country. One hour from the Pacific Ocean. Our beautiful historic Victorian can be your home away from home. Award-winning decor; gourmet chef; complimentary high tea. Your hosts delight in providing the extraordinary. Free color brochure.

Hosts: Mary & Richard Sauter
Singles: 1 (PB) $32.70
Doubles: 6 (4 PB; 2 SB) $103.55
Type of Beds: 3 Twin; 5 Double
Full Breakfast
Credit Cards: A, B (4% service charge)
Wine sold on premises
Notes: 2, 4 (with notice), 5, 8, 9, 14

NW B&B #359

NW Bed & Breakfast Travel Unlimited
610 SW Broadway, Portland, OR, 97205
(503) 243-7616

English-style home built fifty years ago. Close-in central location. Furnished and decorated with casual elegance. Wooded setting, well-maintained garden. Air-conditioning in bedrooms, down pillows, down comforters.

Doubles: 2 (SB) $45-50
Type of Beds: 1 Double; 1 King
Continental Breakfast
Credit Cards: No
Notes: 7 (outside)

NW B&B #391B

NW Bed & Breakfast Travel Unlimited
610 SW Broadway, Portland, OR, 97205
(503) 243-7616

Federal colonial-style home, custom-built in 1921, all newly decorated. Convenient location ten minutes from city center, opposite a large city park near Lloyds Center. On bus route. Pleasant garden and gazebo. Host enjoys travel, music, decorating, gardening.

Doubles: 2 (SB) $30-40
Type of Beds: 2 Queen
Continental Breakfast
Credit Cards: No
Notes: 7 (outside)

Pacific B&B 2

Pacific B&B Agency
701 NW 60th, Seattle, WA, 98107
(206) 784-0539

Built in 1911, this three-story arts-n-crafts home is located in the residential Irvington district. Guests may use the living room or recreation room with TV, VCR, and a large selection of books, music, and videos. Three guest rooms, two with shared bath, one private. Jacuzzi and sauna. Full breakfast, off-street parking, limited smoking, cats in residence. Children over ten are welcome. $40-65.

Pacific B&B 3

Pacific B&B Agency
701 NW 60th, Seattle, WA, 98107
(206) 784-0539

6 Pets welcome: 7 Smoking allowed: 8 Children welcome: 9 Social drinking allowed: 10 Tennis available: 11 Swimming available: 12 Golf available: 13 Skiing available: 14 May be booked through travel agents

This 1924 Georgian colonial has been lovingly restored and furnished with antiues, Oriental rugs, leaded and stained glass. Fireplace in the living room. Guests will enjoy the TV and VCR in the sun room, as well as the deck with lounge chairs in the garden. Three doubles, full breakfast, limited smoking. Children over eight are welcome; resident dog. $40-50.

Pacific B&B 4

Pacific B&B Agency
701 NW 60th, Seattle, WA, 98107
(206) 784-0539

This 1899 colonial overlooks the city. Four guest rooms, one with private bath, share the front room and library. Full breakfast; fine dining within walking distance. Smoking outside only. $45-70.

Portland Guest House

1720 NE 15th, 97212
(503) 282-1402

Portland's most convenient address; a 100-year-old restored Victorian home with great beds, private phones, gourmet breakfasts. Adjacent to Lloyd Center Shopping Mall, ten-theater cinemaplex, and gourmet food market. Quick transit to the Coliseum, convention center, and downtown.

Host: Susan Gisvold
Doubles: 4 (2 PB; 2 SB) $40-55
Type of Beds: 2 Double; 2 Queen
Full Breakfast
Credit Cards: A, B, C
No smoking
Notes: 2, 5, 9, 10, 14

PORT ORFORD

Home by the Sea

444 Jackson, Box 606-N, 97465
(503) 332-2855

Dramatic ocean views and beach access are just outside the windows of this contemporary owner-built home. Its two bedrooms overlook historic Battle Rock Beach with its miles of unspoiled public beaches gracing a quiet Oregon coast fishing village. Laundry privileges, phone in room, TV available.

Hosts: Brenda & Alan Mitchell
Doubles: 2 (PB) $40-50
Type of Beds: 1 Twin; 2 Queen
Full Breakfast
Credit Cards: A, B, D
Notes: 2, 5, 8 (advance notice), 10, 12, 14

Portland Guest House

ROCKAWAY BEACH

Beach House Bed & Breakfast

115 N. Miller, 97136
(503) 355-2411; 355-8282

Comfortable seventy-year-old home on the ocean, within walking distance of shops, restaurants, and recreational facilities. Breakfast served in owner's restaurant across the street any time of day. Fireplace, color TV, games, beach combing, walking, or running on seven miles of beach.

Host: Margie Tiegs
Doubles: 5 (SB) $36.75-47.25
Type of Beds: 1 Twin; 3 Double; 1 Queen
Full Breakfast
Minimum stay weekends & holidays: 2
Credit Cards: A, B
Notes: 2, 4, 5, 9, 10, 11, 12, 14

ROSEBURG

The Woods

428 Oakview Drive, 97470
(503) 672-2927

The Woods is snuggled into 7 southwestern Oregon wooded acres. Fish, swim, or raft the scenic North Umpqua River; visit several famous boutique wineries; or unwind in a Douglas County park. Your world-traveling hosts will make you feel welcome.

Hosts: Wiley & Judy Wood
Doubles: 3 (2 PB; 1 SB) $45-50
Type of Beds: 3 Queen
Full Breakfast
Credit Cards: No
Closed Thanksgiving & Christmas
Notes: 2, 4, 5, 8, 11, 12

The Umpqua House

7338 Oak Hill Road, 97470
(503) 459-4700

Situated on a hillside in a rural setting overlooking beautiful Umpqua Valley, the Umpqua House offers privacy, quiet, and a little pampering to the traveler after a long drive. The house is ideally located midway between San Francisco and Seattle, 170 miles south of Portland. Breakfast includes freshly squeezed juice, seasonal fruits, homemade baked breads, and eggs from our own chickens. Excellent fishing and hunting area.

Hosts: Allen & Rhoda Mozorosky
Doubles: 2 (SB) $35-45
Type of Beds: 1 Double; 1 Queen
Full Breakfast

Credit Cards: No
Notes: 2, 4, 5, 8, 9, 10, 11, 12, 14

ST. HELENS

NW B&B #449

NW Bed & Breakfast Travel Unlimited
610 SW Broadway, Portland, OR, 97205
(503) 243-7616

Restored turn-of-the-century Dutch colonial with a view of Mt. St. Helens and Mt. Hood across the Columbia River. Located in the historic district, the home is within walking distance to shops, museum, restaurants, theater. Arrival by boat; moorage in private or public docks available.

Doubles: 3 (SB) $30-60
Type of Beds: 4 Twin; 2 Double
Continental Breakfast
Credit Cards: No

SALEM

NW B&B #412

NW Bed & Breakfast Travel Unlimited
610 SW Broadway, Portland, OR, 97205
(503) 243-7616

Colonial home on Fairmount Hill, close to city center and within walking distance to Bush Park. Bus service at the door. Warm, friendly, elegant, yet casual atmosphere. A place to take off your shoes, sit by the fire, and relax. Bikes available for exploring Park and nearby Minto Island. TV in family room. Hosts speak English and German.

Singles: 1 (SB) $30
Doubles: 2 (SB) $36
Type of Beds: 1 Twin; 1 Double; 1 Queen
Continental Breakfast
Credit Cards: No
Notes: 7, 13 (XC)

SEAL ROCK

Blackberry Inn

6575 Pacific Coast Highway 101, 97376
(503) 563-2259

Twelve miles south of Newport on the central Oregon coast. Walk to beach and tide pools; outside Jacuzzi; separate entrance and sitting area for guests; massage available. Near restaurants. A country home in a wooded setting.

Host: Barbara Tarter
Singles: 1 (PB) $50
Doubles: 2 (PB) $65
Type of Beds: 2 Twin; 2 Queen; 1 King
Full Breakfast
Minimum stay holidays: 2
Credit Cards: A, B
Closed Thanksgiving-Christmas
Notes: 2, 9,

Victoriana

SEASIDE

"Victoriana" B&B

606 12th Avenue, 97138
(503) 738-8449

"Victoriana" B&B offers country hospitality in the European tradition. Built in 1899, "Victoriana" is one of Seaside's oldest homes. Conveniently located one-half mile from downtown shopping; two and a half blocks to the beach and promenade. River-view location, with easy access to fishing and crabbing. A relaxing, peaceful atmosphere.

Host: LaRee Johnson
Singles: 1 (SB) $30
Doubles: 1 (SB) $50
Type of Beds: 2 Twin; 1 Double
Continental Breakfast
Credit Cards: No
Notes: 2, 5, 8 (over 12), 9, 10, 11, 12, 14

STAYTON

Horncroft

42156 Kingston-Lyons Drive, 97383
(503) 769-6287

Quiet rural home 4.5 miles southeast of Stayton. In the Willamett Valley are berry, fruit, vegetable, and grain farms; vineyards; wineries; holly and nut orchards. Salmon and steelhead fishing in season. Mt. Jefferson Wilderness area is one hour east; the Pacific is 1.5 hours west. Bicycle trails. Traveler's checks accepted.

Hosts: Dr. & Mrs. Kenneth H. Horn
Doubles: 3 (1 PB; 2 SB) $30-45
Type of Beds: 4 Twin; 1 Queen
Full Breakfast
Credit Cards: No
Closed holidays
Notes: 2 (sometimes), 9, 10, 11, 12

TILLAMOOK

Blue Haven Inn

3025 Gienger Road, 97141
(503) 842-2265

Built in 1916, newly refurbished and decorated with antiques that are for sale, Blue Haven Inn is situated in a quiet country setting, surrounded by spacious gardens and tall evergreens. Each room is individually decorated, offering a distinctly unique atmosphere, with books, games, music, and television in the library.

Hosts: Ray & Joy Still
Doubles: 3 (1 PB; 2 SB) $40-50
Type of Beds: 1 Double; 2 Queen
Full Breakfast
Minimum stay weekends & holidays: 2
Credit Cards: No
Notes: 2, 4, 5, 9, 10, 11, 12

WALDPORT

Cliff House

Adahi Street-Yaquina John Point, Box 436, 97394
(503) 563-2506

NOTES: Credit cards accepted: A Master Card; B Visa; C American Express; D Discover Card; E Diners Club; F Other: 2 Personal checks accepted: 3 Lunch available: 4 Dinner available: 5 Open all year

The Cliff House overlooks the ocean. Each room is uniquely decorated with antiques, chandeliers, carpeting, remote color TV; all have private cedar baths and balconies. Elegant lodging coupled with magnificent panoramic ocean view. Deep-sea fishing, river fishing, crabbing, golf club (half a mile), croquet. Horseback riding close by; massage by appointment.

Hosts: Gabrielle Duvall & Debra J. Novgrod
Doubles: 5 (PB) $60-150
Type of Beds: 4 Twin; 3 Queen; 2 King
Full Breakfast
Minimum stay weekends: 2; holidays, 3
Credit Cards: A, B
Closed Oct. 15-March 31
Notes: 2, 4, 9, 10, 11, 12

WELCHES

Mountain Shadows Bed & Breakfast
20390 W. Angelsey Road, Box 147, 97067
(503) 622-4746

A log home built in 1978 by the owners. Situated in a wooded setting at the end of a dead-end street, with panoramic views of Mt. Hood and the surrounding foothills. In the heart of Mt. Hood Recreation Area: fishing, golf, hiking, skiing, tennis are all nearby. Featured in *Northwest Discoveries*

Dec. 7, 1988; *This Week* magazine; *Northwest Best Places;* and *Best Places to Stay in the Pacific Northwest.*

Hosts: Juanita & Wes Post
Doubles: 3 (1 PB; 2 SB) $40-60
Type of Beds: 3 Queen
Full Breakfast
Minimum stay holidays: 2
Credit Cards: A, B
Notes: 2, 5, 6 (call first), 8 (call first), 9, 10, 11, 12, 13, 14

YACHATS

Ziggurat
95330 Hwy. 101, 97498
(503) 547-3925

Ziggurat means terraced pyramid, and this one is spectacular, contemporary, four-story sculpture by the sea. Guests have the privacy of the entire first floor, with a sauna, solarium, and library/living room. There are glass-enclosed decks on the second floor for ocean viewing, where superb food is served. Your hosts are world meanderers. Dunes, parks, and coastal activities are nearby.

Hosts: Mary Lou Cavendish & Irv Tebor
Doubles: 2 (SB) $58-68.90
Full Breakfast
Credit Cards: No
Closed Dec. 20-27
Notes: 2, 8 (over 14), 9, 14

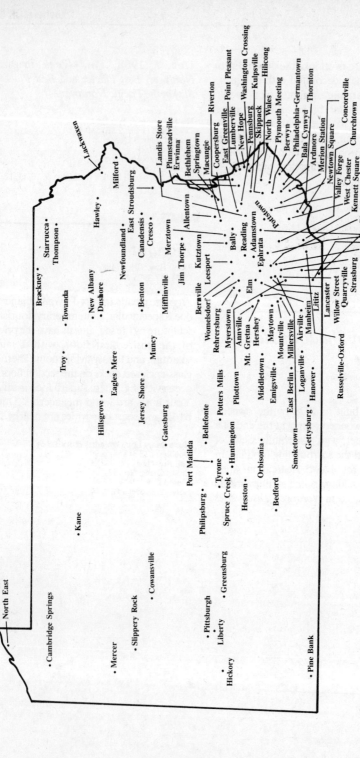

PENNSYLVANIA

Pennsylvania

AIRVILLE

Spring House
Muddy Creek Forks, 17302
(717)927-6906

Built in 1798 of fieldstone, the house is named for the pure spring it protects in the tranquil pre-Revolutionary river- valley village. Lovingly restored to stenciled whitewashed walls, furnished with antiques and art, the inn offers full breakfast of local specialties, wine by the fire or on the front porch, Amish-made cheese, and caring hospitality. Horseback riding, wineries, hiking, trout fishing in immediate area. Near Amish.

Host: Ray Constance Hearne
Doubles: 5 (2 PB; 3 SB) $52-95
Type of Beds: 2 Twin; 5 Double
Full Breakfast
Minimum stay weekends & holidays: 2
Credit Cards: No
Notes: 2, 5, 8, 9, 11, 12, 14

ALLENTOWN

Irish House
B&B Southeast PA
146 W. Philadelphia Ave., Boyertown, 19512
(215) 367-4688

Irish House offers accommodations on two floors. The lower level, with private entrance if needed, is a suite with sitting room, TV, and gas fireplace. Convenient to Dorney Park, colleges, golf, and swimming, with airport and bus pick up available.

Doubles: 2 (PB) $40-50
Type of Beds: 2 Twin; 1 Double
Full Breakfast
Credit Cards: A, B
Closed Jan. - March
Notes: 5, 7 (limited), 8 (over 12), 10, 11

Row Home on the Park
B&B Southeast PA
146 W. Philadelphia Ave., Boyertown, 19512
(215) 367-4688

This typical row home is opposite a quiet, European-style park. There is a guest sitting with TV, and a telephone can be made available for credit-card calls. This house is very close to downtown, minutes from Dorney Park and the Allentown colleges.

Singles: 1 (SB) $30
Doubles: 2 (SB) $35-40
Type of Beds: 1 Twin; 1 Double; 1 Queen
Continental Breakfast
Credit Cards: A, B
Notes: 5, 6, 8 (5 and over)

Salisbury House
910 East Emmaus Avenue, 18103
(215) 791-4225

Built in 1810, Salisbury House offers gracious lodging and gourmet breakfast in the finest tradition of a small country inn. A country setting just ten minutes from historic downtown Bethlehem, in the heart of the Pennsylvania Dutch Country.

Hosts: Judith & Ollie Orth
Doubles: 5 (2 PB; 3 SB) $133-154
Type of Beds: 5 Double
Full Breakfast
Credit Cards: A, B, C
Notes: 2, 5, 7, 9, 10, 11, 12, 13, 14

6 Pets welcome: 7 Smoking allowed: 8 Children welcome: 9 Social drinking allowed: 10 Tennis available: 11 Swimming available: 12 Golf available: 13 Skiing available: 14 May be booked through travel agents

Salisbury House

ANNVILLE

Swatara Creek Inn

Hershey B&B RSO
Box 208, Hershey, 17033
(717) 533-2928

Only a half mile from I-81 or quarter mile from Rt. 22, this inn is fifteen minutes from Hershey attractions, four miles from Lancaster, and eighteen miles from Harrisburg. The house is a three-story Victorian built in 1860. Hearty Pennsylvania Dutch breakfast is served each morning.

Doubles: 6 (PB) $45-70
Type of Beds: 6 Queen; 4 Trundle beds
Full Breakfast
Credit Cards: A, B
Notes: 2, 5, 8, 10, 11, 12, 14

ARDMORE

B&B Connections #1

Box 21, Devon, 19333
(215) 687-3565

Born and raised in Philadelphia, your warm and gracious hostess knows the area well and will be happy to help you see the area. Her Dutch colonial home dates back to 1910 and is tastefully decorated with a contemporary flair. Paintings by the host are throughout.

Doubles: 1 (PB) $40-50
Type of Beds: 2 Twin
Full Breakfast
Credit Cards: A, B, C
Notes: 5, 8, 9, 10, 11, 12, 14

B&B Connections #2

Box 21, Devon, 19333
(215) 687-3565

Two charming second-floor rooms are available in this 1880 Victorian. Your host is fluent in seven languages and she in Spanish; she's also a culinary-school graduate who will delight you with her breakfasts. The home is convenient to the Main Line universities and a five- to ten-minute walk from the train. Resident cat.

Doubles: 2 (SB) $55-65
Type of Beds: 1 Double; 1 Queen
Full Breakfast
Credit Cards: A, B, C
Closed May - Oct.
Notes: 6 (call), 8, 9, 10, 11, 12, 14

BALA CYNWYD

B&B Connections #3

Box 21, Devon, 19333
(215) 687-3565

This comfortable suburban home provides easy access to center city attractions and Main Line universities. Portacrib is available. Your host, an artist, displays many of his works throughout the home. The hostess is a model you've probably seen in magazine and TV ads.

Doubles: 2 (SB) $50-55
Type of Beds: 2 Twin; 1 Double
Continental Breakfast
Credit Cards: A, B, C
Notes: 5, 7, 8, 9, 10, 11, 12, 14

NOTES: Credit cards accepted: A Master Card; B Visa; C American Express; D Discover Card; E Diners Club; F Other: 2 Personal checks accepted: 3 Lunch available: 4 Dinner available: 5 Open all year

BALLY

Bally Spring Farm
B&B Southeast PA
146 W. Philadelphia Ave., Boyertown, 19512
(215) 367-4688

A 1734 stone house on 100 acres with a private 2,285 foot runway so guests can fly in. There's a 6-acre lake stocked with bass and a stream stocked with trout — bring your fishing equipment. Many antique shops and flea markets in the area; Reading's famous outlets are only thirty minutes away. Spanish and French are spoken here; outdoor dogs and cat in residence.

Doubles: 4 (1 PB; 3 SB) $50-65
Type of Beds: 4 Queen
Full Breakfast
Credit Cards: A, B
Notes: 5, 11

BEDFORD

Conifer Ridge Farm
R. 2, Box 202A, Clearville, 15535

A beautiful contemporary passive solar home with a rustic exterior and interior of exceptional design beauty. Luxury features for comfort combine with thirteen-foot brick walls, oak beams and accent pieces. 126 acres farm includes woodlands, stream, and pond. Enjoy nearby Old Bedrod Village, Bedrod Springs Festival, Raystown Lake, and country auctions.

Hosts: Dan & Myeth Haldeman
Doubles: 2 (1 PB; 1 SB) $40
Type of Beds: 1 Double; 1 Queen
Full Breakfast
Credit Cards: No
Closed Dec. 23 - Jan. 3
Notes: 2, 3, 4, 7, 10

BELLEFONTE

Rebecca's House
Rest & Repast B&B Service

Box 126, Pine Grove Mills, 16868
(814) 238-1484

This restored mid-1800s home is located in the historic district, with a formal dining room and Victorian parlor complete with an 1830s square grand piano, country kitchen, and formal guest area.

Doubles: 2 (SB) $35-45
Type of Beds: 2 Twin; 1 Double
Continental-plus Breakfast
Credit Cards: No
Closed Dec. 24-Jan. 2
Notes: 2, 8, 9, 10, 11, 12

BENTON

Grandmaw's Place
RD 2, Box 239, 17814
(717) 925-2630

Grandmaw's Place is located in a quiet natural box canyon just six miles west of Ricketts Glen State Park, two miles north of Rt. 118, at the entrance of state game lands. Fishing creek flows through Grandmaw's 27 acre farm. Relaxing getaway and year-round sports.

Host: Mary Ellen Frank
Singles: 1 (SB) $25
Doubles: 2 (SB) $50
Type of Beds: 4 Twin; 2 Double
Full Breakfast
Credit Cards: No
Notes: 2, 3, 4, 5, 8, 11, 12, 13

BERNVILLE

Sunday's Mill Farm
B&B Southeast PA
146 W. Philadelphia Ave., Boyertown, 19512
(215) 367-4688

Sunday's Mill Farm was built in 1830, 100 yards from Tulpehocken Creek, a river stocked by the state. There's a friendly dog in residence; boarding facilities for guests' horses. Local antique auctions.

Doubles: 2 (SB) $35-55
Type of Beds: 1 Double; 1 Queen

6 Pets welcome: 7 Smoking allowed: 8 Children welcome: 9 Social drinking allowed: 10 Tennis available: 11 Swimming available: 12 Golf available: 13 Skiing available: 14 May be booked through travel agents

Full Breakfast
Credit Cards: A, B
Notes: 4, 5, 7 (restricted), 8 (over 10 with sleeping bags)

BERWYN

B&B Connections #4

Box 21, Devon, 19333
(215) 687-3565

This charming 1770 fieldstone farmhouse is near the Main Line area, the universities, the Brandywine Valley, and Valley Forge Park. Guest rooms feature stenciled walls, canopy beds, one working fireplace, one wood-burning stove. Guest den with TV, wet bar, refrigerator. Shed and pasture are available for guests' horses. Resident dog.

Doubles: 3 (PB & SB) $75-85
Type of Beds: 2 Queen; 1 King
Full Breakfast
Credit Cards: A, B, C
Notes: 5, 8, 9, 10, 11, 12, 14

BETHLEHEM

The Gaslight House

B&B Southeast PA
146 W. Philadelphia Ave., Boyertown, 19512
(215) 367-4688

The Gaslight House is within the walking tour of historic Bethlehem. This centrally air-conditioned townhouse in a quiet area is an ideal location for exploring the city.

Doubles: 1 (PB) $45-55
Type of Beds: 1 Double
Full Breakfast
Credit Cards: A, B
Notes: 5

BIRD-IN-HAND

Greystone Manor Bed & Breakfast

2658 Old Phila. Pike, Box 270, 17505
(717) 393-4233

Greystone Manor is a lovely old French Victorian mansion and carriage house with Victorian furnishings, decorative windows and doors. Surrounded by Amish farms. Minutes from Lancaster, Intercourse, Strasburg, outlet malls, farmers' market, and local craft shops. Quilt shop in mansion basement.

Hosts: Sally & Ed Davis
Singles: 4 (PB) $48.76
Doubles: 8 (PB) $48.76-76.32
Type of Beds: 8 Double; 3 Queen
Continental Breakfast
Credit Cards: A, B
Notes: 2, 5, 8, 9, 10, 12, 14

BRACKNEY

Indian Mountain Inn Bed & Breakfast

RD 1, Box 68, 18812
(717) 663-2645

A true country inn nestled in the Endless Mountains near Binghamton, New York. Full restaurant, spa, liquor license. Surrounded by rolling mountain acres; ideal for all outdoor activities year round. Cozy sitting room with wood stoves. The inn is newly refurbished, and the innkeepers live on the premises.

Hosts: Howard, Deborah & Henrietta Frierman
Doubles: 9 (7 PB; 2 SB) $42.40-60.42
Type of Beds: 2 Twin; 1 Double; 7 Queen
Full Breakfast
Credit Cards: A, B, C, D
Notes: 2 (as deposit), 4, 5, 7 (limited), 8, 9, 12, 13

CAMBRIDGE SPRINGS

Bethany House

Pittsburgh Bed & Breakfast
2190 Ben Franklin Drive, Pittsburgh, 15237
(412) 367-8080

Well-appointed 1876 Victorian listed on the Historic Register. Pre-1900 furnishings and decor, fine antiques, hand-crafted winding staircase, thirteen-foot ceilings, elaborate

NOTES: Credit cards accepted: A Master Card; B Visa; C American Express; D Discover Card; E Diners Club; F Other: 2 Personal checks accepted: 3 Lunch available: 4 Dinner available: 5 Open all year

woodwork. Double-wide whirlpool attached to one guest room. Close to Presque Isle, National Wildlife Preserve, fishing, boating, historical museum, antique shops.

Singles: 1 (PB) $30-50
Doubles: 4 (PB) $30-50
Full Breakfast
Credit Cards: A, B
Notes: 2, 5, 8, 12

CANADENSIS

Dreamy Acres

Box 7, 18325
(717) 595-7115

Dreamy Acres is situated in the heart of the Pocono Mountain vacationland on 3 acres of land with a stream flowing into a small pond. The house is 500 feet back from the highway, giving a pleasing, quiet atmosphere.

Hosts: Esther & Bill Pickett
Doubles: 6 (4 PB; 2 SB) $32-50 plus tax
Type of Beds: 2 Twin; 4 Double
Continental Breakfast
Minimum stay weekends: 2; holidays, 3
Closed Christmas
Credit Cards: No
Notes: 7, 8 (over 12), 9, 10, 11, 12, 13

The Pine Knob Inn

Box 275, 18325
(717) 595-2532

Step back into yesteryear. Experience the atmosphere of years gone by in our 1840s inn situated on 15 acres abounding with antiques and art. Enjoy gourmet dining. Guests gather on the veranda on summer evenings or by the fireplace after a day on the slopes.

Hosts: Ann & Scott Frankel
Singles: 2 (1 PB; 1 SB) $80
Doubles: 25 (20 PB; 5 SB) $160
Type of Beds: 2 Twin; 25 Queen
Full Breakfast
Minimum stay weekends & holidays: 2
Credit Cards: A, B
Rate includes breakfast & dinner
Notes: 2, 4, 5, 7, 8 (over 5), 9, 10, 11

Pump House Inn

Skytop Road, 18325
(717) 595-7501

High in the Poconos, The Pump House Inn dates from 1842. Antiques, books, and distinctive furnishings grace this friendly country inn. Sophisticated dining is the mainstay at the Pump House, where the chef emphasizes French continental cuisine.

Host: John Keeney
Doubles: 6 (2 PB; 4 SB) $65-100
Type of Beds: 4 Twin; 4 Double
Continental Breakfast
Credit Cards: A, B, C, E, F
Closed January
Notes: 2, 4, 5, 7, 8, 9, 10, 11, 12, 13

CHURCHTOWN

Churchtown Inn B & B

Rt 23, Churchtown
Mail to: RD 3, Box 135, Narvon, PA 17555
(215) 445-7794

Lovely eighteenth-century stone mansion, restored and filled with charm and history. Located in the heart of Pennsylvania Dutch country, near all tourist attractions, antique markets, and outlets. Dine at an Amish home by prior arrangement. Air-conditioned, private bath. Highly recommended.

Hosts: Hermine & Stuart Smith & Jim Kent
Singles: 2 (PB)
Doubles: 6 (4 PB; 2 SB) $49-85
Type of Beds: 2 Twin; 6 Queen
Full Breakfast
Minimum stay weekends: 2 ; holidays: 3
Credit Cards: A, B
Closed Christmas
Notes: 2, 4, 7 (limited), 8 (over 12), 9 (limited), 10, 11, 12, 13 (XC)

Foreman House

B&B Southeast PA
146 W. Philadelphia Ave., Boyertown, 19512
(215) 367-4688

This solid stone house was built before 1920 and is surrounded by large trees. A good base for seeing Lancaster County and shopping at the Reading outlets. There's a sitting room and side porch for your enjoyment. Resident cat.

Doubles: 2 (SB) $35-55
Type of Beds: 2 Twin; 2 Double
Full Breakfast weekends; Continental weekdays
Credit Cards: A, B
Notes: 5, 8 (over 12)

CONCORDVILLE

West-Trimble House

B&B Southeast PA
146 W. Philadelphia Ave., Boyertown, 19512
(215) 367-4688

The original part of this house was built in 1728 and added to in the middle of the nineteenth century. It's listed on the National Historic Register, and the property can be traced back to land grants given by William Penn. Wilmington, Delaware, is a short distance away, as are Longwood Gardens, Winterthur, and West Chester State University. Resident cats.

Doubles: 2 (SB) $57-70
Type of Beds: 2 Twin; 1 Queen
Full Breakfast
Credit Cards: A, B
Notes: 5, 7 (limited), 8 (over 6)

COOPERSBURG

Welcome House

B&B Southeast PA
146 W. Philadelphia Ave., Boyertown, 19512
(215) 367-4688

You'll find peace and quiet here, in your private suite with sitting area, TV, powder room, separate shower, wheel-chair accessible private entrance.

Doubles: 1 (PB) $40-50
Type of Beds: 1 Twin; 1 Double
Full or Continental Breakfast
Credit Cards: A, B
Notes: 5, 8 (over 8)

COWANSVILLE

Garrott's B&B

Pittsburgh Bed & Breakfast
2190 Ben Franklin Drive, Pittsburgh, 15237
(412) 367-8080

Enjoy the quiet elegance of a restored 100-year-old home where antiques abound. Forty acres of rolling fields, gardens, and groves of trees for guests to cross-country ski; ice skating and sliding in the winter. In summer you can pick berries, herbs, and vegetables, or fish in the pond. Various habitats attract migrating birds, and because of the lack of air pollution, amateur astronomers bring their scopes.

Doubles: 3 (SB) $50-60
Type of Beds: 2 Twin; 1 Double; 1 Queen
Full Breakfast
Credit Cards: No
Notes: 2, 5, 7, 12, 13

CRESCO

LaAnna Guest House

RD 2, Box 1051, 18426
(717) 676-4225

Built in the 1870s, this Victorian home welcomes guests with large rooms that are furnished in Empire and Victorian antiques. Located in a quiet mountain village with waterfalls, mountain views, and outdoor activities.

Hosts: Kay Swingle & Julie Wilson
Doubles: 2 (1 PB; 1 SB) $25-30
Type of Beds: 2 Twin; 2 Double
Continental Breakfast
Credit Cards: No
Notes: 2, 5, 7, 8, 9, 10, 11, 12, 13 (XC), 14

DUSHORE

Heritage Guest House

Rt. 87 & 487, 18614
(717) 928-7354

NOTES: Credit cards accepted: A Master Card; B Visa; C American Express; D Discover Card; E Diners Club; F Other: 2 Personal checks accepted: 3 Lunch available: 4 Dinner available: 5 Open all year

Heritage Guest House is located in the heart of the Endless Mountains. Nearby are three state parks, three covered bridges, great fishing and hunting, and great antique shops. The house is furnished with antiques that are all for sale.

Hosts: Bill & Gertrude Wilson
Doubles: 4 (1 PB; 3 SB) $32-48
Type of Beds: 2 Twin; 3 Double
Full Breakfast
Minimum stay holidays: 2
Credit Cards: A, B
Closed Christmas-New Years & 2nd & 3rd weeks of Jan.
Notes: 2, 4, 8, 9

EAGLES MERE

Shady Lane Lodge
Allegheny Avenue, 17731
(717) 525-3394

A quiet bed & breakfast inn in the Victorian resort village of Eagles Mere, known as "the town time forgot." Guests enjoy a quiet, wooded setting overlooking the mountains. The inn is within easy walking distance of the lake, gift, and antique shops. Winter activities include cross-country skiing, ice skating, and the famous (since 1904) Ice Toboggan Slide.

Hosts: Lee & Alma Park
Doubles: 7 (PB) $57-60
Type of Beds: 4 Twin; 2 Double; 1 Queen
Full Breakfast; Continental July & Aug.
Credit Cards: No
Closed Christmas
Notes: 2, 5, 7 (limited), 9, 10, 11, 12, 13

EAST BERLIN

Bechtel Mansion Inn
400 West King Street, 17316
(717) 259-7760

Magnificent restored Victorian mansion with quality period furnishings and handmade quilts. Perfect setting for honeymoons and special occasions! Guest rooms are air-conditioned, with private baths. The man-

sion is on the western frontier of the Pennsylvania Dutch country. Excellent restaurants nearby. Convenient to York, Gettysburg, and Lancaster County.

Hosts: Ruth Spangler, Charles & Mariam Bechtel
Singles: 1 (PB) $47.75-95.50
Doubles: 7 (PB) $82.25-106
Suites: 2 (PB) $116.75-132.50
Type of Beds: 2 Twin; 6 Double; 1 Queen
Continental-plus Breakfast
Minimum stay Oct. weekends & holidays: 2
Credit Cards: A, B, C
Notes: 2, 5, 7 (limited), 8, 9, 10, 12, 13 (18 miles), 14

Bechtel Mansion Inn

EAST GREENVILLE

End of the Winding Lane
B&B Southeast PA
146 W. Philadelphia Ave., Boyertown, 19512
(215) 367-4688

You can experience peace and quiet at the End of the Winding Lane in this split-level with five steps up to the living room and another nine to the bedroom. A small TV and radio are available.

Doubles: 1 (PB) $35-50
Type of Beds: 2 Twin
Full Breakfast
Credit Cards: A, B
Notes: 5

6 Pets welcome: 7 Smoking allowed: 8 Children welcome: 9 Social drinking allowed: 10 Tennis available: 11 Swimming available: 12 Golf available: 13 Skiing available: 14 May be booked through travel agents

The Old Grist Mill

B&B Southeast PA
146 W. Philadelphia Ave., Boyertown, 19512
(215) 367-4688

A lovely Victorian home furnished with antiques on a famous trout stream. Breakfast is served on the screened porch in the summer and by the bay window of the kitchen at other times. Dog in residence.

Singles: 1 (SB) $40
Doubles: 2 (PB) $40-50
Type of Beds: 1 Twin; 2 Double
Full Breakfast
Credit Cards: A, B
Notes: 5

EAST STROUDSBURG

The Inn at Meadowbrook

RD 7, Box 7651, 18301
(717) 629-0296

A quiet country inn on 43 acres of rolling hills and meadows in the heart of the Poconos. Fishing lake, tennis courts, and a large outdoor swimming pool. Enjoy the beauty of a peaceful rural location.

Hosts: Bob & Kathy Overman
Doubles: 16 (10 PB; 6 SB) $45-80
Type of Beds: 2 Twin; 11 Double; 4 Queen
Continental Breakfast
Credit Cards: A, B
Notes: 2, 4, 5, 7, 8 (12 and over), 9, 10, 11, 12, 13

ELM

Elm Country Inn

Box 37, 17521
(717) 664-3623

Located in a small country village in beautiful Lancaster County, we are near the Amish country. The house was built in 1860 and has been refurbished, keeping most of the old character intact. Hosts are knowledgeable about the area and will help guests plan their sightseeing.

Hosts: Berry & Melvin Meck
Doubles: 3 (SB) $45
Type of Beds: 1 Twin; 3 Double
Full Breakfast
Credit Cards: A, B
Notes: 5, 8, 9, 10, 11, 12, 14

EMIGSVILLE

Emig Mansion

Box 486, 17318
(717) 764-3342

This skillfully restored nineteenth-century home now features charming guest rooms, a formal dining room of Philippine mahogany, and a private conference room for seminars and meetings. Leaded and stained-glass windows, intricate moldings, and delightful marble and tile throughout.

Hosts: Jane Llewellyn
Doubles: 7 (3 PB; 4 SB) $90-116.60
Type of Beds: 1 Twin; 7 Double
Full Breakfast
Credit Cards: B
Notes: 2, 5, 8 (over 12), 9, 12, 13

EPHRATA

The Guesthouse and the 1777 House at Doneckers

318-324 North State Street, 17522
(717) 733-8696

Experience the Doneckers' warm hospitality in the picturesque setting of historic Lancaster County. Let us pamper you with country elegance, fine antiques, folk art, hand-stenciled walls, and designer linens. Jacuzzi baths and fireplaces in some rooms. Restaurant and fashion stores.

Host: H. William Donecker
Doubles: 29 (27 PB; 2 SB) $59-130 plus tax
Type of Beds: 1 Twin; 4 Double; 24 Queen
Buffet Breakfast
Credit Cards: All
Closed Christmas Day
Notes: 2, 3, 4, 7, 8, 9, 11

NOTES: Credit cards accepted: A Master Card; B Visa; C American Express; D Discover Card; E Diners Club; F Other: 2 Personal checks accepted: 3 Lunch available: 4 Dinner available: 5 Open all year

swimming pool and offer a refreshing drink on arrival. They will made dinner reservations for you. Two cats and a small dog in residence. Convenient for exploring the Amish country and the antique emporiums in Adamstown.

Doubles: 3 (PB) $65
Type of Beds: 2 Twin; 2 Double
Full Breakfast
Credit Cards: A, B
Notes: 5, 10, 11

ERWINNA

The 1777 House at Doneckers

Evermay on-the-Delaware
River Road, 18920
(215) 294-9100

Lodging in manor house and carriage house. Liquor license. Parlor with fireplace. A significant, distinguished country retreat located on 25 acres of gardens, woodland paths, and pastures between the Delaware River and Canal. Dinner served Friday, Saturday, Sunday, and holidays.

Hosts: Ron Strouse & Fred Cresson
Doubles: 15 (PB) $42-115
Type of Beds: 1 Twin; 12 Double; 2 Queen
Continental-plus Breakfast
Minimum stay weekends: 2
Credit Cards: A, B
Closed Dec. 24
Notes: 2, 7, 8 (over 12)

The Historic Smithton Inn
900 W. Main Street, 17522
(717) 733-6094

A romantic 1763 stone inn with fireplaces in every room, canopy beds, easy chairs, quilts, candles, down pillows, night shirts, flowers, chamber music, and feather beds. Parlor, library, and gardens for guests to enjoy. In Lancaster County, an antique and crafts area settled by the Pennsylvania Dutch, Mennonite, and Amish peoples.

Host: Dorothy Graybill
Doubles: 8 (PB and SB) $55-105
Type of Beds: 2 Twin; 3 Double; 4 Queen; 1 King
Full Breakfast
Credit Cards: A, B, C
Notes: 2, 5, 6, 8, 9, 10, 11, 12

EPHRATA-ADAMSTOWN

Springwoods
B&B Southeast PA
146 W. Philadelphia Ave., Boyertown, 19512
(215) 367-4688

This famous Civil War frame farmhouse straddles the county line of Berks and Lancaster counties. Guest rooms share a sitting room with TV. The house is shaded by tall pines and is well equipped with fans. The hosts allow guests to take a quick dip in the

Golden Pheasant Inn
River Road, 18920
(215) 294-9595

This 1857 fieldstone inn is situated between the Delaware River and the Pennsylvania Canal. Five romantic rooms are furnished with an incredible blend of antiques. Three dining rooms, including a candlelit greenhouse. Masterful classical French cuisine by chef/owner Michel Faure. Extensive wine selections.

Hosts: Michel & Barbara Faure
Doubles: 5 (1 PB; 4 SB) $95-125

6 Pets welcome: 7 Smoking allowed: 8 Children welcome: 9 Social drinking allowed: 10 Tennis available: 11 Swimming available: 12 Golf available: 13 Skiing available: 14 May be booked through travel agents

Type of Beds: 4 Double; 1 Queen
Continental Breakfast
Minimum stay weekends: 2 ; holidays: 3
Credit Cards: A, B
Notes: 2, 4, 5, 7, 9, 10, 11, 12, 13

GATESBURG

Maple Hill Farm

Rest & Repast B&B Service
Box 126, Pine Grove Mills, 16868
(814) 238-1484

This mid-1800s stone and frame farmhouse
with wraparound veranda is located in a very
rural area on a working dairy farm. There
are chickens, turkeys, ducks, and a pig pen
that children seem to delight in. In the middle of some of the best hunting in central
Pennsylvania, minutes from state game
lands. Fifteen minutes from Penn State.

Doubles: 2 (SB) $30-40
Type of Beds: 2 Double
Full Breakfast
Credit Cards: No
Closed Dec. 24 - Jan. 2
Notes: 2, 7, 8, 13

The Golden Pheasant Inn

GERMANTOWN

Germantown Bed & Breakfast

5925 Wayne Avenue, 19144
(215) 848-1375

Your 1900s oak bedroom has a cable TV
and a private bath. This is a homestay with
three young children, where you will become
part of the family. Historic sites and
downtown Philadelphia are nearby; walk to
restaurants and conveniences.

Hosts: Molly & Jeff Smith
Doubles: 1 (PB) $35
Type of Beds: 1 Twin; 1 Double
Continental Breakfast
Credit Cards: No
Notes: 2, 5, 8, 9, 11

GETTYSBURG

Abraham Spangler Inn

264 Baltimore Street, 17325
(717) 337-3997

Small European-style inn with three
bedrooms, furnished with antiques and
Oriental rugs. Located ideally for the tourist,
midway between Lincoln Square's business
district and the National Visitor's Center.
There is a sitting room with bay windows
overlooking the historic district of Baltimore
Street, and a quiet, tree-shaded back porch
provides guests a peaceful retreat after a day
of sightseeing.

Host: Joel C. Nimon
Singles: 1 (SB) $26.50-42.70
Doubles: 2 (SB) $31.80-47.70
Type of Beds: 1 Twin; 2 Double
Continental Breakfast
Credit Cards: A, B
Notes: 2, 5, 8 (12 and up), 9

The Brafferton Inn

44 York Street, 17325
(717) 337-3423

NOTES: Credit cards accepted: A Master Card; B Visa; C American Express; D Discover Card; E Diners
Club; F Other: 2 Personal checks accepted: 3 Lunch available: 4 Dinner available: 5 Open all year

This 1786 stone home is listed on the National Register of Historic Places. Enjoy our colonial antiques, stenciled decor, and full breakfast served by a primitive mural. Experience Gettysburg in the first house built in town. Featured in the February 1988 issue of *Country Living* magazine.

Hosts: Mimi & Jim Agard
Doubles: 10 (6 PB; 4 SB) $55-80
Type of Beds: 4 Twin; 8 Double
Full Breakfast
Credit Cards: A, B
Notes: 2, 4, 5, 7 (limited), 8 (over 7), 9, 10, 11, 12, 13, 14

The Brafferton Inn

The Doubleday Inn

104 Doubleday Avenue, 17325
(717) 334-9119

Located directly on the Gettysburg Battlefield, the inn is a beautifully restored Colonial recalling past century charms with Civil War furnishings and antiques. Tour the battlefield and return for afternoon tea to complete a gracious combination of history and hospitality.

Hosts: Joan & Sal Chandon
Singles: $60-85
Doubles: 11 (6 PB; 5 SB) $65-90
Full Breakfast
Credit Cards: A, B
Checks accepted for advance deposit only
Notes: 3, 4, 5, 8 (over 7), 9, 10, 11, 12, 13, 14

Hickory Bridge Farm

231 Hickory Bridge Road, 17353
(717) 642-5261

Quietly located at the edge of the mountains just eight miles west of Gettysburg. Country cottages in a wooded location by a pure mountain stream. Dinners are offered Friday, Saturday, and Sunday in a restored barn furnished with fine antiques. Family owned and operated for fifteen years.

Hosts: Mary Lynn & Robert Martin, Dr. & Mrs. James Hammett
Doubles: 4 (PB) $40-75
Type of Beds: 4 Queen
Full Breakfast
Minimum stay weekends: 2
Credit Cards: A, B
Notes: 2, 4, 5, 7, 8, 9, 11, 12, 13

The Old Appleford Inn

218 Carlisle Street, 17325
(717) 337-1711

This three-story Victorian mansion, built in 1867 by Judge Robt. McCurdy, has a piano and fireplace in the antique-filled living room, a library with fireplace, apple stenciling in the dining room. Eleven elegant bedrooms, each uniquely decorated. There's a plant-filled sunroom with white wicker, and a large, open front porch. Complimentary sherry and full breakfast. Surrounded by Gettysburg College, the battlefield, places to shop for antiques, and a nearby ski area.

Hosts: Maribeth & Frank Skradski
Doubles: 11 (2 PB; 9 SB) $62-82 plus tax
Type of Beds: 9 Double; 2 Queen
Full Breakfast
Credit Cards: A, B, C
Notes: 2, 5, 8 (over 14), 12, 13, 14

GORDONVILLE

The Osceola Mill House

313 Osceola Mill Road, 17529
(717) 768-3758

6 Pets welcome: 7 Smoking allowed: 8 Children welcome: 9 Social drinking allowed: 10 Tennis available: 11 Swimming available: 12 Golf available: 13 Skiing available: 14 May be booked through travel agents

The Osceola Mill House is located in scenic Lancaster County, surrounded by Amish farms in a quaint, historic setting. Antiques and reproductions, poster beds, fireplaces, and Amish quilts. Close to restaurants, antique and craft shops.

Hosts: Barry & Joy Sawyer
Doubles: 4 (SB) $50-70
Type of Beds: 2 Double; 2 Queen
Full Breakfast
Minimum stay holidays: 2
Credit Cards: No
Closed Dec. 24-Jan. 2
Notes: 2, 8 (over 12), 9

GREENSBURG

Huntland Farm

Pittsburgh Bed & Breakfast .
2190 Ben Franklin Drive, Pittsburgh, 15237
(412) 367-8080

This 1848 house is listed in *Historic Places in Western Pennsylvannia*. The original Egyptian Revival interior woodwork still remains. Large living areas are furnished with antiques. Located in the foothills of Laural Highland, which offer many scenic and historic attractions. Seton Hill and St. Vincent College are near.

Doubles: 4 (SB) $40-65
Type of Beds: 6 Twin; 1 Double
Continental Breakfast
Credit Cards: No
Notes: 5, 7 (limited), 8 (12 and over), 9, 12, 13

HANOVER

Beechmont Inn

315 Broadway, 17331
(717) 632-3013

An elegant 1834 Federal inn with antiques, fireplace, air-conditioning. Enjoy a gourmet breakfast in your room, the dining room, or outdoors under the vine-covered trellis. Enjoy great antiquing in nearby New Oxford. Located thirteen miles from Gettysburg; Pennsylvania Dutch country nearby.

Hosts: Terry & Monna Hormel; Glenn & Maggie Hormel
Doubles: 7 (PB) $67.84-89.04
Type of Beds: 1 Double; 6 Queen
Full Breakfast
Minimum stay holidays: 2
Credit Cards: A, B
Notes: 2, 5, 7 (restricted), 8 (over 12), 9, 10, 11, 12, 13 (XC)

Academy Street B&B

HAWLEY

Academy Street Bed & Breakfast

528 Academy Street, 18428
(717) 226-3430
Winter phone: (201) 316-8148

Outstanding historic 1863 Italianate Victorian built by Civil War hero, the first sheriff of Wayne County. Near largest and most beautiful recreational lake in state, with all activities. Convenient to I-84. Lovely furnished inn; full gourmet breakfast and afternoon tea. Large bright, airy, air-conditioned rooms.

Host: Judith Lazan
Doubles: 7 (3 PB; 4 SB) $40-80

NOTES: Credit cards accepted: A Master Card; B Visa; C American Express; D Discover Card; E Diners Club; F Other: 2 Personal checks accepted: 3 Lunch available: 4 Dinner available: 5 Open all year

The Settlers Inn

Type of Beds: 1 Twin; 2 Double; 4 Queen
Full Breakfast
Credit Cards: A, B
Closed Nov.-April
Notes: 7, 9, 10, 11, 12

The Settlers Inn

4 Main Avenue, 18428
(717) 226-2993

A grand Tudor-style hotel beside the park in the village of Hawley. Near Lake Wallen-paupack and many recreational activities. Elegant dining featuring a creative regional menu. Complimentary afternoon tea is served by the fireplace or on the spacious front porch. Enjoy specialty shopping, antiuing, museums, and summer theaters.

Hosts: Grant & Jeanne Genzlinger
Doubles: 18 (PB) $55-75
Type of Beds: 18 Double
Continental Breakfast
Credit Cards: A, B, C
Notes: 2, 3, 4, 5, 7, 8, 9, 10, 11, 12, 13, 14

HERSHEY

Country Home

Hershey B&B RSO, Box 208, 17033
(717) 533-2928

Enjoy the country feeling while eating breakfast on your hosts' patio. Resident parakeet and small dog. Located seven miles from Hershey, less than one hour from Gettysburg and the main attractions of Lancaster.

Doubles: 2 (SB) $50-55
Type of Beds: 2 Twin; 1 Double
Full Breakfast
Credit Cards: A, B
Notes: 5, 8, 9, 10, 11, 12, 13, 14

Edelweis

Hershey B&B RSO, Box 208, 17033
(717) 533-2928

This lovely German family welcomes you to their friendly home. Right near all the Hershey attractions. Enjoy the hostess's home-baked German recipes each morning. Six miles from Rt. 81; one mile from Rt. 322.

Singles: 1 (SB) $45
Doubles: 2 (SB) $45-55
Continental Breakfast
Credit Cards: A, B
Notes: 5, 7, 8, 10, 11, 12

6 Pets welcome: 7 Smoking allowed: 8 Children welcome: 9 Social drinking allowed: 10 Tennis available: 11 Swimming available: 12 Golf available: 13 Skiing available: 14 May be booked through travel agents

Gibson's Bed & Breakfast

141 W. Caracas Avenue, 17033
(717) 534-1305

Bob and Frances Gibson have a fifty-year-old Cape Cod in the center of Hershey, within walking distance of many local attractions. The atmosphere is friendly and informal, and the Gibsons will help you find local sights such as Hershey Park, Chocolate World, Founders Hall, and the Amish country.

Hosts: Frances & Bob Gibson
Doubles: 3 (SB) $25-35
Type of Beds: 3 Twin; 3 Double
Full Breakfast
Credit Cards: No
Notes: 2, 5, 7, 8 (over 6), 9, 10, 11, 12

Pinehurst Inn

Hershey B&B RSO, Box 208, 17033
(717) 533-2928

This large inn is centrally located near interesting sights and recreational activities. Walk to the Sports Arena, stadium, Hershey Park, Chocolate World, and Hershey Museum. Less than one hour's drive to Gettysburg and Lancaster County. Five miles from Rt. 81.

Doubles: 12 (PB and SB) $50-55
Continental Breakfast
Credit Cards: A, B
Notes: 2, 5, 8, 9, 10, 11, 12, 14

Stone Lock Farm

Hershey B&B RSO, Box 208, 17033
(717) 533-2928

This 1700s log home is situated on a horse farm. Country roads for walking, biking; fields and woods for hiking. Resident dog and cat outside, plus other animals. Close to Hershey attractions; less than one hour from Gettysburg and Lancaster County.

Doubles: 1 (PB) $60-65
Type of Beds: 1 Double

Continental Breakfast
Credit Cards: A, B
Notes: 5, 8, 10, 11, 12, 13, 14

HESSTON

Aunt Susie's Country Vacations

RD 1, Box 225, 16647
(814) 658-3638

Experience country living in a warm, friendly atmosphere in a Victorian parsonage or a renovated country store and post office. All rooms are nicely furnished with antiques and oil paintings. Raystown Lake is nearby for recreation; boating, swimming, and fishing are within three miles. Bring your family to the country.

Hosts: Susan, Bob & John
Doubles: 8 (2 PB; 6 SB) $45-50
Type of Beds: 4 Twin; 1 Double; 3 Queen; 2 King
Continental-plus Breakfast
Credit Cards: No
Notes: 2, 5, 8, 9, 10, 11, 12

HICKORY

Shady Elms Farm Bed & Breakfast

RD 1, Box 188, 15340
(412) 356-7755

Restored early 1800 colonial mansion on 140 acre working farm. Furnished with antiques. Swimming and fishing pond. Winter sledding, skiing, and ice skating. Seven miles from intersection of I-70 and I-79. Close to Washington and Jefferson, Bethany, and West Liberty colleges.

Hosts: Marjorie & Connie Curran
Doubles: 3 (2 PB; 1 SB) $35-40
Type of Beds: 1 Twin; 1 Double; 2 Queen
Full Breakfast
Credit Cards: No
Notes: 2, 5, 6, 7, 8, 9, 10, 11, 12

NOTES: Credit cards accepted: A Master Card; B Visa; C American Express; D Discover Card; E Diners Club; F Other: 2 Personal checks accepted: 3 Lunch available: 4 Dinner available: 5 Open all year

HILLSGROVE

The Tannery House

Box 99, Rt. 87, 18619
(717) 924-3505

Located in picturesque Sullivan County, in
the village of Hillsgrove, our country home
has an old-fashioned wraparound porch.
Summer breakfasts are served in the
gazebo. Furnishings are antiques and collectibles, and there is a Victorian parlor with
player piano. We are surrounded by state
forest where you can enjoy cross-country
skiing, hunting, fly fishing, canoeing, and
hiking.

Hosts: Linda & Dennis Renninger
Singles: 3 (SB) $18.55
Doubles: 4 (1 PB; 3 SB) $37.10-53
Type of Beds: 3 Twin; 3 Double; 1 Queen
Continental Breakfast
Credit Cards: A, B (surcharge)
Notes: 2 (2 weeks in advance), 5, 7 (limited), 8, 9, 13
(XC)

HOLICONG

Ash Mill Farm

Box 202, 18928
(215) 794-5373

Ten sheep-filled bucolic acres in Bucks
County. Enjoy your country breakfast and
afternoon tea with Mozart, Bach, and Vivaldi. Six antique-filled rooms just minutes
from New Hope.

Hosts: Patricia & Jim Auslander
Doubles: 6 (4 PB; 2 SB) $75-110
Full Breakfast
Credit Cards: A, B
Notes: 2, 5, 8 (over 15), 9, 10, 11, 12, 13 (XC)

HOLTWOOD

Country Cottage

B&B Southeast PA
146 W. Philadelphia Ave., Boyertown, 19512
(215) 367-4688

Lancaster County. To reach Country Cottage, you drive through trees, up a winding
lane to a small plateau on top of a hill. This
one-level home has two decks and a ramp
for a wheel chair. Your cottage has a living
room with a large stone fireplace, TV/VCR,
stained-glass windows, kitchen, enclosed sun
porch. Baltimore is 1.5 hours away; Gettysburg a little less.

Cottage: 1 (PB) $65
Type of Beds: 2 Double
Continental Breakfast
Credit Cards: A, B
Notes: 5, 7, 8

HUNTINGDON

Juniata B&B

Rest & Repast B&B Service
Box 126, Pine Grove Mills, 16868
(814) 238-1484

This circa 1860 Greek Revival is largely furnished in period antiques. Within easy walking distance to downtown Huntingdon and
Juniata College, also only minutes away
from state parks and Lake Raystown.

Doubles: 2 (SB) $20-40
Type of Beds: 2 Double
Continental Breakfast
Credit Cards: No
Closed Dec. - April
Notes: 2, 7, 8, 9, 10, 11, 12, 13

JERSEY SHORE

Sommerville Farms Bed & Breakfast

RD 4, Box 22, 17740
(717) 398-2368

A Victorian farmhouse, comfortably furnished with antiques, located on a 200 acre
working farm. Historic area along the West
Branch of the Susquehanna River and
scenic Pine Creek Valley. Fishing, cross-
country skiing, boating, hiking the Ap-

palachian Trail, antique auctions and shops, Penn State football games.

Hosts: Bill & Jane Williams
Singles: 1 (SB) $26.50
Doubles: 5 (SB) $37.10
Type of Beds: 6 Twin; 3 Double
Full Breakfast
Minimum stay during foliage weekends: 2
Credit Cards: No
Notes: 2, 5, 7, 8, 9, 11, 12, 13

JIM THORPE

The Harry Packer Mansion
Packer Hill, 18229
(717) 325-8566

This 1874 Second Empire mansion features original appointments and ultra-Victorian decor. Completely restored for tours, B&B, fabulous Mystery Weekends, and a host of other activities. The adjoining carriage house is elegantly decorated in a hunt motif. The mansion is rated 3 diamonds by AAA.

Hosts: Bob & Patricia Handwerk
Doubles: 13 (8 PB; 5 SB) $65-110 plus tax
Type of Beds: 7 Double; 6 Queen
Full Breakfast
Minimum stay weekends: 2
Credit Cards: A, B
Notes: 2, 5, 9, 10, 11, 12, 13, 14

KINZERS

Sycamore Haven Farm
35 S. Kinzer Road, 17535
(717) 442-4901

We are a dairy farm located fifteen miles east of Lancaster, right in Pennsylvania Dutch country. Our rooms are newly papered and painted, and we have a porch in the back of the house with a lovely swing. We also have a balcony with lounge chairs and forty dairy cows that we milk morning and evening. The children will really enjoy our many kittens and pet sheep, who like a lot of attention.

Hosts: Charles & Janet Groff
Doubles: 3 (SB) $30

Type of Beds: 3 Twin; 3 Double
Continental Breakfast
Credit Cards: No
Notes: 2, 5, 6, 8, 11, 12

Kane Manor B&B

KANE

Kane Manor Bed & Breakfast
230 Clay Street, 16735
(814) 837-6522

We are one of the best-kept secrets in the Alleghenies. Come and discover for yourself the feeling of being surrounded by the Allegheny National Forest. Step inside the inn and you'll find yourself surrounded by history. All ten guest rooms are decorated differently, and all have their own personality. Hiking, boating, swimming, golfing, cross-country skiing. Gathering Room, Gift Shoppe, and Cellar Pub.

Host: Laurie Anne Dalton
Doubles: 10 (6 PB; 4 SB) $45-79
Suite: $95
Type of Beds: 2 Twin; 9 Double
Continental Breakfast weekdays; full on weekends
Minimum stay during Sept.-Oct. and Jan.-Feb. weekends: 2
Credit Cards: A, B, C
Notes: 2, 5, 7, 8, 9, 10, 11, 12, 13, 14

KENNETT SQUARE

Meadow Spring Farm
201 E. Street Road, 19348
(215) 444-3903

NOTES: Credit cards accepted: A Master Card; B Visa; C American Express; D Discover Card; E Diners Club; F Other: 2 Personal checks accepted: 3 Lunch available: 4 Dinner available: 5 Open all year

This B&B, located on a working farm in the Brandywine with cows, pigs, lambs, and horses, has a pool, hot tub, and solarium, Amish quilts, Laura Ashley linens, and a game room for your enjoyment. Dinner is available with advance notice. Some of the available activities in the area include canoeing and tubing, museums, tennis, bicycling, hot-air balloon rides.

Host: Anne Hicks
Singles: 1 (SB) $35
Doubles: 5 (3 PB; 2 SB) $53-68.90
Type of Beds: 2 Twin; 4 Queen
Full Breakfast
Credit Cards: No
Notes: 2, 4, 5, 7, 8, 9, 11, 12, 14

KULPSVILLE

The Pool House

B&B Southeast PA
146 W. Philadelphia Ave., Boyertown, 19512
(215) 367-4688

Pool House is located less than a mile from the NE extension of the PA Turnpike. Converted from an old carriage house, the separate cottage overlooks the in-ground pool. Large living room, kitchen with microwave, dining area, cable TV. You may have a full breakfast in the hosts' home or fix your own continental breakfast from supplies left in the kitchen. Close to Skippack Village.

Doubles: 1 (PB) $65
Type of Beds: 1 Queen
Full or Continental Breakfast
Credit Cards: A, B
Notes: 5, 11

KUTZTOWN

Crystal Cottage

B&B Southeast PA
146 W. Philadelphia Ave., Boyertown, 19512
(215) 367-4688

Separate from the main house on 20 acres of land just four miles north of Kutztown,

this is the old summer kitchen of the farm, which has been turned into a charming self-contained suite. The cottage has a wood-burning stove and small kitchen, TV. You may make arrangements to use the hosts' pool. Resident dog. Near Kutztown State University, Crystal Cave, PA Dutch Folk Festival.

Cottage: 1 (PB) $45-55
Type of Beds: 1 Double
Continental Breakfast
Credit Cards: A, B
Notes: 5, 7 (limited), 8 (with sleeping bags), 10

LACKAWAXEN

Roebling Delaware Inn

Scenic Drive, 18435
(717) 685-7900

An historic 1865 center-hall colonial on the beautiful Delaware River between the Zane Grey Museum and Roebling Bridge. Canoe, fish, or just relax amid mountain scenery. Take a scenic drive along the Delaware. Hunt for antiques or enjoy the fall foliage. Tennis, golf, and skiing are all nearby.

Hosts: Donald & JoAnn Jahn
Doubles: 4 (PB) $58-69
Type of Beds: 2 Twin; 1 Double; 3 Queen
Full Breakfast
Minimum stay holidays: 2
Credit Cards: A, B
Closed Christmas
Notes: 2, 5, 7 (restricted), 9, 10, 13

LANCASTER

Buona Notte Bed & Breakfast

2020 Marietta Avenue, 17603
(717) 295-2597

Turn-of-the-century home with large, comfortable rooms, wraparound porch, large backyard and picnic table. Hershey Park, Gettysburg area and Pennsylvania Dutch country are all nearby. Breakfast includes homemade breads, muffins, coffee cakes,

6 Pets welcome: 7 Smoking allowed: 8 Children welcome: 9 Social drinking allowed: 10 Tennis available: 11 Swimming available: 12 Golf available: 13 Skiing available: 14 May be booked through travel agents

and jams. French and Italian are spoken here.

Hosts: Joe & Anna Predoti
Doubles: 3 (1 PB; 2 SB) $40-45
Type of Beds: 2 Twin; 1 Double; 1 King
Continental Breakfast
Credit Cards: No
Notes: 5, 8, 10, 12

Meadowview Guest House

2169 New Holland Pike, Rt. 23, 17601
(717) 299-4017

Located in the heart of the Pennsylvania Dutch area, close to historic sites, antiques, farmers and flea markets, and excellent restaurants. Large air-conditioned rooms, guest kitchen with coffee and tea. To help you enjoy our beautiful county, personalized maps will be provided.

Hosts: Ed & Sheila Christie
Doubles: 3 (1 PB; 2 SB) $25-40
Type of Beds: 3 Twin; 3 Double
Continental Breakfast
Credit Cards: No
Closed Dec. 1 - March 14
Notes: 2, 8 (over 6), 9, 10, 11, 12

Mennonite Home

Hershey B&B RSO, Box 208, Hershey, 17033
(717) 533-2928

A lovely home near all the Dutch Country attractions. About 23 miles from Hershey, 24 to the Redding outlets, 37 to Longwood Gardens, 48 to Gettysburg.

Doubles: 2 (PB) $50
Type of Beds: 2 Twin; 1 Queen
Continental Breakfast
Credit Cards: A, B
Notes: 5, 8, 12, 14

Witmer's Tavern — Historic 1725 Inn

2014 Old Philadelphia Pike, 17602
(717) 299-5305

Sole survivor of the sixty-two inns that once lined the nation's first turnpike between Philadelphia and Lancaster, Witmer's Tavern still operates as a lodging facility. The four-story blue limestone inn, with its individual room fireplaces, early iron door hinges and latches, nine-over-six bubbly windows, and early woodwork, served to provision early settlers on their way west. Today's guests enjoy fresh flowers, antiques, quilts, fireplaces, and the romance of the old inn.

Host: Brant Hartung
Doubles: 5 (SB) $55-75
Type of Beds: 5 Double
Continental Breakfast
Credit Cards: No
Notes: 2, 5, 7, 9, 10, 11, 12, 13, 14

Whitmer's Tavern

LANDIS STORE

Cottage at the Quiltery

B&B Southeast PA
146 W. Philadelphia Ave., Boyertown, 19512
(215) 367-4688

This cottage will make you think you're in the English Cotswolds with acres of woodland. Skillfully decorated with antiques, handmade furniture and quilts. The living room has a wood-burning stove and bay window. Hand-hewn stairs lead to an air-

NOTES: Credit cards accepted: A Master Card; B Visa; C American Express; D Discover Card; E Diners Club; F Other: 2 Personal checks accepted: 3 Lunch available: 4 Dinner available: 5 Open all year

conditioned bedroom. Cats in residence at the main house.

Cottage: 1 (PB) $60
Type of Beds: 1 Double
Full Breakfast
Minimum stay, winter: 2
Credit Cards: A, B
Notes: 5

LEESPORT

The Loom Room

RD 1, Box 1420, 19533
(215) 926-3217

Furnished with early antiques, this lovely 1812 farmhouse also has a weaving studio in its 1760 log wing. A colonial gazebo, herb and flower gardens, and graceful lawns complete the atmosphere of relaxed tranquility. Nearby are abundant antique and outlet shops, nature trails, and historic sites.

Hosts: Mary & Gene Smith
Doubles: 3 (1 PB; 2 SB) $40-45
Type of Beds: 3 Double
Full Breakfast
Credit Cards: No
Notes: 2, 4, 6, 7 (limited), 9, 10, 11, 12

Sleepy Fir

B&B Southeast PA
146 W. Philadelphia Ave., Boyertown, 19512
(215) 367-4688

Sleepy Fir is situated on 3.5 acres in rural Berks Country north of Reading. Ideally located for Blue Marsh Lake or Hawk Mountain. Reading's outlets are nearby, as are various historical sites. Guest bath features a whirlpool and sauna; game room with pool table; bicycles and canoe available.

Doubles: 2 (SB) $40-50
Type of Beds: 2 Double
Full or Continental Breakfast
Credit Cards: A, B
Notes: 5, 7 (limited), 9, 10, 11, 12

LIBERTY

Hill-Top Haven

RD 1, Box 5-C, 16930
(717) 324-2608

This comfortable rambling ranch house is in a rural mountain area, surrounded by fields, woods, and flower beds. The house is filled with handmade crafts and many antiques. State parks, tennis, skiing, golf, biking, and snow mobile trails are close by.

Hosts: Richard & Betty Landis
Doubles: 2 (SB) $30-35
Type of Beds: 2 Double
Continental Breakfast
Credit Cards: No
Notes: 5, 8, 10, 11

LITITZ

Alden House

62 East Main Street, 17543
(717) 627-3363

Circa 1850 pre-Civil War townhouse, located in the center of the historic district of Lititz, a charming Moravian community. Walk to quaint shops, restaurants, and museums. Ten minutes to Lancaster and the Amish attractions. Three large porches to relax on at day's end.

Hosts: Lori & Jim Wilson
Doubles: 7 (5 PB; 2 SB) $68.90-90.10
Type of Beds: 8 Twin; 3 Double; 2 Queen
Continental-plus Breakfast
Minimum stay weekends & holidays: 2
Credit Cards: A, B
Notes: 2, 5, 7, 8, 9

LOGANVILLE

Amanda's B&B
Reservation Service #19

1428 Park Ave., Baltimore, MD, 21217
(301) 225-0001

You're cordially invited to visit the ewes, lambs, rams, and Daisy the sheep dog on this

---

6 Pets welcome: 7 Smoking allowed: 8 Children welcome: 9 Social drinking allowed: 10 Tennis available: 11 Swimming available: 12 Golf available: 13 Skiing available: 14 May be booked through travel agents

working sheep farm. Enjoy the gardens with flowers and vegetables; visit the farm shop with our own wool hand knits, yarns, and knit kits. Afternoon tea, turn-down service, individually planned day trips. Also available is a cottage separate from the main house that sleeps 6 and has a fireplace.

Doubles: 2 (PB) $65
Type of Beds: 2 Double
Continental Breakfast
Credit Cards: A, B, C
Notes: 2, 5, 8, 9, 10, 11, 12, 13, 14

Country Spun Farm B&B

Box 117, 17342
(717) 428-1162

Delightful countryside accommodations on a working sheep farm afford the visitor a beautiful setting, individually planned day trips, and hospitality-plus. A full breakfast is served in the country kitchen or by the garden. Central to York and Lancaster; one mile from I-83.

Hosts: Greg & Martha Lou
Doubles: 2 (PB) $55-65
Full Breakfast
Credit Cards: A, B, D
Notes: 2, 5, 8 (12 and over), 9, 10, 11, 12, 14

LUMBERVILLE

Black Bass Hotel

River Road, Rt. 32, 18933
(215) 297-5770

Whether you come for lunch, dinner, or for a weekend, you'll feel you're in another era. The Black Bass provides a breathtaking view of the Delaware River and delightful cuisine. The guest rooms are decorated with antiques, and some have balconies where you may enjoy your continental breakfast.

Host: Herbert E. Ward
Doubles: 9 (2 PB; 7 SB) $58.30-185.50
Type of Beds: 2 Twin; 5 Double; 2 Queen
Continental Breakfast
Minimum stay weekdays: 2; holidays: 3
Credit Cards: A, B, C, E

Closed Christmas Day
Notes: 2, 3, 4, 5, 6, 9, 10, 11, 12, 13

MACUNGIE

Victorian Retreat

B&B Southeast PA
146 W. Philadelphia Ave., Boyertown, 19512
(215) 367-4688

Your hosts are in the process of renovating this Victorian and can now offer a room with enclosed porch and private bath. Beach towels are available if guests wish to take a quick dip in the in-ground pool. Guests are welcome from Friday-Sunday; resident cat.

Doubles: 1 (PB) $55
Type of Beds: 1 King
Full Breakfast
Credit Cards: A, B
Closed Mon.-Thurs.
Notes: 5, 11, 12

MANHEIM

Herr Farmhouse Inn

Rt. 7, Box 587, 17545
(717) 653-9852

Historic circa 1738 stone farmhouse nestled on 11.5 scenic acres of farmland. The inn has been tastefully restored, retaining original pine floors, moldings, and six working fireplaces. The perfect retreat, with Lancaster County attractions and fine restaurants nearby.

Hosts: Barry & Ruth Herr
Doubles: 3 (1 PB; 2 SB) $68.90-90.10
Suite: 1 (PB)
Type of Beds: 2 Twin; 3 Double; 1 Queen
Continental-plus Breakfast
Minimum stay weekends & holidays: 2
Credit Cards: A, B
Notes: 2, 5, 7, 8 (over 5), 9

MAYTOWN

Three Center Square Inn

3 Center Square, 17550
(717) 653-4338

NOTES: Credit cards accepted: A Master Card; B Visa; C American Express; D Discover Card; E Diners Club; F Other: 2 Personal checks accepted: 3 Lunch available: 4 Dinner available: 5 Open all year

For fine dining and spirits, visit historic Three Center Square Inn. Originally a 1780 tavern, the annex, a general store, was built in 1840. The floors above the store were originally used for the manufacture of cigars and now house fourteen B&B Victorian rooms and a year-round Christmas shop.

Doubles: 14 (SB) $69-89
Continental Breakfast
Credit Cards: A, B, C
Closed Mondays
Notes: 2, 3, 4, 5, 7, 9, 10, 11, 12, 14

Blair Creek Inn & Lodging

MERCER

The Stranahan House Bed & Breakfast

117 E. Market Street, 16137
(412) 662-4516

Enjoy a peaceful night's rest and a delicious breakfast amid antiques and cherished family heirlooms. The 150-year-old Colonial Empire red brick home is near the center of town and the county courthouse. Close to the historical society, Amish country, antique shops, forges, and colleges.

Hosts: Jim & Ann
Doubles: 2 (1 PB; 1 SB) $45-50
Type of Beds: 2 Double
Full Breakfast

Credit Cards: No
Notes: 2, 5, 8, 9, 10, 11, 12, 14

MERION STATION

B&B Connections #5

Box 21, Devon, 19333
(215) 687-3565

Private back stairs lead to the guest rooms in this comfortable suburban home nestled among the oaks on a quiet street centrally located to center city universities and historic attractions. Guest sitting room with TV and sofabed.

Doubles: 2 (PB) $45-50
Type of Beds: 2 Double
Full Breakfast
Credit Cards: A, B, C
Notes: 5, 8, 9, 10, 11, 12, 14

MERTZTOWN

Blair Creek Inn and Lodging

RD 2, Box 20, 19539
(215) 682-6700

This Mobil four-star-rated restaurant offers lodging, breakfast, and dinners Wednesday through Saturday. Sunday brunch is served. Set on 4.5 acres of beautiful lawn and gardens, the inn also caters to weddings, receptions, business affairs, and private parties.

Hosts: Dr. & Mrs. Joseph A. Miller
Doubles: 2 (PB) $125
Type of Beds: 2 Double; 1 Pullout sofa
Continental Breakfast
Credit Cards: A, B
Closed week of July 4
Notes: 2, 4, 7, 8, 9, 11, 12, 13

Longswamp Bed & Breakfast

RD 2, Box 26, 19539
(215) 682-6197

This 200-year-old-home, furnished with antiques and every comfort, is set in gorgeous countryside, yet is close to Reading, Kurtztown, Allentown, and Amish country. Delicious bountiful breakfasts draw raves from guests.

Hosts: Elsa & Dean Dimick
Doubles: 9 (5 PB; 4 SB) $53-68.90
Type of Beds: 6 Twin; 1 Double; 6 Queen
Full Breakfast
Credit Cards: A, B
Notes: 2, 5, 8, 9, 10, 11, 12, 13

MIDDLETOWN

The Gathering Place

Hershey B&B RSO, Box 208, Hershey, 17033
(717) 533-2928

This family home has an interesting collection of mementos from around the world. It's set on 9 acres and has a large deck facing the woods. Hershey Park is seven miles, Lancaster County, twenty, and Gettysburg about 45 minutes away.

Doubles: 2 (SB) $45
Type of Beds: 2 Double
Full or Continental Breakfast
Credit Cards: A, B
Notes: 5, 8, 10, 11, 12, 14

MIFFLINVILLE

Ye Olde Hotel

124 West 3rd Street, 18631
(717) 752-2383

The oldest public building in Mifflinville, the hotel at one time catered to the riverboat traffic on the Susquehanna and Canal. The structure is built with hand-hewn timbers that date back to the 1790s. Ye Olde Hotel is the only two-story log hotel left in Columbia County. Housed on the first floor are an antique shop and a gun shop. All rooms are decorated with country antiques.

Hosts: Mary Ellen & Curtis Moorhead
Singles: 2 (SB) $37.10

Doubles: 3 (1 PB; 2 SB) $47.70-63.60
Twin Beds
Full Breakfast
Credit Cards: No
Notes: 2, 5, 7 (limited), 8 (over 12), 9, 12

MILFORD

Cliff Park Inn

RR 2, Box 8562, 18337
(717) 296-6491

A Mobil three-star-rated golfers' country inn with gourmet restaurant. Cliff Park is surrounded by an established regulation nine-hole golf course edged by deep woods. Come enjoy gracious hospitality in historic surroundings.

Host: Harry Buchanan
Doubles: 18 (PB) $90-135
Full Breakfast
Credit Cards: A, B, D, E
Notes: 2, 3, 4, 5, 7, 8, 9, 10, 11, 12, 13

MILLERSVILLE

Walnut Hill Bed & Breakfast

113 Walnut Hill Road, 17551
(717) 872-2283

Come and enjoy the quiet country living in our 1815 stone farmhouse. Relax on our screened porch or in your air-conditioned room. Close to attractions, but not in the mainstream. Near Millersville University.

Hosts: Melvin & Kathryn Shertzer
Doubles: 3 (SB) $40
Type of Beds: 3 Double
Full Breakfast
Credit Cards: No
Closed Dec. - Feb.
Notes: 2, 7, 8, 10, 11, 12

MT. GRETNA

Mt. Gretna Inn

Hershey B&B RSO, Box 208, Hershey, 17033
(717) 533-2928

This inn is a magnificent mansion on an acre of beautifully kept grounds. Mt. Gretna is a special community, with wooded mountains, lakes, and streams, plus cultural activities all summer. In the winter, the area is known for its cross-country ski trails.

Doubles: 7 (PB) $65-95
Type of Beds: 7 Queen
Continental Breakfast
Credit Cards: No
Notes: 5, 9, 10, 11, 12, 13

MOUNTVILLE

Mountville Antiques and B&B

Box 19, 17554
(717) 285-7200; 285-5956

Antique shop with six rooms furnished with antiques. Breakfast served around a large mahogany table; herb and flower garden to relax in. Amish and Lancaster County Dutch nearby; Hershey and Gettysburg Battlefield are within easy driving distance.

Host: Pat Reno
Doubles: 6 (SB) $45-65
Type of Beds: 1 Twin; 2 Double; 1 Queen
Full Breakfast
Credit Cards: A, B
Closed Dec. 1-April 1
Notes: 9, 10, 11

MUNCY

The Bodine House

307 S. Main Street, 17750
(717) 546-8949

Built in 1805 and located in the National Historic District of Muncy, the Bodine House offers guests the opportunity to enjoy the atmosphere of an earlier age. The comfortable rooms are furnished with antiques, and candlelight is used in the living room by the fireplace, where guests enjoy complimentary wine and cheese.

Hosts: David & Marie Louise Smith
Singles: 1 (SB) $25 plus tax
Doubles: 3 (PB) $50 plus tax
Type of Beds: 2 Twin; 2 Double
Full Breakfast
Credit Cards: A, B, C
Notes: 2, 5, 8 (over 6), 9, 10, 11, 12, 13, 14

MYERSTOWN

Tulpehocken Manor Inn & Plantation

650 W. Lincoln Avenue, 17067
(717) 866-4926

Tulpehocken Manor Plantation dates back as far as 1732 and is made up of four houses of varying ages, with many original details still intact. Now it's a working farm, raising grain and black angus beef cattle. Wander over the plantation at your leisure and ask to see the room George Washington really did sleep in (several times)!

Hosts: James Henry & Esther Nissly
Doubles: (PB and SB) $53-100
Continental Breakfast
Credit Cards: No
Notes: 2, 5, 8 (12 and over), 14

NEW ALBANY

Waltman's Bed & Breakfast

RD 7, Box 87, 18833
(717) 363-2295

In the Endless Mountains, a retired farm couple welcomes you to their restored century-old home with inviting porches, fireplace, comfortable rooms, and breakfast with homemade muffins and jams. Maple syrup made in spring; foliage festivals in fall. US Rt. 220.

Hosts: Ivan & Mae Waltman
Doubles: 3 (SB) $26.50-31.80
Type of Beds: 1 Twin; 2 Double
Continental Breakfast
Notes: 2, 5, 8, 11

NEWFOUNDLAND

White Cloud

RD 1, Box 215, 18445
(717) 676-3162

We're located three miles south of New-foundland on Route 447 and are a meatless, natural-foods inn and restaurant with 45 acres of wooded land, a tennis court, pool, library, and meditation room.

Hosts: George & Judy Wilkinson
Singles: 3 (1 PB; 2 SB) $27-36.75
Doubles: 17 (6 PB; 11 SB) $34-47.75
Type of Beds: 18 Twin; 17 Double
Full Breakfast
Credit Cards: A, B
Closed December 25
Notes: 2, 3, 4, 5, 6, 8, 9, 10, 11, 12, 12, 14

Backstreet Inn

NEW HOPE

Backstreet Inn

144 Old York Road, 18938
(215) 862-9571

The Backstreet Inn B&B offers the comfort and serenity of a small inn in the town of New Hope, Bucks County, Pennsylvania. We are located in a quiet, tucked-away street, yet within walking distance from the center of town.

Hosts: Bob Puccio & John Hein
Doubles: 7 (5 PB; 2 SB) $75-125
Type of Beds: 7 Double
Full Breakfast
Credit Cards: A, B
Notes: 2, 5

Centre Bridge Inn

River Road, 18938
(215) 862-9139

A romantic country inn overlooking the Delaware River in historic Bucks County, featuring canopy beds and river views. Fine restaurant serving French-Continental cuisine and spirits in an old-world-style dining room with fireplace, or alfresco dining in season.

Host: Stephen R. Dugan
Doubles: 9 (PB) $70-125
Type of Beds: 4 Double; 4 Queen; 1 King
Continental Breakfast
Minimum stay weekends: 2 ; holidays: 3
Credit Cards: A, B, C
Notes: 2, 4, 5, 7, 8 (over 8), 9, 10, 11, 12

Wedgewood Inn of New Hope

111 West Bridge Street, 18938
(215) 862-2570

Voted "Inn of the Year" by readers of inn guidebooks, this historic inn, situated on 2 acres of landscaped grounds, is steps from the village center. Antiques, fresh flowers, and Wedgewood china are the rule at the inn, where all house guests are treated like royalty.

Hosts: Carl A. Glassman & Nadine Silnutzer
Doubles: 12 (10 PB; 2 SB) $58.30/person
Continental-plus Breakfast
Minimum stay weekends: 2 ; holidays: 3
Credit Cards: No
Notes: 2, 5, 8, 9, 10, 11, 12, 13, 14

NOTES: Credit cards accepted: A Master Card; B Visa; C American Express; D Discover Card; E Diners Club; F Other: 2 Personal checks accepted: 3 Lunch available: 4 Dinner available: 5 Open all year

The Whitehall Inn

RD 2, Box 250, 18938
(215) 598-7945

Experience a 1794 estate with fireplaced rooms, heirloom sterling, European crystal and china. Afternoon high tea, chamber music, velour robes, chocolate truffles. Swimming pool on premises, dressage horses, roses, and our legendary four-course candlelight breakfast that *Bon Appetit* called "sumptuous." A very special inn!

Hosts: Mike & Suella Wass
Doubles: 6 (4 PB; 2 SB) $106-148.40
Type of Beds: 4 Double; 2 Queen
Full Breakfast
Minimum stay weekends: 2; holidays: 3
Credit Cards: A, B, C, D, E, F
Notes: 2, 5, 8 (over 12), 9, 10, 11, 12, 13, 14 (weekdays)

NEWTOWN SQUARE

B&B Connections #6

Box 21, Devon, 19333
(215) 687-3565

This lovely suburban home, convenient to Philadelphia, the Brandywine Valley, and Valley Forge Park, was designed to recall the elegance of an earlier era. A fieldstone colonial, it was designed by an architect noted for his replicas of 200-year-old PA farmhouses. On the edge of a woods, it overlooks a pond and 5 acres of rolling hunt country. Resident dog.

Singles: 1 (PB) $65
Doubles: 2 (PB) $75
Type of Beds: 3 Twin; 1 Double
Full Breakfast
Credit Cards: A, B, C
Notes: 5, 7, 8, 9, 10, 11, 12, 14

NORTH EAST

Brown's Village Inn

51 East Main Street, 16428
(814) 725-5522

Located in the restored downtown area of North East (Erie County), the inn, built in 1832, once served as a stagecoach tavern and a station for the underground railroad.

Host: Rebecca Brown
Doubles: 3 (PB) $47.70-58.30
Type of Beds: 2 Twin; 2 Double
Full Breakfast
Credit Cards: A, B
Notes: 2, 3, 4, 5, 6, 7, 8, 9, 10, 11, 12, 13, 14

NORTH WALES

Joseph Ambler Inn

1005 Horsham Road, 19454
(215) 362-7500

Spend the evening in the original stone farmhouse, dating back to 1734, or in the newly converted 1820 stone bank barn also housing the restaurant, or the Corybeck tenant farmer's cottage. All rooms have private baths, telephones, and television, and each is uniquely decorated with antiques and reproductions.

Hosts: Steve & Terry Kratz
Singles: 24 (PB) $85.60-139.10
Doubles: 4 (PB) $93.09-149.80
Type of Beds: 11 Double; 21 Queen
Full Breakfast
Credit Cards: A, B, C, D, F
Notes: 2, 4, 5, 7, 8 (over 12), 9, 10, 11, 12

ORBISONIA

Salvino's Guest House

Box 116, Rt. 522, Huntingdon County, 17243
(814) 447-5616

Our Victorian home is located in central Pennsylvania, one-half mile from a steam-engine railroad and trolley museum. One hour from Lake Raystown, Old Bedrod Village, Amish country, and Cowan's Gap State Park. Quilt shop next door.

Hosts: Elaine & Joe Salvino
Doubles: 5 (SB) $35
Type of Beds: 7 Twin; 2 Double; 2 Single sofabeds
Continental Breakfast

6 Pets welcome: 7 Smoking allowed: 8 Children welcome: 9 Social drinking allowed: 10 Tennis available: 11 Swimming available: 12 Golf available: 13 Skiing available: 14 May be booked through travel agents

Pleasant Grove Farm

Credit Cards: A, B
Notes: 2, 5, 6, 8

PARADISE

Maple Lane Guest House

505 Paradise Lane, 17562
(717) 687-7479

We have clean, comfortable, air-conditioned rooms with canopy and poster beds, handmade quilts, hand stenciling, and antiques. This is a large dairy farm with winding stream and woodland in real Amish country, close to all the Pennsylvania Dutch attractions of Lancaster County.

Hosts: Edwin & Marion Rohrer
Doubles: 4 (2 PB; 2 SB) $45-55
Type of Beds: 2 Twin; 4 Double
Continental Breakfast
Minimum stay weekends: 2; holidays, 3
Credit Cards: No
Notes: 2, 5, 8, 10, 11, 12

PEACH BOTTOM

Pleasant Grove Farm

368 Pilottown Road, 17563
(717) 548-3100

Come and enjoy our large, 175-year-old, Federal style stone home. At one time a country store and post office. Century Farm

Award. Watch the cows being milked or feed the pigs. Full country breakfast.

Hosts: Charles & Labertha Tindall
Doubles: 4 (SB) $37.10-42.40
Full Breakfast
Minimum stay weekdays & weekends: 2 ; holidays: 3
Credit Cards: No
Dinner available by prior arrangement
Notes: 2, 4, 5, 8, 11, 12

PENNSBURG

Chesterfield Farm II

B&B Southeast PA
146 W. Philadelphia Ave., Boyertown, 19512
(215) 367-4688

Set in the middle of parkland, this old stone farmhouse has been refurbished with antiques and collectibles. Fishing and boat rental are within one mile; horseback riding and swimming within two miles. One dog and two cats in residence.

Doubles: 2 (SB) $45-50
Type of Beds: 2 Double
Full Breakfast
Credit Cards: A, B
Notes: 5, 6, 7 (restricted), 8 (over 10), 11

PHILADELPHIA

B&B Connections #7

Box 21, Devon, 19333
(215) 687-3565

NOTES: Credit cards accepted: A Master Card; B Visa; C American Express; D Discover Card; E Diners Club; F Other: 2 Personal checks accepted: 3 Lunch available: 4 Dinner available: 5 Open all year

A lovely 1920s stone colonial on a tree-lined suburban street near quaint chestnut Hill, historic Germantown, the Medical College of PA, and the train to Center City. Your cozy third-floor room has a large desk and color TV. An adjacent room with cot-style bed can sleep a child. Resident cat.

Doubles: 1 (PB) $40
Type of Beds: 3 Twin
Continental Breakfast
Credit Cards: A, B, C
Notes: 5, 8, 9, 14

B&B Connections #8

Box 21, Devon, 19333
(215) 687-3565

Built between 1805 and 1810 and redone after the Civil War in Federal style, this charming Society Hill townhouse was renovated by its owners. One room on the second floor with color TV, phone jack, and thermostat. Two third-floor rooms with TV and individual thermostats. Enjoy breakfast out on the patio in warm weather.

Doubles: 3 (1 PB; 2 SB) $65-75
Type of Beds: 2 Twin; 1 Double; 1 Queen; 1 Trundle
Full Breakfast
Credit Cards: A, B, C
Notes: 5, 6, 7, 8, 14

B&B Connections #9

Box 21, Devon, 19333
(215) 687-3565

This Victorian townhouse is within walking distance of Children's Hospital and the University of Pennsylvania. Three second-floor guest rooms to choose from; resident dog.

Singles: 1 (SB) $25
Doubles: 1 (PB) $35-45
Type of Beds: 1 Twin; 1 Double
Full Breakfast

Credit Cards: A, B, C
Notes: 5, 8, 9, 14

B&B Connections #10

Box 21, Devon, 19333
(215) 687-3565

This historic registered row home provides generous third-floor guest quarters with a bedroom, sitting room, TV, and private bath. Close to the University of Pennsylvania, Drexel, the Civic Center, and Children's Hospital. Laundry facilities and refrigerator space are also available. Resident smoker.

Doubles: 2 (PB) $40-50
Type of Beds: 2 Twin; 2 Double
Full Breakfast
Credit Cards: A, B, C
Notes: 7, 8, 9, 14

B&B Connections #11

Box 21, Devon, 19333
(215) 687-3565

This lovely Society Hill townhouse dates back to 1791 and is ideally located for all historic attractions. One room 2.5 floors up; two on the third floor; nonworking fireplaces in two rooms. Use the second-floor sitting room.

Singles: 1 (SB) $50
Doubles: 2 (1 PB; 1 SB) $55-65
Type of Beds: 1 Twin; 2 Queen
Full Breakfast
Credit Cards: A, B, C
Notes: 5, 7, 8, 9, 14

B&B Connections #12

Box 21, Devon, 19333
(215) 687-3565

An eighteenth-floor penthouse with a forty-mile panoramic view of the city! Elegant French and Victorian furnishings.

6 Pets welcome: 7 Smoking allowed: 8 Children welcome: 9 Social drinking allowed: 10 Tennis available: 11 Swimming available: 12 Golf available: 13 Skiing available: 14 May be booked through travel agents

Doubles: 2-3 (PB) $90-100
Type of Beds: 1 Double; 1 Queen; 1 Sofabed
Full Breakfast
Credit Cards: A, B, C
Notes: 6 (call), 7, 8 (10 and over), 9, 14

B&B Connections #13

Box 21, Devon, 19333
(215) 687-3565

Circa 1885 home offers two second-floor guest rooms with connecting bath, both tastefully appointed. Near historic Germantown and the interesting shops of Chestnut Hill; eighteen minute train ride to the heart of Center City. Resident dog.

Singles: 1 (SB) $25
Doubles: 1 (SB) $35
Type of Beds: 3 Twin
Full Breakfast
Credit Cards: A, B, C
Notes: 5, 8, 9, 14

B&B Connections #14

Box 21, Devon, 19333
(215) 687-3565

This large turn-of-the-century home offers a delightful second-floor guest room furnished with antiques and a day couch for an extra family member. Resident cat.

Doubles: 1 (PB) $40
Type of Beds: 1 Twin; 1 Double
Continental Breakfast
Credit Cards: A, B, C
Notes: 5, 7 (outside), 8, 9, 14

B&B Connections #15

Box 21, Devon, 19333
(215) 687-3565

Rhododendron line the long drive up to this Quaker-built 1870s home. The lovely front porch overlooks the garden. The large, comfortable second-floor guest room has a double bed and desk. Convenient to the train and shuttle service to LeSalle University. Resident dog.

Doubles: 1 (PB) $30-35
Type of Beds: 1 Double
Full Breakfast
Credit Cards: A, B, C
Notes: 5, 8, 9, 14

B&B Connections #16

Box 21, Devon, 19333
(215) 687-3565

Within walking distance of the historic district, this building has recently been redone. Private guest entrance on the fourth level; beamed ceiling and individual thermostat.

Doubles: 1 (PB) $60-65
Type of Beds: 1 Double
Continental Breakfast
Credit Cards: A, B, C
Notes: 5, 9

B&B Connections #17

Box 21, Devon, 19333
(215) 687-3565

This 1811 historically registered townhouse was purchased as a shell and has been renovated with a contemporary Southwestern feel. In the hub of historic Philadelphia, and close to New Market Square and South Street. The third-floor accommodations feature a settee and chairs to use in front of the working fireplace. A second room is available on the second floor.

Doubles: 2 (PB) $50-60
Type of Beds: 2 Double
Full Breakfast
Credit Cards: A, B, C
Notes: 5, 8, 9, 14

B&B Connections #18

Box 21, Devon, 19333
(215) 687-3565

This house was designed by architect I. M. Pei and is located just one block from Independence Park. A spiral staircase leads to the second-floor sitting room with grand piano. Your third-floor guest room has two twin beds and TV. Resident dog.

NOTES: Credit cards accepted: A Master Card; B Visa; C American Express; D Discover Card; E Diners Club; F Other: 2 Personal checks accepted: 3 Lunch available: 4 Dinner available: 5 Open all year

Doubles: 1 (PB) $50-55
Type of Beds: 2 Twin
Full Breakfast
Credit Cards: A, B, C
Notes: 5, 8, 9, 14

B&B Connections #19

Box 21, Devon, 19333
(215) 687-3565

Originally built in 1856 as a dry goods emporium, this five-story, granite facade building has been renovated into a luxury 36-room inn. Within walking distance of Independence Mall, Penns Landing, and many fine restaurants. Each room has poster beds, a writing table, and armoire that houses the TV.

Doubles: 36 (PB) $105-125
Continental Breakfast
Credit Cards: A, B, C
Notes: 5, 8, 9, 14

B&B Connections #20

Box 21, Devon, 19333
(215) 687-3565

Independence Square is only one-half mile from this warm, cozy townhouse. Your guest room is located on the second floor, reached via a spiral staircase.

Doubles: 1 (PB) $35-40
Type of Beds: 2 Twin
Full Breakfast
Credit Cards: A, B, C
Notes: 5, 8, 9, 14

B&B Connections #21

Box 21, Devon, 19333
(215) 687-3565

This townhouse is located along Antique Row, within walking distance of the historic district. The complete third floor is for guests. Sliding glass doors lead to a deck where you can enjoy the city skyline and patio gardens below. Resident cats.

Doubles: 1 (PB) $45-55
Type of Beds: 1 Double
Full Breakfast
Credit Cards: A, B, C
Notes: 5, 7, 8, 9

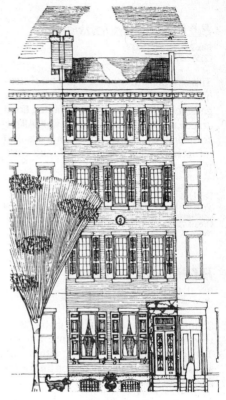

La Reserve

B&B Connections #22

Box 21, Devon, 19333
(215) 687-3565

This magnificent 1902 English Tudor mansion has been featured in area newspapers. Eight very special rooms are available for guests, some with fireplaces, leaded-glass windows, and ceiling fans. A conference room for twelve is available, and special parties may be catered.

6 Pets welcome: 7 Smoking allowed: 8 Children welcome: 9 Social drinking allowed: 10 Tennis available: 11 Swimming available: 12 Golf available: 13 Skiing available: 14 May be booked through travel agents

Doubles: 8 (PB & SB) $55-65
Type of Beds: 4 Twin; 4 Double; 3 Queen
Full Breakfast
Credit Cards: A, B, C
Notes: 5, 8, 9, 14

B&B Connections #23

Box 21, Devon, 19333
(215) 687-3565

This charming townhouse is just off Rittenhouse Square on a lovely city street. Your
guest room features antique furniture, floral
drapes, and bookcases lining the wall. All the
comforts of home, including a small
refrigerator, electric kettle, TV, and desk.
Private entrance. Resident cat.

Doubles: 1 (PB) $65-70
Type of Beds: 1 Double
Continental Breakfast
Credit Cards: A, B, C
Notes: 5, 8, 9, 14

B&B Connections #24

Box 21, Devon, 19333
(215) 687-3565

Southern hospitality awaits you in this 1860s
townhouse just off Rittenhouse Square.
Two third-floor guest rooms, with sitting
areas. A single is also available on the fourth
floor. Resident cat.

Singles: 1 (S2B) $50
Doubles: 2 (S2B) $65-70
Type of Beds: 1 Twin; 1 Double; 1 Queen
Full Breakfast
Credit Cards: A, B, C
Notes: 5, 8, 9, 14

La Reserve

1804 Pine Street, 19103
(215) 735-1137

La Reserve, *grande dame* of Philadelphia
B&Bs, is a well-preserved 140-year-old
private mansion in the Victorian Rittenhouse Square section of center city, which is
the cultural soul of the city. Friendly black
lab in residence. *Bienyenue a La Reserve.*

Host: John T. Lynagh
Doubles: 8 (2 PB; 6 SB) $35-75
Type of Beds: 2 Twin; 2 Double; 3 Queen; 2 King
Continental Breakfast
Credit Cards: No
Closed the day the Phillies win the World Series
Notes: 2, 5, 7, 8, 9, 10, 11, 12, 14

Society Hill Hotel

Society Hill Hotel

301 Chestnut Street, 19106
(215) 925-1394

A twelve-room "urban inn" located in the
heart of historic Philadelphia. Each room is
individually decorated with antiques, fresh
flowers, chocolates, stenciling along the ceiling, and much more. A continental breakfast
is brought to your room each morning.
Downstairs, visit our cafe, where freshly
squeezed juices and a light-fare menu add to
the view of historic Independence Park.

Host: Howard Jacobs
Doubles: 12 (PB) $77-125
Type of Beds: 12 Double
Continental Breakfast
Credit Cards: A, B, C, E
Notes: 2, 3, 4, 5, 7, 8, 9, 14

NOTES: Credit cards accepted: A Master Card; B Visa; C American Express; D Discover Card; E Diners
Club; F Other: 2 Personal checks accepted: 3 Lunch available: 4 Dinner available: 5 Open all year

PILOTTOWN

Pleasant Grove Farm Inn

368 Pilottown Road, 17563
(717) 548-3100

Come relax in warm hospitality in an 1814
Federal style home that has been our family
farm for over one hundred years. Enjoy our
160 acres of rolling hills; watch the milking;
feed the pigs. Or just absorb the history and
antiques of the area. The house has been a
tavern, country store, and post office in the
past.

Hosts: Charles & Labertha Tindall
Doubles: 4 (S2B) $35-45
Type of Beds: 4 Twin; 4 Double
Full Breakfast
Credit Cards: No
Notes: 2, 5, 8, 11, 12

Cole's Log Cabin

PINE BANK

Cole's Log Cabin B&B

RD 1, Box 98, 15354
(412) 451-8521

The Log Cabin B&B is made up of two
colonial log homes joined together to form
one large house. We are located in the ex-
treme southwestern part of Pennsylvania, in
a very rural farming area. Our major activities are hiking, bird watching, antiquing,
and relaxing.

Hosts: Jane & Terry R. Cole
Doubles: 3 (1 PB; 2 SB) $50
Type of Beds: 1 Twin; 2 Double; 1 Queen; 1 3/4 bed
Continental Breakfast
Credit Cards: No
Closed July 5 - Aug. 15
Notes: 2, 9, 11, 12, 14

PITTSBURGH

Adam's House

Pittsburgh Bed & Breakfast
2190 Ben Franklin Drive, 15237
(412) 367-8080

An 1800 Victorian with eclectic decor, a
unique combination of antique and modern
furnishings suggesting sophistication and
style. Outdoor Jacuzzi located in the
landscaped garden. Twenty minutes from
the city and the cultural section of Pittsburgh. Smoker in residence.

Doubles: 2 (PB) $40-55
Type of Beds: 2 Twin
Continental Breakfast
Credit Cards: No
Notes: 5, 7, 8, 9, 10

PHILIPSBURG

Oak Haven

Rest & Repast B&B Service
Box 126, Pine Grove Mills, 16868
(814) 238-1484

An 1890s restored Victorian in the historic
village of Philipsburg, nine miles south of
I-80 and twenty-five miles north of Penn
State. Lots of ornate oak carvings, Victorian
furnishings, and a pretty backyard with
gazebo and gardens.

Singles: 1 (SB) $27
Doubles: 4 (SB) $35-45
Type of Beds: 3 Twin; 3 Double
Continental Breakfast

6 Pets welcome: 7 Smoking allowed: 8 Children welcome: 9 Social drinking allowed: 10 Tennis available: 11
Swimming available: 12 Golf available: 13 Skiing available: 14 May be booked through travel agents

Tattersall Inn

Credit Cards: No
Notes: 2, 5, 7, 8

PLUMSTEADVILLE

Farmhouse 1819

B&B Southeast PA
146 W. Philadelphia Ave., Boyertown, 19512
(215) 367-4688

This restored 1819 farmhouse is on 5 acres in the middle of Bucks County. One guest room features a beamed ceiling and a working fireplace; another also has a fireplace and sitting area. Pets in the house. New Hope and Peddlers Village are fifteen minutes away.

Doubles: 2 (SB) $55-65
Type of Beds: 2 Double
Full Breakfast
Credit Cards: A, B
Notes: 5, 6, 7, 8

PLYMOUTH MEETING

B&B Connections #25

Box 21, Devon, 19333
(215) 687-3565

An 1814 home on 6 acres in a country-like setting overlooking a pond near many of the area businesses. Two second-floor guest rooms in the oldest part of the house. Your host is a military historian and collector of

weapons, as well as a lover of growing orchids. Some French is spoken. Resident dog.

Doubles: 2 (SB) $65
Type of Beds: 2 Twin; 1 Double
Continental Breakfast
Credit Cards: A, B, C
Notes: 5, 8 (14 and over), 9, 10, 11, 12, 14

POINT PLEASANT

Tattersall Inn

Box 569, 18950
(215) 297-8233

Overlooking a river village, this manor house dates to the eighteenth century and features broad porches for relaxation and a walk-in fireplace for cool evenings. Enjoy our antique-furnished rooms and collection of vintage phonographs.

Hosts: Gerry & Berb Moss
Doubles: 7 (PB) $68-93
Type of Beds: 6 Queen; 1 King
Continental Breakfast
Credit Cards: A, B, C
Notes: 2, 5, 7, 8, 9, 10, 11, 14

PORT MATILDA

Skytop Woods

Rest & Repast B&B Service
Box 126, Pine Grove Mills, 16868
(814) 238-1484

NOTES: Credit cards accepted: A Master Card; B Visa; C American Express; D Discover Card; E Diners Club; F Other: 2 Personal checks accepted: 3 Lunch available: 4 Dinner available: 5 Open all year

This architectually unique octagon-shaped home is only a quarter mile from busy Rt. 322 in a beautiful woodland setting. The home has skylights, a woodstove for heat, and a deck for relaxing. The hosts live just down the road and serve breakfast every morning.

Doubles: 2 (S1.5B) $55
Type of Beds: 2 Double
Continental Breakfast
Credit Cards: No
Closed Dec. 24 - Jan. 2
Notes: 2, 8, 9, 10, 11, 13 (XC)

POTTERS MILLS

General Potter Farm
Rest & Repast B&B Service
Box 126, Pine Grove Mills, 16868
(814) 238-1484

This three-story, seventeen-room farmhouse, circa 1800, is the home of one of Centre County's founding fathers. This multi-acre farm has lots of places to explore and a creek with native trout. Nearby state parks and hiking trails.

Doubles: 6 (1 PB; 5 S3B) $30-65
Type of Beds: 6 Twin; 6 Double
Continental Breakfast
Credit Cards: No
Closed Dec. 24 - Jan. 2
Notes: 2, 8, 9, 11, 12, 13

POTTSTOWN

Argyle
B&B Southeast PA
146 W. Philadelphia Ave., Boyertown, 19512
(215) 367-4688

There are reminders of Nova Scotia in this compact home. The hosts are retired but busy entertaining people in retirement homes with sing-alongs and quizzes. One cat in residence.

Doubles: 1 (SB) $30-40
Type of Beds: 1 Double
Full or Continental Breakfast

Credit Cards: A, B
Notes: 5, 9, 10, 11

Foxhill Farm
B&B Southeast PA
146 W. Philadelphia Ave., Boyertown, 19512
(215) 367-4688

The original owner of Foxhill obtained the land grant from William Penn, and the first house was built in 1750 with two later additions in 1800 and 1840. Guest room is upstairs, up very steep steps; resident dog.

Doubles: 1 (PB) $35-45
Type of Beds: 1 Double
Continental Breakfast
Credit Cards: A, B
Notes: 5, 8, 9, 10, 11

QUARRYVILLE

Runnymede Farm Guest House B&B
1030 Robert Fulton Highway, 17566
(717) 786-3626

Enjoy our clean, comfortable farmhouse in southern Lancaster County, with air-conditioning, a lounge with TV, and a pleasant porch. Close to all tourist attractions, but not in the mainstream. Bicycling, hiking, and picnicking.

Hosts: Herb & Sara Hess
Doubles: 3 (SB) $37
Type of Beds: 2 Twin; 2 Double
Continental Breakfast
Credit Cards: No
Notes: 2, 5, 8, 10, 11, 12

READING

Gallery Guest House
B&B Southeast PA
146 W. Philadelphia Ave., Boyertown, 19512
(215) 367-4688

A gallery in this house features the work of a local sculptor. Guest rooms are on the second floor, and there is a resident dog

named Hannah. Convenient to the Reading
outlet stores.

Singles: 1 (SB) $40
Doubles: 2 (1 PB; 1 SB) $40-50
Type of Beds: 3 Twin; 1 Double
Full Breakfast
Credit Cards: A, B
Notes: 5, 8

House on the Old Canal
B&B Southeast PA
146 W. Philadelphia Ave., Boyertown, 19512
(215) 367-4688

This house is within sound of a fifty-foot
waterfall on the Schuylkill River. A 180-
year-old stone farmhouse with a wide porch
and view of the river. The second-floor suite
consists of a bedroom, sitting room with TV,
and private bath. A boat is available for
fishing, and bicycles may be borrowed. With
advance notice, a farm supper will be served.
Resident outside dog.

Doubles: 2 (PB) $50-60
Type of Beds: 1 Double; 1 Queen
Full Breakfast
Credit Cards: A, B
Notes: 4, 5, 7 (limited), 8

New Barn House
B&B Southeast PA
146 W. Philadelphia Ave., Boyertown, 19512
(215) 367-4688

Convenient for the outlets, antique shops,
and flea markets in Adamstown, this house
features the hostess's handmade quilts.
Guest room has a sitting area with TV and
table and chairs if you wish complete privacy.
Three cats in the house.

Doubles: 1 (PB) $40-50
Type of Beds: 1 Double
Full or Continental Breakfast
Credit Cards: A, B
Notes: 5, 8

Studio Guest House
B&B Southeast PA

146 W. Philadelphia Ave., Boyertown, 19512
(215) 367-4688

In a residential section of town near the
Reading Museum and convenient for the
outlets, this potter's house features an extensive collection of contemporary art. A
sauna is available for guests' use, as is the
sitting area with a fireplace.

Doubles: 1 (PB) $45-55
Type of Beds: 1 Double
Continental Breakfast
Credit Cards: A, B
Notes: 5, 7, 8

Windy Hill
B&B Southeast PA
146 W. Philadelphia Ave., Boyertown, 19512
(215) 367-4688

This manor house is on 12 acres eight miles
south of the city. The original farmhouse
(1785) was enlarged in the early 1900s and
is being carefully restored by the owners.
Two small dogs and one cat in the house, but
not in the guest quarters. Second-floor
screened guest porch; living room with
fireplace is available for guests. Each room
has TV and a sitting area. Windy Hill is
fifteen minutes from Adamstown.

Doubles: 2 (PB) $50-60
Type of Beds: 2 Twin; 1 Double
Continental-plus Breakfast
Credit Cards: A, B
Notes: 5, 8

REHRERSBURG

Kurr House
B&B Southeast PA
146 W. Philadelphia Ave., Boyertown, 19512
(215) 367-4688

This log house on the historic register is in
an area settled by Germans who trekked the
300 miles from Schoharie, N.Y. in 1721.
Your hosts live a few doors down the street.
The guest house is furnished with antiques
and collectibles and has two small sitting

NOTES: Credit cards accepted: A Master Card; B Visa; C American Express; D Discover Card; E Diners
Club; F Other: 2 Personal checks accepted: 3 Lunch available: 4 Dinner available: 5 Open all year

rooms, a hidden staircase, antique beds, and garden for relaxing. Perfect for two couples traveling together or one family.

Doubles: 2 (SB) $60
Type of Beds: 1 Twin; 2 Double
Continental Breakfast
Credit Cards: A, B
Notes: 8 (15 and over)

RIVERTON

River House
B&B Southeast PA
146 W. Philadelphia Ave., Boyertown, 19512
(215) 367-4688

This house is on the Pennsylvania side of the Delaware River, with lawns running down to the water. The Victorian home has been carefully restored by your hosts. Guest sitting room, dining room, family room. Boat rental is just one-quarter mile away; nearby beach.

Doubles: 3 (SB) $42-60
Type of Beds: 3 Double
Continental Breakfast
Credit Cards: A, B
Notes: 5, 8, 10, 11

RUSSELVILLE-OXFORD

Hershey's Vacationland B&B
Rt. 10, 19352
(215) 932-9257

Enjoy the peaceful, quiet country of Chester County, a newly constructed home, access to Rt. 5A. Wooded area, bicycling, picnicking, hiking, perhaps hay rides. Enjoy the creatures of the woods and animals of the farm, plus indoor activities in our "barn."

Hosts: Ephraim & Arlene Hershey
Doubles: 2 (PB) $25-35
Type of Beds: 1 Twin; 2 Double
Continental Breakfast
Credit Cards: No
Pets welcome in the barn
Notes: 2, 5, 8, 10, 11, 12

SKIPPACK

Highpoint
B&B Southeast PA
146 W. Philadelphia Ave., Boyertown, 19512
(215) 367-4688

The house is four miles from the village, which is famous for its antique shops, restaurants, and gift shops. It's a large restored Victorian surrounded by fields. Sitting room available for guests; resident English sheep dog. Near ski slopes.

Doubles: 3 (SB) $50-60
Type of Beds: 3 Double
Continental Breakfast
Credit Cards: A, B
Notes: 5, 7 (limited), 8, 13

SLIPPERY ROCK

Applebutter Inn
Pittsburgh Bed & Breakfast
2190 Ben Franklin Drive, Pittsburgh, 15237
(412) 367-8080

The restoration of this 1844 home included attention to the original detail. Fine woodwork, exposed brick fireplaces, original chestnut and poplar flooring serve as gracious settings for country charm. Period furnishings and wall coverings lend a warm atmosphere. It's a short trip to local points of interest: Amish country, McConnell's Mill State Park, Wendall August Forge, Slippery Rock University, Moraine State Park.

Doubles: 11 (PB) $85-115
Type of Beds: 7 Double; 5 Queen; 1 King
Full Breakfast
Credit Cards: A, B, C
Notes: 2, 5, 8, 11, 12

SMOKETOWN

Homestead Lodging
184 E. Brook Road, 17576
(717) 393-6927

Come to our beautiful Lancaster County setting, where you hear the clippity-clop of the Amish buggies go by and can experience the sights and freshness of our farmlands. We are located within walking distance of restaurants and outlets, and within minutes of farmers' markets, quilt shops, antiques, auctions, and craft shops.

Hosts: Robert & Lori Kepiro
Doubles: 5 (PB) $26-46
Type of Beds: 10 Double
Continental Breakfast
Credit Cards: A, B
Notes: 5, 7, 8, 9, 10, 11, 12

SPRINGTOWN

Wildernest

B&B Southeast PA
146 W. Philadelphia Ave., Boyertown, 19512
(215) 367-4688

This house sits on 12 acres of meadow and woods where you'll frequently see deer grazing and borders Cooks Creek, a native trout stream. It's a spectacular cedar contemporary with an orchid solarium, Jacuzzi, wraparound deck, and a twenty-foot bridge connecting upper levels. Five minutes to the Delaware River and Canal and Lake Nockamixon for tubing, boating, hiking, picnicking, cycling, fishing, and hunting. Fifteen minutes to New Hope. One cat and one dog in residence.

Doubles: 3 (1 PB; 2 SB) $75
Type of Beds: 3 Double
Continental Breakfast
Credit Cards: A, B
Notes: 4, 5, 9, 10, 11

SPRUCE CREEK

Eden Croft

Rest & Repast B&B Service
Box 126, Pine Grove Mills, 16868
(814) 238-1484

This house was built around 1820, and many of its original features have been retained and enhanced. It boasts five working fireplaces, deep windowsills, a wide central hall with curving stairs, and much of the original hardware.

Doubles: 2 (SB) $35-40
Type of Beds: 2 Twin; 1 Double
Continental-plus Breakfast
Credit Cards: No
Closed Dec. - March
Notes: 2, 7, 8, 9

STARRUCCA

The Nethercott Inn

1 Main Street, 18462
(717) 727-2211

A lovely Victorian home built around 1893, nestled in the Endless Mountains in the quaint borough of Starrucca. Downhill skiing, cross-country skiing, snowmobiling, hunting, fishing.

Hosts: Ned & Ginny Nethercott
Doubles: 5 (4 PB; 1 SB) $35-60 plus tax
Type of Beds: 2 Twin; 2 Double; 3 Queen
Continental Breakfast
Credit Cards: A. B
Notes: 2, 5, 7, 8, 9, 10, 12, 13 (XC)

STRASBURG

The Decoy

958 Eisenberger Road, 17579
(717) 687-8585

Spectacular view, quiet rural location in Amish farm country. Former Amish home, near local attractions. Bicycle tours available with advance reservations. Two cats in residence.

Hosts: Debby & Hap Joy
Doubles: 4 (PB) $31.80-53
Type of Beds: 4 Double; 4 Day Beds
Full Breakfast
Credit Cards: No
Notes: 2, 5

Limestone Inn B&B

33 E. Main Street, 17579
(717) 687-8392

NOTES: Credit cards accepted: A Master Card; B Visa; C American Express; D Discover Card; E Diners Club; F Other: 2 Personal checks accepted: 3 Lunch available: 4 Dinner available: 5 Open all year

Situated in Strasburg's historic district and the heartland of Amish country, this 203-year-old home is listed in the National Register of Historic Places. A visit to the Limestone Inn promises to be a warm reflection of times past.

Hosts: Jan & Dick Kennell
Singles: 1 (SB) $49
Doubles: 3 (2 PB; 1SB) $59
Type of Beds: 2 Twin; 2 Double, 1 Queen
Continental Breakfast
Minimum stay holidays: 2
Credit Cards: C
Notes: 2, 5, 7 (restricted), 8 (over 14), 9

Limestone Inn B&B

THOMPSON

Jefferson Inn
RD 2, Box 36, 18465
(717) 727-2625

Good food and conversation are provided in the warm atmosphere of the inn, which was built in 1871. We offer reasonably priced accommodations and a full-service restaurant. Situated in the rolling hills of northeast Pennsylvania, with thousands of acres available for fishing, hunting, hiking, touring, cross-country skiing, downhill skiing,

and snow mobiling. Golf and horseback riding are also nearby.

Hosts: Doug & Marge Stark
Doubles: 6 (PB) $25
Type of Beds: 4 Twin; 6 Double
Full Breakfast
Credit Cards: A, B
Notes: 2, 3; 4, 5, 6, 7, 8, 9, 10, 11, 12, 13, 14

THORNTON

Pace One Restaurant & Country Inn
Box 108, 19373
(215) 459-3702

Pace One is a renovated 250-year-old stone barn with rooms on the upper three levels. The ground floor is a restaurant and bar. Beautiful stone, hand-hewn wood beans, old wood floors, and deep-set windows establish a charming rustic atmosphere.

Host: Ted Pace
Singles: 1 (PB) $55
Doubles: 6 (PB) $65-75
Type of Beds: 1 Twin; 7 Queen
Continental Breakfast
Credit Cards: A, B, C, E
Notes: 2, 3, 4, 5, 7, 8, 9, 10, 11, 12

TOWANDA

Victorian Guest House
118 York Avenue, 18848
(717) 265-6972

A charming Victorian guest house, circa 1897, complete with tower rooms, arched windows, and wraparound porches. High-ceilinged guest rooms are furnished in Victorian and turn-of-the-century antiques. Guests are welcome to share the parlor.

Hosts: Tom & Nancy Taylor
Singles: 1 (SB) $32-43
Doubles: 11 (6 PB; 5 SB) $35-46
Type of Beds: 5 Twin; 11 Double
Continental Breakfast
Credit Cards: A, B, C, E
Notes: 2, 5, 7, 8

6 Pets welcome: 7 Smoking allowed: 8 Children welcome: 9 Social drinking allowed: 10 Tennis available: 11 Swimming available: 12 Golf available: 13 Skiing available: 14 May be booked through travel agents

TROY

Silver Oak Leaf B&B

196 Canton Street, 16947
(717) 297-4315

Silver Oak Leaf B&B is in the heart of the
Endless Mountains. The house is a 90-year-
old Victorian that has great charm. There is
a great deal to do and see: antiques, fishing,
auctions, hunting, or just relaxing. Gourmet
breakfasts; wine served in the evening.

Hosts: Steve & June Bahr
Doubles: 4 (SB) $31.80-37.10
Type of Beds: 2 Twin; 4 Double
Full Breakfast
Credit Cards: No
Notes: 2, 5, 6, 8, 9, 10, 11, 12, 13

TYRONE

The White House B&B Inn

Rest & Repast B&B Service
Box 126, Pine Grove Mills, 16868
(814) 238-1484

Built in the late 1890s, this historic home has
been totally restored. Two guest rooms lead
out to a large shared balcony. Honeymoon
suite with a king-sized canopy bed, private
bath, balcony, and small refrigerator.

Doubles: 3 (1 PB; 2 SB) $45-55
Type of Beds: 1 Double; 1 Queen; 1 King
Full Breakfast
Credit Cards: No
Notes: 2, 5, 7, 8, 9, 10, 11, 12, 13

VALLEY FORGE

B&B Connections #26

Box 21, Devon, 19333
(215) 687-3565

Just minutes from Valley Forge Park, this
comfortable old stone home reflects the care
of its carpenter host. Four second-floor
rooms are available with ceiling fans and
portable color TV available. Relax in the
living room in front of the fireplace or in the
den after a day of sightseeing.

Singles: 2 (S2B) $35
Doubles: 3 (S2B) $50-60
Type of Beds: 2 Twin; 2 Double; 1 Queen
Continental Breakfast
Credit Cards: A, B, C
Notes: 5, 9, 10, 11, 12, 14

B&B Connections #27

Box 21, Devon, 19333
(215) 687-3565

A stone colonial pre-Revolutionary home
on 4 acres of wooded land. The original part
of the house was built before 1700; both
additions are over 200 years old. Two third-
floor rooms with refrigerator, microwave,
and telephone on the landing. Full English
breakfast is served in the oldest part of the
house in front of the colonial fireplace with
its huge mantle and eight-foot-wide hearth.
Resident dog; smoker in residence. Pool.

Doubles: 2 (PB) $60-70
Type of Beds: 2 Twin; 1 Double; 1 Queen
Full Breakfast
Credit Cards: A, B, C
Notes: 5, 7, 8, 9, 10, 11, 12, 14

Valley Forge Mountain Home

Box 562, 19481
(215) 783-7838

Nightly and extended stays welcome on this
3 acre country setting adjacent to Valley
Forge National Historical Park. Thirty
minutes to Philadelphia, Longwood Gardens, Reading. Five minutes to Valley Forge
Convention Center, King of Prussia, PA
Turnpike exit 24. For guests' use: TV/VCR,
air-conditioning, parlor/fireplace, Florida
room. Full, hot, hearty breakfast.

Hosts: Carolyn & Dick Williams
Doubles: 3 (PB) $35-65
Type of Beds: 2 Twin; 1 Double; 1 California King
Full Breakfast

NOTES: Credit cards accepted: A Master Card; B Visa; C American Express; D Discover Card; E Diners
Club; F Other: 2 Personal checks accepted: 3 Lunch available: 4 Dinner available: 5 Open all year

Credit Cards: A, B, C
Notes: 2, 5, 6, 7, 8, 9, 10, 11, 12, 13, 14

WASHINGTON CROSSING

Woodhill Farms Inn

150 Glenwood Drive, 18977
(215) 493-1974

Ideally situated on 10 wooded acres in historic Washington Crossing, Bucks County. Just eight years old, our contemporary five-bedroom inn offers quiet seclusion. Guest rooms are tastefully furnished, all have private baths, color TV, individual thermostats, and central air-conditioning. Send for a free brochure.

Hosts: Don & Mary Lou Spagnuolo
Doubles: 5 (PB) $74.20-90.10
Type of Beds: 1 Twin; 1 Double; 3 Queen
Continental Breakfast weekdays; Full weekends
Credit Cards: A, B
Notes: 2, 5, 7 (limited), 8 (under 1 or over 6), 9, 10, 12

WEST CHESTER

B&B Connections #29

Box 21, Devon, 19333
(215) 687-3565

A majestic 1850 farmhouse with a wraparound veranda on top of the highest point in Chester County. Four guest rooms are available, two of which are suites with sitting rooms. All have wonderful views of the rolling farm country. Outdoor cats and indoor dog in residence. Near Longwood Gardens, Winterthur, and the historic Brandywine Valley.

Doubles: 4 (2 PB; 2 SB) $85-95
Type of Beds: 2 Double; 2 Queen
Full Breakfast
Credit Cards: A, B, C
Notes: 5, 8, 9, 10, 11, 12, 14

The Barn

1131 Grove Road, 19380
(215) 436-4544

The Barn is a beautifully restored 1800s stone barn with the stones dramatically exposed on the interior walls. Wide-width pine floors and old beams are a lovely setting for simple furniture, special antiques, and a growing art collection. Right off Route 100, an easy drive to Brandywine attractions and Pennsylvania Dutch country.

Hosts: Susan D. Hager and son
Doubles: 2 (SB) $55
Type of Beds: 2 Twins; 2 Double; 1 King
Full Breakfast
Credit Cards: C
Notes: 2, 5, 6, 7, 8, 9, 10, 14

The Crooked Windsor

409 S. Church Street, 19382
(215) 692-4896

Charming Victorian home centrally located in historic West Chester, within short driving distance of Longwood Gardens, Brandywine Museum, Winterthur, Valley Forge, and other points of interest. Completely furnished with fine antiques. Pool and garden.

Host: Winifred Rupp
Doubles: 4 (S2B) $65
Type of Beds: 4 Double
Full Breakfast
Credit Cards: C
Notes: 2, 5, 9, 10, 11, 12, 14

WILLOW STREET

Green Gables Bed & Breakfast

2532 Willow Street Pike, 17584
(717) 464-5546

Located three miles south of Lancaster, on Route 222N, Green Gables B&B is a 1907 Victorian home with original oak woodwork and stained glass-windows. Be our guest while visiting and touring Lancaster County.

Hosts: Karen & Mike Chiodo
Singles: 1 (SB) $30
Doubles: 3 (SB) $45
Type of Beds: 1 Twin; 3 Double

---

6 Pets welcome: 7 Smoking allowed: 8 Children welcome: 9 Social drinking allowed: 10 Tennis available: 11 Swimming available: 12 Golf available: 13 Skiing available: 14 May be booked through travel agents

Continental-plus Breakfast
Credit Cards: No
Notes: 2, 5, 8, 10

WOMELSDORF

Hiwwelhaus

B&B Southeast PA
146 W. Philadelphia Ave., Boyertown, 19512
(215) 367-4688

This is a new log house with charm and convenience. Guests have the use of the living room and the large front porch on the first floor. Only sixteen miles from Reading, twenty from Hershey, and thirty from Lancaster County.

Doubles: 2 (PB) $40-50
Type of Beds: 2 King
Full or Continental Breakfast
Credit Cards: A, B
Notes: 5, 7, 8 (over 4)

Rhode Island

Atlantic Inn

Box 188, 02807
(401) 466-5883

The Atlantic, with its sweeping panorama of Block Island's pristine coastline and view of the distant mainland, offers an exceptional opportunity to relax. Uncrowded beaches, warm atmosphere, imaginative menus create an unforgettable vacation.

Hosts: Patricia Vincent & Barbara Belniak
Doubles: 21 (PB) $100-165
Type of Beds: 4 Twin; 8 Double; 13 Queen
Continental Breakfast
Minimum stay weekdays: 2 ; holidays: 3
Credit Cards: A, B
Closed Dec.-March
Notes: 2, 4, 7, 8, 9, 10, 11

The Barrington Inn

Beach & Ocean Ave., Box 397, 02807
(401) 466-5510

Recently renovated, century-old farmhouse turned inn on beautiful, picturesque Block Island, located just twelve miles off the coast of Rhode Island. A warm, friendly atmosphere; bright, cheerful rooms; indescribable views and breathtaking sunsets await your visit. Brochure available.

Hosts: Joan & Howard Ballard
Doubles: 6 (PB) $80-110. Off-season rates
Type of Beds: 3 Twin; 4 Double; 2 Queen
Continental-plus Breakfast
Minimum stay summer weekends: 2; holidays: 3
Credit Cards: A, B
Closed Dec.-March
Notes: 2, 7, 8 (over 12), 9, 10, 11

The Blue Dory Inn

Box 488, 02807
(401) 466-5891

The Victorian age is alive and well at the Blue Dory. Located on Crescent Beach, this delightful year-round inn offers an opportunity to revisit a period of time that has long since gone by. The inn is filled with antiques and turn-of-the-century decor, yet has all the modern comforts.

Hosts: Vin McAloon & Julie Cotter
Doubles: 14 (PB) $55-245
Type of Beds: 3 Twin; 10 Double; 4 Queen
Continental Breakfast
Credit Cards: A, B, C, D, E

The Sheffield House

High Street, 02807
(401) 466-2494

An 1888 Victorian house in the historic district. A quiet location just two blocks from beaches, restaurants, and shops. Individually decorated guest rooms, parlor, country kitchen, porch, gardens, and friendly, knowledgeable hosts.

Hosts: Steve & Claire McQueeny
Doubles: 7 (5 PB; 2 SB) $40-110
Type of Beds: 2 Twin; 4 Double; 1 Queen
Continental Breakfast
Minimum stay on weekends & holidays
Credit Cards: A, B
Notes: 2, 5, 7, 9, 10, 11

6 Pets welcome: 7 Smoking allowed: 8 Children welcome: 9 Social drinking allowed: 10 Tennis available: 11 Swimming available: 12 Golf available: 13 Skiing available: 14 May be booked through travel agents

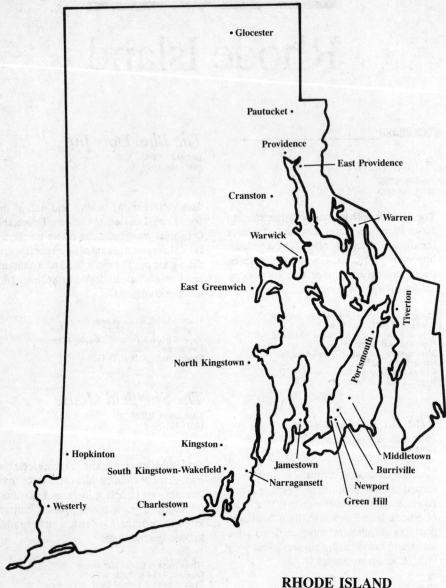

- Glocester

Pautucket •

Providence
• —— East Providence

Cranston •

Warwick
East Providence

Warren

Warwick •

East Greenwich •

North Kingstown •

Portsmouth

Tiverton

Kingston •

Hopkinton •

South Kingstown-Wakefield •

Westerly •

Charlestown •

Jamestown

Narragansett

Middletown

Burriville

Newport

Green Hill

RHODE ISLAND

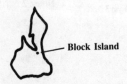

— Block Island

BURRIVILLE

B&B Rhode Island #RI-274
Box 3291-ND, Newport, 02840
(401) 849-1298

Imagine relaxing beside a kidney-shaped pool overlooking a freshwater lake, or exploring the lake by canoe. For the sports minded, there are plenty of places for fishing, hiking, and bicycling nearby. This spacious ranch home has been decorated with country accents and antiques. A sitting room with fireplace and TV, plus a game room with pool table, are available.

Doubles: 3 (PB) $60
Type of Beds: 1 Double; 2 Queen waterbeds
Full Breakfast
Credit Cards: No
Notes: 5, 9, 10, 11, 12, 14

CHARLESTOWN

General Stanton Inn
4115A Old Post Road, Box 222, 02813
(401) 364-8888

We are near the beach and one-half hour from Newport and Mystic, Conn. We have a flea market on the grounds from March through October every Sunday and Monday holidays.

Hosts: Janice & Angelo Falcone
Singles: 9 (7 PB; 2 SB)
Doubles: 6: (PB) 71.50-104.50
Type of Beds: 12 Double; 2 Queen; 1 King
Full Breakfast
Minimum stay holidays: 3
Credit Cards: A, B, C
Notes: 2, 4, 7, 8, 9, 10, 11, 12

CRANSTON

B&B Rhode Island #RI-280
Box 3291-ND, Newport, 02840
(401) 849-1298

A lovely twenty-five-year-old Garrison colonial in the midst of a Christmas-tree and blueberry farm. Only twenty minutes to Providence College and Brown University. Guests may pick their own berries for breakfast in season. The guest room is on the lower level of the home and contains comfortable chairs for reading.

Doubles: 1 (PB) $60
Type of Beds: 2 Twin
Continental Breakfast
Credit Cards: No
Notes: 5, 9, 10, 11, 12, 14

EAST GREENWICH

B&B Rhode Island #RI-114
Box 3291-ND, Newport, 02840
(401) 849-1298

This authentically restored house was built in 1710. It sits on 2.5 acres of wooded property within two miles of I-95. The antique furniture, five working fireplaces, beehive oven, wide plank floors, stenciled walls, and courting door make this home unique. Stay in the main house or in the self-contained cottage.

Doubles: 2 (PB) $60
Continental-plus Breakfast
Credit Cards: No
Notes: 5, 7 (in cottage), 8 (in cottage), 9, 10, 11, 12, 14

B&B Rhode Island #RI-157
Box 3291-ND, Newport, 02840
(401) 849-1298

A reproduction colonial home furnished with antiques and reproduction pieces, family sitting room with wood stove, picnic table, and large yard. Basketball and tennis courts across the road for a more active form of relaxation.

Doubles: 1 (SB) $45
Type of Beds: 1 Double
Continental Breakfast
Credit Cards: No
Notes: 5, 8, 9, 10, 11, 12, 14

EAST PROVIDENCE

B&B Rhode Island #RI-177

Box 3291-ND, Newport, 02840
(401) 849-1298

This Federal-style home is across the street from the waterfront. Guests arriving by boat can dock at one of four marinas within walking distance. Private harborside beach, nearby bike path, and backyard patio.

Doubles: 4 (SB) $55-60
Type of Beds: 4 Twin; 1 Double; 1 King
Continental Breakfast
Credit Cards: No
Notes: 5, 7, 8 (infants or over 10), 9, 10, 11, 12, 14

GLOCESTER

B&B Rhode Island #RI-156

Box 3291-ND, Newport, 02840
(401) 849-1298

Guests who visit this 3-acre farm can help feed the turkeys and sheep or go fishing or swimming in the nearby lake. They also have their choice of hiking, golf, cross-country skiing, snow mobiling, or a horse and buggy ride. The 150-year-old farmhouse is on a quiet road in a rural area.

Doubles: 2 (SB) $38
Type of Beds: 2 Double
Full Breakfast
Credit Cards: No
Notes: 5, 7, 8, 9, 10, 11, 12, 14

GREEN HILL

Fairfield-By-The Sea Bed & Breakfast

527 Green Hill Beach Road, 02879-5703
(401) 789-4717

An artist's contemporary home in a secluded country area. Twenty miles east of Mystic and twenty-five miles west of Newport. Day trips to Plymouth and Block Island. Biking and birding are favorites. Large fireplace and good library for guests. Fine restaurants abound. An informal and relaxed ambience.

Host: Jeanne Lewis
Doubles: 2 (SB) $40-62
Type of Beds: 2 Twin; 1 Double
Continental-plus Breakfast
Minimum stay summer weekends: 2; holidays: 3
Credit Cards: No
Notes: 2, 5, 7, 8, 9, 10, 11, 12

HOPKINTON

B&B Rhode Island #RI-165

Box 3291-ND, Newport, 02840
(401) 849-1298

This 1763 colonial mansion is located in the center of a small New England village of eighteenth- and nineteenth-century homes — a place where you can mail a letter at the post office and have lunch with homemade pie for under $3! Nonworking fireplaces, rough-hewn beamed ceilings, wide plank floors, fresh flowers everywhere in the house. Two sitting rooms for guests, one with a wood stove.

Singles: 1 (SB) $40
Doubles: 6 (2 PB; 4 SB) $50-70
Type of Beds: 3 Twin; 8 Double; 1 King
Full Breakfast
Credit Cards: No
Notes: 5, 8 (over 10), 9, 10, 11, 12, 14

B&B Rhode Island #RI-236

Box 3291-ND, Newport, 02840
(401) 849-1298

Seven acres of gardens and woodlands surround this Victorian farmhouse. Nearby
lakes and ponds for catching local perch. An
idyllic setting for walks past an old barn, an
Indian trading post, and peaceful country
beauty. Bicycles available. Private guest sitting room with stuffed chairs and TV.

Singles: 1 (SB) $35
Doubles: 1 (SB) $50
Type of Beds: 1 Twin; 1 Double
Continental Breakfast
Credit Cards: No
Notes: 5, 7, 8, 9, 10, 11, 12, 14

JAMESTOWN

B&B Rhode Island #RI-205

Box 3291-ND, Newport, 02840
(401) 849-1298

Expansive grounds, an old-fashioned veranda, and comfortable rooms beckon guests to
unwind at this turn-of-the-century, twin-tur-
reted Victorian. The large, sunny rooms feature antique or period furnishings. Two
large sitting rooms offer plenty of space for
relaxing.

Doubles: 4 (SB) $45-50
Type of Beds: 4 Twin; 2 Double; 1 Trundle
Continental-plus Breakfast
Credit Cards: No
Notes: 5, 7, 8, 9, 10, 11, 12, 14

B&B Rhode Island #RI-242

Box 3291-ND, Newport, 02840
(401) 849-1298

A spectacular view of the Newport Bridge
crossing Narragansett Bay dominates nearly
every room in this 1880s Victorian. All
rooms have a view of the water, and there's
plenty of space for relaxing in the sitting
room or on the old-fashioned porch.

Doubles: 4 (PB) $80-140
Type of Beds: 1 Twin or 1 King; 1 Double
Continental Breakfast
Credit Cards: No
Notes: 5, 8 (over 10), 9, 10, 11, 12, 14

The Calico Cat Guest House

14 Union Street, 02835
(401) 423-2641

Located directly across the bay from Newport, we are just 250 feet from the east
harbor, which provides a magnificent view of
the Newport Bridge and Newport Harbor.
It's a short walk to interesting shops and
restaurants, and a short drive to Newport.

Host: Lori Lacaille
Doubles: 10 (SB) $75
Type of Beds: 1 Twin; 6 Double; 3 King
Continental Breakfast
Credit Cards: A, B
Notes: 2, 5, 8, 9, 10, 11, 12, 14

KINGSTON

Hedgerow B&B

Box 1586, 02881
(401) 783-2671

Lovely colonial in Kingston, one-half mile
from the University of Rhode Island campus. Handy for trips to Newport, Block Island, the Rhode Island beaches, Mystic
aquarium and seaport. Happy Hour and full
breakfast are included. Beautiful gardens
and a tennis court on the premises for guests
to enjoy.

Hosts: Ann & Jim Ross
Doubles: 4 (SB) $55-60 plus tax
Type of Beds: 4 Twin; 1 Double; 1 Queen
Full Breakfast
Credit Cards: No
Notes: 2, 5, 8, 9, 10, 11, 12, 14

6 Pets welcome: 7 Smoking allowed: 8 Children welcome: 9 Social drinking allowed: 10 Tennis available: 11
Swimming available: 12 Golf available: 13 Skiing available: 14 May be booked through travel agents

MIDDLETOWN

B&B Rhode Island #RI-192

Box 3291-ND, Newport, 02840
(401) 849-1298

Whimsical touches in every room create a special setting for guests in this 1915 homestead-style home. Guests may enjoy the small alcove just outside their rooms with an ocean view or in the comfortable sitting room. A garden patio surrounded by flowers offers sunshine and ocean breezes. One ocean beach is just a five-minute walk; another is a two-minute drive.

Doubles: 3 (SB) $60-70
Type of Beds: 2 Twin; 2 Queen
Continental Breakfast
Credit Cards: No
Notes: 5, 8 (over 16), 9, 10, 11, 12, 14

B&B Rhode Island #RI-218

Box 3291-ND, Newport, 02840
(401) 849-1298

This ranch is a very private oasis of tranquility set apart from a busy main street by a canopy of low-hanging trees. Just beyond is a small formal garden with goldfish pools, sea-stone paths, and carefully chosen shrubs and flowers. Sun room, sitting room, and deck.

Doubles: 1 (PB) $65
Type of Beds: 1 Double
Continental Breakfast
Credit Cards: No
Notes: 5, 9, 10, 11, 12, 14

NARRAGANSETT

B&B Rhode Island #RI-110

Box 3291-ND, Newport, 02840
(401) 849-1298

This massive stone 1885 house is a delight to the eye. Breakfast is served at the lace-covered dining room table. The 1.5 acre grounds provide an ample outdoor lounge area for relaxing, and the library beckons the curious reader. Hostess will arrange taxi pick-up at Kingston railway station.

Doubles: 4 (2 PB; 2 SB) $50-60
Type of Beds: 1 Double; 1 Queen; 1 King; 2 Three-quarter beds
Full Breakfast
Credit Cards: No
Notes: 5, 9, 10, 11, 12, 14

B&B Rhode Island #RI-213

Box 3291-ND, Newport, 02840
(401) 849-1298

A magnificent view of a meandering river meeting the bay and ocean awaits guests at this outstanding contemporary home. A nearby Audubon Nature Preserve adds to the beauty. Relax on the deck or take the path to the water's edge. One mile to Narragansett Beach. Cathedral ceilings, skylights, and a full wall of glass create an open atmosphere. Sleeping rooms are just off the second-floor gallery that overlooks the sitting room.

Doubles: 2 (SB) $70
Type of Beds: 2 Twin; 1 Double; 1 Rollaway
Continental Breakfast
Credit Cards: No
Closed Nov. - April
Notes: 7, 8 (over 5), 9, 10, 11, 12, 14

B&B Rhode Island #RI-245

Box 3291-ND Newport, 02840
(401) 849-1298

This magnificent 1880s Victorian summer estate sits right on the ocean. Enjoy the parlor with its TV and games, a wonderful player piano, and a telescope for watching boats at sea. An enclosed porch overlooks

NOTES: Credit cards accepted: A Master Card; B Visa; C American Express; D Discover Card; E Diners Club; F Other: 2 Personal checks accepted: 3 Lunch available: 4 Dinner available: 5 Open all year

the ocean. All rooms have an ocean view; some face the water's edge. Guest refrigerator.

Doubles: 8 (PB) $60-125
Type of Beds: 2 Twin; 1 Double; 6 Queen
Full Breakfast
Credit Cards: No
Notes: 5, 8 (over 10), 9, 10, 11, 12, 14

B&B Rhode Island #RI-257

Box 3291-ND, Newport, 02840
(401) 849-1298

This classic Victorian is just half a block from the beach. Plenty of adult toys are available: bicycles, fishing gear, croquet, horseshoes, darts, and more.

Doubles: 3 (SB) $45-60
Type of Beds: 2 Twin; 1 Double; 1 King
Continental-plus Breakfast
Credit Cards: No
Notes: 5, 8 (no infants), 9, 10, 11, 12, 14

The House of Snee

191 Ocean Road, 02882
(401) 783-9494

Turn-of-the-century Dutch colonial with a magnificent view from the front porch, within easy walking distance to the beach. Breakfast is served in the family dining room daily; there's a guest reading room on the second floor and TV in the living room. The house has five fireplaces.

Host: Mildred Snee
Singles: 1 (SB) $35
Doubles: 2 (SB) $45
Type of Beds: 1 Twin; 3 Double
Full Breakfast
Credit Cards: No
Notes: 2, 5, 8, 9, 10, 11, 12

Ilverthorpe Cottage

41 Robinson Street, 02882
(401) 789-2392

Lacy touches, hand-carved moldings, stenciled walls are found throughout this 1896 Victorian "cottage." A convenient three blocks from the beach, so you don't even need a car. Travel to Newport for a day of mansion touring, sailing, and shopping, or take the ferry to nearby Block Island. Whatever your pleasure, you'll enjoy the sumptuous gourmet breakfast each morning.

Hosts: Chris & Jill Raggio
Doubles: 4 (2 PB; 2 SB) $45-65
Type of Beds: 2 Twin; 2 Double; 1 King
Full Breakfast
Credit Cards: No
Notes: 2, 5, 7 (restricted), 8, 9, 10, 11, 12, 14

Murphy's B&B

43 South Pier Road, 02882
(401) 789-1824

Charming 1894 Victorian restored with care by the owners. Situated on a tree-lined residential street one block from the ocean, this makes a perfect base for enjoying our beautiful beaches, historic Newport and Providence, Block Island, the area's many antique shops, art galleries, and fine restaurants. We are known for our gracious ambience and fabulous breakfasts.

Hosts: Kevin & Martha Murphy
Singles: 1 (SB) $50
Doubles: 2 (SB) $65
Type of Beds: 3 Twin; 1 Queen
Full Breakfast
Credit Cards: No
Closed Nov. 15 - April 30
Notes: 2, 3, 4, 7 (outside), 8 (over 10), 9, 10, 11, 12

The Richards

144 Gibson Avenue, 02882
(401) 789-7746

Gracious accommodations in an 1884 historic manse. Relax by the fire in the library or your fireplaced guest room. Enjoy a leisurely full breakfast with homemade muffins, strudels, blintzes. Nancy's many special touches will spoil you — down comforters, canopy beds, flowers from the gardens, etc.

Hosts: Steven & Nancy Richards
Doubles: 4 (2 PB; 2 SB) $47.70-74.20
Type of Beds: 2 Twin; 2 Queen; 1 King
Full Breakfast
Minimum stay weekends: 2; holidays: 3
Credit Cards: No
Notes: 2, 5, 8 (over 12), 9

NEWPORT

B&B Rhode Island #RI-113

Box 3291-ND, 02840
(401) 849-1298

This Queen Anne Victorian has twenty-one rooms with plenty of fireplaces. Featured in *Life* magazine in 1962, this house served as home of the French 12-meter Americas Cup challengers for six summers. Guests enjoy a water view from their rooms and may relax on the large, well-landscaped lawn that's cooled by sea breezes and large shade trees.

Doubles: 8 (PB) $65-125
Type of Beds: 4 Twin; 1 Double; 1 Queen; 4 King or 8 Twin
Continental Breakfast
Credit Cards: No
Notes: 5, 7, 8, 9, 10, 11, 12, 14

B&B Rhode Island #RI-149

Box 3291-ND, 02840
(401) 849-1298

This home was built twenty-five years ago by its present owners. Located minutes from Ocean Drive, Gooseberry Beach, and the Newport mansions, this Cape is nicely landscaped and immaculate. Guests may use the patio for relaxing or the family grill. B&B hosts since 1977.

Doubles: 2 (SB) $60
Type of Beds: 2 Twin; 1 Queen
Continental Breakfast

Credit Cards: No
Notes: 5, 9, 10, 11, 12, 14

B&B Rhode Island #RI-158

Box 3291-ND, 02840
(401) 849-1298

This century-old Victorian, on the National Register of Historic Places, offers leaded-glass windows, open galleries, gracious sitting and dining rooms, a wraparound porch, spacious grounds, and prestigious location.

Doubles: 8 (6 PB; 2 SB) $65-135
Type of Beds: 3 Double; 6 Queen
Full Breakfast
Credit Cards: No
Notes: 5, 7, 8, 9, 10, 11, 12, 14

B&B Rhode Island #RI-178

Box 3291-ND, 02840
(401) 849-1298

Built in 1758 and remodeled in 1840, this lovely Federal colonial has been completely restored. Carved wood balusters, scallop-shell wall niches, and antique French fireplace tiles. Enjoy the harbor view from the sunroom, relax in the sitting room, or stroll the waterfront park just two blocks away.

Doubles: 4 (PB) $70-85
Type of Beds: 2 Twin; 2 Double; 1 Queen
Continental-plus Breakfast
Credit Cards: No
Notes: 5, 8 (over 5), 9, 10, 11, 12, 14

B&B Rhode Island #RI-197

Box 3291-ND, 02840
(401) 849-1298

This gracious 1880s Victorian is the epitome of New England charm. There's a small antique and collectible shop in the first-floor sitting room. The home is an easy walk from most attractions. The second-floor suites all have sitting rooms and antiques; small private flower garden for strolling.

Doubles: 2 (SB) $75-120
Type of Beds: 2 Twin; 1 Double; 1 Futon
Full Breakfast
Credit Cards: No
Notes: 5, 9, 10, 11, 12, 14

B&B Rhode Island #RI-207

Box 3291-ND, 02840
(401) 849-1298

A comfortable 1902 Victorian cottage just a few blocks from the Newport mansions and within walking distance of shops and restaurants. Two beaches one mile away; park across the street. Enjoy the second-floor sun deck that overlooks the park.

Doubles: 3 (SB) $45-60
Type of Beds: 2 Twin; 1 Double; 1 Queen waterbed
Full Breakfast
Credit Cards: A, B (processing fee)
Notes: 5, 8 (over 12), 9, 10, 11, 12, 14

B&B Rhode Island #RI-223

Box 3291-ND, 02840
(401) 849-1298

This 1880s Victorian overlooks Trinity Church and is just two blocks from harborfront shops and restaurants. It's an easy walk or bicycle ride to other attractions. Guests may park on nearby streets or in a paid parking lot. A traditional sitting room features a fireplace and Oriental rugs; informal buffet breakfast is served in the dining room. A private courtyard offers a quiet place to relax.

Doubles: 5 (1 PB; 4 SB) $55-68
Type of Beds: 5 Double
Continental Breakfast

Credit Cards: A, B
Notes: 5, 8 (over 16), 9, 10, 11, 12, 14

B&B Rhode Island #RI-224

Box 3291-ND, 02840
(401) 849-1298

A centrally located 1751 Georgian colonial used as British headquarters during the American Revolution, this house has been meticulously restored. The House has been featured in the books *Architectural Heritage of Newport* and *Newport Restored.* One large suite was originally a ballroom and features a baby grand piano, antique chaise lounge, armoire, and Oriental carpets. All rooms have working fireplaces.

Doubles: 9 (PB) $75-125
Type of Beds: 6 Double; 3 Queen
Full Breakfast
Credit Cards: A, B, C (fee)
Notes: 5, 7, 8 (over 5), 9, 10, 11, 12, 14

B&B Rhode Island #RI-241

Box 3291-ND, 02840
(401) 849-1298

This 1880s Victorian home was once the gardener's cottage for the Astor estate. Within walking distance to Hazard's Beach and central Newport, the house is convenient to the bus line. A bluestone terrace, private deck, and perennial and herb gardens provide a relaxing setting after a busy day. Guests have a private sitting room with TV, VCR, and access to a small balcony.

Doubles: 3 (SB) $60-70
Type of Beds: 2 Twin; 2 Double
Continental Breakfast
Credit Cards: No
Closed Oct. - April
Notes: 8 (over 12), 9, 10, 11, 12, 14

6 Pets welcome: 7 Smoking allowed: 8 Children welcome: 9 Social drinking allowed: 10 Tennis available: 11 Swimming available: 12 Golf available: 13 Skiing available: 14 May be booked through travel agents

B&B Rhode Island #RI-244

Box 3291-ND, 02840
(401) 849-1298

The central location and homey atmosphere of this 1870s Victorian make it ideal for guests who want to be close to attractions. Breakfast is served family style at the large pine table in front of the dining room fireplace.

Doubles: 8 (3 PB; 5 SB) $45-75
Type of Beds: 4 Double; 1 Queen; 3 King or 6 Twin
Continental-plus Breakfast
Credit Cards: No
Notes: 5, 8, 9, 10, 11, 12, 14

B&B Rhode Island #RI-251

Box 3291-ND, 02840
(401) 849-1298

Memories of visiting a favorite great-aunt or grandmother come to mind amid the simple, old-fashioned setting of this early 1900s home. An enclosed front porch overlooking the quiet residential street provides a comfortable respite at the end of the day. There is also a sitting room with TV.

Doubles: 1 (SB) $60
Type of Beds: 2 Twin
Continental Breakfast
Credit Cards: No
Notes: 5, 9, 10, 11, 12, 14

B&B Rhode Island #RI-252

Box 3291-ND, 02840
(401) 849-1298

Tucked into a quiet side street on Historic Hill, this colonial is in a convenient area for walking to all downtown attractions. The house has exposed ceilings and antiques.

Doubles: 1 (PB) $60
Type of Beds: 2 Twin
Continental Breakfast
Credit Cards: No
Notes: 5, 7, 8 (over 12), 9, 10, 11, 12, 14

B&B Rhode Island #RI-270

Box 3291-ND, 02840
(401) 849-2198

Architect William Ralph Emerson, cousin of Ralph Waldo Emerson, designed this magnificent house in 1869. Among some of the extraordinary features are the grand staircase and entrance hall that rises 35 feet from floor to ceiling. Located on the waterfront, this home will afford you the Victorian vacation of a lifetime.

Doubles: 6 (3 PB; 3 SB) $95-145
Type of Beds: 2 Twin; 1 Double; 2 Queen; 3 King
Continental Breakfast
Credit Cards: No
Notes: 5, 7, 8, 9, 10, 11, 12, 14

B&B Rhode Island #RI-272

Box 3291-ND, 02840
(401) 849-1298

This house in Newport's' yachting village. Filled with antiques, Victorian accents, and some country flavor, this home offers a full kitchen for guest use. A help-yourself breakfast is left in the guest kitchen for you convenience.

Doubles: 2 (SB) $75
Type of Beds: 2 Twin; 1 Double
Continental Breakfast
Credit Cards: No
Notes: 5, 9, 10, 11, 12, 14

B&B Rhode Island #RI-281

Box 3291-ND, 02840
(401) 849-1298

NOTES: Credit cards accepted: A Master Card; B Visa; C American Express; D Discover Card; E Diners Club; F Other: 2 Personal checks accepted: 3 Lunch available: 4 Dinner available: 5 Open all year

Located in a pleasant residential area west of Broadway, within a ten-minute walk to the center of town. This turn-of-the-century house has plenty of off-street parking, an old-fashioned porch, and cheery sitting room. Guest frequently join the hosts to watch TV in the family room.

Doubles: 2 (SB) $55-60
Type of Beds: 2 Double
Continental-plus Breakfast
Credit Cards: No
Notes: 5, 7, 8, 9, 10, 11, 12, 14

Brinley Victorian Inn

23 Brinley Street, 02840
(401) 849-7645

Romantic all year long, the inn becomes a Victorian Christmas dream come true. Comfortable antiques and fresh flowers fill every room. Friendly, unpretentious service and attention to detail will make this inn your haven in Newport. Park and walk everywhere.

Hosts: Peter Carlisle & Diane Burke
Doubles: 17 (12 PB; 5 SB) $55-105
Type of Beds: 10 Twin; 17 Double
Continental Breakfast
Minimum stay weekends: 2; holidays: 3
Credit Cards: A, B
Notes: 2, 4, 5, 7, 8 (over 12), 9 10, 11, 12, 13

Harborside Inn

Christie's Landing, 02840
(401) 846-6600

The Harborside Inn blends the charm of colonial Newport with the hustle and bustle of Newport's active waterfront. Each suite provides a view of the harbor and features a wet bar, refrigerator, color TV, sleeping loft, and deck. A short walk to quaint specialty shops, colonial homes and churches, restaurants and antique shops.

Doubles: 14 (PB) $55-165 plus tax
Type of Beds: 14 Queen
Continental Breakfast
Credit Cards: A, B, C
Notes: 2, 4, 5, 7, 8, 9, 10, 11, 12

Inn of Jonathan Bowen

29 Pelham Street, 02840
(401) 846-3324

An elegant inn on a gas-lit historic hill, located in the heart of activity, one-half block to the harborside. Renovated in 1987. Eclectic antique decor, luxurious rooms, safe off-street parking, walk everywhere. Famed mansions, gourmet breakfasts, getaway weekend plan, seminar conference arrangements.

Host: Sally Goddin
Doubles: 8 (6 PB; 2 SB) $65-175
Type of Beds: 2 Double; 6 Queen; 2 King
Continental Breakfast
Minimum stay weekends & holidays: 2
Credit Cards: A, B, D
Notes: 2, 5, 8, 9, 10, 11, 12, 14

The Inntowne

6 Mary Street, 02840
(401) 846-9200

An elegant, reconstructed 26-room inn with colonial reproduction furniture, private baths, telephones, and air-conditioning. Continental breakfast and afternoon tea is served in the antique breakfast room. The perfect location for easy walking to all Newport's shops and restaurants.

Hosts: Betty & Paul McEnroe
Doubles: 26 (PB) $60.50-165
Type of Beds: 5 Twin; 9 Double; 6 Queen; 6 King
Continental Breakfast
Minimum stay in-season weekends: 2 ; holidays: 3
Credit Cards: A, B, C
Notes: 2, 5, 7, 8 (over 12), 9, 10, 11, 12

Jailhouse Inn

13 Marlborough Street, 02840
(401) 847-4638

Built in 1772, the Newport Jail functioned for over 200 years. Now transformed into an inn, The Jail House maintains the nostalgic flavor of the past with modern conveniences and cheerfulness. A stone's throw to restaurants, shops, and the harbor, each room features a refrigerator, telephone, cable TV, private bath, and air-conditioning. Experience the many faces of this quaint and lively town while staying in an authentic piece of its history.

Hosts: Beth Hoban
Doubles: 22 (PB) $45-125
Type of Beds: 22 Queen
Continental Breakfast
Credit Cards: A, B, C
Notes: 2, 4, 5, 7, 8, 9, 10, 11, 12

La Forge Cottage

96 Pelham Street, 02840
(401) 847-4400

La Forge Cottage is a Victorian B&B located in the heart of Newport's Historic Hill area. Close to beaches, downtown. All rooms have private baths, TV, phone, air-conditioning, refrigerators, and full breakfast room service. French and German spoken. Reservations suggested.

Hosts: Louis & Margot Droual
Doubles: 6 (PB) $55-93.50
Suites: 4 (PB) $104-121
Full Breakfast
Minimum stay weekends: 2 ; holidays: 3
Credit Cards: A, B
Notes: 2, 5, 7, 8, 9, 10, 11, 12, 14

The Melville House

The Melville House

39 Clarke Street, 02840
(401) 847-0640

Step back into the past and stay at a colonial inn built circa 1750, located in the heart of Newport's historic district. Homemade breakfast, complimentary sherry hour, off-street parking. Walk to wharfs, shops, restaurants, historic buildings.

Hosts: Rita & Sam Rogers
Doubles: 7 (5 PB; 2 SB) $44-93.50
Type of Beds: 1 Twin; 6 Double
Continental-plus Breakfast
Minimum stay weekends: 2; holidays: 3
Credit Cards: A, B, C
Closed Jan. & Feb.
Notes: 2, 7, 8 (over 12), 9, 10, 11, 12

The Merritt House Guests

57 2nd Street, 02840
(401) 847-4289

Truly a home away from home, picture pretty. Relax on the glider in the yard or play our piano. Full breakfast in a private dining room or in our courtyard. Quiet historical neighborhood ten minutes' walk from town, waterfront, beaches, restaurants, and mansions. Off-street parking. Two dogs in residence.

Hosts: Angela & Joseph Vars
Doubles: 2 (1 PB; 1 SB) $74.20-79.50
Type of Beds: 2 Double
Full Breakfast
Minimum stay weekends & holidays: 2
Credit Cards: No
Notes: 2, 5, 9, 10, 11, 12

Pilgrim House Inn

123 Spring Street, 02840
(401) 846-0040

This Victorian inn, with its comforts and elegance, is located two blocks from the harbor in the midst of the historic district. A fireplaced parlor, immaculate rooms, and wonderful atmosphere await you. Walk to mansions, shops, and restaurants.

Hosts: Pam & Bruce Bayuk
Doubles: 10 (8 PB; 2 SB) $49.50-137.50
Type of Beds: 2 Twin; 8 Double
Continental Breakfast
Minimum stay weekends: 2; holidays: 3
Credit Cards: A, B
Closed January
Notes: 2, 4, 8 (over 12), 9, 10, 11, 12

NOTES: Credit cards accepted: A Master Card; B Visa; C American Express; D Discover Card; E Diners Club; F Other: 2 Personal checks accepted: 3 Lunch available: 4 Dinner available: 5 Open all year

NORTH KINGSTOWN

B&B Rhode Island #RI-121

Box 3291-ND, Newport, 02840
(401) 849-1298

Tasteful country charm characterizes this nineteenth-century colonial with period wall coverings and antiques. Once a dairy farm, the home is located on 2.5 acres surrounded by a picket fence, stone walls, and barns. Close to the village of Wickford and major routes, this home is convenient to Newport, Narragansett, and Providence.

Doubles: 3 (SB) $45-55
Type of Beds: 2 Twin; 2 Double
Continental-plus Breakfast
Credit Cards: No
Notes: 5, 8, 9, 10, 11, 12, 14

B&B Rhode Island #RI-151

Box 3291-ND, Newport, 02840
(401) 849-1298

Built in 1745, this house was confiscated by the patriots during the Revolutionary War because it was owned by a Tory. Care has been taken to keep the decor appropriate to its history. The second-floor guest suite includes two bedrooms, a sitting room, bath, kitchen, and deck overlooking Wickford Harbor and Narragansett Bay. Guests may sun on the small private beach or relax on the deck. Just a few minutes' walk from the town dock and village center.

Doubles: 2 (SB) $45-55
Type of Beds: 2 Twin; 1 Double
Continental Breakfast
Credit Cards: No
Notes: 5, 7, 8, 9, 10, 11, 12, 14

B&B Rhode Island #246

Box 3291-ND, Newport, 02840
(401) 849-1298

This 1920 colonial manor house was built on seventeenth-century stone foundations and is surrounded by ancient stone walls. The 6-acre holly farm has a wooded area, fields, and walking paths. French doors open out to a 200-year-old wisteria-covered arbor and the terrace where summer breakfasts are served overlooking the in-ground pool. French is spoken by your host.

Doubles: 1 (PB) $60
Type of Beds: 1 Double
Continental-plus Breakfast
Credit Cards: No
Notes: 5, 7, 8, 9, 10, 11, 12, 14

B&B Rhode Island #RI-279

Box 3291-ND, Newport, 02840
(401) 849-1298

This mid-1700 colonial farmhouse has a large screened porch and many fine antiues. Its 2.5 acres make it a perfect getaway retreat.

Doubles: 2 (SB) $60
Type of Beds: 2 Double
Continental-plus Breakfast
Credit Cards: No
Notes: 5, 9, 10, 11, 12, 14

PAUTUCKET

B&B Rhode Island #RI-130

Box 3291-ND, Newport, 02840
(401) 849-1298

The architect who built this Cape for himself in 1932 added many unusual architectural details: detailed molding and fireplace mantles, bull's eye glass windows in the front door, and two corner cupboards in the dining room. Both the living room and den have working fireplaces. The home is close to the popular East Side of Providence and two blocks from the bus line to Providence.

6 Pets welcome: 7 Smoking allowed: 8 Children welcome: 9 Social drinking allowed: 10 Tennis available: 11 Swimming available: 12 Golf available: 13 Skiing available: 14 May be booked through travel agents

Doubles: 2 (1 PB; 1 SB) $55
Type of Beds: 4 Twin
Continental-plus Breakfast
Credit Cards: No
Notes: 5, 7, 9, 10, 11, 12, 14

PORTSMOUTH _____

B&B Rhode Island #RI-163

Box 3291-ND Newport, 02840
(401) 849-1298

Built on the foundations of an old 1900 power house, this contemporary is at the end of a quiet street just fifty feet from the water's edge. Enjoy the picturesque view of the Sakonnet River and distant shoreline of Tiverton from the deck, sun room, breakfast area, or balcony outside your room. Outdoor pool, grill, beach.

Doubles: 2 (SB) $50
Type of Beds: 4 Twin
Continental Breakfast
Credit Cards: No
Notes: 5, 8 (over 8), 9, 10, 11, 12, 14

B&B Rhode Island #RI-174

Box 3291-ND Newport, 02840
(401) 849-1298

This new contemporary home is in a residential area on a hilltop with beautiful sunsets over the distant bay. Ancient stone walls enclose two sides of the spacious yard, and colorful flowers border the front walkway.

Doubles: 1 (PB) $50-55
Type of Beds: 2 Twin
Continental Breakfast
Credit Cards: No
Notes: 5, 9, 10, 11, 12, 14

B&B Rhode Island #RI-186

Box 3291-ND, Newport, 02840
(401) 849-1298

Old-fashioned country charm abounds in this new colonial-style house located in a quiet hilltop neighborhood. Several rooms of the house have a beautiful view of the distant bay. An outdoor deck overlooks the spacious back yard.

Doubles: 2 (SB) $55-65
Type of Beds: 2 Twin; 1 Double
Continental Breakfast
Credit Cards: No
Notes: 5, 8 (under 6 months and over 9 years), 9, 10, 11, 12, 14

B&B Rhode Island #RI-214

Box 3291-ND, Newport, 02840
(401) 849-1298

This neat ranch home is in a quiet residential neighborhood and has a large back yard and convenient location. Breakfast is served in the dining room where musically inclined guests may play the piano. Guests are always welcome in the family room.

Doubles: 2 (SB) $40-48
Type of Beds: 2 Double
Full Breakfast
Credit Cards: No
Notes: 5, 8, 9, 10, 11, 12, 14

B&B Rhode Island #RI-231

Box 3291-ND, Newport, 02840
(401) 849-1298

Forty acres of open fields surround this apartment at the rear of a 1700s farmhouse that has been modernized. An exterior stairway leads to a small, sunny deck and private entrance. The apartment has a sitting/kitchen/dining room with cathedral ceiling, skylight, and ceiling fan. Fully equipped kitchen and bedroom.

Doubles: 1 (PB) $95
Type of Beds: 1 Double; 2 Single sofabeds
Continental-plus Breakfast

NOTES: Credit cards accepted: A Master Card; B Visa; C American Express; D Discover Card; E Diners Club; F Other: 2 Personal checks accepted: 3 Lunch available: 4 Dinner available: 5 Open all year

Credit Cards: No
Notes: 5, 8 (no toddlers), 9, 10, 11, 12, 14

PROVIDENCE

B&B Rhode Island #RI-118

Box 3291-ND, Newport, 02840
(401) 849-1298

The hostess here is an historic conservationist who has created a showplace of the Federal Period in her home. Located on the historic East Side, within walking distance of Brown and Rhode Island School of Design. A cozy suite on the third floor is for guests: bedroom, full kitchen, sitting room with table and chairs. Another room on the second floor is for extra guests in the same party.

Doubles: 2 (1 PB; 1 SB) $75
Type of Beds: 2 Twin; 1 Double
Continental-plus Breakfast
Credit Cards: No
Notes: 5, 8, 9, 10, 11, 12, 14

B&B Rhode Island #RI-119

Box 3291-ND, Newport, 02840
(401) 849-1298

This 1849 Greek Revival is an interesting blend of contemporary and traditional styling. It's ideally located near Brown University and the Rhode Island School of Design. Guests have an informal sitting room with TV and a daybed, and the rooms have a commanding view of the surrounding cityscape.

Singles: 1 (PB) $60
Suite: 1 (PB) $75
Type of Beds: 3 Twin; 1 Daybed
Continental Breakfast
Credit Cards: No
Notes: 5, 8, 9, 10, 11, 12, 14

B&B Rhode Island #RI-122

Box 3291-ND Newport, 02840
(401) 849-1298

Graciousness is a way of life in this lovely century-old Victorian with tasteful furnishings and artwork. Guests have two sitting room; the music room has antiques and a grand piano, while the library has TV and a fireplace. Each bedroom has a desk, and one has a private sitting area. Guests have their own second-floor porch. Brown and Rhode Island School of Design are nearby, and off-street parking is provided.

Doubles: 2 (PB) $50-65
Type of Beds: 4 Twin
Full Breakfast
Credit Cards: No
Closed July - Aug.
Notes: 9, 10, 11, 12, 14

B&B Rhode Island #RI-164

Box 3291-ND Newport, 02840
(401) 849-1298

This 1920 home is a showplace of eighteenth-century period furniture reproductions and impressionistic and contemporary art. Sleeping rooms feature antique handmade quilts or European eiderdowns, wall-to-wall carpeting, brass and iron beds, and heirloom antiques. There is a second-floor guest sitting room with an adjoining rooftop deck.

Doubles: 3 (SB) $70
Type of Beds: 2 Twin; 2 Double
Continental Breakfast
Credit Cards: No
Notes: 5, 7, 9, 10, 11, 12, 14

B&B Rhode Island #RI-184

Box 3291-ND, Newport, 02840
(401) 849-1298

6 Pets welcome: 7 Smoking allowed: 8 Children welcome: 9 Social drinking allowed: 10 Tennis available: 11 Swimming available: 12 Golf available: 13 Skiing available: 14 May be booked through travel agents

This comfortable 1930s home is located near Wayland Square, not far from Brown University and the Rhode Island School of Design. The third-floor guest rooms have been thoughtfully appointed in wicker and rattan.

Singles: 2 (SB) $50
Doubles: 1 (SB) $65
Type of Beds: 4 Twin
Continental-plus Breakfast
Credit Cards: No
Notes: 5, 8, 9, 10, 11, 12, 14

B&B Rhode Island #RI-202

Box 3291-NS, Newport, 02840
(401) 849-1298

This house is located three blocks from Miriam Hospital and just a mile north of Brown University, in a pleasant residential area. Guests have a comfortable den with VCR, plus a second-story balcony with lounge chairs..

Singles: 2 (SB) $40-50
Doubles: 1 (SB) $60
Type of Beds: 2 Twin; 1 Double
Continental-plus Breakfast
Credit Cards: No
Notes: 5, 8, 9, 10, 11, 12, 14

B&B Rhode Island #RI-208

Box 3291-ND, Newport, 02840
(401) 849-1298

This beautiful 1860 Italianate home is in the historic East Side, in an area known for its outstanding architecture. Wide plank floors, marble fireplaces, and tasteful Oriental antiques, carpets, and paintings create an elegant atmosphere. Guests take a steep stairway to their third-floor suites that includes a large sitting room with a view of the State House dome. Hostess speaks French and Korean; host speaks Chinese.

Suite: 1 (PB) $75
Type of Beds: 1 Double; 1 Double sofabed
Continental Breakfast
Credit Cards: No
5, 8, 9, 10, 11, 12, 14

B&B Rhode Island #RI-211

Box 3291-ND Newport, 02840
(401) 849-1298

Two hundred years ago, the Federal part of this colonial stood on a large farm. Today the farmland is in the historic East Side of Providence, and the house is still true to its colonial heritage. The guest suite includes two antique-filled bedrooms and a bath. The single room features a circa 1795 single canopy bed. The bath has authentic French wallpaper manufactured in the 1790s and recently found in rolls, still like new.

Suite: 1 (PB) $70
Type of Beds: 1 Twin; 1 Double
Continental-plus Breakfast
Credit Cards: No
Notes: 5, 9, 10, 11, 12, 14

B&B Rhode Island #RI-232

Box 3291-ND, Newport, 02840
(401) 849-1298

This 1846 colonial is on a quiet, narrow side street within walking distance to Brown University. Renovation is still in progress. One corner room has an attached private bath and writing desk. Another suite includes a private sitting room with working fireplace, and shared bath.

Doubles: 2 (1 PB; 1 SB) $50
Type of Beds: 1 Double; 1 King or 2 Twins
Continental-plus Breakfast
Credit Cards: No
Notes: 5, 9, 10, 11, 12, 14

NOTES: Credit cards accepted: A Master Card; B Visa; C American Express; D Discover Card; E Diners Club; F Other: 2 Personal checks accepted: 3 Lunch available: 4 Dinner available: 5 Open all year

B&B Rhode Island #RI-234

Box 3291-ND, Newport, 02840
(401) 849-1298

This 1900s home is close to Wayland Square and Brown University. A second-floor informal den has a fireplace, book-laden shelves, and comfortable furniture. A more formal sitting room with antiques is available on the first floor.

Singles: 1 (SB) $45
Type of Beds: 1 Twin
Full Breakfast
Credit Cards: No
Notes: 5, 9, 10, 11, 12, 14

B&B Rhode Island #RI-242

Box 3291-ND, Newport, 02840
(401) 849-1298

From its hilltop vantage point, this 1850s Greek Revival provides a magnificent view of the domed State House. In the historic East Side, just one block east of Benefit Street. The hosts own a rare-book store; one is a theatrical producer and performer, and the other is a TV host and state representative.

Singles: 1 (SB) $65
Doubles: 1 (SB) $65
Type of Beds: 1 Twin; 1 Double
Continental Breakfast
Credit Cards: No
Notes: 5, 9, 10, 11, 12, 14

B&B Rhode Island #RI-250

Box 3291-ND, Newport, 02840
(401) 849-1298

This lovely circa 1905 gambrel-roofed home sits in a quiet residential neighborhood about one mile from the Brown campus.

Two bedrooms, one with a fireplace and an exquisite oak mantle, share an adjoining bath.

Doubles: 3 (SB) $65
Type of Beds: 2 Twin; 1 Double; 1 Queen
Continental Breakfast
Credit Cards: No
Notes: 5, 8, 9, 10, 11, 12, 14

B&B Rhode Island #RI-256

Bos 3291-ND, Newport, 02840
(401) 749-1298

This adorable colonial is set back from the street and surrounded by beautiful gardens. Two blocks from Benefit Street and Brown University, the house is air-conditioned and decorated throughout with antiques. Guest sitting room with fireplace and bedroom with fireplace, four-poster bed, and Hitchcock chair.

Doubles: 2 (SB) $65
Type of Beds: 1 Double; 1 Queen
Continental Breakfast
Credit Cards: No
Notes: 5, 8 (over 5), 9, 10, 11, 12, 14

B&B Rhode Island #RI-282

Box 3291-ND, Newport, 02840
(401) 849-1298

A large brick Victorian in the East Side, within walking distance of Brown. Plenty of off-street parking. Nine working fireplaces, tall ceilings, antiques. Four bedrooms on the second and third floors, plus a guest parlor with working fireplace, TV, books, desk, and Victorian settee. Your hostess speaks Polish; host speaks French.

Doubles: 4 (1 PB; 3 SB) $75-150
Type of Beds: 2 Double; 2 Queen
Continental Breakfast
Credit Cards: No
Notes: 5, 7, 8 (over 10), 9, 10, 11, 12, 14

6 Pets welcome: 7 Smoking allowed: 8 Children welcome: 9 Social drinking allowed: 10 Tennis available: 11 Swimming available: 12 Golf available: 13 Skiing available: 14 May be booked through travel agents

The Old Court Bed & Breakfast

144 Benefit Street, 02903
(401) 751-2002

In the heart of Providence's historic Benefit Street area, you'll find the Old Court, where tradition is combined with contemporary standards of luxury. The Old Court was built in 1863 and reflects early Victorian styles. In rooms that overlook downtown Providence and Brown University, you'll feel as if you've entered a more gracious era.

Host: Diane Thiel
Doubles: 10 (PB) $105-115
Type of Beds: 1 Twin; 1 Double; 6 Queen; 2 King
Continental Breakfast
Credit Cards: A, B, C
Notes: 2, 5, 7, 10, 11, 12, 14

SOUTH KINGSTOWN-WAKEFIELD

B&B Rhode Island #RI-109

Box 3291-ND, Newport, 02840
(401) 849-1298

This contemporary home is a gallery of artwork produced by family members. Spiral stairs lead to the balcony overlooking the sitting room, where a corner fireplace blazes in cool weather. On 3.5 acres near a salt pond, within walking distance of an un-crowded ocean beach, with an outdoor deck, gas grill, and picnic table.

Doubles: 2 (SB) $62
Type of Beds: 2 Twin; 1 Double
Continental-plus Breakfast
Credit Cards: No
Notes: 5, 7, 8 (no toddlers), 9, 10, 11, 12, 14

B&B Rhode Island #RI-235

Box 3291-ND, Newport, 02840
(401) 849-1298

Close to the University of Rhode Island, this 1930s colonial offers a lounge area, gardens, vine-covered arbor, and tennis court. The sitting room has a baby grand piano and fireplace; den with TV and game room.

Doubles: 4 (SB) $50-60
Type of Beds: 4 Twin; 1 Double; 1 Queen
Full Breakfast
Credit Cards: No
Notes: 5, 7, 8, 9, 10, 11, 12, 14

B&B Rhode Island #RI-237

Box 3291-ND, Newport, 02840
(401) 849-1298

This is an exquisite 1818 Federal house with true New England charm. One of the oldest houses in Wakefield, it was once the home of a Rhode Island governor. Game room, TV, library, in-ground pool.

Doubles: 2 (PB) $65-75
Type of Beds: 2 Double
Full Breakfast
Credit Cards: No
Notes: 5, 8 (over 14), 9, 10, 11, 12, 14

B&B Rhode Island #RI-255

Box 3291-ND Newport, 02840
(401) 849-1298

This quiet farmhouse borders the Great Swamp Reservation and shores of Worden's Pond. Guests may bring their own canoe or go fishing. A large living room offers plenty of space and a piano for musical guests. Hostess speaks Spanish and Portuguese.

Doubles: 1 (SB) $35-40
Type of Beds: 2 Twin
Full Breakfast
Credit Cards: No
Notes: 5, 7, 8, 9, 10, 11, 12, 14

NOTES: Credit cards accepted: A Master Card; B Visa; C American Express; D Discover Card; E Diners Club; F Other: 2 Personal checks accepted: 3 Lunch available: 4 Dinner available: 5 Open all year

B&B Rhode Island #RI-259

Box 3291-ND, Newport, 02840
(401) 849-1298

This 1898 Victorian has been totally restored and furnished with Victorian antiques. Wraparound porch, parlor. Near Theatre-by-the-Sea, Trustom Wildlife Refuge, and many antique shops; shuttle bus to the Block Island Ferry or the airport. Hostess speaks Polish; host speaks French.

Doubles: 10 (8 PB; 2 SB) $60-120
Type of Beds: 4 Twin; 1 Double; 7 Queen
Continental Breakfast
Credit Cards: No
Notes: 5, 8 (over 10), 9, 10, 11, 12, 14

Blueberry Bush B&B

128 South Road, 02879
(401) 783-0907

Over-sized Cape Cod with a large backyard containing cooking facilities for families. Central location for Mystic Village and Seaport, Newport, Block Island, and all the "South County" beaches in Rhode Island. Hosts for eight years.

Hosts: June & Peter Nielsen
Doubles: 2 (SB) $50-55
Type of Beds: 2 Twin; 1 Double
Full Breakfast
Credit Cards: No
Notes: 2, 5, 8, 9, 10, 11, 12, 14

Highland Farm

4145 Tower Hill Road, Rt. 1, 02879
(401) 783-2408

Early 1800s farmhouse on 28 acres. Come and be treated like one of the family. Information and maps available on the surrounding area, which includes historic sites, good beaches, and everything you need for a wonderful family vacation.

Hosts: Edith & Richard Sumner
Doubles: 2 (SB) $42-50
Type of Beds: 1 Double; 1 Queen
Full Breakfast
Credit Cards: No
Closed Oct.-April
Notes: 2, 6, 8

TIVERTON

B&B Rhode Island #RI-134

Box 3291-ND, Newport, 02840
(401) 849-1298

Blueberry Bush B&B

6 Pets welcome: 7 Smoking allowed: 8 Children welcome: 9 Social drinking allowed: 10 Tennis available: 11 Swimming available: 12 Golf available: 13 Skiing available: 14 May be booked through travel agents

A private cottage for two in a rural setting where you can play tennis on the private clay court, ride bikes, jog, or swim at the nearby beach. The cottage has a combined living/kitchen/dining area on the first floor and an upstairs sleeping area. Enjoy breakfast in the cottage or on the bricked backyard terrace. Hostess is fluent in American sign language.

Cottage: 1 (PB) $55-65
Type of Beds: 2 Twin
Continental-plus Breakfast
Credit Cards: No
Closed Jan. - March
Notes: 9, 10, 11, 12, 14

Highland Farm

WAKEFIELD

Highland Farm

4145 Tower Hill Road, 02879
(401) 783-2408

A 150-year-old farmhouse on 28 acres. Hosts are interested in crafts and quilts. Near beaches, Newport, Block Island, and historical points of interest.

Hosts: Richard & Edith Sumner
Doubles: 2 (SB) $42-50
Type of Beds: 1 Double; 1 Queen
Continental Breakfast
Credit Cards: No
Closed Nov. - April
Notes: 2, 6, 8, 11

WARREN

B&B Rhode Island #RI-162

Box 3291-ND, Newport, 02840
(401) 849-1298

Refreshing sea breezes from Mt. Hope Bay cool guests relaxing on the screened porch of this large Dutch colonial just four houses from the water. Close to Newport and Providence, the home is surrounded on three sides by water.

Doubles: 2 (SB) $50-55
Type of Beds: 1 Twin; 2 Double
Full Breakfast
Credit Cards: No
Notes: 5, 8, 9, 10, 11, 12, 14

WARWICK

B&B Rhode Island #RI-275

Box 3291-ND, Newport, 02840
(401) 849-1298

A century-old Cape Anne on a quiet street with water view, within minutes to Providence airport. One room with shared bath.

Doubles: 1 (SB) $40-50
Type of Beds: 1 Twin; 1 Double
Continental Breakfast
Credit Cards: No
Notes: 5, 8 (over 12), 9, 10, 11, 12, 14

B&B Rhode Island #RI-283

Box 3291-ND Newport, 02840
(401) 849-1298

Located in historic Pawtuxet Village, this refinished Victorian features a wraparound porch, sitting with antiques, dining room

NOTES: Credit cards accepted: A Master Card; B Visa; C American Express; D Discover Card; E Diners Club; F Other: 2 Personal checks accepted: 3 Lunch available: 4 Dinner available: 5 Open all year

with fireplace, and a spacious yard for relaxing.

Doubles: 2 (SB) $50-55
Type of Beds: 2 Twin; 1 Double
Continental-plus Breakfast
Credit Cards: No
Notes: 5, 9, 10, 11, 12, 14

WESTERLY

B&B Rhode Island #RI-141

Box 3291-ND Newport, 02840
(401) 849-1298

Located on 20 acres in a country setting 2 miles from the ocean, this home is on a hilltop surrounded by rolling fields and informal gardens. Fireplaces, wide plank floors, antiques, and old-fashioned furnishings.

Doubles: 3 (SB) $60
Type of Beds: 1 Twin; 3 Double
Continental-plus Breakfast
Credit Cards: No
Notes: 5, 8, 9, 10, 11, 12, 14

B&B Rhode Island #RI-172

Box 3291-ND, Newport, 02840
(401) 849-1298

This 1835 Classic Greek Revival is in the heart of the city's cultural center, just a few minutes' walk from the Colonial Theatre, Westerly Center for the Arts, and downtown shopping and dining. Resident manager is only on the premises during breakfast and when guests arrive.

Doubles: 3 (SB) $45-65
Type of Beds: 2 Twin; 1 Double; 1 King or 2 Twin
Continental-plus Breakfast
Credit Cards: No
Notes: 5, 8, 9, 10, 11, 12, 14

B&B Rhode Island #RI-180

Box 3291-ND, Newport, 02840
(401) 849-1298

This early twentieth-century home has a wraparound stone porch overlooking the ocean, Block Island, and Montauk Point. Two golf courses and one tennis club are within walking distance. Misquamicut Beach and Watch Hill are minutes away; Mystic is just a short drive.

Doubles: 12 (2 PB; 10 SB) $45-80
Type of Beds: 8 Twin; 8 Double
Continental-plus Breakfast
Credit Cards: No
Notes: 5, 7, 8, 9, 10, 11, 12, 14

Woody Hill Guest House B&B

RR #3, Box 676E, 02891
(401) 322-0452

Your hostess, a high-school English teacher, invites you to share her reproduction colonial home with antiques and gardens. You may snuggle under quilts, relax on the porch swing, visit nearby Newport and Mystic, or swim at beautiful ocean beaches. Westerly has it all!

Host: Dr. Ellen L. Madison
Doubles: 3 (1 PB; 2 SB) $55-60
Type of Beds: 2 Double
Full Breakfast
Credit Cards: No
Closed one week in Feb.
Notes: 2, 5, 8, 9, 10, 11, 12

6 Pets welcome: 7 Smoking allowed: 8 Children welcome: 9 Social drinking allowed: 10 Tennis available: 11 Swimming available: 12 Golf available: 13 Skiing available: 14 May be booked through travel agents

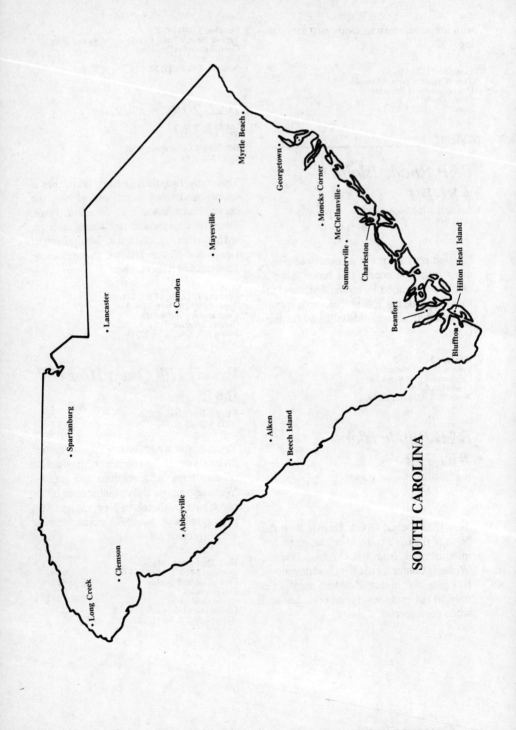

SOUTH CAROLINA

• Myrtle Beach

Georgetown •

• Moncks Corner

McClellanville •

Summerville •

Charleston •

Hilton Head Island

Beaufort

Bluffton •

• Mayesville

• Camden

• Lancaster

• Spartanburg

• Aiken

• Beech Island

• Abbeyville

• Clemson

• Long Creek

South Carolina

ABBEVILLE

The Belmont Inn
106 E. Pickens Street, 29620
(803) 459-9625

The Belmont Inn has its own special ambience and provides it guests the finest in intimacy and privacy. Your stay will be marked by graceful personal service and attention to detail in an atmosphere of Southern elegance. Full dining, lounge, and meeting rooms.

Hosts: Mr. & Mrs. Joseph Harden
Doubles: 24 (PB) $50-65
Type of Beds: 8 Twin; 11 Queen
Continental Breakfast
Credit Cards: A, B, C
Notes: 2, 3, 4, 5, 7, 8, 9, 10, 11, 12, 14

AIKEN

The Willcox Inn
100 Colleton Avenue, 29801
(803) 649-1377; 1-800-288-6754

Beautiful, spacious rooms that have been occupied by Winston Churchill, President Roosevelt, and Elizabeth Arden. Our dining room is known for its fine cuisine, including pheasant in whiskey sauce, rack of lamb, etc. Beautiful town with a lot to offer: golf, polo matches, antique shopping, etc.

Hosts: Stig Jorgensen & Joyce Phillips
Singles: 19 (PB) $69.55-117
Doubles: 11 (PB) $69.55-117
Type of Beds: 5 Twin; 25 Queen
Continental or Full Breakfast
Credit Cards: A, B, C
Notes: 4, 5, 7, 8, 9, 10, 11, 12, 14

BEAUFORT

Bay Street Inn
601 Bay Street, 29902
(803) 524-7720

Fourteen-room Sams Mansion on the inland waterway, once a planter's townhouse and now on the National Register. Five bedrooms with water views; gardens, library, golf, tennis, beach, bikes available. Featured in *Antiques* magazine.

Hosts: Gene & Kathleen Roe
Doubles: 5 (PB) $55.60-65
Type of Beds: 2 Twin; 2 Double; 2 Queen
Continental Breakfast
Credit Cards: A, B
Notes: 2, 5, 7, 8, 9, 10, 11, 12

The Rhett House Inn
1009 Craven Street, 29902
(803) 524-9030

All the guest rooms have been created for your comfort and convenience. They are authentically furnished with homespun quilts and freshly cut flowers, adding to their warmth and individuality. Our inn beautifully recreates the feeling of the Old South. You'll fall in love with the warmth and graciousness of an earlier way of life.

Hosts: Marianne & Steve Harrison
Doubles: 8 (PB) $64.20-100.95
Type of Beds: 2 Twin; 1 Double; 5 Queen
Full Breakfast
Minimum stay weekends & holidays: 2
Credit Cards: A, B
Notes: 2, 5, 7, 8 (over 8), 9, 10, 11, 12

---

6 Pets welcome: 7 Smoking allowed: 8 Children welcome: 9 Social drinking allowed: 10 Tennis available: 11 Swimming available: 12 Golf available: 13 Skiing available: 14 May be booked through travel agents

The Cedars B&B Inn

BEECH ISLAND

The Cedars Bed & Breakfast Inn

1325 Williston Road, Box 117, 29841
(803) 827-0248

An 1820s country manor house on 12 parklike acres, six miles east of Augusta, Ga. Beautifully decorated with antiques and reproductions; modern baths. Close by are Redcliffe Plantation State Park, fine dining, antique shops, and historic districts.

Hosts: Ralph & Maggie Zieger
Doubles: 4 (3 PB; 1 SB) $43-48
Type of Beds: 2 Twin; 1 Double; 2 Queen
Continental-plus Breakfast
Credit Cards: A, B
Notes: 2, 5, 7, 8 (over 12), 9, 14

BLUFFTON

The Fripp House Inn

Box 857, 29910
(803) 757-2139

Built in 1835, Fripp House is a landmark of this historic village on the May River. Private gardens with pool and fountains; spacious home with warm hospitality and hearty breakfast. Five minutes from Hilton Head Island.

Hosts: Grant & Dana Tuttle
Doubles: 4 (3 PB; 1 SB) $46-81
Type of Beds: 1 Twin; 2 Double; 1 Queen
Full Breakfast
Minimum stay holidays: 2
Credit Cards: A, B
Notes: 2, 5, 7 (restricted), 8, 9, 10, 11, 12

CAMDEN

The Carriage House

1413 Lyttleton Street, 29020
(803) 432-2430

This antebellum cottage (circa 1840) reflects the hosts' interest in antiques and interior design and is complete with window boxes and picket fence. Camden, a very cosmopolitan small town, is known as a center for training and racing horses. Excellent restaurants, boutiques, and antique shops abound in this lovely, historic town.

Hosts: Appie & Bob Watkins
Doubles: $50
Full Breakfast
Credit Cards: No
Closed Christmas week
Notes: 2, 3, 4, 5, 6, 7 (limited), 8, 9, 10, 11, 12, 14

The Carriage House

NOTES: Credit cards accepted: A Master Card; B Visa; C American Express; D Discover Card; E Diners Club; F Other: 2 Personal checks accepted: 3 Lunch available: 4 Dinner available: 5 Open all year

CHARLESTON_____

Anne Harper's Bed & Breakfast

56 Smith Street, 29401
(803) 723-3947

This circa 1870 home is located in Charleston's historic district. Two connecting rooms with connecting bath and sitting area with TV. The owner is a retired medical technologist and enjoys serving a full breakfast.

Host: Ann D. Harper
Singles: 1 (PB) $40
Doubles: 1 (PB) $55
Type of Beds: 1 Twin; 1 Double
Full Breakfast
Minimum stay: 2
Credit Cards: No
Notes: 2, 5, 7 (limited), 8 (over 10), 9, 10, 11, 12

Barksdale House Inn

27 George Street, 29401
(803) 577-4800

One of Charleston's most luxurious ten-room inns. A 200-year-old home featuring individually designed rooms, some with whirlpool tubs and fireplaces. Flowers, daily newspaper, wine, tea, sherry, turndown service with chocolates, fountain in the courtyard, and parking.

Host: Suzanne W. Chestnut
Doubles: 10 (PB) $75-150
Type of Beds: 1 Double; 5 Queen; 5 King
Continental Breakfast
Credit Cards: A, B
Closed Dec. 24-25
Notes: 2 (deposit), 5, 7, 8 (over 12), 9, 10, 11, 12, 14

The Battery Carriage House

20 South Battery, 29401
(803) 723-9881; 1-800-845-7638

The Battery Carriage House has ten rooms located in the carriage house overlooking a private courtyard. The rooms are decorated in eighteenth-century reproductions. We serve a continental breakfast and a bottle of wine each day. We also have bicycles for touring.

Doubles: 10 (PB) $96
Type of Beds: 2 Twin; 10 Queen
Continental Breakfast
Credit Cards: A, B, C
Notes: 2, 5, 6, 7, 8, 9

The Cannonboro Inn

Cannonboro Inn

184 Ashley Avenue, 29403
(803) 723-8572

Traditional B&B inn recognized by the City of Charleston as an architecturally significant structure. Guests enjoy a full American breakfast in the formal dining room or on the columned piazza overlooking a low-country garden. Located within the historic district.

Hosts: Robert Warley & James Hare
Doubles: 5 (PB) $49-69
Type of Beds: 1 Twin; 2 Double; 3 Queen
Full Breakfast
Minimum stay weekends: 2
Credit Cards: A, B
Notes: 2, 5, 8, 9, 11, 12, 14

Charleston Society B&B #1

84 Murray Blvd., 29401
(803) 723-4949

6 Pets welcome: 7 Smoking allowed: 8 Children welcome: 9 Social drinking allowed: 10 Tennis available: 11 Swimming available: 12 Golf available: 13 Skiing available: 14 May be booked through travel agents

Carriage house, upstairs, with private entrance, piazza, living room with fireplace, small kitchen. One double, private bath, $100.

Charleston Society B&B #2
84 Murray Blvd., 29401
(803) 723-4949

First floor: living room, kitchen, private entrance. Second floor: two bedrooms, one with a queen canopy bed and the other with a double canopy bed. Full bath. Two doubles, private bath, $65.

Charleston Society B&B #3
84 Murray Blvd., 29401
(803) 723-4949

In the heart of the Old Market area. One bedroom with fireplace and double bed, recently decorated in reproduction period furniture. Private bath, private entrance. One double, private bath, $75.

Charleston Society B&B #4
84 Murray Blvd., 29401
(803) 723-4949

Lovely carriage house with a private entrance, living room with fireplace, full kitchen, two bedrooms, private bath. $90-150.

Charleston Society B&B #5
84 Murray Blvd., 29401
(803) 723-4949

On Orange Street, with a private entrance, bedroom with twin beds, private bath and shower. $70.

Charleston Society B&B #6
84 Murray Blvd., 29401
(803) 723-4949

Carriage house. Private entrance, living room, full kitchen, one bedroom with double bed, bath. $70.

Charleston Society B&B #7
84 Murray Blvd., 29401
(803) 723-4949

A carriage house with private entrance, living room, toaster over and refrigerator, bedroom with twin beds, bath with shower, patio, and garden. $90.

Charleston Society B&B #8
84 Murray Blvd., 29401
(803) 723-4948

Small room and bath on Todd Street. Located in the Historic District, within easy walking distance of shops, restaurants, and historic points of interest. $50.

Charleston Society B&B #1A
84 Murray Blvd., 29401
(803) 723-4949

On Legare Street. Large bedroom with four-poster Rice bed, private bath. $65.

Charleston Society B&B #2A
84 Murray Blvd., 29401
(803) 723-4949

On Tradd Street. Third floor: bedroom with fireplace, twin beds, shared bath with other bedroom on third floor. $45.

NOTES: Credit cards accepted: A Master Card; B Visa; C American Express; D Discover Card; E Diners Club; F Other: 2 Personal checks accepted: 3 Lunch available: 4 Dinner available: 5 Open all year

Charleston Society B&B #3A

84 Murray Blvd., 29401
(803) 723-4949

On Tradd Street. Two bedrooms on the third floor, one with twin, one with double beds. Private bath. $50-60.

Charleston Society B&B #4A

84 Murray Blvd., 29401
(803) 723-4949

On East Battery. Historic home with a beautiful view of Charleston Harbor. Pool. Two bedrooms with double bed. $80.

Charleston Society B&B #7A

84 Murray Blvd., 29401
(803) 723-4948

On Gibbs Street. Large bedroom furnished with antiques. House built in 1850. Lovely rose garden. $65.

1837 Bed & Breakfast

126 Wentworth Street, 29401
(803) 723-7166

Accommodations in a wealthy cotton planter's home and brick carriage house. Centrally located in the historic district, within walking distance of boat tours, Old Market, antique shops, restaurants, and main attractions. Full gourmet breakfast is served in the formal dining room.

Hosts: Richard Dunn & Sherri Weaver
Doubles: 8 (PB) $39-85
Type of Beds: 4 Double; 4 Queen
Full Breakfast
Credit Cards: A, B, C
Notes: 2, 5, 7, 9, 10, 11, 12

The Hayne House

30 King Street, 29412
(803) 577-2633

One of the city's oldest inns, established in 1935. We are located one block from the Battery in the very heart of the historic district. Host shares breakfast with the guests and provides information about Charleston history, which is very entertaining.

Host: Ben Chapman
Singles: 1 (PB)
Doubles: 3 (PB) $55-80
Type of Beds: 2 Twin; 4 Double
Continental Breakfast
Minimum stay weekends & holidays: 2
Credit Cards: No
Notes: 2, 4, 5, 7, 8, 9, 10, 11, 12

Historic Charleston B&B #1

43 Legare Street, 29401
(803) 722-6606

Beaufain Street 1837 home overlooking Colonial Lake. Complimentary wine and goodies; refrigerator, toaster oven. Affectionate dachshund in residence. Convenient to house museums, historic churches, theater, antiquing, outstanding restaurants.

Doubles: 1 (PB) $95-105
Type of Beds: 1 Twin; 1 King
Continental Breakfast
Credit Cards: A, B
Notes: 1, 5, 8 (over 16), 9, 10, 11, 12

Historic Charleston B&B #2

43 Legare Street, 29401
(803) 722-6606

Broad and King streets. Carriage house of a large pre-Revolutionary home set in the middle of the downtown area. Two fireplaces and a charming courtyard. Golden retriever in residence.

6 Pets welcome: 7 Smoking allowed: 8 Children welcome: 9 Social drinking allowed: 10 Tennis available: 11 Swimming available: 12 Golf available: 13 Skiing available: 14 May be booked through travel agents

Doubles: 4 (PB) $75-85
Type of Beds: 4 Twin; 1 Double; 1 Queen
Continental Breakfast
Credit Cards: A, B, C
Notes: 2, 5, 8, 9, 10, 11, 12

Historic Charleston B&B #3

43 Legare Street, 29401
(803) 722-6606

Broad Street at Meeting. A charming carriage house converted to a two-bedroom B&B. Full kitchen, living room, antiques, air-conditioning, fireplace. Within walking distance of most of Charleston's historic attractions.

Doubles: 2 (PB) $90-170
Type of Beds: 1 Double; 1 Queen
Full Breakfast
Credit Cards: A, B, C
Notes: 2, 5, 7, 8, 9, 10, 11, 12

Historic Charleston B&B #4

43 Legare Street, 29401
(803) 722-6606

Broad at Savage. Classic Charleston single house with double side verandas, built in 1868. Jacuzzi, bikes available. College of Charleston, the Citadel, and the Medical University of South Carolina are all within a five to ten-minute drive. Dog in residence.

Doubles: 1 (PB) $80-90
Type of Beds: 1 Queen
Continental Breakfast
Credit Cards: A, B, C
Notes: 2, 5, 9, 10, 11, 12

Historic Charleston B&B #5

43 Legare Street, 29401
(803) 722-6606

Broad Street. Circa 1880 house, within walking distance of everything. All rooms have fireplaces, antiques, TV, air-conditioning.

Doubles: 4 (PB) $75-90
Type of Beds: 2 Double; 1 Queen; 1 King
Continental Breakfast
Credit Cards: A, B, C
Notes: 2, 5, 7, 8, 9, 10, 11, 12

Historic Charleston B&B #8

43 Legare Street, 29401
(803) 722-6606

Meeting Street. A 1740 single house where each suite has a canopy bed, private bath, and fireplace. Fresh fruit, flowers, and the morning paper are provided. One dog in residence.

Doubles: 3 (PB) $75-100
Type of Beds: 3 Double
Continental Breakfast
Credit Cards: A, B, C
Notes: 2, 5, 9

Historic Charleston B&B #9

43 Legare Street, 29401
(803) 722-6606

Orange Street. This house, built in the 1770s, is within walking distance of many attractions. Private entrance, sitting room, kitchen, air-conditioning. German and French are spoken.

Doubles: 1 (PB) $90-110
Type of Beds: 1 Twin; 1 Double
Full Breakfast
Credit Cards: A, B, C
Notes: 2, 5, 8, 9, 10, 11

Historic Charleston B&B #11

43 Legare Street, 29401
(803) 722-6606

Orange Street. Located in the former slave quarters of a 1770 home. Off-street parking and walled garden; air-conditioning, bikes, and piano available.

Doubles: 1 (PB) $70-80
Type of Beds: 1 Queen
Continental Breakfast
Credit Cards: A, B, C
Notes: 2, 5, 9, 10, 11, 12

Historic Charleston B&B #12
43 Legare Street, 29401
(803) 722-6606

Rutledge Avenue. Brick carriage house overlooking a fish pond. Thirty-minute drive to historic gardens or beaches.

Doubles: 1 (PB) $75-85
Type of Beds: 2 Double
Continental Breakfast
Credit Cards: A, B, C
Notes: 2, 5, 8, 9, 10, 11, 12

Historic Charleston B&B #13
43 Legare Street, 29401
(803) 722-6606

South Hampton Street. One room in the main house with canopy bed; another in a cottage with beamed ceiling and fireplace. Pool on premises; kitchen in cottage. Air-conditioning, piano, bikes.

Doubles: 2 (PB) $60-90
Type of Beds: 2 Double
Continental Breakfast
Credit Cards: A, B, C
Notes: 2, 5, 7 (cottage only), 9, 10, 11, 12

Historic Charleston B&B #14
43 Legare Street, 29401
(803) 722-6606

Tradd Street at Church. Main house is pre-Revolutionary, located in the center of the Historic District. Guest rooms are in a separate outbuilding with private entrance. French spoken; one dog in residence.

Doubles: 2 (PB) $55-65
Type of Beds: 4 Twin
Continental Breakfast
Credit Cards: A, B, C
Notes: 2, 5, 7, 8, 9, 10, 11

Historic Charleston B&B #17
43 Legare Street, 29401
(803) 722-6066

Wentworth Street. A grand 1838 Greek Revival mansion. Near the College of Charleston and the Medical University of South Carolina; four blocks from the Charleston Convention Center. Large, formal terraces and garden for your enjoyment.

Doubles: 3 (PB) $80-145
Type of Beds: 2 Double; 1 Queen; 2 King
Full Breakfast
Credit Cards: A, B, C
Notes: 2, 5, 8 (over 12), 9, 10, 11, 12

Indigo Inn
1 Maiden Lane, 29401
(803) 577-5900

Located in the heart of Charleston's historic district The Indigo Inn is renown for its Southern hospitality. All rooms are appointed in eighteenth-century antiques and antique reproductions. The complimentary Hunt Breakfast is best enjoyed in our intimate courtyard. Private parking and complimentary newspaper.

Hosts: Buck & Frankie Limehouse
Singles: 13 (PB) $80.25-101.65
Doubles: 27 (PB) $80.25-112.35
Type of Beds: 40 Queen
Continental Breakfast
Credit Cards: A, B, C
Notes: 2, 5, 6, 7, 8, 9, 12, 14

6 Pets welcome: 7 Smoking allowed: 8 Children welcome: 9 Social drinking allowed: 10 Tennis available: 11 Swimming available: 12 Golf available: 13 Skiing available: 14 May be booked through travel agents

John Rutledge House Inn

116 Broad Street, 29401
(803) 723-7999; 1-800-845-6119

This National Landmark was built in 1763 by John Rutledge, coauthor and signer of the U.S. Constitution. Large rooms and suites located in the main and carriage houses offer the ambience of historic Charleston. Rates include wine and sherry upon arrival, turndown service with brandy and chocolate, and breakfast with newspaper delivered to your room.

Host: Richard Widman
Doubles: 19 (PB) $101.65-181.90
Type of Beds: 8 Double; 2 Queen; 9 King
Continental Breakfast
Credit Cards: A, B, C
Notes: 2, 4, 5, 7, 8, 9, 10, 11, 12, 14

Kings Courtyard Inn

198 King Street, 29401
(803) 723-7000; 1-800-845-6119

Kings Courtyard Inn, circa 1853, is located in the heart of the antique and historic district. Convenient to attractions, shops, and restaurants. Rate includes continental breakfast and newspaper, wine and sherry served in the lobby. Turndown service with chocolate and brandy. AAA four diamond.

Host: Laura Fox
Doubles: 34 (PB) $85.60-128.40
Type of Beds: 10 Double;10 Queen; 14 King
Continental Breakfast
Credit Cards: A, B, C
Notes: 2, 5, 7, 8, 9, 10, 11, 12, 14

King's Inn

136 Tradd Street, 29401
(803) 577-3683

Located in the heart of the historic district, this private home includes two B&B units with separate entrances. House museums, shops, and the waterfront are minutes away. All the historic area can be covered on foot from here. Enjoy the Spoleto Festival in late May or drive to the magnificent plantations or beautiful beaches in half an hour. Your hostess is a registered tour guide.

Host: Hazel King
Doubles: 2 (PB) $85-95
Type of Beds: 2 Twin; 1 Queen
Continental Breakfast
Credit Cards: No
Notes: 2, 5, 8, 9, 10, 11, 12, 14

King's Inn

Maison DuPre

East Bay & George Streets, 29401
(803) 723-8691

Three restored Charleston "single houses" and two carriage houses comprise Maison DuPre, originally built in 1804. The inn features period furniture and antiques and is ideally located in the historic Ansonborough district. Complimentary continental breakfast and a "Lowcountry Tea Party" are served. "Maison DuPre with its faded stucco, pink brick and gray shutters is one of the city's best-looking small inns" — *New York Times*.

Hosts: Lucille, Bob & Mark Mulholland
Doubles: 15 (PB) $108.07-214
Type of Beds: 2 Twin; 13 Queen
Continental Breakfast
Credit Cards: A, B, C
Notes: 2, 5, 8, 9, 10, 11, 12

133 Broad Street B&B

133 Broad Street, 29401
(803) 577-0392

This house was built circa 1870 and is in the historic district, with everything within walking distance. The lovely double bedroom has antiques, a fireplace, wide floor boards, ten-foot ceilings, and a sitting room with a queen sofabed. Wine, crib, cot, bicycles, and parking are available.

Host: Trudy Gary
Suite: 1 (PB) $59-100
Type of Beds: 1 Double; 1 Queen
Continental Breakfast
Credit Cards: A, B, C
Notes: 2, 5, 7, 8, 9, 14

Vendue Inn

29 East Battery, 29401
(803) 577-7970; 1-800-845-7900

At Vendue Inn, located in the heart of the historic district, you will experience the elegance of a small European eighteenth-century inn, coupled with the charm and gentility of the Old South. Continental breakfast, wine and cheese.

Hosts: Evelyn & Morton Needle
Doubles: 34 (PB) $80-180
Continental Breakfast
Credit Cards: A, B, C
Notes: 4, 5, 7, 8, 9, 10, 12

Villa de La Fontaine Bed & Breakfast

138 Wentworth Street, 29401
(803) 577-7709

Villa de La Fontaine is a columned Greek Revival mansion in the heart of the historic district. It was built in 1838, and boasts a half-acre garden with fountain and terraces. It has been restored to impeccable condition and furnished with museum-quality furniture and accessories. Your hosts are retired A.S.I.D. interior designers and have decorated the rooms with eighteenth-century American antiques. Several of the rooms feature canopy beds. Breakfast is prepared by a master chef who prides himself on serving a different menu every day.

Hosts: William Fontaine & Aubrey Hancock
Doubles: 4 (PB) $85
Suites: 2 (PB) $135
Type of Beds: 2 Twin; 2 Queen; 2 King
Full Breakfast
Minimum stay weekends 2 ; holidays: 3 ; Spoleto: 3
Credit Cards: A, B, C
Notes: 2, 5, 8 (12 and over), 9, 10, 11, 12, 14

CLEMSON

Nord-Lac

Box 1111, 29633
(803) 639-2939

Located in a rural setting in the Smoky Mountain foothills, this B&B has two structures. One is a fairly modern home with three exquisitely antique-furnished rooms; the other is an 1826 log cabin that sleeps four. Tennis, billiards, and an antique museum are on the premises.

Hosts: Elaine & Jim Chisman
Doubles: 4 (2 PB; 2 SB) $40-100
Type of Beds: 2 Twin; 4 Double
Full Breakfast
Credit Cards: No
Notes: 2, 5, 8, 9, 10, 11, 12, 14

GEORGETOWN

The Shaw House

8 Cypress Court, 29440
(803) 546-9663

Lovely view overlooking Willowbank Marsh; wonderful bird watching. Many antiques throughout the house; rocking chairs on porch. Within walking distance of the historical district and many wonderful restaurants. Fresh fruits and Southern breakfast. One hour drive to Myrtle Beach or Charleston.

Hosts: Mary & Joe Shaw
Doubles: 3 (PB) $45
Full Breakfast
Credit Cards: No
Notes: 2, 5, 7, 8, 9, 10, 11, 12, 14

HILTON HEAD ISLAND

Halcyon

Shipyard Plantation Harbour Master 604, 29928
(803) 785-7912

Living room, dining room, music room, and sun deck are all available to our guests. Halcyon House is close to the pool, bike trails, beach, and bird-watching sites. Transportation and historic tours of Charleston, Savannah, and Beaufort may be arranged on request.

Host: Maybelle Wayburn
Double: 1 (PB) $65
Type of Beds: 1 Double
Continental Breakfast
Credit Cards: No
Notes: 2, 4, 7, 9, 10, 11, 12

LANCASTER

Wade-Beckham House

Box 348, 29720
(803) 285-1105

The Wade-Beckham house is one of Lancaster County's few surviving plantation homes. The original portion of the home was built between 1802 and 1811, possibly as a summer house where the family could move inland to escape the heat and insects. Guests may choose among three distinctive rooms.

Host: Jan Suke
Doubles: 3 $38-48
Type of Beds: 1 Twin; 1 Double; 1 Queen
Continental Breakfast

Credit Cards: No
Closed holidays
Notes: 2, 8 (over 16), 11

LONG CREEK

Chauga River House Inn

Box 100, 29658
(803) 647-9587

Situated in the country, above the lovely shoals of the scenic Chana River, the River House specializes in offering white-water rafting packages on the nearby Chattooga National Wild and Scenic River. Decorated in French country antiques. Swim and wade in the river, spend time in the game room, and enjoy our Scandinavian breakfast.

Hosts: Jim & Jeanette Greiner
Doubles: 5 (3 PB; 2 SB) $39-59
Continental Breakfast
Credit Cards: A, B
Closed Nov. 1 - March 1
Notes: 2, 7, 8, 9, 10, 11, 12

Windsong

MAYESVILLE

Windsong

Rt. 1, Box 300, 29104
(803) 453-5004

Situated in open farmland, this large house has balconies and porches, plus an open fireplace in the large den. Private entrance.

NOTES: Credit cards accepted: A Master Card; B Visa; C American Express; D Discover Card; E Diners Club; F Other: 2 Personal checks accepted: 3 Lunch available: 4 Dinner available: 5 Open all year

A quail hunting preserve is operated by your host. An excellent place to stop over, whether you're traveling north or south.

Hosts: Lynda & Billy Dabbs
Doubles: 2 (PB) $35-45
Type of Beds: 2 Double
Full Breakfast
Credit Cards: No
Notes: 2, 4, 5, 7, 8, 9

McCLELLANVILLE

Laurel Hill Plantation

8913 North Hwy. 17, Box 182, 29458
(803) 887-3708

Laurel Hill Plantation was built in 1850 and is on the National Register of Historic Places. It faces the Intracoastal Waterway, and is furnished in country and primitive antiques of the period. Featured in the May 1986 issue of *Country Living* magazine; in the book *Plantations of the Low Country*. Thirty miles north of Charleston.

Hosts: Jackie & Lee Morrison
Singles: 2 (SB) $35-40
Doubles: 2 (SB) $45-50
Type of Beds: 2 Twin; 4 Double
Full Breakfast
Credit Cards: No
Notes: 2, 5, 8 (over 7), 9

MONCKS CORNER

Rice Hope Plantation Inn

Box 355, 29461
(803) 761-4832

An old forty-room plantation house on the Cooper River thirty-eight miles from Charleston. Historic sites nearby, antiques in rooms, fishing and canoeing available.

Hosts: Gene & Sue Lanier
Doubles: 4 (PB) $65
Type of Beds: 2 Double; 2 Queen
Full Breakfast
Credit Cards: No
Closed July & August
Notes: 2, 3, 8, 9, 10, 11, 12, 14

MYRTLE BEACH

Serendipity

407-71 Avenue N, 29577
(803) 449-5268

Award-winning Mission style inn, one and one-half blocks from the beach. Pool, Jacuzzi, shuffleboard, Ping-Pong, bicycles. Near sixty golf courses, tennis, pier, and deep sea fishing. Air conditioning, color TV, refrigerator, private baths in all rooms. Historic Charleston 90 miles; great shopping, restaurants are nearby.

Hosts: Cos & Ellen Ficarra
Doubles: 2 (PB) $45-65
Efficiencies: 4 (PB) $57-65
Suites: 4 (PB) $65-82
Type of Beds: 3 Twin; 4 Double; 5 Queen
Continental-plus Breakfast
Credit Cards: A, B, C
Closed Dec.-Jan.
Notes: 7, 8, 9, 10, 11, 12, 14

SPARTANBURG

The Nicholls-Crook Plantation House

Box 5812, 29304
(803) 583-7337

A circa 1800 Georgian-style, up-country plantation house with period antiques. Listed on the National Register of Historic Places. Restful rural setting with easy access from Interstates 26 and 85. Gourmet breakfast in the tavern room.

Hosts: Suzanne & Jim Brown
Doubles: 3 (1 PB; 2 SB) $70-90
Type of Beds: 2 Double; 1 Queen
Full Breakfast
Closed Christmas
Credit Cards: No
Notes: 2, 8 (over 12), 9, 14

---

6 Pets welcome: 7 Smoking allowed: 8 Children welcome: 9 Social drinking allowed: 10 Tennis available: 11 Swimming available: 12 Golf available: 13 Skiing available: 14 May be booked through travel agents

SUMMERVILLE

Bed & Breakfast of Summerville

304 S. Hampton Street, 29483
(803) 871-5275

A restored 1865 house on the Register of Historic Places in a quiet setting. Weather permitting, breakfast can be served in the greenhouse, gazebo, by the pool, or self-prepared from a stocked refrigerator. Wine, soft drinks, fruit, bikes, charcoal grill are available.

Hosts: Dusty & Emmagene Rhodes
Doubles: 2 (PB) $50
Type of Beds: 2 Double
Continental Breakfast
Credit Cards: No
Notes: 2, 5, 7, 8 (12 or over), 9, 10, 11, 12

South Dakota

BERESFORD

Ryger Union House
South Dakota B&B
903 North Dakota Street, Canton, 57013
(605) 987-2834

Lovely oak woodwork and lace curtains are yours to enjoy in this retired school administrator's home. Your host has made twelve trips to Europe and lead tour groups — let him help you explore the area. Hunting package available.

Doubles: 3 (1 PB; 2 SB) $35
Type of Beds: 3 Double
Full Breakfast
Credit Cards: No
Notes: 2, 5, 9, 10, 11

BRUCE

Klernjan B&B
South Dakota B&B
903 North Dakota Street, Canton, 57013
(605) 987-2834

A large three-story farmhouse, with a game room in the basement, on an operating pig and crop family farm. Fishing and hunting area. Special hunting package, including three meals a day and hunting rights on 1,800 acres of land, is also available.

Singles: 1 (SB) $25-35
Doubles: 3 (SB) $25-35
Type of Beds: 2 Twin; 3 Double
Full Breakfast
Credit Cards: No
Notes: 2, 5, 6, 8, 11, 13

BUFFALO

Real Ranch Living
HCR 2, Box 112, 57720
(605) 375-3306

Enjoy Western hospitality at its best! Ride a ranch horse, join a cattle drive, take a buckboard ride, or just relax and watch the sunset. Vacation on a working ranch of 40,000 acres; stay in our cowboy bunk house. Enjoy yourself!

Host: Laurie Routier
Cabins: (SB) $25-40
Type of Beds: 4 Twin; 1 Double
Full Breakfast
Credit Cards: No
Closed Dec.-May
Notes: 2, 4, 6, 7, 8, 9, 14

CANOVA

Skoglund Farm
Rt. 1, Box 45, 57321
(605) 247-3445

Enjoy yourself on the S.D. prairie: cattle, fowl, peacocks, horses, home-cooked evening meal, and full breakfast. Visit nearby attractions: "Little House on the Prairie," "Corn Palace," "Doll House," "Prairie Village," or just relax, hike, and enjoy a family farm. Rate includes evening meal and breakfast.

Hosts: Alden & Delores Skoglund
Doubles: 5 (SB) Adults: $30; Teens: $20; Children: $15; under five, free
Full Breakfast
Credit Cards: No
Notes: 2, 4, 5, 6, 7, 8, 9, 10, 11, 12, 14

6 Pets welcome: 7 Smoking allowed: 8 Children welcome: 9 Social drinking allowed: 10 Tennis available: 11 Swimming available: 12 Golf available: 13 Skiing available: 14 May be booked through travel agents

SOUTH DAKOTA

- Watertown
- Bruce
- Crooks
- Canton
- Beresford
- Canova
- Mitchell
- Vivian
- Okaton
- Milesville
- Philip
- Wall
- Rapid City
- Hill City
- Buffalo

CANTON

Kennedy Rose Inn
South Dakota B&B
903 North Dakota Street, Canton, 57013
(605) 987-2834

A huge Georgian Revival house on 5 acres of wooded grounds, where you can recapture the gracious living of another era. Your host enjoys hunting and wildlife art; the hostess is interested in music, crafts, and gourmet cooking.

Doubles: 4 (1 PB; 3 SB) $35-75
Type of Beds: 2 Twin; 2 Double; 2 Queen; 1 King
Continental Breakfast
Credit Cards: A, B
Notes: 2, 3, 4, 5, 7, 8, 10, 11, 12, 13

CROOKS

Janet's B&B
South Dakota B&B
903 North Dakota Street, Canton, 57013
(605) 987-2834

An eighty-year-old house, remodeled in 1959. Your hostess is a former teacher and outreach worker for the elderly. She enjoys golf, music, and traveling. The house is located in the country, approximately ten miles from Sioux Falls.

Doubles: 2 (SB) $25-35
Type of Beds: 2 Queen
Full Breakfast
Credit Cards: No
Notes: 2, 5, 6, 8, 10, 11, 12, 13

HILL CITY

Bed & Breakfast Heart of the Hills
517 Main Street, 57745
(605) 574-2704

Within walking distance of the 1880 train, gift shops, and restaurants. Mt. Rushmore and the Crazy Horse Memorial are just minutes away. Queen bed, large sitting room with a studio couch that makes into a double bed; private bath, private entrance. Breakfast is served on the deck by the water fountain or in the dining room.

Hosts: Carol Ball Shafer & Wes Shafer
Doubles: 2 (PB) $26-36
Type of Beds: 1 Double; 1 Queen
Full Breakfast
Credit Cards: No
Notes: 2, 5, 7, 8, 9, 10, 11, 12

Peaceful Valley B&B
South Dakota B&B
903 North Dakota Street, Canton, 57013
(605) 987-2834

Nestled in the pines with a beautiful view of Mt. Rushmore and Elkhorn Mountain, near lakes, trout streams, hiking trails, Custer State Park, Custer City, Deadwood, and Lead. Six miles to Mt. Rushmore.

Doubles: 3 (PB) $25-35
Type of Beds: 2 Twin; 1 Double; 1 Queen
Full Breakfast
Credit Cards: No
Notes: 5, 7, 8, 9, 11, 13

MILESVILLE

Fitch's B&B
Old West & Badlands B&B Association
Rt. 2, Box 100A, Philip, SD, 57567
(605) 859-2120

Located three miles south of Milesville, this is a western farm home. The lady of the house quilts and weaves on a floor loom. Two baths. Full breakfast is served family-style. Joggers and walkers welcome. Free ballroom dancing lessons. $30-35.

MITCHELL

Welcome Inn
South Dakota B&B
903 North Dakota Street, Canton, 57013
(605) 987-2834

6 Pets welcome: 7 Smoking allowed: 8 Children welcome: 9 Social drinking allowed: 10 Tennis available: 11 Swimming available: 12 Golf available: 13 Skiing available: 14 May be booked through travel agents

Near the Corn Palace, Doll Museum, Indian Village. Lake Mitchell offers fishing, boating, and golf. A buffalo farm is within a mile of the house. Your host was in social work for twenty-five years and taught school for eighteen years.

Doubles: 3 (SB) $25-35
Type of Beds: 3 Double
Full Breakfast
Credit Cards: No
Notes: 5, 8 (over 4), 10, 11, 12

OKATON

Roghair's B&B
Old West & Badlands B&B Association
Rt. 2, Box 100A, Philip, SD, 57567
(605) 859-2120

Located 6.5 miles northwest of Okaton, this family with six children offers guide service and baby-sitting for your children. Guest rooms are in a separate house. Wheat and all kinds of farm animals on the premises, including a horse for experienced riders. Continental breakfast. $25-40.

PHILIP

Emerson's B&B
Old West & Badlands B&B Association
Rt. 2, Box 100A, Philip, SD, 57567
(605) 859-2120

Located 2.5 miles north of Philip on highway 73, this is a new subterranean home, heated by passive solar heat, on Lake Waggoner. Great fishing and bird watching; only thirty minutes from the Badlands. Local interests include Horne Farms and Scotchman Industries. $30-35.

Fairchild's B&B
Old West & Badlands B&B Association
Rt. 2, Box 100A, Philip, SD, 57567
(605) 859-2120

Located 23 miles north of Philip on highway 73, this family operation raises grain and livestock. Wheat, sheep, pigs, and chickens are the farm's main endeavors. $30-50.

Hewitt's B&B
Old West & Badlands B&B Association
Rt. 2, Box 100A, Philip, SD, 57567
(605) 859-2120

Located two miles north of Philip on highway 73, this modern ranch-style home was designed to harmonize with its natural setting. Grain fields, a meandering creek, grazing livestock, and a popular fishing and boating lake are nearby. Wildlife is frequently seen from the house; golf course within walking distance. Two bedrooms with private bath and family room, plus two additional bedrooms. No smoking or pets. $30-40.

Petersen's B&B
Old West & Badlands B&B Association
Rt. 2, Box 100A, Philip, SD, 57567
(605) 859-2120

Located 2.5 miles north of Philip on highway 73, this is an ideal stop on your way to the Black Hills. A new ranch-style home next to Lake Waggoner, known for its game fish; golf one mile away. Cable TV and HBO. Nonsmokers preferred, pets allowed. $30-45.

Sumpter's B&B
Old West & Badlands B&B Association
Rt. 2, Box 100A, Philip, SD, 57567
(605) 859-2120

A large, newer home with private bath, air-conditioning, and family room with pool table on a working farm with pigs, sheep, and wheat. Corrals available for livestock; lots of space for campers. $30-50.

NOTES: Credit cards accepted: A Master Card; B Visa; C American Express; D Discover Card; E Diners Club; F Other: 2 Personal checks accepted: 3 Lunch available: 4 Dinner available: 5 Open all year

Swift's B&B

Old West & Badlands B&B Association
Rt. 2, Box 100A, Philip, SD, 57567
(605) 859-2120

Located eight miles northwest of Philip. Enjoy a peaceful walk by the creek, volleyball, badminton, or a game of horseshoes. Family room with piano. Only thirty minutes from the Badlands. $25-35.

Thorson's B&B

Old West & Badlands B&B Association
Rt. 2, Box 100A, Philip, SD, 57567
(605) 859-2120

Located twelve miles north of highway 14, between Philip and Wall and near historic Old Deadwood Trail. Watch the farm's operations, walk a country mile. Laundry facilities available; no smoking. $20-35.

RAPID CITY

Audrie's Cranbury Corner B & B

RR 8, Box 2400, 57702
(605) 342-7788

Spacious rooms are furnished in comfortable European antiques, each room featuring a private entrance, private bath, fireplace, patio, hot tub, and full Black Hills style breakfast. Rapid Creek flows almost at your front door for trout fishing. Your back door opens to scenic hiking trails.

Hosts: Hank & Audry Kuhnhauser
Doubles: 3 (PB) $62.40-67.60
Type of Beds: 2 Double; 1 Queen
Full Breakfast
Notes: 2, 4, 5, 9, 11, 12

Black Forest Inn Bed & Breakfast Lodge

HC 33, Box 3123, 57702
(605) 574-2000

The beautiful main lodge has ten guest rooms and outdoor Jacuzzi, while the great room features a large stone fireplace and picture windows framing the beauty of the outdoors. Located in the heart of the Black Hills, near lakes, golf, hiking, swimming, and fishing. One-half hour from Mr. Rushmore and other historic sites.

Hosts: Bruce & Polly Ashland
Doubles: 10 (8 PB; 2 SB) $45-75
Type of Beds: 2 Twin; 4 Double; 4 Queen; 2 King
Full Breakfast
Credit Cards: A, B
Notes: 2, 7, 10, 12

VIVIAN

Moore Ranch

South Dakota B&B
903 North Dakota Street, Canton, 57013
(605) 987-2834

Fifty miles from the state capital, halfway between Sioux Falls and Rapid City, this working farm ranch is a mom and pop operation raising beef cattle. Your hosts love meeting and entertaining people.

Doubles: 3 (SB) $25-35
Type of Beds: 3 Double
Full Breakfast
Credit Cards: No
Notes: 3, 4, 5, 8

WALL

Shearer's B&B

Old West & Badlands B&B Association
Rt. 2, Box 100A, Philip, SD, 57567
(605) 859-2120

Located nine miles north of Wall, this ranch-style home has a rec room, box stalls and corrals for livestock, and a beautiful view. Private entrance and private bath are available. Extended stays could include daily ranch chores, brandings, covered-wagon and trail rides to the Badlands and Indian reservation. $30-40.

6 Pets welcome: 7 Smoking allowed: 8 Children welcome: 9 Social drinking allowed: 10 Tennis available: 11 Swimming available: 12 Golf available: 13 Skiing available: 14 May be booked through travel agents

Talty's B&B

Old West & Badlands B&B Association
Rt. 2, Box 100A, Philip, SD, 57567
(605) 859-2120

Located twenty miles southwest of Wall on a scenic road, two miles west of Badlands National Park and close to the Indian reservation and lots of wildlife. Rock and fossil hunting trips available. Bunkhouse with outside bathroom; shower in main house. Deer and antelope hunters are welcome. No smoking. $25-35.

WATERTOWN

Blue Fountain Inn

South Dakota B&B
903 North Dakota Street, Canton, 57013
(605) 987-2834

The Blue Fountain Inn features one of the finest collections of authentic Victorian furnishing in the Midwest. Near antique shops, Bramble Park Zoo, Lake Kampeska, bike trails, and two eighteen-hole golf courses. Your host is a retired magician and antique collector.

Doubles: 4 (1 PB; 3 SB) $30-55
Type of Beds: 3 Double; 1 Queen
Continental Breakfast
Credit Cards: A, B
Notes: 2, 7, 9, 10, 11, 12, 13

NOTES: Credit cards accepted: A Master Card; B Visa; C American Express; D Discover Card; E Diners Club; F Other: 2 Personal checks accepted: 3 Lunch available: 4 Dinner available: 5 Open all year

Tennessee

B&B Host Homes of Tennessee #35
Box 110227, Nashville, 37222
(800) 458-2421

Housewife and doctor in an affluent section near Maryland Farms offer a side entrance, deck, queen room with antiques and private bath, plus two single rooms upstairs with a shared bath. $28-40.

B&B Host Homes of Tennessee #36
Box 110227, Nashville, 37222
(800) 458-2421

Retired space scientist and homemaker have one queen room with single bed and couch, private bath, plus one double with antiques and a private bath. $30-40.

B&B Host Homes of Tennessee #37
Box 110227, Nashville, 37222
(800) 458-2421

Near Brentwood, this home offers one king and one double room with private balcony. Private or shared bath. $30-40.

B&B Host Homes of Tennessee #38
Box 110227, Nashville, 37222
(800) 458-2421

In Brentwood. Double room, private bath. Can also accommodate one child. No smokers; resident dog; pool in summer. $30-40.

B&B Host Homes of Tennessee #39
Box 110227, Nashville, 37222
(800) 458-2421

Log house, reviewed in a recent magazine, is furnished with antiques. Owned by an antique dealer and college professor. Three rooms, two with private baths. Lovely setting. $50-75.

B&B Host Homes of Tennessee #40
Box 110227, Nashville, 37222
(800) 458-2421

Marketing director and French teacher have one king room and two double rooms, each with private bath. $30-40.

B&B Host Homes of Tennessee #41
Box 110227, Nashville, 37222
(800) 458-2421

6 Pets welcome: 7 Smoking allowed: 8 Children welcome: 9 Social drinking allowed: 10 Tennis available: 11 Swimming available: 12 Golf available: 13 Skiing available: 14 May be booked through travel agents

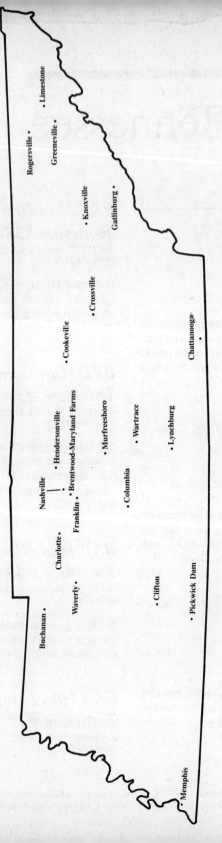

TENNESSEE

Limestone •

Rogersville •   • Greeneville

Knoxville •

Gatlinburg •

Crossville •

Cookeville •   Chattanooga •

Hendersonville •   Murfreesboro •   Wartrace •

Brentwood-Maryland Farms •   Lynchburg •

Nashville
Charlotte •   Franklin •   Columbia •

Waverly •

Buchanan •

Clifton •

Pickwick Dam •

Memphis •

Art lover has a spacious home with a double room with antiques, full bath. Plus a large bedroom with shower only and one single with shared bath. $40-55.

B&B Host Homes of Tennessee #42

Box 110227, Nashville, 37222
(800) 458-2421

Brentwood hosts have a large suite with private bath, private entrance, queen bed, patio off large pool, and backyard garden. $40-60.

B&B Host Homes of Tennessee #43

Box 110227, Nashville, 37222
(800) 458-2421

Doctor and homemaker have a beautiful home in a wooded area. There is one large twin room with private bath and one twin room with a half bath and shared tub. $45-70.

BUCHANAN

B&B Host Homes of Tennessee #B1

Box 110227, Nashville, 37222
(800) 458-2421

Near lakes and hunting areas, this host offers one large queen room and one single with sleeping loft for children. Full breakfast served. $40-65.

CHARLOTTE

B&B Host Homes of Tennessee #C1

Box 110227, Nashville, 37222
(800) 458-2421

Built in the early 1800s, this restored hotel was on the old stagecoach line. Three rooms, one with kitchen. Fifty-five miles east of Nashville and seven miles from Dickson. $35-45.

CHATTANOOGA

B&B Host Homes of Tennessee CH1

Box 110227, Nashville, 37222
(800) 458-2421

Hilltop country Victorian with porches around house, view of Lookout Mountain. Near Chicamauga and Pigeon Mountains, Rock City, and other attractions. Four rooms, three baths. $35-50.

B&B Host Homes of Tennessee CH2

Box 110227, Nashville, 37222
(800) 458-2421

Beautiful mountain-top view. Full upstairs of home with three bedrooms, bath, kitchen. No pets. $30-40.

B&B Host Homes of Tennessee CH3

Box 110227, Nashville, 37222
(800) 458-2421

6 Pets welcome: 7 Smoking allowed: 8 Children welcome: 9 Social drinking allowed: 10 Tennis available: 11 Swimming available: 12 Golf available: 13 Skiing available: 14 May be booked through travel agents

Home with view of lake, near public access for boating and fishing. Public swimming and picnic area. Food is provided, and guests prepare own breakfast. Private twin suite with bath and living room, kitchen. Near attractions, Lookout Mountain, I-24 and I-75. $50.

B&B Host Homes of Tennessee CH5

Box 110227, Nashville, 37222
(800) 458-2421

Near the Ocoee River and Deer Park; hunting and fishing. One double and one single room, bath. $26-40.

CLIFTON

B&B Host Homes of Tennessee CLF1

Box 110227, Nashville, 37222
(800) 458-2421

Two-story log cabin with four beds and bath, kitchen, living area. Porches on both sides. Hearty country breakfast served. Near the Buffalo River. Farm vacation with riding, fishing, swimming. $57-70.

COLUMBIA

B&B Host Homes of Tennessee CO1

Box 110227, Nashville, 37222
(800) 458-2421

Country home has suite with large double bedroom, private bath, private entrance, large sitting room with TV and wood-burning stove. Also one twin room with private half bath. $28-40.

B&B Host Homes of Tennessee CO2

Box 110227, Nashville, 37222
(800) 458-2421

Traditional American four-square home, circa 1900, beautiful entry hall, furnished in Eastlake and Victorian furniture. Double room with shared bath. Host is an artist. $35-45.

COOKEVILLE

B&B Host Homes of Tennessee CK1

Box 110227, Nashville, 37222
(800) 458-2421

Log house with three bedrooms, one private bath. Furnished in antiques. House has great room and three porches. $30-40.

CROSSVILLE

B&B Host Homes of Tennessee C2

Box 110227, Nashville, 37222
(800) 458-2421

Real estate broker/homemaker have a country French home with three double rooms, private baths, and two powder rooms. Six miles from I-40 on Cumberland Plateau. $45-60.

FRANKLIN

B&B Host Homes of Tennessee #44

Box 110227, Nashville, 37222
(800) 458-2421

NOTES: Credit cards accepted: A Master Card; B Visa; C American Express; D Discover Card; E Diners Club; F Other: 2 Personal checks accepted: 3 Lunch available: 4 Dinner available: 5 Open all year

Raising cattle and Arabian horses on this working farm, an actress and homemaker has one double with an antique iron bed, one single, and a unique Japanese room complete with sleeping mats and Japanese garden. Prefers nonsmokers. $30-40.

B&B Host Homes of Tennessee #45

Box 110227, Nashville, 37222
(800) 458-2421

Retired schoolteacher who loves to cook has one double room with private bath. Guests may enjoy TV in the den and explore the large yard. $30-40.

B&B Host Homes of Tennessee #46

Box 110227, Nashville, 37222
(800) 458-2421

TV manager and nurse have a cottage in a walled garden with swimming pool. Cottage is done in wicker, has a full kitchen, living room, and loft bedroom. Two night minimum; weekly rate available. $75.

Buckhorn Inn

B&B Host Homes of Tennessee #47

Box 110227, Nashville, 37222
(800) 458-2421

Historical Register home, furnished with antiques, is owned by a music professional who has a recording studio attached. One double and one twin antique room with sitting areas. $60-75.

GATLINBURG

B&B Host Homes of Tennessee GA1

Box 110227, Nashville, 37222
(800) 458-2421

Twelve miles from Gatlinburg, this three-bedroom chalet has a hot tub, wood stove, full kitchen. Can sleep eight. $70-125.

B&B Host Homes of Tennessee GA3

Box 110227, Nashville, 37222
(800) 458-2421

Contractor and homemaker have two complete suites with private baths, double beds, kitchen, living room. Secluded, with lots of trees — nice walking area. Seven miles from Gatlinburg. $75.

Buckhorn Inn

Rt. 3, Box 393, 37738
(615) 436-4668

Buckhorn Inn is set in the seclusion of quiet woodlands, its white-columned porch overlooking a wide vista of Mt. LeConte, blue-gray mountains, and green hills. The inn was built in 1938 on 25 acres of grass meadows, woodlands, and a spring-fed lake.

6 Pets welcome: 7 Smoking allowed: 8 Children welcome: 9 Social drinking allowed: 10 Tennis available: 11 Swimming available: 12 Golf available: 13 Skiing available: 14 May be booked through travel agents

Monthaven

Hosts: John & Connie Burns
Doubles: 11 (PB) $65-95
Full Breakfast
Credit Cards: No
Closed Christmas Eve and Day
Notes: 2, 4, 5, 7 (restricted), 8, 9, 10, 11, 12, 13

Tudor Mountain Inn

Rt. 3, Box 409, Tudor Mt. Road, 37738
(615) 436-4947

Located on the side of a small mountain
2,000 feet above sea level. Less than a mile
from the Great Smoky Mountain National
Park. Superb vistas of the highest peaks in
the Smokies from the bedroom and deck.
Quiet, secluded setting. Hiking information
available.

Hosts: Kathy & Hugh Welch
Doubles: 1 (PB) $75
Full Breakfast
Credit Cards: No
Notes: 2, 3, 5, 8, 9, 10, 11, 12, 13, 14

GREENEVILLE

B&B Host Homes of Tennessee G2

Box 110227, Nashville, 37222
(800) 458-2421

Country home close to Crockett birthplace
and Jonesboro. Home built in 1815, full of
antiques. Back porch with view of the mountains. Two double rooms, private or shared
bath. $35-40.

Big Spring Inn

315 N. Main Street, 37743
(615) 638-2917

A three-story circa 1905 manor house in the
historic district that includes homes built
from 1783 to 1900 and the home of President Andrew Johnson. The inn has nearly 2
acres of trees and gardens, and a pool. We
love to cook, and our breakfast is definitely
a treat. Near the Smokies, white-water rafting, hiking, riding, and antiques.

Hosts: Jeanne Driese & Cheryl Van Dyck
Doubles: 5 (3 PB; 2 SB) $55-75
Type of Beds: 1 Twin; 6 Double; 1 King
Full Breakfast
Credit Cards: A, B, C
Notes: 2, 4, 5, 7 (limited), 9, 10, 11, 12, 14

HENDERSONVILLE

Monthaven

1154 Main Street West, 37075
(615) 824-6319

NOTES: Credit cards accepted: A Master Card; B Visa; C American Express; D Discover Card; E Diners
Club; F Other: 2 Personal checks accepted: 3 Lunch available: 4 Dinner available: 5 Open all year

On the National Register of Historic Places, Monthaven offers both a heritage of nearly 200 years and a 75 acre estate for the enjoyment of visitors to Nashville and middle Tennessee. The main house served as a field hospital during the Civil War.

Host: Hugh Waddell
Doubles: 4 (2 PB; 2 SB) $40
Log Cabin: $75
Suite: $60
Type of Beds: 3 Twin; 1 Double; 4 Queen
Continental Breakfast
Credit Cards: Most major cards accepted
Notes: 2, 5, 6, 7, 8, 9, 10, 11, 12

KNOXVILLE

B&B Host Homes of Tennessee K1

Box 110227, Nashville, 37222
(800) 458-2421

This is an eighteenth-century hotel. Some units have Jacuzzi. Near the University and downtown; walking distance to good restaurants. Concierge service. $60-125.

B&B Host Homes of Tennessee K2

Box 110227, Nashville, 37222
(800) 458-2421

One king room with private bath and one double room with crib. Residential area; swimming pool in season. $30-40.

B&B Host Homes of Tennessee K3

Box 110227, Nashville, 37222
(800) 458-2421

Caterer and her husband have a charming home in a wooded area with a hot tub. One suite with private bath. Lake privileges. An intimate gourmet dinner will be served by appointment at an additional charge.

Stained-glass windows, cathedral ceilings, boat dock, free canoe. $70.

LIMESTONE

Snapp Inn Bed & Breakfast

Rt. 3, Box 102, 37681
(615) 257-3986

Your hosts will welcome you into this gracious 1815 Federal home furnished with antiques and set in farm country. Enjoy the mountain view from the full back porch or play a game of pool or horseshoes. Close to Davy Crockett Birthplace Park; fifteen-minute drive to historic Jonesborough or Greeneville.

Hosts: Dan & Ruth Dorgan
Doubles: 2 (SB) $40-50
Type of Beds: 2 Double; 1 Cot
Full Breakfast
Credit Cards: No
Notes: 2, 4, 5, 6, 8, 9, 11, 12

LYNCHBURG

Lynchburg Bed & Breakfast

Box 34, 37352
(615) 759-7158

This nineteenth-century home is located within walking distance of the Jack Daniel distillery. Each spacious room features carefully selected antiques. Formerly the home of the first Moore County sheriff (1877).

Host: Virginia Tipps
Doubles: 2 (PB) $38-45
Type of Beds: 1 Double; 1 Queen
Continental Breakfast
Credit Cards: A, B
Notes: 5, 7, 9, 10, 12, 14

MEMPHIS

April House

1320 Central/Lamar, 38104
(901) 726-6970

6 Pets welcome: 7 Smoking allowed: 8 Children welcome: 9 Social drinking allowed: 10 Tennis available: 11 Swimming available: 12 Golf available: 13 Skiing available: 14 May be booked through travel agents

Located in the Central Gardens area of Memphis, five minutes from major hospitals; Memphis International Airport, fifteen minutes; Beale Street and the Mississippi River, fifteen minutes; Elvis's Graceland, twenty minutes.

Host: Nate Bedford
Singles: 3 (PB) $60
Doubles: 5 (PB) $75
Type of Beds: 8 Double
Full Breakfast
Minimum Stay: 2
Credit Cards: No
Notes: 4, 5, 7, 8, 9

B&B Host Homes of Tennessee M1

Box 110227, Nashville, 37222
(800) 458-2421

This mansion, originally built in 1901, is in the National Registry of Homes. Three large rooms, private baths. One extra-large room. All rooms have period furniture and share a bright sitting room. $50-55.

B&B Host Homes of Tennessee M2

Box 110227, Nashville, 37222
(800) 458-2421

Private studio, bath, pullman kitchen, TV, twin beds, and cot. Children welcome; crib available. Porch and garden patio. $32-40.

B&B Host Homes of Tennessee M3

Box 110227, Nashville, 37222
(800) 458-2421

Whitehaven area guest house sleeps four. Refrigerator, private sitting room, private entrance. $30-40.

B&B Host Homes of Tennessee M4

Box 110227, Nashville, 37222
(800) 458-2421

Private bedroom and bath in Germantown. Two double rooms with private or shared bath. Resident dog; no smoking. $30-40.

B&B Host Homes of Tennessee M5

Box 110227, Nashville, 37222
(800) 458-2421

Raleigh. One large twin room, TV, couch. Double room also available. Dog in residence. Hosts are avid travelers. Ten minutes from the medical center and downtown. $30-40.

B&B Host Homes of Tennessee M6

Box 110227, Nashville, 37222
(800) 458-2421

Guest house with one twin and one double room. There is also a double room in the main house with a private bath. $30-45.

B&B Host Homes of Tennessee M7

Box 110227, Nashville, 37222
(800) 458-2421

Victorian double room, with private bath and TV. Also available are one double and one twin with private or shared bath. $30-40.

B&B Host Homes of Tennessee M9

Box 110227, Nashville, 37222
(800) 458-2421

NOTES: Credit cards accepted: A Master Card; B Visa; C American Express; D Discover Card; E Diners Club; F Other: 2 Personal checks accepted: 3 Lunch available: 4 Dinner available: 5 Open all year

Quiet elegance in the center of midtown. An Indiana stone home constructed in 1911, near the downtown area and other attractions. Two double rooms with private baths; two with shared bath. $45-50.

B&B in Memphis #D-0305
Box 41621, Memphis, 38174
(901) 726-5920

On the bluff overlooking the mighty Mississippi River, this condo allows you to watch the spectacular sunsets and riverboats from a plant-filled patio. Panoramic view from windows spanning two stories. Modern luxury condominium with 24-hour security. Your hostess is a small-business owner. One Queen room, $80.

B&B in Memphis #E-1712
Box 41621, Memphis, 38174
(901) 726-5920

Gracious East Memphis home with private suite. Separate entrance, large living room, bedroom, each with bay window overlooking lush trees. Sun-drenched kitchen, full bath, laundry room shared with delightful host family. Near Laurelwood shopping, fine restaurants, Dixon Gallery & Gardens, Licherman Nature Center, Botanical Gardens, expressway. One Queen, $50.74.

B&B in Memphis #G-1903
Box 41621, Memphis, 38174
(901) 726-5920

This friendly executive and his wife enjoy welcoming out-of-town travelers to their large home in Germantown. Spacious guest room with pineapple twin beds, office area with copy machine, typewriter, and phone. No indoor smoking. One twin-bedded room, $38.33-45.10.

B&B in Memphis #G-3801
Box 41621, Memphis, 38174
(901) 726-5920

Elegant country home in fashionable Germantown. Enjoy the 5-acre lake view, formal English gardens, gazebo, library, and Grecian pool. Choice of upstairs or downstairs suite with sitting room. Hostess is a popular interior designer. Near excellent shopping, fine restaurants, Lichterman Nature Center, and the Germantown business center. Two double-bedded rooms, $73.28.

B&B in Memphis #M-0403
Box 41621, Memphis, 38174
(901) 726-5920

On a quiet, tree-lined street in a charming midtown neighborhood. Private upstairs area of a tastefully furnished bungalow. Newly redecorated and fresh, this is a favorite respite for weary businesswomen, who feel right at home here. Hostess is a savvy marketing pro. Enjoy the lush trees, inviting porch swing, and more. Near downtown, the expressway, and the medical center. One room, $38.33-45.10.

B&B of Memphis #M-1106
Box 41621, Memphis, 38174-1621
(901) 726-5920

Walk to Memphis State campus from this beautifully furnished home with private entrance. Suite upstairs features bedroom, refreshment area where your continental breakfast will be stocked, living room, full bath. No smoking. Close to Memphis Pink Palace, Theatre Memphis, Memphis State Theatre, Rhodes College. Two twins and one queen sleeper, $38.33-45.10.

6 Pets welcome: 7 Smoking allowed: 8 Children welcome: 9 Social drinking allowed: 10 Tennis available: 11 Swimming available: 12 Golf available: 13 Skiing available: 14 May be booked through travel agents

B&B of Memphis #M-1200

Box 41621, Memphis, 38174
(901) 726-5920

Walk to Rhodes College and the wonderful Memphis Zoo from this beautiful older home in prestigious Hein Park. Formal gardens off-street parking. Choice of upstairs suite with kitchen or downstairs king bedroom. Two twin, one double, one king, $29.31-45.10.

Lowenstein-Long House

Lowenstein-Long House

217 N. Waldran, 38105
(901) 527-7174

A beautifully restored Victorian mansion near downtown, listed on the National Registry of Historic Places. Convenient to all major tourist attractions: Mississippi River, Graceland, Beale Street, the Memphis Zoo, Brooks Museum, and Victorian Village. Free off-street parking.

Hosts: Walter & Samantha Long
Doubles: 4 (PB) $50
Type of Beds: 4 Queen
Continental-plus Breakfast
Credit Cards: A, B, C
Notes: 2, 5, 7 (limited), 8, 9, 10, 11, 12, 14

MURFREESBORO

Clardy's Guest House

435 E. Main Street, 37130
(615) 893-6030

Located in the historic district, this twenty-room Victorian Romanesque home is filled with antiques and features ornate woodwork and fireplaces. An eight-by-eight-foot stained-glass window overlooks the magnificent staircase. The area has much to offer history buffs and antique shoppers. We are thirty miles from Nashville, just two miles off I-24.

Hosts: Robert & Barbara Deaton
Doubles: 6 (2 PB; 4 SB) $20-35
Type of Beds: 6 Double
Continental Breakfast
Credit Cards: No
Notes: 2, 5, 7, 8, 9, 10, 11, 12

NASHVILLE

B&B Host Homes of Tennessee #1

Box 110227, Nashville, 37222
(800) 458-2421

Retired couple has one king room with TV and one double room with a private bath. Near bus and shopping; Opryland three miles. One double and one king, $28-40.

B&B Host Homes of Tennessee #2

Box 110227, Nashville, 37222
(800) 458-2421

This house, once used as a hospital in the Civil War, is on the Historical Registry. Furnished in antiques. Two double rooms, one private bath, one shared bath, $65-75.

NOTES: Credit cards accepted: A Master Card; B Visa; C American Express; D Discover Card; E Diners Club; F Other: 2 Personal checks accepted: 3 Lunch available: 4 Dinner available: 5 Open all year

B&B Host Homes of Tennessee #3

Box 110227, Nashville, 37222
(800) 458-2421

Hosts like cards and crafts. Dog in residence. Two miles from Opryland. Two double rooms, one private bath, one shared bath, $30-40.

B&B Host Homes of Tennessee #4

Box 110227, Nashville, 37222
(800) 458-2421

Large new home with a lovely view. Near large shopping center, park, country music sights, and Opryland. Also available: trailer that sleeps four. Three rooms: one private bath, two shared bath, $32-50.

B&B Host Homes of Tennessee #5

Box 110227, Nashville, 37222
(800) 458-2421

Luxury guest house with great room, fireplace, grand piano, exercise room with Jacuzzi and sauna, kitchen, swimming pool, lake. Five rooms: three private bath, two shared bath, $45-80.

B&B Host Homes of Tennessee #6

Box 110227, Nashville, 37222
(800) 458-2421

Suite with two double rooms, large bath, private entrance, TV, large den, private pond for fishing. $45-60.

B&B Host Homes of Tennessee #7

Box 110227, Nashville, 37222
(800)458-2421

Log house, made of cedar logs, sitting on the Cumberland. One double room with private bath. Sit and watch all the river activity. $40-50.

B&B Host Homes of Tennessee #8

Box 110227, Nashville, 37222
(800) 458-2421

Twin room with private bath, sitting room with two sofas, double room with private bath. No smoking. $30-40.

B&B Host Homes of Tennessee #9

Box 110227, Nashville, 37222
(800) 458-2421

Near Opryland. Twin room in new condo with private bath. One couple or woman only. $30-40.

B&B Host Homes of Tennessee #9A

Box 110227, Nashville, 37222
(800) 458-2421

Newly built guest house with large bedroom/den, private bath, and walk-in closet. TV. Beautifully decorated. $50-75.

B&B Host Homes of Tennessee #10

Box 110227, Nashville, 37222
(800) 458-2421

6 Pets welcome: 7 Smoking allowed: 8 Children welcome: 9 Social drinking allowed: 10 Tennis available: 11 Swimming available: 12 Golf available: 13 Skiing available: 14 May be booked through travel agents

International sales manager and homemaker have one twin room with private bath. Near lake for boating and fishing. Guests may swim and play tennis on the property. Opryland seven miles. $30-40.

B&B Host Homes of Tennessee #11

Box 110227, Nashville, 37222
(800) 458-2421

Conveniently located near the airport, this house has one twin, one double, one queen, with a private or shared bath. Swimming pool in summer. Also available: suite with double room, sitting area, private entrance, bath, Jacuzzi, and swimming pool. $28-50.

B&B Host Homes of Tennessee #12

Box 110227, Nashville, 37222
(800) 458-2421

Near Nissan, this host has a double room and single hide-a-bed with desk. Private or shared bath. $28-38.

B&B Host Homes of Tennessee #13

Box 110227, Nashville, 37222
(800) 458-2421

The only house in downtown Nashville. Built in 1859, this house has twelve-foot ceilings and fireplaces. One block from the convention center; Opryland fifteen minutes. Rooms furnished in antiques. Private or shared bath. $45-65.

B&B Host Homes of Tennessee #14

Box 110227, Nashville, 37222
(800) 458-2421

Large, airy sun porch in the treetops in a downtown flat. Single lady host requests women guests only. Shared bath. Three flights up, near Vanderbilt and good restaurants. $32-42.

B&B Host Homes of Tennessee #15

Box 110227, Nashville, 37222
(800) 458-2421

Condo on the river near Riverfront Park. Double room with private bath. City view is lovely at night. Den with fireplace. $37-50.

B&B Host Homes of Tennessee #16

Box 110227, Nashville, 37222
(800) 458-2421

Near Vanderbilt, this house has a large double room with sitting area, dressing room, private bath. Beautifully furnished; near Belle Meade Shopping Center. Another large upstairs room is also available. $38-50.

B&B Host Homes of Tennessee #17

Box 110227, Nashville, 37222
(800) 458-2421

Three blocks from Vanderbilt. Twin room with private bath. Ladies or couples only. $28-38.

NOTES: Credit cards accepted: A Master Card; B Visa; C American Express; D Discover Card; E Diners Club; F Other: 2 Personal checks accepted: 3 Lunch available: 4 Dinner available: 5 Open all year

B&B Host Homes of Tennessee #18

Box 110227, Nashville, 37222
(800) 458-2421

Retired school consultant will take one lady, nonsmoker. Across street from bus. Shared bath. $35.

B&B Host Homes of Tennessee #19

Box 110227, Nashville, 37222
(800) 458-2421

Lovely Tudor in the desirable Green Hills area, charmingly filled with antiques. Host likes traveling and meeting people, prefers nonsmokers. Two double rooms with private bath; near bus line. $40-50.

B&B Host Homes of Tennessee #20

Box 110227, Nashville, 37222.
(800) 458-2421

Movie studio art director has one double master bedroom with private bath that shares a sunny sitting room with a suite with pullman kitchen and fireplace. House done in antiques. Well located. $45-70.

B&B Host Homes of Tennessee #21

Box 110227, Nashville, 37222
(800) 458-2421

West Nashville condo owned by an interior designer. Two rooms with private or shared bath. $30-40.

B&B Host Homes of Tennessee #22

Box 110227, Nashville, 37222
(800) 458-2421

Luxury suite west of Nashville with a beautiful view. French Provincial suite with private entrance, patio, marble bath, large kitchen, living room with fireplace, king bedroom. No smokers, no pets; one child okay. Near private lake for swimming, golf, and hiking. $70-80.

B&B Host Homes of Tennessee #23

Box 110227, Nashville, 37222
(800) 458-2421

Small guesthouse with twin beds, bath, TV. Adjoins 24' aboveground pool. Wooded area, very quiet. $35-65.

B&B Host Homes of Tennessee #24

Box 110227, Nashville, 37222
(800) 458-2421

Interior designer has an elegantly decorated, chalet-type condo on a babbling brook. Two-story deck, beautiful pool, two tennis courts, hiking, and playground. $40-60.

B&B Host Homes of Tennessee #25

Box 110227, Nashville, 37222
(800) 458-2421

Restored church in the historical register. One antique double with sitting area and private bath; one Louis XIV double with private bath; contemporary loft that can sleep four with double bed, Jacuzzi. $50-60.

6 Pets welcome: 7 Smoking allowed: 8 Children welcome: 9 Social drinking allowed: 10 Tennis available: 11 Swimming available: 12 Golf available: 13 Skiing available: 14 May be booked through travel agents

B&B Host Homes of Tennessee #26

Box 110227, Nashville, 37222
(800) 458-2421

Furniture sales rep and homemaker have two double rooms with private or shared bath. Horses on premises that may be ridden when hosts are present. $30-40.

B&B Host Homes of Tennessee #27

Box 110227, Nashville, 37222
(800) 458-2421

Retired sales rep and homemaker have a twin room with private bath near a large shopping center and Vanderbilt. Den with TV is shared with hosts. $30-40.

B&B Host Homes of Tennessee #28

Box 110227, Nashville, 37222
(800) 458-2421

Near I-65 South, this home has one king room, one queen room, one double room with private or shared bath. Host is a teacher who loves music and prefers nonsmokers. $30-40.

B&B Host Homes of Tennessee #29

Box 110227, Nashville, 37222
(800) 458-2421

Teacher shares two double rooms with private baths in a beautiful home. Large yard with patio for relaxing. $30-40.

B&B Host Homes of Tennessee #30

Box 110227, Nashville, 37222
(800) 458-2421

Librarian and printer have two double rooms with antiques. History buffs, ham radio, Spanish-speaking. Nonsmokers. Resident cat. $32-40.

B&B Host Homes of Tennessee #31

Box 110227, Nashville, 37222
(800) 458-2421

Insurance broker and nurse have one double and one twin room near major interstates and convenient to colleges. $30-40.

B&B Host Homes of Tennessee #32

Box 110227, Nashville, 37222
(800) 458-2421

Hosts who are rose growers have one double room and one twin with private or shared bath. $30-40.

Hachland Hill Inn

Hachland Hill Inn

5396 Rawlings Road, 37222
(615) 255-1727

A secluded dining inn 15 minutes from downtown Nashville. A perfect executive retreat or for family reunions or honeymooners. Each day, renowned author and chef Phila Hach will provide you with unforgettable cuisine from the grand old South. Accommodations are in a historic log house brimming with museum antiques.

Host: Phila Hach
Singles: 10 (PB) $48.50
Doubles: 15 (PB) $60
Type of Beds: 8 Twin; 10 Double
Full Breakfast
Credit Cards: C
Notes: 2, 4, 5, 6, 7, 8, 9, 14

Ledford Mill

Miss Anne's Bed & Breakfast

3033 Windemere Circle, 37214
(615) 885-1899

Miss Anne's is a cozy little place filled with antiques and collectibles. Breakfast includes home-baked goodies and southern cooking. We are located one and one-half miles from Opryland and are convenient to all other Nashville attractions.

Hosts: Robin & Ann Cowell
Doubles: 4 (SB) $35-40
Type of Beds: 3 Twin; 2 Double; 1 Queen
Full Breakfast
Minimum stay weekends: 2
Credit Cards: No
Notes: 2, 5, 9, 11, 12

Homestead House Inn

PICKWICK DAM

Homestead House Inn

Box 76, 38365
(901) 689-5500

The Homestead House Inn is a 75-year-old house located approximately twenty miles from Shiloh Military Park and Battleground. The original house was built in 1843 and served as a hospital for both Union and Confederate troops during the Civil War. Jesse and Frank James also stayed here between bank robberies. The hosts serve a continental breakfast and offer quiet surroundings and a peaceful night's rest.

Hosts: Stephen & Mary Lee Virginia
Doubles: 5 (2 PB; 3 SB) $32.50-45
Type of Beds: 6 Twin; 2 Queen
Continental Breakfast
Credit Cards: A, B, C
Closed Jan. & Feb.
Notes: 7 (restricted), 8 (12 and over), 9, 10, 11, 12

ROGERSVILLE

Hale Springs Inn

110 W. Main Street, 37857
(615) 272-5171

Elegant, three-story Federal brick building built in 1824; the oldest continuously run inn in Tennessee. Beautifully furnished with antiques from the period. Some of the rooms feature four-poster canopy beds, and all rooms have working fireplaces.

Host: Sharon Jaques
Doubles: 9 (PB) $32.48-64.95
Type of Beds: 3 Twin; 10 Double
Continental Breakfast
Credit Cards: A, B, C
Notes: 2, 4, 5, 7, 8, 10, 11

WARTRACE

Ledford Mill

R2, Box 152, 37183
(615) 455-2546

A private hideaway where you are the only guests in our cozy, open suite with kitchenette. Spend the night in a nineteenth-century grist mill, listening to the waterfalls and murmuring waters of Shippmaus Creek.

Hosts: Norma & Bill Rigler
Suite: 1 (PB) $60
Type of Beds: 1 Double; 1 Queen higdaway
Continental Breakfast

Credit Cards: A, B, C
Notes: 2, 5, 6, 7, 8, 9, 10, 11

WAVERLY

Nolan House Bed & Breakfast Inn

Rt. 4, Box 164, Highway 13N, 37185
(615) 296-2511

The Nolan House is an 1870 restored Victorian on the National Register. It has a dog trot, cisterns, cellars, original gardens, and old family graveyard. Located 7.5 miles from Loretta Lynn's Dude Ranch and 10 from Nathan Bedford Forest State Park.

Hosts: Gordon & LaVerne Turner
Doubles: 4 (PB) $30-35
Type of Beds: 3 Double
Full Breakfast
Credit Cards: No
Closed Jan. & Feb.
Notes: 2, 8, 9, 14

NOTES: Credit cards accepted: A Master Card; B Visa; C American Express; D Discover Card; E Diners Club; F Other: 2 Personal checks accepted: 3 Lunch available: 4 Dinner available: 5 Open all year

Texas

Betty Ann's Ranch B&B

B&B Texas Style
4224 W. Red Bird Lane
Dallas, TX, 75237
(214) 298-5433; (214) 298-8586

This large home just north of Abilene has a swimming pool, lighted tennis courts, a weight room, and three bedrooms in a separate suite. One room has a private bath with either a king bed or twins. The other two rooms share a bath, and each has a queen bed. TV in the guest room, fishing in the nearby creek, and great restaurants just minutes away. Full breakfast. $45-50.

Parkview House

AMARILLO

Parkview House

1311 S. Jefferson, 79101
(806) 373-9464

This turn-of-the-century Prairie Victorian located in the heart of the Texas Panhandle has been lovingly restored by the present owners to capture its original charm. Furnished with antiques and comfortably updated, it has a large family TV room and parlor for reading or listening to music. Convenient to a park, biking, jogging, hiking, and the prize-winning musical drama, "Texas" in Pale Duro State Park. Near the Panhandle Historical Museum and Lake Meredith.

Hosts: Nabil & Carol Dia
Doubles: 4 (SB) $45-55
Suite: 1 (PB) $75
Type of Beds: 1 Double; 4 Queen
Continental-plus Breakfast
Credit Cards: A, B
Notes: 2, 5, 8, 9, 10, 11, 12

ARLINGTON

Meadow Brook

B&B Texas Style
4224 W. Red Bird Lane
Dallas, TX, 75237
(214) 298-5433; (214) 298-8586

Right next to a golf course and convenient to both Dallas and Fort Worth. Near the Texas Ranger Stadium, the University of Texas, and Six Flags Amusement Park, this B&B has one guest room with a pull-down bed and private bath in a private wing. Continental-plus breakfast, two dogs in residence, no smoking. $45-48.

Texas Hacienda

B&B Texas Style
4224 W. Red Bird Lane
Dallas, TX, 75237
(214) 298-5433; (214) 298-8586

6 Pets welcome: 7 Smoking allowed: 8 Children welcome: 9 Social drinking allowed: 10 Tennis available: 11 Swimming available: 12 Golf available: 13 Skiing available: 14 May be booked through travel agents

TEXAS

A magnificent home on the edge of Arlington near east Fort Worth and Arlington Lake. This home has four guest rooms, a swimming pool, and a hot tub. Two rooms with private baths, and two rooms that share a bath. Continental breakfast. $50-60.

AUSTIN

The Brook House

B&B Texas Style
4224 W. Red Bird Lane
Dallas, TX, 75237
(214) 298-5433; (214) 298-8586

A charming country inn just seven blocks from the university and ten minutes from downtown. Two bedrooms in the main home share a hall bath and open out to the upstairs veranda. The carriage house and an apartment are across the back garden. All guests have their breakfast in the main house's family kitchen or may request a tray in their rooms. $49.50-75.

LaPrelle Place Bed & Breakfast

B&B Texas Style
4224 W. Red Bird Lane
Dallas, TX, 75237
(214) 298-5433; (214) 298-8586

Discover the magic of Austin's past while experiencing the beauty of the present in this premier home just south of the Colorado River. Victorian decor with fine antiques. Four guest bedrooms, each with a private bath; hot tub; deck overlooking the garden. Continental breakfast is served in the formal dining room or in the common area upstairs that overlooks the garden. From $45-65.

The McCallum House

613 West 32nd Street, 78705
(512) 451-6744

The historic McCallum House, an Austin landmark, is ten blocks north of the University of Texas, twenty blocks north of the Texas Capitol. All rooms have period furnishings and telephones. Three have private porches; three have kitchen facilities; one is a large, three-room apartment.

Hosts: Nancy & Roger Danley
Doubles: 4 (PB) $40-60
Type of Beds: 6 Twin; 1 Double; 2 Queen
Full Breakfast
Minimum stay holidays: 2
Credit Cards: A, B
Notes: 2, 5, 8, 9, 10, 11, 12

Onion Creek

B&B Texas Style
4224 W. Red Bird Lane
Dallas, TX, 75237
(214) 298-5433; (214) 298-8586

On the south side of Austin, located near the Onion Creek golf course, this lovely condominium is hosted by a world traveler who enjoys needlework and crafts. The condo is just twenty-five minutes from San Marcos and fifteen from downtown Austin. One guest room with twin beds and a private bath. A continental breakfast is served weekdays and a hearty full Texas breakfast on weekends. The community offers a swimming pool, tennis courts, jogging trails. Smoking is allowed. $40-45.

Zilker Park

B&B Texas Style
4224 W. Red Bird Lane
Dallas, TX, 75237
(214) 298-5433; (214) 298-8586

This hostess is willing to give guided tours of the city — she works as a tour guide for a local agent. The guest room has a double bed, private bath, and a sofa. There's a pool out back, and the home sits on a hill. Full breakfast, no smoking. $40-45.

---

6 Pets welcome: 7 Smoking allowed: 8 Children welcome: 9 Social drinking allowed: 10 Tennis available: 11 Swimming available: 12 Golf available: 13 Skiing available: 14 May be booked through travel agents

BACLIFF

Small Inn

4815 S. Bayshore, 77518
(713) 339-3489

See ocean freighters, sailboats, and pelicans
from poolside while enjoying your breakfast,
then fish from our private pier, spend the
day touring NASA, the Astrodome in Houston, or head for Galveston and Sea-Arama,
Victorian homes, a railroad museum, or the
beach. Boat rental, jet skiing, and parasailing
are all minutes away. This home welcomes
families.

Hosts: George & Harriet Small
Doubles: 1 (PB) $50
Type of Beds: 1 King
Full Breakfast
Credit Cards: No
Notes: 3, 4, 5, 7, 8, 9, 10, 11, 12, 14

BAYSIDE

Bayside Inn

B&B Texas Style
4224 W. Red Bird Lane
Dallas, TX, 75237
(214) 298-5433; (214) 298-8586

Right on the water at Copano Bay, this inn
was built about 1870. There are ten
bedrooms, eight with double beds and two
with twins. Nearby attractions include
Arkansas Pass Wildlife Refuge, with whooping cranes, and Goose Island, well-know for
its huge trees. Full country breakfast is
served; dinner is available with reservations.
Sun on the upstairs deck; fish off the wharf
in front, play pool, or watch TV in the den.
$30-35.

BELTON

The Belle of Belton

B&B Texas Style
4224 W. Red Bird Lane

Dallas, TX, 75237
(214) 298-5433; (214) 298-8586

A beautiful antebellum home right in town
with five bedrooms, three with private baths.
The downstairs bedroom has a fireplace that
actually works — a wonder for most restored
historical buildings. Breakfast is an
elaborate continental, with quiche or croissants, fresh fruit, and specially blended cof-
fees or teas, served in the dining room.
$40-50.

BIG SANDY

Annie's Bed & Breakfast

B&B Texas Style
4224 W. Red Bird Lane
Dallas, TX, 75237
(214) 298-5433; (214) 298-8586

This fascinating inn has thirteen bedrooms,
each individually decorated with cozy quilts,
floral wallpapers, and special antiques.
There are small refrigerators in each room
for soft drinks and fruit. Breakfast is served
in Annie's Tea Room, a historical home that
has been converted into a charming restaurant. Crafts and festivals on the premises;
no smoking. $48-173.

BRYAN

Creekway

B&B Texas Style
4224 W. Red Bird Lane
Dallas, TX, 75237
(214) 298-5433; (214) 298-8586

A contemporary home right in the middle of
town and just ten minutes or less from Texas
A&M University. Three guest rooms share
two bathrooms. Resident cats are confined
to the owners' area; smoking outside only.
Continental breakfast, $40-45.

NOTES: Credit cards accepted: A Master Card; B Visa; C American Express; D Discover Card; E Diners
Club; F Other: 2 Personal checks accepted: 3 Lunch available: 4 Dinner available: 5 Open all year

BURNET

Rocky Rest Bed & Breakfast

B&B Texas Style
4224 W. Red Bird Lane
Dallas, TX, 75237
(214) 298-5433; (214) 298-8586

This stone historical home is a fine example of early Texas architecture, built in 1860 by Civil War General Adam Johnson. It has thick walls and high windows to protect against Indian attacks and once served as a schoolhouse. There are four guest bedrooms and two shared baths. A full Texas breakfast is served in the grand dining room, the cozy kitchen, or the warm den. $55-60.

BURTON-BRENHAM

The Long Point Inn

B&B Texas Style
4224 W. Red Bird Lane
Dallas, TX, 75237
(214) 298-5433; (214) 298-8586

This new inn on a 160 acre cattle ranch is owned by a retired colonel and his wife. Two guest rooms, one with antique German sleigh twin beds covered with Texas quilts. The upstairs room has a double bed, a balcony, and private bath. The downstairs room also has a private bath. Breakfast is full gourmet with Texas grits, sausage and eggs, homemade breads or rolls, fruit cup, and beverages, all served on china, sterling, and crystal. Limited smoking, children welcome. $50-65.

CANYON

The Hudspeth House

B&B Texas Style
4224 W. Red Bird Lane
Dallas, TX, 75237
(214) 298-5433; (214) 298-8586

This house was once occupied by Georgia O'Keefe, famous American artist who taught at West Texas State University in town. It has six guest rooms, two with private baths. Breakfast is served in the main dining hall on the first floor and includes homemade breads, special jam and honey, fresh fruit, juice, coffee, or milk. No indoor smoking. $55-85.

Pine Colony Inn

CARROLLTON

Oriental Delight

B&B Texas Style
4224 W. Red Bird Lane
Dallas, TX, 75237
(214) 298-5433; (214) 298-8586

An outgoing couple who have lived for many years in the Far East now open their home and one bedroom to guests. Just ten minutes to Addison and fifteen to downtown Dallas, this B&B offers a queen bedroom with private bath. A full breakfast is served, and there are small dogs in residence. $40-50.

CEDAR CREEK LAKE

Lakeside

B&B Texas Style
4224 W. Red Bird Lane
Dallas, TX, 75237
(214) 298-5433; (214) 298-8586

6 Pets welcome: 7 Smoking allowed: 8 Children welcome: 9 Social drinking allowed: 10 Tennis available: 11 Swimming available: 12 Golf available: 13 Skiing available: 14 May be booked through travel agents

This new home is right on the water. It features two bedrooms with an adjoining bath and a hot tub on the deck just outside the private entrance of the main guest room. Fish off the wharf, swim, or just sit and watch the water. There's a fireplace for cool evenings and a bowl of popcorn. Small dog in residence, smoking outside only. $55-65.

CENTER

Pine Colony Inn

500 Shelbyville Street, 75935
(409) 598-7700

This gracious old hotel is located a few short miles from the Texas State Railroad between Rusk and Palestine. The Pine Colony Inn has enough room to house a B&B convention, with twelve guest rooms, each with unique decor, antiques, collectibles, and lace curtains.

Hosts: Regina Wright & Marcille Hughes
Doubles: 12 (1 PB; 11 SB) $27-55
Type of Beds: 12 Double
Full Breakfast
Credit Cards: A, B
Notes: 5, 8, 9, 10, 11, 12

CHAPPELL HILL

The Browning Plantation

Rt. 1, Box 8, 77426
(409) 836-6144

This three-story antebellum home on a 220-acre working plantation is in the National Register. All antique furnishings, pool, and model railroad. The area is known for its antiques, horse farms, and historical significance. Sixty miles northwest of Houston on Highway 290.

Hosts: Dick & Mildred Ganchan
Doubles: 6 (2 PB; 4 SB) $75-110
Type of Beds: 4 Twin; 2 Double; 4 Queen
Full Breakfast
Credit Cards: No
Notes: 2, 5, 8 (over 12), 9, 11, 12, 14

The Browning Plantation

CLEBURNE

The Cleburne Guesthouse

B&B Texas Style
4224 W. Red Bird Lane
Dallas, TX, 75237
(214) 298-5433; (214) 298-8586

This historic home has been restored and beautifully furnished by the owners. There are three bedrooms, one with a private bath. Two rooms have verandas with big rocking chairs. Lake Cleburne is only five miles away. Full breakfast, children over twelve welcome, smoking outside only. $45-60.

COLLEGE STATION

Aggieland

B&B Texas Style
4224 W. Red Bird Lane
Dallas, TX, 75237
(214) 298-5433; (214) 298-8586

This home has one bedroom for guests and a private bath. Within walking distance of the university and available all year. Hosts enjoy meeting and talking to parents of students visiting for parents' night, graduation, and football games. There are no pets here,

NOTES: Credit cards accepted: A Master Card; B Visa; C American Express; D Discover Card; E Diners Club; F Other: 2 Personal checks accepted: 3 Lunch available: 4 Dinner available: 5 Open all year

and smoking is only allowed outside. A full Texas breakfast is served. $35-50.

COLUMBUS

Raumonda

B&B Texas Style
4224 W. Red Bird Lane
Dallas, TX, 75237
(214) 298-5433; (214) 298-8586

This large, two-story antebellum home has been beautifully and carefully restored and now has air-conditioning and fans in every bedroom. There's a lovely pool in the back garden. An enhanced continental breakfast buffet is arranged on the gallery that overlooks the pool and garden. The host owns an antique shop. Beds here are all doubles, with private baths. $80.

COPPELL

Morning Glory

B&B Texas Style
4224 W. Red Bird Lane
Dallas, TX, 75237
(214) 298-5433; (214) 298-8586

Near the Dallas-Fort Worth Airport and Las Colinas, this new townhome has a bright, cheery upstairs room with a double bed and private bath for guests. A full breakfast is served by your realtor hostess, who will suggest restaurants, attractions, museums, and so forth. Smoking is allowed, but no pets. $30-40.

DALLAS

The Cloisters

B&B Texas Style
4224 W. Red Bird Lane
Dallas, TX, 75237
(214) 298-5433; (214) 298-8586

This lovely home is right on White Rock Lake, in one of the most secluded and little-

known areas of the city. Two bedrooms, each with a private bath. One room has a double bed, the other has one single bed, TV, and sitting area. Full breakfast. A bicycle is available for riding around the lake, or you may want to join the joggers, sailors, and fishermen. $50-60.

Coral Cove

B&B Texas Style
4224 W. Red Bird Lane
Dallas, TX, 75237
(214) 298-5433; (214) 298-8586

Spacious home near Olla Podrida and Richardson has three bedrooms, one with private bath. Hosts are very outgoing and make it easy for guests to enjoy themselves. Breakfast is full or continental — your choice. Smokers are allowed, and cats are in residence. $35-40.

East Dallas

B&B Texas Style
4224 W. Red Bird Lane
Dallas, TX, 75237
(214) 298-5433; (214) 298-8586

An exciting blend of fine artwork and California modern furnishings, convenient to museums, downtown, the Cotton Bowl and Fair Park, and Market Center. Bus line is half a block away. Pool for summer guests, fireplace for the winter. Continental breakfast. One double room with a private bath is available, and smokers are welcome. $35-40.

Fan Room

B&B Texas Style
4224 W. Red Bird Lane
Dallas, TX, 75237
(214) 298-5433; (214) 298-8586

An antique fan displayed in this lovely twin bedroom is the focal point of a large collection of fans. The home is located near Prestonwood, Marshall Fields, and the Galleria.

Southfork Ranch is a fifteen-minute drive north. Another bedroom for guests has a double bed and private bath. Your hosts serve a full country breakfast and will help you plan your visit to Dallas. $38-45.

Iris Canopy

B&B Texas Style
4224 W. Red Bird Lane
Dallas, TX, 75237
(214) 298-5433; (214) 298-8586

This historic home has a lovely double bedroom featuring an iris coverlet, canopy, and prints on the wall. An adjoining king room shares the guest bath. Many antiques in the large, two-story home built in the prairie style. Convenient to the bus line, Convention Center, and Arts District. $60-75.

McKinney Place

B&B Texas Style
4224 W. Red Bird Lane
Dallas, TX, 75237
(214) 298-5433; (214) 298-8586

This new condo near downtown and Highland Park is perfect for "Market People" or business travelers. The gourmet continental breakfast is served in the formal dining room. The bedroom has a king bed, desk, telephone, and TV, as well as private bath. The McKinney Trolley runs right in front of the condo, or you can park your car in the off-street parking provided. $40-50.

Misty Glen

B&B Texas Style
4224 W. Red Bird Lane
Dallas, TX, 75237
(214) 298-5433; (214) 298-8586

A charming German lady has two bedrooms in her lovely contemporary home for guests, one with a queen bed, the other a double. They share an adjoining bath. Ten to fifteen

minutes from downtown (twenty to twenty-five by public transportation). Convenient to the West End Market Place and the Convention Center. Full country breakfast; dog in residence; nonsmokers preferred. $40-45.

Province

B&B Texas Style
4224 W. Red Bird Lane
Dallas, TX, 75237
(214) 298-5433; (214) 298-8586

Your hosts here are health-food enthusiasts who will serve you carrot juice if you're willing to try it, or more conventional breakfast foods. The house is twenty-five minutes from downtown Dallas, two blocks from the public bus line. Nonsmokers preferred, children discouraged. $40-45.

Regal

B&B Texas Style
4224 W. Red Bird Lane
Dallas, TX, 75237
(214) 298-5433; (214) 298-8586

Located in far northern Dallas, near Southfork, Richardson, and Plano, this house offers a queen room with private bath. The public bus is half a block away, about thirty minutes to downtown. Continental breakfast, smokers welcome. Tennis courts and public pool are nearby. $35-40.

Serendipity

B&B Texas Style
4224 W. Red Bird Lane
Dallas, TX, 75237
(214) 298-5433; (214) 298-8586

This B&B resembles an English countryside home. It was built in 1925 and has been completely renovated. Near White Rock Lake, the Lakewood Shopping Center, and many restaurants; about ten to twelve minutes from downtown. Full breakfast, no smoking. One bedroom with a queen bed

NOTES: Credit cards accepted: A Master Card; B Visa; C American Express; D Discover Card; E Diners Club; F Other: 2 Personal checks accepted: 3 Lunch available: 4 Dinner available: 5 Open all year

and private bath; back deck; living room with fireplace. $40-45.

Tudor Mansion

B&B Texas Style
4224 W. Red Bird Lane
Dallas, TX, 75237
(214) 298-5433; (214) 298-8586

Built in 1933 in an exclusive neighborhood in the shadow of downtown, this mansion offers a queen bed and private bath. Your hosts served a full gourmet breakfast of either Cheddar on Toast, Texas Style Creamed Eggs with Jalapeno, or Fresh Vegetable Omelet. Spanish and French are also spoken here. $50-60.

White Rock Lake

B&B Texas Style
4224 W. Red Bird Lane
Dallas, TX, 75237
(214) 298-5433; (214) 298-8586

An upstairs bedroom with a double bed and private bath, plus a twin bedroom. Breakfast is continental. Resident cat. $40-45.

DUNCANVILLE

Rainbow

B&B Texas Style
4224 W. Red Bird Lane
Dallas, TX, 75237
(214) 298-5433; (214) 298-8586

A large upstairs room with queen bed and private bath, stereo, and sitting area, plus off-street parking on a quiet, tree-lined street. Easy access from a major freeway; just fifteen minutes to downtown Dallas. A full breakfast is served. $28-32.

EL PASO

Mexican Retreat

B&B Texas Style

4224 W. Red Bird Lane
Dallas, TX, 75237
(214) 298-5433; (214) 298-8586

There are lots of collectibles from Mexico in this cozy B&B, plus a hostess who is willing to escort guests to her favorite Mexican shopping markets and restaurants. The guest room has a lovely antique bed with high headboard, and a private bath. Full breakfast on weekends, continental on weekdays. Cat in residence. Located eight miles from Juarez, Mexico. $35-40.

A Room With a View

821 Rim Road, 79902
(915) 534-4400; 779-1259

Unique view of two countries, two cities, and three states! European hospitality with American luxury. Hosts have traveled the world and share their international experiences with guests. Come celebrate the El Paso-Mexico border tradition. Mi Casa Es Su Casa.

Hosts: Joan & Roy Forman
Doubles: 3 (PB) $40-85
Type of Beds: 2 Double; 1 King
Full Breakfast
Credit Cards: A, B, C
Notes: 2, 4, 5, 8, 10, 11, 12

FREDERICKSBURG

Country Cottage Inn

405 East Main, 78624
(512) 997-8549

Wonderfully charming rooms in a lovingly restored Texas frontier home (circa 1850). Two-foot-thick stone walls, exposed hand cut beams, high ceilings, period Texas antiues, porch swings, Laura Ashley linens, bathrobes, whirlpool tubs, fireplace, and complimentary wine insure your comfort.

Host: Jeffery Webb
Doubles: 5 (PB) $65-95
Type of Beds: 1 Double; 5 King

6 Pets welcome: 7 Smoking allowed: 8 Children welcome: 9 Social drinking allowed: 10 Tennis available: 11 Swimming available: 12 Golf available: 13 Skiing available: 14 May be booked through travel agents

Continental Breakfast
Credit Cards: A, B
No smoking
Notes: 2, 4, 5, 8, 9, 10, 11, 12

Froehliche Heim

B&B Texas Style
4224 W. Red Bird Lane
Dallas, TX, 75237
(214) 298-5433; (214) 298-8586

An historic home, newly restored and redecorated, on a large lot with huge oak trees. The owner lives nearby. Four bedrooms share two baths. Ceiling fans and other country amenities. Full breakfast. $39.50-49.50.

J Bar K Ranch Bed & Breakfast

HC-10, Box 53-A, 78624
(512) 669-2471

Large historic German rock home on Texas hill-country ranch seventeen miles northwest of Fredericksburg. Near LBJ's ranch, Enchanted Rock, and Nimitz Naval Museum and many other historic attractions. Two rooms with living room, kitchen, and large outside upstairs porch.

Hosts: Kermit & Naomi Kothe
Doubles: 2 (SB) $63.60
Type of Beds: 2 Double; 1 Sofabed
Full Breakfast
Credit Cards: A, B (surcharge)
Closed Jan. & Feb.
Notes: 2, 7, 8 (10 and over), 9

GALVESTON

Hazelwood House

B&B Texas Style
4224 W. Red Bird Lane
Dallas, TX, 75237
(214) 298-5433; (214) 298-8586

This romantic 1877 Victorian is located about ten minutes from the Strand and twelve to fifteen minutes from the beach.

Three lovely rooms, two with private baths. The large verandah has table and chairs for breakfast on sunny mornings, or a hammock to relax in. $75-85.

GARLAND

Catnip Creek

B&B Texas Style
4224 W. Red Bird Lane
Dallas, TX, 75237
(214) 298-5433; (214) 298-8586

Right on Spring Creek, with a hot tub on the deck overlooking the wooded creek. The guest bedroom has a queen bed, private bath, and private entrance. Cats in residence, but they stay in their own area. Breakfast is continental on weekdays and full on weekends. Users of the hot tub may enjoy a wine cooler and cuddle on the deck in the large terry robes that are provided; bicycles also available. About thirty minutes from downtown Dallas and fifteen from Southfork. $35-45.

Morningside

B&B Texas Style
4224 W. Red Bird Lane
Dallas, TX, 75237
(214) 298-5433; (214) 298-8586

Located close to Southfork Ranch in a quiet neighborhood, this house offers a double bed with private bath and a second room with an extra-long bed. Antique furnishings and collectibles, continental breakfast, no smoking. $30-35.

GLEN ROSE

Inn on the River

209 S.W. Barnard Street, 76043
(817) 897-2101

This 1860 inn on the Paluxy River near the town square is a designated Historic Texas

---

NOTES: Credit cards accepted: A Master Card; B Visa; C American Express; D Discover Card; E Diners Club; F Other: 2 Personal checks accepted: 3 Lunch available: 4 Dinner available: 5 Open all year

Landmark. The 21 rooms and 3 suites are individually designed and all have private baths. This area of Texas is noted for its scenic hills, rivers, Dinosaur Valley State Park, and Fossil Rim Wildlife Conservation Ranch.

Hosts: Steve & Peggy Allman
Suites: 3 (PB) $100-125
Doubles: 21 (PB) $80-90
Type of Beds: 1 Twin; 4 Double; 17 Queen
Full Breakfast
Credit Cards: A, B, C
Closed Thanksgiving & Christmas week
Notes: 2, 10, 11, 12, 14

GOLIAD

The White House Inn
203 N. Commercial, 77963
(512) 645-2701

Spanish missions, Court House Square, huge oaks, excellent bird watching and wild game hunting make the Goliad area unique. This artistically decorated inn (with gift shop) is country elegance at its best and most comfortable.

Hosts: Don & Marian Harvey
Doubles: 3 (PB) $45.20-56.50
Type of Beds: 2 Twin; 2 King
Full Breakfast
Credit Cards: No
Closed Thanksgiving & Christmas
Notes: 2, 8, 9, 11, 12

GRANBURY

Pecan Plantation
B&B Texas Style
4224 W. Red Bird Lane
Dallas, TX, 75237
(214) 298-5433; (214) 298-8586

This large fine home in the controlled community of Pecan Plantation was golf course, tennis, swimming, and country-club dining available. The bedroom has twin beds and a private bath. There is a hot tub on the enclosed porch, and breakfast is a full Western breakfast of omelets or scrambled

eggs. Resident outside cat; smokers welcome. $40-50.

GRANITE SHOALS

La Casita
B&B Texas Style
4224 W. Red Bird Lane
Dallas, TX, 75237
(214) 298-5433; (214) 298-8586

This charming guesthouse offers a double bedroom with bath, plus another room for larger parties. A full breakfast will be served either in the main house or in the private guesthouse. Picnic lunches are available for taking along on the Vanishing River Cruise, which is on Lake Buchanan about thirty minutes away. There is a special fishing guide who will show you around Horse Shoe Bay. $55.

HOUSTON

Baroque, Georgetown Style
B&B Texas Style
4224 W. Red Bird Lane
Dallas, TX, 75237
(214) 298-5433; (214) 298-8586

Fantastic antiques abound in this interesting home near the Galleria Mall and twenty minutes from downtown Houston. Two guest rooms upstairs with an adjoining bath, one room with a double bed, the other with twins. Breakfast is continental and is served in the atrium room, where the flowing fountain will make you feel you're in an exotic getaway. $40-50.

Bayside
B&B Texas Style
4224 W. Red Bird Lane
Dallas, TX, 75237
(214) 298-5433; (214) 298-8586

This fine home is right on the water, halfway between Houston and Galveston. The glass wall across the entire side of the home allows you to watch the sailboats and pelicans in comfort. Pool available for guests to use. The guest room has a king bed (or two twins), private entrance, and private bath. Full breakfast. $50-60.

Sara's Bed & Breakfast Inn

941 Heights Blvd., 77008
(713) 868-1130

This two-story mansion was once a one-story Victorian cottage. Renovation was completed in 1986. Twelve bedrooms are beautifully decorated with antiques and collectibles.

Hosts: Donna & Tillman Arledge
Doubles: 12 (3 PB; 9 SB) $46-96
Type of Beds: 4 Twin; 4 Double; 3 Queen; 3 King
Continental Breakfast
Credit Cards: A, B, C, E, F
Notes: 2, 5, 7, 8, 9

INGRAM

Guadalupe Retreat

B&B Texas Style
4224 W. Red Bird Lane
Dallas, TX, 75237
(214) 298-5433; (214) 298-8586

Swimming, tubing, or canoeing in the river is available at this wonderful B&B near Kerrville, about one hour from San Antonio. The large mansion has a complete apartment with kitchen, two bedrooms, and bath, private entrance. Smokers are welcome, as are children; and a full breakfast is served. $40-50.

JEFFERSON

McKay House Bed & Breakfast Inn

306 East Delta Street, 75657
(214) 665-7322

Jefferson is a riverport town from the frontier days of the Republic of Texas. It has historic mule-drawn tours, boat rides on the river, a narrow-gauge train, and thirty antique shops. The house, a recently restored 1851 Greek Revival cottage, offers cool lemonade, porch swings, fireplace, and a full gentleman's breakfast.

Host: Peggy Taylor
Doubles: 6 (4 PB; 2 SB) $55-80
Type of Beds: 6 Double
Full Breakfast
Credit Cards: A, B
Notes: 2, 5, 9, 12, 14

Wise Manor

312 Houston Street, 75657
(214) 665-2386

A gem of a Victorian home that looks as if it has just stepped out of a fairy tale. The little two-story cottage is painted in salmon tones with crisp, white gingerbread trim. Surrounded by large pecan trees, it peers out from behind a wrought-iron fence. It is furnished in Victorian pieces with marble-top tables and ruffled curtains at the windows. Antique white bedspreads and folded appliqued quilts adorn the ornate walnut beds.

Host: Katherine Ramsay Wise
Doubles: 3 (2 PB; 1 SB) $27.50-49.50
Type of Beds: 1 Twin; 2 Double
Continental Breakfast
Credit Cards: No
Notes: 2, 4, 5, 7, 8, 9, 11

LAKE RAY HUBBARD

Texas Queen

B&B Texas Style
4224 W. Red Bird Lane
Dallas, TX, 75237
(214) 298-5433; (214) 298-8586

Enjoy nature, owls hooting, butterflies, squirrels, and the peace and quiet that a lakeside can offer. The large scenic boat attraction, *Texas Queen*, offers tours around the lake for a reasonable fee. There's a king

---

NOTES: Credit cards accepted: A Master Card; B Visa; C American Express; D Discover Card; E Diners Club; F Other: 2 Personal checks accepted: 3 Lunch available: 4 Dinner available: 5 Open all year

bed in the upstairs guest area and another room with twin beds. Private bath. Full breakfast is served. Located twenty minutes from Dallas; resident cat and dog; smokers welcome. $35-40.

Wise Manor

MARSHALL

The Belle-Fry-Gaines House

B&B Texas Style
4224 W. Red Bird Lane
Dallas, TX, 75237
(214) 298-5433; (214) 298-8586

Originally built in 1870, this Greek Revival house has only had three owners in the past 118 years. There are three guest bedrooms, one downstairs with a working fireplace and two upstairs. Two upstairs rooms share a bath. Your continental breakfast will be served in the formal dining room. $75-85.

Three Oaks B & B

609 N. Washington Avenue, 75670
(214) 938-6123

Victorian home built in 1895, located in a national historic district. Two three-room private suites are offered, including formal areas furnished with oak and walnut antiues. Breakfast is wheeled to guests' room on a tea cart adorned with antique linens, silver, china, and crystal.

Hosts: Sandra & Bob McCoy
Doubles: 2 (PB) $68.50
Type of Beds: 1 Double; 1 Queen
Full Breakfast
Minimum stay holidays: 2
Credit Cards: No
Notes: 2, 5, 8 (over 11), 9, 10, 11, 12

Wood Boone Norrell House

215 E. Rusk Street, 75670
(214) 935-1800

Restored 1884 Queen Anne with verandas and a large balcony. Each room is decorated with turn-of-the-century antiques. All rooms have private baths with showers. Nestled in the piney wood of East Texas, just minutes from antique shopping and fishing.

Hosts: Michael & Patsy Norrell
Doubles: 5 (PB) $65
Type of Beds: 4 Double; 1 Queen
Full Breakfast
Credit Cards: A, B
Notes: 2, 5, 6, 8, 14

MIDLAND

Ranch Town Home

B&B Texas Style
4224 W. Red Bird Lane
Dallas, TX, 75237
(214) 298-5433; (214) 298-8586

A large bedroom and private bath in a spacious home with a hot tub and pool that may be used by guests. Midland is the home of many fine museums, a symphony and ballet. Two large, well-behaved dogs who have had obedience training reside here; there is also a stable for guests who need a B&B for their horses. No smoking. $30-40.

6 Pets welcome: 7 Smoking allowed: 8 Children welcome: 9 Social drinking allowed: 10 Tennis available: 11 Swimming available: 12 Golf available: 13 Skiing available: 14 May be booked through travel agents

MINEOLA

The Homestead

B&B Texas Style
4224 W. Red Bird Lane
Dallas, TX, 75237
(214) 298-5433; (214) 298-8586

A tour of East Texas wouldn't be complete without an overnight at this fine historical B&B one block from the center of town and I-80. Three guest rooms share one hall bath. A full Texas breakfast is served, with biscuits and gravy, eggs and bacon, coffee and juice. $50-60.

NASA - SEABROOK

High Tide

B&B Texas Style
4224 W. Red Bird Lane
Dallas, TX, 75237
(214) 298-5433; (214) 298-8586

Right on Galveston Bay at the channel where shrimp boats and ocean liners go in and out, this Cape Cod cottage will sleep seven to nine people. A large deck with chairs is perfect for catching the sea breezes, sunning, and bird and boat watching. Continental breakfast. $50.

PALESTINE

Grandma's House

B&B Texas Style
4224 W. Red Bird Lane
Dallas, TX, 75237
(214) 298-5433; (214) 298-8586

Nestled in the heart of East Texas is a country Christmas tree farm with a guesthouse furnished with twin beds and private bath. Relax on the front porch and watch the deer graze in the field, stroll among the Christmas trees, or ride a paddle board around the pond. Hearty full breakfast. $35-45.

PLANO

Los Rios

B&B Texas Style
4224 W. Red Bird Lane
Dallas, TX, 75237
(214) 298-5433; (214) 298-8586

Exclusive residential area in east Plano, the "hot air balloon capital" of Texas. One bedroom with a double bed and private bath. A second room has twin beds. Three miles to Southfork; golf and tennis are nearby. A full breakfast is served. $35-40.

PORT ISABEL

South Padre Waterfront

B&B Texas Style
4224 W. Red Bird Lane
Dallas, TX, 75237
(214) 298-5433; (214) 298-8586

This large home right on the water with a heated pool/Jacuzzi indoors offers two bedrooms and an adjoining sitting room upstairs that can sleep ten. There is a deck over the water for watching the shrimp boats plying the channel in and out of the Gulf. Full breakfast. $40-50.

ROCKPORT

Key Largo

B&B Texas Style
4224 W. Red Bird Lane
Dallas, TX, 75237
(214) 298-5433; (214) 298-8586

This home is on a canal in a special residential section of Rockport. The hostess has a large suite upstairs with twin beds, private bath, and a large sitting room with TV. The Whooping Crane Boat Trips are popular, as are trips to Mustang Island. Continental breakfast. $50.

NOTES: Credit cards accepted: A Master Card; B Visa; C American Express; D Discover Card; E Diners Club; F Other: 2 Personal checks accepted: 3 Lunch available: 4 Dinner available: 5 Open all year

SAN ANTONIO

B&B Hosts of San Antonio #A

166 Rockhill, 78209
(512) 824-4034

A charming Cape Cod guest house in Alamo Heights near McNay Art Museum, beautifully decorated in antiques. Cathedral ceilings, fireplace, full kitchen, queen canopy bed. Large sun deck in the treetops overlooking the landscaped grounds and swimming pool. Nonsmokers; no pets. $79.50.

B&B Hosts of San Antonio #B

166 Rockhill, 78209
(512) 824-4034

This fifty-year-old family home on one acre in quiet Alamo Heights offers one bedroom with twin bed and private bath and one room with twin beds and private bath. Two blocks to shopping center and VIA bus. Hosts offer airport transportation; convenient access to downtown. Full or Continental breakfast; nonsmokers. $50.35-68.90.

B&B Hosts of San Antonio #C

166 Rockhill, 78209
(512) 824-4034

Retired army couple living in a northwest suburb have two guest rooms with double beds and private bath. Beautifully furnished, full breakfast. The hosts' interests include golf and Oriental rugs. $48.03-62.15.

B&B Hosts of San Antonio #D

166 Rockhill, 78209
(512) 824-4034

Large family home in North San Antonio Hills near Sea World offers guests the entire second floor. Sitting room with fireplace, two bedrooms — one with balcony — adjoining bath. Third bedroom is adjacent to a hall bath. Quiet estate atmosphere with oak trees and a vista of the hill country. $50.35-63.60.

B&B Hosts of San Antonio #E

166 Rockhill, 78209
(512) 824-4034

New, modern guest house in the Cross Mountain Ranch subdivision in the northwest hills, on 2.2 acres. Living room, bedroom, kitchen, dinette. One double bed, daybed, and trundle; central air-conditioning. Enjoy watching deer, rabbits, and birds in this remote atmosphere. Airport pick up can be arranged; children welcome; pets permitted outside. Breakfast provided in guest quarters. $45.05-63.60.

B&B Hosts of San Antonio #F

166 Rockhill, 78209
(512) 824-4034

Charming country home thirty minutes from downtown San Antonio. Two bedrooms with double beds, antiques, real handmade quilts, private bath. Your host is a custom furniture builder with his workshop on the grounds. Walk to the creek to visit the wild ducks; air-conditioning in summer, wood-burning fireplace and stove in winter. $45.05-58.30.

6 Pets welcome: 7 Smoking allowed: 8 Children welcome: 9 Social drinking allowed: 10 Tennis available: 11 Swimming available: 12 Golf available: 13 Skiing available: 14 May be booked through travel agents

B&B Hosts of San Antonio #G
166 Rockhill, 78209
(512) 824-4034

Near Sea World, this house has a large master suite with king bed and eighteenth-century furnishings, dressing room, and private bath. Extra room for teenagers has a queen sleeper sofa. Hosts welcome families, and your continental breakfast will be served on the patio overlooking the swimming pool. $52.47-68.90.

B&B Hosts of San Antonio #1
166 Rockhill, 78209
(512) 824-4034

A lovely restored home offering affordable comfort and a peaceful atmosphere. Special continental breakfast of home-baked rolls and muffins. Six blocks from River Walk. Four rooms available with queen beds, plus a double room with private bath and a double room with shower bath and kitchenette. $67.80-79.10.

B&B Hosts of San Antonio #2
166 Rockhill, 78209
(512) 824-4034

This charming couple has restored their beautiful Victorian in the historic King William area, within walking distance of downtown San Antonio. Airport transportation on request. Upstairs room with double and single beds, balcony, and bath. $48.03-62.15.

B&B Hosts of San Antonio #3
166 Rockhill, 78209
(512) 824-4034

A new guest house in the King William area, with all modern conveniences. Loft bedroom with twin beds; downstairs room with double bed and bath. Sofa bed in the living room; full kitchen with continental breakfast provided. Two bicycles are available. $59.33-79.10.

B&B Hosts of San Antonio #4
166 Rockhill, 78209
(512) 824-4034

Restored carriage house apartment with a private entrance. Charming cathedral-ceiling bedroom with double bed, furnished in white wicker with blue and coral chintz. Kitchenette, full bath, balcony overlooking the landscaped grounds. Continental breakfast provided in the kitchenette. Non-smokers. $90.40.

B&B Hosts of San Antonio #5
166 Rockhill, 78209
(512) 824-4034

Spacious apartment in an historic house. Living room with a fourteen-foot ceiling, fireplace. Large bedroom with queen bed, walk-in closet, and full bath. Middle room has kitchenette, bar, dining area, and sofa bed (double). Business guests may arrange meetings, catered social gatherings and tours with advance notice. Full American or Mexican breakfast. Smoking outside only. $81.93-90.40.

B&B Hosts of San Antonio #6

166 Rockhill, 78209
(512) 824-4034

Children are most welcome at this 100-year-old restored Victorian. Guest room with double bed, private bath in hallway, and TV room. Queen sofa bed in TV room for children or extra couple. Located near Ten Cent Trolley and VIA bus; within walking distance of the Riverwalk and restaurants. Continental or full breakfast; evening snacks. $53.68-67.80.

Bullis House Inn

621 Pierce Street, Box 8059, 78208
(512) 223-9426

Lovely historic white-columned mansion. Wide veranda, swimming pool, spacious guest rooms with fireplaces, queen beds, color TV, French windows — all individually decorated. Downstairs parlors have decorative fourteen-foot plaster ceilings, marble fireplaces, lovely patterned wood floors, and more. Weekend and honeymoon packages available.

Hosts: Steve & Alma Cross
Doubles: 8 (2 PB; 6 SB) $29-89
Type of Beds: 8 Twin; 4 Double; 4 Queen; 7 Trundle
Continental Breakfast
Credit Cards: A, B, C, D
Checks accepted in advance only
Notes: 5, 7, 8, 9, 10, 11, 14

Cardinal Cliff

3806 Highcliff, 78218
(512) 655-2939

Comfortable home in a quiet residential area. The backyard overlooks a wooded river valley. Porta-crib available for infants. Five minutes from the airport; twenty minutes from downtown attractions. Homemade bread, jams, and jellies are a normal breakfast feature.

Hosts: Roger & Alice Sackett
Singles: 2 (SB) $23 ·
Doubles: 1 (SB) $30
Type of Beds: 2 Twin; 1 Double
Full Breakfast
Credit Cards: No
Notes: 2, 5, 8, 9, 11

Terrell Castle

950 East Grayson Street, 78208
(512) 824-8036

Near the Alamo, Riverwalk, River Center Mall, missions, the Mexican Market, Sea World, Terrell Castle offers eight rooms and suites. Five rooms have private baths; three share baths. A full gourmet breakfast is included. No charge for children under 6; crib available at no charge. Well-behaved pets are welcome with advance notice. Meeting rooms are available, as are facilities for groups, weddings, and parties with advance notice. $56.50-107.35.

SHEPHERD

D-Bar-X Tree Farm

B&B Texas Style
4224 W. Red Bird Lane
Dallas, TX, 75237
(214) 298-5433; (214) 298-8586

Shepherd is just north of Houston, less than an hour's drive. If you would like to choose your Christmas tree when you visit, you may go back in December and cut it yourself. The bedroom has a double bed with private bath. There is a second room with a sofabed for children. A pond for fishing, walking trails through the acreage and woods, full breakfast. Others meals available by arrangement. $35-40.

STEPHENVILLE

The Oxford House

563 N. Graham Street, 76401
(817) 965-6885

6 Pets welcome: 7 Smoking allowed: 8 Children welcome: 9 Social drinking allowed: 10 Tennis available: 11 Swimming available: 12 Golf available: 13 Skiing available: 14 May be booked through travel agents

Stephenville is the northern tip of the beautiful Texas hill country. Located on Highway 67 west of Lake Granbury and east of Proctor Lake. Tarleton State University is located in town. The Oxford House was built in 1898 by Judge W. J. Oxford, Sr., and the completely restored two-story Victorian, presently owned by the grandson of the judge, has antique furnishings. Enjoy a quiet, peaceful atmosphere, home-cooked country breakfast, and shopping within walking distance.

Hosts: Bill & Paula Oxford
Doubles: 5 (4 PB; 1 SB) $50-65
Type of Beds: 4 Double; 1 Queen
Continental Breakfast weekdays; Full on weekends
Credit Cards: A, B
Notes: 2, 4, 5, 7 (restricted), 8 (over 10), 9, 14

The Oxford House

SUNNYVALE

The Durant Star Inn
B&B Texas Style
4224 W. Red Bird Lane
Dallas, TX, 75237
(214) 298-5433; (214) 298-8586

Antique cars are the theme at this new inn near Dallas and Forney. The inn is on about 10 acres of wooded land, with a pond right outside the back door. There are five bedrooms, three upstairs and two downstairs, with three guest baths. Full breakfast; children welcome; limited smoking. $65-75.

TYLER

Rosevine Inn Bed & Breakfast
415 South Vine, 75702
(214) 592-?221

Rosevine Inn is located on a historical "brick street" area of Tyler. There are several shops within walking distance. We have a lovely courtyard and a hot tub for guests to enjoy. We serve wine and cheese on arrival and a wonderful formal-style breakfast in the dining room. The innkeepers love visiting with the guests and welcoming them to Tyler, the "Rose Capital of the World."

Hosts: Bert & Rebecca Powell
Doubles: 5 (PB) $62.21-71.83
Type of Beds: 5 Full
Full Breakfast
Credit Cards: A, B
Notes: 2, 5, 8 (over 12), 9, 10, 12, 14

VILLAGE MILLS

Big Thicket Guest House
Box 810, 77663
(409) 834-2875

This resort is set in the center of the Big Thicket two hours northeast of Houston and thirty miles north of Beaumont on highway 69, in a real country setting where you can bird watch, golf, or swim.

Host: Mary Betzner
Doubles: 2 (PB) $55
Type of Beds: 2 Twin; 1 Double
Full Breakfast

NOTES: Credit cards accepted: A Master Card; B Visa; C American Express; D Discover Card; E Diners Club; F Other: 2 Personal checks accepted: 3 Lunch available: 4 Dinner available: 5 Open all year

Credit Cards: No
Notes: 2, 5, 7, 8, 9, 10, 11, 12

WESLACO

Rio Grande Bed & Breakfast

Box 16, 78596
(512) 968-9646

This home is located in the tropical Rio Grande Valley, in a citrus grove with tropical plants and flowers. Fourteen miles to Mexico; sixty miles to the Padre Island beaches; between Santa Ana and Atascosa wildlife refuges.

Doubles: 3 (2 PB; 1 SB) $25-30
Type of Beds: 2 Twin; 2 Double
Continental Breakfast
Credit Cards: No
Notes: 5, 8 (over 8), 11

WIMBERLEY

The Chalet

B&B Of Wimberley, Box 589, 78676
(512) 847-9666

Located on a private estate overlooking crystal-clear Cypress Creek. A large paneled living room overlooks the deck. Amenities include a spacious bedroom, attractive bath with whirlpool tub, fireplace, kitchenette, TV, and air-conditioning. Complimentary wine. One double, private bath, $85.

Deer Lake Cottage

B&B of Wimberley, Box 589, 78676
(512) 847-9666

Located on Lone Man Creek, with a creek and dam right in front of the cottage. Good swimming and fishing. Genial hosts provide a continental breakfast, or you may do your own cooking. Kitchen, dining area, sitting area, bath, air-conditioning, heat, TV.

Sleeps two-four people. One double, private bath, $60.

Flite Acres River Lodge 1

B&B of Wimberley, Box 589, 78676
(512) 847-9666

This newly furnished unit features air-conditioning, living room, modern kitchen, deck with barbecue. Walk to the river. Sleeps four. One double, private bath, $65.

Flite Acres River Lodge 2

B&B of Wimberley, Box 589, 78676
(512) 847-9666

Cozy apartment, great for the budget-minded, has kitchen, bath, air-conditioning. All grounds and riverfront available to guests. Sleeps three. One double, private bath, $60.

Guest House of the Golden Pavilion

B&B of Wimberley, Box 589, 78676
(512) 847-9666

Two miles from the town square, this unit has a large playroom with four single beds, fireplace, pool table, grand piano, TV, stereo, kitchenette, fridge, and washer/dryer. Air-conditioned. Separate parents' room. Sleeps six. One double, private bath, twin beds, $85.

Lone Man Guest House

B&B of Wimberley, Box 589, 78676
(512) 847-9666

Near restaurants, shops, banks, and Post Office; one mile from town square. This house is air-conditioned, with kitchen, refrigerator, telephone, and lobby on first floor. Two doubles, private bath, $35.

The Ranch Room

B&B of Wimberley, Box 589, 78676
(512) 847-9666

All decks and grounds of a private estate overlooking Cypress Creek are available to guests. There is a large sitting room/bedroom/kitchenette with a cozy sitting area. Sleeps four. One double, private bath, $65.

Southwind

Southwind

Rt. 2, Box 15, 78676
(512) 847-5277

This Hill Country inn serves hearty Southwestern breakfasts and offers modern comforts in an Early Texas style home built in 1985. Located on 25 wooded acres, Southwind provides seclusion and quiet, yet is located just three miles from the resort community of Wimberley and is convenient to Austin and San Antonio.

Hosts: Herb & Carla Felsted
Doubles: 2 (PB) $60
Type of Beds: 2 Queen
Full Breakfast
Credit Cards: No
Closed Christmas Day
Notes: 2, 5, 9, 10, 11, 12, 14

Sundown Acres

B&B of Wimberley, Box 589, 78676
(512) 847-9666

Beautiful location on crystal-clear Cypress Creek. Immaculate accommodations, genial hosts. Sun deck, fishing, swimming; close to town for shopping and restaurants. Sleeps six. One double, private bath, $65.

The Tree House

B&B of Wimberley, Box 589, 78676
(512) 847-9666

High up, with a private entrance, this unit offers an attractive bedroom and sitting room, kitchen with refrigerators, full bath, and private deck. One double, private bath, $75.

White Hawk Lodge

B&B of Wimberley, Box 589, 78676
(512) 847-9666

White Hawk Lodge is an experiment in self-sufficiency: windmill, passive solar living, organic garden, chickens, and dairy goats. Secluded, yet only twenty-five minutes south of Austin. Amenities include a hot tub and wood-fired sauna. The guest house can accommodate four to five people. Refrigerator, TV, air-conditioning, wood stove. Full breakfast; additional meals are available at a modest extra cost. One double, private bath, $60.

NOTES: Credit cards accepted: A Master Card; B Visa; C American Express; D Discover Card; E Diners Club; F Other: 2 Personal checks accepted: 3 Lunch available: 4 Dinner available: 5 Open all year

WICHITA FALLS

Guest House Bed & Breakfast

2209 Miramar Street, 76308
(817) 322-7252

This is a separate three-room guest house located on the grounds of our colonial home. Decorated in Early American and Victorian antiques, the rooms feature unusual touches such as antique doll furniture. We serve afternoon refreshments. There are twelve public tennis courts within a half mile and golf within one mile.

Hosts: Mr. & Mrs. Robert Vinson
Cottage: 1 (PB) $40-60
Type of Beds: 2 Twin
Full Breakfast
Credit Cards: No
Notes: 2, 5, 7, 8, 9, 10, 11, 12

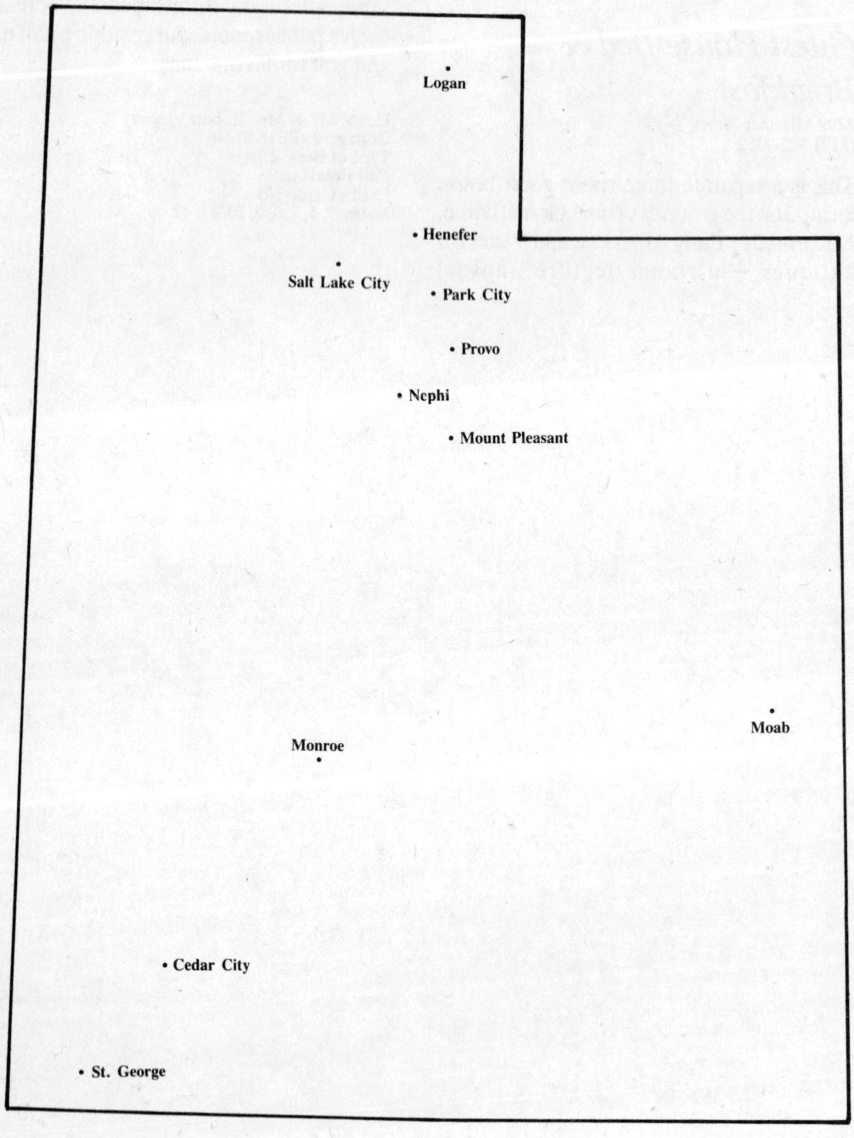

Logan

Henefer

Salt Lake City

Park City

Provo

Nephi

Mount Pleasant

Moab

Monroe

Cedar City

St. George

UTAH

Utah

Paxman Summer House

170 N. 400 W., 84720
(801) 586-3755

The Paxman Summer House is a turn-of-the-century Victorian on a quiet street two blocks from the Shakespearean Festival. Tastefully decorated with antiques. A short drive to Cedar Mountain, Brian Head Ski Resort, Zion National Park, and Bryce Canyon National Park. Local golf course, pool, and tennis courts are nearby.

Host: Karlene Paxman
Doubles: 4 (2 PB; 2 SB) $35-55
Continental Breakfast
Credit Cards: A, B
Reservations required in winter
Notes: 5, 7 (outside), 10, 11, 12, 13, 14

Rocky Mt. #100

B&B Rocky Mountains.
Box 804, Colorado Springs, CO, 80901
(719) 630-3433

Resting peacefully on a quiet residential street, this little guest house was built in 1898 and restored to offer four romantic guest rooms with English antiques and Victorian touches. All have private baths. Near Brian Head Ski area. Cozy down comforters in winter, TV in two rooms, full breakfast. $35-65.

Rocky Mt. #101

B&B Rocky Mountains.
Box 804, Colorado Springs, CO, 80901
(719) 630-3433

This three-bedroom home boasts lovely old antique beds, three bedrooms with shared bath and one with private bath. Short drive to Brian Head, Zion, and Bryce. Continental breakfast. $34-50.

HENEFER

Dearden Bed & Breakfast Inn

20 W. 100 N., 84033
(801) 336-5698

The Dearden Bed and Breakfast Inn is nestled in the foothills of the Wasatch Mountains. Beautiful scenery. All sports are within thirty minutes to one hour. Heneger is the only town on the Mormon Pioneer Trail, and offers a warm, friendly atmosphere.

Host: Wilhelmina Dearden
Singles: 5 (SB) $19.50
Doubles: 3 (SB) $28.50
Type of Beds: 5 Twin; 3 Double
Continental-plus Breakfast
Credit Cards: B
Notes: 2, 3, 5, 6, 7, 9, 10, 11, 13

LOGAN

Center Street Bed & Breakfast Inn

169 East Center Street, 84321
(801) 752-3443

Our inn, a step into the past and the unusual, features fantasy rooms: the Jungle Bungalow, the Arabian Nights Suite, Aphrodite's Court, Garden Suite, Victorian

---

6 Pets welcome: 7 Smoking allowed: 8 Children welcome: 9 Social drinking allowed: 10 Tennis available: 11 Swimming available: 12 Golf available: 13 Skiing available: 14 May be booked through travel agents

Suite, and the Pirate's Paradise. They have exotic decor such as waterfalls, wild animals, Grecian statues, stars, huge aquariums, etc. Also Jacuzzis, free movies, and private breakfasts. Skiing, hiking, boating, theater, and entertainment are nearby.

Hosts: Clyne & Ann Long
Doubles: 6 (PB) $35-70
Type of Beds: 2 Queen; 4 King
Continental-plus Breakfast
Credit Cards: A, B
Notes: 2, 5, 8 (babies only), 9, 10, 11, 12, 13, 14

MOAB

Sistelita

CVSR 2105, 484 Amber Lane, 84532
(801) 259-6012, (800) 842-6622

Discover the red-rock country in scenic southwestern Utah. Come to John Wayne country at Sistelita, a unique ranch-style country inn with deep-jet bath and sauna. Our seven-bedroom home is located in the historic Castle Valley, surrounded by national and state parks.

Hosts: Paul Swanatrom & Lori May
Singles: 4 (SB) $35
Doubles: 2 (PB) $55
Type of Beds: 2 Twin; 1 Double; 2 Queen; 1 King
Full Breakfast
Credit Cards: A, B, C
Notes: 2, 4, 5, 6, 8, 9, 10, 11, 12, 13, 14

MONROE

Petersons Bed & Breakfast

Box 142, 84754
(801) 527-4830

Halfway between Denver and Los Angeles. King-size featherbed room has a private entrance, bath, refrigerator stocked with cold drinks, color TV. There's a suite with twin beds, and a canopy double-bed room. Near five national parks and four national forests. Seven blocks to restaurant.

Host: Mary Ann Peterson
Doubles: 3 (2 PB; 1 SB) $35

Type of Beds: 2 Twin; 1 Double; 1 King; 2 Daybeds
Full Breakfast
Credit Cards: No
Notes: 4, 5, 8, 10, 11, 12, 14

MOUNT PLEASANT

The Mansion House Bed & Breakfast Inn

298 S. State Street, #13, 84647
(801) 462-3031

The town of Mt. Pleasant, in the heart of rural Utah, was given its name because of the pleasant, open views of the surrounding countryside. The Mansion House was built in 1897 by a prominent sheepman and features a carved oak staircase, hand-painted ceiling, and stained-glass windows.

Hosts: Denis & Terri Andelin
Doubles: 4 (PB) $39-49
Type of Beds: 1 Twin; 3 Double
Full Breakfast
Credit Cards: A, B
Notes: 2, 5, 9, 11, 13 (XC)

The Whitmore Mansion

NEPHI

The Whitmore Mansion B&B Inn

110 South Main Street, 84648
(801) 623-2047

NOTES: Credit cards accepted: A Master Card; B Visa; C American Express; D Discover Card; E Diners Club; F Other: 2 Personal checks accepted: 3 Lunch available: 4 Dinner available: 5 Open all year

This Queen Anne Victorian mansion, built in 1898, represents the warmth and charm of days past. A visit to the mansion is truly a memorable experience. Easy access from I-15; just 85 miles south of Salt Lake City.

Hosts: Bob & Dorothy Gliske
Doubles: 6 (PB) $49.05-70.85
Type of Beds: 7 Queen
Full Breakfast
Credit Cards: A, B
Notes: 2, 4, 5, 8, 9, 11, 12, 14

The Old Miners' Lodge

PARK CITY

The Old Miners' Lodge

615 Woodside Avenue, Box 2639, 84060
(801) 645-8068

A restored 1893 miners' boarding house in the national historic district of Park City, with ten individually decorated rooms filled with antiques and older pieces. Close to historic Main Street, with the Park City ski area in its backyard, the lodge is "more like staying with friends than at a hotel!"

Hosts: Hugh Daniels, Jeff Sadowsky, Susan Wynne
Doubles: 10 (PB) $40-160
Type of Beds: 4 Twin; 3 Double; 8 Queen; 1 King
Full Breakfast
Minimum stay, Christmas: 4-6
Credit Cards: A, B, C, D
Notes: 2, 4, 5, 8, 9, 10, 11, 12, 13, 14

PROVO

The Pullman Bed & Breakfast Inn

415 s. University Avenue, 84601
(801) 374-8141

Built in 1898, this magnificent Victorian was named after the luxurious Pullman railroad cars typical of the era. On Friday and Saturday evenings you can enjoy an elegant meal accompanied by a musical variety show.

Hosts: Tim, Kelly & Dennis Morganson
Doubles: 6 (4 PB; 2 SB) $30.59-54.08
Type of Beds: 1 Double; 4 Queen; 1 King
Full Breakfast
Credit Cards: A, B, C
Notes: 2, 4, 5, 8, 9, 10, 11, 12, 13, 14

ST. GEORGE

Greene Gate Village

76 W. Tabernacle Street, 84770
(719) 628-6999

Eight comfortable rooms, all dating back to the time of the pioneers, each lovingly restored with attention to detail. Green Gate Village can cater parties, receptions, conventions, or family reunions. Close to Zion and Bryce national parks, ten golf courses. Forty-five minutes away from skiing. Mild climate year round.

Hosts: Mark & Barbara Greene
Singles: 2 (PB) $40-45
Doubles: 9 (PB) $40-74
Type of Beds: 2 Twin; 1 Double; 13 Queen; 1 King
Full Breakfast
Credit Cards: A, B, C
Notes: 2, 3, 4, 5, 6, 8, 9, 10, 11, 12, 14

Seven Wives Inn

217 N. 100 W, 84770
(801) 628-3737

The inn consists of two adjacent pioneer adobe homes with massive hand-grained moldings framing windows and doors.

Bedrooms are furnished in period antiques and handmade quilts. Some rooms have fireplaces; one has a whirlpool tub. Swimming pool on premises.

Hosts: Donna & Jay Curtis, Alison & Jon Bowcutt
Singles: 1 (PB) $25-$65
Doubles: 13 (PB) $35-$65
Full Breakfast
Credit Cards: A, B
Notes: 2, 4, 5, 6, 8, 9, 10, 11, 12, 14

Seven Wives Inn

SALT LAKE CITY

Rocky Mt. #98
B&B Rocky Mountains

Box 804, Colorado Springs, CO, 80901
(719) 630-3433

One of Salt Lake's most architecturally and historically significant homes, a newly restored three-story Victorian. Each of the five guest rooms is furnished in art deco and contemporary 1920s and 1930s styles. Seven minutes from downtown Salt Lake and twenty from ski areas. Continental-plus breakfast. $47-77.

Rocky Mt. #103
B&B Rocky Mountains
Box 804, Colorado Springs, CO, 80901
(719) 630-3433

Built in 1903 as a residence, this Gothic Victorian was renovated in 1985 as a bed and breakfast. Set amid giant spruces and surrounded by a farm, yet just minutes from downtown. Excellent access to skiing (twenty minutes to Alta and Snowbird); Jacuzzi in one room; continental breakfast brought to your room. $40-85.

Vermont

Auberge Alburg
RD 1, Box 3, 05440
(802) 796-3169

A cozy multigabled house overlooking Lake
Champlain, plus a renovated barn with
newly built garden suite or loft room for
utter privacy. Cosmopolitan atmosphere:
eight languages spoken, books, grand piano,
authentic Russian Gypsy entertainment.
Espresso coffee on porch. Mini-conference
facilities and space for summer theater.
Montreal tours and lodging are also available. Very informal.

Hosts: Gabrielle Tyrnauer & Charles Stastny
Singles: 1 (SB) $40
Doubles: 5 (1 PB; 4 SB) $45-75
Continental Breakfast
Credit Cards: No
Notes: 2, 3, 4, 5, 6, 7, 8, 9, 10, 11, 12, 13

ARLINGTON

The Arlington Inn
Historic Route 7A, 05250
(802) 375-6532

An elegant Victorian inn with antique-filled
guest rooms in one of Vermont's finest
Greek Revival homes. Candlelight dining on
creative American cuisine that has been
awarded numerous Taste of Vermont
Awards as well as the Travel Holiday Dining
Award.

Hosts: Paul & Madeline Kruzel
Doubles: 13 (PB) $60-150
Type of Beds: 1 Twin; 12 Double
Continental Breakfast
Minimum stay weekends: 2 ; holidays: 3

Credit Cards: A, B, C
Notes: 2, 4, 5, 7, 8, 9, 10, 11, 12, 13

The Evergreen Inn
Sandgate Road, Box 2480, 05250
(802) 375-2272

Old-fashioned colonial country inn in the
Green River Valley and Green Mountains.
Off the beaten path, casual, relaxed atmosphere. Family owned and operated for over
fifty years. Close to art centers, summer
theaters, antiques, auctions, fairs, golf courses. Home cooking and baking.

Host: Mathilda Kenny
Singles: 3 (SB) $25-30
Doubles: 16 (PB and SB) $50-60
Type of Beds: 11 Twin; 7 Double; 1 King
Full Breakfast
Credit Cards: No
Closed Oct. 15 - May 15
Notes: 2, 3 (July & Aug.), 4, 6, 7, 8, 9, 10, 11, 12

Hill Farm Inn
RR 2, Box 2015, 05250
(802) 375-2269

Visit one of Vermont's original farmsteads
that has also been an inn since 1905. Stay in
a 1790 or 1830 farmhouse and enjoy hearty
home cooking and homegrown vegetables,
plus a jar of homemade jam to take home.
Nestled at the foot of Mt. Equinox and surrounded by 50 acres of farmland with the
Battenkill River bordering the lower pasture.

Hosts: George & Joanne Hardy
Doubles: 13 (7 PB; 6 SB) $40-83
Type of Beds: 2 Twin; 1 Double; 4 Queen; 6 King
Full Breakfast
Minimum stay weekends: 2; Holidays: 3

6 Pets welcome: 7 Smoking allowed: 8 Children welcome: 9 Social drinking allowed: 10 Tennis available: 11
Swimming available: 12 Golf available: 13 Skiing available: 14 May be booked through travel agents

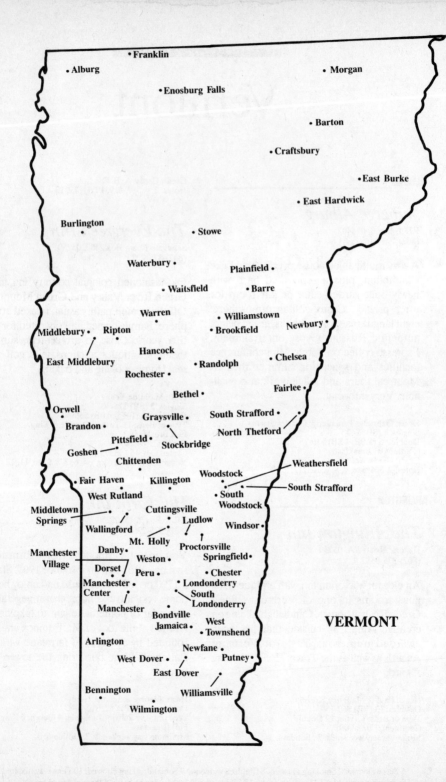

• Franklin

• Alburg

• Morgan

• Enosburg Falls

• Barton

• Craftsbury

• East Burke

• East Hardwick

Burlington •

• Stowe

Waterbury •

Plainfield •

• Waitsfield

• Barre

Warren •

• Williamstown

Middlebury •   • Ripton

• Brookfield

Newbury •

Hancock •

• Chelsea

East Middlebury •

• Randolph

Rochester •

Bethel •

Fairlee •

Orwell •

Graysville •

South Strafford •

Brandon •

North Thetford •

Pittsfield •

Goshen •   • Stockbridge

Chittenden •

Weathersfield

Fair Haven •

Killington •

Woodstock

South Strafford

West Rutland •

• South
Woodstock

Middletown
Springs

Cuttingsville •

Wallingford •

• Ludlow

Windsor •

Mt. Holly •

Proctorsville

Manchester
Village

Danby •

Weston •

Springfield •

Dorset •

Peru •

• Chester

Manchester
Center •

• Londonderry

• South
Londonderry

Manchester •

Bondville •

West
• Townshend

Arlington •

Jamaica •

Newfane •

West Dover •

Putney •

East Dover •

Bennington •

Williamsville •

Wilmington •

VERMONT

Credit Cards: A, B, C, D
Notes: 2, 4, 5, 7 (restricted), 8, 9, 10, 11, 12, 14

Ira Allen House

RD 2, Box 2485, 05250
(802) 362-2284

Vermont state historic site, home of Ira Allen (Ethan's brother, who lived here with him). Norman Rockwell Museum, Hildene, hiking, canoeing, biking, skiing, antiques. Enjoy the experience of a relaxing stay at our historic inn and a bountiful home-cooked breakfast.

Hosts: Rowland & Sally Bryant
Singles: 4 (2 PB; 2 SB) $37-42
Doubles: 7 (3 PB; 4 SB) $58-64
Type of Beds: 8 Twin; 7 Double
Full Breakfast
Credit Cards: A, B, C
Closed April
Dinner available on winter Saturdays
Notes: 2, 8 (over 10), 9, 10, 11, 12, 13

Hill Farm Inn

Shenandoah Farm

05250
(802) 375-6372

This colonial home near the Battenkill River is located five miles from Rt. 7A on Rt. 313. Close to Norman Rockwell museum and recreational activities. Five antique-filled guest rooms are offered with private or shared baths.

Hosts: Woody & Diana Masterson
Singles: 1 (SB) $35-40
Doubles: 4 (1 PB; 3 SB) $60-65
Type of Beds: 2 Twin; 3 Double
Full Breakfast
Minimum stay holidays: 2
Credit Cards: No
Notes: 2, 5, 7, 8, 9, 10, 11, 12, 13

BARRE

Woodruff House

13 East Street, 05641
(802) 476-7745; 479-9381

Large Victorian 1883 home located on a quiet park close to downtown shops and restaurants. Barre is the "Granite Center of the World." Great scenery, fantastic fall foliage. Halfway between Boston and Montreal, off I-89. Friendly and warm, like coming home to Grandma's.

Hosts: Robert & Terry Somaini & Katie
Doubles: 2 (SB) $40-55
Type of Beds: 1 Queen; 1 King
Full Breakfast
Notes: 2, 5, 8 (12 and over), 10, 11, 12, 13

BARTON

B&B Registry #VT-05822LAF

Box 8174, St. Paul, MN, 55108
(612) 646-4238

Secluded rural home on a working dairy farm. Quiet, scenic getaway with good cross-country skiing all around and downhill within twenty miles. Guided nature walks.

Doubles: 2 (SB) $25-30
Type of Beds: 2 Double; 1 Cot
Full Breakfast
Credit Cards: No
Notes: 3, 4, 5, 12, 13 (XC)

BENNINGTON

American Country Collection 041
984 Gloucester Place
Schenectady, N.Y., 12309
(518) 370-4948

Relaxation beckons at this carefully landscaped Victorian just one mile from the center of Bennington. There is a stream in the back of the property and a large front porch for rocking. Bennington College is five miles away; Prospect Mountain, for downhill and cross-country skiing, is six miles away. Antique stores, the Norman Rockwell Museum, and mountain views are features of this lovely old town.

Doubles: 6 (2 PB; 6 SB) $60-90
Type of Beds: 5 Double; 2 Queen
Full Breakfast
Credit Cards: A, B, C
Notes: 2, 5, 8 (0-12), 11, 13, 14

BETHEL

Eastwood House
River Street, 05032
(802) 234-9686

Eastwood House is a Federal brick mansion originally built as a stagecoach stop and tavern in 1816. Hand-sewn quilts, hand-stenciled walls, tab curtains, dried flower wreaths give it a country atmosphere. Located in the White River Valley, the house is close to downhill and cross-country skiing, boating, golf, sightseeing, horseback riding, and antiquing.

Hosts: Christine & Ron Diamond
Doubles: 7 (5 PB; 2 SB) $40-55
Type of Beds: 7 Double
Full Breakfast
Credit Cards: A, B, C
Notes: 2, 5, 8, 9, 11, 12, 13

BONDVILLE

Alpenrose Inn
Winhall Hollow Road, 05340
(802) 297-2750

Small country inn on a quiet road. All rooms are furnished with antiques, some with canopy beds. Cozy lounge with large fireplace. Free tennis to house guests, golf, horseback riding, fishing are within minutes. Near ski lifts and the Appalachian Trail.

Hosts: Rosemarie & Bob Strine
Doubles: 9 (PB) $37.50-49/person
Type of Beds: 8 Twin; 4 Double; 2 Queen
Full Breakfast
Credit Cards: No
Closed 4/1-6/15; 10/23-11/22
Notes: 2, 3, 7 (limited), 9, 10, 11, 12, 13

BRANDON

The Brandon Inn
On the Village Green, 05733
(802) 247-5766

Restored 1786 inn on the village green in Brandon, a typical Vermont village. Individually decorated guest rooms have private baths. Relax in the beautifully appointed, spacious public rooms or around the large, secluded pool. Fine dining, outside terrace. Chef owned and operated.

Hosts: Sarah & Louis Pattis
Doubles: 28 (PB) $58-115; with dinner:$74-150
Type of Beds: 10 Twin; 8 Double; 6 Queen; 4 King
Full Breakfast
Minimum stay some weekends: 2
Credit Cards: A, B, C
Notes: 2, 4, 5, 7, 8, 9, 10, 11, 12, 13, 14

The Moffett House
69 Park Street, 05733
(802) 247-3843

Experience the charm and old-fashioned hospitality of this wonderfully restored Victorian. Each bedroom is a delightful collection of period pieces. Short walk to town for shopping and fine dining.

Hosts: Elliot & Nancy Phillips
Doubles: 6 (2 PB; 4 SB) $55-75
Type of Beds: 4 Twin; 3 Double; 1 Queen; 1 King
Full Breakfast
Credit Cards: No
Notes: 2, 5, 7, 8, 9, 10, 11, 12, 13

Moffett House

BROOKFIELD

Green Trails Country Inn

By the Floating Bridge, 05036
(802) 276-3412

Cozy, relaxing, informal, "Like going home to Grandma's." Home-cooked meals at hearthside, guest rooms decorated with quilts and antiques. Hiking and biking, with serene vistas. In winter, enjoy horse-drawn sleigh rides, cross-country skiing (34 km tracked trails), and fireside friendship. "The epitome of a country inn" — NBC's "Today." B&B or MAP available.

Hosts: Pat & Peter Simpson
Singles: 1 (PB) $53.75
Doubles: 14 (8 PB; 6 SB) $65.25-73.50
Type of Beds: 10 Twin; 10 Double
Full Breakfast
Credit Cards: No
Closed April
Notes: 2, 4, 8, 9, 10, 11, 12, 13, 14

BURLINGTON

Howden Cottage Bed & Breakfast

32 N. Champlain Street, 05401
(802) 864-7198

Howden Cottage offers cozy lodging and warm hospitality in the home of a local artist. Located in downtown Burlington, the house is convenient to shopping, Lake Champlain, movies, night spots, churches, and some of Burlington's best restaurants.

Host: Bruce Howden
Doubles: 2 (SB) $35-45
Type of Beds: 2 Twin; 1 Double
Continental Breakfast
Credit Cards: A, B
Notes: 5, 9, 10, 11, 12

Pineapple Hospitality VT 631

Box F-821, New Bedford, MA 02742-0821
(508) 990-1696

This contemporary split-level home is located one-half mile from downtown Burlington. Walk only a few blocks and you'll find Lake Champlain. A neighborhood association has a portion of a beach along the lake. The home is beautifully furnished with heirloom Oriental rugs, traditional furniture, and some collectibles.

Doubles: 3 (SB) $45
Full Breakfast
Credit Cards: No
Closed July & Aug.
Notes: 2, 3, 4, 8, 9, 10, 11, 12, 13

CHELSEA

Shire Inn

8 Main Street, 05038
(802) 685-3031

An 1832 historic brick Federal, "Very Vermont," inn. Eighteenth-century accommodations with twentieth-century bathrooms. Small & intimate, some rooms have working fireplaces. Chef-owned and operated, with five-course dining available. Centrally located: thirty miles north of Woodstock/Queeche, thirty-four miles to Hanover/Dartmouth, thirty miles south of Montpelier.

Hosts: James & Mary Lee Papa
Doubles: 6 (PB) $65-$95
Type of Beds: 3 Double; 2 Queen; 1 King
Minimum stay weekends & holidays: 2
Full Breakfast
Credit Cards: A, B
Notes: 2, 4, 5, 8 (over 6), 9, 10, 11, 13

Shire Inn

CHESTER

Greenleaf Inn
Depot Street, Box 188, 05143
(802) 875-3171

Lovely 1880s home, now a comfortable village inn facing an expansive lawn. Just five charming rooms, each with private bath. Art gallery on premises features Vermont scenes — browse or buy. Walk to antiques, village green attractions. Bicycle tourists welcome. Full breakfast in our sunny dining room.

Hosts: Elizabeth & Dan Duffield
Doubles: 5 (PB) $60-70
Type of Beds: 2 Twin; 4 Queen
Full Breakfast

Credit Cards: No
Notes: 2, 5, 7, 8 (over 6), 9, 10, 11, 12, 13

Henry Farm Inn
Green Mountain Turnpike, Box 646, 05143
(802) 875-2674

This 1780s farmhouse, newly renovated, sits on 50 acres of rolling meadows and hills. Come by and enjoy the peace and quiet that is Vermont at this early stagecoach stop.

Doubles: 7 (PB) $49.70-78.20
Type of Beds: 2 Twin; 5 Queen
Full Breakfast
Minimum stay weekends & holidays: 2
Credit Cards: A, B
Notes: 2, 5, 7, 8, 9, 10, 11, 12, 13, 14

The Hugging Bear Inn & Shoppe
Main Street, 05143
(802) 875-2412

Charming Victorian home on the village green. The shop has over 3,500 bears, and guests may "adopt" a bear for the night as long as he's back to work in the shop by 9:00 the next morning. Puppet show often performed at breakfast; breakfast music provided by an 1890 music box. Thanksgiving and Christmas dinners available. One friendly dog and two lovable cats in residence.

Host: Georgette Thomas
Singles: 1 (PB) $55-65
Doubles: 5 (PB) $75-95
Type of Beds: 3 Twin; 7 Double; cribs available
Full Breakfast
Minimum stay weekends: 2; holidays: 2-3
Credit Cards: A, B, D
Notes: 2, 5, 6, 8, 9, 10, 11, 12, 13

The Inn at Long Last
Main Street, 05143
(802) 875-2444

A warm and welcoming inn where all the rooms have individual themes, where the

NOTES: Credit cards accepted: A Master Card; B Visa; C American Express; D Discover Card; E Diners Club; F Other: 2 Personal checks accepted: 3 Lunch available: 4 Dinner available: 5 Open all year

decor is highly personal, and where the staff hospitality is exceptional. Gardens, tennis courts, and food that draws raves. Modified American Plan meals.

Host: Jack Coleman
Doubles: 30 (25 PB; 5 SB) $75-95/person MAP
Type of Beds: 12 Twin; 14 Double; 4 Queen
Full Breakfast
Credit Cards: A, B, C
Closed April
Notes: 2, 4, 8, 9, 10, 11, 12, 13, 14

The Stone Hearth Inn

Rt. 11 West, 05143
(802) 875-2525

Built in 1810, The Stone Hearth Inn is widely known for its old-fashioned, informal hospitality. All of the guest rooms retain the romance of the period with antique furnishings, exposed beams, and wide pine floors. Fully licensed pub, dining room, library, and recreation room with whirlpool spa. Gift shop.

Hosts: Janet & Don Strohmeyer
Singles: 1 (PB) $36-60
Doubles: 9 (8 PB; 1 SB) $48-82
Type of Beds: 1 Twin; 7 Double; 1 Queen; 1 King
Full Breakfast
Credit Cards: A, B, D
Notes: 2, 4, 5, 7, 8, 9, 10, 11, 12, 13

CHITTENDEN

Tulip Tree Inn

Chittenden Dam Road, 05737
(802) 483-6213

You'll smell fresh bread baking when you walk in the door of this rambling country inn. The inn has eight guest rooms with private baths; two have their own Jacuzzi tubs. Located next door to a 110-kilometer cross-country ski area and within a thirty-minute drive of another 150 kilometers of trails. Close to Killington and Pico downhill ski areas. In summer, the Chittenden Reservoir is the ideal spot to swim, fish, or canoe.

Wonderful dinners are in the inn's dining room are included in the room rates.

Hosts: Ed & Rosemary McDowell
Doubles: 8 (PB) $60-95
Type of Beds: 2 Twin; 1 Double; 6 Queen
Full Breakfast
Credit Cards: A, B
Closed April - Memorial Day
Notes: 2, 4, 7, 9, 10, 11, 12, 13, 14

The Craftsbury Inn

CRAFTSBURY

The Craftsbury Inn

Main Street, 05826
(802) 586-2848

An 1850 country inn located in Vermont's unique Northeast Kingdom. The ten guest rooms have custom quilts and best-sellers. In summer and fall one may canoe, fish, bike, hike, swim, sail, and play tennis or golf. Winter offers the finest and most consistent cross-country skiing in the East.

Hosts: Blake & Rebecca Gleason
Doubles: 10 (6 PB; 4 SB) $50-90
Type of Beds: 3 Twin; 7 Double
Full Breakfast
Credit Cards: A, B
Closed April & Nov.
Notes: 2, 4, 7, 8, 9, 10, 11, 12, 13, 14

CUTTINGSVILLE

Buckmaster Inn

Lincoln Hill Road, Box 118, Shrewsbury, 05738
(802) 492-3485

Country charm in a picturesque Green Mountain village overlooking a farm. Wide board floors gracefully show off family antiues. Homemade baked goodies served each morning in the dining room or on the porch in the summer. Wood-burning stone fireplaces. In a rural setting, this 1801 stagecoach stop is eight miles southeast of Rutland.

Hosts: Sam & Grace Husselman
Doubles: 4 (1 PB; 3 SB) $35-55 plus tax
Full Breakfast
Minimum stay weekends & holidays: 2
Credit Cards: No
Notes: 5, 8 (over 9), 12, 13, 14

Maple Crest Farm

Lincoln Hill Road, Box 120, 05738
(802) 492-3367

Located high in the Green Mountains, ten miles south of Rutland and twelve miles north of Ludlow, this 1808 twenty-seven-room historic home has been lovingly preserved for five generations. Cross-country skiing and hiking are offered on the farm. Close to major ski areas, Rutland, and places of historic interest. A real taste of true old Vermont hospitality. Maple syrup made on premises.

Hosts: William & Donna Smith
Singles: 1 (SB) $25
Doubles: 5 (1 PB; 4 SB) $50
Full Breakfast
Credit Cards: No
Closed Jan., Feb.
Notes: 2, 7, 9, 10, 11, 12

DANBY

Quails Nest B&B Inn

Box 221, 05739
(802) 293-5099

Nestled in a quiet mountain village, the inn offers its guests friendly conversation around the fireplace, rooms filled with cozy quilts and antiques, tips about local attractions, and a hearty, home-cooked breakfast in the morning.

Hosts: Anharad & Chip Edson
Doubles: 5 (1 PB; 4 SB) $40-65
Type of Beds: 2 Twin; 5 Double
Full Breakfast
Credit Cards: A, B
Notes: 2, 5, 7, 8 (over 6), 9, 10, 11, 12, 13

Silas Griffith Inn

S. Main Street, 05739
(802) 293-5567

Built in 1891 by Vermont's first millionaire, a now lovingly restored Victorian mansion and carriage house. Relax in antique-filled guest rooms with spectacular Green Mountain views. Dinner available.

Hosts: Paul & Lois Dansereau
Doubles: 17 (11 PB; 6 SB) $53-82.68
Type of Beds: 4 Twin; 4 Double; 12 Queen
Full Breakfast
Minimum stay holidays: 2
Credit Cards: A, B, C
Notes: 2, 4, 5, 7 (limited), 8, 9, 11, 14

DORSET

The Little Lodge at Dorset

Rt. 30, Box 673, 05251
(802) 867-4040

On a hillside back from the road, overlooking the pond and mountain view. Lawn chairs, inviting barnboard den with fireplace, picture window, wet bar, guest refrigerator. Screened porch. Beds turned down; mints on pillows; flowers in all rooms.

Hosts: Allan & Nancy Norris
Doubles: 5 (PB) $68.90-95.40
Type of Beds: 5 Twin or 5 King
Continental-plus Breakfast
Minimum stay some weekends & holidays: 2
Credit Cards: C
Notes: 2, 5, 8, 9, 10, 11, 12, 13, 14

NOTES: Credit cards accepted: A Master Card; B Visa; C American Express; D Discover Card; E Diners Club; F Other: 2 Personal checks accepted: 3 Lunch available: 4 Dinner available: 5 Open all year

Maplewood Colonial Inn

Box 1200, 05251
(802) 867-4470

This twenty-room white colonial is in a
beautiful valley surrounded by mountains,
with a swimming pond complete with canoe
and fishing hole. The five corner bedrooms
are comfortably furnished with antiques,
and the dining table is pre-Civil War. Skiing
at nearby Bromley and Stratton. Come and
enjoy.

Hosts: Marge & Leon Edgerton
Doubles: 3 (PB) $50-75
Type of Beds: 1 Twin; 2 Double; 2 Queen
Full Breakfast
Credit Cards: A, B, C
Notes: 2, 5, 6, 7 (outside), 8, 9, 10, 11, 12, 13, 14

Marble West Inn

Dorset West Road, 05251
(802) 867-4155

Marble West Inn is a Greek Revival home
built in the 1840s. The house remained in
the family of Helen "Honey" West until she
sold it to be an inn in 1985. Listed in the
National Register of Historic Places, the inn
features marble-columned porches overlooking the surrounding hills. Maple and
white birch trees provide shade, and a little
pond reflects the dark woodlands. The interior decor features beautiful stenciling that
can be seen in the main hallway, polished
hardwood floors covered with Oriental carpets, and displays of local artwork.

Hosts: Bill & Diane Coleman
Doubles: 7 (PB) $75-150
Type of Beds: 2 Twin; 3 Queen; 1 King
Continental Breakfast
Credit Cards: A, B
Closed April & November
Notes: 2, 11, 12, 13, 14

EAST BARNET

Inwood Manor

Lower Waterford Road, 05821
(802) 633-4047

"Creating" a country inn before it became
chic and approaching it as a life-style, not a
business, has helped keep Ron and Peter
going for ten years in rural northeast Vermont. An abandoned building before they
bought it, Inwood Manor was restored from
its boardinghouse/stage-coach-stop past to a
charming, comfortable, old-style country inn
on 20 private acres with a pond for swimming and ice skating.

Hosts: Ron Kaczor & Peter Embarrato
Doubles: 9 (SB) $45-65
Type of Beds: 2 Twin; 7 Double
Full Breakfast
Credit Cards: A, B
Closed Christmas Day
Notes: 2, 4, 5, 9, 11, 12, 13, 14

Marble West Inn

---

6 Pets welcome: 7 Smoking allowed: 8 Children welcome: 9 Social drinking allowed: 10 Tennis available: 11
Swimming available: 12 Golf available: 13 Skiing available: 14 May be booked through travel agents

Inwood Manor

EAST BURKE

Burke Green Guest House

RR 1, Box 81, 05832
(802) 467-3472

Enjoy our quiet country setting and comfortable, spacious, circa 1840 farmhouse,
remodeled with modern conveniences but
featuring original wooden beams and
relaxed atmosphere. The view of Burke Mt.
is spectacular. Located on 35 acres. Host is
a civil engineer enjoying his own consulting
firm in retirement. Both hosts like to travel
and meet people.

Hosts: Harland & Beverly Lewin
Doubles: 3 (1 PB; 2 SB) $43-48
Types of Beds: 6 Twin; 1 Double
Minimum stay holidays: 2
Continental Breakfast
Credit Cards: B
Notes: 2, 5, 7, 8, 9, 10, 11, 13

EAST DOVER

Cooper Hill Inn

Cooper Hill Rd., Box 146, 05341
(802) 348-6333

Informal and cozy hilltop inn with "one of
the most spectacular mountain panoramas
in all New England." Quiet country-road
location. Hearty home-cooked meals are a
tradition here. Double rooms and family
suites all feature private baths. Dinner and
breakfast included in the daily rate.

Hosts: Pat & Marilyn Hunt
Singles: 2 (PB) $63.60-79.70 MAP
Doubles: 5 (PB) $42.40-52 per person MAP
Suites: 3 (PB) $42.40-52 per person MAP
Type of Beds: 6 Twin; 5 Double; 3 Queen
Full Breakfast
Credit Cards: No
Closed for 1 week in April & November
Notes: 2, 4, 7, 8, 9, 10, 11, 12, 13, 14

EAST HARDWICK

Brick House Guests

Box 128, Brick House Road, 05836
(802) 472-5512

Federal brick house with comfortable Victorian furnishings, sitting on the edge of a
small village with open farmland and woods
nearby. Beautiful gardens, perennial
flowers, and herb nursery. The area is unspoiled, hilly and rural. Nearby you'll find

NOTES: Credit cards accepted: A Master Card; B Visa; C American Express; D Discover Card; E Diners
Club; F Other: 2 Personal checks accepted: 3 Lunch available: 4 Dinner available: 5 Open all year

tennis and golf, horseback riding, swimming in clear lakes, canoeing, and good local restaurants.

Hosts: Thomas & Judith Kane
Doubles: 3 (SB) $40
Type of Beds: 2 Double; 1 Queen
Full Breakfast
Credit Cards: A, B
Closed Dec. 24-26
Notes: 2, 5, 6, 7, 8, 9, 10, 11, 12, 13 (XC)

EAST MIDDLEBURY

Waybury Inn

Rt. 125, 05740
(802) 388-6480

The Waybury Inn stands for the tradition of the old-fashioned country inn. Recognized as a national historical place, the Waybury Inn is featured on the "Bob Newhart Show." Come see Robert Frost's country and enjoy skiing or hiking.

Host: Kimberly Smith
Doubles: 14 (PB) $80-115
Type of Beds: 8 Twin; 4 Double; 3 Queen; 3 King
Full Breakfast
Minimum stay weekends & holidays: 2
Credit Cards: A, B, C
Closed Christmas Eve & Christmas
Notes: 2, 4, 7, 8, 9, 10, 11, 12, 13

ENOSBURG FALLS

Berkson Farms

RD 1 Route 108, 05450
(802) 933-2522

Homey, relaxed atmosphere in a century-old restored farmhouse situated on a 600-acre working dairy farm, surrounded by a large variety of animals and all the simple, wonderful joys of nature and life itself. Warm hospitality and country home cooking.

Hosts: Dick & Joanne Keesler
Doubles: 4 (1 PB; 3 SB) $37.10-$53
Type of Beds: 4 Double; 2 Cots and a Crib available
Full Breakfast
Credit Cards: No
Notes: 2, 4, 5, 6, 7, 8, 9, 10, 11, 12, 13

FAIR HAVEN

Maplewood Inn

Rt. 22A South, 05743
(802) 265-8039

This beautifully restored 1850s Greek Revival inn has exquisitely appointed rooms and suites and common areas that include a TV room with fireplace, BYOB tavern, formal parlor furnished in various period styles and antiques. Many extras; near lakes, shops, and restaurants.

Hosts: Cindy & Paul Soder
Doubles: 5 (4 PB; 1 SB) $65-95 (suites)
Type of Beds: 3 Doubles; 2 Queens; 1 Twin Sofabed; 2 Cots
Full Breakfast
Credit Cards: A, B
Notes: 2, 5, 7, 8 (over 5, call), 9, 10, 11, 12, 13, 14

FAIRLEE

Silver Maple Lodge

Rt. 5, 05045
(802) 333-4326

Historic B&B country inn. Cozy rooms with antiques, or knotty pine cottages. Enjoy beach, boating, fishing, and swimming at Lake Morey, one mile away. Golf, tennis, skiing, and hot-air balloon rides nearby. Dartmouth College, seventeen miles. Walk to restaurant.

Hosts: Scott & Sharon Wright
Doubles: 15 (8 PB; 7 SB) $30-52
Type of Beds: 14 Twin; 11 Double
Continental Breakfast
Minimum stay holidays: 2
Credit Cards: A, B, C
Closed Christmas Eve
Notes: 2, 8, 9, 10, 11, 12, 13, 14

FRANKLIN

Fair Meadow Farm B&B

Box 430 Rt. 235, 05457
(802) 285-2132

In the family since 1853, Fair Meadows is nestled in the northwest corner of Vermont. Peace, quiet, and comfort. When guests arrive, they are invited to "make themselves at home." North of Burlington, sixty-five miles south of Montreal.

Hosts: Terry & Philip Pierce
Singles: 1 (SB) $35
Doubles: 4 (SB) $45
Type of Beds: 1 Twin; 4 Double
Full Breakfast
Credit Cards: No
Notes: 2, 5, 6, 7, 8, 9, 10, 11, 12, 13, 14

GAYSVILLE

Cobble House Inn

Box 49, 05746
(802) 234-5458

The inn sits secluded on a hilltop overlooking the Green Mountains. The White River flows along our boundary, offering swimming and fishing. Each room is decorated in antiques and country furnishings, and we have a dining room that features Northern Italian cuisine prepared by our chef/owners. Complimentary afternoon hors d'ouevres are served.

Hosts: Beau, Phil & Sam Benson
Doubles: 6 (PB) $65-95
Type of Beds: 2 Double; 4 Queen
Full Breakfast
Credit Cards: A, B
Notes: 2 (for deposit), 4, 5, 8 (over 5), 9, 10, 11, 12, 13, 14

GOSHEN

Blueberry Hill Inn

RD 3, 05733
(802) 247-6735

Nestled in the Green Mountain National Forest, Blueberry Hill offers the ultimate country inn experience. Seventy-five kilometers of cross-country and hiking trails, gourmet cuisine, and antique-filled rooms make this an unforgettable stop.

Homemade goodies and fine Vermont handcrafts.

Host: Tony Clark
Singles: 2 (PB)
Doubles: 10 (PB) $136-192
Type of Beds: 12 Twin; 10 Double
Full Breakfast
Credit Cards: A, B
Closed weekdays in April
Notes: 2, 4, 5, 8, 9, 10, 11, 12, 13, 14

HANCOCK

Kincraft Inn

Rt. 100, Box 96, 05748
(802) 767-3734

An 1800s refurbished farmhouse with homemade quilts and Shaker reproduction furniture made by hosts. Full breakfast; dinner by reservation. Midway between five major ski areas; hiking, hunting, fishing nearby. Craft shop on premises. A country inn filled with country hospitality.

Hosts: Irene & Ken Neitzel
Doubles: 6 (SB) $28-50
Type of Beds: 3 Twin; 6 Double
Full Breakfast
Minimum stay holidays: 2
Credit Cards: A, B, C
Notes: 2, 4, 5, 8, 9, 10, 11, 12, 13

JAMAICA

Three Mountain Inn

Box 180, 05343
(802) 874-4140

Small, romantic, 1780s authentic country inn. Fine food, comfortable rooms. Located in the village, just four blocks to hiking in a state park and cross-country skiing. Ten minutes to Stratton. Your innkeepers plan special day trips with detailed local maps of the southern Vermont area. Special midweek rates; honeymoon suites available.

Hosts: Charles & Elaine Murray
Doubles: 16 (14 PB; 2 SB) $110-200
Type of Beds: 4 Twin; 5 Double; 8 Queen; 1 King
Full Breakfast

NOTES: Credit cards accepted: A Master Card; B Visa; C American Express; D Discover Card; E Diners Club; F Other: 2 Personal checks accepted: 3 Lunch available: 4 Dinner available: 5 Open all year

Minimum stay weekends: 2
Credit Cards: No
Closed April, Nov. 1-20, Dec. 1-15
Notes: 2, 4, 8 (over 12), 9, 10, 11, 12, 13

KILLINGTON

The Inn at Long Trail

Rt. 4, Sherburne Pass, Box 767, 05751
(802) 775-7181

Historic country inn, high in the ski country of Vermont, located at the junction of the historic Appalachian & Long Trails, for excellent hiking in the mountains. Irish pub, wood-paneled public rooms, and fireplace suites. Hot tub. Ideal for hiking and skiing. Open summer, fall, and winter.

Hosts: Kyran, Murray & Rosemary McGrath
Singles: 4 (PB)
Doubles: 18 (PB)
Seasonal rates
Minimum stay weekends: 2; holidays: 3
Type of Beds: 12 Twin; 2 Double; 14 Queen
Full Breakfast
Credit Cards: A, B
Closed April 15 - June 30
Notes: 2 (with CC) 4, 7, 8, 9, 10,11, 12, 13, 14

The Vermont Inn

Route 4, 05751
(802) 775-0708

A small country inn built as a farmhouse in 1840. Country charm, warm atmosphere, and gourmet dining on a 5-acre mountain setting. Dining room, open to public, has a three diamond award from AAA. Package plans are available.

Hosts: Susan & Judd Levy
Doubles: 17 (13 PB; 4 SB) $40-85 p.p. MAP
Type of Beds: 13 Double; 4 Queen
Full Breakfast
Minimum stay weekends: 2
Credit Cards: A, B, C
Closed April, May, Oct. 25-Nov. 23
Notes: 2, 4, 7, 8 (over 6), 9, 10, 11, 12, 13, 14

LONDONDERRY

Blue Gentian Lodge

Magic Mountain Road, 05148
(802) 824-5908

Walk to the ski lifts of Magic Mountain. Lounge/library with fireplace. Full country breakfast. All large rooms have private bath, color TV. Fire walls separate rooms. Game rooms, BYOB, ice machine, soda machine, outdoor pool. Near excellent hiking, shopping, antiquing.

Hosts: Dick & June Kidde
Doubles: 14 (PB) $37-91
Type of Beds: 15 Twin; 14 Double
Full Breakfast
Minimum stay weekdays & weekends: 2; holidays: 3
Credit Cards: C
Notes: 2, 4, 5, 7, 8 (over 9), 9, 10, 11, 12, 13

The Highland House

Rt. 100, 05148
(802) 824-3019

An 1842 inn, with swimming pool and tennis court, set on 32 acres. Seventeen rooms, fifteen with private baths. Classic candlelight dining with homemade soups, breads, and desserts. Within minutes to skiing, hiking, horseback riding, shopping, and points of interest.

Hosts: Claire Letch & John Mehan
Doubles: 17 (15 PB; 2 SB) $55-95
Type of Beds: 5 Twin; 6 Double; 6 Queen
Full Breakfast
Minimum stay weekends: 2; holidays: 3
Credit Cards: A, B
Closed one week in Nov., three in April
Notes: 2, 4, 7, 8, 9, 10, 11, 12

The Village Inn at Landgrove

215 Landgrove Road, 05148
(802) 824-6673

This renovated farmstead was featured in *Country Inns and Back Roads*. Rooms and

---

6 Pets welcome: 7 Smoking allowed: 8 Children welcome: 9 Social drinking allowed: 10 Tennis available: 11 Swimming available: 12 Golf available: 13 Skiing available: 14 May be booked through travel agents

meals, pool, tennis courts, pitch-and-putt golf. Families welcome.

Hosts: Else & Don Snyder
Doubles: 20 (16 PB; 4 SB) $60-65
Type of Beds: 16 Twin; 12 Double
Full Breakfast
Credit Cards: A, B, D
Closed April 1 - May 26 & Oct. 30 - Dec. 15
Notes: 2, 4, 7 (limited), 8, 9, 10, 11, 12, 13, 14

LUDLOW

The Andrie Rose Inn

13 Pleasant Street, 05149
(802) 228-4846

Enjoy our elegant circa 1830 village inn. Sip cocktails by the fire, partake in board or card games. Escape to one of our guest rooms with private bath, some with whirlpool or claw-foot tubs, cathedral ceilings, skylights, and views of Okemo Mountain. Savor delectable breakfasts and dinners by candlelight. Minutes from skiing and lakes; walk to shops. MAP available.

Hosts: Rich & Carolyn Bentzinger
Doubles: 8 (PB) $95
Type of Beds: 8 Double
Full Breakfast
Credit Cards: A, B
Closed April
Notes: 2, 3, 4, 9, 11, 12, 13, 14

The Combes Family Inn

RFD 1, Box 275, 05149
(802) 228-8799

Bring your family home to ours at The Combes Family Inn. Located on a quiet country back road with 50 acres of meadows to explore. Brownie, reported to be the friendliest goat around, shares the farm with lots of equally friendly cats, dogs, innkeepers, and guests.

Hosts: Ruth & Bill Combes
Doubles: 12 (8 PB; 4 SB) $60.40-86.90
Type of Beds: 1 Twin; 11 Doubles
Full Breakfast
Minimum stay, fall & winter weekends: 2; holidays: 4
Credit Cards: A, B, C

Closed April 15-May 15
Notes: 2, 4, 6, 7, 8, 9, 10, 11, 12, 13, 14

Echo Lake Inn

Box 154, 05149
(802) 228-8602

Surrounded by Echo Lake, the Black River, and the mountains, near the birthplace of President Coolidge, the inn offers a pool, tennis, boating, fishing, hiking, and cycling. Porch dining. Minutes to Killington and Okemo ski centers; short distance from Woodstock, Weston, and Manchester.

Hosts: Phil & Kathy Cocco
Doubles: 26 (14 PB; 12 SB) $45-65
Full Breakfast
Credit Cards: A, B
Closed April
Notes: 2, 3, 4, 8, 9, 10, 11, 12, 13, 14

Echo Lake Inn

The Governor's Inn

86 Main Street, 05149
(802) 228-8830

An extraordinary reputation for excellence surrounds this premier eight-guestroom Victorian country house. Snuggle in a century-old brass four-poster, wake up to a wonderful English breakfast. Enjoy Vermont all day, then come home to Mozart, afternoon tea, and a crackling fire. Gather for hors d'oeuvres and a six-course dinner. Sip brandy in the late evening. The winner of eleven national culinary awards. Rates include breakfast, tea, and dinner.

Hosts: Charlie & Deedy Marble
Doubles: 8 (PB) $170
Type of Beds: 2 Twin; 6 Double; 1 King
Full Breakfast
Credit Cards: A, B
Notes: 2, 3 (picnic basket), 4, 5, 7, 9, 10, 11, 12, 13, 14

The Governor's Inn

MANCHESTER

American Country Collection 080

984 Gloucester Place
Schenectady, N.Y., 12309
(518) 370-4948

Built in 1890 on a 5-acre lot as a tenant farmer's house, this home has seen many additions throughout the years. The barn and many original features of the house are still intact. Each guest room has a magnificent view, one of the brook, the other of the mountains. Enjoy afternoon tea on the deck beside the brook or by the woodstove or fireplace in cooler weather. Six miles from Bromley, fifteen from Stratton.

Doubles: 2 (PB) $60
Type of Beds: 2 Twin; 1 Double
Continental Breakfast
Credit Cards: A, B, C
Notes: 2, 5, 7 (limited), 10, 11, 13, 14

Equinox Sky Line Inn

Box 325, Equinox Toll Road, 05254
(802) 362-1113; 375-6394

The inn is located atop Mt. Equinox and affords a breathtaking five-state panoramic view. Our guests can relax in peaceful seclusion in a world apart. The inn's restaurant offers one of the finest cuisines in New England. We pride ourselves on our quality, service, and reasonable prices.

Hosts: J. A. Rudd
Doubles: 18 (PB) $34-65
Type of Beds: 10 Twin; 6 Double; 2 Queen; 4 King
Full Breakfast
Minimum stay foliage season & holidays: 2
Credit Cards: A, B
Closed Oct. 31-April 28
Notes: 2, 4, 7, 8, 9, 10, 11, 12, 13

The Inn at Manchester

Box 41, 05254
(802) 362-1793

Beautifully restored turn-of-the-century Victorian set on 4 acres in the picture-book village of Manchester. Elegant rooms with bay windows, brass beds, antiques, and an extensive art collection. Luscious full country breakfast. Secluded pool, skiing, shops, theater in the area. Come for peace, pancakes, and pampering.

Hosts: Stan & Harriet Rosenberg
Doubles: 20 (13 PB; 7 SB) $70-100

Type of Beds: 7 Twin; 13 Double; 7 Queen; 1 King
Full Breakfast
Credit Cards: A, B, C
Notes: 2, 5, 7 (limited), 8 (over 8), 9, 10, 11, 12, 13, 14

MANCHESTER CENTER

Brook-N-Hearth Inn

SR 11 & 30, Box 508, 05255
(802) 362-3604

Homey colonial-style inn 2.5 miles east of
the town center on Routes 11 and 30. Features full breakfast, cozy rooms, private
baths, family suite, cable TV, lounge,
BYOB, recreation rooms, outdoor heated
swimming pool, cross-country and walking
trails by brook.

Hosts: Larry & Terry Greene
Doubles: 4 (2 PB; 2 SB) $35-64
Type of Beds: 3 Twin; 4 Double
Full Breakfast
Minimum stay weekends & holidays: 2
Credit Cards: A, B, C
Closed early Nov. & early May
Notes: 2, 7, 8, 9, 10, 11, 12, 13

Manchester Highlands Inn

Manchester Highlands Inn

Box 1754, 05255
(802) 362-4565

A graceful Queen Anne Victorian inn on a
hilltop overlooking Manchester. Front
porch with rocking chairs, large outdoor
pool, game room, and pub with stone
fireplace. Each room is individually
decorated, most with private bath. Gourmet
country breakfast and afternoon snacks are
served.

Hosts: Robert & Patricia Eichorn
Doubles: 15 (12 PB; 3 SB) $76-86
Type of Beds: 2 Twin; 6 Double; 5 Queen; 1 King
Full Breakfast
Credit Cards: A, B, C
Notes: 2, 5, 7 (limited), 8, 9, 10, 11, 12, 13, 14

MANCHESTER VILLAGE

Village Country Inn

Historic Route 7A, 05254
(802) 362-1792

A French country inn decorated in shades of
mauve, celery, and ecru. Long porch with
chintz rockers, wicker, and flowers. Elegant
candlelight dining and cocktails are available
in our tavern. Guest rooms are a fantasy of
ice-cream colors, each one different. Swimming pool; tennis court. Dinner included in
daily rates.

Hosts: Anne & Jay Megen
Singles: 3 (PB) $90-100 MAP
Doubles: 27 (PB) $125-175 MAP
Type of Beds: 1 Twin; 7 Double; 14 Queen; 8 King
Continental midweek and Full Breakfast week-ends
Credit Cards: A, B, C
Notes: 2, 4, 5, 7, 9, 10, 11, 12, 13, 14

MIDDLEBURY

Brookside Meadows

RD 3, Box 2460, 05753
(802) 388-6429

Attractive farmhouse built in 1979. Quiet
rural setting, but only three miles from village center and many excellent restaurants.
Best downhill and cross-country skiing. Special two-bedroom suite has living room with
wood stove and private entrance.

NOTES: Credit cards accepted: A Master Card; B Visa; C American Express; D Discover Card; E Diners
Club; F Other: 2 Personal checks accepted: 3 Lunch available: 4 Dinner available: 5 Open all year

Hosts: Linda & Roger Cole
Doubles: 2 (PB) $63-95.40
Suite (4 people) $106-127.20
Type of Beds: 2 Twin; 2 Queen
Full Breakfast
Credit Cards: No
Notes: 2, 5, 8 (over 5), 9, 10, 11, 12, 13, 14

Swift House Inn

Route 7, 05753
(802) 388-9925

A warm and gracious Federal style estate
with window seats overlooking the formal
gardens, fireplaces in eight of the rooms, and
whirlpool tubs. Relax in our cozy pub room
and then enjoy award-winning cuisine in our
elegant cherry-paneled dining room. Walking distance to shopping and Middlebury
College; just a short drive to skiing, golf, and
swimming.

Hosts: John & Andrea Nelson
Doubles: 14 (PB) $60-115
Type of Beds: 4 Twin; 8 Queen; 2 King
Full Breakfast
Credit Cards: A, B, C, D, E
Notes: 2, 4, 5, 7, 8, 9, 10, 11, 12, 13, 14

The Hortonville Inn

MIDDLETOWN SPRINGS

Middletown Springs Inn

Box 1068, 05757
(802) 235-2198

An 1879 Victorian mansion in a Vermont
village in a national historic district. Ten
guest rooms and five large common rooms
are decorated in Victorian style and furnished in antiques. Experience rural Vermont and an exceptional country inn. The
food, the hospitality, and the area offer
everything you hope for.

Hosts: Jane & Steve Sax
Doubles: 10 (8 PB; 2 SB) $35-55
Type of Beds: 5 Twin; 6 Double; 3 Queen
Full Breakfast
Credit Cards: A, B
Notes: 2, 4, 5, 7 (limited), 8 (over 6), 9, 10, 11, 12, 13
(XC), 14

MORGAN

Hunt's Hideaway

Mail to: RR 1, Box 570
West Charleston, 05872
(802) 895-4432; 334-8322

Our B&B was started in 1981 after the hosts
stayed in B&Bs in Europe during their many
years of traveling. Contemporary split level
on 100 acres; brook, pond, in-ground pool.
Located in Morgan, six miles from I-91 near
Canadian border.

Host: Pat Hunt
Doubles: 3 (SB) $20-30 plus tax
Type of Beds: 1 Twin; 1 Double; 2 Bunks
Full Breakfast
Credit Cards: No
Kitchen Privileges
Notes: 2, 5, 6, 7, 8, 9, 10, 11, 12, 13

MT. HOLLY

The Hortonville Inn

Box 14, 05758
(802) 259-2587

A 13-acre hilltop retreat, beautifully
decorated and abounding with seasonal activities. Minutes to Okemo, Killington, and
Weston. Porch dining with breathtaking
mountain views. Fireplace in lounge/game
room and dining room. In-room movies,
freshly baked cookies, country breakfasts,
hot mulled cider, hors d'oeuvres.

6 Pets welcome: 7 Smoking allowed: 8 Children welcome: 9 Social drinking allowed: 10 Tennis available: 11
Swimming available: 12 Golf available: 13 Skiing available: 14 May be booked through travel agents

Hosts: Ray & Mary Maglione
Doubles: 5 (2 PB; 3 SB) $50-70
Type of Beds: 2 Twin; 3 Double; 1 Queen; 1 King
Full Breakfast
Minimum stay weekends: 2; holidays: 3
Credit Cards: A, B
Notes: 2, 4, 5, 7 (limited), 8 (over 6), 9, 10, 11, 12, 13, 14

NEWBURY

A Century Past

Box 186 Route 5, 05051
(802) 866-3358

A charming historic house dating back to 1790, nestled in the tranquility of a quaint Vermont village. A cozy sitting room with fireplace: chat with newfound friends or curl up with a good book. Wake up to fresh baked muffins, hot coffee or tea, great French toast — all served in a comfortable dining room.

Hosts: Patricia Smith
Doubles: 4 (2S1B) $47.70
Type of Beds: 4 Twin; 2 Double
Full Breakfast
Credit Cards: A, B
Closed Christmas
Notes: 2, , 8 (over 12), 9, 10, 11, 12, 13

NEWFANE

West River Lodge

RR 1, Box 693, 05345
(802) 365-7745

West River Lodge is a small country inn with farmhouse charm, furnished with antiques. Located in the Green Mountains close to various country pastimes: hiking, swimming, skiing, English riding, trail riding. Riding clinic held in May; watercolor workshop in July. Close to flea markets and antique centers. MAP plan available at extra charge.

Hosts: Jack & Gill Winner
Doubles: 5 (2 PB; 3 SB) $45-75
Type of Beds: 6 Twin; 3 Double
Full Breakfast
Credit Cards: No
Notes: 2, 3, 4, 5, 7 (limited), 8, 9, 10, 11, 12, 13, 14

NORTH THETFORD

Stone House Inn

Rt. 5, Box 47, 05054
(802) 333-9124

An 1835 stone farmhouse on the banks of the Connecticut River in central Vermont. The furnishing of the inn are cheerful and comfortable. Its central location and proximity to Dartmouth College make the inn a good base for touring.

Hosts: Art & Dianne Sharkey
Doubles: 6 (SB) $28-45
Type of Beds: 2 Twin; 4 Double
Continental Breakfast
Credit Cards: A, B
Closed two weeks in April
Notes: 2, 7 (limited), 8, 9, 10, 11, 12, 13

ORWELL

Historic Brookside Farms

Rt. 22A, 05760
(802) 948-2727

In 1989, we celebrated the 200th anniversary of Brookside Farms, a 300-acre estate with its Greek Revival mansion. All rooms are furnished with antiques. On the premises are cross-country skiing; hiking and golf are nearby.

Singles: 3 (2 PB; 1 SB) $62-95
Doubles: 5 (2 PB; 3 SB) $65-152
Type of Beds: 5 Twin; 6 Double
Full Breakfast
Credit Cards: No
Notes: 2, 4, 5, 7, 8, 9, 13

PERU

Johnny Seesaw's

Rt. 11, Bromley Mt., 05152
(802) 824-5533

The essential Vermont Experience. A unique log lodge featuring cozy rooms, charming cottages with fireplaces, game room, casual, candlelit country cuisine, all in the beautiful Green Mountains.

NOTES: Credit cards accepted: A Master Card; B Visa; C American Express; D Discover Card; E Diners Club; F Other: 2 Personal checks accepted: 3 Lunch available: 4 Dinner available: 5 Open all year

Hosts: Nancy & Gary Okun
Doubles: 25 (23 PB; 5 SB) $30.25-44.77; MAP:
$54.45-96.80
Type of Beds: 28 Twin; 4 Double; 5 Queen; 4 King
Full Breakfast
Minimum stay weekends: 2; holidays: 5
Credit Cards: A, B, C
Closed April, May, Nov.
Notes: 2, 4, 6, 7, 8, 9, 10, 11, 12, 13

PITTSFIELD

The Inn at Pittsfield

Box 526, 05762
(802) 746-8943

Hospitality, warmth, and good food have
been a watchword at our inn since 1830. We
are dedicated to continuing the tradition.
Our central location on Vermont's most
scenic highway makes us convenient to four-
season activities. Hiking, biking, fishing, antiquing, skiing, or just plain relaxing. We
have it all.

Hosts: Vikki Budasi & Barbara Morris
Doubles: 9 (PB) $100
Type of Beds: 3 Twin; 6 Double
Full Breakfast
Credit Cards: A, B, C
Notes: 2, 4, 5, 7 (limited), 8, 9, 10, 11, 12, 13, 14

PLAINFIELD

Yankees' Northview Bed & Breakfast

RD 2, 05667
(802) 454-7191

Roomy colonial located on a quiet country
road in picturesque Calais. Antique-filled
rooms, quilts, stenciled walls, sitting room
with fireplace. Enjoy your breakfast on the
garden patio with mountain views.
Museums, antiques, quaking bog, and year-
round recreation are nearby. Cross-country

ski rentals available. Picnic area with
fireplace for guest use.

Hosts: Joani & Glen Yankee
Doubles: 3 (SB) $40-45
Full Breakfast
Credit Cards: No
Notes: 2, 5, 8, 9, 10, 11, 12, 13 (XC)

PROCTORSVILLE

The Golden Stage Inn

Box 218, 05153
(802) 226-7744

The tradition of hospitality continues in our
200-year-old stagecoach stop. The warmth
of grandmother's quilts, antiques, greenery,
favorite books, and a blazing fire comfort
you while Marcel prepares silken sauces and
Kirsten bakes delectable chocolate desserts.
The pool and gardens provide summertime
delights, and the cookie jar is always full.

Hosts: Kirsten Murphy & Marcel Perret
Doubles: 10 (6 PB; 4 SB) $130-140 MAP
Type of Beds: 9 Twin; 6 Double; 1 Queen
Full Breakfast
Credit Cards: A, B
Closed April & November
Notes: 2, 4, 7, 8, 9, 10, 11, 12, 13, 14

PUTNEY

Hickory Ridge House

RR 3, Box 1410, 05346
(802) 387-5709

Gracious 1808 Federal brick manor surrounded by fields and woods on a quiet
country road near Putney. Connecticut
River and I-91 convenient. Six working
fireplaces, high ceilings, original tamarack
floors, antique furnishings throughout. Area
offers fine crafts and music, hiking, XC
skiing, boating, swimming.

Hosts: Jacquie Walker & Steve Anderson
Doubles: 7 (3 PB; 4 SB) $42-70
Type of Beds: 2 Twin; 4 Double; 1 Queen
Full Breakfast

Credit Cards: A, B
Notes: 2, 4, 5, 8, 9, 11, 13

RANDOLPH

Placidia Farm Bed & Breakfast

RD 1, Box 275, 05060
(802) 728-9883

Six miles north of Randolph on 81 acres with mountain views, pond, and brook. Lovely hand-hewn log home with private apartment for B&B guests. Large deck for enjoying the view; TV, hi-fi, books, and games.

Host: Viola A. Frost
Private apartment: bedroom, living room, kitchen, bath, & deck. $64-69
Type of Beds: 1 Twin; 1 Double; 1 Double sleeper sofa
Minimum stay weekends & holidays: 2
Full Breakfast
Credit Cards: No
Notes: 2, 5, 8, 9, 10, 11, 12, 13

RIPTON

The Chipman Inn

Route 125, 05766
(802) 388-2390

A traditional Vermont inn built in 1828, situated in the Green Mountain National Forest. Fine food, wine, and spirits for guests. Nine rooms, all with private bath. One of the two sitting rooms was originally the structure's kitchen, and features a fully-licensed bar and large fireplace.

Hosts: Joyce Henderson & Bill Pierce
Doubles: 9 (PB) $63.60-103.88
Type of Beds: 7 Twin; 9 Double
Full Breakfast
Credit Cards: A, B, C
Closed Nov. 15 - Dec. 26 & Apr. 1 - May 15
Notes: 2, 4, 7, 8 (over 12), 9, 12, 13

ROCHESTER

Liberty Hill Farm

Liberty Hill Road, 05767
(802) 767-3926

Working dairy farm nestled between the White River and Green Mountain National Forest, with year-round activities. The 1820 farmhouse, where hearty, home-cooking is served family style at dinner and breakfast, has eighteen rooms of old-fashioned charm. Families are always welcome to visit the barn. Breakfast and dinner included in the daily rate.

Hosts: Bob & Beth Kennett
Singles: 2 (SB) $42.40 MAP
Doubles: 5 (SB) $85 MAP
Type of Beds: 8 Twin; 4 Double; 1 Queen
Full Breakfast
Credit Cards: No
Notes: 2, 4, 5, 7, 8, 9, 10, 11, 12, 13, 14

SOUTH LONDONDERRY

The Londonderry Inn

Rt. 100, Box 301A, 05155
(802) 824-5226

An 1826 homestead that has been welcoming guests for nearly fifty years. Special family accommodations. Huge living room, billiards and Ping-Pong rooms, and cozy tavern. Well-known dining room with dinner menu that changes nightly. May we send you our brochure?

Hosts: Jim & Jean Cavanagh
Doubles: 23 (18 PB; 5 SB) $25.50-73.15
Type of Beds: 10 Twin; 8 Double; 1 Queen; 4 King
Continental-plus Breakfast
Credit Cards: No
Notes: 2, 4, 5, 7, 8, 9, 10, 11, 12, 13, 14

SOUTH STRAFFORD

Watercourse Way Bed & Breakfast

Rt. 132, 05070
(802) 765-4314

An 1850 country guest house on the banks of the Ompompanoosuc River. Angora goats, Christmas trees, brook trout, vegetable and flower gardens, fireside breakfast, warm atmosphere. Fine dining,

NOTES: Credit cards accepted: A Master Card; B Visa; C American Express; D Discover Card; E Diners Club; F Other: 2 Personal checks accepted: 3 Lunch available: 4 Dinner available: 5 Open all year

shopping in Hanover, NH, and Woodstock, VT. Skiing, hiking, riding, swimming nearby. Simple satisfaction.

Hosts: Lincoln and Anna Alden
Doubles: 3 (SB) $30-$55
Type of Beds: 2 Twin; 3 Double
Full Breakfast
Credit Cards: No
Closed Thanksgiving and Christmas
Notes: 2, 6, 7 (limited), 8, 9, 10, 11, 13, 14

SOUTH WOODSTOCK

Kedron Valley Inn
Rt. 106, 05071
(802) 457-1473

Our 1800s inn is scenically located, yet we're near much fun, including sleigh rides and trail rides. We're known for our queen canopy beds, fireplaces in the rooms, luscious food, and a large heirloom quilt collection. Featured in *Country Living, Good Housekeeping,* and *Yankee.*

Hosts: Max & Merrily Comins
Doubles: 28 (PB) $90-155
Type of Beds: 13 Double; 11 Queen canopy; 2 King
Full Breakfast
Minimum stay weekends & holidays: 2
Credit Cards: A, B, C
Closed April
Notes: 2, 4, 6, 7, 8, 9, 10, 11, 12, 13

SPRINGFIELD

Hartness House Inn
30 Orchard St., 05156
(802) 885-2115

The inn is a Vermont Landmark built in 1904 by the Hartness family. Our facilities include: 45 guest rooms, each with private bath, TV, and telephone; full dining facilities; cocktail lounge; meeting rooms; outdoor pool; tennis court; and our underground museum and operating telescope.

Host: Robert Staudter
Singles: 23 (PB) $54
Doubles: 22 (PB) $64
Suites: (PB) $83
Type of Beds: 13 Twin; 20 Double; 12 Queen

Full Breakfast
Credit Cards: A, B, C, E
Notes: 2, 3, 4, 5, 6, 7, 8, 9, 10, 11, 12, 13 (30 min), 14

STOCKBRIDGE

B&B Registry #VT-05772DUR
Box 8174, St. Paul, MN, 55108
(612) 646-4238

This 1780 colonial was the first house built in town. Located on 2 scenic acres, it's only twelve miles from Killington and Pico ski areas and close to several cross-country ski trails. Antique furnishings and a lovely common room for guests.

Doubles: 7 (2 PB; 5 SB) $58-100
Type of Beds: 7 Twin; 3 Double; 1 Queen; 1 King; 1 Sleep sofa
Full Breakfast
Credit Cards: A, B
Notes: 5, 8 (13 and over), 11, 13

STOWE

Andersen Lodge — An Austrian Inn
RD 1, Box 1450, 05672
(802) 253-7336

A small, friendly Tyrolean inn in a quiet setting. Heated swimming pool, tennis court, living rooms with fireplaces, TV, and air-conditioning. Near a major ski area, eighteen-hole golf course, riding, hiking, fishing.

Hosts: Dietmar & Trude Heiss
Singles: 28 (PB) $58
Doubles: 48 (PB) $78
Full Breakfast
Credit Cards: A, B, C
Closed 4/10-6/1 & 10/25-12/10
Notes: 2, 4, 9, 12, 13

Bittersweet Inn
RR 2, Box 2900, 05672
(802) 253-7787

Bittersweet Inn is a brick cape with a converted carriage house dating back to 1835. The house is on 9 acres overlooking Camel's Hump Mountain, just a half mile to the center of town and minutes to ski lifts and cross-country touring. A good-sized swimming pool is located out back with plenty of room for just taking it easy.

Hosts: Barbara & Paul Hansel
Doubles: 8 (PB and SB) $54-76
Continental Breakfast
Credit Cards: A, B, C
Closed April 9-22 & Nov. 19-27
Notes: 2, 6, 7, 8, 9, 10, 11, 12, 13, 14

Golden Kitz Lodge

RD #3, Box 2980, 05672
(802) 253-4217

At the Golden Kitz, everyone shares legendary Old World antique family treasures in Yankee style. Cozy, caring comfort, with yummy, chummy breakfasts; piano, guitar, and other musical instruments for you to have fun with. Fireside soups and wine; front porch; art studio. Romantic riverside path for walking, biking, or cross-country skiing to shops, dining, and dancing. Family members are painters, writers, potters, skiers, bikers, world travelers, and adventurers.

Hosts: Sam, Annette, Alyce & Margie MacElwee Jones
Singles: 1 (SB) $25
Doubles: 15 (7 PB; 8 SB) $70
Type of Beds: 18 Twin; 17 Double
Full Breakfast
Minimum stay holidays: 2
Credit Cards: A, B, C, D, E, F
Notes: 2, 5, 6, 7 (restricted), 8, 9, 10, 11, 12, 13, 14

Logwood Inn & Chalets

Rt. 1, Box 2290, 05672
1-800-426-6697

Handsome main lodge with fifteen guest rooms; two separate, fully equipped, chalets. Large, quiet living room with large fieldstone fireplace, library, TV room with cable, heated swimming pool, clay tennis court. Spacious lawns with flowers and white birches. Near major ski area, eighteen-hole golf course, riding, hiking, fishing.

Hosts: Len & Ruth Shetler
Singles: 2 (PB) $50-70
Doubles: 23 (20 PB; 3 SB) $60-120
Type of Beds: 10 Twin; 13 Double; 1 Queen; 1 King
Full Breakfast
Minimum stay weekends: 2; holidays: 5
Credit Cards: A, B
Dinner served winter only
Notes: 2, 4, 5, 7, 8, 9, 10, 11, 13, 14

The Siebeness

Mountain Road, Box 1490, 05672
(802) 253-8942; (800) 426-9001

A warm welcome awaits you at our charming country inn! Antiques, private baths, homemade quilts, air-conditioning. Fireplace lounge, BYOB bar, hot tub, pool with beautiful mountain views. Famous for outstanding food. Near skiing, golf. Packages available.

Hosts: Nils & Sue Andersen
Doubles: 10 (PB) $58-87
Type of Beds: 8 Twin; 5 Double; 4 Queen
Full Breakfast
Minimum stay weekends:2
Credit Cards: A, B, C, D, E, F
Notes: 2, 4 (winter), 5, 7, 8, 9, 10, 11, 12, 13, 14

Ski Inn

Rt. 108, 05672
(802) 253-4050

This comfortable inn, noted for good food and good conversation, is a great gathering place for interesting people. Guests enjoy themselves and one another. Nearest lodge to all Stowe ski lifts.

Hosts: Larry & Harriet Heyer
Doubles: 10 (5 PB; 5 SB) $30-80
Type of Beds: 10 Twin; 10 Double
Continental Breakfast; full in winter
Minimum stay holidays: 2-3
Credit Cards: No
Notes: 2, 4 (winter), 5, 7, 8, 9, 10, 11, 12, 13

NOTES: Credit cards accepted: A Master Card; B Visa; C American Express; D Discover Card; E Diners Club; F Other: 2 Personal checks accepted: 3 Lunch available: 4 Dinner available: 5 Open all year

Timberholm Inn

Cottage Club Road, RR 1, Box 810, 05672
(802) 253-7603

Nestled in a quiet location in the woods, the
Timberholm Inn welcomes guests from all
over the world. Warm up after a day of skiing
with a complimentary cup of soup by a large
fieldstone fireplace and enjoy the spectacular mountain views. Rooms finely appointed with antiques and quilts.

Hosts: Wes & Susan Jenson
Doubles: 8 (PB) $65-100
Suites: 2 (PB)
Type of Beds: 3 Twin; 9 Double; 1 Queen
Buffet Breakfast
Credit Cards: A, B
Notes: 2, 5, 7 (restricted), 8, 9, 10, 11, 12, 13

Ye Olde England Inne

The Mountain Rd., Box 320B, 05672
(802) 253-7558

A beautiful inn restored in the English tradition with charming Laura Ashley rooms and
many four-poster beds. The English experience is complete in Mr. Picwick's pub,
famous for its friendly atmosphere and superb selection of the finest ales, wines, and
entertainment amid beams, brass, copper,
and stone.

Hosts: Christopher & Linda Francis
Doubles: 18 (18 PB; 6 w/Jacuzzi) $60-$115
Cottages: 3 (PB)
Minimum stay weekends: 2
Type of Beds: 6 Twin; 2 Double; 18 Queen
Full Breakfast
Credit Cards: A, B
Notes: 2, 4, 5, 7, 8, 10, 11, 12, 13

WAITSFIELD

Hyde Away

RR 1, Box 65, 05673
(802) 496-2322

One of the oldest (c. 1830) and most comfortable inns in the valley. Centrally located
less than five minutes from Sugarbush, Mad

River Glen, Mt. Ellen, historic Waitsfield,
the Long and Catamount trails. Full public
restaurant and rustic tavern; hearty country
meals. Families and children are welcome.
Hiking, biking, swimming, fishing, tennis,
and golf nearby.

Hosts: Bruce & Kathy Hyde
Singles: 1 (SB) $50
Doubles: 14 (SB) $70
Type of Beds: 18 Twin; 7 Double
Full Breakfast
Credit Cards: A, B, C
Notes: 2, 4, 5, 7, 8, 9, 10, 11, 12, 13, 14

Mad River Barn

Rt. 17, Box 88, 05673
(802) 496-3310

Classic Vermont country lodge. Spacious
rooms with private baths, grand stone
fireplace, landscaped grounds, and pool.
Discover mountain streams, visit Lake
Champlain (thirty minutes), Shelburne
Museum, the Vermont State House, or the
Rock of Ages Quarry. Mountain views.

Host: Betsy Pratt
Doubles: 15 (PB) $40-65
Type of Beds: 28 Twin; 5 Double; 8 Queen
Continental Breakfast
Credit Cards: A, B, C
Notes: 2, 4 (winter), 5, 7, 8, 10, 11, 12, 13, 14

Millbrook Inn

Rt. 17, RFD, Box 62, 05673
(802) 496-2405

Relax in the friendly, unhurried atmosphere
of our cozy 1850s inn. Seven guest rooms are
decorated with hand stenciling, antique
bedsteads, and handmade quilts. Breakfast
and dinner included in daily rate. Dine in our
romantic small restaurant that features
hand-rolled pasta, fresh fish, veal, shrimp,
and homemade desserts from our varied
menu. Rates include breakfast and dinner.

Hosts: Joan & Thom Gorman
Doubles: 7 (4 PB; 3 SB) $48-60 per person MAP
Type of Beds: 2 Twin; 6 Double

6 Pets welcome: 7 Smoking allowed: 8 Children welcome: 9 Social drinking allowed: 10 Tennis available: 11
Swimming available: 12 Golf available: 13 Skiing available: 14 May be booked through travel agents

Full Breakfast
Minimum stay weekends: 2; holidays: 3
Closed April 20-June 20; Oct. 25-Thanksgiving
Credit Cards: A, B, C, E
Notes: 2, 4, 7, 8 (over 10), 9, 10, 11, 12, 13

Mountain View Inn

RFD, Box 69, Rt. 17, 05673
(802) 496-2426

Mountain View Inn, a small country inn,
circa 1826, has seven guest rooms, each with
private bath, accommodating two people.
The rooms are decorated with stenciling,
quilts, braided rugs, and antique furniture.
Meals are served family style around an antique harvest table. Good fellowship is enjoyed around the wood-burning fire in the
living room.

Hosts: Fred & Susan Spencer
Doubles: 7 (PB) $50.88-63.60
Type of Beds: 1 Twin; 5 Double; 1 Queen
Full Breakfast
Minimum stay weekends: 2
Credit Cards: No
Notes: 2, 4, 5, 7 (restricted), 8, 9, 10, 11, 12, 13, 14

Tucker Hill Lodge

RD1 , Box 147, 05673
(800) 451-4580

Tucker Hill Lodge is nestled on a wooded
hillside overlooking Rt. 17 in the Mad River
Valley in north central Vermont, one of the
East's most beautiful resort areas. Bike, fish,
golf, ride. Tennis and swimming on the
premises.

Doubles: 22 (16 PB; 6 SB) $60-86/person
Continental Breakfast
Notes: 11, 12

Valley Inn

RR 1, Box 8, 05673
(802) 496-3450

Our recipe for a great Vermont vacation:
take an exceptional country inn in a lovely
Vermont village, add cozy bedrooms with

private baths, stir in some conversation
around a warm fire, add great meals, a sauna
and hot tub, and mix in nice people like you.

Hosts: The Stinson Family
Doubles: 20 (PB) $35-90/person, breakfast & dinner
Type of Beds: 16 Twin; 14 Double; 1 Queen
Full Breakfast
Credit Cards: A, B, C
Notes: 2, 4 (winter), 5, 7 (limited), 8, 9, 10, 11, 12, 13, 14

WALLINGFORD

The Green Mountain Tea Room

RR 1, Box 400, 05773
(802) 446-2611

Whether you like skiing, hiking, antiquing,
hunting, fishing, or just relaxing, our 200-
year-old inn is just the place. Easy to get to,
centrally located, superb breakfasts and
lunches. Come lounge on the picturesque
banks of Otter Creek.

Hosts: Tracy & Ed Crelin
Doubles: 5 (SB) $42.40-53
Type of Beds: 4 Twin; 5 Double
Full Breakfast
Credit Cards: A, B
Notes: 2, 3, 5, 6, 7, 8, 9, 10, 11, 12, 13

Wallingford Inn

N. Main Street, Box 404, 05773
(802) 446-2849

Charming 1876 Victorian mansion offers
ten elegantly appointed guest rooms, eight
with private bath, two with connecting bath.
Antiques, oak woodwork, and polished
wood floors. Enjoy candlelight dining. Full-
service bar.

Hosts: Kathleen & Joseph Lombardo
Singles: 3 (2 PB; 1 SB) $53
Doubles: 7 (6 PB; 1 SB) $74.20
Type of Beds: 3 Twin; 7 Double
Full Breakfast
Minimum stay weekends & holidays: 2
Credit Cards: A, B
Notes: 2, 4, 5, 7, 8 (over 5), 9, 10, 11, 13

NOTES: Credit cards accepted: A Master Card; B Visa; C American Express; D Discover Card; E Diners
Club; F Other: 2 Personal checks accepted: 3 Lunch available: 4 Dinner available: 5 Open all year

White Rocks Inn

RR 1, Box 297, 05773
(802) 446-2077

Circa 1840s farmhouse inn, listed on the National Register of Historic Places, beautifully furnished with antiques, Oriental rugs, canopy beds. All rooms have private baths. Close to four major ski areas, hiking, horseback riding, canoeing, summer theater, and good restaurants. Nonsmokers only.

Hosts: June & Alfred Matthews
Doubles: 5 (PB) $60-90
Type of Beds: 1 Twin; 1 Double; 2 Queen; 1 King
Full Breakfast
Minimum stay weekends: 2; holidays: 2-3
Credit Cards: A, B
Closed November
Notes: 2 (for deposit), 8 (over 10), 9, 10, 11, 12, 13

White Rocks Inn

WARREN

Sugartree Inn

RR Box 38, 05674
(802) 583-3211

An intimate mountainside country inn featuring handmade quilts atop canopy, brass, and antique beds. Oil lamps, original art, antiques, stained glass, and country curtains. Full country breakfast. Enchanting

gazebo amid myriad flowers in summer, blazing foliage in fall, and downhill skiing in winter.

Hosts: Howard & Janice Chapman
Singles: 1 (PB) $50-75
Doubles: 9 (PB) $75-110
Type of Beds: 7 Twin; 7 Double; 2 Queen
Minimum stay holidays: 2
Full Breakfast
Credit Cards: A, B, C
Closed the last two weeks in May
Notes: 2, 7, 8 (over 6), 9, 10, 11, 12, 13, 14

WATERBURY

Inn at Blush Hill

Blush Hill Road, Box 1266, 05676
(802) 244-7529

A circa 1790 restored cape on five acres with beautiful mountain views. The inn has four fireplaces, a large sitting room, and lots of antiques. It is located across from a golf course, and all summer sports are nearby. Enjoy skiing at Stowe, Sugarbush, and Bolton Valley, only minutes away. AAA approved.

Hosts: Gary & Pam Gosselin
Doubles: 6 (2 PB; 4 SB) $55-85
Type of Beds: 3 Twin; 4 Double; 1 Queen
Full Breakfast
Minimum stay holidays: 3
Credit Cards: A, B
Notes: 2, 5, 8, 9, 10, 11, 12, 13, 14

WEATHERSFIELD

The Inn at Weathersfield

Rt. 106, Box 165, 05151
(802) 263-9217

An eighteenth-century stagecoach stop offering bedrooms with private baths, most with working fireplaces. The inn serves American Nouvelle cuisine dinners, has a full bar and extensive wine cellar, and features live piano music nightly. Dinner, high tea, and full breakfast are included in the room rate. On the 21-acre premises is a pond, a grass tennis court, horse-drawn sleigh or carriage rides, box stall, and paddock facilities. An indoor recreation area features a sauna, aerobics equipment, and a pool table. Nearby is alpine and cross-country skiing, golf, hiking, and many points of interest.

Hosts: Mary Louise & Ron Thorburn
Doubles: 12 (PB) $150-160 couple, MAP
Type of Beds: 10 Twin; 7 Double; 11 Queen
Full Breakfast
Credit Cards: A, B, C
Notes: 2, 4, 5, 6, 7, 8 (8 and over), 9, 10, 11, 12, 13, 14

The Sugartree

WEST DOVER

Doveberry Inn

HCR 63, Box 9, Rt. 100, 05356
(802) 464-5652

A small country inn with eight rooms, run by two sisters who are graduates of the New England Culinary Institute. There is a living room with fireplace, books, games, and VCR for guest use. All rooms have private baths, cable TV, and VCrs. Full liquor license.

Host: Patricia Rossi
Doubles: 8 (PB) $75-120
Type of Beds: 1 Twin; 9 Double; 1 King
Full Breakfast
Credit Cards: A, B, C
Closed early spring and late fall
Notes: 4, 7 (restricted), 8 (over 8), 9, 10, 11, 12, 13

WESTON

1830 Inn on the Green

Rt. 100, 05161
(802) 824-6789

Colonial building built in 1830 as a blacksmith/wheelwright shop, located in the center of town overlooking the delightful village green. Parlor with fireplace, slate terrace overlooking the gardens and pond. Furnished with traditional and family antiques.

Hosts: Sandy & Dave Granger
Doubles: 4 (PB) $55-75
Type of Beds: 1 Double; 1 Queen; 2 King
Full Breakfast
Credit Cards: A, B
Notes: 2, 5, 9, 10, 11, 12, 12, 14

The Inn at Weston

Box 56, 05161
(802) 824-5804

Enjoy beautifully appointed guest rooms and continental cuisine in this country inn nestled in the Green Mountains in the picturebook village of Weston. Take a pleasant walk to the Weston Playhouse for professional summer theater or visit the nearby Benedictine Priory. Cross-country skiing from the door and four downhill ski areas within twenty minutes.

Hosts: Jeanne & Bob Wilder
Doubles: 19 (12 PB; 7 SB) $60-78
Type of Beds: 11 Twin; 9 Double; 5 Queen
Full Breakfast
Credit Cards: A, B
Notes: 2, 4, 5, 7, 8 (over 6), 9, 10, 11, 12, 13, 14

The Wilder Homestead Inn

RR 1, Box 106D, 05161
(802) 824-8172

An 1827 brick home listed on the National Register of Historic Places. Walk to shops, museums, summer theater. Crackling fires in common rooms, canopy beds, down comforters. Rooms have original Moses Eaton

The Inn at Weston

stenciling and are furnished with antiques and reproductions. Weston Priory nearby.

Hosts: Peggy & Roy Varner
Doubles: 7 (5 PB; 2 SB) $63.60-84.80
Type of Beds: 2 Twin; 3 Double; 3 Queen
Full Breakfast
Minimum stay weekends: 2; holidays: 2-3
Credit Cards: A, B
Notes: 2, 5, 7 (restricted), 8 (over 6), 9, 10, 11, 12, 13

WEST RUTLAND

The Silver Fox, a Country Inn

RFD 1, Box 1222, Rt. 133, 05777
(802) 438-5555

A 1768 country inn on over 30 acres bordering the Clarendon River. Spacious, individually decorated guest rooms and suites. Original wide-board floors, four-post cherry beds, antiques, quilted bedspreads. Two-course country breakfast and four-course candlelit dinners are available; bar on premises. Fishing, biking, cross-country skiing. Twenty minutes to Killington-Pico downhill skiing.

Host: Frank Kranich
Doubles: 8 (PB) $45-65

Type of Beds: 4 Double; 4 Queen
Full Breakfast
Minimum stay weekends: 2; holidays: 3
Credit Cards: A, B
Closed April
Notes: 2, 4, 7 (restricted), 8 (14 and over), 9, 10, 11, 12, 13

WEST TOWNSHEND

Windham Hill Inn

RR1, Box 44, 05359
(802) 874-4080

Circa 1825 farmhouse and barn located at the end of a dirt road high in the mountains on 150 acres. Spectacular views, hiking trails, XC ski-learning center. Summer concerts are given in the barn. Fifteen guest chambers — antiques, quilts, old-fashioned shoe collection. Wonderful candlelit dinners with six courses on fine china and antique silverware. Warm, caring innkeepers. A true country inn experience.

Hosts: Ken & Linda Busteed
Doubles: 15 (PB) $75-115
Full Breakfast
Credit Cards: A, B, C
Closed: April 1 - May 15 & Nov. 1 - Thanksgiving
Notes: 2, 4, 7 (restricted), 8 (over 12), 9, 10, 11, 12 (XC)

WILLIAMSTOWN

Rosewood Inn Bed & Breakfast

Box 31, 05679
(802) 433-5822

Charmingly gracious Victorian, centrally located in a quiet Vermont village. Spacious antique-filled rooms, elegant wraparound porches. All seasonal activities are nearby. We feature a full gourmet breakfast.

Hosts: John & Elaine Laveroni
Doubles: 4 (PB and SB) $45-80
Continental Breakfast
Closed 2, 5, 11, 12

The Country Inn

WILLIAMSVILLE

The Country Inn at Williamsville

Grimes Hill Road, Box 166, 05362
(802) 348-7148

A 1795 home with living room, library, fireplaces, antiques, and fine art, plus 115 acres of scenic Vermont land for hiking and cross-country skiing. Bicycles are available for touring the scenic back roads. Candlelit

gourmet dining and full Vermont breakfasts. B&B every day, with MAP option on weekends.

Hosts: Bill & Sandra Cassill
Doubles: 6 (PB) $57-116
Type of Beds: 1 Twin; 2 Double; 2 Queen; 1 King
Full Breakfast
Credit Cards: A, B, C
Closed mid-April - mid-May
Notes: 2, 4, 7, 8, 9, 10, 11, 12, 13, 14

WILMINGTON

Darcroft's Schoolhouse

Rt. 100, 05363
(802) 464-2631

A remodeled 1837 one-room schoolhouse with full fireplace in the large living room lounge area. Kitchen facilities available for evening meals. Color TV with cable and VCR. On main road with easy access to downhill or cross-country skiing, golf, tennis, and swimming. No pets allowed in the house, but they can be boarded in a small kennel on the premises.

Host: Doris Meadowcroft
Doubles: 3 (1 PB; 2 SB) $30-65
Type of Beds: 3 Double
Continental Breakfast
Credit Cards: A, B
Limited vacancies Dec.-March
Notes: 2, 5, 6, 7, 8, 9, 10, 11, 12, 13

Misty Mountain Lodge

Stowe Hill Road, Box 114, 05363
(802) 464-3961

A small family inn built in 1803, with a beautiful view of the Green Mountains. We accommodate twenty people; home cooked meals prepared by the owners. Our cozy living room has a large fireplace where guests gather to visit, read, or join in a hearty singalong with your host. Summer walking trails. Close to several major southern Vermont ski areas and Marlboro Music for summer enjoyment.

NOTES: Credit cards accepted: A Master Card; B Visa; C American Express; D Discover Card; E Diners Club; F Other: 2 Personal checks accepted: 3 Lunch available: 4 Dinner available: 5 Open all year

Hosts: Buzz & Elizabeth Cole
Doubles: 9 (S4B) $44-50
Type of Beds: 6 Twin; 7 Double
Full Breakfast
Credit Cards: No
Notes: 2, 4, 5, 7, 8, 9, 10, 11, 12, 13, 14

Nordic Hills Lodge

179 Coldbrook Road, 05363
(802) 464-5130

Come let yourself be spoiled at our family-
operated lodge that offers the nostalgia of a
country inn with all the modern conveniences. Skiing, championship golf, tennis, and
horseback riding are within minutes. Immaculate rooms, sauna, game room, BYOB
bar, and outdoor heated pool complete your
stay.
Hosts: George & Sandra Molner & Marianne Cop-
pola
Doubles: 27 (PB) $42-110
Type of Beds: 28 Twin; 27 Double
Full Breakfast
Credit Cards: A, B, C, E
Notes: 2, 4 (winter), 5, 7, 8, 9, 10, 11, 12, 13

Juniper Hill Inn

Trail's End

Smith Road, 05363
(802) 464-2727

Tucked along a country road, Trail's End
offers traditional New England hospitality in
a secluded, tranquil setting. The inn
provides a warm, cozy atmosphere with a
mix of antiques and family pieces. The
rooms vary in size and have been decorated

with oak dressers, brass headboards, and
fluffy comforters.

Hosts: Bill & Mary Kilburn
Doubles: 18 (PB) $65-100
Type of Beds: 4 Twin; 12 Double; 7 Queen
Full Breakfast
Credit Cards: No
Closed 4/3-5/25 & 11/1-11/21
Notes: 2, 4, 7, 8, 9, 10, 11, 12, 13

The White House of Wilmington

Rt. 9, 05363
(802) 464-2135

Turn-of-the-century mansion set high on a
rolling hill features elegant accommodations, award-winning continental cuisine,
outdoor pool, sauna, indoor pool, and
whirlpool. Complete cross-country ski touring center. Three star Mobil rating. Rate
includes breakfast and dinner.

Host: Robert B. Grinold
Doubles: 12 (PB) $109-212
Type of Beds: 6 Double; 5 Queen; 1 King
Full Breakfast
Minimum stay weekends and holidays
Credit Cards: A, B, C, E (5% service fee)
Notes: 2, 4, 5, 7, 8 (over 10), 9, 10, 11, 12

WINDSOR

Juniper Hill Inn

RR1, Box 79, 05089
(802) 674-5273

Lavish yourself in our elegant but informal
inn with antique-furnished guest rooms, all
with private baths and some with working
fireplaces. We serve sumptuous dinners by
candlelight and hearty, full breakfasts. Cool
off in our outdoor pool or visit antique
shops, covered bridges, museums, and craft
shops. Central to Woodstock and Quechee
in Vermont and Hanover, New Hampshire.
A perfectly romantic inn.

Hosts: Jim & Krisha Pennino
Doubles: 15 (PB) $75-100

6 Pets welcome: 7 Smoking allowed: 8 Children welcome: 9 Social drinking allowed: 10 Tennis available: 11
Swimming available: 12 Golf available: 13 Skiing available: 14 May be booked through travel agents

Type of Beds: 6 Twin; 7 Double; 6 Queen
Full Breakfast
Credit Cards: A, B, C
Closed Nov. 1 - Dec. 15 & mid-March - April 30
Notes: 2, 4, 9, 10, 11, 12, 13

WOODSTOCK_____

Canterbury House

43 Pleasant Street, 05091
(802) 457-3077

Lovely 100-year-old village home just four blocks east of the village green. Furnished with authentic Victorian antiques. Comfortable rooms with private baths; within walking distance of shops and restaurants.

Hosts: Barbara & Bill Hough
Doubles: 7 (PB) $90-115
Type of Beds: 2 Twin; 2 Double; 4 Queen
Full Breakfast
Minimum stay weekends & holidays: 2
Credit Cards: A, B
Notes: 2, 8 (9 and older), 9, 10, 11, 12, 13

The Charleston House

21 Pleasant St., 05091
(802) 457-3843

This circa 1835 Greek Revival home has been authentically restored. Listed in the National Register of Historic Homes. Furnished with antiques combined with a hospitality reminiscent of a family homecoming. Located in the picturesque village of Woodstock — "one of the most beautiful villages in America."

Hosts: Barb, Bill & John Hough
Doubles: 7 (PB) $100-125
Type of Beds: 2 Twin; 2 Double; 4 Queen
Full Breakfast
Minimum stay weekends & holidays
Credit Cards: A, B
Notes: 2, 5, 8 (over 9), 9, 10, 11, 12, 13, 14

Village Inn of Woodstock

41 Pleasant Street, 05091
(802) 457-1255

Walk to shops and galleries. Restored Victorian mansion, circa 1899, has working fireplaces, tin ceilings, oak and chestnut woodwork, stained glass. Candlelight dining on premises; chef-owned inn. Cocktail lounge; warm, friendly staff.

Hosts: Kevin & Anita Clark
Doubles: 8 (6 PB; 2 SB) $53-106
Type of Beds: 2 Twin; 1 Double; 3 Queen; 1 King
Full Breakfast
Minimum stay 9/20-10/20 weekdays: 2; weekends & holidays: 2
Credit Cards: A, B
Notes: 2, 4, 5, 8, 9, 10, 11, 12, 13

Virginia

Summerfield Inn

101 West Valley Street, 24210
(703) 628-5905

Summerfield Inn is located in the Abingdon historic district, just two blocks from world-famous Barter Theatre. We're near the Appalachian Trail, Mount Rogers National Recreation Area, South Holston Lake, the Blue Ridge Parkway, Virginia Creeper Trail, excellent restaurants, and marvelous shops. Just off I-81 at Exit 8.

Hosts: Champe & Don Hyatt
Doubles: 4 (PB) $55-70 plus tax
Type of Beds: 1 Twin; 2 Double; 1 King
Continental Breakfast
Credit Cards: A, B
Notes: 2, 7 (limited), 8 (over 12), 9, 10, 12

ALEXANDRIA

The Little House

719 Gibbon Street, 22314
(703) 548-9654

The entire 1600-square-foot house is rented to the guests, with no hosts on the premises. Breakfast food is stocked, so guests prepare their own meal. Privacy is assured, but should guests need help with reservations or sightseeing, the off-premises manager will provide these services.

Hosts: Tucker Taylor
Doubles: 2 (PB) $200
Type of Beds: 2 Twin; 1 King
Stocked refrigerator
Minimum stay: 2
Credit Cards: No
Notes: 2, 5, 6, 7, 8, 9

Morrison House

116 S. Alfred Street, 22314
(703) 838-8000

Located in the midst of Alexandria's historic Old Town, Morrison House combines the elegance of a Federal Period inn with the intimacy and charm of a small European hotel. Our elegant rooms, English butlers, and French dining provide for a memorable experience.

Hosts: Robert & Rosemary Morrison
Suites: 3 (PB) $230-285
Doubles: 42 (PB) $135-230
Type of Beds: 5 Twin; 28 Queen; 12 King
Full Breakfast on weekends
Credit Cards: A, B, C, E, F
Notes: 2, 4, 5, 7, 8, 9, 11

BOSTON

Thistle Hill B&B

Rt. 1, Box 291, 22713
(703) 987-9142

Situated in Rappahannock County just 65 miles west of Washington, D.C. Guests enjoy cozy antique-furnished rooms. Relax and stroll through tree-filled acreage. Many seasonal activities. Located near the Blue Ridge Mountains, midway between Culpeper and Sperryville on Rt. 522.

Hosts: Charles & Marianne Wilson
Doubles: 3 (1 PB; 2 SB) $55-70
Type of Beds: 2 Twin; 1 Queen; 1 Daybed
Full Breakfast
Minimum stay: 2
Credit Cards: No
Closed Jan. - March
Notes: 2, 8 (12 or over), 9, 10, 11, 12, 13

6 Pets welcome: 7 Smoking allowed: 8 Children welcome: 9 Social drinking allowed: 10 Tennis available: 11 Swimming available: 12 Golf available: 13 Skiing available: 14 May be booked through travel agents

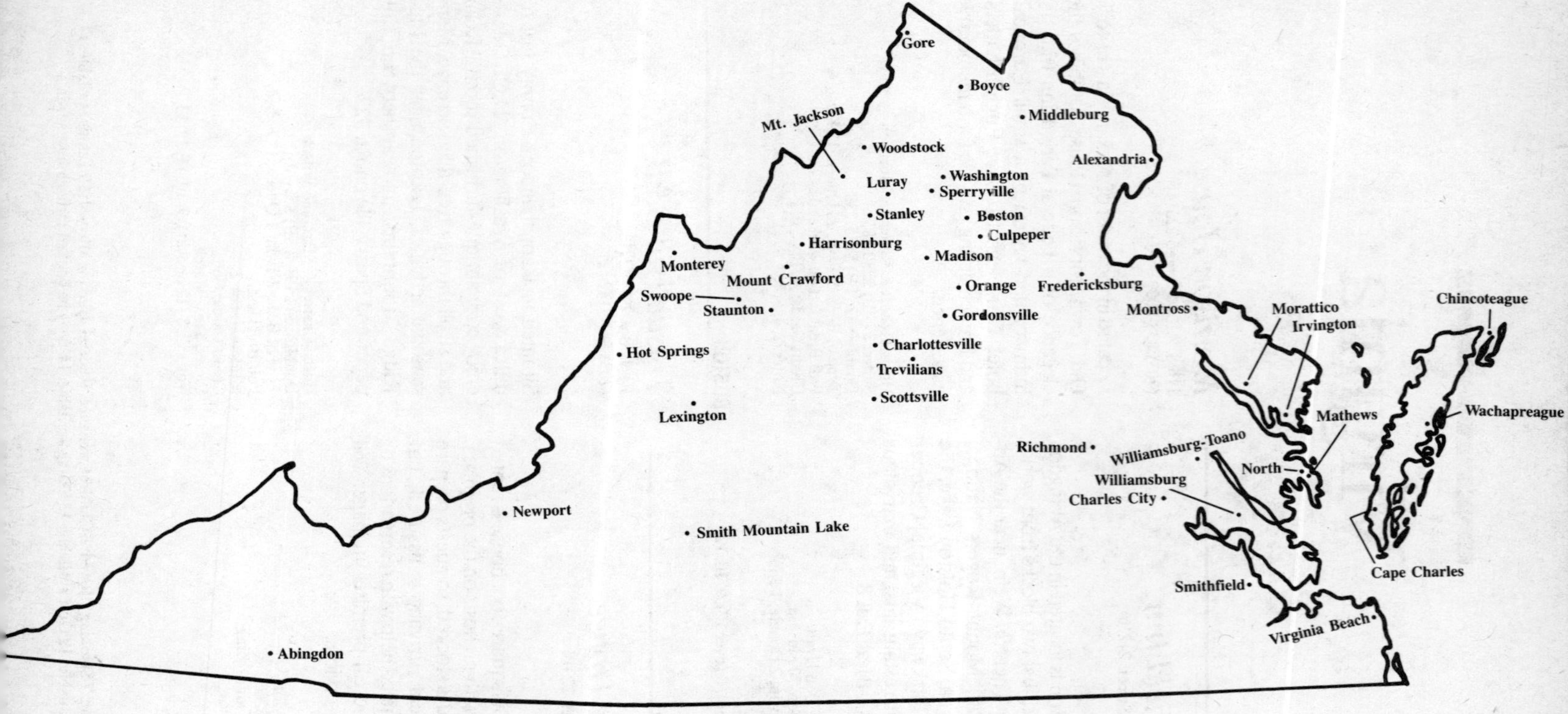

Chincoteague

Wachapreague

Cape Charles

Morattico

Irvington

Mathews

North

Virginia Beach

Williamsburg-Toano

Richmond

Williamsburg

Smithfield

Charles City

Montross

Fredericksburg

Alexandria

Middleburg

Boyce

Washington

Sperryville

Culpeper

Orange

Gordonsville

Beston

Madison

Charlottesville

Woodstock

Luray

Stanley

Trevilians

Harrisonburg

Scottsville

Gore

Mt. Jackson

Mount Crawford

Monterey

Staunton

Swoope

Hot Springs

Lexington

Smith Mountain Lake

Newport

Abingdon

VIRGINIA

BOYCE

The River House

Rt. 2, Box 135, 22620
(703) 837-1476

A rural getaway on the Shenandoah River, built in 1780 and 1820. Convenient to scenic, historic, and recreational areas, we also offer special features and programs for house parties, small workshops, and family reunions. Accommodations are available for small, two or three day business conferences and executive retreats during the week. Relaxing, book-filled bed/sitting rooms have fireplaces, air-conditioning, and private baths.

Host: Cornelia S. Niemann
Doubles: 5 (PB) $65-80
Type of Beds: 2 Twin; 2 Double; 1 Queen
Full Breakfast
Credit Cards: A, B
Closed Christmas Day
Notes: 2 (by arrangement), 3 (on request), 4 (by arrangement), 5, 6, 7, 8, 9, 10, 11, 12

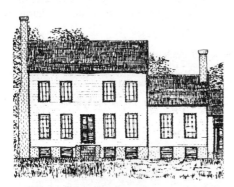

Pickett's Harbor

CAPE CHARLES

Pickett's Harbor

Box 97AA, 23310
(804) 331-2212

The perfect place for rest and relaxation! A colonial home in a secluded wooded setting, with all rooms overlooking 17 acres of private wide beach on Chesapeake Bay. The home is decorated with antiques and reproductions, and natural flora and fauna abound on Virginia's Eastern Shore.

Hosts: Sara & Cooke Goffigon
Singles: 1 (SB) $50
Doubles: 3 (SB) $60
Type of Beds: 1 Twin; 1 Double; 2 Queen
Full Breakfast
Credit Cards: No
Notes: 2, 5, 8 (over 6), 9, 11, 12

CHARLES CITY

Edgewood Plantation

Rt. Box 490, 23030
(804) 829-2962

A unique national landmark Gothic with fourteen rooms, ten fireplaces, old canopy beds, period clothes, antiques, and candlelight breakfast. Refreshments are served, and the house has a swimming pool and hot tub. Many historic attractions are nearby. Located between Richmond and Williamsburg, in plantation country.

Host: Dot Boulware
Doubles: 4 (2 PB; 2SB) $92
Type of Beds: 6 Double; 1 Queen; 1 King
Full Breakfast
Credit Cards: A, B
Notes: 5, 9, 10, 11, 12, 13, 14

CHARLOTTESVILLE

Carrsbrook

Box 5737, 22905
(804) 979-7264

Peter Carr built this estate home in 1798, using many of the architectural innovations of his uncle and guardian, Thomas Jefferson, including fifteen-foot ceilings and Jefferson's characteristic way of hiding stairways. Private entrance to the suite is from a large patio overlooking a formal boxwood garden with the deepest hand-dug well in Albermarle County. Downstairs is the sitting room with a pull-out sofa, adjacent bath, and small refrigerator.

Suite: (PB) $72-120
Type of Beds: 1 Double; 1 Cot
Full or Continental Breakfast
Credit Cards: A, B, C (deposit only)
Notes: 2, 5, 7, 8, 9, 10, 11, 12

Clifton

Clifton — The Country Inn

Rt. 9, Box 412, 22901
(804) 971-1800

A Virginia historic landmark, Clifton is among the few remaining large plantation properties in Albemarle County. On 45 secluded acres with endless walking trails, private lake, small pool, and tennis court. All rooms feature woodburning fireplaces, private bath, large sitting areas, canopy or four-poster beds. Five minutes to Charlottesville.

Host: Nancy Keel
Doubles: 9 (PB) $115-145
Full Breakfast
Credit Cards: A, B
Notes: 2, 3 (by arrangement), 4, (by arrangement), 5, 8, 9, 10, 11, 12, 12, 14

Oxbridge Inn

316 14th Street NW, 22903
(804) 295-7707

Handsome Victorian house centrally located for touring. Three blocks from the university and hospital, minutes from the historic downtown district, Jefferson's Monticello, Monroe's Ashlawn, and the surrounding Blue Ridge mountains. Large parlor with fireplace, TV, and guest refrigerator. Veranda, gardens, and picnic area.

Hosts: Randy McNamara & Gwen Gulliksen
Singles: 1 (SB) $40
Doubles: 7 (PB and SB) $50-85
Type of Beds: 3 Twin; 5 Double; 1 King; 1 Sleeper sofa
Continental Breakfast
Credit Cards: A, B
Notes: 2, 5, 8, 9, 10, 11, 12, 13, 14

Silver Thatch Inn

3001 Hollymead Drive, 22901
(804) 978-4686

We are a small, intimate inn on the outskirts of Charlottesville, dating back to 1780. We have seven beautifully decorated guest rooms, each with private bath and four with working fireplaces. Our restaurant is famous for its modern country cuisine and features an eclectic menu that showcases Virginia wines and produce. We're proud to offer the first entirely smoke-free inn and restaurant in the state.

Hosts: Joe & Mickey Geller
Doubles: 7 (PB) $75-115
Type of Beds: 1 Twin; 3 Double; 4 Queen
Continental-plus Breakfast
Credit Cards: A, B
Closed Dec. 24-26 & first two weeks in Jan.
Notes: 2, 4, 8, 9, 10, 11, 12

Silver Thatch Inn

NOTES: Credit cards accepted: A Master Card; B Visa; C American Express; D Discover Card; E Diners Club; F Other: 2 Personal checks accepted: 3 Lunch available: 4 Dinner available: 5 Open all year

200 South Street Inn

200 South Street, 22901
(804) 979-0200

Lovely restored inn, garden terrace, sweeping veranda, located in historic downtown Charlottesville, with English and Belgian antiques, six Jacuzzi tubs, eleven fireplaces, canopy and four-poster beds. Revolving art exhibit. Continental breakfast and afternoon tea (with wine) and canapes. Near Monticello and Ash Lawn.

Host: Donna Deibert
Doubles: 20 (PB) $92-172.50
Type of Beds: 4 Twin; 16 Queen
Continental Breakfast
Minimum Stay April & May, Sept. & Oct.
Credit Cards: A, B, C
Closed Christmas Day
Notes: 2, 4, 7, 8, 9, 10, 11, 12, 13, 14

Woodstock Hall

Woodstock Hall

Rt. 3, Box 40, 22901
(804) 293-8977

A faithfully restored 1757 inn on the Historic National Register. Located off I-64, close to the University of Virginia, Monticello, and other historic landmarks. Experience all the eighteenth-century charm of a fine inn, including gourmet breakfast; yet be provided with the modern conveniences demanded by today's discriminating traveler.

Hosts: Jean Wheby & Mary Ann Elder
Doubles: 4 (PB) $101.18-138.45
Type of Beds: 1 Double; 2 Queen; 1 King
Full Breakfast
Credit Cards: No
Notes: 2, 5, 8 (over 10), 9, 10, 11, 12, 13 (18 miles)

CHINCOTEAGUE

Miss Molly's Inn

113 N. Main Street, 23336
(804) 336-6686

A charming Victorian inn on the bay five miles from Chincoteague National Wildlife Refuge and Assateague National Seashore. All rooms are air-conditioned and furnished with period antiques. Room rate includes breakfast and afternoon tea. Marguerite Henry stayed here while writing *Misty of Chincoteague.*

Hosts: Dr. & Mrs. James Stam
Singles: 2 (SB) $45
Doubles: 11 (PB and SB) $55-95
Full Breakfast
Credit Cards: No
Closed Dec. 1 - March 30
Notes: 2, 7 (limited), 8 (over 12), 9, 10, 11, 12, 14

Year of the Horse Inn

600 S. Main Street, 23336
(804) 336-3221

Three guest rooms with private bath and balcony, right on the water, plus a two-bedroom apartment that sleeps six. One-hundred-foot pier for fishing or crabbing. Located just ten minutes from the ocean beach, wildlife refuge, and wild ponies of Chincoteague.

Host: Carlton Bond
Doubles: 5 (PB) $70-90
Type of Beds: 2 Twin; 4 Double; 2 Queen
Continental Breakfast
Credit Cards: A, B
Closed Dec. & Jan.
Notes: 2, 7, 8, 9, 10, 11, 12, 14

6 Pets welcome: 7 Smoking allowed: 8 Children welcome: 9 Social drinking allowed: 10 Tennis available: 11 Swimming available: 12 Golf available: 13 Skiing available: 14 May be booked through travel agents

CULPEPER

Fountain Hall Bed & Breakfast

609 South East Street, 22701
(703) 825-8200

Built in 1859, this grand B&B is within walking distance of historic downtown Culpeper. The inn is furnished with antiques and warmly welcomes business and leisure travelers. Area activities and attractions include wineries, historic battlefields, antique shops, the Skyline Drive, tennis, swimming, golf, and more.

Hosts: Steve & Kathi Walker
Doubles: 5 (3 PB; 2 SB) $45-75
Type of Beds: 1 Twin; 4 Double; 2 Queen; Bunk, Crib, & Cot
Continental-plus Breakfast
Credit Cards: A, B, C
Notes: 2, 5, 7, 8, 9, 10, 11, 12, 14

Miss Molly's Inn

FREDERICKSBURG

Kenmore Inn

1200 Princess Anne Street, 22401
(703) 371-7622

Elegant inn built in the late 1700s. On the historical walking tour, near shops and the river. Grand dining and a relaxing pub for your enjoyment. Serving lunch and dinner daily.

Hosts: Ed & Alice Bannan
Doubles: 13 (PB) $78-99
Type of Beds: 4 Twin; 7 Double; 3 Queen
Continental Breakfast
Credit Cards: A, B, C
Closed Jan. 3-13
Notes: 2, 3, 4, 5, 7, 8, 9, 10, 11, 12, 14

Lavista Plantation

4420 Guinea Station Road, 22401
(703) 898-8444

Classical Revival circa 1838 manor house located on 10 quiet country acres. Surrounded by farm fields and mature trees. Stocked pond, six fireplaces, antiques, rich Civil War past, radio, phone, TV, bicycles, nearby historic attractions. Fresh eggs and homemade jams; air-conditioned.

Hosts: Edward & Michele Schiesser
Double: 1 (PB) $53.25-69.23
Suite: 1 (PB)
Full Breakfast
Credit Cards: A, B
Notes: 5, 7, 8, 9, 10, 11, 12

Richard Johnston Inn

711 Caroline Street, 22401
(703) 899-7606

In the downtown historical area, near many antique shops, Civil War battlefield, and the homes of George Washington and Robert E. Lee. Close to Amtrak and hiking.

Hosts: Dennis & Libby Gowin
Doubles: 9 (5 PB; 4 SB) $55-85
Type of Beds: 8 Twin; 3 Double
Continental Breakfast
Credit Cards: A, B, C
Notes: 2, 5, 14

GORDONSVILLE

Sleepy Hollow Farm

Rt. 3, Box 43, 22942
(703) 832-5555

NOTES: Credit cards accepted: A Master Card; B Visa; C American Express; D Discover Card; E Diners Club; F Other: 2 Personal checks accepted: 3 Lunch available: 4 Dinner available: 5 Open all year

This is a two-story, eighteenth-century farmhouse with flower and herb gardens, a pond, gazebo, and restored slave cottage. Antiques and lovely things fill the rooms. Located near Montpelier in Orange County's western historic district, amid cattle and horse farms.

Host: Beverley Allison
Doubles: 6 (PB) $45-80
Type of Beds: 3 Twin; 5 Double
Full Breakfast
Credit Cards: A, B
Notes: 2, 3 (by arrangement), 4 (by arrangement), 5, 6 (by invitation), 7, 8, 9, 10, 11, 12, 14

GORE

Rainbow's End

Rt. 1, Box 335, 22637
(703) 858-2808

Enjoy your stay at this comfortable country home on Timber Ridge in the Appalachian Mountains. Nearby Winchester provides quaint shops, historic attractions, antiquing, and fairs. The area provides hiking, fishing, and hunting in season. Every season has much to offer in this quiet apple country.

Hosts: Thom & Eleanor McKay
Singles: 1 (SB) $35
Doubles: 1 (SB) $40
Type of Beds: 1 Double; 1 King
Continental Breakfast
Credit Cards: No
Notes: 2, 5, 9

HARRISONBURG

Kingsway B & B

3581 Singers Glen Road, 22801
(703) 867-9696

Visit nearby George Washington Forest, Shenandoah National Park with scenic Skyline Drive, caverns, hiking, and skiing. Nearby are Monticello, New Market Battlefield, Natural Bridge, antique shops, flea markets, and Valley Mall. This modern country home is 4.5 miles west of downtown.

Hosts: Chester & Verna Leaman
Singles: 2 (SB) $35
Doubles: 2 (SB) $45-55
Type of Beds: 1 Double; 1 Queen; floor mattress for children
Continental-plus Breakfast
No smoking or alcohol, please
Credit Cards: No
Notes: 2, 5, 6, 11, 12

HOT SPRINGS

Vine Cottage Inn

U.S. Route 220, 24445
(703) 839-2422

A rambling and charming country inn situated in a mountain spa resort village. Twelve uniquely decorated rooms with large, inviting pedestal tub baths. Spacious and comfortable sitting room with fireplace, reading/writing alcove, and large TV.

Hosts: Pat & Wendell Lucas
Singles: 5 (3 PB; 2 SB) $30
Doubles: 7 (6 PB; 1 SB) $85
Type of Beds: 17 Twin; 8 Double
Continental Breakfast
Credit Cards: A, B
Closed Dec. 24-25
Notes: 2, 4, 5, 7, 8, 9, 10, 11, 12, 13

IRVINGTON

King Carter Inn

King Carter Drive, 22480
(804) 438-6053

Victorian inn in the historic Northern Neck of Virginia. Bicycles for use of guests; golf, sailing, and fishing are nearby. Many fine restaurants in the area.

Host: Marilyn Taylor
Doubles: 8 (4 PB; 4 SB) $47.03-62.70
Type of Beds: 4 Twin; 5 Double; 1 King
Full Breakfast
Credit Cards: No
Notes: 2, 5, 7, 8, 9, 10, 12, 14

LEXINGTON

Fassifern Bed & Breakfast

Rt. 5, Box 87, 24450
(703) 463-1013

Cozy 1867 antique-filled manor house on 3.5 park-like acres near quaint, historic Lexington in the beautiful Shenandoah Valley. Convenient to I-81 and I-64 on Scenic Byway 39. Numerous sights nearby. For travelers with discriminating taste. Ambience and comfort are our trademarks!

Hosts: Pat & Jim Tichenor
Doubles: 6 (4 PB; 2 SB) $45-73
Type of Beds: 4 Twin; 3 Double; 1 Queen
Continental-plus Breakfast
Credit Cards: A, B, C
Notes: 2, 5, 8 (over 16), 9, 10, 11, 12, 13

Historic Country Inns

11 North Main Street, 24450
(703) 463-2044

Three lovely historic homes: Alexander-Winrow House (1789); McCampbell Inn (1809), located in Lexington's historic district; and Maple Hall (1850), a plantation home six miles north of Lexington, offer unique overnight accommodations. Maple Hall provides gourmet dining for guests.

Hosts: the Peter Meredith family & Don Fredenburg
Doubles: 29 (PB) $70-110
Suites: 8 (PB)
Type of Beds: 4 Twin; 18 Double; 15 Queen
Continental-plus Breakfast
Credit Cards: A, B
Notes: 2, 4, 5, 7, 8, 9, 10, 11, 12

Irish Gap Inns

Rt. 1, Box 40, Vesuvius, 24483
(804) 922-7701

Situated on 285 mountaintop acres bordering the Blue Ridge Parkway, the Bee Skep Inn and the Gatehouse B&B offer old-world charm with modern comfort. Hiking, fishing, swimming, wild flowers, and farm animals. Handicap facilities. Send for brochure.

Hosts: Dillard Saunders & Martha Shewey
Doubles: 7 (6 PB; 1 SB) $48-92
Type of Beds: 4 Twin; 5 Double; 2 Queen
Full Breakfast

Minimum stay weekends & holidays: 2
Credit Cards: A, B
Notes: 2, 4 (with reservations), 5, 6, 7, 8, 9, 11

Llewellyn Doge at Lexington

603 S. Main Street, 24450
(703) 463-3235

A warm and friendly atmosphere awaits guests to this lovely brick colonial. Upon arrival, guests are welcomed with refreshments. A hearty gourmet breakfast is served that includes omelets, Belgian waffles, sausage, bacon, and homemade muffins. The decor combines traditional and antique furnishing. Within walking distance of the Lee Chapel, Stonewall Jackson House, Washington and Lee University, and Virginia Military Institute.

Host: Ellen P. Thornber
Singles: 1 (PB) $45
Doubles: 4 (PB) $53-68
Type of Beds: 1 Twin; 1 Double; 2 Queen; 1 King
Full Breakfast
Credit Cards: A, B, C
Notes: 2, 5, 7, 8, 9, 10, 11, 12, 14

LURAY

Shenandoah Countryside

Route 2, Box 370, 22835
(703) 743-6434

A custom built brick farmhouse located on 45 acres overlooking the Shenandoah Valley, with a magnificent view of the Blue Ridge. Has a Finnish sauna and bicycles. Shenandoah National Park, Luray Caverns, hiking, horseback riding, canoeing, and antiquing are all nearby.

Hosts: Phel & Bob Jacobsen
Doubles: 3 (1 PB; 2 S2B) $53.25-63.90
Type of Beds: 2 Twin; 1 Double; 1 Queen; 1 King
Full Breakfast
Credit Cards: No
Notes: 2, 5, 8 (over 12), 9, 10, 11, 12

NOTES: Credit cards accepted: A Master Card; B Visa; C American Express; D Discover Card; E Diners Club; F Other: 2 Personal checks accepted: 3 Lunch available: 4 Dinner available: 5 Open all year

Shenandoah River Roost

Route 3, Box 566, 22835
(703) 743-3467

Country log home facing the Shenandoah River. Three miles from famous Luray Caverns, ten minutes from the Skyline Drive, fishing, swimming, tubing, and hiking. Close to two golf courses and horseback riding. Beautiful view of the Blue Ridge Mountains from all bedroom windows.

Hosts: Gerry and Rubin McNab
Singles: 1 (SB) $45
Doubles: 1 (SB) $55
Type of Beds: 2 Twin; 1 Queen
Full Country Breakfast
Credit Cards: No
Closed Nov. 1st - May 1st
Notes: 2, 6, 7, 8 (over 12), 9, 10, 11, 12

Red Fox Inn

MADISON

Shenandoah Springs Country Inn

Box 122, 22727
(703) 923-4300

On Shenandoah Springs estate you will enjoy swimming, canoeing, fishing, and horseback riding. You may rent one of our cottages or stay at the Inn.

Hosts: Anne & Douglas Farmer
Doubles: 7 (2PB; 5SB) $75-100
Full Breakfast
Credit Cards: No
Notes: 2, 4, 5, 8 (over 6), 10, 11, 13

MATHEWS

RiverFront House Bed & Breakfast

Rt. 14 East, Box 310, 23109
(804) 725-9975

Waterfront setting and Williamsburg, too (55 minute trip). Nineteenth-century house, set on 10 acres in Chesapeake Country — the perfect place to laze around, use as a base for exploring, for day cruises across the Bay or down river. Biking, craft and antique shops, berry picking. Ideal for family reunions and retreats.

Host: Annette Waldman Goldreyer
Doubles: 8 (PB) $50-70
Type of Beds: 4 Twin; 2 Double; 3 Queen; 1 King
Full Breakfast
Credit Cards: No
Closed Thanksgiving - April 1
Notes: 2, 3, 7, 8 (over 4), 9, 10, 14

MIDDLEBURG

Red Fox Inn & Mosby's Tavern

Box 385, 22117
(800) 223-1728

Built in 1728 as Chinn's Ordinary, the inn was a popular stopping place for travelers between Winchester and Alexandria. The inn's twenty-seven guest rooms are decorated with period reproductions; most have canopied beds; some have working fireplaces. Color TV, private baths, telephones, thick cotton bathrobes, bedside sweets, and fresh flowers. Complimentary breakfast is offered in the room or dining room, with a complimentary copy of the *Washington Post*.

6 Pets welcome: 7 Smoking allowed: 8 Children welcome: 9 Social drinking allowed: 10 Tennis available: 11 Swimming available: 12 Golf available: 13 Skiing available: 14 May be booked through travel agents

Hosts: Turner & Dan Reuter
Doubles: 27 (PB) $125-145
Type of Beds: 4 Twin; 2 Double; 15 Queen; 6 King
Continental Breakfast
Credit Cards: A, B, C
Notes: 2, 3, 4, 5, 7, 8, 9, 14

Welbourne

22117
(703) 687-3201

A seven-generation antebellum plantation home in the middle of Virginia's fox-hunting country. On a 600-acre working farm. Full Southern breakfasts, working fireplaces, cottages. On the National Register of Historic Places.

Hosts: Nat & Sherry Morison
Doubles: 11 (PB) $47-94
Type of Beds: 4 Twin; 7 Queen
Full Breakfast
Credit Cards: C
Notes: 2, 5, 6, 7, 8, 9

MONTEREY

Highland Inn

Main Street, 24465
(703) 468-2143

Highland Inn, built in 1904 and on the National Historic Register, has Eastlake wraparound porches. Wonderful "Country Cookin'," maple pecan pie, and fresh trout are our specialties at this Pride of the Mountains Hotel that boasts of no phones and no TVs (well, maybe a few!).

Hosts: John & Joanne Crow
Singles: 2 (PB) $36.58
Doubles: 16 (PB) $40.76
Type of Beds: 4 Twin; 12 Double; 2 King
Continental Breakfast
Minimum stay holidays: 2
Credit Cards: A, B
Notes: 2, 4, 5, 7, 8, 9, 11, 12

MONTROSS

The Inn at Montross

Courthouse Square, 22520
(804) 493-9097

On the site of a seventeenth-century tavern, this house has been in continuous use for over three hundred years. Guest rooms feature four-poster beds (some with canopies) and antiques. A restaurant featuring fine dining, pub room, and English tavern are on the premises. Historic area near Washington's birthplace and Stratford Hall.

Hosts: Eileen & Michael Longman
Doubles: 6 (PB) $60-75
Type of Beds: 3 Twin; 1 Full; 4 Queen
Continental Breakfast
Credit Cards: A, B, C, D, E
Notes: 2, 3, 4, 5, 6, 7, 9, 10, 11, 12, 14

Highland Inn

MORATTICO

Holly Point

Box 64, 22523
(804) 462-7759

Besides the many historical sites in the area, Holly Point has 120 acres of pine forest and looks out on a lovely view of the Rappahanock River. There are many land and water activities: hiking, biking, swimming, boating, water skiing, fishing, and crabbing.

Host: Mary Chilton Graham
Doubles: 4 (1 PB; 3 SB) $30-35
Type of Beds: 1 Twin; 6 Double
Continental Breakfast

NOTES: Credit cards accepted: A Master Card; B Visa; C American Express; D Discover Card; E Diners Club; F Other: 2 Personal checks accepted: 3 Lunch available: 4 Dinner available: 5 Open all year

Credit Cards: No
Closed Nov.1-May 1
Notes: 2, 6, 7, 8, 9

MOUNT CRAWFORD

The Pumpkin House Inn

Rt. 2, Box 155, 22841
(703) 434-6963

An 1847 restored brick home featuring Victorian and country rooms furnished with antiques.

Hosts: J. Thomas Kidd, Jr. & Elizabeth K. Umstott
Doubles: 7 (3 PB; 4 SB) $50-70
Type of Beds: 1 Twin; 3 Double; 2 Queen
Continental Breakfast
Credit Cards: A, B, C
Notes: 2, 5, 7, 8, 9

The Inn at Montross

MT. JACKSON

The Widow Kip's

Rt. 1, Box 117, 22842
(703) 477-2400

A stately 1830 colonial on 7 acres in the Shenandoah Valley overlooking the mountains. Friendly rooms filled with family photographs, bric-a-brac, and antiques (all for sale). Each bedroom has a working fireplace, canopy, sleigh, or Lincoln bed. Two cozy cottages are also available. Pool, nearby battlefields to explore, caverns,

canoeing, hiking, or downhill skiing. Bicycles, picnics, grill available.

Host: Rosemary Kip
Doubles: 7 (PB) $47.20-69.10
Type of Beds: 5 Double; 2 Queen
Full Breakfast
Minimum stay holidays: 2
Credit Cards: A, B
Notes: 2, 5, 6, 10, 11, 12, 13

NEWPORT

The Newport House

Rt. 1, Box 102, 24128
(703) 961-2480

A country inn with new private baths and air-conditioning on 30 well-maintained acres in southwest Virginia. Antebellum farmhouse offers porches, patios, mountain stream, gracious private accommodations, and country breakfasts.

Hosts: Harold & Pamela Kurstedt
Doubles: 7 (PB) $75-80
Type of Beds: 1 Twin; 2 Double; 3 Queen; 1 King
Full Breakfast
Credit Cards: A, B
Notes: 2, 4, 5, 8 (over 10), 9, 10, 11, 12, 13

NORTH

Cedar Point Inn

Rt. 617, Box 369, 23128
(804) 725-9535

An 80-acre country estate located on one-third mile of river and bay front. Finest accommodations; elegantly appointed rooms. Relax by the pool, watch Arabian horses play, or observe sailboats go by while you swing in a hammock. Close to Williamsburg and colonial areas. Brochure available.

Hosts: Ernie & Renate Hux
Doubles: 4 (PB) $68-78
Type of Beds: 1 Twin; 2 Queen; 1 King
Full Country Breakfast
Credit Cards: No
Notes: 2, 4, 5, 9, 11, 14

6 Pets welcome: 7 Smoking allowed: 8 Children welcome: 9 Social drinking allowed: 10 Tennis available: 11
Swimming available: 12 Golf available: 13 Skiing available: 14 May be booked through travel agents

ORANGE

Hidden Inn

249 Caroline Street, 22960
(703) 672-3625

A romantic Victorian featuring nine guest rooms, all with private bath. Jacuzzi tubs, working fireplaces, and private verandas are available. Wicker and rocking chairs on the wraparound verandas, hand-made quilts and canopied beds enhance the Victorian flavor. Full country breakfast, afternoon tea, and gourmet dinners are served. Located minutes from Montpelier and Virginia wineries.

Hosts: Ray & Barbara Lonick
Doubles: 9 (PB) $69-119
Type of Beds: 3 Twin; 2 Double; 6 Queen; 1 King
Full Breakfast
Credit Cards: A, B
Notes: 2, 3, 4, 5, 8, 9, 10, 14

Mayhurst Inn

Box 707, U.S. 15 S., 22960
(703) 672-5597

Mayhurst is a fanciful Italianate Victorian plantation home on 36 acres in historic Orange County. Some rooms have fireplaces, and the inn is air-conditioned. There is a fishing pond, fields for strolling, and an antique shop. A full country breakfast is served every day, and dinner is available on Saturday evenings.

Hosts: Stephen & Shirley Ramsey
Doubles: 7 (PB) $149
Type of Beds: 4 Twin; 5 Double; 2 Queen
Full Breakfast
Credit Cards: A, B
Closed Christmas Day
Notes: 2, 4 (Sat.), 5, 8 (12 and over), 9, 10

The Shadows

Rt. 1, Box 535, 22960
(703) 672-5057

A restored 1913 stone farmhouse on 44 acres, featuring a large stone fireplace, guest rooms filled with antiques, flowers and lace. Romantic getaway in a country Victorian setting. Near Montpelier on Rt. 20.

Hosts: Barbara & Pat Loffredo
Doubles: 4 (PB) $69.22-90.52
Type of Beds: 2 Double; 1 Queen; 1 King
Full Breakfast
Credit Cards: No
Notes: 2, 5, 8 (over 12), 14

The Catlin-Abbott House

RICHMOND

The Catlin-Abbott House

2304 East Broad Street, 23223
(804) 780-3746

Elegantly restored 1845 house in the historic district. Community rooms have Czechoslovakian crystal chandeliers, Chinese Oriental rugs, and many handsome pieces of furniture passed down through the family. Enjoy the luxury of triple sheeting, turndown service at night, coffee served in your room in the morning, canopy beds, and working fireplaces.

Hosts: Dr. & Mrs. James L. Abbott
Doubles: 5 (3 PB; 3 SB) $72.50-82.50
Type of Beds: 2 Twin; 1 Double; 3 Queen
Full Breakfast
Credit Cards: A, B, C
Notes: 2, 5, 7, 14

NOTES: Credit cards accepted: A Master Card; B Visa; C American Express; D Discover Card; E Diners Club; F Other: 2 Personal checks accepted: 3 Lunch available: 4 Dinner available: 5 Open all year

Hanover Hosts in the Fan

Hanover Hosts in the Fan

Box 25145, 23260
(804) 355-5855

Desirable for tourists and corporate travelers alike, this elegant 1907 Colonial Revival townhouse, located in Richmond's most prestigious historic district, is near convention and corporate centers, museums, restaurants, shopping, historic sites. Enjoy exquisite period decor, hearty Virginia breakfasts by the fire. Laundry facilities available, TV in rooms, afternoon tea and sherry.

Hosts: Barbara & Bill Fleming
Singles: 2 (PB) $35-45
Doubles: 4 (2 PB; 2 SB) $55-85
Suites available: $140
Type of Beds: 3 Twin; 3 Double; 3 Queen
Full Breakfast
Credit Cards: No
Notes: 2, 5, 8 (over 12), 9

SCOTTSVILLE

Chester Bed & Breakfast

Rt. 4, Box 57, 24590
(804) 286-3960

An 1847 Greek Revival estate on 7 acres abounding with shaded lawns, century-old boxwood, antiques, and Oriental rugs. Four guest rooms have fireplaces, as so the living room, dining room, and library. Monticello, Ashlawn, Montpelier, the University of Virginia, Appomattox, and the Blue Ridge Mountains are all within an easy hour's drive of historic Scottsville.

Hosts: Gordon Anderson & Dick Shaffer
Doubles: 5 (1 PB; 4 SB) $55-70
Type of Beds: 2 Twin; 2 Double; 1 Queen; 3/4 antique
Full Breakfast
Credit Cards: No
Notes: 2, 4, 5, 6, 7, 9, 11, 14

High Meadows — Virginia's Vineyard Inn

Rt. 4, Box 6, 24590
(804) 286-2218

Enchanting nineteenth-century European-style auberge with tastefully appointed, spacious guest rooms, private baths, period antiques. Several common rooms, fireplaces, and tranquility. Pastoral setting on 23 acres. Privacy, relaxing walks, gourmet picnics. Virginia wine tasting and weekend candlelight dining.

Hosts: Peter & Mary Jae Abbitt Sushka
Doubles: 7 (PB) $78.38-88.82
Type of Beds: 4 Twin; 4 Double; 2 Queen
Full Breakfast
Minimum stay weekends & holidays: 2
Credit Cards: No
Closed two weeks early March & early Aug.
Notes: 2, 4, 5, 6, 8 (over 8), 9, 10, 11, 14

SMITHFIELD

Isle of Wight Inn

345 S. Church Street, 23430
(804) 357-3176

Luxurious colonial B&B inn located in a delightful, historic river port. Several suites feature fireplaces and Jacuzzi. Antique shop, featuring tallcase clocks and period furniture. Over sixty old homes in town dating from 1750. Thirty minutes and a ferry ride from Williamsburg and Jamestown; less than one hour from James River plantations, Norfolk, Hampton, and Virginia Beach.

Hosts: Marcella Hoffman, Sam Earl & Robert Hart
Doubles: 12 (PB) $49-79
Type of Beds: 12 Queen
Continental-plus Breakfast
Credit Cards: A, B
Notes: 2, 5, 7, 8, 9, 10, 11, 12, 14

SMITH MOUNTAIN LAKE

Holland-Duncan House

Rt. 5, Box 681, 24121
(703) 721-8510

Historic 1820 brick farmhouse on 28 acres of woods. Centrally located for access to all recreational activities at Smith Mountain Lake. Enjoy our "old timey" log cabin with "walk-in" fireplace, loft, and private bath.

Hosts: Kathryn & Clint Shay
Doubles: 4 (2 PB; 2 SB) $40.80-61.20
Type of Beds: 2 Double; 2 Queen; 1 King
Full Breakfast
Credit Cards: A, B
Closed January
Notes: 2, 6 (cabin only), 8, 9, 10, 11, 12

The Manor at Taylor's Store

Rt. 1, Box 533, Wirtz, 24184
(703) 721-3951

Circa 1799, 100-acre estate near Smith Mountain Lake, Roanoke, and the Blue Ridge Parkway. On-premises hiking, fishing, canoeing, swimming, hot tub. Picnic lunches and six-course gourmet dinners also available.

Hosts: Lee & Mary Lynn Tucker
Doubles: 4 (PB) $50-100
Cottage sleeping 6-8 available
Type of Beds: 4 Double; 1 Queen
Full Breakfast
Notes: 2, 4, 5, 8 (in cottages), 9, 10, 11, 12, 13

SPERRYVILLE

The Conyers House

Box 157, Rt. 707, 22740
(703) 987-8025

Nestled in the foothills of the Blue Ridge Mountains, The Conyers House is in the middle of Virginia's most beautiful hunt country. The hostess is an avid fox hunter who will encourage you to ride cross country. The host collects old cars and is an old film buff. An elegant candlelight fireside five-course dinner may be ordered at extra charge. Innkeeping seminars are offered for those thinking of becoming hosts.

Doubles: 8 (4 PB; 4 SB) $90-160
Full Breakfast
Credit Cards: No
Notes: 2, 4, 5, 6 (call), 7 (limited), 8 (weekdays), 9, 10, 11, 13

STANLEY

Jordan Hollow Farm Inn

Route 2, Box 375, 22851
(703) 778-2209; 778-2285

A restored colonial horse farm. Sixteen rooms with private bath; one suite. Full-service restaurant and pub. Horseback riding — trails, lessons, clinics, English and Western. In the Shenandoah Valley just ten miles from Skyline Drive, six miles from Luray Caverns.

Hosts: Jetze & Marley Beers
Doubles: 16
Suites: 5
Type of Beds: 12 Twin; 14 Double; 12 Queen
Full or Continental Breakfast
Credit Cards: A, B, E
Notes: 2, 3, 4, 5, 6, 7, 8, 9, 10, 11, 12, 13, 14

STAUNTON

Frederick House

18 E. Frederick Street, 24401
(703) 885-4220

NOTES: Credit cards accepted: A Master Card; B Visa; C American Express; D Discover Card; E Diners Club; F Other: 2 Personal checks accepted: 3 Lunch available: 4 Dinner available: 5 Open all year

An historic townhouse hotel in the European tradition. Large, comfortable rooms or suites, private baths, cable television, air-conditioning, telephones, and antique furnishings. Convenient to fine restaurants, shopping, museums, and the Blue Ridge Mountains.

Hosts: Joe & Evy Harman
Doubles: 11 (PB) $37-63.90
Type of Beds: 2 Twin; 7 Queen; 2 King
Full Breakfast
Credit Cards: A, B, C, D, E
Notes: 2, 4, 5, 8, 9, 10, 11, 12, 14

Thornrose House at Gypsy Hill

531 Thornrose Avenue, 24401
(703) 885-7026

A wraparound veranda and Greek colonnades distinguish this turn-of-the-century Georgian residence. Family antiques, a grand piano, and fireplaces create an elegant, restful atmosphere. Breakfast specialties served in a formal dining room energize you for sight-seeing in the beautiful Shenandoah Valley. Located at a 300-acre park with golf, tennis, swimming, and trails. Other attractions include Woodrow Wilson's birthplace, The Museum of American Frontier Culture, and nearby Skyline Drive and the Blue Ridge Parkway.

Hosts: Carolyn & Ray Hoaster
Doubles: 3 (PB) $45-55
Type of Beds: 1 Double; 1 Queen; 1 King; Cot available
Full Breakfast
Credit Cards: No
Notes: 2, 5, 8, 9, 10, 11, 12, 13

SWOOPE

Lambsgate Bed & Breakfast

Rt. 1, Box 63, 24479
(703) 337-6929

Six miles west of Staunton on routes 254 and 833. Restored 1816 farmhouse in the historic Shenandoah Valley. Mountain view; Shenandoah National Park; Skyline Drive; Monticello; Luray Caverns; Natural Bridge all nearby. British tradition with gracious Virginia hospitality.

Hosts: Dan & Elizabeth Fannon
Doubles: 3 (SB) $31.35-36.58
Type of Beds: 1 Twin; 2 Double
Full Breakfast
Minimum stay July 4: 2
Credit Cards: No
Notes: 2, 5, 8, 9

TREVILIANS

Prospect Hill

Rt. 3, Box 430, 23093
(703) 967-0844

Prospect Hill is a 1732 plantation just fifteen miles east of Charlottesville. Lodgings are in the manor house and renovated outbuildings featuring working fireplaces, Jacuzzis, and breakfast in bed. Candlelight dinners are served every evening by reservation.

Hosts: Mireille & Bill Sheehan
Doubles: 12 (PB) $110-160
Type of Beds: 1 Twin; 9 Double; 2 Queen
Full Breakfast
Credit Cards: A, B
Closed Dec. 24 & 25
Notes: 2, 4, 5, 7, 8, 14

VIRGINIA BEACH

Angie's Guest Cottage

302 24th Street, 23451
(804) 428-4690

Located in the heart of the resort area, one block from the ocean. Large beach house that former guest describes as "cute, clean, comfortable, and convenient." All rooms are air-conditioned; some have small refrigerators and private entrances. Breakfast is served on the front porch, and there is also a sun deck, barbecue pit, and picnic tables.
Host: Barbara G. Yates

6 Pets welcome: 7 Smoking allowed: 8 Children welcome: 9 Social drinking allowed: 10 Tennis available: 11 Swimming available: 12 Golf available: 13 Skiing available: 14 May be booked through travel agents

Singles: 1 (SB) $34.88
Doubles: 5 (1 PB; 4 SB) $43.60-56.68
Type of Beds: 3 Twin; 3 Double
Continental-plus Breakfast
Minimum stay in season: 2
Credit Cards: No
Closed Oct. 1-April 1
Notes: 7 (limited), 8, 9, 10, 11, 12

WACHAPREAGUE

The Burton House

11 Brooklyn Street, 23480
(804) 787-4560

Recently restored 1883 Victorian overlooking the Barrier Islands. Spacious rooms with period furnishings. Gazebo porch. Fully air-conditioned when needed. Bikes to ride; rental boats available. Complimentary home-cooked breakfast and evening refreshments are served.

Hosts: Pat, Tom, and Mike Hart
Doubles: 7 (PB) $53.25-63.90
Type of Beds: 2 Twin; 4 Double; 1 Queen
Full Breakfast
Credit Cards: No
Notes: 2, 5, 7 (on porches) 8 (over 12), 10, 11, 12

WASHINGTON

Caledonia Farm B & B

Rt. 1, Box 2080, 22627
(703) 675-3693

Beautifully restored 1812 stone home and romantic guest house on farm adjacent to Shenandoah National Park. Splendor for all seasons in Virginia's Blue Ridge Mountains. Skyline Drive, wineries, caves, historic sites, superb dining. Fireplaces, air-conditioning, bicycles. Only 68 miles to Washington, D.C.

Host: Phil Irwin
Doubles: 3 (1 PB; 2 SB) $70-100 plus tax
Type of Beds: 1 Twin; 3 Double
Full Breakfast
Credit Cards: A, B for confirmation only
Dinner available by reservation weekdays
Notes: 2, 3, 4, 5, 8 (over 12,) 9, 10, 11, 12, 13, 14

The Foster-Harris House

Main Street, Box 333, 22747
(703) 675-3757

A charming farmhouse Victorian in a tiny historic village just sixty-five miles from Washington, D. C. World-acclaimed five-star restaurant three blocks away. Antiques, fresh flowers, outstanding views of the Blue Ridge Mountains. Fireplace stoves in some rooms. Near Skyline Drive and Luray Caverns.

Hosts: Camille Harris & Patrick Foster
Doubles: 3 (1 PB; 2 SB) $53.50-90.96 (suite)
Type of Beds: 3 Queen
Continental Breakfast
Credit Cards: A, B
Notes: 2, 5, 6, 7, 8, 9, 10, 11, 12, 14

WILLIAMSBURG

The Cedars

616 Jamestown Road, 23185
(804) 229-3591

This brick Georgian colonial has air-conditioning, traditional antiques, and colonial reproductions. Nine rooms and a cottage with kitchen, located just one-quarter mile from the historic area and across from the College of William and Mary.

Host: Gil Horne
Doubles: 9 (SB) $48 and up
Continental Breakfast
Credit Cards: A, B
Notes: 2, 5, 6, 7, 8, 9, 10, 11, 12, 14

For Cant Hill Guest Home

4 Canterbury Lane, 23185
(804) 229-6623

Our home is only six to eight blocks from the restored area of Williamsburg, yet very secluded and quiet in a lovely wooded setting overlooking a lake that joins the College of William and Mary campus. The rooms are beautifully decorated, and the hosts are happy to make dinner reservations for you and provide helpful information on the many area attractions.

Hosts: Martha & Hugh Easler
Doubles: 2 (PB) $50
Type of Beds: 2 Twin; 1 Double
Continental Breakfast
Credit Cards: No
Notes: 2, 5, 8 (10 and over), 9, 10, 11, 12

Fox Grape

701 Monumental Avenue, 23185
(804) 229-6914

A brick Cape Cod home within a ten minute walk of Colonial Williamsburg. The home features antiques, stained glass, needlepoint wall hangings, and a decoy collection. Pat's interests include counted cross stitch and needlepoint. Bob makes duck-head walking sticks.

Hosts: Bob & Pat Orendorff
Doubles: 4 (2 PB; 2 SB) $42.60-53.25
Type of Beds: Double
Continental Breakfast
Credit Cards: A, B
Notes: 2, 5, 7, 8, 9, 10, 11, 12

Himmel-Bed & Breakfast

706 Richmond Road, 23185
(804) 229-6421

Himmel-bed, which means "heavenly bed" in German, is a cozy country Cape Cod stuffed to the brim with a classic collection of Dutch country antiques, stenciled walls, canopied beds. A hearty breakfast is served. Located just four blocks from the historic area and William and Mary College.

Host: Mary Peters
Doubles: 3 (PB) $55-65
Full Breakfast
Credit Cards: No
Notes: 2, 5, 8, 9, 10, 11, 12, 14

The Travel Tree 2

Box 838, Williamsburg, VA, 23187
(804) 253-1571

For the traveling family wanting cozy accommodations, this home provides a suite of three bedrooms and a breakfast/sitting room. Located in a quiet residential neighborhood, a separate entrance to the suite affords privacy and convenience.

Suite: 1 (PB) $45
Type of Beds: 2 Twin; 1 Double
Continental Breakfast
Credit Cards: No
Notes: 2, 5, 8, 10, 12

The Travel Tree 9

Box 838, Williamsburg, VA, 23187
(804) 253-1571

Spacious two-bedroom and bath suite with private entrance in a brick colonial-style home. Attractively decorated, accented with antique pieces. Dining area with small refrigerator and toaster oven.

Doubles: 2 (PB) $70
Type of Beds: 1 Double; 1 Queen
Continental Breakfast
Credit Cards: No
Notes: 2, 5, 8, 10, 12

The Travel Tree 10

Box 838, Williamsburg, VA, 23187
(804) 253-1571

In a unique colonial setting just 1.5 miles from Colonial Williamsburg, you'll enjoy the utmost in privacy with your own sitting room, kitchenette, bedroom, and bath. Relax over a leisurely breakfast as you enjoy the view from your bay window. Return to peace and quiet in the evening.

Doubles: 1 (PB) $90
Type of Beds: 1 Queen
Continental Breakfast
Credit Cards: No
Notes: 2, 5, 8, 10, 12

The Travel Tree 133

Box 838, Williamsburg, VA, 23187
(804) 253-1571

6 Pets welcome: 7 Smoking allowed: 8 Children welcome: 9 Social drinking allowed: 10 Tennis available: 11 Swimming available: 12 Golf available: 13 Skiing available: 14 May be booked through travel agents

A beautifully landscaped property in a wooded residential area provides a quiet, relaxed atmosphere welcome after a day of touring. This sprawling brick home offers a spacious bedroom with private bath, a dining area with small refrigerator, microwave, and coffee maker, and a private entrance. A wonderful getaway for two.

Doubles: 1 (PB) $60
Type of Beds: 1 King
Continental Breakfast
Credit Cards: No
Notes: 2, 5, 8, 10, 12

The Travel Tree 605

Box 838, Williamsburg, VA, 23187
(804) 253-1571

Conveniently located near Colonial Williamsburg and the College of William and Mary, this small B&B inn has accommodations to meet your every need. Breakfast is served in the dining room and afternoon tea in the parlor.

Doubles: 4 (PB) $65-90
Type of Beds: 3 Twin; 3 Queen
Continental Breakfast
Credit Cards: No
Notes: 2, 5, 8, 10, 12

The Travel Tree 616

Box 838, Williamsburg, VA, 23187
(804) 253-1571

Walk or bike to the historic area from this charming traditional white frame home. Your gracious hosts serve tea and wine in the spacious plantation parlor at 4:00 P.M. Two guest rooms with private baths are available, one with a queen-sized canopied waterbed.

Doubles: 2 (PB) $55-70
Type of Beds: 2 Twin; 2 Double; 1 Queen
Full Breakfast
Credit Cards: No
Notes: 2, 5, 8, 10, 12

The Travel Tree 710

Box 838, Williamsburg, VA, 23187
(804) 253-1571

Within walking distance of the historic area, this replica of an eighteenth-century home offers two double rooms, each with private bath. Furnished with period pieces, these accommodations extend your colonial experience right on through the night.

Doubles: 2 (PB) $75
Type of Beds: 2 Twin; 2 Queen
Continental Breakfast
Credit Cards: No
Notes: 2, 5, 8, 10, 12

War Hill Inn

4560 Long Hill Road, 23185
(804) 565-0248

Eighteenth-century home on 32-acre farm three miles off Rt. 60. Close to Colonial Williamsburg, William & Mary College, Busch Gardens, shopping outlets. Eight antique-furnished guest rooms with private baths.

Hosts: Shirley, Billy Lee, Cherie & Will Lee
Doubles: 8 (PB) $50-85
Suite: 3 (PB)
Continental Breakfast
Credit Cards: A, B, C
Notes: 2, 5, 8, 9

WILLIAMSBURG-TOANO

Blue Bird Haven

8691 Barhamsville Road, Toano, 23168
(804) 566-0177

Nine miles from Colonial Williamsburg, five minutes to Williamsburg Pottery. Friendly, at-home atmosphere, "inside tips" for visitors. Comfortable, traditionally furnished guest rooms in private wing. Homemade buffet breakfasts feature granola, quiche, stradas, blueberry pancakes, Virginia ham, muffins, spoonbread, cheese grits.

NOTES: Credit cards accepted: A Master Card; B Visa; C American Express; D Discover Card; E Diners Club; F Other: 2 Personal checks accepted: 3 Lunch available: 4 Dinner available: 5 Open all year

Hosts: June & Ed Cottle
Doubles: 3 (1 PB; 2 SB) $38-48
Type of Beds: 2 Twin; 2 Double
Full Breakfast
Minimum stay holidays: 2
Credit Cards: No
Closed January
Notes: 2, 4, 6, 7, 8 (over 6), 9, 10, 11, 12

WOODSTOCK

The Country Fare

402 N. Main Street, 22664
(703) 459-4828

A small, cozy country inn where old-fashioned hospitality has not gone out of style, within walking distance of the village of Woodstock. Relax and unwind in one of the three hand-stenciled bedrooms furnished with a comfortable blend of family antiques and country collectibles with touches of greenery throughout. Original house built in 1772 with addition in 1840 of log and brick. Used as a hospital between 1861 and 1864. A stay will surprise and delight you.

Host: Bette Hallgren
Doubles: 3 (1PB; 2SB) $48-58.75
Types of Beds: 1 Twin; 2 Doubles
Continental-plus Breakfast
Credit Cards: B
Notes: 2, 5, 7 (restricted), 8 (call), 9

Inn at Narrow Passage

US 11 South, 22664
(703) 459-8000

Historic 250-year-old log inn with 5 acres on the Shenandoah River. Two new wings have been added. Early American style rooms, most with private baths and fireplaces. Two miles from I-81; 1.5 hours from Washington, DC, Charlottesville, VA, and Lexington, VA. Fishing, hiking, caverns, and historic sites close by.

Hosts: Ellen & Ed Markel
Doubles: 12 (8PB; 4SB) $48-79
Type of Beds: 2 Twin; 13 Double
Full Breakfast
Credit Cards: A, B
Notes: 2, 4, 5, 8, 9, 10, 11, 12, 13 (30 min), 14

---

6 Pets welcome: 7 Smoking allowed: 8 Children welcome: 9 Social drinking allowed: 10 Tennis available: 11 Swimming available: 12 Golf available: 13 Skiing available: 14 May be booked through travel agents

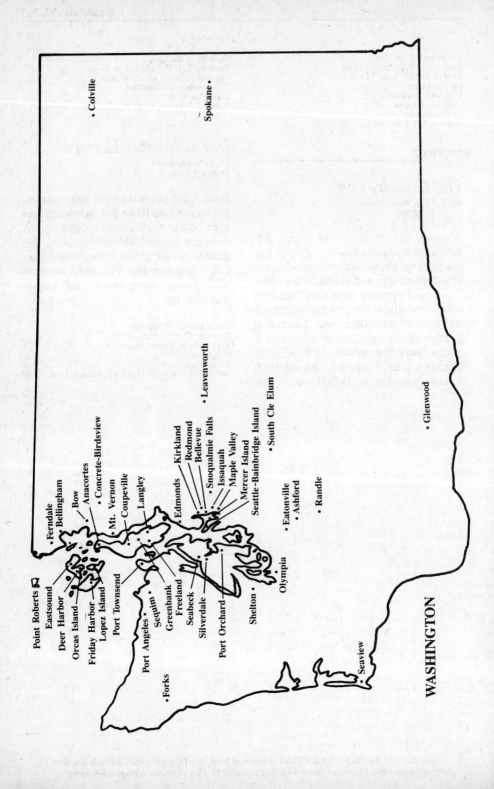

WASHINGTON

Colville •

Spokane •

Glenwood •

Leavenworth •

South Cle Elum •

Eatonville •
Ashford •
Randle •

Ferndale •
Bellingham •
Bow •
Anacortes •
Concrete-Birdsview •
Mt. Vernon •
Coupeville •
Langley •

Edmonds •
Kirkland •
Redmond •
Bellevue •
Snoqualmie Falls •
Issaquah •
Maple Valley •
Mercer Island •
Seattle-Bainbridge Island •

Point Roberts
Eastsound •
Deer Harbor •
Orcas Island •
Friday Harbor •
Lopez Island •
Port Townsend •

Port Angeles •
Sequim •
Greenbank •
Freeland •
Seabeck •
Silverdale •
Port Orchard •

Forks •

Shelton •
Olympia •

Seaview •

Washington

ANACORTES

Channel House Bed & Breakfast

2902 Oakes Avenue, 98221
(206) 293-9382

A classic island home built in 1902, the Channel House offers large, comfortable rooms, two with fireplaces, and lovely water and island views. The outdoor hot tub is a treat after a busy day of hiking or biking on the islands. Pat's oatmeal-raisin cookies are baked fresh every day. Anacortes is the beginning of the San Juan Island and Sydney, B.C., ferry routes and a center for chartering of sail and power boats for wonderful vacation trips.

Hosts: Dennis & Patricia McIntyre
Doubles: 6 (4 PB; 2 SB) $65-75
Type of Beds: 2 Twin; 4 Double; 2 Queen
Full Breakfast
Credit Cards: A, B
Notes: 2, 5, 8 (over 12), 9, 10, 11, 12, 14

Dutch Treat House

1220 31st Street, 98221
(206) 293-8154

Dutch Treat House offers comfortable, attractively furnished, large, bright corner rooms and tastefully prepared breakfasts. Ideally located and surrounded by some of the finest fishing and boating waters anywhere. Visitors enjoy many nearby attractions such as San Juan Islands, Victoria, and the Olympic Peninsula.

Hosts: Bill & Mary O'Connor
Singles: 1 (SB) $37.50

Doubles: 4 (SB) $53.75
Type of Beds: 1 Twin; 1 Double; 3 Queen
Full Breakfast
Credit Cards: A, B
Notes: 2, 5, 8 (over 8), 9, 10, 11, 12

Channel House B&B

ASHFORD

Ashford Mansion

Box G, 98304
(206) 569-2739

This twelve-room dwelling was built at the turn of the century and is located on an old mountain road six miles from Mt. Rainier National Park. There is a parlor with fireplace, grand piano, old-fashioned porch, and nearby Ashford Creek to lull you to sleep.

Host: Jan Green
Doubles: 4 (SB) $48-80
Type of Beds: 1 Double; 3 Queen
Full Breakfast
Credit Cards: A, B
Notes: 2, 5, 8 (12 and over), 9, 13 (XC)

6 Pets welcome: 7 Smoking allowed: 8 Children welcome: 9 Social drinking allowed: 10 Tennis available: 11 Swimming available: 12 Golf available: 13 Skiing available: 14 May be booked through travel agents

Ashford Mansion

Growly Bear Bed & Breakfast

37311 SR 706, 98304
(206) 569-2339

Experience a bit of history and enjoy your mountain stay at a rustic homestead house built in 1890. Secluded location near Mt. Rainier National Park. Listen to Goat Creek just outside your window; indulge in fresh pastries from the Growly Bear Bakery.

Host: Susan Jenny
Doubles: 2 (1 PB; 1 SB) $50-80
Type of Beds: 2 Twin; 3 Double
Full Breakfast
Credit Cards: No
Notes: 2, 5, 7 (restricted), 13

Mountain Meadows Inn

28912 SR 706 E., 98304
(206) 569-2788

Gracious hospitality, unique, quiet country atmosphere. Relax while absorbing nature's colors and sounds from our full veranda overlooking the pond. Friendly farm animals, including Oscar the llama. Nearby

Mt. Ranier National Park offers all-season recreation.

Hosts: Tanna Barney & Chad Darrah
Doubles: 3 (1 PB; 2 SB) $54.75-76.65
Type of Beds: 2 Twin; 2 Queen; 1 King
Full Breakfast
Minimum stay holidays: 2
Credit Cards: A, B
Notes: 2, 5, 8 (over 10), 9, 13, 14

BAINBRIDGE ISLAND

Bombay House

8490 Beck Road, 98110
(206) 842-3926

The Bombay House is a spectacular 35-minute ferry ride from downtown Seattle. The house was built in 1907 and sits high on a hillside in the country overlooking Rich Passage. Widow's walk, rustic, rough-cedar gazebo, masses of gardens exploding with seasonal color. Watch the ferry pass and see the lights of Bremerton in the distance. Just a few blocks from the beach, a country theater, and fine dining. A great spot for the visiting Seattle business traveler or vacationer.

Hosts: Bunny Cameron & Roger Kanchuk
Doubles: 5 (3 PB; 2 SB) $49-84
Type of Beds: 1 Twin; 2 Double; 2 Queen; 1 King
Continental Breakfast
Credit Cards: A, B, C
Notes: 2, 4, 5, 8, 9, 10, 11, 12

BELLEVUE

The Bed & Breakfast Cottage

8022 NE 27th Street, 98004
(206) 455-4140

The cottage is conveniently located to downtown Bellevue, Kirkland, and the University of Washington in Seattle. Newly renovated and very comfortable, the cottage has an atmosphere of casual graciousness.

NOTES: Credit cards accepted: A Master Card; B Visa; C American Express; D Discover Card; E Diners Club; F Other: 2 Personal checks accepted: 3 Lunch available: 4 Dinner available: 5 Open all year

Hosts: Arden Sweeting & Mary Rusk
Singles: 1 (PB) $50-60
Type of Beds: 1 Twin
Continental Breakfast
Credit Cards: No
Notes: 2, 5, 10, 11, 12

Petersen Bed & Breakfast

10228 SE 8th, 98004
(206) 454-9334

Petersen B&B is located in a well-established neighborhood five minutes from the Bellevue Shopping Square and twenty minutes from Seattle. It offers two rooms, one with a queen waterbed, and a spa on the deck off the atrium kitchen. Homestyle breakfast; airport pick-up can be arranged.

Hosts: Eunice & Carl Petersen
Doubles: 2 (SB) $35-45
Type of Beds: 2 Twin; 1 Queen
Full Breakfast
Credit Cards: No
Notes: 2, 5, 7 (outside), 8, 9, 10, 11

BELLINGHAM

Bellingham's DeCann House Bed & Breakfast

2610 Eldridge Avenue, 98225
(206) 734-9172

A Victorian B&B that combines the best of European hospitality and American convenience. Featuring family heirlooms, private baths, and a billiard room for mingling. Ask us about excursions to Vancourver, the San Juan Islands, or the Alaska ferry. Our breakfast will start your day with a smile.

Hosts: Van & Barbara Hudson
Doubles: 2 (PB) $35-55
Type of Beds: 2 Queen
Full Breakfast
Credit Cards: No
Notes: 2, 5, 8 (over 12), 9, 10, 11, 12

North Garden Inn

1014 North Garden, 98225
(206) 671-7828

North Garden Inn is an 1897 Queen Anne Victorian on the National Register. Many of the guest rooms have splendid views of Bellingham Bay. The inn features two studio grand pianos in performance condition and is located close to shopping, fine dining, and Western Washington University.

Hosts: Frank & Barbara De Freytas
Doubles (winter): 6 (1 PB; 5 SB) $42.04-52.82
Doubles (summer): 10 (2 PB; 8 SB) $42.04-52.82
Type of Beds: 1 Double; 4 Queen; 1 King
Continental Breakfast
Credit Cards: A, B
Notes: 2, 5, 8, 9, 14

Schnauzer Crossing

4421 Lakeway Drive, 98226
(206) 733-0055

Schnauzer Crossing is a luxury B&B located between Seattle and Vancourver, B.C. Enjoy this destination B&B, with its lakeside beauty, swimming, canoeing, and tennis, its master suite with fireplace and Jacuzzi tub. Sail in the San Juan Islands or climb 10,000-foot Mt. Baker. Experience Washington State!

Hosts: Vermont & Donna McAllister
Doubles: 2 (PB) $60-90
Type of Beds: 1 Queen; 1 King
Full Breakfast
Credit Cards: A, B
Notes: 2, 5, 6 (outdoors), 7 (outside), 8, 9, 10, 11, 12

BOW

Alice Bay Bed & Breakfast

982 Scott Road, Samish Island, Bow 98232
(206) 766-6396

Samish Island is a refuge for wildlife, and Alice Bay shelters a blue heron rookery. A restful room overlooks the bay, and a Finnish sauna and hot tub are available for guests. In the morning, you'll be served food from the *Alice Bay Cookbook* in our summer kitchen, which is warmed by a southern exposure.

Hosts: Terry & Julie Rousseau
Doubles: 1 (PB) $55
Type of Beds: 2 Twin; 1 Queen
Continental Breakfast
Credit Cards: No
Notes: 2, 5, 8, 10, 11

COLVILLE

Lakeside Manor Bed & Breakfast

Tiger Star Rt., Box 194, 99114
(509) 584-8741

The mansion is on a tiny peninsula with one lake at the front door and another at the back. Large indoor Jacuzzi, fireplace, panoramic views of the lakes and mountains. Centered in the Colville National Forest in northeast Washington.

Host: Pat Thomas
Doubles: 2 (SB) $60
Type of Beds: 2 King
Continental Breakfast
Credit Cards: A, B
Notes: 2, 5, 9, 11, 12, 13, 14

CONCRETE-BIRDSVIEW

Cascade Mountain Inn

3840 Pioneer Lane, 98237
(206) 826-4333

The inn is located close to the Skagit River, Baker Lake, and the North Cascades National Park, just off Highway 20 in a pastoral setting. Easy access to hiking, fishing, and sightseeing in one of the nation's most scenic mountain areas.

Hosts: Ingrid & Gerhard Meyer
Singles: 1 (PB) $55.90
Doubles: 5 (PB) $73.10
Type of Beds: 4 Twin; 3 Double; 1 Queen; 1 Rollaway
Full Breakfast
Credit Cards: A, B
Notes: 2, 5, 8 (over 10), 9, 14

COUPEVILLE

The Victorian Bed & Breakfast

602 North Main, Box 761, 98239
(206) 678-5305

This Victorian bed and breakfast provides gracious accommodations all year to Whidbey Island visitors. Guests may choose from either of the charming upstairs bedrooms or hideaway in the guest cottage. Hiking, boating, biking, and fishing available.

Host: Dolores Fresh
Doubles: 2 (PB) $80.85
Guest Cottage: 1
Type of Beds: 1 Twin; 3 Queen
Full Breakfast
Minimum stay in-season weekends & holidays: 2
Credit Cards: A, B
Notes: 2, 5

DEER HARBOR

Palmer's Chart House

Box 51, 98243
(206) 376-4231

The first B&B on Orcas Island (since 1975), with a magnificent water view. The 33-foot private yacht *Amante* is available for a minimal fee with Skipper Don. Low-key, private, personal attention makes this B&B unique and attractive. Well-traveled hosts speak Spanish.

Hosts: Majean & Donald Palmer
Doubles: 2 (PB) $45-60
Full Breakfast
Credit Cards: No
Notes: 2, 4 (by arrangement), 5, 8 (over 10), 9, 10, 11, 12, 14

EATONVILLE

Old Mill House Bed & Breakfast

116 Oak Street, Box 543, 98328
(206) 832-6506

NOTES: Credit cards accepted: A Master Card; B Visa; C American Express; D Discover Card; E Diners Club; F Other: 2 Personal checks accepted: 3 Lunch available: 4 Dinner available: 5 Open all year

Your password to the twenties! Indulge in spacious guest rooms complete with costumes and memorabilia, a shower with seven heads, a library leading to a secret prohibition bar and dance room. On the National Historic Register. Just say, "Joe sent me."

Hosts: Catharine & Michael Gallagher
Doubles: 4 (1PB; 3SB) $54-77
Type of Beds: 1 Double; 2 Queen; 1 King
Full Breakfast
Credit Cards: A, B
Notes: 2, 5, 8, 9, 11, 13, 14

Old Mill House B&B

EASTSOUND

Kangaroo House

Box 334, 98245
(206) 376-2175

Restful 1907 home on Orcas Island, gem of the San Juans. Period furnishings, extensive lawns and flower gardens. Gourmet breakfasts. Walk to village shops, galleries, and restaurants. Panoramic view of the islands from Moran State Park. Pick-up from ferry or airport.

Hosts: Jan & Mike Russillo
Doubles: 5 (SB) $50-60
Type of Beds: 3 Double; 2 Queen
Full Breakfast
Credit Cards: A, B
Notes: 2, 5, 7 (limited), 8, 9, 10, 11, 12

EDMONDS

Harrison House

210 Sunset Avenue, 98020
(206) 776-4748

New waterfront home with sweeping view of Puget Sound and the Olympic Mountains. Many fine restaurants within walking distance. Your spacious room has a private bath, private deck, TV, wet bar, telephone, and king-size bed. University of Washington is nearby.

Hosts: Jody & Harve Harrison
Doubles: 2 (PB) $35-45
Type of Beds: 1 Queen; 1 King
Continental Breakfast
Credit Cards: No
Notes: 2, 5, 9, 10, 11, 12, 13

FERNDALE

Hill Top Bed & Breakfast

5832 Church Road, 98248
(206) 384-3619

Large, comfortable rooms with sitting areas, one with fireplace. Beds and walls warmed with an array of quilts made by your hostess. Private entry and patio, hearty breakfast, panoramic mountain view.

Hosts: Paul & Doris Matz
Singles: 1 $36.55
Doubles: 2 (1 PB; 1 SB) $47.30
Type of Beds: 2 Twin; 2 Queen
Continental Breakfast
Credit Cards: A, B
Closed Christmas
Notes: 2, 8, 9, 10, 11, 12

FORKS

Miller Tree Inn

Box 953, 98331
(206) 374-6806

Quaint, comfortable 1917 farmhouse offers warm hospitality, choice of breakfast, and quiet country atmosphere. It's the Olympic Peninsula's best location for hiking, steelhead fishing, Hoh Rain Forest, or Rialto Beach. Listed in Brewster's *Northwest Best Places*. Guided fishing trips our specialty.

Hosts: Ted & Prue Miller
Doubles: 6 (2 PB; 4 SB) $35-60
Type of Beds: 4 Twin; 5 Double
Full Breakfast
Credit Cards: A, B
Notes: 2, 5, 6, 7, 8 (over 4), 9

FREELAND

Cliff House

5440 Windmill Road, 98249
(206) 321-1566

On Whidbey Island. Daringly different! In a private world of luxury, this stunning home is yours alone. Secluded in a forest on the very edge of Puget Sound, the views are breathtaking! Stone fireplace, spa, beach. King-sized feather bed, gourmet kitchen.

Hosts: Peggy Moore & Walter O'Toole
Doubles: 2 (PB) $225-242.55
Type of Beds: 1 Queen; 1 King
Continental-plus Breakfast
Minimum stay: 2
Credit Cards: No
Closed Christmas through January
Notes: 2, 9, 12

Pillars by the Sea

1367 East Bayview Avenue, 98249
(206) 221-7738

Turn-of-the-century home, restored to its beautiful original condition. Rooms have queen beds with private baths. This historic home overlooks beautiful Holmes Harbor.

You can hike, beach walk, relax. Tennis, golf, horseback riding, bicycling. Restaurants nearby.

Hosts: Richard & Andree Ploss
Doubles: 3 (PB) $60-70
Type of Beds: 3 Queen
Full Breakfast
Minimum stay weekends: 2; holidays: 3
Credit Cards: A, B
Closed January
Notes: 2, 9, 10, 11, 12

FRIDAY HARBOR

Tucker House Bed & Breakfast

260 "B" Street, 98250
(206) 378-2783

Located on San Juan Island, Tucker House offers three private cottages, three rooms in the main house, and a hot tub. Walking distance to ferry, shops, restaurants, galleries, marina, and whale museum. Two of the rooms accommodate four people.

Hosts: John & Evelyn Lackey & Mitzi Stack
Doubles: 6 (3 PB; 3 SB) $53.75-86
Type of Beds: 2 Twin; 2 Double; 5 Queen
Full Breakfast
Credit Cards: A, B
Notes: 2, 5, 7, 8, 14

GLENWOOD

Flying L Ranch

25 Flying L Lane, 98619
(509) 364-3488

Built in 1945 by the Lloyds and operated by them ever since. On 160 beautiful acres with trails, wild flowers, wildlife, pond, in a tranquil, secluded valley at the base of 12,276-foot Mt. Adams. Intimate lodge, guest house with views, fireplaces, common kitchens, cabin. Restaurant, stores nearby.

Hosts: Darvel & Ilse Lloyd
Singles: 2 (1 PB; 1 SB) $34-44
Doubles: 10 (7 PB; 3 SB) $49-64
Type of Beds: 10 Twin; 9 Double; 3 Queen
Full Breakfast

NOTES: Credit cards accepted: A Master Card; B Visa; C American Express; D Discover Card; E Diners Club; F Other: 2 Personal checks accepted: 3 Lunch available: 4 Dinner available: 5 Open all year

Minimum stay certain weekends & holidays: 2
Credit Cards: A, B
Notes: 2, 5, 6, 8, 9, 11, 12, 13, 14

GREENBANK

Guest House Cottages

835 E. Christenson Road, 98253
(206) 678-3115

Luxurious couples' retreat on Whidbey Island. Beautiful log lodge for 2; four cozy cottages; Wildflower Suite in 1920s farmhouse. Each accommodates two adults. Outdoor pool, hot tub, exercise room, Jacuzzis, wildlife pond, and 25 acres of land. All cottages have kitchens, VCRs, complimentary movies, fireplaces, and antiques.

Hosts: The Creger Family
Doubles: 6 (PB) $70-195 plus tax
Type of Beds: 1 Twin; 3 Double; 1 Queen; 2 King
Continental Breakfast
Minimum stay weekends: 2 ; holidays: 2-3
Credit Cards: A, B, C, D
Notes: 2, 5, 7 (restricted), 9, 10, 11, 14

Guest House Cottages

ISSAQUAH

Wildflower Bed & Breakfast Inn

25237 SE Issaquah-Fall City Road, 98027
(206) 392-1196

Quiet country charm in a small, delightful suburb of Seattle. Two-story log home nestled in acres of evergreens offers the comfort of spacious rooms, antique furnishings, home-cooked breakfasts. Nearby are Gilman Shopping Village, a small theater, and excellent restaurants. Close to state and county recreational parks; thirty-five minutes from skiing.

Host: Laureita Caldwell
Doubles: 4 (2 PB; 2 SB) $45-50
Type of Beds: 1 Twin; 1 Double; 3 Queen
Full Breakfast
Notes: 2, 5, 8 (over 11), 10, 11, 12

KIRKLAND

Shumway Mansion

11410 99th Place NE 98033
(206) 823-2303

Overlook Lake Washington from this award-winning 1909, twenty-three-room mansion. Seven individually decorated guest rooms with private baths. Variety-filled breakfast. Complimentary use of athletic club. Short distance to all forms of shopping; twenty minutes to downtown Seattle. Water and snow recreation close at hand.

Hosts: Richard & Salli Harris
Doubles: 7 (PB) $57-78
Type of Beds: 7 Queen
Full Breakfast
Credit Cards: A, B
Notes: 2, 5, 7 (restricted), 8 (over 12), 9, 10, 11, 14

LANGLEY

Country Cottage of Langley

Box 459, 98260
(206) 221-8709

6 Pets welcome: 7 Smoking allowed: 8 Children welcome: 9 Social drinking allowed: 10 Tennis available: 11 Swimming available: 12 Golf available: 13 Skiing available: 14 May be booked through travel agents

Country Cottage of Langley

Old-fashioned hospitality in country elegance. Remodeled 1926 farmhouse on 3 acres of manicured lawn with a view of Puget Sound and the Cascades Mountains. Five rooms or suites with private baths, full breakfast. Two blocks to the water and downtown Langley, the art capital of Whidbey Island. Bicycling, strolling wooded parks, and water sports are all island activities.

Hosts: Trudy & Whitey Marten
Doubles: 5 (PB) $65-85
Type of Beds: 5 Queen
Full Breakfast
Credit Cards: A, B
Notes: 2, 5, 9, 10, 11, 12, 14

Eagles Nest Inn

3236 East Saratoga Road, 98260
(206) 321-5331

The inn's rural setting on Whidbey Island offers a sweeping view of Saratoga Passage and Mount Baker. Casual elegance abounds. Relax and enjoy the wood stove fireplace, spa, library/lounge, and bottomless chocolate chip cookie jar. Write or call for brochure. Canoeing and horseback riding available.

Hosts: Nancy & Dale Bowman
Doubles: 3 (PB) $80.85
Type of Beds: 1 Queen; 2 King
Full Breakfast
Minimum stay weekends & holidays: 2
Credit Cards: A, B

Closed Thanksgiving & Christmas
Notes: 2, 4, 10

Log Castle

3273 East Saratoga Road, 98260
(206) 321-5483

Located on Whidbey Island, thirty miles north of Seattle. Log lodge on secluded beach. Big stone fireplace, turret bedrooms, panoramic views of Puget Sound and the Cascade Mountains. Norma's breakfast is a legend. Watch for bald eagles and Orca whales from our widow's walk.

Hosts: Senator Jack & Norma Metcalf
Doubles: 4 (PB) $60-80
Type of Beds: 1 Double; 1 Queen; 2 King
Full Breakfast
Minimum stay holidays: 2
Credit Cards: A, B
Notes: 2, 5, 8 (over 11), 10

The Saratoga Inn

4850 South Coles Road, 98260
(206) 221-7526

A Cape Cod inn on 25 peaceful acres overlooking Saratoga Passage. Spacious rooms with private baths and fireplace. English cottage garden. Five minutes to beach, tennis, or shopping. Located on the south end of Whidbey Island, one hour north of Seattle.

Host: Debbie Jones
Doubles: 5 (PB) $75-95
Type of Beds: 2 Twin; 4 Queen

NOTES: Credit cards accepted: A Master Card; B Visa; C American Express; D Discover Card; E Diners Club; F Other: 2 Personal checks accepted: 3 Lunch available: 4 Dinner available: 5 Open all year

Continental-plus Breakfast
Minimum stay weekends: 2
Credit Cards: No
Notes: 2, 5, 9

LEAVENWORTH

Brown's Farm Bed & Breakfast

11150 Highway 209, 98826
(509) 548-7863

Our country farmhouse, nestled among towering pines and grand firs, offers year-round country delight. Come cuddle a kitten, gather fresh eggs, snuggle under a down comforter. Brown's Farm is a rare experience in homespun hospitality.

Host: Wendi Krieg
Doubles: 3 (SB) $55-65
Type of Beds: 1 Twin; 1 Double; 2 Queen
Full Breakfast
Credit Cards: A, B
Notes: 2, 5, 8, 9, 11, 12, 13, 14

Brown's Farm B&B

LOPEZ ISLAND

MacKaye Harbor Inn

Rt. 1, Box 1940, 98261
(206) 468-2253

The ideal beachfront getaway! Lopez's only B&B on the water, this Victorian home is full of charm and nostalgia. Beautiful grounds, beach combing, biking, rowing, and kayaking. Eagles, deer, seals, and otters frequent the area. Waterfront dining on island-fresh seafood or steaks. Totally non-smoking facility not suitable for small children.

Hosts: Rick & Terri Hickox
Doubles: 5 (PB and SB) $49-69
Full Breakfast
Credit Cards: A, B
Notes: 2, 4, 5, 9, 10, 11, 12, 14

MAPLE VALLEY

Maple Valley Bed & Breakfast

20020 SE 228, 98038
(206) 432-1409

Welcome to our warm cedar home in the wooded Northwest. Spacious grounds, wildlife pond, and finely feathered friends. Experience hootenanny pancakes, "hot babies," and gracious family hospitality. Celebrate 100 years "Inn" Washington with AVA Volkswalking from our threshold. Crest Airpark is just minutes away. Be special; be our guest!

Hosts: Jayne Hurlbut & Shana Clarke
Doubles: 2 (SB) $45
Type of Beds: 2 Twin; 1 Queen; 2 Cots
Full Breakfast
Credit Cards: No
Closed Christmas Day & Easter
Notes: 2, 5, 8, 9, 10, 11, 12, 14

MERCER ISLAND

Pacific B&B 6

Pacific B&B Agency
701 NW 60th, Seattle, WA, 98107
(206) 784-0539

This modern cedar home offers two private suites with private entrances, deck or patio overlooking the lake. Just one block to a beach and five miles to Seattle. Your German hostess serves an extraordinary breakfast. Great place for joggers and walkers. $45-50.

Pacific B&B 7

Pacific B&B Agency
701 NW 60th, Seattle, WA, 98107
(206) 784-0539

The guest home offers two guest rooms, patio, and gardens with a waterfall. Both rooms share one bath. Fine breakfast is served in the dining room under a chandelier that once hung in a French castle. Your hosts are world travelers. $50-70.

MT. VERNON

The White Swan Guest House

1388 Moore Road, 98273
(206) 445-6805

The White Swan is a very special "storybook" farmhouse six miles from the historic waterfront town of La Conner. Fine restaurants, great antiquing, and interesting shops in Washington's favorite artist community. Just one hour north of Seattle and ninety miles south of Vancouver.

Host: Peter Goldfarb
Doubles: 3 (S2B) $48-55
Type of Beds: 2 Queen; 1 King
Continental Breakfast
Credit Cards: A, B
Notes: 2, 5

OLYMPIA

Harbinger Inn

1136 East Bay Drive, 98506
(206) 754-0389

Completely restored National Historic Landmark. View of East Bay Marina, Capitol, and Olympic Mountains. Ideally located for boating, bicycling, jogging, fine dining, and business ventures. A "Northwest Best Place."

Hosts: Dave & Emmy Mathes
Doubles: 4 (1 PB; 3 SB) $37-63
Type of Beds: 2 Double; 1 Queen; 1 King
Full Breakfast
Credit Cards: A, B, C
Notes: 2, 5, 8 (over 12), 9

ORCAS ISLAND

Turtleback Farm

Rt. 1, Box 650, Eastsound, 98245
(206) 376-4914

A meticulously restored farmhouse set on 80 acres in Crow Valley on Orcas Island in the San Juan Islands. Seven antique-filled guest rooms, each with a private bath. An award-winning full breakfast is served.

Hosts: William & Susan C. Fletcher
Doubles: 7 (PB) $55-120
Type of Beds: 2 Twin; 1 Double; 5 Queen; 1 King
Full Breakfast
Credit Cards: A, B
Notes: 2, 5, 9, 10, 11, 14

Woodsong Bed & Breakfast

Box 32, 98280
(206) 376-2340

A remodeled country schoolhouse on 4 acres of woods and meadows provides a peaceful setting for your stay on this unspoiled island off the coast of Washington. Explore our back roads, hike, bike, kayak, or just relax. Good restaurants, craft shops, and a community theater are available. Arrival is by ferry.

Hosts: Carol & Alby Meyer
Doubles: 2 (1 PB; 1 SB) $55
Type of Beds: 2 Twin; 1 Double; 1 Queen
Full Breakfast
Credit Cards: No
Closed Nov., Dec., & Jan.
Notes: 2, 8, 9, 12

NOTES: Credit cards accepted: A Master Card; B Visa; C American Express; D Discover Card; E Diners Club; F Other: 2 Personal checks accepted: 3 Lunch available: 4 Dinner available: 5 Open all year

Tudor Inn

Tudor Inn

1108 S. Oak, 98362
(206) 452-3138

Located between the mountains and the sea, this half-timbered Tudor home was built by an Englishman in 1910 and has been tastefully restored and furnished with European antiques. Tea is served in the lounge, the library, or the gazebo overlooking the English garden.

Hosts: Jane & Jerry Glass
Doubles: 5 (1 PB; 4 S2B) $48.50-73.30
Type of Beds: 1 Double; 2 Queen; 2 King
Full Breakfast
Minimum stay weekends & holidays: 2
Credit Cards: A, B
Notes: 2, 5, 8 (over 10), 9, 12, 11, 12, 13, 14

PORT ORCHARD

Ogle's Bed & Breakfast

1307 Dogwood Hill SW, 98366
(206) 876-9170

Secluded single-level, stairless hillside home overlooking Puget Sound. View anchored navy ships. Secure off-street parking. Charming Port Orchard is a gateway to the beautiful Olympic Peninsula. Excellent restaurants, antique shops, large marinas nearby. Quiet, restful setting.

Hosts: Quentin & Louise Ogle
Singles: 1 (SB) $33
Doubles: 2 (SB) $43
Type of Beds: 1 Twin; 1 Double; 1 Queen
Full Breakfast
Credit Cards: A, B
Notes: 5, 7 (restricted), 8 (over 12), 9, 10, 12

POINT ROBERTS

The Old House Bed & Breakfast Inn

674 Kendor Road, 98281
(206) 945-5210

A large historic home nestled in a parklike setting on the warm southern slope of Point Roberts, fronted by a private beach available to guests. Guest rooms share a second-story sun deck with an unparalleled view of the San Juan Islands and the Canadian Gulf Islands. Ten minutes from the Victoria ferry terminal and twenty-five from downtown Vancouver.

Hosts: Glenda Fraser & Jim Day
Singles: $29-30
Doubles: $39-49
Type of Beds: 2 Twin; 2 Queen
Full Breakfast
Credit Cards: No
Notes: 2, 5, 7 (restricted), 8 (over 12), 11, 12, 14

PORT TOWNSEND

The James House

1238 Washington Street, 98368
(206) 385-1238

A grand Victorian mansion built by Francis James in 1889, the James House became the first bed and breakfast guest house in the Northwest in 1973. Its fine tradition of warmth and hospitality continues in this splendid seaport setting.

Hosts: Lowell & Barbara Bogart
Doubles: 12 (4 PB; 8 SB) $45-125
Type of Beds: 1 Twin; 14 Double
Continental Breakfast
Minimum stay weekends & holidays: 2
Credit Cards: A, B
Notes: 2, 5, 8, 9, 10, 11, 12

6 Pets welcome: 7 Smoking allowed: 8 Children welcome: 9 Social drinking allowed: 10 Tennis available: 11 Swimming available: 12 Golf available: 13 Skiing available: 14 May be booked through travel agents

The Lincoln Inn

538 Lincoln, 98368
(206) 385-6677

An 1888 historic inn located in the West Coast's famous Victorian seaport of Port Townsend. Antique-filled rooms, water views, private baths (some with Jacuzzis), full sumptuous breakfast, and gourmet dining available at night.

Hosts: Robert & Joan Allen
Doubles: 6 (PB) $65
Type of Beds: 3 Double; 3 Queen
Full Breakfast
Credit Cards: A, B
Closed Christmas-Jan. 31
Notes: 2 (in advance), 4, 7 (restricted), 8 (over 12), 9, 10, 12

Starrett House Inn

744 Clay Street, 98368
(206) 385-3205

Situated on a bluff overlooking the Olympic Mountains, the Cascades, Puget Sound, and historic Port Townsend. The house is internationally renowned for its Victorian architecture, free-hung staircase, frescoed domed ceiling with a solar calendar, and sumptuous breakfasts.

Hosts: Edel & Bob Sokol
Doubles: 9 (PB and SB) $45-85
Full Breakfast
Credit Cards: A, B
Notes: 2, 5, 9, 10, 11, 12

RANDLE

Hampton House Bed & Breakfast

409 Silverbrook Road, 98377
(206) 497-2907

Country charm in a restored 1906 local landmark on 1.5 acres. Near Mt. St. Helens and Mt. Rainier. Two large bedrooms with queen beds. Friendly hosts help you plan sightseeing in the area. Full breakfast features N.W. fruit and berries in season. Two-hour drive from either Seattle or Portland airports.

Hosts: Sylvia & Jack Wasson
Singles: 2 (SB) $45
Doubles: 2 (SB) $55
Type of Beds: Twin; Queen
Full Breakfast
Credit Cards: No
Closed Oct. 15 - Apr. 15
Notes: 2, 12, 13

REDMOND

Cedarym — A Colonial Bed & Breakfast

1011 - 240th Avenue N.E., 98053
(206) 868-4159

"... a few minutes and a couple centuries away" from Seattle, this authentic colonial reproduction home is situated on over 2 acres of landscaped grounds. Enjoy the gazebo-covered spa, walk in the woods, and breakfast by candlelight.

Hosts: Mary Ellen & Walt Brown
Doubles: 2 (SB) $48.65
Type of Beds: 2 Double
Full Breakfast
Credit Cards: A, B
Notes: 2, 5, 9, 10, 11, 12, 14

SEABECK

Summer Song

Box 82, 98380
(206) 830-5089

The majestic Olympic Mountains reflecting on Hood Canal provide a quiet, spectacular setting for this private waterfront cottage with its gentle touch of country comfort. The cottage will accommodate up to four guests and features a bedroom, living room, kitchen, bath, fireplace, TV, and VCR. A perfect place to relax, swim, boat, fish, or hike.

NOTES: Credit cards accepted: A Master Card; B Visa; C American Express; D Discover Card; E Diners Club; F Other: 2 Personal checks accepted: 3 Lunch available: 4 Dinner available: 5 Open all year

Hosts: Ron & Sharon Barney
Cottage: 1 (PB) $55
Type of Beds: 1 Double; 1 Queen
Full Breakfast
Credit Cards: A, B
Notes: 2, 5, 7, 9, 10, 11, 14

SEATTLE

Beech Tree Manor

Seattle B&B Assoc., Box 95853, 98145
(206) 547-1020

A 1904 Victorian five minutes from city center. Scrumptious breakfast; sherry served in Irish crystal. Original art in all rooms, plus a lazy back porch with wicker chairs. Dog in residence.

Doubles: 4 (2 PB; 2 SB) $59-75
Type of Beds: 2 Twin; 3 Double
Full Breakfast
Credit Cards: A, B, C, E
Notes: 5, 7 (outside), 8

Chambered Nautilus

5005 22nd Avenue NE 98105
(206) 522-2536

A gracious 1915 Georgian colonial nestled high on a hill, furnished with a mixture of American and English antiques and reproductions. Offers excellent access to Seattle's theaters, restaurants, public transportation, shopping, bike and jogging trails, and the University of Washington campus.

Hosts: Bunny & Bill Hagemeyer
Doubles: 6 (2 PB; 4 SB) $65-85
Triples: 2 (PB) $85-95
Type of Beds: 1 Double; 5 Queen
Full Breakfast
Minimum stay holidays: 3
Credit Cards: A, B, C
Notes: 2, 5, 8, 9, 10, 11, 12

Chelsea Station Bed & Breakfast Inn

4915 Linden Avenue North, 98103
(206) 547-6077

For a quiet, comfortable, and private accommodation, nothing beats Chelsea Station. With Seattle's rose gardens at our doorstep, you can breathe in the restorative calm. Try a soothing cup of tea or a nap in the afternoon. That's our style, and we welcome you to it.

Hosts: Dick & Marylou Jones
Doubles: 5 (PB) $59-80
Type of Beds: 5 King
Full Breakfast
Minimum stay holidays: 3
Credit Cards: A, B, C, E, F
Notes: 2, 5, 8 (over 11), 9, 10, 11, 12, 14

Galer Place B&B

Galer Place Bed & Breakfast

318 W. Galer, 98119
(206) 282-5339

Quiet, cozy 1906 Victorian, close to downtown and Seattle center. Delicious full

6 Pets welcome: 7 Smoking allowed: 8 Children welcome: 9 Social drinking allowed: 10 Tennis available: 11 Swimming available: 12 Golf available: 13 Skiing available: 14 May be booked through travel agents

breakfasts. Four guest rooms, all furnished with antiques and private baths. Peace and tranquility within the city.

Hosts: Chris & Terry Giles
Doubles: 4 (PB) $70-80
Type of Beds: 1 Twin; 1 Double; 1 Queen; 1 King
Full Breakfast
Minimum stay weekends: 2
Credit Cards: A, B, C, E
Notes: 2, 5, 6, 7 (limited), 8 (over 12), 9, 10, 11, 12

Hainsworth House

Seattle B&B Assoc., Box 95853, 98145
(206) 547-1020

An historic 1906 Tudor mansion offering coffee/tea trolley service and a formal gourmet champagne breakfast. Each room has a private bath, deck, and city view. Two dogs in residence. No children, pets, smoking or unmarried couples, please.

Doubles: 2 (PB) $75-85
Full Breakfast
Credit Cards: A, B, C

Hanson House

Seattle B&B Assoc., Box 95853, 98145
(206) 547-1020

Romantic getaway overlooking Elliott Bay and Seattle's unparalleled skyline. Lounge in the guest solarium and enjoy the nightly city-glitter watching. One dog, two cats in residence in this 1904 Tudor. Children 14 and over welcome; no pets; limited smoking.

Doubles: 2 (PB) $70
Type of Beds: 2 King
Continental-plus Breakfast
Credit Cards: A, B

Marit's B&B

Seattle B&B Assoc., Box 95853, 98145
(206) 547-1020

Enjoy Scandinavian hospitality in a brick, ivy-covered Tudor. Awaken to the smell of freshly brewed coffee and home-baked rolls, which are just part of the full breakfast.

Enjoy the view of Puget Sound and the Olympic Mountains; walk to the park, zoo, and lake. No pets; no smoking.

Doubles: 2 (SB) $45
Type of Beds: 1 Double; 1 Queen
Full Breakfast
Credit Cards: No

Mildred's Bed & Breakfast

1202 15th Avenue East, 98112
(206) 325-6072

A traditional 1890 Victorian gem in an elegant style. Old-fashioned hospitality awaits: red carpets, lace curtains, fireplace, grand piano, and wraparound porch. Across the street is the Seattle Art Museum, Flower Conservatory, and historic 44-acre Volunteer Park. Electric trolley at the front door. Minutes to city center, freeways, and all points of interest.

Host: Mildred Sarver
Doubles: 3 (SB) $45-55
Type of Beds: 2 Twin or 1 King; 2 Double
Full Breakfast
Credit Cards: A, B, C
Notes: 2, 5, 8, 9, 10, 11, 12, 14

Mildred's B&B

NW B&B #152

NW Bed & Breakfast Travel Unlimited
610 SW Broadway, Portland, OR, 97205
(503) 243-7616

Handsome old New England style house
with extensive gardens and lawns, spacious
living room with cathedral ceiling, and an
antique organ. Nearby Puget Sound access
by steep trail or drive to Seahurst Park. Near
SeaTac Airport and a major shopping center. One dog in residence.

Singles: 1 (SB) $35
Doubles: 1 (PB) $48
Type of Beds: 1 Twin; 1 Queen
Continental Breakfast
Credit Cards: No

NW B&B #176A

NW Bed & Breakfast Travel Unlimited
610 SW Broadway, Portland, OR, 97205
(503) 243-7616

Modest home on 1 acre, including orchard,
very convenient to SeaTac airport, fifteen
minutes to downtown, three blocks to the
bus. Short walk to lovely small park with
ducks. Fireplace in the living room. Pick-up
from airport with advance notice.

Doubles: 2 (SB) $30-40
Type of Beds: 2 Double
Continental Breakfast
Credit Cards: No
Notes: 6 (call), 7

NW B&B #177

NW Bed & Breakfast Travel Unlimited
610 SW Broadway, Portland, OR, 97205
(503) 243-7616

Contemporary home on a secluded lot overlooking Puget Sound and the Olympics, in a
quiet residential community twelve miles
south of downtown. Convenient to SeaTac
Airport, Des Moines Marina and Fishing
Pier, Saltwater Park, shopping centers, and
bus. Guest rooms, living room, and deck all
offer a lovely view of Puget Sound.

Doubles: 1 (PB) $32-38
Type of Beds: 1 Queen; 1 Crib
Continental Breakfast
Credit Cards: No
Notes: 7 (limited)

Pacific B&B 8

Pacific B&B Agency
701 NW 60th, Seattle, WA, 98107
(206) 784-0539

A gracious brick Georgian in a most convenient location. Walk to restaurants, shops,
bus lines, a city park, and the museum. Spacious rooms on the first floor with sitting
areas and queen beds; shared bath. Enjoy
your breakfast on the patio or in the oversized kitchen, lounge in the huge living room
with its extensive art collection. $50-65.

Queen Anne Hill

Seattle B&B Assoc., Box 95853, 98145
(206) 547-1020

Cozy, turn-of-the-century home near
downtown and Seattle center. Spectacular
mountain and water views and sunsets.
Filled with art and antiques, this home is only
minutes from historic Pike Place Market.
Two dogs in residence. No children, pets, or
smoking, please.

Doubles: 5 (SB) $60
Type of Beds: 5 Double
Full Breakfast
Credit Cards: No

Roberta's Bed & Breakfast Inn

1147 16th Avenue East, 98112
(206) 329-3326

A classic turn-of-the century home nestled
on a tree-lined street in Seattle's historic
Capitol Hill neighborhood. Five minutes
from downtown, the University of
Washington, two lakes, and public transportation. The hosts will gladly fill you in on all

6 Pets welcome: 7 Smoking allowed: 8 Children welcome: 9 Social drinking allowed: 10 Tennis available: 11
Swimming available: 12 Golf available: 13 Skiing available: 14 May be booked through travel agents

the local attractions, restaurants, and available activities.

Host: Roberta C. Barry
Doubles: 4 (1 PB; 3 SB) $50-75
Type of Beds: 1 Twin; 3 Queen
Full Breakfast
Minimum stay holidays: 2
Credit Cards: A, B, C, E
Notes: 2, 5, 8 (over 12), 9, 10, 11, 12

Salisbury House

750 16th Ave. E., 98112
(206) 328-8682

An elegant turn-of-the-century home on Capitol Hill, just minutes from Seattle's cultural and business activities. The spacious library, living room, and wraparound porch invite relaxation. We're just two blocks from a park and the Seattle Art Museum.

Hosts: Mary & Cathryn Wiese
Doubles: 4 (S2B) $46.48-68.10
Type of Beds: 2 Twin; 3 Queen
Full Breakfast
Minimum stay weekends: 2; holidays: 3
Credit Cards: A, B
Notes: 2, 5, 8 (over 12), 9, 10, 11, 12, 14

Seattle Guest Cottage

701 N.W. 60th, 98107
(206) 784-0539

A 1925 cottage in a quiet neighborhood close to downtown, the University of Washington, a beach, lakes, and city parks. Comfortably furnished with brass and oak accents, it has two bedrooms and sleeps up to six. One room has a lovely antique mahogany bedroom set; the second has two twin beds. Crib available; fully furnished and equipped kitchen, color TV, free phone, fireplace. Ideal for vacations, visiting relatives, honeymooners, business persons.

Hosts: Inge Pokrandt
Doubles: 2 (SB) $69 plus $10 each additional person
Type of Beds: 2 Twin; 1 Double
Stocked kitchen
Credit Cards: A, B, C
Notes: 2, 5, 8, 9, 10, 11, 12, 13, 14

The Shafer Mansion

907- 14th Avenue East, 98112
(206) 329-4628

Large English manor house on beautiful tree-lined street. Within walking distance to some of Seattle's best shops and restaurants. Comfortably quiet, spacious rooms with antique double beds and tile baths.

Host: H. Lee Vennes
Doubles: 5 (3 PB: 2 SB) $55-95
Type of Beds: 5 Double
Continental Breakfast
Credit Cards: C
Notes: 2, 5, 9, 10, 12

Tugboat Challenger

Tugboat Challenger

809 Fairview Place North, 98109
(206) 340-1201

Restored 1944 tugboat in downtown Seattle. Carpeted, granite fireplace; bar; laundry. Refrigerators, TV, phone, VCR, sinks, sprinkler system, private entrance for each room. Restaurants, bars, classic and modern sail boats, power boats, row boats, and kayak rentals. Swimming. Featured in *Travel & Leisure, Cosmopolitan,* and many major papers.

Hosts: Jerry Brown
Doubles: 5 (2PB; 3SB) $54-$125

NOTES: Credit cards accepted: A Master Card; B Visa; C American Express; D Discover Card; E Diners Club; F Other: 2 Personal checks accepted: 3 Lunch available: 4 Dinner available: 5 Open all year

Type of Beds: 4 Twin; 2 Double; 1 Queen
Full Breakfast
Credit Cards: A, B, C
Notes: 2, 5, 7, 9, 10, 11, 12, 14

Villa Heidelberg

Seattle B&B Assoc., Box 95853, 98145
(206) 547-1020

A 1909 country home in West Seattle with leaded glass, beamed ceiling, fireplaces, wraparound porch, sound and mountain view. Convenient location. Cat in residence. Children welcome; limited smoking.

Doubles: 2 (SB) $45-55
Type of Beds: 1 Double; 1 King
Full Breakfast
Credit Cards: No

Williams House B&B

1505 4th Ave. North, 98109
(206) 285-0810

A family bed and breakfast in an Edwardian home with much of the original woodwork and original gas-light fixtures. Decorated with antiques, most guest rooms have views of Seattle, the mountains, or the water. A sunny enclosed porch is shared by all, as well as the first and second floors. Close to downtown, the Space Needle, Public Market. Public transportation available.

Hosts: Susan, Doug & Danielle
Doubles: 5 (1PB; 4SB) $60-80
Type of Beds: 4 Queen; 5 King
Full Breakfast
Minimum stay holidays: 2
Credit Cards: A, B, C, E
Notes: 2, 5, 7 (limited to porches), 8 (by prior arrangement), 10, 11

SEAVIEW

Shelburne County Inn

Box 250, 98644
(206) 642-2442

Come, enjoy the beauty of Washington's oldest country inn, nestled between the Columbia River and Pacific Ocean. We'll pamper you with great food, friendly innkeepers, and exquisite furnishings. Restaurant on the premises.

Hosts: Laurie Anderson & David Campiche
Doubles: 16 (13 PB; 3 SB) $67.91-139
Type of Beds: 1 Twin; 6 double; 9 Queen
Full Breakfast
Minimum stay weekends & holidays: 2
Credit Cards: A, B, C
Notes: 2, 4, 5, 7, 8, 9, 14

SEQUIM

Margie's Bed & Breakfast

120 Forrest Road, 98382
(206) 683-7011

A spacious, contemporary ranch home on beautiful Sequim Bay. The fantastic water view is enhanced by year-round lush green surroundings, and the peace and quiet of country life. View of Mt. Baker.

Doubles: 6 (1 PB; 5 SB) $49-79
Type of Beds:1 Twin; 2 Double; 3 Queen
Full Breakfast
Minimum stay holidays: 2
Credit Cards: A, B
Notes: 2, 8 (over 12), 9, 10, 11, 12

SHELTON

Twin River Ranch B&B

E5730 Highway 3, 98584
(206) 426-1023

Grand old farmhouse with stone fireplace, beamed ceilings, rooms tucked under eves. Salmon stream right outside. This 140-acre Angus ranch borders a saltwater bay just five miles north of Shelton. Southern Olympic Peninsula, Olympic National Park, Hood Canal, hiking all nearby.

Hosts: Bjorn & Phlorence Rohde
Doubles: 2 (SB) $37.50-48.50
Type of Beds: 2 Twin; 1 Double
Full Breakfast
Credit Cards: No
Closed Jan.
Notes: 2, 7 (limited), 9 (limited), 10, 11, 12

---

6 Pets welcome: 7 Smoking allowed: 8 Children welcome: 9 Social drinking allowed: 10 Tennis available: 11 Swimming available: 12 Golf available: 13 Skiing available: 14 May be booked through travel agents

Seabreeze Beach Cottage

SILVERDALE

Seabreeze Beach Cottage

16609 Olympic View Road NW, 98383
(206) 692-4648

Challenged by lapping waves at high tide, this private retreat will awaken your five senses with the smell of salty air, a taste of fresh oysters and clams, views of the Olympic Mountains, and the exhilaration of sun, surf, and sand. Free brochure.

Host: Dennis Fulton
Doubles: 2 (PB) $44-64
Type of Beds: 2 Twin; 2 Double
Continental Breakfast
Credit Cards: A, B
Notes: 2, 4, 5, 6, 8, 9, 11, 12

SNOQUALMIE FALLS

The Old Honey Farm Country Inn

8910 384th Avenue, SE, 98065
(206) 888-9399

Stay the night in Washington's newest country inn. Beautiful pastoral setting less than two miles from famous Snoqualmie Falls, Salish Lodge, and Snoqualmie Winery. Walking distance to historic depot and train rides. Many recreational activities, including golf, are nearby.

Hosts: Conrad & Mary Jean Potter & Marilyn Potter Olsen
Doubles: 10 (PB) $55-110
Type of Beds: 9 Queen; 1 King
Full Breakfast
Minimum stay weekends: 2
Credit Cards: A, B
Notes: 2 (in advance), 3, 4, 5, 8 (over 14), 9, 12, 13

SOUTH CLE ELUM

The Moore House Country Bed & Breakfast

526 Marie Street, Box 2861, 98943
(509) 674-5939

The Moore House offers ten bright and airy rooms in a renovated railroad-crew hotel recently placed on the Historic Register. Accommodations range from economical to exquisite, including one that is a real caboose. They each capture the essence of the bygone era of railroading. Old print wallpaper, oak antiques, artifacts combine with the peaceful language of nature to cre-

NOTES: Credit cards accepted: A Master Card; B Visa; C American Express; D Discover Card; E Diners Club; F Other: 2 Personal checks accepted: 3 Lunch available: 4 Dinner available: 5 Open all year

ate an ideal romantic interlude. Adjacent to Iron Horse Trail State Park.

Hosts: Connie & Monty Moore
Doubles: 10 (5 PB; 5 SB) $30-79
Type of Beds: 3 Twin; 8 Double; 3 Queen
Full Breakfast
Minimum stay winter weekends & holidays: 2
Credit Cards: A, B, C
Notes: 2, 5, 7 (restricted), 8, 9, 12, 13, 14

SPOKANE

Blakely Estate B&B

E. 7710 Hodin Drive, 99212
(509) 926-9426

Our bed and breakfast is located in a beautiful parklike setting just fifteen minutes from downtown Spokane. Amenities include an outdoor hot tub, canoe, and the Centennial Trail, which passes just outside our private entrance. The host of this home serves a full breakfast on the upper deck overlooking the Spokane River.

Hosts: John & Kathy Smith
Doubles: 2 (SB) $38-43
Type of Beds: 2 Twin; 1 Double
Full Breakfast
Credit Cards: A, B
Notes: 2, 5, 9, 12, 14

Durocher House Bed & Breakfast

W. 4000 Randolph Road, 99204
(509) 325-4739

Enjoy the hospitality of Durocher House, the 1899 Victorian residence of Fort Wright, on the National Register of Historic Places. Relax in the tranquil atmosphere of this gracious home that overlooks the Spokane River and the mountains beyond. Located just ten minutes from downtown and the airport.

Hosts: Mary E. Dunton & Bernadette Carlson
Singles: 2 (SB) $35
Doubles: 3 (1 PB; 2 SB) $45
Type of Beds: 4 Twin; 2 Double; 1 King
Continental Breakfast
Credit Cards: A, B
Notes: 2, 5, 8 (call)

Luckey's Residence

West 828 28th Avenue, 99203
(509) 747-5774

This house, which resembles an English cottage, was built in the 1930s on the South Hill, among pine trees and volcanic rock. Two miles from downtown; two blocks from a scenic drive overlooking a canyon; two blocks to public swimming pool, tennis court, and children's play area. City bus one block.

Hosts: Royden & Patricia Luckey
Singles: 2 (SB) $25
Doubles: 2 (SB) $35
Type of Beds: 2 Twin; 2 Queen
Full Breakfast
Credit Cards: No
Notes: 2, 5, 8, 10, 11, 12

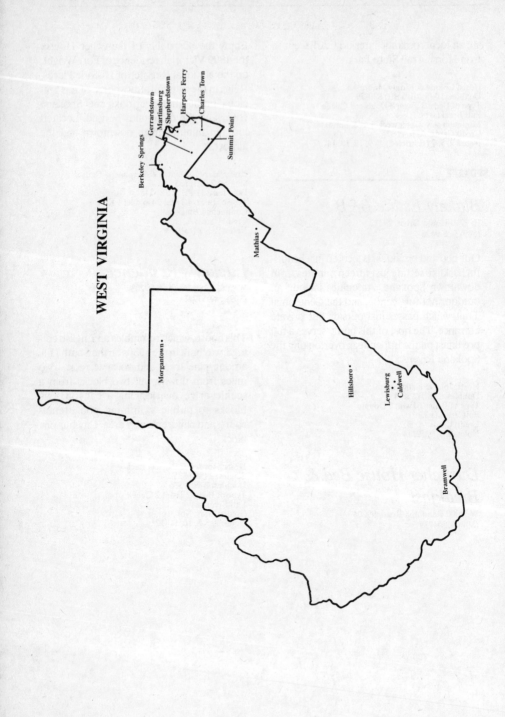

WEST VIRGINIA

Berkeley Springs
Gerrardstown
Martinsburg
Shepherdstown
Harpers Ferry
Charles Town
Summit Point

Mathias

Morgantown •

Hillsboro •
Lewisburg •
Caldwell •

Bramwell •

West Virginia

Highlawn Inn

304 Market Street, 25411
(304) 258-5700

Highlawn Inn, a restored Victorian, is located in a quaint mountain town famous for its historic mineral baths. Only two hours from Washington, DC, we specialize in romantic getaways for adults only. Antiques, decorator linens, private baths, color TVs and air-conditioning in all rooms. All kinds of recreation nearby.

Hosts: Sandra M. Kauffman
Doubles: 6 (PB) $77-$99
Type of Beds: 2 Twin; 4 Double
Full Breakfast
Credit Cards: A, B
Notes: 2, 4 (some holidays & weekends), 5, 7, 9, 10, 11, 12

Highlawn Inn

Folkestone Bed & Breakfast

Rt. 2, Box 404, 25411
(304) 258-3743

Folkestone is an English-style residence built in 1929 on 10 acres of wooded land. Guest accommodations are on the second floor with a sitting room and bath. Two miles from Berkeley Springs State Park, where Roman baths and massages are available.

Host: Hettie Hawvermale
Singles: 1 (PB) $35
Doubles: 2 (SB) $50-60
Type of Beds: 1 Twin; 2 Double
Full Breakfast
Credit Cards: No
Closed Nov. 1 - April 1
Notes: 2, 7, 9, 10, 11, 12

Maria's Garden & Inn

201 Independence Street, 25411
(304) 258-2021

Nestled in the heart of the town of Bath, two blocks from the famed mineral springs and Roman baths, Berkeley Castle, and the antique mall. Our inn is in two brick colonial homes built in the 1920s. A family-run restaurant featured homemade Italian dishes.

Hosts: Peg, Curtis & Alesa Perry
Doubles: 10 (4 PB; 6 SB) $35-55
Type of Beds: 2 Twin; 9 Double
Full Breakfast
Credit Cards: A, B, C, D, E
Notes: 2, 3, 4, 5, 8, 10, 11, 12, 13, 14

Three Oaks & A Quilt

Box 84, 24715
(304) 248-8316

---

6 Pets welcome: 7 Smoking allowed: 8 Children welcome: 9 Social drinking allowed: 10 Tennis available: 11 Swimming available: 12 Golf available: 13 Skiing available: 14 May be booked through travel agents

Visitors to historic Bramwell come to view a most unique town of mansions built by bituminous coal operators in the early 1900s. Three Oaks & A Quilt is a delightfully relaxing Victorian experience. Quilts are artfully displayed; a "Whig Rose" hangs on the front porch wall. Reservations, please.

Host: B. J. Kahle
Doubles: 2 (PB and SB) $55
Type of Beds: 2 Twin; 2 Double
Full Breakfast
Credit Cards: No
Notes: 2, 5, 7 (limited), 8 (12 and over), 9, 10, 11, 12

CALDWELL

The Greenbrier River Inn

Box 133, 24925
(304) 647-5652; 647-5712

Constructed in 1824, The Greenbrier River Inn is on the National Registry of Historic Places. Twenty-five acres of land near the Greenbrier Hotel, with fishing on the premises in the Greenbrier River. Homemade jams and breads, cable TV, near antique shops. Available for family reunions.

Hosts: Joan & Jim Jeter
Doubles: 7 (PB) $55-65
Type of Beds: 7 Twin; 6 Double; 1 King
Continental Breakfast
Credit Cards: A, B
Notes: 2, 5, 6, 7, 8, 9, 10, 11, 12

CHARLES TOWN

The Carriage Inn

417 E. Washington Street, 25414
(304) 728-8003

Each of the five bedrooms is large and airy, with its own private bath and queen canopy bed, and four of the rooms have working fireplaces. Charles Town is the home of the Charles Town races, the Jefferson County Museum, Old Oprah House, and the site of the John Brown Gallows. The inn is located eight miles from Harpers Ferry.

Hosts: Bob & Virginia Kaetzel
Doubles: 5 (PB) $65-85
Type of Beds: 5 Queen
Full Breakfast
Credit Cards: A, B, D
Notes: 2, 5, 9, 10, 11, 12

Cottonwood Inn

Rt. 2, Box 61-S, 25414
(304) 725-3371

The Cottonwood Inn offers B&B accommodations in a restored Georgian farmhouse (circa 1800). The inn is located on Bullskin Run in the historic Shenandoah Valley, near Harpers Ferry and Charles Town, and is furnished in antiques and period reproductions. Fireplaces in the dining room, parlor/library, and one guest room. We invite you to join us and enjoy the inn's peaceful secluded acres, memorable country breakfasts, and warm hospitality.

Hosts: Colin & Eleanor Simpson
Doubles: 6 (PB) 62-92
Type of Beds: 2 Twin; 5 Queen
Full Breakfast
Minimum stay holidays: 2
Credit Cards: A, B
Notes: 2, 4, 5, 7, 8, 9, 10, 11, 12, 13 (XC), 14

Gilbert House B&B

Box 1104, 25414
(304) 725-0637

Comfort, hospitality, and elegance describe this grand historic home, a magnificent greystone (circa 1760) on the National Register. Located in a quaint village near Harpers Ferry, Antietam battlefield, and I-81. Large rooms with private baths and fireplaces; tasteful antiques. Honeymoon suite available. Some say this little village has its own private ghost!

Hosts: Jean & Bernie Heiler
Doubles: 3 (PB) $75-125
Type of Beds: 2 Double; 1 Queen
Full Breakfast
Minimum stay weekends & holidays: 2
Credit Cards: A, B, F
Notes: 2, 5, 7, 9, 10, 11, 12

NOTES: Credit cards accepted: A Master Card; B Visa; C American Express; D Discover Card; E Diners Club; F Other: 2 Personal checks accepted: 3 Lunch available: 4 Dinner available: 5 Open all year

GERRARDSTOWN

Prospect Hill Bed & Breakfast

Box 135, 25420
(304) 229-3346

Prospect Hill is a Georgian mansion set on 225 acres and listed on the National Register of Historic Places. Once a well-to-do gentleman's home, it has a permanent Franklin fireplace, antiques, and a hall mural depicting life in the early Republic. Guests may choose one of the beautifully appointed rooms in the main house or the former slave quarters, where rooms are complete with country kitchen and fireplace. There is much to do on this working farm near Harpers Ferry, Martinsburg, and Winchester.

Hosts: Charles & Hazel Hudock
Cottage: $85-125
Doubles: (PB) $65-85
Full Breakfast
Credit Cards: A, B
Notes: 2, 5, 7, 8 (in cottage), 9, 10, 11, 12, 14

HARPERS FERRY

Fillmore Street Bed & Breakfast

Fillmore Street, 25425
(301) 377-0070; (304) 535-2619

Mountain view, antique-furnished Victorian home known for its hospitality, service, and gourmet breakfast. Private accommodations and baths, in-room television, air conditioning, complimentary sherry and tea, and a blazing fire on cool mornings.

Hosts: Alden & James Addy
Singles: 2 (PB) $57
Doubles: 2 (PB) $68
Full Breakfast
Credit Cards: No
Closed Thanksgiving, Christmas, and New Year's Day
Notes: 2, 7, 8 (over 12), 9

HILLSBORO

The Current

HC 64, Box 135, 24946
(304) 653-4722

A country home surrounded by a Morgan horse farm just a short walk from the Greenbrier River and a 75-mile trail. Near state parks, national forest, Cranberry Wilderness, and the Pearl S. Buck home. Mountain biking, cross-country skiing, golf trips arranged. Large deck with outdoor hot tub; antiques and quilts.

Hosts: Leslee McCarty & John Walkup
Doubles: 3 (SB) $30-40
Type of Beds: 3 Double
Full Breakfast
Credit Cards: A, B
Notes: 2, 5, 8, 9, 10, 11, 12, 13

LEWISBURG

Lynn's Inn Bed & Breakfast

Rt. 4, Box 40, 24901
(304) 645-2003

A comfortable home in a farm setting with fully country breakfast. Downtown historic Lewisburg is three miles away; the state fair, 4.5 miles, Green Brier Hotel, 10 miles. Within easy driving distance to some of the best hiking, fishing, hunting, golfing, spelunking, white water, and skiing places in the east.

Hosts: Richard & Lynn McLaughlin
Singles: 1 (PB) $25
Doubles: 2 (PB) $40-50
Type of Beds: 3 Double; 1 Queen
Full Breakfast
Credit Cards: No
Notes: 2, 5, 8, 9, 10, 11, 12

6 Pets welcome: 7 Smoking allowed: 8 Children welcome: 9 Social drinking allowed: 10 Tennis available: 11 Swimming available: 12 Golf available: 13 Skiing available: 14 May be booked through travel agents

MARTINSBURG

Boydville, The Inn at Martinsburg

601 S. Queen Street, 25401
(304) 263-1448

This historic manor house on 10 acres still contains the original wallpaper and woodwork. Described by *Travel & Leisure* as "a country inn as stupendous as any Relais and Chateaux lodging on the other side of the Atlantic." Only 1.5 hours from downtown Washington, in the heart of Civil War country.

Hosts: Owen Sullivan & Ripley Hotch
Doubles: 7 (4 PB; 3 SB) $75-100
Type of Beds: 3 Double; 4 Queen
Full Breakfast
Credit Cards: A, B, C
Notes: 2, 5, 9, 10, 11, 12, 14

Boydville

MATHIAS

Valley View Farm

Rt. 1, Box 467, 26812
(304) 897-5229

National Geographic's America's Great Hideaways calls Valley View Farm "Your home away from home." This cattle and sheep farm of 250 acres specializes in excellent food and friendly hosts. Near Lost River

State Park; horseback riding and other recreation available in season. Craft shops.

Hosts: Ernest & Edna Shipe
Singles: 2 (SB)
Doubles: 2 (SB)
Adults: $15 each; children $8
With all meals: adults $20, children $12
Type of Beds: 2 Twin; 3 Double
Full Breakfast
Credit Cards: No
Notes: 2, 4, 5, 6, 7, 8, 9, 10, 11

MORGANTOWN

Chestnut Ridge School

1000 Stewartstown Road, 26505
(304) 598-2262

A restored 1920s elementary school welcomes you with warm hospitality. We are surrounded by outstanding scenic attractions and recreational areas. Come "back to school," and enjoy personal attention, our special muffins, and beautiful sunsets.

Hosts: Sam & Nancy Bonasso
Doubles: 4 (PB) $52.32-58.86
Type of Beds: 4 Queen; 1 Portacrib
Continental Breakfast
Minimum stay football weekends: 2
Credit Cards: No
Notes: 2, 5, 8, 9, 10, 11, 12

SHEPHERDSTOWN

Shang-Ra-La B & B

Terrapin Neck, Rt. 1, Box 156, 25443
(304) 876-2391

Enjoy the farm and wildlife preserved on the Potomac River in the beautiful and peaceful Shenandoah Valley. Four duplex efficiency cottages. Walk the nature trails or sightsee in Shepherdstown, the oldest town in the state, or Harpers Ferry. Sixty-five miles from Washington, D.C. or Baltimore.

Hosts: Richard & Sandy Hessenauer
Singles: 2 (PB) $48.90
Doubles: 4 (PB) $59.65
Type of Beds: 3 Twin; 10 Double
Full Breakfast
Minimum stay holidays: 2

NOTES: Credit cards accepted: A Master Card; B Visa; C American Express; D Discover Card; E Diners Club; F Other: 2 Personal checks accepted: 3 Lunch available: 4 Dinner available: 5 Open all year

Thomas Shepherd Inn

Credit Cards: A, B
Closed Jan. & Feb.
Notes: 2, 4, 7, 8, 9, 10, 11, 12

Thomas Shepherd Inn

Box 1162, 25443
(304) 876-3715

Small, charming inn in a quaint, historic Civil War town that offers that special hospitality of the past. Guests find Belgian chocolates at their bedsides, fluffy towels and special soaps in their baths, complimentary beverage by the fireside, memorable breakfasts. Bicycles, picnics available.

Hosts: Ed & Carol Ringoot
Doubles: 6 (4 PB; 2 SB) $67-94
Type of Beds: 2 Twin; 2 Double; 3 Queen
Full Breakfast
Credit Cards: A, B
Notes: 2, 5, 7 (limited), 8 (over 12), 9, 10, 11, 12, 13

SUMMIT POINT

Countryside

Box 57, 25446
(304) 725-2614

Countryside is located in a charming village near historic Harpers Ferry and is decorated with items old and new: quilts, baskets, books, and collectibles. Guests are welcomed with a cheerful room, bath, and breakfast amid lovely rural scenery.

Hosts: Lisa & Daniel Hileman
Doubles: 2 (PB) $42.40-53
Type of Beds: 2 Double
Continental Breakfast
Minimum stay holidays: 2
Children over 8 welcome weekdays only
Credit Cards: A, B
Notes: 2, 5, 8, 9, 10, 11, 12

6 Pets welcome: 7 Smoking allowed: 8 Children welcome: 9 Social drinking allowed: 10 Tennis available: 11 Swimming available: 12 Golf available: 13 Skiing available: 14 May be booked through travel agents

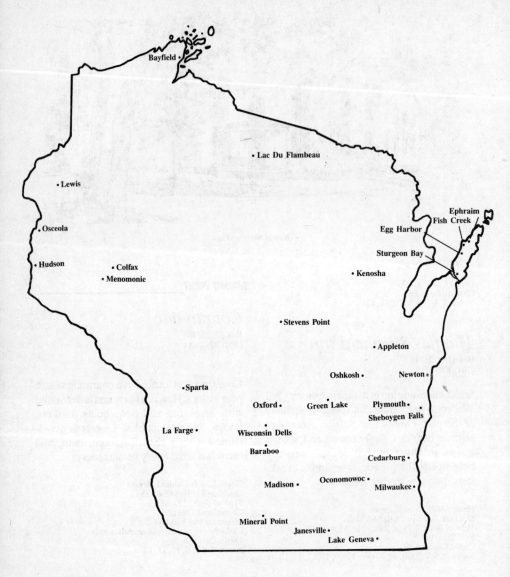

WISCONSIN

Wisconsin

APPLETON

The Parkside Bed & Breakfast
402 East North Street, 54911
(414) 733-0200

Relax in Old World elegance and look out onto Appleton's historic city park. Guests can take a short walk to Lawrence University and downtown shops and restaurants. The expansive, private accommodations afford many amenities to the business traveler.

Host: Bonnie Riley
Suite: 1 (PB) $51.50-61.80
Type of Beds: 1 King; 2 Twin
Full Breakfast
Minimum stay during EAA Fly-in: 7
Credit Cards: No
Notes: 2, 5, 7, 8 (over 8), 9, 10, 11, 12, 13

The Parkside B&B

BARABOO

The Barrister's House
226 9th Avenue, Box 166, 53913
(608) 356-3344

Colonial charm and simple elegance in a parklike setting. Unique guest rooms; library with fireplace; sitting room with game table, piano and fireplace; screened porch, veranda, and terrace. Gracious continental breakfast. Located in the heart of the Baraboo/Wisconsin Dells/Devils Lake vacationland.

Hosts: Glen & Mary Schulz
Doubles: 4 (PB) $42-57.75
Type of Beds: 3 Double; 1 Queen
Continental Breakfast
Credit Cards: No
Closed Midweek Nov. - April
Notes: 2, 8 (over 6), 9, 10, 11, 12, 13

BAYFIELD

Old Rittenhouse Inn
Box 584, 54814
(715) 779-5111

Our inn is a beautiful Victorian mansion built in 1890 overlooking Lake Superior. Guest rooms are furnished with antiques and working fireplaces. Dinner, offered nightly by reservation, features fine formal service.

Hosts: Jerry & Mary Phillips
Doubles: 20 (PB) $69-119
Continental Breakfast (full available at extra charge)
Minimum stay May-Oct. weekends: 2
Credit Cards: A, B
Notes: 2, 5, 8, 9, 10, 11, 12, 13

6 Pets welcome: 7 Smoking allowed: 8 Children welcome: 9 Social drinking allowed: 10 Tennis available: 11 Swimming available: 12 Golf available: 13 Skiing available: 14 May be booked through travel agents

CEDARBURG

The Washington House Inn

W62 N573 Washington Avenue, 53012
(414) 375-3550

Built in 1884 and listed on the National Registry, The Washington House Inn is located in the heart of the Cedarburg historic district. Rooms feature antique furnishings, whirlpool baths, fireplaces. Walking distance to Cedar Creek Settlement antique shops and fine dining.

Host: Judith I. Drefahl
Singles: 20 (PB) $61.95-135.45
Doubles: 9 (PB) $82.95-135.45
Type of Beds: 25 Queen; 4 King
Continental Breakfast
Credit Cards: A, B, C, D, E, F
Notes: 2, 4, 5, 7, 8, 9, 10, 11, 12, 13

The Washington House Inn

COLFAX

Son-Ne-Vale Farm

Rt. 1, Box 132, 54730
(715) 962-4342

Enjoy staying in the large farmhouse or one of the two duplex cottages available. Nearby bowling, golf, fishing, restaurants, historical sites, and museums. Tainter Lake is only fourteen miles away for boating and fishing.

Host: Lillian Sonnenberg
Singles: 2 (SB) $35
Doubles: 2 (PB) $45
Type of Beds: 2 Twin; 5 Queen
Full Breakfast
Credit Cards: No
Closed Oct. 15-April 15
Notes: 2, 4, 6, 7, 8, 9, 11, 12

EGG HARBOR

Country Gardens Bed & Breakfast

6421 Highway 42, 54209
(414) 743-7434

Enjoy the fields and forests of this 160-acre Door Country fruit and grain farm. This 1900s home radiates warmth and comfort. Four bedrooms share two baths. Balcony; full breakfast in striking country kitchen varies daily. Preferred Host Award in 1987 and 1988. Located close to the many and varied activities that Door County is famous for. Brochure available; reservations preferred.

Hosts: Jim & Crystal Barnard
Doubles: 4 (S2B) $55-85
Type of Beds: 2 Double; 3 Queen
Full Breakfast
Minimum stay holidays: 2
Credit Cards: A, B
Notes: 2, 5, 8, 10, 11, 12, 13

EPHRAIM

Eagle Harbor Inn

9914 Water Street, Box 72, 54211
(414) 854-2121

Nestled in the heart of historic Ephraim, Eagle Harbor is a gracious, antique-filled country inn. Centrally located, across from the lake, and close to the boat ramp, golf course, park, beach and cross-country ski trails.

Hosts: Ronald & Barbara Schultz
Doubles: 9 (PB) $59-89

Type of Beds: 2 Doubles; 7 Queen
Continental-plus Breakfast
Minimum stay: 2; holidays: 3
Credit Cards: A, B
Notes: 2, 4, 5, 7, 9, 14

FISH CREEK

Thorp House Inn
Box 90, 54212
(414) 868-2444

A turn-of-the-century historic home with a
bay view. Four romantic guest rooms, parlor
with stone fireplace, and cozy library, all furnished in fine antiques and lots of authentic
detail. Also available, fireplace cottages
done in country antiques.

Hosts: Christine & Sverre Falck-Pedersen
Doubles: 4 (SB) $51.70-65.41
Type of Beds: 3 Double; 1 Queen
Continental Breakfast
Minimum stay weekends:2 ; holidays: 3
Credit Cards: No
Closed winter, except for weekends
Notes: 2, 9, 10, 11, 12, 13

Thorp House Inn

Strawberry Hill B&B

GREEN LAKE

Strawberry Hill Bed & Breakfast
Rt. 1, Box 524-D, 54941
(414) 294-3450

Relax in the country quiet of this large, comfortably furnished old farmhouse. Fully air-
conditioned. Four guest rooms share two
full baths. Three excellent golf courses
within eight miles. Hot tub for guests' enjoyment. Hearty country breakfasts begin with
strawberry daiquiris. Twenty-eight miles to
EAA.

Host: Patricia Spencer
Doubles: 4 (4 S2B) $29-40
Type of Beds: 2 Twin; 2 Double; 1 King
Full Breakfast
Credit Cards: A, B
Closed two weeks in March and November
Notes: 2, 8 (over 12), 9, 10, 11, 12, 13, 14

HUDSON

Jefferson-Day House
1109 3rd Street, 54016
(715) 386-7111

This 1857 home offers antique collections,
air-conditioned rooms, and three-course
fireside breakfasts. The pleasing decor and

friendly atmosphere will relax you, while the nearby St. Croix River, Octagon House Museum, and Phipps Theatre for the Arts will bring you enjoyment.

Hosts: Sharon, Wally, and Marjorie Miller
Doubles: 4 (2PB; 2SB) $55-95
Type of Beds: 2 Double; 2 Queen
Full Breakfast weekends, Continental weekdays
Credit Cards: No
Notes: 2, 5, 8 (over 9), 9, 11, 12, 13, 14

JANESVILLE

Jackson Street Inn B&B

210 S. Jackson Street, 53545
(608) 754-7250, (800) 222-3209

Comfortable Victorian air-conditioned home. Leaded-glass windows and cushioned window seats in the spacious, cheerful sleeping rooms. Sitting room with books, games, magazines, and menus from nearby restaurants. Marble fireplaces, intricate oak paneling, coffered ceilings in the dining and TV rooms. Putting green, shuffleboard court, attractive landscaped lawn and gardens; near I-90 on Hwy 11; off-street parking.

Hosts: Ilah & Bob Sessler
Singles: $30-45
Doubles: 4 (2PB; 2SB) $40-55
Type of Beds: 2 Twin; 1 Double; 3 Queen
Full Breakfast
Credit Cards: A, B
Notes: 2, 5, 7, 8, 9, 10, 11, 12, 13 (XC), 14

KENOSHA

The Manor House

6536 3rd Avenue, 53140
(414) 658-0014

Stately brick Georgian mansion overlooking Lake Michigan in the heart of Kenosha's lakeshore historical district. Listed on the National Register of Historic Places, furnished with carefully selected antiques, surrounded by beautifully landscaped grounds. Midway between Chicago and Milwaukee.

Meeting rooms available. Weekday discounts and corporate rates.

Hosts: Ron & Mary Rzeplinski
Doubles: 4 (PB) $83.25-122.10
Type of Beds: 2 Twin; 2 Queen; 1 King
Continental Breakfast
Credit Cards: A, B, C
Notes: 2, 5, 7 (restricted), 8 (12 and over), 9, 10, 11, 12, 13, 14

LAC DU FLAMBEAU

Ty-Bach B&B

3104 Simpson Lane, 54538
(715) 588-7851

For a relaxing getaway anytime of the year, share our modern home on the shore of a tranquil northwoods lake. Guest quarters include a large living area and a deck overlooking our "Golden Pond." Eighty acres of woods to explore, Native American cultural attractions; listen to the loons!

Hosts: Janet & Kermit Bekkum
Doubles: 2 (PB) $45-50
Full Breakfast
Credit Cards: No
Notes: 2, 5, 6, 11, 12, 13 (XC)

LA FARGE

Trillium

Rt. 2, Box 121, 54639
(608) 625-4492

Your own private cottage located on our farm amid 85 acres of fields and woods, near a tree-lined brook. Situated in a thriving Amish farming community just thirty-five miles southeast of La Crosse.

Host: Rosanne Boyett
Cottage: 1 (PB) $52.50-63
Type of Beds: 2 Twin; 2 Double
Full Breakfast
Children under 12 stay without charge
Credit Cards: No
Notes: 2, 5, 7, 8, 9, 10, 11, 12, 13

NOTES: Credit cards accepted: A Master Card; B Visa; C American Express; D Discover Card; E Diners Club; F Other: 2 Personal checks accepted: 3 Lunch available: 4 Dinner available: 5 Open all year

LAKE GENEVA

Elizabethian Inn

463 Wrigley Drive, 53147
(414) 248-9131

The inn, on the lakefront of Lake Geneva, has its own pier for swimming, sunbathing, boating, and fishing. Enjoy the comfortable, warm atmosphere of an old New England inn with high poster beds, beautiful old quilts, and antique furniture.

Host: Elizabeth Farrell
Doubles: 10 (PB) $82.50-99
Type of Beds: 2 Twin; 10 Double
Full Breakfast
Minimum stay weekends & holidays: 2
Credit Cards: A, B
Notes: 2, 5, 8 (over 12), 9, 10, 11, 12, 13

The Greene House Bed & Breakfast

Rt. 2, Box 214, Whitewater, 53190
(414) 495-8771

Put your feet up and relax in an authentic 1850s farmhouse or enjoy one of the many available activities. Superb cross-country skiing, hiking, horseback riding, bicycling, antiquing, outdoor music theater. Fifteen minutes north of Lake Geneva; a short drive from Chicago, Milwaukee, or Madison.

Hosts: Lynn & Mayner Greene
Doubles: 6 (SB) $49-75
Type of Beds: 2 Twin; 4 Double; 2 Queen
Full Breakfast
Credit Cards: A, B, C
Notes: 2, 4, 5, 7, 8, 9, 10, 11, 12, 13 (XC), 14

LEWIS

7 Pines Lodge

Box 4, 54851
(715) 653-2323

Rejuvenate amid nature on this 57 acre country estate. Listed on the National Register of Historic Places, 7 Pines offers unusual warmth and hospitality set in a time and era gone by.

Host: Joan Simpson
Doubles: 8 (5 PB; 3 SB) $58-74
Continental or Full Breakfast
Minimum stay weekends: 2
Credit Cards: No
Notes: 2, 4, 5, 8, 10, 11, 12

MADISON

The Collins House

704 E. Gorham Street, 53703
(608) 255-4230

On the shores of Lake Mendota in downtown Madison, this restored home of the Prairie School of Architecture is listed on the National Register of Historic Places.

Hosts: Barb & Mike Pratzel
Doubles: 4 (PB) $66.08-95.20
Type of Beds: 2 Double; 3 Queen
Full Breakfast weekends; Continental weekdays
Minimum stay holidays: 2
Credit Cards: A, B
Notes: 2, 5, 6 (restricted), 7 (restricted), 8, 9 (restricted), 10, 11, 12, 13

Mansion Hill Inn

424 N. Pinchney Street, 53703
(608) 255-3999

Eleven luxurious rooms, each with private bath. Whirlpool tubs, fireplaces, stereo systems, remote cable television, and mini-bars. Private wine cellar. VCRs and access to athletic club available on request. Refreshments served daily in the parlour.

Host: Polly Elder
Doubles: 11 (PB) $89.60-280
Type of Beds: 11 Queen
Continental Breakfast
Credit Cards: A, B, C
Notes: 2, 4 (with notice), 5, 7, 9, 10, 11, 12

MENOMONIE

Cedar Trail Guesthouse

Rt. 4, Box 175, 54751
(715) 664-8828

6 Pets welcome: 7 Smoking allowed: 8 Children welcome: 9 Social drinking allowed: 10 Tennis available: 11 Swimming available: 12 Golf available: 13 Skiing available: 14 May be booked through travel agents

Comfortable modern home on the fringe of a small rural community. Relax on the deck with cookies from the cookie jar and watch the livestock. Snuggle under a handmade wool comforter. Scout out cheese, maple syrup, and other products from local farmers. Ski or bike the Red Cedar Trail.

Hosts: Barb Anderson & Judy Schalow
Doubles: 4 (1 PB; 3 SB) $40-55
Type of Beds: 4 Queen
Full Breakfast
Credit Cards: A, B
Notes: 2, 5, 8, 9, 10, 11, 12, 13, 14

MILWAUKEE

B&B of Milwaukee #1

Box 20715, 53220
(414) 327-1338

Ideal location within walking distance to all major attractions. Turn-of-the-century Victorian renovated in 1982 with a beautiful contemporary interior. Guests may use the entire first floor with sitting room, fireplace, kitchen, dining room. Resident cat.

Doubles: 2 (PB) $60-70
Continental Breakfast
Credit Cards: A, B, C
Notes: 2, 5, 9

B&B of Milwaukee #2

Box 20715, 53220
(414) 327-1338

This unique penthouse has it all: spectacular views of the city skyline and Lake Michigan, walking distance to downtown, solarium with large whirlpool spa, roof garden and deck. Secured building with private elevator and heated indoor parking.

Doubles: 1 (PB) $125
Type of Beds: 1 Queen
Full Breakfast
Credit Cards: A, B, C
Notes: 2, 5, 9

B&B of Milwaukee #3

Box 20715, 53220
(414) 327-1338

Lovely Tudor home in the city featuring leaded-glass windows and natural woodwork. British hosts offer their special touches.

Doubles: 1 (PB) $40-45
Type of Beds: 2 Twin
Continental Breakfast
Credit Cards: A, B, C
Notes: 2, 5, 9

B&B of Milwaukee #4

Box 20715, 53220
(414) 327-1338

This home, on the Historic Register offers one suite and another room on the second floor. Breakfast is served on heirloom china in the dining room.

Doubles: 2 (PB) $65-75
Type of Beds: 2 Queen
Continental Breakfast
Credit Cards: A, B, C
Notes: 2, 5, 7, 9

B&B Milwaukee #5

Box 20715, 53220
(414) 327-1338

This two-story colonial has easy access to the freeway or bus. Lovely furnishings feature antiques and traditional furniture. Screened porch for breakfast. Hosts enjoy long-distance biking and cross-country skiing.

Doubles: 1 (SB) $40-45
Type of Beds: 1 Double
Continental Breakfast
Credit Cards: A, B, C
Notes: 2, 5, 9

B&B of Milwaukee #6

Box 20715, 53220
(414) 327-1338

NOTES: Credit cards accepted: A Master Card; B Visa; C American Express; D Discover Card; E Diners Club; F Other: 2 Personal checks accepted: 3 Lunch available: 4 Dinner available: 5 Open all year

An 1878 remodeled farmhouse twenty minutes from downtown Milwaukee on a heavily wooded lot with pond. Sun porch with wicker furniture. Your hostess enjoys art, and the home is filled with it.

Doubles: 2 (SB) $40-45
Type of Beds: 4 Twin
Continental Breakfast
Credit Cards: A, B, C
Notes: 2, 5, 9

B&B of Milwaukee #7

Box 20715, 53220
(414) 327-1338

This house is located in Waukesha, seventeen miles from downtown Milwaukee and 1.5 blocks from Waukesha Memorial Hospital. cat in residence.

Doubles: 2 (SB) $35-40
Type of Beds: 2 Double
Continental Breakfast
Credit Cards: A, B, C
Notes: 2, 5, 7, 9

B&B of Milwaukee #8

Box 20715, 53220
(414) 327-1338

A newer colonial in the affluent western suburb of Bookfield. Central air-conditioning, sun room, screened porch. Near shops, zoo, stadium, state fairgrounds, and Mount Mary College.

Doubles: 1 (PB) $45-50
Type of Beds: 1 Queen
Continental Breakfast
Credit Cards: A, B, C
Notes: 2, 5, 9

B&B of Milwaukee #9

Box 20715, 53220
(414) 327-1338

This home, in the suburb of Waukesha, features an in-ground pool with slide and separate whirlpool spa, plus a sauna. Breakfast is served in the screened sun room.

Doubles: 1 (SB) $45-50
Type of Beds: 1 Double
Continental Breakfast
Credit Cards: A, B, C
Notes: 2, 5, 9

B&B of Milwaukee #10

Box 20715, 53220
(414) 327-1338

This suburban home is close to the botanical gardens, a shopping center, cross-country skiing, and golf courses. Two-acre natural wooded lot. Guests may enjoy the quiet room with books, fireplace, and chess set. Two cats and a dog in residence.

Doubles: 2 (PB) $40-55
Type of Beds: 1 Double; 1 King
Continental Breakfast
Credit Cards: A, B, C
Notes: 2, 5, 9

B&B of Milwaukee #11

Box 20715, 53220
(414) 327-1338

A modest duplex in historic Bay View ten minutes from downtown on the city bus line. Your hostess is an RN with interest in music and art.

Doubles: 1 (SB) $30-35
Type of Beds: 1 Double
Continental Breakfast
Credit Cards: A, B, C
Notes: 2, 5, 9

B&B of Milwaukee #12

Box 20715, 53220
(414) 327-1338

Located on 3.5 acres of rolling countryside, this 23-year-old two-story home offers an in-ground pool and bicycles. Near many lakes, golf, cross-country skiing trails, and fine restaurants.

Doubles: 1 (PB) $35-40
Type of Beds: 1 Double
Continental Breakfast
Credit Cards: A, B, C
Notes: 2, 5, 9

B&B of Milwaukee #13

Box 20715, 53220
(414) 327-1338

Close to many lakes, ski trails, and golf courses, this spacious contemporary with manicured grounds has a spa, exercise room, and fire pit. World-traveling hosts and an engineer and a teacher.

Doubles: 1 (PB) $40-45
Type of Beds: 1 Double
Continental Breakfast
Credit Cards: A, B, C
Notes: 2, 5, 9

B&B of Milwaukee #14

Box 20715, 53220
(414) 327-1338

An 1848 country farmhouse filled with beautiful antiques and collectibles. Bike, hike, or ski in this natural wonderland. Prearrange a wine tasting, sing-a-long, or dinner with your music-teacher host and professional-chef hostess. Restricted smoking.

Doubles: 4 (S2B) $40-59
Full Breakfast
Credit Cards: A, B, C
Notes: 2, 5, 9

Ogden House

2237 N. Lake Drive, 53202
(414) 272-2740

Located just two blocks from Lake Michigan and one mile north of downtown, Ogden House is in the historic district of Milwaukee's early mansions. We offer the charm of fireplaces, high canopy beds, and old-fashioned hospitality. Our home is your home.

Hosts: Mary Jane & John Moss
Doubles: 2(PB) $68.25-78.75
Type of Beds: 2 Queen
Continental-plus Breakfast
Credit Cards: No
Notes: 2, 5, 7, 8 (call), 9, 10, 11, 12, 13 (XC),14

MINERAL POINT

Duke House

618 Maiden Street
(608) 987-2821

An 1870 Federal house furnished with hardwood floors, Oriental rugs, four-poster or canopy beds, windback chairs, tie-back curtains. A perfect blend of antiques and reproduction furniture. Evening social hour and a full breakfast that always includes homemade coffee cake, muffins, tea biscuits, and scones.

Hosts: Tom & Darlene Duke
Doubles: 3 (SB) $47
Full Breakfast
Credit Cards: A, B
Notes: 2, 5, 9, 10, 11, 12, 13

The Duke House

NOTES: Credit cards accepted: A Master Card; B Visa; C American Express; D Discover Card; E Diners Club; F Other: 2 Personal checks accepted: 3 Lunch available: 4 Dinner available: 5 Open all year

NEWTON

Rambling Hills Tree Farm
8825 Willever Lane, 53063
(414) 726-4388

Enjoy the serenity of country living in a comfortable newer home with a panoramic view of 50 acres of rolling hills, small lake, marsh, meadows, and forest with a network of trails and boardwalks to hike or ski. Three miles from Lake Michigan.

Hosts: Pete & Judie Stuntz
Doubles: 3 (SB) $31.50-42
Type of Beds: 1 Twin; 2 Double; 1 King; 1 Rollaway
Full Breakfast
Credit Cards: No
Notes: 2, 5, 6, 7, 8, 9, 11, 13

OCONOMOWOC

The Inn at Pine Terrace
351 E. Lisbon Road, 53066
(414) 567-7463

This thirteen-room inn is furnished to reflect the opulent graciousness of a highly decorative arts period. Modern amenities such as double whirlpool baths, cable TV, telephones, and a new swimming pool have been blended into the period setting. Pine Terrace overlooks Fowler Lake and is a short walk or bike ride to the downtown area's shops and restaurants. There are historic walking tours around the lake, boating, sailing, fishing, biking, skiing, and community events to enjoy.

Host: Linda Moore
Doubles: 13 (PB) $59-129
Type of Beds: 3 Twin; 10 Queen
Continental Breakfast
Credit Cards: A, B, C
Notes: 2, 5, 6, 7, 8, 9, 11, 12, 13, 14

OSCEOLA

St. Croix River Inn
1305 River Street, 54020
(715) 294-4248

A meticulously restored eighty-year-old stone home nestled in one of the region's finest recreational areas. Ski at Wild Mountain or Trollhaugen. Canoe or fish in the lovely St. Croix River. Or visit the scenic Taylors Falls area. Then relax in the B&B suites of the St. Croix River Inn, some with fireplaces, all with Jacuzzi whirlpool baths.

Host: Vickie Farnham
Doubles: 7 (PB) $75-150
Type of Beds: 7 Queen
Full Breakfast
Credit Cards: A, B, C
Notes: 2, 5, 7 (limited), 9, 10, 11, 12, 13, 14

OSHKOSH

The Tiffany Inn
206 Algoma Blvd., 54901
(414) 231-0909

The inn is named after the famous American art glass creator Louis Comfort Tiffany, whose work is represented in the Episcopal church across the street. The inn has eleven rooms with cable TV and is within walking distance of the University of Wisconsin, the Aircraft Association Museum, paddlewheel lake cruises, Oshkosh clothing outlets, the Paine Art Center and Arboretum, plus many fine restaurants.

Hosts: Mary & Tom Rossow
Doubles: 11 (PB) $45-75
Type of Beds: 2 Twin; 10 Queen
Continental Breakfast
Credit Cards: A, B, C
Notes: 2, 5, 6, 7, 8, 9, 10, 11, 12, 13, 14

OXFORD

Halfway House Bed & Breakfast
Rt. 2, Box 80, 53952
(608) 586-5489

Our house was a stopping place for travelers on an old logging road and has been called Halfway House since the 1800s. In a quiet, rural setting with a large lawn, flower beds, birds, and game. The hosts, a veterinarian and his wife, have traveled to Africa and Europe. Skiing within 25 miles.

Hosts: Dr. J. A. & Geneviere Hines
Singles: 1 (SB) $29.40
Doubles: 3 (SB) $44.10
Type of Beds: 1 Twin; 2 Double; 1 Queen
Full Breakfast
Credit Cards: No
Notes: 2, 5, 9, 12

PLYMOUTH

52 Stafford, An Irish Guest House
52 Stafford Street, 53073
(414) 893-0552

Listed on the National Register of Historic Places, this inn has twenty rooms, seventeen of which have whirlpool baths and cable TV. 52 Stafford features one of the most beautiful pubs in America, which serves lunch and dinner. There are 35,000 acres of public recreation land nearby, cross-country skiing, hiking, biking, sports fishing, boating, swimming, golfing. Crystal-clear lakes and beautiful fall colors.

Hosts: Rip & Christine O'Dwanny
Doubles: 20 (PB) $65-85
Continental Breakfast
Credit Cards: A, B, C, D, E
Notes: 2, 3, 4, 5, 6, 7, 8, 9, 10, 11, 12, 13, 14

SHEBOYGEN FALLS

The Rochester Inn
504 Water Street, 53085
(414) 467-3123

The Rochester Inn is listed on the National Register of Historic Places. the region features a championship golf course, excellent restaurants and shops, hiking, cross-country

skiing in the Northern Kettle Morraine State Park, and Great Lakes sport fishing centers.

Host: Jacquelyn Zorn
Doubles: 5 (PB) $69-99
Type of Beds: 5 Queen
Continental Breakfast
Credit Cards: A, B, C, D
Notes: 2, 5, 6, 7, 8, 9, 10, 11, 12, 13, 14

SPARTA

Just-N-Trails Bed & Breakfast
Route 1, Box 263, 54656
(608) 269-4522

Unwind in a 1920 farmhouse on a working dairy farm. Four bedrooms — two private and two shared baths. Laura Ashley linens; full breakfast. Near the safe, scenic Elroy-Sparta Bike Trail and Amish community. New "Little House on the Prairie" log cabin with bath.

Hosts: Don & Donna Justin
Doubles: 2 (2PB; 2SB) $40-60
Type of Beds: 4 Double
Full Breakfast
Credit Cards: A, B
Notes: 2, 5, 8, 10, 11, 12, 13, 14

STEVENS POINT

Victorian Swan on Water
1716 Water Street, 54481
(715) 345-0595

Explore this romantic, historic house at the gateway to Wisconsin vacationland. Cozy nooks, fireplace, bountiful breakfasts in the plant-filled sun room. There is also a TV room, and meeting rooms are available. River walkways, forest preserves, scenic cross-country ski trails, golf, tennis close. Air-conditioned.

Host: Joan Ouellette
Doubles: 4 (PB) $45-60 plus tax
Type of Beds: 2 Twin; 2 Double; 1 Queen; 1 King
Full Breakfast

NOTES: Credit cards accepted: A Master Card; B Visa; C American Express; D Discover Card; E Diners Club; F Other: 2 Personal checks accepted: 3 Lunch available: 4 Dinner available: 5 Open all year

Credit Cards: A, B, C
Notes: 2, 5, 9, 10, 12, 13, 14

STURGEON BAY

The Gray Goose Bed & Breakfast

4258 Bay Shore Drive, 54235
(414) 743-9100

Enjoy warm hospitality in our Civil War home in Door County. Authentic antique furnishings. Large, comfortable rooms. Guest sitting room with a water/sunset view to remember. Beautiful dining room. Quiet, wooded site north of town.

Hosts: Jack & Jessie Burkhardt
Doubles: 4 (S2B) $47.48-68.58
Type of Beds: 2 Twin; 1 Double; 2 Queen
Full Breakfast
Minimum stay holidays: 2
Credit Cards: A, B, C
Notes: 2, 5, 7, 8 (over 16), 9, 10, 11, 12, 13

White Lace Inn

16 N. 5th Avenue, 54235
(414) 743-1105

The White Lace Inn is a romantic getaway featuring three restored turn-of-the-century houses brought together by a winding garden pathway. The fifteen elegant guest rooms are furnished in fine antiques. Three rooms have double whirlpool tubs, six have fireplaces, and four have both fireplace and whirlpool.

Hosts: Dennis & Bonnie Statz
Doubles: 15 (PB) $60-130
Type of Beds: 5 Double; 10 Queen
Continental Breakfast
Credit Cards: A, B
Notes: 2, 5, 9, 10, 11, 12, 13

WISCONSIN DELLS

Bennett House

825 Oak Street, 53965
(608) 254-2500

Elegantly restored home of pioneer photographer H. H. Bennett, on the National Register of Historic Places. Victorian charm of lace, crystal, wood. One block from the river, shops, attractions. Full breakfast served in the country kitchen; sunsets on the screened porch; conversation in the parlor.

Hosts: Gail & Rich Obermeyer
Doubles: 3 (1 PB; 2 SB) $53.50-80.25
Type of Beds: 1 Double; 2 Queen
Full Breakfast
Credit Cards: No
Notes: 2, 5, 7, 8 (over 13), 9, 10, 11, 12, 13, 14

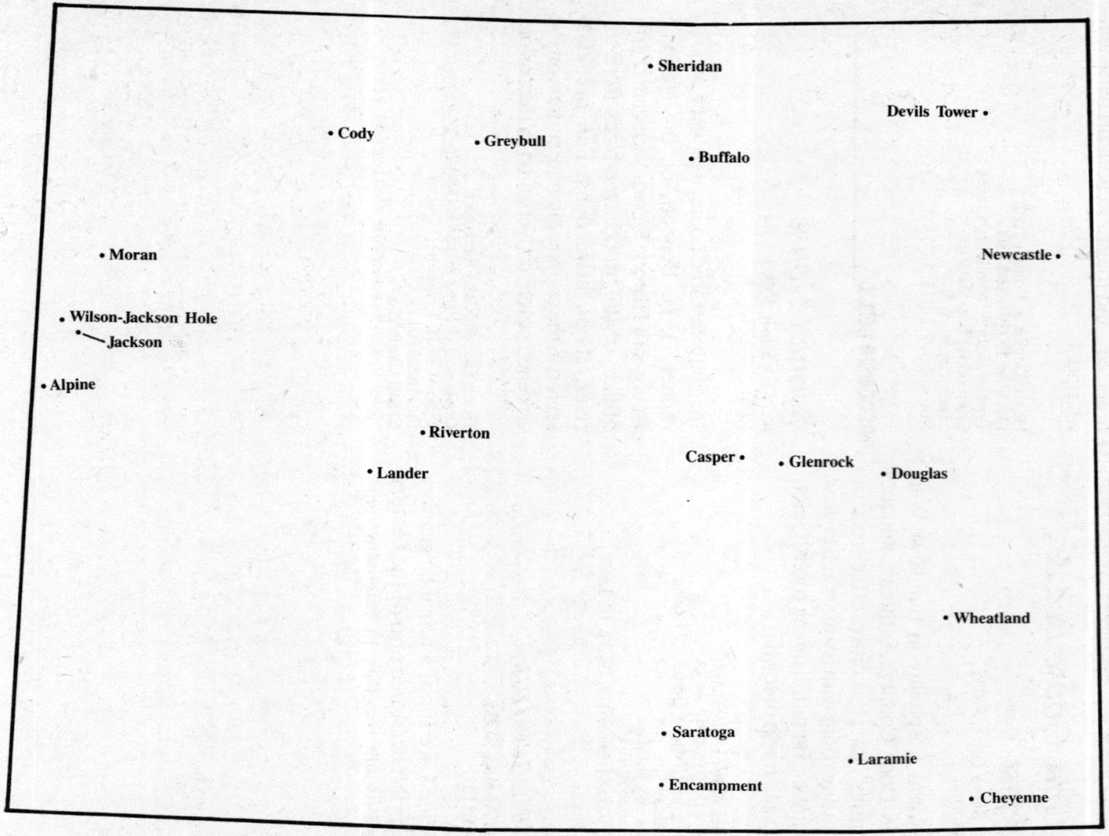
Sheridan
Devils Tower
Cody
Greybull
Buffalo
Moran
Newcastle
Wilson-Jackson Hole
Jackson
Alpine
Riverton
Lander
Casper
Glenrock
Douglas
Wheatland
Saratoga
Laramie
Encampment
Cheyenne

WYOMING

Wyoming

ALPINE

B&B Western Adventure #220

Box 20972, Billings, MT, 59104
(406) 259-7993

This beautiful alpine log home looks out onto the rugged beauty of the Freys River area. A haven for fisherman (host-guided tours), 38 miles southwest of Jackson Hole. Within three miles, guests can fish the Snake, the Greys, or the Salt River and Palisades Lake. Float fishing and white-water rafting are close, as is skiing in Jackson. One room with private shower, two share a bath. Children over 12 welcome; no smoking. $50-60.

BUFFALO

Paradise Guest Ranch

Box 790, 82834
(307) 684-7876

This guest ranch, tucked into a secluded valley in the Big Horn area, offers family enjoyment for all. Each person has his "own" horse to use during daily trips and lessons. Wilderness fishing camp; rodeo; heated pool, enclosed spa; evening bonfires; childrens' program; evening activities. Weekly rates include three meals a day and activities. Reduced rates for children six to twelve.

Hosts: Jim & Leah Anderson
1 bedroom cabins: 4(PB) $700-800 per week AP
2 bedroom cabins: 11(PB) $700-800 per week AP
3 bedroom cabins: 3(PB) $700-800 per week AP

Type of Beds: 32 Twin; 19 Queen
Full Breakfast
Credit Cards: No
Closed Oct. 1 - Mid May
Notes: 2, 3, 4, 7, 8, 9, 11

South Fork Inn

Box 854, 82834
(307) 684-9609 (radio phone)

Located in the Big Horn National Forest, South Fork Inn is a rustic mountain lodge. We have ten guest cabins and a main lodge with our dining room and game room. Activities include horseback riding, fishing, hiking, biking, skiing, and many others.

Hosts: Ken & Patty Reid
Cabins: 10 (3 PB; 7 SB) $25-45
Type of Beds: 8 Twin; 18 Double
Full Breakfast
Credit Cards: No
From Nov. 1 - Jan. 15 only open weekends
Notes: 2, 3, 4, 6, 7, 8, 9, 13 (XC)

South Fork Inn

CASPER

B&B Western Adventure #245

Box 20972, Billings, MT, 59104
(406) 259-7993

A two-level ranch-style home overlooking the North Platte River. Abundant wildlife: deer in residence all year, ducks and geese, eagles, pelicans, herons. Two bedrooms with private baths. Float trips, fishing, skiing, snowmobiling. Host will serve as your river guide. Full breakfast 7:00 to 8:00; continental for late risers. No smoking. $35-45.

CHEYENNE

B&B Western Adventure #242

Box 20972, Billings, MT, 59104
(406) 259-7993

A modern rustic home on 10 country acres. Near antelope, deer, and elk hunting, fishing. Three bedrooms, one with private bath. Museums, the state capitol, Frontier Days, and rodeos at nearby Frontier Park. Full breakfast at 6:30; continental for late risers. $30-40.

CODY

Hunter Peak Ranch

Box 1731, Painter Road, 82414
(307) 587-3711

Hunter Peak Ranch, at 6,700-feet elevation, is located in the Shoshone National Forest, with access to North Absaroka and Beartooth Wilderness Areas and Yellowstone. Come enjoy the area's photographic opportunities, hiking, horseback riding.

Hosts: Louis & Shelley Cary
Doubles: 8 (PB) $50
Type of Beds: 17 Twin; 11 Double

Full Breakfast
Minimum stay: 3
Credit Cards: No
Closed Dec. 15 - May 15
Notes: 2 (deposit), 3, 4, 6, 7, 8, 9, 11, 14

Trout Creek Inn

North Fork Rt., 82414
(307) 587-6288

Imagine basking in the morning sunshine, a sumptuous breakfast on a lawn table, scenic mountains all around (unless you prefer privacy in your deluxe room). Located in the valley Theodore Roosevelt called "world's most scenic." Private trout fishing, swimming, horseback riding, picture taking. Four kitchenettes available: accessible to the handicapped.

Hosts: Bert & Norma Sowerwine
Singles: 4 (PB) $31.50-42
Doubles: 17 (PB) $37.80-52.5
Type of Beds: 38 Queen
All you can eat Country Breakfast
Credit Cards: A, B, C, D
Notes: 5, 6, 7, 8, 9, 11, 13

DEVILS TOWER

B&B Western Adventure #241

Box 20972, Billings, MT, 59104
(406) 259-7993

Country home at the foot of Devils Tower in the Black Hills. One bedroom with king bed, private shower, private entrance, and deck. Free evening campfire programs, abundant wildlife, XC skiing, and hunting in the fall. Children over 16 welcome; no smoking inside. $45.

DOUGLAS

B&B Western Adventure #243

Box 20972, Billings, MT, 59104
(406) 259-7993

NOTES: Credit cards accepted: A Master Card; B Visa; C American Express; D Discover Card; E Diners Club; F Other: 2 Personal checks accepted: 3 Lunch available: 4 Dinner available: 5 Open all year

Hotel Higgins

A working cattle ranch with a cabin and bunkhouse for guests. Bunkhouse has three bedrooms and one bath, kitchen, living and dining area. The cabin has a small living room and private bath. Resident dog and cat. Children welcome. If you feel like it, join in feeding the calves, branding, mending fences, feeding the horses, or baking bread. Full breakfast. No pets; smoking is allowed. $35-40. Senior citizen discount.

ENCAMPMENT

Platt's Rustic Mountain Lodge
Star Route 49, 82325
(307) 327-5539

A peaceful mountain view and wholesome country atmosphere with lots of western hospitality, hay rides, horseback riding, fishing, hiking, rock hounding; fully guided tours available to scenic mountain area. Enjoy the flora and fauna, historic trails, old mining camps, plus snowmobiling and cross-

country skiing in the winter. By reservation only.

Hosts: Mayvon & Ron Platt
Singles: 2 (SB) $65
Doubles: 1: (SB) $75
Type of Beds: 9 Twin; 1 Double
Continental or Full Breakfast
Minimum stay: 2
Credit Cards: No
Closed Thanksgiving & Christmas
Notes: 4, 8, 9, 13

GLENROCK

Hotel Higgins
416 West Birch, 82637
(307) 436-9212

A grand old hotel in its heyday (1916), the Hotel Higgins has been restored to its original grandeur, using original pieces of furniture and many collectibles. The hotel is listed on the National Historic Register and has hosted regionally famous people from the early 1900s to present-day governors, senators, and congressmen. A full gourmet breakfast is served in sunny, private dining areas. The hotel boasts the award-winning Paisley Shawl Restaurant.

6 Pets welcome: 7 Smoking allowed: 8 Children welcome: 9 Social drinking allowed: 10 Tennis available: 11 Swimming available: 12 Golf available: 13 Skiing available: 14 May be booked through travel agents

Hosts: Jack & Margaret Doll
Doubles: 10 (7 PB; 3 SB) $36-55
Type of Beds: 2 Twin; 8 Double
Full Breakfast
Credit Cards: A, B, C
Notes: 2, 3, 4, 5, 7, 8, 9, 10, 11, 12, 14

GREYBULL

B&B Western Adventure #240

Box 20972, Billings, MT, 59104
(406) 259-7993

This authentic cattle and horse ranch sits on the western slope of the Big Horn Mountains in Shell Canyon. Hosts are licensed outfitters and know the habits of the abundant wildlife in the area. Bunkhouse with two rooms, private baths, common room with TV, games, and laundry facilities. Two more rooms in the house. Children over twelve welcome; no smoking inside. $30-40.

JACKSON

B&B Western Adventures #50

Box 20972, Billings, MT, 59104
(406) 259-7993

This four-story home has fabulous views of the Jackson Hole Valley below. Six rooms with private showers, ideal for active people who want to experience nature firsthand. Continental-plus breakfast. May not be appropriate for the physically handicapped. $75-95.

B&B Western Adventures #79

Box 20972, Billings, MT, 59104
(406) 259-7993

A lovely ranch home at the foot of the Teton Mountains. One room with private bath upstairs, another with private bath

downstairs. Private entrance, TV, pool table, sitting area. Full breakfast. Children over 6 welcome; small dogs; smoking allowed. $35-55.

B&B Western Adventure #80

Box 20972, Billings, MT, 59104
(406) 259-7993

Two-story modern log home bordering the national forest. Secluded area with abundant wildlife — bighorn sheep, deer, elk in the backyard. Resident dog. River access to trout stream, picnic area; guided fishing trips can be arranged. Full breakfast; no pets or smoking. $45-60.

B&B Western Adventure #204

Box 20972, Billings, MT, 59104
(406) 259-7993

An early 1900s inn, secluded in the middle of 7 forested acres with a view of the Grand Tetons. Five bedrooms with private baths, TV, antique furniture. Three miles from Teton Village Ski Resort; four from Jackson. Racquet club, swimming, tennis, health club, and fine restaurants nearby. Full breakfast, restricted smoking. $85-135 (high season).

B&B Western Adventure #205

Box 20972, Billings, MT, 59104
(406) 259-7993

A lovely new home with two bedrooms sharing a bath. Children are welcome. Four miles from Teton Village Ski Resort; five from Jackson Hole. Fine restaurants, shopping, tennis, swimming, racquet club and fishing

NOTES: Credit cards accepted: A Master Card; B Visa; C American Express; D Discover Card; E Diners Club; F Other: 2 Personal checks accepted: 3 Lunch available: 4 Dinner available: 5 Open all year

guides within a mile. Full breakfast; smoking outdoors only. $45-70.

Big Mountain Inn
Box 7453, 83001
(307) 733-1981

A quality inn located near the base of the Tetons. Five rooms with private baths and color TV; two rooms with Japanese soaking tubs. Daily maid service. Close to Teton Ski Resort and Aspen Golf Course.

Host: Penny Foster
Doubles: 5 (PB) $85-135
Type of Beds: 2 Double; 5 Queen
Full Breakfast
Minimum stay: 2
Credit Cards: A, B
Closed Nov. & April
Notes: 2, 4, 8 (over 5), 9, 10, 12, 13

LANDER

Black Mountain Ranch
548 North Fork Road, 82520
(307) 332-6442

Discover the treasures and country comfort of Black Mountain Ranch. The ranch is nestled along the Popo Agie River in the foothills of the Wind River Mountains, on the way to Yellowstone. Trout fishing, horseback riding, hiking, llama picnics, and interesting local tours available.

Hosts: Dan & Rosie Ratigan
Singles: 4 (2 PB; 2 SB) $25-30
Doubles: 2 (SB) $40-50
Full Breakfast
Credit Cards: A, B
Closed Oct. 1-April 30
Notes: 2, 4, 8, 9, 14

Country Fare Bed & Breakfast
904 Main Street, 82520
(307) 332-9604

Country Fare...an adventure in old-fashioned charm! Enjoy our delicious English breakfasts, traditional Cream Tea, antique-filled bedrooms, and warm hospitality. Lander is the sports enthusiast's dream: hunting, fishing, hiking, snow sports, and more. On direct route to Yellowstone.

Hosts: A. R. & Mary Ann Hoyt
Doubles: 3 (SB) $30-45 plus tax
Type of Beds: 1 Double; 2 Queen
Full English Breakfast
Credit Cards: A, B
Notes: 2, 5, 8 (over 8), 9, 10, 11, 12, 13, 14

LARAMIE

Alvina's Townhouse Inn Bed & Breakfast
1107 Lewis, 82070
(307) 742-4836

Located right across the street from the University of Wyoming. Guests will enjoy being served breakfast at private tables in our dining room. The craftsmanship of our hardwood floors, antique china, and other collectibles is part of the charm of this lovely home.

Hosts: George & Terri Lucy
Doubles: 3 (PB) $21-36.75
Type of Beds: 3 Double; 1 Youth Daybed
Full Breakfast
Credit Cards: A, B
Notes: 2, 4, 5, 8, 9, 10, 11, 12

Annie Moore's Guest House
819 University, 82070
(307) 721-4177

Six individually decorated guest rooms, four with sink. Large, sunny common living rooms, second-story sun deck. Across the street from the University of Wyoming; two blocks from the Laramie Plains Museum; six blocks from downtown. Fifteen to thirty minutes from skiing, hiking, camping, fishing, uncrowded wilderness area.

Host: Diana Kopulos
Doubles: 6 (SB) $35-52
Continental Breakfast
Credit Cards: A, B, C
Closed Thanksgiving & Christmas
Notes: 2, 8 (over 4), 9, 14

MORAN

Box K Ranch

Box 110, 83013
(307) 543-2407

Located in the beautiful Buffalo Valley, surrounded by national forest, with Grand Teton Park outside our front door and a short drive to Yellowstone. Horseback riding, float trips, hiking, fishing — all with great Western hospitality.

Host: Walter M. Korn
Singles: 2 (SB) $30
Doubles: 1 (PB) $60
Type of Beds: 2 Twin; 1 Double
Full Breakfast
Credit Cards: No
Closed Nov. - April
Notes: 3, 4, 8, 9, 11

Hotel Wolf

NEWCASTLE

4W Ranch Recreation

1162 Lynch Road, 82701
(307) 746-2815

Looking for the unbeaten path? Spend a few days on our working cattle ranch with 20,000 acres of diversified rangeland to explore at your leisure. Rates include three meals a day.

Hosts: Bob Harshbarger & Jean Sears
Doubles: 2 (SB) $60 for 1, $100 for 2 AP
Type of Beds: 2 Twin; 1 Double
Full Breakfast
Credit Cards: B
Notes: 2, 3, 4, 5, 7, 8, 9

RIVERTON

B&B Western Adventure #218

Box 20972, Billings, MT, 59104
(406) 259-7993

This working ranch is surrounded by the Wind River Reservation, home of the Shoshone and Arapaho tribes. Three rooms share a bath. Excellent fishing, hunting, and snowmobiling. Full breakfast with homemade breads and preserves. No indoor smoking. $35-40.

SARATOGA

Hotel Wolf

Box 1298, 82331
(307) 326-5525

The Hotel Wolf, built in 1893, served as a stagecoach stop, During its early years, the hotel was the hub of the community and noted for its fine food and convivial atmosphere. The same holds true today. The dining room is acclaimed as one of the finest in the region. Nearby is a mineral hot springs.

Hosts: Doug & Kathleen Campbell
Singles: 7 (5 PB; 2 SB) $23-35
Doubles: 3 (1 PB; 2 SB) $21-28
Suite: 1 (PB) $75
Type of Beds: 2 Twin; 1 Double; 1 Queen; 1 Hidabed
Continental Breakfast
Credit Cards: A, B, C, E
Notes: 2, 3, 4, 5, 7, 8, 9, 10, 11, 12

NOTES: Credit cards accepted: A Master Card; B Visa; C American Express; D Discover Card; E Diners Club; F Other: 2 Personal checks accepted: 3 Lunch available: 4 Dinner available: 5 Open all year

SHERIDAN

B&B Western Adventure #250

Box 20972, Billings, MT, 59104
(406) 259-7993

This gracious log home in the pines has hiking trails leading directly to the adjacent Big Horn National Forest. With a 100-mile view and abundant wildlife, including deer and moose. Two rooms with private baths. A secluded cabin sleeps six. Host will take you gold panning or Jeeping in the wilderness. Children are welcome; no indoor smoking. $35-75.

Kilbourne Kastle

320 South Main, 82801
(307) 674-8716

On Sheridan's historic district walking tour, Kilbourne Kastle is near a golf course and good fishing areas. A convenient stopover on your way to Cody, Yellowstone, and Glacier national parks. One block from downtown Sheridan; convenient parking in rear.

Hosts: Jack & Pat Roush
Doubles: 3 (SB) $25.75-30.90
Continental Breakfast
Credit Cards: A, B
Notes: 2, 5, 8, 9, 10, 11, 12

WHEATLAND

Edwards Bed & Breakfast

846 Cooney Hills Road, 82201
(307) 322-3921

We offer a remote retreat in the mountains of Wyoming. We only take one party or family at a time. Lots of wildlife, great fishing, Jeep rides, and home cooking with a friendly atmosphere.

Hosts: Richard & Dodie Edwards
Doubles: 2 (PB) $30-35
Type of Beds: 2 Twin; 2 Double
Full Breakfast
Credit Cards: No
Notes: 2, 4, 5, 6, 7, 8, 9, 11

WILSON-JACKSON HOLE

Teton Tree House

Box 550, 83014
(307) 733-3233

Helpful, longtime mountain and river guides offer a special four-story, open-beam home on a forested mountainside. Large, rustic, but elegant rooms have exceptional views of the Jackson Hole Valley and mountains beyond. Generous, tasty, healthy breakfasts.

Hosts: Chris & Denny Becker
Doubles: 5 (PB) $58.85-101.65
Type of Beds: 2 Double; 2 Queen; 2 King
Full Breakfast (low cholesterol)
Credit Cards: A, B, D
Notes: 5, 8 (no infants), 9, 10, 11, 12, 13, 14

Teton View Bed and Breakfast

2136 Coyote Loop, Box 652, 83014
(307) 733-7954

Rooms have mountain views, cozy country decor. Lounge area — where homemade pastries, fresh fruit and coffee are served — connects to private deck overlooking Teton Mountain range. Own entrance. Many added personal touches. Convenient location to Yellowstone/Grand Teton national parks.

Hosts: Jane and Tom Neil
Doubles: 2 (SB) $37.45-69.55 for 1; $42.80-74.90 for 2
Type of Beds: 2 Queen; 2 Sofa sleepers
Continental Breakfast
Credit Cards: A, B
Notes: 2, 3, 4, 5, 6, 8, 9, 10, 11, 12, 13, 14

6 Pets welcome: 7 Smoking allowed: 8 Children welcome: 9 Social drinking allowed: 10 Tennis available: 11 Swimming available: 12 Golf available: 13 Skiing available: 14 May be booked through travel agents

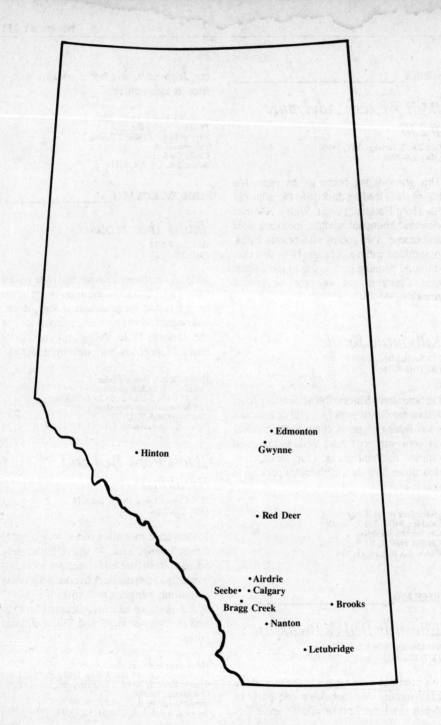

• Edmonton
• Gwynne

• Hinton

• Red Deer

• Airdrie
Seebe • • Calgary
Bragg Creek
                    • Brooks
• Nanton

• Letubridge

ALBERTA

Alberta

Alberta B&B 1

Box 15477, M.P.O., Vancouver
British Columbia, Canada, V6B 5B2
(604) 682-4610

This home, in a country setting, is a ten-minute drive to the outskirts of Calgary and hour's drive to Banff. A five-level split with one guest room and a shared bath.

Doubles: 1 (SB) $30-40
Type of Beds: 1 Double
Continental Breakfast
Credit Cards: No
Notes: 2, 9, 10, 11, 12, 13

BRAGG CREEK_____

Alberta B&B 2

Box 15477, M.P.O., Vancouver
British Columbia, Canada, V6B 5B2
(604) 682-4610

This home is in a lovely area of Redwood Meadows, twenty minutes from Calgary's city limits. A short, scenic drive takes you to beautiful Elbow Falls. One guest room and private bath.

Doubles: 1 (PB) $30-40
Type of Beds: 2 Twin
Continental-plus Breakfast
Credit Cards: No
Notes: 2, 9, 10, 11, 12, 13

BROOKS_____

Alberta B&B 3

Box 15477, M.P.O., Vancouver
British Columbia, Canada, V6B 5B2
(604) 682-4610

This country inn offers four rooms, each with private bath and air-conditioning. A full country breakfast is served in the solarium. The "Gathering Room" with fireplace is for the use of guests. Pets are welcome to stay in the heated kennels. Sportsmen have on-site facilities for cleaning their catch, with freezer storage.

Doubles: 4 (PB) $60-75
Type of Beds: 4 Double
Full Breakfast
Credit Cards: No
Notes: 2, 6, 9, 10, 11, 12, 13

CALGARY_____

Alberta B&B 4

Box 15477, M.P.O., Vancouver
British Columbia, Canada, V6B 5B2
(604) 682-4610

This multilevel home has a family room with a fireplace and a cedar-lined hot tub that guests are welcome to use. Guest room has a double bed and private bath.

Doubles: 1 (PB) $35-45
Type of Beds: 1 Double
Continental Breakfast
Credit Cards: No
Notes: 2, 9, 10, 11, 12, 13

CHEMAINUS_____

Moyers

All Season B&B Agency
Box 5511, Station B, Victoria, B.C.
Canada V8R 6S4
(604) 595-BEDS

NOTES: Credit cards accepted: A Master Card; B Visa; C American Express; D Discover Card; E Diners Club; F Other: 2 Personal checks accepted: 3 Lunch available: 4 Dinner available: 5 Open all year

Enjoy a peaceful seaview from the shaded veranda of a century-old farmhouse with antique furnishings. Near a pub, golf course, art galleries, and ferries to nearby islands.

Doubles: (SB) $40-48
Full Breakfast
Credit Cards: A, B

EDMONTON

Alberta B&B 5

Box 15477, M.P.O., Vancouver
British Columbia, Canada, V6B 5B2
(604) 682-4610

A beautiful red brick home designated as an historical home. Built in 1910 for James Gibbons, who fought in the 1885 Riel Rebellion, and for whom the town of Gibbons is named, the home is owned by professional musicians. One upstairs guest room with double bed and one guest bath. Hosts has two cats.

Doubles: 1 (PB) $30-40
Type of Beds: 1 Double
Continental Breakfast
Credit Cards: No
Notes: 2, 9, 10, 11, 12

GWYNNE

Gwynalta Farm

T0C 1L0
(403) 352-3587

Experience life on a dairy farm, walk along the shore of a secluded lake, or fish. Enjoy many species of birds and perhaps see some wild animals or the Northern Lights. Great for camera buffs. Close to Edmonton International Airport.

Singles: 1 (SB) $20
Doubles: 1 (SB) $30
Type of Beds: 2 Twin; 1 Queen
Full Breakfast
Credit Cards: No
Notes: 4, 5, 6, 7, 8, 9, 10, 11, 12, 13

HINTON

Black Cat Guest Ranch

Box 976, T0E 1B0
(403) 865-3084

The Black Cat Guest Ranch offers horseback riding and hiking in summer, cross-country skiing in winter, and relaxation year-round. Home-style meals and sociable surroundings. No children's program or baby-sitting available. In a beautiful mountain setting one hour's drive from Jasper.

Hosts: Amber & Perry Hayward
Doubles: 16 (PB) $35-100 (Canadian)
Type of Beds: 15 Twin; 16 Double; 1 Queen
Full Breakfast
Credit Cards: A, B
Notes: 2, 3, 4, 5, 7, 8, 9, 13

LETUBRIDGE

Heritage House

1115 8th Avenue, T1J 1P7
(403) 328-9011

This 1937 home is a provincial historic site, situated on a large lot near the city center. Designated a provincial historic site because of its architecture and hand-painted inside decorations. Close to two world heritage sites. Breakfasts reflect western Canadian taste. Hosts have written several books about western Canadian history.

Hosts: Bruce & Joan Haig
Doubles: 3 (SB) $29-40
Type of Beds: 2 Twin; 3 Queen
Full Breakfast
Credit Cards: A, B
Notes: 2, 5, 8, 9, 10, 11, 12, 14

NANTON

Alberta B&B 6

Box 15477, M.P.O., Vancouver
British Columbia, Canada, V6B 5B2
(604) 682-4610

NOTES: Credit cards accepted: A Master Card; B Visa; C American Express; D Discover Card; E Diners Club; F Other: 2 Personal checks accepted: 3 Lunch available: 4 Dinner available: 5 Open all year

A small ranch in the beautiful foothills of the Canadian Rockies, this home is owned by hosts who keep cattle, horses, and sheep. Two guest rooms and shared bath. Horseback riding is available, and fishing is good in the nearby lake and mountain streams.

Doubles: 2 (SB) $30-40
Type of Beds: 2 Twin; 1 Queen
Continental Breakfast
Credit Cards: No
Notes: 2, 8, 9

RED DEER

Alberta B&B 7

Box 15477, M.P.O., Vancouver
British Columbia, Canada, V6B 5B2
(604) 682-4610

Situated approximately midway between Edmonton and Calgary, the bungalow has an upstairs guest room, downstairs guest room with adjacent sitting room, and one guest bath. Host is a registered nurse.

Doubles: 2 (1 PB; 1 SB) $30-40
Type of Beds: 2 Double

Continental Breakfast
Credit Cards: No
Notes: 2

SEEBE

Brewster's Kananaskis Guest Ranch

General Delivery, T0L 0C0
(403) 673-3737

Relax in the old Brewster family homestead forty-five minutes west of Calgary, just off the Trans-Canada Highway. Ride to the ridge of Yamnuska Mountain, explore the Bow River, soak in our whirlpool, or tee off on one of the four golf courses that are minutes from the ranch.

Hosts: The Brewster Family
Doubles: 27 (PB) $65-72
Full Breakfast
Credit Cards: A, B
Closed Oct. 15-April 30
Notes: 3, 4, 7, 8, 11, 12, 14

6 Pets welcome: 7 Smoking allowed: 8 Children welcome: 9 Social drinking allowed: 10 Tennis available: 11 Swimming available: 12 Golf available: 13 Skiing available: 14 May be booked through travel agents

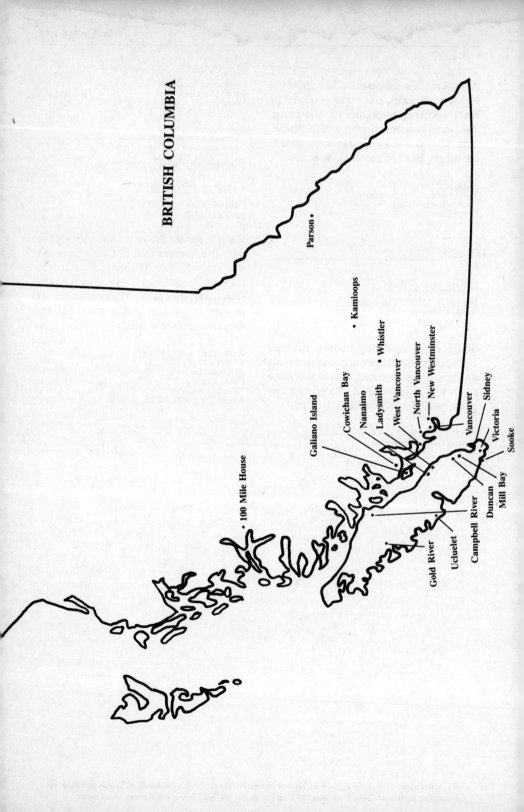

BRITISH COLUMBIA

Parson •

Kamloops •

• Whistler

West Vancouver

North Vancouver

New Westminster

Vancouver

Sidney

Victoria

Sooke

Galiano Island

Cowichan Bay

Nanaimo

Ladysmith

Duncan

Mill Bay

100 Mile House •

Campbell River

Gold River

Ucluelet

British Columbia

CAMPBELL RIVER

April Point Lodge and Fishing Resort

Box 1, V9W 4Z1
(604) 285-2222; 285-2411

April Point Lodge is located on Quadra Island, approximately 100 miles north of Vancouver. April Point features world-class salmon fishing and gourmet dining in a pristine natural setting. The lodge is easily reached by plane or car.

Hosts: Phyllis, Eric, & Warren Peterson
Doubles: 38 (SB) $129.50-179.50 plus tax
Children under 16, no charge
Type of Beds: 60 Twin; 13 Double; 56 Queen; 6 King
Full Breakfast
Credit Cards: A, B, C, E
Closed Oct. 16-April 14
Notes: 2, 4, 6, 7, 8, 9, 11

Campbell River Lodge & Fishing Resort

1760 Island Highway, V9W 2E7
(604) 287-7446

Campbell River's oldest fishing lodge, located on the banks of the famous Campbell River. Experienced guides for salt-water salmon fishing; dining room, Olde English-style pub; squash court; sauna, and whirlpool (seasonal).

Hosts: Ted & Sharon Arbour
Doubles: 30 (PB) $39-$70 plus 8% tax.
Type of Beds: 12 Twin; 18 Queen
Continental Breakfast
Credit Cards: A, B

Closed Christmas Day
Notes: 4, 6, 7, 8, 9

The Dogwoods

302 Birch Street, V9W 2S6
(604) 287-4213

Come join your fellow travelers in a charming older home centrally located in the "salmon-fishing capital of the world" on Vancouver Island. Good company — good times. Salmon fishing charters readily available. Send $5(US) for Peter's fishing book.

Hosts: Peter Johnson
Doubles: 2 (PB) $25-$40
Type of Beds: 2 Double
Continental Breakfast
Credit Cards: No
Notes: 9, 10, 11, 12, 13

COWICHAN BAY

Caterham Court

Town & Country B&B in B.C.
Box 46544, Stn. G, Vancouver, B.C., V6R 4G6
(604) 731-5942

Nestled in the trees overlooking beautiful Cowichan Bay, this turn-of-the-century home offers three charming, spacious rooms with private baths. Stroll the quaint country roads, take the rowboat for a paddle on the bay, or relax by the fireplace in our guest lounge.

Doubles: 3 (PB) $45-65
Type of Beds: 2 Twin; 2 Queen
Full Breakfast
Credit Cards: No
Notes: 2, 5, 7, 8, 10, 11, 12

6 Pets welcome: 7 Smoking allowed: 8 Children welcome: 9 Social drinking allowed: 10 Tennis available: 11 Swimming available: 12 Golf available: 13 Skiing available: 14 May be booked through travel agents

DUNCAN

Fairburn Farm Country Manor
3310 Jackson Road, RR#7, V9L 4W4
(604) 746-4637

A nineteenth-century manor house on a 130-acre traditional farm in a secluded valley. We organically grow grain, fruits and vegetables; raise sheep and have dairy cows. Our property includes a mountain stream and trails where wildlife abounds. We have a dining room, large rooms with log fires, and a self-contained cottage which is available by the week. We welcome children with parental supervision.

Hosts: Darrell and Anthea Archer
Doubles: 6 (2 PB; 4 SB) $53.60 for 1; 70.10 for 2 (Canadian)
Types of Beds: 6 Twin; 1 Double; 3 Queen
Full Breakfast
Credit Cards: No
Notes: 2, 3, 4, 5, 8, 10, 11, 12, 14

GALIANO ISLAND

La Berengerie
Montague Road, V0N 1P0
(604) 539-5392

Set in the forest, a ten-minute walk from Montague Harbour, this charming home is furnished with antiques and decorated with local artists' paintings. European atmosphere.

Hosts: Huguette & Andrew Benger
Doubles: 3 (1 PB; 2 SB) $55
Type of Beds: 2 Twin; 2 Double
Full Breakfast
Minimum stay weekends & holidays: 2
Credit Cards: No
Notes: 2, 4, 5, 8, 9, 10, 11, 12

GOLD RIVER

Kozy Korner
All Season B&B Agency
Box 5511, Station B, Victoria, B.C.

Canada V8R 6S4
(604) 595-BEDS

Right on the doorstep of historic Nootka Sound, our home offers a large rec room with pool table, games, books, TV, and a cozy woodstove. Large sun deck with barbeque and picnic table to enjoy.

Doubles: (SB) $25-45
Full Breakfast
Credit Cards: A, B

KAMLOOPS

Alberta B&B 8
Box 15477, M.P.O., Vancouver
British Columbia, Canada, V6B 5B2
(604) 682-4610

This lovely home is on the South Thompson River. Weather permitting, breakfast will be served on the patio that overlooks the swimming pool and private dock with canoe available for boating. Children are most welcome. Hostess is a weaver with an interesting studio. Three guest rooms with two guest baths.

Doubles: 3 (PB and SB) $30-40
Type of Beds: 3 Double
Continental Breakfast
Credit Cards: No
Notes: 2, 8, 9, 10, 11, 12

LADYSMITH

Aneverly by the Sea
All Season B&B Agency
Box 5511, Station B, Victoria, B.C.
Canada V8R 6S4
(604) 595-BEDS

Beautiful oceanfront setting in the Yellow Point resort area, halfway between Ladysmith and Nanaimo. Comfortable home with 7 acres of forest and a mile of beach to explore. Fishing, crabbing, boating, canoeing, wildlife. On-line computer and word processor available.

NOTES: Credit cards accepted: A Master Card; B Visa; C American Express; D Discover Card; E Diners Club; F Other: 2 Personal checks accepted: 3 Lunch available: 4 Dinner available: 5 Open all year

Doubles: 4 (PB) $35-48
Continental Breakfast
Credit Cards: A, B

Yellow Point Lodge

RR 3, V0R 2E0
(604) 245-7422

Set on 180 acres of private natural forest land surrounded by the Gulf Islands, the lodge and cottages have been a rustic favorite for fifty years. No phones or TV. All meals and recreational activities included in daily rate.

Hosts: Richard Hill & Millie Hogg
Singles: 2 (SB) $45-95 (Canadian)
Doubles: 53 (25 PB; 28 SB) $80-145 (Canadian)
Type of Beds: 14 Twin; 24 Double; 12 Queen; 3 King
All Meals Included
Minimum stay weekends:2; holidays:3
Credit Cards: A, B
Closed Dec. 20-23
Notes: 2, 7, 8 (16 and over), 9, 10, 11

MILL BAY

Pine Lodge Farm

3191 Mutter Road, V0R 2P0
(604) 743-4083

An antique-filled pine lodge built on a 30-acre farm overlooking the ocean, with majestic arbutus trees and breath-taking views of the sea and islands. Walking trails, fields, and farm animals add to the paradise-like setting. Located in historic Mill Bay. No smoking.

Hosts: Barbara & Cliff Clarke
Doubles: 7 (PB) $65-75 Canadian
Type of Beds: 2 Twin; 2 Double; 4 Queen
Full Breakfast
Credit Cards: A, B
Notes: 2, 5, 8, 9, 12, 13

NANAIMO

Carey House

All Season B&B Agency
Box 5511, Station B, Victoria, B.C.
Canada V8R 6S4
(604) 595-BEDS

We have a character home with many interesting antiques, comfortably furnished and situated in a beautiful garden of flowers, trees, and shrubs. Within easy walking distance of downtown, the harbor, parks, and so forth.

Doubles: 2 (PB) $35-50
Continental Breakfast
Credit Cards: A, B

NEW WESTMINSTER

The Dutch Touch

325 Pine Street, V3L 2T1
(604) 526-0978

Welcome to our turn-of-the-century home! Close to stores, parks, restaurants, and the Sky Skytrain, which takes you to downtown Vancouver in 25 minutes. Experience all the many exciting sites of Greater Vancouver while enjoying morning and evening quiet amid heritage homes in charming New Westminster.

Host: Mrs. Alice Van Kessel
Doubles: 2 (SB) $25-35
Type of Beds: 1 Twin; 1 Queen
Full Breakfast
Credit Cards: No
Closed Dec. - Feb.
Notes: 2, 7, 9, 10, 11

The Phillips House

Town & Country B&B in B.C.
Box 46544, Stn. G, Vancouver, B.C., V6R 4G6
(604) 731-5942

A grand old Victorian house built in 1892, with leaded-glass windows and antique furnishings. Walk two blocks to the Skytrain for the twenty-minute ride to Vancouver, or drive. Within walking distance to a number of New Westminster's finest restaurants.

Singles: 1 (SB) $40
Doubles: 2 (PB) $50-60
Type of Beds: 1 Twin; 1 Double; 1 Queen
Full Breakfast
Credit Cards: No
Notes: 8 (call), 10, 11, 12

6 Pets welcome: 7 Smoking allowed: 8 Children welcome: 9 Social drinking allowed: 10 Tennis available: 11 Swimming available: 12 Golf available: 13 Skiing available: 14 May be booked through travel agents

NORTH VANCOUVER

Helen's Bed & Breakfast

302 East 5th Street, V7L 1L1
(604) 985-4869

Welcome to our old Victorian home, its charm and comfort enhanced by antiques, wonderful views, and color cable TV in each room. Five blocks to the Pacific; twenty minutes to the Horseshoe Bay Ferries; minutes to Grouse Mountain, Whister Sea-Bus, restaurants, and shopping. Gourmet breakfast served in elegant dining room.

Host: Helen Boire
Doubles: 3 (1 PB; 2 SB) From $40-50
Type of Beds: 3 Double
Full Breakfast
Credit Cards: No
Closed Christmas
Notes: 7, 8, 9, 10, 11, 12, 13

The Nelsons'

470 West St. James Road, V7N 2P5
(604) 985-1178

Tastefully appointed home on a quiet residential street, with a restful patio and sun deck overlooking the heated pool, in a garden setting. Full breakfast menu offers various choices of home-cooked food. Minutes from Vancouver's many attractions. Sorry, no smoking or pets.

Hosts: Roy & Charlotte Nelson
Singles: 1 (PB) $35
Doubles: 2 (PB) $50
Type of Beds: 1 Twin; 2 Double
Full Breakfast
Credit Cards: No
Closed Nov.-March
Notes: 2, 8 (over 10), 10, 11, 12, 13

Sue's Victorian Bed & Breakfast

152 East 3rd Street, V7L 1E6
(604) 985-1523

This lovely restored 1909 home has a gorgeous harbour view. It is centrally located for public transportation, shopping, and restaurants. No smoking. Long-term rates available. Guest refrigerator, shared kitchen, and laundry facilities available. Choice of full, continental, or no breakfast.

Host: Sue Chalmers
Singles: 1 (SB) $35 (Canadian)
Doubles: 3 (2 PB; 1 SB) $50 (Canadian)
Also available: 2 cots, youth bed, baby cot
Continental Breakfast (full available)
Minimum stay: 2
Credit Cards: No
Notes: 2, 5, 8

100 MILE HOUSE

Cariboo Lakeside B&B

Town & Country B&B in B.C.
Box 46544, Stn. G, Vancouver, B.C., V6R 4G6
(604) 731-5942

This waterfront home is in a very quiet location ideal for fishing, walking, cross-country skiing, and swimming. Minutes from town, a major health spa, and public beach. Hosts speak German. About 400 miles north of Vancouver.

Doubles: 2 (1 PB; 1 SB) $30-45
Type of Beds: 2 Twin
Full Breakfast
Credit Cards: No
Notes: 2, 8, 11, 12, 13

PARSON

Taliesin Guest House

V0A 1L0

Taliesin nestles among the Rocky Mountains on the forested benchlands overlooking the beautiful Columbia River Valley. The forested land around the cabin hosts a display of wild flowers, and the majestic mountains and valley surrounding us are home to many animals, birds, and waterfowl. Taliesin is a picture of peacefulness in all seasons. No smoking, no pets.

Hosts: Marilyn & Bryan Kelly-McArthur
Singles: 1 (SB) $30

NOTES: Credit cards accepted: A Master Card; B Visa; C American Express; D Discover Card; E Diners Club; F Other: 2 Personal checks accepted: 3 Lunch available: 4 Dinner available: 5 Open all year

Doubles: 2 (SB) $40
Type of Beds: 2 Twin; 2 Double
Full Breakfast
Minimum stay weekends: 2
Credit Cards: B
Notes: 5, 8

The Grahams' Cedar House B&B

SIDNEY

The Grahams' Cedar House B&B

Town & Country B&B in B.C.
Box 46544, Stn. G, Vancouver, B.C., V6R 4G6
(604) 731-5942

A quiet country setting, yet close to the village of Sidney by the sea. One or two bedroom accommodations with full kitchen, bath, and ground-level private entrance. Close to fishing, beach, tennis, golf, ferries to Vancouver, and the U.S. Thirty-five minutes to Victoria.

Doubles: 2 (SB) $35-60
Type of Beds: 3 Double
Full Breakfast
Credit Cards: No
Notes: 2, 5, 8, 10, 11, 12

SOOKE

Rose Cottage Bed & Breakfast

Town & Country B&B in B.C.
Box 46544, Stn. G, Vancouver, B.C., V6R 4G6
(604) 731-5942

Rose Cottage is forty minutes from Victoria, set amid lawns and a rose garden in a quiet country area. Furnished with antiques. Excellent location for fishing, beaches, and watching sea life.

Doubles: 2 (SB) $35-45
Type of Beds: 2 Twin; 1 Double
Full Breakfast
Credit Cards: No
Notes: 2, 5, 8 (5 and up), 10, 11, 12

UCLUELET

Barry & Bernice's

All Season B&B Agency
Box 5511, Station B, Victoria, B.C.
Canada V8R 6S4
(604) 595-BEDS

Enjoy the most fantastic beaches in Canada, just a twenty-minute walk from this home on park-maintained trails. Or take rough trails to isolated beaches where few find their way. Hosts will pick up passengers from the *Lady Rose* ferry that docks in Ucluelet.

Doubles: (PB) $40-45
Full Breakfast
Credit Cards: A, B

VANCOUVER

Diana Luxury Suites

1019 East 38th Avenue, N5W 1J4
(604) 321-2855

Comfortable, spacious suites at attractive rates. Free transportation to airport or downtown locations.

Singles: 4 (PB) $50 (US)
Doubles: 4 (PB) $55 (US)
Full Breakfast
Credit Cards: A, B
Notes: 5, 7, 10, 11, 12

May's B&B

Town & Country B&B in B.C.
Box 46544, Stn. G, Vancouver, B.C., V6R 4G6
(604) 731-5942

6 Pets welcome: 7 Smoking allowed: 8 Children welcome: 9 Social drinking allowed: 10 Tennis available: 11 Swimming available: 12 Golf available: 13 Skiing available: 14 May be booked through travel agents

This Austrian chalet-type home in a quiet area offers Viennese charm. Well located on the popular west side of town, one block from a bus stop, ten minutes from Vancouver International Airport, and fifteen minutes from downtown. Enjoy the patio and secluded garden or watch TV in the cozy den.

Doubles: 2 (PB) $35-60
Type of Beds: 2 Twin; 1 Queen
Full Breakfast
Credit Cards: No
Notes: 2, 5, 7 (outside), 8 (over 6), 10, 11, 12, 13

NW B&B #902

NW Bed & Breakfast Travel Unlimited
610 SW Broadway, Portland, OR, 97205
(503) 243-7616

Traditional colonial, built in the 1920s, with sun deck, garden, den, private breakfast room. On a beautiful tree-lined street in a fine, residential west-side area. Conveniently located near many Vancouver attractions, close to the University of British Columbia campus. Good for city bus; a few minutes from the airport.

Doubles: 2 (SB) $40-50
Type of Beds: 2 Twin; 1 Double
Continental Breakfast
Credit Cards: No
Notes: 7

Peloquin's B&B

Town & Country B&B in B.C.
Box 46544, Stn. G, Vancouver, B.C., V6R 4G6
(604) 731-5942

This comfortable, newly decorated home is located in a quiet, central neighborhood. Guests have a private entrance and TV. Your hospitable hosts speak French and Ukrainian and enjoy sharing helpful information on the city. Close to restaurants, shops, parks, major bus lines.

Doubles: 2 (SB) $40-50
Type of Beds: 2 Double; 1 Cot; 1 Rollaway
Full Breakfast

Credit Cards: No
Notes: 2, 5, 8, 10, 11, 12, 13

The Platt's Bed & Breakfast

4393 Quinton Place
V7R-4A8
(604) 987-4100

Fifteen to twenty minutes to the heart of town and famous Stanley Park. Close to the Capilano suspension bridge, fish hatchery, and the Cleveland dam. Quiet parklike area, ideal for cycling. Homemade bread and jams featured at breakfast.

Hosts: Nancy & Elwood Platt
Singles: 1 (PB) $25 US
Doubles: 1 (PB) $35 US
Type of Beds: 2 Twin; 1 Double
Full Breakfast
Credit Cards: No
Notes: 2, 5, 8 (over 10), 9, 10, 11, 12

Storwick House

Town & Country B&B in B.C.
Box 46544, Stn. G, Vancouver, B.C., V6R 4G6
(604) 731-5942

Centrally located on a quiet, tree-lined street in the lovely Shaughnessy residential area. Ideal for travelers without a car, as there is a direct bus to downtown just a short block away. Easy access to shopping, Queen Elizabeth Park, Granville Island, Stanley Park and Aquarium, theaters, ocean beaches. Only fifteen minutes from the airport.

Doubles: 3 (SB) $35-55
Type of Beds: 2 Twin; 2 Double; 1 Cot
Full Breakfast
Credit Cards: No
Notes: 2, 5, 8, 10, 11, 12, 13

West End Guest House

1362 Haro Street, V6E 1G2
(604) 681-2889

Quiet, central 1906 historic home of Vancouver's first photographers. Recent renovations by an award-winning architect

NOTES: Credit cards accepted: A Master Card; B Visa; C American Express; D Discover Card; E Diners Club; F Other: 2 Personal checks accepted: 3 Lunch available: 4 Dinner available: 5 Open all year

include modern comfort and safety features while maintaining the ambience and style of the original home, elegantly blended with the artistic talents of your host. All rooms have private baths and direct-dial telephones.

Host: George Christie
Singles: 1 (PB) $45-65
Doubles: 6 (PB) $65-80
Type of Beds: 2 Twin; 6 Queen
Full Breakfast
Credit Cards: A, B
Notes: 5, 9, 10, 11, 12, 13, 14

West End Guest House

VICTORIA

Battery Street Guesthouse

670 Battery Street, V8V 1E5
(604) 385-4632

Guesthouse (1898) in downtown Victoria. Within walking distance of town and sites. Park and ocean are one block away. Clean, quiet, comfortable, and centrally located. Hostess speaks Dutch.

Host: Mrs. Pamela Verduyn
Singles: 1 (SB) $25-45
Doubles: 6 (SB) $40-60

Full Breakfast
Credit Cards: No
Notes: 2, 5, 10, 11, 12

Bed & Breakfast in Victoria

Town & Country B&B in B.C.
Box 46544, Stn. G, Vancouver, B.C., V6R 4G6
(604) 731-5942

Located in the suburb of Gordon Head, on the edge of Mount Douglas Park only fifteen minutes from downtown Victoria. Convenient to in-coming visitors because of its location on the airport and ferry side of Victoria. Near the University of Victoria.

Doubles: 2 (1 PB; 1 SB) $35-50
Type of Beds: 2 Twin; 1 Double
Full Breakfast
Credit Cards: No
Notes: 2, 5, 7, 10, 11, 12

Carriage Stop

All Season B&B Agency
Box 5511, Station B, Victoria, B.C.
Canada V8R 6S4
(604) 595-BEDS

In the heart of James Bay, close to everything. Walk to the beach or the heart of the city. This charming older home offers a relaxed atmosphere with full or continental breakfast.

Doubles: 1 (SB) $45-60
Full Breakfast
Credit Cards: A, B

Elk Lake Lodge

5259 Patricia Bay Hwy., V8Y 1S8
(604) 658-8879

Originally built in 1910 as a country chapel, Elk Lake Lodge has been beautifully restored. Four individually decorated guest rooms, a magnificent lounge, and outdoor hot tub are available for guests. Just steps to the lake for trout fishing, sailing, and wind surfing.

Hosts: Ken & Brenda Hicks
Doubles: 4 (2 PB; 2 SB) $45-60 Canadian, plus tax

6 Pets welcome: 7 Smoking allowed: 8 Children welcome: 9 Social drinking allowed: 10 Tennis available: 11 Swimming available: 12 Golf available: 13 Skiing available: 14 May be booked through travel agents

Type of Beds: 2 Twin; 1 Double; 2 Queen; 1 King
Full Breakfast
Credit Cards: A, B
Notes: 5, 6, 7 (restricted), 8 (over 5), 9, 11

Great-Snoring-On-Sea

10858 Madrona Dr., RR#1, Sidney, V8L 3R9
(604) 656-9549

Let us spoil you in our luxurious English-antique-furnished villa, perched high on a cliff overlooking the sea. Lie in bed and watch the sea-lions, bald eagles, and Orca whales. Beautiful Butchart gardens, quaint Empress Hotel, and ferries nearby.

Hosts: Sharon & Bill Flavelle
Doubles: 2 (PB) $85-155(US)
Type of Beds: 1 Double; 1 Queen
Full English Breakfast
Credit Cards: No
Closed Christmas, Jan 15. - March 15
Notes: 2, 7, 8 (call), 9, 10, 11, 12, 14

Heritage House B&B

3808 Heritage Lane, V82 7A7
(604) 479-0892

1910 mansion on 3/4 acre in a country setting, elegantly furnished. Convenient to ferry and downtown Victoria. On bus route, but off main road. Choice of home-made breakfasts; large rooms; guest parlor with fireplace; lounging veranda; off-road parking.

Hosts: Mike & Marlene Gilbert
Singles: 4 (SB) $40-47
Doubles: 4 (SB) $50-59
Type of Beds: 8 Twin; 5 Double; 1 Queen
Full Breakfast
Credit Cards: A, B
Notes: 2 (deposits only), 4, 5, 7, 8 (over 6), 9, 10, 11, 12, 14

Hibernia Bed & Breakfast

747 Helvetia Cr., V8Y 1M1
(604) 658-5519

Large country residence located on a cul-de-sac, surrounded by lawns, trees, and vines. Antique furnishings, comfortable beds. Full

Irish breakfast is served on our vine covered patio. Fifteen minutes from the airport or ferries, Victoria Butchart Gardens, beaches, restaurants, golf, and tennis.

Host: Aideen Lydon
Singles: 1 (SB) $25(US) $30(CAN)
Doubles: 2 (SB) $40(US) $48(CAN)
Type of Beds: 2 Twin; 1 Double; 1 Queen
Full Breakfast
Credit Cards: No
Closed Dec. 20 - Jan. 4
Notes: 2, 8, 9, 10, 11, 12, 14

Joan Brown's B&B

Town & Country B&B in B.C.
Box 46544, Stn. G, Vancouver, B.C., V6R 4G6
(604) 731-5942

In Victoria's grand old Rockland district, two blocks from Government House and Craigdarroch Castle, less than five minutes from ocean beaches, Beaconhill Park, and the center of town. Bedrooms feature Laura Ashley touches and handmade quilts.

Singles: 1 (SB) $50
Doubles: 4 (3 PB; 1 SB) $80-90
Type of Beds: 1 Double; 1 Queen; 3 King
Full Breakfast
Credit Cards: No
Notes: 2, 5, 10, 11, 12

Laird House

All Season B&B Agency
Box 5511, Station B, Victoria, B.C.
Canada V8R 6S4
(604) 595-BEDS

This 1912 heritage-style home is in the peaceful setting of James Bay, just a fifteen minute walk from downtown, the ferries, museum, shopping, and tea rooms.

Doubles: 3 (S2B) $45-65
Full Breakfast
Credit Cards: A, B

Niagara Nook

All Season B&B Agency
Box 5511, Station B, Victoria, B.C.
Canada V8R 6S4
(604) 595-BEDS

NOTES: Credit cards accepted: A Master Card; B Visa; C American Express; D Discover Card; E Diners Club; F Other: 2 Personal checks accepted: 3 Lunch available: 4 Dinner available: 5 Open all year

This nineteenth-century gem is a stone's throw from famous Beacon Hill Park and Mile "O," while beaches just beyond offer grandstand views of ships and seals and those majestic Olympic peaks.

Doubles: 1 (SB) $45-60
Full Breakfast
Credit Cards: A, B

NW B&B #955A

NW Bed & Breakfast Travel Unlimited
610 SW Broadway, Portland, OR, 97205
(503) 243-7616

Elegant, spacious Tudor on 6 acres of attractive grounds on Elk Lake, close to Butchart Gardens. Twenty minutes from the ferry terminal and fifteen minutes from downtown. English hosts particularly enjoy hosting families. One resident dog and three cats; horses on premises.

Suite: 1 (PB) $50-60
Type of Beds: 2 Twin; 2 Double; 1 Crib; 1 Cot
Continental Breakfast
Credit Cards: No

Scholefield House

All Season B&B Agency
Box 5511, Station B, Victoria, B.C.
Canada V8R 6S4
(604) 595-BEDS

This Victorian Italianate, circa 1892, offers the warmth and comforts of home. On a city bus route and located within easy walking distance of the Inner Harbour, U.S. ferries, Royal British Columbia Museum, Antique Row, and restaurants.

Doubles: 4 (S2B) $45-65
Full Breakfast
Credit Cards: A, B

Sea Rose Bed & Breakfast

Town & Country B&B in B.C.
Box 46544, Stn. G, Vancouver, B.C., V6R 4G6
(604) 731-5942

Enjoy the tranquility of the ocean and mountains. Located along Victoria's scenic marine drive, just five minutes by car from downtown.

Doubles: 4 (PB) $76-98
Type of Beds: 2 Twin; 1 Double; 2 Queen
Full Breakfast
Credit Cards: A, B
Notes: 5, 10, 11, 12

WEST VANCOUVER

Beachside Bed & Breakfast

Town & Country B&B in B.C.
Box 46544, Stn. G, Vancouver, B.C., V6R 4G6
(604) 731-5942

Situated at the end of a quiet cul-de-sac, this beautiful home fronts the ocean, with a beach at its doorstep. Share the patio overlooking the seashore, watch the waves wash on the beach and the cruise ships as they make their way to the harbor.

Doubles: 3 (PB) $65-95
Type of Beds: 1 Twin; 3 Queen
Full Breakfast
Credit Cards: A, B
Notes: 5, 10, 11, 12, 13

WHISTLER

Alberta B&B 10

Box 15477, M.P.O., Vancouver
British Columbia, Canada, V6B 5B2
(604) 682-4610

Your French and German hosts offer European hospitality at this chalet. Enjoy the guest sitting room with wood stove or the sun deck with a view of Whistler and Blackcomb Mountains. In summer you can hike, horseback ride, swim, bike, golf, play tennis, go canoeing, fishing, or wind surfing. In winter, ski Whistler and Blackcomb mountains. Ski storage and sauna are available.

Doubles: 6 (PB) $59-85
Type of Beds: 3 Twin; 3 Double
Continental Breakfast
Credit Cards: No
Notes: 2, 8, 9, 10, 11, 12, 13

6 Pets welcome: 7 Smoking allowed: 8 Children welcome: 9 Social drinking allowed: 10 Tennis available: 11 Swimming available: 12 Golf available: 13 Skiing available: 14 May be booked through travel agents

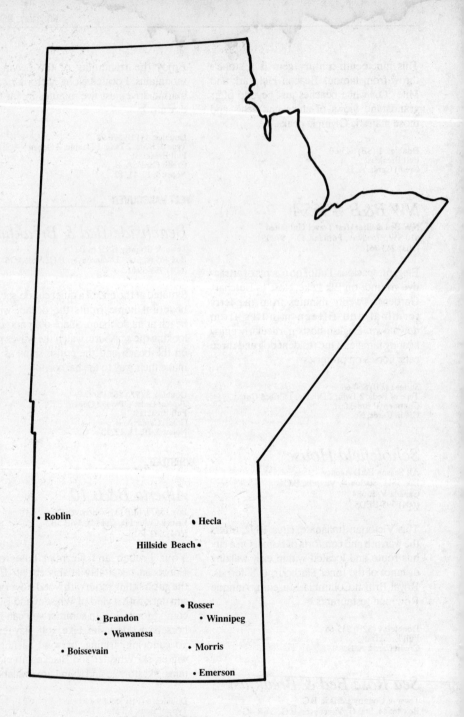

- Roblin

- Hecla

Hillside Beach •

- Rosser
- Brandon   • Winnipeg
- Wawanesa
- Boissevain   • Morris

- Emerson

MANITOBA

Manitoba

BOISSEVAIN

B&B of Manitoba
93 Healy Crescent
Winnipeg, Manitoba, R2N 2S2, Canada
(204) 256-6151

Dueck's Cedar Chalet offers a large, all-cedar bedroom with private in-room Jacuzzi. Close to Turtle Mountain Provincial Park, the International Peace Gardens, good beaches. $50.

B&B of Manitoba
93 Healy Crescent
Winnipeg, Manitoba, R2N 2S2, Canada
(204) 256-6151

The Dycks are close to popular Turtle Derby, good beaches, fishing, and the Turtle Mountains. Come enjoy our country home and hospitality, good home-cooked food, and various farm animals. English, German, and some French spoken. $20-30.

B&B of Manitoba
93 Healy Crescent
Winnipeg, Manitoba, R2N 2S2, Canada
(204) 256-6151

The Neufelds' grain farm offers a quiet retreat in the Turtle Mountain countryside. Close to good beaches, cross-country ski trails, good hunting. $25-35.

BRANDON

B&B of Manitoba
93 Healy Crescent
Winnipeg, Manitoba, R2N 2S2, Canada
(204) 256-6151

Dr. Whidden's Queen Anne Victorian mansion offers Palladian windows, a veranda with enclosed balconies, grand entrance foyer, and a sitting room off two bedrooms. Close to City Centre Mall, Centennial Auditorium, Via Rail, library, and the YMCA. $28-38.

Casa Maley
1605 Victoria Ave., R7A 1C1
(204) 728-0812

A three-story Tudor-style home, built in 1912 with a red brick exterior. The spacious interior is in beautiful quarter-cut golden-oak, with hardwood floors. Two bedrooms feature a fireplace. Casa Maley is located just off the two main roads of Brandon (the second largest city in Manitoba), a multi-cultural city with a genuine, made-on-the-prairies history.

Host: William Shwaluk
Singles: 1 (SB) $30
Doubles: 2 (SB) $40
Type of Beds: 2 Twin; 2 Double
Full Breakfast
Credit Cards: No
Notes: 2, 4, 5, 8, 9, 10, 11, 12, 13

---

6 Pets welcome: 7 Smoking allowed: 8 Children welcome: 9 Social drinking allowed: 10 Tennis available: 11 Swimming available: 12 Golf available: 13 Skiing available: 14 May be booked through travel agents

EMERSON

B&B of Manitoba

93 Healy Crescent
Winnipeg, Manitoba, R2N 2S2, Canada
(204) 256-6151

Tanglewood is a peaceful neighborhood town on the Canada-US border. The 1881 home is located in a country-like setting with flowers and fruit trees on the banks of the Red River. $25-35.

HECLA

B&B of Manitoba

93 Healy Crescent
Winnipeg, Manitoba, R2N 2S2, Canada
(204) 256-6151

The Solmundson Gesta Hus is located on Hecla Island, originally settled by Icelanders over one hundred years ago. The house overlooks Lake Winnipeg and the historic Icelandic village, in the center of some of the finest recreational lands in Manitoba. Bring your fishing equipment, bathing suits, golf clubs, and hiking boots. $49-69.

HILLSIDE BEACH

B&B of Manitoba

93 Healy Crescent
Winnipeg, Manitoba, R2N 2S2, Canada
(204) 256-6151

Located on Lake Winnipeg, in a beautiful resort area. Come for the weekend and cross-country ski, water ski, boat, fish, sun on the beach, go bicycling, or just relax. $30-40.

MORRIS

Deerbank Farm

RR 2, Box 23, R0G 1K0
(204) 746-8395

Our farm is a mixed operation with different crops as well as a variety of livestock. In May and June we host school groups daily, so there is a variety of small animals and poultry for children to see and pet. In the Red River Valley: a flat, grain-growing area. July features the Manitoba Stampede and Exhibition. One hour from Winnipeg. One dog in residence.

Hosts: Kathleen & Ed Jorgenson
Doubles: 3 (SB) $35 (Canadian)
Type of Beds: 3 Double
Full Breakfast
Credit Cards: No
Closed Christmas & Easter
Notes: 2, 4 (with advance notice), 6, 7, 8, 9, 10, 11, 12, 13

ROBLIN

B&B of Manitoba

93 Healy Crescent
Winnipeg, Manitoba, R2N 2S2, Canada
(204) 256-6151

Relax on the huge deck or in the luxurious sitting lounge overlooking beautiful Shell Valley. Enjoy our games room, swimming, hiking, cross-country skiing, fishing, and sightseeing. A hunter's and honeymooners' paradise. Try our homemade German sausage! $28-38.

ROSSER

B&B of Manitoba

93 Healy Crescent
Winnipeg, Manitoba, R2N 2S2, Canada
(204) 256-6151

Families are welcome to enjoy our peaceful country home and warm hospitality. Spacious outdoor area for children, delicious home-baked buns. Quick access to the airport, Assiniboia Downs Racetrack, Birds Hill Park. $20-28.

NOTES: Credit cards accepted: A Master Card; B Visa; C American Express; D Discover Card; E Diners Club; F Other: 2 Personal checks accepted: 3 Lunch available: 4 Dinner available: 5 Open all year

WAWANESA

B&B of Manitoba
93 Healy Crescent
Winnipeg, Manitoba, R2N 2S2, Canada
(204) 256-6151

Spruce Shadows Farm is in a beautiful area near the junction of the Souris and Assiniboine rivers. Relax in our beautifully landscaped backyard with a patio, sun deck, fire pit, and childrens' play area. Delicious home-cooked meals. $25-35.

WINNIPEG

B&B of Manitoba #1
93 Healy Crescent
Winnipeg, Manitoba, R2N 2S2, Canada
(204) 256-6151

A luxurious home just off the north bypass. Enjoy warm Canadian hospitality and our delicious muffins. Quick access to Birds Hill Park, popular beaches, Rainbow Stage, Kildonan Park, Kildonan Place Mall. $25-35.

B&B of Manitoba #2
93 Healy Crescent
Winnipeg, Manitoba, R2N 2S2, Canada
(204) 256-6151

Enjoy our modern home and large, shaded lot, or take a walk in Fraser Grove Park on the Red River. Excellent bus service, restaurants, and shopping. $25-32.

B&B of Manitoba #3
93 Healy Crescent
Winnipeg, Manitoba, R2N 2S2, Canada
(204) 256-6151

Warm hospitality at its best! Enjoy mint tea, choice music, and intelligent conversation in the Old English decor of warm wood, burnished brass, leaded glass, and live greenery. Close to Polo Park and Portage Place malls, Folkorama, arena, and stadium. On express bus route. $24-34.

B&B of Manitoba #4
93 Healy Crescent
Winnipeg, Manitoba, R2N 2S2, Canada
(204) 256-6151

Enjoy the relaxing atmosphere of this unique house, built in 1900. Adjacent to the guest bedroom is a sitting room; can accommodate a family of four. Lunch and dinner available on request. $25-35.

B&B of Manitoba #5
93 Healy Crescent
Winnipeg, Manitoba, R2N 2S2, Canada
(204) 256-6151

Come and enjoy our lovely colonial home, evening tea, and quiet walks in St. Johns Park or along the Red River. Seven Oaks Museum, Rainbow Stage, Planetarium, and the Concert Hall are nearby. $25-35.

B&B of Manitoba #6
93 Healy Crescent
Winnipeg, Manitoba, R2N 2S2, Canada
(204) 256-6151

A lovely two-story home (1911) in a quiet treed neighborhood. Go for a relaxing evening walk to the banks of the Red River. Within walking distance of downtown. $25-34.

B&B of Manitoba #7
93 Healy Crescent
Winnipeg, Manitoba, R2N 2S2, Canada
(204) 256-6151

A unique, beautifully preserved English home in a prestigious neighborhood. Enjoy warm hospitality over a cup of tea in our cozy sun room or on the veranda. $25-35.

6 Pets welcome: 7 Smoking allowed: 8 Children welcome: 9 Social drinking allowed: 10 Tennis available: 11 Swimming available: 12 Golf available: 13 Skiing available: 14 May be booked through travel agents

B&B of Manitoba #8

93 Healy Crescent
Winnipeg, Manitoba, R2N 2S2, Canada
(204) 256-6151

Located in a nice community setting close to
the Trans-Canada Highway and local attractions. Your hostess loves crafts and needlework hobbies. $22-30.

B&B of Manitoba #9

93 Healy Crescent
Winnipeg, Manitoba, R2N 2S2, Canada
(204) 256-6151

English, German, and French are all spoken
here. Located on the banks of the historic
Red River, this beautiful Tudor home has
an English garden in the backyard and a
riverbank walkway. Dinners are available at
additional charge. $39-59.

B&B of Manitoba #10

93 Healy Crescent
Winnipeg, Manitoba, R2N 2S2, Canada
(204) 256-6151

Relax in our family den, enjoy a hearty full
breakfast in a unique Ukrainian home. Located downtown close to the bus route, the
house has good access to the airport, Via
Rail, Polo Park, museums, concerts, and
theater. $25-35.

B&B of Manitoba #11

93 Healy Crescent
Winnipeg, Manitoba, R2N 2S2, Canada
(204) 256-6151

Located in a quiet residential area with a
very private yard for sunbathing. Private
kitchen available. Close to two public swimming pool, racing, shopping, and museums.
Children are welcome. $24-32.

B&B of Manitoba #12

93 Healy Crescent
Winnipeg, Manitoba, R2N 2S2, Canada
(204) 256-6151

Your hosts here speak English and German
and are interested in antiques. Home
baking, fresh strawberries and raspberries in
season. Relax with tea on the deck. Within
walking distance of a park for cycling, cross-
country skiing. $25-32.

B&B of Manitoba #13

93 Healy Crescent
Winnipeg, Manitoba, R2N 2S2, Canada
(204) 256-6151

Enjoy this spacious four-level split home
with spacious bedrooms, located on .5 acre
of landscaped hardens and lawns. Within
walking distance of shopping, parks, and
good restaurants. English, French, and
Polish spoken. $25-32.

B&B of Manitoba #14

93 Healy Crescent
Winnipeg, Manitoba, R2N 2S2, Canada
(204) 256-6151

This spacious modern home is next to the
Assiniboine River. It has a screened porch,
large backyard in a country-like setting.
Near parks, hiking, bird watching, and cross-
country skiing. $25-35.

B&B of Manitoba #15

93 Healy Crescent
Winnipeg, Manitoba, R2N 2S2, Canada
(204) 256-6151

Enjoy a pleasant stay in this very attractive,
quiet home in the prestigious River Heights
area. Relax in the lovely backyard or in the
privacy of the family room. Near parks, the
zoo, malls, and downtown. $25-35.

NOTES: Credit cards accepted: A Master Card; B Visa; C American Express; D Discover Card; E Diners
Club; F Other: 2 Personal checks accepted: 3 Lunch available: 4 Dinner available: 5 Open all year

B&B of Manitoba #16

93 Healy Crescent
Winnipeg, Manitoba, R2N 2S2, Canada
(204) 256-6151

This wheel-chair accessible home is only .5 mile from the Perimeter Highway, an ideal location for tourists not enjoying city driving. Close to parks, the mint, museum. Excellent bus route. $20-28.

B&B of Manitoba #17

93 Healy Crescent
Winnipeg, Manitoba, R2N 2S2, Canada
(204) 256-6151

Enjoy the relaxed atmosphere of this cozy home on a quiet street off the express bus route. Quick access to malls, downtown, airport, bus depot. $22-30.

B&B of Manitoba #18

93 Healy Crescent
Winnipeg, Manitoba, R2N 2S2, Canada
(204) 256-6151

This Tudor home was designed by the owner. All oak trim, eighteen-foot family-room ceiling, second-floor den overlooking the family room. English, Ukrainian, and French are spoken here. $25-38.

B&B of Manitoba #19

93 Healy Crescent
Winnipeg, Manitoba, R2N 2S2, Canada
(204) 256-6151

Quiet, comfortable, relaxing! Enjoy interesting conversation with your well-traveled hosts. Convenient location on three bus routes; close to legislative buildings, downtown commercial area, art gallery, hospital, museum, and zoo. $22-32.

B&B of Manitoba #20

93 Healy Crescent
Winnipeg, Manitoba, R2N 2S2, Canada
(204) 256-6151

A spacious, quiet home on the banks of the Assiniboine River. Enjoy a lovely evening walk, bird watching, tennis, games room. Close to the racetrack, parks, mall, winter cross-country skiing. $25-35.

B&B of Manitoba #21

93 Healy Crescent
Winnipeg, Manitoba, R2N 2S2, Canada
(204) 256-6151

Very private facilities can accommodate a family of four in this luxurious home in a prestigious area. Children are welcome. Quick access to the Trans-Canada Highway, mall, race track, and swimming pool. $25-35.

B&B of Manitoba #22

93 Healy Crescent
Winnipeg, Manitoba, R2N 2S2, Canada
(204) 256-6151

Enjoy warm hospitality and quiet relaxation on our screened porch. Can accommodate a family of five; English and German are spoken here. Close to express bus route, mall, race track, good restaurants. $24-32.

B&B of Manitoba #23

93 Healy Crescent
Winnipeg, Manitoba, R2N 2S2, Canada
(204) 256-6151

Our well-kept home is located in the prestigious River Heights area. Guest sitting room with TV and coffee and tea making facilities. The queen bedroom has an adjoining powder room. Ten minutes from downtown and a shopping center; five minutes from Assiniboine Park and Zoo. $25-36.

6 Pets welcome: 7 Smoking allowed: 8 Children welcome: 9 Social drinking allowed: 10 Tennis available: 11 Swimming available: 12 Golf available: 13 Skiing available: 14 May be booked through travel agents

B&B of Manitoba #24

93 Healy Crescent
Winnipeg, Manitoba, R2N 2S2, Canada
(204) 256-6151

We live in a condominium in a beautifully
treed downtown area within walking distance of Osborne Village and the legislative
buildings. Relax on our balcony or go for a
swim in our sun-roof pool. $24-32.

B&B of Manitoba #25

93 Healy Crescent
Winnipeg, Manitoba, R2N 2S2, Canada
(204) 256-6151

Located in a quiet residential area. Come
and enjoy our relaxing atmosphere. TV sit-

ting room available. Easy access to main city
route and highways. Close to Crescent Park
on the historic Red River, University of
Manitoba, good restaurants and shopping.
$24-40.

B&B of Manitoba #26

93 Healy Crescent
Winnipeg, Manitoba, R2N 2S2, Canada
(204) 256-6151

Located in an attractive, quiet neighborhood with quick access to the airport. Close
to Grace Hospital, museum, restaurants,
public swimming pools. $25-35.

New Brunswick

GRAND MANAN ISLAND

Shorecrest Lodge
North Head, E0G 2M0
(506) 662-3216

A charming country inn overlooking the sea. We cater to nature lovers on an island blessed with an abundance of birds, whales, and wild flowers. Grand Manan has a reputation as the best natural-history destination in Maritime Canada. Whale watching arranged.

Hosts: Gillian Malins & Frank Longstaff
Singles: 3 (SB) $45
Doubles: 12 (1 PB; 11 SB) $65
Type of Beds: 10 Twin; 10 Double
Continental Breakfast
Credit Cards: A, B
Closed mid Oct.-mid May
Notes: 4, 7, 8, 9, 10, 11, 12

LOWER JEMSEG

Oakley House
E0E 1S0
(506) 488-3113; FAX: (506) 488-2785

Enjoy a warm stay in a graciously rebuilt home in the peaceful lower Saint John River valley. Organic food; eclectic library; music; canoeing, swimming, bird watching. The area is rich in loyalist history. We also have a lovely fully furnished suite available by the week. French and Spanish spoken. No smoking.

Hosts: Max M. & Willi Evans Wolfe
Singles: 2 (SB) $27(Can)
Doubles: 1 (SB) $45(Can)
Type of Beds: 4 Twin; 2 Double
Full Breakfast

Credit Cards: B
Notes: 2, 5, 9, 11, 13

PLASTER ROCK

Northern Wilderness Lodge
Box 571, E0J 1W0
(506) 356-8327

Stay as little or as long as you want while enjoying our lounge with satellite TV and fireplace, our game room, or the cross-country ski and snow-mobile trails — which become great walking trails during the summer. We serve buffet style breakfast, lunch and dinner.

Hosts: Sheila and Bill Linton
Singles: 3 (PB) $44.40 (Canadian)
Doubles: 10 (PB) $49.95 (Canadian)
Continental Breakfast
Credit Cards: A, B, C
Notes: 3, 4, 5, 6, 7, 8, 9, 10, 11, 12, 13

ST. ANDREW'S

Pansy Patch
59 Carleton Street, E0G 2X0
(506) 529-3834

Our unique home is a combination bookshop, antique store, and bed and breakfast. All rooms are furnished in lovely antiques and overlook the Bay of Fundy. Our breakfasts are prepared with imagination: French toast, waffles, pancakes, quiche. We cater to special diets and try to help our guests truly enjoy the beauty of our area.

Hosts: Kathleen & Michael Lazare
Doubles: 4 (SB) $66.60-72.15 (Canadian)
Type of Beds: 2 Twin; 3 Double

6 Pets welcome: 7 Smoking allowed: 8 Children welcome: 9 Social drinking allowed: 10 Tennis available: 11 Swimming available: 12 Golf available: 13 Skiing available: 14 May be booked through travel agents

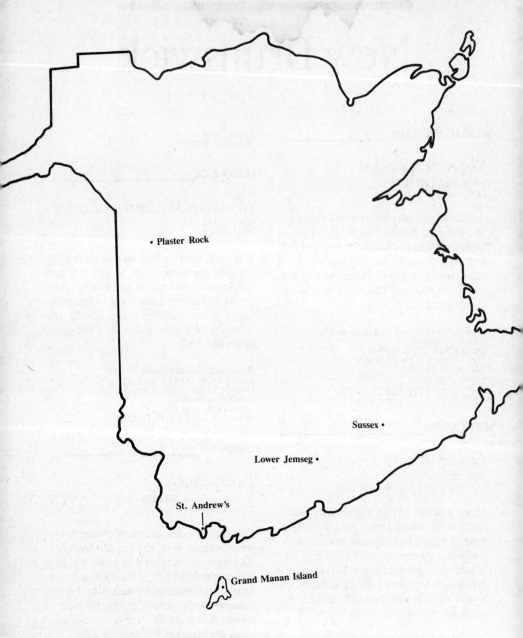

- Plaster Rock

Sussex •

Lower Jemseg •

St. Andrew's

Grand Manan Island

NEW BRUNSWICK

Full Breakfast
Credit Cards: A, B, C
Closed Oct. 1-April 30
Notes: 2, 4, 6, 7, 8 (over 6), 9, 10, 11, 12

SUSSEX

Anderson Country Vacation Farm

RR 2, E0E 1P0
(506) 433-3786

A working farm of 200 acres with sheep and beef cattle, a wide variety of fowl, colorful pheasants and peacocks, wild Canadian geese, swans, ducks, donkey, goat, and friendly dog. Pond stocked with native trout and nature trail on premises. Fundy National Park is one hour away, as are the reversing falls at Saint John and the magnetic hill at Moncton.

Hosts: Tom & Laura Anderson
Doubles: 3 (SB) $25-30
Type of Beds: 2 Twin; 1 Double
Full Breakfast
Credit Cards: No
Notes: 5, 8, 11, 12

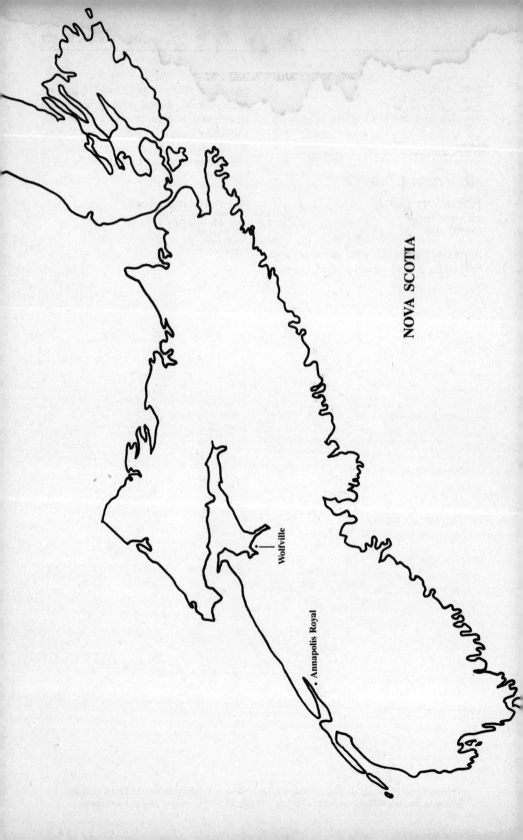

NOVA SCOTIA

Wolfville

Annapolis Royal

Nova Scotia

ANNAPOLIS ROYAL

Garrison House Inn

350 St. George Street, B0S 1A0
(902) 532-5750

An historic 1854 roadside inn located opposite Fort Anne in the heart of Annapolis
Royal, Canada's oldest town (1605). Our
three intimate dining rooms offer fresh local
fare from the sea and the fertile Annapolis
Valley, served and prepared with verve and
imagination to our guests and the traveling
public.

Host: Patrick Redgrave
Doubles: 7 (5 PB; 2 SB) $35-125
Continental Breakfast
Credit Cards: A, B, C
Notes: 3, 4, 7, 8, 9, 10, 11, 12, 13

WOLFVILLE

Blomidon Inn

127 Main Street, Box 839, B0P 1X0
(902) 542-2291

Offering the gracious comforts of a
nineteenth-century sea captain's mansion,
with a reputation for elegant accommodations and hospitable country cuisine — a

reputation that extends far beyond the
province of Nova Scotia.

Hosts: Jim & Donna Laceby
Doubles: 27 (25 PB; 2 SB) $42.90-97.90
Type of Beds: 9 Twin; 18 Double; 3 Queen; 2 3/4
Continental Breakfast
Credit Cards: A, B, C, F
Notes: 3, 4, 5, 7, 8, 9, 10, 11, 12, 13, 14

Victoria's Historic Inn

416 Main Street, Box 819, B0P 1X0
(902) 542-5744

This fine Victorian home and restaurant
featuring Cajun food is a true tribute to the
craftsmanship of the late nineteenth century, with its gingerbread verandas, sheltered entries, and ornamented eaves.
Walking distance to Acadia University, Randall House Museum, Mermaid Puppet
Theatre. Minutes from Grand Pre National
Park, Bay of Fundy fishing villages.

Hosts: Ron & Doreen Cook
Singles: 2(1 PB; 1 SB) $38.50-53.90
Doubles: 13 (7 PB; 6 SB) $53.90-75.90
Type of Beds: 6 Twin; 10 Double; 2 Queen; 1 King
Full Breakfast
Credit Cards: A, B, C
Closed Jan.-April 15
Notes: 4, 7, 8, 9, 10, 11, 12

6 Pets welcome: 7 Smoking allowed: 8 Children welcome: 9 Social drinking allowed: 10 Tennis available: 11
Swimming available: 12 Golf available: 13 Skiing available: 14 May be booked through travel agents

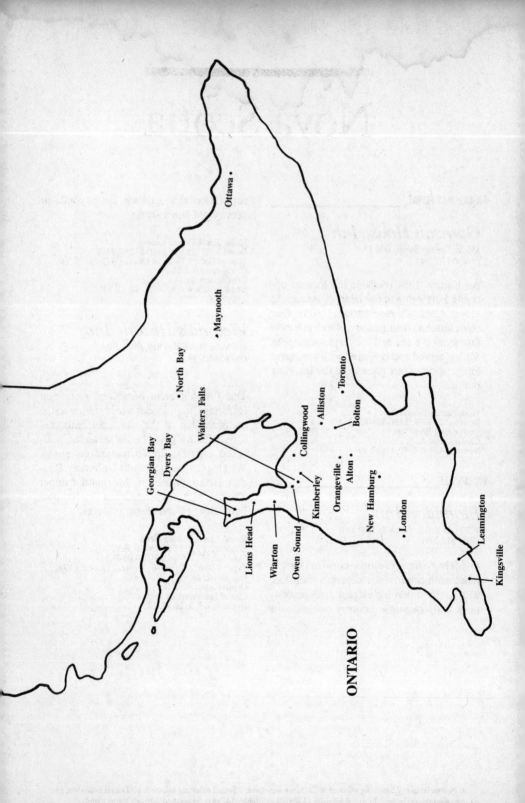

Ottawa •

• Maynooth

• North Bay

Walters Falls

Georgian Bay
Dyers Bay

Collingwood •
• Alliston
• Toronto
Bolton

Kimberley •
Orangeville •
Alton •
New Hamburg

Lions Head
Wiarton
Owen Sound

• London

Leamington

Kingsville

ONTARIO

Ontario

Country Host #5

R.R. #1, Palgrave, Ontario
L0N 1P0, Canada
(519) 941-7633

Fintona, meaning "beautiful green place," is
the Irish name of this 1874 restored
farmhouse on 197 acres between Alliston
and Shelburne, south of Highway 89. It
boasts a landing field for private planes and
a fine collection of antiques in the house.
Hosts will transport hikers to and from the
Bruce Trail; excellent skiing and craft shops
nearby. Resident cat.

Doubles: 2 (1 PB; 1 SB) $35-50
Type of Beds: 2 Double
Full Breakfast
Credit Cards: No
Closed Dec. 25, 26, Jan. 1
Notes: 3, 5, 7, 9, 10, 11, 12, 13

ALTON

Cataract Inn

RR 2, L0N 1A0
(519) 927-5779

Cataract Inn is surrounded by a country
playground of unparalleled scenery. We
have three unique dining rooms, and
whether you choose the warmth of the
fireside room, the charm of the floral room,
or the comfort of our lounge chairs, Cataract
Inn makes dining a pleasure.

Hosts: Rodney & Jennifer Hough, Alice Smith
Singles: 2 (S2B) $70-113
Doubles: 4 (S2B) $70-113
Type of Beds: 4 Twin; 4 Double
Continental Breakfast
Minimum stay weekends & holidays: 2

Credit Cards: A, B, C
Closed Christmas
Notes: 3, 4, 8 (over 5), 11, 12, 13

BOLTON

Country Host #1

R.R. #1, Palgrave, Ontario
L0N 1P0, Canada
(519) 941-7633

This heavily wooded property of 11 acres is
less than an hour's drive from Toronto off
Highway 50 north of Bolton. The architect-
designed house has a greenhouse, and there
is a view from every window. A circular staircase leads to the main floor with a sun room
overlooking the pond. Nearby conservation
areas have year-round activities; horse
shows spring and fall; good dining nearby.
Children welcome.

Doubles: 3 (2 PB; 1 SB) $35-50
Type of Beds: 4 Twin; 1 Queen
Full Breakfast
Credit Cards: No
Notes: 3, 5, 7 (restricted), 8, 9, 10, 11, 12, 13

Country Host #2

R.R. #1, Palgrave, Ontario
L0N 1P0, Canada
(519) 941-7633

This 1888 restored Victorian brick
farmhouse with a pool on 7 acres is forty-five
minutes north of Toronto, off Highway 50
northwest of Bolton. Plank flooring and antiques throughout. Close to conservation
areas with year-round activities; horse shows
spring and fall; good dining. Half an hour
from Canada's Wonderland. Friendly resident dog.

6 Pets welcome: 7 Smoking allowed: 8 Children welcome: 9 Social drinking allowed: 10 Tennis available: 11
Swimming available: 12 Golf available: 13 Skiing available: 14 May be booked through travel agents

Doubles: 3 (SB) $35-50
Type of Beds: 1 Twin; 1 Double; 1 Queen
Full Breakfast
Credit Cards: No
Notes: 3, 4, 5, 7 (restricted), 8 (over 12), 9, 10, 11, 12, 13

COLLINGWOOD

Country Host #6

R.R. #1, Palgrave, Ontario
L0N 1P0, Canada
(519) 941-7633

This 1857 brick mansion is on 5 acres and offers a self-contained apartment in one wing. Georgian Bay and the ski slopes are less than a half hour away, and the Bruce Trail is much closer. Guests enjoy gleaming pine floors, sweeping spiral staircases, sparkling chandeliers and antiques in the main house, with its friendly dogs. Private entrance to the apartment. English and French are spoken here. Fishing in three rivers, swimming at Wasaga Beach, sleigh rides, and sports are nearby.

Doubles: 2 (1 PB; 1 SB) $35-50
Full Breakfast
Credit Cards: No
Closed Dec. 25, 26, Jan. 1
Notes: 5, 8, 9, 10, 11, 12, 13

Country Host #7

R.R. #1, Palgrave, Ontario
L0N 1P0, Canada
(519) 941-7633

The Old Poplar Country Inn, circa 1867, is close to Collingwood and Georgian Bay. It has a private, self-contained apartment available with its own entrance. Close to all attractions and the ski hills of Blue Mountain.

Doubles: 1 (PB) $35-50
Type of Beds: 1 Queen
Full Breakfast
Credit Cards: No
Notes: 5, 7, 8, 9, 10, 11, 12, 13

Country Host #8

R.R. #1, Palgrave, Ontario
L0N 1P0, Canada
(519) 941-7633

Wildgoose Landing is a turn-of-the-century brick farmhouse on 240 acres a half hour south of Collingwood and Georgian Bay. Hiking trails, downhill and cross-country skiing, snowmobiling. Resident dog and cat.

Doubles: 2 (SB) $35-50
Type of Beds: 2 Double
Full Breakfast
Credit Cards: No
Closed Dec. 25, 26, Jan. 1
Notes: 5, 8, 9, 10, 11, 12, 13

Country Host #9

R.R. #1, Palgrave, Ontario
L0N 1P0, Canada
(519) 941-7633

This modern house on Highway 24 near Collingwood is open in the winter only, to cater to skiers, snowmobilers, and ice fishermen. It's a cozy home with acreage outside Nottawa. Open Nov. 1 - April 1.

Doubles: 1 (SB) $35-50
Type of Beds: 1 Double
Full Breakfast
Credit Cards: No
Closed April 1 - Oct. 31
Notes: 7, 9, 13

Country Host #10

R.R. #1, Palgrave, Ontario
L0N 1P0, Canada
(519) 941-7633

Your Dutch hostess welcomes you to this spotless home on 25 acres, located five minutes from the ski area north of Collingwood, with its four-season activities. Close to the world-famous Bruce Trail for hikers, birders, and nature lovers; near Beaver River for fishing, and Georgian Bay for swimming and boating. Resident friendly dog.

NOTES: Credit cards accepted: A Master Card; B Visa; C American Express; D Discover Card; E Diners Club; F Other: 2 Personal checks accepted: 3 Lunch available: 4 Dinner available: 5 Open all year

Doubles: 3 (1 PB; 2 SB) $35-50
Type of Beds: 1 Twin; 1 Full; 1 Queen
Full Breakfast
Credit Cards: No
Notes: 3, 5, 7 (restricted), 8, 9, 10, 11, 12, 13

DYERS BAY

Country Host #20

R.R. #1, Palgrave, Ontario
L0N 1P0, Canada
(519) 941-7633

Original Irish settlers built this pre-1900 log house on 25 acres up in Bruce County near Dyers Bay. Subsequent owners have added wings to accommodate growing families, and your host has added antiques. This comfortable home is close to the most challenging part of the Bruce Trail for hikers, and half an hour from Tobermory, with its attractions. Winter weekend specials for cross-country skiers, snow mobilers, and city folk needing to relax (all meals available then). One friendly resident poodle.

Doubles: 3 (SB) $35-50
Type of Beds: 1 Twin; 2 Double
Full Breakfast
Credit Cards: No
Notes: 3, 4, 5, 7, 8, 9, 13

Country Host #21

R.R. #1, Palgrave, Ontario
L0N 1P0, Canada
(519) 941-7633

High on the bluffs near Dyers Bay in the Bruce Peninsula, with a magnificent view of Georgian Bay, is this traditional home with flowers galore. The Mennonite owners built this home themselves. The entire upper floor with full-length balcony is one room for families, and all meals are available if requested when making reservations. Main-floor accommodation is also available. Close to the Bruce Trail, swimming, boating.

Doubles: 2 (1 PB; 1 SB) $35-50
Full Breakfast
Credit Cards: No

Closed holy days
Notes: 3, 4, 8, 11, 13

GEORGIAN BAY

Country Host #11

R.R. #1, Palgrave, Ontario
L0N 1P0, Canada
(519) 941-7633

A turn-of-the-century brick farmhouse on 100 acres, with the Niagara Escarpment and Bruce Trail running through the bush and meadows for hikers and nature lovers. Located northwest of Collingwood on Georgian Bay, with its four-season activities. All meals available if requested in advance.

Doubles: 3 (SB) $35-50
Type of Beds: 1 Twin; 2 Double
Full Breakfast
Credit Cards: No
Closed Dec. 1 - March 15
Notes: 3, 4, 6, 7 (restricted), 8, 9, 10, 11, 12, 13

KIMBERLEY

Country Host #12

R.R. #1, Palgrave, Ontario
L0N 1P0, Canada
(519) 941-7633

A spacious bungalow with inground pool in the beautiful Beaver Valley at Kimberley. The Niagara Escarpment runs on both sides of the valley, with its Bruce Trail for hikers, birders, camera buffs, and naturalists. The Beaver River is close for fishing, and good restaurants for dining. Cross-country and downhill skiing nearby at Talisman.

Doubles: 4 (SB) $35-50
Type of Beds: 2 Twin; 2 Double
Full Breakfast
Credit Cards: No
Closed Dec. 25, 26, Jan. 1
Notes: 3, 5, 7 (restricted), 8, 9, 10, 11, 12, 13

Country Host #13

R.R. #1, Palgrave, Ontario
L0N 1P0, Canada
(519) 941-7633

6 Pets welcome: 7 Smoking allowed: 8 Children welcome: 9 Social drinking allowed: 10 Tennis available: 11 Swimming available: 12 Golf available: 13 Skiing available: 14 May be booked through travel agents

An 1881 inn with eight rooms where stage coaches used to stop now accommodates up to seventeen people. Located south of Kinberley in the lovely Beaver Valley, three miles from the challenging Bruce Trail, which can be walked nine months of the year. Bicyclists find its meandering gravel roads perfect. Good skiing and all summer activities nearby.

Doubles: 8 (SB) $35-50
Type of Beds: 1 Twin; 8 Double
Full Breakfast
Credit Cards: No
Notes: 3, 4, 5, 7, 8, 9, 10, 11, 12, 13

KINGSVILLE

Country Host #25

R.R. #1, Palgrave, Ontario
L0N 1P0, Canada
(519) 941-7633

Outside Kingsville on Lake Erie, this is a self-contained, heated and air-conditioned cottage accommodating four to five people. Available from September to June only. In an excellent location for watching bird migrations spring and fall, plus the Monarch butterflies in September and October. Woods and canal nearby; fishing and relaxing. Kingsville is a five- to seven-minute drive, and Point Plee National Park is about half an hour.

Doubles: 2 (SB) $35-50
Type of Beds: 2 Double
Full Breakfast
Credit Cards: No
Closed July & Aug.
Notes: 3, 6, 7, 8, 9, 10, 11, 12, 13

Country Host #26

R.R. #1, Palgrave, Ontario
L0N 1P0, Canada
(519) 941-7633

Outside Kingsville on Lake Erie, this is an efficiency apartment for two facing the lake. Heated. Available year-round for birders,

artists, naturalists, and quiet folk who like to relax.

Doubles: 1 (1 PB) $35-50
Type of Beds: 1 Double
Full Breakfast
Credit Cards: No
Notes: 3, 5, 6, 7, 8, 9, 10, 11, 12, 13

Country Host #27

R.R. #1, Palgrave, Ontario
L0N 1P0, Canada
(519) 941-7633

In Kingsville, home of the famous Pelee Island Wines, this air-conditioned, turn-of-the-century home is available from April to September for bird watchers and the Monarch butterfly migration. An outside barbeque and microwave are available to guests who want to prepare their own dinners. A short drive takes you to Jack Miner's bird sanctuary, Colisanti's tropical gardens, crafts, and shops.

Doubles: 3 (SB) $35-50
Type of Beds: 1 Double; 2 Queen
Full Breakfast
Credit Cards: No
Closed Sept. 1 - April 1
Notes: 7, 8, 9, 10, 11, 12, 13

LEAMINGTON

Country Host #23

R.R. #1, Palgrave, Ontario
L0N 1P0, Canada
(519) 941-7633

In Leamington, on Lake Erie, thirty-five miles from the US/Canada border. This architect-designed brick home has large rooms and air-conditioning. It is a favorite of bird watchers who flock to nearby Point Pelee National Park for North America's most spectacular bird migrations spring and fall, as well as the Monarch butterfly migration in September. Open year-round, Leamington's shops and surrounding areas have many attractions.

NOTES: Credit cards accepted: A Master Card; B Visa; C American Express; D Discover Card; E Diners Club; F Other: 2 Personal checks accepted: 3 Lunch available: 4 Dinner available: 5 Open all year

London, ONT 865

Doubles: 2 (PB) $35-50
Type of Beds: 2 Queen
Full Breakfast
Credit Cards: No
Closed Dec. 25, 26, Jan. 1
Notes: 5, 8, 10, 11, 12, 13

Country Host #24

R.R. #1, Palgrave, Ontario
L0N 1P0, Canada
(519) 941-7633

On the outskirts of Leamington on Lake
Erie, this home is available Oct. 15 - Dec. 15
and April 1 - July 1. This two-story brick
home with air-conditioning caters mainly to
bird watchers. Point Plee National Park is
only a five-minute drive away, and Hillman
Marsh is not far.

Doubles: 2 (SB) $35-50
Type of Beds: 2 Double
Full Breakfast
Credit Cards: No
Closed July 1 - Oct. 15; Dec. 15 - April 1
Notes: 3, 7, 8, 9, 10, 11, 12, 13

LIONS HEAD

Country Host #19

R.R. #1, Palgrave, Ontario
L0N 1P0, Canada
(519) 941-7633

An original settler's log farmhouse on 100
acres north of Lions Head in Bruce County,
this house has been extended and tastefully
furnished with antiques. The property is a
naturalist's paradise, with 23 wetlands, 7
rock ridges, wildlife, birds, and rare orchids.
Tobermory, at the tip of the Bruce Peninsula, is thirty minutes away.

Doubles: 3 (1 PB; 2 SB) $35-50
Type of Beds: 1 Twin; 3 Double
Full Breakfast
Credit Cards: No
Notes: 5, 6, 7, 8, 9, 11, 13

LONDON

Annigan's

194 Elmwood Avenue E., N6C 1K2
(519) 439-9196

Owned by an interior designer, this turn-of-
the-century house features a turret,
fireplace, and fine architectural details. Two
double and one twin rooms; full bath, powder room, smoking lounge. Downtown,
Grand Theatre, U.W.O. bus routes, and antique stores are close by. Adults preferred.
Master Card accepted. $30-45.

Christophe House

398 Piccadilly Street, N6A 1S7
(519) 673-6878

For the warmth and charm of yesterday,
come visit us at Christophe House. Built in
1895, maintained in period style, and furnished with fine Canadiana. Located in
central core, within walking distance of
theater, restaurants, shopping. Suite with
whirlpool available. $39-49.

Corsaut

RR 3, Ilderton, N0M 2A0
(519) 666-1876

Quiet, tree-shaded farm located just six
miles north of London offers two attractive
rooms, one with double bed and one with a
single. Guests may enjoy the ponies and see
our antique John Deere tractors. Nonsmokers preferred. Air-conditioned. $25-
30.

Cozy Corners

87 Askin Street, N6C 1E5
(519) 673-4598

Our 1871 Victorian home is in the core area of London. We have lovingly restored it to maintain the warm glow of wood and stained glass. Three bedrooms, kitchenette, and bath. English and French spoken. Full breakfast is served between 7:30-9:00 only. $30-38. Children under 10: $10.

Dillon's Place

56 Gerrard Street, N6C 4C7
(519) 439-9666

Air-conditioned old home in South London has comfortable people and a large, friendly Labrador. Guest rooms with double or twin beds and bath nearby. Very close to downtown, Wellington Road, Victoria Hospital, and bus service. Nonsmoking adults preferred. $20-30.

Eileen's

433 Hyde Park Road, N6H 3R9
(519) 471-1107

Comfortable Cape Cod home on an acre of land with trees. One double, one twin, and one single bedroom. Five minutes to Thames Valley golf course and Springbank Park. Ten minutes to downtown, theaters, shopping and U.W.O. Bus service. Lots of parking; use of swimming pool; central air-conditioning. $25-40.

Ferndale West

53 Longbow Road, N6G 1Y5
(519) 471-8038

Ferndale West offers central air, extra-large rooms, two with queen beds, one of which is a two-room suite; other is a twin. Very close to the university, cross-country skiing, and there is a nature walk at the end of the street. Use of swimming pool. $30-50.

Hindhope

RR 2, Lucan, N0M 2J0
(519) 227-4514

Century-old country home twenty minutes from London on Highway 7. Thirty-minute drive to Lake Huron and Grand Bend. Children and pets welcome; no smoking in bedrooms. Additional meals on request. $25-30.

Johnson B&B

308 Princess Avenue, N6B 2A6
(519) 672-2394

Lovely old home offering a room with double beds and nearby bath. Also a suite of rooms with private bath and kitchenette. Nonsmokers, please. $30-40.

Koch B&B

250 Epworth Avenue, N6A 2M1
(519) 434-4045

Share an artist's home of white-washed walls and old beams in London North with air-conditioning, patio, fireplace. Within walking distance of U.W.O., University and St. Joseph's Hospitals. Five minutes to downtown. Sorry, no small children. English, Spanish, Italian, French, and Polish spoken. $25-38.

Lambert House

231 Cathcart Street, N6C 3M8
(519) 672-8996 (after 6:00 P.M.)

Quiet turn-of-the-century home in the heart of Old South London. Close to downtown, parks, golf, and six antique shops. Guests are served welcome snacks. Afternoon tea and champagne with breakfast on weekends. No pets; adults preferred. $30-40.

NOTES: Credit cards accepted: A Master Card; B Visa; C American Express; D Discover Card; E Diners Club; F Other: 2 Personal checks accepted: 3 Lunch available: 4 Dinner available: 5 Open all year

McLellan Place
880 Farnham Road, N6K 1R9
(519) 473-3709
Lovely tri-level home with air-conditioning, three bedrooms, two baths. Breakfast in formal dining room or on the back patio. Near Westmount shopping mall, Wally World, mini-golf. No smoking. Visa and Mastercard accepted. $25-45.

Overdale
2 Normandy Gardens, N6H 4A9
(519) 641-0236

Air-conditioned home in mature, residential West London. Near parks and golf courses; easily accessible to U.W.O. and downtown. Guest floor has three bedrooms with full bath. Separate suite with bath and kitchen. Twin, double, or king beds. Only open April 1 - Dec. 31. $30-48.

Rolling Ridge Farm
RR 1, Arva, N0M 1C0
(519) 666-0896

Unwind in our big old country home ten miles northwest of London and five miles west of Arva. Two double bedrooms, one with a private bath. See our maple-syrup making and products. Use of swimming pool; hayloft fun. No pets. $25-35.

Rose's Bed & Breakfast
526 Dufferin Avenue, N6B 2A2
(519) 433-9978

Welcome to London's finest B&B home, located in a quiet, exclusive residential area of century-old homes in the downtown area. London is midway between Detroit and Toronto and is a theatre, recreational, and shopping center for southwest Ontario.

Hosts: Betty & Doug Rose
Doubles: 3 (1 PB; 2 SB) $30-40

Type of Beds: 1 Twin; 2 Double
Full Breakfast
Credit Cards: No
Notes: 5, 9, 10, 11, 12, 13

Searchover Farm
RR 1, Denfield, N0M 1O0
(519) 666-0520

A rustic farmhouse in a beautiful country setting with a winding creek offers three large bedrooms with double beds. No pets. Located just twenty minutes from London, thirty-five from Stratford and Grand Bend. $25-30.

Serena's Place
720 Headley Drive, N6H 3V6
(519) 471-6228

Air-conditioned home in the prestigious residential area of West London. Three bedrooms and full bath. Sun room for relaxation. Near Springbank Park and Thames Valley Golf Course. Ten minutes from Theatre London. Bus service at the door. $25-35.

Trillium
71 Trillium Cres., N5Y 4T3
(519) 453-3801

Restful, modern, air-conditioned home offers two guest rooms — one with queen bed, one with twins — on a quiet crescent just off highway 126. Close to U.W.O., hospitals, airport, Fanshaw Pioneer Village, golf course, bus routes, and shopping. No smoking, please. Home-cooked meals on request. $25-35

Tudor Lane
141 Windsor Cres., N6K 1V9
(519) 439-9984

Tudor-style home in South London offers three guest rooms; one with two-piece bath.

6 Pets welcome: 7 Smoking allowed: 8 Children welcome: 9 Social drinking allowed: 10 Tennis available: 11 Swimming available: 12 Golf available: 13 Skiing available: 14 May be booked through travel agents

Close to 401; near downtown area. Children and pets welcome. $25-35.

MAYNOOTH

Bed & Breakfast House

Main Street, K0L 2S0
(613) 338-2239

Our bed and breakfast house is on a 2-acre lot, peaceful and quiet, with lots of sightseeing places to visit in the area. Fishing, swimming, and hiking are close by, and in winter there is a ski hill 33 km away.

Host: Bea Leveque
Doubles: 3 (SB) $30-35
Type of Beds: 2 Twin; 1 Double; 1 Queen
Continental or Full Breakfast
Credit Cards: No
Open weekends only
Notes: 2, 7, 8, 9, 13

NEW HAMBURG

The Waterlot Inn

17 Huron Street, N0B 2G0
(519) 662-2020

Two large and very comfortably appointed rooms, one under each of the 1840 peaks at the front of the house. Marble shower, bidet, sink, and sitting area, plus a suite.

Hosts: W. Gordon Elkeer
Singles: 2 (SB) $65
Doubles: 1 (PB) $100
Type of Beds: 1 Double; 1 Queen; 2 King
Continental Breakfast
Credit Cards: A, B, C, F
Closed Mondays and Christmas Day
Notes: 2, 4, 9, 10, 11, 12, 13

NORTH BAY

Country Host #22

R.R. #1, Palgrave, Ontario
L0N 1P0, Canada
(519) 941-7633

On Lake Nipissing, close to North Bay, with its own private sandy beach and a dock for sun bathing. The Manitou Islands sunsets are famous here, and a canoe and fishing boat are available to guests. There is year-round fishing, a shopping center three miles away, carnivals, regattas, downhill and cross-country skiing. Friendly resident poodles and two cats.

Doubles: 3 (1 PB; 2 SB) $35-50
Type of Beds: 1 Double; 3 Queen
Full Breakfast
Credit Cards: No
Notes: 5, 8, 9, 10, 11, 12, 13

ORANGEVILLE

Country Host #3

R.R. #1, Palgrave, Ontario
L0N 1P0, Canada
(519) 941-7633

A comfortable home full of antiques on 2 acres of manicured lawns; one of fifteen homes around a community pond. Country lanes and the Bruce Trail are nearby for hikers and nature lovers. Craft and antique shops, good dining; nearby horse shows spring and fall.

Doubles: 3 (1 PB; 2 SB) $35-50
Type of Beds: 2 Twin; 1 Queen
Full Breakfast
Credit Cards: No
Closed Christmas & Boxing Day
Notes: 3, 4, 5, 7 (restricted), 8 (over 12), 9, 10, 11, 12, 13

Country Host #4

R.R. #1, Palgrave, Ontario
L0N 1P0, Canada
(519) 941-7633

A sprawling country house with fireplaces, located on a hill with rolling hills and the Niagara Escarpment views. Fishing, hiking, swimming, skiing. Craft and antique shops nearby, good dining. One friendly resident dog.

Doubles: 1 (PB) $35-50
Type of Beds: 2 Twin
Full Breakfast

NOTES: Credit cards accepted: A Master Card; B Visa; C American Express; D Discover Card; E Diners Club; F Other: 2 Personal checks accepted: 3 Lunch available: 4 Dinner available: 5 Open all year

Credit Cards: No
Closed Christmas & New Years Day
Notes: 3, 5, 9, 10, 11, 12, 13

OTTAWA

Auberge McGee's Inn

185 Daly Avenue, K1N 6E8
(613) 237-6089

Welcome to McGees! A handsomely restored Victorian mansion centrally located and within walking distance to all downtown attractions. Featuring rooms with private bath, telephone, cable TV, fireplaces, Jacuzzi suites. Free parking. Recommended by *Country Inns,* Frommer's, AAA/CAA, OHMA.

Hosts: Ann Schutte & Mary Unger
Doubles: 14 (10 PB; 4 SB) $52-108
Type of Beds: 9 Twin; 4 Double; 6 Queen; 1 King
Full Breakfast
Minimum stay holidays: 2
Credit Cards: A, B
Notes: 5, 8 (over 5), 11, 12, 13

Australis Guest House

35 Marlborough Avenue, K1N 8E6
(613) 235-8461

Our sixty-year-old home is a classic residence with fireplaces and leaded windows in a lovely part of downtown Ottawa. Near parks, embassies, and the river. Our breakfasts are hearty and friendly and famous for their conversation.

Hosts: Brian & Carol Waters
Doubles: 3 (1 PB; 2 SB) From $32-40 (Canadian)
Type of Beds: 1 Twin; 1 Double; 1 Queen
Full Breakfast
Credit Cards: No
Notes: 5, 7, 8

Cartier House Inn

46 Cartier Street, K2P 1J3
(613) 236-4667

Eleven exquisite rooms/suites with antique furniture, rich draperies, carefully selected

works of art in a restored turn-of-the-century mansion. Jacuzzis in suites; turn-down service; morning newspaper. On a quiet street within walking distance of Parliament buildings, National Arts Center, shopping, and restaurants.

Host: Noreen Spanier
Doubles: 11 (PB) $93.45-135.45 Canadian
Type of Beds: 11 Queen
Continental Breakfast
Credit Cards: A, B, E, F
Notes: 2, 5, 7 (limited), 8, 9, 10, 11, 12, 13, 14

Constance House

62 Sweetland Avenue, K1N 7T6
(613) 235-8888

A heritage home (1895) in downtown Ottawa that boasts antique chandeliers and original maple wood staircase. Year-round comfort with air-conditioning and fireplace. Each room has its own sink, terry robes, hair dryer. Suite available for extended visits.

Host: Esther M. Peterson
Singles: 2 (SB) $42
Doubles: 3 (1 PB; 2 SB) $92.40
Type of Beds: 2 Twin; 2 Double; 1 Queen
Full Breakfast
Minimum stay holidays: 2
Credit Cards: A, B, C
Notes: 2, 5, 8, 9, 10, 11, 12, 13, 14

Gasthaus Switzerland Inn

89 Daly Avenue, K1N 6E6
(613) 237-0335

We are located in the heart of Ottawa, within walking distance to Parliament Hill, the old market, the Rideau Center, Congress Center, Ottawa University, and the Rideau Canal.

Hosts: Sabine & Josef Sauter
Doubles: 17 (5 PB; 12 SB) $35.70-63
Type of Beds: 5 Twin; 1 Double; 16 Queen
Full Swiss Country Breakfast
Minimum stay weekdays & weekends: 2
Credit Cards: A, B
Notes: 5, 12, 13

6 Pets welcome: 7 Smoking allowed: 8 Children welcome: 9 Social drinking allowed: 10 Tennis available: 11 Swimming available: 12 Golf available: 13 Skiing available: 14 May be booked through travel agents

Leclerc's Residence

253 McLeod, K2P 1A1
(613) 234-7577

A lovely 1871 Victorian home, graciously
decorated, located in the center of town on
a quiet street facing a park. Within walking
distance of all major points of interest, many
fine restaurants, and shopping. Your hosts
speak both English and French. Free parking, limited smoking. A TV sitting room is
available for guests' use.

Hosts: J-J & Clemence Leclerc
Singles (SB) $45-50
Doubles: 2 (SB) $55-60
Type of Beds: 3 Twin; 2 Double
Full Breakfast
Minimum stay weekends & holidays: 2 ; summer week-
days: 2
Credit Cards: No
Notes: 2, 4, 5, 9, 10, 11, 12, 13

O'Connor House Downtown

172 O'Connor Street, K2P 1T5
(613) 236-4221

Located in downtown Ottawa, within walking distance of Canada's Parliament buildings, Rideau Canal, National Gallery,
National Arts Center, major shopping and
tourist attractions. Less than one-half hour
to several ski resorts. Warm, courteous staff,
common dining/TV room for guests.

Host: Donna Bradley
Singles: 4 (SB) $47 (Canadian)
Doubles: 30 (SB) $49-53 (Canadian)
Type of Beds: 6 Twin; 28 Double; 2 Queen
Full Breakfast
Credit Cards: A, B, C, E, F
Notes: 2, 5, 7, 8, 10, 11, 12, 13, 14

Rideau View Inn

177 Frank Street, K2P 0X4
(613) 236-9309

Rideau View Inn is located near the Rideau
Canal on a quiet residential street within
easy walking distance to fine restaurants,

shopping, parliament hill, and public
transportation. Our guests are encouraged
to relax in front of the fireplace in the living
room, enjoy a leisurely stroll beside the
Rideau Canal or a game of tennis at nearby
public courts.

Host: George Hartsgrove
Doubles: 6 (SB) $49-61
Type of Beds: 4 Double; 3 Queen
Full Breakfast
Credit Cards: A, B, C
Notes: 5, 10, 11, 12, 13

Robert's Bed & Breakfast

Box 4848, Station E, K1S 5J1
(613) 563-0161

Robert's Bed & Breakfast is a large and
most comfortable home over 100 years old.
Furnished with a pleasant blend of Canadian
and American pieces. Large en-suite with
bathroom, sitting room, balcony. Within
walking distance of Parliament buildings and
museums.

Host: Robert Rivoire
Singles: 1 (SB) $34 Canadian
Doubles: 1 (SB) $44 Canadian
Suite: 1 (PB) $58 Canadian
Type of Beds: 1 Twin; 1 Double; 1 Queen
Full or Continental Breakfast
Credit Cards: No
Notes: 2, 5, 9, 10, 11, 12, 13, 14

OWEN SOUND

Country Host #15

R.R. #1, Palgrave, Ontario
L0N 1P0, Canada
(519) 941-7633

In Owen Sound, this 1904 stone mansion is
an outstanding example of Edwardian architecture. Tastefully furnished and air-conditioned, with fire alarm system. Swiss hosts
are knowledgeable about the area's many
attractions and will transport Bruce Trail
hikers to and from the trail.

Doubles: 4 (SB) $35-50
Type of Beds: 3 Twin; 2 Double

NOTES: Credit cards accepted: A Master Card; B Visa; C American Express; D Discover Card; E Diners
Club; F Other: 2 Personal checks accepted: 3 Lunch available: 4 Dinner available: 5 Open all year

Full Breakfast
Credit Cards: No
Notes: 3, 5, 8, 9, 10, 11, 12, 13

TORONTO

Burken Guest House

322 Palmerston Blvd., M6G 2N6
(416) 920-7842

Splendidly situated in a charming residential neighborhood adjacent to downtown. Eight tastefully appointed rooms with shared bathrooms. Limited parking on premises; public transportation nearby. Friendly, capable service in a relaxed, Old World atmosphere.

Hosts: Burke & Ken
Singles: 3 (SB) $48-58
Doubles: 5 (SB) $58-63
Type of Beds: 7 Twin; 4 Double
Continental Breakfast
Credit Cards: A, B
Notes: 5, 8, 9, 14

Oppenheims

153 Huron Street, M5T 2B6
(416) 598-4562

Oppenheims is now beginning its ninth year of operation. The four eclectic rooms and "special" breakfasts have been featured on national TV, CNN Travel News, and over twenty-five magazines and newspapers. The house, built in 1890, features four pianos, a turn-of-the-century general store, and huge kitchen. It is downtown, halfway between the art gallery and the Royal Ontario Museum. No smoking. One dog in residence.

Host: Susan Oppenheim
Singles: 1 (SB) $40-50
Doubles: 3 (SB) $50-55
Type of Beds: 3 Double; 1 Queen
Full Breakfast
Minimum stay: 3
Notes: 2 (deposit only), 5, 8 (over 12), 9, 10, 11, 12

WALTERS FALLS

Country Host #14

R.R. #1, Palgrave, Ontario
L0N 1P0, Canada
(519) 941-7633

A passive-solar guest house with pine decor, nestled in the peaceful, rolling countryside near Walters Falls, southeast of Owen Sound, on 42 acres. Macrobiotic cooking only, and all meals are available with yoga, if desired. Wooded trails for solitude and stillness; fishing and canoeing. Many craftsmen in the area.

Doubles: 2 (SB) $35-50
Type of Beds: 2 Double
Full Breakfast
Credit Cards: No
Notes: 3, 4, 5, 10, 11, 12, 13

WIARTON

Country Host #16

R.R. #1, Palgrave, Ontario
L0N 1P0, Canada
(519) 941-7633

In Wiarton, at the start of the Bruce Peninsula, this Victorian mansion dates from 1896. The Peninsula section of the Bruce Trial for hikers starts here and extends to Tobermory. An hour's drive will take you there to see the many craft shops, the world's only underwater park with shipwrecks, flower-pot islands, and to catch the ferry to Manitoulin Island.

Doubles: 4 (SB) $35-50
Type of Beds: 2 Twin; 2 Double
Full Breakfast
Credit Cards: No
Notes: 3, 5, 7 (restricted), 8, 9, 10, 11, 12, 13

Country Host #17

R.R. #1, Palgrave, Ontario
L0N 1P0, Canada
(519) 941-7633

6 Pets welcome: 7 Smoking allowed: 8 Children welcome: 9 Social drinking allowed: 10 Tennis available: 11 Swimming available: 12 Golf available: 13 Skiing available: 14 May be booked through travel agents

In Wiarton, gateway to the Bruce Peninsula, this 1883 Victorian offers you year-round fishing in Colpoys Bay, Bruce Trail and conservation-area hiking, swimming, snow mobiling, and cross-country skiing. Tobermory is an hour's drive. Friendly resident poodle.

Doubles: 3 (1 PB; 2 SB) $35-50
Type of Beds: 2 Double; 1 King
Full Breakfast
Credit Cards: No
Closed Dec. 25, 26, Jan. 1
Notes: 3, 5, 7, 8, 9, 10, 11, 12, 13

Country Host #18

R.R. #1, Palgrave, Ontario
L0N 1P0, Canada
(519) 941-7633

This huge 1889 stone farmhouse has an in-ground pool. Located on 800 acres of grain and beef cattle, with four ponds. The Bruce Trail runs through the property, which adjoins the Crocker Indian Reserve. Accommodation for ten people is available, with all meals, if requested in advance. Groomed cross-country ski trails on the property, as well as snow mobiling. An hour's drive to Tobermory.

Doubles: 5 (2 PB; 3 SB) $35-50
Type of Beds: 1 Twin; 3 Double; 2 Queen
Full Breakfast
Credit Cards: No
Closed Dec. 25, 26, Jan. 1
Notes: 3, 5, 7 (restricted), 8, 9, 11, 12, 13

NOTES: Credit cards accepted: A Master Card; B Visa; C American Express; D Discover Card; E Diners Club; F Other: 2 Personal checks accepted: 3 Lunch available: 4 Dinner available: 5 Open all year

Prince Edward Island

MONTAGUE

Partridge's

Panmure Island, RR2, C0A 1R0
(902) 838-4687

Partridge's Bed & Breakfast, surrounded by sandy beaches, is near Panmure Island Provincial Park, where well-trained lifeguards patrol one of the most beautiful beaches on P.E.I. A leisurely walk through the woods to our beach offers quiet relaxation. Wild strawberries and raspberries can be picked, clams can be dug, and Graham's Lobster Factory is nearby. Baby sitting, as well as cribs and kitchen privileges, are available. Bicycles, a canoe, and row boats are a few of the other added attractions offered for rent. Hostess has two cats, and pets are permitted.

Host: Mrs. Gertrude Partridge
Singles: 1 (PB) $33 plus 10% tax
Doubles: 6 (4PB; 2SB) $33-44 plus 10% tax
Type of Beds: 11 Twin; 6 Double
Full Breakfast
Credit Cards: B
Notes: 2, 5, 6, 8, 9, 10, 11, 12, 13 (XC),14

MURRAY RIVER

Bayberry Cliff Inn Bed & Breakfast

RR 4, Little Sands, C0A 1W0
(902) 962-3395

Situated on the edge of a 40-foot cliff, the inn consists of two converted post-and-beam barns decorated with antiques and marine art. Stairs to the shore. Seals, restaurants, craft shops nearby.

Hosts: Don & Nancy Perkins
Singles: 1 (SB) $29.50
Doubles: 6 (SB) $44
Type of Beds: 7 Twin; 9 Double
Full Breakfast
Credit Cards: A, B
Closed Oct. 15-May 1
Notes: 8, 9, 11

SUMMERSIDE

Faye & Eric's Bed & Breakfast

380 MacEwen Road,
(902) 436-6847

All rooms tastefully decorated; crib, high chair, and cots available. Two suites available — one with Jacuzzi and whirlpool bath. Housekeeping unit sleeps four and has private entrance and bath. Private kitchen for guests, patio, and barbecue. Beach about three miles away; restaurant and shopping within walking distance.

Hosts: Faye & Eric Oulton
Doubles: 9 (2 PB; 7 S4B) $35-75
Type of Beds: 2 Twin; 7 Double
Continental Breakfast (full available)
Credit Cards: A
Notes: 5, 7, 9, 12

Silver Fox Inn

61 Granville Street, C1N 2Z3
(902) 436-4033

For nearly a century, proud owners have carefully preserved the beauty of the spacious rooms with their fireplaces and fine woodwork. Combining modern comfort with the cherished past, the Silver Fox Inn offers accommodation for twelve guests. Its

6 Pets welcome: 7 Smoking allowed: 8 Children welcome: 9 Social drinking allowed: 10 Tennis available: 11 Swimming available: 12 Golf available: 13 Skiing available: 14 May be booked through travel agents

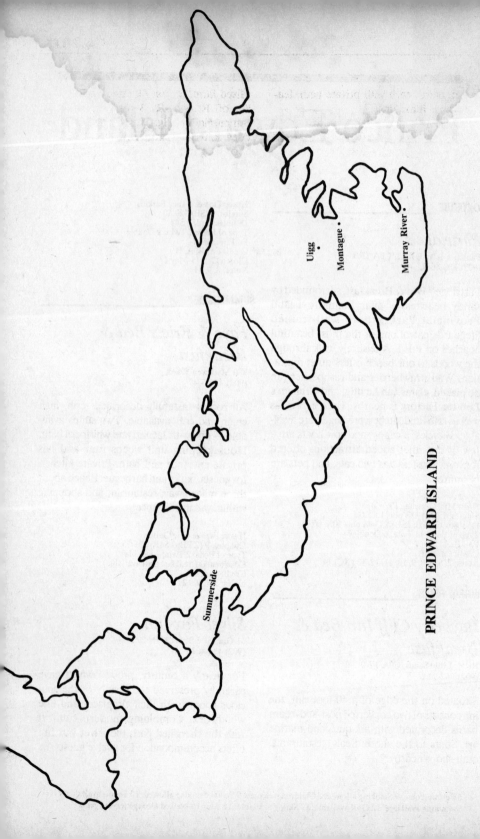

Uigg •

Montague •

Murray River •

Summerside •

PRINCE EDWARD ISLAND

six bedrooms, each with private bath, feature period furnishings.

Host: Julie Simmons
Doubles: 6 (PB) $48-53
Type of Beds: 2 Twin; 3 Double; 1 Queen
Continental Breakfast
Credit Cards: A, B, C
Closed Christmas
Notes: 5, 7, 8 (over 10), 9, 10, 11, 12, 13

UIGG

MacLeod's Farm Bed & Breakfast
 Vernon Post Office C0A 2E0
 (902) 651-2303

Mixed farm, centrally located on Rt. 24, 3 km. off Rt. 1 or Rt. 3 in the quiet, scenic community of Uigg. Large play area, hay rides, kittens, bunnies, and Newfoundland dog for guests' enjoyment. Beaches and music festival twenty minutes away. Home-baked breads and homemade jams.

Hosts: Malcolm & Margie Mac Leod
Doubles: 3 (SB) $25-35
Type of Beds: 2 Twin; 1 Double; 1 Queen
Continental Breakfast
Credit Cards: No
Closed Sept. 30
Notes: 2, 8, 9, 11, 12, 13

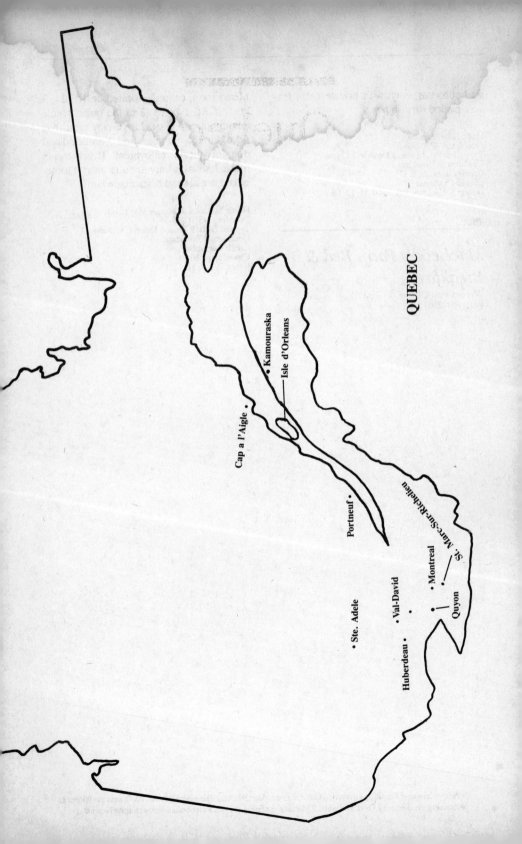

QUEBEC

Kamouraska

Isle d'Orleans

Cap a l'Aigle

Portneuf

St. Marc-Sur-Richelieu

Ste. Adele

Val-David

Montreal

Huberdeau

Quyon

Quebec

La Pinsonniere
124 St. Raphael, G0T 1B0
(418) 665-4431

A small deluxe inn located in Charlevoix, a haven for artists and dreamers. This beautiful country stretches from Quebec City to Baie Ste-Catherine along the St-Laurent River, and offers a world of discoveries, from exquisite cuisine to whale watching.

Hosts: Janine & Jean Authier
Doubles: 28 (PB) $145-350, dinner included
Type of Beds: 5 Twin; 2 Double; 19 Queen; 2 King
Full Breakfast
Minimum stay weekends: 2; holidays: 3
Credit Cards: A, B
Closed 11/11-12/24
Notes: 4, 7, 8, 10, 11, 12, 13

HUBERDEAU

Auberge Otter Lake Haus
122 Chemin Trudeu, J0T 1G0
(819) 687-2767

Twenty-two guest rooms in a family-owned inn operated since 1927. Great surroundings for boating, fishing, swimming, wind surfing, and paddle boating on the lake. Cross-country ski trails and downhill slopes nearby. Just 115 km from Montreal, in the heart of the Laurentians.

Hosts: The Thiel Family
Singles: 2 (SB) $35-47
Doubles: 19 (8 PB; 11 SB) $58-70
Type of Beds: 16 Twin; 16 Double
Full Breakfast
Minimum stay weekends: 2; holidays: 3
Credit Cards: A, B
Closed Oct. 15-Dec. 1
Notes: 4, 6, 7, 8, 9, 10, 11, 12, 13

Le Vigie du Pilote
170, Chemin des Ormes, St.-Jean, G0A 3W0
(418) 829-2613

Come and enjoy the peaceful and relaxed atmosphere of the river pilot's home. A luxurious house on beautiful Orleans Island, only thirty-five minutes from Quebec. Quiet country surroundings with magnificent views over the St. Lawrence River. Non-smokers only.

Hosts: John & Lorraine Godolphin
Doubles: 3 (PB) $40-70 (Canadian)
Type of Beds: 3 Double
Full Breakfast
Closed Nov. 1-April 30
Credit Cards: No
Notes: 2, 8, 9, 11, 12

Gite du Passant
81 Ave. Morel, C. P. 174, G0L 1M0
(418) 492-2921

Nineteenth-century home situated on a patch of land on the south shore of the St. Lawrence River. Watch the glorious sunsets. Very quiet.

Host: Mariette Le Blanc
Singles: 1 (SB) $20
Doubles: 3 (1 PB; 2 SB) $30
Type of Beds: 1 Twin; 2 Double
Full Breakfast
Maximum stay: 3
Credit Cards: No
Closed Nov. 1-April 30
Notes: 8, 9, 11

6 Pets welcome: 7 Smoking allowed: 8 Children welcome: 9 Social drinking allowed: 10 Tennis availab[le]
Swimming available: 12 Golf available: 13 Skiing available: 14 May be booked through travel agents

MONTREAL

A B&B-A Downtown Network #1

3458 Laval Avenue, H2X 3C8
(514) 289-9749

Downtown Sherbrooke Street. Sylvie offers a double in her attractive and uniquely designed split-level duplex. Only a few minutes' walk to Old Montreal and fascinating St. Denis Street. In the summer, enjoy Sylvie's homemade rhubarb-strawberry preserves with your croissants. Be her guest at the health club.

Doubles: 1 (SB) $55
Type of Beds: 1 Queen
Full Breakfast
Credit Cards: A, B, C
Notes: 2 (for deposit), 5, 8, 9, 10, 11, 12, 13

A B&B-A Downtown Network #2

3458 Laval Avenue, H2X 3C8
(514) 289-9749

Downtown, in the heart of the Latin Quarter. Enjoy the superb location of this restored traditional Quebecoise home. Your host, active in the restaurant business, offers two sunlit doubles and one triple with a bay window opening onto typical Montreal scene. The privacy of this tastefully furnished home is perfect for first or second honeymooners.

Triple: 1 (SB) $75
Doubles: 2 (SB) $55
Type of Beds: 1 Twin; 3 Queen
full Breakfast
dit Cards: A, B, C
 2 (for deposit), 5, 7, 9, 10, 11, 12, 13

1 Downtown

2
C8

When traveling to Quebec City, stop at this listed landmark home, built in 1671, which faces the beautiful St. Lawrence River. Your hostess, a blue-ribbon chef, offers guests a memorable breakfast featuring "Quiche Floriane." Experience the warmth and hospitality of a typical Quebecoise home.

Doubles: 2 (SB) $55
Type of Beds: 1 Twin; 1 Queen
Full Breakfast
Credit Cards: A, B, C
Notes: 5, 7, 8, 9, 10, 11, 12, 13

A B&B-A Downtown Network #4

3458 Laval Avenue, H2X 3C8
(514) 289-9749

Downtown double off Sherbrooke Street. This antique-filled apartment on Drummond Street is tastefully decorated and only two minutes to the Museum of Fine Arts and all shopping. Mount Royal Park is nearby, and McGill University is just two blocks. Your hosts will pamper you with a gourmet breakfast and invite you to join them for a sherry in the evening.

Doubles: 1 (SB) $55
Type of Beds: 1 Queen
Full Breakfast
Credit Cards: A, B, C
Notes: 2 (for deposit), 5, 7, 9, 10, 11, 12, 13

A B&B-A Downtown Network #5

3458 Laval Avenue, H2X 3C8
(514) 289-9749

Downtown, near St. Denis Street. Be in the heart of everything! The big bay window of this ninety-year-old, restored home overlooks the city's most historic park. Original woodwork and detail add to the charm of this home. The neighborhood is famous for

s accepted: A Master Card; B Visa; C American Express; D Discover Card; E Diners
ersonal checks accepted: 3 Lunch available: 4 Dinner available: 5 Open all year

its excellent "bring your own wine" restaurants, and your host knows them all.

Doubles: 2 (SB) $55
Triples: 2 (SB) $75
Type of Beds: 4 Queen
Full Breakfast
Credit Cards: A, B, C
Notes: 2 (for deposit), 5, 8, 9, 10, 11, 12, 13

A B&B-A Downtown Network #6

3458 Laval Avenue, H2X 3C8
(514) 289-9749

Old Montreal. Your hosts spoil their guests with Quebecoise hospitality. As a city councillor, the host was instrumental in the preservation of the Latin Quarter. They'll be glad to suggest one of the city's sensational restaurants and have personal knowledge of the antique district.

Doubles: 1 (PB) $75
Type of Beds: 1 Queen
Full Breakfast
Credit Cards: A, B, C
Notes: 2 (for deposit), 5, 7, 8, 9, 10, 11, 12, 13

A B&B-A Downtown Network #7

3458 Laval Avenue, H2X 3C8
(514) 289-9749

Downtown, turn-of-the-century home. This restored Victorian features a marble fireplace, original hardwood floors, and a skylight. Your host offers two charmingly decorated singles and two doubles (one with a brass bed), and grandma's quilt in the winter. You can bird watch on the balcony or have a challenging game of Scruples in the evening.

Doubles: 2 (SB) $40-55
Type of Beds: 1 Twin; 1 Queen
Full Breakfast
Credit Cards: A, B, C
Notes: 2 (for deposit), 5, 9, 10, 11, 12, 13

Anne's B&B

Anne's B&B

4912 Victoria Avenue, H3W 2N1
(514) 738-9410

Anne's large Georgian home is filled with fine objects and a wonderful collection of Canadian art. Large grounds include a shady patio with lawn furniture. St. Joseph's Oratory and the Universite of Montreal are neighbors.

Singles: 1 (SB) $40 Canadian
Doubles: 2 (SB) $60-65 Canadian
Type of Beds: 3 Twin; 1 Double
Full Breakfast
Credit Cards: A, B, C
Notes: 5, 7, 9, 10, 12, 13, 14

Brigette's B&B

4912 Victoria Avenue, H3W 2N1
(514) 738-9410

Brigette's love of art and antiques is obvious in her fabulous three-story townhouse, located in the Latin Quarter area of downtown Montreal. Cozy living room with fireplace and view of the city's most historic park all add to the charm of this home. Walk to the chic boutiques, international restaurants, and jazz clubs that are a feature of the neighborhood.

6 Pets welcome: 7 Smoking allowed: 8 Children welcome: 9 Social drinking allowed: 10 Tennis available: 11 Swimming available: 12 Golf available: 13 Skiing available: 14 May be booked through travel agents

Doubles: 1 (PB) $80 Canadian
Type of Beds: 1 Double
Full Breakfast
Credit Cards: A, B, C
Notes: 5, 7, 9, 10, 12, 13, 14

Johanne's B&B

4912 Victoria Avenue, H3W 2N1
(514) 738-9410

In this most unusual renovated Victorian row house, guests have the first level to themselves, including double bedroom with bath, living area, interior skylit patio, and quaint dining area. One block from St. Denis Street, the heart of Montreal's Latin Quarter, with its cafes, restaurants, shops, and exciting nightlife. Five-course gourmet breakfasts.

Doubles: 1 (PB) $100 Canadian
Type of Beds: 1 Double
Full Breakfast
Credit Cards: A, B, C
Notes: 5, 9, 10, 12, 13, 14

Manoir Ambrose

3422 Stanley, H3A 1R8
(514) 288-6922

Situated on the quiet and restful slope of beautiful Mount-Royal, within walking distance of Montreal's restaurants, theatres, shopping districts, metro system. Comfortably furnished rooms in a Victorian setting.

Host: Lucie Seguin
Singles: 16 (9 PB; 7 SB) $35-55
Doubles: 21 (14 PB; 7 SB) $40-60
Type of Beds: 4 Twin; 18 Double
Continental Breakfast
Credit Cards: A, B
Notes: 5, 6, 7, 8, 9, 14

Martha's B&B

4912 Victoria Avenue, H3W 2N1
(514) 738-9410

Stencilled glass windows, original woodwork and detail, and smart period furnishings are just some of the features of this B&B.

Martha's home is a few minutes from the Forum, site of national hockey games, and just one street from a very fashionable shopping mall.

Doubles: 1 (SB) $60 Canadian
Type of Beds: 1 Double
Full Breakfast
Credit Cards: A, B, C
Notes: 5, 9, 10, 12, 13, 14

PORTNEUF

Edale Place

Edale Place, G0A 2Y0
(418) 286-3168

A family home of the Victorian era, quiet and comfortable, in open countryside only forty-five minutes from downtown Quebec. Flowers in summer, clean snow in winter.

Hosts: Mary & Tam Farnsworth
Singles: 1 (SB) $25-30
Doubles: 3 (SB) $40-50
Type of Beds: 5 Twin; 2 Double
Full Breakfast
Credit Cards: No
Dinner available on request
Notes: 4, 5, 7, 8, 9, 11, 12, 13

QUYON

Memory Lane Farm

RR#1, J0X 2V0
(819) 458-2479

Modern farmhouse close to Gatineau Hills, just thirty miles from our nation's capital, Ottawa, with museums, art galleries, and festivals. Antique car enthusiasts, sugarbush, and other hobbies. Groomed snowmobile trails start at the door.

Hosts: Blair & Laura Prior
Singles: 1 (SB) $25
Doubles: 2 (SB) $35
Type of Beds: 1 Twin; 2 Double; 1 Rollaway
Full Breakfast
Credit Cards: No
Notes: 2, 4, 5, 7, 8, 9, 11, 12, 13 (15mi)

NOTES: Credit cards accepted: A Master Card; B Visa; C American Express; D Discover Card; E Diners Club; F Other: 2 Personal checks accepted: 3 Lunch available: 4 Dinner available: 5 Open all year